Course   Introduction to Management
Rutgers Business School
New Brunswick and Newark

http://create.mheducation.com

This McGraw-Hill Create text may include materials submitted to
McGraw-Hill for publication by the instructor of this course.
The instructor is solely responsible for the editorial content of such
materials. Instructors retain copyright of these additional materials.

ISBN-10: 1307093345   ISBN-13: 9781307093346

Contents

Credits

HBR.ORG

Harvard Business Review

NOVEMBER 2012
REPRINT R1211D

NOVEMBER 2012
REPRINT R1211D

SPOTLIGHT ON HBR AT 90

Does Management Really Work?

How three essential practices can address even the most complex global problems
by Nicholas Bloom, Raffaella Sadun, and John Van Reenen

SPOTLIGHT ON HBR AT 90

Spotlight

ARTWORK Man Ray
Rayography 2 Cones
1927, rayograph

Does Management Really Work?

FOR ARTICLE REPRINTS CALL 800-988-0886 OR 617-783-7500, OR VISIT **HBR.ORG**

Nicholas Bloom is a professor of economics at Stanford University.

Raffaella Sadun is an assistant professor at Harvard Business School.

John Van Reenen is the director of the Centre for Economic Performance at the London School of Economics and Political Science.

How three essential practices can address even the most complex global problems *by Nicholas Bloom, Raffaella Sadun, and John Van Reenen*

HBR's 90th anniversary seems like a good time to back up and ask a basic question: Are organizations more likely to succeed if they adopt good management practices? For a decade we've been conducting research to find out. That may seem like a foolish endeavor—isn't the obvious answer yes? But as classically trained economists, we believe in reexamining long-held assumptions to see whether they stand the test of time.

At least since Frederick Winslow Taylor published *The Principles of Scientific Management* in 1911, businesses have been trying to follow formalized sets of best practices. Academic disciplines such as complexity and contingency theory have sprung up, as have numerous practical innovations, from decentralized budgets to performance reviews to lean manufacturing. To formulate a testable hypothesis for our research effort, we asked whether or not the thousands of organizations we studied adhere to three practices that are generally considered to be the essential elements of good management:

• Targets: Does the organization support long-term goals with tough but achievable short-term performance benchmarks?

• Incentives: Does the organization reward high performers with promotions and bonuses while retraining or moving underperformers?

• Monitoring: Does the organization rigorously collect and analyze performance data to identify opportunities for improvement?

Our teams of researchers asked managers a targeted list of open-ended questions, designed to ferret out details about how their companies were—or were not—implementing these practices. Overall, we learned three things. First, according to our criteria, many organizations throughout the world are very badly managed. Well-run companies set stretch targets on productivity and other parameters, base the compensation and promotions they offer on meeting those targets, and constantly measure results—but many firms do none of those things. Second, our indicators of better management and superior performance are strongly correlated with measures such as productivity, return on capital employed, and firm survival. Indeed, a one-point increment in a five-point management score that we created—the equivalent of going from the bottom third to the top third of the group—was associated with 23% greater productivity. (See the exhibit "The Return on Good Management.") Third, management makes a difference in shaping national performance. Our analysis shows, for example, that variation in management accounts for nearly a quarter of the roughly 30% productivity gap between the U.S. and Europe.

Having established that good management can yield practical improvements, we turned to a tougher question: Can these simple principles be applied to complex worldwide problems, including deficiencies in education and health care? A huge question, obviously. To approach it, we did what we had done with manufacturers: We looked at whether or not schools and hospitals showed a correlation between performance and implementation of the three basic management principles. On the basis of interviews conducted in local managers' own languages, we found that effective management can indeed improve performance, even beyond the private sector.

Transforming Manufacturers

When we began assessing management practices, we focused on medium-sized manufacturers, both independent and multinational-owned companies that had 50 to 5,000 workers. With more than 100 researchers accumulating data since 2004, our sample has come to include more than 8,000 firms in 20 countries in the developed and developing worlds.

Examples of bad management were all too easy to find. A manager at a privately held manufacturer in France, with about 500 workers, was hamstrung by his firm's inability to motivate apathetic employees. Union pressure and labor regulations meant that workers effectively had jobs for life. The only way he could balance his production line was to team up poor employees with star performers, but this practice prevented stars from earning team bonuses and eventually drove them out of the company. He said his firm was turning into an asylum for the chronically lazy. At another company, the bonus scheme for managers was so complex that it was nearly useless. There were more than 20 targets—including profit margins, sales growth, inventory turns, and employee turnover—with many measured over different time periods and weighted inconsistently. Managers told us that they ignored the targets and felt unmotivated by "seemingly random" annual bonuses.

Using a business-assessment tool we developed with McKinsey partners John Dowdy and Stephen Dorgan, we looked closely at 18 practices that fall into the three broad categories: targets, incentives, and monitoring. (See the sidebar "What to Ask Your Managers.") After interviewing managers by telephone, we rated each plant's implementation of each practice on our five-point scale and determined an average overall score for each organization. Low management scores abounded. Only 15% of U.S. companies—and fewer than 5% outside the U.S.—scored above a four. More than 30% of U.S. firms and more than 70% in Brazil, China, and India scored a three or lower. These firms fail to collect even the most basic performance data and offer few employee incentives.

In a related initiative, we partnered with the World Bank to offer 66 manufacturers in the textile-hub city of Tarapur, India, the opportunity to participate in an experiment involving management practices. Twenty-eight plants (at 17 firms) accepted the invitation, and we randomly assigned them to either an intervention group or a control group. The 14 plants in the intervention group got free, high-quality advice from a consultant who was on site half-time for five months to diagnose problems, teach managers, and implement practices. The advice focused on the basics of lean manufacturing—nothing cutting-edge or sophisticated. Essentially, the companies were taught the three aforementioned fundamentals: setting targets, establishing incentives, and monitoring performance. For follow-up, all 28 factories were visited one day each month for more than a year.

What to Ask Your Managers

Interviews with plant managers at more than 8,000 manufacturers in 20 countries revealed what management practices are actually being used on the front lines. Here is a small sampling of interview topics and related questions. For more detail, go to **worldmanagementsurvey.org**.

INTERCONNECTION OF TARGETS
How are goals cascaded down to the individual workers?

CLARITY AND COMPARABILITY OF GOALS
Does anyone complain that the targets are too complex?

CONSEQUENCE MANAGEMENT
How do you deal with repeated failures in a specific business segment?

INSTILLING A TALENT MIND-SET
How do senior managers show that attracting and developing talent is a top priority?

REMOVING POOR PERFORMERS
How long is underperformance tolerated?

UNIQUE EMPLOYEE-VALUE PROPOSITION
What makes it distinctive to work at your company?

RETAINING TALENT
What does the company do about a star performer who wants to leave?

CONTINUOUS IMPROVEMENT
How do problems typically get exposed and fixed?

PERFORMANCE TRACKING
What key indicators do you use for performance tracking?

PERFORMANCE DIALOGUE
For a given problem, how do you identify the root cause?

Idea in Brief

Are organizations more likely to succeed if they adopt good management practices?

The answer to that question may seem obvious, but economists prefer to test such long-held assumptions. An economist-led, international research effort conducted for the past decade reveals that poor management is rampant and that most leaders of poorly managed institutions are unaware of the deficiencies. When manufacturers were systematically taught how to implement good management's basic features—targets, incentives, and monitoring—performance improved measurably and dramatically.

Bringing these fundamental best practices to the wide array of companies, schools, and hospitals that need them can ultimately increase wealth and can substantially improve education and health care. A call for "better management" may not seem like a cutting-edge idea, but given the potentially large effects on incomes, productivity, and delivery of critically needed services worldwide, it may actually be a radical one.

When we started, facilities were often dirty and unproductive. Many workers received $5 a day for brutal 12-hour shifts, and accidents were common. At one textile plant, we heard that a worker had broken his leg when a faulty restraining strap allowed a beam to fall off a trolley. With no sick pay, he and his family experienced severe financial hardship. Even though wages were low, the company's profits were meager. It was common for companies in the area to default on their loans and go out of business.

The intervention transformed the plants that had received help. On average, they cut defects by more than 50%, reduced inventory by 20%, and raised output by 10%. They also became far easier for their CEOs to manage, which allowed for the addition of new facilities and the expansion of product lines. Productivity at the factory where the worker had broken his leg increased by almost 20%, and average profits rose by what we estimate to be roughly 30% (profit is often a closely guarded secret at these companies). That company is opening a second factory and hiring 100 more weavers, after attracting them away from rival firms with the promise of 10% higher pay. Safety also improved: For example, daily monitoring of cleanliness at the factory avoided the buildup of oil and cotton waste around weaving machines, thereby preventing life-threatening fires.

Beyond the Factory Floor

Having seen the effect on manufacturing operations, we expanded our research to other kinds of organizations. So far we have conducted interviews at 1,000 schools in the U.S., UK, Germany, Italy, Sweden, and India, and at 1,300 hospitals in those countries and in France, ranking each of the organizations in much the same way as we ranked the manufacturers.

Our management scores showed that, overall, schools and hospitals are even more poorly managed than manufacturing companies. In one illustrative example, a nurse in the UK told us that her hospital didn't store bed linens on each floor, despite the obvious advantages of such a policy. One evening, when she was overseeing a ward, she went to a different floor to get new linens for a patient; upon returning, she found that another patient had died from a seizure. With no process for monitoring or correcting problems like this, the linens policy persisted two years later.

The public sector is also strikingly bad at rewarding good employees and dealing with underperformers. One U.S. high school principal confided to us about a teacher who spoke so quietly that her pupils struggled to hear her. According to the principal, grades were often poor, and parents complained if their kids were seated at the back of the class. The principal had repeatedly offered training to help the teacher, to no avail. Removing the individual was impossible under union rules, so the poor teaching continued year after year.

Of course, some educational organizations regularly evaluate pupils and teachers against clear goals and provide appropriate incentives. Similarly, many

On average, firms that received the management intervention cut defects by half, reduced inventory by 20%, and raised output by 10%.

health care institutions establish targets for various kinds of processes, such as order entry and error reduction, and compensate employees on the basis of rigorous monitoring. Comparing management practices with outcomes, we found that high-scoring schools have better exam results: A one-point improvement in the management score is associated with about a 10% jump in student test performance. Similarly, at hospitals, a one-point management-score increase is associated with a 0.5% lower 30-day mortality rate for heart attack victims who are admitted to emergency rooms.

We didn't conduct interventions in the schools and hospitals we studied, but other researchers have. For example, Harvard's Roland Fryer ran management experiments in schools in Houston, Texas. In one study, nine schools in the city's worst-performing district adopted simple techniques such as collecting and analyzing weekly grading data—a surprisingly uncommon practice—so that teachers could rapidly assist underperforming students. Target measures such as math grades, attendance, and graduation rates soared past those of a control group of schools that stuck to their old ways, and the percentage of failing students dropped by more than 70%. Monetary incentives for teachers have been successful at increasing achievement in developing countries such as India and Kenya (results in the U.S. have been more mixed).

The example of Virginia Mason Medical Center, in Seattle, illustrates what can happen when a health care organization makes a concerted effort to improve management practices. In 2002 it introduced procedures, such as extensive performance monitoring and weekly team meetings, inspired by the Toyota Production System. These changes dramatically improved patient care. In the breast clinic, for example, the average elapsed time between a patient's first call and a diagnosis dropped from three weeks to three days. The changes also bolstered employee morale and returned the hospital to profitability after years of losses.

Raising Consciousness

At the companies in Tarapur where we conducted interventions, we easily made a convincing case for the value of good management. But the need to spread the word to the thousands of other underperforming companies, schools, and hospitals worldwide is urgent. Awareness is very low: 79% of the organizations in our study claimed to have above-average manage-

The Return on Good Management

A one-point increment on a five-point management score correlated with better performance at manufacturers around the globe. The score was based on how well the firms adhered to three basic management practices: targets, incentives, and monitoring.

1

POINT INCREMENT ON A MANAGEMENT SCORE WAS ASSOCIATED WITH

+23%
PRODUCTIVITY

+14%
MARKET CAPITALIZATION

+1.4 PERCENTAGE POINTS
ANNUAL SALES GROWTH

ment practices, yet no correlation existed between our scores and the institutions' self-scores, either in management practices or in overall performance.

Much of the opportunity for improvement is in the hands of local managers. To see how far behind their organizations are, they must rigorously evaluate their own practices and compare themselves with others'. Managers can quickly benchmark themselves by country and industry on our management scoring grid at worldmanagementsurvey.org.

FOR ARTICLE REPRINTS CALL 800-988-0886 OR 617-783-7500, OR VISIT **HBR.ORG**

Awareness is only the beginning, of course. Having seen where they need to improve, managers should begin working toward slow but steady progress. We've seen organizations make a good start by identifying which processes they need to change (for example, is product development too slow?) and then devising metrics for monitoring progress over the short and long terms. Ideally, goals should be visible to everyone—one company we studied posted its goals on the CEO's door—and should be translated into companywide, group, and individual targets that are tracked frequently and meaningfully. That approach helps companies replace finger-pointing with timely, effective action plans across all organizational functions.

But you shouldn't expect immediate results. GE, McDonald's, Nike, and Toyota didn't become top performers overnight. They established well-focused targets and powerful incentives, and they continuously monitored performance for many years, always seeking to improve. Small changes can be very effective in driving larger shifts later. In the Indian textile factories we studied, for example, we typically overcame resistance to lean manufacturing by piloting changes on a few machines in one corner of the factory. The positive results then opened the way for overhauling the whole plant.

In many instances, poor management is reinforced by national policies such as production quotas and tariff barriers, which reduce competition. In India, for example, hefty tariffs keep low-cost Chinese textiles out of the market and shelter domestic firms from international competition. Governments can play a positive role by reducing subsidies for certain sectors, eliminating tax breaks for favored companies, and lowering barriers to trade.

In education and health care, better management practices usually take especially long to have transformational effects. After Mastery Charter Schools took over three middle schools in Philadelphia, for instance, test scores increased by 50% and violence declined by 80% over three years. And Virginia Mason's CEO Gary Kaplan and his management team spent several years turning around that health center's performance. Teams of managers and frontline workers traveled to Japan to study the Toyota Production System; when they returned, they worked with other staff people to transform patient care.

ANOTHER QUESTION we addressed in our research is why some organizations are motivated to change and others aren't. We eventually found a pattern: Leaders often initiate transformations in response to extremely challenging conditions. For example, because of its location in a seismically active zone, Virginia Mason had to upgrade its outdated buildings to make them safe against earthquakes. Facing huge costs for this overhaul, the hospital's leaders realized they needed to turn their losses into profits. That initiative, combined with managers' desire to improve the hospital's delivery of health care, led Virginia Mason to embark on the management initiatives that transformed the organization.

The recent global recession is just that kind of extreme challenge. It has generated tough conditions that will undoubtedly spur at least some companies, schools, and hospitals to examine and overhaul their management practices. A call for "better management" may sound prosaic, but given the potential effect on incomes, productivity, and delivery of critically needed services worldwide, it's actually quite radical. ⬧ **HBR Reprint** R1211D

"Yes, I finally landed a corner office and, no, I'd rather not discuss it."

HBR.ORG

Harvard Business Review

NOVEMBER 2012
REPRINT R1211C

The Management Century

by Walter Kiechel III

SPOTLIGHT ON HBR AT 90

Spotlight

ARTWORK Man Ray, *Rayography "Champs délicieux" n°o8,* 1922, rayograph

Walter Kiechel III is a former editorial director of Harvard Business Publishing, a former managing editor of *Fortune,* and the author of *The Lords of Strategy* (Harvard Business Review Press, 2010).

The Management Century

by Walter Kiechel III

If you want to pinpoint a place and time that the first glints of the Management Century appeared on the horizon, you could do worse than Chicago, May 1886. There, to the recently formed American Society of Mechanical Engineers, Henry R. Towne, a cofounder of the Yale Lock Manufacturing Company, delivered an address titled "The Engineer as an Economist."

Towne argued that there were good engineers and good businessmen, but seldom were they one and the same. He went on to assert that "the *management of works* has become a matter of such great and far-reaching importance as perhaps to justify its classification also as one of the modern arts."

Towne's speech heralded a new reality in at least three respects. Call the first consciousness raising: Management was to be viewed as a set of practices that could be studied and improved. It was to be rooted in economics, which to this crowd meant achieving maximum efficiency with the resources provided. And the members of the audience were engineers. In the decades to come, such masters of the material universe, from Frederick Winslow Taylor to Michael Porter, Tom Peters, and Michael Hammer, would have a disproportionate effect on management's history.

Towne was catching a wave. During the century that followed, management as we know it would come into being and shape the world in which we work. Three eras punctuate the period from the 1880s until today. In the first, the years until World War II, aspirations to scientific exactitude gave wings to the ambitions of a new, self-proclaimed managerial elite. The second, from the late 1940s until about 1980, was managerialism's era of good feelings, its apogee of self-confidence and widespread public support. The third and ongoing era has been marked by a kind of retreat—into specialization, servitude to market forces, and declining moral ambitions. But it has also been an era of global triumph, measured by agreement on certain key ideas, steadily improving productivity, the worldwide march of the MBA degree, and a general elevation of expectations about how workers should be treated.

Americans and a few other Anglophones dominated management's early history, in the sense that their ideas on the subject gained the greatest cur-

rency. There were exceptions: In 1908 Henri Fayol, an engineer who had run one of France's largest mining companies, enumerated a list of management principles, which included a hierarchical chain of command, a separation of functions, and an emphasis on planning and budgeting. Still, his 1916 magnum opus, *Administration Industrielle et Générale,* took decades to be translated and to have much effect beyond France. Although globalization promises more-diverse sources of thinking on management, most of our story so far takes place in the United States. (See the sidebar "Saving Ourselves from Global Provincialism.")

The Age of "Scientific Management"

In the last two decades of the 19th century, the U.S. was shifting—uneasily—from a loosely connected world of small towns, small businesses, and agriculture to an industrialized network of cities, factories, and large companies linked by rail. A rising middle class was professionalizing—early incarnations of the American Medical Association and the American Bar Association date from this era—and mounting a progressive push against corrupt political bosses and the finance capitalists, who were busy consolidating industries such as oil and steel in the best robber-baron style.

Progressives claimed special wisdom rooted in science and captured in processes. Frederick Taylor, who wrote that "the best management is a true science, resting upon clearly defined laws, rules, and principles," clearly counted himself in their camp (fans such as Louis Brandeis and Ida Tarbell agreed). His stated goal was the "maximum prosperity for the employer, coupled with the maximum prosperity for each employee," through "a far more equal division of the responsibility between the management and the workmen." Translation (lest the reader overestimate Taylor's respect for workers' potential

Idea in Brief

In the early years of the last century, "improving the practice of management" meant making it more scientific.

A new managerial elite studied factory-floor operations and the psychology of workers. Managers streamlined operations and significantly increased productivity as a result.

In the middle years of the century, the study of management became more sophisticated and self-confident. Managers learned to think of corporations as social institutions and of employees as "knowledge workers." Executives started to apply the principles of strategy (conceived for warfare) to how companies were run.

Since 1980 businesses have faced extraordinary change, driven by global trade, emerging markets, and fast-developing information technology. In response to this disequilibrium, a "thought leadership" industry has evolved—but it has sometimes been hard to distinguish between profound insight and hyped-up trivia. One challenge going forward will be to define more fully what "good management" in the 21st century consists of.

---

contributions): The laborer should work according to a process analyzed and designed by management for optimum efficiency, "the one best way," allowing him to do as much as humanly possible within a specific time period.

The publication, in 1911, of Taylor's *Principles of Scientific Management*—originally a paper presented to that same American Society of Mechanical Engineers—set off a century-long quest for the right balance between the "things of production" and the "humanity of production," as the Englishman Oliver Sheldon put it in 1923. Or, as some would have it, between the "numbers people" and the "people people." It's the key tension that has defined management thinking.

The cartoon version of management history depicts the human relations movement, begun in the 1920s and 1930s, as a reaction to Taylor's relentless, reductive emphasis on the quantifiable. A better view regards the two as complementary. As evidence, consider the research of Elton Mayo and the other men behind the pathbreaking Hawthorne studies. Their work shares Taylor's overarching ambition to improve productivity and cooperation with management through the application of science, though in this case the science was psychology and, to a lesser extent, sociology.

The studies, which were mostly conducted at Western Electric's Hawthorne plant in Cicero, Illinois, began in 1924 and ran through 1932; eventually they involved other factories and other companies. The analysis was largely done at Harvard Business School, including outposts such as its Fatigue Lab. (If tired workers were the problem, how to design operations to lessen exhaustion but still achieve maximum output?) The Hawthorne studies were easily the most important social science research ever done on industry. The project is worth unpacking a bit, if only to dispel the popular myth about what was learned.

("They turned the lights up, productivity improved. They turned the lights down, same thing. Any sign of attention from management was enough to improve productivity.") Essentially the studies progressed through a succession of hypotheses, dismantling each one. Neither changes in physical conditions (better illumination), nor in work schedules (more rest breaks), nor even in incentive systems could fully explain why productivity steadily improved among a set of young women—always labeled "the girls"—assembling parts in a test room.

After years of experiments it began to dawn on Mayo, an Australian psychologist who had joined the HBS faculty, that at least two factors were driving the

> ## The Principles of Scientific Management
> *(1911) set off a century-long quest to balance "the things of production" and "the humanity of production."*

results. First, the women had forged themselves into a group, and group dynamics—members encouraging one another—were proving a strong determinant of output. Second, "the girls" had been consulted by the researchers at every step of the way: The intention of the experiment had been explained to them, and their suggestions had been solicited. From such heady stuff were distilled the basic insights of the human relations school—that workers were not mere automatons to be measured and goosed with a stopwatch; that it was probably helpful to inquire after what they knew and felt; and that a group had substantial control over how much it was prepared to produce.

Those insights sound humane, and they were. Still, the aim of the experiments was always to discover how psychology could be used to raise productivity, resist unionization, and increase workers' cooperation with management. Behind the effort of Taylor and the so-called "Harvard Circle" was an elitism, a class arrogance, almost incomprehensible by today's standards. Dean Wallace B. Donham, who founded HBR, ardently believed that an educated managerial cadre—a "new managing class"—was the answer to the nation's problems: to the Depression, to inept government, to social upheaval. He and others on the banks of the Charles looked down on the typical worker as a lesser being, one to be manipulated in service of higher purposes (or as Taylor said of the type of man best suited to load pig iron, "so stupid and so phlegmatic that he more nearly resembles in his mental make-up the ox").

Management Triumphant

Then into these stuffy rooms blew a blast of fresh, cleansing air. Call it Hurricane Drucker. Personal confession: Although I, like every other right-thinking student of management, have long tugged my forelock in ritual homage to the great man, I never fully appreciated what a revolutionary thinker he was until I steeped myself in the work of his predecessors.

The application of humanistic psychology to social institutions. Beginning with *Concept of the Corporation* (1946) and continuing through *The Practice of Management* (1954) and *Managing for Results* (1964), Peter Drucker laid out a vision of the corporation as a social institution—indeed, a social network—in which the capacity and potential of everyone involved were to be respected. Out with the vocabulary (and mind-set) of "boss," "foreman," and "worker"; in with "manager" and "employee." If Drucker didn't invent the concept of "management," he did more than anyone else to introduce the "m" word and all its iterations into how we think about running organizations.

Drucker didn't foment the managerial revolution alone. Fritz Roethlisberger, in his masterly 1937 summation of the Hawthorne experiments, described organizations as "social systems." Management's job, he stated, was to maintain their equilibrium. In the 1950s Drucker began to revive interest in the work of Mary Parker Follett, a largely forgotten figure from the 1920s whose ideas about management—"power with" rather than "power over," "constructive confrontation," and the pursuit of "win-win" solutions—found new resonance in the postwar era.

Others chimed in. Douglas McGregor, first as a management professor at MIT's Sloan School, then

PHOTOGRAPHY: © BETTMANN/CORBIS PORTRAITS: ANTONY HARE

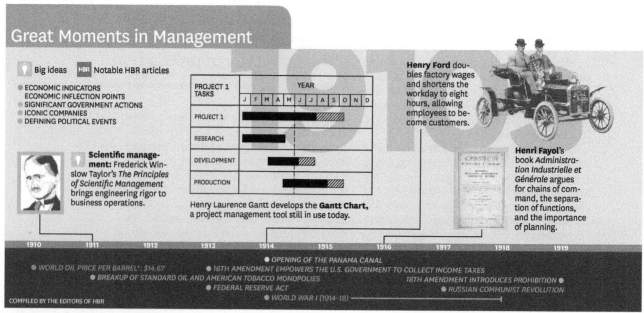

Great Moments in Management

💡 Big ideas   🅗🅑🅡 Notable HBR articles

- ECONOMIC INDICATORS
- ECONOMIC INFLECTION POINTS
- SIGNIFICANT GOVERNMENT ACTIONS
- ICONIC COMPANIES
- DEFINING POLITICAL EVENTS

Scientific management: Frederick Winslow Taylor's *The Principles of Scientific Management* brings engineering rigor to business operations.

PROJECT 1 TASKS	YEAR
	J F M A M J J A S O N D
PROJECT 1	
RESEARCH	
DEVELOPMENT	
PRODUCTION	

Henry Laurence Gantt develops the **Gantt Chart,** a project management tool still in use today.

Henry Ford doubles factory wages and shortens the workday to eight hours, allowing employees to become customers.

Henri Fayol's book *Administration Industrielle et Générale* argues for chains of command, the separation of functions, and the importance of planning.

| 1910 | 1911 | 1912 | 1913 | 1914 | 1915 | 1916 | 1917 | 1918 | 1919 |

- OPENING OF THE PANAMA CANAL
- WORLD OIL PRICE PER BARREL*: $14.67
- 16TH AMENDMENT EMPOWERS THE U.S. GOVERNMENT TO COLLECT INCOME TAXES
- BREAKUP OF STANDARD OIL AND AMERICAN TOBACCO MONOPOLIES
- 18TH AMENDMENT INTRODUCES PROHIBITION
- FEDERAL RESERVE ACT
- RUSSIAN COMMUNIST REVOLUTION
- WORLD WAR I (1914-18)

COMPILED BY THE EDITORS OF HBR

*IN U.S. DOLLARS, ADJUSTED TO 2011 VALUE. **IN 1990 INTERNATIONAL DOLLARS.

FOR ARTICLE REPRINTS CALL 800-988-0886 OR 617-783-7500, OR VISIT **HBR.ORG**

as the president of Antioch College, drew on the humanistic psychology of Abraham Maslow—he of the hierarchy of human needs—to propound the famous Theory X (people are inherently lazy and will shirk their duties if they aren't closely policed) and Theory Y (people want to find meaning in their work and will contribute in positive ways if the work is well designed). X and Y, McGregor took pains to assert, were "different cosmologies [that is, beliefs about the nature of man]...but not managerial strategies." To his dismay, nobody much listened to him on that detail.

The overall thrust of the postwar managerial thinkers was to elevate the "humanity of production." Workers will be most productive, the reasoning went, if they're respected and if managers rely on them to motivate themselves and solve problems on their own.

Not that the old order went down without a fight. After researching General Motors for *Concept of the Corporation*, Drucker persuaded rising GM executive Charlie Wilson to propose a set of reforms including greater autonomy for plant managers and what we'd call "worker empowerment" today. Two forces killed the idea. One was the rest of GM management,

including CEO Alfred P. Sloan. The other was the United Auto Workers, in the person of Walter Reuther, who wanted no blurring of the line between management and labor.

More-enlightened managerial attitudes combined with other forces—a democratization of American society following World War II; an explosion of deferred demand for economic goods—to usher in two decades of good spirits and seeming contentment with corporations and their conduct. The number of strikes and other job actions dropped precipitously from the nasty levels seen just after the war; union membership, as a percentage of the workforce, peaked and then began the long, slow decline that continues to this day. (Managerial solicitude was probably stimulated by an unemployment rate that fell below 3% in 1953.)

The rise of strategic thinking. In addition to its more-enlightened attitudes toward employees, the postwar period brought a heightened sense of what managers could accomplish. Here again Drucker led the way.

From our perch in the 21st century, when every company has a strategy and every executive a set of

PHOTOGRAPHY: HBS ARCHIVES, ALCATEL-LUCENT ARCHIVES, MURRAY HILL, NEW JERSEY

> *"The development, strengthening, and multiplication of socially minded business men is the central problem of business."* —DEAN WALLACE B. DONHAM

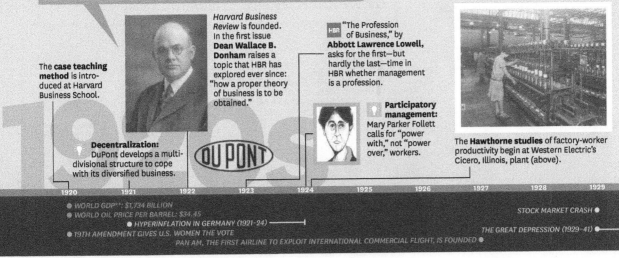

The **case teaching method** is introduced at Harvard Business School.

Harvard Business Review is founded. In the first issue **Dean Wallace B. Donham** raises a topic that HBR has explored ever since: "how a proper theory of business is to be obtained."

"The Profession of Business," by **Abbott Lawrence Lowell**, asks for the first—but hardly the last—time in HBR whether management is a profession.

Decentralization: DuPont develops a multidivisional structure to cope with its diversified business.

DUPONT

Participatory management: Mary Parker Follett calls for "power with," not "power over," workers.

The **Hawthorne studies** of factory-worker productivity begin at Western Electric's Cicero, Illinois, plant (above).

1920   1921   1922   1923   1924   1925   1926   1927   1928   1929

● WORLD GDP**: $1,734 BILLION
● WORLD OIL PRICE PER BARREL: $34.45   *STOCK MARKET CRASH* ●
● HYPERINFLATION IN GERMANY (1921-24)
● 19TH AMENDMENT GIVES U.S. WOMEN THE VOTE   *THE GREAT DEPRESSION (1929-41)* ●
        PAN AM, THE FIRST AIRLINE TO EXPLOIT INTERNATIONAL COMMERCIAL FLIGHT, IS FOUNDED ●

key objectives, it's difficult to comprehend the lack of direction that is said to have characterized earlier generations. But, as Drucker pointed out in *The Practice of Management,* "the early economist"—and, by implication, other students of management— "conceived of the businessman and his behavior as purely passive: success in business meant rapid and intelligent adaptation to events occurring outside, in an economy shaped by impersonal, objective forces that were neither controlled by the businessman nor influenced by his reaction to them." (Whether real-live businesspeople felt quite that powerless is debatable.)

This was not good enough, Drucker proclaimed. "[M]anagement has to manage. And managing is not just passive, adaptive behaviour." Managers had to take charge; they should be "attempting to change the economic environment...constantly pushing back the limitations of economic circumstances on the enterprise's freedom of action." To aid in the effort, he argued, managers should have objectives and should manage according to them.

Drucker's 1964 book, *Managing for Results,* set the bar higher, arguing that "businesses exist to produce results" and that managers should systematically scan their markets for opportunities to grow the enterprise. In a 1985 preface to a new edition, the author would claim that the book was the first one on business "strategy" but also recall that he and his publisher had been dissuaded from using that word.

Consultants felt no such hesitation. In 1963 Bruce Henderson, a former Westinghouse executive and a true American original, started what was to become the Boston Consulting Group. In short order the firm would take as its mission defining *corporate strategy*—before then the term had barely been used— and bringing the light of its gospel to corporations.

This was no mere shift in vocabulary. The rise of corporate strategy represented a bold new reach by those concerned with the "things of production." BCG's building-block concepts—the experience curve, the growth-share matrix—were enormously influential, but even more important was the analytical passion that lay underneath. The consultants insisted on delving into the numbers behind costs, customers, and competitors to a depth that few companies had plumbed before. Strategy's constant companion and facilitator was what I've elsewhere called Greater Taylorism—the imperative to take a sharp pencil and a stopwatch not just to some poor schlub's daily labor but to every aspect of the company's operations.

Strategy was aggressive. The point of gathering all those numbers was to figure out where you stood in

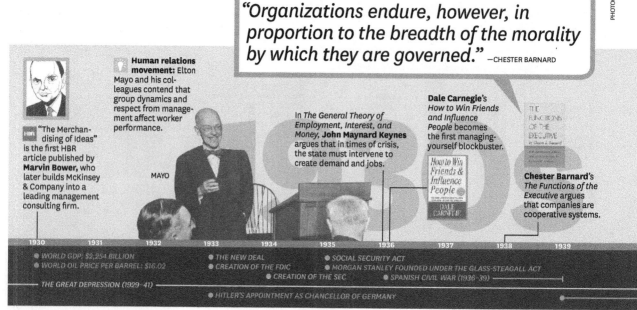

"*Organizations endure, however, in proportion to the breadth of the morality by which they are governed.*" —CHESTER BARNARD

"The Merchandising of Ideas" is the first HBR article published by **Marvin Bower,** who later builds McKinsey & Company into a leading management consulting firm.

Human relations movement: Elton Mayo and his colleagues contend that group dynamics and respect from management affect worker performance.

MAYO

In *The General Theory of Employment, Interest, and Money,* **John Maynard Keynes** argues that in times of crisis, the state must intervene to create demand and jobs.

Dale Carnegie's *How to Win Friends and Influence People* becomes the first managing-yourself blockbuster.

Chester Barnard's *The Functions of the Executive* argues that companies are cooperative systems.

| 1930 | 1931 | 1932 | 1933 | 1934 | 1935 | 1936 | 1937 | 1938 | 1939 |

- WORLD GDP: $2,254 BILLION
- WORLD OIL PRICE PER BARREL: $16.02
- THE NEW DEAL
- CREATION OF THE FDIC
- CREATION OF THE SEC
- SOCIAL SECURITY ACT
- MORGAN STANLEY FOUNDED UNDER THE GLASS-STEAGALL ACT
- SPANISH CIVIL WAR (1936–39)
- THE GREAT DEPRESSION (1929–41)
- HITLER'S APPOINTMENT AS CHANCELLOR OF GERMANY

FOR ARTICLE REPRINTS CALL 800-988-0886 OR 617-783-7500, OR VISIT **HBR.ORG**

Saving Ourselves from Global Provincialism

The worldwide lingua franca of management is English—at least until Chinese takes its place. English is also the dominant language of management literature.

Although the French have their *grandes écoles* and the Japanese their celebrated "Toyota way," most of the managerial ideas that make it into print arrive courtesy of Anglophones. Thinkers born outside the U.S. or Great Britain who achieve gurudom—Kenichi Ohmae, C.K. Prahalad, W. Chan Kim—have typically spent time at an English-speaking university or consulting firm.

Where are the voices of indigenous Indian, Chinese, and African business leaders who have original ideas, rooted in their cultures, to add new perspectives to the worldwide conversation about management? So far they're found mostly in interviews with CEOs of successful global companies. But then, most CEOs aren't management thinkers first and foremost.

Expect to see more ideas bubbling up through at least two channels as heretofore Western notions of management spread. The first is the academy. The best estimates indicate that more than 100,000 MBAs and other graduate management degrees are awarded in India each year, almost all from programs conducted in English. Second, consulting firms such as McKinsey and the Boston Consulting Group are now authentically global organizations, with their leadership and the bulk of their revenue coming from outside the U.S. If partners get to the point where they aren't so busy building their firms' practices in new lands, perhaps they'll start capturing some of what they've learned and translating it into articles and books.

relation to competitors and how you might seize advantage over them. With graphs and diagrams, BCG relentlessly brought home the importance of being number one or number two in your line of business.

By 1967, when John Kenneth Galbraith published *The New Industrial State,* some had begun to worry that American companies and their leadership had perhaps become *too* aggressive. Galbraith decried the fact that firms had grown so large and successful—by 1974 the 200 largest U.S. manufacturing companies controlled two-thirds of the country's manufacturing assets and more than three-fifths of its sales, employment, and income. He argued that social goals increasingly were adapted to corporate goals. A largely anonymous "technostructure" of business leaders could dictate to consumers what to buy and, implicitly, how to live—or so the theory went.

The Era of Nervous Globalism

After two decades without serious recession, the oil shocks of the 1970s and an accompanying economic malaise put paid to the notion of managerialism triumphant. A 1966 Harris poll had found 55% of Americans voicing "a great deal of confidence" in the leaders of large companies. By 1975 the percentage had dropped to 15.

Forces for change. Multiple new forces confronted American executives, unleashing heightened competition and eventually disrupting the relative amity that had prevailed among business, labor, and government.

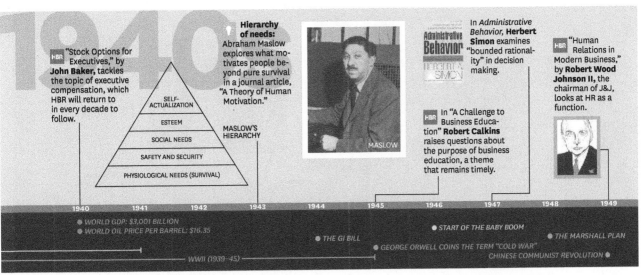

"Stock Options for Executives," by **John Baker,** tackles the topic of executive compensation, which HBR will return to in every decade to follow.

Hierarchy of needs: Abraham Maslow explores what motivates people beyond pure survival in a journal article, "A Theory of Human Motivation."

MASLOW'S HIERARCHY

SELF-ACTUALIZATION
ESTEEM
SOCIAL NEEDS
SAFETY AND SECURITY
PHYSIOLOGICAL NEEDS (SURVIVAL)

MASLOW

In *Administrative Behavior,* **Herbert Simon** examines "bounded rationality" in decision making.

In "A Challenge to Business Education" **Robert Calkins** raises questions about the purpose of business education, a theme that remains timely.

"Human Relations in Modern Business," by **Robert Wood Johnson II,** the chairman of J&J, looks at HR as a function.

1940 1941 1942 1943 1944 1945 1946 1947 1948 1949

● WORLD GDP: $3,001 BILLION
● WORLD OIL PRICE PER BARREL: $16.35
● START OF THE BABY BOOM
● THE GI BILL ● THE MARSHALL PLAN
● GEORGE ORWELL COINS THE TERM "COLD WAR"
CHINESE COMMUNIST REVOLUTION ●
WWII (1939–45)

In an attempt to fight runaway inflation, U.S. President Jimmy Carter launched efforts to deregulate airlines, railroads, and trucking. His successors would leap onto the deregulatory bandwagon, turning their attention to telecommunications and finance. Meanwhile, U.S. attempts to encourage global trade were succeeding all too well. As imported cars, steel, and consumer electronics piled into domestic markets, doubts snuck in, too: "Could it be that a bunch of foreigners, particularly the Japanese, know more about management than we do?"

Technology, especially computer technology, steadily increased the calculating power available to the numbers people, in the form of the integrated circuit (late 1950s), the minicomputer (mid 1960s), the microprocessor (early 1970s), and then the microcomputer (mid 1970s), soon to morph into the ubiquitous PC. Greater Taylorism, launched in the era of slide rules, had found the means to create ever more precise models of how a business should perform.

As stocks began to heat up again in 1982—it had taken the Dow Jones Industrial Average 10 years to crawl back to its 1972 high of 1,000—a lively market

for corporate control developed. Old constraints against hostile takeovers fell away, new sources of funds became available to potential acquirers (think junk bonds), and financiers realized there was money to be made in buying up companies that had a dog's breakfast of businesses and selling off the parts. More than 25% of the firms on the *Fortune* 500 list in 1980 were acquired by 1989.

Shareholder capitalism's ascent over stakeholder capitalism. During this period of intense change, the purpose of strategy, and indeed of corporate management, took on new clarity: It was to create wealth for shareholders. To be sure, that idea had always been around, dating back to the buccaneering financiers of the 19th century. But during management's era of good feelings, a more inclusive notion had taken root in some quarters. As Michael Lind notes in *Land of Promise,* his recent economic history of the United States, in 1951 the chairman of Standard Oil of New Jersey had proclaimed, "The job of management is to maintain an equitable and working balance among the claims of the various directly affected interest groups...stockholders, employees, customers, and the public at large." Some-

> *"There is only one valid definition of business purpose: To create a customer."* —PETER DRUCKER

In *The Changing Culture of a Factory,* organizational psychologist **Elliott Jaques** suggests that managers should be measured on the long-term impact of their decisions.

"Barriers and Gateways to Communication," by **Carl Rogers** (above) and **F.J. Roethlisberger,** applies insights from psychotherapy to managerial work.

"How to Deal with Resistance to Change," by **Paul Lawrence,** introduces the notion that implementing change in organizations is an uphill battle.

LAWRENCE

Peter Drucker's *Concept of the Corporation* (1946), *The Practice of Management* (1954), and *Managing for Results* (1964) develop a more humanistic vocabulary for management.

| 1950 | 1951 | 1952 | 1953 | 1954 | 1955 | 1956 | 1957 | 1958 | 1959 |

● WORLD GDP: $4,082 BILLION
● WORLD OIL PRICE PER BARREL: $15.97
● BROWN V. BOARD OF EDUCATION
● SOVIET LAUNCH OF SPUTNIK
● FOUNDING OF NASA
● MCDONALD'S OPENS ITS FIRST FRANCHISE
CASTRO'S RISE TO POWER IN CUBA ●
● KOREAN WAR (1950–53)
● VIETNAM WAR (1954–75)

FOR ARTICLE REPRINTS CALL 800-988-0886 OR 617-783-7500, OR VISIT **HBR.ORG**

How to *Really* Get Management's Attention

One constant throughout the century has been that corporate leadership focuses on the wants and needs of employees in direct proportion to the scarcity of labor.

times labeled "stakeholder capitalism," this broader-minded conception would be steadily chipped away at by partisans of "shareholder capitalism," to the point that it almost disappeared from discussions of corporate purpose.

Management thinkers responded to the new pressures besetting corporations by sharpening their focus. With his 1980 book, *Competitive Strategy,* Michael Porter did more than anyone else to give strategy an academic rigor it sometimes lacked among consultants. His next book, *Competitive Advantage* (1985), would arm companies with concepts such as the value chain, enabling them to break down every stage of their operations into units that could be costed out, benchmarked, and measured for competitiveness.

As the economy quickened and the deal making and excitement on Wall Street mounted, more people sought to join the ranks of management—or at least to obtain the entry credential, the MBA, whose luster was burnished by the salaries paid degree-holders by investment banks and management consulting firms. Some 26,000 MBAs had been awarded in the United States in 1970; by 1985 the number was up to 67,000.

At business schools, strategy experts such as Porter displaced the faculty who had been teaching "business policy." Professors of finance assumed greater pride of place, shoving toward the periphery teachers of the "softer" subjects—human behavior, organizational dynamics—once central to Don-

World War I took about 5 million men out of the workforce temporarily, and when it ended, the gates slammed shut against the tide of low-cost immigrant labor. Only shortly after that did social science initiatives such as the Hawthorne studies try to divine what was on workers' minds.

Labor shortages during World War II, combined with wage controls, prompted companies to begin offering health insurance benefits to employees, saddling the U.S. with the employment-based system that bedevils us today.

In 2001 three McKinsey consultants published *The War for Talent.* The book reflected the fact that during the internet boom of the prior few years, corporate management had become worried that a lack of tech-savvy employees would limit their companies' growth or leave their business models at risk. But with the popping of the tech bubble, the talent war was mostly called

off—or it was fought selectively—and swaths of what had once been thought of as talent were mowed down by layoffs.

These days solicitude can be even more finely targeted, with business analytics enabling companies to parse their human resources to precisely identify which individuals or positions generate the most profit. To hear one executive at a corporation renowned for its HR prowess tell it, "We want someone with just the right skills exactly when we need them, and no longer than that." During the recent recession many companies discovered that they could indeed do just fine with fewer employees than they'd had in the past—leaving only the question of where these lean, mean enterprises are to find enough customers with well-paying jobs to buy their products.

PHOTOGRAPHY: HESS ARCHIVES

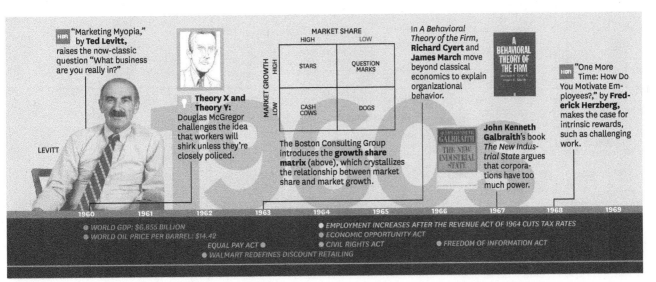

"Marketing Myopia," by **Ted Levitt,** raises the now-classic question "What business are you really in?"

LEVITT

Theory X and Theory Y: Douglas McGregor challenges the idea that workers will shirk unless they're closely policed.

MARKET SHARE
HIGH — LOW

MARKET GROWTH — HIGH / LOW

| STARS | QUESTION MARKS |
| CASH COWS | DOGS |

The Boston Consulting Group introduces the **growth share matrix** (above), which crystallizes the relationship between market share and market growth.

In *A Behavioral Theory of the Firm,* **Richard Cyert** and **James March** move beyond classical economics to explain organizational behavior.

A BEHAVIORAL THEORY OF THE FIRM

John Kenneth Galbraith's book *The New Industrial State* argues that corporations have too much power.

"One More Time: How Do You Motivate Employees?," by **Frederick Herzberg,** makes the case for intrinsic rewards, such as challenging work.

1960 — 1961 — 1962 — 1963 — 1964 — 1965 — 1966 — 1967 — 1968 — 1969

● WORLD GDP: $6.855 BILLION
● WORLD OIL PRICE PER BARREL: $14.42
EQUAL PAY ACT ●
● WALMART REDEFINES DISCOUNT RETAILING

● EMPLOYMENT INCREASES AFTER THE REVENUE ACT OF 1964 CUTS TAX RATES
● ECONOMIC OPPORTUNITY ACT
● CIVIL RIGHTS ACT   ● FREEDOM OF INFORMATION ACT

ham's and Mayo's visions of management education. Across the board, both in the corporate world and in academics, the numbers people seemed to be winning, bringing greater quantitative precision to increasingly specialized domains of expertise.

But they weren't necessarily winning the hearts of the wider managerial population. In 1982 two McKinsey consultants, Tom Peters and Bob Waterman, published *In Search of Excellence.* It was a paean to the importance of culture in organizations, an attack on strategy as a merely quantitative exercise, and a celebration of the human element in making companies successful. "Soft is hard," Peters observed. The book sold more than 6 million copies, astonishing its authors and alerting the publishing industry to the existence of a huge audience for books on managerial wisdom. It didn't hurt that *Excellence* extolled U.S. companies and their practices, this shortly before President Ronald Reagan would announce "It's morning again in America" and well after everyone outside Japan had grown tired of being lectured on the superiority of that country's management methods.

For the next 30 years, right down to our own day, the two strains of thought—the numbers-driven push for greater profitability, and the cry for more respect for the "humanity of production"—would coexist in uneasy tension. And not just on the commanding heights of management thought, where ideas, books, gurus, and academics battle for attention. The debate has also taken place in conference rooms and offices—and in the minds of executives deliberating tough choices—where the fates of businesses, and people, are decided.

Fueled by tax cuts and deficit spending under President Reagan, the U.S. economy surged ahead after 1982. But, unlike in the 1950s, this rising tide didn't lift all boats. In the name of beating foreign competition, completing (or avoiding) takeovers, and serving the interests of shareholders, it became acceptable to sell off businesses that didn't fit the new corporate strategy and to lay off battalions of workers. Most famously at General Electric under Jack Welch, the old employer-employee contract, with its implicit assurance of something like lifetime employment, was ripped up. And the stock market cheered, as did many an individual investor lured back into the action by rising share prices and a dazzling variety of mutual funds, 401(k) plans, and individual retirement accounts.

Management literature provided the intellectual undergirding for the new aggressiveness. Since the 1960s, strategists had sounded a wake-up call about the need to know your competition, an adjuration almost totally neglected by the big thinkers of the prior era. Exploiting tools such as the Freedom of Information Act (1966) and databases such as Lexis-Nexis (1970s), consultants helped clients fill in the details to see how their situations fit the frameworks devised by Porter and others.

In two notable HBR articles in the 1980s, Michael Jensen resurrected agency theory, providing

PHOTOGRAPHY: TSUTOMU SUYAMA

In *The Concept of Corporate Strategy,* **Kenneth Andrews** identifies strategy as the primary work of executives.

HBR "Evolution and Revolution as Organizations Grow," by **Larry Greiner,** posits that organizations go through predictable developmental stages.

HBR "The Manager's Job: Folklore and Fact," by **Henry Mintzberg,** reveals how managers use intuition and relationships in their work.

Agency theory: Michael Jensen (above) and William Meckling introduce the idea that managers' and stockholders' interests need to be aligned.

Rosabeth Moss Kanter publishes *Men and Women of the Corporation,* a landmark work on corporate power as it relates to women.

KANTER

THE FIVE FORCES

POTENTIAL ENTRANTS

SUPPLIERS → INDUSTRY COMPETITORS ← BUYERS

SUBSTITUTES

HBR "How Competitive Forces Shape Strategy," by **Michael Porter,** outlines the five forces that affect competitive positioning.

1970 · 1971 · 1972 · 1973 · 1974 · 1975 · 1976 · 1977 · 1978 · 1979

● WORLD GDP: $12,138 Billion
● WORLD OIL PRICE PER BARREL: $10.42
● OCCUPATIONAL SAFETY AND HEALTH ACT
CHINA JOINS THE UN ●
● OPEC OIL EMBARGO SETS OFF ERA OF STAGFLATION
● ELECTRONIC CREDIT-CARD AUTHORIZATION BEGINS
● WATERGATE SCANDAL (1972–74)
─ VIETNAM WAR (1954–75) ─
● AIRLINE DEREGULATION ACT
CHINA PERMITS FOREIGN DIRECT INVESTMENT ●
IRAN HOSTAGE CRISIS (1979–81) ●

Who Made You the Boss?

One question that has percolated throughout the Management Century, sometimes just below the surface, is, What are the sources, moral and otherwise, of a corporate executive's authority?

We know how Frederick Taylor would have answered ("his superior knowledge of scientific management") and what Wallace Donham would have said ("his membership in an educated, civic-minded elite"). But in an era when many forward-looking organizations aspire to flatter structures and distributed decision making, deference to authority based merely on a place in the hierarchy seems outmoded, hypocritical, or even comic (take a look at *Dilbert* or any episode of *The Office*, British or American).

The source-of-authority question presents itself with equal or greater urgency to those at the top of the political, educational, and financial heaps. Answers built on efficacy ("she gets results") or even inspiration ("he provides a vision") lack the moral resonance earlier managerial generations would have hoped for. Recovering or reimagining authentic, satisfying sources of executive authority will be high on the to-do list for management's next century.

a rationale for takeover activity. The idea held that although companies existed to enrich shareholders, too often their managers developed interests of their own, particularly if they didn't have a sufficiently large ownership stake in the enterprise. To keep their eyes on the prize, they needed both the stick of potentially being acquired and the carrot of incentives linked to stock price.

Conveniently, in 1993 the U.S. Congress changed the tax code to encourage the grant of stock options as executive compensation. As Lind points out, by the end of the decade more than half the payout to the typical *Fortune* 500 executive took that form. So what if the ratio of CEO pay to that of the humble cubicle worker was climbing to Olympian heights? Think of all the value the CEO was creating. OK, per-

haps this wasn't the kind of moral leadership that Wallace Donham had had in mind for the managerial class, but he was long dead, his voice largely forgotten.

With the reengineering movement, the imperative to exploit the latest information technology turbocharged the push for efficiency and competitiveness. Obliterate your existing processes, admonished Michael Hammer in a celebrated 1990 HBR article and then with coauthor James Champy in a best-selling book. Redesign them with your ultimate customer in view, the sight line provided by the wonders of new electronic communications. Companies flocked to reengineering's banner, but too often merely as a lofty-sounding justification for layoffs. Eventually so many corporate innocents had been

PHOTOGRAPHY: EVGENIA ELISEEVA

"Strategy is about making choices, trade-offs; it's about deliberately choosing to be different." —MICHAEL PORTER

Michael Porter's *Competitive Strategy* (1980) and *Competitive Advantage* (1985) bring new rigor to the study of strategy.

"Managing Our Way to Economic Decline," by **Robert Hayes** and **William Abernathy,** delivers a scathing critique of U.S. managers' focus on short-term financial gain.

Tom Peters and **Robert Waterman Jr.**'s *In Search of Excellence* lionizes strong organizational cultures.

"Quality on the Line," by **David Garvin,** describes the results of a two-year study revealing huge differences in quality between U.S. and Japanese manufacturers.

"Management Women and the New Facts of Life," by **Felice Schwartz,** starts a conversation about "the mommy track," though those words don't appear in the article.

"The Discipline of Innovation," by **Peter Drucker,** offers a systematic approach to the creative process.

1980 | 1981 | 1982 | 1983 | 1984 | 1985 | 1986 | 1987 | 1988 | 1989

● WORLD GDP: $18,818 BILLION
● WORLD OIL PRICE PER BARREL: $100.54
● FIRING OF AIR TRAFFIC CONTROLLERS
● CHRYSLER TURNS ITSELF AROUND WITH MASSIVE GOVERNMENT ASSISTANCE (1980-83)
● UNION CARBIDE POISON GAS LEAK IN BHOPAL, INDIA
● BREAKUP OF AT&T
● BLACK MONDAY ON THE NYSE
● REAGANOMICS (TAX REFORM ACT OF 1986)
S&L BANK BAILOUT ●
FALL OF THE BERLIN WALL ●

slaughtered in its name that the movement was discredited, to be held up later as a chief example of a management fad gone horribly wrong.

The shift toward leadership and innovation. Advocates for the humanity of production, meanwhile, pursued a blurrier line. Within a couple of years of the publication of *In Search of Excellence,* *BusinessWeek* reported that a third of the companies held up in the book no longer met the authors' criteria for superiority. This embarrassment suggested a more general confusion that was to dog the humanists—namely, just what were the managerial practices that would bring out the best from employees, and how were they to be measured and their value to the company calculated?

Strategy at least had a fairly clear paradigm and set of frameworks for successive generations of thinkers to build on. Champions of shareholder value gloried in their single yardstick, the stock price, as the measure of all things. By comparison, students of human behavior in organizations were all over the landscape. Scholars in the field decried what one of them, Jeffrey Pfeffer, called its "fairly low level of paradigm development" and the fact that they couldn't agree among themselves about which problems most needed to be addressed.

Such eclecticism, to put it charitably, was mirrored on the list of business best sellers. Books on how to be a learning organization jostled with ones on the wisdom of teams, the power of corporate loyalty, the necessity of core competences, the impor-

tance of delighting customers, and the imperative to navigate change, as in figuring out who'd moved your cheese.

If the thinking on the human side coalesced at all, it was around two themes: leadership and innovation. Over the last two decades of the 20th century, business schools revised their mission from "educating general managers" to "helping leaders develop." Unfortunately, despite some inspiring writing on how leaders differ from managers, no consensus has formed on exactly what constitutes a leader or how those exalted beings come to exist. (The current downturn has raised questions about corporate leaders' sources of authority as well. See the sidebar "Who Made You the Boss?")

Innovation invites less controversy. Both humanists and numbers people recognize its critical, company-saving importance in an era when new rivals can emerge suddenly from nowhere, industry leadership can change hands in a trice, and competitive advantages once thought unassailable are eroded in months. Books by Richard Foster and Clayton Christensen demonstrated to a wide managerial audience how new technologies systematically displace old ones, in the process overthrowing the pecking order of entire industries.

Innovation is where satisfying the fierce demands of the market depends, as never before, on eliciting the best from the humanity of production. No one yet appears to have been able to automate the invention of the new or to come up with ma-

PHOTOGRAPHY: GANGFENG WANG

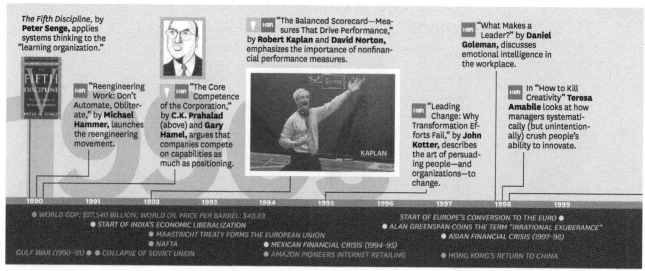

The Fifth Discipline, by **Peter Senge,** applies systems thinking to the "learning organization."

"Reengineering Work: Don't Automate, Obliterate," by **Michael Hammer,** launches the reengineering movement.

"The Core Competence of the Corporation," by **C.K. Prahalad** (above) and **Gary Hamel,** argues that companies compete on capabilities as much as positioning.

"The Balanced Scorecard—Measures That Drive Performance," by **Robert Kaplan** and **David Norton,** emphasizes the importance of nonfinancial performance measures.

KAPLAN

"Leading Change: Why Transformation Efforts Fail," by **John Kotter,** describes the art of persuading people—and organizations—to change.

"What Makes a Leader?" by **Daniel Goleman,** discusses emotional intelligence in the workplace.

In "How to Kill Creativity" **Teresa Amabile** looks at how managers systematically (but unintentionally) crush people's ability to innovate.

| 1990 | 1991 | 1992 | 1993 | 1994 | 1995 | 1996 | 1997 | 1998 | 1999 |

● WORLD GDP: $27,540 BILLION; WORLD OIL PRICE PER BARREL: $40.83   START OF EUROPE'S CONVERSION TO THE EURO ●
● START OF INDIA'S ECONOMIC LIBERALIZATION   ● ALAN GREENSPAN COINS THE TERM "IRRATIONAL EXUBERANCE"
● MAASTRICHT TREATY FORMS THE EUROPEAN UNION   ● ASIAN FINANCIAL CRISIS (1997–98)
● NAFTA   ● MEXICAN FINANCIAL CRISIS (1994–95)
GULF WAR (1990–91) ● ● COLLAPSE OF SOVIET UNION   ● AMAZON PIONEERS INTERNET RETAILING   ● HONG KONG'S RETURN TO CHINA

   SOURCES WORLD GDP: "ESTIMATES OF WORLD GDP, ONE MILLION B.C.–PRESENT," J. BRADFORD DE LONG, DEPARTMENT OF ECONOMICS, U.C. BERKELEY, 1998. WORLD OIL PRICES: BP STATISTICAL REVIEW OF WORLD ENERGY, 2012.

FOR ARTICLE REPRINTS CALL 800-988-0886 OR 617-783-7500, OR VISIT **HBR.ORG**

chine-replicable substitutes for the spark of human imagination. Perhaps the biggest managerial challenge facing the 21st-century company will be finding ways to free that spark, resident in employees, from the organization's tidal pull to keep doing the same old things.

THE AGE OF MANAGEMENT isn't over, of course. Management thought is spreading to wherever capitalism and more-or-less free markets find a home. By some counts that home has welcomed 3 billion new inhabitants over the past two decades, with the fall of Soviet communism and the economic liberalization of China and India. Capitalism and the managerial ideas that struggle to make it more productive have indisputably rendered the world richer and better educated. And not just the capitalist and managerial elite, including the estimated half million people awarded an MBA or its foreign equivalent last year: The percentage of people worldwide living below the poverty line has dropped dramatically in the past 50 years, while literacy rates have steadily climbed.

In the world of offices, factories, stores, and even cubicle farms, particularly those of large organizations, people expect to be treated with fairness and respect (even if their long-term job security is less assured). Blatant sexism, naked bullying, and outrageous managerial behavior are more likely to be called out, even if they haven't been totally eliminated. Upon going through the front door of a company almost anywhere in the capitalist world,

a visitor can typically assume that certain rules will be followed, certain procedures observed.

True, managerialism hasn't solved all the problems in the workplace. Most notably, it hasn't figured out a way to employ everyone who wants a job, though achieving that goal probably requires the efforts of government and economists as well, along with a public consensus. Ironies, occasionally cruel, have accompanied managerialism's rise. As Peter Drucker observed, when he was a boy growing up in Vienna the people who put in the longest hours were those at the bottom of the economic ladder—the lady's maid expected to wait up for her mistress to return home from the opera. Nowadays it's the executive elite, fielding 300 e-mails a day and calls from around the world, who toil into the night.

And managerialism's work is not finished. Because management is, finally, about how to make humans and their organizations more effective—and because humans stubbornly cling to their propensity to be, well, human—there will never be "the one best way." But there's almost always a better way. Management will keep looking for it. ▢

HBR Reprint R1211C

> "If you only do what worked in the past, you will wake up one day and find that you've been passed by." —CLAYTON CHRISTENSEN

MARKET PYRAMID

PURCHASING POWER		POPULATION (China)
>$20,000	TIER 1	2 million
$10,000 to $20,000	TIER 2	60 million
$5,000 to $10,000	TIER 3	330 million
<$5,000	TIER 4	800 million

In "The End of Corporate Imperialism," **C.K. Prahalad** and **Kenneth Lieberthal** note the huge business opportunities near the bottom of the pyramid.

In *Creative Destruction*, **Richard Foster** and **Sarah Kaplan** explain how companies can better sustain their performance by acting more like markets.

Disruptive innovation: Clayton Christensen explains how disruptive technologies cause great firms to fail.

Analytics: Thomas Davenport and others examine firms whose competitive advantage comes from understanding data better.

"How GE Is Disrupting Itself," by **Jeffrey Immelt, Vijay Govindarajan,** and **Chris Trimble,** introduces the idea of "reverse innovation."

2000 2001 2002 2003 2004 2005 2006 2007 2008 2009 2010 2011

- WORLD GDP: $41,017 BILLION; WORLD OIL PRICE PER BARREL: $37.22
- DOT-COM BUBBLE BURSTS AFTER NASDAQ PEAK OF 5046.86
- SEPTEMBER 11 ATTACKS ON WORLD TRADE CENTER AND PENTAGON
- START OF U.S. WAR IN AFGHANISTAN
- CHINA JOINS THE WTO
- IRAQ WAR (2003-11)
- FACEBOOK IS FOUNDED, AND SOCIAL NETWORKING TAKES OFF
- CHINA PASSES JAPAN AS THE WORLD'S SECOND-LARGEST ECONOMY
- GREAT RECESSION (2007-09)
- TOYOTA DISPLACES GM AS THE #1 AUTOMAKER
- ARAB SPRING BEGINS IN TUNISIA

CHAPTER 2

The Evolution of Management Thought

Learning Objectives

After studying this chapter, you should be able to:

LO2-1 Describe how the need to increase organizational efficiency and effectiveness has guided the evolution of management theory.

LO2-2 Explain the principle of job specialization and division of labor, and tell why the study of person–task relationships is central to the pursuit of increased efficiency.

LO2-3 Identify the principles of administration and organization that underlie effective organizations.

LO2-4 Trace the changes in theories about how managers should behave to motivate and control employees.

LO2-5 Explain the contributions of management science to the efficient use of organizational resources.

LO2-6 Explain why the study of the external environment and its impact on an organization has become a central issue in management thought.

A MANAGER'S CHALLENGE

Simplifying Business Strategies at GE

What is the best way to maintain a competitive edge? More than ever before, companies must learn how to adapt and remain competitive in a changing global marketplace. And sometimes companies have to completely re-think their corporate strategies when their business becomes too diverse and somewhat unwieldy. General Electric is one example of a company that grew at a fast pace by acquiring different types of businesses. However, in recent years, senior management has made some strategic moves to simplify its business mix in an effort to increase value to shareholders and to position the company for continued success.

The company was created in 1892 from the merger of two companies: the Edison General Electric Company and the Thomas-Houston Company. (It is the only company included in the original 1896 Dow Jones Industrial Index that is still included today.) Thomas Edison and Charles Coffin pioneered the development of the incandescent lightbulb, which heats a filament wire, using electricity, until it emits light. The filament is protected from oxidation by a glass bulb that contains inert gas or a vacuum. GE was not the first company to produce and sell such bulbs and related electrical equipment. However, Edison and Coffin used their combined expertise and patents to produce practical, affordable lightbulbs relatively easily, which gave them a competitive advantage.

Originally, GE produced lightbulbs and related electrical equipment at its headquarters in Schenectady, New York. Over the years it expanded to serve customers in more than 160 nations with a lineup of multiple businesses and several hundred products. To do this, GE draws on the talents of more than 300,000 employees.

GE's birth as a merger established a pattern for quick growth by diversifying its businesses through merger and acquisition of other firms, as well as development of new business

GE CEO Jeffrey Immelt has refocused the company's competitive strategies by simplifying its business mix.
© Bloomberg/Getty Images

portfolios. In 1911 GE bought the National Electric Lamp Association, which strengthened its distribution and product portfolio. A few short years later, in 1919, GE formed the Radio Corporation of America (RCA). RCA was intended to operate as a retailer for General Electric's radios but grew into a large business of its own. Since then, GE has diversified into aircraft engines, computers, medical technology, entertainment, wind power, appliances, and even petroleum extraction products. It also branched out into banking and financial services as part of its growth strategy.

One challenge inherent in this growth is the incredible complexity of managing multiple businesses in different industries across the globe. As businesses like GE grow in size and scope, they often become cumbersome to manage. To be consistent across operations, these businesses can become highly formalized and bureaucratic. This management style enables a company to maintain control over its operations. However, it can also impede the company's ability to respond to changing market dynamics and is likely to hinder innovation. Because GE competes in multiple industries, it must work hard to stay agile in the face of multiple competitors and a large global footprint.

Large companies also struggle to maintain a competitive edge with innovation because new products or offerings must be approved by layers of formal bureaucracy, which slows down the process. Because companies often compete to bring products to market first, the size and formal bureaucracy of an organization can be a stumbling block. For example, even though a GE engineer, Edward Hammer, developed the spiral compact fluorescent light (CFL) in the 1970s, GE's management decided to shelve the project due to cost concerns. Today incandescent bulbs are being phased out in favor of CFLs, and GE has lost ground to competitors like Philips.

It is this competitive and challenging business environment that caused General Electric CEO Jeffrey Immelt and his management team to take a long, critical look at the company's diverse portfolio of businesses and make some drastic changes. Focusing on the goal of becoming a "digital industrial company," Immelt has simplified GE's business by selling off GE Capital (sold to various financial entities for more than $200 billion); its home appliance business (sold to China's Haier for more than $5 billion); its share of NBCUniversal (sold to Comcast for $16.7 billion), and other businesses that no longer fit the industrial focus Immelt sees as fertile ground for GE's future success.[1]

But GE is not just shedding businesses for the sake of becoming lean and mean. It's also buying companies that support Immelt's vision of a digital industrial company. In 2015 GE completed its largest acquisition ever, buying Alstom, a French power and grid business, for more than $9 billion. GE believes that Alstom will extend the company's global reach in the power generation business. In addition, the company recently announced the creation of Current—a start-up business that will focus on developing products and services in energy efficiency for large customers, like hospitals, universities, retailers, and even cities.[2]

Time will tell whether GE's dramatic simplification will help keep the company on a continued path of success. According to Immelt, GE is leaving a world of disconnected businesses, financial spreadsheets, and bureaucratic workflows and taking a giant leap to agile teams that are mission-based. He also acknowledges that he needs to make the "new" GE a place where young, talented leaders will want to work and continue to innovate. In this digital, quick-paced business environment, he believes that speed and simplification are synonymous with quality and innovation. For GE to succeed, a culture of simplification is essential for investors, customers, and employees.[3]

Overview

As this sketch of the evolution of management thinking at GE suggests, changes in management practices occur as managers, theorists, researchers, and customers look for ways to increase how efficiently and effectively products can be made. The driving force behind the evolution of management theory is the search for better ways to use organizational resources to make goods and services. Advances in management thought typically occur as managers and researchers find better ways to perform the principal management tasks: planning, organizing, leading, and controlling human and other organizational resources.

In this chapter we examine how management thought has evolved in modern times and the central concerns that have guided ongoing advances in management theory. First we examine the so-called classical management theories that emerged around the turn of the 20th century. These include scientific management, which focuses on matching people and tasks to maximize efficiency, and administrative management, which focuses on identifying the principles that will lead to the creation of the most efficient system of organization and management. Next we consider behavioral management theories, developed both before and after World War II; these focus on how managers should lead and control their workforces to increase performance. Then we discuss management science theory, which developed during World War II and has become increasingly important as researchers have developed rigorous analytical and quantitative techniques to help managers measure and control organizational performance. Finally, we discuss changes in management practices from the middle to the late 20th century and focus on the theories developed to help explain how the external environment affects the way organizations and managers operate.

By the end of this chapter you will understand how management thought and theory have evolved over time. You will also understand how economic, political, and cultural forces have affected the development of these theories and how managers and their organizations have changed their behavior as a result. In Figure 2.1 we summarize the chronology of the management theories discussed in this chapter.

Scientific Management Theory

The evolution of modern management began in the closing decades of the 19th century, after the industrial revolution had swept through Europe and America. In the new economic climate, managers of all types of organizations—political, educational, and economic—were trying to find better ways to satisfy customers' needs. Many major economic, technical, and cultural changes were taking place. The introduction of steam power and the development of sophisticated machinery and equipment changed how goods were produced, particularly in the weaving and clothing industries. Small workshops run by skilled workers who produced hand-manufactured products (a system called *crafts production*) were being replaced by large factories in which sophisticated machines controlled by hundreds or even thousands of unskilled or semiskilled workers made

Figure 2.1

The Evolution of Management Theory

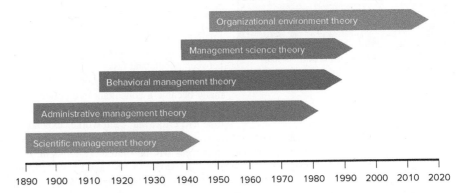

LO2-1 Describe how the need to increase organizational efficiency and effectiveness has guided the evolution of management theory.

LO2-2 Explain the principle of job specialization and division of labor, and tell why the study of person–task relationships is central to the pursuit of increased efficiency.

job specialization The process by which a division of labor occurs as different workers specialize in different tasks over time.

products. For example, raw cotton and wool, which in the past had been spun into yarn by families or whole villages working together, were now shipped to factories, where workers operated machines that spun and wove large quantities of yarn into cloth.

Owners and managers of the new factories found themselves unprepared for the challenges accompanying the change from small-scale crafts production to large-scale, mechanized manufacturing. Moreover, many managers and supervisors in these workshops and factories were engineers who had only a technical orientation. They were unprepared for the social problems that occur when people work together in large groups in a factory or shop system. Managers began to search for new techniques to manage their organizations' resources, and soon they started focusing on ways to increase the efficiency of the worker–task mix.

Job Specialization and the Division of Labor

Initially, management theorists were interested in why the new machine shops and factory system were more efficient and produced greater quantities of goods and services than older, crafts-style production operations. Nearly 200 years before, Adam Smith had been one of the first writers to investigate the advantages associated with producing goods and services in factories. A famous economist, Smith journeyed around England in the 1700s, studying the effects of the industrial revolution.[4] In a study of factories that produced various pins or nails, Smith identified two different manufacturing methods. The first was similar to crafts-style production, in which each worker was responsible for all the 18 tasks involved in producing a pin. The other had each worker performing only one or a few of these 18 tasks.

Smith found that the performance of the factories in which workers specialized in only one or a few tasks was much greater than the performance of the factory in which each worker performed all 18 pin-making tasks. In fact, Smith found that 10 workers specializing in a particular task could make 48,000 pins a day, whereas those workers who performed all the tasks could make only a few thousand.[5] Smith reasoned that this performance difference occurred because the workers who specialized became much more skilled at their specific tasks and as a group were thus able to produce a product faster than the group of workers who each performed many tasks. Smith concluded that increasing the level of job specialization—the process by which a division of labor occurs as different workers specialize in tasks—improves efficiency and leads to higher organizational performance.[6]

Armed with the insights gained from Adam Smith's observations, other managers and researchers began to investigate how to improve job specialization to increase performance. Management practitioners and theorists focused on how managers should organize and control the work process to maximize the advantages of job specialization and the division of labor.

F. W. Taylor and Scientific Management

Frederick W. Taylor (1856–1915) is best known for defining the techniques of scientific management, the systematic study of relationships between people and tasks for the purpose of redesigning the work process to increase efficiency. Taylor was a manufacturing manager who eventually became a consultant and taught other managers how to apply his scientific management techniques. Taylor believed that if the amount of time and effort that each worker expends to produce a unit of output (a finished good or service) can be reduced by increasing specialization and the division of labor, the production process will become more efficient. According to Taylor, the way to create the most efficient division of labor could best be determined by scientific management techniques rather than by intuitive or informal, rule-of-thumb knowledge. Based on his

Frederick W. Taylor, founder of scientific management and one of the first people to study the behavior and performance of people at work.
© Bettmann/Getty Images

scientific management The systematic study of relationships between people and tasks for the purpose of redesigning the work process to increase efficiency.

experiments and observations as a manufacturing manager in a variety of settings, he developed four principles to increase efficiency in the workplace:

- Principle 1: *Study the way workers perform their tasks, gather all the informal job knowledge that workers possess, and experiment with ways of improving how tasks are performed.*

To discover the most efficient method of performing specific tasks, Taylor studied in great detail and measured the ways different workers went about performing their tasks. One of the main tools he used was a time-and-motion study, which involves the careful timing and recording of the actions taken to perform a particular task. Once Taylor understood the existing method of performing a task, he then experimented to increase specialization. He tried different methods of dividing and coordinating the various tasks necessary to produce a finished product. Usually, this meant simplifying jobs and having each worker perform fewer, more routine tasks, as at a pin factory or on a car assembly line. Taylor also sought to find ways to improve each worker's ability to perform a particular task—for example, by reducing the number of motions workers made to complete the task, by changing the layout of the work area or the type of tools workers used, or by experimenting with tools of different sizes.

- Principle 2: *Codify the new methods of performing tasks into written rules and standard operating procedures.*

Once the best method of performing a particular task was determined, Taylor specified that it should be recorded so this procedure could be taught to all workers performing the same task. These new methods further standardized and simplified jobs—essentially making jobs even more routine. In this way efficiency could be increased throughout an organization.

- Principle 3: *Carefully select workers who possess skills and abilities that match the needs of the task, and train them to perform the task according to the established rules and procedures.*

To increase specialization, Taylor believed workers had to understand the tasks that were required and be thoroughly trained to perform the tasks at the required level. Workers who could not be trained to this level were to be transferred to a job where they were able to reach the minimum required level of proficiency.[7]

- Principle 4: *Establish a fair or acceptable level of performance for a task, and then develop a pay system that rewards performance above the acceptable level.*

To encourage workers to perform at a high level of efficiency, and to give them an incentive to reveal the most efficient techniques for performing a task, Taylor advocated that workers benefit from any gains in performance. They should be paid a bonus and receive some percentage of the performance gains achieved through the more efficient work process.[8]

By 1910 Taylor's system of scientific management had become nationally known and in many instances was faithfully and fully practiced.[9] However, managers in many organizations chose to implement the new principles of scientific management selectively. This decision ultimately resulted in problems. For example, some managers using scientific management obtained increases in performance, but rather than sharing performance gains with workers through bonuses, as Taylor had advocated, they simply increased the amount of work that each worker was expected to do. Many workers experiencing the reorganized work system found that as their performance increased, managers required that they do more work for the same pay. Workers also learned that performance increases often meant fewer jobs and a greater threat of layoffs, because fewer workers were needed. In addition, the specialized, simplified jobs were often monotonous and repetitive, and many workers became dissatisfied with their jobs.

Scientific management brought many workers more hardship than gain and a distrust of managers who did not seem to care about workers' well-being.[10] These dissatisfied workers resisted attempts to use the new scientific management techniques and at times even withheld their job knowledge from managers to protect their jobs and pay. It is not difficult for workers to conceal the true potential efficiency of a work system to protect their interests. Experienced machine operators, for example, can slow their machines in undetectable ways by adjusting the tension in the belts or misaligning the gears.

Unable to inspire workers to accept the new scientific management techniques for performing tasks, some organizations increased the mechanization of the work process. For example, one reason Henry Ford introduced moving conveyor belts in his factory was the realization that when a conveyor belt controls the pace of work (instead of workers setting their own pace), workers can be pushed to perform at higher levels—levels that they may have thought were beyond their reach. Charlie Chaplin captured this aspect of mass production in one of the opening scenes of his famous movie *Modern Times* (1936). In the film Chaplin caricatured a new factory employee fighting to work at the machine-imposed pace but losing the battle to the machine. Henry Ford also used the principles of scientific management to identify the tasks that each worker should perform on the production line and, thus, to determine the most effective division of labor to suit the needs of a mechanized production system.

From a performance perspective, the combination of the two management practices—(1) achieving the right worker–task specialization and (2) linking people and tasks by the speed of the production line—makes sense. It produces the huge cost savings and dramatic output increases that occur in large, organized work settings. For example, in 1908 managers at the Franklin Motor Company using scientific management principles redesigned the work process, and the output of cars increased from 100 cars a *month* to 45 cars a *day;* workers' wages, however, increased by only 90 percent.[11] From other perspectives, however, scientific management practices raise many concerns. Some companies, like McDonald's in the accompanying "Ethics in Action" feature, have codified management practices to protect workers.

ETHICS IN ACTION

McDonald's and Workers' Rights

When most individuals think about McDonald's, they might think of a Big Mac, a McChicken Sandwich, or perhaps Ronald McDonald, the lovable clown. Workers' rights probably would be far down the list.

However, McDonald's, like other global companies, has faced increased scrutiny about the way its employees are treated. McDonald's estimates that one in eight Americans has worked for the fast-food giant. Public figures such as Sharon Stone, Jay Leno, Shania Twain, Rachel McAdams, and Pink have been employed at McDonald's.

Fast-food work is not well paid, and it sometimes places employees in uncomfortable and stressful situations. In one case, a McDonald's franchise owner in Pennsylvania faced charges for requiring his foreign workers to live in expensive company-owned housing while underpaying them.[12]

In response to the increased scrutiny, the McDonald's corporation issued a report on the sustainability and corporate responsibility of its businesses. The McDonald's Corporation operates approximately 35,000 restaurants worldwide. Of these, 80 percent are owned by independent businesses or franchisees. This means that McDonald's has only indirect control over the majority of its restaurants. Yet the company has put in place a number of managerial controls designed to help ensure that all McDonald's employees are treated humanely and fairly.[13]

For example, McDonald's has hired a global chief compliance officer to ensure that its businesses comply with local and international regulations regarding the treatment of employees. This officer maintains a staff that travels to stores throughout the world to interview employees and ensure that each restaurant is complying with the standards the company has developed. McDonald's also conducts training on the humane treatment of employees. Finally, McDonald's maintains a hotline for employees to report instances of mistreatment. To ensure that employees are not afraid to report violations, the company has a "nonretaliation policy" that protects employees from retaliation by management.[14]

Recently, however, the fast-food giant came under pressure in a case currently before the National Human Relations Board (NLRB), which suggests that McDonald's should be considered a "joint-employer" of the workers employed by company franchisees. This case has far-reaching implications for McDonald's as well as its competitors in the fast-food industry. A ruling against the Golden Arches could increase pressure on the company to boost wages and accept more responsibility for working conditions at franchise stores.[15]

Although the NLRB case is far from settled, McDonald's continues to work with company-owned outlets and franchise owners to ensure that all employees are treated well, and that any human rights violations will be quickly reported and resolved.

The Gilbreths

Two prominent followers of Taylor were Frank Gilbreth (1868–1924) and Lillian Gilbreth (1878–1972), who refined Taylor's analysis of work movements and made many contributions to time-and-motion study.[16] Their aims were to (1) analyze every individual action necessary to perform a particular task and break it into each of its component actions, (2) find better ways to perform each component action, and (3) reorganize each of the component actions so that the action as a whole could be performed more efficiently—at less cost in time and effort.

The Gilbreths often filmed a worker performing a particular task and then separated the task actions, frame by frame, into their component movements. Their goal was to maximize the efficiency with which each individual task was performed so that gains across tasks would add up to enormous savings of time and effort. Their attempts to develop improved management principles were captured—at times quite humorously—in the movie *Cheaper by the Dozen,* a new version of which appeared in 2004, which depicts how the Gilbreths (with their 12 children) tried to live their own lives according to these efficiency principles and apply them to daily actions such as shaving, cooking, and even raising a family.[17]

Eventually, the Gilbreths became increasingly interested in the study of fatigue. They studied how physical characteristics of the workplace contribute to job stress that often leads to fatigue and, thus, poor performance. They isolated factors that result in worker fatigue, such as lighting, heating, the color of walls, and the design of tools and machines. Their pioneering studies paved the way for new advances in management theory.

In workshops and factories, the work of the Gilbreths, Taylor, and many others had a major effect on the practice of management. In comparison with the old crafts system, jobs in the new system were more repetitive, boring, and monotonous as a result of the application of scientific management principles, and workers became increasingly dissatisfied. Frequently, the management of work settings became a game between workers and managers: Managers tried to initiate work practices to increase performance, and workers tried to hide the true potential efficiency of the work setting to protect their own well-being.[18] The story of how John D. Rockefeller built Standard Oil is another illustration of the same kind of management thinking (see the accompanying "Manager as a Person" feature).

This scene from the 2003 version of *Cheaper by the Dozen* illustrates how "efficient families" such as the Gilbreths use formal family courts to solve problems, such as assigning chores to different family members.
© Collection Christophel/Alamy

John D. Rockefeller

On July 8, 1839, John D. Rockefeller was born. As a child, he showed an aptitude for finance. He earned money doing odd jobs and was able to save $50. Then, instead of spending the money, Rockefeller lent it to a farmer at a 7 percent interest rate.[19] This transaction was the beginning of Rockefeller's career.

In 1855 at the age of 16, Rockefeller attended Folsom's Commercial College, where he studied accounting and banking, among other subjects. That same year, he began seeking work in Cleveland, Ohio, as a clerk or accountant.[20] Eventually, he landed a job as an assistant bookkeeper.[21] Rockefeller's mathematical ability and conscientiousness soon gained him additional responsibilities at his company. This included helping manage the company's supply chain and attempting to optimize the profit from moving freight.

At the age of 19, Rockefeller created a commodities partnership with Maurice Clark. The American Civil War began in 1861, and prices and demand for commodities soared. Rockefeller's exposure to rail shipping showed him the potential of railroads as a mode of transferring freight and the importance of petroleum as a commodity. In 1862 Rockefeller entered the industry for which he would become famous: oil refining. As he learned the business, he devoted a significant amount of energy to increasing the efficiency of his refineries.

In February 1865 Rockefeller bought out his partners and then hired his brother, William, to help manage the operation, which he called the "Standard Works." He set up his business so that the refinery increased the scope and efficiency of production to develop and maintain economies of scale.[22]

In 1870 Rockefeller, along with his associates, founded the Standard Oil Company of Ohio.[23] At the time of its creation, the Standard Oil Company of Ohio serviced about 10 percent of the oil market. That same year, Rockefeller began implementing his vision to unite the area's oil producers and consolidate the industry. He handled negotiations with rival firms himself.

By 1872 Rockefeller had acquired nearly all the oil refineries in Cleveland. Inefficient operations were closed, while Rockefeller worked to improve the quality of the rest. By 1879, just eight years after its creation, Standard Oil had grown to managing almost 90 percent of the oil refining business. The business would make Rockefeller among the wealthiest men of his day. In response, Rockefeller gave most of his fortune away to charitable groups before his death.[24]

Administrative Management Theory

LO2-3 Identify the principles of administration and organization that underlie effective organizations.

While scientific managers like Rockefeller were studying the person–technology mix to increase efficiency, other managers and researchers were focusing on **administrative management**, the study of how to create an organizational structure and control system that leads to high efficiency and effectiveness. *Organizational structure* is the system of task and authority relationships that controls how employees use resources to achieve the organization's goals. Two of the most influential early views regarding the creation of efficient systems of organizational administration were developed in Europe: Max Weber, a German sociology professor, developed one theory; and Henri Fayol, the French manager who developed the model of management introduced in Chapter 1, developed the other.

administrative management The study of how to create an organizational structure and control system that leads to high efficiency and effectiveness.

The Theory of Bureaucracy

Max Weber (1864–1920) wrote at the turn of the 20th century, when Germany was undergoing its industrial revolution.[25] To help Germany manage its growing industrial enterprises while it was striving to become a world power, Weber developed the principles of

Figure 2.2

Weber's Principles of Bureaucracy

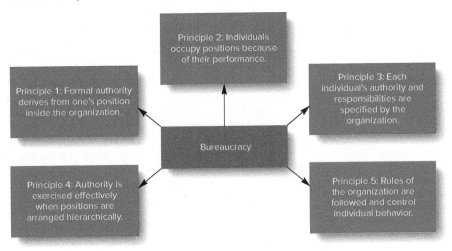

Principle 2: Individuals occupy positions because of their performance.

Principle 1: Formal authority derives from one's position inside the organization.

Principle 3: Each individual's authority and responsibilities are specified by the organization.

Bureaucracy

Principle 4: Authority is exercised effectively when positions are arranged hierarchically.

Principle 5: Rules of the organization are followed and control individual behavior.

bureaucracy A formal system of organization and administration designed to ensure efficiency and effectiveness.

bureaucracy—a formal system of organization and administration designed to ensure efficiency and effectiveness. A bureaucratic system of administration is based on the five principles summarized in Figure 2.2:

- Principle 1: *In a bureaucracy, a manager's formal authority derives from the position he or she holds in the organization.*

authority The power to hold people accountable for their actions and to make decisions concerning the use of organizational resources.

Authority is the power to hold people accountable for their actions and to make decisions concerning the use of organizational resources. Authority gives managers the right to direct and control their subordinates' behavior to achieve organizational goals. In a bureaucratic system of administration, obedience is owed to a manager not because of any personal qualities—such as personality, wealth, or social status—but because the manager occupies a position that is associated with a certain level of authority and responsibility.[26]

- Principle 2: *In a bureaucracy, people should occupy positions because of their performance, not because of their social standing or personal contacts.*

This principle was not always followed in Weber's time and is often ignored today. Some organizations and industries are still affected by social networks in which personal contacts and relations, not job-related skills, influence hiring and promotion decisions.

- Principle 3: *The extent of each position's formal authority and task responsibilities, and its relationship to other positions in an organization, should be clearly specified.*

When the tasks and authority associated with various positions in the organization are clearly specified, managers and workers know what is expected of them and what to expect from each other. Moreover, an organization can hold all its employees strictly accountable for their actions when they know their exact responsibilities.

- Principle 4: *Authority can be exercised effectively in an organization when positions are arranged hierarchically so employees know whom to report to and who reports to them.*[27]

Managers must create an organizational hierarchy of authority that makes it clear who reports to whom and to whom managers and workers should go if conflicts or problems arise. This principle is especially important in the armed forces, the FBI, the CIA, and other organizations that deal with sensitive issues involving possible major repercussions. It is vital that managers at high levels of the hierarchy be able to hold subordinates accountable for their actions.

Max Weber developed the principles of bureaucracy during Germany's burgeoning industrial revolution to help organizations increase their efficiency and effectiveness.

© akg-images/The Image Works

● Principle 5: *Managers must create a well-defined system of rules, standard operating procedures, and norms so they can effectively control behavior within an organization.*

rules Formal, written instructions that specify actions to be taken under different circumstances to achieve specific goals.

standard operating procedures (SOPs) Specific sets of written instructions about how to perform a certain aspect of a task.

norms Unwritten, informal codes of conduct that prescribe how people should act in particular situations and are considered important by most members of a group or an organization.

Rules are formal, written instructions that specify actions to be taken under different circumstances to achieve specific goals (for example, if A happens, do B). **Standard operating procedures (SOPs)** are specific sets of written instructions about how to perform a certain aspect of a task. A rule might state that at the end of the workday employees are to leave their machines in good order, and a set of SOPs would specify exactly how they should do so, itemizing which machine parts must be oiled or replaced. **Norms** are unwritten, informal codes of conduct that prescribe how people should act in particular situations and are considered important by most members of a group or an organization. For example, an organizational norm in a restaurant might be that waiters should help each other if time permits.

Rules, SOPs, and norms provide behavioral guidelines that increase the performance of a bureaucratic system because they specify the best ways to accomplish organizational tasks. Companies such as McDonald's and Walmart have developed extensive rules and procedures to specify the behaviors required of their employees, such as "Always greet the customer with a smile." For example, Walmart, the world's largest retailer, automatically tracks inventory levels of products at its stores. When inventory is too low, the retailer sends an automatic request to a supplier to purchase an item and have it shipped. These items are then routed as efficiently as possible to the store where they are needed. Thus, Walmart incorporates bureaucratic controls in its operations to make employees as efficient as possible.[28]

Weber believed organizations that implement all five principles establish a bureaucratic system that improves organizational performance. The specification of positions and the use of rules and SOPs to regulate how tasks are performed make it easier for managers to organize and control the work of subordinates. Similarly, fair and equitable selection and promotion systems improve managers' feelings of security, reduce stress, and encourage organizational members to act ethically and further promote the interests of the organization.[29]

If bureaucracies are not managed well, however, many problems can result. Sometimes managers allow rules and SOPs, "bureaucratic red tape," to become so cumbersome that decision making is slow and inefficient and organizations cannot change. When managers rely too much on rules to solve problems and not enough on their own skills and judgment, their behavior becomes inflexible. A key challenge for managers is to use bureaucratic principles to benefit, rather than harm, an organization.

Fayol's Principles of Management

Henri Fayol (1841–1925) was the CEO of Comambault Mining. Working at the same time as Weber, but independently, Fayol identified 14 principles (summarized in Table 2.1) that he believed essential to increasing the efficiency of the management process.[30] We discuss these principles in detail here because, although they were developed at the turn of the 20th century, they remain the bedrock on which much of recent management theory and research is based. In fact, as the "Management Insight" feature following this discussion suggests, modern writers, such as well-known management guru Jim Collins, continue to extol these principles.

DIVISION OF LABOR   A champion of job specialization and the division of labor for reasons already mentioned, Fayol was nevertheless among the first to point out the downside of too much specialization: boredom—a state of mind likely to diminish product quality, worker initiative, and flexibility. As a result, Fayol advocated that workers be given more job duties to perform or be encouraged to assume more responsibility for work outcomes—a principle increasingly applied today in organizations that empower their workers. Modern grocery stores, like Publix, use division of labor in their operations. For example, in the bakery and deli, employees focus on creating cakes, pies, and ready-to-eat meals. In the meat section, a butcher provides fresh cuts of poultry and beef. In the produce section, workers place fresh vegetables and fruits. Shelf stockers ensure that store shelves have the products customers want. Finally, customer service employees help customers bag, purchase, and carry groceries out to their automobiles. By using division of labor, Publix employees are able to develop expertise they might not otherwise gain.[31]

Table 2.1

Fayol's 14 Principles of Management

Division of labor Job specialization and the division of labor should increase efficiency, especially if managers take steps to lessen workers' boredom.

Authority and responsibility Managers have the right to give orders and the power to exhort subordinates for obedience.

Unity of command An employee should receive orders from only one superior.

Line of authority The length of the chain of command that extends from the top to the bottom of an organization should be limited.

Centralization Authority should not be concentrated at the top of the chain of command.

Unity of direction The organization should have a single plan of action to guide managers and workers.

Equity All organizational members are entitled to be treated with justice and respect.

Order The arrangement of organizational positions should maximize organizational efficiency and provide employees with satisfying career opportunities.

Initiative Managers should allow employees to be innovative and creative.

Discipline Managers need to create a workforce that strives to achieve organizational goals.

Remuneration of personnel The system that managers use to reward employees should be equitable for both employees and the organization.

Stability of tenure of personnel Long-term employees develop skills that can improve organizational efficiency.

Subordination of individual interests to the common interest Employees should understand how their performance affects the performance of the whole organization.

Esprit de corps Managers should encourage the development of shared feelings of comradeship, enthusiasm, or devotion to a common cause.

AUTHORITY AND RESPONSIBILITY Like Weber, Fayol emphasized the importance of authority and responsibility. Fayol, however, went beyond Weber's formal authority, which derives from a manager's position in the hierarchy, to recognize the *informal* authority that derives from personal expertise, technical knowledge, moral worth, and the ability to lead and to generate commitment from subordinates. (The study of authority is the subject of recent research into leadership, discussed in Chapter 14.)

unity of command A reporting relationship in which an employee receives orders from, and reports to, only one superior.

UNITY OF COMMAND The principle of unity of command specifies that an employee should receive orders from, and report to, only one superior. Fayol believed that *dual command*, the reporting relationship that exists when two supervisors give orders to the same subordinate, should be avoided except in exceptional circumstances. Dual command confuses subordinates, undermines order and discipline, and creates havoc within the formal hierarchy of authority. Assessing any manager's authority and responsibility in a system of dual command is difficult, and the manager who is bypassed feels slighted and angry and may be uncooperative in the future. For example, the U.S. Army maintains unity of command for its soldiers. Clearly defined ranks range from private to five-star general, and each soldier answers to a commanding officer with a higher rank. While operating in the field, it is critical that soldiers understand their objectives, and consistent unity of command enables each soldier to know exactly whom he or she should follow to get the job done.[32]

line of authority The chain of command extending from the top to the bottom of an organization.

LINE OF AUTHORITY The line of authority is the chain of command extending from the top to the bottom of an organization. Fayol was one of the first management theorists to point out the importance of limiting the length of the chain of command by controlling the number of levels in the managerial hierarchy. The more levels in the hierarchy, the longer communication takes between managers at the top and bottom and the slower the pace of planning and organizing. Restricting the number of hierarchical levels to lessen these communication problems lets an organization act quickly and flexibly; this is one reason for the recent trend toward restructuring (discussed in Chapter 1).

Fayol also pointed out that when organizations are split into different departments or functions, each with its own hierarchy, it is important to allow middle and first-line managers in each department to interact with managers at similar levels in other departments. This interaction helps speed decision making because managers know each other and know whom to go to when problems arise. For cross-departmental integration to work, Fayol noted the importance of keeping one's superiors informed about what is taking place so that lower-level decisions do not harm activities taking place in other parts of the organization. One alternative to cross-departmental integration is to create cross-departmental teams controlled by a team leader (see Chapter 1).

CENTRALIZATION   Fayol also was one of the first management writers to focus on centralization, the concentration of authority at the top of the managerial hierarchy. Fayol believed authority should not be concentrated at the top of the chain of command. One of the most significant issues that top managers face is how much authority to centralize at the top of the organization and what authority to decentralize to managers and workers at lower hierarchical levels. This important issue affects the behavior of people at all levels in the organization.

If authority is very centralized, only managers at the top make important decisions and subordinates simply follow orders. This arrangement gives top managers great control over organizational activities and helps ensure that the organization is pursuing its strategy, but it makes it difficult for the people who are closest to problems and issues to respond to them in a timely manner. It also can reduce the motivation of middle and first-line managers and make them less flexible and adaptable because they become reluctant to make decisions on their own, even when doing so is necessary. They get used to passing the buck. The pendulum is now swinging toward decentralization as organizations seek to empower middle managers and create self-managed teams that monitor and control their own activities, both to increase organizational flexibility and to reduce operating costs and increase efficiency. The U.S. Department of State is responsible for maintaining diplomatic relations between America and nearly 180 other nations. Although the Department of State operates embassies and consulates throughout the world, the secretary of state is based at its headquarters in Washington, DC, so that major policy decisions are centralized.[33]

UNITY OF DIRECTION   Just as there is a need for unity of command, there is also a need for unity of direction, the singleness of purpose that makes possible the creation of one plan of action to guide managers and workers as they use organizational resources. An organization without a single guiding plan becomes inefficient and ineffective; its activities become unfocused, and individuals and groups work at cross-purposes. Successful planning starts with top managers working as a team to craft the organization's strategy, which they communicate to middle managers, who decide how to use organizational resources to implement the strategy.

EQUITY   As Fayol wrote, "For personnel to be encouraged to carry out their duties with all the devotion and loyalty of which they are capable, they must be treated with respect for their own sense of integrity, and equity results from the combination of respect and justice."[34] Equity—the justice, impartiality, and fairness to which all organizational members are entitled—is receiving much attention today; the desire to treat employees fairly is a primary concern of managers. (Equity theory is discussed in Chapter 13.)

ORDER   Like Taylor and the Gilbreths, Fayol was interested in analyzing jobs, positions, and individuals to ensure that the organization was using resources as efficiently as possible. To Fayol, order meant the methodical arrangement of positions to provide the organization with the greatest benefit and to provide employees with career opportunities that satisfy their needs. Thus Fayol recommended the use of organizational charts to show the position and duties of each employee and to indicate which positions an employee might move to or be promoted into in the future. He also advocated that managers engage in extensive career

centralization The concentration of authority at the top of the managerial hierarchy.

unity of direction The singleness of purpose that makes possible the creation of one plan of action to guide managers and workers as they use organizational resources.

equity The justice, impartiality, and fairness to which all organizational members are entitled.

order The methodical arrangement of positions to provide the organization with the greatest benefit and to provide employees with career opportunities.

planning to help ensure orderly career paths. Career planning is of primary interest today as organizations increase the resources they are willing to devote to training and developing their workforces.

INITIATIVE Although order and equity are important means to fostering commitment and loyalty among employees, Fayol believed managers must also encourage employees to exercise initiative, the ability to act on their own without direction from a superior. Used properly, initiative can be a major source of strength for an organization because it leads to creativity and innovation. Managers need skill and tact to achieve the difficult balance between the organization's need for order and employees' desire for initiative. Fayol believed the ability to strike this balance was a key indicator of a superior manager.

initiative The ability to act on one's own without direction from a superior.

DISCIPLINE In focusing on the importance of discipline—obedience, energy, application, and other outward marks of respect for a superior's authority—Fayol was addressing the concern of many early managers: how to create a workforce that was reliable and hardworking and would strive to achieve organizational goals. According to Fayol, discipline results in respectful relationships between organizational members and reflects the quality of an organization's leadership and a manager's ability to act fairly and equitably.

discipline Obedience, energy, application, and other outward marks of respect for a superior's authority.

REMUNERATION OF PERSONNEL Fayol proposed reward systems including bonuses and profit-sharing plans, which are increasingly used today as organizations seek improved ways to motivate employees. Convinced from his own experience that an organization's payment system has important implications for organizational success, Fayol believed effective reward systems should be equitable for both employees and the organization, encourage productivity by rewarding well-directed effort, not be subject to abuse, and be uniformly applied to employees. PayScale Incorporated is a company dedicated to helping its clients effectively compensate their employees. The company works with highly competitive IT customers to track employee performance and effectively reward talent, increasing employee morale and productivity while reducing employee attrition.[35]

STABILITY OF TENURE OF PERSONNEL Fayol also recognized the importance of long-term employment, and this idea has been echoed by contemporary management gurus such as Tom Peters, Jeff Pfeffer, and Jim Collins. When employees stay with an organization for extended periods, they develop skills that improve the organization's ability to use its resources.

SUBORDINATION OF INDIVIDUAL INTERESTS TO THE COMMON INTEREST The interests of the organization as a whole must take precedence over the interests of any individual or group if the organization is to survive. Equitable agreements must be established between the organization and its members to ensure that employees are treated fairly and rewarded for their performance and to maintain the disciplined organizational relationships so vital to an efficient system of administration.

ESPRIT DE CORPS As this discussion of Fayol's ideas suggests, the appropriate design of an organization's hierarchy of authority and the right mix of order and discipline foster cooperation and commitment. Likewise, a key element in a successful organization is the development of esprit de corps, a French expression that refers to shared feelings of comradeship, enthusiasm, or devotion to a common cause among members of a group. Esprit de corps can result when managers encourage personal, verbal contact between managers and workers and encourage communication to solve problems and implement solutions. (Today the term *organizational culture* is used to refer to these shared feelings; this concept is discussed at length in Chapter 3.)

esprit de corps Shared feelings of comradeship, enthusiasm, or devotion to a common cause among members of a group.

Some of the principles that Fayol outlined have faded from contemporary management practices, but most have endured. The characteristics of successful organizations that Jim Collins presents in his best-selling book *Good to Great* (2001) are discussed in the accompanying "Management Insight."

How to Get from *Good to Great*

In his book *Good to Great,* Jim Collins, noted consultant and business coach, reports on a case study of firms with exemplary performance. He is seeking to shed light on the factors that contributed to these firms' rise to excellence.[36] Collins says that several principles predict a firm's success.

The first is that of Level 5 leadership. These leaders possess great humility but also an intense professional will. Although Level 5 leadership is applicable to all levels of the organization, Collins proposes that its application only by top managers is enough to raise an organization from mediocrity to greatness.

Second, Collins argues that having the right people in place is more important than establishing the values and strategy of the firm. Firms should focus on hiring the right people, and getting rid of the wrong people, to move firms in an upward trajectory.

Third, Collins says that confrontation and conflict are important drivers of decision success. Thus it is critical for managers to establish a climate of trust where information can be readily shared. Furthermore, Collins asserts that attempting to motivate others is wrong because the right employees will be self-motivated—rewards may actually be counterproductive.

Fourth, Collins argues for the Hedgehog Principle, which says that companies should stick to what they know; companies should do what they can excel at, make money at, and be passionate about. Fifth, Collins says that great companies are disciplined companies. Here *discipline* means adhering to only those opportunities that accommodate the Hedgehog Principle. Opportunities that violate the Hedgehog Principle should be avoided.

Finally, *Good to Great* proposes that great companies do not chase technological fads but, instead, seek incremental improvements in technology that complement core businesses. According to Collins, great companies pursue incremental change and improvement instead of radical change.[37]

LO2-4 Trace the changes in theories about how managers should behave to motivate and control employees.

As this insight into contemporary management suggests, the basic concerns that motivated Fayol continue to inspire management theorists.[38] The principles that Fayol and Weber set forth still provide clear and appropriate guidelines that managers can use to create a work setting that efficiently and effectively uses organizational resources. These principles remain the bedrock of modern management theory; recent researchers have refined or developed them to suit modern conditions. For example, Weber's and Fayol's concerns for equity and for establishing appropriate links between performance and reward are central themes in contemporary theories of motivation and leadership.

Behavioral Management Theory

behavioral management The study of how managers should behave to motivate employees and encourage them to perform at high levels and be committed to the achievement of organizational goals.

Because the writings of Weber and Fayol were not translated into English and published in the United States until the late 1940s, American management theorists in the first half of the 20th century were unaware of the contributions of these European pioneers. American management theorists began where Taylor and his followers left off. Although their writings were different, these theorists all espoused a theme that focused on behavioral management, the study of how managers should personally behave to motivate employees and encourage them to perform at high levels and be committed to achieving organizational goals.

The Work of Mary Parker Follett

If F. W. Taylor is considered the father of management thought, Mary Parker Follett (1868–1933) serves as its mother.[39] Much of her writing about management and about the way managers should behave toward workers was a response to her concern that Taylor was

Mary Parker Follett, an early management thinker who advocated, "Authority should go with knowledge . . . whether it is up the line or down."

ignoring the human side of the organization. She pointed out that management often overlooks the multitude of ways in which employees can contribute to the organization when managers allow them to participate and exercise initiative in their everyday work lives.[40] Taylor, for example, never proposed that managers should involve workers in analyzing their jobs to identify better ways to perform tasks or should even ask workers how they felt about their jobs. Instead he used time-and-motion experts to analyze workers' jobs for them. Follett, in contrast, argued that because workers know the most about their jobs, they should be involved in job analysis and managers should allow them to participate in the work development process.

Follett proposed that "authority should go with knowledge . . . whether it is up the line or down." In other words, if workers have the relevant knowledge, then workers, rather than managers, should be in control of the work process itself, and managers should behave as coaches and facilitators—not as monitors and supervisors. In making this statement, Follett anticipated the current interest in self-managed teams and empowerment. She also recognized the importance of having managers in different departments communicate directly with each other to speed decision making. She advocated what she called "cross-functioning": members of different departments working together in cross-departmental teams to accomplish projects—an approach that is increasingly used today.[41]

Fayol also mentioned expertise and knowledge as important sources of managers' authority, but Follett went further. She proposed that knowledge and expertise, not managers' formal authority deriving from their position in the hierarchy, should decide who will lead at any particular moment. She believed, as do many management theorists today, that power is fluid and should flow to the person who can best help the organization achieve its goals. Follett took a horizontal view of power and authority, in contrast to Fayol, who saw the formal line of authority and vertical chain of command as being most essential to effective management. Follett's behavioral approach to management was very radical for its time.

The Hawthorne Studies and Human Relations

Probably because of its radical nature, Follett's work was unappreciated by managers and researchers until quite recently. Most continued to follow in the footsteps of Taylor and the Gilbreths. To increase efficiency, they studied ways to improve various characteristics of the work setting, such as job specialization or the kinds of tools workers used. One series of studies was conducted from 1924 to 1932 at the Hawthorne Works of the Western Electric Company.[42] This research, now known as the *Hawthorne studies,* began as an attempt to investigate how characteristics of the work setting—specifically, the level of lighting, or illumination— affect worker fatigue and performance. The researchers conducted an experiment in which they systematically measured worker productivity at various levels of illumination.

The experiment produced some unexpected results. The researchers found that regardless of whether they raised or lowered the level of illumination, productivity increased. In fact, productivity began to fall only when the level of illumination dropped to the level of moonlight—a level at which workers could presumably no longer see well enough to do their work efficiently.

The researchers found these results puzzling and invited a noted Harvard psychologist, Elton Mayo, to help them. Mayo proposed another series of experiments to solve the mystery. These experiments, known as the *relay assembly test experiments,* were designed to investigate the effects of other aspects of the work context on job performance, such as the effect of the number and length of rest periods and hours of work on fatigue and monotony.[43] The goal was to raise productivity.

During a two-year study of a small group of female workers, the researchers again observed that productivity increased over time, but the increases could not be solely attributed to the effects of changes in the work setting. Gradually, the researchers discovered that, to some degree, the results they were obtaining were influenced by the fact that the researchers themselves had become part of the experiment. In other words, the presence of the researchers was affecting the results because the workers enjoyed receiving attention and being the subject of study and were willing to cooperate with the researchers to produce the results they believed the researchers desired.

Subsequently, it was found that many other factors also influence worker behavior, and it was not clear what was actually influencing the Hawthorne workers' behavior. However, this particular effect—which became known as the Hawthorne effect—seemed to suggest that workers' attitudes toward their managers affect the level of workers' performance. In particular, the significant finding was that each manager's personal behavior or leadership approach can affect performance. This finding led many researchers to turn their attention to managerial behavior and leadership. If supervisors could be trained to behave in ways that would elicit cooperative behavior from their subordinates, productivity could be increased. From this view emerged the human relations movement, which advocates that supervisors be behaviorally trained to manage subordinates in ways that elicit their cooperation and increase their productivity.

The importance of behavioral, or human relations, training became even clearer to its supporters after another series of experiments—the *bank wiring room experiments*. In a study of workers making telephone switching equipment, researchers Elton Mayo and F. J. Roethlisberger discovered that the workers, as a group, had deliberately adopted a norm of output restriction to protect their jobs. Workers who violated this informal production norm were subjected to sanctions by other group members. Those who violated group performance norms and performed above the norm were called "ratebusters"; those who performed below the norm were called "chiselers."

The experimenters concluded that both types of workers threatened the group as a whole. Ratebusters threatened group members because they revealed to managers how fast the work could be done. Chiselers were looked down on because they were not doing their share of the work. Work group members disciplined both ratebusters and chiselers to create a pace of work that the workers (not the managers) thought was fair. Thus, a work group's influence over output can be as great as the supervisors' influence. Because the work group can influence the behavior of its members, some management theorists argue that supervisors should be trained to behave in ways that gain the goodwill and cooperation of workers so that supervisors, not workers, control the level of work group performance.

One implication of the Hawthorne studies was that the behavior of managers and workers in the work setting is as important in explaining the level of performance as the technical aspects of the task. Managers must understand the workings of the informal organization, the system of behavioral rules and norms that emerge in a group, when they try to manage or change behavior in organizations. Many studies have found that as time passes, groups often develop elaborate procedures and norms that bond members together, allowing unified action either to cooperate with management to raise performance or to restrict output and thwart the attainment of organizational goals.[44] The Hawthorne studies demonstrated the importance of understanding how the feelings, thoughts, and behavior of work group members and managers affect performance. It was becoming increasingly clear to researchers that understanding behavior in organizations is a complex process that is critical to increasing performance.[45] Indeed, the increasing interest in the area of management known as organizational behavior, the study of the factors that have an impact on how individuals and groups respond to and act in organizations, dates from these early studies.

Theory X and Theory Y

Several studies after World War II revealed how assumptions about workers' attitudes and behavior affect managers' behavior. Perhaps the most influential approach was developed by Douglas McGregor. He proposed two sets of assumptions about how work attitudes and behaviors not only dominate the way managers think but also affect how they behave in organizations. McGregor named these two contrasting sets of assumptions *Theory X* and *Theory Y* (see Figure 2.3).[46]

THEORY X According to the assumptions of Theory X, the average worker is lazy, dislikes work, and will try to do as little as possible. Moreover, workers have little ambition and wish to avoid responsibility. Thus, the manager's task is to counteract workers' natural

Hawthorne effect The finding that a manager's behavior or leadership approach can affect workers' level of performance.

human relations movement A management approach that advocates the idea that supervisors should receive behavioral training to manage subordinates in ways that elicit their cooperation and increase their productivity.

informal organization The system of behavioral rules and norms that emerge in a group.

organizational behavior The study of the factors that have an impact on how individuals and groups respond to and act in organizations.

Theory X A set of negative assumptions about workers that leads to the conclusion that a manager's task is to supervise workers closely and control their behavior.

Figure 2.3

Theory X versus Theory Y

THEORY X	THEORY Y
The average employee is lazy, dislikes work, and will try to do as little as possible.	Employees are not inherently lazy. Given the chance, employees will do what is good for the organization.
To ensure that employees work hard, managers should closely supervise employees.	To allow employees to work in the organization's interest, managers must create a work setting that provides opportunities for workers to exercise initiative and self-direction.
Managers should create strict work rules and implement a well-defined system of rewards and punishments to control employees.	Managers should decentralize authority to employees and make sure employees have the resources necessary to achieve organizational goals.

Source: From D. McGregor, The Human Side of Enterprise. Copyright © McGraw-Hill Companies, Inc. Reprinted with permission.

tendencies to avoid work. To keep workers' performance at a high level, the manager must supervise workers closely and control their behavior by means of "the carrot and stick"— rewards and punishments.

Managers who accept the assumptions of Theory X design and shape the work setting to maximize their control over workers' behaviors and minimize workers' control over the pace of work. These managers believe workers must be made to do what is necessary for the success of the organization, and they focus on developing rules, SOPs, and a well-defined system of rewards and punishments to control behavior. They see little point in giving workers autonomy to solve their own problems because they think the workforce neither expects nor desires cooperation. Theory X managers see their role as closely monitoring workers to ensure that they contribute to the production process and do not threaten product quality. Henry Ford, who closely supervised and managed his workforce, fits McGregor's description of a manager who holds Theory X assumptions.

Theory Y A set of positive assumptions about workers that leads to the conclusion that a manager's task is to create a work setting that encourages commitment to organizational goals and provides opportunities for workers to be imaginative and to exercise initiative and self-direction.

THEORY Y   In contrast, Theory Y assumes that workers are not inherently lazy, do not naturally dislike work, and, if given the opportunity, will do what is good for the organization. According to Theory Y, the characteristics of the work setting determine whether workers consider work to be a source of satisfaction or punishment, and managers do not need to closely control workers' behavior to make them perform at a high level because workers exercise self-control when they are committed to organizational goals. The implication of Theory Y, according to McGregor, is that "the limits of collaboration in the organizational setting are not limits of human nature but of management's ingenuity in discovering how to realize the potential represented by its human resources."[47] It is the manager's task to create a work setting that encourages commitment to organizational goals and provides opportunities for workers to be imaginative and to exercise initiative and self-direction.

When managers design the organizational setting to reflect the assumptions about attitudes and behavior suggested by Theory Y, the characteristics of the organization are quite different from those of an organizational setting based on Theory X. Managers who believe workers are motivated to help the organization reach its goals can decentralize authority and give more control over the job to workers, both as individuals and in groups. In this setting, individuals and groups are still accountable for their activities; however, the manager's role is not to control employees but to provide support and advice, to make sure employees have the resources they need to perform their jobs, and to evaluate them on their ability to help the organization meet its goals. Henri Fayol's approach to administration more closely reflects the assumptions of Theory Y rather than Theory X. Companies such as 3M, Apple, and Google exemplify those that follow Theory Y.

Herb Kelleher, former CEO and chairman of Southwest Airlines, built a company known for customer service by following an open-door policy and giving employees flexible job descriptions and significant discretion in interacting with customers.

© Jon Freilich/Bloomberg via Getty Images

Southwest Airlines has long been the darling of the airline industry, and Southwest's leadership cites their Theory Y culture as a driving force. Inspired by former CEO and Chairman Herb Kelleher, Southwest Airlines emphasizes a culture of fun, creativity, and camaraderie.[48] Southwest employees note how Kelleher maintained an open-door policy of contact, which enabled him to stay in touch with problems facing the airline and find solutions faster.

Employees have highly flexible job descriptions that enable them to chip in and help where needed. Unlike many of its competitors, which use highly regimented and formalized employee roles, Southwest employees are encouraged to help solve problems where they see them. Thus, it's not uncommon to see a Southwest manager helping move passenger luggage into aircraft or check in passengers at a gate.

Southwest also gives its employees significant discretion, enabling them to solve problems quickly. In an industry dominated by tight schedules and narrow windows to resolve problems, these actions enable employees to serve customers better.

Finally, Southwest Airlines views its unions as partners rather than adversaries. It works with independent unions to ensure that employees are compensated and treated fairly, and it routinely solicits input from its employees on how to improve operations.[49] As a result of this innovative culture dominated by Theory Y thinking, Southwest Airlines has become the most consistently profitable company among its U.S. competitors.

Management Science Theory

Management science theory is a contemporary approach to management that focuses on the use of rigorous quantitative techniques to help managers make maximum use of organizational resources to produce goods and services. In essence, management science theory is a contemporary extension of scientific management, which, as developed by Taylor, also took a quantitative approach to measuring the worker–task mix to raise efficiency. There are many branches of management science, and IT, which is having a significant impact on all kinds of management practices, is affecting the tools managers use to make decisions.[50] Each branch of management science deals with a specific set of concerns:

LO2-5 Explain the contributions of management science to the efficient use of organizational resources.

management science theory An approach to management that uses rigorous quantitative techniques to help managers make maximum use of organizational resources.

- *Quantitative management* uses mathematical techniques—such as linear and nonlinear programming, modeling, simulation, queuing theory, and chaos theory—to help managers decide, for example, how much inventory to hold at different times of the year, where to locate a new factory, and how best to invest an organization's financial capital. IT offers managers new and improved ways of handling information so they can make more accurate assessments of the situation and better decisions.

- *Operations management* gives managers a set of techniques they can use to analyze any aspect of an organization's production system to increase efficiency. IT, through the Internet and through growing B2B networks, is transforming how managers acquire inputs and dispose of finished products.

- *Total quality management (TQM)* focuses on analyzing an organization's input, conversion, and output activities to increase product quality.[51] Once again, through sophisticated software packages and computer-controlled production, IT is changing how managers and employees think about the work process and ways of improving it.

- *Management information systems (MISs)* give managers information about events occurring inside the organization as well as in its external environment—information that is vital for effective decision making. IT gives managers access to more and better information and allows more managers at all levels to participate in the decision-making process.

All these subfields of management science, enhanced by sophisticated IT, provide tools and techniques that managers can use to help improve the quality of their decision making and increase efficiency and effectiveness. For example, Toyota applied management science theory with its "Toyota Production System (TPS)." The TPS emphasizes continuous improvement in quality and the reduction of waste through learning. TPS was a major catalyst for the "lean revolution" in global manufacturing, and manufacturing companies worldwide have embraced this philosophy and adapted it for their own operations.[52] We discuss many important developments in management science theory in this book. In particular, Chapter 9 focuses on how to use operations management and TQM to improve quality, efficiency, and responsiveness to customers. And Chapter 18 describes the many ways managers use information systems and technologies to improve their planning, organizing, and controlling functions.

Organizational Environment Theory

An important milestone in the history of management thought occurred when researchers went beyond the study of how managers can influence behavior within organizations to consider how managers control the organization's relationship with its external environment, or **organizational environment**—the set of forces and conditions that operate beyond an organization's boundaries but affect a manager's ability to acquire and utilize resources. Resources in the organizational environment include the raw materials and skilled people that an organization requires to produce goods and services, as well as the support of groups, including customers who buy these goods and services and provide the organization with financial resources. One way of determining the relative success of an organization is to consider how effective its managers are at obtaining scarce and valuable resources.[53] The importance of studying the environment became clear after the development of open-systems theory and contingency theory during the 1960s.

LO2-6 Explain why the study of the external environment and its impact on an organization has become a central issue in management thought.

organizational environment The set of forces and conditions that operate beyond an organization's boundaries but affect a manager's ability to acquire and utilize resources.

open system A system that takes in resources from its external environment and converts them into goods and services that are then sent back to that environment for purchase by customers.

closed system A system that is self-contained and thus not affected by changes occurring in its external environment.

entropy The tendency of a closed system to lose its ability to control itself and thus to dissolve and disintegrate.

The Open-Systems View

One of the most influential views of how an organization is affected by its external environment was developed by Daniel Katz, Robert Kahn, and James Thompson in the 1960s.[54] These theorists viewed the organization as an **open system**—a system that takes in resources from its external environment and converts or transforms them into goods and services that are sent back to that environment, where they are bought by customers (see Figure 2.4).

At the *input stage* an organization acquires resources such as raw materials, money, and skilled workers to produce goods and services. Once the organization has gathered the necessary resources, conversion begins. At the *conversion stage* the organization's workforce, using appropriate tools, techniques, and machinery, transforms the inputs into outputs of finished goods and services such as cars, hamburgers, or flights to Hawaii. At the *output stage* the organization releases finished goods and services to its external environment, where customers purchase and use them to satisfy their needs. The money the organization obtains from the sales of its outputs allows the organization to acquire more resources so the cycle can begin again.

The system just described is said to be open because the organization draws from and interacts with the external environment in order to survive; in other words, the organization is open to its environment. A **closed system**, in contrast, is a self-contained system that is not affected by changes in its external environment. Organizations that operate as closed systems, that ignore the external environment, and that fail to acquire inputs are likely to experience **entropy**, which is the tendency of a closed system to lose its ability to control itself and thus to dissolve and disintegrate.

Management theorists can model the activities of most organizations by using the open-systems view. For example, manufacturing companies, like Ford and General Electric, buy inputs such as component parts, skilled and semiskilled labor, and robots and computer-controlled manufacturing equipment; then at the conversion stage they use their

Figure 2.4

The Organization as an Open System

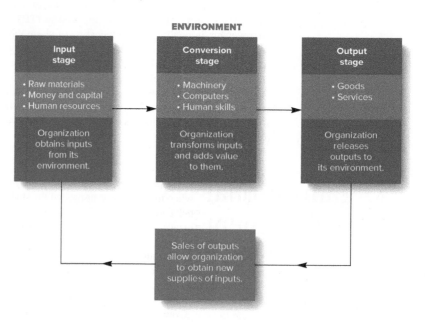

manufacturing skills to assemble inputs into outputs of cars and appliances. As we discuss in later chapters, competition between organizations for resources is one of several major challenges to managing the organizational environment.

Researchers using the open-systems view are also interested in how the various parts of a system work together to promote efficiency and effectiveness. Systems theorists like to argue that the whole is greater than the sum of its parts; they mean that an organization performs at a higher level when its departments work together rather than separately. Synergy, the performance gains that result from the *combined* actions of individuals and departments, is possible only in an organized system. The recent interest in using teams combined or composed of people from different departments reflects systems theorists' interest in designing organizational systems to create synergy and thus increase efficiency and effectiveness.

synergy Performance gains that result when individuals and departments coordinate their actions.

Contingency Theory

contingency theory The idea that the organizational structures and control systems managers choose depend on (are contingent on) characteristics of the external environment in which the organization operates.

Another milestone in management theory was the development of contingency theory in the 1960s by Tom Burns and G. M. Stalker in Britain and Paul Lawrence and Jay Lorsch in the United States.[55] The crucial message of contingency theory is that *there is no one best way to organize:* The organizational structures and the control systems that managers choose depend on (are contingent on) characteristics of the external environment in which the organization operates. According to contingency theory, the characteristics of the environment affect an organization's ability to obtain resources; to maximize the likelihood of gaining access to resources, managers must allow an organization's departments to organize and control their activities in ways most likely to allow them to obtain resources, given the constraints of the environment they face. In other words, how managers design the organizational hierarchy, choose a control system, and lead and motivate their employees is contingent on the characteristics of the organizational environment (see Figure 2.5).

An important characteristic of the external environment that affects an organization's ability to obtain resources is the degree to which the environment is changing. Changes in the organizational environment include changes in technology, which can lead to the creation of new products (such as Apple TV) and result in the obsolescence of existing products (Blu-ray players); the entry of new competitors (such as foreign organizations that compete for available resources); and unstable economic conditions. In general, the more quickly the

Figure 2.5

Contingency Theory of Organizational Design

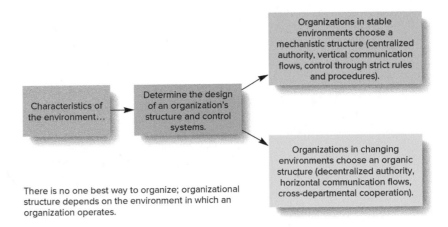

Organizations in stable environments choose a mechanistic structure (centralized authority, vertical communication flows, control through strict rules and procedures).

Characteristics of the environment...

Determine the design of an organization's structure and control systems.

Organizations in changing environments choose an organic structure (decentralized authority, horizontal communication flows, cross-departmental cooperation).

There is no one best way to organize; organizational structure depends on the environment in which an organization operates.

organizational environment is changing, the greater are the problems associated with gaining access to resources, and the greater is managers' need to find ways to coordinate the activities of people in different departments to respond to the environment quickly and effectively.

MECHANISTIC AND ORGANIC STRUCTURES   Drawing on Weber's and Fayol's principles of organization and management, Burns and Stalker proposed two basic ways in which managers can organize and control an organization's activities to respond to characteristics of its external environment: They can use a *mechanistic structure* or an *organic structure*.[56] As you will see, a mechanistic structure typically rests on Theory X assumptions, and an organic structure typically rests on Theory Y assumptions.

When the environment surrounding an organization is stable, managers tend to choose a mechanistic structure to organize and control activities and make employee behavior predictable. In a mechanistic structure, authority is centralized at the top of the managerial hierarchy, and the vertical hierarchy of authority is the main means used to control subordinates' behavior. Tasks and roles are clearly specified, subordinates are closely supervised, and the emphasis is on strict discipline and order. Everyone knows his or her place, and there is a place for everyone. A mechanistic structure provides the most efficient way to operate in a stable environment because it allows managers to obtain inputs at the lowest cost, giving an organization the most control over its conversion processes and enabling the most efficient production of goods and services with the smallest expenditure of resources. McDonald's restaurants operate with a mechanistic structure. Supervisors make all important decisions; employees are closely supervised and follow well-defined rules and standard operating procedures.

In contrast, when the environment is changing rapidly, it is difficult to obtain access to resources, and managers need to organize their activities in a way that allows them to cooperate, to act quickly to acquire resources (such as new types of inputs to produce new kinds of products), and to respond effectively to the unexpected. In an organic structure, authority is decentralized to middle and first-line managers to encourage them to take responsibility and act quickly to pursue scarce resources. Departments are encouraged to take a cross-departmental or functional perspective, and cross-functional teams composed of people from different departments are formed. As in Mary Parker Follett's model, the organization operates in an organic way because authority rests with the individuals, departments, and teams best positioned to control the current problems the organization is facing. As a result, managers in an organic structure can react more quickly to a changing environment than can managers in a mechanistic structure. However, an organic structure is generally more expensive to operate because it requires that more managerial time, money, and effort be spent on coordination. So it is used only when needed—when the organizational environment is unstable and changing rapidly.[57] Google, Apple, and IBM are examples of companies that operate with organic structures. For

mechanistic structure An organizational structure in which authority is centralized, tasks and rules are clearly specified, and employees are closely supervised.

organic structure An organizational structure in which authority is decentralized to middle and first-line managers and tasks and roles are left ambiguous to encourage employees to cooperate and respond quickly to the unexpected.

example, at Apple, all employees have the opportunity to provide and receive feedback from management, and even junior-level designers receive input from Apple executives. By using an organic managerial structure, Apple is able to clarify exactly what is expected of employees and to ensure that its employees are making needed progress on the company's objectives. Apple's management is also able to stay abreast of technological developments and changing competitive conditions that bear on the company's products and services.[58]

Summary and Review

In this chapter we examined the evolution of management theory and research over the last century. Much of the material in the rest of this book stems from developments and refinements of this work. Indeed, the rest of this book incorporates the results of the extensive research in management that has been conducted since the development of the theories discussed here.

LO2-1, 2-2   SCIENTIFIC MANAGEMENT THEORY   The search for efficiency started with the study of how managers could improve person–task relationships to increase efficiency. The concept of job specialization and division of labor remains the basis for the design of work settings in modern organizations. New developments such as lean production and total quality management are often viewed as advances on the early scientific management principles developed by Taylor and the Gilbreths.

LO2-3   ADMINISTRATIVE MANAGEMENT THEORY   Max Weber and Henri Fayol outlined principles of bureaucracy and administration that are as relevant to managers today as they were when developed at the turn of the 20th century. Much of modern management research refines these principles to suit contemporary conditions. For example, the use of cross-departmental teams and the empowerment of workers are issues that managers also faced a century ago.

LO2-4   BEHAVIORAL MANAGEMENT THEORY   Researchers have described many different approaches to managerial behavior, including Theories X and Y. Often the managerial behavior that researchers suggest reflects the context of their own historical eras and cultures. Mary Parker Follett advocated managerial behaviors that did not reflect accepted modes of managerial behavior at the time, and her work was largely ignored until conditions changed.

LO2-5   MANAGEMENT SCIENCE THEORY   The various branches of management science theory provide rigorous quantitative techniques that give managers more control over each organization's use of resources to produce goods and services.

LO2-6   ORGANIZATIONAL ENVIRONMENT THEORY   The importance of studying the organization's external environment became clear after the development of open-systems theory and contingency theory during the 1960s. A main focus of contemporary management research is to find methods to help managers improve how they use organizational resources and compete in the global environment. Strategic management and total quality management are two important approaches intended to help managers make better use of organizational resources.

Management in Action

Topics for Discussion and Action

Discussion

1. Choose a fast-food restaurant, a department store, or some other organization with which you are familiar, and describe the division of labor and job specialization it uses to produce goods and services. How might this division of labor be improved? [LO2-1, 2-2]

2. Apply Taylor's principles of scientific management to improve the performance of the organization you chose in topic 1. [LO2-2]

3. In what ways are Weber's and Fayol's ideas about bureaucracy and administration similar? How do they differ? [LO2-3]

4. Which of Weber's and Fayol's principles seem most relevant to the creation of an ethical organization? [LO2-4, 2-6]

5. How are companies using management science theory to improve their processes? Is this theory equally applicable for manufacturing and service companies? If so, how? [LO2-4, 2-5]

6. What is contingency theory? What kinds of organizations familiar to you have been successful or unsuccessful in dealing with contingencies from the external environment? [LO2-6]

7. Why are mechanistic and organic structures suited to different organizational environments? [LO2-4, 2-6]

Action

8. Question a manager about his or her views of the relative importance of Fayol's 14 principles of management. [LO2-3, 2-4]

9. Visit at least two organizations in your community, and identify those that seem to operate with a Theory X or a Theory Y approach to management. [LO2-4]

Building Management Skills

Managing Your Own Business [LO2-2, 2-4]

Now that you understand the concerns addressed by management thinkers over the last century, use this exercise to apply your knowledge to developing your management skills.

Imagine that you are the founding entrepreneur of a software company that specializes in developing games for mobile devices. Customer demand for your games has increased so much that over the last year your company has grown from a busy one-person operation to one with 16 employees. In addition to yourself, you employ six software developers to produce the software, three graphic artists, two computer technicians, two marketing and sales personnel, and two assistants. In the next year you expect to hire 30 new employees, and you are wondering how best to manage your growing company.

1. Use the principles of Weber and Fayol to decide on the system of organization and management that you think will be most effective for your growing organization. How many levels will the managerial hierarchy of your organization have? How much authority will you decentralize to your subordinates? How will you establish the division of labor between subordinates? Will your subordinates work alone and report to you or work in teams?

2. Which management approach (for example, Theory X or Y) do you propose to use to run your organization? In 50 or fewer words, write a statement describing the management approach you believe will motivate and coordinate your subordinates, and tell why you think this style will be best.

Managing Ethically [LO2-3, 2-4]

How Unethical Behavior Shut Down a Meatpacking Plant

By all appearances the Westland/Hallmark Meat Co. based in Chico, California, was considered to be an efficient and sanitary meatpacking plant. Under the control of its owner and CEO, Steven Mendell, the plant regularly passed inspections by the U.S. Dept. of Agriculture (USDA). Over 200 workers were employed to slaughter cattle and prepare the beef for shipment to fast-food restaurants such as Burger King and Taco Bell. Also, millions of pounds of meat the plant produced yearly were delivered under contract to one of the federal government's most coveted accounts: the National School Lunch Program.[59]

When the Humane Society turned over a videotape (secretly filmed by one of its investigators, who had taken a job as a plant employee) to the San Bernardino County district attorney, showing major violations of health procedures, an uproar followed. The videotape showed two workers dragging sick cows up the ramp that led to the slaughterhouse using metal chains and forklifts, and shocking them with electric prods and shooting streams of water in their noses and faces. Not only did the tape show inhumane treatment of animals, but it also provided evidence that the company was flouting the ban on allowing sick animals to enter the food supply chain—something that federal regulations explicitly outlaw because of concerns for human health and safety.

Once the USDA was informed that potentially contaminated beef products had entered the supply chain—especially the one to the nation's schools—it issued a notice for the recall of the 143 million pounds of beef processed in the plant over the last two years, the largest recall in history. In addition, the plant was shut down as the investigation proceeded. CEO Steven Mendell was subpoenaed to appear before the House Panel on Energy and Commerce Committee. He denied that these violations had taken place and that diseased cows had entered the food chain. However, when panel members demanded that he view the videotape, which he claimed he had not seen, he was forced to acknowledge that inhumane treatment of animals had occurred.[60] Moreover, federal investigators turned up evidence that as early as 1996 the plant had been cited for overuse of electric prods to speed cattle through the plant and had been cited for other violations since, suggesting that these abuses had been going on for a long period.

Not only were consumers and schoolchildren harmed by these unethical actions, but the plant itself was permanently shut down and all 220 workers lost their jobs. In addition, the employees directly implicated in the video were prosecuted and one, who pleaded guilty to animal abuse, was convicted and sentenced to six months' imprisonment.[61] Clearly, all the people and groups affected by the meatpacking plant have suffered from its unethical and inhumane organizational behaviors and practices.

Questions

1. Use the theories discussed in the chapter to debate the ethical issues involved in the way the Westland/Hallmark Meat Co. business operated.

2. Use theories to discuss the ethical issues involved in the way the meatpacking business is being conducted today.

3. Search the web for changes occurring in the meatpacking business.

Small Group Breakout Exercise [LO2-6]

Modeling an Open System

Form groups of three to five people, and appoint one group member as the spokesperson who will communicate your findings to the class when called on by the instructor. Then discuss the following scenario:

Think of an organization with which you are all familiar, such as a local restaurant, store, or bank. After choosing an organization, model it from an open-systems perspective. Identify its input, conversion, and output processes, and identify forces in the external environment that help or hurt the organization's ability to obtain resources and dispose of its goods or services.

Exploring the World Wide Web [LO2-3, 2-6]

Explore General Electric's corporate history by reviewing the innovation timeline at http://www.ge.com/transformation, and then answer the following questions:

1. What do you think precipitated General Electric's growth strategy based on merger and acquisition?

2. How were early acquisitions and mergers related to one another?

3. What are some of the challenges faced by GE's current leadership team?

Be the Manager [LO2-2, 2-4]

How to Manage a Hotel

You have been called in to advise the owners of an exclusive new luxury hotel. For the venture to succeed, hotel employees must focus on providing customers with the highest-quality customer service possible. The challenge is to devise a way of organizing and controlling employees that will promote high-quality service, that will encourage employees to be committed to the hotel, and that will reduce the level of employee turnover and absenteeism—which are typically high in the hotel business.

Questions

1. How do the various management theories discussed in this chapter offer clues for organizing and controlling hotel employees?

2. Which parts would be the most important for an effective system to organize and control employees?

Bloomberg Case in the News [LO 2-1, 2-3, 2-4, 2-6]

Welcome, Olympic Tourists, to Brazil. Please Don't Mind the Mess

When Rio de Janeiro won the rights in 2009 to host the Olympics, Brazil planned a blitz of projects to showcase just how far it had risen. But when tourists start showing up in two months to attend the games, it'll be the bust and not Brazil's best that'll be on display.

That sewage-filled harbor that visitors will pass on the way from the airport—and the spot where Olympic sailing events will be staged—was supposed to be a shimmering, clean bay. That new metro line they'll take from the posh Ipanema beach neighborhood to the games will at best run on a limited schedule, having started operations just four days before the opening ceremony. And what about the state-of-the-art gear that police were supposed to get to help keep travelers safe? A top official says it never happened.

Welcome to Brazil, a land of political, economic and fiscal crisis.

"When you look back at the bid documents from 2009, the Olympics were definitely designed and pitched as a way of showcasing Brazil as this thriving democracy and burgeoning economy," said Jules Boykoff, the author of a book on Olympics history that's critical about the legacy of major sporting events. "How big a difference seven years make."

To be fair, most of the 39 billion reais ($11 billion) in arenas and infrastructure being built ahead of the Olympics will be ready in time and, besides a few eyesores and commuting delays, most tourists may not even notice all that should have been. But the unfinished work is an indication of a much bigger problem that will last long after the visitors jet out: Rio state is all but broke.

No one knows that better than Joao Vitor da Silva and his father, Rodrigo da Silva. The scrawny nine-year-old in an Iron Man T-shirt is a hemophiliac, and Batista said they've been warned that public-health spending cuts may disrupt supplies of prophylaxis, the shots that prevent Joao from bleeding out whenever he's injured or sick.

"If there's money for the Olympics, there has to be money for health," said Da Silva, a 34-year-old former forklift-operator who's on medical leave.

Brazil's hardly the first nation to host the Olympics games from a hotbed of chaos. (Russia, Mexico and South Korea are all part of the club.)

Even so, the tumultuous backdrop when the games begin Aug. 5 is a far cry from the image of the up-and-coming powerhouse organizers had envisioned when hosting rights were awarded.

These days, Brazil is stuck in a crushing recession and Lula's successor, Dilma Rousseff, was stripped of power while she faces an impeachment trial on allegations she illegally financed budget deficits. Rio state missed debt payments last month and is delaying public-worker salaries after oil prices collapsed, a primary source of revenue. And at least six companies contracted for Olympic projects and related infrastructure have been crippled by allegations they paid kickbacks to win lucrative public-works deals.

Three of those companies—builders Queiroz Galvao SA, OAS SA, and Andrade Gutierrez SA—were responsible for a project to dredge four polluted lagoons and plant 500,000 mangrove trees in Barra da Tijuca, the key staging ground for the games. But work won't be ready after public prosecutors requested delays and then the state faced cash shortages, according to the Environment Secretariat. A press official for the builders group confirmed that the pace of work has been "reduced" and declined to comment further.

"Rio is the showcase of Brazil—of its incompetence and impunity," said Mario Moscatelli, the biologist subcontracted by the construction firms to plant the mangroves. He says he'll be able to finish less than 10 percent of the work.

Queiroz is also part of the group building the subway line from Ipanema to Barra, which still awaits a nearly 1 billion-real loan from the Rio-based national development bank before it can finish works.

Rio state projects a 20 billion-real deficit this year, of which 12 billion relate to the underwater pension system, and Thursday announced a new round of spending cuts. Almost 70 percent of public-school teachers and workers have been on strike since March as salaries are delayed, their union says. Rio city was forced to take control of two public hospitals, and a doctors' group warns others may soon close for lack of funding.

The state also slashed its security budget by 32 percent this year and has delayed payments to police and their families. New equipment police expected for the games never materialized, and instead many officers are saddled with obsolete gear, said a high-ranking military police official, who asked not to be identified criticizing the budget cuts.

All major security investments for the Olympics have been carried out since 2012 or are in their final phase, and any personnel or equipment shortage during the games will be covered by federal security agencies, according to the press office of Rio's security secretariat.

Leonardo Espindola, chief of staff to Rio's governor, told the Supreme Court in April that the state is on the verge of "social collapse." State Finance Secretary Julio Bueno agrees. At the outset of an hour-long interview last month, Bueno claimed to have "the worst job in Rio de Janeiro."

"We're unable to maintain essential services like police and health," he said. "That's what defines the health of a society."

Questions for Discussion

1. Describe how the contingency theory of management would help or hinder Brazilian officials with getting the country ready to host the Olympic Games.

2. Do you consider Brazil's approach to managing the Olympics a closed or open system? Explain your answer.

3. Would a management science theory approach to staging the Olympics ensure success? Why or why not?

Notes

1. "Letter to Shareowners," *GE 2015 Annual Report*, www.ge.com, accessed June 9, 2016.

2. "GE & Alstom Energy: Powering a Sustainable Energy Future," www.ge-alstom .com, accessed June 9, 2016; J. Passeri, "Why GE's $10 Billion Alstom Purchases Is Its Best Deal in a Century," *The Street*, https://www.thestreet.com, December 4, 2015; L. Beilfuss, "GE Completes Alstom Power Acquisition," *The Wall Street Journal*, www.wsj.com, November 2, 2015; D. Cardwell, "G.E. to Spin Off New Energy Technologies in One Company," *The New York Times*, www.nytimes.com, October 7, 2015.

3. "Letter to Shareowners."

4. A. Smith, *The Wealth of Nations* (London: Penguin, 1982).

5. Ibid., 110.

6. J.G. March and H.A. Simon, *Organizations* (New York: Wiley, 1958).

7. L.W. Fry, "The Maligned F.W. Taylor: A Reply to His Many Critics," *Academy of Management Review* 1 (1976), 124–29.

8. F.W. Taylor, *Shop Management* (New York: Harper, 1903); F.W. Taylor, *The Principles of Scientific Management* (New York: Harper, 1911).

9. J.A. Litterer, *The Emergence of Systematic Management as Shown by the Literature from 1870–1900* (New York: Garland, 1986).

10. H.R. Pollard, *Developments in Management Thought* (New York: Crane, 1974).

11. D. Wren, *The Evolution of Management Thought* (New York: Wiley, 1994), 134.

12. M.A. Johnson, "Pennsylvania McDonald's Franchisee Accused of Abusing Foreign Workers," *NBCNews,* usnews.nbcnews .com/_news/2013/03/08/17227684-pennsylvania-mcdonalds-franchisee-accused-of-abusing-foreign-workers?lite, March 8, 2013.

13. J. Lawrence, "McDonald's Commitment to Building Trust and Unity," *Great Place to Work,* www.greatplacetowork.co.uk, August 22, 2013; "McDonald's USA National Employee Scholarship Program," www.scholarships.com.

14. Lawrence, "McDonald's Commitment to Building Trust and Unity."

15. K. Gibson, "Should McDonald's Be Responsible for How Its Franchises Treat Workers?" *CBS Money Watch,* www.cbsnews.com, March 11, 2016.

16. F.B. Gilbreth, *Primer of Scientific Management* (New York: Van Nostrand Reinhold, 1912).

17. F.B. Gilbreth Jr. and E.G. Gilbreth, *Cheaper by the Dozen* (New York: Crowell, 1948).

18. D. Roy, "Efficiency and the Fix: Informal Intergroup Relations in a Piece Work Setting," *American Journal of Sociology* 60 (1954), 255–66.

19. K. Poole, "Biography of John D. Rockefeller, Senior," *Public Broadcasting Service,* www.pbs.org/wgbh/ americanexperience/features/biography/ rockefellers-john/.

20. Ibid.

21. R. Chernow, *Titan: The Life of John D. Rockefeller, Sr.* (New York: Random House, 2004).

22. Poole, "Biography of John D. Rockefeller, Senior.

23. E.G. Coffey and N. Shuker, *John D. Rockefeller, Empire Building* (Silver Burdett, 1989).

24. Poole, "Biography of John D. Rockefeller, Senior."

25. M. Weber, *From Max Weber: Essays in Sociology,* ed. H.H. Gerth and C.W. Mills (New York: Oxford University Press, 1946); M. Weber, *Economy and Society,* ed. G. Roth and C. Wittich (Berkeley: University of California Press, 1978).

26. C. Perrow, *Complex Organizations,* 2nd ed. (Glenview, IL: Scott, Foresman, 1979).

27. Weber, *From Max Weber,* 331.

28. Trefis Team, "Why Are Wal-Mart's Margins Gradually Declining?" *Forbes,* www.forbes.com, September 9, 2014.

29. See Perrow, *Complex Organizations,* chap. 1, for a detailed discussion of these issues.

30. H. Fayol, *General and Industrial Management* (New York: IEEE Press, 1984).

31. "Innovative Technology Companies Rely on PayScale to Attract and Retain Talent: Impressive List of More Than 400 Technology Companies That Depend on Highly Skilled Professionals Use PayScale's Real-Time Market Data and Cloud Software to Get Pay Right," *Ein News,* www.einnews.com/pr_news/197824565/ innovative-technology-companies-rely-on-payscale-to-attract-and-retain-talent, March 31, 2014.

32. Ibid.

33. Ibid.

34. Fayol, *General and Industrial Management,* 79.

35. "Innovative Technology Companies Rely on PayScale to Attract and Retain Talent."

36. J. Collins, "Good to Great," jimcollins .com, www.jimcollins.com/article_topics/ articles/good-to-great.html, October 2001.

37. K. Weisul, "Jim Collins: Good to Great in 10 Steps," *Inc.,* www.inc.com/kimberly-weisul/jim-collins-good-to-great-in-ten-steps.html, May 7, 2012.

38. R.E. Eccles and N. Nohira, *Beyond the Hype: Rediscovering the Essence of Management* (Boston: Harvard Business School Press, 1992).

39. L.D. Parker, "Control in Organizational Life: The Contribution of Mary Parker Follett," *Academy of Management Review* 9 (1984), 736–45.

40. P. Graham, *M.P. Follett—Prophet of Management: A Celebration of Writings from the 1920s* (Boston: Harvard Business School Press, 1995).

41. M.P. Follett, *Creative Experience* (London: Longmans, 1924).

42. E. Mayo, *The Human Problems of Industrial Civilization* (New York: Macmillan, 1933); F.J. Roethlisberger and W.J. Dickson, *Management and the Worker* (Cambridge: Harvard University Press, 1947).

43. D.W. Organ, "Review of *Management and the Worker,* by F.J. Roethlisberger and W.J. Dickson," *Academy of Management Review* 13 (1986), 460–64.

44. D. Roy, "Banana Time: Job Satisfaction and Informal Interaction," *Human Organization* 19 (1960), 158–61.

45. For an analysis of the problems in distinguishing cause from effect in the Hawthorne studies and in social settings in general, see A. Carey, "The Hawthorne Studies: A Radical Criticism," *American Sociological Review* 33 (1967), 403–16.

46. D. McGregor, *The Human Side of Enterprise* (New York: McGraw-Hill, 1960).

47. Ibid., 48.

48. "Southwest Citizenship," https://www. southwest.com, accessed June 9, 2016.

49. "Labor Relations: FAQs," http://swamedia .com, accessed June 9, 2016.

50. T. Dewett and G.R. Jones, "The Role of Information Technology in the Organization: A Review, Model, and Assessment," *Journal of Management* 27 (2001), 313–46.

51. W.E. Deming, *Out of the Crisis* (Cambridge: MIT Press, 1986).

52. Company website, "Toyota Production System," www.toyota-global.com, accessed June 9, 2016.

53. J.D. Thompson, *Organizations in Action* (New York: McGraw-Hill, 1967).

54. D. Katz and R.L. Kahn, *The Social Psychology of Organizations* (New York: Wiley, 1966); Thompson, *Organizations in Action.*

55. T. Burns and G.M. Stalker, *The Management of Innovation* (London: Tavistock, 1961); P.R. Lawrence and J.R. Lorsch, *Organization and Environment* (Boston: Graduate School of Business Administration, Harvard University, 1967).

56. Burns and Stalker, *The Management of Innovation.*

57. C.W.L. Hill and G.R. Jones, *Strategic Management: An Integrated Approach,* 8th ed. (Florence, KY: Cengage, 2010).

58. A. Lashinsky, "How Apple Works: Inside the World's Biggest Startup," *Fortune,* tech.fortune.cnn.com/2011/08/25/how-apple-works-inside-the-worlds-biggest-startup/, August 25, 2011.

59. E. Werner, "Slaughterhouse Owner Acknowledges Abuse," www. pasadenastarnews.com, March 13, 2008.

60. D. Bunis and N. Luna, "Sick Cows Never Made Food Supply, Meat Plant Owner Says," www.ocregister.com, March 12, 2008.

61. "Worker Sentenced in Slaughterhouse Abuse," www.yahoo.com, March 22, 2008.

CHAPTER 1

What Is Strategy and Why Is It Important?

© Fanatic Studio/Getty Images

Learning Objectives

THIS CHAPTER WILL HELP YOU UNDERSTAND:

LO 1   What we mean by a company's *strategy*.

LO 2   The concept of a *sustainable competitive advantage*.

LO 3   The five most basic strategic approaches for setting a company apart from rivals and winning a sustainable competitive advantage.

LO 4   That a company's strategy tends to evolve because of changing circumstances and ongoing efforts by management to improve the strategy.

LO 5   Why it is important for a company to have a viable business model that outlines the company's customer value proposition and its profit formula.

LO 6   The three tests of a winning strategy.

Strategy means making clear-cut choices about how to compete.

    Jack Welch—*Former CEO of General Electric*

I believe that people make their own luck by great preparation and good strategy.

    Jack Canfield—*Corporate trainer and entrepreneur*

The underlying principles of strategy are enduring, regardless of technology or the pace of change.

    Michael Porter—*Professor and consultant*

According to *The Economist,* a leading publication on business, economics, and international affairs, "In business, strategy is king. Leadership and hard work are all very well and luck is mighty useful, but it is strategy that makes or breaks a firm."[1] Luck and circumstance can explain why some companies are blessed with initial, short-lived success. But only a well-crafted, well-executed, constantly evolving strategy can explain why an elite set of companies somehow manage to rise to the top and stay there, year after year, pleasing their customers, shareholders, and other stakeholders alike in the process. Companies such as Apple, Disney, Microsoft, Alphabet (parent company of Google), Berkshire Hathaway, General Electric, and Amazon come to mind—but long-lived success is not just the province of U.S. companies. Diverse kinds of companies, both large and small, from many different countries have been able to sustain strong performance records, including Korea's Samsung (in electronics), the United Kingdom's HSBC (in banking),

Dubai's Emirates Airlines, Switzerland's Swatch Group (in watches and luxury jewelry), China Mobile (in telecommunications), and India's Tata Steel.

In this opening chapter, we define the concept of strategy and describe its many facets. We explain what is meant by a competitive advantage, discuss the relationship between a company's strategy and its business model, and introduce you to the kinds of competitive strategies that can give a company an advantage over rivals in attracting customers and earning above-average profits. We look at what sets a winning strategy apart from others and why the caliber of a company's strategy determines whether the company will enjoy a competitive advantage over other firms. By the end of this chapter, you will have a clear idea of why the tasks of crafting and executing strategy are core management functions and why excellent execution of an excellent strategy is the most reliable recipe for turning a company into a standout performer over the long term.

WHAT DO WE MEAN BY *STRATEGY?*

A company's **strategy** is the set of actions that its managers take to outperform the company's competitors and achieve superior profitability. The objective of a well-crafted strategy is not merely temporary competitive success and profits in the short run, but rather the sort of lasting success that can support growth and secure the

4 PART 1 Concepts and Techniques for Crafting and Executing Strategy

company's future over the long term. Achieving this entails making a managerial commitment to a coherent array of well-considered choices about how to compete.[2] These include:

- *How* to position the company in the marketplace.
- *How* to attract customers.
- *How* to compete against rivals.
- *How* to achieve the company's performance targets.
- *How* to capitalize on opportunities to grow the business.
- *How* to respond to changing economic and market conditions.

LO 1

What we mean by a company's *strategy*.

In most industries, companies have considerable freedom in choosing the *hows* of strategy.[3] Some companies strive to achieve lower costs than rivals, while others aim for product superiority or more personalized customer service dimensions that rivals cannot match. Some companies opt for wide product lines, while others concentrate their energies on a narrow product lineup. Some deliberately confine their operations to local or regional markets; others opt to compete nationally, internationally (several countries), or globally (all or most of the major country markets worldwide).

Strategy Is about Competing Differently

Mimicking the strategies of successful industry rivals—with either copycat product offerings or maneuvers to stake out the same market position—rarely works. Rather, every company's strategy needs to have some distinctive element that draws in customers and provides a competitive edge. Strategy, at its essence, is about competing differently— doing what rival firms *don't* do or what rival firms *can't* do.[4] This does not mean that the key elements of a company's strategy have to be 100 percent different, but rather that they must differ in at least *some important respects*. A strategy stands a better chance of succeeding when it is predicated on actions, business approaches, and competitive moves aimed at (1) appealing to buyers in ways that *set a company apart from its rivals* and (2) staking out a market position that is not crowded with strong competitors.

Strategy is about competing differently from rivals—doing what competitors don't do or, even better, doing what they can't do!

A company's strategy provides direction and guidance, in terms of not only what the company *should* do but also what it *should not* do. Knowing what not to do can be as important as knowing what to do, strategically. At best, making the wrong strategic moves will prove a distraction and a waste of company resources. At worst, it can bring about unintended long-term consequences that put the company's very survival at risk.

Figure 1.1 illustrates the broad types of actions and approaches that often characterize a company's strategy in a particular business or industry. For a more concrete example of the specific actions constituting a firm's strategy, see Illustration Capsule 1.1 describing Starbucks's strategy in the specialty coffee market.

LO 2

The concept of a *sustainable competitive advantage*.

Strategy and the Quest for Competitive Advantage

The heart and soul of any strategy are the actions in the marketplace that managers are taking to gain a competitive advantage over rivals. A company achieves a **competitive advantage** whenever it has some type of edge over rivals in attracting buyers and coping with competitive forces. There are many routes to competitive advantage, but they all involve either giving buyers what they perceive as superior value compared to the offerings of rival sellers or giving buyers the same value as others at a lower cost to the firm. Superior value can mean a good product at a lower price, a superior product that

FIGURE 1.1   Identifying a Company's Strategy—What to Look For

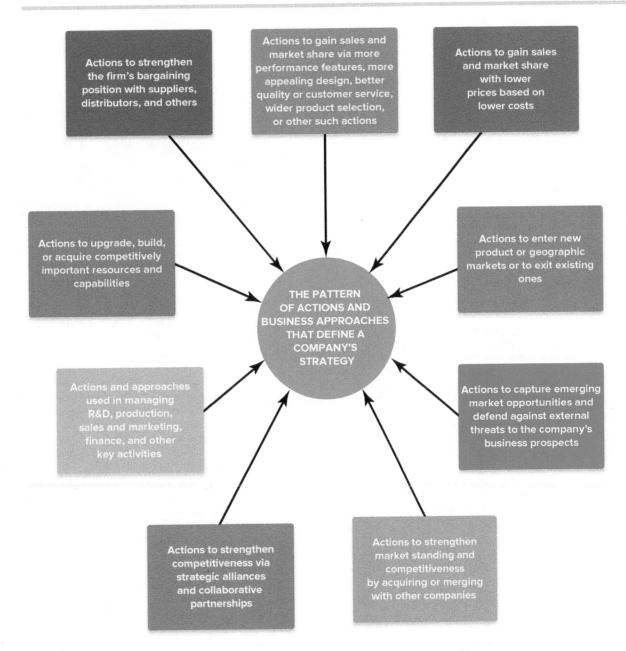

is worth paying more for, or a best-value offering that represents an attractive combination of price, features, quality, service, and other attributes. Delivering superior value or delivering value more efficiently—whatever form it takes—nearly always requires performing value chain activities differently than rivals and building capabilities that are not readily matched. In Illustration Capsule 1.1, it's evident that Starbucks has gained a competitive advantage over its rivals in the coffee shop industry through its efforts to create an upscale experience for coffee drinkers by catering to individualized tastes, enhancing the atmosphere and comfort of the shops, and delivering a premium product

Starbucks's Strategy in the Coffeehouse Market

Since its founding in 1985 as a modest nine-store operation in Seattle, Washington, Starbucks had become the premier roaster and retailer of specialty coffees in the world, with nearly 23,000 store locations as of October 2015. In fiscal 2015, its annual sales were expected to exceed $19 billion—an all-time high for revenues and net earnings. The key elements of Starbucks's strategy in the coffeehouse industry included:

- *Train "baristas" to serve a wide variety of specialty coffee drinks that allow customers to satisfy their individual preferences in a customized way.* Starbucks essentially brought specialty coffees, such as cappuccinos, lattes, and macchiatos, to the mass market in the United States, encouraging customers to personalize their coffee-drinking habits. Requests for such items as an "Iced Grande Hazelnut Macchiato with Soy Milk, and *no* Hazelnut Drizzle" could be served up quickly with consistent quality.

- *Emphasize store ambience and elevation of the customer experience at Starbucks stores.* Starbucks's management viewed each store as a billboard for the company and as a contributor to building the company's brand and image. Each detail was scrutinized to enhance the mood and ambience of the store to make sure everything signaled "best-of-class" and reflected the personality of the community and the neighborhood. The thesis was "everything mattered." The company went to great lengths to make sure the store fixtures, the merchandise displays, the artwork, the music, and the aromas all blended to create an inviting environment that evoked the romance of coffee and signaled the company's passion for coffee. Free Wi-Fi drew those who needed a comfortable place to work while they had their coffee.

- *Purchase and roast only top-quality coffee beans.* The company purchased only the highest-quality Arabica beans and carefully roasted coffee to exacting standards of quality and flavor. Starbucks did not use chemicals or artificial flavors when preparing its roasted coffees.

© Craig Warga/Bloomberg via Getty Images

- *Foster commitment to corporate responsibility.* Starbucks was protective of the environment and contributed positively to the communities where Starbucks stores were located. In addition, Starbucks promoted fair trade practices and paid above-market prices for coffee beans to provide its growers and suppliers with sufficient funding to sustain their operations and provide for their families.

- *Expand the number of Starbucks stores domestically and internationally.* Starbucks operated stores in high-traffic, high-visibility locations in the United States and abroad. The company's ability to vary store size and format made it possible to locate stores in settings such as downtown and suburban shopping areas, office buildings, and university campuses. The company also focused on making Starbucks a global brand, expanding its reach to more than 65 countries in 2015.

- *Broaden and periodically refresh in-store product offerings.* Non-coffee products by Starbucks included teas, fresh pastries and other food items, candy, juice drinks, music CDs, and coffee mugs and accessories.

- *Fully exploit the growing power of the Starbucks name and brand image with out-of-store sales.* Starbucks's Consumer Packaged Goods division included domestic and international sales of Frappuccino, coffee ice creams, and Starbucks coffees.

Sources: Company documents, 10-Ks, and information posted on Starbucks's website.

produced under environmentally sound fair trade practices. By differentiating itself in this manner from other coffee purveyors, Starbucks has been able to charge prices for its coffee that are well above those of its rivals and far exceed the low cost of its inputs. Its expansion policies have allowed the company to make it easy for customers to find a Starbucks shop almost anywhere, further enhancing the brand and cementing customer loyalty. A creative *distinctive* strategy such as that used by Starbucks is a company's most reliable ticket for developing a competitive advantage over its rivals. If a strategy is not distinctive, then there can be no competitive advantage, since no firm would be meeting customer needs better or operating more efficiently than any other.

If a company's competitive edge holds promise for being *sustainable* (as opposed to just temporary), then so much the better for both the strategy and the company's future profitability. What makes a competitive advantage **sustainable** (or durable), as opposed to temporary, are elements of the strategy that give buyers lasting reasons to prefer a company's products or services over those of competitors—*reasons that competitors are unable to nullify or overcome despite their best efforts*. In the case of Starbucks, the company's unparalleled name recognition, its reputation for high-quality specialty coffees served in a comfortable, inviting atmosphere, and the accessibility of the shops make it difficult for competitors to weaken or overcome Starbucks's competitive advantage. Not only has Starbucks's strategy provided the company with a sustainable competitive advantage, but it has made Starbucks one of the most admired companies on the planet.

Five of the most frequently used and dependable strategic approaches to setting a company apart from rivals, building strong customer loyalty, and winning a competitive advantage are:

1. *A low-cost provider strategy*—achieving a cost-based advantage over rivals. Walmart and Southwest Airlines have earned strong market positions because of the low-cost advantages they have achieved over their rivals. Low-cost provider strategies can produce a durable competitive edge when rivals find it hard to match the low-cost leader's approach to driving costs out of the business.

2. *A broad differentiation strategy*—seeking to differentiate the company's product or service from that of rivals in ways that will appeal to a broad spectrum of buyers. Successful adopters of differentiation strategies include Apple (innovative products), Johnson & Johnson in baby products (product reliability), LVMH (luxury and prestige), and BMW (engineering design and performance). One way to sustain this type of competitive advantage is to be sufficiently innovative to thwart the efforts of clever rivals to copy or closely imitate the product offering.

3. *A focused low-cost strategy*—concentrating on a narrow buyer segment (or market niche) and outcompeting rivals by having lower costs and thus being able to serve niche members at a lower price. Private-label manufacturers of food, health and beauty products, and nutritional supplements use their low-cost advantage to offer supermarket buyers lower prices than those demanded by producers of branded products.

4. *A focused differentiation strategy*—concentrating on a narrow buyer segment (or market niche) and outcompeting rivals by offering buyers customized attributes that meet their specialized needs and tastes better than rivals' products. Lululemon, for example, specializes in high-quality yoga clothing and the like, attracting a devoted set of buyers in the process. Jiffy Lube International in quick oil changes, McAfee in virus protection software, and The Weather Channel in cable TV provide some other examples of this strategy.

5. *A best-cost provider strategy*—giving customers more value for the money by satisfying their expectations on key quality features, performance, and/or service attributes while beating their price expectations. This approach is a hybrid strategy that blends elements of low-cost provider and differentiation strategies; the aim is to have lower costs than rivals while simultaneously offering better differentiating attributes. Target is an example of a company that is known for its hip product design (a reputation it built by featuring limited edition lines by designers

CORE CONCEPT

A company achieves a **competitive advantage** when it provides buyers with superior value compared to rival sellers or offers the same value at a lower cost to the firm. The advantage is **sustainable** if it persists despite the best efforts of competitors to match or surpass this advantage.

LO 3

The five most basic strategic approaches for setting a company apart from rivals and winning a sustainable competitive advantage.

such as Jason Wu), as well as a more appealing shopping ambience for discount store shoppers. Its dual focus on low costs as well as differentiation shows how a best-cost provider strategy can offer customers great value for the money.

Winning a *sustainable* competitive edge over rivals with any of the preceding five strategies generally hinges as much on building competitively valuable expertise and capabilities that rivals cannot readily match as it does on having a distinctive product offering. Clever rivals can nearly always copy the attributes of a popular product or service, but for rivals to match the experience, know-how, and specialized capabilities that a company has developed and perfected over a long period of time is substantially harder to do and takes much longer. FedEx, for example, has superior capabilities in next-day delivery of small packages, while Apple has demonstrated impressive product innovation capabilities in digital music players, smartphones, and e-readers. Hyundai has become the world's fastest-growing automaker as a result of its advanced manufacturing processes and unparalleled quality control systems. Capabilities such as these have been hard for competitors to imitate or best.

Why a Company's Strategy Evolves over Time

LO 4

A company's strategy tends to evolve because of changing circumstances and ongoing efforts by management to improve the strategy.

The appeal of a strategy that yields a sustainable competitive advantage is that it offers the potential for an enduring edge over rivals. However, managers of every company must be willing and ready to modify the strategy in response to changing market conditions, advancing technology, unexpected moves by competitors, shifting buyer needs, emerging market opportunities, and new ideas for improving the strategy. Most of the time, a company's strategy evolves incrementally as management fine-tunes various pieces of the strategy and adjusts the strategy in response to unfolding events.[5] However, on occasion, major strategy shifts are called for, such as when the strategy is clearly failing or when industry conditions change in dramatic ways. Industry environments characterized by high-velocity change require companies to repeatedly adapt their strategies.[6] For example, companies in industries with rapid-fire advances in technology like medical equipment, shale fracking, and smartphones often find it essential to adjust key elements of their strategies several times a year, sometimes even finding it necessary to "reinvent" their approach to providing value to their customers.

Regardless of whether a company's strategy changes gradually or swiftly, the important point is that the task of crafting strategy is not a one-time event but always a work in progress. Adapting to new conditions and constantly evaluating what is working well enough to continue and what needs to be improved are normal parts of the strategy-making process, resulting in an *evolving strategy*.[7]

A Company's Strategy Is Partly Proactive and Partly Reactive

Changing circumstances and ongoing management efforts to improve the strategy cause a company's strategy to evolve over time—a condition that makes the task of crafting strategy a *work in progress*, not a one-time event.

A company's strategy is shaped partly by management analysis and choice and partly by the necessity of adapting and learning by doing.

The evolving nature of a company's strategy means that the typical company strategy is a blend of (1) *proactive*, planned initiatives to improve the company's financial performance and secure a competitive edge and (2) *reactive* responses to unanticipated developments and fresh market conditions. The biggest portion of a company's current strategy flows from previously initiated actions that have proven themselves in the marketplace and newly launched initiatives aimed at edging out rivals and boosting financial performance. This part of management's action plan for running the company is its **deliberate strategy,** consisting of proactive strategy elements that

FIGURE 1.2   A Company's Strategy Is a Blend of Proactive Initiatives and Reactive Adjustments

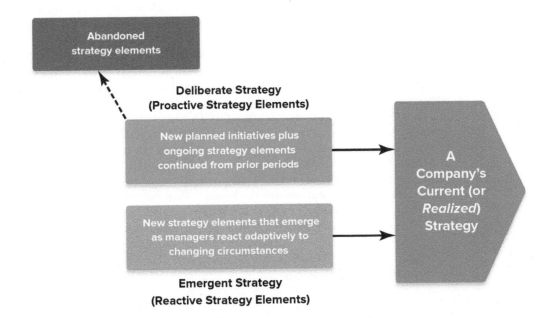

are both planned and realized as planned (while other planned strategy elements may not work out and are abandoned in consequence)—see Figure 1.2.[8]

But managers must always be willing to supplement or modify the proactive strategy elements with as-needed reactions to unanticipated conditions. Inevitably, there will be occasions when market and competitive conditions take an unexpected turn that calls for some kind of strategic reaction. Hence, *a portion of a company's strategy is always developed on the fly,* coming as a response to fresh strategic maneuvers on the part of rival firms, unexpected shifts in customer requirements, fast-changing technological developments, newly appearing market opportunities, a changing political or economic climate, or other unanticipated happenings in the surrounding environment. These adaptive strategy adjustments make up the firm's **emergent strategy.** A company's strategy *in toto* (its *realized strategy*) thus tends to be a *combination* of proactive and reactive elements, with certain strategy elements being *abandoned* because they have become obsolete or ineffective. A company's realized strategy can be observed in the pattern of its actions over time, which is a far better indicator than any of its strategic plans on paper or any public pronouncements about its strategy.

CORE CONCEPT

A company's **deliberate strategy** consists of *proactive* strategy elements that are planned; its **emergent strategy** consists of *reactive* strategy elements that emerge as changing conditions warrant.

A COMPANY'S STRATEGY AND ITS BUSINESS MODEL

At the core of every sound strategy is the company's **business model.** A business model is management's blueprint for delivering a valuable product or service to customers in a manner that will generate revenues sufficient to cover costs and yield an attractive profit.[9] The two elements of a company's business model are (1) its *customer value proposition* and (2) its *profit formula.* The customer value proposition lays out

10

the company's approach to satisfying buyer wants and needs at a price customers will consider a good value. The profit formula describes the company's approach to determining a cost structure that will allow for acceptable profits, given the pricing tied to its customer value proposition. Figure 1.3 illustrates the elements of the business model in terms of what is known as the *value-price-cost framework*.[10] As the framework indicates, the customer value proposition can be expressed as $V - P$, which is essentially the customers' perception of how much value they are getting for the money. The profit formula, on a per-unit basis, can be expressed as $P - C$. Plainly, from a customer perspective, the greater the value delivered (V) and the lower the price (P), the more attractive is the company's value proposition. On the other hand, the lower the costs (C), given the customer value proposition ($V - P$), the greater the ability of the business model to be a moneymaker. Thus the profit formula reveals how efficiently a company can meet customer wants and needs and deliver on the value proposition. The nitty-gritty issue surrounding a company's business model is whether it can execute its customer value proposition profitably. Just because company managers have crafted a strategy for competing and running the business does not automatically mean that the strategy will lead to profitability—it may or it may not.

Aircraft engine manufacturer Rolls-Royce employs an innovative "power-by-the-hour" business model that charges airlines leasing fees for engine use, maintenance, and repairs based on actual hours flown. The company retains ownership of the engines and is able to minimize engine maintenance costs through the use of sophisticated sensors that optimize maintenance and repair schedules. Gillette's business model in razor blades involves selling a "master product"—the razor—at an attractively low price and then making money on repeat purchases of razor blades that can be produced cheaply and sold at high profit margins. Printer manufacturers like Hewlett-Packard, Canon, and Epson pursue much the same business model as Gillette—selling printers at a low (virtually break-even) price and making large profit margins on the repeat purchases of ink cartridges and other printer supplies.

McDonald's invented the business model for fast food—providing value to customers in the form of economical quick-service meals at clean, convenient locations. Its profit formula involves such elements as standardized cost-efficient store design, stringent specifications for ingredients, detailed operating procedures for each unit, sizable investment in human resources and training, and heavy reliance on advertising and in-store promotions to drive volume. Illustration Capsule 1.2 describes three contrasting business models in radio broadcasting.

FIGURE 1.3   The Business Model and the Value-Price-Cost Framework

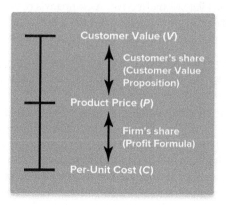

Pandora, SiriusXM, and Over-the-Air Broadcast Radio: Three Contrasting Business Models

© Rob Kim/Getty Images

	Pandora	SiriusXM	Over-the-Air Radio Broadcasters
Customer value proposition	• Through free-of-charge Internet radio service, allowed PC, tablet computer, and smartphone users to create up to 100 personalized music and comedy stations. • Utilized algorithms to generate playlists based on users' predicted music preferences. • Offered programming interrupted by brief, occasional ads; eliminated advertising for Pandora One subscribers.	• For a monthly subscription fee, provided satellite-based music, news, sports, national and regional weather, traffic reports in limited areas, and talk radio programming. • Also offered subscribers streaming Internet channels and the ability to create personalized commercial-free stations for online and mobile listening. • Offered programming interrupted only by brief, occasional ads.	• Provided free-of-charge music, national and local news, local traffic reports, national and local weather, and talk radio programming. • Included frequent programming interruption for ads.
Profit formula	*Revenue generation:* Display, audio, and video ads targeted to different audiences and sold to local and national buyers; subscription revenues generated from an advertising-free option called Pandora One. *Cost structure:* Fixed costs associated with developing software for computers, tablets, and smartphones. Fixed and variable costs related to operating data centers to support streaming network, content royalties, marketing, and support activities.	*Revenue generation:* Monthly subscription fees, sales of satellite radio equipment, and advertising revenues. *Cost structure:* Fixed costs associated with operating a satellite-based music delivery service and streaming Internet service. Fixed and variable costs related to programming and content royalties, marketing, and support activities.	*Revenue generation:* Advertising sales to national and local businesses. *Cost structure:* Fixed costs associated with terrestrial broadcasting operations. Fixed and variable costs related to local news reporting, advertising sales operations, network affiliate fees, programming and content royalties, commercial production activities, and support activities.

Pandora	SiriusXM	Over-the-Air Radio Broadcasters
Profit margin: Profitability dependent on generating sufficient advertising revenues and subscription revenues to cover costs and provide attractive profits.	*Profit margin:* Profitability dependent on attracting a sufficiently large number of subscribers to cover costs and provide attractive profits.	*Profit margin:* Profitability dependent on generating sufficient advertising revenues to cover costs and provide attractive profits.

WHAT MAKES A STRATEGY A WINNER?

LO 6

The three tests of a winning strategy.

Three tests can be applied to determine whether a strategy is a *winning strategy:*

1. ***The Fit Test:*** *How well does the strategy fit the company's situation?* To qualify as a winner, a strategy has to be well matched to industry and competitive conditions, a company's best market opportunities, and other pertinent aspects of the business environment in which the company operates. No strategy can work well unless it exhibits good *external fit* with respect to prevailing market conditions. At the same time, a winning strategy must be tailored to the company's resources and competitive capabilities and be supported by a complementary set of functional activities (i.e., activities in the realms of supply chain management, operations, sales and marketing, and so on). That is, it must also exhibit *internal fit* and be compatible with a company's ability to execute the strategy in a competent manner. Unless a strategy exhibits good fit with both the external and internal aspects of a company's overall situation, it is likely to be an underperformer and fall short of producing winning results. Winning strategies also exhibit *dynamic fit* in the sense that they evolve over time in a manner that maintains close and effective alignment with the company's situation even as external and internal conditions change.[11]

> To pass the *fit test*, a strategy must exhibit fit along three dimensions: (1) external, (2) internal, and (3) dynamic.

2. ***The Competitive Advantage Test:*** *Is the strategy helping the company achieve a sustainable competitive advantage?* Strategies that fail to achieve a persistent competitive advantage over rivals are unlikely to produce superior performance for more than a brief period of time. Winning strategies enable a company to achieve a competitive advantage over key rivals that is long-lasting. The bigger and more durable the competitive advantage, the more powerful it is.

3. ***The Performance Test:*** *Is the strategy producing superior company performance?* The mark of a winning strategy is strong company performance. Two kinds of performance indicators tell the most about the caliber of a company's strategy: (1) competitive strength and market standing and (2) profitability and financial strength. Above-average financial performance or gains in market share, competitive position, or profitability are signs of a winning strategy.

> A **winning strategy** must pass three tests:
> 1. The fit test
> 2. The competitive advantage test
> 3. The performance test

Strategies—either existing or proposed—that come up short on one or more of the preceding tests are plainly less appealing than strategies passing all three tests with flying colors. New initiatives that don't seem to match the company's internal and external situations should be scrapped before they come to fruition, while existing strategies must be scrutinized on a regular basis to ensure they have good fit, offer a competitive advantage, and are contributing to above-average performance or performance improvements. Failure to pass one or more of the three tests should prompt managers to make immediate changes in an existing strategy.

WHY CRAFTING AND EXECUTING STRATEGY ARE IMPORTANT TASKS

Crafting and executing strategy are top-priority managerial tasks for two big reasons. First, a clear and reasoned strategy is management's prescription for doing business, its road map to competitive advantage, its game plan for pleasing customers, and its formula for improving performance. High-performing enterprises are nearly always the product of astute, creative, and proactive strategy making. Companies don't get to the top of the industry rankings or stay there with flawed strategies, copycat strategies, or timid attempts to try to do better. Only a handful of companies can boast of hitting home runs in the marketplace due to lucky breaks or the good fortune of having stumbled into the right market at the right time with the right product. Even if this is the case, success will not be lasting unless the companies subsequently craft a strategy that capitalizes on their luck, builds on what is working, and discards the rest. So there can be little argument that the process of crafting a company's strategy matters—and matters a lot.

Second, even the best-conceived strategies will result in performance shortfalls if they are not executed proficiently. The processes of crafting and executing strategies must go hand in hand if a company is to be successful in the long term. The chief executive officer of one successful company put it well when he said:

> In the main, our competitors are acquainted with the same fundamental concepts and techniques and approaches that we follow, and they are as free to pursue them as we are. More often than not, the difference between their level of success and ours lies in the relative thoroughness and self-discipline with which we and they develop and execute our strategies for the future.

Good Strategy + Good Strategy Execution = Good Management

Crafting and executing strategy are thus core management tasks. Among all the things managers do, nothing affects a company's ultimate success or failure more fundamentally than how well its management team charts the company's direction, develops competitively effective strategic moves, and pursues what needs to be done internally to produce good day-in, day-out strategy execution and operating excellence. Indeed, *good strategy and good strategy execution are the most telling and trustworthy signs of good management.* The rationale for using the twin standards of good strategy making and good strategy execution to determine whether a company is well managed is therefore compelling: *The better conceived a company's strategy and the more competently it is executed, the more likely the company will be a standout performer in the marketplace.* In stark contrast, a company that lacks clear-cut direction, has a flawed strategy, or can't execute its strategy competently is a company whose financial performance is probably suffering, whose business is at long-term risk, and whose management is sorely lacking.

THE ROAD AHEAD

How well a company performs is directly attributable to the caliber of its strategy and the proficiency with which the strategy is executed.

Throughout the chapters to come and in Part 2 of this text, the spotlight is on the foremost question in running a business enterprise: *What must managers do, and do well, to make a company a winner in the marketplace?* The answer that emerges is that doing a good job of managing inherently requires good strategic thinking and good management of the strategy-making, strategy-executing process.

The mission of this book is to provide a solid overview of what every business student and aspiring manager needs to know about crafting and executing strategy. We will explore what good strategic thinking entails, describe the core concepts and tools of strategic analysis, and examine the ins and outs of crafting and executing strategy. The accompanying cases will help build your skills in both diagnosing how well the strategy-making, strategy-executing task is being performed and prescribing actions for how the strategy in question or its execution can be improved. The strategic management course that you are enrolled in may also include a strategy simulation exercise in which you will run a company in head-to-head competition with companies run by your classmates. Your mastery of the strategic management concepts presented in the following chapters will put you in a strong position to craft a winning strategy for your company and figure out how to execute it in a cost-effective and profitable manner. As you progress through the chapters of the text and the activities assigned during the term, we hope to convince you that first-rate capabilities in crafting and executing strategy are essential to good management.

As you tackle the content and accompanying activities of this book, ponder the following observation by the essayist and poet Ralph Waldo Emerson: "Commerce is a game of skill which many people play, but which few play well." If your efforts help you become a savvy player and better equip you to succeed in business, the time and energy you spend here will indeed prove worthwhile.

KEY POINTS

1. A company's strategy is its game plan to attract customers, outperform its competitors, and achieve superior profitability.

2. The central thrust of a company's strategy is undertaking moves to build and strengthen the company's long-term competitive position and financial performance by *competing differently* from rivals and gaining a sustainable competitive advantage over them.

3. A company achieves a *competitive advantage* when it provides buyers with superior value compared to rival sellers or offers the same value at a lower cost to the firm. The advantage is *sustainable* if it persists despite the best efforts of competitors to match or surpass this advantage.

4. A company's strategy typically evolves over time, emerging from a blend of (1) proactive deliberate actions on the part of company managers to improve the strategy and (2) reactive emergent responses to unanticipated developments and fresh market conditions.

5. A company's business model sets forth the logic for how its strategy will create value for customers and at the same time generate revenues sufficient to cover costs and realize a profit. Thus, it contains two crucial elements: (1) the *customer value proposition*—a plan for satisfying customer wants and needs at a price

customers will consider good value, and (2) the *profit formula*—a plan for a cost structure that will enable the company to deliver the customer value proposition profitably. These elements are illustrated by the value-price-cost framework.

6. A winning strategy will pass three tests: (1) *fit* (external, internal, and dynamic consistency), (2) *competitive advantage* (durable competitive advantage), and (3) *performance* (outstanding financial and market performance).

7. Crafting and executing strategy are core management functions. How well a company performs and the degree of market success it enjoys are directly attributable to the caliber of its strategy and the proficiency with which the strategy is executed.

ASSURANCE OF LEARNING EXERCISES

1. Based on your experiences as a coffee consumer, does Starbucks's strategy (as described in Illustration Capsule 1.1) seem to set it apart from rivals? Does the strategy seem to be keyed to a cost-based advantage, differentiating features, serving the unique needs of a niche, or some combination of these? What is there about Starbucks's strategy that can lead to sustainable competitive advantage?

LO 1, LO 2, LO 3

2. Elements of the Hershey Company's strategy have evolved in meaningful ways since the company's founding as an American chocolate manufacturer in 1900. After reviewing the company's history at www.thehersheycompany.com/about-hershey/our-story/hersheys-history.aspx and the links at the company's investor relations site (www.thehersheycompany.com/investors/company-profile.aspx), prepare a one- to two-page report that discusses how its strategy has evolved. Your report should also assess how well Hershey's strategy passes the three tests of a winning strategy.

LO 4, LO 6

3. Go to investor.siriusxm.com and check whether Sirius XM's recent financial reports indicate that its business model is working. Are its subscription fees increasing or declining? Are its revenue stream advertising and equipment sales growing or declining? Does its cost structure allow for acceptable profit margins?

LO 5

EXERCISE FOR SIMULATION PARTICIPANTS

Three basic questions must be answered by managers of organizations of all sizes as they begin the process of crafting strategy:

- What is our present situation?
- Where do we want to go from here?
- How are we going to get there?

After you have read the Participant's Guide or Player's Manual for the strategy simulation exercise that you will participate in during this academic term, you and your co-managers should come up with brief one- or two-paragraph answers to these three questions *prior to* entering your first set of decisions. While your answer to the first of the three questions can be developed from your reading of the manual, the second and third questions will require a collaborative discussion among the members of your company's management team about how you intend to manage the company you have been assigned to run.

1. *What is our company's current situation?* A substantive answer to this question should cover the following issues:
   - Is your company in a good, average, or weak competitive position vis-à-vis rival companies?
   - Does your company appear to be in a sound financial condition?
   - Does it appear to have a competitive advantage, and is it likely to be sustainable?
   - **LO 1, LO 2, LO 3** What problems does your company have that need to be addressed?

2. *Where do we want to take the company during the time we are in charge?* A complete answer to this question should say something about each of the following:
   - What goals or aspirations do you have for your company?
   - What do you want the company to be known for?
   - What market share would you like your company to have after the first five decision rounds?
   - By what amount or percentage would you like to increase total profits of the company by the end of the final decision round?
   - **LO 4, LO 6** What kinds of performance outcomes will signal that you and your co-managers are managing the company in a successful manner?

3. *How are we going to get there?* Your answer should cover these issues:
   - Which one of the basic strategic and competitive approaches discussed in this chapter do you think makes the most sense to pursue?
   - What kind of competitive advantage over rivals will you try to achieve?
   - How would you describe the company's business model?
   - **LO 4, LO 5** What kind of actions will support these objectives?

ENDNOTES

[1] B. R, "Strategy," *The Economist*, October 19, 2012, www.economist.com/blogs/schumpeter/2012/10/z-business-quotations-1 (accessed January 4, 2014).

[2] Jan Rivkin, "An Alternative Approach to Making Strategic Choices," Harvard Business School case 9-702-433, 2001.

[3] Michael E. Porter, "What Is Strategy?" *Harvard Business Review* 74, no. 6 (November–December 1996), pp. 65–67.

[4] Ibid.

[5] Eric T. Anderson and Duncan Simester, "A Step-by-Step Guide to Smart Business Experiments," *Harvard Business Review* 89, no. 3 (March 2011).

[6] Shona L. Brown and Kathleen M. Eisenhardt, *Competing on the Edge: Strategy as Structured Chaos* (Boston, MA: Harvard Business School Press, 1998).

[7] Cynthia A. Montgomery, "Putting Leadership Back into Strategy," *Harvard Business Review* 86, no. 1 (January 2008).

[8] Henry Mintzberg and J. A. Waters, "Of Strategies, Deliberate and Emergent," *Strategic Management Journal* 6 (1985); Costas Markides, "Strategy as Balance: From 'Either-Or' to 'And,' " *Business Strategy Review* 12, no. 3 (September 2001).

[9] Mark W. Johnson, Clayton M. Christensen, and Henning Kagermann, "Reinventing Your Business Model," *Harvard Business Review* 86, no. 12 (December 2008); Joan Magretta, "Why Business Models Matter," *Harvard Business Review* 80, no. 5 (May 2002).

[10] A. Brandenburger and H. Stuart, "Value-Based Strategy," *Journal of Economics and Management Strategy* 5 (1996), pp. 5–24; D. Hoopes, T. Madsen, and G. Walker, "Guest Editors' Introduction to the Special Issue: Why Is There a Resource-Based View? Toward a Theory of Competitive Heterogeneity," *Strategic Management Journal* 24 (2003), pp. 889–992; M. Peteraf and J. Barney, "Unravelling the Resource-Based Tangle," *Managerial and Decision Economics* 24 (2003), pp. 309–323.

[11] Rivkin, "An Alternative Approach to Making Strategic Choices."

CHAPTER 2

Charting a Company's Direction

Its Vision, Mission, Objectives, and Strategy

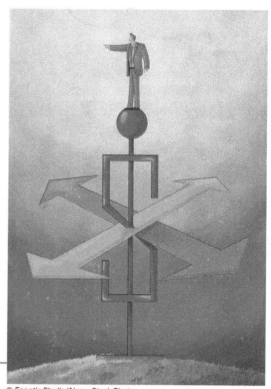

© Fanatic Studio/Alamy Stock Photo

Learning Objectives

THIS CHAPTER WILL HELP YOU UNDERSTAND:

LO 1 Why it is critical for company managers to have a clear strategic vision of where a company needs to head.

LO 2 The importance of setting both strategic and financial objectives.

LO 3 Why the strategic initiatives taken at various organizational levels must be tightly coordinated to achieve companywide performance targets.

LO 4 What a company must do to achieve operating excellence and to execute its strategy proficiently.

LO 5 The role and responsibility of a company's board of directors in overseeing the strategic management process.

Sound strategy starts with having the right goal.

Michael Porter—*Professor and consultant*

Good business leaders create a vision, articulate the vision, passionately own the vision, and relentlessly drive it to completion.

Jack Welch—*Former CEO of General Electric*

Apple is so focused on its vision that it does things in a very careful, deliberate way.

John Sculley—*Former CEO of Apple*

Crafting and executing strategy are the heart and soul of managing a business enterprise. But exactly what is involved in developing a strategy and executing it proficiently? What goes into charting a company's strategic course and long-term direction? Is any analysis required? Does a company need a strategic plan? What are the various components of the strategy-making, strategy-executing process and to what extent are company personnel—aside from senior management—involved in the process?

This chapter presents an overview of the ins and outs of crafting and executing company strategies.

The focus is on management's direction-setting responsibilities—charting a strategic course, setting performance targets, and choosing a strategy capable of producing the desired outcomes. There is coverage of why strategy making is a task for a company's entire management team and which kinds of strategic decisions tend to be made at which levels of management. The chapter concludes with a look at the roles and responsibilities of a company's board of directors and how good corporate governance protects shareholder interests and promotes good management.

WHAT DOES THE STRATEGY-MAKING, STRATEGY-EXECUTING PROCESS ENTAIL?

Crafting and executing a company's strategy is an ongoing process that consists of five interrelated stages:

1. *Developing a strategic vision* that charts the company's long-term direction, a *mission statement* that describes the company's purpose, and a set of *core values* to guide the pursuit of the vision and mission.
2. *Setting objectives* for measuring the company's performance and tracking its progress in moving in the intended long-term direction.
3. *Crafting a strategy* for advancing the company along the path management has charted and achieving its performance objectives.
4. *Executing the chosen strategy* efficiently and effectively.

20   PART 1   Concepts and Techniques for Crafting and Executing Strategy

FIGURE 2.1   The Strategy-Making, Strategy-Executing Process

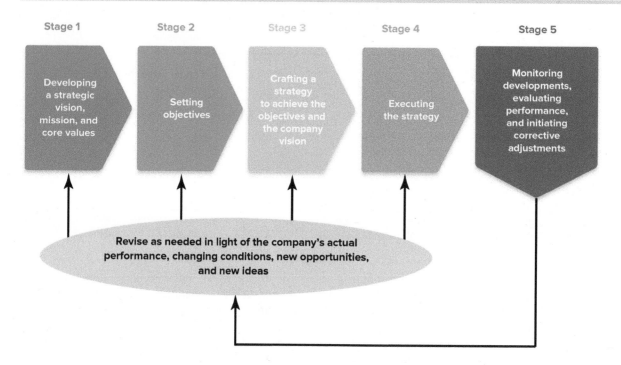

5. *Monitoring developments, evaluating performance, and initiating corrective adjustments* in the company's vision and mission statement, objectives, strategy, or approach to strategy execution in light of actual experience, changing conditions, new ideas, and new opportunities.

Figure 2.1 displays this five-stage process, which we examine next in some detail. The first three stages of the strategic management process involve making a strategic plan. A **strategic plan** maps out where a company is headed, establishes strategic and financial targets, and outlines the competitive moves and approaches to be used in achieving the desired business results.[1] We explain this more fully at the conclusion of our discussion of stage 3, later in this chapter.

STAGE 1: DEVELOPING A STRATEGIC VISION, MISSION STATEMENT, AND SET OF CORE VALUES

LO 1

Why it is critical for company managers to have a clear strategic vision of where a company needs to head.

Very early in the strategy-making process, a company's senior managers must wrestle with the issue of what directional path the company should take. Can the company's prospects be improved by changing its product offerings, or the markets in which it participates, or the customers it aims to serve? Deciding to commit the company to one path versus another pushes managers to draw some carefully reasoned conclusions about whether the company's present strategic course offers attractive opportunities for growth and profitability or whether changes of one kind or another in the company's strategy and long-term direction are needed.

Developing a Strategic Vision

Top management's views about the company's long-term direction and what product-market-customer business mix seems optimal for the road ahead constitute a **strategic vision** for the company. A strategic vision delineates management's aspirations for the company's future, providing a panoramic view of "where we are going" and a convincing rationale for why this makes good business sense. A strategic vision thus points an organization in a particular direction, charts a strategic path for it to follow, builds commitment to the future course of action, and molds organizational identity. A clearly articulated strategic vision communicates management's aspirations to stakeholders (customers, employees, stockholders, suppliers, etc.) and helps steer the energies of company personnel in a common direction. The vision of Google's cofounders Larry Page and Sergey Brin "to organize the world's information and make it universally accessible and useful" provides a good example. In serving as the company's guiding light, it has captured the imagination of stakeholders and the public at large, served as the basis for crafting the company's strategic actions, and aided internal efforts to mobilize and direct the company's resources.

Well-conceived visions are *distinctive* and *specific* to a particular organization; they avoid generic, feel-good statements like "We will become a global leader and the first choice of customers in every market we serve."[2] Likewise, a strategic vision proclaiming management's quest "to be the market leader" or "to be the most innovative" or "to be recognized as the best company in the industry" offers scant guidance about a company's long-term direction or the kind of company that management is striving to build.

A surprising number of the vision statements found on company websites and in annual reports are vague and unrevealing, saying very little about the company's future direction. Some could apply to almost any company in any industry. Many read like a public relations statement—high-sounding words that someone came up with because it is fashionable for companies to have an official vision statement.[3] An example is Hilton Hotel's vision "to fill the earth with light and the warmth of hospitality," which simply borders on the incredulous. The real purpose of a vision statement is to serve as a management tool for giving the organization a sense of direction.

For a strategic vision to function as a valuable management tool, it must convey what top executives want the business to look like and provide managers at all organizational levels with a reference point in making strategic decisions and preparing the company for the future. It must say something definitive about how the company's leaders intend to position the company beyond where it is today. Table 2.1 provides some dos and don'ts in composing an effectively worded vision statement. Illustration Capsule 2.1 provides a critique of the strategic visions of several prominent companies.

> **CORE CONCEPT**
>
> A **strategic vision** describes management's aspirations for the company's future and the course and direction charted to achieve them.

> An effectively communicated vision is a valuable management tool for enlisting the commitment of company personnel to actions that move the company in the intended long-term direction.

Communicating the Strategic Vision

A strategic vision has little value to the organization unless it's effectively communicated down the line to lower-level managers and employees. A vision cannot provide direction for middle managers or inspire and energize employees unless everyone in the company is familiar with it and can observe senior management's commitment to the vision. It is particularly important for executives to provide a compelling rationale for a dramatically *new* strategic vision and company direction. When company personnel don't understand or accept the need for redirecting organizational efforts, they are prone to resist change. Hence, explaining the basis for the new direction,

TABLE 2.1   Wording a Vision Statement—the Dos and Don'ts

The Dos	The Don'ts
Be graphic. Paint a clear picture of where the company is headed and the market position(s) the company is striving to stake out.	**Don't be vague or incomplete.** Never skimp on specifics about where the company is headed or how the company intends to prepare for the future.
Be forward-looking and directional. Describe the strategic course that will help the company prepare for the future.	**Don't dwell on the present.** A vision is not about what a company once did or does now; it's about "where we are going."
Keep it focused. Focus on providing managers with guidance in making decisions and allocating resources.	**Don't use overly broad language.** Avoid all-inclusive language that gives the company license to pursue any opportunity.
Have some wiggle room. Language that allows some flexibility allows the directional course to be adjusted as market, customer, and technology circumstances change.	**Don't state the vision in bland or uninspiring terms.** The best vision statements have the power to motivate company personnel and inspire shareholder confidence about the company's future.
Be sure the journey is feasible. The path and direction should be within the realm of what the company can accomplish; over time, a company should be able to demonstrate measurable progress in achieving the vision.	**Don't be generic.** A vision statement that could apply to companies in any of several industries (or to any of several companies in the same industry) is not specific enough to provide any guidance.
Indicate why the directional path makes good business sense. The directional path should be in the long-term interests of stakeholders (especially shareholders, employees, and suppliers).	**Don't rely on superlatives.** Visions that claim the company's strategic course is the "best" or "most successful" usually lack specifics about the path the company is taking to get there.
Make it memorable. A well-stated vision is short, easily communicated, and memorable. Ideally, it should be reducible to a few choice lines or a one-phrase slogan.	**Don't run on and on.** A vision statement that is not concise and to the point will tend to lose its audience.

Sources: John P. Kotter, *Leading Change* (Boston: Harvard Business School Press, 1996); Hugh Davidson, *The Committed Enterprise* (Oxford: Butterworth Heinemann, 2002); Michel Robert, *Strategy Pure and Simple II* (New York: McGraw-Hill, 1992).

addressing employee concerns head-on, calming fears, lifting spirits, and providing updates and progress reports as events unfold all become part of the task in mobilizing support for the vision and winning commitment to needed actions.

Winning the support of organization members for the vision nearly always requires putting "where we are going and why" in writing, distributing the statement organizationwide, and having top executives personally explain the vision and its rationale to as many people as feasible. Ideally, executives should present their vision for the company in a manner that reaches out and grabs people. An engaging and convincing strategic vision has enormous motivational value—for the same reason that a stonemason is more inspired by the opportunity to build a great cathedral for the ages than a house. Thus, executive ability to paint a convincing and inspiring picture of a company's journey to a future destination is an important element of effective strategic leadership.

ILLUSTRATION CAPSULE 2.1

Examples of Strategic Visions— How Well Do They Measure Up?

© Jeff Greenberg/UIG via Getty Images

Vision Statement	Effective Elements	Shortcomings
Whole Foods Whole Foods Market is a dynamic leader in the quality food business. We are a mission-driven company that aims to set the standards of excellence for food retailers. We are building a business in which high standards permeate all aspects of our company. Quality is a state of mind at Whole Foods Market. Our motto—Whole Foods, Whole People, Whole Planet—emphasizes that our vision reaches far beyond just being a food retailer. Our success in fulfilling our vision is measured by customer satisfaction, team member happiness and excellence, return on capital investment, improvement in the state of the environment and local and larger community support. Our ability to instill a clear sense of interdependence among our various stakeholders (the people who are interested and benefit from the success of our company) is contingent upon our efforts to communicate more often, more openly, and more compassionately. Better communication equals better understanding and more trust.	• Forward-looking • Graphic • Focused • Makes good business sense	• Long • Not memorable
Keurig Become the world's leading personal beverage systems company.	• Focused • Flexible • Makes good business sense	• Not graphic • Lacks specifics • Not forward-looking
Nike NIKE, Inc. fosters a culture of invention. We create products, services and experiences for today's athlete* while solving problems for the next generation. *If you have a body, you are an athlete.	• Forward-looking • Flexible	• Vague and lacks detail • Not focused • Generic • Not necessarily feasible

Note: Developed with Frances C. Thunder.

Source: Company websites (accessed online February 12, 2016).

Expressing the Essence of the Vision in a Slogan The task of effectively conveying the vision to company personnel is assisted when management can capture the vision of where to head in a catchy or easily remembered slogan. A number of organizations have summed up their vision in a brief phrase. Ben & Jerry's vision is "Making the best possible ice cream, in the nicest possible way," while Charles Schwab's is simply "Helping investors help themselves." Disney's overarching vision for its five business groups—theme parks, movie studios, television channels, consumer products, and interactive media entertainment—is to "create happiness by providing the finest in entertainment for people of all ages, everywhere." Even Scotland Yard has a catchy vision, which is to "make London the safest major city in the world." Creating a short slogan to illuminate an organization's direction and using it repeatedly as a reminder of "where we are headed and why" helps rally organization members to maintain their focus and hurdle whatever obstacles lie in the company's path.

Why a Sound, Well-Communicated Strategic Vision Matters
A well-thought-out, forcefully communicated strategic vision pays off in several respects: (1) It crystallizes senior executives' own views about the firm's long-term direction; (2) it reduces the risk of rudderless decision making; (3) it is a tool for winning the support of organization members to help make the vision a reality; (4) it provides a beacon for lower-level managers in setting departmental objectives and crafting departmental strategies that are in sync with the company's overall strategy; and (5) it helps an organization prepare for the future. When top executives are able to demonstrate significant progress in achieving these five benefits, the first step in organizational direction setting has been successfully completed.

Developing a Company Mission Statement

The defining characteristic of a strategic vision is what it says about the company's *future strategic course*—"the direction we are headed and the shape of our business in the future." It is aspirational. In contrast, a **mission statement** describes the enterprise's *present business and purpose*—"who we are, what we do, and why we are here." It is purely descriptive. Ideally, a company mission statement (1) identifies the company's products and/or services, (2) specifies the buyer needs that the company seeks to satisfy and the customer groups or markets that it serves, and (3) gives the company its own identity. The mission statements that one finds in company annual reports or posted on company websites are typically quite brief; some do a better job than others of conveying what the enterprise's current business operations and purpose are all about.

Consider, for example, the mission statement of Singapore Airlines, which is consistently rated among the world's best in terms of passenger safety and comfort:

> Singapore Airlines is a global company dedicated to providing air transportation services of the highest quality and to maximizing returns for the benefit of its shareholders and employees.

Note that Singapore Airlines's mission statement does a good job of conveying "who we are, what we do, and why we are here," but it provides no sense of "where we are headed."

An example of a well-stated mission statement with ample specifics about what the organization does is that of St. Jude Children's Research Hospital: "to advance cures, and means of prevention, for pediatric catastrophic diseases through research and treatment. Consistent with the vision of our founder Danny Thomas, no child is

The distinction between a strategic vision and a mission statement is fairly clear-cut: A **strategic vision** *portrays a company's aspirations for its* future *("where we are going"), whereas a company's* **mission** *describes the scope and purpose of its* present *business ("who we are, what we do, and why we are here").*

denied treatment based on race, religion or a family's ability to pay." Facebook's mission statement, while short, still captures the essence of what the company is about: "to give people the power to share and make the world more open and connected." An example of a not-so-revealing mission statement is that of Microsoft: "To empower every person and every organization on the planet to achieve more." It says nothing about the company's products or business makeup and could apply to many companies in many different industries. A person unfamiliar with Microsoft could not discern from its mission statement that it is a globally known provider of PC software and a leading maker of video game consoles (the popular Xbox 360). Coca-Cola, which markets more than 500 beverage brands in over 200 countries, also has an uninformative mission statement: "to refresh the world; to inspire moments of optimism and happiness; to create value and make a difference." The usefulness of a mission statement that cannot convey the essence of a company's business activities and purpose is unclear.

Occasionally, companies couch their mission in terms of making a profit. This, too, is flawed. Profit is more correctly an *objective* and a *result* of what a company does. Moreover, earning a profit is the obvious intent of every commercial enterprise. Companies such as Gap Inc., Edward Jones, Honda, The Boston Consulting Group, Citigroup, DreamWorks Animation, and Intuit are all striving to earn a profit for shareholders; but plainly the fundamentals of their businesses are substantially different when it comes to "who we are and what we do." It is management's answer to "make a profit doing what and for whom?" that reveals the substance of a company's true mission and business purpose.

> To be well worded, a company mission statement must employ language specific enough to distinguish its business makeup and purpose from those of other enterprises and give the company its own identity.

Linking the Vision and Mission with Company Values

Many companies have developed a set of values to guide the actions and behavior of company personnel in conducting the company's business and pursuing its strategic vision and mission. By **values** (or **core values,** as they are often called) we mean certain designated beliefs, traits, and behavioral norms that management has determined should guide the pursuit of its vision and mission. Values relate to such things as fair treatment, honor and integrity, ethical behavior, innovativeness, teamwork, a passion for top-notch quality or superior customer service, social responsibility, and community citizenship.

> ### CORE CONCEPT
>
> A company's **values** are the beliefs, traits, and behavioral norms that company personnel are expected to display in conducting the company's business and pursuing its strategic vision and mission.

Most companies have articulated four to eight core values that company personnel are expected to display and that are supposed to be mirrored in how the company conducts its business. At Samsung, five core values are linked to its desire to contribute to a better global society by creating superior products and services: (1) giving people opportunities to reach their full potential, (2) developing the best products and services on the market, (3) embracing change, (4) operating in an ethical way, and (5) being dedicated to social and environmental responsibility. American Express embraces seven core values: (1) respect for people, (2) commitment to customers, (3) integrity, (4) teamwork, (5) good citizenship, (6) a will to win, and (7) personal accountability.

Do companies practice what they preach when it comes to their professed values? Sometimes no, sometimes yes—it runs the gamut. At one extreme are companies with window-dressing values; the values are given lip service by top executives but have little discernible impact on either how company personnel behave or how the company operates. Such companies have value statements because they are in vogue and make the company look good. At the other extreme are companies whose executives are committed to grounding company operations on sound values and principled ways of doing business. Executives at these companies deliberately seek to ingrain the designated core values into the corporate culture—the core values thus become an integral part of the company's DNA and what makes the company tick. At such values-driven companies, executives "walk the talk" and company personnel are held accountable for embodying the stated values in their behavior.

At companies where the stated values are real rather than cosmetic, managers connect values to the pursuit of the strategic vision and mission in one of two ways. In companies with long-standing values that are deeply entrenched in the corporate culture, senior managers are careful to craft a vision, mission, strategy, and set of operating practices that match established values; moreover, they repeatedly emphasize how the value-based behavioral norms contribute to the company's business success. If the company changes to a different vision or strategy, executives make a point of explaining how and why the core values continue to be relevant. Few companies with sincere commitment to established core values ever undertake strategic moves that conflict with ingrained values. In new companies, top management has to consider what values and business conduct should characterize the company and then draft a value statement that is circulated among managers and employees for discussion and possible modification. A final value statement that incorporates the desired behaviors and that connects to the vision and mission is then officially adopted. Some companies combine their vision, mission, and values into a single statement or document, circulate it to all organization members, and in many instances post the vision, mission, and value statement on the company's website. Illustration Capsule 2.2 describes how core values underlie the company's mission at Patagonia, Inc., a widely known and quite successful outdoor clothing and gear company.

STAGE 2: SETTING OBJECTIVES

LO 2

The importance of setting both strategic and financial objectives.

CORE CONCEPT

Objectives are an organization's performance targets—the specific results management wants to achieve.

The managerial purpose of setting **objectives** is to convert the vision and mission into specific performance targets. Objectives reflect management's aspirations for company performance in light of the industry's prevailing economic and competitive conditions and the company's internal capabilities. Well-stated objectives must be *specific, quantifiable* or *measurable,* and *challenging* and must contain a *deadline for achievement.* As Bill Hewlett, cofounder of Hewlett-Packard, shrewdly observed, "You cannot manage what you cannot measure. . . . And what gets measured gets done."[4] Concrete, measurable objectives are managerially valuable for three reasons: (1) They focus organizational attention and align actions throughout the organization, (2) they serve as *yardsticks* for tracking a company's performance and progress, and (3) they motivate employees to expend greater effort and perform at a high level.

The Imperative of Setting Stretch Objectives

The experiences of countless companies teach that one of the best ways to promote outstanding company performance is for managers to set performance targets high enough to *stretch an organization to perform at its full potential and deliver the best possible results.* Challenging company personnel to go all out and deliver "stretch" gains in performance pushes an enterprise to be more inventive, to exhibit more urgency in improving both its financial performance and its business position,

ILLUSTRATION CAPSULE 2.2

Patagonia, Inc.: A Values-Driven Company

PATAGONIA'S MISSION STATEMENT

Build the best product, cause no unnecessary harm, use business to inspire and implement solutions to the environmental crisis.

PATAGONIA'S CORE VALUES

Quality: Pursuit of ever-greater quality in everything we do.

Integrity: Relationships built on integrity and respect.

Environmentalism: Serve as a catalyst for personal and corporate action.

Not Bound by Convention: Our success—and much of the fun—lies in developing innovative ways to do things.

© Robert Alexander/Getty Images

Patagonia, Inc. is an American outdoor clothing and gear company that clearly "walks the talk" with respect to its mission and values. While its mission is relatively vague about the types of products Patagonia offers, it clearly states the foundational "how" and "why" of the company. The four core values individually reinforce the mission in distinct ways, charting a defined path for employees to follow. At the same time, each value is reliant on the others for maximum effect. The values' combined impact on internal operations and public perception has made Patagonia a strong leader in the outdoor gear world.

While many companies espouse the pursuit of **quality** as part of their strategy, at Patagonia quality must come through honorable practices or not at all. Routinely, the company opts for more expensive materials and labor to maintain internal consistency with the mission. Patagonia learned early on that it could not make good products in bad factories, so it holds its manufacturers accountable through a variety of auditing partnerships and alliances. In this way, the company maintains relationships built on **integrity** and respect. In addition to keeping faith with those

who make its products, Patagonia relentlessly pursues integrity in sourcing production inputs. Central to its **environmental** mission and core values, it targets for use sustainable and recyclable materials, ethically procured. Demonstrating leadership in environmentalism, Patagonia established foundations to support ecological causes, even **defying convention** by giving 1 percent of profits to conservation causes. These are but a few examples of the ways in which Patagonia's core values fortify each other and support the mission.

For Patagonia, quality would not be possible without integrity, unflinching environmentalism, and the company's unconventional approach. Since its founding in 1973 by rock climber Yvon Chouinard, Patagonia has remained remarkably consistent to the spirit of these values. This has endeared the company to legions of loyal customers while leading other businesses in protecting the environment. More than an apparel and gear company, Patagonia inspires everyone it touches to do their best for the planet and each other, in line with its mission and core values.

Note: Developed with Nicholas J. Ziemba.

Sources: Patagonia, Inc., "Corporate Social Responsibility," *The Footprint Chronicles,* 2007; "Becoming a Responsible Company," www.patagonia.com/us/patagonia.go?assetid=2329 (accessed February 28, 2014).

and to be more intentional and focused in its actions. Stretch objectives spur exceptional performance and help build a firewall against contentment with modest gains in organizational performance.

Manning Selvage & Lee (MS&L), a U.S. public relations firm, had originally set a goal of tripling its revenues to $100 million in five years, but managed to hit its target in just three years using ambitious stretch objectives. A company exhibits *strategic intent* when it relentlessly pursues an ambitious strategic objective, concentrating the full force of its resources and competitive actions on achieving that objective. MS&L's strategic intent was to become one of the leading global PR firms, which it achieved with the help of its stretch objectives. Both Google and Amazon have had the strategic intent of developing drones, Amazon's for delivery and Google's for both delivery of goods and access to high-speed Internet service from the skies. As of 2015, both companies had tested their systems and filed for Federal Aviation Administration registration of their drones. Elon Musk, CEO of both Tesla Motors and SpaceX, is well known for his ambitious stretch goals and strategic intent. In 2016, he said that his commercial flight program, SpaceX, should be ready to send people to Mars in 10 years.

What Kinds of Objectives to Set

Two distinct types of performance targets are required: those relating to financial performance and those relating to strategic performance. **Financial objectives** communicate management's goals for financial performance. **Strategic objectives** are goals concerning a company's marketing standing and competitive position. A company's set of financial and strategic objectives should include both near-term and longer-term performance targets. Short-term (quarterly or annual) objectives focus attention on delivering performance improvements in the current period and satisfy shareholder expectations for near-term progress. Longer-term targets (three to five years off) force managers to consider what to do *now* to put the company in position to perform better later. Long-term objectives are critical for achieving optimal long-term performance and stand as a barrier to a near-sighted management philosophy and an undue focus on short-term results. When trade-offs have to be made between achieving long-term objectives and achieving short-term objectives, long-term objectives should take precedence (unless the achievement of one or more short-term performance targets has unique importance). Examples of commonly used financial and strategic objectives are listed in Table 2.2.

The Need for a Balanced Approach to Objective Setting

The importance of setting and attaining financial objectives is obvious. Without adequate profitability and financial strength, a company's long-term health and ultimate survival are jeopardized. Furthermore, subpar earnings and a weak balance sheet alarm shareholders and creditors and put the jobs of senior executives at risk. However, good financial performance, by itself, is not enough. Of equal or greater importance is a company's strategic performance—outcomes that indicate whether a company's market position and competitiveness are deteriorating, holding steady, or improving. *A stronger market standing and greater competitive vitality—especially when accompanied by competitive advantage—is what enables a company to improve its financial performance.*

Moreover, a company's financial performance measures are really *lagging indicators* that reflect the results of past decisions and organizational activities.[5] But a company's past or current financial performance is not a reliable indicator of its future prospects—poor financial performers often turn things around and do

TABLE 2.2   Common Financial and Strategic Objectives

Financial Objectives	Strategic Objectives
• An *x* percent increase in annual revenues • Annual increases in after-tax profits *of x* percent • Annual increases in earnings per share of *x* percent • Annual dividend increases of *x* percent • Profit margins of *x* percent • An *x* percent return on capital employed (ROCE) or return on shareholders' equity (ROE) investment • Increased shareholder value in the form of an upward-trending stock price • Bond and credit ratings of *x* • Internal cash flows of *x* dollars to fund new capital investment	• Winning an *x* percent market share • Achieving lower overall costs than rivals • Overtaking key competitors on product performance, quality, or customer service • Deriving *x* percent of revenues from the sale of new products introduced within the past five years • Having broader or deeper technological capabilities than rivals • Having a wider product line than rivals • Having a better-known or more powerful brand name than rivals • Having stronger national or global sales and distribution capabilities than rivals • Consistently getting new or improved products to market ahead of rivals

better, while good financial performers can fall upon hard times. The best and most reliable *leading indicators* of a company's future financial performance and business prospects are strategic outcomes that indicate whether the company's competitiveness and market position are stronger or weaker. The accomplishment of strategic objectives signals that the company is well positioned to sustain or improve its performance. For instance, if a company is achieving ambitious strategic objectives such that its competitive strength and market position are on the rise, then there's reason to expect that its *future* financial performance will be better than its current or past performance. If a company is losing ground to competitors and its market position is slipping—outcomes that reflect weak strategic performance (and, very likely, failure to achieve its strategic objectives)—then its ability to maintain its present profitability is highly suspect.

Consequently, it is important to use a performance measurement system that strikes a *balance* between financial objectives and strategic objectives.[6] The most widely used framework of this sort is known as the **Balanced Scorecard**.[7] This is a method for linking financial performance objectives to specific strategic objectives that derive from a company's business model. It provides a company's employees with clear guidelines about how their jobs are linked to the overall objectives of the organization, so they can contribute most productively and collaboratively to the achievement of these goals. A 2013 survey by Bain & Company of 12,300 companies worldwide found that balanced scorecard methodology was one of the top-five management tools.[8] In 2015, nearly 50 percent of companies in the United States, Europe, and Asia employed a balanced scorecard approach to measuring strategic and financial performance.[9] Organizations that have adopted the balanced scorecard approach include 7-Eleven, Ann Taylor Stores, Allianz Italy, Wells Fargo Bank, Ford Motor Company, Verizon, ExxonMobil, Pfizer, DuPont, Royal Canadian Mounted Police, U.S. Army Medical Command, and over 30 colleges and universities.[10] Illustration Capsule 2.3 provides selected strategic and financial objectives of three prominent companies.

Examples of Company Objectives

UPS

Increase the percentage of business-to-consumer package deliveries from 46 percent of domestic deliveries in 2014 to 51 percent of domestic deliveries in 2019; increase intraregional export shipments from 66 percent of exported packages in 2014 to 70 percent of exported packages in 2019; lower U.S. domestic average cost per package by 40 basis points between 2014 and 2019; increase total revenue from $58.2 billion in 2014 to $74.3–$81.6 billion in 2019; increase total operating profit from $4.95 billion in 2014 to $7.62–$9.12 billion by 2019; increase capital expenditures from 4 percent of revenues in 2014 to 5 percent of revenues in 2019.

ALCOA

Increase revenues from higher margin aero/defense and transportation aluminum products from 31 percent of revenues in 2014 to 41 percent of revenues in 2016; increase automotive sheet shipments from $340 million in 2014 to $1.05 billion in 2016; increase alumina price index/spot pricing from 68 percent of third-party shipments in 2014 to 84 percent of third-party shipments in 2016; reduce product development to market cycle time from 52 weeks to 25 weeks.

YUM! BRANDS (KFC, PIZZA HUT, TACO BELL, WINGSTREET)

Add 1,000 new Taco Bell units in the United States by 2020; increase Taco Bell revenues from $7 billion in 2012

© Luke Sharrett/Bloomberg via Getty Images

to $14 billion in 2022; achieve a number-two ranking in quick-service chicken in western Europe, the United Kingdom, and Australia; increase the percentage of franchised KFC units in China from 6 percent in 2013 to 10 percent in 2017; expand the number of Pizza Hut locations in China by 300 percent by 2020; increase the number of Pizza Hut Delivery stores in the United States from 235 in 2014 to 500 in 2016; expand the digital ordering options in all quick-service concepts; increase the number of restaurant locations in India from 705 in 2013 to 2,000 by 2020; increase the operating margin for KFC, Pizza Hut, and Taco Bell from 24 percent in 2014 to 30 percent in 2017; sustain double-digit EPS growth from 2015 through 2020.

Sources: Information posted on company websites.

Setting Objectives for Every Organizational Level

Objective setting should not stop with top management's establishing companywide performance targets. Company objectives need to be broken down into performance targets for each of the organization's separate businesses, product lines, functional departments, and individual work units. Employees within various functional areas and operating levels will be guided much better by specific objectives relating directly to their departmental activities than broad organizational-level goals. Objective setting is thus a *top-down process* that must extend to the lowest organizational levels. This means that each organizational unit must take care to set performance targets that support—rather than conflict with or negate—the achievement of companywide strategic and financial objectives.

The ideal situation is a team effort in which each organizational unit strives to produce results that contribute to the achievement of the company's performance targets and strategic vision. Such consistency signals that organizational units know their strategic role and are on board in helping the company move down the chosen strategic path and produce the desired results.

STAGE 3: CRAFTING A STRATEGY

As indicated in Chapter 1, the task of stitching a strategy together entails addressing a series of "hows": *how* to attract and please customers, *how* to compete against rivals, *how* to position the company in the marketplace, *how* to respond to changing market conditions, *how* to capitalize on attractive opportunities to grow the business, and *how* to achieve strategic and financial objectives. Astute entrepreneurship is called for in choosing among the various strategic alternatives and in proactively searching for opportunities to do new things or to do existing things in new or better ways.[11] The faster a company's business environment is changing, the more critical it becomes for its managers to be good entrepreneurs in diagnosing the direction and force of the changes under way and in responding with timely adjustments in strategy. Strategy makers have to pay attention to early warnings of future change and be willing to experiment with dare-to-be-different ways to establish a market position in that future. When obstacles appear unexpectedly in a company's path, it is up to management to adapt rapidly and innovatively. *Masterful strategies come from doing things differently from competitors where it counts—out-innovating them, being more efficient, being more imaginative, adapting faster—rather than running with the herd.* Good strategy making is therefore inseparable from good business entrepreneurship. One cannot exist without the other.

LO 3

Why the strategic initiatives taken at various organizational levels must be tightly coordinated to achieve companywide performance targets.

Strategy Making Involves Managers at All Organizational Levels

A company's senior executives obviously have lead strategy-making roles and responsibilities. The chief executive officer (CEO), as captain of the ship, carries the mantles of chief direction setter, chief objective setter, chief strategy maker, and chief strategy implementer for the total enterprise. Ultimate responsibility for *leading* the strategy-making, strategy-executing process rests with the CEO. And the CEO is always fully accountable for the results the strategy produces, whether good or bad. In some enterprises, the CEO or owner functions as chief architect of the strategy, personally deciding what the key elements of the company's strategy will be, although he or she may seek the advice of key subordinates and board members. A CEO-centered approach to strategy development is characteristic of small owner-managed companies and some large corporations that were founded by the present CEO or that have a CEO with strong strategic leadership skills. Elon Musk at Tesla Motors and SpaceX, Mark Zuckerberg at Facebook, Jeff Bezos at Amazon, Indra Nooyi at PepsiCo, Jack Ma of Alibaba, Warren Buffett at Berkshire Hathaway, and Irene Rosenfeld at Kraft Foods are examples of high-profile corporate CEOs who have wielded a heavy hand in shaping their company's strategy.

In most corporations, however, strategy is the product of more than just the CEO's handiwork. Typically, other senior executives—business unit heads, the chief financial officer, and vice presidents for production, marketing, and other functional departments—have influential strategy-making roles and help fashion the chief strategy components. Normally, a company's chief financial officer is in charge of devising and implementing an appropriate financial strategy; the production vice president takes the lead in developing the company's production strategy; the marketing vice president orchestrates sales and marketing strategy; a brand manager is in charge of the strategy for a particular brand in the company's product lineup; and so on. Moreover, the strategy-making efforts of top managers are complemented by advice and counsel from the company's board of directors; normally, all major strategic decisions are submitted to the board of directors for review, discussion, perhaps modification, and official approval.

In most companies, crafting and executing strategy is a collaborative team effort in which every manager has a role for the area he or she heads; it is rarely something that only high-level managers do.

But strategy making is by no means solely a *top* management function, the exclusive province of owner-entrepreneurs, CEOs, high-ranking executives, and board members. The more a company's operations cut across different products, industries, and geographic areas, the more that headquarters executives have little option but to delegate considerable strategy-making authority to down-the-line managers in charge of particular subsidiaries, divisions, product lines, geographic sales offices, distribution centers, and plants. On-the-scene managers who oversee specific operating units can be reliably counted on to have more detailed command of the strategic issues for the particular operating unit under their supervision since they have more intimate knowledge of the prevailing market and competitive conditions, customer requirements and expectations, and all the other relevant aspects affecting the several strategic options available. Managers with day-to-day familiarity of, and authority over, a specific operating unit thus have a big edge over headquarters executives in making wise strategic choices for their unit. The result is that, in most of today's companies, crafting and executing strategy is a *collaborative team effort* in which *every company manager plays a strategy-making role*—ranging from minor to major—for the area he or she heads.

The larger and more diverse the operations of an enterprise, the more points of strategic initiative it has and the more levels of management that have a significant strategy-making role.

Take, for example, a company like General Electric, a $150 billion global corporation with over 300,000 employees, operations in some 170 countries, and businesses that include jet engines, lighting, power generation, electric transmission and distribution equipment, oil and gas equipment, medical imaging and diagnostic equipment, locomotives, security devices, water treatment systems, and financial services. While top-level headquarters executives may well be personally involved in shaping GE's *overall* strategy and fashioning *important* strategic moves, they simply cannot know enough about the situation in every GE organizational unit to direct every strategic move made in GE's worldwide organization. Rather, it takes involvement on the part of GE's whole management team—top executives, business group heads, the heads of specific business units and product categories, and key managers in plants, sales offices, and distribution centers—to craft the thousands of strategic initiatives that end up composing the whole of GE's strategy.

A Company's Strategy-Making Hierarchy

In diversified companies like GE, where multiple and sometimes strikingly different businesses have to be managed, crafting a full-fledged strategy involves four distinct types of strategic actions and initiatives. Each of these involves different facets of the company's overall strategy and calls for the participation of different types of managers, as shown in Figure 2.2.

As shown in Figure 2.2, **corporate strategy** is orchestrated by the CEO and other senior executives and establishes an overall strategy for managing a *set of businesses*

CHAPTER 2   Charting a Company's Direction   33

FIGURE 2.2   A Company's Strategy-Making Hierarchy

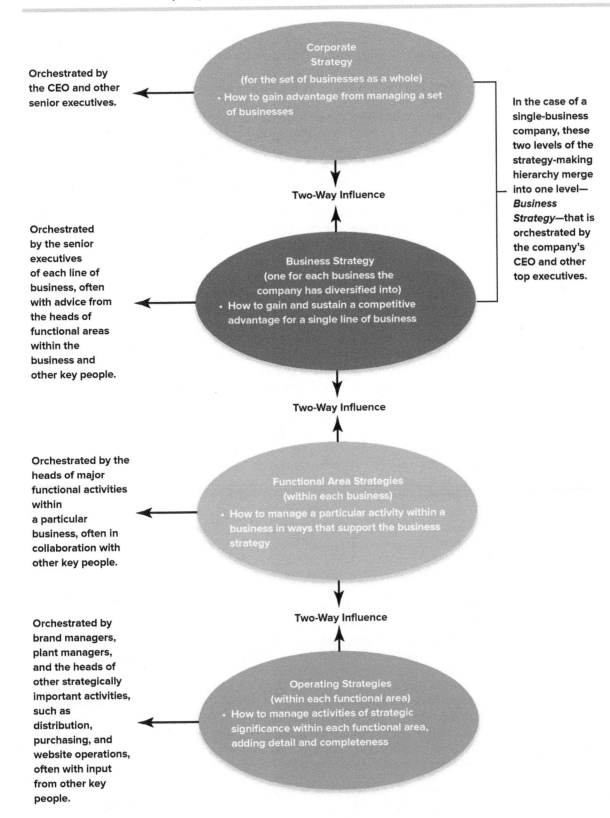

Orchestrated by the CEO and other senior executives.

Corporate Strategy
(for the set of businesses as a whole)
- How to gain advantage from managing a set of businesses

In the case of a single-business company, these two levels of the strategy-making hierarchy merge into one level—*Business Strategy*—that is orchestrated by the company's CEO and other top executives.

Two-Way Influence

Orchestrated by the senior executives of each line of business, often with advice from the heads of functional areas within the business and other key people.

Business Strategy
(one for each business the company has diversified into)
- How to gain and sustain a competitive advantage for a single line of business

Two-Way Influence

Orchestrated by the heads of major functional activities within a particular business, often in collaboration with other key people.

Functional Area Strategies
(within each business)
- How to manage a particular activity within a business in ways that support the business strategy

Two-Way Influence

Orchestrated by brand managers, plant managers, and the heads of other strategically important activities, such as distribution, purchasing, and website operations, often with input from other key people.

Operating Strategies
(within each functional area)
- How to manage activities of strategic significance within each functional area, adding detail and completeness

in a diversified, multibusiness company. Corporate strategy concerns how to improve the combined performance of the set of businesses the company has diversified into by capturing cross-business synergies and turning them into competitive advantage. It addresses the questions of what businesses to hold or divest, which new markets to enter, and how to best enter new markets (by acquisition, creation of a strategic alliance, or through internal development, for example). Corporate strategy and business diversification are the subjects of Chapter 8, in which they are discussed in detail.

Business strategy is concerned with strengthening the market position, building competitive advantage, and improving the performance of a single line of business unit. Business strategy is primarily the responsibility of business unit heads, although corporate-level executives may well exert strong influence; in diversified companies it is not unusual for corporate officers to insist that business-level objectives and strategy conform to corporate-level objectives and strategy themes. The business head has at least two other strategy-related roles: (1) seeing that lower-level strategies are well conceived, consistent, and adequately matched to the overall business strategy; and (2) keeping corporate-level officers (and sometimes the board of directors) informed of emerging strategic issues.

Functional-area strategies concern the approaches employed in managing particular functions within a business—like research and development (R&D), production, procurement of inputs, sales and marketing, distribution, customer service, and finance. A company's marketing strategy, for example, represents the managerial game plan for running the sales and marketing part of the business. A company's product development strategy represents the game plan for keeping the company's product lineup in tune with what buyers are looking for.

Functional strategies flesh out the details of a company's business strategy. Lead responsibility for functional strategies within a business is normally delegated to the heads of the respective functions, with the general manager of the business having final approval. Since the different functional-level strategies must be compatible with the overall business strategy and with one another to have beneficial impact, there are times when the general business manager exerts strong influence on the content of the functional strategies.

Operating strategies concern the relatively narrow approaches for managing key operating units (e.g., plants, distribution centers, purchasing centers) and specific operating activities with strategic significance (e.g., quality control, materials purchasing, brand management, Internet sales). A plant manager needs a strategy for accomplishing the plant's objectives, carrying out the plant's part of the company's overall manufacturing game plan, and dealing with any strategy-related problems that exist at the plant. A company's advertising manager needs a strategy for getting maximum audience exposure and sales impact from the ad budget. Operating strategies, while of limited scope, add further detail and completeness to functional strategies and to the overall business strategy. Lead responsibility for operating strategies is usually delegated to frontline managers, subject to the review and approval of higher-ranking managers.

Even though operating strategy is at the bottom of the strategy-making hierarchy, its importance should not be downplayed. A major plant that fails in its strategy to achieve production volume, unit cost, and quality targets can damage the company's reputation for quality products and undercut the achievement of company sales and profit objectives. Frontline managers are thus an important part of an organization's strategy-making team. One cannot reliably judge the strategic importance of a given action simply by the strategy level or location within the managerial hierarchy where it is initiated.

In single-business companies, the uppermost level of the strategy-making hierarchy is the business strategy, so a single-business company has three levels of strategy: business strategy, functional-area strategies, and operating strategies. Proprietorships, partnerships, and owner-managed enterprises may have only one or two strategy-making levels since it takes only a few key people to craft and oversee the firm's strategy. The larger and more diverse the operations of an enterprise, the more points of strategic initiative it has and the more levels of management that have a significant strategy-making role.

> A company's strategy is at full power only when its many pieces are united.

Uniting the Strategy-Making Hierarchy

Ideally, the pieces of a company's strategy up and down the strategy hierarchy should be cohesive and mutually reinforcing, fitting together like a jigsaw puzzle. *Anything less than a unified collection of strategies weakens the overall strategy and is likely to impair company performance.*[12] It is the responsibility of top executives to achieve this unity by clearly communicating the company's vision, objectives, and major strategy components to down-the-line managers and key personnel. Midlevel and frontline managers cannot craft unified strategic moves without first understanding the company's long-term direction and knowing the major components of the corporate and/or business strategies that their strategy-making efforts are supposed to support and enhance. Thus, as a general rule, strategy making must start at the top of the organization and then proceed downward from the corporate level to the business level and then from the business level to the associated functional and operating levels. Once strategies up and down the hierarchy have been created, lower-level strategies must be scrutinized for consistency with and support of higher-level strategies. Any strategy conflicts must be addressed and resolved, either by modifying the lower-level strategies with conflicting elements or by adapting the higher-level strategy to accommodate what may be more appealing strategy ideas and initiatives bubbling up from below.

A Strategic Vision + Mission + Objectives + Strategy = A Strategic Plan

Developing a strategic vision and mission, setting objectives, and crafting a strategy are basic direction-setting tasks. They map out where a company is headed, delineate its strategic and financial targets, articulate the basic business model, and outline the competitive moves and operating approaches to be used in achieving the desired business results. Together, these elements constitute a **strategic plan** for coping with industry conditions, competing against rivals, meeting objectives, and making progress along the chosen strategic course.[13] Typically, a strategic plan includes a commitment to allocate resources to carrying out the plan and specifies a time period for achieving goals.

In companies that do regular strategy reviews and develop explicit strategic plans, the strategic plan usually ends up as a written document that is circulated to most managers. Near-term performance targets are the part of the strategic plan most often communicated to employees more generally and spelled out explicitly. A number of companies summarize key elements of their strategic plans in the company's annual report to shareholders, in postings on their websites, or in statements provided to the

CORE CONCEPT

A company's **strategic plan** lays out its future direction, business model, performance targets, and competitive strategy.

business media; others, perhaps for reasons of competitive sensitivity, make only vague, general statements about their strategic plans.[14] In small, privately owned companies it is rare for strategic plans to exist in written form. Small-company strategic plans tend to reside in the thinking and directives of owner-executives; aspects of the plan are revealed in conversations with company personnel about where to head, what to accomplish, and how to proceed.

STAGE 4: EXECUTING THE STRATEGY

LO 4

What a company must do to achieve operating excellence and to execute its strategy proficiently.

Managing the implementation of a strategy is easily the most demanding and time-consuming part of the strategy management process. Converting strategic plans into actions and results tests a manager's ability to direct organizational change, motivate company personnel, build and strengthen competitive capabilities, create and nurture a strategy-supportive work climate, and meet or beat performance targets. Initiatives to put the strategy in place and execute it proficiently must be launched and managed on many organizational fronts.

Management's action agenda for executing the chosen strategy emerges from assessing what the company will have to do to achieve the targeted financial and strategic performance. Each company manager has to think through the answer to the question "What needs to be done in my area to execute my piece of the strategic plan, and what actions should I take to get the process under way?" How much internal change is needed depends on how much of the strategy is new, how far internal practices and competencies deviate from what the strategy requires, and how well the present work culture supports good strategy execution. Depending on the amount of internal change involved, full implementation and proficient execution of the company strategy (or important new pieces thereof) can take several months to several years.

In most situations, managing the strategy execution process includes the following principal aspects:

- Creating a strategy-supporting structure.
- Staffing the organization to obtain needed skills and expertise.
- Developing and strengthening strategy-supporting resources and capabilities.
- Allocating ample resources to the activities critical to strategic success.
- Ensuring that policies and procedures facilitate effective strategy execution.
- Organizing the work effort along the lines of best practice.
- Installing information and operating systems that enable company personnel to perform essential activities.
- Motivating people and tying rewards directly to the achievement of performance objectives.
- Creating a company culture conducive to successful strategy execution.
- Exerting the internal leadership needed to propel implementation forward.

Good strategy execution requires diligent pursuit of operating excellence. It is a job for a company's whole management team. Success hinges on the skills and cooperation of operating managers who can push for needed changes in their organizational units and consistently deliver good results. Management's handling of the strategy implementation process can be considered successful if things go smoothly enough that the company meets or beats its strategic and financial performance targets and shows good progress in achieving management's strategic vision.

STAGE 5: EVALUATING PERFORMANCE AND INITIATING CORRECTIVE ADJUSTMENTS

The fifth component of the strategy management process—monitoring new external developments, evaluating the company's progress, and making corrective adjustments—is the trigger point for deciding whether to continue or change the company's vision and mission, objectives, strategy, and/or strategy execution methods.[15] As long as the company's strategy continues to pass the three tests of a winning strategy discussed in Chapter 1 (good fit, competitive advantage, strong performance), company executives may decide to stay the course. Simply fine-tuning the strategic plan and continuing with efforts to improve strategy execution are sufficient.

But whenever a company encounters disruptive changes in its environment, questions need to be raised about the appropriateness of its direction and strategy. If a company experiences a downturn in its market position or persistent shortfalls in performance, then company managers are obligated to ferret out the causes—do they relate to poor strategy, poor strategy execution, or both?—and take timely corrective action. A company's direction, objectives, and strategy have to be revisited anytime external or internal conditions warrant.

Likewise, managers are obligated to assess which of the company's operating methods and approaches to strategy execution merit continuation and which need improvement. Proficient strategy execution is always the product of much organizational learning. It is achieved unevenly—coming quickly in some areas and proving troublesome in others. Consequently, top-notch strategy execution entails vigilantly searching for ways to improve and then making corrective adjustments whenever and wherever it is useful to do so.

> A company's vision, mission, objectives, strategy, and approach to strategy execution are never final; reviewing whether and when to make revisions is an ongoing process.

CORPORATE GOVERNANCE: THE ROLE OF THE BOARD OF DIRECTORS IN THE STRATEGY-CRAFTING, STRATEGY-EXECUTING PROCESS

Although senior managers have the *lead responsibility* for crafting and executing a company's strategy, it is the duty of a company's board of directors to exercise strong oversight and see that management performs the various tasks involved in each of the five stages of the strategy-making, strategy-executing process in a manner that best serves the interests of shareholders and other stakeholders.[16] A company's board of directors has four important obligations to fulfill:

1. *Oversee the company's financial accounting and financial reporting practices.* While top executives, particularly the company's CEO and CFO (chief financial officer), are primarily responsible for seeing that the company's financial statements fairly and accurately report the results of the company's operations,

LO 5

The role and responsibility of a company's board of directors in overseeing the strategic management process.

board members have a *legal obligation* to warrant the accuracy of the company's financial reports and protect shareholders. It is their job to ensure that generally accepted accounting principles (GAAP) are used properly in preparing the company's financial statements and that proper financial controls are in place to prevent fraud and misuse of funds. Virtually all boards of directors have an audit committee, always composed entirely of *outside directors* (*inside directors* hold management positions in the company and either directly or indirectly report to the CEO). The members of the audit committee have the lead responsibility for overseeing the decisions of the company's financial officers and consulting with both internal and external auditors to ensure accurate financial reporting and adequate financial controls.

2. *Critically appraise the company's direction, strategy, and business approaches.* Board members are also expected to guide management in choosing a strategic direction and to make independent judgments about the validity and wisdom of management's proposed strategic actions. This aspect of their duties takes on heightened importance when the company's strategy is failing or is plagued with faulty execution, and certainly when there is a precipitous collapse in profitability. But under more normal circumstances, many boards have found that meeting agendas become consumed by compliance matters with little time left to discuss matters of strategic importance. The board of directors and management at Philips Electronics hold annual two- to three-day retreats devoted exclusively to evaluating the company's long-term direction and various strategic proposals. The company's exit from the semiconductor business and its increased focus on medical technology and home health care resulted from management-board discussions during such retreats.[17]

3. *Evaluate the caliber of senior executives' strategic leadership skills.* The board is always responsible for determining whether the current CEO is doing a good job of strategic leadership (as a basis for awarding salary increases and bonuses and deciding on retention or removal).[18] Boards must also exercise due diligence in evaluating the strategic leadership skills of other senior executives in line to succeed the CEO. When the incumbent CEO steps down or leaves for a position elsewhere, the board must elect a successor, either going with an insider or deciding that an outsider is needed to perhaps radically change the company's strategic course. Often, the outside directors on a board visit company facilities and talk with company personnel personally to evaluate whether the strategy is on track, how well the strategy is being executed, and how well issues and problems are being addressed by various managers. For example, independent board members at GE visit operating executives at each major business unit once a year to assess the company's talent pool and stay abreast of emerging strategic and operating issues affecting the company's divisions. Home Depot board members visit a store once per quarter to determine the health of the company's operations.[19]

4. *Institute a compensation plan for top executives that rewards them for actions and results that serve stakeholder interests, and most especially those of shareholders.* A basic principle of corporate governance is that the owners of a corporation (the shareholders) delegate operating authority and managerial control to top management in return for compensation. In their role as *agents* of shareholders, top executives have a clear and unequivocal duty to make decisions and operate the company in accord with shareholder interests. (This does not mean disregarding

the interests of other stakeholders—employees, suppliers, the communities in which the company operates, and society at large.) Most boards of directors have a compensation committee, composed entirely of directors from *outside* the company, to develop a salary and incentive compensation plan that rewards senior executives for boosting the company's *long-term* performance on behalf of shareholders. The compensation committee's recommendations are presented to the full board for approval. But during the past 10 to 15 years, many boards of directors have done a poor job of ensuring that executive salary increases, bonuses, and stock option awards are tied tightly to performance measures that are truly in the long-term interests of shareholders. Rather, compensation packages at many companies have increasingly rewarded executives for short-term performance improvements—most notably, for achieving quarterly and annual earnings targets and boosting the stock price by specified percentages. This has had the perverse effect of causing company managers to become preoccupied with actions to improve a company's near-term performance, often motivating them to take unwise business risks to boost short-term earnings by amounts sufficient to qualify for multimillion-dollar compensation packages (that many see as obscenely large). The focus on short-term performance has proved damaging to long-term company performance and shareholder interests—witness the huge loss of shareholder wealth that occurred at many financial institutions in 2008–2009 because of executive risk taking in subprime loans, credit default swaps, and collateralized mortgage securities. As a consequence, the need to overhaul and reform executive compensation has become a hot topic in both public circles and corporate boardrooms. Illustration Capsule 2.4 discusses how weak governance at Volkswagen contributed to the 2015 emissions cheating scandal, which cost the company billions of dollars and the trust of its stakeholders.

Every corporation should have a strong independent board of directors that (1) is well informed about the company's performance, (2) guides and judges the CEO and other top executives, (3) has the courage to curb management actions the board believes are inappropriate or unduly risky, (4) certifies to shareholders that the CEO is doing what the board expects, (5) provides insight and advice to management, and (6) is intensely involved in debating the pros and cons of key decisions and actions.[20] Boards of directors that lack the backbone to challenge a strong-willed or "imperial" CEO or that rubber-stamp almost anything the CEO recommends without probing inquiry and debate abdicate their fiduciary duty to represent and protect shareholder interests.

Effective corporate governance requires the board of directors to oversee the company's strategic direction, evaluate its senior executives, handle executive compensation, and oversee financial reporting practices.

ILLUSTRATION
CAPSULE 2.4

Corporate Governance Failures at Volkswagen

In 2015, Volkswagen admitted to installing "defeat devices" on at least 11 million vehicles with diesel engines. These devices enabled the cars to pass emission tests, even though the engines actually emitted pollutants up to 40 times above what is allowed in the United States. Current estimates are that it will cost the company at least €7 billion to cover the cost of repairs and lawsuits. Although management must have been involved in approving the use of cheating devices, the Volkswagen supervisory board has been unwilling to accept any responsibility. Some board members even questioned whether it was the board's responsibility to be aware of such problems, stating "matters of technical expertise were not for us" and "the scandal had nothing, not one iota, to do with the advisory board." Yet governing boards do have a responsibility to be well informed, to provide oversight, and to become involved in key decisions and actions. So what caused this corporate governance failure? Why is this the third time in the past 20 years that Volkswagen has been embroiled in scandal?

© Paul J. Richards/AFP/Getty Images

The key feature of Volkswagen's board that appears to have led to these issues is a lack of independent directors. However, before explaining this in more detail it is important to understand the German governance model. German corporations operate two-tier governance structures, with a management board, and a separate supervisory board that does not contain any current executives. In addition, German law requires large companies to have at least 50 percent supervisory board representation from workers. This structure is meant to provide more oversight by independent board members and greater involvement by a wider set of stakeholders.

In Volkswagen's case, these objectives have been effectively circumvented. Although Volkswagen's supervisory board does not include any current management, the chairmanship appears to be a revolving door of former senior executives. Ferdinand Piëch, the chair during the scandal, was CEO for 9 years prior to becoming chair in 2002. Martin Winterkorn, the recently ousted

CEO, was expected to become supervisory board chair prior to the scandal. The company continues to elevate management to the supervisory board even though they have presided over past scandals. Hans Dieter Poetsch, the newly appointed chair, was part of the management team that did not inform the supervisory board of the EPA investigation for two weeks.

VW also has a unique ownership structure where a single family, Porsche, controls more than 50 percent of voting shares. Piëch, a family member and chair until 2015, forced out CEOs and installed unqualified family members on the board, such as his former nanny and current wife. He also pushed out independent-minded board members, such as Gerhard Cromme, author of Germany's corporate governance code. The company has lost numerous independent directors over the past 10 years, leaving it with only one non-shareholder, non-labor representative. Although Piëch has now been removed, it is unclear that Volkswagen's board has solved the underlying problem. Shareholders have seen billions of dollars wiped away and the Volkswagen brand tarnished. As long as the board continues to lack independent directors, change will likely be slow.

Note: Developed with Jacob M. Crandall.

Sources: "Piëch under Fire," *The Economist*, December 8, 2005; Chris Bryant and Richard Milne, "Boardroom Politics at Heart of VW Scandal," *Financial Times*, October 4, 2015; Andreas Cremer and Jan Schwartz, "Volkswagen Mired in Crisis as Board Members Criticize Piech," Reuters, April 24, 2015; Richard Milne, "Volkswagen: System Failure," *Financial Times*, November 4, 2015.

KEY POINTS
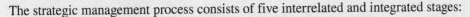

The strategic management process consists of five interrelated and integrated stages:

1. *Developing a strategic vision* of the company's future, a *mission statement* that defines the company's current purpose, and a set of *core values* to guide the pursuit of the vision and mission. This stage of strategy making provides direction for the company, motivates and inspires company personnel, aligns and guides actions throughout the organization, and communicates to stakeholders management's aspirations for the company's future.

2. *Setting objectives* to convert the vision and mission into performance targets that can be used as yardsticks for measuring the company's performance. Objectives need to spell out *how much* of *what kind* of performance *by when*. Two broad types of objectives are required: *financial objectives* and *strategic objectives*. A *balanced scorecard* approach for measuring company performance entails setting both financial objectives and strategic objectives. *Stretch objectives* spur exceptional performance and help build a firewall against complacency and mediocre performance. A company exhibits *strategic intent* when it relentlessly pursues an ambitious strategic objective, concentrating the full force of its resources and competitive actions on achieving that objective.

3. *Crafting a strategy* to achieve the objectives and move the company along the strategic course that management has charted. Masterful strategies come from doing things differently from competitors where it counts—out-innovating them, being more efficient, being more imaginative, adapting faster—rather than running with the herd. In large diversified companies, the strategy-making hierarchy consists of four levels, each of which involves a corresponding level of management: corporate strategy (multibusiness strategy), business strategy (strategy for individual businesses that compete in a single industry), functional-area strategies within each business (e.g., marketing, R&D, logistics), and operating strategies (for key operating units, such as manufacturing plants). Thus, strategy making is an inclusive collaborative activity involving not only senior company executives but also the heads of major business divisions, functional-area managers, and operating managers on the frontlines.

4. *Executing the chosen strategy* and converting the strategic plan into action. Management's agenda for executing the chosen strategy emerges from assessing what the company will have to do to achieve the targeted financial and strategic performance. Management's handling of the strategy implementation process can be considered successful if things go smoothly enough that the company meets or beats its strategic and financial performance targets and shows good progress in achieving management's strategic vision.

5. *Monitoring developments, evaluating performance, and initiating corrective adjustments* in light of actual experience, changing conditions, new ideas, and new opportunities. This stage of the strategy management process is the trigger point for deciding whether to continue or change the company's vision and mission, objectives, strategy, and/or strategy execution methods.

The sum of a company's strategic vision, mission, objectives, and strategy constitutes a *strategic plan* for coping with industry conditions, outcompeting rivals, meeting objectives, and making progress toward aspirational goals.

Boards of directors have a duty to shareholders to play a vigilant role in overseeing management's handling of a company's strategy-making, strategy-executing process.

This entails four important obligations: (1) Ensure that the company issues accurate financial reports and has adequate financial controls; (2) critically appraise the company's direction, strategy, and strategy execution; (3) evaluate the caliber of senior executives' strategic leadership skills; and (4) institute a compensation plan for top executives that rewards them for actions and results that serve stakeholder interests, most especially those of shareholders.

ASSURANCE OF LEARNING EXERCISES

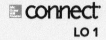

LO 1

1. Using the information in Table 2.1, critique the adequacy and merit of the following vision statements, listing effective elements and shortcomings. Rank the vision statements from best to worst once you complete your evaluation.

Vision Statement	Effective Elements	Shortcomings
American Express • We work hard every day to make American Express the world's most respected service brand.		
Hilton Hotels Corporation Our vision is to be the first choice of the world's travelers. Hilton intends to build on the rich heritage and strength of our brands by: • Consistently delighting our customers • Investing in our team members • Delivering innovative products and services • Continuously improving performance • Increasing shareholder value • Creating a culture of pride • Strengthening the loyalty of our constituents		
MasterCard • A world beyond cash.		
BASF We are "The Chemical Company" successfully operating in all major markets. • Our customers view BASF as their partner of choice. • Our innovative products, intelligent solutions and services make us the most competent worldwide supplier in the chemical industry. • We generate a high return on assets. • We strive for sustainable development. • We welcome change as an opportunity. • We, the employees of BASF, together ensure our success.		

Sources: Company websites and annual reports.

2. Go to the company investor relations websites for Starbucks (investor.starbucks .com), Pfizer (www.pfizer.com/investors), and Salesforce (investor.salesforce .com) to find examples of strategic and financial objectives. List four objectives for each company, and indicate which of these are strategic and which are financial.   **LO 2**

3. American Airlines's Chapter 11 reorganization plan filed in 2012 involved the company reducing operating expenses by $2 billion while increasing revenues by $1 billion. The company's strategy to increase revenues included expanding the number of international flights and destinations and increasing daily departures for its five largest markets by 20 percent. The company also intended to upgrade its fleet by spending $2 billion to purchase new aircraft and refurbish the first-class cabins for planes not replaced. A final component of the restructuring plan included a merger with US Airways (completed in 2015) to create a global airline with more than 56,700 daily flights to 336 destinations in 56 countries. The merger was expected to produce cost savings from synergies of more than $1 billion and result in a stronger airline capable of paying creditors and rewarding employees and shareholders. Explain why the strategic initiatives at various organizational levels and functions require tight coordination to achieve the results desired by American Airlines.   **LO 3**

4. Go to the investor relations website for Walmart (investors.walmartstores .com) and review past presentations Walmart has made during various investor conferences by clicking on the Events option in the navigation bar. Prepare a one- to two-page report that outlines what Walmart has said to investors about its approach to strategy execution. Specifically, what has management discussed concerning staffing, resource allocation, policies and procedures, information and operating systems, continuous improvement, rewards and incentives, corporate culture, and internal leadership at the company?   **LO 4**

5. Based on the information provided in Illustration Capsule 2.4, describe the ways in which Volkswagen did not fulfill the requirements of effective corporate governance. In what ways did the board of directors sidestep its obligations to protect shareholder interests? How could Volkswagen better select its board of directors to avoid mistakes such as the emissions scandal in 2015?   **LO 5**

EXERCISE FOR SIMULATION PARTICIPANTS

1. Meet with your co-managers and prepare a strategic vision statement for your company. It should be at least one sentence long and no longer than a brief paragraph. When you are finished, check to see if your vision statement meets the conditions for an effectively worded strategic vision set forth in Table 2.1. If not, then revise it accordingly. What would be a good slogan that captures the essence of your strategic vision and that could be used to help communicate the vision to company personnel, shareholders, and other stakeholders?   **LO 1**

2. What are your company's financial objectives? What are your company's strategic objectives?   **LO 2**

3. What are the three to four key elements of your company's strategy?   **LO 3**

ENDNOTES

[1] Gordon Shaw, Robert Brown, and Philip Bromiley, "Strategic Stories: How 3M Is Rewriting Business Planning," *Harvard Business Review* 76, no. 3 (May–June 1998); David J. Collis and Michael G. Rukstad, "Can You Say What Your Strategy Is?" *Harvard Business Review* 86, no. 4 (April 2008) pp. 82–90.

[2] Hugh Davidson, *The Committed Enterprise: How to Make Vision and Values Work* (Oxford: Butterworth Heinemann, 2002); W. Chan Kim and Renée Mauborgne, "Charting Your Company's Future," *Harvard Business Review* 80, no. 6 (June 2002), pp. 77–83; James C. Collins and Jerry I. Porras, "Building Your Company's Vision," *Harvard Business Review* 74, no. 5 (September–October 1996), pp. 65–77; Jim Collins and Jerry Porras, *Built to Last: Successful Habits of Visionary Companies* (New York: HarperCollins, 1994); Michel Robert, *Strategy Pure and Simple II: How Winning Companies Dominate Their Competitors* (New York: McGraw-Hill, 1998).

[3] Davidson, *The Committed Enterprise*, pp. 20 and 54.

[4] As quoted in Charles H. House and Raymond L. Price, "The Return Map: Tracking Product Teams," *Harvard Business Review* 60, no. 1 (January–February 1991), p. 93.

[5] Robert S. Kaplan and David P. Norton, *The Strategy-Focused Organization* (Boston: Harvard Business School Press, 2001); Robert S. Kaplan and David P. Norton, *The Balanced Scorecard: Translating Strategy into Action* (Boston: Harvard Business School Press, 1996).

[6] Kaplan and Norton, *The Strategy-Focused Organization;* Kaplan and Norton, *The Balanced Scorecard;* Kevin B. Hendricks, Larry Menor, and Christine Wiedman, "The Balanced Scorecard: To Adopt or Not to Adopt," *Ivey Business Journal* 69, no. 2 (November–December 2004), pp. 1–7; Sandy Richardson, "The Key Elements of Balanced Scorecard Success," *Ivey Business Journal* 69, no. 2 (November–December 2004), pp. 7–9.

[7] Kaplan and Norton, *The Balanced Scorecard.*

[8] Ibid.

[9] Ibid.

[10] Information posted on the website of the Balanced Scorecard Institute, balancedscorecard.org (accessed October, 2015).

[11] Henry Mintzberg, Bruce Ahlstrand, and Joseph Lampel, *Strategy Safari: A Guided Tour through the Wilds of Strategic Management* (New York: Free Press, 1998); Bruce Barringer and Allen C. Bluedorn, "The Relationship between Corporate Entrepreneurship and Strategic Management," *Strategic Management Journal* 20 (1999), pp. 421–444; Jeffrey G. Covin and Morgan P. Miles, "Corporate Entrepreneurship and the Pursuit of Competitive Advantage," *Entrepreneurship: Theory and Practice* 23, no. 3 (Spring 1999), pp. 47–63; David A. Garvin and Lynne C. Levesque, "Meeting the Challenge of Corporate Entrepreneurship," *Harvard Business Review* 84, no. 10 (October 2006), pp. 102–112.

[12] Joseph L. Bower and Clark G. Gilbert, "How Managers' Everyday Decisions Create or Destroy Your Company's Strategy," *Harvard Business Review* 85, no. 2 (February 2007), pp. 72–79.

[13] Gordon Shaw, Robert Brown, and Philip Bromiley, "Strategic Stories: How 3M Is Rewriting Business Planning," *Harvard Business Review* 76, no. 3 (May–June 1998), pp. 41–50.

[14] Collis and, "Can You Say What Your Strategy Is?".

[15] Cynthia A. Montgomery, "Putting Leadership Back into Strategy," *Harvard Business Review* 86, no. 1 (January 2008), pp. 54–60.

[16] Jay W. Lorsch and Robert C. Clark, "Leading from the Boardroom," *Harvard Business Review* 86, no. 4 (April 2008), pp. 105–111.

[17] Ibid.

[18] Stephen P. Kaufman, "Evaluating the CEO," *Harvard Business Review* 86, no. 10 (October 2008), pp. 53–57.

[19] Ibid.

[20] David A. Nadler, "Building Better Boards," *Harvard Business Review* 82, no. 5 (May 2004), pp. 102–105; Cynthia A. Montgomery and Rhonda Kaufman, "The Board's Missing Link," *Harvard Business Review* 81, no. 3 (March 2003), pp. 86–93; John Carver, "What Continues to Be Wrong with Corporate Governance and How to Fix It," *Ivey Business Journal* 68, no. 1 (September–October 2003), pp. 1–5. See also Gordon Donaldson, "A New Tool for Boards: The Strategic Audit," *Harvard Business Review* 73, no. 4 (July–August 1995), pp. 99–107.

CHAPTER 3 ●

Evaluating a Company's External Environment

© Bull's Eye/Image Zoo/Getty Images

Learning Objectives

THIS CHAPTER WILL HELP YOU UNDERSTAND:

LO 1   How to recognize the factors in a company's broad macro-environment that may have strategic significance.

LO 2   How to use analytic tools to diagnose the competitive conditions in a company's industry.

LO 3   How to map the market positions of key groups of industry rivals.

LO 4   How to determine whether an industry's outlook presents a company with sufficiently attractive opportunities for growth and profitability.

No matter what it takes, the goal of *strategy* is to beat the competition.

    Kenichi Ohmae—*Consultant and author*

There is no such thing as weak competition; it grows all the time.

    Nabil N. Jamal—*Consultant and author*

Sometimes by losing a battle you find a new way to win the war.

    Donald Trump—*President of the United States and founder of Trump Entertainment Resorts*

In order to chart a company's strategic course wisely, managers must first develop a deep understanding of the company's present situation. Two facets of a company's situation are especially pertinent: (1) its external environment—most notably, the competitive conditions of the industry in which the company operates; and (2) its internal environment—particularly the company's resources and organizational capabilities.

Insightful diagnosis of a company's external and internal environments is a prerequisite for managers to succeed in crafting a strategy that is an excellent *fit* with the company's situation—the first test of a winning strategy. As depicted in Figure 3.1, strategic thinking begins with an appraisal of the company's external and internal environments (as a basis for deciding on a long-term direction and developing a strategic vision), moves toward an evaluation of the most promising alternative strategies and business models, and culminates in choosing a specific strategy.

This chapter presents the concepts and analytic tools for zeroing in on those aspects of a company's external environment that should be considered in making strategic choices. Attention centers on the broad environmental context, the specific market arena in which a company operates, the drivers of change, the positions and likely actions of rival companies, and the factors that determine competitive success. In Chapter 4, we explore the methods of evaluating a company's internal circumstances and competitive capabilities.

THE STRATEGICALLY RELEVANT FACTORS IN THE COMPANY'S MACRO-ENVIRONMENT

Every company operates in a broad **"macro-environment"** that comprises six principal components: political factors; economic conditions in the firm's general environment (local, country, regional, worldwide); sociocultural forces; technological factors; environmental factors (concerning the natural environment); and legal/regulatory conditions. Each of these components has the potential to affect the firm's more immediate industry and competitive environment, although some are likely to have a more important effect than others (see Figure 3.2). An analysis of the impact of these factors is often referred to as **PESTEL analysis,** an acronym that serves as a reminder of the six components involved (political, economic, sociocultural, technological, environmental, legal/regulatory).

LO 1

How to recognize the factors in a company's broad macro-environment that may have strategic significance.

FIGURE 3.1   From Thinking Strategically about the Company's Situation to Choosing a Strategy

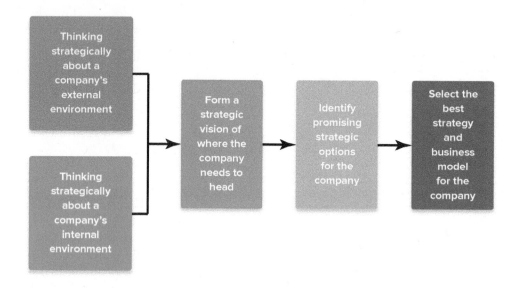

Since macro-economic factors affect different industries in different ways and to different degrees, it is important for managers to determine which of these represent the most *strategically relevant factors* outside the firm's industry boundaries. By *strategically relevant,* we mean important enough to have a bearing on the decisions the company ultimately makes about its long-term direction, objectives, strategy, and business model. The impact of the outer-ring factors depicted in Figure 3.2 on a company's choice of strategy can range from big to small. But even if those factors change slowly or are likely to have a low impact on the company's business situation, they still merit a watchful eye.

For example, the strategic opportunities of cigarette producers to grow their businesses are greatly reduced by antismoking ordinances, the decisions of governments to impose higher cigarette taxes, and the growing cultural stigma attached to smoking. Motor vehicle companies must adapt their strategies to customer concerns about high gasoline prices and to environmental concerns about carbon emissions. Companies in the food processing, restaurant, sports, and fitness industries have to pay special attention to changes in lifestyles, eating habits, leisure-time preferences, and attitudes toward nutrition and fitness in fashioning their strategies. Table 3.1 provides a brief description of the components of the macro-environment and some examples of the industries or business situations that they might affect.

As company managers scan the external environment, they must be alert for potentially important outer-ring developments, assess their impact and influence, and adapt the company's direction and strategy as needed. However, the factors in a company's environment having the *biggest* strategy-shaping impact typically pertain to the company's immediate industry and competitive environment. Consequently, it is on a company's industry and competitive environment that we concentrate the bulk of our attention in this chapter.

CHAPTER 3 'Evaluating a Company's External Environment

49

FIGURE 3.2 The Components of a Company's Macro-Environment

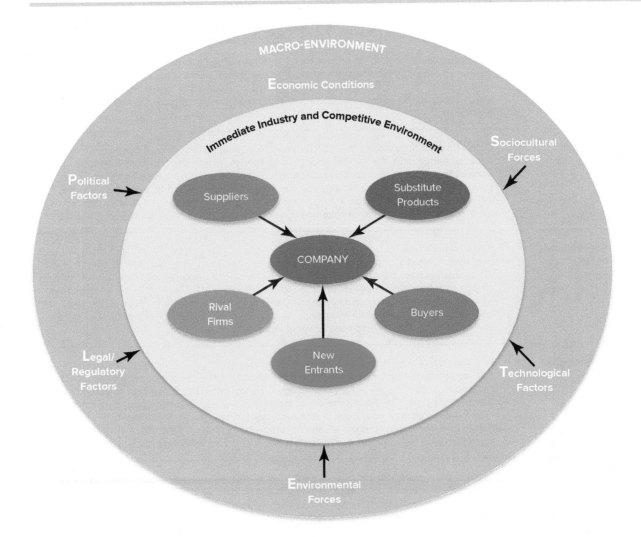

ASSESSING THE COMPANY'S INDUSTRY AND COMPETITIVE ENVIRONMENT

Thinking strategically about a company's industry and competitive environment entails using some well-validated concepts and analytic tools. These include the five forces framework, the value net, driving forces, strategic groups, competitor analysis, and key success factors. Proper use of these analytic tools can provide managers with the understanding needed to craft a strategy that fits the company's situation within their industry environment. The remainder of this chapter is devoted to describing how managers can use these tools to inform and improve their strategic choices.

LO 2

How to use analytic tools to diagnose the competitive conditions in a company's industry.

TABLE 3.1 The Six Components of the Macro-Environment

Component	Description
Political factors	Pertinent political factors include matters such as tax policy, fiscal policy, tariffs, the political climate, and the strength of institutions such as the federal banking system. Some political policies affect certain types of industries more than others. An example is energy policy, which clearly affects energy producers and heavy users of energy more than other types of businesses.
Economic conditions	Economic conditions include the general economic climate and specific factors such as interest rates, exchange rates, the inflation rate, the unemployment rate, the rate of economic growth, trade deficits or surpluses, savings rates, and per-capita domestic product. Some industries, such as construction, are particularly vulnerable to economic downturns but are positively affected by factors such as low interest rates. Others, such as discount retailing, benefit when general economic conditions weaken, as consumers become more price-conscious.
Sociocultural forces	Sociocultural forces include the societal values, attitudes, cultural influences, and lifestyles that impact demand for particular goods and services, as well as demographic factors such as the population size, growth rate, and age distribution. Sociocultural forces vary by locale and change over time. An example is the trend toward healthier lifestyles, which can shift spending toward exercise equipment and health clubs and away from alcohol and snack foods. The demographic effect of people living longer is having a huge impact on the health care, nursing homes, travel, hospitality, and entertainment industries.
Technological factors	Technological factors include the pace of technological change and technical developments that have the potential for wide-ranging effects on society, such as genetic engineering, nanotechnology, and solar energy technology. They include institutions involved in creating new knowledge and controlling the use of technology, such as R&D consortia, university-sponsored technology incubators, patent and copyright laws, and government control over the Internet. Technological change can encourage the birth of new industries, such as the connected wearable devices, and disrupt others, such as the recording industry.
Environmental forces	These include ecological and environmental forces such as weather, climate, climate change, and associated factors like water shortages. These factors can directly impact industries such as insurance, farming, energy production, and tourism. They may have an indirect but substantial effect on other industries such as transportation and utilities.
Legal and regulatory factors	These factors include the regulations and laws with which companies must comply, such as consumer laws, labor laws, antitrust laws, and occupational health and safety regulation. Some factors, such as financial services regulation, are industry-specific. Others, such as minimum wage legislation, affect certain types of industries (low-wage, labor-intensive industries) more than others.

THE FIVE FORCES FRAMEWORK

The character and strength of the competitive forces operating in an industry are never the same from one industry to another. The most powerful and widely used tool for diagnosing the principal competitive pressures in a market is the *five forces framework*.[1] This framework, depicted in Figure 3.3, holds that competitive pressures on

FIGURE 3.3   The Five Forces Model of Competition: A Key Analytic Tool

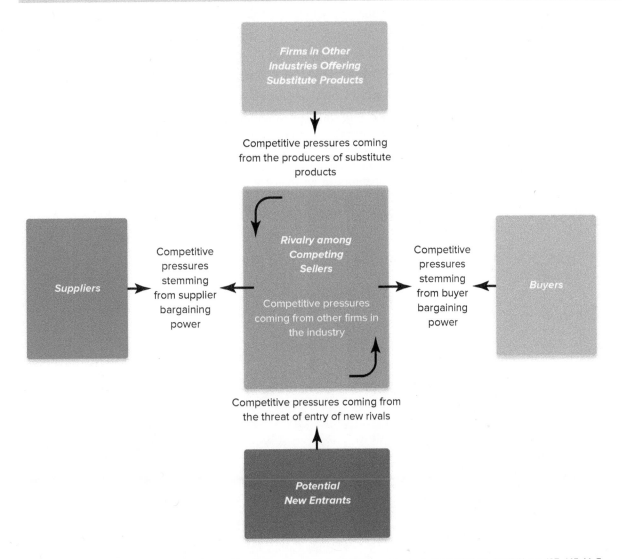

Sources: Adapted from M. E. Porter, "How Competitive Forces Shape Strategy," *Harvard Business Review* 57, no. 2 (1979), pp. 137–145; M. E. Porter, "The Five Competitive Forces That Shape Strategy," *Harvard Business Review* 86, no. 1 (2008), pp. 80–86.

companies within an industry come from five sources. These include (1) competition from *rival sellers,* (2) competition from *potential new entrants* to the industry, (3) competition from producers of *substitute products,* (4) *supplier* bargaining power, and (5) *customer* bargaining power.

Using the five forces model to determine the nature and strength of competitive pressures in a given industry involves three steps:

- *Step 1:* For each of the five forces, identify the different parties involved, along with the specific factors that bring about competitive pressures.

- *Step 2:* Evaluate how strong the pressures stemming from each of the five forces are (strong, moderate, or weak).
- *Step 3:* Determine whether the five forces, overall, are supportive of high industry profitability.

Competitive Pressures Created by the Rivalry among Competing Sellers

The strongest of the five competitive forces is often the rivalry for buyer patronage among competing sellers of a product or service. The intensity of rivalry among competing sellers within an industry depends on a number of identifiable factors. Figure 3.4 summarizes these factors, identifying those that intensify or weaken rivalry among direct competitors in an industry. A brief explanation of why these factors affect the degree of rivalry is in order:

FIGURE 3.4   Factors Affecting the Strength of Rivalry

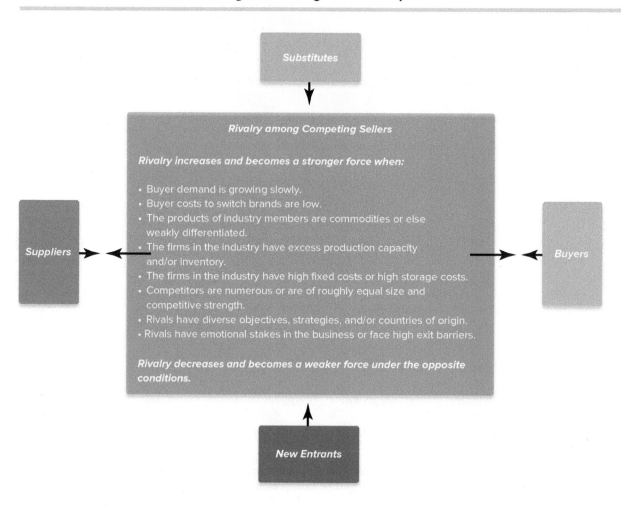

- *Rivalry increases when buyer demand is growing slowly or declining.* Rapidly expanding buyer demand produces enough new business for all industry members to grow without having to draw customers away from rival enterprises. But in markets where buyer demand is slow-growing or shrinking, companies eager to gain more business are likely to engage in aggressive price discounting, sales promotions, and other tactics to increase their sales volumes at the expense of rivals, sometimes to the point of igniting a fierce battle for market share.

- *Rivalry increases as it becomes less costly for buyers to switch brands.* The less costly it is for buyers to switch their purchases from one seller to another, the easier it is for sellers to steal customers away from rivals. When the cost of switching brands is higher, buyers are less prone to brand switching and sellers have protection from rivalrous moves. Switching costs include not only monetary costs but also the time, inconvenience, and psychological costs involved in switching brands. For example, retailers may not switch to the brands of rival manufacturers because they are hesitant to sever long-standing supplier relationships or incur the additional expense of retraining employees, accessing technical support, or testing the quality and reliability of the new brand.

- *Rivalry increases as the products of rival sellers become less strongly differentiated.* When the offerings of rivals are identical or weakly differentiated, buyers have less reason to be brand-loyal—a condition that makes it easier for rivals to convince buyers to switch to their offerings. Moreover, when the products of different sellers are virtually identical, shoppers will choose on the basis of price, which can result in fierce price competition among sellers. On the other hand, strongly differentiated product offerings among rivals breed high brand loyalty on the part of buyers who view the attributes of certain brands as more appealing or better suited to their needs.

- *Rivalry is more intense when industry members have too much inventory or significant amounts of idle production capacity, especially if the industry's product entails high fixed costs or high storage costs.* Whenever a market has excess supply (overproduction relative to demand), rivalry intensifies as sellers cut prices in a desperate effort to cope with the unsold inventory. A similar effect occurs when a product is perishable or seasonal, since firms often engage in aggressive price cutting to ensure that everything is sold. Likewise, whenever fixed costs account for a large fraction of total cost so that unit costs are significantly lower at full capacity, firms come under significant pressure to cut prices whenever they are operating below full capacity. Unused capacity imposes a significant cost-increasing penalty because there are fewer units over which to spread fixed costs. The pressure of high fixed or high storage costs can push rival firms into offering price concessions, special discounts, and rebates and employing other volume-boosting competitive tactics.

- *Rivalry intensifies as the number of competitors increases and they become more equal in size and capability.* When there are many competitors in a market, companies eager to increase their meager market share often engage in price-cutting activities to drive sales, leading to intense rivalry. When there are only a few competitors, companies are more wary of how their rivals may react to their attempts to take market share away from them. Fear of retaliation and a descent into a damaging price war leads to restrained competitive moves. Moreover, when rivals are of comparable size and competitive strength, they can usually compete on a fairly equal footing—an evenly matched contest tends to be fiercer than a contest in which one or more industry members have commanding market shares and substantially greater resources than their much smaller rivals.

- *Rivalry becomes more intense as the diversity of competitors increases in terms of long-term directions, objectives, strategies, and countries of origin.* A diverse group of sellers often contains one or more mavericks willing to try novel or rule-breaking market approaches, thus generating a more volatile and less predictable competitive environment. Globally competitive markets are often more rivalrous, especially when aggressors have lower costs and are intent on gaining a strong foothold in new country markets.

- *Rivalry is stronger when high exit barriers keep unprofitable firms from leaving the industry.* In industries where the assets cannot easily be sold or transferred to other uses, where workers are entitled to job protection, or where owners are committed to remaining in business for personal reasons, failing firms tend to hold on longer than they might otherwise—even when they are bleeding red ink. Deep price discounting of this sort can destabilize an otherwise attractive industry.

The previous factors, taken as whole, determine whether the rivalry in an industry is relatively strong, moderate, or weak. When rivalry is *strong,* the battle for market share is generally so vigorous that the profit margins of most industry members are squeezed to bare-bones levels. When rivalry is *moderate,* a more normal state, the maneuvering among industry members, while lively and healthy, still allows most industry members to earn acceptable profits. When rivalry is *weak,* most companies in the industry are relatively well satisfied with their sales growth and market shares and rarely undertake offensives to steal customers away from one another. Weak rivalry means that there is no downward pressure on industry profitability due to this particular competitive force.

The Choice of Competitive Weapons

Competitive battles among rival sellers can assume many forms that extend well beyond lively price competition. For example, competitors may resort to such marketing tactics as special sales promotions, heavy advertising, rebates, or low-interest-rate financing to drum up additional sales. Rivals may race one another to differentiate their products by offering better performance features or higher quality or improved customer service or a wider product selection. They may also compete through the rapid introduction of next-generation products, the frequent introduction of new or improved products, and efforts to build stronger dealer networks, establish positions in foreign markets, or otherwise expand distribution capabilities and market presence. Table 3.2 displays the competitive weapons that firms often employ in battling rivals, along with their primary effects with respect to price (P), cost (C), and value (V)—the elements of an effective business model and the value-price-cost framework, discussed in Chapter 1.

Competitive Pressures Associated with the Threat of New Entrants

New entrants into an industry threaten the position of rival firms since they will compete fiercely for market share, add to the number of industry rivals, and add to the industry's production capacity in the process. But even the *threat* of new entry puts added competitive pressure on current industry members and thus functions as an important competitive force. This is because credible threat of entry often prompts industry members to lower their prices and initiate defensive actions in an attempt

TABLE 3.2   Common "Weapons" for Competing with Rivals

Types of Competitive Weapons	Primary Effects
Discounting prices, holding clearance sales	Lowers price (P), increases total sales volume and market share, lowers profits if price cuts are not offset by large increases in sales volume
Offering coupons, advertising items on sale	Increases sales volume and total revenues, lowers price (P), increases unit costs (C), may lower profit margins per unit sold (P – C)
Advertising product or service characteristics, using ads to enhance a company's image	Boosts buyer demand, increases product differentiation and perceived value (V), increases total sales volume and market share, but may increase unit costs (C) and lower profit margins per unit sold
Innovating to improve product performance and quality	Increases product differentiation and value (V), boosts buyer demand, boosts total sales volume, likely to increase unit costs (C)
Introducing new or improved features, increasing the number of styles to provide greater product selection	Increases product differentiation and value (V), strengthens buyer demand, boosts total sales volume and market share, likely to increase unit costs (C)
Increasing customization of product or service	Increases product differentiation and value (V), increases buyer switching costs, boosts total sales volume, often increases unit costs (C)
Building a bigger, better dealer network	Broadens access to buyers, boosts total sales volume and market share, may increase unit costs (C)
Improving warranties, offering low-interest financing	Increases product differentiation and value (V), increases unit costs (C), increases buyer switching costs, boosts total sales volume and market share

to deter new entrants. Just how serious the threat of entry is in a particular market depends on two classes of factors: (1) the *expected reaction of incumbent firms to new entry* and (2) what are known as *barriers to entry*. The threat of entry is low in industries where incumbent firms are likely to retaliate against new entrants with sharp price discounting and other moves designed to make entry unprofitable (due to the expectation of such retaliation). The threat of entry is also low when entry barriers are high (due to such barriers). Entry barriers are high under the following conditions:[2]

- *There are sizable economies of scale in production, distribution, advertising, or other activities.* When incumbent companies enjoy cost advantages associated with large-scale operations, outsiders must either enter on a large scale (a costly and perhaps risky move) or accept a cost disadvantage and consequently lower profitability.

- *Incumbents have other hard to replicate cost advantages over new entrants.* Aside from enjoying economies of scale, industry incumbents can have cost advantages that stem from the possession of patents or proprietary technology, exclusive partnerships with the best and cheapest suppliers, favorable locations, and low fixed costs (because they have older facilities that have been mostly depreciated). Learning-based cost savings can also accrue from experience in performing certain activities such as manufacturing or new product development or inventory management. The extent of such savings can be measured with learning/experience curves. The steeper the learning/experience curve, the bigger the cost advantage of the company with the largest *cumulative* production volume. The microprocessor industry provides an excellent example of this:

> *Manufacturing unit costs for microprocessors tend to decline about 20 percent each time cumulative production volume doubles. With a 20 percent experience curve effect, if the first 1 million chips cost $100 each, once production volume reaches 2 million, the unit cost would fall to $80 (80 percent of $100), and by a production volume of 4 million, the unit cost would be $64 (80 percent of $80).*[3]

- *Customers have strong brand preferences and high degrees of loyalty to seller.* The stronger the attachment of buyers to established brands, the harder it is for a newcomer to break into the marketplace. In such cases, a new entrant must have the financial resources to spend enough on advertising and sales promotion to overcome customer loyalties and build its own clientele. Establishing brand recognition and building customer loyalty can be a slow and costly process. In addition, if it is difficult or costly for a customer to switch to a new brand, a new entrant may have to offer a discounted price or otherwise persuade buyers that its brand is worth the switching costs. Such barriers discourage new entry because they act to boost financial requirements and lower expected profit margins for new entrants.

- *Patents and other forms of intellectual property protection are in place.* In a number of industries, entry is prevented due to the existence of intellectual property protection laws that remain in place for a given number of years. Often, companies have a "wall of patents" in place to prevent other companies from entering with a "me too" strategy that replicates a key piece of technology.

- *There are strong "network effects" in customer demand.* In industries where buyers are more attracted to a product when there are many other users of the product, there are said to be "network effects," since demand is higher the larger the network of users. Video game systems are an example because users prefer to have the same systems as their friends so that they can play together on systems they all know and can share games. When incumbents have a large existing base of users, new entrants with otherwise comparable products face a serious disadvantage in attracting buyers.

- *Capital requirements are high.* The larger the total dollar investment needed to enter the market successfully, the more limited the pool of potential entrants. The most obvious capital requirements for new entrants relate to manufacturing facilities and equipment, introductory advertising and sales promotion campaigns, working capital to finance inventories and customer credit, and sufficient cash to cover startup costs.

- *There are difficulties in building a network of distributors/dealers or in securing adequate space on retailers' shelves.* A potential entrant can face numerous distribution-channel challenges. Wholesale distributors may be reluctant to take on a product that lacks buyer recognition. Retailers must be recruited and convinced to give a new brand ample display space and an adequate trial period. When existing sellers have strong, well-functioning distributor–dealer networks, a newcomer has an uphill struggle in squeezing its way into existing distribution channels. Potential entrants sometimes have to "buy" their way into wholesale or retail channels by cutting their prices to provide dealers and distributors with higher markups and profit margins or by giving them big advertising and promotional allowances. As a consequence, a potential entrant's own profits may be squeezed unless and until its product gains enough consumer acceptance that distributors and retailers are willing to carry it.

- *There are restrictive regulatory policies.* Regulated industries like cable TV, telecommunications, electric and gas utilities, radio and television broadcasting, liquor retailing, nuclear power, and railroads entail government-controlled entry. Government agencies can also limit or even bar entry by requiring licenses and permits, such as the medallion required to drive a taxicab in New York City. Government-mandated safety regulations and environmental pollution standards also create entry barriers because they raise entry costs. Recently enacted banking regulations in many countries have made entry particularly difficult for small new bank startups—complying with all the new regulations along with the rigors of competing against existing banks requires very deep pockets.

- *There are restrictive trade policies.* In international markets, host governments commonly limit foreign entry and must approve all foreign investment applications. National governments commonly use tariffs and trade restrictions (anti-dumping rules, local content requirements, quotas, etc.) to raise entry barriers for foreign firms and protect domestic producers from outside competition.

Figure 3.5 summarizes the factors that cause the overall competitive pressure from potential entrants to be strong or weak. An analysis of these factors can help managers determine whether the threat of entry into their industry is high or low, *in general*. But certain kinds of companies—those with sizable financial resources, proven competitive capabilities, and a respected brand name—may be able to hurdle an industry's entry barriers even when they are high.[4] For example, when Honda opted to enter the U.S. lawn-mower market in competition against Toro, Snapper, Craftsman, John Deere, and others, it was easily able to hurdle entry barriers that would have been formidable to other newcomers because it had long-standing expertise in gasoline engines and a reputation for quality and durability in automobiles that gave it instant credibility with homeowners. As a result, Honda had to spend relatively little on inducing dealers to handle the Honda lawn-mower line or attracting customers. Similarly, Samsung's brand reputation in televisions, DVD players, and other electronics products gave it strong credibility in entering the market for smartphones—Samsung's Galaxy smartphones are now a formidable rival of Apple's iPhone.

It is also important to recognize that the barriers to entering an industry can become stronger or weaker over time. For example, key patents that had prevented new entry in the market for functional 3-D printers expired in February 2014, opening the way for new competition in this industry. Use of the Internet for shopping has made it much easier for e-tailers to enter into competition against some of the best-known retail chains. On the other hand, new strategic actions by incumbent firms to increase advertising, strengthen distributor–dealer relations, step up R&D, or improve product quality can erect higher roadblocks to entry.

Whether an industry's entry barriers ought to be considered high or low depends on the resources and capabilities possessed by the pool of potential entrants.

High entry barriers and weak entry threats today do not always translate into high entry barriers and weak entry threats tomorrow.

FIGURE 3.5   Factors Affecting the Threat of Entry

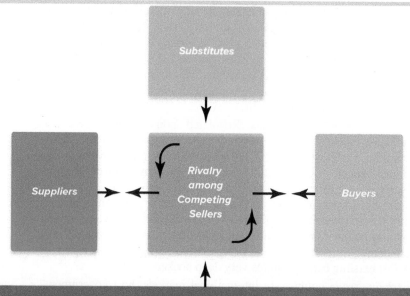

Substitutes

Suppliers

Rivalry among Competing Sellers

Buyers

Competitive Pressures from Potential Entrants

Threat of entry is a stronger force when incumbents are unlikely to make retaliatory moves against new entrants and entry barriers are low. Entry barriers are high (and threat of entry is low) when:
- Incumbents have large cost advantages over potential entrants due to:
  - High economies of scale
  - Significant experience-based cost advantages or learning curve effects
  - Other cost advantages (e.g., favorable access to inputs, technology, location, or low fixed costs)
- Customers have strong brand preferences and/or loyalty to incumbent sellers.
- Patents and other forms of intellectual property protection are in place.
- There are strong network effects.
- Capital requirements are high.
- There is limited new access to distribution channels and shelf space.
- Government policies are restrictive.
- There are restrictive trade policies.

Competitive Pressures from the Sellers of Substitute Products

Companies in one industry are vulnerable to competitive pressure from the actions of companies in a closely adjoining industry whenever buyers view the products of the two industries as good substitutes. For instance, the producers of eyeglasses and contact lens face competitive pressures from the doctors who do corrective laser surgery. Similarly, the producers of sugar experience competitive pressures from the producers of sugar substitutes (high-fructose corn syrup, agave syrup, and artificial sweeteners). Internet providers of news-related information have put brutal competitive pressure on the publishers of newspapers.

As depicted in Figure 3.6, three factors determine whether the competitive pressures from substitute products are strong or weak. Competitive pressures are stronger when:

1. *Good substitutes are readily available and attractively priced.* The presence of readily available and attractively priced substitutes creates competitive pressure by placing a ceiling on the prices industry members can charge without risking sales erosion. This price ceiling, at the same time, puts a lid on the profits that industry members can earn unless they find ways to cut costs.

2. *Buyers view the substitutes as comparable or better in terms of quality, performance, and other relevant attributes.* The availability of substitutes inevitably invites customers to compare performance, features, ease of use, and other attributes besides price. The users of paper cartons constantly weigh the

FIGURE 3.6   Factors Affecting Competition from Substitute Products

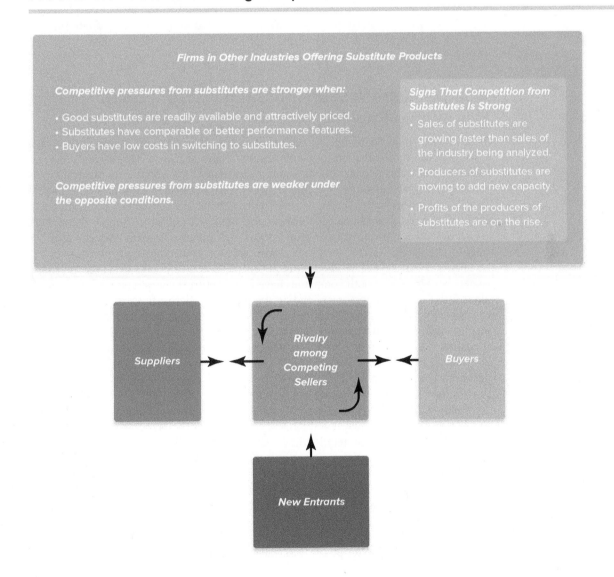

price-performance trade-offs with plastic containers and metal cans, for example. Movie enthusiasts are increasingly weighing whether to go to movie theaters to watch newly released movies or wait until they can watch the same movies streamed to their home TV by Netflix, Amazon Prime, cable providers, and other on demand sources.

3. *The costs that buyers incur in switching to the substitutes are low.* Low switching costs make it easier for the sellers of attractive substitutes to lure buyers to their offerings; high switching costs deter buyers from purchasing substitute products.

Before assessing the competitive pressures coming from substitutes, company managers must identify the substitutes, which is less easy than it sounds since it involves (1) determining where the industry boundaries lie and (2) figuring out which other products or services can address the same basic customer needs as those produced by industry members. Deciding on the industry boundaries is necessary for determining which firms are direct rivals and which produce substitutes. This is a matter of perspective—there are no hard-and-fast rules, other than to say that other brands of the same basic product constitute rival products and not substitutes.

Competitive Pressures Stemming from Supplier Bargaining Power

Whether the suppliers of industry members represent a weak or strong competitive force depends on the degree to which suppliers have sufficient *bargaining power* to influence the terms and conditions of supply in their favor. Suppliers with strong bargaining power are a source of competitive pressure because of their ability to charge industry members higher prices, pass costs on to them, and limit their opportunities to find better deals. For instance, Microsoft and Intel, both of which supply PC makers with essential components, have been known to use their dominant market status not only to charge PC makers premium prices but also to leverage their power over PC makers in other ways. The bargaining power of these two companies over their customers is so great that both companies have faced antitrust charges on numerous occasions. Prior to a legal agreement ending the practice, Microsoft pressured PC makers to load only Microsoft products on the PCs they shipped. Intel has defended itself against similar antitrust charges, but in filling orders for newly introduced Intel chips, it continues to give top priority to PC makers that use the biggest percentages of Intel chips in their PC models. Being on Intel's list of preferred customers helps a PC maker get an early allocation of Intel's latest chips and thus allows the PC maker to get new models to market ahead of rivals.

Small-scale retailers often must contend with the power of manufacturers whose products enjoy well-known brand names, since consumers expect to find these products on the shelves of the retail stores where they shop. This provides the manufacturer with a degree of pricing power and often the ability to push hard for favorable shelf displays. Supplier bargaining power is also a competitive factor in industries where unions have been able to organize the workforce (which supplies labor). Air pilot unions, for example, have employed their bargaining power to increase pilots' wages and benefits in the air transport industry.

As shown in Figure 3.7, a variety of factors determine the strength of suppliers' bargaining power. Supplier power is stronger when:

FIGURE 3.7   Factors Affecting the Bargaining Power of Suppliers

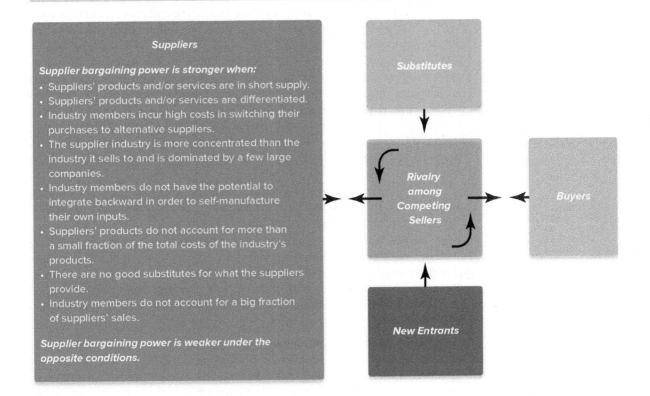

Suppliers

Supplier bargaining power is stronger when:
- Suppliers' products and/or services are in short supply.
- Suppliers' products and/or services are differentiated.
- Industry members incur high costs in switching their purchases to alternative suppliers.
- The supplier industry is more concentrated than the industry it sells to and is dominated by a few large companies.
- Industry members do not have the potential to integrate backward in order to self-manufacture their own inputs.
- Suppliers' products do not account for more than a small fraction of the total costs of the industry's products.
- There are no good substitutes for what the suppliers provide.
- Industry members do not account for a big fraction of suppliers' sales.

Supplier bargaining power is weaker under the opposite conditions.

Substitutes

Rivalry among Competing Sellers

Buyers

New Entrants

- *Demand for suppliers' products is high and the products are in short supply.* A surge in the demand for particular items shifts the bargaining power to the suppliers of those products; suppliers of items in short supply have pricing power.

- *Suppliers provide differentiated inputs that enhance the performance of the industry's product.* The more valuable a particular input is in terms of enhancing the performance or quality of the products of industry members, the more bargaining leverage suppliers have. In contrast, the suppliers of commodities are in a weak bargaining position, since industry members have no reason other than price to prefer one supplier over another.

- *It is difficult or costly for industry members to switch their purchases from one supplier to another.* Low switching costs limit supplier bargaining power by enabling industry members to change suppliers if any one supplier attempts to raise prices by more than the costs of switching. Thus, the higher the switching costs of industry members, the stronger the bargaining power of their suppliers.

- *The supplier industry is dominated by a few large companies and it is more concentrated than the industry it sells to.* Suppliers with sizable market shares and strong demand for the items they supply generally have sufficient bargaining power to charge high prices and deny requests from industry members for lower prices or other concessions.

- *Industry members are incapable of integrating backward to self-manufacture items they have been buying from suppliers.* As a rule, suppliers are safe from the threat of self-manufacture by their customers until the volume of parts a customer needs becomes large enough for the customer to justify backward integration into self-manufacture of the component. When industry members can threaten credibly to self-manufacture suppliers' goods, their bargaining power over suppliers increases proportionately.

- *Suppliers provide an item that accounts for no more than a small fraction of the costs of the industry's product.* The more that the cost of a particular part or component affects the final product's cost, the more that industry members will be sensitive to the actions of suppliers to raise or lower their prices. When an input accounts for only a small proportion of total input costs, buyers will be less sensitive to price increases. Thus, suppliers' power increases when the inputs they provide do *not* make up a large proportion of the cost of the final product.

- *Good substitutes are not available for the suppliers' products.* The lack of readily available substitute inputs increases the bargaining power of suppliers by increasing the dependence of industry members on the suppliers.

- *Industry members are not major customers of suppliers.* As a rule, suppliers have less bargaining leverage when their sales to members of the industry constitute a big percentage of their total sales. In such cases, the well-being of suppliers is closely tied to the well-being of their major customers, and their dependence upon them increases. The bargaining power of suppliers is stronger, then, when they are *not* bargaining with major customers.

In identifying the degree of supplier power in an industry, it is important to recognize that different types of suppliers are likely to have different amounts of bargaining power. Thus, the first step is for managers to identify the different types of suppliers, paying particular attention to those that provide the industry with important inputs. The next step is to assess the bargaining power of each type of supplier separately.

Competitive Pressures Stemming from Buyer Bargaining Power and Price Sensitivity

Whether buyers are able to exert strong competitive pressures on industry members depends on (1) the degree to which buyers have bargaining power and (2) the extent to which buyers are price-sensitive. Buyers with strong bargaining power can limit industry profitability by demanding price concessions, better payment terms, or additional features and services that increase industry members' costs. Buyer price sensitivity limits the profit potential of industry members by restricting the ability of sellers to raise prices without losing revenue due to lost sales.

As with suppliers, the leverage that buyers have in negotiating favorable terms of sale can range from weak to strong. Individual consumers seldom have much bargaining power in negotiating price concessions or other favorable terms with sellers. However, their price sensitivity varies by individual and by the type of product they are buying (whether it's a necessity or a discretionary purchase, for example). Similarly, small businesses usually have weak bargaining power because of the small-size orders they place with sellers. Many relatively small wholesalers and retailers join buying groups to pool their purchasing power and approach manufacturers for better terms than could be gotten individually. Large business buyers, in contrast, can have considerable bargaining power. For example, large retail chains like

Walmart, Best Buy, Staples, and Home Depot typically have considerable bargaining power in purchasing products from manufacturers, not only because they buy in large quantities, but also because of manufacturers' need for access to their broad base of customers. Major supermarket chains like Kroger, Albertsons, Hannaford, and Aldi have sufficient bargaining power to demand promotional allowances and lump-sum payments (called *slotting fees*) from food products manufacturers in return for stocking certain brands or putting them in the best shelf locations. Motor vehicle manufacturers have strong bargaining power in negotiating to buy original-equipment tires from tire makers such as Goodyear, Michelin, and Pirelli, partly because they buy in large quantities and partly because consumers are more likely to buy replacement tires that match the tire brand on their vehicle at the time of its purchase.

Figure 3.8 summarizes the factors determining the strength of buyer power in an industry. Note that the first five factors are the mirror image of those determining the bargaining power of suppliers, as described next.

Buyer bargaining power is stronger when:

- *Buyer demand is weak in relation to the available supply.* Weak or declining demand and the resulting excess supply create a "buyers' market," in which bargain-hunting buyers have leverage in pressing industry members for better deals and special treatment. Conversely, strong or rapidly growing market demand creates a "sellers'

FIGURE 3.8   Factors Affecting the Bargaining Power of Buyers

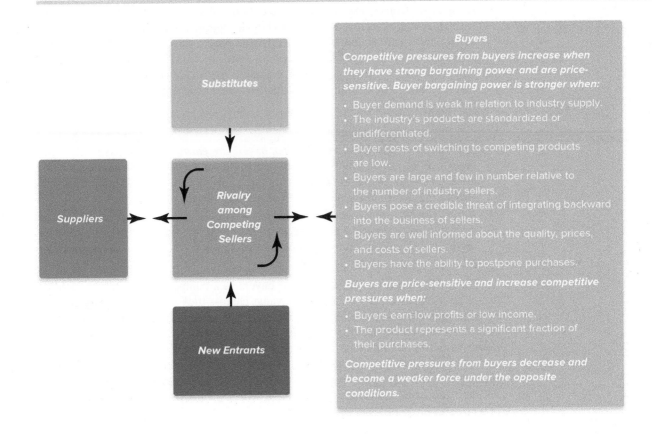

market" characterized by tight supplies or shortages—conditions that put buyers in a weak position to wring concessions from industry members.

- *Industry goods are standardized or differentiation is weak.* In such circumstances, buyers make their selections on the basis of price, which increases price competition among vendors.

- *Buyers' costs of switching to competing brands or substitutes are relatively low.* Switching costs put a cap on how much industry producers can raise prices or reduce quality before they will lose the buyer's business.

- *Buyers are large and few in number relative to the number of sellers.* The larger the buyers, the more important their business is to the seller and the more sellers will be willing to grant concessions.

- *Buyers pose a credible threat of integrating backward into the business of sellers.* Companies like Anheuser-Busch, Coors, and Heinz have partially integrated backward into metal-can manufacturing to gain bargaining power in obtaining the balance of their can requirements from otherwise powerful metal-can manufacturers.

- *Buyers are well informed about the product offerings of sellers (product features and quality, prices, buyer reviews) and the cost of production (an indicator of markup).* The more information buyers have, the better bargaining position they are in. The mushrooming availability of product information on the Internet (and its ready access on smartphones) is giving added bargaining power to consumers, since they can use this to find or negotiate better deals.

- *Buyers have discretion to delay their purchases or perhaps even not make a purchase at all.* Consumers often have the option to delay purchases of durable goods (cars, major appliances), or decline to buy discretionary goods (massages, concert tickets) if they are not happy with the prices offered. Business customers may also be able to defer their purchases of certain items, such as plant equipment or maintenance services. This puts pressure on sellers to provide concessions to buyers so that the sellers can keep their sales numbers from dropping off.

The following factors increase buyer price sensitivity and result in greater competitive pressures on the industry as a result:

- *Buyer price sensitivity increases when buyers are earning low profits or have low income.* Price is a critical factor in the purchase decisions of low-income consumers and companies that are barely scraping by. In such cases, their high price sensitivity limits the ability of sellers to charge high prices.

- *Buyers are more price-sensitive if the product represents a large fraction of their total purchases.* When a purchase eats up a large portion of a buyer's budget or represents a significant part of his or her cost structure, the buyer cares more about price than might otherwise be the case.

The starting point for the analysis of buyers as a competitive force is to identify the different types of buyers along the value chain—then proceed to analyzing the bargaining power and price sensitivity of each type separately. It is important to recognize that *not all buyers of an industry's product have equal degrees of bargaining power with sellers, and some may be less sensitive than others to price, quality, or service differences.* For example, apparel manufacturers confront significant bargaining power when selling to big retailers like Nordstrom, Macy's, or Bloomingdale's, but they can command much better prices selling to small owner-managed apparel boutiques.

Is the Collective Strength of the Five Competitive Forces Conducive to Good Profitability?

Assessing whether each of the five competitive forces gives rise to strong, moderate, or weak competitive pressures sets the stage for evaluating whether, overall, the strength of the five forces is conducive to good profitability. Is any of the competitive forces sufficiently powerful to undermine industry profitability? Can companies in this industry reasonably expect to earn decent profits in light of the prevailing competitive forces?

The most extreme case of a "competitively unattractive" industry occurs when all five forces are producing strong competitive pressures: Rivalry among sellers is vigorous, low entry barriers allow new rivals to gain a market foothold, competition from substitutes is intense, and both suppliers and buyers are able to exercise considerable leverage. Strong competitive pressures coming from all five directions drive industry profitability to unacceptably low levels, frequently producing losses for many industry members and forcing some out of business. But an industry can be competitively unattractive without all five competitive forces being strong. In fact, *intense competitive pressures from just one of the five forces may suffice to destroy the conditions for good profitability and prompt some companies to exit the business.*

As a rule, *the strongest competitive forces determine the extent of the competitive pressure on industry profitability.* Thus, in evaluating the strength of the five forces overall and their effect on industry profitability, managers should look to the strongest forces. Having more than one strong force will not worsen the effect on industry profitability, but it does mean that the industry has multiple competitive challenges with which to cope. In that sense, an industry with three to five strong forces is even more "unattractive" as a place to compete. Especially intense competitive conditions seem to be the norm in tire manufacturing, apparel, and commercial airlines, three industries where profit margins have historically been thin.

In contrast, when the overall impact of the five competitive forces is moderate to weak, an industry is "attractive" in the sense that the *average* industry member can reasonably expect to earn good profits and a nice return on investment. The ideal competitive environment for earning superior profits is one in which both suppliers and customers are in weak bargaining positions, there are no good substitutes, high barriers block further entry, and rivalry among present sellers is muted. Weak competition is the best of all possible worlds for also-ran companies because even they can usually eke out a decent profit—if a company can't make a decent profit when competition is weak, then its business outlook is indeed grim.

> **CORE CONCEPT**
>
> The strongest of the five forces determines the extent of the downward pressure on an industry's profitability.

Matching Company Strategy to Competitive Conditions

Working through the five forces model step by step not only aids strategy makers in assessing whether the intensity of competition allows good profitability but also promotes sound strategic thinking about how to better match company strategy to the specific competitive character of the marketplace. Effectively matching a company's business strategy to prevailing competitive conditions has two aspects:

1. Pursuing avenues that shield the firm from as many of the different competitive pressures as possible.
2. Initiating actions calculated to shift the competitive forces in the company's favor by altering the underlying factors driving the five forces.

> A company's strategy is increasingly effective the more it provides some insulation from competitive pressures, shifts the competitive battle in the company's favor, and positions the firm to take advantage of attractive growth opportunities.

But making headway on these two fronts first requires identifying competitive pressures, gauging the relative strength of each of the five competitive forces, and gaining a deep enough understanding of the state of competition in the industry to know which strategy buttons to push.

COMPLEMENTORS AND THE VALUE NET

Not all interactions among industry participants are necessarily competitive in nature. Some have the potential to be cooperative, as the value net framework demonstrates. Like the five forces framework, the value net includes an analysis of buyers, suppliers, and substitutors (see Figure 3.9). But it differs from the five forces framework in several important ways.

First, the analysis focuses on the interactions of industry participants with a particular company. Thus it places that firm in the center of the framework, as Figure 3.9 shows. Second, the category of "competitors" is defined to include not only the focal firm's direct competitors or industry rivals but also the sellers of substitute products and potential entrants. Third, the value net framework introduces a new category of industry participant that is not found in the five forces framework—that of "complementors." **Complementors** are the producers of complementary products, which are products that enhance the value of the focal firm's products when they are used together. Some examples include snorkels and swim fins or shoes and shoelaces.

The inclusion of complementors draws particular attention to the fact that success in the marketplace need not come at the expense of other industry participants.

> **CORE CONCEPT**
>
> **Complementors** are the producers of complementary products, which are products that enhance the value of the focal firm's products when they are used together.

FIGURE 3.9   The Value Net

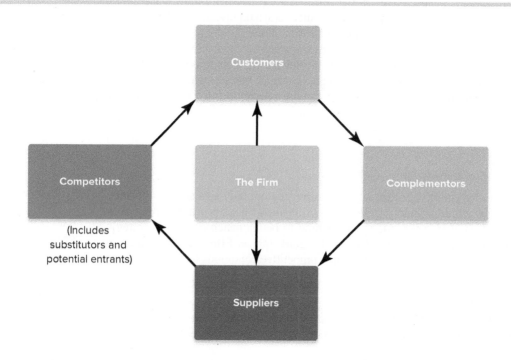

Interactions among industry participants may be cooperative in nature rather than competitive. In the case of complementors, an increase in sales for them is likely to increase the sales of the focal firm as well. But the value net framework also encourages managers to consider other forms of cooperative interactions and realize that value is created jointly by all industry participants. For example, a company's success in the marketplace depends on establishing a reliable supply chain for its inputs, which implies the need for cooperative relations with its suppliers. Often a firm works hand in hand with its suppliers to ensure a smoother, more efficient operation for both parties. Newell-Rubbermaid, for example, works cooperatively as a supplier to companies such as Kmart and Kohl's. Even direct rivals may work cooperatively if they participate in industry trade associations or engage in joint lobbying efforts. Value net analysis can help managers discover the potential to improve their position through cooperative as well as competitive interactions.

INDUSTRY DYNAMICS AND THE FORCES DRIVING CHANGE

While it is critical to understand the nature and intensity of competitive and cooperative forces in an industry, it is equally critical to understand that the intensity of these forces is fluid and subject to change. All industries are affected by new developments and ongoing trends that alter industry conditions, some more speedily than others. The popular hypothesis that industries go through a life cycle of takeoff, rapid growth, maturity, market saturation and slowing growth, followed by stagnation or decline is but one aspect of industry change—many other new developments and emerging trends cause industry change.[5] Any strategies devised by management will therefore play out in a dynamic industry environment, so it's imperative that managers consider the factors driving industry change and how they might affect the industry environment. Moreover, with early notice, managers may be able to influence the direction or scope of environmental change and improve the outlook.

Industry and competitive conditions change because forces are enticing or pressuring certain industry participants (competitors, customers, suppliers, complementors) to alter their actions in important ways. The most powerful of the change agents are called **driving forces** because they have the biggest influences in reshaping the industry landscape and altering competitive conditions. Some driving forces originate in the outer ring of the company's macro-environment (see Figure 3.2), but most originate in the company's more immediate industry and competitive environment.

> **CORE CONCEPT**
>
> **Driving forces** are the major underlying causes of change in industry and competitive conditions.

Driving-forces analysis has three steps: (1) identifying what the driving forces are; (2) assessing whether the drivers of change are, on the whole, acting to make the industry more or less attractive; and (3) determining what strategy changes are needed to prepare for the impact of the driving forces. All three steps merit further discussion.

Identifying the Forces Driving Industry Change

Many developments can affect an industry powerfully enough to qualify as driving forces. Some drivers of change are unique and specific to a particular industry situation, but most drivers of industry and competitive change fall into one of the following categories:

- *Changes in an industry's long-term growth rate.* Shifts in industry growth up or down have the potential to affect the balance between industry supply and buyer demand, entry and exit, and the character and strength of competition. Whether demand is growing or declining is one of the key factors influencing the intensity of rivalry in an industry, as explained earlier. But the strength of this effect will depend on how changes in the industry growth rate affect entry and exit in the industry. If entry barriers are low, then growth in demand will attract new entrants, increasing the number of industry rivals and changing the competitive landscape.

- *Increasing globalization.* Globalization can be precipitated by such factors as the blossoming of consumer demand in developing countries, the availability of lower-cost foreign inputs, and the reduction of trade barriers, as has occurred recently in many parts of Latin America and Asia. The forces of globalization are sometimes such a strong driver that companies find it highly advantageous, if not necessary, to spread their operating reach into more and more country markets.

- *Emerging new Internet capabilities and applications.* The Internet of the future will feature faster speeds, dazzling applications, and over a billion connected gadgets performing an array of functions, thus driving a host of industry and competitive changes. But Internet-related impacts vary from industry to industry. The challenges are to assess precisely how emerging Internet developments are altering a particular industry's landscape and to factor these impacts into the strategy-making equation.

- *Shifts in who buys the products and how the products are used.* Shifts in buyer demographics and the ways products are used can greatly alter competitive conditions. Longer life expectancies and growing percentages of relatively well-to-do retirees, for example, are driving demand growth in such industries as cosmetic surgery, assisted living residences, and vacation travel. The burgeoning popularity of streaming video has affected broadband providers, wireless phone carriers, and television broadcasters, and created opportunities for such new entertainment businesses as Hulu and Netflix.

- *Technological change and manufacturing process innovation.* Advances in technology can cause disruptive change in an industry by introducing substitutes or can alter the industry landscape by opening up whole new industry frontiers. For instance, revolutionary change in self-driving technology has enabled even companies such as Google to enter the motor vehicle market.

- *Product innovation.* An ongoing stream of product innovations tends to alter the pattern of competition in an industry by attracting more first-time buyers, rejuvenating industry growth, and/or increasing product differentiation, with concomitant effects on rivalry, entry threat, and buyer power. Product innovation has been a key driving force in the smartphone industry, which in an ever more connected world is driving change in other industries. Phillips Company, for example, has introduced a new wireless lighting system (Hue) that allows homeowners to use a smartphone app to remotely turn lights on and off and program them to blink if an intruder is detected. Wearable action-capture cameras and unmanned aerial view drones are rapidly becoming a disruptive force in the digital camera industry by enabling photography shots and videos not feasible with handheld digital cameras.

- *Entry or exit of major firms.* Entry by a major firm thus often produces a new ball game, not only with new key players but also with new rules for competing. Similarly, exit of a major firm changes the competitive structure by reducing the number of market leaders and increasing the dominance of the leaders who remain.

- *Diffusion of technical know-how across companies and countries.* As knowledge about how to perform a particular activity or execute a particular manufacturing technology spreads, products tend to become more commodity-like. Knowledge diffusion can occur through scientific journals, trade publications, onsite plant tours, word of mouth among suppliers and customers, employee migration, and Internet sources.

- *Changes in cost and efficiency.* Widening or shrinking differences in the costs among key competitors tend to dramatically alter the state of competition. Declining costs of producing tablets have enabled price cuts and spurred tablet sales (especially lower-priced models) by making them more affordable to lower-income households worldwide. Lower-cost e-books are cutting into sales of costlier hardcover books as increasing numbers of consumers have laptops, iPads, Kindles, and other brands of tablets.

- *Reductions in uncertainty and business risk.* Many companies are hesitant to enter industries with uncertain futures or high levels of business risk because it is unclear how much time and money it will take to overcome various technological hurdles and achieve acceptable production costs (as is the case in the solar power industry). Over time, however, diminishing risk levels and uncertainty tend to stimulate new entry and capital investments on the part of growth-minded companies seeking new opportunities, thus dramatically altering industry and competitive conditions.

- *Regulatory influences and government policy changes.* Government regulatory actions can often mandate significant changes in industry practices and strategic approaches—as has recently occurred in the world's banking industry. New rules and regulations pertaining to government-sponsored health insurance programs are driving changes in the health care industry. In international markets, host governments can drive competitive changes by opening their domestic markets to foreign participation or closing them to protect domestic companies.

- *Changing societal concerns, attitudes, and lifestyles.* Emerging social issues as well as changing attitudes and lifestyles can be powerful instigators of industry change. Growing concern about the effects of climate change has emerged as a major driver of change in the energy industry. Concerns about the use of chemical additives and the nutritional content of food products have been driving changes in the restaurant and food industries. Shifting societal concerns, attitudes, and lifestyles alter the pattern of competition, favoring those players that respond with products targeted to the new trends and conditions.

While many forces of change may be at work in a given industry, *no more than three or four* are likely to be true driving forces powerful enough to qualify as the *major determinants* of why and how the industry is changing. Thus, company strategists must resist the temptation to label every change they see as a driving force. Table 3.3 lists the most common driving forces.

The most important part of driving-forces analysis is to determine whether the collective impact of the driving forces will increase or decrease market demand, make competition more or less intense, and lead to higher or lower industry profitability.

TABLE 3.3 The Most Common Drivers of Industry Change

- Changes in the long-term industry growth rate
- Increasing globalization
- Emerging new Internet capabilities and applications
- Shifts in buyer demographics
- Technological change and manufacturing process innovation
- Product and marketing innovation
- Entry or exit of major firms
- Diffusion of technical know-how across companies and countries
- Changes in cost and efficiency
- Reductions in uncertainty and business risk
- Regulatory influences and government policy changes
- Changing societal concerns, attitudes, and lifestyles

Assessing the Impact of the Forces Driving Industry Change

The second step in driving-forces analysis is to determine whether the prevailing change drivers, on the whole, are acting to make the industry environment more or less attractive. Three questions need to be answered:

1. Are the driving forces, on balance, acting to cause demand for the industry's product to increase or decrease?
2. Is the collective impact of the driving forces making competition more or less intense?
3. Will the combined impacts of the driving forces lead to higher or lower industry profitability?

The real payoff of driving-forces analysis is to help managers understand what strategy changes are needed to prepare for the impacts of the driving forces.

Getting a handle on the collective impact of the driving forces requires looking at the likely effects of each factor separately, since the driving forces may not all be pushing change in the same direction. For example, one driving force may be acting to spur demand for the industry's product while another is working to curtail demand. Whether the net effect on industry demand is up or down hinges on which change driver is the most powerful.

Adjusting the Strategy to Prepare for the Impacts of Driving Forces

The third step in the strategic analysis of industry dynamics—where the real payoff for strategy making comes—is for managers to draw some conclusions about *what strategy adjustments will be needed to deal with the impacts of the driving forces.* But taking the "right" kinds of actions to prepare for the industry and competitive changes being wrought by the driving forces first requires accurate diagnosis of the forces driving industry change and the impacts these forces will have on both the industry environment and the company's business. To the extent that managers are unclear about the drivers of industry change and their impacts, or if their views are off-base, the chances of making astute and timely strategy adjustments are slim. So driving-forces analysis is not something to take lightly; it has practical value and is basic to the task of thinking strategically about where the industry is headed and how to prepare for the changes ahead.

STRATEGIC GROUP ANALYSIS

Within an industry, companies commonly sell in different price/quality ranges, appeal to different types of buyers, have different geographic coverage, and so on. Some are more attractively positioned than others. Understanding which companies are strongly positioned and which are weakly positioned is an integral part of analyzing an industry's competitive structure. The best technique for revealing the market positions of industry competitors is **strategic group mapping.**

> **LO 3**
>
> How to map the market positions of key groups of industry rivals.

Using Strategic Group Maps to Assess the Market Positions of Key Competitors

A **strategic group** consists of those industry members with similar competitive approaches and positions in the market. Companies in the same strategic group can resemble one another in a variety of ways. They may have comparable product-line breadth, sell in the same price/quality range, employ the same distribution channels, depend on identical technological approaches, compete in much the same geographic areas, or offer buyers essentially the same product attributes or similar services and technical assistance.[6] Evaluating strategy options entails examining what strategic groups exist, identifying the companies within each group, and determining if a competitive "white space" exists where industry competitors are able to create and capture altogether new demand. As part of this process, the number of strategic groups in an industry and their respective market positions can be displayed on a strategic group map.

> **CORE CONCEPT**
>
> **Strategic group mapping** is a technique for displaying the different market or competitive positions that rival firms occupy in the industry.

The procedure for constructing a *strategic group map* is straightforward:

- Identify the competitive characteristics that delineate strategic approaches used in the industry. Typical variables used in creating strategic group maps are price/quality range (high, medium, low), geographic coverage (local, regional, national, global), product-line breadth (wide, narrow), degree of service offered (no frills, limited, full), use of distribution channels (retail, wholesale, Internet, multiple), degree of vertical integration (none, partial, full), and degree of diversification into other industries (none, some, considerable).

- Plot the firms on a two-variable map using pairs of these variables.

- Assign firms occupying about the same map location to the same strategic group.

- Draw circles around each strategic group, making the circles proportional to the size of the group's share of total industry sales revenues.

> **CORE CONCEPT**
>
> A **strategic group** is a cluster of industry rivals that have similar competitive approaches and market positions.

This produces a two-dimensional diagram like the one for the U.S. casual dining industry in Illustration Capsule 3.1.

Several guidelines need to be observed in creating strategic group maps. First, the two variables selected as axes for the map should *not* be highly correlated; if they are, the circles on the map will fall along a diagonal and reveal nothing more about the relative positions of competitors than would be revealed by comparing the rivals

Comparative Market Positions of Selected Companies in the Casual Dining Industry: A Strategic Group Map Example

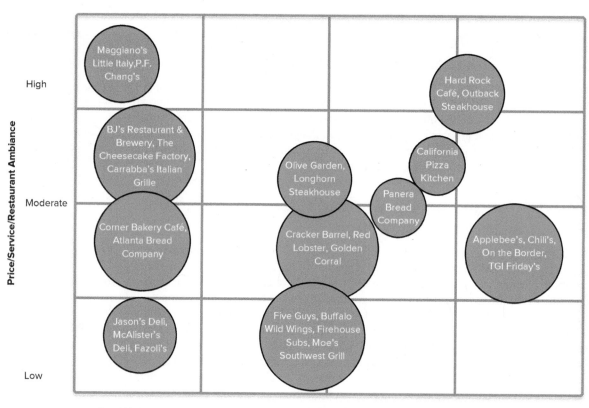

Note: Circles are drawn roughly proportional to the sizes of the chains, based on revenues.

on just one of the variables. For instance, if companies with broad product lines use multiple distribution channels while companies with narrow lines use a single distribution channel, then looking at the differences in distribution-channel approaches adds no new information about positioning.

Second, the variables chosen as axes for the map should reflect important differences among rival approaches—when rivals differ on both variables, the locations of the rivals will be scattered, thus showing how they are positioned differently. Third, the variables used as axes don't have to be either quantitative or continuous; rather, they can be discrete variables, defined in terms of distinct classes and combinations. Fourth, drawing the sizes of the circles on the map proportional to the combined sales of the firms in each strategic group allows the map to reflect the relative sizes of each strategic group. Fifth, if more than two good variables can be used as axes for the map, then it is wise to draw several maps to give different exposures to the competitive positioning relationships present in the industry's structure—there is not necessarily one best map for portraying how competing firms are positioned.

The Value of Strategic Group Maps

Strategic group maps are revealing in several respects. The most important has to do with identifying which industry members are close rivals and which are distant rivals. Firms in the same strategic group are the closest rivals; the next closest rivals are in the immediately adjacent groups. Often, firms in strategic groups that are far apart on the map hardly compete at all. For instance, Walmart's clientele, merchandise selection, and pricing points are much too different to justify calling Walmart a close competitor of Neiman Marcus or Saks Fifth Avenue. For the same reason, the beers produced by Yuengling are really not in competition with the beers produced by Pabst.

Strategic group maps reveal which companies are close competitors and which are distant competitors.

The second thing to be gleaned from strategic group mapping is that *not all positions on the map are equally attractive.*[7] Two reasons account for why some positions can be more attractive than others:

1. *Prevailing competitive pressures from the industry's five forces may cause the profit potential of different strategic groups to vary.* The profit prospects of firms in different strategic groups can vary from good to poor because of differing degrees of competitive rivalry within strategic groups, differing pressures from potential entrants to each group, differing degrees of exposure to competition from substitute products outside the industry, and differing degrees of supplier or customer bargaining power from group to group. For instance, in the ready-to-eat cereal industry, there are significantly higher entry barriers (capital requirements, brand loyalty, etc.) for the strategic group comprising the large branded-cereal makers than for the group of generic-cereal makers or the group of small natural-cereal producers. Differences among the branded rivals versus the generic cereal makers make rivalry stronger within the generic strategic group. In the retail chain industry, the competitive battle between Walmart and Target is more intense (with consequently smaller profit margins) than the rivalry among Prada, Versace, Gucci, Armani, and other high-end fashion retailers.

2. *Industry driving forces may favor some strategic groups and hurt others.* Likewise, industry driving forces can boost the business outlook for some strategic groups and adversely impact the business prospects of others. In the news industry, for example, Internet news services and cable news networks are gaining ground at the expense of newspapers and networks due to changes in technology and changing social lifestyles. Firms in strategic groups that are being adversely impacted by driving forces may try to shift to a more favorably situated position. If certain firms are known to be trying to change their competitive positions on the map, then attaching arrows to the circles showing the targeted direction helps clarify the picture of competitive maneuvering among rivals.

Some strategic groups are more favorably positioned than others because they confront weaker competitive forces and/or because they are more favorably impacted by industry driving forces.

Thus, part of strategic group map analysis always entails drawing conclusions about where on the map is the "best" place to be and why. Which companies/strategic groups are destined to prosper because of their positions? Which companies/strategic groups seem destined to struggle? What accounts for why some parts of the map are better than others?

COMPETITOR ANALYSIS

Studying competitors' past behavior and preferences provides a valuable assist in anticipating what moves rivals are likely to make next and outmaneuvering them in the marketplace.

Unless a company pays attention to the strategies and situations of competitors and has some inkling of what moves they will be making, it ends up flying blind into competitive battle. As in sports, scouting the opposition is an essential part of game plan development. Gathering competitive intelligence about the strategic direction and likely moves of key competitors allows a company to prepare defensive countermoves, to craft its own strategic moves with some confidence about what market maneuvers to expect from rivals in response, and to exploit any openings that arise from competitors' missteps. The question is where to look for such information, since rivals rarely reveal their strategic intentions openly. If information is not directly available, what are the best indicators?

Michael Porter's **Framework for Competitor Analysis** points to four indicators of a rival's likely strategic moves and countermoves. These include a rival's *current strategy, objectives, resources and capabilities,* and *assumptions* about itself and the industry, as shown in Figure 3.10. A strategic profile of a rival that provides good clues to its behavioral proclivities can be constructed by characterizing the rival along these four dimensions.

Current Strategy   To succeed in predicting a competitor's next moves, company strategists need to have a good understanding of each rival's current strategy, as an indicator of its pattern of behavior and best strategic options. Questions to consider include: How is the competitor positioned in the market? What is the basis for

FIGURE 3.10   A Framework for Competitor Analysis

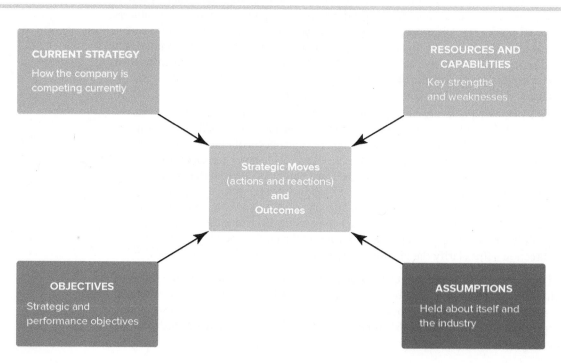

its competitive advantage (if any)? What kinds of investments is it making (as an indicator of its growth trajectory)?

Objectives   An appraisal of a rival's objectives should include not only its financial performance objectives but strategic ones as well (such as those concerning market share). What is even more important is to consider the extent to which the rival is meeting these objectives and whether it is under pressure to improve. Rivals with good financial performance are likely to continue their present strategy with only minor fine-tuning. Poorly performing rivals are virtually certain to make fresh strategic moves.

Resources and Capabilities   A rival's strategic moves and countermoves are both enabled and constrained by the set of resources and capabilities the rival has at hand. Thus a rival's resources and capabilities (and efforts to acquire new resources and capabilities) serve as a strong signal of future strategic actions (and reactions to your company's moves). Assessing a rival's resources and capabilities involves sizing up not only its strengths in this respect but its weaknesses as well.

Assumptions   How a rival's top managers think about their strategic situation can have a big impact on how the rival behaves. Banks that believe they are "too big to fail," for example, may take on more risk than is financially prudent. Assessing a rival's assumptions entails considering its assumptions about itself as well as about the industry it participates in.

Information regarding these four analytic components can often be gleaned from company press releases, information posted on the company's website (especially the presentations management has recently made to securities analysts), and such public documents as annual reports and 10-K filings. Many companies also have a competitive intelligence unit that sifts through the available information to construct up-to-date strategic profiles of rivals. Doing the necessary detective work can be time-consuming, but scouting competitors well enough to anticipate their next moves allows managers to prepare effective countermoves (perhaps even beat a rival to the punch) and to take rivals' probable actions into account in crafting their own best course of action.

KEY SUCCESS FACTORS

An industry's **key success factors (KSFs)** are those competitive factors that most affect industry members' ability to survive and prosper in the marketplace: the particular strategy elements, product attributes, operational approaches, resources, and competitive capabilities that spell the difference between being a strong competitor and a weak competitor—and between profit and loss. KSFs by their very nature are so important to competitive success that *all firms* in the industry must pay close attention to them or risk becoming an industry laggard or failure. To indicate the significance of KSFs another way, how well the elements of a company's strategy measure up against an industry's KSFs determines whether the company can meet the basic criteria for surviving and thriving in the industry. Identifying KSFs, in light of the prevailing and anticipated industry and competitive conditions, is therefore always a top priority in analytic and strategy-making considerations. Company strategists need to understand the industry landscape well enough to separate the factors most important to competitive success from those that are less important.

CORE CONCEPT

Key success factors are the strategy elements, product and service attributes, operational approaches, resources, and competitive capabilities that are essential to surviving and thriving in the industry.

Key success factors vary from industry to industry, and even from time to time within the same industry, as change drivers and competitive conditions change. But regardless of the circumstances, an industry's key success factors can always be deduced by asking the same three questions:

1. On what basis do buyers of the industry's product choose between the competing brands of sellers? That is, what product attributes and service characteristics are crucial?

2. Given the nature of competitive rivalry prevailing in the marketplace, what resources and competitive capabilities must a company have to be competitively successful?

3. What shortcomings are almost certain to put a company at a significant competitive disadvantage?

Only rarely are there more than five key factors for competitive success. And even among these, two or three usually outrank the others in importance. Managers should therefore bear in mind the purpose of identifying key success factors—to determine which factors are most important to competitive success—and resist the temptation to label a factor that has only minor importance as a KSF.

In the beer industry, for example, although there are many types of buyers (wholesale, retail, end consumer), it is most important to understand the preferences and buying behavior of the beer drinkers. Their purchase decisions are driven by price, taste, convenient access, and marketing. Thus the KSFs include a *strong network of wholesale distributors* (to get the company's brand stocked and favorably displayed in retail outlets, bars, restaurants, and stadiums, where beer is sold) and *clever advertising* (to induce beer drinkers to buy the company's brand and thereby pull beer sales through the established wholesale and retail channels). Because there is a potential for strong buyer power on the part of large distributors and retail chains, competitive success depends on some mechanism to offset that power, of which advertising (to create demand pull) is one. Thus the KSFs also include *superior product differentiation* (as in microbrews) or *superior firm size and branding capabilities* (as in national brands). The KSFs also include *full utilization of brewing capacity* (to keep manufacturing costs low and offset the high costs of advertising, branding, and product differentiation).

Correctly diagnosing an industry's KSFs also raises a company's chances of crafting a sound strategy. The key success factors of an industry point to those things that every firm in the industry needs to attend to in order to retain customers and weather the competition. If the company's strategy cannot deliver on the key success factors of its industry, it is unlikely to earn enough profits to remain a viable business.

THE INDUSTRY OUTLOOK FOR PROFITABILITY

Each of the frameworks presented in this chapter—PESTEL, five forces analysis, driving forces, strategy groups, competitor analysis, and key success factors—provides a useful perspective on an industry's outlook for future profitability. Putting them all together provides an even richer and more nuanced picture. Thus, the final step in evaluating the industry and competitive environment is to use the results of each of the analyses performed to determine whether the industry presents the company with strong prospects for competitive success and attractive profits. The important factors on which to base a conclusion include:

- How the company is being impacted by the state of the macro-environment.
- Whether strong competitive forces are squeezing industry profitability to subpar levels.
- Whether the presence of complementors and the possibility of cooperative actions improve the company's prospects.
- Whether industry profitability will be favorably or unfavorably affected by the prevailing driving forces.
- Whether the company occupies a stronger market position than rivals.
- Whether this is likely to change in the course of competitive interactions.
- How well the company's strategy delivers on the industry key success factors.

As a general proposition, *the anticipated industry environment is fundamentally attractive if it presents a company with good opportunity for above-average profitability; the industry outlook is fundamentally unattractive if a company's profit prospects are unappealingly low.*

However, it is a mistake to think of a particular industry as being equally attractive or unattractive to all industry participants and all potential entrants.[8] Attractiveness is relative, not absolute, and conclusions one way or the other have to be drawn from the perspective of a particular company. For instance, a favorably positioned competitor may see ample opportunity to capitalize on the vulnerabilities of weaker rivals even though industry conditions are otherwise somewhat dismal. At the same time, industries attractive to insiders may be unattractive to outsiders because of the difficulty of challenging current market leaders or because they have more attractive opportunities elsewhere.

When a company decides an industry is fundamentally attractive and presents good opportunities, a strong case can be made that it should invest aggressively to capture the opportunities it sees and to improve its long-term competitive position in the business. When a strong competitor concludes an industry is becoming less attractive, it may elect to simply protect its present position, investing cautiously—if at all—and looking for opportunities in other industries. A competitively weak company in an unattractive industry may see its best option as finding a buyer, perhaps a rival, to acquire its business.

LO 4

How to determine whether an industry's outlook presents a company with sufficiently attractive opportunities for growth and profitability.

The degree to which an industry is attractive or unattractive is not the same for all industry participants and all potential entrants.

KEY POINTS

Thinking strategically about a company's external situation involves probing for answers to the following questions:

1. *What are the strategically relevant factors in the macro-environment, and how do they impact an industry and its members?* Industries differ significantly as to how they are affected by conditions and developments in the broad macro-environment. Using PESTEL analysis to identify which of these factors is strategically relevant is the first step to understanding how a company is situated in its external environment.

2. *What kinds of competitive forces are industry members facing, and how strong is each force?* The strength of competition is a composite of five forces: (1) rivalry within the industry, (2) the threat of new entry into the market, (3) inroads being made by the sellers of substitutes, (4) supplier bargaining power, and (5) buyer bargaining power. All five must be examined force by force, and their collective strength evaluated. One strong force, however, can be sufficient to keep average industry profitability low. Working through the five forces model aids strategy makers in assessing how to insulate the company from the strongest forces, identify attractive arenas for expansion, or alter the competitive conditions so that they offer more favorable prospects for profitability.

3. *What cooperative forces are present in the industry, and how can a company harness them to its advantage?* Interactions among industry participants are not only competitive in nature but cooperative as well. This is particularly the case when complements to the products or services of an industry are important. The value net framework assists managers in sizing up the impact of cooperative as well as competitive interactions on their firm.

4. *What factors are driving changes in the industry, and what impact will they have on competitive intensity and industry profitability?* Industry and competitive conditions change because certain forces are acting to create incentives or pressures for change. The first step is to identify the three or four most important drivers of change affecting the industry being analyzed (out of a much longer list of potential drivers). Once an industry's change drivers have been identified, the analytic task becomes one of determining whether they are acting, individually and collectively, to make the industry environment more or less attractive.

5. *What market positions do industry rivals occupy—who is strongly positioned and who is not?* Strategic group mapping is a valuable tool for understanding the similarities, differences, strengths, and weaknesses inherent in the market positions of rival companies. Rivals in the same or nearby strategic groups are close competitors, whereas companies in distant strategic groups usually pose little or no immediate threat. The lesson of strategic group mapping is that some positions on the map are more favorable than others. The profit potential of different strategic groups may not be the same because industry driving forces and competitive forces likely have varying effects on the industry's distinct strategic groups.

6. *What strategic moves are rivals likely to make next?* Anticipating the actions of rivals can help a company prepare effective countermoves. Using the Framework for Competitor Analysis is helpful in this regard.

7. *What are the key factors for competitive success?* An industry's key success factors (KSFs) are the particular strategy elements, product attributes, operational approaches, resources, and competitive capabilities that all industry members must have in order to survive and prosper in the industry. For any industry, they can be deduced by answering three basic questions: (1) On what basis do buyers of the industry's product choose between the competing brands of sellers, (2) what resources and competitive capabilities must a company have to be competitively successful, and (3) what shortcomings are almost certain to put a company at a significant competitive disadvantage?

8. *Is the industry outlook conducive to good profitability?* The last step in industry analysis is summing up the results from applying each of the frameworks employed

in answering questions 1 to 6: PESTEL, five forces analysis, driving forces, strategic group mapping, competitor analysis, and key success factors. Applying multiple lenses to the question of what the industry outlook looks like offers a more robust and nuanced answer. If the answers from each framework, seen as a whole, reveal that a company's profit prospects in that industry are above-average, then the industry environment is basically attractive *for that company*. What may look like an attractive environment for one company may appear to be unattractive from the perspective of a different company.

Clear, insightful diagnosis of a company's external situation is an essential first step in crafting strategies that are well matched to industry and competitive conditions. To do cutting-edge strategic thinking about the external environment, managers must know what questions to pose and what analytic tools to use in answering these questions. This is why this chapter has concentrated on suggesting the right questions to ask, explaining concepts and analytic approaches, and indicating the kinds of things to look for.

ASSURANCE OF LEARNING EXERCISES

1. Prepare a brief analysis of the organic food industry using the information provided by the Organic Trade Association at www.ota.com and the *Organic Report* magazine at theorganicreport.com. That is, based on the information provided on these websites, draw a five forces diagram for the organic food industry and briefly discuss the nature and strength of each of the five competitive forces.

   connect
   LO 2

2. Based on the strategic group map in Illustration Capsule 3.1, which casual dining chains are Applebee's closest competitors? With which strategic group does California Pizza Kitchen compete the least, according to this map? Why do you think no casual dining chains are positioned in the area above the Olive Garden's group?

   connect
   LO 3

3. The National Restaurant Association publishes an annual industry fact book that can be found at imis.restaurant.org/store/detail.aspx?id=FOR2016FB. Based on information in the latest report, does it appear that macro-environmental factors and the economic characteristics of the industry will present industry participants with attractive opportunities for growth and profitability? Explain.

   LO 1, LO 4

EXERCISE FOR SIMULATION PARTICIPANTS

1. Which of the factors listed in Table 3.1 might have the most strategic relevance for your industry?

   LO 1, LO 2, LO 3, LO 4

2. Which of the five competitive forces is creating the strongest competitive pressures for your company?

3. What are the "weapons of competition" that rival companies in your industry can use to gain sales and market share? See Table 3.2 to help you identify the various competitive factors.

4. What are the factors affecting the intensity of rivalry in the industry in which your company is competing? Use Figure 3.4 and the accompanying discussion to help you in pinpointing the specific factors most affecting competitive intensity. Would you characterize the rivalry and jockeying for better market position, increased sales, and market share among the companies in your industry as fierce, very strong, strong, moderate, or relatively weak? Why?

5. Are there any driving forces in the industry in which your company is competing? If so, what impact will these driving forces have? Will they cause competition to be more or less intense? Will they act to boost or squeeze profit margins? List at least two actions your company should consider taking in order to combat any negative impacts of the driving forces.

6. Draw a strategic group map showing the market positions of the companies in your industry. Which companies do you believe are in the most attractive position on the map? Which companies are the most weakly positioned? Which companies do you believe are likely to try to move to a different position on the strategic group map?

7. What do you see as the key factors for being a successful competitor in your industry? List at least three.

8. Does your overall assessment of the industry suggest that industry rivals have sufficiently attractive opportunities for growth and profitability? Explain.

ENDNOTES

[1] Michael E. Porter, *Competitive Strategy* (New York: Free Press, 1980); Michael E. Porter, "The Five Competitive Forces That Shape Strategy," *Harvard Business Review* 86, no. 1 (January 2008), pp. 78–93.
[2] J. S. Bain, *Barriers to New Competition* (Cambridge, MA: Harvard University Press, 1956); F. M. Scherer, *Industrial Market Structure and Economic Performance* (Chicago: Rand McNally, 1971).
[3] Ibid.
[4] C. A. Montgomery and S. Hariharan, "Diversified Expansion by Large Established Firms,"

Journal of Economic Behavior & Organization 15, no. 1 (January 1991).
[5] For a more extended discussion of the problems with the life-cycle hypothesis, see Porter, *Competitive Strategy*, pp. 157–162.
[6] Mary Ellen Gordon and George R. Milne, "Selecting the Dimensions That Define Strategic Groups: A Novel Market-Driven Approach," *Journal of Managerial Issues* 11, no. 2 (Summer 1999), pp. 213–233.
[7] Avi Fiegenbaum and Howard Thomas, "Strategic Groups as Reference Groups: Theory, Modeling and Empirical Examination of

Industry and Competitive Strategy," *Strategic Management Journal* 16 (1995), pp. 461–476; S. Ade Olusoga, Michael P. Mokwa, and Charles H. Noble, "Strategic Groups, Mobility Barriers, and Competitive Advantage," *Journal of Business Research* 33 (1995), pp. 153–164.
[8] B. Wernerfelt and C. Montgomery, "What Is an Attractive Industry?" *Management Science* 32, no. 10 (October 1986), pp. 1223–1230.

CHAPTER 4

Evaluating a Company's Resources, Capabilities, and Competitiveness

© Ikon Images/Alamy Stock Photo

Learning Objectives

THIS CHAPTER WILL HELP YOU UNDERSTAND:

LO 1   How to take stock of how well a company's strategy is working.

LO 2   Why a company's resources and capabilities are centrally important in giving the company a competitive edge over rivals.

LO 3   How to assess the company's strengths and weaknesses in light of market opportunities and external threats.

LO 4   How a company's value chain activities can affect the company's cost structure and customer value proposition.

LO 5   How a comprehensive evaluation of a company's competitive situation can assist managers in making critical decisions about their next strategic moves.

Crucial, of course, is having a difference that matters in the industry.

Cynthia Montgomery—*Professor and author*

If you don't have a competitive advantage, don't compete

Jack Welch—*Former CEO of General Electric*

Organizations succeed in a competitive marketplace over the long run because they can do certain things their customers value better than can their competitors.

Robert Hayes, Gary Pisano, and David Upton— *Professors and consultants*

Chapter 3 described how to use the tools of industry and competitor analysis to assess a company's external environment and lay the groundwork for matching a company's strategy to its external situation. This chapter discusses techniques for evaluating a company's internal situation, including its collection of resources and capabilities and the activities it performs along its value chain. Internal analysis enables managers to determine whether their strategy is likely to give the company a significant competitive edge over rival firms. Combined with external analysis, it facilitates an understanding of how to reposition a firm to take advantage of new opportunities and to cope with emerging competitive threats. The analytic spotlight will be trained on six questions:

1. How well is the company's present strategy working?

2. What are the company's most important resources and capabilities, and will they give the

company a lasting competitive advantage over rival companies?

3. What are the company's strengths and weaknesses in relation to the market opportunities and external threats?

4. How do a company's value chain activities impact its cost structure and customer value proposition?

5. Is the company competitively stronger or weaker than key rivals?

6. What strategic issues and problems merit front-burner managerial attention?

In probing for answers to these questions, five analytic tools—resource and capability analysis, SWOT analysis, value chain analysis, benchmarking, and competitive strength assessment—will be used. All five are valuable techniques for revealing a company's competitiveness and for helping company managers match their strategy to the company's particular circumstances.

QUESTION 1: HOW WELL IS THE COMPANY'S PRESENT STRATEGY WORKING?

In evaluating how well a company's present strategy is working, the best way to start is with a clear view of what the strategy entails. Figure 4.1 shows the key components of a single-business company's strategy. The first thing to examine is the company's competitive approach. What moves has the company made recently to attract customers and improve its market position—for instance, has it cut prices, improved the

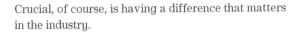

LO 1

How to take stock of how well a company's strategy is working.

design of its product, added new features, stepped up advertising, entered a new geographic market, or merged with a competitor? Is it striving for a competitive advantage based on low costs or a better product offering? Is it concentrating on serving a broad spectrum of customers or a narrow market niche? The company's functional strategies in R&D, production, marketing, finance, human resources, information technology, and so on further characterize company strategy, as do any efforts to establish alliances with other enterprises.

The three best indicators of how well a company's strategy is working are (1) whether the company is achieving its stated financial and strategic objectives, (2) whether its financial performance is above the industry average, and (3) whether it is gaining customers and gaining market share. Persistent shortfalls in meeting company performance targets and weak marketplace performance relative to rivals are reliable warning signs that the company has a weak strategy, suffers from poor strategy execution, or both. Specific indicators of how well a company's strategy is working include:

- Trends in the company's sales and earnings growth.
- Trends in the company's stock price.
- The company's overall financial strength.
- The company's customer retention rate.

FIGURE 4.1 Identifying the Components of a Single-Business Company's Strategy

- The rate at which new customers are acquired.
- Evidence of improvement in internal processes such as defect rate, order fulfillment, delivery times, days of inventory, and employee productivity.

The stronger a company's current overall performance, the more likely it has a well-conceived, well-executed strategy. The weaker a company's financial performance and market standing, the more its current strategy must be questioned and the more likely the need for radical changes. Table 4.1 provides a compilation of the financial ratios most commonly used to evaluate a company's financial performance and balance sheet strength.

> Sluggish financial performance and second-rate market accomplishments almost always signal weak strategy, weak execution, or both.

TABLE 4.1   Key Financial Ratios: How to Calculate Them and What They Mean

Ratio	How Calculated	What It Shows
Profitability ratios		
1. Gross profit margin	$\dfrac{\text{Sales revenues} - \text{Cost of goods sold}}{\text{Sales revenues}}$	Shows the percentage of revenues available to cover operating expenses and yield a profit.
2. Operating profit margin (or return on sales)	$\dfrac{\text{Sales revenues} - \text{Operating expenses}}{\text{Sales revenues}}$ *or* $\dfrac{\text{Operating income}}{\text{Sales revenues}}$	Shows the profitability of current operations without regard to interest charges and income taxes. Earnings before interest and taxes is known as *EBIT* in financial and business accounting.
3. Net profit margin (or net return on sales)	$\dfrac{\text{Profits after taxes}}{\text{Sales revenues}}$	Shows after-tax profits per dollar of sales.
4. Total return on assets	$\dfrac{\text{Profits after taxes} + \text{Interest}}{\text{Total assets}}$	A measure of the return on total investment in the enterprise. Interest is added to after-tax profits to form the numerator, since total assets are financed by creditors as well as by stockholders.
5. Net return on total assets (ROA)	$\dfrac{\text{Profits after taxes}}{\text{Total assets}}$	A measure of the return earned by stockholders on the firm's total assets.
6. Return on stockholders' equity (ROE)	$\dfrac{\text{Profits after taxes}}{\text{Total stockholders' equity}}$	The return stockholders are earning on their capital investment in the enterprise. A return in the 12%–15% range is average.
7. Return on invested capital (ROIC)— sometimes referred to as return on capital employed (ROCE)	$\dfrac{\text{Profits after taxes}}{\text{Long-term debt} + \text{Total stockholders' equity}}$	A measure of the return that shareholders are earning on the monetary capital invested in the enterprise. A higher return reflects greater bottom-line effectiveness in the use of long-term capital.
Liquidity ratios		
1. Current ratio	$\dfrac{\text{Current assets}}{\text{Current liabilities}}$	Shows a firm's ability to pay current liabilities using assets that can be converted to cash in the near term. Ratio should be higher than 1.0.

(continued)

TABLE 4.1   *(continued)*

Ratio	How Calculated	What It Shows
2. Working capital	Current assets − Current liabilities	The cash available for a firm's day-to-day operations. Larger amounts mean the company has more internal funds to (1) pay its current liabilities on a timely basis and (2) finance inventory expansion, additional accounts receivable, and a larger base of operations without resorting to borrowing or raising more equity capital.
Leverage ratios		
1. Total debt-to-assets ratio	$\dfrac{\text{Total debt}}{\text{Total assets}}$	Measures the extent to which borrowed funds (both short-term loans and long-term debt) have been used to finance the firm's operations. A low ratio is better—a high fraction indicates overuse of debt and greater risk of bankruptcy.
2. Long-term debt-to-capital ratio	$\dfrac{\text{Long-term debt}}{\text{Long-term debt} + \text{Total stockholders' equity}}$	A measure of creditworthiness and balance sheet strength. It indicates the percentage of capital investment that has been financed by both long-term lenders and stockholders. A ratio below 0.25 is preferable since the lower the ratio, the greater the capacity to borrow additional funds. Debt-to-capital ratios above 0.50 indicate an excessive reliance on long-term borrowing, lower creditworthiness, and weak balance sheet strength.
3. Debt-to-equity ratio	$\dfrac{\text{Total debt}}{\text{Total stockholders' equity}}$	Shows the balance between debt (funds borrowed both short term and long term) and the amount that stockholders have invested in the enterprise. The further the ratio is below 1.0, the greater the firm's ability to borrow additional funds. Ratios above 1.0 put creditors at greater risk, signal weaker balance sheet strength, and often result in lower credit ratings.
4. Long-term debt-to-equity ratio	$\dfrac{\text{Long-term debt}}{\text{Total stockholders' equity}}$	Shows the balance between long-term debt and stockholders' equity in the firm's *long-term* capital structure. Low ratios indicate a greater capacity to borrow additional funds if needed.
5. Times-interest-earned (or coverage) ratio	$\dfrac{\text{Operating income}}{\text{Interest expenses}}$	Measures the ability to pay annual interest charges. Lenders usually insist on a minimum ratio of 2.0, but ratios above 3.0 signal progressively better creditworthiness.
Activity ratios		
1. Days of inventory	$\dfrac{\text{Inventory}}{\text{Cost of goods sold} \div 365}$	Measures inventory management efficiency. Fewer days of inventory are better.
2. Inventory turnover	$\dfrac{\text{Cost of goods sold}}{\text{Inventory}}$	Measures the number of inventory turns per year. Higher is better.
3. Average collection period	$\dfrac{\text{Accounts receivable}}{\text{Total sales} \div 365}$ *or* $\dfrac{\text{Accounts receivable}}{\text{Average daily sales}}$	Indicates the average length of time the firm must wait after making a sale to receive cash payment. A shorter collection time is better.

(continued)

TABLE 4.1   *(continued)*

Ratio	How Calculated	What It Shows
Other important measures of financial performance		
1. Dividend yield on common stock	$\dfrac{\text{Annual dividends per share}}{\text{Current market price per share}}$	A measure of the return that shareholders receive in the form of dividends. A "typical" dividend yield is 2%–3%. The dividend yield for fast-growth companies is often below 1%; the dividend yield for slow-growth companies can run 4%–5%.
2. Price-to-earnings (P/E) ratio	$\dfrac{\text{Current market price per share}}{\text{Earnings per share}}$	P/E ratios above 20 indicate strong investor confidence in a firm's outlook and earnings growth; firms whose future earnings are at risk or likely to grow slowly typically have ratios below 12.
3. Dividend payout ratio	$\dfrac{\text{Annual dividends per share}}{\text{Earnings per share}}$	Indicates the percentage of after-tax profits paid out as dividends.
4. Internal cash flow	After-tax profits + Depreciation	A rough estimate of the cash a company's business is generating after payment of operating expenses, interest, and taxes. Such amounts can be used for dividend payments or funding capital expenditures.
5. Free cash flow	After-tax profits + Depreciation – Capital expenditures – Dividends	A rough estimate of the cash a company's business is generating after payment of operating expenses, interest, taxes, dividends, and desirable reinvestments in the business. The larger a company's free cash flow, the greater its ability to internally fund new strategic initiatives, repay debt, make new acquisitions, repurchase shares of stock, or increase dividend payments.

QUESTION 2: WHAT ARE THE COMPANY'S MOST IMPORTANT RESOURCES AND CAPABILITIES, AND WILL THEY GIVE THE COMPANY A LASTING COMPETITIVE ADVANTAGE OVER RIVAL COMPANIES?

An essential element of deciding whether a company's overall situation is fundamentally healthy or unhealthy entails examining the attractiveness of its resources and capabilities. A company's resources and capabilities are its **competitive assets** and determine whether its competitive power in the marketplace will be impressively strong or disappointingly weak. Companies with second-rate competitive assets nearly always are relegated to a trailing position in the industry.

Resource and capability analysis provides managers with a powerful tool for sizing up the company's competitive assets and determining whether they can provide the foundation necessary for competitive success in the marketplace. This is a two-step process. The first step is to identify the company's resources and

CORE CONCEPT

A company's resources and capabilities represent its **competitive assets** and are determinants of its competitiveness and ability to succeed in the marketplace.

Resource and capability analysis is a powerful tool for sizing up a company's competitive assets and determining whether the assets can support a sustainable competitive advantage over market rivals.

LO 2

Why a company's resources and capabilities are centrally important in giving the company a competitive edge over rivals.

CORE CONCEPT

A **resource** is a competitive asset that is owned or controlled by a company; a **capability** (or **competence**) is the capacity of a firm to perform some internal activity competently. Capabilities are developed and enabled through the deployment of a company's resources.

capabilities. The second step is to examine them more closely to ascertain which are the most competitively important and whether they can support a sustainable competitive advantage over rival firms.[1] This second step involves applying the *four tests of a resource's competitive power.*

Identifying the Company's Resources and Capabilities

A firm's resources and capabilities are the fundamental building blocks of its competitive strategy. In crafting strategy, it is essential for managers to know how to take stock of the company's full complement of resources and capabilities. But before they can do so, managers and strategists need a more precise definition of these terms.

In brief, a **resource** is a productive input or competitive asset that is owned or controlled by the firm. Firms have many different types of resources at their disposal that vary not only in kind but in quality as well. Some are of a higher quality than others, and some are more competitively valuable, having greater potential to give a firm a competitive advantage over its rivals. For example, a company's brand is a resource, as is an R&D team—yet some brands such as Coca-Cola and Xerox are well known, with enduring value, while others have little more name recognition than generic products. In similar fashion, some R&D teams are far more innovative and productive than others due to the outstanding talents of the individual team members, the team's composition, its experience, and its chemistry.

A **capability** (or **competence**) is the capacity of a firm to perform some internal activity competently. Capabilities or competences also vary in form, quality, and competitive importance, with some being more competitively valuable than others. American Express displays superior capabilities in brand management and marketing; Starbucks's employee management, training, and real estate capabilities are the drivers behind its rapid growth; LinkedIn relies on superior software innovation capabilities to increase new user memberships. *Organizational capabilities are developed and enabled through the deployment of a company's resources.*[2] For example, Nestlé's brand management capabilities for its 2,000+ food, beverage, and pet care brands draw on the knowledge of the company's brand managers, the expertise of its marketing department, and the company's relationships with retailers in nearly 200 countries. W. L. Gore's product innovation capabilities in its fabrics and medical and industrial product businesses result from the personal initiative, creative talents, and technological expertise of its associates and the company's culture that encourages accountability and creative thinking.

Types of Company Resources   A useful way to identify a company's resources is to look for them within categories, as shown in Table 4.2. Broadly speaking, resources can be divided into two main categories: **tangible** and **intangible** resources. Although *human resources* make up one of the most important parts of a company's resource base, we include them in the intangible category to emphasize the role played by the skills, talents, and knowledge of a company's human resources.

Tangible resources are the most easily identified, since tangible resources are those that can be *touched* or *quantified* readily. Obviously, they include various types of *physical resources* such as manufacturing facilities and mineral resources, but they also include a company's *financial resources, technological resources,* and *organizational resources* such as the company's communication and control systems. Note

CHAPTER 4   Evaluating a Company's Resources, Capabilities, and Competitiveness   **89**

TABLE 4.2   Types of Company Resources

Tangible resources

- *Physical resources:* land and real estate; manufacturing plants, equipment, and/or distribution facilities; the locations of stores, plants, or distribution centers, including the overall pattern of their physical locations; ownership of or access rights to natural resources (such as mineral deposits)

- *Financial resources:* cash and cash equivalents; marketable securities; other financial assets such as a company's credit rating and borrowing capacity

- *Technological assets:* patents, copyrights, production technology, innovation technologies, technological processes

- *Organizational resources:* IT and communication systems (satellites, servers, workstations, etc.); other planning, coordination, and control systems; the company's organizational design and reporting structure

Intangible resources

- *Human assets and intellectual capital:* the education, experience, knowledge, and talent of the workforce, cumulative learning, and tacit knowledge of employees; collective learning embedded in the organization, the intellectual capital and know-how of specialized teams and work groups; the knowledge of key personnel concerning important business functions; managerial talent and leadership skill; the creativity and innovativeness of certain personnel

- *Brands, company image, and reputational assets:* brand names, trademarks, product or company image, buyer loyalty and goodwill; company reputation for quality, service, and reliability; reputation with suppliers and partners for fair dealing

- *Relationships:* alliances, joint ventures, or partnerships that provide access to technologies, specialized know-how, or geographic markets; networks of dealers or distributors; the trust established with various partners

- *Company culture and incentive system:* the norms of behavior, business principles, and ingrained beliefs within the company; the attachment of personnel to the company's ideals; the compensation system and the motivation level of company personnel

that technological resources are included among tangible resources, *by convention,* even though some types, such as copyrights and trade secrets, might be more logically categorized as intangible.

Intangible resources are harder to discern, but they are often among the most important of a firm's competitive assets. They include various sorts of *human assets and intellectual capital,* as well as a company's *brands, image, and reputational assets.* While intangible resources have no material existence on their own, they are often embodied in something material. Thus, the skills and knowledge resources of a firm are embodied in its managers and employees; a company's brand name is embodied in the company logo or product labels. Other important kinds of intangible resources include a company's *relationships* with suppliers, buyers, or partners of various sorts, and the *company's culture and incentive system.* A more detailed listing of the various types of tangible and intangible resources is provided in Table 4.2.

Listing a company's resources category by category can prevent managers from inadvertently overlooking some company resources that might be competitively important. At times, it can be difficult to decide exactly how to categorize certain types of resources. For example, resources such as a work group's specialized expertise in developing innovative products can be considered to be technological assets or human assets or intellectual capital and knowledge assets; the work ethic and drive of a company's workforce could be included under the company's human assets or its culture and incentive system. In this regard, it is important to remember that *it is not exactly how a resource is categorized that matters but, rather, that all of the company's different types of resources are included in the inventory.* The real purpose of using categories in identifying a company's resources is *to ensure that none of a company's resources go unnoticed when sizing up the company's competitive assets.*

Identifying Capabilities   Organizational capabilities are more complex entities than resources; indeed, they are built up through the use of resources and draw on some combination of the firm's resources as they are exercised. Virtually all organizational capabilities are *knowledge-based, residing in people and in a company's intellectual capital, or in organizational processes and systems, which embody tacit knowledge.* For example, Amazon's speedy delivery capabilities rely on the knowledge of its fulfillment center managers, its relationship with the United Postal Service, and the experience of its merchandisers to correctly predict inventory flow. Bose's capabilities in auditory system design arise from the talented engineers that form the R&D team as well as the company's strong culture, which celebrates innovation and beautiful design.

Because of their complexity, capabilities are harder to categorize than resources and more challenging to search for as a result. There are, however, two approaches that can make the process of uncovering and identifying a firm's capabilities more systematic. The first method takes the completed listing of a firm's resources as its starting point. Since capabilities are built from resources and utilize resources as they are exercised, a firm's resources can provide a strong set of clues about the types of capabilities the firm is likely to have accumulated. This approach simply involves looking over the firm's resources and considering whether (and to what extent) the firm has built up any related capabilities. So, for example, a fleet of trucks, the latest RFID tracking technology, and a set of large automated distribution centers may be indicative of sophisticated capabilities in logistics and distribution. R&D teams composed of top scientists with expertise in genomics may suggest organizational capabilities in developing new gene therapies or in biotechnology more generally.

The second method of identifying a firm's capabilities takes a functional approach. Many capabilities relate to fairly specific functions; these draw on a limited set of resources and typically involve a single department or organizational unit. Capabilities in injection molding or continuous casting or metal stamping are manufacturing-related; capabilities in direct selling, promotional pricing, or database marketing all connect to the sales and marketing functions; capabilities in basic research, strategic innovation, or new product development link to a company's R&D function. This approach requires managers to survey the various functions a firm performs to find the different capabilities associated with each function.

A problem with this second method is that many of the most important capabilities of firms are inherently *cross-functional.* Cross-functional capabilities draw on a number of different kinds of resources and are multidimensional in nature—they spring from the effective collaboration among people with different types of expertise working in different organizational units. Warby Parker draws from its cross-functional design process to create its popular eyewear. Its design capabilities are not just due to its creative designers, but are the product of their capabilities in market research and engineering as well as their relations with suppliers and manufacturing companies. Cross-functional capabilities and other complex capabilities involving numerous linked and closely integrated competitive assets are sometimes referred to as **resource bundles.**

It is important not to miss identifying a company's resource bundles, since they can be the most competitively important of a firm's competitive assets. Resource bundles can sometimes pass the four tests of a resource's competitive power (described below) even when the individual components of the resource bundle cannot. Although PetSmart's supply chain and marketing capabilities are matched well by rival Petco, the company has and continues to outperform competitors through its customer service capabilities (including animal grooming and veterinary and day care services). Nike's bundle of styling expertise, marketing research skills, professional endorsements, brand name, and managerial know-how has allowed it to remain number one in the athletic footwear and apparel industry for more than 20 years.

> **CORE CONCEPT**
>
> A **resource bundle** is a linked and closely integrated set of competitive assets centered around one or more cross-functional capabilities.

Assessing the Competitive Power of a Company's Resources and Capabilities

To assess a company's competitive power, one must go beyond merely identifying its resources and capabilities to probe its *caliber*.[3] Thus, the second step in resource and capability analysis is designed to ascertain which of a company's resources and capabilities are competitively superior and to what extent they can support a company's quest for a sustainable competitive advantage over market rivals. When a company has competitive assets that are central to its strategy and superior to those of rival firms, they can support a competitive advantage, as defined in Chapter 1. If this advantage proves durable despite the best efforts of competitors to overcome it, then the company is said to have a *sustainable* **competitive advantage.** While it may be difficult for a company to achieve a sustainable competitive advantage, it is an important strategic objective because it imparts a potential for attractive and long-lived profitability.

The Four Tests of a Resource's Competitive Power   The competitive power of a resource or capability is measured by how many of four specific tests it can pass.[4] These tests are referred to as the **VRIN tests for sustainable competitive advantage**—*VRIN* is a shorthand reminder standing for *Valuable, Rare, Inimitable,* and *Nonsubstitutable.* The first two tests determine whether a resource or capability can support a competitive advantage. The last two determine whether the competitive advantage can be sustained.

> **CORE CONCEPT**
>
> The **VRIN tests for sustainable competitive advantage** ask whether a resource is valuable, rare, inimitable, and nonsubstitutable.

1. *Is the resource or capability competitively **Valuable?*** To be competitively valuable, a resource or capability must be directly relevant to the company's strategy, making the company a more effective competitor. Unless the resource or capability contributes to the effectiveness of the company's strategy, it cannot pass this first test. An indicator of its effectiveness is whether the resource enables the company to strengthen its business model by improving its customer value proposition and/or profit formula (see Chapter 1). Companies have to guard against contending that something they do well is necessarily competitively valuable. Apple's OS X operating system for its personal computers by some accounts is superior to Microsoft's Windows 10, but Apple has failed in converting its resources devoted to operating system design into anything more than moderate competitive success in the global PC market.

2. *Is the resource or capability **Rare**—is it something rivals lack?* Resources and capabilities that are common among firms and widely available cannot be a source of competitive advantage. All makers of branded cereals have valuable marketing

capabilities and brands, since the key success factors in the ready-to-eat cereal industry demand this. They are not rare. However, the brand strength of Oreo cookies is uncommon and has provided Kraft Foods with greater market share as well as the opportunity to benefit from brand extensions such as Double Stuf Oreos and Mini Oreos. A resource or capability is considered rare if it is held by only a small number of firms in an industry or specific competitive domain. Thus, while general management capabilities are not rare in an absolute sense, they are relatively rare in some of the less developed regions of the world and in some business domains.

3. *Is the resource or capability **Inimitable**—is it hard to copy?* The more difficult and more costly it is for competitors to imitate a company's resource or capability, the more likely that it can also provide a *sustainable* competitive advantage. Resources and capabilities tend to be difficult to copy when they are unique (a fantastic real estate location, patent-protected technology, an unusually talented and motivated labor force), when they must be built over time in ways that are difficult to imitate (a well-known brand name, mastery of a complex process technology, years of cumulative experience and learning), and when they entail financial outlays or large-scale operations that few industry members can undertake (a global network of dealers and distributors). Imitation is also difficult for resources and capabilities that reflect a high level of *social complexity* (company culture, interpersonal relationships among the managers or R&D teams, trust-based relations with customers or suppliers) and *causal ambiguity,* a term that signifies the hard-to-disentangle nature of the complex resources, such as a web of intricate processes enabling new drug discovery. Hard-to-copy resources and capabilities are important competitive assets, contributing to the longevity of a company's market position and offering the potential for sustained profitability.

4. *Is the resource or capability **Nonsubstitutable**—is it invulnerable to the threat of substitution from different types of resources and capabilities?* Even resources that are competitively valuable, rare, and costly to imitate may lose much of their ability to offer competitive advantage if rivals possess equivalent substitute resources. For example, manufacturers relying on automation to gain a cost-based advantage in production activities may find their technology-based advantage nullified by rivals' use of low-wage offshore manufacturing. Resources can contribute to a sustainable competitive advantage only when resource substitutes aren't on the horizon.

> ## CORE CONCEPT
>
> *Social complexity* and *causal ambiguity* are two factors that inhibit the ability of rivals to imitate a firm's most valuable resources and capabilities. Causal ambiguity makes it very hard to figure out how a complex resource contributes to competitive advantage and therefore exactly what to imitate.

The vast majority of companies are not well endowed with standout resources or capabilities, capable of passing all four tests with high marks. Most firms have a mixed bag of resources—one or two quite valuable, some good, many satisfactory to mediocre. Resources and capabilities that are valuable pass the first of the four tests. As key contributors to the effectiveness of the strategy, they are relevant to the firm's competitiveness but are no guarantee of competitive advantage. They may offer no more than competitive parity with competing firms.

Passing both of the first two tests requires more—it requires resources and capabilities that are not only valuable but also rare. This is a much higher hurdle that can be cleared only by resources and capabilities that are *competitively superior.* Resources and capabilities that are competitively superior are the company's true strategic assets. They provide the company with a competitive advantage over its competitors, if only in the short run.

To pass the last two tests, a resource must be able to maintain its competitive superiority in the face of competition. It must be resistant to imitative attempts and efforts by competitors to find equally valuable substitute resources. Assessing the availability of substitutes is the most difficult of all the tests since substitutes are harder to recognize, but the key is to look for resources or capabilities held by other firms or being developed that *can serve the same function* as the company's core resources and capabilities.[5]

Very few firms have resources and capabilities that can pass all four tests, but those that do enjoy a sustainable competitive advantage with far greater profit potential. Costco is a notable example, with strong employee incentive programs and capabilities in supply chain management that have surpassed those of its warehouse club rivals for over 35 years. Lincoln Electric Company, less well known but no less notable in its achievements, has been the world leader in welding products for over 100 years as a result of its unique piecework incentive system for compensating production workers and the unsurpassed worker productivity and product quality that this system has fostered.

A Company's Resources and Capabilities Must Be Managed Dynamically

Even companies like Costco and Lincoln Electric cannot afford to rest on their laurels. Rivals that are initially unable to replicate a key resource may develop better and better substitutes over time. Resources and capabilities can depreciate like other assets if they are managed with benign neglect. Disruptive changes in technology, customer preferences, distribution channels, or other competitive factors can also destroy the value of key strategic assets, turning resources and capabilities "from diamonds to rust."[6]

Resources and capabilities must be continually strengthened and nurtured to sustain their competitive power and, at times, may need to be broadened and deepened to allow the company to position itself to pursue emerging market opportunities.[7] Organizational resources and capabilities that grow stale can impair competitiveness unless they are refreshed, modified, or even phased out and replaced in response to ongoing market changes and shifts in company strategy. Management's challenge in managing the firm's resources and capabilities dynamically has two elements: (1) attending to the ongoing modification of existing competitive assets, and (2) casting a watchful eye for opportunities to develop totally new kinds of capabilities.

> A company requires a dynamically evolving portfolio of resources and capabilities to sustain its competitiveness and help drive improvements in its performance.

The Role of Dynamic Capabilities

Companies that know the importance of recalibrating and upgrading their most valuable resources and capabilities ensure that these activities are done on a continual basis. By incorporating these activities into their routine managerial functions, they gain the experience necessary to be able to do them consistently well. At that point, their ability to freshen and renew their competitive assets becomes a capability in itself—a **dynamic capability.** A dynamic capability is the ability to modify, deepen, or augment the company's existing resources and capabilities.[8] This includes the capacity to improve existing resources and capabilities incrementally, in the way that Toyota aggressively upgrades the company's capabilities in fuel-efficient hybrid engine technology and constantly fine-tunes its famed Toyota production system. Likewise, management at BMW developed new organizational capabilities in hybrid engine design that allowed the company to launch its highly touted i3 and i8 plug-in hybrids.

> ### CORE CONCEPT
>
> A **dynamic capability** is an ongoing capacity of a company to modify its existing resources and capabilities or create new ones.

A dynamic capability also includes the capacity to add new resources and capabilities to the company's competitive asset portfolio. One way to do this is through alliances and acquisitions. An example is Bristol-Meyers Squibb's famed "string of pearls" acquisition capabilities, which have enabled it to replace degraded resources such as expiring patents with new patents and newly acquired capabilities in drug discovery for new disease domains.

QUESTION 3: WHAT ARE THE COMPANY'S STRENGTHS AND WEAKNESSES IN RELATION TO THE MARKET OPPORTUNITIES AND EXTERNAL THREATS?

LO 3

How to assess the company's strengths and weaknesses in light of market opportunities and external threats.

SWOT analysis is a simple but powerful tool for sizing up a company's strengths and weaknesses, its market opportunities, and the external threats to its future well-being.

Basing a company's strategy on its most competitively valuable strengths gives the company its best chance for market success.

In evaluating a company's overall situation, a key question is whether the company is in a position to pursue attractive market opportunities and defend against external threats to its future well-being. The simplest and most easily applied tool for conducting this examination is widely known as **SWOT analysis**, so named because it zeros in on a company's internal Strengths and Weaknesses, market Opportunities, and external Threats. A first-rate SWOT analysis provides the basis for crafting a strategy that capitalizes on the company's strengths, overcomes its weaknesses, aims squarely at capturing the company's best opportunities, and defends against competitive and macro-environmental threats.

Identifying a Company's Internal Strengths

A **strength** is something a company is good at doing or an attribute that enhances its competitiveness in the marketplace. A company's strengths depend on the quality of its resources and capabilities. Resource and capability analysis provides a way for managers to assess the quality objectively. While resources and capabilities that pass the VRIN tests of sustainable competitive advantage are among the company's greatest strengths, other types can be counted among the company's strengths as well. A capability that is not potent enough to produce a sustainable advantage over rivals may yet enable a series of temporary advantages if used as a basis for entry into a new market or market segment. A resource bundle that fails to match those of top-tier competitors may still allow a company to compete successfully against the second tier.

Assessing a Company's Competencies—What Activities Does It Perform Well? One way to appraise the degree of a company's strengths has to do with the company's skill level in performing key pieces of its business—such as supply chain management, R&D, production, distribution, sales and marketing, and customer service. A company's skill or proficiency in performing different facets of its operations can range from the extreme of having minimal ability to perform an activity (perhaps having just struggled to do it the first time) to the other extreme of being able to perform the activity better than any other company in the industry.

When a company's proficiency rises from that of mere ability to perform an activity to the point of being able to perform it consistently well and at acceptable cost, it is said to have a **competence**—a true *capability,* in other words. If a company's competence level in some activity domain is superior to that of its rivals it is known as a **distinctive competence.** A **core competence** is a proficiently performed internal activity that is *central* to a company's strategy and is typically distinctive as well. A core competence is a more competitively valuable strength than a competence because of the activity's key role in the company's strategy and the contribution it makes to the company's market success and profitability. Often, core competencies can be leveraged to create new markets or new product demand, as the engine behind a company's growth. Procter and Gamble has a core competence in brand management, which has led to an ever increasing portfolio of market-leading consumer products, including Charmin, Tide, Crest, Tampax, Olay, Febreze, Luvs, Pampers, and Swiffer. Nike has a core competence in designing and marketing innovative athletic footwear and sports apparel. Kellogg has a core competence in developing, producing, and marketing breakfast cereals.

Identifying Company Weaknesses and Competitive Deficiencies

A **weakness,** or *competitive deficiency,* is something a company lacks or does poorly (in comparison to others) or a condition that puts it at a disadvantage in the marketplace. A company's internal weaknesses can relate to (1) inferior or unproven skills, expertise, or intellectual capital in competitively important areas of the business; (2) deficiencies in competitively important physical, organizational, or intangible assets; or (3) missing or competitively inferior capabilities in key areas. *Company weaknesses are thus internal shortcomings that constitute competitive liabilities.* Nearly all companies have competitive liabilities of one kind or another. Whether a company's internal weaknesses make it competitively vulnerable depends on how much they matter in the marketplace and whether they are offset by the company's strengths.

Table 4.3 lists many of the things to consider in compiling a company's strengths and weaknesses. Sizing up a company's complement of strengths and deficiencies is akin to constructing a *strategic balance sheet,* where strengths represent *competitive assets* and weaknesses represent *competitive liabilities.* Obviously, the ideal condition is for the company's competitive assets to outweigh its competitive liabilities by an ample margin—a 50–50 balance is definitely not the desired condition!

Identifying a Company's Market Opportunities

Market opportunity is a big factor in shaping a company's strategy. Indeed, managers can't properly tailor strategy to the company's situation without first identifying its market opportunities and appraising the growth and profit potential each one holds. Depending on the prevailing circumstances, a company's opportunities can be plentiful or scarce, fleeting or lasting, and can range from wildly attractive to marginally interesting to unsuitable. Table 4.3 displays a sampling of potential market opportunities.

Newly emerging and fast-changing markets sometimes present stunningly big or "golden" opportunities, but it is typically hard for managers at one company to peer into "the fog of the future" and spot them far ahead of managers at other companies.[9]

CORE CONCEPT

A **competence** is an activity that a company has learned to perform with proficiency.

A **distinctive competence** is a capability that enables a company to perform a particular set of activities better than its rivals.

CORE CONCEPT

A **core competence** is an activity that a company performs proficiently and that is also central to its strategy and competitive success.

CORE CONCEPT

A company's **strengths** represent its competitive assets; its **weaknesses** are shortcomings that constitute competitive liabilities.

TABLE 4.3   What to Look for in Identifying a Company's Strengths, Weaknesses, Opportunities, and Threats

Potential Strengths and Competitive Assets	Potential Weaknesses and Competitive Deficiencies
• Competencies that are well matched to industry key success factors • Ample financial resources to grow the business • Strong brand-name image and/or company reputation • Economies of scale and/or learning- and experience-curve advantages over rivals • Other cost advantages over rivals • Attractive customer base • Proprietary technology, superior technological skills, important patents • Strong bargaining power over suppliers or buyers • Resources and capabilities that are valuable and rare • Resources and capabilities that are hard to copy and for which there are no good substitutes • Superior product quality • Wide geographic coverage and/or strong global distribution capability • Alliances and/or joint ventures that provide access to valuable technology, competencies, and/or attractive geographic markets	• No clear strategic vision • No well-developed or proven core competencies • No distinctive competencies or competitively superior resources • Lack of attention to customer needs • A product or service with features and attributes that are inferior to those of rivals • Weak balance sheet, insufficient financial resources to grow the firm • Too much debt • Higher overall unit costs relative to those of key competitors • Too narrow a product line relative to rivals • Weak brand image or reputation • Weaker dealer network than key rivals and/or lack of adequate distribution capability • Lack of management depth • A plague of internal operating problems or obsolete facilities • Too much underutilized plant capacity • Resources that are readily copied or for which there are good substitutes
Potential Market Opportunities	**Potential External Threats to a Company's Future Profitability**
• Meeting sharply rising buyer demand for the industry's product • Serving additional customer groups or market segments • Expanding into new geographic markets • Expanding the company's product line to meet a broader range of customer needs • Utilizing existing company skills or technological know-how to enter new product lines or new businesses • Taking advantage of falling trade barriers in attractive foreign markets • Taking advantage of an adverse change in the fortunes of rival firms • Acquiring rival firms or companies with attractive technological expertise or capabilities • Taking advantage of emerging technological developments to innovate • Entering into alliances or joint ventures to expand the firm's market coverage or boost its competitive capability	• Increased intensity of competition among industry rivals—may squeeze profit margins • Slowdowns in market growth • Likely entry of potent new competitors • Growing bargaining power of customers or suppliers • A shift in buyer needs and tastes away from the industry's product • Adverse demographic changes that threaten to curtail demand for the industry's product • Adverse economic conditions that threaten critical suppliers or distributors • Changes in technology—particularly disruptive technology that can undermine the company's distinctive competencies • Restrictive foreign trade policies • Costly new regulatory requirements • Tight credit conditions • Rising prices on energy or other key inputs

But as the fog begins to clear, golden opportunities are nearly always seized rapidly—and the companies that seize them are usually those that have been actively waiting, staying alert with diligent market reconnaissance, and preparing themselves to capitalize on shifting market conditions by patiently assembling an arsenal of resources to enable aggressive action when the time comes. In mature markets, unusually attractive market opportunities emerge sporadically, often after long periods of relative calm—but future market conditions may be more predictable, making emerging opportunities easier for industry members to detect.

In evaluating a company's market opportunities and ranking their attractiveness, managers have to guard against viewing every *industry* opportunity as a *company* opportunity. Rarely does a company have the resource depth to pursue all available market opportunities simultaneously without spreading itself too thin. Some companies have resources and capabilities better-suited for pursuing some opportunities, and a few companies may be hopelessly outclassed in competing for any of an industry's attractive opportunities. *The market opportunities most relevant to a company are those that match up well with the company's competitive assets, offer the best prospects for growth and profitability, and present the most potential for competitive advantage.*

> A company is well advised to pass on a particular market opportunity unless it has or can acquire the resources and capabilities needed to capture it.

Identifying the Threats to a Company's Future Profitability

Often, certain factors in a company's external environment pose *threats* to its profitability and competitive well-being. Threats can stem from such factors as the emergence of cheaper or better technologies, the entry of lower-cost foreign competitors into a company's market stronghold, new regulations that are more burdensome to a company than to its competitors, unfavorable demographic shifts, and political upheaval in a foreign country where the company has facilities. Table 4.3 shows a representative list of potential threats.

External threats may pose no more than a moderate degree of adversity (all companies confront some threatening elements in the course of doing business), or they may be imposing enough to make a company's situation look tenuous. On rare occasions, market shocks can give birth to a *sudden-death* threat that throws a company into an immediate crisis and a battle to survive. Many of the world's major financial institutions were plunged into unprecedented crisis in 2008–2009 by the aftereffects of high-risk mortgage lending, inflated credit ratings on subprime mortgage securities, the collapse of housing prices, and a market flooded with mortgage-related investments (collateralized debt obligations) whose values suddenly evaporated. It is management's job to identify the threats to the company's future prospects and to evaluate what strategic actions can be taken to neutralize or lessen their impact.

> Simply making lists of a company's strengths, weaknesses, opportunities, and threats is not enough; the payoff from SWOT analysis comes from the conclusions about a company's situation and the implications for strategy improvement that flow from the four lists.

What Do the SWOT Listings Reveal?

SWOT analysis involves more than making four lists. The two most important parts of SWOT analysis are *drawing conclusions* from the SWOT listings about the company's overall situation and *translating these conclusions into strategic actions* to better match the company's strategy to its internal strengths and market opportunities, to correct important weaknesses, and to defend against external threats. Figure 4.2 shows the steps involved in gleaning insights from SWOT analysis.

FIGURE 4.2   The Steps Involved in SWOT Analysis: Identify the Four Components of SWOT, Draw Conclusions, Translate Implications into Strategic Actions

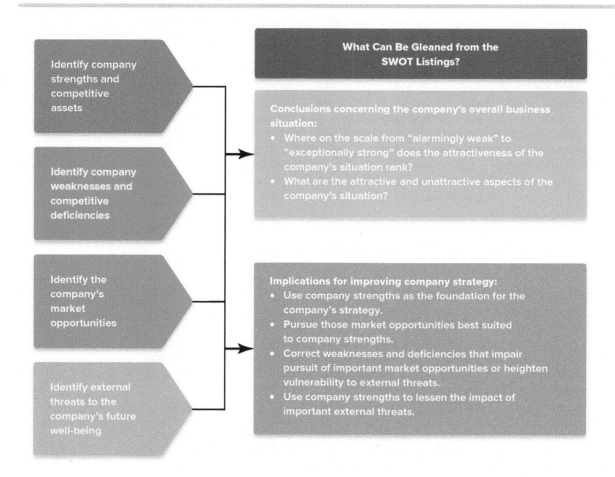

The final piece of SWOT analysis is to translate the diagnosis of the company's situation into actions for improving the company's strategy and business prospects. *A company's internal strengths should always serve as the basis of its strategy— placing heavy reliance on a company's best competitive assets is the soundest route to attracting customers and competing successfully against rivals.*[10] As a rule, strategies that place heavy demands on areas where the company is weakest or has unproven competencies should be avoided. Plainly, managers must look toward correcting competitive weaknesses that make the company vulnerable, hold down profitability, or disqualify it from pursuing an attractive opportunity. Furthermore, a company's strategy should be aimed squarely at capturing attractive market opportunities that are suited to the company's collection of capabilities. How much attention to devote to defending against external threats to the company's future performance hinges on how vulnerable the company is, whether defensive moves can be taken to lessen their impact, and whether the costs of undertaking such moves represent the best use of company resources.

QUESTION 4: HOW DO A COMPANY'S VALUE CHAIN ACTIVITIES IMPACT ITS COST STRUCTURE AND CUSTOMER VALUE PROPOSITION?

Company managers are often stunned when a competitor cuts its prices to "unbelievably low" levels or when a new market entrant introduces a great new product at a surprisingly low price. While less common, new entrants can also storm the market with a product that ratchets the quality level up so high that customers will abandon competing sellers even if they have to pay more for the new product. This is what seems to have happened with Apple's iPhone 6 and iMac computers; it is what Apple is betting on with the Apple Watch.

Regardless of where on the quality spectrum a company competes, it must remain competitive in terms of its customer value proposition in order to stay in the game. Patagonia's value proposition, for example, remains attractive to customers who value quality, wide selection, and corporate environmental responsibility over cheaper outerwear alternatives. Since its inception in 1925, the *New Yorker*'s customer value proposition has withstood the test of time by providing readers with an amalgam of well-crafted, rigorously fact-checked, and topical writing.

The value provided to the customer depends on how well a customer's needs are met for the price paid. How well customer needs are met depends on the perceived quality of a product or service as well as on other, more tangible attributes. The greater the amount of customer value that the company can offer profitably compared to its rivals, the less vulnerable it will be to competitive attack. For managers, the key is to keep close track of how *cost-effectively* the company can deliver value to customers relative to its competitors. If it can deliver the same amount of value with lower expenditures (or more value at the same cost), it will maintain a competitive edge.

Two analytic tools are particularly useful in determining whether a company's costs and customer value proposition are competitive: value chain analysis and benchmarking.

The Concept of a Company Value Chain

Every company's business consists of a collection of activities undertaken in the course of producing, marketing, delivering, and supporting its product or service. All the various activities that a company performs internally combine to form a **value chain**—so called because the underlying intent of a company's activities is ultimately to *create value for buyers*.

As shown in Figure 4.3, a company's value chain consists of two broad categories of activities: the *primary activities* foremost in creating value for customers and the requisite *support activities* that facilitate and enhance the performance of the primary activities.[11] The kinds of primary and secondary activities that constitute a company's value chain vary according to the specifics of a company's business; hence, the listing of the primary and support activities in Figure 4.3 is illustrative rather than definitive. For example, the primary activities at a hotel operator like Starwood Hotels and Resorts mainly consist of site selection and construction, reservations, and hotel operations (check-in and check-out, maintenance and housekeeping, dining and room service, and conventions and meetings); principal support

LO 4

How a company's value chain activities can affect the company's cost structure and customer value proposition.

The higher a company's costs are above those of close rivals, the more competitively vulnerable the company becomes.

The greater the amount of customer value that a company can offer profitably relative to close rivals, the less competitively vulnerable the company becomes.

CORE CONCEPT

A company's **value chain** identifies the primary activities and related support activities that create customer value.

FIGURE 4.3   A Representative Company Value Chain

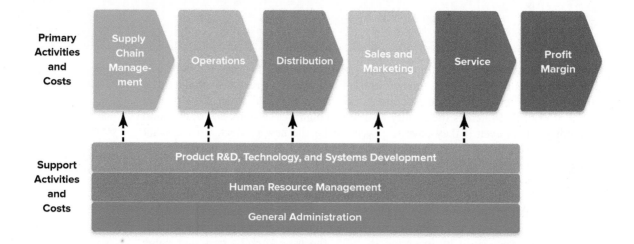

PRIMARY ACTIVITIES

- **Supply Chain Management**—Activities, costs, and assets associated with purchasing fuel, energy, raw materials, parts and components, merchandise, and consumable items from vendors; receiving, storing, and disseminating inputs from suppliers; inspection; and inventory management.

- **Operations**—Activities, costs, and assets associated with converting inputs into final product form (production, assembly, packaging, equipment maintenance, facilities, operations, quality assurance, environmental protection).

- **Distribution**—Activities, costs, and assets dealing with physically distributing the product to buyers (finished goods warehousing, order processing, order picking and packing, shipping, delivery vehicle operations, establishing and maintaining a network of dealers and distributors).

- **Sales and Marketing**—Activities, costs, and assets related to sales force efforts, advertising and promotion, market research and planning, and dealer/distributor support.

- **Service**—Activities, costs, and assets associated with providing assistance to buyers, such as installation, spare parts delivery, maintenance and repair, technical assistance, buyer inquiries, and complaints.

SUPPORT ACTIVITIES

- **Product R&D, Technology, and Systems Development**—Activities, costs, and assets relating to product R&D, process R&D, process design improvement, equipment design, computer software development, telecommunications systems, computer-assisted design and engineering, database capabilities, and development of computerized support systems.

- **Human Resource Management**—Activities, costs, and assets associated with the recruitment, hiring, training, development, and compensation of all types of personnel; labor relations activities; and development of knowledge-based skills and core competencies.

- **General Administration**—Activities, costs, and assets relating to general management, accounting and finance, legal and regulatory affairs, safety and security, management information systems, forming strategic alliances and collaborating with strategic partners, and other "overhead" functions.

Source: Based on the discussion in Michael E. Porter, *Competitive Advantage* (New York: Free Press, 1985), pp. 37–43.

activities that drive costs and impact customer value include hiring and training hotel staff and handling general administration. Supply chain management is a crucial activity for J.Crew and Boeing but is not a value chain component at Facebook, LinkedIn, or Goldman Sachs. Sales and marketing are dominant activities at GAP and Match.com but have only minor roles at oil-drilling companies and natural gas pipeline companies. Customer delivery is a crucial activity at Domino's Pizza but insignificant at Starbucks.

With its focus on value-creating activities, the value chain is an ideal tool for examining the workings of a company's customer value proposition and business model. It permits a deep look at the company's cost structure and ability to offer low prices. It reveals the emphasis that a company places on activities that enhance differentiation and support higher prices, such as service and marketing. It also includes a profit margin component, since profits are necessary to compensate the company's owners and investors, who bear risks and provide capital. Tracking the profit margin along with the value-creating activities is critical because unless an enterprise succeeds in delivering customer value profitably (with a sufficient return on invested capital), it can't survive for long. Attention to a company's profit formula in addition to its customer value proposition is the essence of a sound business model, as described in Chapter 1.

Illustration Capsule 4.1 shows representative costs for various value chain activities performed by Boll & Branch, a maker of luxury linens and bedding sold directly to consumers online.

Comparing the Value Chains of Rival Companies   Value chain analysis facilitates a comparison of how rivals, activity by activity, deliver value to customers. Even rivals in the same industry may differ significantly in terms of the activities they perform. For instance, the "operations" component of the value chain for a manufacturer that makes all of its own parts and components and assembles them into a finished product differs from the "operations" of a rival producer that buys the needed parts and components from outside suppliers and performs only assembly operations. How each activity is performed may affect a company's relative cost position as well as its capacity for differentiation. Thus, even a simple comparison of how the activities of rivals' value chains differ can reveal competitive differences.

A Company's Primary and Secondary Activities Identify the Major Components of Its Internal Cost Structure   The combined costs of all the various primary and support activities constituting a company's value chain define its internal cost structure. Further, the cost of each activity contributes to whether the company's overall cost position relative to rivals is favorable or unfavorable. The roles of value chain analysis and benchmarking are to develop the data for comparing a company's costs activity by activity against the costs of key rivals and to learn which internal activities are a source of cost advantage or disadvantage.

Evaluating a company's cost-competitiveness involves using what accountants call *activity-based costing* to determine the costs of performing each value chain activity.[12] The degree to which a company's total costs should be broken down into costs for specific activities depends on how valuable it is to know the costs of specific activities versus broadly defined activities. At the very least, cost estimates are needed for each broad category of primary and support activities, but

A company's cost-competitiveness depends not only on the costs of internally performed activities (its own value chain) but also on costs in the value chains of its suppliers and distribution-channel allies.

ILLUSTRATION CAPSULE 4.1

The Value Chain for Boll & Branch

© belchonock/iStock/Getty Images

A king-size set of sheets from Boll & Branch is made from 6 meters of fabric, requiring 11 kilograms of raw cotton.

Raw Cotton	$ 28.16	
Spinning/Weaving/Dyeing	12.00	
Cutting/Sewing/Finishing	9.50	
Material Transportation	3.00	
Factory Fee	15.80	
Cost of Goods		**$ 68.46**
Inspection Fees	5.48	
Ocean Freight/Insurance	4.55	
Import Duties	8.22	
Warehouse/Packing	8.50	
Packaging	15.15	
Customer Shipping	14.00	
Promotions/Donations*	30.00	
Total Cost		**$154.38**
Boll & Brand Markup	About 60%	
Boll & Brand Retail Price		**$250.00**
Gross Margin**	**$ 95.62**	

Source: Adapted from Christina Brinkley, "What Goes into the Price of Luxury Sheets?" *The Wall Street Journal,* March 29, 2014, www.wsj.com/articles/SB10001424052702303725404579461953672838672 (accessed February 16, 2016).

cost estimates for more specific activities within each broad category may be needed if a company discovers that it has a cost disadvantage vis-à-vis rivals and wants to pin down the exact source or activity causing the cost disadvantage. However, a company's own *internal costs* may be insufficient to assess whether its product offering and customer value proposition are competitive with those of rivals. Cost and price differences among competing companies can have their origins in activities performed by suppliers or by distribution allies involved in getting the product to the final customers or end users of the product, in which case the company's entire *value chain system* becomes relevant.

The Value Chain System

A company's value chain is embedded in a larger system of activities that includes the value chains of its suppliers and the value chains of whatever wholesale distributors and retailers it utilizes in getting its product or service to end users. This *value chain system* (sometimes called a vertical chain) has implications that extend far beyond the company's costs. It can affect attributes like product quality that enhance differentiation and have importance for the company's customer value proposition, as well as its profitability.[13] Suppliers' value chains are relevant because suppliers perform activities and incur costs in creating and delivering the purchased inputs utilized in a company's own value-creating activities. The costs, performance features, and quality of these inputs influence a company's own costs and product differentiation capabilities. Anything a company can do to help its suppliers drive down the costs of their value chain activities or improve the quality and performance of the items being supplied can enhance its own competitiveness—a powerful reason for working collaboratively with suppliers in managing supply chain activities.[14] For example, automakers have encouraged their automotive parts suppliers to build plants near the auto assembly plants to facilitate just-in-time deliveries, reduce warehousing and shipping costs, and promote close collaboration on parts design and production scheduling.

Similarly, the value chains of a company's distribution-channel partners are relevant because (1) the costs and margins of a company's distributors and retail dealers are part of the price the ultimate consumer pays and (2) the activities that distribution allies perform affect sales volumes and customer satisfaction. For these reasons, companies normally work closely with their distribution allies (who are their direct customers) to perform value chain activities in mutually beneficial ways. For instance, motor vehicle manufacturers have a competitive interest in working closely with their automobile dealers to promote higher sales volumes and better customer satisfaction with dealers' repair and maintenance services. Producers of kitchen cabinets are heavily dependent on the sales and promotional activities of their distributors and building supply retailers and on whether distributors and retailers operate cost-effectively enough to be able to sell at prices that lead to attractive sales volumes.

As a consequence, *accurately assessing a company's competitiveness entails scrutinizing the nature and costs of value chain activities throughout the entire value chain system for delivering its products or services to end-use customers.* A typical value chain system that incorporates the value chains of suppliers and forward-channel allies (if any) is shown in Figure 4.4. As was the case with company value chains, the specific activities constituting value chain systems vary significantly from industry to industry. The primary value chain system activities in the pulp and paper industry (timber farming, logging, pulp mills, and papermaking) differ from the primary value

FIGURE 4.4   A Representative Value Chain System

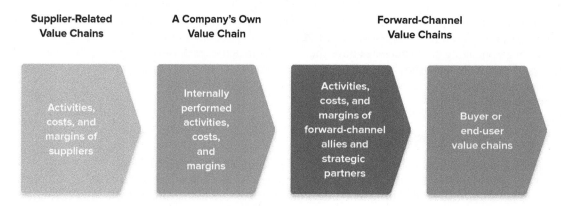

Supplier-Related Value Chains	A Company's Own Value Chain	Forward-Channel Value Chains
Activities, costs, and margins of suppliers	Internally performed activities, costs, and margins	Activities, costs, and margins of forward-channel allies and strategic partners	Buyer or end-user value chains

Source: Based in part on the single-industry value chain displayed in Michael E. Porter, *Competitive Advantage* (New York: Free Press, 1985), p. 35.

chain system activities in the home appliance industry (parts and components manufacture, assembly, wholesale distribution, retail sales) and yet again from the computer software industry (programming, disk loading, marketing, distribution).

Benchmarking: A Tool for Assessing Whether the Costs and Effectiveness of a Company's Value Chain Activities Are in Line

Benchmarking entails comparing how different companies (both inside and outside the industry) perform various value chain activities—how materials are purchased, how inventories are managed, how products are assembled, how fast the company can get new products to market, how customer orders are filled and shipped—and then making cross-company comparisons of the costs and effectiveness of these activities.[15] The objectives of benchmarking are to identify the best means of performing an activity and to emulate those best practices.

A **best practice** is a method of performing an activity or business process that consistently delivers superior results compared to other approaches.[16] To qualify as a legitimate best practice, the method must have been employed by at least one enterprise and shown to be *consistently more effective* in lowering costs, improving quality or performance, shortening time requirements, enhancing safety, or achieving some other highly positive operating outcome. Best practices thus identify a path to operating excellence with respect to value chain activities.

Xerox pioneered the use of benchmarking to become more cost-competitive, quickly deciding not to restrict its benchmarking efforts to its office equipment rivals but to extend them to *any company regarded as "world class"* in performing *any activity* relevant to Xerox's business. Other companies quickly picked up on Xerox's approach. Toyota managers got their idea for just-in-time inventory deliveries by studying how U.S. supermarkets replenished their shelves. Southwest Airlines reduced the turnaround time of its aircraft at each scheduled stop by studying pit crews on the auto racing circuit. More than 80 percent of Fortune 500 companies reportedly use benchmarking for comparing themselves against rivals on cost and other competitively important measures.

The tough part of benchmarking is not whether to do it but, rather, how to gain access to information about other companies' practices and costs. Sometimes benchmarking can be accomplished by collecting information from published reports, trade groups, and industry research firms or by talking to knowledgeable industry analysts, customers, and suppliers. Sometimes field trips to the facilities of competing or noncompeting companies can be arranged to observe how things are done, compare practices and processes, and perhaps exchange data on productivity and other cost components. However, such companies, even if they agree to host facilities tours and answer questions, are unlikely to share competitively sensitive cost information. Furthermore, comparing two companies' costs may not involve comparing apples to apples if the two companies employ different cost accounting principles to calculate the costs of particular activities.

However, a third and fairly reliable source of benchmarking information has emerged. The explosive interest of companies in benchmarking costs and identifying best practices has prompted consulting organizations (e.g., Accenture, A. T. Kearney, Benchnet—The Benchmarking Exchange, and Best Practices, LLC) and several associations (e.g., the QualServe Benchmarking Clearinghouse, and the Strategic Planning Institute's Council on Benchmarking) to gather benchmarking data, distribute information about best practices, and provide comparative cost data without identifying the names of particular companies. Having an independent group gather the information and report it in a manner that disguises the names of individual companies protects competitively sensitive data and lessens the potential for unethical behavior on the part of company personnel in gathering their own data about competitors. Illustration Capsule 4.2 describes benchmarking practices in the cement industry.

> Benchmarking the costs of company activities against those of rivals provides hard evidence of whether a company is cost-competitive.

Strategic Options for Remedying a Cost or Value Disadvantage

The results of value chain analysis and benchmarking may disclose cost or value disadvantages relative to key rivals. Such information is vital in crafting strategic actions to eliminate any such disadvantages and improve profitability. Information of this nature can also help a company find new avenues for enhancing its competitiveness through lower costs or a more attractive customer value proposition. There are three main areas in a company's total value chain system where company managers can try to improve its efficiency and effectiveness in delivering customer value: (1) a company's own internal activities, (2) suppliers' part of the value chain system, and (3) the forward-channel portion of the value chain system.

Improving Internally Performed Value Chain Activities Managers can pursue any of several strategic approaches to reduce the costs of internally performed value chain activities and improve a company's cost-competitiveness. They can *implement best practices* throughout the company, particularly for high-cost activities. They can *redesign the product and/or some of its components* to eliminate high-cost components or facilitate speedier and more economical manufacture or assembly. They can *relocate high-cost activities* (such as manufacturing) to geographic areas where they can be performed more cheaply or *outsource activities* to lower-cost vendors or contractors.

Delivered-Cost Benchmarking in the Cement Industry

Cement is a dry powder that creates concrete when mixed with water and sand. People interact with concrete every day. It is often the building material of choice for sidewalks, curbs, basements, bridges, and municipal pipes. Cement is manufactured at billion-dollar continuous-process plants by mining limestone, crushing it, scorching it in a kiln, and then milling it again.

About 24 companies (CEMEX, Holcim, and Lafarge are some of the biggest) manufacture cement at 90 U.S. plants with the capacity to produce 110 million tons per year. Plants serve tens of markets distributed across multiple states. Companies regularly benchmark "delivered costs" to understand whether their plants are cost leaders or laggards.

Delivered-cost benchmarking studies typically subdivide manufacturing and logistics costs into five parts: fixed-bin, variable-bin, freight-to-terminal, terminal operating, and freight-to-customer costs. These cost components are estimated using different sources.

Fixed- and variable-bin costs represent the cost of making a ton of cement and moving it to the plant's storage silos. They are the hardest to estimate. Fortunately, the Portland Cement Association, or PCA (the cement industry's association), publishes key data for every plant that features plant location, age, capacity, technology, and fuel. Companies combine the industry data, satellite imagery revealing quarry characteristics, and news reports with the company's proprietary plant-level financial data to develop their estimates of competitors' costs. The basic assumption is that plants of similar size utilizing similar technologies and raw-material inputs will have similar cost performance.

Logistics costs (including freight-to-terminal, terminal operating, and freight-to-customer costs) are much easier to accurately estimate. Cement companies use common

© Ulrich Doering/Alamy Stock Photo

carriers to move their product by barge, train, and truck transit modes. Freight pricing is competitive on a per-mile basis by mode, meaning that the company's per-ton-mile barge cost applies to the competition. By combining the per-ton-mile cost with origin-destination distances, freight costs are easily calculated. Terminal operating costs, the costs of operating barge or rail terminals that store cement and transfer it to trucks for local delivery, represent the smallest fraction of total supply chain cost and typically vary little within mode type. For example, most barge terminals cost $10 per ton to run, whereas rail terminals are less expensive and cost $5 per ton.

By combining all five estimated cost elements, the company benchmarks its estimated relative cost position by market. Using these data, strategists can identify which of the company's plants are most exposed to volume fluctuations, which are in greatest need of investment or closure, which markets the company should enter or exit, and which competitors are the most likely candidates for product or asset swaps.

Note: Developed with Peter Jacobson.

Source: www.cement.org (accessed January 25, 2014).

To improve the effectiveness of the company's customer value proposition and enhance differentiation, managers can take several approaches. They can *adopt best practices for quality, marketing, and customer service.* They can *reallocate resources to activities that address buyers' most important purchase criteria,* which will have the biggest impact on the value delivered to the customer. They can *adopt new technologies that spur innovation, improve design, and enhance creativity.* Additional approaches to managing value chain activities to lower costs and/or enhance customer value are discussed in Chapter 5.

Improving Supplier-Related Value Chain Activities   Supplier-related cost disadvantages can be attacked by pressuring suppliers for lower prices, switching to lower-priced substitute inputs, and collaborating closely with suppliers to identify mutual cost-saving opportunities.[17] For example, just-in-time deliveries from suppliers can lower a company's inventory and internal logistics costs and may also allow suppliers to economize on their warehousing, shipping, and production scheduling costs—a win–win outcome for both. In a few instances, companies may find that it is cheaper to integrate backward into the business of high-cost suppliers and make the item in-house instead of buying it from outsiders.

Similarly, a company can enhance its customer value proposition through its supplier relationships. Some approaches include selecting and retaining suppliers that meet higher-quality standards, providing quality-based incentives to suppliers, and integrating suppliers into the design process. Fewer defects in parts from suppliers not only improve quality throughout the value chain system but can lower costs as well since less waste and disruption occur in the production processes.

Improving Value Chain Activities of Distribution Partners

Any of three means can be used to achieve better cost-competitiveness in the forward portion of the industry value chain:

1. Pressure distributors, dealers, and other forward-channel allies to reduce their costs and markups.
2. Collaborate with them to identify win–win opportunities to reduce costs—for example, a chocolate manufacturer learned that by shipping its bulk chocolate in liquid form in tank cars instead of as 10-pound molded bars, it could not only save its candy bar manufacturing customers the costs associated with unpacking and melting but also eliminate its own costs of molding bars and packing them.
3. Change to a more economical distribution strategy, including switching to cheaper distribution channels (selling direct via the Internet) or integrating forward into company-owned retail outlets.

The means to enhancing differentiation through activities at the forward end of the value chain system include (1) engaging in cooperative advertising and promotions with forward allies (dealers, distributors, retailers, etc.), (2) creating exclusive arrangements with downstream sellers or utilizing other mechanisms that increase their incentives to enhance delivered customer value, and (3) creating and enforcing standards for downstream activities and assisting in training channel partners in business practices. Harley-Davidson, for example, enhances the shopping experience and perceptions of buyers by selling through retailers that sell Harley-Davidson motorcycles exclusively and meet Harley-Davidson standards.

Translating Proficient Performance of Value Chain Activities into Competitive Advantage

A company that does a *first-rate job* of managing its value chain activities *relative to competitors* stands a good chance of profiting from its competitive advantage. A company's value-creating activities can offer a competitive advantage in one of two ways (or both):

1. They can contribute to greater efficiency and lower costs relative to competitors.
2. They can provide a basis for differentiation, so customers are willing to pay relatively more for the company's goods and services.

Achieving a cost-based competitive advantage requires determined management efforts to be cost-efficient in performing value chain activities. Such efforts have to be ongoing and persistent, and they have to involve each and every value chain activity. The goal must be continuous cost reduction, not a one-time or on-again–off-again effort. Companies like Dollar General, Nucor Steel, Irish airline Ryanair, T.J.Maxx, and French discount retailer Carrefour have been highly successful in managing their value chains in a low-cost manner.

Ongoing and persistent efforts are also required for a competitive advantage based on differentiation. Superior reputations and brands are built up slowly over time, through continuous investment and activities that deliver consistent, reinforcing messages. Differentiation based on quality requires vigilant management of activities for quality assurance throughout the value chain. While the basis for differentiation (e.g., status, design, innovation, customer service, reliability, image) may vary widely among companies pursuing a differentiation advantage, companies that succeed do so on the basis of a commitment to coordinated value chain activities aimed purposefully at this objective. Examples include Cartier (status), Room and Board (craftsmanship), American Express (customer service), Dropbox (innovation), and FedEx (reliability).

How Value Chain Activities Relate to Resources and Capabilities

There is a close relationship between the value-creating activities that a company performs and its resources and capabilities. An organizational capability or competence implies a *capacity* for action; in contrast, a value-creating activity *initiates* the action. With respect to resources and capabilities, activities are "where the rubber hits the road." When companies engage in a value-creating activity, they do so by drawing on specific company resources and capabilities that underlie and enable the activity. For example, brand-building activities depend on human resources, such as experienced brand managers (including their knowledge and expertise in this arena), as well as organizational capabilities in advertising and marketing. Cost-cutting activities may derive from organizational capabilities in inventory management, for example, and resources such as inventory tracking systems.

Because of this correspondence between activities and supporting resources and capabilities, value chain analysis can complement resource and capability analysis as another tool for assessing a company's competitive advantage. Resources and capabilities that are *both valuable and rare* provide a company with *what it takes* for competitive advantage. For a company with competitive assets of this sort, the potential is there. When these assets are deployed in the form of a value-creating activity, that potential is realized due to their competitive superiority. Resource analysis is one tool for identifying competitively superior resources and capabilities. But their value and the competitive superiority of that value can be assessed objectively only *after* they are deployed. Value chain analysis and benchmarking provide the type of data needed to make that objective assessment.

There is also a dynamic relationship between a company's activities and its resources and capabilities. Value-creating activities are more than just the embodiment of a resource's or capability's potential. They also contribute to the formation and development of capabilities. The road to competitive advantage begins with management efforts to build organizational expertise in performing certain competitively important value chain activities. With consistent practice and continuous investment of company resources, these activities rise to the level of a reliable organizational capability or a competence. To the extent that top management makes the growing capability a cornerstone of the company's strategy, this capability becomes a core competence for the company. Later, with further organizational

Performing value chain activities with capabilities that permit the company to either outmatch rivals on differentiation or beat them on costs will give the company a competitive advantage.

learning and gains in proficiency, the core competence may evolve into a distinctive competence, giving the company superiority over rivals in performing an important value chain activity. Such superiority, if it gives the company significant competitive clout in the marketplace, can produce an attractive competitive edge over rivals. Whether the resulting competitive advantage is on the cost side or on the differentiation side (or both) will depend on the company's choice of which types of competence-building activities to engage in over this time period.

QUESTION 5: IS THE COMPANY COMPETITIVELY STRONGER OR WEAKER THAN KEY RIVALS?

Using resource analysis, value chain analysis, and benchmarking to determine a company's competitiveness on value and cost is necessary but not sufficient. A more comprehensive assessment needs to be made of the company's *overall* competitive strength. The answers to two questions are of particular interest: First, how does the company rank relative to competitors on each of the important factors that determine market success? Second, all things considered, does the company have a *net* competitive advantage or disadvantage versus major competitors?

LO 5

How a comprehensive evaluation of a company's competitive situation can assist managers in making critical decisions about their next strategic moves.

An easy-to-use method for answering these two questions involves developing quantitative strength ratings for the company and its key competitors on each industry key success factor and each competitively pivotal resource, capability, and value chain activity. Much of the information needed for doing a competitive strength assessment comes from previous analyses. Industry and competitive analyses reveal the key success factors and competitive forces that separate industry winners from losers. Benchmarking data and scouting key competitors provide a basis for judging the competitive strength of rivals on such factors as cost, key product attributes, customer service, image and reputation, financial strength, technological skills, distribution capability, and other factors. Resource and capability analysis reveals which of these are competitively important, given the external situation, and whether the company's competitive advantages are sustainable. SWOT analysis provides a more comprehensive and forward-looking picture of the company's overall situation.

Step 1 in doing a competitive strength assessment is to make a list of the industry's key success factors and other telling measures of competitive strength or weakness (6 to 10 measures usually suffice). Step 2 is to assign weights to each of the measures of competitive strength based on their perceived importance. (The sum of the weights for each measure must add up to 1.) Step 3 is to calculate weighted strength ratings by scoring each competitor on each strength measure (using a 1-to-10 rating scale, where 1 is very weak and 10 is very strong) and multiplying the assigned rating by the assigned weight. Step 4 is to sum the weighted strength ratings on each factor to get an overall measure of competitive strength for each company being rated. Step 5 is to use the overall strength ratings to draw conclusions about the size and extent of the company's net competitive advantage or disadvantage and to take specific note of areas of strength and weakness.

Table 4.4 provides an example of competitive strength assessment in which a hypothetical company (ABC Company) competes against two rivals. In the example, relative cost is the most telling measure of competitive strength, and the other strength measures are of lesser importance. The company with the highest rating on a given measure has an implied competitive edge on that measure, with the size of its edge reflected in the difference between its weighted rating and rivals' weighted ratings.

TABLE 4.4 **A Representative Weighted Competitive Strength Assessment**

| Key Success Factor/Strength Measure | Importance Weight | Competitive Strength Assessment (rating scale: 1 = very weak, 10 = very strong) | | | | | |
| | | ABC Co. | | Rival 1 | | Rival 2 | |
		Strength Rating	Weighted Score	Strength Rating	Weighted Score	Strength Rating	Weighted Score
Quality/product performance	0.10	8	0.80	5	0.50	1	0.10
Reputation/image	0.10	8	0.80	7	0.70	1	0.10
Manufacturing capability	0.10	2	0.20	10	1.00	5	0.50
Technological skills	0.05	10	0.50	1	0.05	3	0.15
Dealer network/ distribution capability	0.05	9	0.45	4	0.20	5	0.25
New product innovation capability	0.05	9	0.45	4	0.20	5	0.25
Financial resources	0.10	5	0.50	10	1.00	3	0.30
Relative cost position	0.30	5	1.50	10	3.00	1	0.30
Customer service capabilities	0.15	5	0.75	7	1.05	1	0.15
Sum of importance weights	**1.00**						
Overall weighted competitive strength rating			**5.95**		**7.70**		**2.10**

For instance, Rival 1's 3.00 weighted strength rating on relative cost signals a considerable cost advantage over ABC Company (with a 1.50 weighted score on relative cost) and an even bigger cost advantage over Rival 2 (with a weighted score of 0.30). The measure-by-measure ratings reveal the competitive areas in which a company is strongest and weakest, and against whom.

The overall competitive strength scores indicate how all the different strength measures add up—whether the company is at a net overall competitive advantage or disadvantage against each rival. The higher a company's *overall weighted strength rating,* the stronger its *overall competitiveness* versus rivals. The bigger the difference between a company's overall weighted rating and the scores of *lower-rated* rivals, the greater is its implied *net competitive advantage*. Thus, Rival 1's overall weighted score of 7.70 indicates a greater net competitive advantage over Rival 2 (with a score of 2.10) than over ABC Company (with a score of 5.95). Conversely, the bigger the difference between a company's overall rating and the scores of *higher-rated* rivals, the greater its implied *net competitive disadvantage*. Rival 2's score of 2.10 gives it a smaller net competitive disadvantage against ABC Company (with an overall score of 5.95) than against Rival 1 (with an overall score of 7.70).

> High-weighted competitive strength ratings signal a strong competitive position and possession of competitive advantage; low ratings signal a weak position and competitive disadvantage.

Strategic Implications of Competitive Strength Assessments

In addition to showing how competitively strong or weak a company is relative to rivals, the strength ratings provide guidelines for designing wise offensive and defensive strategies. For example, if ABC Company wants to go on the offensive to win additional sales and market share, such an offensive probably needs to be aimed directly at winning customers away from Rival 2 (which has a lower overall strength score) rather than Rival 1 (which has a higher overall strength score). Moreover, while ABC has high ratings for technological skills (a 10 rating), dealer network/distribution capability (a 9 rating), new product innovation capability (a 9 rating), quality/product performance (an 8 rating), and reputation/image (an 8 rating), these strength measures have low importance weights—meaning that ABC has strengths in areas that don't translate into much competitive clout in the marketplace. Even so, it outclasses Rival 2 in all five areas, plus it enjoys substantially lower costs than Rival 2 (ABC has a 5 rating on relative cost position versus a 1 rating for Rival 2)—and relative cost position carries the highest importance weight of all the strength measures. ABC also has greater competitive strength than Rival 3 regarding customer service capabilities (which carries the second-highest importance weight). Hence, because ABC's strengths are in the very areas where Rival 2 is weak, ABC is in a good position to attack Rival 2. Indeed, ABC may well be able to persuade a number of Rival 2's customers to switch their purchases over to its product.

> A company's competitive strength scores pinpoint its strengths and weaknesses against rivals and point directly to the kinds of offensive and defensive actions it can use to exploit its competitive strengths and reduce its competitive vulnerabilities.

But ABC should be cautious about cutting price aggressively to win customers away from Rival 2, because Rival 1 could interpret that as an attack by ABC to win away Rival 1's customers as well. And Rival 1 is in far and away the best position to compete on the basis of low price, given its high rating on relative cost in an industry where low costs are competitively important (relative cost carries an importance weight of 0.30). Rival 1's strong relative cost position vis-à-vis both ABC and Rival 2 arms it with the ability to use its lower-cost advantage to thwart any price cutting on ABC's part. Clearly ABC is vulnerable to any retaliatory price cuts by Rival 1—Rival 1 can easily defeat both ABC and Rival 2 in a price-based battle for sales and market share. If ABC wants to defend against its vulnerability to potential price cutting by Rival 1, then it needs to aim a portion of its strategy at lowering its costs.

The point here is that a competitively astute company should utilize the strength scores in deciding what strategic moves to make. When a company has important competitive strengths in areas where one or more rivals are weak, it makes sense to consider offensive moves to exploit rivals' competitive weaknesses. When a company has important competitive weaknesses in areas where one or more rivals are strong, it makes sense to consider defensive moves to curtail its vulnerability.

QUESTION 6: WHAT STRATEGIC ISSUES AND PROBLEMS MERIT FRONT-BURNER MANAGERIAL ATTENTION?

The final and most important analytic step is to zero in on exactly what strategic issues company managers need to address—and resolve—for the company to be more financially and competitively successful in the years ahead. This step involves drawing on the results of both industry analysis and the evaluations of the company's internal situation. The task here is to get a clear fix on exactly what strategic and competitive challenges confront the company, which of the company's competitive shortcomings need fixing, and what specific problems merit company managers' front-burner attention. *Pinpointing the specific issues that management needs to address sets the agenda for deciding what actions to take next to improve the company's performance and business outlook.*

Compiling a "priority list" of problems creates an agenda of strategic issues that merit prompt managerial attention.

The "priority list" of issues and problems that have to be wrestled with can include such things as *how* to stave off market challenges from new foreign competitors, *how* to combat the price discounting of rivals, *how* to reduce the company's high costs, *how* to sustain the company's present rate of growth in light of slowing buyer demand, *whether* to correct the company's competitive deficiencies by acquiring a rival company with the missing strengths, *whether* to expand into foreign markets, *whether* to reposition the company and move to a different strategic group, *what to do* about growing buyer interest in substitute products, and *what to do* to combat the aging demographics of the company's customer base. The priority list thus always centers on such concerns as "how to . . . ," "what to do about . . . ," and "whether to . . ." The purpose of the priority list is to identify the specific issues and problems that management needs to address, not to figure out what specific actions to take. Deciding what to do—which strategic actions to take and which strategic moves to make—comes later (when it is time to craft the strategy and choose among the various strategic alternatives).

A good strategy must contain ways to deal with all the strategic issues and obstacles that stand in the way of the company's financial and competitive success in the years ahead.

If the items on the priority list are relatively minor—which suggests that the company's strategy is mostly on track and reasonably well matched to the company's overall situation—company managers seldom need to go much beyond fine-tuning the present strategy. If, however, the problems confronting the company are serious and indicate the present strategy is not well suited for the road ahead, the task of crafting a better strategy needs to be at the top of management's action agenda.

KEY POINTS

There are six key questions to consider in evaluating a company's ability to compete successfully against market rivals:

1. *How well is the present strategy working?* This involves evaluating the strategy in terms of the company's financial performance and market standing. The stronger a company's current overall performance, the less likely the need for radical strategy changes. The weaker a company's performance and/or the faster the

changes in its external situation (which can be gleaned from PESTEL and industry analysis), the more its current strategy must be questioned.

2. *What are the company's most important resources and capabilities and can they give the company a sustainable advantage over competitors?* A company's resources can be identified using the tangible/intangible typology presented in this chapter. Its capabilities can be identified either by starting with its resources to look for related capabilities or looking for them within the company's different functional domains.

   The answer to the second part of the question comes from conducting the four tests of a resource's competitive power—the VRIN tests. If a company has resources and capabilities that are competitively *valuable* and *rare,* the firm will have a competitive advantage over market rivals. If its resources and capabilities are also hard to copy *(inimitable),* with no good substitutes *(nonsubstitutable),* then the firm may be able to sustain this advantage even in the face of active efforts by rivals to overcome it.

3. *Is the company able to seize market opportunities and overcome external threats to its future well-being?* The answer to this question comes from performing a SWOT analysis. The two most important parts of SWOT analysis are (1) drawing conclusions about what strengths, weaknesses, opportunities, and threats tell about the company's overall situation; and (2) acting on the conclusions to better match the company's strategy to its internal strengths and market opportunities, to correct the important internal weaknesses, and to defend against external threats. A company's strengths and competitive assets are strategically relevant because they are the most logical and appealing building blocks for strategy; internal weaknesses are important because they may represent vulnerabilities that need correction. External opportunities and threats come into play because a good strategy necessarily aims at capturing a company's most attractive opportunities and at defending against threats to its well-being.

4. *Are the company's cost structure and value proposition competitive?* One telling sign of whether a company's situation is strong or precarious is whether its costs are competitive with those of industry rivals. Another sign is how the company compares with rivals in terms of differentiation—how effectively it delivers on its customer value proposition. Value chain analysis and benchmarking are essential tools in determining whether the company is performing particular functions and activities well, whether its costs are in line with those of competitors, whether it is differentiating in ways that really enhance customer value, and whether particular internal activities and business processes need improvement. They complement resource and capability analysis by providing data at the level of individual activities that provide more objective evidence of whether individual resources and capabilities, or bundles of resources and linked activity sets, are competitively superior.

5. *On an overall basis, is the company competitively stronger or weaker than key rivals?* The key appraisals here involve how the company matches up against key rivals on industry key success factors and other chief determinants of competitive success and whether and why the company has a *net* competitive advantage or disadvantage. Quantitative competitive strength assessments, using the method

presented in Table 4.4, indicate where a company is competitively strong and weak and provide insight into the company's ability to defend or enhance its market position. As a rule, a company's competitive strategy should be built around its competitive strengths and should aim at shoring up areas where it is competitively vulnerable. When a company has important competitive strengths in areas where one or more rivals are weak, it makes sense to consider offensive moves to exploit rivals' competitive weaknesses. When a company has important competitive weaknesses in areas where one or more rivals are strong, it makes sense to consider defensive moves to curtail its vulnerability.

6. *What strategic issues and problems merit front-burner managerial attention?* This analytic step zeros in on the strategic issues and problems that stand in the way of the company's success. It involves using the results of industry analysis as well as resource and value chain analysis of the company's competitive situation to identify a "priority list" of issues to be resolved for the company to be financially and competitively successful in the years ahead. Actually deciding on a strategy and what specific actions to take is what comes after developing the list of strategic issues and problems that merit front-burner management attention.

Like good industry analysis, solid analysis of the company's competitive situation vis-à-vis its key rivals is a valuable precondition for good strategy making.

ASSURANCE OF LEARNING EXERCISES

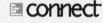

LO 1

1. Using the financial ratios provided in Table 4.1 and the financial statement information presented below for Costco Wholesale Corporation, calculate the following ratios for Costco for both 2013 and 2014:

    a. Gross profit margin

    b. Operating profit margin

    c. Net profit margin

    d. Times-interest-earned (or coverage) ratio

    e. Return on stockholders' equity

    f. Return on assets

    g. Debt-to-equity ratio

    h. Days of inventory

    i. Inventory turnover ratio

    j. Average collection period

    Based on these ratios, did Costco's financial performance improve, weaken, or remain about the same from 2013 to 2014?

Consolidated Income Statements for Costco Wholesale Corporation, 2013–2014 (in millions, except per share data)

	2014	2013
Net sales	$110,212	$102,870
Membership fees	2,428	2,286
Total revenue	112,640	105,156
Merchandise costs	98,458	$ 91,948
Selling, general, and administrative	10,899	10,155
Operating income	3,220	3,053
Other income (expense)		
Interest expense	(113)	(99)
Interest income and other, net	90	97
Income before income taxes	3,197	3,051
Provision for income taxes	1,109	990
Net income including noncontrolling interests	2,088	2,061
Net income attributable to noncontrolling interests	(30)	(22)
Net income	$ 2,058	$ 2,039
Basic earnings per share	$ 4.69	$ 4.68
Diluted earnings per share	$ 4.65	$ 4.63

Source: Costco Wholesale Corporation 2014 10-K.

Consolidated Balance Sheets for Costco Wholesale Corporation, 2013–2014 (in millions, except per share data)

	August 31, 2014	September 1, 2013
Assets		
Current Assets		
Cash and cash equivalents	$ 5,738	$ 4,644
Short-term investments	1,577	1,480
Receivables, net	1,148	1,026
Merchandise inventories	8,456	7,894

(continued)

	August 31, 2014	September 1, 2013
Deferred income taxes and other current assets	669	621
Total current assets	17,588	$15,840
Property and Equipment		
Land	$ 4,716	$ 4,409
Buildings and improvements	12,522	11,556
Equipment and fixtures	4,845	4,472
Construction in progress	592	585
	22,675	21,022
Less accumulated depreciation and amortization	(7,845)	(7,141)
Net property and equipment	14,830	13,881
Other assets	606	562
Total assets	$33,024	$30,283
Liabilities and Equity		
Current Liabilities		
Accounts payable	$ 8,491	$ 7,872
Accrued salaries and benefits	2,231	2,037
Accrued member rewards	773	710
Accrued sales and other taxes	442	382
Deferred membership fees	1,254	1,167
Other current liabilities	1,221	1,089
Total current liabilities	14,412	13,257
Long-term debt, excluding current portion	5,093	4,998
Deferred income taxes and other liabilities	1,004	1,016
Total liabilities	20,509	$19,271
Commitments and Contingencies		
Equity		
Preferred stock $0.005 par value; 100,000,000 shares authorized; no shares issued and outstanding	0	0
Common stock $0.005 par value; 900,000,000 shares authorized; 436,839,000 and 432,350,000 shares issued and outstanding	2	2
Additional paid-in capital	$ 4,919	$ 4,670
Accumulated other comprehensive (loss) income	(76)	(122)

(continued)

CHAPTER 4   Evaluating a Company's Resources, Capabilities, and Competitiveness   117

	August 31, 2014	September 1, 2013
Retained earnings	7,458	6,283
Total Costco stockholders' equity	12,303	10,833
Noncontrolling interests	212	179
Total equity	12,515	11,012
Total Liabilities and Equity	$33,024	$30,283

Source: Costco Wholesale Corporation 2014 10-K.

2. Panera Bread operates more than 1,900 bakery-cafés in more than 45 states and Canada. How many of the four tests of the competitive power of a resource does the store network pass? Using your general knowledge of this industry, perform a SWOT analysis. Explain your answers.   **LO 2, LO 3**

3. Review the information in Illustration Capsule 4.1 concerning Boll & Branch's average costs of producing and selling a king-size sheet set, and compare this with the representative value chain depicted in Figure 4.3. Then answer the following questions: **connect**

   LO 4

   a. Which of the company's costs correspond to the primary value chain activities depicted in Figure 4.3?

   b. Which of the company's costs correspond to the support activities described in Figure 4.3?

   c. What value chain activities might be important in securing or maintaining Boll & Branch's competitive advantage? Explain your answer.

4. Using the methodology illustrated in Table 4.3 and your knowledge as an automobile owner, prepare a competitive strength assessment for General Motors and its rivals Ford, Chrysler, Toyota, and Honda. Each of the five automobile manufacturers should be evaluated on the key success factors and strength measures of cost-competitiveness, product-line breadth, product quality and reliability, financial resources and profitability, and customer service. What does your competitive strength assessment disclose about the overall competitiveness of each automobile manufacturer? What factors account most for Toyota's competitive success? Does Toyota have competitive weaknesses that were disclosed by your analysis? Explain.   **LO 5**

EXERCISE FOR SIMULATION PARTICIPANTS

1. Using the formulas in Table 4.1 and the data in your company's latest financial statements, calculate the following measures of financial performance for your company: **LO 1**

   a. Operating profit margin

   b. Total return on total assets

    c. Current ratio

    d. Working capital

    e. Long-term debt-to-capital ratio

    f. Price-to-earnings ratio

LO 1   **2.** On the basis of your company's latest financial statements and all the other available data regarding your company's performance that appear in the industry report, list the three measures of financial performance on which your company did best and the three measures on which your company's financial performance was worst.

LO 1   **3.** What hard evidence can you cite that indicates your company's strategy is working fairly well (or perhaps not working so well, if your company's performance is lagging that of rival companies)?

LO 2, LO 3   **4.** What internal strengths and weaknesses does your company have? What external market opportunities for growth and increased profitability exist for your company? What external threats to your company's future well-being and profitability do you and your co-managers see? What does the preceding SWOT analysis indicate about your company's present situation and future prospects—where on the scale from "exceptionally strong" to "alarmingly weak" does the attractiveness of your company's situation rank?

LO 2, LO 3   **5.** Does your company have any core competencies? If so, what are they?

LO 4   **6.** What are the key elements of your company's value chain? Refer to Figure 4.3 in developing your answer.

LO 5   **7.** Using the methodology presented in Table 4.4, do a weighted competitive strength assessment for your company and two other companies that you and your co-managers consider to be very close competitors.

ENDNOTES

[1] Birger Wernerfelt, "A Resource-Based View of the Firm," *Strategic Management Journal* 5, no. 5 (September–October 1984), pp. 171–180; Jay Barney, "Firm Resources and Sustained Competitive Advantage," *Journal of Management* 17, no. 1 (1991), pp. 99–120.

[2] R. Amit and P. Schoemaker, "Strategic Assets and Organizational Rent," *Strategic Management Journal* 14 (1993).

[3] Jay B. Barney, "Looking Inside for Competitive Advantage," *Academy of Management Executive* 9, no. 4 (November 1995), pp. 49–61; Christopher A. Bartlett and Sumantra Ghoshal, "Building Competitive Advantage through People," *MIT Sloan Management Review* 43, no. 2 (Winter 2002), pp. 34–41; Danny Miller, Russell Eisenstat, and Nathaniel Foote, "Strategy from the Inside Out: Building Capability-Creating

Organizations," *California Management Review* 44, no. 3 (Spring 2002), pp. 37–54.

[4] M. Peteraf and J. Barney, "Unraveling the Resource-Based Tangle," *Managerial and Decision Economics* 24, no. 4 (June–July 2003), pp. 309–323.

[5] Margaret A. Peteraf and Mark E. Bergen, "Scanning Dynamic Competitive Landscapes: A Market-Based and Resource-Based Framework," *Strategic Management Journal* 24 (2003), pp. 1027–1042.

[6] C. Montgomery, "Of Diamonds and Rust: A New Look at Resources," in C. Montgomery (ed.), *Resource-Based and Evolutionary Theories of the Firm* (Boston: Kluwer Academic, 1995), pp. 251–268.

[7] Constance E. Helfat and Margaret A. Peteraf, "The Dynamic Resource-Based View:

Capability Lifecycles," *Strategic Management Journal* 24, no. 10 (2003).

[8] D. Teece, G. Pisano, and A. Shuen, "Dynamic Capabilities and Strategic Management," *Strategic Management Journal* 18, no. 7 (1997), pp. 509–533; K. Eisenhardt and J. Martin, "Dynamic Capabilities: What Are They?" *Strategic Management Journal* 21, no. 10–11 (2000), pp. 1105–1121; M. Zollo and S. Winter, "Deliberate Learning and the Evolution of Dynamic Capabilities," *Organization Science* 13 (2002), pp. 339–351; C. Helfat et al., *Dynamic Capabilities: Understanding Strategic Change in Organizations* (Malden, MA: Blackwell, 2007).

[9] Donald Sull, "Strategy as Active Waiting," *Harvard Business Review* 83, no. 9 (September 2005), pp. 121–126.

[10] M. Peteraf, "The Cornerstones of Competitive Advantage: A Resource-Based View," *Strategic Management Journal,* March 1993, pp. 179–191.

[11] Michael Porter in his 1985 best seller *Competitive Advantage* (New York: Free Press).

[12] John K. Shank and Vijay Govindarajan, *Strategic Cost Management* (New York: Free Press, 1993), especially chaps. 2–6, 10, and 11; Robin Cooper and Robert S. Kaplan, "Measure Costs Right: Make the Right Decisions," *Harvard Business Review* 66, no. 5 (September–October, 1988), pp. 96–103; Joseph A. Ness and Thomas G. Cucuzza, "Tapping the Full Potential of ABC," *Harvard Business Review* 73, no. 4 (July–August 1995), pp. 130–138.

[13] Porter, *Competitive Advantage,* p. 34.

[14] Hau L. Lee, "The Triple-A Supply Chain," *Harvard Business Review* 82, no. 10 (October 2004), pp. 102–112.

[15] Gregory H. Watson, *Strategic Benchmarking: How to Rate Your Company's Performance against the World's Best* (New York: Wiley, 1993); Robert C. Camp, *Benchmarking: The Search for Industry Best Practices That Lead to Superior Performance* (Milwaukee: ASQC Quality Press, 1989); Dawn Iacobucci and Christie Nordhielm, "Creative Benchmarking," *Harvard Business Review* 78 no. 6 (November–December 2000), pp. 24–25.

[16] www.businessdictionary.com/definition/best-practice.html (accessed December 2, 2009).

[17] Reuben E. Stone, "Leading a Supply Chain Turnaround," *Harvard Business Review* 82, no. 10 (October 2004), pp. 114–121.

CHAPTER 5

The Five Generic Competitive Strategies

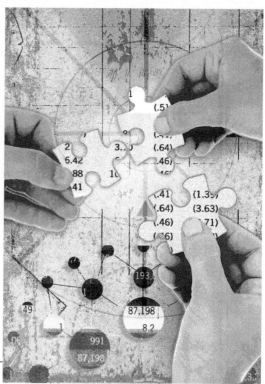

© Roy Scott/Ikon Images/SuperStock

Learning Objectives

THIS CHAPTER WILL HELP YOU UNDERSTAND:

LO 1   What distinguishes each of the five generic strategies and why some of these strategies work better in certain kinds of competitive conditions than in others.

LO 2   The major avenues for achieving a competitive advantage based on lower costs.

LO 3   The major avenues to a competitive advantage based on differentiating a company's product or service offering from the offerings of rivals.

LO 4   The attributes of a best-cost provider strategy—a hybrid of low-cost provider and differentiation strategies.

Strategy 101 is about choices: You can't be all things to all people.

  Michael E. Porter—*Professor, author, and cofounder of Monitor Consulting*

Strategy is all about combining choices of what to do and what not to do into a system that creates the requisite fit between what the environment needs and what the company does.

  Costas Markides—*Professor and consultant*

I learnt the hard way about positioning in business, about catering to the right segments.

  Shaffi Mather—*Social entrepreneur*

A company can employ any of several basic approaches to competing successfully and gaining a competitive advantage over rivals, but they all involve *delivering more value* to customers than rivals or *delivering value more efficiently* than rivals (or both). More value for customers can mean a good product at a lower price, a superior product worth paying more for, or a best-value offering that represents an attractive combination of price, features, service, and other appealing attributes. Greater efficiency means delivering a given level of value to customers at a lower cost to the company. But whatever approach to delivering value the company takes, it nearly always requires performing value chain activities differently than rivals and building competitively valuable resources and capabilities that rivals cannot readily match or trump.

This chapter describes the five *generic competitive strategy options*. Which of the five to employ is a company's first and foremost choice in crafting an overall strategy and beginning its quest for competitive advantage.

TYPES OF GENERIC COMPETITIVE STRATEGIES

A company's competitive strategy *deals exclusively with the specifics of management's game plan for competing successfully*—its specific efforts to position itself in the marketplace, please customers, ward off competitive threats, and achieve a particular kind of competitive advantage. The chances are remote that any two companies—even companies in the same industry—will employ competitive strategies that are exactly alike in every detail. However, when one strips away the details to get at the real substance, the two biggest factors that distinguish one competitive strategy from another boil down to (1) whether a company's market target is broad or narrow and (2) whether the company is pursuing a competitive advantage linked to lower costs or differentiation. These two factors give rise to five competitive strategy options, as shown in Figure 5.1 and listed next.[1]

LO 1

What distinguishes each of the five generic strategies and why some of these strategies work better in certain kinds of competitive conditions than in others.

1. *A low-cost provider strategy*—striving to achieve lower overall costs than rivals on comparable products that attract a broad spectrum of buyers, usually by underpricing rivals.

FIGURE 5.1   The Five Generic Competitive Strategies

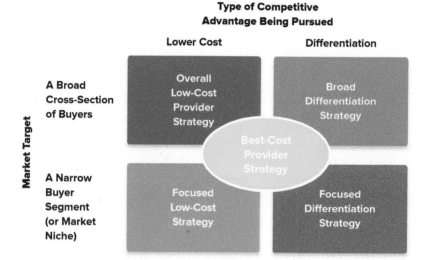

Source: This is an expanded version of a three-strategy classification discussed in Michael E. Porter, *Competitive Strategy* (New York: Free Press, 1980).

2. *A broad differentiation strategy*—seeking to differentiate the company's product offering from rivals' with attributes that will appeal to a broad spectrum of buyers.

3. *A focused low-cost strategy*—concentrating on the needs and requirements of a narrow buyer segment (or market niche) and striving to meet these needs at lower costs than rivals (thereby being able to serve niche members at a lower price).

4. *A focused differentiation strategy*—concentrating on a narrow buyer segment (or market niche) and outcompeting rivals by offering niche members customized attributes that meet their tastes and requirements better than rivals' products.

5. *A best-cost provider strategy*—striving to incorporate upscale product attributes at a lower cost than rivals. Being the "best-cost" producer of an upscale, multifeatured product allows a company to *give customers more value for their money* by underpricing rivals whose products have similar upscale, multifeatured attributes. This competitive approach is a *hybrid* strategy that *blends elements of the previous four options* in a unique and often effective way.

The remainder of this chapter explores the ins and outs of these five generic competitive strategies and how they differ.

LOW-COST PROVIDER STRATEGIES

Striving to achieve lower overall costs than rivals is an especially potent competitive approach in markets with many price-sensitive buyers. A company achieves **low-cost leadership** when it becomes the industry's lowest-cost provider rather than just being one of perhaps several competitors with comparatively low costs. A low-cost provider's foremost strategic objective is meaningfully lower costs than rivals—*but not* *necessarily the absolutely lowest possible cost.* In striving for a cost advantage over rivals, company managers must incorporate features and services that buyers consider essential. A product offering that is too frills-free can be viewed by consumers as offering little value regardless of its pricing.

A company has two options for translating a low-cost advantage over rivals into attractive profit performance. Option 1 is to use the lower-cost edge to underprice competitors and attract price-sensitive buyers in great enough numbers to increase total profits. Option 2 is to maintain the present price, be content with the present market share, and use the lower-cost edge to earn a higher profit margin on each unit sold, thereby raising the firm's total profits and overall return on investment.

While many companies are inclined to exploit a low-cost advantage by using option 1 (attacking rivals with lower prices), this strategy can backfire if rivals respond with retaliatory price cuts (in order to protect their customer base and defend against a loss of sales). A rush to cut prices can often trigger a price war that lowers the profits of all price discounters. The bigger the risk that rivals will respond with matching price cuts, the more appealing it becomes to employ the second option for using a low-cost advantage to achieve higher profitability.

The Two Major Avenues for Achieving a Cost Advantage

To achieve a low-cost edge over rivals, a firm's cumulative costs across its overall value chain must be lower than competitors' cumulative costs. There are two major avenues for accomplishing this:[2]

1. Perform value chain activities more cost-effectively than rivals.
2. Revamp the firm's overall value chain to eliminate or bypass some cost-producing activities.

Cost-Efficient Management of Value Chain Activities   For a company to do a more cost-efficient job of managing its value chain than rivals, managers must diligently search out cost-saving opportunities in every part of the value chain. No activity can escape cost-saving scrutiny, and all company personnel must be expected to use their talents and ingenuity to come up with innovative and effective ways to keep down costs. Particular attention must be paid to a set of factors known as **cost drivers** that have a strong effect on a company's costs and can be used as levers to lower costs. Figure 5.2 shows the most important cost drivers. Cost-cutting approaches that demonstrate an effective use of the cost drivers include:

1. *Capturing all available economies of scale.* Economies of scale stem from an ability to lower unit costs by increasing the scale of operation. Economies of scale may be available at different points along the value chain. Often a large plant is more economical to operate than a small one, particularly if it can be operated round the clock robotically. Economies of scale may be available due to a large warehouse operation on the input side or a large distribution center on the output side. In global industries, selling a mostly standard product world-wide tends to lower unit costs as opposed to making separate products for each country market, an approach in which costs are typically higher due to an inability to reach the most economic scale of production for each country. There are economies of scale in advertising as well. For example, Anheuser-Busch could

CORE CONCEPT

A **low-cost provider's** basis for competitive advantage is lower overall costs than competitors. Successful **low-cost leaders,** who have the lowest industry costs, are exceptionally good at finding ways to drive costs out of their businesses and still provide a product or service that buyers find acceptable.

A low-cost advantage over rivals can translate into better profitability than rivals attain.

CORE CONCEPT

A **cost driver** is a factor that has a strong influence on a company's costs.

FIGURE 5.2   Cost Drivers: The Keys to Driving Down Company Costs

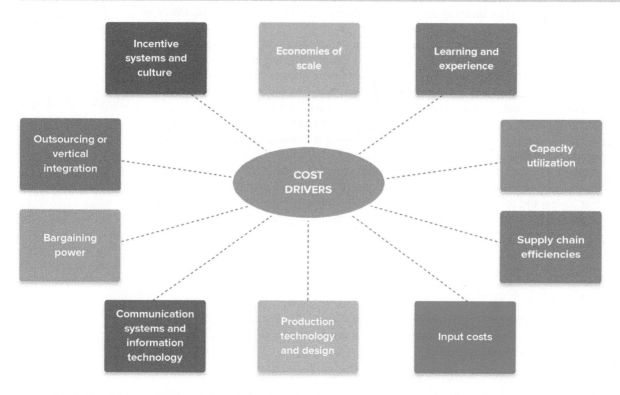

Source: Adapted from Michael E. Porter, *Competitive Advantage: Creating and Sustaining Superior Performance* (New York: Free Press, 1985).

afford to pay the $5 million cost of a 30-second Super Bowl ad in 2016 because the cost could be spread out over the hundreds of millions of units of Budweiser that the company sells.

2. *Taking full advantage of experience and learning-curve effects.* The cost of performing an activity can decline over time as the learning and experience of company personnel build. Learning and experience economies can stem from debugging and mastering newly introduced technologies, using the experiences and suggestions of workers to install more efficient plant layouts and assembly procedures, and the added speed and effectiveness that accrues from repeatedly picking sites for and building new plants, distribution centers, or retail outlets.

3. *Operating facilities at full capacity.* Whether a company is able to operate at or near full capacity has a big impact on unit costs when its value chain contains activities associated with substantial fixed costs. Higher rates of capacity utilization allow depreciation and other fixed costs to be spread over a larger unit volume, thereby lowering fixed costs per unit. The more capital-intensive the business and the higher the fixed costs as a percentage of total costs, the greater the unit-cost penalty for operating at less than full capacity.

4. *Improving supply chain efficiency.* Partnering with suppliers to streamline the ordering and purchasing process, to reduce inventory carrying costs via just-in-time inventory practices, to economize on shipping and materials handling, and to

ferret out other cost-saving opportunities is a much-used approach to cost reduction. A company with a distinctive competence in cost-efficient supply chain management, such as BASF (the world's leading chemical company), can sometimes achieve a sizable cost advantage over less adept rivals.

5. *Substituting lower-cost inputs wherever there is little or no sacrifice in product quality or performance.* If the costs of certain raw materials and parts are "too high," a company can switch to using lower-cost items or maybe even design the high-cost components out of the product altogether.

6. *Using the company's bargaining power vis-à-vis suppliers or others in the value chain system to gain concessions.* Home Depot, for example, has sufficient bargaining clout with suppliers to win price discounts on large-volume purchases.

7. *Using online systems and sophisticated software to achieve operating efficiencies.* For example, sharing data and production schedules with suppliers, coupled with the use of enterprise resource planning (ERP) and manufacturing execution system (MES) software, can reduce parts inventories, trim production times, and lower labor requirements.

8. *Improving process design and employing advanced production technology.* Often production costs can be cut by (1) using design for manufacture (DFM) procedures and computer-assisted design (CAD) techniques that enable more integrated and efficient production methods, (2) investing in highly automated robotic production technology, and (3) shifting to a mass-customization production process. Dell's highly automated PC assembly plant in Austin, Texas, is a prime example of the use of advanced product and process technologies. Many companies are ardent users of total quality management (TQM) systems, business process reengineering, Six Sigma methodology, and other business process management techniques that aim at boosting efficiency and reducing costs.

9. *Being alert to the cost advantages of outsourcing or vertical integration.* Outsourcing the performance of certain value chain activities can be more economical than performing them in-house if outside specialists, by virtue of their expertise and volume, can perform the activities at lower cost. On the other hand, there can be times when integrating into the activities of either suppliers or distribution-channel allies can lower costs through greater production efficiencies, reduced transaction costs, or a better bargaining position.

10. *Motivating employees through incentives and company culture.* A company's incentive system can encourage not only greater worker productivity but also cost-saving innovations that come from worker suggestions. The culture of a company can also spur worker pride in productivity and continuous improvement. Companies that are well known for their cost-reducing incentive systems and culture include Nucor Steel, which characterizes itself as a company of "20,000 teammates," Southwest Airlines, and Walmart.

Revamping of the Value Chain System to Lower Costs   Dramatic cost advantages can often emerge from redesigning the company's value chain system in ways that eliminate costly work steps and entirely bypass certain cost-producing value chain activities. Such value chain revamping can include:

- *Selling direct to consumers and bypassing the activities and costs of distributors and dealers.* To circumvent the need for distributors and dealers, a company can (1) create its own direct sales force (which adds the costs of maintaining and supporting a sales force but which may well be cheaper than using independent distributors and dealers to access buyers) and/or (2) conduct sales operations at the company's website (incurring costs for website operations and shipping may be a substantially cheaper way to make sales than going through distributor–dealer channels). Costs in the wholesale and retail portions of the value chain frequently represent 35 to 50 percent of the final price consumers pay, so establishing a direct sales force or selling online may offer big cost savings.

- *Streamlining operations by eliminating low-value-added or unnecessary work steps and activities.* At Walmart, some items supplied by manufacturers are delivered directly to retail stores rather than being routed through Walmart's distribution centers and delivered by Walmart trucks. In other instances, Walmart unloads incoming shipments from manufacturers' trucks arriving at its distribution centers and loads them directly onto outgoing Walmart trucks headed to particular stores without ever moving the goods into the distribution center. Many supermarket chains have greatly reduced in-store meat butchering and cutting activities by shifting to meats that are cut and packaged at the meatpacking plant and then delivered to their stores in ready-to-sell form.

- *Reducing materials handling and shipping costs by having suppliers locate their plants or warehouses close to the company's own facilities.* Having suppliers locate their plants or warehouses close to a company's own plant facilitates just-in-time deliveries of parts and components to the exact workstation where they will be used in assembling the company's product. This not only lowers incoming shipping costs but also curbs or eliminates the company's need to build and operate storerooms for incoming parts and components and to have plant personnel move the inventories to the workstations as needed for assembly.

Illustration Capsule 5.1 describes the path that Amazon.com, Inc. has followed on the way to becoming not only the largest online retailer (as measured by revenues) but also the lowest-cost provider in the industry.

Examples of Companies That Revamped Their Value Chains to Reduce Costs

Nucor Corporation, the most profitable steel producer in the United States and one of the largest steel producers worldwide, drastically revamped the value chain process for manufacturing steel products by using relatively inexpensive electric arc furnaces and continuous casting processes. Using electric arc furnaces to melt recycled scrap steel eliminated many of the steps used by traditional steel mills that made their steel products from iron ore, coke, limestone, and other ingredients using costly coke ovens, basic oxygen blast furnaces, ingot casters, and multiple types of finishing facilities—plus Nucor's value chain system required far fewer employees. As a consequence, Nucor produces steel with a far lower capital investment, a far smaller workforce, and far lower operating costs than traditional steel mills. Nucor's strategy to replace the traditional steelmaking value chain with its simpler, quicker value chain approach has made it one of the world's lowest-cost producers of steel, allowing it to take a huge amount of market share away from traditional steel companies and earn attractive profits. (Nucor reported a profit in 188 out of 192 quarters during 1966–2014—a remarkable feat in a mature and cyclical industry notorious for roller-coaster bottom-line performance.)

Southwest Airlines has achieved considerable cost savings by reconfiguring the traditional value chain of commercial airlines, thereby permitting it to offer travelers dramatically lower fares. Its mastery of fast turnarounds at the gates (about 25 minutes

ILLUSTRATION CAPSULE 5.1

Amazon's Path to Becoming the Low-Cost Provider in E-commerce

In 1996, shortly after founding Amazon.com, CEO Jeff Bezos told his employees, *"When you are small, someone else that is bigger can always come along and take away what you have."* Since then, the company has relentlessly pursued growth, aiming to become the global cost leader in "customer-centric E-commerce" across nearly all consumer merchandise lines. Amazon.com now offers over 230 million items for sale in America—approximately 30 times more than Walmart—and its annual sales are greater than the next five largest e-retailers combined.

In scaling up, Amazon has achieved lower costs not only through economies of scale, but also by increasing its bargaining power over its supplies and distribution partners. With thousands of suppliers, Amazon.com is not reliant on any one relationship. Suppliers, however, have few other alternative e-retailers that can match Amazon's reach and popularity. This gives Amazon bargaining power when negotiating revenue sharing and payment schedules. Amazon has even been able to negotiate for space inside suppliers' warehouses, reducing their own inventory costs.

On the distribution side, Amazon has been developing its own capabilities to reduce reliance on third-party delivery services. Unlike most mega retailers, Amazon's distribution operation was designed to send small orders to residential customers. Amazon.com attained proximity to its customers by building a substantial network of warehousing facilities and processing capability—249 fulfillment and delivery stations globally. This wide footprint decreases the marginal cost of quick delivery, as well as Amazon's reliance on cross-country delivery services. In addition, Amazon has adopted innovative delivery services to further lower costs and extend its reach. In India and the UK, for example, through Easy

© Sean Gallup/Getty Images

Ship Amazon's crew picks up orders directly from sellers, eliminating the time and cost of sending goods to a warehouse and the need for more space.

Amazon's size has also enabled it to spread the fixed costs of its massive up-front investment in automation across many units. Amazon.com was a pioneer of algorithms generating customized recommendations for customers. While developing these algorithms was resource-intensive, the costs of employing them are low. The more Amazon uses its automated sales tools to drive revenue, the more the up-front development cost is spread thin across total revenue. As a result, the company has lower capital intensity for each dollar of sales than other large retailers (like Walmart and Target). Other proprietary tools that increase the volume and speed of sales—without increasing variable costs—include Amazon.com's patented One Click Buy feature. All in all, these moves have been helping secure Amazon's position as the low-cost provider in this industry.

Note: Developed with Danielle G. Garver.

Sources: Company websites; seekingalpha.com/article/2247493-amazons-competitive-advantage-quantified; Brad Stone, *The Everything Store* (New York: Back Bay Books, 2013); www.reuters.com/article/us-amazon-com-india-logistics-idUSKCN0T12PL20151112 (accessed February 16, 2016).

versus 45 minutes for rivals) allows its planes to fly more hours per day. This translates into being able to schedule more flights per day with fewer aircraft, allowing Southwest to generate more revenue per plane on average than rivals. Southwest does not offer assigned seating, baggage transfer to connecting airlines, or first-class seating and service, thereby eliminating all the cost-producing activities associated with these features. The company's fast and user-friendly online reservation system facilitates e-ticketing and reduces staffing requirements

Success in achieving a low-cost edge over rivals comes from out-managing rivals in finding ways to perform value chain activities faster, more accurately, and more cost-effectively.

at telephone reservation centers and airport counters. Its use of automated check-in equipment reduces staffing requirements for terminal check-in. The company's carefully designed point-to-point route system minimizes connections, delays, and total trip time for passengers, allowing about 75 percent of Southwest passengers to fly nonstop to their destinations and at the same time reducing Southwest's costs for flight operations.

The Keys to Being a Successful Low-Cost Provider

While low-cost providers are champions of frugality, they seldom hesitate to spend aggressively on resources and capabilities *that promise to drive costs out of the business.* Indeed, having competitive assets of this type and ensuring that they remain competitively superior is essential for achieving competitive advantage as a low-cost provider. Walmart, for example, has been an early adopter of state-of-the-art technology throughout its operations; however, the company *carefully estimates the cost savings of new technologies before it rushes to invest in them.* By continuously investing in complex, cost-saving technologies that are hard for rivals to match, Walmart has sustained its low-cost advantage for over 30 years.

Other companies noted for their successful use of low-cost provider strategies include Vizio in big-screen TVs, EasyJet and Ryanair in airlines, Huawei in networking and telecommunications equipment, Bic in ballpoint pens, Stride Rite in footwear, and Poulan in chain saws.

When a Low-Cost Provider Strategy Works Best

A low-cost provider strategy becomes increasingly appealing and competitively powerful when:

1. *Price competition among rival sellers is vigorous.* Low-cost providers are in the best position to compete offensively on the basis of price, to gain market share at the expense of rivals, to win the business of price-sensitive buyers, to remain profitable despite strong price competition, and to survive price wars.

2. *The products of rival sellers are essentially identical and readily available from many eager sellers.* Look-alike products and/or overabundant product supply set the stage for lively price competition; in such markets, it is the less efficient, higher-cost companies whose profits get squeezed the most.

3. *It is difficult to achieve product differentiation in ways that have value to buyers.* When the differences between product attributes or brands do not matter much to buyers, buyers are nearly always sensitive to price differences, and industry-leading companies tend to be those with the lowest-priced brands.

4. *Most buyers use the product in the same ways.* With common user requirements, a standardized product can satisfy the needs of buyers, in which case low price, not features or quality, becomes the dominant factor in causing buyers to choose one seller's product over another's.

5. *Buyers incur low costs in switching their purchases from one seller to another.* Low switching costs give buyers the flexibility to shift purchases to lower-priced sellers having equally good products or to attractively priced substitute products. A low-cost leader is well positioned to use low price to induce potential customers to switch to its brand.

Pitfalls to Avoid in Pursuing a Low-Cost Provider Strategy

Perhaps the biggest mistake a low-cost provider can make is getting carried away with overly aggressive price cutting. *Higher unit sales and market shares do not automatically translate into higher profits.* Reducing price results in earning a lower profit margin on each unit sold. Thus reducing price improves profitability *only if* the lower price increases unit sales enough to offset the loss in revenues due to the lower per unit profit margin. A simple numerical example tells the story: Suppose a firm selling 1,000 units at a price of $10, a cost of $9, and a profit margin of $1 opts to cut price 5 percent to $9.50—which reduces the firm's profit margin to $0.50 per unit sold. If unit costs remain at $9, then it takes a 100 percent sales increase to 2,000 units just to offset the narrower profit margin and get back to total profits of $1,000. Hence, whether a price cut will result in higher or lower profitability depends on how big the resulting sales gains will be and how much, if any, unit costs will fall as sales volumes increase.

A second pitfall is *relying on cost reduction approaches that can be easily copied by rivals.* If rivals find it relatively easy or inexpensive to imitate the leader's low-cost methods, then the leader's advantage will be too short-lived to yield a valuable edge in the marketplace.

A third pitfall is *becoming too fixated on cost reduction.* Low costs cannot be pursued so zealously that a firm's offering ends up being too feature-poor to generate buyer appeal. Furthermore, a company driving hard to push down its costs has to guard against ignoring declining buyer sensitivity to price, increased buyer interest in added features or service, or new developments that alter how buyers use the product. Otherwise, it risks losing market ground if buyers start opting for more upscale or feature-rich products.

Even if these mistakes are avoided, a low-cost provider strategy still entails risk. An innovative rival may discover an even lower-cost value chain approach. Important cost-saving technological breakthroughs may suddenly emerge. And if a low-cost provider has heavy investments in its present means of operating, then it can prove costly to quickly shift to the new value chain approach or a new technology.

> A low-cost provider is in the best position to win the business of price-sensitive buyers, set the floor on market price, and still earn a profit.

> Reducing price does not lead to higher total profits unless the added gains in unit sales are large enough to offset the loss in revenues due to lower margins per unit sold.

> A low-cost provider's product offering must always contain enough attributes to be attractive to prospective buyers—low price, by itself, is not always appealing to buyers.

BROAD DIFFERENTIATION STRATEGIES

Differentiation strategies are attractive whenever buyers' needs and preferences are too diverse to be fully satisfied by a standardized product offering. Successful product differentiation requires careful study to determine what attributes buyers will find appealing, valuable, and worth paying for.[3] Then the company must incorporate a combination of these desirable features into its product or service that will be different enough to stand apart from the product or service offerings of rivals. A broad differentiation strategy achieves its aim when a wide range of buyers find the company's offering more appealing than that of rivals and worth a somewhat higher price.

Successful differentiation allows a firm to do one or more of the following:

LO 3

The major avenues to a competitive advantage based on differentiating a company's product or service offering from the offerings of rivals.

- Command a premium price for its product.
- Increase unit sales (because additional buyers are won over by the differentiating features).

- Gain buyer loyalty to its brand (because buyers are strongly attracted to the differentiating features and bond with the company and its products).

Differentiation enhances profitability whenever a company's product can command a sufficiently higher price or generate sufficiently bigger unit sales *to more than cover the added costs of achieving the differentiation.* Company differentiation strategies fail when buyers don't place much value on the brand's uniqueness and/or when a company's differentiating features are easily matched by its rivals.

Companies can pursue differentiation from many angles: a unique taste (Red Bull, Listerine); multiple features (Microsoft Office, Apple Watch); wide selection and one-stop shopping (Home Depot, Alibaba.com); superior service (Ritz-Carlton, Nordstrom); spare parts availability (John Deere; Morgan Motors); engineering design and performance (Mercedes, BMW); high fashion design (Prada, Gucci); product reliability (Whirlpool and Bosch in large home appliances); quality manufacture (Michelin); technological leadership (3M Corporation in bonding and coating products); a full range of services (Charles Schwab in stock brokerage); and wide product selection (Campbell's soups).

Managing the Value Chain to Create the Differentiating Attributes

Differentiation is not something hatched in marketing and advertising departments, nor is it limited to the catchalls of quality and service. Differentiation opportunities can exist in activities all along an industry's value chain. The most systematic approach that managers can take, however, involves focusing on the **value drivers,** a set of factors—analogous to cost drivers—that are particularly effective in creating differentiation. Figure 5.3 contains a list of important value drivers. Ways that managers can enhance differentiation based on value drivers include the following:

1. *Create product features and performance attributes that appeal to a wide range of buyers.* The physical and functional features of a product have a big influence on differentiation, including features such as added user safety or enhanced environmental protection. Styling and appearance are big differentiating factors in the apparel and motor vehicle industries. Size and weight matter in binoculars and mobile devices. Most companies employing broad differentiation strategies make a point of incorporating innovative and novel features in their product or service offering, especially those that improve performance and functionality.

2. *Improve customer service or add extra services.* Better customer services, in areas such as delivery, returns, and repair, can be as important in creating differentiation as superior product features. Examples include superior technical assistance to buyers, higher-quality maintenance services, more and better product information provided to customers, more and better training materials for end users, better credit terms, quicker order processing, and greater customer convenience.

3. *Invest in production-related R&D activities.* Engaging in production R&D may permit custom-order manufacture at an efficient cost, provide wider product variety and selection through product "versioning," or improve product quality. Many manufacturers have developed flexible manufacturing systems that allow different models and product versions to be made on the same assembly line. Being able to provide buyers with made-to-order products can be a potent differentiating capability.

FIGURE 5.3 Value Drivers: The Keys to Creating a Differentiation Advantage

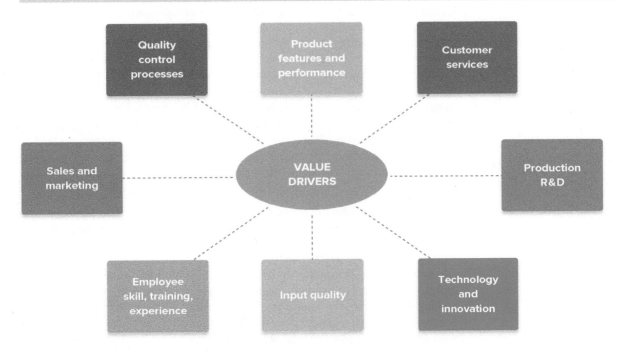

Source: Adapted from Michael E. Porter, *Competitive Advantage: Creating and Sustaining Superior Performance* (New York: Free Press, 1985).

4. *Strive for innovation and technological advances.* Successful innovation is the route to more frequent first-on-the-market victories and is a powerful differentiator. If the innovation proves hard to replicate, through patent protection or other means, it can provide a company with a first-mover advantage that is sustainable.

5. *Pursue continuous quality improvement.* Quality control processes reduce product defects, prevent premature product failure, extend product life, make it economical to offer longer warranty coverage, improve economy of use, result in more end-user convenience, or enhance product appearance. Companies whose quality management systems meet certification standards, such as the ISO 9001 standards, can enhance their reputation for quality with customers.

6. *Increase marketing and brand-building activities.* Marketing and advertising can have a tremendous effect on the value perceived by buyers and therefore their willingness to pay more for the company's offerings. They can create differentiation even when little tangible differentiation exists otherwise. For example, blind taste tests show that even the most loyal Pepsi or Coke drinkers have trouble telling one cola drink from another.[4] Brands create customer loyalty, which increases the perceived "cost" of switching to another product.

7. *Seek out high-quality inputs.* Input quality can ultimately spill over to affect the performance or quality of the company's end product. Starbucks, for example, gets high ratings on its coffees partly because it has very strict specifications on the coffee beans purchased from suppliers.

8. *Emphasize human resource management activities that improve the skills, expertise, and knowledge of company personnel.* A company with high-caliber intellectual capital often has the capacity to generate the kinds of ideas that drive product innovation, technological advances, better product design and product performance, improved production techniques, and higher product quality. Well-designed incentive compensation systems can often unleash the efforts of talented personnel to develop and implement new and effective differentiating attributes.

Revamping the Value Chain System to Increase Differentiation

Just as pursuing a cost advantage can involve the entire value chain system, the same is true for a differentiation advantage. Activities performed upstream by suppliers or downstream by distributors and retailers can have a meaningful effect on customers' perceptions of a company's offerings and its value proposition. Approaches to enhancing differentiation through changes in the value chain system include:

- *Coordinating with channel allies to enhance customer value.* Coordinating with downstream partners such as distributors, dealers, brokers, and retailers can contribute to differentiation in a variety of ways. Methods that companies use to influence the value chain activities of their channel allies include setting standards for downstream partners to follow, providing them with templates to standardize the selling environment or practices, training channel personnel, or cosponsoring promotions and advertising campaigns. Coordinating with retailers is important for enhancing the buying experience and building a company's image. Coordinating with distributors or shippers can mean quicker delivery to customers, more accurate order filling, and/or lower shipping costs. The Coca-Cola Company considers coordination with its bottler-distributors so important that it has at times taken over a troubled bottler to improve its management and upgrade its plant and equipment before releasing it again.[5]

- *Coordinating with suppliers to better address customer needs.* Collaborating with suppliers can also be a powerful route to a more effective differentiation strategy. Coordinating and collaborating with suppliers can improve many dimensions affecting product features and quality. This is particularly true for companies that engage only in assembly operations, such as Dell in PCs and Ducati in motorcycles. Close coordination with suppliers can also enhance differentiation by speeding up new product development cycles or speeding delivery to end customers. Strong relationships with suppliers can also mean that the company's supply requirements are prioritized when industry supply is insufficient to meet overall demand.

Delivering Superior Value via a Broad Differentiation Strategy

Differentiation strategies depend on meeting customer needs in unique ways or creating new needs through activities such as innovation or persuasive advertising. The objective is to offer customers something that rivals can't—at least in terms of the level of satisfaction. There are four basic routes to achieving this aim.

The first route is to incorporate product attributes and user features that *lower the buyer's overall costs* of using the company's product. This is the least obvious and most overlooked route to a differentiation advantage. It is a differentiating factor since it can help business buyers be more competitive in their markets and more profitable. Producers of materials and components often win orders for their products by reducing a buyer's raw-material waste (providing cut-to-size components), reducing a buyer's inventory requirements (providing just-in-time deliveries), using online systems to reduce a buyer's procurement and order processing costs, and providing free technical support. This route to differentiation can also appeal to individual consumers who are looking to economize on their overall costs of consumption. Making a company's product more economical for a buyer to use can be done by incorporating energy-efficient features (energy-saving appliances and lightbulbs help cut buyers' utility bills; fuel-efficient vehicles cut buyer costs for gasoline) and/or by increasing maintenance intervals and product reliability to lower buyer costs for maintenance and repairs.

A second route is to incorporate *tangible* features that increase customer satisfaction with the product, such as product specifications, functions, and styling. This can be accomplished by including attributes that add functionality; enhance the design; save time for the user; are more reliable; or make the product cleaner, safer, quieter, simpler to use, more portable, more convenient, or longer-lasting than rival brands. Smartphone manufacturers are in a race to introduce next-generation devices capable of being used for more purposes and having simpler menu functionality.

A third route to a differentiation-based competitive advantage is to incorporate *intangible* features that enhance buyer satisfaction in noneconomic ways. Toyota's Prius appeals to environmentally conscious motorists not only because these drivers want to help reduce global carbon dioxide emissions but also because they identify with the image conveyed. Bentley, Ralph Lauren, Louis Vuitton, Burberry, Cartier, and Coach have differentiation-based competitive advantages linked to buyer desires for status, image, prestige, upscale fashion, superior craftsmanship, and the finer things in life. Intangibles that contribute to differentiation can extend beyond product attributes to the reputation of the company and to customer relations or trust.

Differentiation can be based on *tangible* or *intangible* attributes.

The fourth route is to *signal the value* of the company's product offering to buyers. Typical signals of value include a high price (in instances where high price implies high quality and performance), more appealing or fancier packaging than competing products, ad content that emphasizes a product's standout attributes, the quality of brochures and sales presentations, and the luxuriousness and ambience of a seller's facilities (important for high-end retailers and for offices or other facilities frequented by customers). They make potential buyers aware of the professionalism, appearance, and personalities of the seller's employees and/or make potential buyers realize that a company has prestigious customers. Signaling value is particularly important (1) when the nature of differentiation is based on intangible features and is therefore subjective or hard to quantify, (2) when buyers are making a first-time purchase and are unsure what their experience with the product will be, (3) when repurchase is infrequent, and (4) when buyers are unsophisticated.

Regardless of the approach taken, achieving a successful differentiation strategy requires, first, that the company have capabilities in areas such as customer service, marketing, brand management, and technology that can create and support differentiation. That is, the resources, competencies, and value chain activities of the company must be well matched to the requirements of the strategy. For the strategy to result in competitive advantage, the company's competencies must also be sufficiently unique in delivering value to buyers that they help set its product offering apart from those of rivals. They must be competitively superior. There are numerous examples of companies that have differentiated themselves on the basis of distinctive capabilities. Health care facilities like M.D. Anderson, Mayo Clinic, and Cleveland Clinic have specialized expertise and equipment for treating certain diseases that most hospitals and health care providers cannot afford to emulate. When a major news event occurs, many people turn to Fox News and CNN because they have the capabilities to get reporters on the scene quickly, break away from their regular programming (without suffering a loss of advertising revenues associated with regular programming), and devote extensive air time to newsworthy stories.

The most successful approaches to differentiation are those that are difficult for rivals to duplicate. Indeed, this is the route to a sustainable differentiation advantage. While resourceful competitors can, in time, clone almost any tangible product attribute, socially complex intangible attributes such as company reputation, long-standing relationships with buyers, and image are much harder to imitate. Differentiation that creates switching costs that lock in buyers also provides a route to sustainable advantage. For example, if a buyer makes a substantial investment in learning to use one type of system, that buyer is less likely to switch to a competitor's system. (This has kept many users from switching away from Microsoft Office products, despite the fact that there are other applications with superior features.) As a rule, differentiation yields a longer-lasting and more profitable competitive edge when it is based on a well-established brand image, patent-protected product innovation, complex technical superiority, a reputation for superior product quality and reliability, relationship-based customer service, and unique competitive capabilities.

> Easy-to-copy differentiating features cannot produce sustainable competitive advantage.

When a Differentiation Strategy Works Best

Differentiation strategies tend to work best in market circumstances where:

- *Buyer needs and uses of the product are diverse.* Diverse buyer preferences allow industry rivals to set themselves apart with product attributes that appeal to particular buyers. For instance, the diversity of consumer preferences for menu selection, ambience, pricing, and customer service gives restaurants exceptionally wide latitude in creating a differentiated product offering. Other industries with diverse buyer needs include magazine publishing, automobile manufacturing, footwear, and kitchen appliances.

- *There are many ways to differentiate the product or service that have value to buyers.* Industries in which competitors have opportunities to add features to products and services are well suited to differentiation strategies. For example, hotel chains can differentiate on such features as location, size of room, range of guest services, in-hotel dining, and the quality and luxuriousness of bedding and furnishings. Similarly, cosmetics producers are able to differentiate based on prestige and image, formulations that fight the signs of aging, UV light protection, exclusivity of retail locations, the inclusion of antioxidants and natural ingredients, or prohibitions against animal testing. Basic commodities, such as chemicals, mineral deposits, and agricultural products, provide few opportunities for differentiation.

- *Few rival firms are following a similar differentiation approach.* The best differentiation approaches involve trying to appeal to buyers on the basis of attributes that rivals are not emphasizing. A differentiator encounters less head-to-head rivalry when it goes its own separate way in creating value and does not try to out-differentiate rivals on the very same attributes. When many rivals base their differentiation efforts on the same attributes, the most likely result is weak brand differentiation and "strategy overcrowding"—competitors end up chasing much the same buyers with much the same product offerings.

- *Technological change is fast-paced and competition revolves around rapidly evolving product features.* Rapid product innovation and frequent introductions of next-version products heighten buyer interest and provide space for companies to pursue distinct differentiating paths. In smartphones and wearable Internet devices, drones for hobbyists and commercial use, automobile lane detection sensors, and battery-powered cars, rivals are locked into an ongoing battle to set themselves apart by introducing the best next-generation products. Companies that fail to come up with new and improved products and distinctive performance features quickly lose out in the marketplace.

Pitfalls to Avoid in Pursuing a Differentiation Strategy

Differentiation strategies can fail for any of several reasons. *A differentiation strategy keyed to product or service attributes that are easily and quickly copied is always suspect.* Rapid imitation means that no rival achieves differentiation, since whenever one firm introduces some value-creating aspect that strikes the fancy of buyers, fast-following copycats quickly reestablish parity. This is why a firm must seek out sources of value creation that are time-consuming or burdensome for rivals to match if it hopes to use differentiation to win a sustainable competitive edge.

Differentiation strategies can also falter when buyers see little value in the unique attributes of a company's product. Thus, even if a company succeeds in setting its product apart from those of rivals, its strategy can result in disappointing sales and profits if the product does not deliver adequate value to buyers. Anytime many potential buyers look at a company's differentiated product offering with indifference, the company's differentiation strategy is in deep trouble.

The third big pitfall is overspending on efforts to differentiate the company's product offering, thus eroding profitability. Company efforts to achieve differentiation nearly always raise costs—often substantially, since marketing and R&D are expensive undertakings. The key to profitable differentiation is either to keep the unit cost of achieving differentiation below the price premium that the differentiating attributes can command (thus increasing the profit margin per unit sold) or to offset thinner profit margins per unit by selling enough additional units to increase total profits. If a company goes overboard in pursuing costly differentiation, it could be saddled with unacceptably low profits or even losses.

Other common mistakes in crafting a differentiation strategy include:

- *Offering only trivial improvements in quality, service, or performance features vis-à-vis rivals' products.* Trivial differences between rivals' product offerings may not be visible or important to buyers. If a company wants to generate the fiercely loyal customer following needed to earn superior profits and open up a differentiation-based competitive advantage over rivals, then its strategy must result in *strong rather than weak product differentiation.* In markets where differentiators do no better than achieve weak product differentiation, customer loyalty is weak, the costs of brand switching are low, and no one company has enough of a differentiation edge to command a price premium over rival brands.

- *Over-differentiating so that product quality, features, or service levels exceed the needs of most buyers.* A dazzling array of features and options not only drives up product price but also runs the risk that many buyers will conclude that a less deluxe and lower-priced brand is a better value since they have little occasion to use the deluxe attributes.

- *Charging too high a price premium.* While buyers may be intrigued by a product's deluxe features, they may nonetheless see it as being overpriced relative to the value delivered by the differentiating attributes. A company must guard against

Any differentiating feature that works well is a magnet for imitators.

Over-differentiating and overcharging are fatal differentiation strategy mistakes.
A low-cost provider strategy can defeat a differentiation strategy when buyers are satisfied with a basic product and don't think "extra" attributes are worth a higher price.

turning off would-be buyers with what is perceived as "price gouging." Normally, the bigger the price premium for the differentiating extras, the harder it is to keep buyers from switching to the lower-priced offerings of competitors.

FOCUSED (OR MARKET NICHE) STRATEGIES

What sets focused strategies apart from low-cost provider and broad differentiation strategies is concentrated attention on a narrow piece of the total market. The target segment, or niche, can be in the form of a geographic segment (such as New England), or a customer segment (such as urban hipsters), or a product segment (such as a class of models or some version of the overall product type). Community Coffee, the largest family-owned specialty coffee retailer in the United States, has a geographic focus on the state of Louisiana and communities across the Gulf of Mexico. Community holds only a small share of the national coffee market but has recorded sales in excess of $100 million and has won a strong following in the 20-state region where its coffee is distributed. Examples of firms that concentrate on a well-defined market niche keyed to a particular product or buyer segment include Zipcar (car rental in urban areas), Airbnb and VRBO (by-owner lodging rental), Comedy Central (cable TV), Blue Nile (online jewelry), Tesla Motors (electric cars), and CGA, Inc. (a specialist in providing insurance to cover the cost of lucrative hole-in-one prizes at golf tournaments). Microbreweries, local bakeries, bed-and-breakfast inns, and retail boutiques have also scaled their operations to serve narrow or local customer segments.

A Focused Low-Cost Strategy

A focused low-cost strategy aims at securing a competitive advantage by serving buyers in the target market niche at a lower cost and lower price than those of rival competitors. This strategy has considerable attraction when a firm can lower costs significantly by limiting its customer base to a well-defined buyer segment. The avenues to achieving a cost advantage over rivals also serving the target market niche are the same as those for low-cost leadership—use the cost drivers to perform value chain activities more efficiently than rivals and search for innovative ways to bypass nonessential value chain activities. The only real difference between a low-cost provider strategy and a focused low-cost strategy is the size of the buyer group to which a company is appealing—the former involves a product offering that appeals broadly to almost all buyer groups and market segments, whereas the latter aims at just meeting the needs of buyers in a narrow market segment.

Focused low-cost strategies are fairly common. Producers of private-label goods are able to achieve low costs in product development, marketing, distribution, and advertising by concentrating on making generic items imitative of name-brand merchandise and selling directly to retail chains wanting a low-priced store brand. The Perrigo Company has become a leading manufacturer of over-the-counter health care products, with 2014 sales of over $4 billion, by focusing on producing private-label brands for retailers such as Walmart, CVS, Walgreens, Rite Aid, and Safeway. Budget motel chains, like Motel 6, Sleep Inn, and Super 8, cater to price-conscious travelers who just want to pay for a clean, no-frills place to spend the night. Illustration Capsule 5.2 describes how Clinícas del Azúcar's focus on lowering the costs of diabetes care is allowing it to address a major health issue in Mexico.

ILLUSTRATION CAPSULE 5.2

Clinícas del Azúcar's Focused Low-Cost Strategy

Though diabetes is a manageable condition, it is the leading cause of death in Mexico. Over 14 million adults (14 percent of all adults) suffer from diabetes, 3.5 million cases remain undiagnosed, and more than 80,000 die due to related complications each year. The key driver behind this public health crisis is limited access to affordable, high-quality care. Approximately 90 percent of the population cannot access diabetes care due to financial and time constraints; private care can cost upwards of $1,000 USD per year (approximately 45 percent of Mexico's population has an annual income less than $2,000 USD) while average wait times alone at public clinics surpass five hours. Clinícas del Azúcar (CDA), however, is quickly scaling a solution that uses a *focused low-cost strategy* to provide affordable and convenient care to low-income patients.

By relentlessly focusing only on the needs of its target population, CDA has reduced the cost of diabetes care by more than 70 percent and clinic visit times by over 80 percent. The key has been the use of proprietary technology and a streamlined care system. First, CDA leverages evidence-based algorithms to diagnose patients for a fraction of the costs of traditional diagnostic tests. Similarly, its mobile outreach significantly reduces the costs of supporting patients in managing their diabetes after leaving CDA facilities. Second, CDA has redesigned the care process to implement a streamlined "patient process flow" that eliminates the need for multiple referrals to other care providers and brings together the necessary professionals and equipment into one facility. Consequently, CDA has become a one-stop shop for diabetes care, providing every aspect of diabetes treatment under one roof.

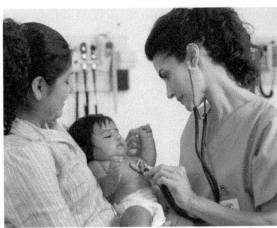

© Ariel Skelley/Blend Images/Getty Images

The bottom line: CDA's cost structure allows it to keep its prices for diabetes treatment very low, saving patients both time and money. Patients choose from three different care packages, ranging from preventive to comprehensive care, paying an annual fee that runs between approximately $70 and $200 USD. Given this increase in affordability and convenience, CDA estimates that it has saved its patients over $2 million USD in medical costs and will soon increase access to affordable, high-quality care for 10 to 80 percent of the population. These results have attracted investment from major funders including Endeavor, Echoing Green, and the Clinton Global Initiative. As a result, CDA and others expect CDA to grow from 5 clinics serving approximately 5,000 patients to more than 50 clinics serving over 100,000 patients throughout Mexico by 2020.

Note: Developed with David B. Washer.

Sources: www.clinicasdelazucar.com; "Funding Social Enterprises Report," *Echoing Green,* June 2014; Jude Webber, "Mexico Sees Poverty Climb Despite Rise in Incomes," *Financial Times* online, July 2015, www.ft.com/intl/cms/s/3/98460bbc-31e1-11e5-8873-775ba7c2ea3d.html#axzz3zz8grtec; "Javier Lozano," Schwab Foundation for Social Entrepreneurship online, 2016, www.schwabfound.org/content/javier-lozano.

A Focused Differentiation Strategy

Focused differentiation strategies involve offering superior products or services tailored to the unique preferences and needs of a narrow, well-defined group of buyers. Successful use of a focused differentiation strategy depends on (1) the existence of a buyer segment that is looking for special product attributes or seller capabilities and (2) a firm's ability to create a product or service offering that stands apart from that of rivals competing in the same target market niche.

Companies like L.A. Burdick (gourmet chocolates), Rolls-Royce, and Ritz-Carlton Hotel Company employ successful differentiation-based focused strategies targeted at upscale buyers wanting products and services with world-class attributes. Indeed, most markets contain a buyer segment willing to pay a big price premium for the very finest items available, thus opening the strategic window for some competitors to pursue differentiation-based focused strategies aimed at the very top of the market pyramid. Whole Foods Market, which bills itself as "America's Healthiest Grocery Store," has become the largest organic and natural foods supermarket chain in the United States (2014 sales of $14.2 billion) by catering to health-conscious consumers who prefer organic, natural, minimally processed, and locally grown foods. Whole Foods prides itself on stocking the highest-quality organic and natural foods it can find; the company defines quality by evaluating the ingredients, freshness, taste, nutritive value, appearance, and safety of the products it carries. Illustration Capsule 5.3 describes how Canada Goose has been gaining attention with a focused differentiation strategy.

When a Focused Low-Cost or Focused Differentiation Strategy Is Attractive

A focused strategy aimed at securing a competitive edge based on either low costs or differentiation becomes increasingly attractive as more of the following conditions are met:

- The target market niche is big enough to be profitable and offers good growth potential.
- Industry leaders have chosen not to compete in the niche—in which case focusers can avoid battling head to head against the industry's biggest and strongest competitors.
- It is costly or difficult for multisegment competitors to meet the specialized needs of niche buyers and at the same time satisfy the expectations of their mainstream customers.
- The industry has many different niches and segments, thereby allowing a focuser to pick the niche best suited to its resources and capabilities. Also, with more niches there is room for focusers to concentrate on different market segments and avoid competing in the same niche for the same customers.
- Few if any rivals are attempting to specialize in the same target segment—a condition that reduces the risk of segment overcrowding.

The advantages of focusing a company's entire competitive effort on a single market niche are considerable, especially for smaller and medium-sized companies that may lack the breadth and depth of resources to tackle going after a broader customer base with a more complex set of needs. YouTube has become a household name by concentrating on short video clips posted online. Papa John's and Domino's Pizza have created impressive businesses by focusing on the home delivery segment.

The Risks of a Focused Low-Cost or Focused Differentiation Strategy

Focusing carries several risks. One is the chance that competitors outside the niche will find effective ways to match the focused firm's capabilities in serving the target niche—perhaps by coming up with products or brands specifically designed to

ILLUSTRATION CAPSULE 5.3

Canada Goose's Focused Differentiation Strategy

Open up a winter edition of *People* and you will probably see photos of a celebrity sporting a Canada Goose parka. Recognizable by a distinctive red, white, and blue arm patch, the brand's parkas have been spotted on movie stars like Emma Stone and Bradley Cooper, on New York City streets, and on the cover of *Sports Illustrated*. Lately, Canada Goose has become extremely successful thanks to a focused differentiation strategy that enables it to thrive within its niche in the $1.2 trillion fashion industry. By targeting upscale buyers and providing a uniquely functional and stylish jacket, Canada Goose can charge nearly $1,000 per jacket and never need to put its products on sale.

While Canada Goose was founded in 1957, its recent transition to a focused differentiation strategy allowed it to rise to the top of the luxury parka market. In 2001, CEO Dani Reiss took control of the company and made two key decisions. First, he cut private-label and non-outerwear production in order to focus on the branded outerwear portion of Canada Goose's business. Second, Reiss decided to remain in Canada despite many North American competitors moving production to Asia to increase profit margins. Fortunately for him, these two strategy decisions have led directly to the company's current success. While other luxury brands, like Moncler, are priced similarly, no competitor's products fulfill the promise of handling harsh winter weather quite like a Canada Goose "Made in Canada" parka. The Canadian heritage, use of down sourced from rural Canada, real coyote fur (humanely trapped), and promise to provide warmth in sub-25°F temperatures have

© Richard Lautens/Toronto Star via Getty Images

let Canada Goose break away from the pack when it comes to selling parkas. The company's distinctly Canadian product has made it a hit among buyers, which is reflected in the willingness to pay a steep premium for extremely high-quality and warm winter outerwear.

Since Canada Goose's shift to a focused differentiation strategy, the company has seen a boom in revenue and appeal across the globe. Prior to Reiss's strategic decisions in 2001, Canada Goose had annual revenue of about $3 million. Within a decade, the company had experienced over 4,000 percent growth in annual revenue; by the end of 2015, sales were expected to exceed $300 million in more than 50 countries. At this pace, it looks like Canada Goose will remain a hot commodity as long as winter temperatures remain cold.

Note: Developed with Arthur J. Santry.

Sources: Drake Bennett, "How Canada Goose Parkas Migrated South," *Bloomberg Businessweek*, March 13, 2015, www.bloomberg.com; Hollie Shaw, "Canada Goose's Made-in-Canada Marketing Strategy Translates into Success," *Financial Post*, May 18, 2012, www.financialpost.com; "The Economic Impact of the Fashion Industry," *The Economist*, June 13, 2015, www.maloney.house.gov; and company website (accessed February 21, 2016).

appeal to buyers in the target niche or by developing expertise and capabilities that offset the focuser's strengths. In the lodging business, large chains like Marriott and Hilton have launched multibrand strategies that allow them to compete effectively in several lodging segments simultaneously. Marriott has flagship JW Marriott and Ritz-Carlton hotels with deluxe accommodations for business travelers and resort vacationers. Its Courtyard by Marriott and SpringHill Suites brands cater to business travelers looking for moderately priced lodging, whereas Marriott Residence Inns and TownePlace Suites are designed as a "home away from home" for travelers staying five or more nights. Its Fairfield Inn & Suites is intended to appeal to travelers looking for quality lodging at an "affordable" price. Marriott has also added Edition, AC Hotels by Marriott, and Autograph Collection hotels that offer stylish, distinctive decors and personalized services that appeal to young profession-als seeking distinctive lodging alternatives. Multibrand strategies are attractive to large companies like Marriott, Procter & Gamble, and Nestlé precisely because they enable entry into smaller market segments and siphon away business from compa-nies that employ a focused strategy.

A second risk of employing a focused strategy is the potential for the preferences and needs of niche members to shift over time toward the product attributes desired by buyers in the mainstream portion of the market. An erosion of the differences across buyer segments lowers entry barriers into a focuser's market niche and provides an open invitation for rivals in adjacent segments to begin competing for the focuser's customers. A third risk is that the segment may become so attractive that it is soon inundated with competitors, intensifying rivalry and splintering segment profits. And there is always the risk for segment growth to slow to such a small rate that a focuser's prospects for future sales and profit gains become unacceptably dim.

BEST-COST PROVIDER STRATEGIES

As Figure 5.1 indicates, **best-cost provider strategies** stake out a middle ground between pursuing a low-cost advantage and a differentiation advantage and between appealing to the broad market as a whole and a narrow market niche. This permits companies to aim squarely at the sometimes great mass of value-conscious buyers looking for a better product or service at an economical price. Value-conscious buy-ers frequently shy away from both cheap low-end products and expensive high-end products, but they are quite willing to pay a "fair" price for extra features and func-tionality they find appealing and useful. The essence of a best-cost provider strategy is giving customers *more value for the money* by satisfying buyer desires for appeal-ing features and charging a lower price for these attributes compared to rivals with similar-caliber product offerings.[6] From a competitive-positioning standpoint, best-cost strategies are thus a *hybrid,* balancing a strategic emphasis on low cost against a strategic emphasis on differentiation (desirable features delivered at a relatively low price).

To profitably employ a best-cost provider strategy, a company *must have the capability to incorporate upscale attributes into its product offering at a lower cost than rivals.* When a company can incorporate more appealing features, good to excellent product performance or quality, or more satisfying customer service into its product offering *at a lower cost than rivals,* then it enjoys "best-cost" status—it is the low-cost provider of a product or service with *upscale attributes.* A best-cost provider can use its low-cost advantage to underprice rivals whose products or services have similarly upscale attributes and it still earns attractive profits.

Being a best-cost provider is different from being a low-cost provider because the additional attractive attributes entail additional costs (which a low-cost pro-vider can avoid by offering buyers a basic product with few frills). Moreover, the two strategies aim at a distinguishably different market target. *The target market for a best-cost provider is value-conscious buyers*—buyers who are looking for appeal-ing extras and functionality at a comparatively low price. Value-hunting buyers (as distinct from *price-conscious buyers* looking for a basic product at a bargain-basement price) often constitute a very sizable part of the overall market for a product or service.

Toyota has employed a classic best-cost provider strategy for its Lexus line of motor vehicles. It has designed an array of high-performance characteristics and upscale features into its Lexus models to make them comparable in performance and luxury to Mercedes, BMW, Audi, Jaguar, Cadillac, and Lincoln models. To further draw buyer attention, Toyota established a network of Lexus dealers, separate from Toyota dealers, dedicated to providing exceptional customer service. Most important, though, Toyota has drawn on its considerable know-how in making high-quality vehicles at low cost to produce its high-tech upscale-quality Lexus models at substantially lower costs than other luxury vehicle makers have been able to achieve in producing their models. To capitalize on its lower manufacturing costs, Toyota prices its Lexus models below those of comparable Mercedes, BMW, Audi, and Jaguar models to induce value-conscious luxury car buyers to purchase a Lexus instead. The price differential has typically been quite significant. For example, in 2015 the Lexus RX 350, a mid-sized SUV, had a sticker price of $43,395 for the all-wheel-drive model with standard equipment, whereas the base price of a comparable Mercedes M-class SUV was $51,725 and the base price of a comparable BMW X5 SUV was $57,150.

When a Best-Cost Provider Strategy Works Best

A best-cost provider strategy works best in markets where product differentiation is the norm and an attractively large number of value-conscious buyers can be induced to purchase midrange products rather than cheap, basic products or expensive, top-of-the-line products. A best-cost provider needs to position itself *near the middle of the market* with either a medium-quality product at a below-average price or a high-quality product at an average or slightly higher price. Best-cost provider strategies also work well in recessionary times, when masses of buyers become value-conscious and are attracted to economically priced products and services with more appealing attributes. But unless a company has the resources, know-how, and capabilities to incorporate upscale product or service attributes at a lower cost than rivals, adopting a best-cost strategy is ill-advised. Illustration Capsule 5.4 describes how American Giant has applied the principles of the best-cost provider strategy in producing and marketing its hoodie sweatshirts.

LO 4

The attributes of a best-cost provider strategy—a hybrid of low-cost provider and differentiation strategies.

The Risk of a Best-Cost Provider Strategy

A company's biggest vulnerability in employing a best-cost provider strategy is getting squeezed between the strategies of firms using low-cost and high-end differentiation strategies. Low-cost providers may be able to siphon customers away with the appeal of a lower price (despite less appealing product attributes). High-end differentiators may be able to steal customers away with the appeal of better product attributes (even though their products carry a higher price tag). Thus, to be successful, a best-cost provider must achieve significantly lower costs in providing upscale features so that it can outcompete high-end differentiators on the basis of a *significantly* lower price. Likewise, it must offer buyers *significantly* better product attributes to justify a price above what low-cost leaders are charging. In other words, it must offer buyers a more attractive customer value proposition.

American Giant's Best-Cost Provider Strategy

Bayard Winthrop, founder and owner of American Giant, set out to make a hoodie like the soft, ultra-thick Navy sweatshirts his dad used to wear in the 1950s. But he also had two other aims: He wanted it to have a more updated look with a tailored fit, and he wanted it produced cost-effectively so that it could be sold at a great price. To accomplish these aims, he designed the sweatshirt with the help of a former industrial engineer from Apple and an internationally renowned pattern maker, rethinking every aspect of sweatshirt design and production along the way. The result was a hoodie differentiated from others on the basis of extreme attention to fabric, fit, construction, and durability. The hoodie is made from heavy-duty cotton that is run through a machine that carefully picks loops of thread out of the fabric to create a thick, combed, ring-spun fleece fabric that feels three times thicker than most sweatshirts. A small amount of spandex paneling along the shoulders and sides creates the fitted look and maintains the shape, keeping the sweatshirt from looking slouchy or sloppy. It has double stitching with strong thread on critical seams to avoid deterioration and boost durability. The zippers and draw cord are customized to match the sweatshirt's color—an uncommon practice in the business.

American Giant sources yarn from Parkdale, South Carolina, and turns it into cloth at the nearby Carolina Cotton Works. This reduces transport costs, creates a more dependable, durable product that American Giant can easily quality-check, and shortens product turnaround to about a month, lowering inventory costs. This process also enables the company to use a genuine "Made in the U.S.A." label, a perceived quality driver.

American Giant disrupts the traditional, expensive distribution models by having no stores or resellers.

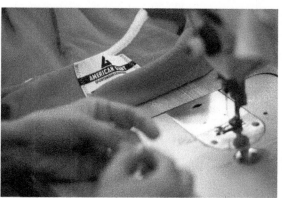

© David Paul Morris/Getty Images

Instead, it sells directly to customers from its website, with free two-day shipping and returns. Much of the company's growth comes from word of mouth and a strong public relations effort that promotes the brand in magazines, newspapers, and key business-oriented television programs. American Giant has a robust refer-a-friend program that offers a discount to friends of, and a credit to, current owners. Articles in popular media proclaiming its product "the greatest hoodie ever made" have made demand for its sweatshirts skyrocket.

At $89 for the original men's hoodie, American Giant is not cheap but offers customers value in terms of both price and quality. The price is higher than what one would pay at The Gap or American Apparel and comparable to Levi's, J.Crew, or Banana Republic. But its quality is more on par with high-priced designer brands, while its price is far more affordable.

Note: Developed with Sarah Boole.

Sources: www.nytimes.com/2013/09/20/business/us-textile-factories-return.html?emc=eta1&_r=0; www.american-giant.com; www.slate.com/articles/technology/technology/2012/12/american_giant_hoodie_this_is_the_greatest_sweatshirt_known_to_man.html; www.businessinsider.com/this-hoodie-is-so-insanely-popular-you-have-to-wait-months-to-get-it-2013-12.

THE CONTRASTING FEATURES OF THE FIVE GENERIC COMPETITIVE STRATEGIES: A SUMMARY

Deciding which generic competitive strategy should serve as the framework on which to hang the rest of the company's strategy is not a trivial matter. Each of the five generic competitive strategies *positions* the company differently in its market and competitive environment. Each establishes a *central theme* for how the company will endeavor to outcompete rivals. Each creates some boundaries or guidelines for maneuvering as market circumstances unfold and as ideas for improving the strategy are debated. Each entails differences in terms of product line, production emphasis, marketing emphasis, and means of maintaining the strategy, as shown in Table 5.1.

A company's competitive strategy should be well matched to its internal situation and predicated on leveraging its collection of competitively valuable resources and capabilities.

Thus a choice of which generic strategy to employ spills over to affect many aspects of how the business will be operated and the manner in which value chain activities must be managed. Deciding which generic strategy to employ is perhaps the most important strategic commitment a company makes—it tends to drive the rest of the strategic actions a company decides to undertake.

Successful Competitive Strategies Are Resource-Based

For a company's competitive strategy to succeed in delivering good performance and gain a competitive edge over rivals, it has to be well matched to a company's internal situation and underpinned by an appropriate set of resources, know-how, and competitive capabilities. To succeed in employing a low-cost provider strategy, a company must have the resources and capabilities to keep its costs below those of its competitors. This means having the expertise to cost-effectively manage value chain activities better than rivals by leveraging the cost drivers more effectively, and/or having the innovative capability to bypass certain value chain activities being performed by rivals. To succeed in a differentiation strategy, a company must have the resources and capabilities to leverage value drivers more effectively than rivals and incorporate attributes into its product offering that a broad range of buyers will find appealing. Successful focus strategies (both low cost and differentiation) require the capability to do an outstanding job of satisfying the needs and expectations of niche buyers. Success in employing a best-cost strategy requires the resources and capabilities to incorporate upscale product or service attributes at a lower cost than rivals. *For all types of generic strategies, success in sustaining the competitive edge depends on having resources and capabilities that rivals have trouble duplicating and for which there are no good substitutes.*

TABLE 5.1 Distinguishing Features of the Five Generic Competitive Strategies

	Low-Cost Provider	Broad Differentiation	Focused Low-Cost Provider	Focused Differentiation	Best-Cost Provider
Strategic target	• A broad cross-section of the market.	• A broad cross-section of the market.	• A narrow market niche where buyer needs and preferences are distinctively different.	• A narrow market niche where buyer needs and preferences are distinctively different.	• Value-conscious buyers. • A middle-market range.
Basis of competitive strategy	• Lower overall costs than competitors.	• Ability to offer buyers something attractively different from competitors' offerings.	• Lower overall cost than rivals in serving niche members.	• Attributes that appeal specifically to niche members.	• Ability to offer better goods at attractive prices.
Product line	• A good basic product with few frills (acceptable quality and limited selection).	• Many product variations, wide selection; emphasis on differentiating features.	• Features and attributes tailored to the tastes and requirements of niche members.	• Features and attributes tailored to the tastes and requirements of niche members.	• Items with appealing attributes and assorted features; better quality, not best.
Production emphasis	• A continuous search for cost reduction without sacrificing acceptable quality and essential features.	• Build in whatever differentiating features buyers are willing to pay for; strive for product superiority.	• A continuous search for cost reduction for products that meet basic needs of niche members.	• Small-scale production or custom-made products that match the tastes and requirements of niche members.	• Build in appealing features and better quality at lower cost than rivals.
Marketing emphasis	• Low prices, good value. • Try to make a virtue out of product features that lead to low cost.	• Tout differentiating features. • Charge a premium price to cover the extra costs of differentiating features.	• Communicate attractive features of a budget-priced product offering that fits niche buyers' expectations.	• Communicate how product offering does the best job of meeting niche buyers' expectations.	• Emphasize delivery of best value for the money.
Keys to maintaining the strategy	• Economical prices, good value. • Strive to manage costs down, year after year, in every area of the business.	• Stress constant innovation to stay ahead of imitative competitors. • Concentrate on a few key differentiating features.	• Stay committed to serving the niche at the lowest overall cost; don't blur the firm's image by entering other market segments or adding other products to widen market appeal.	• Stay committed to serving the niche better than rivals; don't blur the firm's image by entering other market segments or adding other products to widen market appeal.	• Unique expertise in simultaneously managing costs down while incorporating upscale features and attributes.
Resources and capabilities required	• Capabilities for driving costs out of the value chain system. • *Examples:* large-scale automated plants, an efficiency-oriented culture, bargaining power.	• Capabilities concerning quality, design, intangibles, and innovation. • *Examples:* marketing capabilities, R&D teams, technology.	• Capabilities to lower costs on niche goods. • *Examples:* lower input costs for the specific product desired by the niche, batch production capabilities.	• Capabilities to meet the highly specific needs of niche members. • *Examples:* custom production, close customer relations.	• Capabilities to simultaneously deliver lower cost and higher-quality/differentiated features. • *Examples:* TQM practices, mass customization.

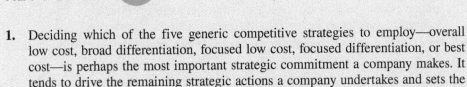

KEY POINTS

1. Deciding which of the five generic competitive strategies to employ—overall low cost, broad differentiation, focused low cost, focused differentiation, or best cost—is perhaps the most important strategic commitment a company makes. It tends to drive the remaining strategic actions a company undertakes and sets the whole tone for pursuing a competitive advantage over rivals.

2. In employing a low-cost provider strategy and trying to achieve a low-cost advantage over rivals, a company must do a better job than rivals of cost-effectively managing value chain activities and/or it must find innovative ways to eliminate cost-producing activities. An effective use of cost drivers is key. Low-cost provider strategies work particularly well when price competition is strong and the products of rival sellers are virtually identical, when there are not many ways to differentiate, when buyers are price-sensitive or have the power to bargain down prices, when buyer switching costs are low, and when industry newcomers are likely to use a low introductory price to build market share.

3. Broad differentiation strategies seek to produce a competitive edge by incorporating attributes that set a company's product or service offering apart from rivals in ways that buyers consider valuable and worth paying for. This depends on the appropriate use of value drivers. Successful differentiation allows a firm to (1) command a premium price for its product, (2) increase unit sales (if additional buyers are won over by the differentiating features), and/or (3) gain buyer loyalty to its brand (because some buyers are strongly attracted to the differentiating features and bond with the company and its products). Differentiation strategies work best when buyers have diverse product preferences, when few other rivals are pursuing a similar differentiation approach, and when technological change is fast-paced and competition centers on rapidly evolving product features. A differentiation strategy is doomed when competitors are able to quickly copy the appealing product attributes, when a company's differentiation efforts fail to interest many buyers, and when a company overspends on efforts to differentiate its product offering or tries to overcharge for its differentiating extras.

4. A focused strategy delivers competitive advantage either by achieving lower costs than rivals in serving buyers constituting the target market niche or by developing a specialized ability to offer niche buyers an appealingly differentiated offering that meets their needs better than rival brands do. A focused strategy based on either low cost or differentiation becomes increasingly attractive when the target market niche is big enough to be profitable and offers good growth potential, when it is costly or difficult for multisegment competitors to meet the specialized needs of the target market niche and at the same time satisfy the expectations of their mainstream customers, when there are one or more niches that present a good match for a focuser's resources and capabilities, and when few other rivals are attempting to specialize in the same target segment.

5. Best-cost strategies create competitive advantage by giving buyers *more value for the money*—delivering superior quality, features, performance, and/or service attributes while also beating customer expectations on price. To profitably employ a best-cost provider strategy, a company *must have the capability to incorporate*

attractive or upscale attributes at a lower cost than rivals. A best-cost provider strategy works best in markets with large numbers of value-conscious buyers desirous of purchasing better products and services for less money.

6. In all cases, competitive advantage depends on having competitively superior resources and capabilities that are a good fit for the chosen generic strategy. A sustainable advantage depends on maintaining that competitive superiority with resources, capabilities, and value chain activities that rivals have trouble matching and for which there are no good substitutes.

ASSURANCE OF LEARNING EXERCISES

LO 1, LO 2, LO 3, LO 4

1. Best Buy is the largest consumer electronics retailer in the United States, with 2015 sales of over $50 billion. The company competes aggressively on price with such rivals as Costco, Sam's Club, Walmart, and Target, but it is also known by consumers for its first-rate customer service. Best Buy customers have commented that the retailer's sales staff is exceptionally knowledgeable about the company's products and can direct them to the exact location of difficult-to-find items. Best Buy customers also appreciate that demonstration models of PC monitors, digital media players, and other electronics are fully powered and ready for in-store use. Best Buy's Geek Squad tech support and installation services are additional customer service features that are valued by many customers.

   How would you characterize Best Buy's competitive strategy? Should it be classified as a low-cost provider strategy? A differentiation strategy? A best-cost strategy? Explain your answer.

connect

LO 2

2. Illustration Capsule 5.1 discusses Amazon's low-cost position in the electronic commerce industry. Based on information provided in the capsule, explain how Amazon has built its low-cost advantage in the industry and why a low-cost provider strategy is well suited to the industry.

LO 1, LO 2, LO 3, LO 4

3. USAA is a Fortune 500 insurance and financial services company with 2014 annual sales exceeding $24 billion. The company was founded in 1922 by 25 Army officers who decided to insure each other's vehicles and continues to limit its membership to active-duty and retired military members, officer candidates, and adult children and spouses of military-affiliated USAA members. The company has received countless awards, including being listed among *Fortune*'s World's Most Admired Companies in 2014 and 2015 and 100 Best Companies to Work For in 2010 through 2015. USAA was also ranked as the number-one Bank, Credit Card, and Insurance Company by Forrester Research from 2013 to 2015. You can read more about the company's history and strategy at www.usaa.com.

   How would you characterize USAA's competitive strategy? Should it be classified as a low-cost provider strategy? A differentiation strategy? A best-cost strategy? Also, has the company chosen to focus on a narrow piece of the market, or does it appear to pursue a broad market approach? Explain your answer.

4. Explore lululemon athletica's website at info.lululemon.com and see if you can identify at least three ways in which the company seeks to differentiate itself from rival athletic apparel firms. Is there reason to believe that lululemon's differentiation strategy has been successful in producing a competitive advantage? Why or why not?

LO 3

EXERCISE FOR SIMULATION PARTICIPANTS

1. Which one of the five generic competitive strategies best characterizes your company's strategic approach to competing successfully?

    LO 1, LO 2, LO 3, LO 4

2. Which rival companies appear to be employing a low-cost provider strategy?
3. Which rival companies appear to be employing a broad differentiation strategy?
4. Which rival companies appear to be employing a best-cost provider strategy?
5. Which rival companies appear to be employing some type of focused strategy?
6. What is your company's action plan to achieve a sustainable competitive advantage over rival companies? List at least three (preferably more than three) specific kinds of decision entries on specific decision screens that your company has made or intends to make to win this kind of competitive edge over rivals.

ENDNOTES

[1] Michael E. Porter, *Competitive Strategy: Techniques for Analyzing Industries and Competitors* (New York: Free Press, 1980), chap. 2; Michael E. Porter, "What Is Strategy?" *Harvard Business Review* 74, no. 6 (November–December 1996).
[2] Michael E. Porter, *Competitive Advantage: Creating and Sustaining Superior Performance* (New York: Free Press, 1985).

[3] Richard L. Priem, "A Consumer Perspective on Value Creation," *Academy of Management Review* 32, no. 1 (2007), pp. 219–235.
[4] jrscience.wcp.muohio.edu/nsfall01/FinalArticles/Final-IsitWorthitBrandsan.html.
[5] D. Yoffie, "Cola Wars Continue: Coke and Pepsi in 2006," Harvard Business School case 9-706-447.

[6] Peter J. Williamson and Ming Zeng, "Value-for-Money Strategies for Recessionary Times," *Harvard Business Review* 87, no. 3 (March 2009), pp. 66–74.

Chapter 1

What Do We Mean by Leadership?

Introduction

In the spring of 1972, an airplane flew across the Andes mountains carrying its crew and 40 passengers. Most of the passengers were members of an amateur Uruguayan rugby team en route to a game in Chile. The plane never arrived. It crashed in snow-covered mountains, breaking into several pieces on impact. The main part of the fuselage slid like a toboggan down a steep valley, coming to rest in waist-deep snow. Although a number of people died immediately or within a day of the impact, the picture for the 28 survivors was not much better. The fuselage offered little protection from the extreme cold, food supplies were scant, and a number of passengers had serious injuries from the crash. Over the next few days, several surviving passengers became psychotic and several others died from their injuries. The passengers who were relatively uninjured set out to do what they could to improve their chances of survival.

Several worked on "weatherproofing" the wreckage; others found ways to get water; and those with medical training took care of the injured. Although shaken by the crash, the survivors initially were confident they would be found. These feelings gradually gave way to despair as search and rescue teams failed to find the wreckage. With the passing of several weeks and no sign of rescue in sight, the remaining passengers decided to mount expeditions to determine the best way to escape. The most physically fit were chosen to go on the expeditions because the thin mountain air and the deep snow made the trips difficult. The results of the trips were both frustrating and demoralizing: the expedition members determined they were in the middle of the Andes mountains, and walking out to find help was believed to be impossible. Just when the survivors thought nothing worse could possibly happen, an avalanche hit the wreckage and killed several more of them.

The remaining survivors concluded they would not be rescued, and their only hope was for someone to leave the wreckage and find help. Three of the fittest passengers were chosen for the final expedition, and everyone else's work was directed toward improving the expedition's chances of success. The three expedition members were given more food and were exempted from routine survival activities; the rest spent most of their energies securing supplies for the trip. Two months after the plane crash, the expedition members set out on their final attempt to find help. After hiking for 10 days through some of the most rugged terrain in the world, the expedition stumbled across a group of Chilean peasants tending cattle. One of the expedition members stated, "I come from a plane that fell in the mountains. I am Uruguayan . . ." Eventually 14 other survivors were rescued.

When the full account of their survival became known, it was not without controversy. It had required extreme and unsettling measures: the survivors had lived only by eating the flesh of their deceased comrades. Nonetheless, their story is one of the most moving survival dramas of all time, magnificently told by Piers Paul Read in *Alive*.[1] It is a story of tragedy and courage, and it is a story of leadership.

Perhaps a story of survival in the Andes is so far removed from everyday experience that it does not seem to hold any relevant lessons about leadership for you personally. But consider some of the basic issues the Andes survivors faced: tension between individual and group goals, dealing with the different needs and personalities of group members, and keeping hope alive in the face of adversity. These issues are not so different from those facing many groups we're a part of. We can also look at the Andes experience for examples of the emergence of informal leaders in groups. Before the flight, a boy named Parrado was awkward and shy, a "second-stringer" both athletically and socially. Nonetheless, this unlikely hero became the best loved and most respected among the survivors for his courage, optimism, fairness, and emotional support. Persuasiveness in group decision making also was an important part of leadership among the Andes survivors. During the difficult discussions preceding the agonizing decision to survive on the flesh of their deceased comrades, one of the rugby players made his reasoning clear: "I know that if my dead body could help you stay alive, then I would want you to use it. In fact, if I do die and you don't eat me, then I'll come back from wherever I am and give you a good kick in the ass."[2]

Lives of great men all remind us
We can make our lives sublime
And, departing, leave behind us
Footprints on the sands of time.
Henry Wadsworth Longfellow

What Is Leadership?

The Andes story and the experiences of many other leaders we'll introduce to you in a series of profiles sprinkled throughout the chapters provide numerous examples of leadership. But just what *is* leadership?

4 Part One *Leadership Is a Process, Not a Position*

People who do research on leadership disagree more than you might think about what leadership really is. Most of this disagreement stems from the fact that **leadership** is a complex phenomenon involving the leader, the followers, and the situation. Some leadership researchers have focused on the personality, physical traits, or behaviors of the leader; others have studied the relationships between leaders and followers; still others have studied how aspects of the situation affect how leaders act. Some have extended the latter viewpoint so far as to suggest there is no such thing as leadership; they argue that organizational successes and failures often get falsely attributed to the leader, but the situation may have a much greater impact on how the organization functions than does any individual, including the leader.[3]

Perhaps the best way for you to begin to understand the complexities of leadership is to see some of the ways leadership has been defined. Leadership researchers have defined leadership in many different ways:

- The process by which an agent induces a subordinate to behave in a desired manner.[4]
- Directing and coordinating the work of group members.[5]
- An interpersonal relation in which others comply because they want to, not because they have to.[6]
- The process of influencing an organized group toward accomplishing its goals.[7]
- Actions that focus resources to create desirable opportunities.[8]
- Creating conditions for a team to be effective.[9]
- The ability to get results and the ability to build teams; these represent the what and the how of leadership.[10]
- A complex form of social problem solving.[11]

As you can see, definitions of leadership differ in many ways, and these differences have resulted in various researchers exploring disparate aspects of leadership. For example, if we were to apply these definitions to the Andes survival scenario described earlier, some researchers would focus on the behaviors Parrado used to keep up the morale of the survivors. Researchers who define leadership as influencing an organized group toward accomplishing its goals would examine how Parrado managed to convince the group to stage and support the final expedition. One's definition of leadership might also influence just *who* is considered an appropriate leader for study. Thus each group of researchers might focus on a different aspect of leadership, and each would tell a different story regarding the leader, the followers, and the situation.

Although having many leadership definitions may seem confusing, it is important to understand that there is no single correct definition. The various definitions can help us appreciate the multitude of factors that affect leadership, as well as different perspectives from which to view it. For example, in the first definition just listed, the word *subordinate* seems to confine leadership to downward influence in hierarchical relationships; it seems to exclude informal leadership. The second definition emphasizes the directing and controlling aspects of leadership, and thereby may deemphasize emotional aspects of leadership. The emphasis placed in the third definition on subordinates' "wanting to" comply with a leader's wishes seems to exclude any kind of coercion as a leadership tool. Further, it becomes problematic to identify ways in which a leader's actions are really leadership if subordinates voluntarily comply when a leader with considerable potential coercive power merely asks others to do something without explicitly threatening them. Similarly, a key reason behind using the phrase *desirable opportunities* in one of the definitions was precisely to distinguish between leadership and tyranny. And partly because there are many different definitions of leadership, there is also a wide range of individuals we consider leaders. In addition to stories about leaders and leadership we will sprinkle through this book, we will highlight several in each chapter in a series of Profiles in Leadership. The first of these is Profiles in Leadership 1.1, which highlights Peter Jackson.

All considered, we find that defining leadership as "the process of influencing an organized group toward accomplishing its goals" is fairly comprehensive and helpful. Several implications of this definition are worth further examination.

Leadership Is Both a Science and an Art

Saying leadership is both a science and an art emphasizes the subject of leadership as a field of scholarly inquiry, as well as certain aspects of the practice of leadership. The scope of the science of leadership is reflected in the number of studies—approximately 8,000—cited in an authoritative reference work, *Bass & Stogdill's Handbook of Leadership: Theory, Research, and Managerial Applications.*[12] However, being an expert on leadership research is neither necessary nor sufficient for being a good leader. Some managers may be effective leaders without ever having taken a course or training program in leadership, and some scholars in the field of leadership may be relatively poor leaders themselves.

However, knowing something about leadership research is relevant to leadership effectiveness. Scholarship may not be a prerequisite for leadership effectiveness, but understanding some of the major research findings can help individuals better analyze situations using a variety of perspectives. That, in turn, can tell leaders how to be more effective. Even so, because skills in analyzing and responding to situations vary greatly across leaders, leadership will always remain partly an art as well as a science.

Any fool can keep a rule. God gave him a brain to know when to break the rule.
General Willard W. Scott

6   Part One   *Leadership Is a Process, Not a Position*

Peter Jackson

PROFILES IN LEADERSHIP 1.1

When Peter Jackson read *The Lord of the Rings* trilogy at the age of 18, he couldn't wait until it was made into a movie; 20 years later he made that movie himself. In 2004 *The Lord of the Rings: The Return of the King* took home 11 Academy Awards, winning the Oscar in every category for which it was nominated. This tied the record for the most Oscars ever earned by one motion picture. Such an achievement might seem unlikely for a producer/director whose film debut was titled *Bad Taste,* which it and subsequent works exemplified in spades. Peter Jackson made horror movies so grisly and revolting that his fans nicknamed him the "Sultan of Splatter." Nonetheless, his talent was evident to discerning eyes—at least among horror film aficionados. *Bad Taste* was hailed as a cult classic at the Cannes Film Festival, and horror fans tabbed Jackson as a talent to follow.

When screenwriter Costa Botes heard that *The Lord of the Rings* would be made into a live action film, he thought those responsible were crazy. Prevailing wisdom was that the fantastic and complex trilogy simply could not be believably translated onto the screen. But he also believed that "there was no other director on earth who could do it justice" (Botes, 2004). And do it justice he obviously did. What was it about the "Sultan of Splatter's" leader-

ship that gave others such confidence in his ability to make one of the biggest and best movies of all time? What gave him the confidence to even try? And what made others want to share in his vision?

Peter Jackson's effectiveness as a leader has been due in large part to a unique combination of personal qualities and talents. One associate, for example, called him "one of the smartest people I know," as well as a maverick willing to buck the establishment. Jackson is also a tireless worker whose early successes were due in no small part to the combination of his ambition and dogged perseverance (Botes, 2004). His initial success was driven largely by his budding genius in making films on a low budget and with virtually no other staff. In reading others' comments who worked with him on the *LOTR* project, however, it's clear that his leadership continued to develop over the years. It was his ability to communicate a shared vision and inspire such extraordinary work from an incredibly large staff that made *LOTR* so spectacularly successful.

Not one to rest on his laurels, in 2012 Jackson released the first installment of *The Hobbit*, another technologically standard-breaking and popular film trilogy.

Source: Adapted from Costa Botes, *Made in New Zealand: The Cinema of Peter Jackson,* NZEDGE.com, May 2004.

Highlight 1.1 provides further perspective on how the art and science of leadership are represented in somewhat distinctive research traditions.

> *A democracy cannot follow a leader unless he is dramatized. A man to be a hero must not content himself with heroic virtues and anonymous action. He must talk and explain as he acts—drama.*
>
> **William Allen White, American writer and editor,** *Emporia Gazette*

Leadership Is Both Rational and Emotional

Leadership involves both the rational and emotional sides of human experience. Leadership includes actions and influences based on reason and logic as well as those based on inspiration and passion. We do not want to cultivate merely intellectualized leaders who respond with only logical predictability. Because people differ in their thoughts and feelings, hopes and dreams, needs and fears, goals and ambitions, and strengths and weaknesses, leadership situations can be complex. People are both rational and emotional, so leaders can use rational techniques and emotional appeals to influence followers, but they must also weigh the rational and emotional consequences of their actions.

The Academic and Troubadour Traditions of Leadership Research

HIGHLIGHT 1.1

On a practical level, leadership is a topic that almost everyone is interested in at one time or another. People have a vested interest in who is running their government, schools, company, or church, and because of this interest thousands of books and articles have been written about the topic of leadership. Curphy and Hogan believe these works can be divided into two major camps. The **academic tradition** consists of articles that use data and statistical techniques to make inferences about effective leadership. Because the academic tradition is research based, for the most part these findings are written for other leadership researchers and are virtually uninterpretable to leadership *practitioners*. As such, leadership practitioners are often unfamiliar with the research findings of the academic tradition.

The second camp of leadership literature is the **troubadour tradition.** These books and articles often consist of nothing more than the opinions or score-settling reminiscences of former leaders. Books in the troubadour tradition, such as *Who Moved My Cheese?, What the CEO Wants You to Know, Winning,* and *Lead Like Jesus: Lessons from the Greatest Leadership Role Model of all Time,* are wildly popular, but it is difficult to separate fact from fiction or determine whether these opinions translate to other settings. People who are unfamiliar with the findings of the academic tradition and the limitations of the troubadour tradition find it difficult to differentiate research findings from opinion.

Perhaps the biggest challenge to improving the practice of leadership is to give practitioners timely, easily digestible, research-grounded advice on how to effectively lead others. The knowledge accumulated from 90 years of leadership research is of tremendous value, yet scientists have paid little attention to the ultimate consumers of their work—leaders and leaders-to-be. Leadership practitioners often want fast answers about how to be more effective or successful and understandably turn to popular books and articles that *appear* to provide timely answers to their practical concerns. Unfortunately, however, the claims in the popular literature are rarely based on sound research; they oversimplify the complexities of the leadership process; and many times they actually offer bad advice. Relatively little weight is given to well-researched leadership studies, primarily because the arcane requirements of publishing articles in scholarly journals make their content virtually unreadable (and certainly uninteresting) to actual leadership practitioners. One of the primary objectives of this book is to make the results of leadership research more usable for leaders and leaders-to-be.

Sources: G. J. Curphy, M. J. Benson, A. Baldrica, and R. T. Hogan, *Managerial Incompetence* (unpublished manuscript, 2007); G. J. Curphy, "*What We Really Know about Leadership (But Seem Unwilling to Implement)*" (presentation given to the Minnesota Professionals for Psychology and Applied Work, Minneapolis, MN, January 2004); R. T. Hogan, *Personality and the Fate of Organizations* (Mahwah, NJ: Lawrence Erlbaum Associates, 2007).

A full appreciation of leadership involves looking at both these sides of human nature. Good leadership is more than just calculation and planning, or following a checklist, even though rational analysis can enhance good leadership. Good leadership also involves touching others' feelings; emotions play an important role in leadership too. Just one example of this is the civil rights movement of the 1960s, which was based on emotions as well as on principles. Dr. Martin Luther King Jr. inspired many people to action; he touched people's hearts as well as their heads.

Aroused feelings, however, can be used either positively or negatively, constructively or destructively. Some leaders have been able to inspire others to deeds of great purpose and courage. On the other hand, as images of Adolf Hitler's mass rallies or present-day angry mobs attest, group frenzy can readily become group mindlessness. As another example, emotional appeals by the Reverend Jim Jones resulted in approximately 800 of his followers volitionally committing suicide.

The mere presence of a group (even without heightened emotional levels) can also cause people to act differently than when they are alone. For example, in airline cockpit crews, there are clear lines of authority from the captain down to the first officer (second in command) and so on. So strong are the norms surrounding the authority of the captain that some first officers will not take control of the airplane from the captain even in the event of impending disaster. Foushee[13] reported a study wherein airline captains in simulator training intentionally feigned incapacitation so the response of the rest of the crew could be observed. The feigned incapacitations occurred at a predetermined point during the plane's final approach in landing, and the simulation involved conditions of poor weather and visibility. Approximately 25 percent of the first officers in these simulated flights allowed the plane to crash. For some reason, the first officers did not take control even when it was clear the captain was allowing the aircraft to deviate from the parameters of a safe approach. This example demonstrates how group dynamics can influence the behavior of group members even when emotional levels are *not* high. (Believe it or not, airline crews are so well trained that this is *not* an emotional situation.) In sum, it should be apparent that leadership involves followers' feelings and nonrational behavior as well as rational behavior. Leaders need to consider *both* the rational and the emotional consequences of their actions.

Leadership and Management

In trying to answer "What is leadership?" it is natural to look at the relationship between leadership and management. To many, the word **management** suggests words like *efficiency, planning, paperwork, procedures, regulations, control,* and *consistency.* Leadership is often more associated with words like *risk taking, dynamic, creativity, change,* and *vision.* Some say leadership is fundamentally a value-choosing, and thus a value-laden, activity, whereas management is not. Leaders are thought to *do the right things,* whereas managers are thought to *do things right.*[14,15] Here are some other distinctions between managers and leaders:[16]

If you want some ham, you gotta go into the smokehouse.

Huey Long, governor of Louisiana, 1928–1932

- Managers administer; leaders innovate.
- Managers maintain; leaders develop.
- Managers control; leaders inspire.

- Managers have a short-term view; leaders, a long-term view.
- Managers ask how and when; leaders ask what and why.
- Managers imitate; leaders originate.
- Managers accept the status quo; leaders challenge it.

Zaleznik[17] goes so far as to say these differences reflect fundamentally different personality types: leaders and managers are basically different kinds of people. He says some people are managers *by nature;* other people are leaders *by nature.* One is not better than the other; they are just different. Their differences, in fact, can be useful because organizations typically need both functions performed well. For example, consider again the U.S. civil rights movement in the 1960s. Dr. Martin Luther King Jr. gave life and direction to the civil rights movement in America. He gave dignity and hope of freer participation in national life to people who before had little reason to expect it. He inspired the world with his vision and eloquence, and he changed the way we live together. America is a different nation today because of him. Was Dr. Martin Luther King Jr. a leader? Of course. Was he a manager? Somehow that does not seem to fit, and the civil rights movement might have failed if it had not been for the managerial talents of his supporting staff. Leadership and management complement each other, and both are vital to organizational success.

With regard to the issue of leadership versus management, the authors of this book take a middle-of-the-road position. We think of leadership and management as closely related but distinguishable functions. Our view of the relationship is depicted in Figure 1.1, which shows leadership and management as two overlapping functions. Although some functions performed by leaders and managers may be unique, there is also an area of overlap. In reading Highlight 1.2, do you see more good management in the response to the 1906 San Francisco earthquake, more good leadership, or both?

FIGURE 1.1
Leadership and Management Overlap

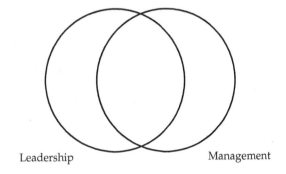

Leadership   Management

The Response of Leadership to a Natural Disaster

HIGHLIGHT 1.2

Much has been written about the inadequate response of local, state, and federal agencies to Hurricane Katrina. It may be instructive to compare the response of government agencies to a natural disaster on a different coast a century earlier: the San Francisco earthquake and fire of 1906.

While the precipitant disaster was the earthquake itself, much destruction resulted from the consequent fire, one disaster aggravating the impact of the other. Because of the earthquake, utility poles throughout the city fell, taking the high-tension wires they were carrying with them. Gas pipes broke; chimneys fell, dropping hot coals into thousands of gallons of gas spilled by broken fuel tanks; stoves and heaters in homes toppled over; and in moments fires erupted across the city. And because the earthquake's first tremors also broke water pipes throughout the city, fire hydrants everywhere suddenly went dry, making fighting the fires virtually impossible. In objective terms, the disaster is estimated to have killed as many as 3,000 people, rendered more than 200,000 homeless, and by some measures caused $195 billion in property loss as measured by today's dollars.

How did authorities respond to the crisis when there were far fewer agencies with presumed response plans to combat disasters, and when high-tech communication methods were unheard of? Consider these two examples:

- The ranking officer assigned to a U.S. Army post in San Francisco was away when the earthquake struck, so it was up to his deputy to help organize the army's and federal government's response. The deputy immediately cabled Washington, D.C., requesting tents, rations, and medicine. Secretary of War William Howard Taft, who would become the next U.S. president, responded by immediately dispatching 200,000 rations from Washington State. In a matter of days, every tent in the U.S. Army had been sent to San Francisco, and the longest hospital train in history was dispatched from Virginia.

- Perhaps the most impressive example of leadership initiative in the face of the 1906 disaster was that of the U.S. Post Office. It recovered its ability to function in short order without losing a single item that was being handled when the earthquake struck. And because the earthquake had effectively destroyed the city's telegraphic connection (telegrams inside the city were temporarily being delivered by the post office), a critical question arose: How could people struck by the disaster communicate with their families elsewhere? The city postmaster immediately announced that all citizens of San Francisco could use the post office to inform their families and loved ones of their condition and needs. He further stipulated that for outgoing private letters *it would not matter whether the envelopes bore stamps.* This was what was needed: Circumstances demanded that people be able to communicate with friends and family whether or not they could find or pay for stamps.

Perhaps this should remind us that modern leadership is not necessarily better leadership, and that leadership in government is not always bureaucratic and can be both humane and innovative.

Source: Adapted from S. Winchester, *A Crack in the Edge of the World: America and the Great California Earthquake of 1906* (New York: Harper Perennial, 2006).

The Romance of Leadership

HIGHLIGHT 1.3

This text is predicated on the idea that leaders can make a difference. Interestingly, though, while businesspeople generally agree, not all scholars do.

People in the business world attribute much of a company's success or failure to its leadership. One study counted the number of articles appearing in *The Wall Street Journal* that dealt with leadership and found nearly 10 percent of the articles about representative target companies addressed that company's leadership. Furthermore, there was a significant positive relationship between company performance and the number of articles about its leadership; the more a company's leadership was emphasized in *The Wall Street Journal,* the better the company was doing. This might mean the more a company takes leadership seriously (as reflected by the emphasis in *The Wall Street Journal*), the better it does.

However, the study authors were skeptical about the real utility of leadership as a concept.

They suggested leadership is merely a romanticized notion—an obsession people want and need to believe in. Belief in the potency of leadership may be a cultural myth that has utility primarily insofar as it affects how people create meaning about causal events in complex social systems. The behavior of leaders, the authors contend, does not account for much of the variance in an organization's performance. Nonetheless, people seem strongly committed to a basic faith that individual leaders shape organizational destiny for good or ill.

As you read this book and come to appreciate how many factors affect a group's success *besides* the talents of the individual leader, you might pay a price for that understanding. As you appreciate the *complexity* of leadership more, the *romance* of leadership might slightly diminish.

Source: J. R. Meindl, S. B. Ehrlich, and J. M. Dukerich, "The Romance of Leadership," *Administrative Science Quarterly* 30 (1985), pp. 78–102.

Leadership Myths

Few things pose a greater obstacle to leadership development than certain unsubstantiated and self-limiting beliefs about leadership. Therefore, before we begin examining leadership and leadership development in more detail, we will consider what they are not. We will examine several beliefs (we call them myths) that stand in the way of fully understanding and developing leadership.

Myth: Good Leadership Is All Common Sense

At face value, this myth says one needs only common sense to be a good leader. It also implies, however, that most if not all of the studies of leadership reported in scholarly journals and books only confirm what anyone with common sense already knows.

The problem, of course, is with the ambiguous term *common sense*. It implies a common body of practical knowledge about life that virtually any reasonable person with moderate experience has acquired. A simple experiment, however, may convince you that common sense may be less common than you think. Ask a few friends or acquaintances whether the old folk wisdom "Absence makes the heart grow fonder" is true or false. Most will say it is true. After that ask a different group whether the old folk wisdom "Out of sight, out of mind" is true or false. Most of that group will answer true as well, even though the two proverbs are contradictory.

A similar thing sometimes happens when people hear about the results of studies concerning human behavior. On hearing the results, people may say, "Who needed a study to learn that? I knew it all the time." However, several experiments[18,19] showed that events were much more surprising when subjects had to guess the outcome of an experiment than when subjects were told the outcome. What seems obvious after you know the results and what you (or anyone else) would have predicted beforehand are not the same thing. Hindsight is always 20/20.

The point might become clearer with a specific example; read the following paragraph:

> After World War II, the U.S. Army spent enormous sums of money on studies only to reach conclusions that, many believed, should have been apparent at the outset. One, for example, was that southern soldiers were better able to stand the climate in the hot South Sea islands than northern soldiers were.

This sounds reasonable, but there is a problem: the statement here is exactly contrary to the actual findings. Southerners were no better than northerners in adapting to tropical climates.[20] Common sense can often play tricks on us.

Put a little differently, one challenge of understanding leadership may be to know when common sense applies and when it does not. Do leaders need to act confidently? Of course. But they also need to be humble enough to recognize that others' views are useful, too. Do leaders need to persevere when times get tough? Yes. But they also need to recognize when times change and a new direction is called for. If leadership were nothing more than common sense, there should be few, if any, problems in the workplace. However, we venture to guess you have noticed more than a few problems between leaders and followers. Effective leadership must be something more than just common sense.

If you miss seven balls out of ten, you're batting three hundred and that's good enough for the Hall of Fame. You can't score if you keep the bat on your shoulder.
Walter B. Wriston, chairman of Citicorp, 1970–1984

Myth: Leaders Are Born, Not Made

Some people believe being a leader is either in one's genes or not; others believe that life experiences mold the individual and that no one is born a leader. Which view is right? In a sense, both and neither. Both views are right in that innate factors as well as formative experiences influence many sorts of behavior, including leadership. Yet both views are wrong to the extent they imply leadership is *either* innate *or* acquired; what matters more is how these factors *interact*. It does not seem useful, we believe, to think of the world as composed of two mutually exclusive types of people, leaders and nonleaders. It is more useful to address how each person can make the most of leadership opportunities he or she faces.

It may be easier to see the pointlessness of asking whether leaders are born or made by looking at an alternative question of far less popular interest: Are *college professors* born or made? Conceptually the issues are the same, and here too the answer is that every college professor is both born *and* made. It seems clear enough that college professors are partly "born" because (among other factors) there is a genetic component to intelligence, and intelligence surely plays some part in becoming a college professor (well, at least a *minor* part!). But every college professor is also partly "made." One obvious way is that college professors must have advanced education in specialized fields; even with the right genes one could not become a college professor without certain requisite experiences. Becoming a college professor depends partly on what one is born with and partly on how that inheritance is shaped through experience. The same is true of leadership.

More specifically, research indicates that many cognitive abilities and personality traits are at least partly innate.[21] Thus natural talents or characteristics may offer certain advantages or disadvantages to a leader. Consider physical characteristics: A man's above-average height may increase others' tendency to think of him as a leader; it may also boost his own self-confidence. But it doesn't make him a leader. The same holds true for psychological characteristics that seem related to leadership. The stability of certain characteristics over long periods (for example, at school reunions people seem to have kept the same personalities we remember them as having years earlier) may reinforce the impression that our basic natures are fixed, but different environments nonetheless may nurture or suppress different leadership qualities.

Never reveal all of yourself to other people; hold back something in reserve so that people are never quite sure if they really know you.
Michael Korda, author, editor

Myth: The Only School You Learn Leadership from Is the School of Hard Knocks

Some people skeptically question whether leadership can develop through formal study, believing instead it can be acquired only through actual experience. It is a mistake, however, to think of formal study and learning from experience as mutually exclusive or antagonistic. In fact, they complement each other. Rather than ask whether leadership develops from formal study or from real-life experience, it is better to ask what kind of study will help students learn to discern critical lessons about leadership from their own experience. Approaching the issue in such a way recognizes the vital role of experience in leadership development, but it also admits that certain kinds of study and training can improve a person's ability to discern important lessons about leadership

Progress always involves risks. You can't steal second base and keep your foot on first.
Frederick B. Wilcox

from experience. It can, in other words, accelerate the process of learning from experience.

We argue that one advantage of formally studying leadership is that formal study provides students with a variety of ways of examining a particular leadership situation. By studying the different ways researchers have defined and examined leadership, students can use these definitions and theories to better understand what is going on in any leadership situation. For example, earlier in this chapter we used three different leadership definitions as a framework for describing or analyzing the situation facing Parrado and the survivors of the plane crash, and each definition focused on a different aspect of leadership. These frameworks can similarly be applied to better understand the experiences one has as both a leader and a follower. We think it is difficult for leaders, particularly novice leaders, to examine leadership situations from multiple perspectives; but we also believe developing this skill can help you become a better leader. Being able to analyze your experiences from multiple perspectives may be the greatest single contribution a formal course in leadership can give you. Maybe you can reflect on your own leadership over a cup of coffee in Starbucks as you read about the origins of that company in Profiles in Leadership 1.2.

Howard Schultz

PROFILES IN LEADERSHIP 1.2

Starbucks began in 1971 as a very different company than we know it as today. The difference is due in large part to the way its former CEO, Howard Schultz, reframed the kind of business Starbucks should be. Schultz joined Starbucks in 1981 to head its marketing and retail store operations. While on a trip to Italy in 1983, Schultz was amazed by the number and variety of espresso bars there—1,500 in the city of Turin alone. He concluded that the Starbucks stores in Seattle had missed the point: *Starbucks should be not just a store but an experience—a gathering place.*

Everything looks clearer in hindsight, of course, but the Starbucks owners resisted Schultz's vision; Starbucks was a retailer, they insisted, not a restaurant or bar. Schultz's strategic reframing of the Starbucks opportunity was ultimately vindicated when—after having departed Starbucks to pursue the same idea with another company—Schultz had the opportunity to purchase the whole Starbucks operation in Seattle, including its name.

Despite today's pervasiveness of Starbucks across the world, however, and the seeming obviousness of Schultz's exemplary leadership, the Starbucks story has not been one of completely consistent success. After Schultz retired as Starbucks CEO when it was a global megabrand, the company's performance suffered to the point Schultz complained that it was "losing its soul." He was asked to return as CEO in 2008 and has tried to resurrect Starbucks by bringing new attention to the company's operating efficiency and by admitting, in effect, that some of his own earlier instinctive approach to company strategy and management would no longer be sufficient for the new global scale of Starbucks operation. In fact, Schultz discovered the challenges and the road to recovery even more daunting than he expected. Leadership—even for one with a proven track record—is never easy.

The Interactional Framework for Analyzing Leadership

Perhaps the first researcher to formally recognize the importance of the leader, follower, and situation in the leadership process was Fred Fiedler.[22] Fiedler used these three components to develop his contingency model of leadership, a theory of leadership that will be discussed in more detail in Chapter 13. Although we recognize Fiedler's contributions, we owe perhaps even more to Hollander's[23] transactional approach to leadership. We call our approach the **interactional framework.**

Several aspects of this derivative of Hollander's approach are worthy of additional comment. First, as shown in Figure 1.2, the framework depicts leadership as a function of three elements—the **leader,** the **followers,** and the **situation.** Second, a particular leadership scenario can be examined using each level of analysis separately. Although this is a useful way to understand the leadership process, we can understand the process even better if we also examine the **interactions** among the three elements, or lenses, represented by the overlapping areas in the figure. For example, we can better understand the leadership process if we not only look at the leaders and the followers but also examine how leaders and followers affect each other in the leadership process. Similarly, we can examine the leader and the situation separately, but we can gain even further understanding of the leadership process by looking at how the situation can constrain or facilitate a leader's actions and how the leader can change different aspects of the situation to be more effective. Thus a final important aspect of the framework is that leadership is the result of a complex set of interactions among the leader, the followers, and the situation. These complex interactions may be why broad generalizations about leadership are problematic: many factors influence the leadership process (see Highlight 1.3 on page 11).

FIGURE 1.2
An Interactional Framework for Analyzing Leadership

Source: Adapted from E. P. Hollander, *Leadership Dynamics: A Practical Guide to Effective Relationships* (New York: Free Press, 1978).

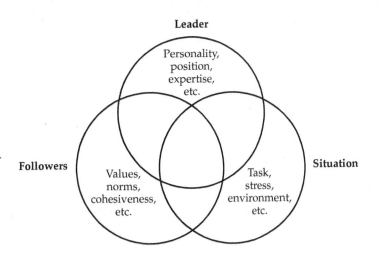

An example of one such complex interaction between leaders and followers is evident in what have been called in-groups and out-groups. Sometimes there is a high degree of mutual influence and attraction between the leader and a few subordinates. These subordinates belong to the **in-group** and can be distinguished by their high degree of loyalty, commitment, and trust felt toward the leader. Other subordinates belong to the **out-group.** Leaders have considerably more influence with in-group followers than with out-group followers. However, this greater degree of influence has a price. If leaders rely primarily on their formal authority to influence their followers (especially if they punish them), then leaders risk losing the high levels of loyalty and commitment followers feel toward them.[24]

The Leader

This element examines primarily what the leader brings *as an individual* to the leadership equation. This can include unique personal history, interests, character traits, and motivation.

Leaders are *not* all alike, but they tend to share many characteristics. Research has shown that leaders differ from their followers, and effective leaders differ from ineffective leaders, on various personality traits, cognitive abilities, skills, and values.[25-30] Another way personality can affect leadership is through temperament, by which we mean whether a leader is generally calm or is instead prone to emotional outbursts. Leaders who have calm dispositions and do not attack or belittle others for bringing bad news are more likely to get complete and timely information from subordinates than are bosses who have explosive tempers and a reputation for killing the messenger.

Another important aspect of the leader is how he or she achieved leader status. Leaders who are appointed by superiors may have less credibility with subordinates and get less loyalty from them than leaders who are elected or emerge by consensus from the ranks of followers. Often emergent or elected officials are better able to influence a group toward goal achievement because of the power conferred on them by their followers. However, both elected and emergent leaders need to be sensitive to their constituencies if they wish to remain in power.

More generally, a leader's experience or history in a particular organization is usually important to her or his effectiveness. For example, leaders promoted from within an organization, by virtue of being familiar with its culture and policies, may be ready to "hit the job running." In addition, leaders selected from within an organization are typically better known by others in the organization than are leaders selected from the outside. That is likely to affect, for better or worse, the latitude others in the organization are willing to give the leader; if the leader is widely respected for a history of accomplishment, she may be given more latitude than a newcomer whose track record is less well known. On the other hand, many people tend to give new leaders a fair chance to succeed, and newcomers to an organization often take time to learn the organization's informal rules, norms, and "ropes" before they make any radical or potentially controversial decisions.

A leader's legitimacy also may be affected by the extent to which followers participated in the leader's selection. When followers have had a say in the selection or election of a leader, they tend to have a heightened sense of psychological identification with her, but they also may have higher expectations and make more demands on her.[31] We also might wonder what kind of support a leader has from his own boss. If followers sense their boss has a lot of influence with the higher-ups, subordinates

"I'll be blunt, coach. I'm having a problem with this 'take a lap' thing of yours . . ."

18   Part One   *Leadership Is a Process, Not a Position*

I must follow the people. Am I not their leader?

Benjamin Disraeli, 19th-century British prime minister

The crowd will follow a leader who marches twenty steps in advance; but if he is a thousand steps in front of them, they do not see and do not follow him.

Georg Brandes

may be reluctant to take their complaints to higher levels. On the other hand, if the boss has little influence with higher-ups, subordinates may be more likely to make complaints to these levels.

The foregoing examples highlight the sorts of insights we can gain about leadership by focusing on the individual leader as a level of analysis. Even if we were to examine the individual leader completely, however, our understanding of the leadership process would be incomplete.

The Followers

Followers are a critical part of the leadership equation, but their role has not always been appreciated, at least in empirical research (but read Highlight 1.4 to see how the role of followers has been recognized in literature). For a long time, in fact, "the common view of leadership was that leaders actively led and subordinates, later called followers, passively and obediently followed."[32] Over time, especially in the last century, social change shaped people's views of followers, and leadership theories gradually recognized the active and important role that followers play in the leadership process.[33] Today it seems natural to accept the important role

The *First* Band of Brothers

HIGHLIGHT 1.4

Many of you probably have seen, or at least heard of, the award-winning series *Band of Brothers* that followed a company of the famous 101st Airborne division during World War II. You may not be aware that an earlier band of brothers was made famous by William Shakespeare in his play *Henry V*.

In one of the most famous speeches by any of Shakespeare's characters, the young Henry V tried to unify his followers when their daring expedition to conquer France was failing. French soldiers followed Henry's army along the rivers, daring them to cross over and engage the French in battle. Just before the battle of Agincourt, Henry's rousing words rallied his vastly outnumbered, weary, and tattered troops to victory. Few words of oratory have ever better bonded a leader with his followers than Henry's call for unity among "we few, we happy few, we band of brothers."

Hundreds of years later, Henry's speech is still a powerful illustration of a leader who emphasized the importance of his followers. Modern leadership concepts like vision, charisma, relationship orientation, and empowerment are readily evident

in Henry's interactions with his followers. Here are the closing lines of Henry's famous speech:

> *From this day to the ending of the world,*
> *But we in it shall be remembered—*
> *We few, we happy few, we band of brothers;*
> *For he today that sheds his blood with me*
> *Shall be my brother; be he ne'er so vile,*
> *This day shall gentle his condition;*
> *And gentlemen in England now-a-bed*
> *Shall think themselves accurs'd they were not here,*
> *And hold their manhoods cheap whiles any speaks*
> *That fought with us upon Saint Crispin's day.*

Shakespeare's insights into the complexities of leadership should remind us that while modern research helps enlighten our understanding, it does not represent the only, and certainly not the most moving, perspective on leadership to which we should pay attention.

Source: N. Warner, "Screening Leadership through Shakespeare: Paradoxes of Leader–Follower Relations in *Henry V* on Film," *The Leadership Quarterly* 18 (2007), pp. 1–15.

A Student's Perspective on Leadership and Followership

HIGHLIGHT 1.5

Krista Kleiner, a student at Claremont-McKenna College and active in its Kravis Leadership Institute, has offered these reflections on the importance for both students and college administrators of taking seriously the opportunities provided in the classroom for developing leadership and followership skills.

She notes that the admissions process to college (as well, we might add, as postcollege job searches) typically places significant emphasis on a person's leadership experience and abilities. Usually this is reflected in something like a list of "leadership positions held." Unfortunately, however, this system tends to overemphasize the mere acquisition of leadership titles and pays insufficient attention to the domain that is the most central and common element of student life: the classroom learning environment. Outstanding learning, she argues, is to a significant degree a collaborative experience between the formal leader (the teacher) and the informal followers (the students). The learning experience is directly enhanced by the degree to which effective participation by students contributes to their classroom groups, and this requires good leadership and good followership. The quality of one's contribution to the group could be

assessed via peer surveys, the results of which would be made available to the teacher. The surveys would assess dimensions of student contributions like these:

- Which students displayed particularly helpful leadership in work groups you participated in, and what did they do that was effective?

- Which students displayed particularly helpful followership in work groups you participated in that supported or balanced the leadership that emerged in the group or that was helpful to fellow group members?

- How have you contributed to the learning experience of your peers through your leadership–followership role in the classroom? How have you grown as a constructive leader and constructive follower through these experiences?

We hope these ideas challenge you to be a leader in your own student life and especially in this leadership course.

Source: K. Kleiner, "Rethinking Leadership and Followership: A Student's Perspective," in R. Riggio, I. Chaleff, and J. Lipman-Blumen (eds.), *The Art of Followership: How Great Followers Create Great Leaders and Organizations* (San Francisco: Jossey-Bass, 2008), pp. 89–93.

All men have some weak points, and the more vigorous and brilliant a person may be, the more strongly these weak points stand out. It is highly desirable, even essential, therefore, for the more influential members of a general's staff not to be too much like the general.

Major General Hugo Baron von Freytag-Loringhoven, anti-Hitler conspirator

followers play. Highlight 1.5 suggests some interesting interactions between leadership and followership in an arena familiar to you.

One aspect of our text's definition of leadership is particularly worth noting in this regard: Leadership is a social influence process shared among *all* members of a group. Leadership is not restricted to the influence exerted by someone in a particular position or role; followers are part of the leadership process, too. In recent years both practitioners and scholars have emphasized the relatedness of leadership and **followership.** As Burns[34] observed, the idea of "one-man leadership" is a contradiction in terms.

Obvious as this point may seem, it is also clear that early leadership researchers paid relatively little attention to the roles followers play in the leadership process.[35,36] However, we know that the followers' expectations, personality traits, maturity levels, levels of competence, and motivation affect the leadership process too. Highlight 1.6 describes a systematic approach to classifying different kinds of followers that has had a major impact on research.[37-40]

Followership Styles

HIGHLIGHT 1.6

The concept of different styles of leadership is reasonably familiar, but the idea of different styles of followership is relatively new. The very word *follower* has a negative connotation to many, evoking ideas of people who behave like sheep and need to be told what to do. Robert Kelley, however, believes that followers, rather than representing the antithesis of leadership, are best viewed as collaborators with leaders in the work of organizations.

Kelley believes that different types of followers can be described in terms of two broad dimensions. One of them ranges from **independent, critical thinking** at one end to **dependent, uncritical thinking** on the other end. According to Kelley, the best followers think for themselves and offer constructive advice or even creative solutions. The worst followers need to be told what to do. Kelley's other dimension ranges from whether people are **active followers** or **passive followers** in the extent to which they are engaged in work. According to Kelley, the best followers are self-starters who take initiative for themselves, whereas the worst followers are passive, may even dodge responsibility, and need constant supervision.

Using these two dimensions, Kelley has suggested five basic styles of followership:

1. *Alienated followers* habitually point out all the negative aspects of the organization to others. While alienated followers may see themselves as mavericks who have a healthy skepticism of the organization, leaders often see them as cynical, negative, and adversarial.

2. *Conformist followers* are the "yes people" of organizations. While very active at doing the organization's work, they can be dangerous if their orders contradict societal standards of behavior or organizational policy. Often this style is the result of either the demanding and authoritarian style of the leader or the overly rigid structure of the organization.

3. *Pragmatist followers* are rarely committed to their group's work goals, but they have learned not to make waves. Because they do not like to stick out, pragmatists tend to be mediocre performers who can clog the arteries of many organizations. Because it can be difficult to discern just where they stand on issues, they present an ambiguous image with both positive and negative characteristics. In organizational settings, pragmatists may become experts in mastering the bureaucratic rules which can be used to protect them.

4. *Passive followers* display none of the characteristics of the exemplary follower (discussed next). They rely on the leader to do all the thinking. Furthermore, their work lacks enthusiasm. Lacking initiative and a sense of responsibility, passive followers require constant direction. Leaders may see them as lazy, incompetent, or even stupid. Sometimes, however, passive followers adopt this style to help them cope with a leader who expects followers to behave that way.

5. *Exemplary followers* present a consistent picture to both leaders and co-workers of being independent, innovative, and willing to stand up to superiors. They apply their talents for the benefit of the organization even when confronted with bureaucratic stumbling blocks or passive or pragmatist co-workers. Effective leaders appreciate the value of exemplary followers. When one of the authors was serving in a follower role in a staff position, he was introduced by his leader to a conference as "my favorite subordinate because he's a loyal 'No-Man.' "

Exemplary followers—high on both critical dimensions of followership—are essential to organizational success.

Leaders, therefore, would be well advised to select people who have these characteristics and, perhaps even more importantly, *create the conditions that encourage these behaviors.*

Source: Adapted from R. Kelley, *The Power of Followership* (New York: Doubleday Currency, 1992).

The nature of followers' motivation to do their work is also important. Workers who share a leader's goals and values, and who feel intrinsically rewarded for performing a job well, might be more likely to work extra hours on a time-critical project than those whose motivation is solely monetary.

Even the number of followers reporting to a leader can have significant implications. For example, a store manager with three clerks working for him can spend more time with each of them (or on other things) than can a manager responsible for eight clerks and a separate delivery service; chairing a task force with 5 members is a different leadership activity than chairing a task force with 18 members. Still other relevant variables include followers' trust in the leader and their degree of confidence that he or she is interested in their well-being. Another aspect of followers' relations to a leader is described in Profiles in Leadership 1.3.

Paul Revere

PROFILES IN LEADERSHIP 1.3

A fabled story of American history is that of Paul Revere's ride through the countryside surrounding Boston, warning towns that the British were coming so local militia could be ready to meet them. As a result, when the British did march toward Lexington on the following day, they faced unexpectedly fierce resistance. At Concord the British were beaten by a ragtag group of locals, and so began the American Revolutionary War.

It has been taken for granted by generations of Americans that the success of Paul Revere's ride lay in his heroism *and* in the self-evident importance of the news itself. A little-known fact, however, is that Paul Revere was not the only rider that night. A fellow revolutionary by the name of William Dawes had the same mission: to ride simultaneously through a separate set of towns surrounding Boston to warn them that the British were coming. He did so, carrying the news through just as many towns as Revere did. But his ride was not successful; those local militia leaders weren't aroused and did not rise up to confront the British. If they had been, Dawes would be as famous today as Paul Revere.

Why was Revere's ride successful when Dawes's ride was not? Paul Revere started a word-of-mouth epidemic, and Dawes did not, *because of differing kinds of relationships the two men had with others.* It wasn't, after all, the nature of the news itself that proved ultimately important so much as the nature of the men who carried it. Paul Revere was a gregarious and social person—what Malcolm Gladwell calls a *connector.* Gladwell writes that Revere was "a fisherman and a hunter, a cardplayer and a theater-lover, a frequenter of pubs and a successful businessman. He was active in the local Masonic Lodge and was a member of several select social clubs." He was a man with a knack for always being at the center of things. So when he began his ride that night, it was Revere's nature to stop and share the news with anyone he saw on the road, and he would have known who the key players were in each town to notify.

Dawes was not by nature so gregarious as Revere, and he did not have Revere's extended social network. It's likely he *wouldn't* have known whom to share the news with in each town and whose doors to knock on. Dawes did notify some people, but not enough to create the kind of impact that Revere did. Another way of saying this is simply to note that the people Dawes notified didn't know *him* the way that Revere was known by those *he* notified.

It isn't just the information or the ideas you have as a leader that make a difference. It's also whom you know, and how many you know—and what they know about you.

Source: Adapted from Malcolm Gladwell, *The Tipping Point* (New York: Little, Brown and Company, 2002).

22   Part One   *Leadership Is a Process, Not a Position*

Never try to teach a pig to sing; it wastes your time and it annoys the pig.

Paul Dickson, baseball writer

In the context of the interactional framework, the question "What is leadership?" cannot be separated from the question "What is followership?" There is no simple line dividing them; they merge. The relationship between leadership and followership can be represented by borrowing a concept from topographical mathematics: the Möbius strip. You are probably familiar with the curious properties of the Möbius strip: when a strip of paper is twisted and connected in the manner

Source: © *Tribune Media Services, Inc. All Rights Reserved. Reprinted with permission.*

FIGURE 1.3
The Leadership/
Followership
Möbius Strip

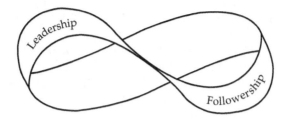

depicted in Figure 1.3, it has only one side. You can prove this to your-self by putting a pencil to any point on the strip and tracing continuously. Your pencil will cover the entire strip (that is, both "sides"), eventually returning to the point at which you started. To demonstrate the relevance of this curiosity to leadership, cut a strip of paper. On one side write *leadership,* and on the other side write *followership*. Then twist the strip and connect the two ends in the manner of the figure. You will have created a leadership/followership Möbius strip wherein the two concepts merge, just as leadership and followership can become indistinguishable in organizations.[41]

This does not mean leadership and followership are the same thing. When top-level executives were asked to list qualities they most look for and admire in leaders and followers, the lists were similar but not identical.[42] Ideal leaders were characterized as honest, competent, forward-looking, and inspiring; ideal followers were described as honest, competent, independent, and cooperative. The differences could become critical in certain situations, as when a forward-looking and inspiring subordinate perceives a significant conflict between his own goals or ethics and those of his superiors. Such a situation could become a crisis for the individual and the organization, demanding a choice between leading and following.

As the complexity of the leadership process has become better understood, the importance placed on the leader–follower relationship itself has undergone dynamic change.[43,44] One reason for this is an increasing pressure on all kinds of organizations to function with reduced resources. Reduced resources and company downsizing have reduced the number of managers and increased their span of control, which in turn leaves followers to pick up many of the functions traditionally performed by leaders. Another reason is a trend toward greater power sharing and decentralized authority in organizations, which create greater interdependence among organizational subunits and increase the need for collaboration among them. Furthermore, the nature of problems faced by many organizations is becoming so complex and the changes are becoming so rapid that more and more people are required to solve them.

These trends suggest several different ways in which followers can take on new leadership roles and responsibilities in the future. For one thing, followers can become much more proactive in their stance toward organizational problems. When facing the discrepancy between the way things are in an organization and the way they could or should be, followers can play an active and constructive role collaborating with leaders in solving problems. In general, making organizations better is a task that needs to be "owned" by followers as well as by leaders. With these changing roles for followers, it should not be surprising to find that qualities of good followership are statistically correlated with qualities typically associated with good leadership. One recent study found positive correlations between the followership qualities of active engagement and independent thinking and the leadership qualities of dominance, sociability, achievement orientation, and steadiness.[45]

In addition to helping solve organizational problems, followers can contribute to the leadership process by becoming skilled at "influencing upward." Because followers are often at the levels where many organizational problems occur, they can give leaders relevant information so good solutions are implemented. Although it is true that some leaders need to become better listeners, it is also true that many followers need training in expressing ideas to superiors clearly and positively. Still another way followers can assume a greater share of the leadership challenge in the future is by staying flexible and open to opportunities. The future portends more change, not less, and followers who face change with positive anticipation and an openness to self-development will be particularly valued and rewarded.[46]

Thus, to an ever-increasing degree, leadership must be understood in terms of both leader variables and follower variables, as well as the interactions among them. But even that is not enough—we must also understand the particular situations in which leaders and followers find themselves.

The Situation

You've got to give loyalty down, if you want loyalty up.

Donald T. Regan, former CEO and White House chief of staff

The situation is the third critical part of the leadership equation. Even if we knew all we could know about a given leader and a given set of followers, leadership often makes sense only in the context of how the leader and followers interact in a particular situation (see Profiles in Leadership 1.4 and 1.5).

This view of leadership as a complex interaction among leader, follower, and situational variables was not always taken for granted. To the contrary, most early research on leadership was based on the assumption that leadership is a general personal trait expressed independently of the situation in which the leadership is manifested. This view, commonly known as the **heroic theory,** has been largely discredited

Aung San Suu Kyi

PROFILES IN LEADERSHIP 1.4

In 1991 Aung San Suu Kyi already had spent two years under house arrest in Burma for "endangering the state." That same year she won the Nobel Peace Prize. She was not released from house arrest until 2010, and in 2012 was elected to Parliament. Like Nelson Mandela, Suu Kyi is an international symbol of heroic and peaceful resistance to government oppression.

Until the age of 43, Suu Kyi led a relatively quiet existence in England as a professional working mother. Her life changed dramatically in 1988 when she returned to her native country of Burma to visit her sick mother. That visit occurred during a time of considerable political unrest in Burma. Riot police had recently shot to death hundreds of demonstrators in the capital city of Rangoon (the demonstrators had been protesting government repression). Over the next several months, police killed nearly 3,000 people who had been protesting government policies.

When hundreds of thousands of pro-democracy demonstrators staged a protest rally at a prominent pagoda in Rangoon, Suu Kyi spoke to the crowd. Overnight she became the leading voice for freedom and democracy in Burma.

Today she is the most popular and influential leader in her country.

What prepared this woman, whose life was once relatively simple and contented, to risk her life by challenging an oppressive government? What made her such a magnet for popular support? Impressive as Aung San Suu Kyi is as a populist leader, it is impossible to understand her effectiveness purely in terms of her own personal characteristics. It is impossible to understand it independent of her followers—the people of Burma. Her rapid rise to prominence as the leading voice for democracy and freedom in Burma must be understood in terms of the living link she represented to the country's greatest modern hero—her father. He was something of a George Washington figure in that he founded the Burmese Army in 1941 and later made a successful transition from military leadership to political leadership. At the height of his influence, when he was the universal choice to be Burma's first president, he was assassinated. Suu Kyi was two years old. Stories about his life and principles indelibly shaped Suu Kyi's own life, but his life and memory also created a readiness among the Burmese people for Suu Kyi to take up her father's mantle of leadership.

but for a long time represented the dominant way of conceptualizing leadership.[47]

In the 1950s and 1960s a different approach to conceptualizing leadership dominated research and scholarship. It involved the search for effective leader *behaviors* rather than the search for universal *traits* of leadership. That approach proved too narrow because it neglected important contextual, or situational, factors in which presumably effective or ineffective behaviors occur. Over time, the complexities of interactions among leader, follower, and situational variables increasingly have been the focus of leadership research.[48] (See Chapters 6, 7, and 13 for more detailed discussions of leader attributes, leader behaviors, and formal theories of leadership that examine complex interdependencies between leader, follower, and situational variables.) Adding the situation to the mix of variables that make up leadership is complicated. The

Bill Gates's Head Start

PROFILES IN LEADERSHIP 1.5

Belief in an individual's potential to overcome great odds and achieve success through talent, strength, and perseverance is common in America, but usually there is more than meets the eye in such success stories. Malcolm Gladwell's best seller *Outliers* presents a fascinating exploration of how situational factors contribute to success in addition to the kinds of individual qualities we often assume are all-important. Have you ever thought, for example, that Bill Gates was able to create Microsoft because he's just brilliant and visionary?

Well, let's take for granted he *is* brilliant and visionary—there's plenty of evidence of that. The point here, however, is that's not always enough (and maybe it's *never* enough). Here are some of the things that placed Bill Gates, with all his intelligence and vision, at the right time in the right place:

- Gates was born to a wealthy family in Seattle that placed him in a private school for seventh grade. In 1968, his second year there, the school started a computer club—even before most *colleges* had computer clubs.

- In the 1960s virtually everyone who was learning about computers used computer cards, a tedious and mind-numbing process. The computer at Gates's school, however, was linked to a mainframe in downtown Seattle. Thus in 1968 Bill Gates was practicing computer programming via time-sharing as an eighth grader; few others in the world then had such opportunity, whatever their age.

- Even at a wealthy private school like the one Gates attended, however, funds ran out to cover the high costs of buying time on a mainframe computer. Fortunately, at about the same time, a group called the Computer Center Corporation was formed at the University of Washington to lease computer time. One of its founders, coincidentally a parent at Gates's own school, thought the school's computer club could get time on the computer in exchange for testing the company's new software programs. Gates then started a regular schedule of taking the bus after school to the company's offices, where he programmed long into the evening. During one seven-month period, Gates and his fellow computer club members averaged eight hours a day, seven days a week, of computer time.

- When Gates was a high school senior, another extraordinary opportunity presented itself. A major national company (TRW) needed programmers with specialized experience—exactly, as it turned out, the kind of experience the kids at Gates's school had been getting. Gates successfully lobbied his teachers to let him spend a spring doing this work in another part of the state for independent study credit.

- By the time Gates dropped out of Harvard after his sophomore year, he had accumulated more than *10,000 hours* of programming experience. It was, he's said, a better exposure to software development than anyone else at a young age could have had—and all because of a lucky series of events.

It appears that Gates's success is at least partly an example of the right person being in the right place at just the right time.

Source: Malcolm Gladwell, *Outliers: The Story of Success* (New York: Little, Brown and Company, 2008).

situation may be the most ambiguous aspect of the leadership framework; it can refer to anything from the specific task a group is engaged in to broad situational contexts such as the remote predicament of the Andes survivors. One facet of the complexity of the situation's role in leadership is examined in Highlight 1.7.

Decision Making in a Complex World

HIGHLIGHT 1.7

Decision making is a good example of how leaders need to behave differently in various situations. Until late in the 20th century, decision making in government and business was largely based on an implicit assumption that the world was orderly and predictable enough for virtually all decision making to involve a series of specifiable steps: assessing the facts of a situation, categorizing those facts, and then responding based on established practice. To put that more simply, decision making required managers to *sense, categorize,* and *respond.*

The Situation	The Leader's Job
Simple: predictable and orderly; right answers exist.	Ensure that proper processes are in place, follow best practices, and communicate in clear and direct ways.
Complex: flux, unpredictability, ambiguity, many competing ideas, lots of unknowns.	Create environments and experiments that allow patterns to emerge; increase levels of interaction and communication; use methods that generate new ideas and ways of thinking among everyone.

That process is actually still effective in simple contexts characterized by stability and clear cause-and-effect relationships that are readily apparent. Not all situations in the world, however, are so simple, and new approaches to decision making are needed for situations that have the elements of what we might call complex systems: large numbers of interacting elements, nonlinear interactions among those elements by which small changes can produce huge effects, and interdependence among the elements so that the whole is more than the sum of the parts. The challenges of dealing with the threat of terrorism are one example of the way complexity affects decision making, but it's impacting how we think about decision making in business as well as government. To describe this change succinctly, the decision-making process in complex contexts must change from sense, categorize, and respond to probe, sense, and respond.

In other words, making good decisions is about both *what* decisions one makes and understanding the role of the situation in affecting *how* one makes decisions.

Source: D.F. Snowden and M.E. Boone, "A Leader's Framework for Decision Making," *Harvard Business Review,* November 2007, pp. 69–76.

Illustrating the Interactional Framework: Women in Leadership Roles

Not long ago if people were asked to name a leader they admired, most of the names on the resulting list could be characterized as "old white guys." Today the names on that same list would be considerably more heterogeneous. That change—which we certainly consider progress—represents a useful illustration of the power of using the interactional framework to understand the complexities of the leadership process.

A specific example is women in leadership roles, and in this section we'll examine the extent to which women have been taking on new leadership roles, whether there are differences in the effectiveness of men and women in leadership roles, and what explanations have been offered for differences between men and women in being selected for and succeeding in positions of leadership. This is an area of considerable academic research and popular polemics, as evident in many recent articles in the popular press that claim a distinct advantage for women in leadership roles.[49]

It is clear that women are taking on leadership roles in greater numbers than ever before. On the other hand, the actual percentage of women in leadership positions has stayed relatively stable. For example, a report released in 2010 by the U.S. Government Accountability Office indicated that women comprised an estimated 40 percent of managers in the U.S. workforce in 2007 compared with 39 percent in 2000.[50] And the percentage of women in top executive positions is considerably less encouraging. In a 2009 study by the nonprofit organization Catalyst, women made up only 13.5 percent of senior executive positions; almost 30 percent of companies in the Fortune 500 had no women in those top positions.[51]

Although these statistics are important and promising, problems still exist that constrain the opportunity for capable women to rise to the highest leadership roles in organizations. Many studies have considered this problem, a few of which we'll examine here.

One recent study reported that a higher percentage of women executives now receive on-the-job mentoring than men. The same study, however, found that the mentors of those women executives had less organizational influence and clout than did the mentors of their male counterparts. While such mentoring can still provide invaluable psychosocial support for personal and professional development, it does not seem sufficient to assure promotion to higher level jobs (mentoring will be explored in greater detail in the next chapter).[52] Another recent study examined differences in the networking patterns of men and women. Compared to men, women's trust in each other tends to decrease when work situations become more professionally risky. Such a pattern of behavior could potentially become a kind of self-imposed promotion disadvantage by women on themselves.[53]

In a classic study of sex roles, Schein[54,55] demonstrated how bias in sex role stereotypes created problems for women moving up through managerial roles. Schein asked male and female middle managers to complete a survey in which they rated various items on a five-point scale in terms of how characteristic they were of men in general, women in general, or successful managers. Schein found a high correlation between the ways both male and female respondents perceived "males" and "managers," but no correlation between the ways the respondents perceived "females" and "managers." It was as though being a manager was defined by attributes thought of as masculine.

Furthermore, it does not appear that the situation has changed much over the past two decades. In 1990 management students in the United

States, Germany, and Great Britain, for example, still perceived successful middle managers in terms of characteristics more commonly ascribed to men than to women.[56] A 2011 meta-analysis of studies of gender stereotyping continued to find strong evidence of a tendency for leadership to be viewed as culturally masculine. It involved sophisticated statistical analyses of the results of 40 separate studies similar to Schein's paradigm of *think manager–think male*; of 22 other studies that looked at gender stereotyping in an *agency-communion* paradigm; and of a third group of 7 studies that looked at stereotyping through the lens of occupational stereotyping. The study concluded that a strong masculine stereotype of leadership continues to exist in the workplace and that it will continue to challenge women for some time to come.[57] One area where views *do* seem to have changed over time involves women's perceptions of their own roles. In contrast to the earlier studies, women today see as much similarity between "female" and "manager" as between "male" and "manager."[58] To women, at least, being a woman and being a manager are not contradictory.

There have been many other studies of the role of women in management. In one of these, *Breaking the Glass Ceiling*,[59] researchers documented the lives and careers of 78 of the highest-level women in corporate America. A few years later the researchers followed up with a small sample of those women to discuss any changes that had taken place in their leadership paths. The researchers were struck by the fact that the women were much like the senior men they had worked with in other studies. Qualitatively, they had the same fears: They wanted the best for themselves and for their families. They wanted their companies to succeed. And not surprisingly, they still had a drive to succeed. In some cases (also true for the men) they were beginning to ask questions about life balance—was all the sacrifice and hard work worth it? Were 60-hour workweeks worth the cost to family and self?

More quantitatively, however, the researchers expected to find significant differences between the women who had broken the glass ceiling and the men who were already in leadership positions. After all, the popular literature and some social scientific literature had conditioned them to expect that there is a feminine versus a masculine style of leadership, the feminine style being an outgrowth of a consensus/team-oriented leadership approach. Women, in this view, are depicted as leaders who, when compared to men, are better listeners, more empathic, less analytical, more people oriented, and less aggressive in pursuit of goals.

In examining women in leadership positions, the researchers collected behavioral data, including ratings by both self and others, assessment center data, and their scores on the California Psychological Inventory. Contrary to the stereotypes and popular views, however, there were no statistically significant differences between men's and women's leadership styles. Women and men were equally analytical, people oriented, forceful, goal oriented, empathic, and skilled at listening. There were other differences between the men and women, however, beyond the question of leadership styles. The researchers did find (and these results must be interpreted cautiously because of the relatively small numbers involved) that women had significantly lower well-being scores, their commitment to the organizations they worked for was more guarded than that of their male counterparts, and the women were much more likely to be willing to take career risks associated with going to new or unfamiliar areas of the company where women had not been before.

Continued work with women in corporate leadership positions has both reinforced and clarified these findings. For example, the lower scores for women in general well-being may reflect the inadequacy of their support system for dealing with day-to-day issues of living. This is tied to the reality for many women that in addition to having roles in their companies they remain chief caretakers for their families. Further, there may be additional pressures of being visibly identified as proof that the organization has women at the top.

Other types of differences—particularly those around "people issues"—are still not evident. In fact, the hypothesis is that such supposed differences may hinder the opportunities for leadership development of women in the future. For example, turning around a business that is in trouble or starting a new business are two of the most exciting opportunities a developing leader has to test her leadership abilities. If we apply the "women are different" hypothesis, the type of leadership skills needed for successful completion of either of these assignments may leave women off the list of candidates. However, if we accept the hypothesis that women and men are more alike as leaders than they are different, women will be found in equal numbers on the candidate list.

Research on women leaders from medium-sized, nontraditional organizations has shown that successful leaders don't all come from the same mold. Such women tended to be successful by drawing on their shared experience as women, rather than by adhering to the "rules of conduct" by which men in larger and more traditional organizations have been successful.[60] Survey research by Judith Rosener identified several differences in how men and women described their leadership experiences. Men tended to describe themselves in somewhat transactional terms, viewing leadership as an exchange with subordinates for services rendered. They influenced others primarily through their organizational position and authority. The women, on the other hand, tended to describe themselves in transformational terms. They helped subordinates develop commitment to broader goals than their own self-interest, and they described their influence more in terms of personal characteristics like charisma and interpersonal skill than mere organizational position.

According to Rosener, such women leaders encouraged participation and shared power and information, but went far beyond what is commonly thought of as participative management. She called it **interactive leadership.** Their leadership self-descriptions reflected an approach based on enhancing others' self-worth and believing that the best performance results when people are excited about their work and feel good about themselves.

How did this interactive leadership style develop? Rosener concluded it was due to these women's socialization experiences and career paths. As we have indicated, the social role expected of women has emphasized that they be cooperative, supportive, understanding, gentle, and service-oriented. As they entered the business world, they still found themselves in roles emphasizing these same behaviors. They found themselves in staff, rather than line, positions, and in roles lacking formal authority over others so that they had to accomplish their work without reliance on formal power. What they had to do, in other words, was employ their socially acceptable behavioral repertoire to survive organizationally.

What came easily to women turned out to be a survival tactic. Although leaders often begin their careers doing what comes naturally and what fits

"*That's what they all say, honey.*"

Source: © Tom Cheney, *The New Yorker Collection*, *www.cartoonbank.com*.

32   Part One   *Leadership Is a Process, Not a Position*

Neither shall you allege the example of the many as an excuse for doing wrong.

Exodus 23.2

within the constraints of the job, they also develop their skills and styles over time. The women's use of interactive leadership has its roots in socialization, and the women interviewees believe that it benefits their organizations. Through the course of their careers, they have gained conviction that their style is effective. In fact, for some it was their own success that caused them to formulate their philosophies about what motivates people, how to make good decisions, and what it takes to maximize business performance.

Rosener has called for organizations to expand their definitions of effective leadership—to create a *wider* band of acceptable behavior so both men and women will be freer to lead in ways that take advantage of their true talents. There is further discussion of stereotype-based "bands of acceptable behavior" in Highlight 1.8.

The Narrow Band of Acceptable Behavior

HIGHLIGHT 1.8

One of the most important factors that seems to impede the advance of women and other minorities into leadership roles is bias. A bias that might be labeled "the narrow band of acceptable behavior" is depicted below.

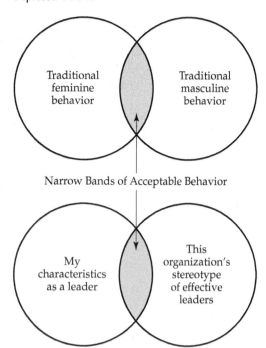

Narrow Bands of Acceptable Behavior

The characteristics and behaviors in the right-hand circle are those associated with traditional masculine behavior, and the characteristics and behaviors in the left-hand circle are those associated with traditional feminine behavior. The narrow band of overlap between the two circles can be thought of as a "hoop" women executives need to pass through.

The concept of a narrow band of acceptable behavior is not limited to women. It may be applied to any individual's deviation from organizationally defined standards. The more a person looks like, acts like, dresses like, and talks like other leaders in the organization, the wider the band of acceptable behavior (the greater the overlap of the two circles). The less one looks like, acts like, dresses like, and talks like other leaders in the organization (some aspects of which, such as gender and race, are beyond a person's control) the narrower the band of acceptable behavior. One implication of this view is that an individual who differs in obvious ways from the prototypical image of a leader (as with gender) has less "wiggle room" available; it's as though there are already one or two strikes against that person. It's like walking a tightrope.

Source: Adapted from A. M. Morrison, R.P. White, and E. Van Velsor, *Breaking the Glass Ceiling* (Reading, MA: Addison-Wesley, 1987).

A more recent study sheds additional light on factors that affect the rise of women in leadership positions.[61] It identifies four general factors that explain the shift toward more women leaders.

The first of these is that *women themselves have changed*. That's evident in the ways women's aspirations and attitudes have become more similar to those of men over time. This is illustrated in findings about the career aspirations of female university students;[62] in women's self-reports of traits such as assertiveness, dominance, and masculinity;[63,64] and in the value that women place on characteristics of work such as freedom, challenge, leadership, prestige, and power.[65] The second factor is that *leadership roles have changed,* particularly with regard to a trend toward less stereotypically masculine characterizations of leadership. Third, *organizational practices have changed*. A large part of this can be attributed to legislation prohibiting gender-based discrimination at work, as well as changes in organizational norms that put a higher priority on results than on an "old boy" network. Finally, the *culture has changed*. This is evident, for example, in the symbolic message often intended by appointment of women to important leadership positions, one representing a departure from past practices and signaling commitment to progressive change.

Finally, in addition to the glass ceiling, another recently identified challenge for women is called the **glass cliff**. The glass cliff refers to the intriguing finding that female candidates for an executive position are *more* likely to be hired than equally qualified male candidates when an organization's performance is declining. At first that may seem like good news for women, but the picture is not quite so positive. When an organization's performance is declining, there is inherently an increased risk of failure. The increased likelihood of women being selected in those situations may actually reflect a greater willingness to put women in precarious positions;[66] it could also, of course, represent an increased willingness to take some chances when nothing else seems to be working.

There Is No Simple Recipe for Effective Leadership

To fill the gaps between leadership research and practice, this book will critically review major findings about the nature of leadership as well as provide practical advice for improving leadership. As our first step in that journey, the next chapter of the book will describe how leadership develops through experience. The remainder of the book uses the leader–follower–situation interaction model as a framework for organizing and discussing various theories and research findings related to leadership. In this study, it will become clear that while there is no simple recipe for effective leadership, there *are* many different paths to effective leadership.

34   Part One   *Leadership Is a Process, Not a Position*

As noted previously, it is important to understand how the three domains of leadership interact—how the leader, the followers, and the situation are all part of the leadership process. Understanding their interaction is necessary before you can draw valid conclusions from the leadership you observe around you. When you see a leader's behavior (even when it may appear obviously effective or ineffective to you), you should not automatically conclude something good or bad about the leader, or what is the right way or wrong way leaders should act. You need to think about the effectiveness of that behavior in *that* context with *those* followers.

As obvious as this advice sounds, we often ignore it. Too frequently we look at just the leader's behavior and conclude that he or she is a good leader or a bad leader apart from the context. For example, suppose you observe a leader soliciting advice from subordinates. Obviously it seems unreasonable to conclude that good leaders always ask for advice or that leaders who do not frequently ask for advice are not good leaders. The appropriateness of seeking input from subordinates depends on many factors, such as the nature of the problem or the subordinates' familiarity with the problem. Perhaps the subordinates have a lot more experience with this particular problem, and soliciting their input is the correct action to take in this situation.

Consider another example. Suppose you hear that a leader did not approve a subordinate's request to take time off to attend to family matters. Was this bad leadership because the leader did not appear to be taking care of her people? Was it good leadership because she did not let personal matters interfere with the mission? Again, you cannot make an intelligent decision about the leader's actions by looking at the behavior itself. You must always assess leadership in the context of the leader, the followers, and the situation.

The following statements about leaders, followers, and the situation make these points a bit more systematically:

- A leader may need to respond to various followers differently in the same situation.
- A leader may need to respond to the same follower differently in different situations.
- Followers may respond to various leaders quite differently.
- Followers may respond to each other differently with different leaders.
- Two leaders may have different perceptions of the same followers or situations.

All of these points lead to one conclusion: the right behavior in one situation is not necessarily the right behavior in another situation. It does *not* follow, however, that any behavior is appropriate in any situation. Although we may not be able to agree on the one best behavior in a given situation, we often can agree on some clearly inappropriate behaviors.

Saying that the right behavior for a leader depends on the situation is not the same thing as saying it does not matter what the leader does. It merely recognizes the complexity among leaders, followers, and situations. This recognition is a helpful first step in drawing meaningful lessons about leadership from experience.

Summary

We have defined leadership as the process of influencing an organized group toward achieving its goals. The chapter also looked at the idea that leadership is both a science and an art. Because leadership is an immature science, researchers are still struggling to find out what the important questions in leadership are; we are far from finding conclusive answers to them. Even individuals with extensive knowledge of leadership research may be poor leaders. Knowing what to do is not the same as knowing when, where, and how to do it. The art of leadership concerns the skill of understanding leadership situations and influencing others to accomplish group goals. Formal leadership education may give individuals the skills to better understand leadership situations, and mentorships and experience may give individuals the skills to better influence others. Leaders must also weigh both rational and emotional considerations when attempting to influence others. Leadership sometimes can be accomplished through relatively rational, explicit, rule-based methods of assessing situations and determining actions.

Nevertheless, the emotional side of human nature must also be acknowledged. Leaders are often most effective when they affect people at both the emotional level and the rational level. The idea of leadership as a whole-person process can also be applied to the distinction often made between leaders and managers. Although leadership and management can be distinguished as separate functions, there is considerable overlap between them in practice.

Leadership is a process in which leaders and followers interact dynamically in a particular situation or environment. Leadership is a broader concept than that of leaders, and the study of leadership must involve more than just the study of leaders as individuals. The study of leadership must also include two other areas: the followers and the situation. In addition, the interactive nature of these three domains has become increasingly important in recent years and can help us to better understand the changing nature of leader–follower relationships and the increasing complexity of situations leaders and followers face. Because of this complexity, now, more than ever before, effective leadership cannot be boiled down to a simple recipe. It is still true, however, that good leadership makes a difference, and it can be enhanced through greater awareness of the important factors influencing the leadership process.

36   Part One   *Leadership Is a Process, Not a Position*

Key Terms

leadership, 4
academic tradition, 7
troubadour
    tradition, 7
management, 8
interactional
    framework, 15
leader, 15

followers, *15*
situation, *15*
interactions, *15*
in-group, *16*
out-group, *16*
followership, *19*
independent, critical
    thinking, *20*

dependent, uncritical
    thinking, *20*
active followers, *20*
passive followers, *20*
heroic theory, *24*
interactive
    leadership, *30*
glass cliff, *33*

Questions

1. We say leadership involves influencing organized groups toward goals. Do you see any disadvantages to restricting the definition to organized groups?

2. How would you define *leadership*?

3. Are some people the "leader type" and others not the "leader type"? If so, what in your judgment distinguishes them?

4. Identify several "commonsense" notions about leadership that, to you, are self-evident.

5. Does every successful leader have a valid theory of leadership?

6. Would you consider it a greater compliment for someone to call you a good manager or a good leader? Why? Do you believe you can be both?

7. Do you believe leadership can be studied scientifically? Why or why not?

8. To the extent that leadership is an art, what methods come to mind for improving one's "art of leadership"?

9. According to the interactional framework, effective leader behavior depends on many variables. It follows that there is no simple prescription for effective leader behavior. Does this mean effective leadership is merely a matter of opinion or subjective preference?

10. Generally leaders get most of the credit for a group's or an organization's success. Do you believe this is warranted or fair?

11. What are some other characteristics of leaders, followers, and situations you could add to those listed in Figure 1.2?

Activities

1. Describe the best leader you have personally known or a favorite leader from history, a novel, or a movie.

2. In this activity you will explore connotations of the words *leadership* and *management*. Divide yourselves into small groups and have each group brainstorm different word associations to the terms *leader* and *leadership* or *manager* and *management*. In addition, each group should discuss whether they would prefer to work for a manager or for a leader, and why. Then the whole group should discuss similarities and differences among the respective perceptions and feelings about the two concepts.

Minicase

Richard Branson Shoots for the Moon

The Virgin Group is the umbrella for a variety of business ventures ranging from air travel to entertainment. With close to 200 companies in over 30 countries, it is one of the largest companies in the world. At the head of this huge organization is Richard Branson. Branson founded Virgin over 30 years ago and has built the organization from a small student magazine to the multibillion-dollar enterprise it is today.

Branson is not your typical CEO. Branson's dyslexia made school a struggle and sabotaged his performance on standard IQ tests. His teachers and tests had no way of measuring his greatest strengths—his uncanny knack for uncovering lucrative business ideas and his ability to energize the ambitions of others so that they, like he, could rise to the level of their dreams.

Richard Branson's true talents began to show themselves in his late teens. While a student at Stowe School in England in 1968, Branson decided to start his own magazine, *Student*. Branson was inspired by the student activism on his campus in the 1960s and decided to try something different. *Student* differed from most college newspapers or magazines; it focused on the students and their interests. Branson sold advertising to major corporations to support his magazine. He included articles by ministers of Parliament, rock stars, intellectuals, and celebrities. *Student* grew to become a commercial success.

In 1970 Branson saw an opportunity for *Student* to offer records cheaply by running ads for mail-order delivery. The subscribers to *Student* flooded the magazine with so many orders that his spin-off discount music venture proved more lucrative than the magazine subscriptions. Branson recruited the staff of *Student* for his discount music business. He built a small recording studio and signed his first artist. Mike Oldfield recorded "Tubular Bells" at Virgin in 1973; the album sold 5 million copies, and Virgin Records and the Virgin brand name were born. Branson has gone on to start his own airline (Virgin Atlantic Airlines was launched in 1984), build hotels (Virgin Hotels started in 1988), get into the personal finance business (Virgin Direct Personal Finance Services was launched in 1995), and even enter the cola wars (Virgin Cola was introduced in 1994). And those are just a few highlights of the Virgin Group—all this while Branson has attempted to break world speed records for crossing the Atlantic Ocean by boat and by hot air balloon.

As you might guess, Branson's approach is nontraditional—he has no giant corporate office or staff and few if any board meetings. Instead he keeps each enterprise small and relies on his skills of empowering people's ideas to fuel success. When a flight attendant from Virgin Airlines approached him with her vision of a wedding business, Richard told her to go do it. He even put on a wedding dress himself to help launch the publicity. Virgin Brides was born. Branson relies heavily on the creativity of his staff; he is more a supporter of new ideas than a creator of them. He encourages searches for new business ideas everywhere he goes and even has a spot on the Virgin website called "Got a Big Idea?"

In December 1999 Richard Branson was awarded a knighthood in the Queen's Millennium New Year's Honours List for "services to entrepreneurship." What's next on Branson's list? It's Virgin Galactic, Branson's company designed in part to make space tourism available to private citizens. He has announced that the company's first space flight will take place in 2013 on its *Spaceship Two* traveling 62 miles above the earth. The first passengers will be Branson himself and his two adult sons; you can take a later flight yourself for a mere $200,000 for a two-hour trip. Not everyone is convinced that space tourism can become a fully fledged part of the travel industry, but with Branson behind the idea it just might fly.

1. Would you classify Richard Branson as a manager or a leader? What qualities distinguish him as one or the other?

2. As mentioned earlier in this chapter, followers are part of the leadership process. Describe the relationship between Branson and his followers.

3. Identify the myths of leadership development that Richard Branson's success helps to disprove.

Sources: http://www.johnshepler.com/articles/branson.html;
http://www.wma.com/richard_branson/summary/;
http://www.virgin.com/aboutvirgin/allaboutvirgin/thewholestory/;
http://www.virgin.com/aboutvirgin/allaboutvirgin/whosrichardbranson/;
http://www.qksrv.net/click-310374-35140;
http://www.guardian.co.uk/space/article/0,14493,1235926,00.html.

End Notes

1. P. P. Read, *Alive* (New York: J. B. Lippincott, 1974).

2. Ibid., p. 77.

3. J. R. Meindl and S. B. Ehrlich, "The Romance of Leadership and the Evaluation of Organizational Performance," *Academy of Management Journal* 30 (1987), pp. 90–109.

4. W. G. Bennis, "Leadership Theory and Administrative Behavior: The Problem of Authority," *Administrative Science Quarterly* 4 (1959), pp. 259–60.

5. F. Fiedler, *A Theory of Leadership Effectiveness* (New York: McGraw-Hill, 1967).

6. R. K. Merton, *Social Theory and Social Structure* (New York: Free Press, 1957).

7. C. F. Roach and O. Behling, "Functionalism: Basis for an Alternate Approach to the Study of Leadership," in *Leaders and Managers: International Perspectives on Managerial Behavior and Leadership*, eds. J. G. Hunt, D. M. Hosking, C. A. Schriesheim, and R. Stewar (Elmsford, NY: Pergamon, 1984).

8. D. P. Campbell, *Campbell Leadership Index Manual* (Minneapolis: National Computer Systems, 1991).

9. R. C. Ginnett, "Team Effectiveness Leadership Model: Identifying Leverage Points for Change," *Proceedings of the 1996 National Leadership Institute Conference* (College Park, MD: National Leadership Institute, 1996).

10. G. J. Curphy and R. T. Hogan, *The Rocket Model: Practical Advice for Building High Performing Teams* (Tulsa, OK: Hogan Press, 2012).

11. M. D. Mumford, S. J. Zaccaro, F. D. Harding, T. O. Jacobs, and E. A. Fleishman, "Leadership Skills for a Changing World," *Leadership Quarterly* 11, no. 1 (2000), pp. 11–35.

12. B. M. Bass, *Bass and Stogdill's Handbook of Leadership*, 3rd ed. (New York: Free Press, 1990).

13. H. C. Foushee, "Dyads and Triads at 35,000 Feet: Factors Affecting Group Process and Aircrew Performance," *American Psychologist* 39 (1984), pp. 885–93.

14. W. G. Bennis and B. Nanus, *Leaders: The Strategies for Taking Charge* (New York: Harper & Row, 1985).

15. A. Zaleznik, "The Leadership Gap," *Washington Quarterly* 6, no. 1 (1983), pp. 32–39.

16. W. G. Bennis, *On Becoming a Leader* (Reading, MA: Addison-Wesley, 1989).

17. Zaleznik, "The Leadership Gap."

18. P. Slovic and B. Fischoff, "On the Psychology of Experimental Surprises," *Journal of Experimental Social Psychology* 22 (1977), pp. 544–51.

19. G. Wood, "The Knew-It-All-Along Effect," *Journal of Experimental Psychology: Human Perception and Performance* 4 (1979), pp. 345–53.

20. P. E. Lazarsfeld, "The American Soldier: An Expository Review," *Public Opinion Quarterly* 13 (1949), pp. 377–404.

21. For example, A. Tellegen, D. T. Lykken, T. J. Bouchard, K. J. Wilcox, N. L. Segal, and S. Rich, "Personality Similarity in Twins Reared Apart and Together," *Journal of Personality and Social Psychology* 54 (1988), pp. 1031–39.

22. Fiedler, *A Theory of Leadership Effectiveness.*

23. E. P. Hollander, *Leadership Dynamics: A Practical Guide to Effective Relationships* (New York: Free Press, 1978).

24. G. B. Graen and J. F. Cashman, "A Role-Making Model of Leadership in Formal Organizations: A Developmental Approach," in *Leadership Frontiers*, eds. J. G. Hunt and L. L. Larson (Kent, OH: Kent State University Press, 1975).

25. R. M. Stogdill, "Personal Factors Associated with Leadership: A Review of the Literature," *Journal of Psychology* 25 (1948), pp. 35–71.

26. R. M. Stogdill, *Handbook of Leadership* (New York: Free Press, 1974).

27. R. T. Hogan, G. J. Curphy, and J. Hogan, "What We Know about Personality: Leadership and Effectiveness," *American Psychologist* 49 (1994), pp. 493–504.

28. R. G. Lord, C. L. DeVader, and G. M. Allinger, "A Meta-Analysis of the Relationship between Personality Traits and Leadership Perceptions: An Application of Validity Generalization Procedures," *Journal of Applied Psychology* 71 (1986), pp. 402–10.

29. R. M. Kanter, *The Change Masters* (New York: Simon & Schuster, 1983).

30. E. D. Baltzell, *Puritan Boston and Quaker Philadelphia* (New York: Free Press, 1980).

31. E. P. Hollander and L. R. Offermann, "Power and Leadership in Organizations," *American Psychologist* 45 (1990), pp. 179–89.

32. S. D. Baker, "Followership: The Theoretical Foundation of a Contemporary Construct," *Journal of Leadership & Organizational Studies* 14, no. 1 (2007), p. 51.

33. Baker, "Followership."

34. J. M. Burns, *Leadership* (New York: Harper & Row, 1978).

35. B. M. Bass, *Bass and Stogdill's Handbook of Leadership,* 3rd ed. (New York: Free Press, 1990).

36. Stogdill, *Handbook of Leadership.*

37. C. D. Sutton and R. W. Woodman, "Pygmalion Goes to Work: The Effects of Supervisor Expectations in the Retail Setting," *Journal of Applied Psychology* 74 (1989), pp. 943–50.

38. L. I. Moore, "The FMI: Dimensions of Follower Maturity," *Group and Organizational Studies* 1 (1976), pp. 203–22.

39. T. A. Scandura, G. B. Graen, and M. A. Novak, "When Managers Decide Not to Decide Autocratically: An Investigation of Leader-Member Exchange and Decision Influence," *Journal of Applied Psychology* 52 (1986), pp. 135–47.

40. C. A. Sales, E. Levanoni, and D. H. Saleh, "Satisfaction and Stress as a Function of Job Orientation, Style of Supervision, and the Nature of the Task," *Engineering Management International* 2 (1984), pp. 145–53.

41. Adapted from K. Macrorie, *Twenty Teachers* (Oxford: Oxford University Press, 1984).

42. J. M. Kouzes and B. Z. Posner, *The Leadership Challenge: How to Get Extraordinary Things Done in Organizations* (San Francisco: Jossey-Bass, 1987).

43. R. Lippitt, "The Changing Leader–Follower Relationships of the 1980s," *Journal of Applied Behavioral Science* 18 (1982), pp. 395–403.

44. P. Block, *Stewardship* (San Francisco: Berrett-Koehler, 1992).

45. G. F. Tanoff and C. B. Barlow, "Leadership and Followership: Same Animal, Different Spots?" *Consulting Psychology Journal: Practice and Research,* Summer 2002, pp. 157–65.

46. P. M. Senge, *The Fifth Discipline: The Art and Practice of the Learning Organization* (New York: Doubleday/Currency, 1990).

47. V. Vroom and A. G. Jago, "The Role of the Situation in Leadership," *American Psychologist* 62, no. 1 (2007), pp. 17–24.

48. Vroom and Jago, "The Role of the Situation in Leadership."

49. For example, M. Conlin, "The New Gender Gap: From Kindergarten to Grad School, Boys Are Becoming the Second Sex," *BusinessWeek,* May 26, 2003.

50. GAO, Women in Management: Female Managers' Representation, Characteristics, and Pay, GAO-10-1064T (Washington, D.C.: September 28, 2010).

51. http://catalyst.org/press-release/161/2009-catalyst-census-of-the-fortune-500-reveals-women-missing-from-critical-business-leadership. 10/05/2010.

52. H. Ibarra, N. M. Carter, and C. Silva, "Why Men Still Get More Promotions Than Women," *Harvard Business Review,* September 2010, pp. 80–85.

53. D. Bevelander and M. J. Page, "Ms. Trust: Gender, Networks and Trust—Implications for Management and Education," *Academy of Management Learning & Education* 10, no. 4 (2011), pp. 623–42.

54. V. Schein, "The Relationship between Sex Role Stereotypes and Requisite Management Characteristics," *Journal of Applied Psychology* 57 (1973), pp. 95–100.

55. V. Schein, "Relationships between Sex Role Stereotypes and Requisite Management Characteristics among Female Managers, *Journal of Applied Psychology* 60 (1975), pp. 340–44.

56. V. Schein and R. Mueller, "Sex Role Stereotyping and Requisite Management Characteristics: A Cross Cultural Look," *Journal of Organizational Behavior* 13 (1992), pp. 439–47.

57. A. M. Koenig, A. H. Eagly, A. A. Mitchell, and T. Ristikari, "Are Leader Stereotypes Masculine? A Meta-analysis of Three Research Paradigms," *Psychological Bulletin* 137, no. 4, (2011), pp. 616–42.

58. O. C. Brenner, J. Tomkiewicz, and V. E. Schein, "The Relationship between Sex Role Stereotypes and Requisite Management Characteristics Revisited," *Academy of Management Journal* 32 (1989), pp. 662–69.

59. A. M. Morrison, R. P. White, and E. Van Velsor, *Breaking the Glass Ceiling* (Reading, MA: Addison-Wesley, 1987).

60. J. B. Rosener, "Ways Women Lead," *Harvard Business Review* 68 (1990), pp. 119–25.

61. A. H. Eagly and L. L. Carli, "The Female Leadership Advantage: An Evaluation of the Evidence," *The Leadership Quarterly* 14 (2003), pp. 807–34.

62. A. W. Astin, S. A. Parrrott, W. S. Korn, and L. J. Sax, *The American Freshman: Thirty Year Trends* (Los Angeles: Higher Education Research Institute, University of California, 1997).

63. J. M. Twenge, "Changes in Masculine and Feminine Traits over Time: A Meta-analysis," *Sex Roles* 36 (1997), pp. 305–25.

64. J. M. Twenge, "Changes in Women's Assertiveness in Response to Status and Roles: A Cross-Temporal Meta-analysis, 1931–1993," *Journal of Personality and Social Psychology* 81 (2001), pp. 133–45.

65. A. M. Konrad, J. E. Ritchie, Jr., P. Lieb, and E. Corrigall, "Sex Differences and Similarities in Job Attribute Preferences: A Meta-analysis," *Psychological Bulletin* 126 (2000), pp. 593–641.

66. S. A. Haslam and M. K. Ryan, "The Road to the Glass Cliff: Differences in the Perceived Suitability of Men and Women for Leadership Positions in Succeeding and Failing Organizations," *The Leadership Quarterly* 19 (2008), pp. 530–46.

Strategic Control and Corporate Governance

chapter 9

After reading this chapter, you should have a good understanding of the following learning objectives:

LO9.1 The value of effective strategic control systems in strategy implementation.

LO9.2 The key difference between "traditional" and "contemporary" control systems.

LO9.3 The imperative for contemporary control systems in today's complex and rapidly changing competitive and general environments.

LO9.4 The benefits of having the proper balance among the three levers of behavioral control: culture, rewards and incentives, and boundaries.

LO9.5 The three key participants in corporate governance: shareholders, management (led by the CEO), and the board of directors.

LO9.6 The role of corporate governance mechanisms in ensuring that the interests of managers are aligned with those of shareholders from both the United States and international perspectives.

Learning from Mistakes

Just a few years ago, Tesco was a high-flying global retailer. Throughout the 1990s and early 2000s, Tesco grew to dominate the U.K. retailing market, attaining a 33 percent market share, and successfully expanded into new geographic markets. However, over the last several years, Tesco has faced increasing pressures at home and large struggles outside the U.K. This included a failed entry into the U.S. market and increasing pressure at home from hard-discounting competitors, most notably Lidl and Aldi. In recent years, Tesco has seen its stock price drop by nearly 40 percent, major investors including Warren Buffett bail out, and pressures from investors that forced the ousting of the firm's CEO.

In September 2014, the situation for Tesco got much worse.[1] After an employee alerted the firm's general counsel of accounting irregularities, a full-blown accounting scandal erupted. Senior managers in the U.K. food business had been booking income early and delaying the booking of costs to shore up the financial performance of the firm. The firm was forced to restate its earnings for the first half of 2014, initially to the tune of $408 million, which was later increased to $431 million as the scope of the problem increased. The scandal led to the suspension or dismissal of eight senior executives at Tesco, the suspension of retirement packages for the firm's prior CEO and CFO, and the eventual resignation of the chairman of the board of Tesco. It also triggered an investigation by the U.K.'s accounting watchdog, the Financial Reporting Council, into Tesco's accounting practices for the years 2012, 2013, and 2014.

The scandal has triggered commentators to reassert some long-standing concerns about Tesco's governance and also led them to point out some new concerns. Industry analysts have long been critical of Tesco's board of directors, especially noting that the board lacks retail experience. This likely played a role in the scandal, since the board would have had limited ability to notice the arcane, retail-related accounting practices at the center of the accounting deception. Interestingly, four months before the scandal arose, Tesco's auditor, PricewaterhouseCoopers, warned of the "risk of manipulation" in the accounting of promotional events, the areas that were manipulated, but the board appeared to take no action in its following meeting. The accounting irregularities also arose at a time of limited oversight within the firm. Laurie McIlwee, the firm's chief financial officer, stepped down in April 2014, but her replacement didn't take up the CFO position until December 2014. During that time, Tesco's finances were managed by the CEO's office. Thus, the firm did not have a senior executive whose primary task was to ensure the validity of the firm's financial reporting. Finally, the most senior leadership of the firm was distracted by other tasks. The firm's prior CEO was dismissed in July, and the new CEO took the reins in August 2014. Thus, Dave Lewis, the new CEO, was focusing on learning the business and the firm's operations just as the scandal broke.

The scandal has been quite damaging to the firm, with Tesco's already battered stock price plunging an additional 28 percent during the period the scandal unfolded.

Discussion Questions

1. What changes should Tesco make to avoid future similar scandals?
2. To what degree do you think the scandal at Tesco was related to how the firm had been performing?

strategic control
the process of monitoring
and correcting a firm's
strategy and performance.

We first explore two central aspects of **strategic control:**[2] (1) *informational control,* which is the ability to respond effectively to environmental change, and (2) *behavioral control,* which is the appropriate balance and alignment among a firm's culture, rewards, and boundaries. In the final section of this chapter, we focus on strategic control from a much broader perspective—what is referred to as *corporate governance.*[3] Here, we direct our attention to the need for a firm's shareholders (the owners) and their elected representatives (the board of directors) to ensure that the firm's executives (the management team) strive to fulfill their fiduciary duty of maximizing long-term shareholder value. As we just saw in the Tesco example, poor governance and control can lead to damaging scandals in firms.

LO9.1

The value of effective strategic control systems in strategy implementation.

Ensuring Informational Control: Responding Effectively to Environmental Change

We discuss two broad types of control systems: "traditional" and "contemporary." As both general and competitive environments become more unpredictable and complex, the need for contemporary systems increases.

A Traditional Approach to Strategic Control

traditional approach
to strategic control
a sequential method of
organizational control
in which (1) strategies
are formulated and
top management sets
goals, (2) strategies are
implemented, and (3)
performance is measured
against the predetermined
goal set.

The **traditional approach to strategic control** is sequential: (1) strategies are formulated and top management sets goals, (2) strategies are implemented, and (3) performance is measured against the predetermined goal set, as illustrated in Exhibit 9.1.

Control is based on a feedback loop from performance measurement to strategy formulation. This process typically involves lengthy time lags, often tied to a firm's annual planning cycle. Such traditional control systems, termed "single-loop" learning by Harvard's Chris Argyris, simply compare actual performance to a predetermined goal.[4] They are most appropriate when the environment is stable and relatively simple, goals and objectives can be measured with a high level of certainty, and there is little need for complex measures of performance. Sales quotas, operating budgets, production schedules, and similar quantitative control mechanisms are typical. The appropriateness of the business strategy or standards of performance is seldom questioned.[5]

LO9.2

The key difference between "traditional" and "contemporary" control systems.

James Brian Quinn of Dartmouth College has argued that grand designs with precise and carefully integrated plans seldom work.[6] Rather, most strategic change proceeds incrementally—one step at a time. Leaders should introduce some sense of direction, some logic in incremental steps.[7] Similarly, McGill University's Henry Mintzberg has written about leaders "crafting" a strategy.[8] Drawing on the parallel between the potter at her wheel and the strategist, Mintzberg pointed out that the potter begins work with some general idea of the artifact she wishes to create, but the details of design—even possibilities for a different design—emerge as the work progresses. For businesses facing complex and turbulent business environments, the craftsperson's method helps us deal with the uncertainty about how a design will work out in practice and allows for a creative element.

LO9.3

The imperative for contemporary control systems in today's complex and rapidly changing competitive and general environments.

Mintzberg's argument, like Quinn's, questions the value of rigid planning and goal-setting processes. Fixed strategic goals also become dysfunctional for firms competing in highly unpredictable competitive environments. Strategies need to change frequently and opportunistically. An inflexible commitment to predetermined goals and milestones can prevent the very adaptability that is required of a good strategy.

EXHIBIT 9.1 Traditional Approach to Strategic Control

A Contemporary Approach to Strategic Control

Adapting to and anticipating both internal and external environmental change is an integral part of strategic control. The relationships between strategy formulation, implementation, and control are highly interactive, as suggested by Exhibit 9.2. The exhibit also illustrates two different types of strategic control: informational control and behavioral control. **Informational control** is primarily concerned with whether or not the organization is "doing the right things." **Behavioral control,** on the other hand, asks if the organization is "doing things right" in the implementation of its strategy. Both the informational and behavioral components of strategic control are necessary, but not sufficient, conditions for success. What good is a well-conceived strategy that cannot be implemented? Or what use is an energetic and committed workforce if it is focused on the wrong strategic target?

John Weston is the former CEO of ADP Corporation, the largest payroll and tax-filing processor in the world. He captures the essence of contemporary control systems:

> At ADP, 39 plus 1 adds up to more than 40 plus 0. The 40-plus-0 employee is the harried worker who at 40 hours a week just tries to keep up with what's in the "in" basket. . . . Because he works with his head down, he takes zero hours to think about what he's doing, why he's doing it, and how he's doing it. . . . On the other hand, the 39-plus-1 employee takes at least 1 of those 40 hours to think about what he's doing and why he's doing it. That's why the other 39 hours are far more productive.[9]

informational control
a method of organizational control in which a firm gathers and analyzes information from the internal and external environment in order to obtain the best fit between the organization's goals and strategies and the strategic environment.

behavioral control
a method of organizational control in which a firm influences the actions of employees through culture, rewards, and boundaries.

Informational control deals with the internal environment as well as the external strategic context. It addresses the assumptions and premises that provide the foundation for an organization's strategy. Do the organization's goals and strategies still "fit" within the context of the current strategic environment? Depending on the type of business, such assumptions may relate to changes in technology, customer tastes, government regulation, and industry competition.

This involves two key issues. First, managers must scan and monitor the external environment, as we discussed in Chapter 2. Also, conditions can change in the internal environment of the firm, as we discussed in Chapter 3, requiring changes in the strategic direction of the firm. These may include, for example, the resignation of key executives or delays in the completion of major production facilities.

In the contemporary approach, information control is part of an ongoing process of organizational learning that continuously updates and challenges the assumptions that underlie the organization's strategy. In such double-loop learning, the organization's assumptions, premises, goals, and strategies are continuously monitored, tested, and reviewed. The benefits of continuous monitoring are evident—time lags are dramatically shortened, changes in the competitive environment are detected earlier, and the organization's ability to respond with speed and flexibility is enhanced.

Contemporary control systems must have four characteristics to be effective:[10]

1. The focus is on constantly changing information that has potential strategic importance.
2. The information is important enough to demand frequent and regular attention from all levels of the organization.

EXHIBIT 9.2 Contemporary Approach to Strategic Control

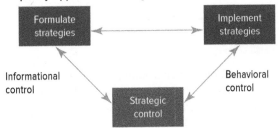

STRATEGY **SPOTLIGHT**

HOW DO MANAGERS AND EMPLOYEES VIEW THEIR FIRM'S CONTROL SYSTEM?

Top executives of organizations often assert that they are pushing for more contemporary control systems. The centralized, periodic setting of objectives and rules with top-down implementation processes is ineffective for organizations facing heterogeneous and dynamic environments. For example, Walmart has, in recent years, realized its top-down, rule-based leadership system was too rigid for a firm emphasizing globalization and technological change. Like many other firms, Walmart is moving to a more decentralized, values-based leadership system where lower-level managers make key decisions, keeping the values of the firm in mind as they do so.

Managers of firms see the need to make this transition, but do lower-level managers and workers see a change in the control systems at their organizations? To get at this question, the Boston Research Group conducted a study of 36,000 managers and employees to get their views on their firm's control systems. Their findings are enlightening. Only 3 percent of employees saw their firm's culture as "self-governing," in which decision making is driven by a "set of core principles and values." In contrast, 43 percent of employees saw their firm as operating using a top-down, command-and-control decision process, what the authors of the study labeled as the "blind-obedience" model; and 53 percent of employees saw their firm following an "informed-acquiescence" model, in which the overall style is top-down but with skilled management that used a mix of rewards and rules to get the desired behavior. In total, 97 percent of employees saw their firm's culture and decision style as being top-down.

Interestingly, managers had a different view. The survey found that 24 percent of managers believed their organizations used the values-driven, decentralized "self-governing" model. Thus, managers were eight times more likely than employees to see the firm employing a contemporary, values-driven control system. Similarly, while 41 percent of managers said that their firm rewarded performance based on values and not just financial outcomes, only 14 percent of employees saw this.

The cynicism employees expressed regarding the control systems in their firms had important consequences for the firm. Almost half of the employees who had described their firms as blind-obedience firms had witnessed unethical behavior in the firm within the last year. Only one in four employees in firms with the other two control types said they had witnessed unethical behavior. Additionally, only one-fourth of the employees in blind-obedience firms would blow the whistle on unethical behavior, but this rate went up to nine in ten if the firm relied on self-governance. Finally, the impressions of employees influence the ability of the firm to be responsive and innovative. Among those surveyed, 90 percent of employees in self-governing and 67 percent of employees in informed-acquiescence firms agreed with the statement that "good ideas are readily adopted by my company." Less than 20 percent of employees in blind-obedience firms agreed with the same statement.

These findings indicate that managers need to be aware of how the actions they take to improve the control systems in their firms are being received by employees. If the employees see the pronouncements of management regarding moving toward a decentralized, culture-centered control system as simply propaganda, the firm is unlikely to experience the positive changes it desires.

Sources: Anonymous. 2011. The view from the top and bottom. *The Economist*, September 24: 76; and Levit, A. 2012. Your employees aren't wearing your rose colored glasses. *openforum.com*, November 12: np.

3. The data and information generated are best interpreted and discussed in face-to-face meetings.

4. The control system is a key catalyst for an ongoing debate about underlying data, assumptions, and action plans.

An executive's decision to use the control system interactively—in other words, to invest the time and attention to review and evaluate new information—sends a clear signal to the organization about what is important. The dialogue and debate that emerge from such an interactive process can often lead to new strategies and innovations. Strategy Spotlight 9.1 discusses how managers and employees each see the control systems at work in their companies and identifies some of the consequences of those impressions.

LO9.4

The benefits of having the proper balance among the three levers of behavioral control: culture, rewards and incentives, and boundaries.

Attaining Behavioral Control: Balancing Culture, Rewards, and Boundaries

Behavioral control is focused on implementation—doing things right. Effectively implementing strategy requires manipulating three key control "levers": culture, rewards, and boundaries (see Exhibit 9.3). There are two compelling reasons for an increased emphasis on culture and rewards in a system of behavioral controls.[11]

EXHIBIT 9.3 Essential Elements of Behavioral Control

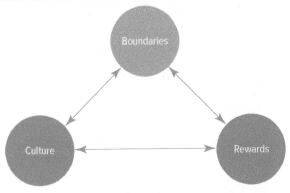

First, the competitive environment is increasingly complex and unpredictable, demanding both flexibility and quick response to its challenges. As firms simultaneously downsize and face the need for increased coordination across organizational boundaries, a control system based primarily on rigid strategies, rules, and regulations is dysfunctional. The use of rewards and culture to align individual and organizational goals becomes increasingly important.

Second, the implicit long-term contract between the organization and its key employees has been eroded.[12] Today's younger managers have been conditioned to see themselves as "free agents" and view a career as a series of opportunistic challenges. As managers are advised to "specialize, market yourself, and have work, if not a job," the importance of culture and rewards in building organizational loyalty claims greater importance.

Each of the three levers—culture, rewards, and boundaries—must work in a balanced and consistent manner. Let's consider the role of each.

Building a Strong and Effective Culture

Organizational culture is a system of shared values (what is important) and beliefs (how things work) that shape a company's people, organizational structures, and control systems to produce behavioral norms (the way we do things around here).[13] How important is culture? Very. Over the years, numerous best sellers, such as *Theory Z, Corporate Cultures, In Search of Excellence,* and *Good to Great,*[14] have emphasized the powerful influence of culture on what goes on within organizations and how they perform.

Collins and Porras argued in *Built to Last* that the key factor in sustained exceptional performance is a cultlike culture.[15] You can't touch it or write it down, but it's there in every organization; its influence is pervasive; it can work for you or against you.[16] Effective leaders understand its importance and strive to shape and use it as one of their important levers of strategic control.[17]

The Role of Culture Culture wears many different hats, each woven from the fabric of those values that sustain the organization's primary source of competitive advantage. Some examples are:

- FedEx and Amazon focus on customer service.
- Lexus (a division of Toyota) and Apple emphasize product quality.
- Google and 3M place a high value on innovation.
- Nucor (steel) and Walmart are concerned, above all, with operational efficiency.

Culture sets implicit boundaries—unwritten standards of acceptable behavior—in dress, ethical matters, and the way an organization conducts its business.[18] By creating a

> **organizational culture**
> a system of shared values and beliefs that shape a company's people, organizational structures, and control systems to produce behavioral norms.

framework of shared values, culture encourages individual identification with the organization and its objectives. Culture acts as a means of reducing monitoring costs.[19]

Strong culture can lead to greater employee engagement and provide a common purpose and identity. Firms have typically relied on economic incentives for workers, using a combination of rewards (carrots) and rules and threats (sticks) to get employees to act in desired ways. But these systems rely on the assumption that individuals are fundamentally self-interested and selfish. However, research suggests that this assumption is overstated.[20] When given a chance to act selfishly or cooperatively with others, over half of employees choose to cooperate, while only 30 percent consistently choose to act selfishly. Thus, cultural systems that build engagement, communication, and a sense of common purpose and identity would allow firms to leverage these collaborative workers.

Sustaining an Effective Culture   Powerful organizational cultures just don't happen overnight, and they don't remain in place without a strong commitment—in terms of both words and deeds—by leaders throughout the organization.[21] A viable and productive organizational culture can be strengthened and sustained. However, it cannot be "built" or "assembled"; instead, it must be cultivated, encouraged, and "fertilized."[22]

Storytelling is one way effective cultures are maintained. 3M is a company that uses powerful stories to reinforce the culture of the firm. One of those is the story of Francis G. Okie.[23] In 1922 Okie came up with the idea of selling sandpaper to men as a replacement for razor blades. The idea obviously didn't pan out, but Okie was allowed to remain at 3M. Interestingly, the technology developed by Okie led 3M to develop its first blockbuster product: a waterproof sandpaper that became a staple of the automobile industry. Such stories foster the importance of risk taking, experimentation, freedom to fail, and innovation—all vital elements of 3M's culture. Strategy Spotlight 9.2 discusses the power of pictures and stories in building a customer-centric culture.

Rallies or "pep talks" by top executives also serve to reinforce a firm's culture. The late Sam Walton was known for his pep rallies at local Walmart stores. Four times a year, the founders of Home Depot—Bernard Marcus and Arthur Blank—used to don orange aprons and stage Breakfast with Bernie and Arthur, a 6:30 a.m. pep rally, broadcast live over the firm's closed-circuit TV network to most of its 45,000 employees.[24]

Southwest Airlines' "Culture Committee" is a unique vehicle designed to perpetuate the company's highly successful culture. The following excerpt from an internal company publication describes its objectives:

> The goal of the Committee is simple—to ensure that our unique Corporate Culture stays alive. . . . Culture Committee members represent all regions and departments across our system and they are selected based upon their exemplary display of the "Positively Outrageous Service" that won us the first-ever Triple Crown; their continual exhibition of the "Southwest Spirit" to our Customers and to their fellow workers; and their high energy level, boundless enthusiasm, unique creativity, and constant demonstration of teamwork and love for their fellow workers.[25]

Motivating with Rewards and Incentives

Reward and incentive systems represent a powerful means of influencing an organization's culture, focusing efforts on high-priority tasks, and motivating individual and collective task performance.[26] Just as culture deals with influencing beliefs, behaviors, and attitudes of people within an organization, the **reward system**—by specifying who gets rewarded and why—is an effective motivator and control mechanism.[27] The managers at Not Your Average Joe's, a Massachusetts-based restaurant chain, changed their staffing procedures both to let their servers better understand their performance and to better motivate them.[28] The chain uses sophisticated software to track server performance—in both per customer sales and customer satisfaction as seen in tips. Highly rated servers are given more tables

reward system
policies that specify who gets rewarded and why.

9.2 STRATEGY SPOTLIGHT

USING PICTURES AND STORIES TO BUILD A CUSTOMER-ORIENTED CULTURE

Most firms tout that customers are their most important stakeholders. In firms that have value statements, these statements typically list the firms' responsibilities to their customers first. But it is hard to build and maintain a customer-centric culture. Using visual imagery and stories can help firms put customers at the center of their culture.

The old saying is that "a picture is worth a thousand words." This is certainly true when building a culture. A simple snapshot of a customer or end user can be a powerful motivating tool for workers to care about that customer. For example, radiologists rarely see patients. They look at X-rays from the files of patients, but these patients are typically faceless and anonymous to them. However, when pictures of the patients were added to their files, one study found that radiologists increased the length of their reports on the patients' X-rays by 29 percent and improved the accuracy of their diagnoses by 46 percent. Other firms have found the same effect. Microfinance provider Kiva includes pictures of the entrepreneurs whom it is trying to fund, believing that potential donors feel more of a connection with an entrepreneur when they have seen a picture of him or her.

Stories can also help build a customer-centric culture. Inside the firm, the stories that employees share with each other become imprinted on the organizational mind. Thus, as employees share their positive stories of experiences with customers, they not only provide encouragement for other employees to better meet the needs of customers but also reinforce the storytelling employee's desire to work hard to serve customers. For example, at Ritz-Carlton hotels, employees meet each day for 15 minutes to share stories about how they went the extra yard to meet customers' needs. These stories can even be more significant for new employees, helping them learn about the values of the firm. With outside stories, firms can draw on the accounts of customers to reinvigorate their employees. These can be based on personal statements from customers or even from news stories. To test these effects, one researcher gave lifeguards a few short news stories about swimmers who were saved by lifeguards on other beaches. The lifeguards who heard these stories reported that they found their job more meaningful, volunteered to work more hours, and were rated by their supervisors as being more vigilant in their work one month later.

Managers can help ensure that the stories told support the firm's customer-centric culture by taking the following steps:

- Tell positive stories about employees' interactions with customers.
- Share positive customer feedback with employees.
- Tie employee recognition to positive employee actions.
- Weave stories into the employee handbook and new employee orientation.
- Make sure that mentors in the firm know about the importance of using stories in their mentoring efforts.

The "short story" here is that firms can help build and reinforce a customer-centric culture if they just keep the customer in the center of the stories they tell and make the customer personally relevant to workers.

Sources: Grant, A. 2011. How customers rally your troops. *Harvard Business Review*, 89(6): 96–103; and Heathfield, S. 2014. How stories strengthen your work culture—or not. *humanresources.about.com*, December 29: np.

and preferred schedules. In shifting more work and better schedules to the best workers, the chain hopes to improve profitability and motivate all workers.

The Potential Downside   While they can be powerful motivators, reward and incentive policies can also result in undesirable outcomes in organizations. At the individual level, incentives can go wrong for multiple reasons. First, if individual workers don't see how their actions relate to how they are compensated, incentives can be demotivating. For example, if the rewards are related to the firm's stock price, workers may feel that their efforts have little if any impact and won't perceive any benefit from working harder. On the other hand, if the incentives are too closely tied to their individual work, they may lead to dysfunctional outcomes. For example, if a sales representative is rewarded for sales volume, she will be incentivized to sell at all costs. This may lead her to accept unprofitable sales or push sales through distribution channels the firm would rather avoid. Thus, the collective sum of individual behaviors of an organization's employees does not always result in what is best for the organization; individual rationality is no guarantee of organizational rationality.

Reward and incentive systems can also cause problems across organizational units. As corporations grow and evolve, they often develop different business units with multiple reward systems. These systems may differ based on industry contexts, business situations, stage of product life cycles, and so on. Subcultures within organizations may reflect differences among functional areas, products, services, and divisions. To the extent that reward systems reinforce such behavioral norms, attitudes, and belief systems, cohesiveness is reduced; important information is hoarded rather than shared, individuals begin working at cross-purposes, and they lose sight of overall goals.

Such conflicts are commonplace in many organizations. For example, sales and marketing personnel promise unrealistically quick delivery times to bring in business, much to the dismay of operations and logistics; overengineering by R&D creates headaches for manufacturing; and so on. Conflicts also arise across divisions when divisional profits become a key compensation criterion. As ill will and anger escalate, personal relationships and performance may suffer.

Creating Effective Reward and Incentive Programs   To be effective, incentive and reward systems need to reinforce basic core values, enhance cohesion and commitment to goals and objectives, and meet with the organization's overall mission and purpose.[29]

At General Mills, to ensure a manager's interest in the overall performance of his or her unit, half of a manager's annual bonus is linked to business unit results and half to individual performance.[30] For example, if a manager simply matches a rival manufacturer's performance, his or her salary is roughly 5 percent lower. However, if a manager's product ranks in the industry's top 10 percent in earnings growth and return on capital, the manager's total pay can rise to nearly 30 percent beyond the industry norm.

Effective reward and incentive systems share a number of common characteristics[31] (see Exhibit 9.4). The perception that a plan is "fair and equitable" is critically important. The firm must have the flexibility to respond to changing requirements as its direction and objectives change. In recent years many companies have begun to place more emphasis on growth. To ensure that managers focus on growth, a number of firms have changed their compensation systems to move from a bottom-line focus to one that emphasizes growth, new products, acquisitions, and international expansion.

However, incentive and reward systems don't have to be all about money. Employees respond not only to monetary compensation but also to softer forms of incentives and rewards. In fact, a number of studies have found that for employees who are satisfied with their base salary, nonfinancial motivators are more effective than cash incentives in building long-term employee motivation.[32] Three key reward systems appear to provide the greatest incentives. First, employees respond to managerial praise. This can include formal recognition policies and events. For example, at Mars Central Europe, the company holds an event twice a year at which they celebrate innovative ideas generated by employees. Recognition at the Mars "Make a Difference" event is designed to motivate the winners and also other employees who want to receive the same recognition. Employees also respond well to informal recognition rewards, such as personal praise, written praise, and public praise. This is especially effective when it includes small perks, such as a gift certificate for dinner, some scheduling flexibility, or even an extra day off. Positive words and actions are especially powerful since almost two-thirds of employees in one study said management was much more likely to criticize them for poor performance than praise them for good work. Second, employees feel rewarded when they receive attention from

EXHIBIT 9.4

Characteristics of
Effective Reward and
Incentive Systems

- Objectives are clear, well understood, and broadly accepted.
- Rewards are clearly linked to performance and desired behaviors.
- Performance measures are clear and highly visible.
- Feedback is prompt, clear, and unambiguous.
- The compensation "system" is perceived as fair and equitable.
- The structure is flexible; it can adapt to changing circumstances.

INSIGHTS FROM RESEARCH

INSPIRE PASSION—MOTIVATE TOP PERFORMANCE

Overview

Often, managers approach and strive to motivate employees with extrinsic rewards. These produce some results; however, employees tend to perform best when their intrinsic needs are met. Think of ways to highlight the purpose of your employees' work. Allow employees to work on projects that ignite their passions.

What the Research Shows

Employees who are passionate about their jobs are more engaged in their jobs. And employees who are more engaged in their jobs perform them better, according to investigators from the University of Richmond, Nanyang Technological University, and Keppel Offshore and Marine Ltd. in Singapore. Their 2011 research, published in the *Journal of Management Studies,* utilized the performance appraisals of 509 headquarters employees of a large insurance company. The employees were given a survey to identify their attitudes toward their jobs. Using structural equations modeling, the researchers found a relationship between the employees' passion for their jobs and their performance of their jobs. However, the effect was significant only when mediated by the employees' absorption in their jobs.

Employees who had job passion identified with their jobs intrinsically and believed their work was meaningful. Therefore, they were able to feel passionate about their jobs while balancing that passion with other aspects of their lives that were also important to them. This resulted in an intensity of focus on and deep immersion in their tasks while they were working. When they were deeply engrossed in work, the employees were not distracted by other activities or roles in their lives. In turn, this job absorption resulted in superior performance on the job.

Why This Matters

While many managers attempt to tap into their employees' passions to motivate them to perform their jobs, external incentives are not the best way to engender internal identification with work. Even positive feedback can become an external incentive if employees work toward receiving that recognition rather than working simply because they identify with and enjoy their jobs. A better way to nurture employees' identification with their work is to provide them with a sense of ownership of their work and, more importantly, to help them see how meaningful their jobs are. For example, to help their employees see the impact of their work on others, Cancer Treatment Centers of America in the Tulsa, Oklahoma, area recruits spouses of employees to

form and run a nonprofit organization to raise money for cancer patients' nonmedical expenses.

Kevin Cleary, CEO of Clif Bar and Co., says success is contingent upon an "engaged, inspired and outrageously committed team." He breaks this down into these steps:

1. Engage your employees with the company's mission and vision. If you don't have a mission and vision statement, get employees' contributions to create one you believe in.

2. Once people understand the mission and vision, trust your employees to work. Do not micromanage or assume they need a held hand.

3. Have a business model in which people come first, second, and third.

Cleary says exceptional talent is valuable only when employees believe in the organization's mission.

Key Takeaways

- Employees who are passionate about their jobs will be more engaged and absorbed in them and will perform better.

- When employees like their jobs and view them as important, they will be more passionate about their work.

- Employees whose jobs are significant to their personal identities—relative to the other roles they play in their lives—will be more passionate about their jobs.

- When employees are passionate about their jobs, they become deeply engrossed in their job tasks and aren't easily distracted by other activities.

- Although job passion must be voluntary and driven by employees' internal identities, managers can encourage it by helping employees see the significance of their work.

Apply This Today

Managers can fuel employees' intrinsic motivation by helping them see the meaning in their tasks, the company, and its mission. If employees can find personal meaning and passion in their jobs, the company will be rewarded with significant improvements in performance. To learn more about motivating your employees, visit *businessminded.com.*

Research Reviewed

Ho, V. T., Wong, S. S., & Lee, C. H. 2011. A tale of passion: Linking job passion and cognitive engagement to employee work performance. *Journal of Management Studies,* 48(1): 26–47.

leaders and, as a result, feel valued and involved. One survey found that the number-one factor employees valued was "managerial support and involvement"—having their managers ask for their opinions, involve them in decisions, and give them authority to complete tasks. Third, managers can reward employees by giving them opportunities to lead projects or task forces. In sum, incentives and rewards can go well beyond simple pay to include formal recognition, praise, and the self-esteem that comes from feeling valued.

The Insights from Research box provides further evidence that employees are motivated more when they feel a sense of purpose in their work and feel valued by their employers than when they are only monetarily rewarded for their work.

Setting Boundaries and Constraints

In an ideal world, a strong culture and effective rewards should be sufficient to ensure that all individuals and subunits work toward the common goals and objectives of the whole organization.[33] However, this is not usually the case. Counterproductive behavior can arise because of motivated self-interest, lack of a clear understanding of goals and objectives, or outright malfeasance. **Boundaries and constraints** can serve many useful purposes for organizations, including:

- Focusing individual efforts on strategic priorities.
- Providing short-term objectives and action plans to channel efforts.
- Improving efficiency and effectiveness.
- Minimizing improper and unethical conduct.

boundaries and constraints
rules that specify behaviors that are acceptable and unacceptable.

Focusing Efforts on Strategic Priorities Boundaries and constraints play a valuable role in focusing a company's strategic priorities. For example, in 2015, GE sold off its financial services businesses in order to refocus on its manufacturing businesses. Similarly, Pfizer sold its infant formula business as it refocused its attention on core pharmaceutical products.[34] This concentration of effort and resources provides the firm with greater strategic focus and the potential for stronger competitive advantages in the remaining areas.

Steve Jobs would use whiteboards to set priorities and focus attention at Apple. For example, he would take his "top 100" people on a retreat each year. One year, he asked the group what 10 things Apple should do next. The group identified ideas. Ideas went up on the board and then got erased or revised; new ones were added, revised, and erased. The group argued about it for a while and finally identified their list of top 10 initiatives. Jobs proceeded to slash the bottom seven, stating, "We can only do three."[35]

Boundaries also have a place in the nonprofit sector. For example, a British relief organization uses a system to monitor strategic boundaries by maintaining a list of companies whose contributions it will neither solicit nor accept. Such boundaries are essential for maintaining legitimacy with existing and potential benefactors.

Providing Short-Term Objectives and Action Plans In Chapter 1 we discussed the importance of a firm having a vision, mission, and strategic objectives that are internally consistent and that provide strategic direction. In addition, short-term objectives and action plans provide similar benefits. That is, they represent boundaries that help to allocate resources in an optimal manner and to channel the efforts of employees at all levels throughout the organization.[36] To be effective, short-term objectives must have several attributes. They should:

- Be specific and measurable.
- Include a specific time horizon for their attainment.
- Be achievable, yet challenging enough to motivate managers who must strive to accomplish them.

Research has found that performance is enhanced when individuals are encouraged to attain specific, difficult, yet achievable, goals (as opposed to vague "do your best" goals).[37]

9.3 STRATEGY SPOTLIGHT ENVIRONMENTAL SUSTAINABILITY

BREAKING DOWN SUSTAINABILITY INTO MEASURABLE GOALS

Marks and Spencer (M&S) laid out an ambitious goal in early 2010 to become "the world's most sustainable retailer" by 2015. To meet this goal, M&S needed to substantially change how it undertook nearly all of its business operations. To make this process more tractable and to provide opportunities to identify a range of actions managers could take, M&S developed an overarching plan for its sustainability efforts, dubbed Plan A. They called it Plan A because, as M&S managers put it, when it comes to building environmental sustainability, there is no Plan B. Everyone in the firm needed to be committed to the one vision. In this plan, M&S identified three broad themes:

- Aim for all M&S products to have at least one Plan A quality.
- Help our customers make a difference to the social and environmental causes that matter to them.
- Help our customers live a more sustainable life.

Thus, M&S aimed not only to improve its own operations but also to change the lives of its customers and the operations of its suppliers and other partners. Marc Bolland, M&S's CEO, fleshed out the general Plan A goal with 180 environmental commitments. These commitments all had time targets associated with them, some short term and some longer term. For example, one commitment was to make the company carbon-neutral, a goal it achieved in 2014. To meet its goal, M&S estimated it needed to achieve a 25 percent reduction in energy use in its stores by 2012 and extended it to 35 percent by 2015. This provided clear targets for store managers to work toward. Similarly, M&S set a goal to improve its water use efficiency in stores by 25 percent by the year 2015. Additionally, M&S set out to design new stores that used 35 percent less water than current stores. These targets provided clear metrics for store managers as well as architects and designers working on new stores.

In working with its suppliers, M&S similarly rolled out a series of time-based commitments. For example, it conducted a review with all suppliers on the Plan A initiatives in the first year of the plan. M&S required all suppliers of fresh meat, dairy, produce, and flowers to engage in a sustainable agriculture program by 2012. All clothing suppliers were required to install energy-efficient lighting and improved insulation by 2015 to attain a 10 percent reduction in energy usage. These types of efforts spanned across the firm and its supply chain. As of 2014, 85 of M&S's top 100 suppliers had introduced energy-efficient best practices.

With its Plan A, M&S broke down a huge initiative into clear targets that were actionable by managers across the firm and in its partner firms. Interestingly, while this initiative was hatched as a means to achieve environmental sustainability gains, it has also turned out to be an economic win for M&S. In the first year of the plan, the firm experienced an $80 million profit on the actions it undertook. The surplus has resulted from gains in energy efficiency, lower packaging costs, lower waste bills, and profit from a sustainable energy business it set up that relies on burning biowaste to generate electricity.

Sources: Felsted, A. 2011. Marks and Spencer's green blueprint. *ft.com,* March 17: np; Anonymous. 2012. Marks & Spencer's ambitious sustainability goals. *sustainablebusiness.com,* March 3: np; and *planareport.marksandspencer.com.*

Short-term objectives must provide proper direction and also provide enough flexibility for the firm to keep pace with and anticipate changes in the external environment, new government regulations, a competitor introducing a substitute product, or changes in consumer taste. Unexpected events within a firm may require a firm to make important adjustments in both strategic and short-term objectives. The emergence of new industries can have a drastic effect on the demand for products and services in more traditional industries.

Action plans are critical to the implementation of chosen strategies. Unless action plans are specific, there may be little assurance that managers have thought through all of the resource requirements for implementing their strategies. In addition, unless plans are specific, managers may not understand what needs to be implemented or have a clear time frame for completion. This is essential for the scheduling of key activities that must be implemented. Finally, individual managers must be held accountable for the implementation. This helps to provide the necessary motivation and "sense of ownership" to implement action plans on a timely basis. Strategy Spotlight 9.3 illustrates how Marks and Spencer puts its sustainability mission into action by creating clear, measurable goals.

Improving Operational Efficiency and Effectiveness Rule-based controls are most appropriate in organizations with the following characteristics:

- Environments are stable and predictable.
- Employees are largely unskilled and interchangeable.

- Consistency in product and service is critical.
- The risk of malfeasance is extremely high (e.g., in banking or casino operations).[38]

McDonald's Corp. has extensive rules and regulations that regulate the operation of its franchises.[39] Its policy manual from a number of years ago stated, "Cooks must turn, never flip, hamburgers. If they haven't been purchased, Big Macs must be discarded in 10 minutes after being cooked and French fries in 7 minutes. Cashiers must make eye contact with and smile at every customer."

Guidelines can also be effective in setting spending limits and the range of discretion for employees and managers, such as the $2,500 limit that hotelier Ritz-Carlton uses to empower employees to placate dissatisfied customers.

Minimizing Improper and Unethical Conduct   Guidelines can be useful in specifying proper relationships with a company's customers and suppliers.[40] Many companies have explicit rules regarding commercial practices, including the prohibition of any form of payment, bribe, or kickback. For example, Singapore Airlines has a 17-page policy outlining its anticorruption and antibribery policies.[41]

Regulations backed up with strong sanctions can also help an organization avoid conducting business in an unethical manner. Since the passing of the Sarbanes-Oxley Act (which provides for stiffer penalties for financial reporting misdeeds) in 2002, many chief financial officers (CFOs) have taken steps to ensure ethical behavior in the preparation of financial statements. For example, Home Depot's CFO, Carol B. Tomé, strengthened the firm's code of ethics and developed stricter guidelines. Now all 25 of her subordinates must sign personal statements that all of their financial statements are correct—just as she and her CEO have to do.[42]

Behavioral Control in Organizations: Situational Factors

Here, the focus is on ensuring that the behavior of individuals at all levels of an organization is directed toward achieving organizational goals and objectives. The three fundamental types of control are culture, rewards and incentives, and boundaries and constraints. An organization may pursue one or a combination of them on the basis of a variety of internal and external factors.

Not all organizations place the same emphasis on each type of control.[43] In high-technology firms engaged in basic research, members may work under high levels of autonomy. An individual's performance is generally quite difficult to measure accurately because of the long lead times involved in R&D activities. Thus, internalized norms and values become very important.

When the measurement of an individual's output or performance is quite straightforward, control depends primarily on granting or withholding rewards. Frequently, a sales manager's compensation is in the form of a commission and bonus tied directly to his or her sales volume, which is relatively easy to determine. Here, behavior is influenced more strongly by the attractiveness of the compensation than by the norms and values implicit in the organization's culture. The measurability of output precludes the need for an elaborate system of rules to control behavior.[44]

Control in bureaucratic organizations is dependent on members following a highly formalized set of rules and regulations. Most activities are routine, and the desired behavior can be specified in a detailed manner because there is generally little need for innovative or creative activity. Managing an assembly plant requires strict adherence to many rules as well as exacting sequences of assembly operations. In the public sector, the Department of Motor Vehicles in most states must follow clearly prescribed procedures when issuing or renewing driver licenses. Strategy Spotlight 9.4 highlights how Digital Reasoning is using data analytics to strengthen control in major financial firms.

Exhibit 9.5 provides alternative approaches to behavioral control and some of the situational factors associated with them.

9.4 STRATEGY SPOTLIGHT

USING DATA ANALYTICS TO ENHANCE ORGANIZATIONAL CONTROL

Tim Estes's goal was to develop cognitive computing as a useful business tool. Cognitive computing strives to integrate raw computing power with natural-language processing and pattern recognition to build powerful computer systems that mimic human problem solving and learning. He first found a ready home for his vision in national security. The U.S. Army's Ground Intelligence Center contracted with Digital Reasoning to develop systems to identify potential terrorists on the basis of analyses of large volumes of different sources of data, including emails, travel information, and other data.

More recently, Digital Reasoning has taken its expertise to the financial services industry and, in doing so, is providing a new type of control system to catch potential rogue traders and market manipulators within the firms. Digital Reasoning provides systems Estes refers to as "proactive compliance" to a number of major financial services providers, including Credit Suisse and Goldman Sachs. Digital Reasoning has developed software that looks for information in and patterns across billions of emails, instant messages, media reports, and memos that suggest an employee's intention to engage in illegal or prohibited behavior before the employee crosses the line. Rather than looking for evidence of actions already taken, Digital Reasoning's software looks into ongoing patterns of correspondence to search for evolving personal relationships within the company, putting up red flags when it sees unexpected patterns, such as people in different units of the firm suddenly communicating with unusual frequency or a heightened level of discussion on topics that may be tied to unethical or illegal behavior. Any unusual patterns are then investigated by analysts in each of the financial services' firms. The goal for the firms is to both control employee behavior to stay on the right side of the law and also to send signals to customers and regulators that they are taking steps to stay on the right side of legal and ethical boundaries.

Sources: McGee, J. 2014. When crisis strikes, Digital Reasoning takes action. *tennessean.com,* October 9: np; McGee, J. 2014. Digital reasoning gains $24M from Goldman, Credit Suisse. *tennessean.com,* October 9: np; and Dillow, C. 2014. Nothing to hide, everything to fear. *Fortune,* September 1: 45–48.

Evolving from Boundaries to Rewards and Culture

In most environments, organizations should strive to provide a system of rewards and incentives, coupled with a culture strong enough that boundaries become internalized. This reduces the need for external controls such as rules and regulations.

First, hire the right people—individuals who already identify with the organization's dominant values and have attributes consistent with them. Kroger, a supermarket chain, uses a preemployment test to assess the degree to which potential employees will be friendly and communicate well with customers.[45] Microsoft's David Pritchard is well aware of the consequences of failing to hire properly:

> If I hire a bunch of bozos, it will hurt us, because it takes time to get rid of them. They start infiltrating the organization and then they themselves start hiring people of lower quality. At Microsoft, we are always looking for people who are better than we are.

Second, training plays a key role. For example, in elite military units such as the Green Berets and Navy SEALs, the training regimen so thoroughly internalizes the culture that

EXHIBIT 9.5 Organizational Control: Alternative Approaches

Approach	Some Situational Factors
Culture: A system of unwritten rules that forms an internalized influence over behavior.	• Often found in professional organizations. • Associated with high autonomy. • Norms are the basis for behavior.
Rules: Written and explicit guidelines that provide external constraints on behavior.	• Associated with standardized output. • Most appropriate when tasks are generally repetitive and routine. • Little need for innovation or creative activity.
Rewards: The use of performance-based incentive systems to motivate.	• Measurement of output and performance is rather straightforward. • Most appropriate in organizations pursuing unrelated diversification strategies. • Rewards may be used to reinforce other means of control.

individuals, in effect, lose their identity. The group becomes the overriding concern and focal point of their energies. At firms such as FedEx, training not only builds skills but also plays a significant role in building a strong culture on the foundation of each organization's dominant values.

Third, managerial role models are vital. Andy Grove, former CEO and cofounder of Intel, didn't need (or want) a large number of bureaucratic rules to determine who is responsible for what, who is supposed to talk to whom, and who gets to fly first class (no one does). He encouraged openness by not having many of the trappings of success—he worked in a cubicle like all the other professionals. Can you imagine any new manager asking whether or not he can fly first class? Grove's personal example eliminated such a need.

Fourth, reward systems must be clearly aligned with the organizational goals and objectives. For example, as part of its efforts to drive sustainability efforts down through its suppliers, Marks and Spencer pushes the suppliers to develop employee reward systems that support a living wage and team collaboration.

The Role of Corporate Governance

LO9.5

The three key participants in corporate governance: shareholders, management (led by the CEO), and the board of directors.

corporate governance
the relationship among various participants in determining the direction and performance of corporations. The primary participants are (1) the shareholders, (2) the management, and (3) the board of directors.

We now address the issue of strategic control in a broader perspective, typically referred to as "corporate governance." Here we focus on the need for both shareholders (the owners of the corporation) and their elected representatives, the board of directors, to actively ensure that management fulfills its overriding purpose of increasing long-term shareholder value.[46]

Robert Monks and Nell Minow, two leading scholars in **corporate governance,** define it as "the relationship among various participants in determining the direction and performance of corporations. The primary participants are (1) the shareholders, (2) the management (led by the CEO), and (3) the board of directors."* Our discussion will center on how corporations can succeed (or fail) in aligning managerial motives with the interests of the shareholders and their elected representatives, the board of directors.[47] As you will recall from Chapter 1, we discussed the important role of boards of directors and provided some examples of effective and ineffective boards.[48]

Good corporate governance plays an important role in the investment decisions of major institutions, and a premium is often reflected in the price of securities of companies that practice it. The corporate governance premium is larger for firms in countries with sound corporate governance practices compared to countries with weaker corporate governance standards.[49]

Sound governance practices often lead to superior financial performance. However, this is not always the case. For example, practices such as independent directors (directors who are not part of the firm's management) and stock options are generally assumed to result in better performance. But in many cases, independent directors may not have the necessary expertise or involvement, and the granting of stock options to the CEO may lead to decisions and actions calculated to prop up share price only in the short term.

At the same time, few topics in the business press are generating as much interest (and disdain!) as corporate governance.

Some recent notable examples of flawed corporate governance include:[50]

- In 2014, three senior executives at Walmart resigned from the firm in the wake of accusations of bribery of government officials in Mexico. In response, Walmart changed both the leadership in this region and its compliance structure.[51]

---

*Management cannot ignore the demands of other important firm stakeholders such as creditors, suppliers, customers, employees, and government regulators. At times of financial duress, powerful creditors can exert strong and legitimate pressures on managerial decisions. In general, however, the attention to stakeholders other than the owners of the corporation must be addressed in a manner that is still consistent with maximizing long-term shareholder returns. For a seminal discussion on stakeholder management, refer to Freeman, R. E. 1984. *Strategic Management: A Stakeholder Approach.* Boston: Pitman.

- In 2012 Japanese camera and medical equipment maker Olympus Corporation and three of its former executives pleaded guilty to charges that they falsified accounting records over a five-year period to inflate the financial performance of the firm. The total value of the accounting irregularities came to $1.7 billion.[52]
- In October 2010, Angelo Mozilo, the cofounder of Countrywide Financial, agreed to pay $67.5 million to the Securities and Exchange Commission (SEC) to settle fraud charges. He was charged with deceiving the home loan company's investors while reaping a personal windfall. He was accused of hiding risks about Countrywide's loan portfolio as the real estate market soured. Former Countrywide president David Sambol and former chief financial officer Eric Sieracki were also charged with fraud, as they failed to disclose the true state of Countrywide's deteriorating mortgage portfolio. The SEC accused Mozilo of insider trading, alleging that he sold millions of dollars worth of Countrywide stock after he knew the company was doomed.

Because of the many lapses in corporate governance, we can see the benefits associated with effective practices.[53] However, corporate managers may behave in their own self-interest, often to the detriment of shareholders. Next we address the implications of the separation of ownership and management in the modern corporation, and some mechanisms that can be used to ensure consistency (or alignment) between the interests of shareholders and those of the managers to minimize potential conflicts.

The Modern Corporation: The Separation of Owners (Shareholders) and Management

Some of the proposed definitions for a *corporation* include:

- "The business corporation is an instrument through which capital is assembled for the activities of producing and distributing goods and services and making investments. Accordingly, a basic premise of corporation law is that a business corporation should have as its objective the conduct of such activities with a view to enhancing the corporation's profit and the gains of the corporation's owners, that is, the shareholders." (Melvin Aron Eisenberg, *The Structure of Corporation Law*)
- "A body of persons granted a charter legally recognizing them as a separate entity having its own rights, privileges, and liabilities distinct from those of its members." (*American Heritage Dictionary*)
- "An ingenious device for obtaining individual profit without individual responsibility." (Ambrose Bierce, *The Devil's Dictionary*)[54]

All of these definitions have some validity and each one reflects a key feature of the corporate form of business organization—its ability to draw resources from a variety of groups and establish and maintain its own persona that is separate from all of them. As Henry Ford once said, "A great business is really too big to be human."

Simply put, a **corporation** is a mechanism created to allow different parties to contribute capital, expertise, and labor for the maximum benefit of each party.[55] The shareholders (investors) are able to participate in the profits of the enterprise without taking direct responsibility for the operations. The management can run the company without the responsibility of personally providing the funds. The shareholders have limited liability as well as rather limited involvement in the company's affairs. However, they reserve the right to elect directors who have the fiduciary obligation to protect their interests.

Over 80 years ago, Columbia University professors Adolf Berle and Gardiner C. Means addressed the divergence of the interests of the owners of the corporation from the professional managers who are hired to run it. They warned that widely dispersed ownership "released management from the overriding requirement that it serve stockholders." The separation of

corporation
a mechanism created to allow different parties to contribute capital, expertise, and labor for the maximum benefit of each party.

ownership from management has given rise to a set of ideas called "agency theory." Central to agency theory is the relationship between two primary players—the *principals,* who are the owners of the firm (stockholders), and the *agents,* who are the people paid by principals to perform a job on their behalf (management). The stockholders elect and are represented by a board of directors that has a fiduciary responsibility to ensure that management acts in the best interests of stockholders to ensure long-term financial returns for the firm.

agency theory
a theory of the relationship between principals and their agents, with emphasis on two problems: (1) the conflicting goals of principals and agents, along with the difficulty of principals to monitor the agents, and (2) the different attitudes and preferences toward risk of principals and agents.

Agency theory is concerned with resolving two problems that can occur in agency relationships.[56] *The first is the agency problem that arises (1) when the goals of the principals and agents conflict and (2) when it is difficult or expensive for the principal to verify what the agent is actually doing.*[57] The board of directors would be unable to confirm that the managers were actually acting in the shareholders' interests because managers are "insiders" with regard to the businesses they operate and thus are better informed than the principals. Thus, managers may act "opportunistically" in pursuing their own interests—to the detriment of the corporation.[58] Managers may spend corporate funds on expensive perquisites (e.g., company jets and expensive art), devote time and resources to pet projects (initiatives in which they have a personal interest but that have limited market potential), engage in power struggles (where they may fight over resources for their own betterment and to the detriment of the firm), and negate (or sabotage) attractive merger offers because they may result in increased employment risk.[59]

The second issue is the problem of risk sharing. This arises when the principal and the agent have different attitudes and preferences toward risk. The executives in a firm may favor additional diversification initiatives because, by their very nature, they increase the size of the firm and thus the level of executive compensation.[60] At the same time, such diversification initiatives may erode shareholder value because they fail to achieve some synergies that we discussed in Chapter 6 (e.g., building on core competencies, sharing activities, or enhancing market power). Agents (executives) may have a stronger preference toward diversification than shareholders because it reduces their personal level of risk from potential loss of employment. Executives who have large holdings of stock in their firms were more likely to have diversification strategies that were more consistent with shareholder interests—increasing long-term returns.[61]

At times, top-level managers engage in actions that reflect their self-interest rather than the interests of shareholders. We provide two examples below:

- Steve Wynn, the CEO of Wynn Resorts, had a great year in 2011, even though his stockholders barely broke even. He received a starting salary of $3.9 million. On top of that, he received two bonuses, one worth $2 million and another for $9 million. In addition to cash compensation, he received over $900,000 worth of personal flying time on the corporate jet and over $500,000 worth of use of the company's villa.[62]
- John Sperling retired as chairman emeritus of Apollo Group in early 2013. He founded Apollo, the for-profit education company best known for its University of Phoenix unit, in 1973. Even though he already owned stock in Apollo worth in excess of $200 million, the board of directors, which includes his son as a member, granted him a "special retirement bonus" of $5 million, gave him two cars, and awarded him a lifetime annuity of $71,000 a month. He received all of these benefits even though Apollo's stock at the time of his retirement was worth one-fourth of its value in early 2009.[63]

LO9.6

The role of corporate governance mechanisms in ensuring that the interests of managers are aligned with those of shareholders from both the United States and international perspectives.

Governance Mechanisms: Aligning the Interests of Owners and Managers

As noted above, a key characteristic of the modern corporation is the separation of ownership from control. To minimize the potential for managers to act in their own self-interest, or "opportunistically," the owners can implement some governance mechanisms.[64] First, there are two primary means of monitoring the behavior of managers. These include (1) a committed and involved *board of directors* that acts in the best interests of the shareholders to create long-term value and (2) *shareholder activism,* wherein the owners view themselves as share*owners* instead of share*holders* and become actively engaged in the governance of the corporation. Finally, there are managerial incentives, sometimes called "contract-based outcomes," which consist of *reward and compensation agreements.* Here the goal is to carefully craft managerial incentive packages to align the interests of management with those of the stockholders.[65]

We close this section with a brief discussion of one of the most controversial issues in corporate governance—duality. Here, the question becomes: Should the CEO also be chairman of the board of directors? In many Fortune 500 firms, the same individual serves in both roles. However, in recent years, we have seen a trend toward separating these two positions. The key issue is what implications CEO duality has for firm governance and performance.

A Committed and Involved Board of Directors   The **board of directors** acts as a fulcrum between the owners and controllers of a corporation. The directors are the intermediaries who provide a balance between a small group of key managers in the firm based at the corporate headquarters and a sometimes vast group of shareholders.[66] In the United States, the law imposes on the board a strict and absolute fiduciary duty to ensure that a company is run consistent with the long-term interests of the owners—the shareholders. The reality, as we have seen, is somewhat more ambiguous.[67]

The Business Roundtable, representing the largest U.S. corporations, describes the duties of the board as follows:

> **board of directors**
> a group that has a fiduciary duty to ensure that the company is run consistently with the long-term interests of the owners, or shareholders, of a corporation and that acts as an intermediary between the shareholders and management.

1. Making decisions regarding the selection, compensation and evaluation of a well-qualified and ethical CEO. The board also appoints or approves other members of the senior management team.
2. Directors monitor management on behalf of the corporation's shareholders. Exercise vigorous and diligent oversight of the corporation's affairs. This includes the following activities.
   a. Plan for senior management development and succession.
   b. Review, understand and monitor the implementation of the corporation's strategic plans.
   c. Review and understand the corporation's risk assessment and oversee the corporation's risk management processes.
   d. Review, understand and oversee annual operating plans and budgets.
   e. Ensure the integrity and clarity of the corporation's financial statements and financial reporting.
   f. Advise management on significant issues facing the corporation.
   g. Review and approve significant corporate actions.
   h. Nominate directors and committee members and oversee effective corporate governance.
   i. Oversee legal and ethical compliance.
3. Represent the interests of all shareholders.[68]

While the roles of the board are fairly clear, following these guidelines does not guarantee that the board will be effective. To be effective, the board needs to allocate its scarce time to the most critical issues to which its members can add value. A survey of several hundred corporate board members revealed dramatic differences in how the most and least effective boards allocated their time. Boards that were seen as being ineffective, meaning they had limited impact on the direction and success of the firm, spent almost all of their time on the basic requirements of ensuring compliance, reviewing financial reports,

9.5 STRATEGY SPOTLIGHT

MOVING THE BOARD FROM AUDITOR TO ADVISER

Boards of directors are given the formal role of representing shareholders of a corporation and overseeing corporate managers to make sure managers act to enhance shareholder value. However, for decades, boards were often little more than cozy clubs, populated by the friends of the CEO who would meet every few months to rubber-stamp the CEO's plans for the firm. Financial scandals and corporate failures in the late 1990s and early 2000s changed this. New regulations came about, pushing for stronger oversight by the board, more independent directors, and greater penalties for boards that failed to fulfill their duties. This has resulted in stronger boards that more diligently oversee and discipline firm management. But it doesn't mean that the firm is leveraging all of the talent on the board, unless the firm finds a way to effectively draw on the experiences and expertise of its board.

Ram Charan, Dennis Carey, and Michael Useem argue in their book *Boards That Lead* that boards need to change, and are dramatically changing, their role, moving away from being auditors that check on the performance of managers and, instead, becoming strategic partners with firm management. The key change is that rather than reviewing and ratifying managers' decisions, the board can serve as a panel of strategic advisers to the firm, aiding in the formulation of the firm's strategy and not simply reviewing the firm's strategy. To do so, board members work to build strong relationships with the firm's CEO, actively mentor the CEO by providing advice from the wealth of their experience, and serve as talent scouts to help identify new executives for the firm. For example, the board of Ford Motor Company was instrumental in the firm's turnaround by convincing the firm's CEO, Bill Ford, of the need for new leadership, recruiting Alan Mulally from Boeing to be Ford's new CEO, and working with and advising Ford management as it worked to reorient the firm. More generally, research on a broad range of companies has found that boards that have the skills and knowledge to advise CEOs on potential key strategic initiatives are able to add more value to the firm.

The potential benefits of a leading board are clear, but so are the risks of this change. Can boards that work with and advise the CEO also serve as effective overseers of firm management, or will they end up in the cozy relationships seen in the past? Will the CEO be comfortable sharing power with the board, or will there be a power struggle as the board weighs in with advice? Finding the right balance will require not only negotiations between the board and the CEO to define the roles effectively but also the efforts of institutional investors and regulators to ensure the board doesn't get too friendly with the CEO.

Sources: McDonald, M., Westphal, J., & Graebner, M. 2008. What do they know? The effects of outside director acquisition experience on firm acquisition performance. *Strategic Management Journal*, 29: 1155–1177; Haynes, K. & Hillman, A. 2010. The effect of board capital and CEO power on strategic change. *Strategic Management Journal*, 31: 1145–1163; and Anonymous. 2013. From cuckolds to captains. *The Economist*, December 7: 72.

assessing corporate diversification, and evaluating current performance metrics. Effective boards examined these issues but also expanded the range of issues they discussed to include more forward-looking strategic issues. Effective boards discussed potential performance synergies and the value of strategic alternatives open to the firm, assessed the firm's value drivers, and evaluated potential resource reallocation options. In the end, effective and ineffective boards spent about the same time on their basic board roles, but effective boards spent additional time together to discuss more forward-looking, strategic issues. As a result, board members of effective boards spent twice as many days, about 40 per year, in their role as a board member compared to only about 19 days per year for members of ineffective boards.[69]

Strategy Spotlight 9.5 extends our discussion of the growing role of the effective boards as strategic advisers to firm management.

Although boards in the past were often dismissed as CEOs' rubber stamps, increasingly they are playing a more active role by forcing out CEOs who cannot deliver on performance.[70] Not only are they dismissing CEOs, but boards are more willing to make strong public statements about CEOs they dismissed. In the past, firms would often announce that a CEO was leaving the position to spend more time with family or pursue new opportunities. More frequently, boards are unambiguously labeling the action a dismissal to signal that they are active and engaged boards. For example, when Symantec's board removed the firm's CEO in March 2014, the board announced it was bringing in an interim CEO following "the termination of Steve Bennett." Sanofi, a French pharmaceutical firm, went even further when it fired CEO Christopher Viehbacher. In a conference call with stock analysts, the firm's board chairman discussed how a "lack of trust" between the board and Viehbacher led to his dismissal. Sometimes even the CEO clarifies the situation. When Andrew Mason was ousted as head of Groupon, he released a humorous statement saying, "After four and a half intense and wonderful years as CEO of Groupon, I've decided to spend more time with my family. Just kidding—I was fired today."[71]

Another key component of top-ranked boards is director independence.[72] Governance experts believe that a majority of directors should be free of all ties to either the CEO or the company.[73] This means that a minimum of "insiders" (past or present members of the management team) should serve on the board and that directors and their firms should be barred from doing consulting, legal, or other work for the company.[74] Interlocking directorships—in which CEOs and other top managers serve on each other's boards—are not desirable. But perhaps the best guarantee that directors act in the best interests of share-holders is the simplest: Most good companies now insist that directors own significant stock in the company they oversee.[75]

Taking it one step further, research and simple observations of boards indicate that simple prescriptions, such as having a majority of outside directors, are insufficient to lead to effective board operations. Firms need to cultivate engaged and committed boards. There are several actions that can have a positive influence on board dynamics as the board works to both oversee and advise management.[76]

1. *Build in the right expertise on the board.* Outside directors can bring in experience that the management team is missing. For example, corporations that are considering expanding into a new region of the globe may want to add a board member who brings expertise on and connections in that region. Similarly, research suggests that firms that are focusing on improving their operational efficiency benefit from having an external board member whose full-time position is as a chief operating officer, a position that typically focuses on operational activities.

2. *Keep your board size manageable.* Small, focused boards, generally with 5 to 11 members, are preferable to larger ones. As boards grow in size, the ability for them to function as a team declines. The members of the board feel less connected with each other, and decision making can become unwieldy.

3. *Choose directors who can participate fully.* The time demands on directors have increased as their responsibilities have grown to include overseeing management, verifying the firm's financial statements, setting executive compensation, and advising on the strategic direction of the firm. As a result, the average number of hours per year spent on board duties has increased to over 350 hours for directors of large firms. Directors have to dedicate significant time to their roles—not just for scheduled meetings but also to review materials between meetings and to respond to time-sensitive challenges. Thus, firms should strive to include directors who are not currently overburdened by their core occupation or involvement on other boards.

4. *Balance the need to focus on the past, the present, and the future.* Boards have a three-tiered role. They need to focus on the recent performance of the firm, how the firm is meeting current milestones and operational targets, and what the strategic direction of the firm will be moving forward. Under current regulations, boards are required to spend a great amount of time on the past as they vet the firm's financials. However, effective boards balance this time and ensure that they give adequate consideration to the present and the future.

5. *Consider management talent development.* As part of their future-oriented focus, effective boards develop succession plans for the CEO but also focus on talent development at other upper echelons of the organization. In a range of industries,

human capital is an increasingly important driver of firm success, and boards should be involved in evaluating and developing the top management core.

6. *Get a broad view.* In order to better understand the firm and make contact with key managers, the meetings of the board should rotate to different operating units and sites of the firm.

7. *Maintain norms of transparency and trust.* Highly functioning boards maintain open, team-oriented dialogue wherein information flows freely and questions are asked openly. Directors respect each other and trust that they are all working in the best interests of the corporation.

Because of financial crises and corporate scandals, regulators and investors have pushed for significant changes in the structure and actions of boards. Exhibit 9.6 highlights some of the changes seen among firms in the S&P 500.

Shareholder Activism As a practical matter, there are so many owners of the largest American corporations that it makes little sense to refer to them as "owners" in the sense of

EXHIBIT 9.6

The Changing Face of the Board of Firms in the S&P 500

Issue	Then and Now		Explanation
	1987	2011	
Percentage of boards that have an average age of 64 or older	3	37	Fewer sitting CEOs are willing to serve on the boards of other firms. As a result, companies are raising the retirement age for directors and pulling in retired executives to their boards.
Average pay for directors	$36,667	$95,262	Board work has taken greater time and commitment. Additionally, the personal liability directors face has increased. As a result, compensation has increased to attract and retain board members.
Percentage of board members who are female	9	16.2	While the number of boards with women and minorities has increased, these groups are still underrepresented. Still, companies have emphasized including female directors in key roles. For example, over half the audit and compensation committees of S&P 500 firms have at least one female member.
Percentage of boards with 12 or fewer members	22	83	As the strategic role and the legal requirements of the board have increased, firms have opted for smaller boards since these smaller boards better operate as true decision-making groups.
Percentage of the directors who are independent	68	84	The Sarbanes-Oxley Act and pressure from investors have led to an increase in the number of independent directors. In fact, over half the S&P 500 firms now have no insiders other than the CEO on the board.

Sources: Anonymous. 2011. Corporate boards: Now and then. *Harvard Business Review,* 89(11): 38–39; and Dalton, D. & Dalton, C. 2010. Women and corporate boards of directors: The promise of increased, and substantive, participation in the post Sarbanes-Oxley era. *Business Horizons,* 53: 257–268.

individuals becoming informed and involved in corporate affairs.[77] However, even an individual shareholder has several rights, including (1) the right to sell the stock, (2) the right to vote the proxy (which includes the election of board members), (3) the right to bring suit for damages if the corporation's directors or managers fail to meet their obligations, (4) the right to certain information from the company, and (5) certain residual rights following the company's liquidation (or its filing for reorganization under bankruptcy laws), once creditors and other claimants are paid off.[78]

Collectively, shareholders have the power to direct the course of corporations.[79] This may involve acts such as being party to shareholder action suits and demanding that key issues be brought up for proxy votes at annual board meetings.[80] The power of shareholders has intensified in recent years because of the increasing influence of large institutional investors such as mutual funds (e.g., T. Rowe Price and Fidelity Investments) and retirement systems such as TIAA-CREF (for university faculty members and school administrative staff).[81] Institutional investors hold over 50 percent of all listed corporate stock in the United States.[82]

Shareholder activism refers to actions by large shareholders, both institutions and individuals, to protect their interests when they feel that managerial actions diverge from shareholder value maximization.

Many institutional investors are aggressive in protecting and enhancing their investments. They are shifting from traders to owners. They are assuming the role of permanent shareholders and rigorously analyzing issues of corporate governance. In the process they are reinventing systems of corporate monitoring and accountability.[83]

Consider the proactive behavior of CalPERS, the California Public Employees' Retirement System, which manages nearly $300 billion in assets and is the third-largest pension fund in the world.[84] Every year CalPERS reviews the performance of the 1,000 firms in which it retains a sizable investment.[85] It reviews each firm's short- and long-term performance, governance characteristics, and financial status, as well as market expectations for the firm. CalPERS then meets with selected companies to better understand their governance and business strategy. If needed, CalPERS requests changes in the firm's governance structure and works to ensure shareholders' rights. If CalPERS does not believe that the firm is responsive to its concerns, it considers filing proxy actions at the firm's next shareholders meeting and possibly even court actions. CalPERS's research suggests that these actions lead to superior performance. The portfolio of firms it has included in its review program produced a cumulative return that was 11.59 percent higher than a respective set of benchmark firms over a three-year period. Thus, CalPERS has seen a real benefit of acting as an interested owner, rather than as a passive investor.

Strategy Spotlight 9.6 discusses how institutional investors have moved beyond only filing proxy actions designed to create shareholder value. In addition to pushing for changes in executive pay and increasing stock buyback initiatives, institutional investors are now pushing social initiatives.

Managerial Rewards and Incentives   As we discussed earlier in the chapter, incentive systems must be designed to help a company achieve its goals.[86] From the perspective of governance, one of the most critical roles of the board of directors is to create incentives that align the interests of the CEO and top executives with the interests of owners of the corporation—long-term shareholder returns.[87] Shareholders rely on CEOs to adopt policies and strategies that maximize the value of their shares.[88] A combination of three basic policies may create the right monetary incentives for CEOs to maximize the value of their companies:[89]

1. Boards can require that the CEOs become substantial owners of company stock.
2. Salaries, bonuses, and stock options can be structured so as to provide rewards for superior performance and penalties for poor performance.
3. Dismissal for poor performance should be a realistic threat.

shareholder activism
actions by large shareholders to protect their interests when they feel that managerial actions of a corporation diverge from shareholder value maximization.

9.6 STRATEGY SPOTLIGHT — ENVIRONMENTAL SUSTAINABILITY

INSTITUTIONAL INVESTORS PUSH SOCIAL CONCERNS

Traditionally, activist investors have been very bottom-line-focused. They've pushed firms to unlock more value for shareholders. This led firms to take actions such as appointing a nonexecutive chairman of the board, altering compensation for top managers, divesting business units, increasing dividends, adding activist representatives to the board of directors, changing CEOs, and undertaking stock buyback programs. However, activist investors are now pushing a broader range of issues with managers, most notably pushing social initiatives. In the first quarter of 2014, 56 percent of shareholder proposals related to environmental and social issues. These proposals have resulted in shareholders voting on issues related to greenhouse gas emissions, political spending, and labor rights.

These initiatives rarely find strong support from shareholders, with environmental and social resolutions garnering only 21 percent support from shareholders when they get to an actual vote. About 30 percent of these proposals never get to a vote. Instead, corporate leaders and the activist investors negotiate an agreement on the issue. Corporations are often open to finding a negotiated solution to avoid unnecessary negative press coverage

of the firm. For example, after being pressured by the $160 billion New York State Common Retirement Fund, Safeway, a major grocery retailer, agreed to buy only palm oil produced in ways that don't harm rainforests. Similarly, after being pressured by Greenpeace and associated activist investors, Lego agreed to not renew a contract with Royal Dutch Shell that had allowed Lego to sell kits with the Shell logo on trucks and gas pumps. The activists were concerned that Shell was not developing Arctic drilling areas in an environmentally responsible way and pressured Lego to disassociate itself from Shell. The effects of such activist investors can be seen more broadly as well. For example, 53 percent of firms in the S&P 500 now publish sustainability reports, and 80 percent publish data on their political giving—both of which are common concerns of social-oriented activist investors.

These pressures also put managers in a difficult position as they potentially face competing pressures. One class of activist investors may be pushing the firm to take aggressive, profitability-oriented actions, while other activist investors may be pushing competing initiatives for the firm to take social or environmental actions.

Sources: Studzinski, J. 2014. Shareholder activists up their game. *Fortune*, April 28: 20; Chasan, E. 2014. More companies bow to investors with a social cause. *wsj.com*, March 31: np; and Hansegard, J. 2014. Lego to stop making Shell play sets after Greenpeace campaign. *wsj.com*, October 9: np.

In recent years the granting of stock options has enabled top executives of publicly held corporations to earn enormous levels of compensation. In 2013, the average CEO in the Standard & Poor's 500 stock index took home 330 times the pay of the average worker—up from 40 times the average in 1980.[90] The counterargument, that the ratio is down from the 514 multiple in 2000, doesn't get much traction.[91]

Many boards have awarded huge option grants despite poor executive performance, and others have made performance goals easier to reach. However, stock options can be a valuable governance mechanism to align the CEO's interests with those of the shareholders. The extraordinarily high level of compensation can, at times, be grounded in sound governance principles.[92] Research by Steven Kaplan at the University of Chicago found that firms with CEOs in the top quintile of pay generated stock returns 60 percent higher than their direct competitors, while firms with CEOs in the bottom quintile of pay saw their stock underperform their rivals by almost 20 percent.[93] For example, Robert Kotik, CEO of video game firm Activision Blizzard, made $64.9 million in 2013, but the firm's stock price rose by over 60 percent that year, producing a strong return for stockholders as well.

That doesn't mean that executive compensation systems can't or shouldn't be improved. Exhibit 9.7 outlines a number of ways to build effective compensation packages for executives.[94]

CEO Duality: Is It Good or Bad?

CEO duality is one of the most controversial issues in corporate governance. It refers to the dual-leadership structure wherein the CEO acts simultaneously as the chair of the board of directors.[95] Scholars, consultants, and executives who are interested in determining the best way to manage a corporation are divided on the issue of the roles and responsibilities of a CEO. Two schools of thought represent the alternative positions.

EXHIBIT 9.7 Six Policies for Effective Top-Management Compensation

Boards need to be diligent in building executive compensation packages that will incentivize executives to build long-term shareholder value and to address the concerns that regulators and the public have about excessive compensation. The key is to have open, fair, and consistent pay plans. Here are six policies to achieve that.

1. **Increase transparency.** Principles and pay policies should be consistent over time and fully disclosed in company documents. For example, Novartis has emphasized making its compensation policies fully transparent and not altering the targets used for incentive compensation in midstream.

2. **Build long-term performance with long-term pay.** The timing of compensation can be structured to force executives to think about the long-term success of the organization. For example, ExxonMobil times two-thirds of its senior executives' incentive compensation so that they don't receive it until they retire or for 10 years, whichever is longer. Similarly, in 2009, Goldman Sachs replaced its annual bonuses for its top managers with restricted stock grants that executives could sell in three to five years.

3. **Reward executives for performance, not simply for changes in the company's stock price.** To keep them from focusing only on stock price, Target includes a component in its executives' compensation plan for same-store sales performance over time.

4. **Have executives put some "skin in the game."** Firms should create some downside risk for managers. Relying more on restricted stock, rather than stock options, can achieve this. But some experts suggest that top executives should purchase sizable blocks of the firm's stock with their own money.

5. **Avoid overreliance on simple metrics.** Rather than rewarding for short-term financial performance metrics, firms should include future-oriented qualitative measures to incentivize managers to build for the future. Companies could include criteria such as customer retention rates, innovation and new product launch milestones, and leadership development criteria. For example, IBM added bonuses for executives who evidenced actions fostering global cooperation.

6. **Increase equity between workers and executives.** Top executives, with their greater responsibilities, should and will continue to make more than frontline employees, but firms can signal equity by dropping special perks, plans, and benefits for top managers. Additionally, companies can give employees the opportunity to share in the success of the firm by establishing employee stock ownership plans.

Sources: George, B. 2010. Executive pay: Rebuilding trust in an era of rage. *Bloomberg Businessweek*, September 13: 56; and Barton, D. 2011. Capitalism for the long term. *Harvard Business Review*, 89(3): 85.

Unity of Command   Advocates of the unity-of-command perspective believe that when one person holds both roles, he or she is able to act more efficiently and effectively. CEO duality provides firms with a clear focus on both objectives and operations as well as eliminates confusion and conflict between the CEO and the chairman. Thus, it enables smoother, more effective strategic decision making. Holding dual roles as CEO/chairman creates unity across a company's managers and board of directors and ultimately allows the CEO to serve the shareholders even better. Having leadership focused in a single individual also enhances a firm's responsiveness and ability to secure critical resources. This perspective maintains that separating the two jobs—that of a CEO and that of the chairperson of the board of directors—may produce all types of undesirable consequences. CEOs may find it harder to make quick decisions. Ego-driven chief executives and chairmen may squabble over who is ultimately in charge. The shortage of first-class business talent may mean that bosses find themselves second-guessed by people who know little about the business.[96] Companies like Coca-Cola, JPMorgan, and Time Warner have refused to divide the CEO's and chairman's jobs and support this duality structure.

Agency Theory   Supporters of agency theory argue that the positions of CEO and chairman should be separate. The case for separation is based on the simple principle of the separation of power. How can a board discharge its basic duty—monitoring the boss—if the boss is chairing its meetings and setting its agenda? How can a board act as a safeguard against corruption or incompetence when the possible source of that corruption and incompetence is sitting at the head of the table? CEO duality can create a conflict of interest that could negatively affect the interests of the shareholders.

Duality also complicates the issue of CEO succession. In some cases, a CEO/chairman may choose to retire as CEO but keep his or her role as the chairman. Although this splits up the roles, which appeases an agency perspective, it nonetheless puts the new CEO in a difficult position. The chairman is bound to question some of the new changes put in place, and the board as a whole might take sides with the chairman they trust and with whom they have a history. This conflict of interest would make it difficult for the new CEO to institute any changes, as the power and influence would still remain with the former CEO.[97]

Duality also serves to reinforce popular doubts about the legitimacy of the system as a whole and evokes images of bosses writing their own performance reviews and setting their own salaries. A number of the largest corporations, including Ford Motor Company, General Motors, Citigroup, Oracle, Apple, and Microsoft, have divided the roles between the CEO and chairman and eliminated duality. Finally, more than 90 percent of S&P 500 companies with CEOs who also serve as chairman of the board have appointed "lead" or "presiding" directors to act as a counterweight to a combined chairman and chief executive.

Research suggests that the effects of going from having a joint CEO/chairman to separating the two positions is contingent on how the firm is doing. When the positions are broken apart, there is a clear shift in the firm's performance. If the firm has been performing well, its performance declines after the separation. If the firm has been doing poorly, it experiences improvement after separating the two roles. This research suggests that there is no one correct answer on duality, but that firms should consider its current position and performance trends when deciding whether to keep the CEO and chairman positions in the hands of one person.[98]

External Governance Control Mechanisms

Thus far, we've discussed internal governance mechanisms. Internal controls, however, are not always enough to ensure good governance. The separation of ownership and control that we discussed earlier requires multiple control mechanisms, some internal and some external, to ensure that managerial actions lead to shareholder value maximization. Further, society-at-large wants some assurance that this goal is met without harming other stakeholder groups. Now we discuss several **external governance control mechanisms** that have developed in most modern economies. These include the market for corporate control, auditors, banks and analysts, governmental regulatory bodies, media, and public activists.

> **external governance control mechanisms**
> methods that ensure that managerial actions lead to shareholder value maximization and do not harm other stakeholder groups that are outside the control of the corporate governance system.

The Market for Corporate Control   Let us assume for a moment that internal control mechanisms in a company are failing. This means that the board is ineffective in monitoring managers and is not exercising the oversight required of it and that shareholders are passive and are not taking any actions to monitor or discipline managers. Under these circumstances managers may behave opportunistically.[99] Opportunistic behavior can take many forms. First, managers can *shirk* their responsibilities. Shirking means that managers fail to exert themselves fully, as is required of them. Second, they can engage in *on-the-job consumption.* Examples of on-the-job consumption include private jets, club memberships, expensive artwork in the offices, and so on. Each of these represents consumption by managers that does not in any way increase shareholder value. Instead, they actually diminish shareholder value. Third, managers may engage in *excessive product-market diversification.*[100] As we discussed in Chapter 6, such diversification serves to reduce only the employment risk of the managers rather than the financial risk of the shareholders, who can more cheaply diversify their risk by owning a portfolio of investments. Is there any external mechanism to stop managers from shirking, consumption on the job, and excessive diversification?

> **market for corporate control**
> an external control mechanism in which shareholders dissatisfied with a firm's management sell their shares.

The **market for corporate control** is one external mechanism that provides at least some partial solution to the problems described. If internal control mechanisms fail and the management is behaving opportunistically, the likely response of most shareholders will be to sell their stock rather than engage in activism.[101] As more stockholders vote with their feet, the value of the stock begins to decline. As the decline continues, at some point the market value of the firm becomes less than the book value. A corporate raider can take over the company for a price less than the book value of the assets of the company. The first thing that the raider may do on assuming control over the company is fire the underperforming management. The risk of being acquired by a hostile raider is often referred to as the **takeover constraint.** The takeover constraint deters management from engaging in opportunistic behavior.[102]

takeover constraint
the risk to management of the firm being acquired by a hostile raider.

Although in theory the takeover constraint is supposed to limit managerial opportunism, in recent years its effectiveness has become diluted as a result of a number of defense tactics adopted by incumbent management (see Chapter 6). Foremost among them are poison pills, greenmail, and golden parachutes. Poison pills are provisions adopted by the company to reduce its worth to the acquirer. An example would be payment of a huge one-time dividend, typically financed by debt. Greenmail involves buying back the stock from the acquirer, usually at an attractive premium. Golden parachutes are employment contracts that cause the company to pay lucrative severance packages to top managers fired as a result of a takeover, often running to several million dollars.

Auditors   Even when there are stringent disclosure requirements, there is no guarantee that the information disclosed will be accurate. Managers may deliberately disclose false information or withhold negative financial information as well as use accounting methods that distort results based on highly subjective interpretations. Therefore, all accounting statements are required to be audited and certified to be accurate by external auditors. These auditing firms are independent organizations staffed by certified professionals who verify the firm's books of accounts. Audits can unearth financial irregularities and ensure that financial reporting by the firm conforms to standard accounting practices.

However, these audits often fail to catch accounting irregularities. In the past, auditing failures played an important part in the failures of firms such as Enron and WorldCom. A recent study by the Public Company Accounting Oversight Board (PCAOB) found that audits conducted by the Big 4 accounting firms were often deficient. For example, 20 percent of the Ernst & Young audits examined by the PCAOB failed. And this was the best of the Big 4! The PCAOB found fault with 45 percent of the Deloitte audits it examined. Why do these reputable firms fail to find all of the issues in audits they conduct? First, auditors are appointed by the firm being audited. The desire to continue that business relationship sometimes makes them overlook financial irregularities. Second, most auditing firms also do consulting work and often have lucrative consulting contracts with the firms that they audit. Understandably, some of them tend not to ask too many difficult questions, because they fear jeopardizing the consulting business, which is often more profitable than the auditing work.

Banks and Analysts   Commercial and investment banks have lent money to corporations and therefore have to ensure that the borrowing firm's finances are in order and that the loan covenants are being followed. Stock analysts conduct ongoing in-depth studies of the firms that they follow and make recommendations to their clients to buy, hold, or sell. Their rewards and reputation depend on the quality of these recommendations. Their access to information, their knowledge of the industry and the firm, and the insights they gain from interactions with the management of the company enable them to alert the investing community of both positive and negative developments relating to a company.

It is generally observed that analyst recommendations are often more optimistic than warranted by facts. "Sell" recommendations tend to be exceptions rather than the norm. Many analysts failed to grasp the gravity of the problems surrounding failed companies such as Lehman Brothers and Countrywide till the very end. Part of the explanation may lie in the fact that most analysts work for firms that also have investment banking relationships with the companies they follow. Negative recommendations by analysts can displease the management, who may decide to take their investment banking business to a rival firm. Otherwise independent and competent analysts may be pressured to overlook negative information or tone down their criticism.

Governmental Regulatory Bodies   The extent of government regulation is often a function of the type of industry. Banks, utilities, and pharmaceuticals are subject to more regulatory oversight because of their importance to society. Public corporations are subject to more regulatory requirements than private corporations.[103]

All public corporations are required to disclose a substantial amount of financial information by bodies such as the Securities and Exchange Commission. These include quarterly and annual filings of financial performance, stock trading by insiders, and details of executive compensation packages. There are two primary reasons behind such requirements. First, markets can operate efficiently only when the investing public has faith in the market system. In the absence of disclosure requirements, the average investor suffers from a lack of reliable information and therefore may completely stay away from the capital market. This will negatively impact an economy's ability to grow. Second, disclosure of information such as insider trading protects the small investor to some extent from the negative consequences of information asymmetry. The insiders and large investors typically have more information than the small investor and can therefore use that information to buy or sell before the information becomes public knowledge.

The failure of a variety of external control mechanisms led the U.S. Congress to pass the Sarbanes-Oxley Act in 2002. This act calls for many stringent measures that would ensure better governance of U.S. corporations. Some of these measures include:[104]

- *Auditors* are barred from certain types of nonaudit work. They are not allowed to destroy records for five years. Lead partners auditing a client should be changed at least every five years.
- *CEOs* and *CFOs* must fully reveal off-balance-sheet finances and vouch for the accuracy of the information revealed.
- *Executives* must promptly reveal the sale of shares in firms they manage and are not allowed to sell when other employees cannot.
- *Corporate lawyers* must report to senior managers any violations of securities law lower down.

Media and Public Activists   The press is not usually recognized as an external control mechanism in the literature on corporate governance. There is no denying that in all developed capitalist economies, the financial press and media play an important indirect role in monitoring the management of public corporations. In the United States, business magazines such as *Bloomberg Businessweek* and *Fortune,* financial newspapers such as *The Wall Street Journal* and *Investor's Business Daily,* as well as television networks like Fox Business Network and CNBC are constantly reporting on companies. Public perceptions about a company's financial prospects and the quality of its management are greatly influenced by the media. Food Lion's reputation was sullied when ABC's *Prime Time Live* in 1992 charged the company with employee exploitation, false package dating, and unsanitary meat-handling practices. Bethany McLean of *Fortune* magazine is often credited as the first to have raised questions about Enron's long-term financial viability.[105]

Similarly, consumer groups and activist individuals often take a crusading role in exposing corporate malfeasance.[106] Well-known examples include Ralph Nader and Erin Brockovich, who played important roles in bringing to light the safety issues related to GM's Corvair and environmental pollution issues concerning Pacific Gas and Electric Company, respectively. Ralph Nader has created over 30 watchdog groups, including:[107]

- *Aviation Consumer Action Project.* Works to propose new rules to prevent flight delays, impose penalties for deceiving passengers about problems, and push for higher compensation for lost luggage.

- *Center for Auto Safety.* Helps consumers find plaintiff lawyers and agitate for vehicle recalls, increased highway safety standards, and lemon laws.
- *Center for Study of Responsive Law.* This is Nader's headquarters. Home of a consumer project on technology, this group sponsored seminars on Microsoft remedies and pushed for tougher Internet privacy rules. It also took on the drug industry over costs.
- *Pension Rights Center.* This center helped employees of IBM, General Electric, and other companies to organize themselves against cash-balance pension plans.

Corporate Governance: An International Perspective

The topic of corporate governance has long been dominated by agency theory and based on the explicit assumption of the separation of ownership and control.[108] The central conflicts are principal–agent conflicts between shareholders and management. However, such an underlying assumption seldom applies outside the United States and the United Kingdom. This is particularly true in emerging economies and continental Europe. Here, there is often concentrated ownership, along with extensive family ownership and control, business group structures, and weak legal protection for minority shareholders. Serious conflicts tend to exist between two classes of principals: controlling shareholders and minority shareholders. Such conflicts can be called **principal–principal (PP) conflicts,** as opposed to *principal–agent* conflicts (see Exhibits 9.8 and 9.9).

Strong family control is one of the leading indicators of concentrated ownership. In East Asia (excluding China), approximately 57 percent of the corporations have board chairmen and CEOs from the controlling families. In continental Europe, this number is 68 percent. A very common practice is the appointment of family members as board chairmen, CEOs, and other top executives. This happens because the families are controlling (not necessarily majority) shareholders. In 2003, 30-year-old James Murdoch was appointed CEO of British Sky Broadcasting (BSkyB), Europe's largest satellite broadcaster. There was very vocal resistance by minority shareholders. Why was he appointed in the first place? James's father just happened to be Rupert Murdoch, who controlled 35 percent of BSkyB and chaired the board. Clearly, this is a case of a PP conflict.

principal–principal conflicts
conflicts between two classes of principals—controlling shareholders and minority shareholders—within the context of a corporate governance system.

EXHIBIT 9.8 Traditional Principal–Agent Conflicts versus Principal–Principal Conflicts: How They Differ along Dimensions

	Principal–Agent Conflicts	Principal–Principal Conflicts
Goal incongruence	Between shareholders and professional managers who own a relatively small portion of the firm's equity.	Between controlling shareholders and minority shareholders.
Ownership pattern	Dispersed—5%–20% is considered "concentrated ownership."	Concentrated—often greater than 50% of equity is controlled by controlling shareholders.
Manifestations	Strategies that benefit entrenched managers at the expense of shareholders in general (e.g., shirking, pet projects, excessive compensation, and empire building).	Strategies that benefit controlling shareholders at the expense of minority shareholders (e.g., minority shareholder expropriation, nepotism, and cronyism).
Institutional protection of minority shareholders	Formal constraints (e.g., judicial reviews and courts) set an upper boundary on potential expropriation by majority shareholders. Informal norms generally adhere to shareholder wealth maximization.	Formal institutional protection is often lacking, corrupted, or unenforced. Informal norms are typically in favor of the interests of controlling shareholders ahead of those of minority investors.

Source: Adapted from Young, M., Peng, M. W., Ahlstrom, D., & Bruton, G. 2002. Governing the Corporation in Emerging Economies: A Principal–Principal Perspective. *Academy of Management Best Papers Proceedings,* Denver.

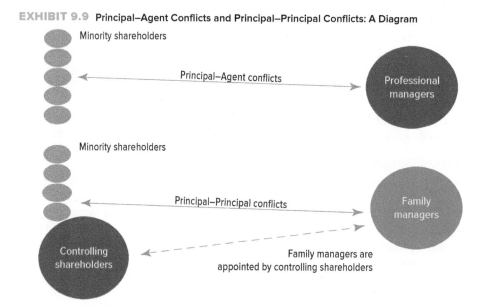

EXHIBIT 9.9   **Principal–Agent Conflicts and Principal–Principal Conflicts: A Diagram**

Source: Young, M. N., Peng, M. W., Ahlstrom, D., Bruton, G. D., & Jiang, 2008. Principal–Principal Conflicts in Corporate Governance. *Journal of Management Studies,* 45(1): 196–220; and Peng, M. V. 2006. *Global Strategy.* Cincinnati: Thomson South-Western. We are very appreciative of the helpful comments of Mike Young of Hong Kong Baptist University and Mike Peng of the University of Texas at Dallas.

In general, three conditions must be met for PP conflicts to occur:

- A dominant owner or group of owners who have interests that are distinct from minority shareholders.
- Motivation for the controlling shareholders to exercise their dominant positions to their advantage.
- Few formal (such as legislation or regulatory bodies) or informal constraints that would discourage or prevent the controlling shareholders from exploiting their advantageous positions.

expropriation of minority shareholders activities that enrich the controlling shareholders at the expense of the minority shareholders.

The result is often that family managers, who represent (or actually are) the controlling shareholders, engage in **expropriation of minority shareholders,** which is defined as activities that enrich the controlling shareholders at the expense of minority shareholders. What is their motive? After all, controlling shareholders have incentives to maintain firm value. But controlling shareholders may take actions that decrease aggregate firm performance if their personal gains from expropriation exceed their personal losses from their firm's lowered performance.

business groups a set of firms that, though legally independent, are bound together by a constellation of formal and informal ties and are accustomed to taking coordinated action.

Another ubiquitous feature of corporate life outside the United States and United Kingdom is *business groups* such as the keiretsus of Japan and the chaebols of South Korea. This is particularly dominant in emerging economies. A **business group** is "a set of firms that, though legally independent, are bound together by a constellation of formal and informal ties and are accustomed to taking coordinated action."[109] Business groups are especially common in emerging economies, and they differ from other organizational forms in that they are communities of firms without clear boundaries.

Business groups have many advantages that can enhance the value of a firm. They often facilitate technology transfer or intergroup capital allocation that otherwise might be impossible because of inadequate institutional infrastructure such as excellent financial services firms. On the other hand, informal ties—such as cross-holdings, board interlocks, and coordinated actions—can often result in intragroup activities and transactions, often at very favorable terms to member firms. Expropriation can be legally done through *related transactions,* which can occur when controlling owners sell firm assets to another firm they own at below-market prices or spin off the most profitable part of a public firm and merge it with another of their private firms.

ISSUE FOR DEBATE

CEO Pay: Appropriate Incentives or Always Dealing the CEO a Winning Hand

Alpha Natural Resources had its worst ever financial performance in 2011. The firm shut six mines, laid off over 1,500 workers, and saw its stock price drop by 66 percent. Still, the board of directors granted the firm's CEO a $528,000 bonus on top of his over $6 million pay package, noting his "tremendous efforts" to improve worker safety. Stories like these leave commentators questioning if the game is stacked to ensure that CEOs receive high pay regardless of their firm's performance.

Most large firms structure the pay packages of their top executives so that the CEO and other senior executives' pay is tied to firm performance. A large part of their pay is stock-based. The value of the stock options they receive goes up and down with the price of the firm's stock. Their annual bonuses are conditional on meeting preset performance targets. However, boards often change the rules if the firm performs poorly. If the stock price drops, leaving the options held by the CEO "underwater" and worthless, they often reprice the options the CEO holds to a lower price, making them potentially much more valuable to the CEO if the stock price bounces back. As noted above, boards also often find reasons to grant bonuses to CEOs even if the firm underperforms.

At first blush, this suggests the boards of directors are ineffective and serve to meet the desires of the CEO. But there is a logical reason why boards reprice options and grant bonuses when firms perform poorly. Boards may reprice options or change the goals that justify bonuses as a means to protect CEOs from being harmed by events out of their control. For example, if a spike in fuel prices hurts the performance of an airline or a major hurricane results in a loss for an insurance firm, the boards of these firms may argue that underperformance isn't the fault of the CEO and shouldn't result in less pay.

However, critics of this practice argue that it's wrong to protect CEOs from bad luck but not withhold benefits if the firm benefits from good luck. Boards rarely, if ever, raise the standards on CEO pay when the firm benefits from an unanticipated event. A study by researchers at Claremont Graduate University and Washington University found that executives lost less pay when their firms experienced bad luck than they gained when the firm experienced good luck. Additionally, critics point out that most workers, such as the 1,500 who were laid off by Alpha, don't receive the same protection from adverse events that the CEO does.

Discussion Questions

1. Is it appropriate for firms to insulate their CEOs' pay from bad luck?
2. How can firms restructure pay to ensure that the CEOs also don't benefit from good luck?

Sources: Mider, Z. & Green, J. 2012. Heads or tails, some CEOs win the pay game. *Bloomberg Businessweek*, October 8: 23; and Devers, C., McNamara, G., Wiseman, R., & Arrfelt, M. 2008. Moving closer to the action: Examining compensation design effects on firm risk. *Organization Science*, 19: 548–566.

Reflecting on Career Implications . . .

▣ **Behavioral Control:** What types of behavioral control does your organization employ? Do you find these behavioral controls helping or hindering you from doing a good job? Some individuals are comfortable with and even desire rules and procedures for everything. Others find that they inhibit creativity and stifle initiative. Evaluate your own level of comfort with the level of behavioral control and then assess the match between your own optimum level of control and the level and type of control used by your organization. If the gap is significant, you might want to consider other career opportunities.

▣ **Setting Boundaries and Constraints:** Your career success depends to a great extent on you monitoring and regulating your own behavior. Setting boundaries and constraints on yourself can help you focus on strategic priorities, generate short-term objectives and action plans, improve efficiency and effectiveness, and minimize improper conduct. Identify the boundaries and constraints you have placed on yourself and evaluate how each of those contributes to your personal growth and career development. If you do not have boundaries and constraints, consider developing them.

▣ **Rewards and Incentives:** Is your organization's reward structure fair and equitable? On what criteria do you base your conclusions? How does the firm define outstanding performance and reward it? Are these financial or nonfinancial rewards? The absence of rewards that are seen as fair and equitable can result in the long-term erosion of morale, which may have long-term adverse career implications for you.

▣ **Culture:** Given your career goals, what type of organizational culture would provide the best work environment? How does your organization's culture deviate from this concept? Does your organization have a strong and effective culture? In the long run, how likely are you to internalize the culture of your organization? If you believe that there is a strong misfit between your values and the organization's culture, you may want to reconsider your relationship with the organization.

For firms to be successful, they must practice effective strategic control and corporate governance. Without such controls, the firm will not be able to achieve competitive advantages and outperform rivals in the marketplace.

We began the chapter with the key role of informational control. We contrasted two types of control systems: what we termed "traditional" and "contemporary" information control systems. Whereas traditional control systems may have their place in placid, simple competitive environments, there are fewer of those in today's economy. Instead, we advocated the contemporary approach wherein the internal and external environment are constantly monitored so that when surprises emerge, the firm can modify its strategies, goals, and objectives.

Behavioral controls are also a vital part of effective control systems. We argued that firms must develop the proper balance between culture, rewards and incentives, and boundaries and constraints. Where there are strong and positive cultures and rewards, employees tend to internalize the organization's strategies and objectives. This permits a firm to spend fewer resources on monitoring behavior, and assures the firm that the efforts and initiatives of employees are more consistent with the overall objectives of the organization.

In the final section of this chapter, we addressed corporate governance, which can be defined as the relationship between various participants in determining the direction and performance of the corporation. The primary participants include shareholders, management (led by the chief executive officer), and the board of directors. We reviewed studies that indicated a consistent relationship between effective corporate governance and financial performance. There are also several internal and external control mechanisms that can serve to align managerial interests and shareholder interests. The internal mechanisms include a committed and involved board of directors, shareholder activism, and effective managerial incentives and rewards. The external mechanisms include the market for corporate control, banks and analysts, regulators, the media, and public activists. We also addressed corporate governance from both a United States and an international perspective.

SUMMARY REVIEW QUESTIONS

1. Why are effective strategic control systems so important in today's economy?
2. What are the main advantages of contemporary control systems over traditional control systems? What are the main differences between these two systems?
3. Why is it important to have a balance between the three elements of behavioral control—culture, rewards and incentives, and boundaries?
4. Discuss the relationship between types of organizations and their primary means of behavioral control.
5. Boundaries become less important as a firm develops a strong culture and reward system. Explain.
6. Why is it important to avoid a "one best way" mentality concerning control systems? What are the consequences of applying the same type of control system to all types of environments?
7. What is the role of effective corporate governance in improving a firm's performance? What are some of the key governance mechanisms that are used to ensure that managerial and shareholder interests are aligned?
8. Define principal–principal (PP) conflicts. What are the implications for corporate governance?

key terms

strategic control 280
traditional approach to
    strategic control 280
informational control 281
behavioral control 281
organizational culture 283
reward system 284
boundaries and constraints 288
corporate governance 292

corporation 293
agency theory 294
board of directors 295
shareholder activism 299
external governance control
    mechanisms 302
market for corporate
    control 302
takeover constraint 303
principal–principal
    conflicts 305
expropriation of minority
    shareholders 306
business groups 306

experiential exercise

McDonald's Corporation, the world's largest fast-food restaurant chain, with 2014 revenues of $27 billion, but the firm has stumbled recently. Sales in 2014 dropped by 2%, and its shareholder value declined by 4% from May 2014 to May 2015. Using the Internet, evaluate the quality of the corporation in terms of management, the board of directors, and shareholder activism. (Fill in the chart below.) Are the issues you list favorable or unfavorable for sound corporate governance?

application questions & exercises

1. The problems of many firms may be attributed to a traditional control system that failed to continuously monitor the environment and make necessary changes in their strategy and objectives. What companies are you familiar with that responded appropriately (or inappropriately) to environmental change?

2. How can a strong, positive culture enhance a firm's competitive advantage? How can a weak, negative culture erode competitive advantages? Explain and provide examples.

3. Use the Internet to research a firm that has an excellent culture and/or reward and incentive system. What are this firm's main financial and nonfinancial benefits?

4. Using the Internet, go to the website of a large, publicly held corporation in which you are interested. What evidence do you see of effective (or ineffective) corporate governance?

ethics questions

1. Strong cultures can have powerful effects on employee behavior. How does this create inadvertent control mechanisms? That is, are strong cultures an ethical way to control behavior?

2. Rules and regulations can help reduce unethical behavior in organizations. To be effective, however, what other systems, mechanisms, and processes are necessary?

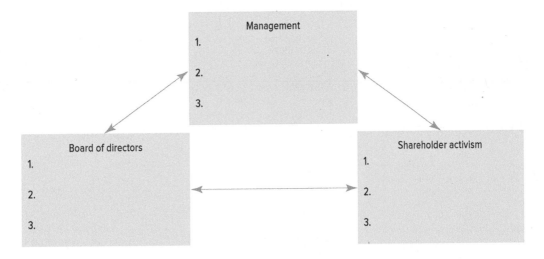

references

1. Anonymous. 2014. Not so funny. *economist.com,* September 27: np; Evans, P. & Fleisher, L. 2014. Tesco investigates accounting error. *wsj.com,* September 23: np; Rosenblum, P. 2014. Tesco's accounting irregularities are mind blowing. *forbes.com,* September 22: np; and Davey, J. 2014. UK watchdog to investigate Tesco accounts and auditor PwC. *reuters.com,* December 22: np.

2. This chapter draws upon Picken, J. C. & Dess, G. G. 1997. *Mission critical.* Burr Ridge, IL: Irwin Professional.

3. For a unique perspective on governance, refer to Carmeli, A. & Markman, G. D. 2011. Capture, governance, and resilience: Strategy implications from the history of Rome. *Strategic Management Journal,* 32(3): 332–341.

4. Argyris, C. 1977. Double-loop learning in organizations. *Harvard Business Review,* 55: 115–125.

5. Simons, R. 1995. Control in an age of empowerment. *Harvard Business Review,* 73: 80–88. This chapter draws on this source in the discussion of informational control.

6. Goold, M. & Quinn, J. B. 1990. The paradox of strategic controls. *Strategic Management Journal,* 11: 43–57.

7. Quinn, J. B. 1980. *Strategies for change.* Homewood, IL: Irwin.

8. Mintzberg, H. 1987. Crafting strategy. *Harvard Business Review,* 65: 66–75.

9. Weston, J. S. 1992. Soft stuff matters. *Financial Executive,* July–August: 52–53.

10. This discussion of control systems draws upon Simons, op. cit.

11. Ryan, M. K., Haslam, S. A., & Renneboog, L. D. R. 2011. Who gets the carrot and who gets the stick? Evidence of gender discrimination in executive remuneration. *Strategic Management Journal,* 32(3): 301–321.

12. For an interesting perspective on this issue and how a downturn in the economy can reduce the tendency toward "free agency" by managers and professionals, refer to Morris, B. 2001. White collar blues. *Fortune,* July 23: 98–110.

13. For a colorful example of behavioral control in an organization, see Beller, P. C. 2009. Activision's unlikely hero. *Forbes,* February 2: 52–58.

14. Ouchi, W. 1981. *Theory Z.* Reading, MA: Addison-Wesley; Deal, T. E. & Kennedy, A. A. 1982. *Corporate cultures.* Reading, MA: Addison-Wesley; Peters, T. J. & Waterman, R. H. 1982. *In search of excellence.* New York: Random House; and Collins, J. 2001. *Good to great.* New York: HarperCollins.

15. Collins, J. C. & Porras, J. I. 1994. *Built to last: Successful habits of visionary companies.* New York: Harper Business.

16. Lee, J. & Miller, D. 1999. People matter: Commitment to employees, strategy, and performance in Korean firms. *Strategic Management Journal,* 6: 579–594.

17. For an insightful discussion of IKEA's unique culture, see Kling, K. & Goteman, I. 2003. IKEA CEO Anders Dahlvig on international growth and IKEA's unique corporate culture and brand identity. *Academy of Management Executive,* 17(1): 31–37.

18. For a discussion of how professionals inculcate values, refer to Uhl-Bien, M. & Graen, G. B. 1998. Individual self-management: Analysis of professionals' self-managing activities in functional and cross-functional work teams. *Academy of Management Journal,* 41(3): 340–350.

19. A perspective on how antisocial behavior can erode a firm's culture can be found in Robinson, S. L. & O'Leary-Kelly, A. M. 1998. Monkey see, monkey do: The influence of work groups on the antisocial behavior of employees. *Academy of Management Journal,* 41(6): 658–672.

20. Benkler, Y. 2011. The unselfish gene. *Harvard Business Review,* 89(7): 76–85.

21. An interesting perspective on organizational culture is in Mehta, S. N. 2009. Under Armour reboots. *Fortune,* February 2: 29–33.

22. For insights on social pressure as a means for control, refer to Goldstein, N. J. 2009. Harnessing social pressure. *Harvard Business Review,* 87(2): 25.

23. Mitchell, R. 1989. Masters of innovation. *BusinessWeek,* April 10: 58–63.

24. Sellers, P. 1993. Companies that serve you best. *Fortune,* May 31: 88.

25. Southwest Airlines Culture Committee. 1993. *Luv Lines* (company publication), March–April: 17–18; for an interesting perspective on the "downside" of strong "cultlike" organizational cultures, refer to Arnott, D. A. 2000. *Corporate cults.* New York: AMACOM.

26. Kerr, J. & Slocum, J. W., Jr. 1987. Managing corporate culture through reward systems. *Academy of Management Executive,* 1(2): 99–107.

27. For a unique perspective on leader challenges in managing wealthy professionals, refer to Wetlaufer, S. 2000. Who wants to manage a millionaire? *Harvard Business Review,* 78(4): 53–60.

28. Netessine, S. & Yakubovich, V. 2012. The Darwinian workplace. *Harvard Business Review,* 90(5): 25–28.

29. For a discussion of the benefits of stock options as executive compensation, refer to Hall, B. J. 2000. What you need to know about stock options. *Harvard Business Review,* 78(2): 121–129.

30. Tully, S. 1993. Your paycheck gets exciting. *Fortune,* November 13: 89.

31. Carter, N. M. & Silva, C. 2010. Why men still get more promotions than women. *Harvard Business Review,* 88(9): 80–86.

32. Sirota, D., Mischkind, L. & Meltzer, I. 2008. Stop demotivating your employees! *Harvard Management Update,* July: 3–5; Nelson, B. 2003. Five questions about employee recognition and reward. *Harvard Management Update;* Birkinshaw, J., Bouquet, C., & Barsaoux, J. 2011. The 5 myths of innovation. *MIT Sloan Management Review.* Winter, 43–50; and Dewhurst, M. Guthridge, M., & Mohr, E. 2009. Motivating people: Getting beyond money. *mckinsey.com.* November: np.

33. This section draws on Picken & Dess, op. cit., chap. 5.

34. Anonymous. 2012. Nestle set to buy Pfizer unit. *Dallas Morning News,* April 19: 10D.

35. Isaacson, W. 2012. The real leadership lessons of Steve Jobs. *Harvard Business Review,* 90(4): 93–101.

36. This section draws upon Dess, G. G. & Miller, A. 1993. *Strategic management.* New York: McGraw-Hill.

37. For a good review of the goal-setting literature, refer to Locke, E. A. & Latham, G. P. 1990. *A theory of goal setting and task performance.* Englewood Cliffs, NJ: Prentice Hall.

38. For an interesting perspective on the use of rules and regulations that is counter to this industry's (software) norms, refer to Fryer, B. 2001. Tom Siebel of Siebel Systems: High tech the old fashioned way. *Harvard Business Review,* 79(3): 118–130.

39. Thompson, A. A., Jr., & Strickland, A. J., III. 1998. *Strategic management: Concepts and cases* (10th ed.): 313. New York: McGraw-Hill.

40. Weaver, G. R., Trevino, L. K., & Cochran, P. L. 1999. Corporate ethics programs as control systems: Influences of executive commitment and environmental factors. *Academy of Management Journal,* 42(1): 41–57.

41. www.singaporeair.com/pdf/media-centre/anti-corruption-policy-procedures.pdf.

42. Weber, J. 2003. CFOs on the hot seat. *BusinessWeek,* March 17: 66–70.

43. William Ouchi has written extensively about the use of clan control (which is viewed as an alternative to bureaucratic or market control). Here, a powerful culture results in people aligning their individual interests with those of the firm. Refer to Ouchi, op. cit.

This section also draws on Hall, R. H. 2002. *Organizations: Structures, processes, and outcomes* (8th ed.). Upper Saddle River, NJ: Prentice Hall.

44. Poundstone, W. 2003. *How would you move Mount Fuji?* New York: Little, Brown: 59.

45. Abby, E. 2012. Woman sues over personality test job rejection. *abcnews.go.com,* October 1: np.

46. Interesting insights on corporate governance are in Kroll, M., Walters, B. A., & Wright, P. 2008. Board vigilance, director experience, and corporate outcomes. *Strategic Management Journal,* 29(4): 363–382.

47. For a brief review of some central issues in corporate governance research, see Hambrick, D. C., Werder, A. V., & Zajac, E. J. 2008. New directions in corporate governance research. *Organization Science,* 19(3): 381–385.

48. Monks, R. & Minow, N. 2001. *Corporate governance* (2nd ed.). Malden, MA: Blackwell.

49. Pound, J. 1995. The promise of the governed corporation. *Harvard Business Review,* 73(2): 89–98.

50. Maurer, H. & Linblad, C. 2009. Scandal at Satyam. *BusinessWeek,* January 19: 8; Scheck, J. & Stecklow, S. 2008. Brocade ex-CEO gets 21 months in prison. *The Wall Street Journal,* January 17: A3; Levine, D. & Graybow, M. 2010. Mozilo to pay millions in Countrywide settlement. *finance. yahoo.com,* October 15: np; Ellis, B. 2010. Countrywide's Mozilo to pay $67.5 million settlement. *cnnmoney .com,* October 15: np; Frank, R., Efrati, A., Lucchetti, A., & Bray, C. 2009. Madoff jailed after admitting epic scam. *The Wall Street Journal,* March 13: A1; and Henriques, D. B. 2009. Madoff is sentenced to 150 years for Ponzi scheme. *www. nytimes.com,* June 29: np.

51. Harris, E. 2014. After bribery scandal, high-level departures at Walmart. *nytimes.com,* June 4: np.

52. Anonymous. 2012. Olympus and ex-executives plead guilty in accounting fraud. *nytimes.com,* September 25: np.

53. Corporate governance and social networks are discussed in McDonald, M. L., Khanna, P., & Westphal, J. D. 2008. *Academy of Management Journal,* 51(3): 453–475.

54. This discussion draws upon Monks & Minow, op. cit.

55. For an interesting perspective on the politicization of the corporation, read Palazzo, G. & Scherer, A. G.

2008. Corporate social responsibility, democracy, and the politicization of the corporation. *Academy of Management Review,* 33(3): 773–774.

56. Eisenhardt, K. M. 1989. Agency theory: An assessment and review. *Academy of Management Review,* 14(1): 57–74. Some of the seminal contributions to agency theory include Jensen, M. & Meckling, W. 1976. Theory of the firm: Managerial behavior, agency costs, and ownership structure. *Journal of Financial Economics,* 3: 305–360; Fama, E. & Jensen, M. 1983. Separation of ownership and control. *Journal of Law and Economics,* 26: 301, 325; and Fama, E. 1980. Agency problems and the theory of the firm. *Journal of Political Economy,* 88: 288–307.

57. Nyberg, A. J., Fulmer, I. S., Gerhart, B., & Carpenter, M. 2010. Agency theory revisited: CEO return and shareholder interest alignment. *Academy of Management Journal,* 53(5): 1029–1049.

58. Managers may also engage in "shirking"—that is, reducing or withholding their efforts. See, for example, Kidwell, R. E., Jr. & Bennett, N. 1993. Employee propensity to withhold effort: A conceptual model to intersect three avenues of research. *Academy of Management Review,* 18(3): 429–456.

59. For an interesting perspective on agency and clarification of many related concepts and terms, visit *www.encycogov.com.*

60. The relationship between corporate ownership structure and export intensity in Chinese firms is discussed in Filatotchev, I., Stephan, J., & Jindra, B. 2008. Ownership structure, strategic controls and export intensity of foreign-invested firms in transition economies. *Journal of International Business,* 39(7): 1133–1148.

61. Argawal, A. & Mandelker, G. 1987. Managerial incentives and corporate investment and financing decisions. *Journal of Finance,* 42: 823–837.

62. Gross, D. 2012. Outrageous CEO compensation: Wynn, Adelson, Dell and Abercrombie shockers. *finance. yahoo.com,* June 7: np.

63. Anonymous. 2013. Too early for the worst footnote of 2013? *footnoted. com,* January 18: np.

64. For an insightful, recent discussion of the academic research on corporate governance, and in particular the role of boards of directors, refer to Chatterjee, S. & Harrison, J. S. 2001. Corporate

governance. In Hitt, M. A., Freeman, R. E., & Harrison, J. S. (Eds.), *Handbook of strategic management:* 543–563. Malden, MA: Blackwell.

65. For an interesting theoretical discussion on corporate governance in Russia, see McCarthy, D. J. & Puffer, S. M. 2008. Interpreting the ethicality of corporate governance decisions in Russia: Utilizing integrative social contracts theory to evaluate the relevance of agency theory norms. *Academy of Management Review,* 33(1): 11–31.

66. Haynes, K. T. & Hillman, A. 2010. The effect of board capital and CEO power on strategic change. *Strategic Management Journal,* 31(110): 1145–1163.

67. This opening discussion draws on Monks & Minow, op. cit. pp. 164, 169; see also Pound, op. cit.

68. Business Roundtable. 2012. Principles of corporate governance.

69. Bhagat, C. & Kehoe, C. 2014. High performing boards: What's on their agenda? *mckinsey.com,* April: np.

70. The role of outside directors is discussed in Lester, R. H., Hillman, A., Zardkoohi, A., & Cannella, A. A., Jr. 2008. Former government officials as outside directors: The role of human and social capital. *Academy of Management Journal,* 51(5): 999–1013.

71. Feintzeig, R. 2014. You're fired! And we really mean it. *The Wall Street Journal,* November 5: B1, B6.

72. For an analysis of the effects of outside directors' compensation on acquisition decisions, refer to Deutsch, T., Keil, T., & Laamanen, T. 2007. Decision making in acquisitions: The effect of outside directors' compensation on acquisition patterns. *Journal of Management,* 33(1): 30–56.

73. Director interlocks are addressed in Kang, E. 2008. Director interlocks and spillover effects of reputational penalties from financial reporting fraud. *Academy of Management Journal,* 51(3): 537–556.

74. There are benefits, of course, to having some insiders on the board of directors. Inside directors would be more aware of the firm's strategies. Additionally, outsiders may rely too often on financial performance indicators because of information asymmetries. For an interesting discussion, see Baysinger, B. D. & Hoskisson, R. E. 1990. The composition of boards of directors and strategic control: Effects on

corporate strategy. *Academy of Management Review,* 15: 72–87.

75. Hambrick, D. C. & Jackson, E. M. 2000. Outside directors with a stake: The linchpin in improving governance. *California Management Review,* 42(4): 108–127.

76. Corsi, C., Dale, G., Daum, J., Mumm, J., & Schoppen, W. 2010. 5 things board directors should be thinking about. *spencerstuart.com,* December: np; Evans, B. 2007. Six steps to building an effective board. *inc.com:* np; Beatty, D. 2009. New challenges for corporate governance. *Rotman Magazine,* Fall: 58–63; and Krause, R., Semadeni, M., & Cannella, A. 2013. External COO/presidents as expert directors: A new look at the service role of boards. *Strategic Management Journal,* 34(13): 1628–1641.

77. A discussion on the shareholder approval process in executive compensation is presented in Brandes, P., Goranova, M., & Hall, S. 2008. Navigating shareholder influence: Compensation plans and the shareholder approval process. *Academy of Management Perspectives,* 22(1): 41–57.

78. Monks and Minow, op. cit., p. 93.

79. A discussion of the factors that lead to shareholder activism is found in Ryan, L. V. & Schneider, M. 2002. The antecedents of institutional investor activism. *Academy of Management Review,* 27(4): 554–573.

80. For an insightful discussion of investor activism, refer to David, P., Bloom, M., & Hillman, A. 2007. Investor activism, managerial responsiveness, and corporate social performance. *Strategic Management Journal,* 28(1): 91–100.

81. There is strong research support for the idea that the presence of large-block shareholders is associated with value-maximizing decisions. For example, refer to Johnson, R. A., Hoskisson, R. E., & Hitt, M. A. 1993. Board of director involvement in restructuring: The effects of board versus managerial controls and characteristics. *Strategic Management Journal,* 14: 33–50.

82. Anonymous. 2011. Institutional ownership nears all-time highs. Good or bad for alpha-seekers? *allaboutalpha.com,* February 2: np.

83. For an interesting perspective on the impact of institutional ownership on a firm's innovation strategies, see Hoskisson, R. E., Hitt, M. A., Johnson, R. A., & Grossman, W. 2002. *Academy of Management Journal,* 45(4): 697–716.

84. *calpers.ca.gov.*

85. *www.calpers-governance.org.*

86. For a study of the relationship between ownership and diversification, refer to Goranova, M., Alessandri, T. M., Brandes, P., & Dharwadkar, R. 2007. Managerial ownership and corporate diversification: A longitudinal view. *Strategic Management Journal,* 28(3): 211–226.

87. Jensen, M. C. & Murphy, K. J. 1990. CEO incentives—It's not how much you pay, but how. *Harvard Business Review,* 68(3): 138–149.

88. For a perspective on the relative advantages and disadvantages of "duality"—that is, one individual serving as both chief executive office and chairman of the board, see Lorsch, J. W. & Zelleke, A. 2005. Should the CEO be the chairman? *MIT Sloan Management Review,* 46(2): 71–74.

89. A discussion of knowledge sharing is addressed in Fey, C. F. & Furu, P. 2008. Top management incentive compensation and knowledge sharing in multinational corporations. *Strategic Management Journal,* 29(12): 1301–1324.

90. Dill, K. 2014. Report: CEOs earn 331 times as much as average workers, 774 times as much as minimum wage earners. *forbes.com,* April 15: np.

91. Sasseen, J. 2007. A better look at the boss's pay. *BusinessWeek,* February 26: 44–45; and Weinberg, N., Maiello, M., & Randall, D. 2008. Paying for failure. *Forbes,* May 19: 114, 116.

92. Research has found that executive compensation is more closely aligned with firm performance in companies with compensation committees and boards dominated by outside directors. See, for example, Conyon, M. J. & Peck, S. I. 1998. Board control, remuneration committees, and top management compensation. *Academy of Management Journal,* 41: 146–157.

93. Anonymous. 2012. American chief executives are not overpaid. *The Economist,* September 8: 67.

94. George, B. 2010. Executive pay: Rebuilding trust in an era of rage. *Bloomberg Businessweek,* September 13: 56.

95. Chahine, S. & Tohme, N. S. 2009. Is CEO duality always negative? An exploration of CEO duality and ownership structure in the Arab IPO context. *Corporate Governance: An International Review,* 17(2): 123–141; and McGrath, J. 2009.

How CEOs work. *HowStuffWorks.com.* January 28: np.

96. Anonymous. 2009. Someone to watch over them. *The Economist,* October 17: 78; Anonymous. 2004. Splitting up the roles of CEO and chairman: Reform or red herring? *Knowledge@Wharton,* June 2: np; and Kim, J. 2010. Shareholders reject split of CEO and chairman jobs at JPMorgan. *FierceFinance.com,* May 18: np.

97. Tuggle, C. S., Sirmon, D. G., Reutzel, C. R., & Bierman, L. 2010. Commanding board of director attention: Investigating how organizational performance and CEO duality affect board members' attention to monitoring. *Strategic Management Journal,* 31: 946–968; Weinberg, N. 2010. No more lapdogs. *Forbes,* May 10: 34–36; and Anonymous. 2010. Corporate constitutions. *The Economist,* October 30: 74.

98. Semadeni, M. & Krause, R. 2012. Splitting the CEO and chairman roles: It's complicated . . . *businessweek.com,* November 1: np.

99. Such opportunistic behavior is common in all principal–agent relationships. For a description of agency problems, especially in the context of the relationship between shareholders and managers, see Jensen, M. C. & Meckling, W. H. 1976. Theory of the firm: Managerial behavior, agency costs, and ownership structure. *Journal of Financial Economics,* 3: 305–360.

100. Hoskisson, R. E. & Turk, T. A. 1990. Corporate restructuring: Governance and control limits of the internal market. *Academy of Management Review,* 15: 459–477.

101. For an insightful perspective on the market for corporate control and how it is influenced by knowledge intensity, see Coff, R. 2003. Bidding wars over R&D-intensive firms: Knowledge, opportunism, and the market for corporate control. *Academy of Management Journal,* 46(1): 74–85.

102. Walsh, J. P. & Kosnik, R. D. 1993. Corporate raiders and their disciplinary role in the market for corporate control. *Academy of Management Journal,* 36: 671–700.

103. The role of regulatory bodies in the banking industry is addressed in Bhide, A. 2009. Why bankers got so reckless. *BusinessWeek,* February 9: 30–31.

104. Wishy-washy: The SEC pulls its punches on corporate-governance rules. 2003. *The Economist,* February 1: 60.

105. McLean, B. 2001. Is Enron overpriced? *Fortune,* March 5: 122–125.

106. Swartz, J. 2010. Timberland's CEO on standing up to 65,000 angry activists. *Harvard Business Review,* 88(9): 39–43.

107. Bernstein, A. 2000. Too much corporate power. *BusinessWeek,* September 11: 35–37.

108. This section draws upon Young, M. N., Peng, M. W., Ahlstrom, D., Bruton, G. D., & Jiang, Y. 2005. Principal–principal conflicts in corporate governance (unpublished manuscript); and, Peng, M. W. 2006. *Global Strategy.* Cincinnati: Thomson South-Western. We appreciate the helpful comments of Mike Young of Hong Kong Baptist University and Mike Peng of the University of Texas at Dallas.

109. Khanna, T. & Rivkin, J. 2001. Estimating the performance effects of business groups in emerging markets. *Strategic Management Journal,* 22: 45–74.

CHAPTER 16

Managerial Control

> More than at any time in the past, companies will not be able to hold themselves together with the traditional methods of control: hierarchy, systems, budgets, and the like. . . . The bonding glue will increasingly become ideological.
>
> —COLLINS AND PORRAS[1]
>
> Use your good judgment in all situations.
>
> —NORDSTROM'S EMPLOYEE MANUAL

LEARNING OBJECTIVES

After studying Chapter 16, you will be able to:

LO 1 Explain why companies develop control systems for employees.

LO 2 Summarize how to design a basic bureaucratic control system.

LO 3 Describe the purposes for using budgets as a control device.

LO 4 Define basic types of financial statements and financial ratios used as controls.

LO 5 List procedures for implementing effective control systems.

LO 6 Identify ways in which organizations use market control mechanisms.

LO 7 Discuss the use of clan control in an empowered organization.

CHAPTER OUTLINE

Bureaucratic Control Systems

The Control Cycle

Approaches to Bureaucratic Control

Management Audits

Budgetary Controls

Financial Controls

The Downside of Bureaucratic Control

Designing Effective Control Systems

The Other Controls: Markets and Clans

Market Control

Clan Control: The Role of Empowerment and Culture

Management in Action

CAN BETTER CONTROLS HELP BEST BUY SURVIVE IN THE INTERNET AGE?

Best Buy once had other stores' managers running scared. Founder Richard Schulze built a St. Paul, Minnesota, electronics store into a retailing giant; today more than 125,000 employees sell $40 billion of merchandise a year. Consumers who once bought a television set at a department or discount store flocked to Best Buy for its wide selection and knowledgeable salespeople. Today, however, consumers have alternatives. They can find product specifications and reviews online, from the comfort of their homes. Those who bother to visit a store are likely to be just taking a look at preselected items; after making their choice, they will return to the Internet and order from the lowest-priced seller.

Best Buy is struggling to stay relevant in this environment. Its revenues at stores open a year or more have been sliding, and it has posted one unprofitable quarter after another. Its market share, though it represents close to one-third of U.S. sales of consumer electronics, is falling. Competing on price with online retailers such as Amazon is difficult because Best Buy has many large stores to maintain.

Management has tried several responses. Trying to keep prices low, the company launched a program to match prices available online. It cut costs by laying off employees. It lured in younger shoppers with low-priced items such as CDs and expanded into services with the Geek Squad. It pressed customers to buy extended warranties, which are very profitable. To its credit, Best Buy has stayed in business while its competitors, Circuit City and Radio Shack, declared bankruptcy.

One of management's most attention-getting efforts was the decision to abandon a policy called Results Only Work Environment (ROWE). The policy granted

© Brendan Smialowski/AFP/Getty Images

employees at headquarters freedom to set work hours; managers, dubbed "results coaches," evaluated these employees only on their achievements, not their attendance. Facilitators were used to help move the organization from a "face time culture to a workplace that is focused on work outcomes." The policy had been announced to great fanfare, with its sponsors saying ROWE helped the company save money that would have been lost to employee turnover. However, CEO Hubert Joly saw ROWE as a failure to lead decisively at a time when Best Buy needs all hands on deck. Eliminating ROWE was just one part of a major restructuring plan, called "Renew Blue," aimed at "enhancing the company's core business, removing management layers, and eliminating operational inefficiencies." Joly's first step was to save $725 million in costs by cutting about 400 jobs from Best Buy headquarters resulting in the elimination of $150 million in administrative costs.[2]

> Survival is difficult in the retailing industry because consumer tastes and habits can change abruptly. Best Buy won over a huge base of customers and is now struggling to keep them without sacrificing profits. As you read this chapter, think about the kinds of control measures and processes that can help a company manage in a turbulent environment.

500   Part Five   Controlling: Learning and Changing

Bottom Line

Control is essential for the attainment of any management objective. *What happens in the absence of control?*

control

Any process that directs the activities of individuals toward the achievement of organizational goals.

Financial measures are signaling Best Buy's managers that they need to make changes to improve performance. Another company that uses measurements to help it improve is La-Z-Boy, where teams of employees constantly find ways to improve productivity and quality. La-Z-Boy also uses systems to prevent problems. It assigns a production engineer to design teams to make sure that new products can be produced efficiently, reducing defects as well as costs.[3] These examples are two sides of one coin: control—a means or mechanism for regulating the behavior of organization members. Left on their own, people may act in ways that they perceive to be beneficial to them individually but that may work to the detriment of the organization as a whole. Even well-intentioned people may not know whether they are directing their efforts toward the activities that are most important. Thus control is one of the fundamental forces that keep the organization together and heading in the right direction.

Control is defined as any process that directs the activities of individuals toward the achievement of organizational goals. It is how effective managers make sure that activities are going as planned. Some managers don't want to admit it (see Exhibit 16.1), but control problems—the lack of controls or the wrong kinds of controls—frequently cause irreparable damage to organizations. Ineffective control systems result in problems ranging from employee theft to peeling tire tread problems. BP has spent billions of dollars to repair damage to the Gulf of Mexico following the Deepwater Horizon disaster; years later, it was still in court, defending charges of negligence. The damage to its reputation could hardly help the company as it more recently responded to safety questions related to oil leaks in Lake Michigan and off the coast of Norway.[4] Employees simply wasting time cost U.S. employers billions of dollars each year![5]

Control has been called one of the conjoined twins of management. The other twin is planning. Some means of control are necessary because once managers form plans and strategies, they must ensure that the plans are carried out. They must make sure that other people are doing what needs to be done and not doing inappropriate things. If plans are not carried out properly, management must take steps to correct the problem. This process is the primary control function of management. By ensuring creativity, enhancing quality, and reducing cost, managers must figure out ways to control the activities in their organizations.

> *Control* has been called one of the conjoined twins of management.

Not surprisingly, effective planning facilitates control, and control facilitates planning. Planning lays out a framework for the future and, in this sense, provides a blueprint for control. Control systems, in turn, regulate the allocation and use of resources and, in so doing, facilitate the process of the next phases of planning. In today's complex organizational environment, both functions have become more difficult to implement while they have become more important in every department of the organization. Managers today

EXHIBIT 16.1

Symptoms of an Out-of-Control Company

- **Lax top management**—senior managers do not emphasize or value the need for controls, or they set a bad example.
- **Absence of policies**—the firm's expectations are not established in writing.
- **Lack of agreed-upon standards**—organization members are unclear about what needs to be achieved.
- **"Shoot the messenger" management**—employees feel their careers would be at risk if they reported bad news.
- **Lack of periodic reviews**—managers do not assess performance on a regular, timely basis.
- **Bad information systems**—key data are not measured and reported in a timely and easily accessible way.
- **Lack of ethics in the culture**—organization members have not internalized a commitment to integrity.

Managerial Control   Chapter 16   501

must control their people, inventories, quality, and costs, to mention just a few of their responsibilities.

According to William Ouchi of the University of California at Los Angeles, managers can apply three broad strategies for achieving organizational control: bureaucratic control, market control, and clan control.[6] **Bureaucratic control** is the use of rules, regulations, and formal authority to guide performance. It includes such items as budgets, statistical reports, and performance appraisals to regulate behavior and results. **Market control** involves the use of pricing mechanisms to regulate activities in organizations as though they were economic transactions. Business units may be treated as profit centers and trade resources (services or goods) with one another via such mechanisms. Managers who run these units may be evaluated on the basis of profit and loss. **Clan control** (also known as *cultural control),* unlike the first two types, does not assume that the interests of the organization and individuals naturally diverge. Instead clan control is based on the idea that employees may share the values, expectations, and goals of the organization and act in accordance with them. When members of an organization have common values and goals—and trust one another—formal controls may be less necessary. Clan control is based on many of the interpersonal processes described in the organization culture section of Chapter 2, in Chapter 12 on leadership, and in Chapter 14 on groups and teams (e.g., group norms and cohesiveness).

Exhibit 16.2 summarizes the main features of bureaucratic, market, and clan controls. We use this framework as a foundation for our discussions throughout the chapter.

bureaucratic control

The use of rules, regulations, and authority to guide performance; see also *control systems.*

market control

Control based on the use of pricing mechanisms and economic information to regulate activities within organizations.

clan control

Control based on the norms, values, shared goals, and trust among group members.

System Control	Features and Requirements
Bureaucratic control	Uses formal rules, standards, hierarchy, and legitimate authority. Works best where tasks are certain and workers are independent.
Market control	Uses prices, competition, profit centers, and exchange relationships. Works best where tangible output can be identified and a market can be established between parties.
Clan control	Involves culture, shared values, beliefs, expectations, and trust. Works best where there is no one best way to do a job, and employees are empowered to make decisions.

EXHIBIT 16.2

Characteristics of Controls

SOURCES: W. G. Ouchi, "A Conceptual Framework for the Design of Organizational Control Mechanisms," *Management Science* 25 (1979), pp. 833–48; W. G. Ouchi, "Markets, Bureaucracies, and Clans," *Administrative Science Quarterly* 25 (1980), pp. 129–41; and R. D. Robey and C. A. Sales, *Designing Organizations* (Burr Ridge, IL: Richard D. Irwin, 1994).

Bureaucratic Control Systems

Bureaucratic (or formal) control systems are designed to measure progress toward set performance goals and, if necessary, to apply corrective measures to ensure that performance achieves managers' objectives. Control systems detect and correct significant variations, or discrepancies, in the results of planned activities.

The Control Cycle

As Exhibit 16.3 shows, a typical control system has four major steps:

1. Setting performance standards.
2. Measuring performance.
3. Comparing performance against the standards and determining deviations.
4. Taking action to correct problems and reinforce successes.

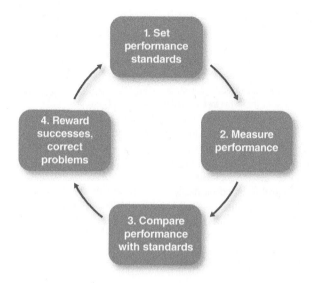

EXHIBIT 16.3
The Control Process

standard

Expected performance for a given goal: a target that establishes a desired performance level, motivates performance, and serves as a benchmark against which actual performance is assessed.

Bottom Line

Standards must be set for all bottom-line practices.
Give an example of a standard for sustainability.

Step 1: Setting Performance Standards Every organization has goals: profitability, innovation, satisfaction of customers and employees, and so on. A **standard** is the level of expected performance for a given goal. Standards are targets that establish desired performance levels, motivate performance, and serve as benchmarks against which to assess actual performance. Standards can be set for any activity—financial activities, operating activities, legal compliance, charitable contributions,[7] and social impact (see the "Social Enterprise" box).

We have discussed setting performance standards in other parts of the text. For example, employee goal setting for motivation is built around the concept of specific, measurable performance standards. Such standards should be challenging and should aim for improvement over past performance. Typically, performance standards are derived from job requirements, such as increasing market share by 10 percent, reducing costs 20 percent, and answering customer complaints within 24 hours. But performance standards don't apply just to people in isolation—they frequently reflect the integration of both human and system performance.

HealthPartners, a Bloomington, Minnesota, nonprofit organization that operates clinics and a hospital and offers health insurance plans, sets ambitious standards for patient care. To achieve a goal of reducing diabetes complications by 30 percent, HealthPartners measured existing practices and results and then set up a standard protocol for exams and treatments, including the requirement that any abnormal results receive an immediate response. To encourage its physicians to follow the protocol, HealthPartners offers financial incentives for compliance. In little more than a decade, HealthPartners exceeded its goal for improved diabetes care. HealthPartners has similar programs for treatment of cardiovascular disease and depression and for improving the health status of patients who are obese or smoke.[8] In a recent year, HealthPartners estimated it saved more than $3.6 million through programs aimed at eliminating health complications that bring patients back to the hospital after being discharged.

Performance standards can be set with respect to (1) quantity, (2) quality, (3) time used, and (4) cost. For example, production activities include volume of output (quantity), defects (quality), on-time availability of finished goods (time use), and dollar expenditures for raw materials and direct labor (cost). Many important aspects of performance, such as customer service, can be measured by the same standards—adequate supply and availability of products, quality of service, speed of delivery, and so forth.

One word of caution: The downside of establishing performance targets and standards is that they may not be supported by other elements of the control system. Each piece of the system is important and depends on the others. Otherwise the system can get terribly out of balance.

Step 2: Measuring Performance The second step in the control process is to measure performance levels. For example, managers can count units produced, websites viewed, days absent, samples distributed, and dollars earned. Performance data commonly are obtained from three sources: written reports, oral reports, and personal observations.

Written reports include computer-generated reports. Thanks to computers' data-gathering and analysis capabilities and decreasing costs, both large and small companies can gather huge amounts of performance data.

One common example of oral reports occurs when a salesperson contacts his or her immediate manager at the close of each business day to report the accomplishments, problems, or customers' reactions during the day. The manager can ask questions to gain

Social Enterprise

Beyond Counting: Alternative Ways to Measure Social Impact

Many social enterprises set ambitious goals such as ending hunger or eradicating diseases in the world. Mohammed Yunus, former recipient of a Nobel Peace Prize and founder of Grameen Bank, set a high standard when he declared that "social business" could lead to a "world without poverty." Before progress toward such objectives can be assessed, social enterprises need to measure more fully the impact they are having on social challenges.

A popular approach among social enterprises is to count the number of people that received the enterprise's product or service. For example, TOMS counts the number of shoes it donates annually to impoverished children (over 35 million in 70 countries at last count). Root Capital has made loans to 600,000 small-scale farmers and over 3 million individuals. Both organizations are certainly making a social impact, but the questions remain: How much of an impact are they making on their recipients? Did all of the recipients wear the shoes or use the loan money as intended? To what degree did the recipients fare better than comparable individuals who didn't receive free shoes or a loan?

Despite its popularity, counting outcomes is an incomplete measure. Progress is being made to develop more comprehensive assessments of social impact, including the following measures:

1. *Impact Value Chain (IVC)*. Developed by Professor Catherine Clark, the IVC takes a holistic approach to measuring social impact. She recommends that social enterprises measure their impact by evaluating the entire process or value chain of their enterprise, including inputs, outputs, and outcomes.
2. *Progress Out of Poverty Index (PPI)*. Created by the Grameen Foundation, the PPI "provides a relatively low-cost and efficient way to evaluate the poverty level of a given community."

© The McGraw-Hill Companies, Inc./Roberts Publishing Services

3. *B Impact Assessment (BIA)*. Developed by B-Lab, a nonprofit that certifies benefit corporations, the BIA evaluates an organization's "impact on its workers, community, environment, and customers."

With better measures, we will all know when a social enterprise changes the world.[9]

Questions

- Assume the role of devil's advocate: Why is counting outcomes, like in the case of TOMS, an adequate way of assessing a social enterprise's social impact?
- If you ran a social enterprise to reduce poverty in India, which of the three measures (IVC, PPI, or BIA) would you likely use to measure your enterprise's social impact?

additional information or clear up any misunderstandings. When necessary, tentative corrective actions can be worked out during the discussion.

Personal observation involves going to the area where activities take place and watching what is occurring. The manager can directly observe work methods, employees' nonverbal signals, and the general operation. Personal observation gives a detailed picture of what is going on, but it also has some disadvantages. It does not provide accurate quantitative data; the information usually is general and subjective. Also, employees can misunderstand the purpose of personal observation as mistrust or lack of confidence. Still, many managers believe in the value of firsthand observation. As you learned in earlier chapters, personal contact can increase leadership visibility

At the Baccarat factory in France, the workers in the quality control area are responsible for the quality and selection of these fine cut crystal glasses.

© Chamussy/Sipa via AP Images

and upward communication. It also provides valuable information about performance to supplement written and oral reports.

Regardless of the performance measure used, the information must be provided to managers on a timely basis. For example, consumer goods companies such as General Foods carefully track new product sales in selected local markets first so they can make any necessary adjustments well before a national rollout. Information that is not available is of little or no use to managers.

Step 3: Comparing Performance with the Standard   The third step in the control process is comparing performance with the standard. In this process, the manager evaluates the performance. For some activities, relatively small deviations from the standard are acceptable, whereas in others a slight deviation may be serious. In many manufacturing processes, a significant deviation in either direction (e.g., drilling a hole that is too small or too large) is unacceptable. In other cases, a deviation in one direction, such as sales or customer satisfaction that fall below the target level, is a problem, but a deviation in the other, exceeding the sales target or customer expectations, is a sign employees are getting better-than-expected results. As a result, managers who perform the oversight must analyze and evaluate the results carefully.

> Managers can save much time and effort if they apply the principle of exception.

principle of exception

A managerial principle stating that control is enhanced by concentrating on the exceptions to or significant deviations from the expected result or standard.

The managerial **principle of exception** states that control is enhanced by concentrating on the exceptions to, or significant deviations from, the expected result or standard. In other words, in comparing performance with the standard, managers need to direct their attention to the exception—for example, a handful of defective components produced on an assembly line or the feedback from customers who are upset or delighted with a service. Virginia-based Accurid Pest Solutions installed GPS tracking software on company-issued smartphones used by its drivers. After monitoring the location and movement of the staff, the owner of the company discovered that two drivers were taking off several hours from work each day (without permission). Consequently, the drivers were let go.[10]

With the principle of exception, only exceptional cases require corrective action. This principle is important in controlling. The manager is not concerned with performance that equals or closely approximates the expected results. Managers can save much time and effort if they apply the principle of exception.

Step 4: Taking Action to Correct Problems and Reinforce Successes   The last step in the control process is to take appropriate action when there are significant deviations. This step ensures that operations are adjusted to achieve the planned results—or to continue exceeding the plan if the manager determines that is possible. In cases in which significant variances are discovered, the manager usually takes immediate and vigorous action.

McDonald's has an extra challenge in introducing corrective action: When it identifies a problem in its restaurants, it has to persuade franchise owners that they should make changes. Most McDonald's restaurants have independent owners (franchisees), so the company cannot simply direct them as it would direct employees.

Recently, McDonald's addressed the problem that its sales had begun to fall after years of solid growth. In looking for the source of the problem, management observed that the data it gathers about customer satisfaction showed an increase in complaints about speed and quality of service.

McDonald's responded by sharing this information with its franchisees. It told them that a survey by the National Restaurant Association showed that customers care almost as much about high-quality service as about value for the price. McDonald's urged franchisees to schedule more employees for peak hours, and it began providing equipment and training for a new dual-point ordering system. Under the system, one employee takes a customer's order and provides a receipt showing an order number. The customer moves to the other end of the counter to pick up the order when the order number displays on a monitor.[11]

When corrective action is needed to solve a systemic problem, such as major delays in work flow, often a team approach is most effective. A corrective action is more likely to have greater acceptance in the organization if it is based on a common effort and takes into account multiple points of view. As we discussed in Chapter 14, teams often bring a greater diversity of resources, ideas, and perspectives to problem solving. Knowledgeable team members can often prevent managers from implementing simplistic solutions that don't address the underlying causes of a problem. They are more likely to take into account the effects of any solution on other parts of the organization, preventing new problems from arising later. And they may well develop solutions that managers might not have considered on their own. As a result, any corrective action that is finally adopted will probably be more effective. An important added benefit of bringing employees together to develop corrective actions is that it helps managers build and reinforce an organizationwide culture of high standards.

The selection of the corrective action depends on the nature of the problem. The corrective action may involve a shift in marketing strategy (if, say, the problem is lower-than-expected sales), a disciplinary action, a new way to check the accuracy of manufactured parts, or a major modification to a process or system. Sometimes managers learn they can get better results if they adjust their own practices. Each year, FedEx surveys employees about their job satisfaction and feelings about management's leadership performance. After the results are tabulated, managers hold feedback sessions to discuss the survey findings with employees. Problems are identified and action plans are developed to resolve them. The survey and subsequent action plans have become a problem-solving tool that operates both horizontally and vertically throughout the organization.[12]

After trying corrective action, a growing number of organizations conduct an **after-action review**, a frank and open-minded discussion of the four questions shown in Exhibit 16.4, aimed at continuous improvement.[13] The process was developed by the U.S. Army to help soldiers learn from their experiences, and many companies find that the method applies equally well to businesses that want to improve. Employees at the J. M. Huber Corporation conduct a review after every planned project and major unplanned event and then post the lessons learned in a database available online. In the public sector, emergency response teams have improved their performance as a result of using after-action reviews. This type of review is most effective if the reviews are scheduled consistently, participation is mandatory, and all participants in the project are included.

Approaches to Bureaucratic Control

The three approaches to bureaucratic control are feedforward, concurrent, and feedback. **Feedforward control** takes place before operations begin and includes policies, procedures, and rules designed to ensure that planned activities are carried out properly. Examples include inspection of raw materials and proper selection and training of employees. **Concurrent control** takes place while plans are being carried out. It includes directing, monitoring, and fine-tuning activities as they occur. **Feedback control** focuses on the use of information about results to correct deviations from the acceptable standard after they arise.

after-action review

A frank and open-minded discussion of four basic questions aimed at continuous improvement.

feedforward control

The control process used before operations begin, including policies, procedures, and rules designed to ensure that planned activities are carried out properly.

concurrent control

The control process used while plans are being carried out, including directing, monitoring, and fine-tuning activities as they are performed.

feedback control

Control that focuses on the use of information about previous results to correct deviations from the acceptable standard.

1. What were our intended results?	2. What were our actual results?	3. What caused our results?	4. What will we sustain? Improve?
(What was planned?)	(What really happened?)	(Why did it happen?)	(What can we do better next time?)

EXHIBIT 16.4

Questions for an After-Action Review

Feedforward Control   Feedforward control (sometimes called *preliminary control*) is future oriented; its aim is to prevent problems before they arise. Instead of waiting for results and comparing them with goals, a manager can exert control by limiting activities in advance. For example, companies have policies defining the scope within which decisions are made. A company may dictate that managers must adhere to clear ethical and legal guidelines when making decisions. Formal rules and procedures also prescribe people's actions before they occur. For example, legal experts advise companies to establish policies forbidding disclosure of proprietary information or making clear that employees are not speaking for the company when they post messages on blogs, microblogging sites such as Tumblr or Twitter, or social networking sites such as LinkedIn or Facebook. Human resource policies defining what forms of body art are acceptable to display at work can avoid awkward case-by-case conversations about a tattoo that offends co-workers or piercings that are incompatible with the company's image.[14]

Recently more managers have grown concerned about the organizational pitfalls of workplace romances, and some have sought a solution in feedforward controls. As wonderful as it is to find love, problems can arise if romantic activities between a supervisor and subordinate create a conflict of interest or charges of sexual harassment. Other employees might interpret the relationship wrongly—that the company sanctions personal relationships as a path to advancement. In addition, romantic ups and downs can spill over into the workplace and affect everyone's mood and motivation. Controls aimed at preventing such problems in an organization include training in appropriate behavior (including how to avoid sexual harassment) and even requiring executives and their romantic interests to sign love contracts in which they indicate that the relationship is voluntary and welcome. A copy of the contract goes into the company's personnel files in case the attachment disintegrates and an unhappy employee wants to blame the company for having allowed it in the first place.[15]

Concurrent Control   Concurrent control, which takes place while plans are carried out, is the heart of any control system. On a manufacturing floor, all efforts are directed toward producing the correct quantity and quality of the right products in the specified amount of time. In an airline terminal, the baggage must get to the right airplanes before flights depart. In factories, materials must be available when and where needed, and breakdowns in the production process must be repaired immediately. Concurrent control also is in effect when supervisors watch employees to ensure they work efficiently and avoid mistakes.

Advances in information technology have created powerful concurrent controls. Computerized systems give managers immediate access to data from the most remote corners of their companies. For example, managers can update budgets instantly based on a continuous flow of performance data. In production facilities, monitoring systems that track errors per hour, machine speeds, and other measures allow managers to correct small production problems before they become disasters. Point-of-sale terminals in store checkout lines send sales data back to a retailer's headquarters to show which products are selling in which locations.

Concurrent control also can be applied to service settings. As part of its efforts to transform safety, quality, and efficiency, Virginia Mason Medical Center authorized employees to issue personal safety alerts (PSAs). If any employee has a concern or question about a patient's safety, that employee may call an alert. The PSA system not only has improved the hospital's safety performance, it also has lowered its costs for professional liability insurance.[16]

> Timing is an important aspect of feedback control.

Feedback Control   Feedback control is involved when performance data have been gathered and analyzed and the results have been returned to someone (or something) in the process to make corrections. When supervisors monitor behavior, they are exercising

Multiple Generations at Work

Is Annual Performance Feedback a Thing of the Past?

Some companies are doing away with annual performance evaluations in favor of continuous coaching and development of employees. Some attribute this change to Millennial employees' desire for greater responsibility and a "feedback-rich" culture in which learning is continuous. Others suggest that today's fast-changing business environment requires more frequent dialogue between managers and employees to ensure alignment between employees' skills and the firm's business strategy.

Tata Consulting Services (TCS) of India has a workforce of 240,000 employees of which over 70 percent are Millennials. Ajoy Mukherjee, the director of human resources, responded to this pressure for change by having managers provide feedback on performance more quickly and giving junior employees more responsibility sooner.

Software maker Adobe used to spend over 80,000 hours per year on administering traditional performance evaluations. After trying to modify the system, the firm decided "it was inconsistent with Adobe's strong culture of teamwork and collaboration." The new feedback system is more effective. Every three months, a manager or employee requests a "check-in" to discuss ways to improve the employee's performance. Prior to the meeting, feedback about his/her performance is collected from

© E. Audras/PhotoAlto

a group of fellow employees. Adobe's goal is to "make coaching and developing a continuous, collaborative process between managers and employees." Since launching the new performance feedback system, Adobe reported a 30 percent reduction in its voluntary employee turnover.

If organizations want to align their highly skilled talent with evolving business strategies, then managers must provide employees with continuous coaching and developmental feedback.[17]

concurrent control. When they point out and correct improper performance, they are using feedback as a means of control.

Timing is an important aspect of feedback control. Long time lags often occur between performance and feedback, such as when actual spending is compared with the quarterly budget, instead of weekly or monthly, or when an employee's annual performance is compared to goals set a year earlier. Yet if feedback on performance is not timely, managers cannot quickly identify and eliminate the problem and prevent more serious harm.[18] The "Multiple Generations at Work" box discusses the trend toward more frequent, timely performance feedback.

Some feedback processes are under real-time (concurrent) control, such as a computer-controlled robot on an assembly line. Such units have sensors that continually determine whether they are in the correct position to perform their functions. If they are not, a built-in control device makes immediate corrections.

In other situations, feedback processes require more time. The feedback used by Hertz includes customer ratings of the company's service and the quality of the cars it rents. Patterns of praise and complaints can help the company reinforce or correct practices at particular facilities or throughout the organization, and if a customer is upset about something, Hertz wants to know as soon as possible so it can correct the problem. In the past, gathering and interpreting customer feedback from surveys and online comments could take about three weeks. Now, however, analytic software collects and tallies data as it flows into the company, and it delivers daily reports to local managers. Armed with the information, the managers are expected to respond to any problems within 24 hours. With these changes, customer satisfaction with Hertz has been rising consistently.[19]

508   Part Five   Controlling: Learning and Changing

The Role of Six Sigma   One of the most important quality control tools to emerge is six sigma, which we first discussed in Chapter 9. It is a particularly robust and powerful application of feedback control. Six sigma is designed to reduce defects in all organization processes—not just product defects but anything that may result in customer dissatisfaction. The system was developed at Motorola in the late 1980s, when the company found it was being beaten consistently in the competitive marketplace by foreign firms that were able to produce higher-quality products at a lower cost. Since then, the technique has been widely adopted and even improved on by many companies, such as GE, AlliedSignal, Ford, and Xerox.

Sigma is the Greek letter used in statistics to designate the estimated standard deviation, or variation, in a process. It indicates how often defects in a process are likely to occur. The higher the sigma number, the lower the level of variation or defects. For example, as you can see in Exhibit 16.5, a two-sigma-level process has more than 300,000 defects per million opportunities (DPMO)—not a very well-controlled process. A three-sigma-level process has 66,807 DPMO, which is roughly a 93 percent level of accuracy. Many organizations operate at this level, which on its face does not sound too bad, until we consider its implications—for example, 7 items of airline baggage lost for every 100 processed. The additional costs to organizations of such inaccuracy are enormous. As you can see in the exhibit, even at just above a 99 percent defect-free rate, or 6,210 DPMO, the accuracy level is often unacceptable.[20]

At a six-sigma level, a process is producing fewer than 3.4 defects per million, which we saw in Chapter 9 is a 99.99966 percent level of accuracy. Six-sigma companies have not only close to zero product or service defects but also substantially lower production costs and cycle times and much higher levels of customer satisfaction. The methodology isn't just for the factory floor, either. Accountants have used six sigma to improve the quality of their audits investigating risks faced by their clients.[21]

The six-sigma approach is based on an intense statistical analysis of business processes that contribute to customer satisfaction. For example, a business process could be assembling a product or delivering products to customers. For the given process, the effort begins by defining the outputs and information that flow through each stage of the process and then measuring performance at each stage. A variety of tools are available for analyzing the results. These might include looking for all the root causes of any problem. Suppose some customers are dissatisfied with a company's customer service. Asking "why?" over and over could reveal that customers are dissatisfied because phone calls go unanswered, which happens because support staff cannot keep up with the call volume, which happens because the department is understaffed, which is the result of frozen hiring levels, the result of budget cuts. Any solution will have to address the budget restrictions, either by increasing the budget or by finding a way that a small department can satisfy customers. After the problems are analyzed, process improvements are identified and implemented, and the new process is evaluated again. This cycle continues until the desired quality level is achieved. In this way, the six-sigma process leads to continuous improvement in an organization's operations.

Bottom Line

Six sigma aims for defect-free performance.
What impact would achieving six-sigma quality have on a company's costs?

EXHIBIT 16.5

Relationship between Sigma Level and Defects per Million Opportunities

Sigma Level	DPMO	Is Four Sigma Good Enough?
2σ	308,537	Consider these everyday examples of four-sigma quality . . .
3σ	66,807	• 20,000 lost articles of mail per hour.
4σ	**6,210**	• Unsafe drinking water 15 minutes per day.
5σ	233	• 5,000 incorrect surgical operations per week.
6σ	3.4	• 200,000 wrong prescriptions each year.
		• No electricity for 7 hours each month.

SOURCE: Tom Rancour and Mike McCracken, "Applying 6 Sigma Methods for Breakthrough Safety Performance," *Professional Safety* 45, no. 10 (October 2000), pp. 29–32. Reprinted with permission.

Six sigma has come under some criticism for not always delivering business results.[22] One likely reason six sigma doesn't always improve the bottom line is that it focuses only on how to eliminate defects in a process, not whether the process is the best one for the organization. So, for example, at 3M, a drive to improve efficiency through six sigma has been blamed for slowing the flow of innovative ideas. At Home Depot, six sigma has been credited with improving such processes as customer checkout and deciding where to place products in stores, but some say the effort took store workers away from customers. One way managers can apply the strengths of six sigma and minimize the drawbacks is by setting different goals and control processes for the company's mature products than for its areas of innovation.

Management Audits

Over the years, **management audits** have developed as a means of evaluating the effectiveness and efficiency of various systems within an organization, from social responsibility programs to accounting control. Management audits may be external or internal. Managers conduct external audits of other companies and internal audits of their own companies. Some of the same tools and approaches are used for both types of audit.[23]

External Audits   An **external audit** occurs when one organization evaluates another organization. Typically an external body such as a CPA firm conducts financial audits of an organization (accounting audits are discussed later). But any company can conduct external audits of competitors or other companies for its own strategic decision-making purposes. This type of analysis (1) investigates other organizations for possible merger or acquisition, (2) determines the soundness of a company that will be used as a major supplier, or (3) discovers the strengths and weaknesses of a competitor to maintain or better exploit the competitive advantage of the investigating organization. Publicly available data usually are used for these evaluations.[24]

External audits provide essential feedback control when they identify legal and ethical lapses that could harm the organization and its reputation. They also are useful for preliminary control because they can prevent problems from occurring. If a company seeking to acquire other businesses gathers adequate, accurate information about possible candidates, it is more likely to acquire the most appropriate companies and avoid unsound acquisitions.

Internal Audits   An organization may assign a group to conduct an **internal audit** to assess (1) what the company has done for itself and (2) what it has done for its customers or other recipients of its goods or services. The company can be evaluated on a number of factors, including financial stability, production efficiency, sales effectiveness, human resources development, earnings growth, energy use, public relations, civic responsibility, and other criteria of organizational effectiveness. The audit reviews the company's past, present, and future, including any risks the organization should be prepared to face.[25] A recent study found that the stock prices of companies with highly rated audit committees tended to rise faster than shares of companies with lower-rated internal auditors. It is likely that the higher-rated audit committees do a better job of finding and eliminating undesirable practices.[26]

To perform a management audit, auditors compile a list of desired qualifications and weight each qualification. Among the most common undesirable practices uncovered by a management audit are the performance of unnecessary work, duplication of work, poor inventory control, uneconomical use of equipment and machines, procedures that are more costly than necessary, and wasted resources. At Coca-Cola, an internal assessment revealed nearly 33 percent of its bottling operations and 24 percent of the suppliers audited had violations related to employee overtime and rest days. This rate increases to nearly 1 in 2 workplaces in some developing countries. To ensure that employees receive adequate time off, Coca-Cola recommends that managers map out production flow and pinpoint "bottlenecks, increase staffing levels to cover peak periods, and provide cross training to employees."[27]

management audit

An evaluation of the effectiveness and efficiency of various systems within an organization.

external audit

An evaluation conducted by one organization, such as a CPA firm, on another.

internal audit

A periodic assessment of a company's own planning, organizing, leading, and controlling processes.

Sustainability Audits and the Triple Bottom Line   Companies that are serious about goals for sustainability conduct audits to evaluate how effectively they are serving all stakeholders and protecting the environment. These sustainability audits typically evaluate performance in terms of a triple bottom line—that is, the company's financial performance, environmental impact, and impact on people in the company and the communities where it operates. Adapting a slogan coined by Shell in the 1990s, an easy way to remember the three bottom lines is with the terms *profit, planet,* and *people.*[28] In practice, reporting a triple bottom line is not standardized and regulated the way financial reporting is. A company might report its profitability in the traditional way, its environmental impact in terms of trends in efficiency of resource use, and its human impact in terms of general policies. As we saw Chapter 13, we can expect the impact of a sustainability audit to be greatest where there are specific goals and rewards for achieving them. However, committing to issue a report based on a sustainability audit can be a first step toward measuring and reinforcing sustainable business practices.

Budgetary Controls

Budgetary control is one of the most widely recognized and commonly used methods of managerial control. It ties together feedforward control, concurrent control, and feedback control, depending on the point at which it is applied. Budgetary control is the process of finding out what's being done and comparing the results with the corresponding budget data to verify accomplishments or remedy differences. Budgetary control is commonly called **budgeting.**

budgeting

The process of investigating what is being done and comparing the results with the corresponding budget data to verify accomplishments or remedy differences; also called budgetary controlling.

Fundamental Budgetary Considerations   In private industry, budgetary control begins with an estimate of sales and expected income. Exhibit 16.6 shows a budget with a forecast of expected sales (the sales budget) on the top row, followed by several categories of estimated expenses for the first three months of the year. In the bottom row, the profit estimate is determined by subtracting each month's budgeted expenses from the sales in that month's sales budget. Columns next to each month's budget provide space to enter the actual accomplishments so that managers can readily compare expected amounts and actual results.

Although this discussion of budgeting focuses on the flow of money into and out of the organization, budgeting information is not confined to finances. The entire enterprise and any of its units can create budgets for their activities, using units other than dollars if appropriate. For example, many organizations use production budgets forecasting physical units produced and shipped, and labor can be budgeted in skill levels or hours of work required.

EXHIBIT 16.6   A Sales Expense Budget

	January		February		March	
	Expectancy	Actual	Expectancy	Actual	Expectancy	Actual
Sales	$1,200,000		$1,350,000		$1,400,000	
Expenses						
General overhead	310,000		310,000		310,000	
Selling	242,000		275,000		288,000	
Producing	327,000		430,000		456,800	
Research	118,400		118,400		115,000	
Office	90,000		91,200		91,500	
Advertising	32,500		27,000		25,800	
Estimated gross profit	80,100		97,900		112,900	

A primary consideration of budgeting is the length of the budget period. All budgets are prepared for a specific time period. Many budgets cover one, three, or six months or one year. The length of time selected depends on the primary purpose of the budgeting. The period chosen should include the enterprise's complete normal cycle of activity. For example, seasonal variations should be included for production and for sales. The budget period commonly coincides with other control devices such as managerial reports, balance sheets, and statements of profit and loss. In addition, the extent to which reasonable forecasts can be made should be considered in selecting the length of the budget period.

Budgetary control proceeds through several stages. Establishing *expectancies* starts with the broad plan for the company and the estimate of sales, and it ends with budget approval and publication. Next, the budgetary operations stage deals with finding out what is being accomplished and comparing the results with expectancies. The last stage, as in any control process, involves responding appropriately with some combination of reinforcing successes and correcting problems.

Although practices differ widely, a member of top management often serves as the chief coordinator for formulating and using the budget. Usually the chief financial officer (CFO) has these duties. He or she needs to be less concerned with the details than with resolving conflicting interests, recommending adjustments when needed, and giving official sanction to the budgetary procedures. In a small company, budgeting responsibility generally rests with the owner.

Types of Budgets   There are many types of budgets. Some of the more common types are as follows:

- *Sales budget.* Usually data for the sales budget include forecasts of sales by month, sales area, and product.
- *Production budget.* The production budget commonly is expressed in physical units. Required information for preparing this budget includes types and capacities of machines, economic quantities to produce, and availability of materials.
- *Cost budget.* The cost budget is used for areas of the organization that incur expenses but no revenue, such as human resources and other support departments. Cost budgets may also be included in the production budget. Costs may be fixed, or independent of the immediate level of activity (such as rent), or variable, rising or falling with the level of activity (such as raw materials).
- *Cash budget.* The cash budget is essential to every business. It should be prepared after all other budget estimates are completed. The cash budget shows the anticipated receipts and expenditures, the amount of working capital available, the extent to which outside financing may be required, and the periods and amounts of cash available.
- *Capital budget.* The capital budget is used for the cost of fixed assets such as plants and equipment. Such costs are usually treated not as regular expenses but as investments because of their long-term nature and importance to the organization's productivity.
- *Master budget.* The master budget includes all the major activities of the business. It brings together and coordinates all the activities of the other budgets and can be thought of as a budget of budgets.

Traditionally, budgets were often imposed top-down, with senior management setting specific targets for the entire organization at the beginning of the budget process. In today's more complex organizations, the budget process is much more likely to be bottom-up, with top management setting the general direction but with lower-level and middle-level managers actually developing the budgets and submitting them for approval. When the budgets are consolidated, senior managers can then determine whether the budget objectives of the organization are being met. The budget will then be either approved or sent back down the organization for additional refinement.

accounting audits

Procedures used to verify accounting reports and statements.

Accounting records must be inspected periodically to ensure they were properly prepared and are correct. **Accounting audits,** which are designed to verify accounting reports and statements, are essential to the control process. This audit is performed by members of an outside firm of public accountants. Knowing that accounting records are accurate, true, and in keeping with generally accepted accounting practices (GAAP) creates confidence that a reliable base exists for sound overall controlling purposes.

Activity-Based Costing   Traditional methods of cost accounting may be inappropriate in today's business environment because they are based on outdated methods of rigid hierarchical organization. Instead of assuming that organizations are bureaucratic machines that can be separated into component functions such as human resources, purchasing, and maintenance, companies such as Hewlett-Packard and GE have used **activity-based costing (ABC)** to allocate costs across business processes.

activity-based costing (ABC)

A method of cost accounting designed to identify streams of activity and then to allocate costs across particular business processes according to the amount of time employees devote to particular activities.

ABC starts with the assumption that organizations are collections of people performing many different but related activities to satisfy customer needs. The ABC system is designed to identify those streams of activity and then to allocate costs across particular business processes. The basic procedure involves assigning expenses to particular processes or areas of activity. In a manufacturing company, for example, a group of employees might process sales orders, buy parts, and request engineering changes. The expenses for their salaries and fringe benefits would be divided among these activities according to the amount of time spent on each activity. A similar approach, illustrated in Exhibit 16.7, is to allocate expenses of providing support services to the functions served. In this example, a medical clinic, administrative expenses such as office workers' salaries, rent, and utilities are divided among the doctors' practices and the clinic's laboratory and radiology services. Options for allocating these expenses include the number of employees served in each group, the number of patients seen, and the square footage occupied by each group. Traditional and ABC systems reach the same bottom line. However, because the ABC method allocates costs across business processes, it provides a more accurate picture of how costs should be charged to products and services.[29]

Bottom Line

Activity-based costing can highlight overspending. *If one activity costs the most, how would you decide whether this is a case of overspending?*

This heightened accuracy can give managers a more realistic picture of how the organization is actually allocating its resources. It can highlight where wasted activities are occurring or whether activities cost too much relative to the benefits provided. Managers can then take action to correct the problem.

EXHIBIT 16.7

Activity-Based Costing Example: ABC Medical Clinic

Administrative expenses		Expenses allocated to services provided	Laboratory	Radiology	Dr. Kent (240 visits)	Dr. Olson (200 visits)	Dr. Lane (160 visits)
Office salaries							
Direct	1,500				600	500	400
Payroll and personnel	1,000		119	39	337	254	251
Supervision	2,000		238	79	673	508	502
Unutilized*	500						
Advertising	600				200	200	200
Rent	1,000		125	125	250	250	250
Utilities	200		25	25	50	50	50
Office supplies	300				100	100	100
Building insurance	100		12	13	25	25	25
Telephone	600				200	200	200
Depreciation	300				100	100	100
Total	8,100		519	281	2,535	2,187	2,078

*Not allocated.

SOURCE: Based on Pam Schuneman, "Master the 'ABCs' of Activity-Based Costing," *Managed Care*, May 1997, http://www.managedcaremag.com.

Financial Controls

LO 4

In addition to budgets, businesses commonly use other statements for financial control. Two financial statements that help control overall organizational performance are the balance sheet and the profit and loss statement.

The Balance Sheet   The **balance sheet** shows the financial picture of a company at a given time. This statement itemizes three elements: (1) assets, (2) liabilities, and (3) stockholders' equity. **Assets** are the values of the various items the corporation owns. **Liabilities** are the amounts the corporation owes to various creditors. **Stockholders' equity** is the amount accruing to the corporation's owners. The relationship among these three elements is as follows:

$$\text{Assets} = \text{Liabilities} + \text{Stockholders' equity}$$

Exhibit 16.8 shows an example of a balance sheet. During the year, the company grew because it enlarged its building and acquired more machinery and equipment by means of long-term debt in the form of a first mortgage. Additional stock was sold to help finance the expansion. At the same time, accounts receivable were increased, and work in process was reduced. Observe that Total assets ($3,053,367) = Total liabilities ($677,204 + $618,600) + Stockholders' equity ($700,000 + $981,943 + $75,620).

Summarizing balance sheet items over a long period of time uncovers important trends and gives a manager further insight into overall performance and areas in which adjustments need to be made. For example, at some point, the company might decide that it would be prudent to slow down its expansion plans.

The Profit and Loss Statement   The **profit and loss statement** is an itemized financial statement of the income and expenses of a company's operations. Exhibit 16.9 shows a comparative statement of profit and loss for two consecutive years. In this illustration, the operating revenue of the enterprise has increased. Expense also has increased but at a lower rate, resulting in a higher net income. Some managers draw up tentative profit and loss statements and use them as goals. Then performance is measured against these goals or standards. From comparative statements of this type, a manager can identify trouble areas and correct them.

Controlling by profit and loss is most commonly used for the entire enterprise and, in the case of a diversified corporation, its divisions. However, if controlling is by departments, as in a decentralized organization in which department managers have control over both revenue and expense, a profit and loss statement is used for each department. Each department's output is measured, and a cost, including overhead, is charged to each department's operation. Expected net income is the standard for measuring a department's performance.

Financial Ratios   An effective approach for checking on the overall performance of an enterprise is to use key financial ratios. Ratios help indicate possible strengths and weaknesses in a company's operations. Key ratios are calculated from selected items on the profit and loss statement and the balance sheet. We will briefly discuss three categories of financial ratios—liquidity, leverage, and profitability:

- *Liquidity ratios.* Liquidity ratios indicate a company's ability to pay short-term debts. The most common liquidity ratio is *current assets to current liabilities,* called the **current ratio** or *net working capital ratio.* This ratio indicates the extent to which current assets can decline and still be adequate to pay current liabilities. Some analysts set a ratio of 2 to 1, or 2.00, as the desirable minimum. For example, referring back to Exhibit 16.8, the liquidity ratio there is about 2.86 ($1,918,455/$667,204). The company's current assets are more than capable of supporting its current liabilities.
- *Leverage ratios.* Leverage ratios show the relative amount of funds in the business supplied by creditors and shareholders. An important example is the **debt–equity ratio,** which indicates the company's ability to meet its long-term

---

balance sheet

A report that shows the financial picture of a company at a given time and itemizes assets, liabilities, and stockholders' equity.

assets

The values of the various items the corporation owns.

liabilities

The amounts a corporation owes to various creditors.

stockholders' equity

The amount accruing to the corporation's owners.

profit and loss statement

An itemized financial statement of the income and expenses of a company's operations.

current ratio

A liquidity ratio that indicates the extent to which short-term assets can decline and still be adequate to pay short-term liabilities.

debt–equity ratio

A leverage ratio that indicates the company's ability to meet its long-term financial obligations.

514   Part Five   Controlling: Learning and Changing

EXHIBIT 16.8
A Comparative Balance
Sheet

Comparative Balance Sheet for the Years Ending December 31		
	This Year	Last Year
Assets		
Current assets:		
Cash	$161,870	$119,200
U.S. Treasury bills	250,400	30,760
Accounts receivable	825,595	458,762
Inventories:		
Work in process and finished products	429,250	770,800
Raw materials and supplies	251,340	231,010
Total current assets	1,918,455	1,610,532
Other assets:		
Land	157,570	155,250
Building	740,135	91,784
Machinery and equipment	172,688	63,673
Furniture and fixtures	132,494	57,110
Total other assets before depreciation	1,202,887	367,817
Less: Accumulated depreciation and amortization	67,975	63,786
Total other assets	1,134,912	304,031
Total assets	$3,053,367	$1,914,563
Liabilities and stockholders' equity		
Current liabilities:		
Accounts payable	$287,564	$441,685
Payrolls and withholdings from employees	44,055	49,580
Commissions and sundry accruals	83,260	41,362
Federal taxes on income	176,340	50,770
Current installment on long-term debt	85,985	38,624
Total current liabilities	667,204	622,021
Long-term liabilities:		
15-year, 9 percent loan, payable in each of the years 2005–2018	210,000	225,000
5 percent first mortgage	408,600	
Registered 9 percent notes payable		275,000
Total long-term liabilities	618,600	500,000
Stockholders' equity:		
Common stock: authorized 1,000,000 shares, outstanding last year 492,000 shares, outstanding this year 700,000 shares at $1 par value	700,000	492,000
Capital surplus	981,943	248,836
Earned surplus	75,620	51,706
Total stockholders' equity	1,757,563	792,542
Total liabilities and stockholders' equity	$3,053,367	$1,914,563

Comparative Statement of Profit and Loss for the Years Ending June 30			
	This Year	Last Year	Increase or Decrease
Income:			
Net sales	$253,218	$257,636	$4,418*
Dividends from investments	480	430	50
Other	1,741	1,773	32*
Total	255,439	259,839	4,400*
Deductions:			
Cost of goods sold	180,481	178,866	1,615
Selling and administrative expenses	39,218	34,019	5,199
Interest expense	2,483	2,604	121*
Other	1,941	1,139	802
Total	224,123	216,628	7,495
Income before taxes	31,316	43,211	11,895*
Provision for taxes	3,300	9,500	6,200*
Net income	$ 28,016	$ 33,711	$5,695*

EXHIBIT 16.9
A Comparative Statement of Profit and Loss

* Decrease

financial obligations. If this ratio is less than 1.5, the amount of debt is not considered excessive. In Exhibit 16.8, the debt–equity ratio is only 0.35 ($618,600/$1,757,563). The company has financed its expansion almost entirely by issuing stock rather than by incurring significant long-term debt.

- *Profitability ratios.* Profitability ratios indicate management's ability to generate a financial return on sales or investment. For example, **return of investment (ROI)** is a ratio of profit to capital used, or a rate of return from capital (equity plus long-term debt). This ratio allows managers and shareholders to assess how well the firm is doing compared with other investments. For example, if the net income of the company in Exhibit 16.8 were $300,000 this year, its return on capital would be 12.6 percent [$300,000/($1,757,563/$618,600)]—normally a very reasonable rate of return.

return on investment (ROI)

A ratio of profit to capital used, or a rate of return from capital.

Using Financial Ratios   Although ratios provide both performance standards and indicators of what has occurred, exclusive reliance on financial ratios can have negative consequences. Because ratios usually are expressed in compressed time horizons (monthly, quarterly, or yearly), they often cause **management myopia**—managers focus on short-term earnings and profits at the expense of their longer-term strategic obligations.[30] Control systems using long-term (e.g., three- to six-year) performance targets can reduce management myopia and focus attention further into the future.

A second negative outcome of ratios is that they relegate other important considerations to a secondary position. Research and development, management development, progressive human resource practices, and other considerations may receive insufficient attention. Therefore, the use of ratios should be supplemented with other control measures. Organizations can hold managers accountable for market share, number of patents granted, sales of new products, human resource development, and other performance indicators. As you read "Management in Action: Progress Report," consider the advantages and limits of financial ratios in helping Best Buy's managers figure out how to improve performance.

management myopia

Focusing on short-term earnings and profits at the expense of longer-term strategic obligations.

Management in Action

BEST BUY AIMS FOR BETTER NUMBERS

Best Buy's financial numbers have raised concern. The company has recently posted losses, with flat sales and falling market share, even after Circuit City closed and RadioShack filed for bankruptcy. A key measure in retailing is same-store sales, the total sales made only at the company's stores that have been open at least one year. By ignoring any other stores, managers can see whether performance has changed within stores, in contrast to sales growth or declines from opening or closing stores. At Best Buy, same-store sales have increased for three straight quarters, but the growth rate in the latest quarter was only 0.6 percent. Sales of smartphones and big screen televisions are helping to keep same-store sales in the black.

To sell more, Best Buy cut prices, but to preserve profits, it must cut costs, too. On the price side, the company promised to match the lowest price charged by any competitor, and it increased the value of rewards issued to customers with loyalty cards. On the cost side, CEO Hubert Joly has cut more than $1 billion since Renew Blue was announced a couple of years ago. In 2015, he announced that he "plans to reduce expenses by another $400 million in the next three years." The cost-cutting measures, along with the sale of higher margin products like smartphones and televisions, have helped the firm turn a small profit. Also, in competing with online retailers, Best Buy remains at a disadvantage. Selling from a warehouse is cheaper than selling from a store, and most of Best Buy's customers shop in its stores, not at its website. To counter this challenge, Best Buy is experimenting with shipping customers' online orders directly from stores.

Another way to sell more is to use persuasive salespeople. In its early years, Best Buy was known for skillful selling, and managers emphasized sales targets. Best Buy recently increased training and began offering incentive pay linked to sales. The ratio of closed to attempted sales did not improve, but surveys showed greater customer satisfaction.

Another way Joly is trying to boost sales is by pursuing a "store within a store" business model. Best Buy will be opening another 60 Pacific Kitchen & Home "stores" that sell premium appliances. Also, 20 more Magnolia design centers will be opened where sales staff help customers design home entertainment theaters.

Management also considered geography. The worst performance has been in Best Buy's European stores, so the company arranged to sell its European operations.[31]

- How well do you think Best Buy's management has analyzed and corrected its performance? Why?

- Besides the measures described here, what other financial measures could help with controlling performance at Best Buy?

The Downside of Bureaucratic Control

So far you have learned about control from a mechanical viewpoint. But organizations are not strictly mechanical; they are composed of people. Although control systems are used to constrain people's behavior and make their future behavior predictable, people are not machines that automatically fall into line as the designers of control systems intend. In fact, control systems can lead to dysfunctional behavior.

> A control system cannot be effective without consideration of how people will react to it.

A control system cannot be effective without consideration of how people will react to it. For effective control of employee behavior, managers should consider three types of potential responses to control: rigid bureaucratic behavior, tactical behavior, and resistance.[32]

Rigid Bureaucratic Behavior   Often people act in ways that will help them look good on the control system's measures. This tendency can be useful because it focuses people on the behaviors management requires. But it can result in rigid, inflexible behavior geared toward doing *only* what the system requires. For example, in the earlier discussion of six sigma, we noted that this control process emphasizes efficiency over innovation. After 3M began using six sigma extensively, it slipped from its goal of having at least one-third of sales come from newly released products. When George Buckley took the CEO post, only one-fourth of sales were coming from new products, and Buckley began relying less extensively on efficiency controls. Buckley explained to a reporter, "Invention is by its very nature a disorderly process."[33] The control challenge, of course, is for 3M to be both efficient and creative.

Rigid bureaucratic behavior occurs when control systems prompt employees to stay out of trouble by following the rules. Unfortunately, such systems often lead to poor customer service and make the entire organization slow to act. (Recall the discussion of bureaucracy in Chapter 10.) General Motors is notorious for having a lumbering bureaucracy, which has often been blamed for making the company unresponsive to changes in consumer tastes. For example, several years ago, GM kept engineers at work on the design for a new Hummer SUV even though many of them doubted the vehicles would ever be built. Their pessimism was correct; GM shut down the Hummer group. The company has been trying to change. For its head of vehicle development, GM selected Mary Barra, who has a background in both manufacturing and human resources as well as a reputation for speaking out and pressing for action. She quickly eliminated layers of management between herself and the top engineer and aggressively supports designers who want to make changes consumers are asking for.[34] Now as CEO, Barra continues to pursue her mission to make GM more responsive and efficient (see the Management in Action boxes in Chapter 8).

We have all been victimized at some time by rigid bureaucratic behavior. Reflect for a moment on this now classic story of a nightmare at a hospital:

> At midnight, a patient with eye pains enters an emergency room at a hospital. At the reception area, he is classified as a nonemergency case and referred to the hospital's eye clinic. Trouble is, the eye clinic doesn't open until the next morning. When he arrives at the clinic, the nurse asks for his referral slip, but the emergency room doctor had forgotten to give it to him. The patient has to return to the emergency room and wait for another physician to screen him. The physician refers him back to the eye clinic and to a social worker to arrange payment. Finally, a third doctor looks into his eye, sees a small piece of metal, and removes it—a 30-second procedure.[35]

Stories such as these have, of course, given bureaucracy a bad name. Some managers will not even use the term *bureaucratic control* because of its potentially negative connotation. That is unfortunate because the control system itself is not the problem. The problems occur when the systems are no longer viewed as tools for running the business but instead as rules for dictating rigid behavior.

Tactical Behavior   Control systems will be ineffective if employees engage in tactics aimed at beating the system. The most common type of tactical behavior is to manipulate information or report false performance data. People may produce two kinds of invalid data: about what *has* been done and about what *can* be done. False reporting about the past is less common because it is easier to identify someone who misreports what happened than someone who gives an erroneous prediction or estimate of what might happen. Still, managers sometimes change their accounting systems to smooth out the numbers. Also, people may intentionally feed false information into a management information system to cover up errors or poor performance. In 2014, allegations surfaced that some employees of the U.S. Department of Veterans Affairs were falsifying records regarding how many days it took for veterans to receive medical help.[36] According to guidelines, new patients were entitled to see a physician within 14 days of completing the necessary paperwork. According to one investigation of the VA medical center in Phoenix, 1,700 veterans were kept waiting an average of 115 days for their first primary care appointment.[37] The VA's inspector general discovered that officials at the medical center hid this fact by falsifying the records.

President Barack Obama and other officials meet to discuss how to correct problems at the U.S. Department of Veterans Affairs.

© Saul Loeb/AFP/Getty Images

Additional evidence of alleged wrongdoing has been linked to other VA medical units in multiple cities.[38] One U.S. senator summed up the scandal: "Poor management is costing the department billions of dollars more and compromising veterans' access to medical care."[39]

More commonly, people falsify their predictions or requests for the future. When asked to give budgetary estimates, employees usually ask for larger amounts than they need. On the other hand, they sometimes submit unrealistically *low* estimates when they believe a low estimate will help them get a budget or a project approved. Budget-setting sessions can become tugs of war between subordinates trying to get slack in the budget and superiors attempting to minimize slack. Similar tactics are exhibited when managers negotiate unrealistically low performance standards so that subordinates will have little trouble meeting them; when salespeople project low forecasts so that they will look good by exceeding them; and when workers slow down the work pace while time-study analysts are setting work pace standards. In these and other cases, people are concerned only with their own performance figures rather than with the overall performance of their departments or companies.

Resistance to Control   Often people strongly resist control systems. They do so for several reasons. First, comprehensive control systems increase the accuracy of performance data and make employees more accountable for their actions. Control systems uncover mistakes, threaten people's job security and status, and decrease people's autonomy.

Second, control systems can change expertise and power structures. For example, management information systems can make the costing, purchasing, and production decisions previously made by managers much quicker. Those individuals may fear a loss of expertise, power, and decision-making authority as a result.

Third, control systems can change the social structure of an organization. They can create competition and disrupt social groups and friendships. People may end up competing against those with whom they formerly had comfortable, cooperative relationships. Because people's social needs are so important, they will resist control systems that reduce social need satisfaction.

Fourth, control systems may be seen as an invasion of privacy, lead to lawsuits, and cause low morale.

Designing Effective Control Systems

Effective control systems maximize potential benefits and minimize dysfunctional behaviors. To achieve this, management needs to design control systems that

1. Establish valid performance standards.
2. Provide adequate information to employees.
3. Ensure acceptability to employees.
4. Maintain open communication.
5. Use multiple approaches.

Establish Valid Performance Standards   An effective control system must be based on valid and accurate performance standards. The most effective standards, as discussed earlier, tend to be expressed in quantitative terms; they are objective rather than subjective. Also, the measures should not be capable of being easily sabotaged or faked. Moreover, the system must incorporate all important aspects of performance. For example, a company that just focused on sales volume without also looking at profitability might soon go out of business. As you learned earlier, unmeasured behaviors are neglected. Often performance standards for delivering training and other HR programs emphasize trainee satisfaction as reported on surveys. But the Philadelphia Department of Licenses and Inspections instead verified that its training actually improved employee performance. The department was notorious for its long lines and rude workers, so it turned for help to the Philadelphia Ritz-Carlton Hotel—part of a chain known for its superb customer service. The hotel's area general manager provided training initially to 40 department workers in how to improve their service skills. As part of its posttraining measurement process, the department checked the wait times for license applicants, which dropped from 82 minutes to 14 minutes. The department is continuing its partnership program with Ritz-Carlton through additional employee training and attendance at each other's management meetings.[40]

But management also must defend against another problem: too many measures that create overcontrol and employee resistance. To make many controls tolerable, managers can devote attention to a few key areas while setting satisfactory performance standards in others. Or they can establish simple priorities. The purchasing agent may have to meet targets in the following sequence: quality, availability, cost, inventory level. Finally, managers can set tolerance ranges. For example, in financial budgeting, optimistic, expected, and minimum levels sometimes are specified.

Many companies' budgets set cost targets only. This causes managers to control spending but also to neglect earnings. At Emerson Electric, profit and growth are key measures. If an unanticipated opportunity to increase market share arises, managers can spend what they need to go after it. The phrase "it's not in the budget" is less likely to stifle people at Emerson than it is at most other companies.

This principle applies to nonfinancial aspects of performance as well. At many customer service call centers, control aims to maximize efficiency by focusing on the average amount of time each agent spends handling each phone call. But the business objectives of call centers should also include other measures such as cross-selling products or improving customer satisfaction and repeat business. Customer service agents at TD bank are trained to solve customers' problems the first time they call. The agents are evaluated by their ability to "achieve first-call issue resolution and receive favorable customer feedback—not by how quickly they can get the customer off the phone."[41]

Business consultant Michael Hammer summarizes these points in terms of what he calls seven "deadly sins" of performance measurement to avoid:[42]

1. *Vanity*—using measures that are sure to make managers and the organization look good. For example, a company might measure order fulfillment in terms of whether products are delivered by the latest date promised by the organization, rather than by the tougher and more meaningful measure of when the customers request to receive the products.

2. *Provincialism*—limiting measures to functional or departmental responsibilities rather than the organization's overall objectives. If a company's transportation department measures only shipping costs, it won't have an incentive to consider that shipping reliability (delivery on a given date) will affect performance at the company's stores or distribution centers.

3. *Narcissism*—measuring from the employee's, manager's, or company's point of view, rather than the customer's. For example, a maker of computer systems measured on-time shipping of each component; if 90 percent of the system's components arrived at the customer on time, it was 90 percent on time. But from the customer's point of view, the system wasn't on time at all because the customer needed *all* the components to use the system.

4. *Laziness*—not expending the effort to analyze what is important to measure. An electric power company simply assumed customers cared about installation speed, but in fact, customers really cared more about receiving an accurate installation schedule.

5. *Pettiness*—measuring just one component of what affects business performance. An example would be clothing manufacturers that assume they should consider just manufacturing cost rather than the overall costs of making exactly the right products available in stores when customers demand them.

6. *Inanity*—failing to consider the way standards will affect real-world human behavior and company performance. A fast-food restaurant targeted waste reduction and was surprised when restaurant managers began slowing down operations by directing their employees to hold off on cooking anything until orders were placed.

7. *Frivolity*—making excuses for poor performance rather than taking performance standards seriously. In some organizations, more effort goes to blaming others than to correcting problems.

According to Hammer, the basic correction to these "sins" is to select standards carefully that look at entire business processes, such as product development or order fulfillment, and identify which actions make those processes succeed. Then managers should measure performance against these standards precisely, accurately, and practically, making individuals responsible for their achievement and rewarding success.

Provide Adequate Information   Management must communicate to employees the importance and nature of the control system. Then people must receive feedback about their performance. Feedback motivates people and provides information that enables them to correct their own deviations from performance standards. Allowing people to initiate their own corrective action encourages self-control and reduces the need for outside supervision. Open-book management, described in Chapter 15, is a powerful use of this control principle.

Information should be as accessible as possible, particularly when people must make decisions quickly and frequently. For example, a national food company with its own truck fleet had a difficult problem. The company wanted drivers to go through customer sales records every night, insert new prices from headquarters every morning, and still make their rounds—an impossible set of demands. To solve this control problem, the company installed personal computers in more than 1,000 delivery trucks. Now drivers use their PCs for constant communication with headquarters. Each night drivers send information about the stores, and each morning headquarters sends prices and recommended stock mixes.

In general, a manager designing a control system should evaluate the information system in terms of the following questions:

1. Does it provide people with data relevant to the decisions they need to make?
2. Does it provide the right amount of information to decision makers throughout the organization?
3. Does it provide enough information to each part of the organization about how other, related parts of the organization are functioning?[43]

Ensure Acceptability to Employees   Employees are less likely to resist a control system and exhibit dysfunctional behaviors if they accept the system. They are more likely to accept systems that have useful performance standards but are not overly controlling. Employees also will find systems more acceptable if they believe the standards are possible to achieve.

The control system should emphasize positive behavior rather than focusing on controlling negative behavior alone. In more than two decades, Johnson & Johnson's Ethicon San Lorenzo facility has never had to recall a product. The company makes sutures, meshes, and other supplies for surgery—an industry in which quality must be perfect but recalls have been all too common. To achieve these outstanding results, the company set up a system it calls the Do It Right Framework, which includes training, employee involvement in process improvements, and open communication about company objectives and the reasons for changes. Most important, employees understand that their work matters. Every employee sees a video about Ethicon's work, highlighted by a cardiovascular surgeon describing how he uses the products and why their quality affects patients' recovery. Thus, doing the job right is something employees genuinely care about.[44]

One of the best ways to establish reasonable standards and thus gain employee acceptance of the control system is to set standards participatively. As we discussed in Chapter 4, participation in decision making secures people's understanding and cooperation and results in better decisions. Allowing employees to collaborate in control system decisions that affect their jobs directly will help overcome resistance and foster acceptance of the system. In addition, employees on the front line are more likely to know which standards are most important and practical, and they can inform a manager's judgment on these issues. Finally, if standards are established in collaboration with employees, managers will more easily obtain cooperation on solving the problem when deviations from standards occur.

Maintain Open Communication   When deviations from standards occur, it is important for employees to feel able to report the deviations so that the problem can be addressed. If employees come to feel that their managers want to hear only good news or, worse, if they fear reprisal for reporting bad news, even if it is not their fault, then any controls that are in place will be much less likely to be effective. Problems may go unreported or, even worse, may reach the point at which they become much more expensive or difficult to solve. But if managers create an environment of openness and honesty, one in which employees feel comfortable sharing even negative information and are appreciated for doing so in a timely fashion, then the control system is much more likely to work effectively.

Nevertheless, managers may sometimes need to discipline employees who are failing to meet important standards. In such cases, an approach called *progressive discipline* is usually most effective. In this approach, clear standards are established, but failure to meet them is dealt with in a progressive or step-by-step process. For example, the first time an employee's sales performance has been worse than it should have been, the supervising manager may offer verbal counseling or coaching. If problems persist, the next step might be a written reprimand. This type of reasonable and considered approach signals to all employees that the manager is interested in improving their performance, not in punishing them.

Use Multiple Approaches   Multiple controls are necessary. For example, banks need controls on risk so that they don't lose a lot of money from defaulting borrowers, as well as profit controls including sales budgets that aim for growth in accounts and customers.

As you learned earlier in this chapter, control systems generally should include both financial and nonfinancial performance targets and incorporate aspects of preliminary, concurrent, and feedback control. In recent years, a growing number of companies are using **strategy maps** to show how they plan to convert their various assets into desired outcomes. Related to these maps is the **balanced scorecard** which holds managers responsible for a combination of four sets of performance measures (see Exhibit 16.10): (1) financial, (2) customer satisfaction, (3) business processes (quality and efficiency), and (4) learning and growth.[45] The goal is generally to broaden management's horizon beyond short-term financial results so that the company's long-term success is more likely. Michael Boo, chief strategy officer of the National Marrow Donor Program (NMDP), wanted to develop new ways of reaching the nonprofit's vision of 10,000 bone marrow transplants per year. Such transplants can prolong the lives of individuals with leukemia and other life-threatening diseases. He and colleagues developed a Balanced Scorecard with four perspectives: stakeholder, financial performance, processes, and people/knowledge/technology. The NMDP has achieved 60 percent of its goal, averaging nearly 500 transplants each month.[46]

Effective control will also require managers and organizations to use many of the other techniques and practices of good management. For example, compensation systems will grant rewards for meeting standards and impose consequences if they are not met. And to gain employee acceptance, managers may also rely on many of the other communication and motivational tools that we discussed in earlier chapters, such as persuasion and positive reinforcement.

strategy map

A visual depiction that shows how an organization plans to convert its various assets into desired outcomes

balanced scorecard

Control system combining four sets of performance measures: financial, customer, business process, and learning and growth.

EXHIBIT 16.10 A Strategy Map and Balanced Scorecard for Performance Improvement at a Hospital

Strategy Map

Financial	Steady growth	Return on investor capital	Productivity
Customer	Service leadership	Patient satisfaction	Operational excellence
Internal	Improve quality and timeliness of services	Continuously improve staff's skills	Improve patient value
Learning & Growth	Promote culture of quality service	Align employee competencies with strategy	Implement technology to support innovation

Balanced Scorecard

	Objectives	Measurement	Target
Financial	Grow sales revenue Increase profit	Balance sheet Profit and loss statement	10% annually 5% annually
Customer	Increase satisfaction Attract repeat patients	Satisfaction surveys Track in database	90% highly satisfied 80% return rate
Internal	Increase expertise of staff Reduce error rates	Completion rate of online training modules Number of incorrect dosages	90% passed with score of 85% or higher 2% or lower
Learning & Growth	Communicate importance of high quality Develop succession plan	Number of e-mails and mentions during meetings Percent completed and times updated	One e-mail and mention per week 90% by year-end and one time per month

SOURCES: Adapted from R. S. Kaplan and D. P. Norton, "Having Trouble with Your Strategy? Then Map It," *Harvard Business Review* (September–October 2000), pp. 167–72; and R. S. Kaplan and D. P. Norton, *The Balanced Scorecard: Translating Strategy into Action* (Boston: Harvard Business School Press, 1996), p. 76.

The Other Controls: Markets and Clans

Although the concept of control has always been a central feature of organizations, the principles and philosophies underlying its use are changing. In the past, control was focused almost exclusively on bureaucratic (and market) mechanisms. Generations of managers were taught that they could maximize productivity by regulating what employees did on the job—through standard operating procedures, rules, regulations, and close supervision. To increase output on an assembly line, for example, managers in the past tried to identify the one best way to approach the work and then to monitor employees' activities to make certain that they followed standard operating procedures. In short, they controlled work by dividing and simplifying tasks, a process we referred to in Chapter 1 as *scientific management*.

> Although formal bureaucratic control systems are perhaps the most pervasive in organizations, they are not always the most effective.

Although formal bureaucratic control systems are perhaps the most pervasive in organizations (and the most talked about in management textbooks), they are not always the most effective. Market controls and clan controls may both represent more flexible, though no less potent, approaches to regulating performance.

Market Control

In contrast to bureaucratic controls, market controls involve the use of economic forces— and the pricing mechanisms that accompany them—to regulate performance. The system works like this: when output from an individual, department, or business unit has value to other people, a price can be negotiated for its exchange. As a market for these transactions becomes established, two effects occur:

- Price becomes an indicator of the value of the good or service.
- Price competition has the effect of controlling productivity and performance.

The basic principles that underlie market controls can operate at the corporate level, the business unit (or department) level, and the individual level. Exhibit 16.11 shows a few ways in which market controls are used in an organization.

Market Controls at the Corporate Level   In large, diversified companies, market controls often are used to regulate independent business units. Particularly in large conglomerate firms that act as holding companies, business units typically are treated as profit centers that compete with one another. Top executives may place very few bureaucratic controls on business unit managers but use profit and loss data for evaluating performance. Although decision making and power are decentralized to the business units, market controls ensure that business unit performance is in line with corporate objectives.

Use of market control mechanisms in this way has been criticized by those who insist that economic measures do not reflect the complete value of an organization adequately. Employees often suffer as diversified companies are repeatedly bought and sold based on market controls.

Market Controls at the Business Unit Level   Market control also can be used within business units to regulate exchanges among departments and functions. Transfer pricing is one method that organizations use to try to reflect market forces for internal transactions. A **transfer price** is the charge by one unit in the organization for a good or service that it supplies to another unit of the same organization. For example, in automobile manufacturing, a transfer price may be affixed to components and subassemblies before they are shipped to subsequent business units for final assembly. Ideally, the transfer price reflects the price that the receiving business unit would have to pay for that product or service in the marketplace.

transfer price

Price charged by one unit for a good or service provided to another unit within the organization.

EXHIBIT 16.11

Examples of Market Control

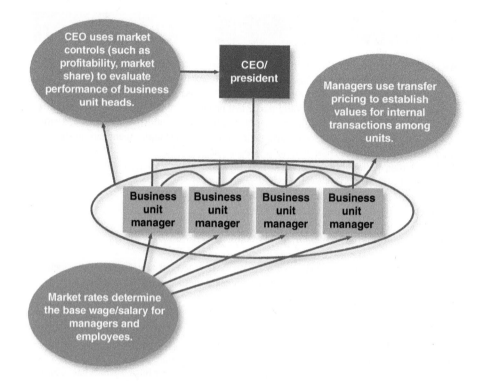

As organizations have more options to outsource goods and services to external part-ners, market controls such as transfer prices provide natural incentives to keep costs down and quality up. Managers stay in close touch with prices in the marketplace to make sure their own costs are in line, and they try to improve the service they provide to increase their department's value to the organization. Consider the situation in which training and development activities can be done internally by the human resources department or out-sourced to a consulting firm. If the human resources department cannot supply quality training at a reasonable price, there may be no reason for that department to exist inside the firm. Similarly, Penske Truck Leasing Company began outsourcing many of its finance processes to a company called Genpact, not only for lower prices but also for the exper-tise developed by that specialized firm to compete in the marketplace. Penske's chief financial officer, Frank Cocuzza, says the department spends $20 million less per year than it did to perform the same functions in-house while it has improved its rate of collections and learned thousands of ways to make his own operation more efficient, modeled after Genpact's lean practices.[47]

Market Controls at the Individual Level   Market controls also are used at the indi-vidual level. For example, when organizations are trying to hire employees, the supply and demand for particular skills influence the wages employees can expect to receive and the rate organizations are likely to pay. Employees or job candidates who have more valuable skills tend to be paid a higher wage. Of course, wages don't always reflect market rates—sometimes they are based (perhaps arbitrarily) on internal resource considerations—but the market rate is often the best indicator of an employee's potential worth to a firm.

Market-based controls such as these are important in that they provide a natural incen-tive for employees to enhance their skills and offer them to potential firms. Even after individuals gain employment, market-based wages are important as controls in that persons with higher economic value may be promoted faster to higher positions in the organization.

Market controls often are used by boards of directors to manage CEOs of major corporations. Ironically, CEOs usually are seen as the ones controlling everyone else in the company; but the CEO is accountable to the board of directors, and the board must devise ways to ensure that the CEO acts in its interest. Absent board control, CEOs may act in ways that make them look good personally (such as making the company bigger or more diversified) but that do not lead to higher profits for the firm. And as recent corporate scandals have shown, without board control, CEOs may also artificially inflate the firm's earnings or not fully declare expenses, making the firm look much more successful than it really is.

As much as it would seem that market controls play a significant role in the salary of a professional baseball player or any other professional athlete, are the sometimes ridiculously high salaries that are paid for players today truly indicative of a player's skill—or something else? If the player doesn't live up to the expectation of the previously perceived skill level or, put another way, has a bad year, should the organization be allowed to cut his pay?

© imac/Alamy

Traditionally, boards have tried to control CEO performance mainly through the use of incentive plans in addition to base salary. These typically include some type of bonus tied to short-term profit targets. In large U.S. companies, most CEO compensation is now at risk, meaning it depends mainly on the performance of the company. In addition to short-term incentives, boards use some type of long-term incentives linked to the firm's share price, usually through stock options, which we discussed in Chapter 10. Also, balanced scorecards are intended to keep CEOs focused on the company's longer-term health. And under the Sarbanes-Oxley Act, described in Chapter 5, board members are expected to exercise careful control over the company's financial performance, including oversight of the CEO's compensation package.

Clan Control: The Role of Empowerment and Culture

Increasingly, managers are discovering that control systems based solely on bureaucratic and market mechanisms are insufficient for directing today's workforce. There are several reasons for this:

- *Employees' jobs have changed.* The nature of work is evolving. Employees working with computers, for example, have more variability in their jobs, and much of their work is intellectual and therefore invisible. Because of this, there is no one best way to perform a task, and programming or standardizing jobs becomes extremely difficult. Close supervision is also unrealistic because it is nearly impossible to supervise activities such as reasoning and problem solving.
- *The nature of management has changed.* The role of managers is evolving, too. Managers used to know more about the job than employees did. Today it is typical for employees to know more about their jobs than anyone else does. We refer to this as the shift from touch labor to knowledge work. When real expertise in organizations exists at the very lowest levels, hierarchical control becomes impractical.[48]
- *The employment relationship has changed.* The social contract at work is being renegotiated. It used to be that employees were most concerned about issues such as pay, job security, and the hours of work. Today, however, more and more employees want to be more fully engaged in their work, taking part in decision making, devising solutions to unique problems, and receiving assignments that are challenging and involving. They want to use their brains.

For these three reasons, the concept of *empowerment* not only has become more popular in organizations but has become a necessary aspect of a manager's repertoire of control. With no one best way to approach a job and no way to scrutinize what employees do every day, managers must empower employees to make decisions and trust that they will act in the best interests of the firm. But this does not mean giving up control. It means creating a strong culture of high standards and integrity so that employees will exercise effective control on their own.

Recall our extensive discussion of organization culture in Chapter 2. If the organization's culture encourages the wrong behaviors, then an effort to impose effective controls will be severely hindered. But if managers create and reinforce a strong culture that encourages correct behavior, one in which everyone understands management's values and expectations and is motivated to act in accordance with them, then clan control can be a very effective control tool.[49] As we noted at the beginning of this chapter, clan control involves creating relationships built on mutual respect and encouraging each individual to take responsibility for his or her actions. Employees work within a guiding framework of values, and they are expected to use good judgment. For example, at NetApp, an IT company specializing in data storage and protection, a commitment to employee empowerment prompted the switch from a 12-page travel policy to some simple guidelines for employees who need to go on a business trip: "We are a frugal company. But don't show up dog-tired to save a few bucks. Use your common sense."[50] The emphasis in an empowered organization is on satisfying customers, not on pleasing the boss. Mistakes are tolerated as the unavoidable by-product of dealing with change and uncertainty and are viewed as opportunities to learn. And team members learn together. Exhibit 16.12 provides a set of guidelines for managing in an empowered world.

The resilience and time investment of clan control are a double-edged sword. Clan control takes a long time to develop and an even longer time to change. This gives an organization stability and direction during periods of upheaval in the environment or the organization (e.g., during changes in the top management). "Management in Action: Onward" provides an example of a company trying to cope with upheaval in the retail industry; consider whether clan control could help Best Buy. Yet if managers want to establish a new culture—a new form of clan control—they must help employees unlearn the old values and embrace the new. We will talk about this transition process more in the final chapter of this book.

Bottom Line

Clan control empowers employees to meet performance standards. *Would you expect more clan control with standardized jobs or creative positions?*

EXHIBIT 16.12

Management Control in an Empowered Setting

1. **Put control where the operation is.** Layers of hierarchy, close supervision, and checks and balances are quickly disappearing and being replaced with self-guided teams. For centuries even the British Empire—as large as it was—never had more than six levels of management, including the queen.

2. **Use real-time rather than after-the-fact controls.** Issues and problems must be solved at the source by the people doing the actual work. Managers become a resource to help out the team.

3. **Rebuild the assumptions underlying management control to build on trust rather than distrust.** Today's high-flex organizations are based on empowerment, not obedience. Information must facilitate decision making, not police it.

4. **Move to control based on peer norms.** Clan control is a powerful thing. Workers in Japan, for example, have been known to commit suicide rather than disappoint or lose face within their team. Although this is extreme, it underlines the power of peer influence. The Japanese have a far more homogeneous culture and set of values than we do. In North America, we must build peer norms systematically and put much less emphasis on managing by the numbers.

5. **Rebuild the incentive systems to reinforce responsiveness and teamwork.** The twin goals of adding value to the customer and team performance must become the dominant raison d'être of the measurement systems.

SOURCE: Gerald. H. B. Ross, "Revolution in Management Control," *Management Accounting*, November 1990, pp. 23–27. Reprinted by permission.

Management in Action

WAS ROWE A PROBLEM FOR BEST BUY—OR PART OF THE SOLUTION?

When Hubert Joly became Best Buy's CEO in 2012, he focused on basic ideas: a company whose name points to great deals should offer customers the merchandise they want at the lowest price. That requires operating efficiently and selling effectively in stores and on the web.

As simple as the principles are, they are extremely hard to carry out in the Internet age. Nevertheless, Joly sees his role as being the leader who points to the basics and the need to be fully engaged. In December 2012, when Joly called "All hands on deck," sending office employees into stores during the evening and weekend hours, he expressed a spirit he wanted to permeate the company.

For Joly, the Results Oriented Work Environment (ROWE) was inconsistent with "all hands on deck." If employees could work wherever and whenever they wanted, perhaps they would not be at the office when needed or would be unavailable in a crisis. Ending ROWE would put employees "in the office as much as possible," to quote Best Buy spokesman Matt Furman. Joly also said ROWE delegates decisions that managers should be involved in making.

The creators of the ROWE policy dispute this understanding. Cali Ressler and Jody Thompson, former Best Buy employees, came up with the idea as a way to improve efficiency while motivating workers. They say Best Buy saved more than $2 million in the first two years of ROWE because employee turnover plummeted and productivity rose. (Based on the interest in ROWE, the two women left Best Buy to spread the idea through a consulting firm,

CultureRx.) They explain that under ROWE, employees discussed goals and work arrangements with their managers and were responsible for achieving the mutually agreed-upon goals. Flexibility involved only the details of *how* they achieved their goals. Also, ROWE applied only to Best Buy's office employees, not to the store workers.

ROWE's emphasis on flexibility contrasts with commentary about decision making and change at Best Buy. According to the *Minneapolis Star Tribune,* former executives say Best Buy developed a bureaucratic style that slowed down its responses to a changing environment. Perhaps more ROWE-style flexibility would have made Best Buy nimbler; clearly, Joly disagrees. In contrast to the bottom-up creation of ROWE, the program's elimination was a swift, top-down decision.

In the three years since Joly's announcement, Best Buy's revenues stopped falling, and its stock price took a long-awaited upward turn. Several other factors have contributed to the improved financial results at Best Buy, most notably the "Renew Blue" plan that resulted in $1 billion in cost reductions, the offering of high-margin smartphones, and the growth of the store-within-a-store concept.[51]

- How well did ROWE meet the criteria of an effective performance system? Will eliminating it be more or less effective? Why?
- How can clan control help Best Buy improve its performance?

KEY TERMS

accounting audits, p. 512

activity-based costing (ABC), p. 512

after-action review, p. 505

assets, p. 513

balance sheet, p. 513

balanced scorecard, p. 521

budgeting, p. 510

bureaucratic control, p. 501

clan control, p. 501

concurrent control, p. 505

control, p. 500

current ratio, p. 513

debt–equity ratio, p. 513

external audit, p. 509

feedback control, p. 505

feedforward control, p. 505

internal audit, p. 509

liabilities, p. 513

management audit, p. 509

management myopia, p. 515

market control, p. 501

principle of exception, p. 504

profit and loss statement, p. 513

return on investment (ROI), p. 515

standard, p. 502

stockholders' equity, p. 513

strategy map, p. 521

transfer price, p. 523

RETAINING WHAT YOU LEARNED

In Chapter 16, you learned that companies develop control systems in order to keep employees focused on achieving organizational goals. The basic bureaucratic control system includes setting, measuring, and comparing performance standards and, when necessary, eliminating unfavorable deviations. Performance standards should cover issues such as quantity, quality, time, and cost. Budgets are a control mechanism that act as an initial guide for allocating resources and using funds. Many companies are changing how they prepare budgets to eliminate waste and improve business processes. Balance sheets compare the value of company assets to the obligations the company owes to owners and creditors. Profit and loss statements show company income relative to costs incurred. Ratios provide a goal for managers as well as a standard against which to evaluate performance. Managers use a variety of procedures to maximize the effectiveness of control systems. Market controls can be used at the level of the corporation, the business unit or department, or the individual. To be responsive to customers, companies are increasingly using clan control to harness the expertise of employees and give them the freedom to act on their own initiative.

LO 1   Explain why companies develop control systems for employees.

- Left to their own devices, employees may act in ways that do not benefit the organization.
- Control systems are designed to eliminate idiosyncratic behavior and keep employees directed toward achieving the goals of the firm.
- Control systems are a steering mechanism for guiding resources and for helping each individual act on behalf of the organization.

LO 2   Summarize how to design a basic bureaucratic control system.

- The design of a basic control system involves four steps: (1) setting performance standards, (2) measuring performance, (3) comparing performance with the standards, and (4) eliminating unfavorable deviations by taking corrective action.
- Performance standards should be valid and should cover issues such as quantity, quality, time, and cost.
- Once performance is compared with the standards, the principle of exception suggests that the manager needs to direct attention to the exceptional cases that have significant deviations. Then the manager takes the action most likely to solve the problem.

LO 3   Describe the purposes for using budgets as a control device.

- Budgets combine the benefits of feedforward, concurrent, and feedback controls. They are used as an initial guide for allocating resources, a reference point for using funds, and a feedback mechanism for comparing actual levels of sales and expenses with their expected levels.

- Recently companies have modified their budgeting processes to allocate costs over basic processes (such as customer service) rather than to functions or departments.
- By changing the way they prepare budgets, many companies have discovered ways to eliminate waste and improve business processes.

LO 4   Define basic types of financial statements and financial ratios used as controls.

- The basic financial statements are the balance sheet and the profit and loss statement.
- The balance sheet compares the value of company assets to the obligations the company owes to owners and creditors.
- The profit and loss statement shows company income relative to costs incurred. In addition to these statements, companies look at liquidity ratios (whether the company can pay its short-term debts), leverage ratios (the extent to which the company is funding operations by going into debt), and profitability ratios (profit relative to investment). These ratios provide a goal for managers as well as a standard against which to evaluate performance.

LO 5   List procedures for implementing effective control systems.

- To maximize the effectiveness of controls, managers should (1) establish valid performance standards, (2) provide adequate information to employees, (3) ensure acceptability, (4) maintain open communication, and (5) see that multiple approaches are used (such as bureaucratic, market, and clan control).

LO 6   Identify ways in which organizations use market control mechanisms.

- Market controls can be used at the level of the corporation, the business unit or department, or the individual.
- At the corporate level, business units are evaluated against one another based on profitability. At times, less profitable businesses are sold while more profitable businesses receive more resources.
- Within business units, transfer pricing may be used to approximate market mechanisms to control transactions among departments.
- At the individual level, market mechanisms control the wage rate of employees and can be used to evaluate the performance of individual managers.

LO 7   Discuss the use of clan control in an empowered organization.

- Approaching control from a centralized, mechanistic viewpoint is increasingly impractical. In today's organizations, it is difficult to program one best way to approach work, and it is often difficult to monitor performance.

- To be responsive to customers, companies must harness the expertise of employees and give them the freedom to act on their own initiative.
- To maintain control while empowering employees, companies should (1) use self-guided teams, (2) allow decision making at the source of the problems, (3) build trust and mutual respect, (4) base control on a guiding framework of norms, and (5) use incentive systems that encourage teamwork.

DISCUSSION QUESTIONS

1. What controls can you identify in the management of your school or at a company where you now work (or recently worked)? If you can, interview a manager or employee of the organization to learn more about the controls in use there. How might the organization's performance change if those controls were not in place?

2. How are leadership and control different? How are planning and control different? How are structure and control different?

3. Imagine you are the sales manager of a company that sells medical supplies to hospitals nationwide. You have 10 salespeople reporting to you. You are responsible for your department achieving a certain level of sales each year. In general terms, how might you go about taking each step in the control cycle?

4. In the situation described in Question 3, what actions would you need to take if sales fell far below the budgeted level? What, if any, actions would you need to take if sales far exceeded the sales budget? If sales are right on target, does effective controlling require any response from you? (Would your answer differ if the department were on target overall, but some salespeople fell short and others exceeded their targets?)

5. Besides sales and expenses, identify five other important control measures for a business. Include at least one nonfinancial measure.

6. What are the pros and cons of bureaucratic controls such as rules, procedures, and supervision?

7. Suppose a company at which executives were rewarded for meeting targets based only on profits and stock price switches to a balanced scorecard that adds measures for customer satisfaction, employee engagement, employee diversity, and ethical conduct. How, if at all, would you expect executives' performance to change in response to the new control system? How, if at all, would you expect the company's performance to change?

8. Google offers Google Apps, such as Gmail, Google Calendar, and Docs & Spreadsheets, as collaboration tools for employees. Describe how the company could use market controls to determine whether Google employees will use these software programs or competing software (e.g., Word and Excel).

9. How effective is clan control as a control mechanism? What are its strengths? Its limitations? When would a manager rely on clan control the most?

10. Does empowerment imply the loss of control? Why or why not?

11. Some people use the concept of personal control to describe the application of business control principles to individual careers. Thinking about your school performance and career plans, which steps of the control process (Exhibit 16.3) have you been applying effectively? How do you keep track of your performance in meeting your career and life goals? How do you measure your success? Does clan control help you meet your personal objectives?

EXPERIENTIAL EXERCISES

16.1   SAFETY PROGRAM

OBJECTIVE
To understand some of the specific activities that fall under the management functions of planning, organizing, controlling and staffing, and directing.

INSTRUCTIONS
Read the following case and then evaluate the likely success of this managerial control effort. Specifically, how well did the manager review the source of the problems? How well designed is the new control system? How effectively is the manager building employee commitment to using the control mechanisms? How could this manager improve the control process? Summarize your findings and recommendations in a paragraph or two.

MANAGING THE VAMP CO. SAFETY PROGRAM
If there are specific things that a manager does, how are they done? What does it look like when one manages? The following describes a typical situation in which a manager performs managerial functions:

As production manager of the Vamp Stamping Company, you've become quite concerned over the metal stamping shop's safety record. Accidents that resulted in operators' missing time on the job have increased quite rapidly in the past year. These more serious accidents have jumped from 3 percent of all accidents reported to a current level of 10 percent.

Because you're concerned about your workers' safety as well as the company's ability to meet its customers' orders, you want to reduce this downtime accident rate to its previous level or lower within the next six months.

You call the accident trend to the attention of your production supervisors, pointing out the seriousness of the situation and their continuing responsibility to enforce the gloves and safety goggles rules. Effective immediately, every supervisor will review his or her accident reports for the past year, file a report summarizing these accidents with you, and state their intended actions to correct recurring causes of the accidents. They will make out weekly safety reports as well as meet with you every Friday to discuss what is being done and any problems they are running into.

You request the union steward's cooperation in helping the safety supervisor set up a short program on shop safety practices.

Because the machine operators are having the accidents, you encourage your supervisors to talk to their workers and find out what they think can be done to reduce the downtime accident rate to its previous level.

While the program is going on, you review the weekly reports, looking for patterns that will tell you how effective the program is and where the trouble spots are. If a supervisor's operators are not decreasing their accident rate, you discuss the matter in considerable detail with the supervisor and his or her key workers.

SOURCE: From Theodore T. Herbert, *The New Management: Study Guide,* 4th ed., p. 41.

16.2   PRELIMINARY, CONCURRENT, AND FEEDBACK CONTROL

OBJECTIVES

1. To demonstrate the need for control procedures.
2. To gain experience in determining when to use preliminary, concurrent, and feedback controls.

INSTRUCTIONS

1. Read the text materials on preliminary, concurrent, and feedback control.
2. Read the Control Problem Situation and be prepared to resolve those control problems in a group setting.
3. Your instructor will divide the class into small groups. Each group completes the Preliminary, Concurrent, and Feedback Control Worksheet by achieving consensus on the types of control that should be applied in each situation. The group also develops responses to the discussion questions.
4. After the class reconvenes, group spokespersons present group findings.

DISCUSSION QUESTIONS

1. For which control(s) was it easier to determine application? For which was it harder?
2. Would this exercise be better assigned to groups or to individuals?

CONTROL PROBLEM SITUATION

Your management consulting team has just been hired by Technocron International, a rapidly growing producer of electronic surveillance devices that are sold to commercial and government end users. Some sales are made through direct selling, and some through industrial resellers. Direct-sale profits are being hurt by what seem to be exorbitant expenses paid to a few of the salespeople, especially those who fly all over the world in patterns that suggest little planning and control. There is trouble among the resellers because standard contracts have not been established and each reseller has an entirely different contractual relationship. Repayment schedules vary widely from customer to customer. Also, profits are reduced by the need to customize most orders, making mass production almost impossible. However, no effort has been made to create interchangeable components. There are also tremendous inventory problems. Some raw materials and parts are bought in such small quantities that new orders are being placed almost daily. Other orders are so large that there is hardly room to store everything. Many of these purchased components are later found to be defective and unusable, causing production delays. Engineering changes are made that make large numbers of old components still in storage obsolete. Some delays result from designs that are very difficult to assemble, and assemblers complain that their corrective suggestions are ignored by engineering. To save money, untrained workers are hired and assigned to experienced worker-buddies who are expected to train them on the job. However, many of the new people are too poorly educated to understand their assignments, and their worker-buddies wind up doing a great deal of their work. This, along with the low pay and lack of consideration from engineering, is causing a great deal of worker unrest and talk of forming a union. Last week alone nine new worker grievances were filed, and the U.S. Equal Employment Opportunity Commission has just announced intentions to investigate two charges of discrimination on the part of the company. There is also a serious cash flow problem because a number of long-term debts are coming due at the same time. The cash flow problem could be relieved somewhat if some of the accounts payable could be collected.

The CEO manages corporate matters through five functional divisions: operations, engineering, marketing, finance, and human resources management and general administration.

Preliminary, Concurrent, and Feedback Control Worksheet

Technocron International is in need of a variety of controls. Complete the following matrix by noting the preliminary, concurrent, and feedback controls that are needed in each of the five functional divisions.

Divisions	Preliminary Controls	Concurrent Controls	Feedback Controls
HRM and general administration			
Operations			
Engineering			
Marketing			
Finance			

CONCLUDING CASE

THE GRIZZLY BEAR LODGE

Diane and Rudy Conrad own a small lodge outside Yellowstone National Park. Their lodge has 15 rooms that can accommodate up to 40 guests, with some rooms set up for families. Diane and Rudy serve a continental breakfast on weekdays and a full breakfast on weekends, included in the room rates they charge. Their busy season runs from May through September, but they remain open until Thanksgiving and reopen in April for a short spring season. They currently employ one cook and two waitpersons for the breakfasts on weekends, handling the other breakfasts themselves. They also have several housekeeping staff members, a groundskeeper, and a front-desk employee. The Conrads take pride in the efficiency of their operation, including the loyalty of their employees, which they attribute to their own form of clan control. If a guest needs something—whether it's a breakfast catered to a special diet or an extra set of towels—Grizzly Bear workers are empowered to supply it.

The Conrads are considering expanding their business. They have been offered the opportunity to buy the property next door, which would give them the space to build an annex containing an additional 20 rooms. Currently their annual sales total $300,000. With expenses running at $230,000—including mortgage, payroll, maintenance, and so forth—the Conrads' annual income is $70,000. They want to expand and make improvements without cutting back on the personal service they offer to their guests. In fact, in addition to hiring more staff to handle the larger facility, they are considering collaborating with more local businesses to offer guided rafting, fishing, hiking, and horseback riding trips. They also want to expand their food service to include dinner during the high season, which means renovating the restaurant area of the lodge and hiring more kitchen and wait staff. Ultimately, the Conrads would like the lodge to be open year-round, offering guests opportunities to cross-country ski, ride snowmobiles, or hike in the winter. They hope to offer holiday packages for Thanksgiving, Christmas, and New Year's celebrations in the great outdoors. The Conrads report that their employees are enthusiastic about their plans and want to stay with them through the expansion process. "This is our dream business," says Rudy. "We're only at the beginning."

QUESTIONS

1. Discuss how Rudy and Diane can use feedforward, concurrent, and feedback controls both now and in the future at the Grizzly Bear Lodge to ensure their guests' satisfaction.

2. What might be some of the fundamental budgetary considerations the Conrads would have as they plan the expansion of their lodge?

3. Describe how the Conrads could use market controls to plan and implement their expansion.

CHAPTER 10

Managing Organizational Structure and Culture

Learning Objectives

After studying this chapter, you should be able to:

LO10-1   Identify the factors that influence managers' choice of an organizational structure.

LO10-2   Explain how managers group tasks into jobs that are motivating and satisfying for employees.

LO10-3   Describe the types of organizational structures managers can design, and explain why they choose one structure over another.

LO10-4   Explain why managers must coordinate jobs, functions, and divisions using the hierarchy of authority and integrating mechanisms.

LO10-5   List the four sources of organizational culture, and explain why and how a company's culture can lead to competitive advantage.

A MANAGER'S CHALLENGE

Warby Parker Keeps an Eye on Company Culture

How does organizational culture influence employee performance and customer service? If you ask the four friends who started Warby Parker, the influence is eye opening. In 2008, Neil Blumenthal, Dave Gilboa, Andy Hunt, and Jeff Raider were MBA students at the Wharton School. Between classes, they got into a conversation about why glasses cost so much and why they weren't sold online. Later that day, actually in the middle of the night, Blumenthal emailed his three friends and proposed they start an online eyewear company.[1]

While researching the eyewear industry, the cofounders discovered a few large companies controlled the business, a fact that kept prices artificially high, reaping huge profits from consumers who had few options. By designing their own frames under their own brand, working closely with suppliers, and dealing directly with customers, Warby Parker could avoid the middleman and provide high-quality, stylish prescription eyewear for $95 a frame—including lenses. While eyewear has become a fashion accessory, some consumers might hesitate to purchase glasses over the Internet. No problem, according to Warby Parker. As part of its innovative business model, the company lets prospective customers pick five frames to be shipped to their homes so they can try them on for size and style—and return shipping is free.[2]

In 2010 the company started selling eyewear online and was featured in *GQ* magazine, in which the writer called Warby Parker "the Netflix of eyewear." Within 48 hours of the magazine being published, the website was flooded with orders. Because the cofounders rushed to get the website up and running, there was no "sold out" function on the site—so customers were placing orders long after inventory had run out.

More than *20,000* people were on the wait list to buy Warby Parker's selection of inexpensive and stylish eyewear.[3]

Initially operating the business out of his apartment, Blumenthal believed engaging

Neil Blumenthal, left, and Dave Gilboa, right, are the visionaries behind Warby Parker, the online retailer that has successfully disrupted the eyewear industry and created a unique organizational culture.
© Carolyn Cole/Los Angeles Times/Getty Images

directly with the 20,000 people waiting to purchase Warby Parker eyewear and apologizing for the lack of merchandise was a good first step in creating a company culture that has become the envy of many successful businesses. "It was this moment of panic, but also a great opportunity for us to provide awesome customer service and write personalized emails to apologize and explain," Blumenthal says, "that really set the tone for how we would run customer service."[4]

Since the beginning, Warby Parker has put organizational culture at the forefront of its business. Within the company, there is a "culture team" responsible for planning company outings and themed luncheons. The team also plays a part in screening job candidates, ensuring Warby Parker culture is evident from the start of any potential employee's tenure with the company. To encourage a cohesive workforce, the company implemented weekly episodes of "lunch roulette"—where four randomly selected employees are sent out to lunch together so they get to know each other away from their desks.[5]

The company has grown dramatically from its early days in Blumenthal's apartment to a workforce of more than 500 employees and 30-plus brick-and-mortar stores—for consumers still unsure about selecting eyewear over the Internet. As part of that quick expansion, Warby Parker management knows its employees need to be agile and ready to jump in at a moment's notice. To underscore the need for agility, every employee at Warby Parker spends a week training on the Customer Experience team—just in case they are called on to wait on customers in the retail stores or answer questions via the website.[6]

As part of the company's culture, Warby Parker founders and a group of employees put together a list of core values of what the company stands for and how it conducts business on a daily basis. The tenets include "act with integrity and tell the whole truth"; "pursue new and creative ideas"; "be biased toward action"; "inject fun and quirkiness into everything we do"; and "treat others as we want to be treated." Participating in brainstorming sessions, employees regularly review the list and have input into updating the core values as the company expands.[7]

Warby Parker is one of a growing number of businesses that have gone the extra mile to become certified as a "B Corporation," making sure company decisions have a positive impact on all of its stakeholders—customers, employees, community, and the environment.[8] The company's "Buy a Pair, Give a Pair" program underscores its commitment to the global community. Based on the number of eyeglasses sold, Warby Parker makes a monthly donation to its nonprofit partners, which covers the cost of sourcing a specific number of glasses. The nonprofits train men and women in developing countries to give basic eye exams and to sell glasses to their communities at affordable prices. To date more than 1 million pairs of glasses have been distributed as a result of the program.[9]

Disrupting the eyewear industry with its innovative business model, Warby Parker continues to stay true to its vision of leading the way for socially conscious companies—with a strong organizational culture and the ability to stay comfortable in an ever-changing business environment.

Overview

As the opening example suggests, organizational culture is a powerful influence on how employees work. In a quickly changing business environment, it is important for managers to identify the best way to organize people and resources to increase efficiency and effectiveness.

In Part 4 of this book, we examine how managers can organize and control human and other resources to create high-performing organizations. To organize and control (two of the four tasks of management identified in Chapter 1), managers must design an organizational architecture that makes the best use of resources to produce the goods and services customers want. **Organizational architecture** is the combination of organizational structure, culture, control systems, and human resource management (HRM) systems that determines how efficiently and effectively organizational resources are used.

By the end of this chapter, you will be familiar not only with various forms of organizational structures and cultures but also with various factors that determine the organizational design choices that managers make. Then, in Chapters 11 and 12, we examine issues surrounding the design of an organization's control systems and HRM systems.

organizational architecture The organizational structure, control systems, culture, and human resource management systems that together determine how efficiently and effectively organizational resources are used.

Designing Organizational Structure

Organizing is the process by which managers establish the structure of working relationships among employees to allow them to achieve an organization's goals efficiently and effectively. **Organizational structure** is the formal system of task and job reporting relationships that determines how employees use resources to achieve an organization's goals.[10] *Organizational culture*, discussed in Chapter 3, is the shared set of beliefs, values, and norms that influence how people and groups work together to achieve an organization's goals. **Organizational design** is the process by which managers create a specific type of organizational structure and culture so a company can operate in the most efficient and effective way.[11]

 LO10-1 Identify the factors that influence managers' choice of an organizational structure.

organizational structure A formal system of task and reporting relationships that coordinates and motivates organizational members so they work together to achieve an organization's goals.

organizational design The process by which managers make specific organizing choices that result in a particular kind of organizational structure.

Once a company decides what kind of work attitudes and behaviors it wants from its employees, managers create a particular arrangement of task and authority relationships, and promote specific cultural values and norms, to obtain these desired attitudes and behaviors. The challenge facing all companies is to design a structure and a culture that (1) *motivate* managers and employees to work hard and to develop supportive job behaviors and attitudes and (2) *coordinate* the actions of employees, groups, functions, and divisions to ensure they work together efficiently and effectively.

As noted in Chapter 2, according to contingency theory, managers design organizational structures to fit the factors or circumstances that are affecting the company the most and causing the most uncertainty.[12] Thus, there is no one best way to design an organization: Design reflects each organization's specific situation, and researchers have argued that stable, mechanistic structures may be most appropriate in some situations, where as in others flexible, organic structures might be the most effective. Four factors are important determinants of the type of organizational structure or culture managers select: the nature of the organizational environment, the type of strategy the organization pursues, the technology (and particularly information technology) the organization uses, and the characteristics of the organization's human resources (see Figure 10.1).[13]

The Organizational Environment

In general, the more quickly the external environment is changing and the greater the uncertainty within it, the greater are the problems managers face in trying to gain access to scarce resources. In this situation, to speed decision making and communication and make it easier to obtain resources, managers typically make organizing choices that result in more flexible structures and entrepreneurial cultures.[14] They are likely to decentralize authority, empower lower-level employees to make important operating decisions, and encourage values and norms that emphasize change and innovation—a more organic form of organizing.

In contrast, if the external environment is stable, resources are readily available, and uncertainty is low, then less coordination and communication among people and functions are needed to obtain resources. Managers can make organizing choices that bring more stability or formality to the organizational structure and can establish values and norms that emphasize obedience and being a team player. Managers in this situation prefer to make decisions within a clearly defined hierarchy of authority and to use detailed rules, standard operating procedures (SOPs), and restrictive norms to guide and govern employees' activities—a more mechanistic form of organizing.

Figure 10.1

Factors Affecting Organizational Structure

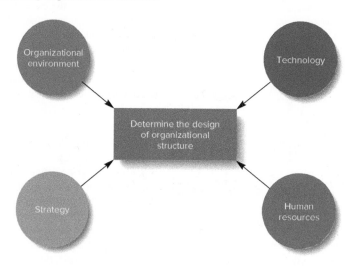

As we discussed in Chapter 6, change is rapid in today's marketplace, and increasing competition both at home and abroad is putting greater pressure on managers to attract customers and increase efficiency and effectiveness. Consequently, interest in finding ways to structure organizations—such as through empowerment and self-managed teams—to allow people and departments to behave flexibly has been increasing.

Strategy

Chapter 8 suggests that once managers decide on a strategy, they must choose the right means to implement it. Different strategies often call for the use of different organizational structures and cultures. For example, a differentiation strategy aimed at increasing the value customers perceive in an organization's goods and services usually succeeds best in a flexible structure with a culture that values innovation; flexibility facilitates a differentiation strategy because managers can develop new or innovative products quickly—an activity that requires extensive cooperation among functions or departments. In contrast, a low-cost strategy that is aimed at driving down costs in all functions usually fares best in a more formal structure with more conservative norms, which gives managers greater control over the activities of an organization's various departments.[15]

In addition, at the corporate level, when managers decide to expand the scope of organizational activities by vertical integration or diversification, for example, they need to design a flexible structure to provide sufficient coordination among the different business divisions.[16] As discussed in Chapter 8, many companies have been divesting businesses because managers have been unable to create a competitive advantage to keep them up to speed in fast-changing industries. By moving to a more flexible structure, managers gain more control over their different businesses. Finally, expanding internationally—operating in many different countries—challenges managers to create organizational structures that allow organizations to be flexible on a global level.[17] As we discuss later, managers can group their departments or divisions in several ways to allow them to effectively pursue an international strategy.

Technology

Recall that technology is the combination of skills, knowledge, machines, and computers that are used to design, make, and distribute goods and services. As a rule, the more complicated the technology that an organization uses, the more difficult it is to regulate or control it because more unexpected events can arise. Thus, the more complicated the technology, the greater is the need for a flexible structure and progressive culture to enhance managers' ability to respond to unexpected situations—and give them the freedom and desire to work out new solutions to the problems they encounter. In contrast, the more routine the technology, the more appropriate is a formal structure because tasks are simple and the steps needed to produce goods and services have been worked out in advance.

What makes a technology routine or complicated? One researcher who investigated this issue, Charles Perrow, argued that two factors determine how complicated or nonroutine technology is: task variety and task analyzability.[18] *Task variety* is the number of new or unexpected problems or situations that a person or function encounters in performing tasks or jobs. *Task analyzability* is the degree to which programmed solutions are available to people or functions to solve the problems they encounter. Nonroutine or complicated technologies are characterized by high task variety and low task analyzability; this means many varied problems occur and solving these problems requires significant nonprogrammed decision making. In contrast, routine technologies are characterized by low task variety and high task analyzability; this means the problems encountered do not vary much and are easily resolved through programmed decision making.

Examples of nonroutine technology are found in the work of scientists in an R&D laboratory who develop new products or discover new drugs, and they are seen in the planning exercises an organization's top management team uses to chart future strategy. Examples of routine technology include typical mass production or assembly operations, where workers perform the same task repeatedly and where managers have already identified the programmed solutions necessary to perform a task efficiently. Similarly, in service organizations such as fast-food restaurants, the tasks that crew members perform in making and serving fast food are routine.

 LO10-2 Explain how managers group tasks into jobs that are motivating and satisfying for employees.

Human Resources

A final important factor affecting an organization's choice of structure and culture is the characteristics of the human resources it employs. In general, the more highly skilled its workforce, and the greater the number of employees who work together in groups or teams, the more likely an organization is to use a flexible, decentralized structure and a professional culture based on values and norms that foster employee autonomy and self-control. Highly skilled employees, or employees who have internalized strong professional values and norms of behavior as part of their training, usually desire greater freedom and autonomy and dislike close supervision.

Flexible structures, characterized by decentralized authority and empowered employees, are well suited to the needs of highly skilled people. Similarly, when people work in teams, they must be allowed to interact freely and develop norms to guide their own work interactions, which also is possible in a flexible organizational structure. Thus, when designing organizational structure and culture, managers must pay close attention to the needs of the workforce and to the complexity and kind of work employees perform.

In summary, an organization's external environment, strategy, technology, and human resources are the factors to be considered by managers seeking to design the best structure and culture for an organization. The greater the level of uncertainty in the organization's environment, the more complex its strategy and technologies, and the more highly qualified and skilled its workforce, the more likely managers are to design a structure and a culture that are flexible, can change quickly, and allow employees to be innovative in their responses to problems, customer needs, and so on. The more stable the organization's environment, the less complex and more well understood its strategy or technology, and the less skilled its workforce, the more likely managers are to design an organizational structure that is formal and controlling and a culture whose values and norms prescribe how employees should act in particular situations.

Later in the chapter we discuss how managers can create different kinds of organizational cultures. First, however, we discuss how managers can design flexible or formal organizational structures. The way an organization's structure works depends on the organizing choices managers make about three issues:

- How to group tasks into individual jobs
- How to group jobs into functions and divisions
- How to allocate authority and coordinate or integrate functions and divisions

Grouping Tasks into Jobs: Job Design

job design The process by which managers decide how to divide tasks into specific jobs.

job simplification The process of reducing the number of tasks that each worker performs.

job enlargement Increasing the number of different tasks in a given job by changing the division of labor.

The first step in organizational design is **job design**, the process by which managers decide how to divide into specific jobs the tasks that have to be performed to provide customers with goods and services. Managers at McDonald's, for example, have decided how best to divide the tasks required to provide customers with fast, cheap food in each McDonald's restaurant. After experimenting with different job arrangements, McDonald's managers decided on a basic division of labor among chefs and food servers. Managers allocated all the tasks involved in actually cooking the food (putting oil in the fryers, opening packages of frozen french fries, putting beef patties on the grill, making salads, and so on) to the job of chef. They allocated all the tasks involved in giving the food to customers (such as greeting customers, taking orders, putting fries and burgers into bags, and taking money) to food servers. In addition, they created other jobs—the job of dealing with drive-through customers, the job of keeping the restaurant clean, and the job of overseeing employees and responding to unexpected events. The result of the job design process is a *division of labor* among employees, one that McDonald's managers have discovered through experience is most efficient.

Establishing an appropriate division of labor among employees is a critical part of the organizing process, one that is vital to increasing efficiency and effectiveness. At McDonald's, the tasks associated with chef and food server were split into different jobs because managers found that, for the kind of food McDonald's serves, this approach was most efficient. It is efficient because when each employee is given fewer tasks to perform (so that each job becomes more specialized), employees become more productive at performing the tasks that constitute each job.

At Subway sandwich shops, however, managers chose a different kind of job design. At Subway there is no division of labor among the people who make the sandwiches, wrap the sandwiches, give them to customers, and take the money. The roles of chef and food server are combined into one. This different division of tasks and jobs is efficient for Subway and not for McDonald's because Subway serves a limited menu of mostly submarine-style sandwiches that are prepared to order. Subway's production system is far simpler than McDonald's; McDonald's menu is much more varied, and its chefs must cook many different kinds of foods. In 2014 Subway changed its children's menu to promote healthful options and trained its employees to encourage children to choose apples as part of their meals.[19]

Managers of every organization must analyze the range of tasks to be performed and then create jobs that best allow the organization to give customers the goods and services they want. In deciding how to assign tasks to individual jobs, however, managers must be careful not to take **job simplification**, the process of reducing the number of tasks that each worker performs, too far.[20] Too much job simplification may reduce efficiency rather than increase it if workers find their simplified jobs boring and monotonous, become demotivated and unhappy, and as a result, perform at a low level.

Job Enlargement and Job Enrichment

In an attempt to create a division of labor and design individual jobs to encourage workers to perform at a higher level and be more satisfied with their work, several researchers have proposed ways other than job simplification to group tasks into jobs: job enlargement and job enrichment.

Job enlargement is increasing the number of different tasks in a given job by changing the division of labor.[21] For example, because Subway food servers make the food as well as serve it, their jobs are "larger" than the jobs of McDonald's food servers. The idea behind job enlargement is that increasing the range of tasks performed by a worker will reduce boredom and fatigue and may increase motivation to perform at a high level—increasing both the quantity and the quality of goods and services provided. The accompanying "Management Insight" feature describes how one Wendy's franchise tried to improve service by enlarging jobs through training.

MANAGEMENT INSIGHT

Employee Training Part of Wendy's Image Makeover

Wendy's is changing its image. It has redesigned its corporate logo and chosen a new look for its restaurants that includes new employee uniforms, Wi-Fi, and flat-screen televisions. It has also added lounge areas with fireplaces and faux leather chairs.[22]

What is the idea behind having a living room area at a fast-food restaurant? "The hearth at home is a gathering place," said Tré Musco, who is the chief executive of Tesser, the design firm hired to oversee Wendy's remodeling efforts. "It's warm, it's comfortable, it says stay and relax, as opposed to, this is fast food, get in and get out as quickly as possible."[23]

Customers who dine in tend to spend a little more money, so having a welcoming environment can increase sales. Wendy's reported a 25 percent jump in sales at the renovated restaurants.[24]

The company has remodeled more than 600 of its restaurants in the new design. The company also has a schedule for when franchise-owned restaurants will be updated. But at least one franchise owner is innovating in a way that has a similar effect, without the remodel.

Meritage Hospitality Group, which owns more than 160 Wendy's locations,[25] is improving customer service through training. First, the company committed to bringing on board 10 well-trained workers to each of its stores in Michigan. That's almost 500 new workers. The company held a job fair and looked for friendly, caring people. Then the company provided extensive training for all employees. In fact, they hired the new position of corporate trainer to do one-on-one training with cashiers.[26] Employees are encouraged to look for ways to initiate a conversation with customers and create a personal connection. They also are encouraged to have a regular customer's order prepared before the customer asks. Finally, the franchise group instituted contests among the staff in the restaurants. One contest between the day shift and the night shift was to see who could get the most customer names in a given day.

As a result of the effort, sales went up, customer complaints went down, and customer compliments went up. "Our biggest tip is to invest the time in training," said Al Pruitt, president of Wendy's for Meritage. "If you spend time on your people, you will always get a return on your investment."[27]

In addition to Wendy's stores getting an image makeover, one of its top franchisees focuses on employee training as a way of improving customer service and enlarging jobs.
© dcwcreations/Shutterstock.com RF

job enrichment Increasing the degree of responsibility a worker has over his or her job.

Job enrichment is increasing the degree of responsibility a worker has over a job by, for example, (1) empowering workers to experiment to find new or better ways of doing the job, (2) encouraging workers to develop new skills, (3) allowing workers to decide how to do the work and giving them the responsibility for deciding how to respond to unexpected situations, and (4) allowing workers to monitor and measure their own performance.[28] The idea behind job enrichment is that increasing workers' responsibility increases their involvement in their jobs and, thus, improves their interest in the quality of the goods they make or the services they provide.

In general, managers who make design choices that increase job enrichment and job enlargement are likely to increase the degree to which people behave flexibly rather than rigidly or mechanically. Narrow, specialized jobs are likely to lead people to behave in predictable ways; workers who perform a variety of tasks and who are allowed and encouraged to discover new and better ways to perform their jobs are likely to act flexibly and creatively. Thus, managers who enlarge and enrich jobs create a flexible organizational structure, and those who simplify jobs create a more formal structure. If workers are grouped into self-managed work teams, the organization is likely to be flexible because team members provide support for each other and can learn from one another.

The Job Characteristics Model

J. R. Hackman and G. R. Oldham's job characteristics model is an influential model of job design that explains in detail how managers can make jobs more interesting and motivating.[29] Hackman and Oldham's model also describes the likely personal and organizational outcomes that will result from enriched and enlarged jobs.

According to Hackman and Oldham, every job has five characteristics that determine how motivating the job is. These characteristics determine how employees react to their work and lead to outcomes such as high performance and satisfaction and low absenteeism and turnover:

- *Skill variety:* The extent to which a job requires that an employee use a wide range of different skills, abilities, or knowledge. Example: The skill variety required by the job of a research scientist is higher than that called for by the job of a McDonald's food server.

- *Task identity:* The extent to which a job requires that a worker perform all the tasks necessary to complete the job, from the beginning to the end of the production process. Example: A craftsworker who takes a piece of wood and transforms it into a custom-made desk has higher task identity than does a worker who performs only one of the numerous operations required to assemble a flat-screen TV.

- *Task significance:* The degree to which a worker feels his or her job is meaningful because of its effect on people inside the organization, such as coworkers, or on people outside the organization, such as customers. Example: A teacher who sees the effect of his or her efforts in a well-educated and well-adjusted student enjoys high task significance compared to a dishwasher who monotonously washes dishes as they come to the kitchen.

- *Autonomy:* The degree to which a job gives an employee the freedom and discretion needed to schedule different tasks and decide how to carry them out. Example: Salespeople who have to plan their schedules and decide how to allocate their time among different customers have relatively high autonomy compared to assembly-line workers, whose actions are determined by the speed of the production line.

- *Feedback:* The extent to which actually doing a job provides a worker with clear and direct information about how well he or she has performed the job. Example: An air traffic controller whose mistakes may result in a midair collision receives immediate feedback on job performance; a person who compiles statistics for a business magazine often has little idea of when he makes a mistake or does a particularly good job.

Hackman and Oldham argue that these five job characteristics affect an employee's motivation because they affect three critical psychological states. The more that employees feel that their work is *meaningful* and that they are *responsible for work outcomes* and *responsible for knowing how those outcomes affect others,* the more motivating work becomes and the more likely employees are to be satisfied and to perform at a high level. Moreover, employees who have jobs that are highly motivating are called on to use their skills more and to perform more tasks, and they are given more responsibility for doing the job. All of the foregoing are characteristic of jobs and employees in flexible structures where authority is decentralized and where employees commonly work with others and must learn new skills to complete the range of tasks for which their group is responsible.

Grouping Jobs into Functions and Divisions: Designing Organizational Structure

Once managers have decided which tasks to allocate to which jobs, they face the next organizing decision: how to group jobs together to best match the needs of the organization's environment, strategy, technology, and human resources. Typically, managers first decide to group jobs into departments and then design a *functional structure* to use organizational resources effectively. As an organization grows and becomes more difficult to control, managers must choose a more complex organizational design, such as a divisional structure or a matrix or product team structure. The different ways in which managers can design organizational structure are discussed next. Selecting and designing an organizational structure to increase efficiency and effectiveness is a significant challenge. As noted in Chapter 8, managers reap the rewards of a well-thought-out strategy only if they choose the right type of structure to implement the strategy. The ability to make the right kinds of organizing choices is often what differentiates effective from ineffective managers and creates a high-performing organization.

 LO10-3 Describe the types of organizational structures managers can design, and explain why they choose one structure over another.

functional structure An organizational structure composed of all the departments that an organization requires to produce its goods or services.

Functional Structure

A *function* is a group of people, working together, who possess similar skills or use the same kind of knowledge, tools, or techniques to perform their jobs. Manufacturing, sales, and research and development are often organized into functional departments. A **functional structure** is an organizational structure composed of all the departments that an organization requires to produce its goods or services. Figure 10.2 shows the functional structure that Pier 1 Imports, a home furnishings company, uses to supply its customers with a range of goods from around the world to satisfy their desires for new and innovative products.

Within Pier 1's organizational structure, the main functions include finance and administration, merchandising (purchasing the goods), the global supply chain (managing the vendors who supply the goods), marketing and sales, planning and allocations (managing credit and product distribution), and human resources. Each job inside a function exists because it helps the function perform the activities necessary for high organizational performance. Thus, within the marketing function are all the jobs necessary to efficiently advertise Pier 1's products to increase their appeal to customers (such as promotion, photography, and visual communication).

There are several advantages to grouping jobs according to function. First, when people who perform similar jobs are grouped together, they can learn from observing one another and thus become more specialized and can perform at a higher level. The tasks associated with one job often are related to the tasks associated with another job, which encourages cooperation within a function. In Pier 1's marketing department, for example, the person designing the photography program for an ad campaign works closely with the person responsible for designing store layouts and with visual communication experts. As a result, Pier 1 can develop a strong, focused marketing campaign to differentiate its products.

Second, when people who perform similar jobs are grouped together, it is easier for managers to monitor and evaluate their performance.[30] Imagine if marketing experts, purchasing experts, and real estate experts were grouped together in one function and supervised by a

Figure 10.2

The Functional Structure of Pier 1 Imports

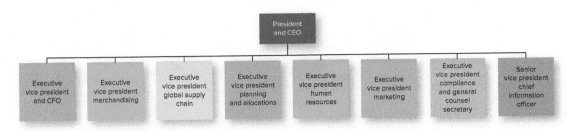

manager from merchandising. Obviously, the merchandising manager would not have the expertise to evaluate all these different people appropriately. A functional structure allows workers to evaluate how well coworkers are performing their jobs, and if some workers are performing poorly, more experienced workers can help them develop new skills.

Finally, managers appreciate functional structure because it lets them create the set of functions they need to scan and monitor the competitive environment and obtain information about how it is changing.[31] With the right set of functions in place, managers are in a good position to develop a strategy that allows the organization to respond to its changing situation. Employees in the marketing group can specialize in monitoring new marketing developments that will allow Pier 1 to better target its customers. Employees in merchandising can monitor all potential suppliers of home furnishings, both at home and abroad, to find the goods most likely to appeal to Pier 1's customers.

As an organization grows, and particularly as its task environment and strategy change because it is beginning to produce a wider range of goods and services for different kinds of customers, several problems can make a functional structure less efficient and effective.[32] First, managers in different functions may find it more difficult to communicate and coordinate with one another when they are responsible for several different kinds of products, especially as the organization grows both domestically and internationally. Second, functional managers may become so preoccupied with supervising their own specific departments and achieving their departmental goals that they lose sight of the organization's goals. If that happens, organizational effectiveness will suffer because managers will be viewing issues and problems facing the organization only from their own, relatively narrow departmental perspectives.[33] Both of these problems can reduce efficiency and effectiveness.

Divisional Structures: Product, Market, and Geographic

divisional structure An organizational structure composed of separate business units, within which are the functions that work together to produce a specific product for a specific customer.

As the problems associated with growth and diversification increase over time, managers must search for new ways to organize their activities to overcome the problems associated with a functional structure. Most managers of large organizations choose a **divisional structure** and create a series of business units to produce a specific kind of product for a specific kind

Pier 1 organizes its operations by function, which means that employees can more easily learn from one another and improve the service they provide to its customers.
© Tim Boyle/Getty Images

of customer. Each *division* is a collection of functions or departments that work together to produce the product. The goal behind the change to a divisional structure is to create smaller, more manageable units within the organization. There are three forms of divisional structure (see Figure 10.3).[34] When managers organize divisions according to the *type of good or service* they provide, they adopt a product structure. When managers organize divisions according to the *area of the country or world* they operate in, they adopt a geographic structure. When managers organize divisions according to *the type of customer* they focus on, they adopt a market structure.

PRODUCT STRUCTURE   Imagine the problems that managers at Pier 1 would encounter if they decided to diversify into producing and selling cars, fast food, and health insurance—in addition to home furnishings—and tried to use their existing set of functional managers to oversee the production of all four kinds of products. No manager would have the necessary skills or abilities to oversee those four products. No individual marketing manager, for example, could effectively market cars, fast food, health insurance, and home furnishings at the same time. To perform a functional activity successfully, managers must have experience in specific markets or industries. Consequently, if managers decide to diversify into new industries or to expand their range of products, they commonly design a product structure to organize their operations (see Figure 10.3A).

Figure 10.3

Product, Market, and Geographic Structures

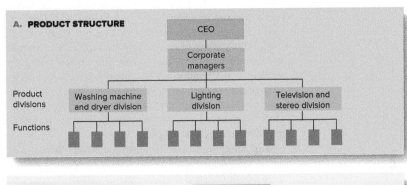

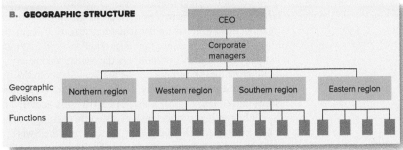

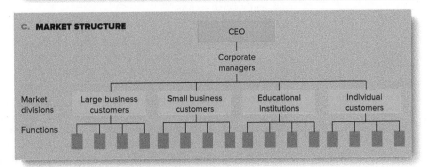

316   Chapter Ten

product structure An organizational structure in which
each product line or business
is handled by a selfcontained
division.

Using a **product structure**, managers place each distinct product line or business in its own, self-contained division and give divisional managers the responsibility for devising an appropriate business-level strategy to allow the division to compete effectively in its industry or market.[35] Each division is self-contained because it has a complete set of all the functions—marketing, R&D, finance, and so on—that it needs to produce or provide goods or services efficiently and effectively. Functional managers report to divisional managers, and divisional managers report to top or corporate managers.

Grouping functions into divisions focused on particular products has several advantages for managers at all levels in the organization. First, a product structure allows functional managers to specialize in only one product area, so they can build expertise and fine-tune their skills in this particular area. Second, each division's managers can become experts in their industry; this expertise helps them choose and develop a business-level strategy to differentiate their products or lower their costs while meeting the needs of customers. Third, a product structure frees corporate managers from the need to supervise directly each division's day-to-day operations; this latitude lets corporate managers create the best corporate-level strategy to maximize the organization's future growth and ability to create value. Corporate managers are likely to make fewer mistakes about which businesses to diversify into or how to best expand internationally, for example, because they can take an organizationwide view.[36] Corporate managers also are likely to evaluate better how well divisional managers are doing, and they can intervene and take corrective action as needed.

The extra layer of management, the divisional management layer, can improve the use of organizational resources. Moreover, a product structure puts divisional managers close to their customers and lets them respond quickly and appropriately to the changing task environment. One pharmaceutical company that successfully adopted a new product structure to better organize its activities is GlaxoSmithKline (GSK). The need to innovate new kinds of prescription drugs to boost performance is a continual battle for pharmaceutical companies. In the 2000s many of these companies have been merging to try to increase their research productivity, and one of them, GlaxoSmithKline, was created from the merger between Glaxo Wellcome and SmithKline Beecham.[37] Prior to the merger, both companies experienced a steep decline in the number of new prescription drugs their scientists were able to invent. The problem facing the new company's top managers was how to best use and combine the talents of the scientists and researchers from both of the former companies to allow them to quickly innovate exciting new drugs.

Top managers realized that after the merger there would be enormous problems associated with coordinating the activities of the thousands of research scientists who were working on hundreds of different drug research programs. Understanding the problems associated with large size, the top managers decided to group the researchers into eight product divisions to allow them to focus on particular clusters of diseases such as heart disease or viral infections. The members of each product division were told they would be rewarded based on the number of new prescription drugs they were able to invent and the speed with which they could bring these new drugs to the market. GlaxoSmithKline's new product structure worked well; its research productivity doubled after the reorganization, and a record number of new drugs moved into clinical trials.[38] In 2015 GSK acquired Novartis' global vaccines business (excluding influenza vaccines), divested its oncology business to Novartis, and then created a new consumer health care joint venture with the Swiss pharmaceutical firm. GSK sees the move as a way to balance its various businesses across the pharmaceutical, consumer health care, and vaccine sectors.[39]

GEOGRAPHIC STRUCTURE   When organizations expand rapidly both at home and abroad, functional structures can create special problems because managers in one central location may find it increasingly difficult to deal with the different problems and issues that may arise in each region of a country or area of the world. In these cases, a **geographic** **structure**, in which divisions are broken down by geographic location, is often chosen (see Figure 10.3B). To achieve the corporate mission of providing next-day mail service, Fred Smith, CEO of FedEx, chose a geographic structure and divided up operations by creating a division in each region. Large retailers such as Macy's, Neiman Marcus, and Brooks Brothers also use a geographic structure. Because the needs of retail customers differ by region—for

geographic structure An
organizational structure in
which each region of a country
or area of the world is served
by a self-contained division.

example, shorts in California and down parkas in the Midwest—a geographic structure gives retail regional managers the flexibility they need to choose the range of products that best meets the needs of regional customers.

In adopting a *global geographic structure,* as shown in Figure 10.4A, managers locate different divisions in each of the world regions where the organization operates. Managers are most likely to do this when they pursue a multidomestic strategy because customer needs vary widely by country or world region. If products that appeal to U.S. customers do not sell in Europe, the Pacific Rim, or South America, managers must customize the products to meet the needs of customers in those different world regions; a global geographic structure with global divisions will allow them to do this. For example, food and beverage companies need to customize the taste of their products to closely match the desires of customers in different countries and world regions. The accompanying "Managing Globally" feature describes how one company reorganized itself to be able to offer more services to customers in each region it serves.

MANAGING GLOBALLY

Firm's Structure Focuses on Client Needs

The Michael Baker Corporation has worked on some high-profile engineering projects. The company had a role in building the 789-mile Trans-Alaska Pipeline in North America, the 135-mile KHMR-American Friendship Highway in Cambodia, the New River Gorge Bridge in West Virginia, the Midfield Terminal Complex at the Pittsburgh International Airport, and a 2,600-mile fiber optic telecommunications network in Mexico.[40] More recently the company was selected to rehabilitate the Pulaski Skyway, the bridge that connects Newark and Jersey City in New Jersey.[41]

As the need for engineering, construction management, and other services expands nationally and internationally, the company launched a national and global expansion program.[42] Michael Baker Corporation merged with Integrated Mission Solutions in 2013 to create Michael Baker International.

The company's vision statement includes the words "Be the go-to company for clients and employees." Its services include architectural, environmental, construction, cybersecurity, planning, and project/program management. The company works with U.S. and foreign allied governments, as well as with commercial customers.[43]

The renovation of the Pulaski Skyway in New Jersey is one of Michael Baker International's projects. The engineering and consulting firm reorganized its operations into seven regions and three business units to offer more services and to focus project leadership on a local basis.
© Mel Evans/AP Images

The firm has more than 6,000 employees in 90 national and international offices. In 2014 it decided to reorganize into an operations-centric structure in seven regions. In its announcement of the reorganization, the company suggested that its new structure would allow it to offer more services to customers in each region. The reorganization also would allow more local leadership of projects.

"This reorganization is a result of extensive review, market analysis, client demand, and discussion with personnel at all levels of the company identifying and highlighting opportunities for building a balanced business in each of our regions," stated Kurt Bergman, chief executive officer. "The new organization promotes empowered business leaders at the office and regional levels, supported by national market and practice leads, to build and manage well-balanced portfolios reflective of the complete continuum of services provided by the Michael Baker International enterprise."[44]

Figure 10.4
Global Geographic and Global Product Structures

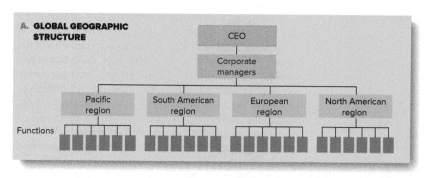

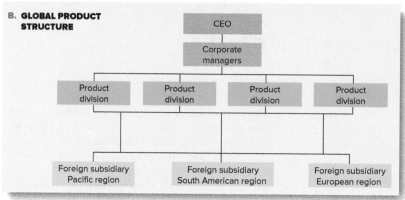

In contrast, to the degree that customers abroad are willing to buy the same kind of product or slight variations thereof, managers are more likely to pursue a global strategy. In this case, they are more likely to use a global product structure. In a *global product structure,* each product division, not the country and regional managers, takes responsibility for deciding where to manufacture its products and how to market them in countries worldwide (see Figure 10.4B). Product division managers manage their own global value chains and decide where to establish foreign subsidiaries to distribute and sell their products to customers in foreign countries.

MARKET STRUCTURE   Sometimes the pressing issue facing managers is to group functions according to the type of customer buying the product in order to tailor the products the organization offers to each customer's unique demands. A PC maker such as Dell, for example, has several kinds of customers, including large businesses (which might demand networks of computers linked to a mainframe computer), small companies (which may need just a few PCs linked together), educational users in schools and universities (which might want thousands of independent PCs for their students), and individual users (who may want a high-quality multimedia PC so they can play the latest video games).

market structure An organizational structure in which each kind of customer is served by a self-contained division; also called *customer structure.*

To satisfy the needs of diverse customers, a company might adopt a **market structure**, which groups divisions according to the particular kinds of customers they serve (see Figure 10.3C). A market structure lets managers respond to the needs of their customers and allows them to act flexibly in making decisions in response to customers' changing needs. To spearhead its turnaround, for example, Dell created four streamlined market divisions that each focus on being responsive to one particular type of customer: individual consumers, small businesses, large companies, and government and state agencies. Organizations need to continually evaluate their structures and make sure that operations are working according to plan. The accompanying "Management Insight" feature provides an example of what can occur in an organization when leaders do not know what is happening.

MANAGEMENT INSIGHT

Restoring a Team-First Culture in Miami

In the middle of the 2013 professional football season, Miami Dolphins offensive lineman Jonathan Martin abruptly quit and entered a hospital to get psychiatric help.[45] He said he had been bullied by three of his teammates.

The National Football League investigated the team and found Martin had been subjected to daily harassment by Richie Incognito, then a guard for the Miami Dolphins, as well as John Jerry and Mike Pouncey, both offensive linemen who also played for the Miami Dolphins at the time. The harassment included racial slurs about Martin being African-American, sexual taunts about his mother and sister, and jokes that Martin was gay.

The owner of the Miami Dolphins, Stephen Ross, said, "When we asked the NFL to conduct this independent review, we felt it was important to take a step back and thoroughly research these serious allegations. As an organization, we are committed to a culture of team-first accountability and respect for one another."[46]

The investigation and subsequent report identified Incognito as the main instigator of the harassment.[47] After the report was released, Jim Turner, who was the coach of the offensive line, was fired for not stopping the harassment and for taking part in some taunting. Additionally, Kevin O'Neill, who was the head athletic trainer at the time, was fired for not cooperating with the investigation.[48] However, the investigation concluded that Joe Philbin, the coach for the Miami Dolphins, did not take part in or know of the harassment that Martin was subjugated to.

After a disastrous 1–3 start to the 2015 NFL season, the Miami Dolphins fired Philbin. Finishing that season with an interim head coach (Dan Campbell), the Dolphins will now be coached by Adam Gase, former offensive coordinator of the Chicago Bears and the youngest head coach in the NFL, at the age of 37.[49] Gase's hiring has received both praise and criticism from players, fans, and the media. Some believe the Dolphins's "broken" culture needs a more experienced head coach to fix it, while others think Gase will bring a sense of unity and quiet leadership to the storied football franchise, helping to bring back the "team-first" culture so important to a successful sports organization.[50] Time will tell whether Gase can control the locker room and convince team members they have what it takes to play championship football.

Matrix and Product Team Designs

Moving to a product, market, or geographic divisional structure allows managers to respond more quickly and flexibly to the particular circumstances they confront. However, when information technology or customer needs are changing rapidly and the environment is uncertain, even a divisional structure may not give managers enough flexibility to respond to the environment quickly. To operate effectively under these conditions, managers must design the most flexible kinds of organizational structure available: a matrix structure or a product team structure (see Figure 10.5).

matrix structure An organizational structure that simultaneously groups people and resources by function and by product.

MATRIX STRUCTURE   In a matrix structure, managers group people and resources in two ways simultaneously: by function and by product.[51] Employees are grouped by *functions* to allow them to learn from one another and become more skilled and productive. In addition, employees are grouped into *product teams* in which members of different functions work together to develop a specific product. The result is a complex network of reporting relationships among product teams and functions that makes the matrix structure very flexible (see Figure 10.5A). Each person in a product team reports to two managers: (1) a functional boss, who assigns individuals to a team and evaluates their performance from a functional

Figure 10.5

Matrix and Product Team Structures

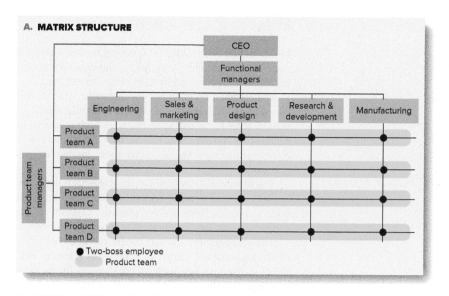

A. MATRIX STRUCTURE

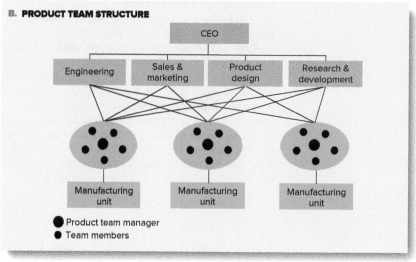

B. PRODUCT TEAM STRUCTURE

perspective, and (2) the boss of the product team, who evaluates their performance on the team. Thus, team members are known as *two-boss employees*. The functional employees assigned to product teams change over time as the specific skills that the team needs change. At the beginning of the product development process, for example, engineers and R&D specialists are assigned to a product team because their skills are needed to develop new products. When a provisional design has been established, marketing experts are assigned to the team to gauge how customers will respond to the new product. Manufacturing personnel join when it is time to find the most efficient way to produce the product. As their specific jobs are completed, team members leave and are reassigned to new teams. In this way the matrix structure makes the most use of human resources.

To keep the matrix structure flexible, product teams are empowered and team members are responsible for making most of the important decisions involved in product development.[52] The product team manager acts as a facilitator, controlling the financial resources and trying to keep the project on time and within budget. The functional managers try to ensure that the product is the best it can be to maximize its differentiated appeal.

High-tech companies that operate in environments where new product development takes place monthly or yearly have used matrix structures successfully for many years, and the need to innovate quickly is vital to the organization's survival. The flexibility afforded by a matrix structure lets managers keep pace with a changing and increasingly complex environment.[53]

PRODUCT TEAM STRUCTURE   The dual reporting relationships that are at the heart of a matrix structure have always been difficult for managers and employees to deal with. Often the functional boss and the product boss make conflicting demands on team members, who do not know which boss to satisfy first. Also, functional and product team bosses may come into conflict over precisely who is in charge of which team members and for how long. To avoid these problems, managers have devised a way of organizing people and resources that still allows an organization to be flexible but makes its structure easier to operate: a product team structure.

product team structure An organizational structure in which employees are permanently assigned to a cross-functional team and report only to the product team manager or to one of his or her direct subordinates.

The product team structure differs from a matrix structure in two ways: (1) It does away with dual reporting relationships and two-boss employees, and (2) functional employees are permanently assigned to a cross-functional team that is empowered to bring a new or redesigned product to market. A cross-functional team is a group of managers brought together from different departments to perform organizational tasks. When managers are grouped into cross-functional teams, the artificial boundaries between departments disappear, and a narrow focus on departmental goals is replaced with a general interest in working together to achieve the organization's goals. For example, when mattress company Sealy saw its sales slipping, it pulled together a cross-functional team that was allowed to work outside the organization's hierarchy and quickly design a new mattress. With everyone focused on the goal, team members created a mattress that broke previous sales records.[54]

cross-functional team A group of managers brought together from different departments to perform organizational tasks.

Members of a cross-functional team report only to the product team manager or to one of his or her direct subordinates. The heads of the functions have only an informal advisory relationship with members of the product teams—the role of functional managers is only to counsel and help team members, share knowledge among teams, and provide new technological developments that can help improve each team's performance (see Figure 10.5B).[55]

Increasingly, organizations are making empowered cross-functional teams an essential part of their organizational architecture to help them gain a competitive advantage in fast-changing organizational environments. For example, Newell Brands, the well-known maker of such products as Rubbermaid, Calphalon, and Sharpies, moved to a product structure to speed up the rate of production innovation.[56] In 2014 the company opened a design center in Kalamazoo, Michigan, as part of its ongoing "growth game plan," which involves making better product portfolio choices and investing in new marketing and innovation approaches to accelerate performance.[57]

Coordinating Functions and Divisions

The more complex the structure a company uses to group its activities, the greater are the problems of *linking and coordinating* its different functions and divisions. Coordination becomes a problem because each function or division develops a different orientation toward the other groups that affects how it interacts with them. Each function or division comes to view the problems facing the company from its own perspective; for example, it may develop different views about the major goals, problems, or issues facing a company.

LO10-4 Explain why managers must coordinate jobs, functions, and divisions using the hierarchy of authority and integrating mechanisms.

At the functional level, the manufacturing function typically has a short-term view; its major goal is to keep costs under control and get the product out the factory door on time. By contrast, the product development function has a long-term viewpoint because developing a new product is a relatively slow process, and high product quality is seen as more important than low costs. Such differences in viewpoint may make manufacturing and product development managers reluctant to cooperate and coordinate their activities to meet company goals. At the divisional level, in a company with a product structure, employees may become concerned more with making *their* division's products a success than with the profitability of the entire company. They may refuse, or simply not see the need, to cooperate and share information or knowledge with other divisions.

The problem of linking and coordinating the activities of different functions and divisions becomes more acute as the number of functions and divisions increases. We look first at how managers design the hierarchy of authority to coordinate functions and divisions so that they work together effectively. Then we focus on integration and examine the integrating mechanisms managers can use to coordinate functions and divisions.

Allocating Authority

As organizations grow and produce a wider range of goods and services, the size and number of their functions and divisions increase. To coordinate the activities of people, functions, and divisions and to allow them to work together effectively, managers must develop a clear hierarchy of authority.[58] Authority is the power vested in a manager to make decisions and use resources to achieve the organization's goals by virtue of his or her position in an organization. The hierarchy of authority is an organization's *chain of command*—the relative authority that each manager has—extending from the CEO at the top, down through the middle managers and first-line managers, to the nonmanagerial employees who actually make goods or provide services. Every manager, at every level of the hierarchy, supervises one or more subordinates. The term span of control refers to the number of subordinates who report directly to a manager.

Figure 10.6 shows a simplified picture of the hierarchy of authority at McDonald's Corporation as of July 2016. The fast-food giant's president and CEO, Steve Easterbrook, has taken bold steps to revise the company's organizational structure in an effort to reset and turnaround the business. Easterbrook, who took over as CEO in March 2015, is the manager who has the ultimate responsibility for the company's overall performance, and he has the authority to decide how to use organizational resources to benefit McDonald's stakeholders. Peter Bensen, the company's former CFO, is now the company's chief administrative officer, responsible for oversight of global departments that support operations, including finance, supply chain and sustainability, restaurant development, franchising, information technology, and restaurant solutions. McDonald's four divisions focus on combining markets with similar needs, challenges, and opportunities for growth—rather than a geographic approach to company operations. Also in the top management hierarchy is Robert Gibbs, executive vice president and chief communications officer. Unlike other managers, Gibbs is not a line manager, someone in the direct line or chain of command who has formal authority over people and resources. Rather, Gibbs is a staff manager, responsible for one of McDonald's specialist functions—communications. He reports directly to Easterbrook.[59]

Managers at each level of the hierarchy confer with managers at the next level down the authority hierarchy to decide how to use organizational resources. Accepting this authority, those lower-level managers are accountable for how well they make those decisions. Managers who make the right decisions are typically promoted, and organizations motivate managers with the prospects of promotion and increased responsibility within the chain of command.

Below Andres are the other main levels, or layers, in the McDonald's USA chain of command—presidents of its Northeast, South, Central, and West zones, regional managers, and supervisors. A hierarchy is also evident in each company-owned McDonald's restaurant. At the top is the store manager; at lower levels are the first assistant, shift managers, and crew

authority The power to hold people accountable for their actions and to make decisions concerning the use of organizational resources.

hierarchy of authority An organization's chain of command, specifying the relative authority of each manager.

span of control The number of subordinates who report directly to a manager.

line manager Someone in the direct line or chain of command who has formal authority over people and resources at lower levels.

staff manager Someone responsible for managing a specialist function, such as finance or marketing.

Figure 10.6

The Hierarchy of Authority and Span of Control at McDonald's Corporation

Figure 10.7

Tall and Flat Organizations

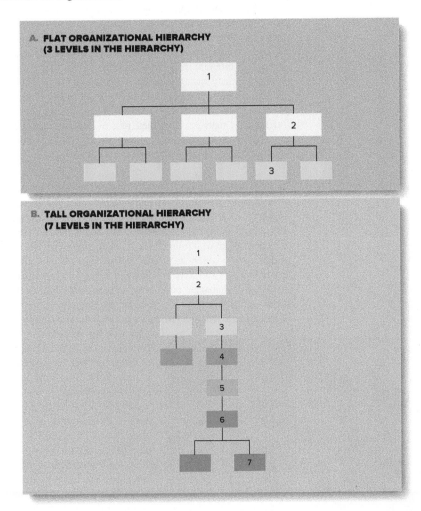

personnel. McDonald's managers have decided that this hierarchy of authority best allows the company to pursue its business-level strategy of providing fast food at reasonable prices—and its stock price has steadily climbed as performance has increased.

TALL AND FLAT ORGANIZATIONS   As an organization grows in size (normally measured by the number of its managers and employees), its hierarchy of authority normally lengthens, making the organizational structure taller. A *tall* organization has many levels of authority relative to company size; a *flat* organization has fewer levels relative to company size (see Figure 10.7).[60] As a hierarchy becomes taller, problems that make the organization's structure less flexible and slow managers' response to changes in the organizational environment may result.

Communication problems may arise when an organization has many levels in the hierarchy. It can take a long time for the decisions and orders of upper-level managers to reach managers further down in the hierarchy, and it can take a long time for top managers to learn how well their decisions worked. Feeling out of touch, top managers may want to verify that lower-level managers are following orders and may require written confirmation from them. Middle managers, who know they will be held strictly accountable for their actions, start devoting too much time to the process of making decisions to improve their chances of being right. They might even try to avoid responsibility by making top managers decide what actions to take.

Another communication problem that can result is the distortion of commands and messages being transmitted up and down the hierarchy, which causes managers at different levels to interpret what is happening differently. Distortion of orders and messages can be accidental, occurring because different managers interpret messages from their own narrow functional perspectives. Or distortion can be intentional, occurring because managers low in the hierarchy decide to interpret information in a way that increases their own personal advantage.

Another problem with tall hierarchies is that they usually indicate that an organization is employing many managers, and managers are expensive. Managerial salaries, benefits, offices, and secretaries are a huge expense for organizations. Large companies such as IBM and GM pay their managers millions of dollars a year. During the recent global recession, hundreds of thousands of managers lost their jobs as companies restructured and downsized their workforces to reduce costs. In 2016, however, a strong economic recovery seemed to be underway, with the U.S. economy experiencing robust hiring gains among workers and managers.[61]

THE MINIMUM CHAIN OF COMMAND   To ward off the problems that result when an organization becomes too tall and employs too many managers, top managers need to ascertain whether they are employing the right number of middle and first-line managers and whether they can redesign their organizational architecture to reduce the number of managers. Top managers might well follow a basic organizing principle—the principle of the minimum chain of command—which states that top managers should always construct a hierarchy with the fewest levels of authority necessary to efficiently and effectively use organizational resources.

Effective managers constantly scrutinize their hierarchies to see whether the number of levels can be reduced—for example, by eliminating one level and giving the responsibilities of managers at that level to managers above and by empowering employees below. One manager who has worked to empower employees is David Novak, former executive chairman and CEO of Yum Brands. Instead of dictating what the company's Taco Bell, KFC, and Pizza Hut brands should do, Novak turned Yum's corporate headquarters into a support center for worldwide operations. Novak also wrote a book called *Taking People with You: The Only Way to Make BIG Things Happen,* which outlines the leadership program Novak developed to motivate and recognize employees, aligning them with the organization's overall goals.[62]

In the United States over 5 million manufacturing jobs have been lost to factories in low-cost countries abroad in the 2000s. While many large U.S. manufacturing companies have given up the battle, some small companies such as electronics maker Plexus Corp. have been able to find ways of organizing that allow them to survive and prosper in a low-cost manufacturing world. They have done this by creating empowered work teams. U.S. companies cannot match the efficiency of manufacturers abroad in producing high volumes of a single product, such as millions of a particular circuit board used in a laptop computer. So Plexus's managers decided to focus their efforts on developing a manufacturing technology, called "low–high," that could efficiently produce low volumes of many different kinds of products. Plexus's managers formed a team to design an organizational structure based on creating four "focused factories" in which control over production decisions is given to the workers, whose managers cross-train them so they can perform all the operations involved in making a product in their "factory." Now, when work slows down at any point in the production of a particular product, a worker further along the production process can move back to help solve the problem that has arisen at the earlier stage.[63]

Furthermore, managers organized workers into self-managed teams that are empowered to make all the decisions necessary

Plexus Corp. uses empowered work teams to help it utilize a "low–high" manufacturing technology that can help produce low volumes of many different kinds of products.
© Maskot/Corbis RF

to make a particular product in one of the four factories. Because each product is different, the ability of the teams to make rapid decisions and respond to unexpected contingencies is vital on a production line, where time is money. At Plexus, managers, by allowing teams to experiment, have reduced changeover time from hours to as little as 30 minutes so the line is making products over 80 percent of the time.[64] The flexibility brought about by self-managed teams is why Plexus is so efficient and can compete against low-cost manufacturers abroad.

CENTRALIZATION AND DECENTRALIZATION OF AUTHORITY   Another way in which managers can keep the organizational hierarchy flat is by decentralizing authority— that is, by giving lower-level managers and nonmanagerial employees the right to make important decisions about how to use organizational resources.[65] If managers at higher levels give lower-level employees the responsibility of making important decisions and only *manage by exception,* then the problems of slow and distorted communication noted previously are kept to a minimum. Moreover, fewer managers are needed because their role is not to make decisions but to act as coach and facilitator and to help other employees make the best decisions. In addition, when decision-making authority is low in the organization and near the customer, employees are better able to recognize and respond to customer needs.

decentralizing authority
Giving lower-level managers and nonmanagerial employees the right to make important decisions about how to use organizational resources.

Decentralizing authority allows an organization and its employees to behave in a flexible way even as the organization grows and becomes taller. This is why managers are so interested in empowering employees, creating self-managed work teams, establishing cross-functional teams, and even moving to a product team structure. These design innovations help keep the organizational architecture flexible and responsive to complex task and general environments, complex technologies, and complex strategies.

Although more and more organizations are taking steps to decentralize authority, *too much* decentralization has certain disadvantages. If divisions, functions, or teams are given too much decision-making authority, they may begin to pursue their own goals at the expense of the organization's goals. Managers in engineering design or R&D, for example, may become so focused on making the best possible product that they fail to realize that the best product may be so expensive few people are willing or able to buy it. Also, too much decentralization can cause lack of communication among functions or divisions; this prevents the synergies of cooperation from ever materializing, and organizational performance suffers.

Top managers must seek the balance between centralization and decentralization of authority that best meets the four major contingencies an organization faces (see Figure 10.1). If managers are in a stable environment, are using well-understood technology, and are producing stable kinds of products (such as cereal, canned soup, or books), there is no pressing need to decentralize authority, and managers at the top can maintain control of much of organizational decision making.[66] However, in uncertain, changing environments where high-tech companies are producing state-of-the-art products, top managers must often empower employees and allow teams to make important strategic decisions so the organization can keep up with the changes taking place. No matter what its environment, a company that fails to control the balance between centralization and decentralization will find its performance suffering. The accompanying "Manager as a Person" feature describes how Microsoft's CEO uses elements of both centralization and decentralization to shift the company's business focus.

MANAGER AS A PERSON

Microsoft's Nadella Pushes for Innovation

In February 2014 Microsoft hired its third CEO in the company's almost 40 years. Satya Nadella had previously headed the company's cloud and enterprise group. When former CEO Steve Ballmer retired in 2013, he sent an email to Microsoft employees, announcing Nadella's appointment and touting Nadella's business, technical, and leadership skills. Ballmer told employees that Nadella, along with a strong leadership team, would drive Microsoft forward in the highly competitive tech sector.[67]

In his first interview as CEO, Nadella discussed elements of centralization and decentralization at Microsoft. First, he said the effectiveness of the leadership team was his top priority, suggesting a focus on centralization. However, he also discussed the need for everyone in the organization to be innovating, suggesting a focus on decentralization.

On centralization, Nadella wants the leadership team "to commit and engage in an authentic way, and for us to feel that energy as a team."[68] Since he has worked with everyone on the team before, he has confidence in their ability to perform. However, he wants to see them come together as a team and lead the organization. The job of the leadership team, according to Nadella, is to clarify what needs to be done, make sure the organization is aligned to be able to do it, and pursue the work with intensity.[69]

On decentralization, Nadella said that the boundaries within the organization are crumbling and the company structure is changing. He wants to create a self-organizing organization in which employees own the innovation agenda and share implementation. An organization chart or structure is not helpful in creating such a company structure, Nadella said, but a change in organizational culture could help achieve such a shift.[70]

In his first email message to Microsoft employees after being named CEO, Nadella stressed the need for innovation. He also called on all employees to pitch in and help lead change in the organizational culture.[71]

Nadella has wasted little time shaking up Microsoft, its organizational culture, and its business focus. He has already made tough calls as a result of the company's earlier decision to acquire Nokia's phone division in 2014—more than 18,000 jobs were eliminated, with another 8,000 job cuts in 2015 and 2016, as well as writing off more than $7 billion it paid to acquire the company. Microsoft recently announced its mission to "reinvent productivity and business processes, build the intelligent cloud platform, and create more personal computing."[72]

In 2016 Microsoft acquired professional social networking site LinkedIn for more than $26 billion. (See the end-of-chapter "Case in the News" for more details.) Nadella believes the deal will open new channels for the company's Office software suite as well as for LinkedIn. He believes that today's work is divided between tools that workers use to get their jobs done (such as Microsoft Office) and professional networks that connect workers (such as LinkedIn). Nadella said the acquisition would weave these two pieces together: "It's really the coming together of the professional cloud and the professional network."[73]

Integrating and Coordinating Mechanisms

Much coordination takes place through the hierarchy of authority. However, several problems are associated with establishing contact among managers in different functions or divisions. As discussed earlier, managers from different functions and divisions may have different views about what must be done to achieve the organization's goals. But if the managers have equal authority (as functional managers typically do), the only manager who can tell them what to do is the CEO, who has the ultimate authority to resolve conflicts. The need to solve everyday conflicts, however, wastes top management time and slows strategic decision making; indeed, one sign of a poorly performing structure is the number of problems sent up the hierarchy for top managers to solve.

integrating mechanisms
Organizing tools that managers can use to increase communication and coordination among functions and divisions.

To increase communication and coordination among functions or between divisions and to prevent these problems from emerging, top managers incorporate various integrating mechanisms into their organizational architecture. The greater the complexity of an organization's structure, the greater is the need for coordination among people, functions, and divisions to make the organizational structure work efficiently and effectively.[74] Thus when managers adopt a divisional, matrix, or product team structure, they must use complex integrating mechanisms to achieve the organization's goals. Several integrating mechanisms are available to managers to increase communication and coordination.[75] Figure 10.8 lists these mechanisms, as well as examples of the individuals or groups who might use them.

Figure 10.8

Types and Examples of Integrating Mechanisms

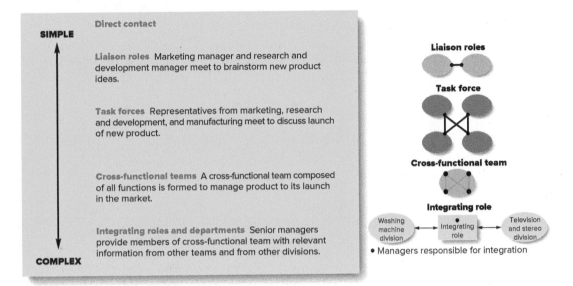

LIAISON ROLES   Managers can increase coordination among functions and divisions by establishing liaison roles. When the volume of contacts between two functions increases, one way to improve coordination is to give one manager in each function or division the responsibility for coordinating with the other. These managers may meet daily, weekly, monthly, or as needed. A liaison role is illustrated in Figure 10.8; the small dot represents the person within a function who has responsibility for coordinating with the other function. Coordinating is part of the liaison's full-time job, and usually an informal relationship develops between the people involved, greatly easing strains between functions. Furthermore, liaison roles provide a way of transmitting information across an organization, which is important in large organizations whose employees may know no one outside their immediate function or division.

TASK FORCES   When more than two functions or divisions share many common problems, direct contact and liaison roles may not provide sufficient coordination. In these cases, a more complex integrating mechanism, a task force, may be appropriate (see Figure 10.8). One manager from each relevant function or division is assigned to a task force that meets to solve a specific, mutual problem; members are responsible for reporting to their departments on the issues addressed and the solutions recommended. Task forces are often called *ad hoc committees* because they are temporary; they may meet on a regular basis or only a few times. When the problem or issue is solved, the task force is no longer needed; members return to their normal roles in their departments or are assigned to other task forces. Typically, task force members also perform many of their normal duties while serving on the task force.

task force A committee of managers from various functions or divisions who meet to solve a specific, mutual problem; also called *ad hoc committee.*

CROSS-FUNCTIONAL TEAMS   In many cases the issues addressed by a task force are recurring problems, such as the need to develop new products or find new kinds of customers. To address recurring problems effectively, managers are increasingly using permanent integrating mechanisms such as cross-functional teams. An example of a cross-functional team is a new product development committee that is responsible for the choice, design, manufacturing, and marketing of a new product. Such an activity obviously requires a great deal of integration among functions if new products are to be successfully introduced, and using a complex integrating mechanism such as a cross-functional team accomplishes this. As discussed earlier, in a product team structure people and resources are grouped into permanent cross-functional teams to speed products to market. These teams assume long-term responsibility for all aspects of development and making the product.

INTEGRATING ROLES An integrating role is a role whose only function is to increase coordination and integration among functions or divisions to achieve performance gains from synergies. Usually, managers who perform integrating roles are experienced senior managers who can envisage how to use the resources of the functions or divisions to obtain new synergies. At PepsiCo, Amy Chen, now senior market director, coordinated with several divisions to help create a program that would deliver meals during the summer months to children from low-income families. The resulting program, Food for Good, now makes healthy meals accessible year round to low-income families. To date, Food for Good has delivered nearly 8 million meals to low-income children.[76] The more complex an organization and the greater the number of its divisions, the more important integrating roles are.

In summary, to keep an organization responsive to changes in its task and general environments as it grows and becomes more complex, managers must increase coordination among functions and divisions by using complex integrating mechanisms. Managers must decide on the best way to organize their structures—that is, choose the structure that allows them to make the best use of organizational resources.

Organizational Culture

organizational culture
The shared set of beliefs, expectations, values, and norms that influence how members of an organization relate to one another and cooperate to achieve the organization's goals.

The second principal issue in organizational design is to create, develop, and maintain an organization's culture. As we discussed in Chapter 3, organizational culture is the shared set of beliefs, expectations, values, and norms that influence how members of an organization relate to one another and cooperate to achieve the organization's goals. Culture influences the work behaviors and attitudes of individuals and groups in an organization because its members adhere to shared values, norms, and expected standards of behavior. Employees *internalize* organizational values and norms and then let these values and norms guide their decisions and actions.[77]

A company's culture is a result of its pivotal or guiding values and norms. A company's *values* are the shared standards that its members use to evaluate whether they have helped the company achieve its vision and goals. The values a company might adopt include any or all of the following standards: excellence, stability, predictability, profitability, economy, creativity, morality, and usefulness. A company's *norms* specify or prescribe the kinds of shared beliefs, attitudes, and behaviors that its members should observe and follow. Norms are informal, but powerful, rules about how employees should behave or conduct themselves in a company if they are to be accepted and help it to achieve its goals. Norms can be equally as constraining as the formal written rules contained in a company's handbook. Companies might encourage workers to adopt norms such as working hard, respecting traditions and authority, and being courteous to others; being conservative, cautious, and a "team player"; being creative and courageous and taking risks; or being honest and frugal and maintaining high personal standards. Norms may also prescribe certain specific behaviors such as keeping one's desk tidy, cleaning up at the end of the day, taking one's turn to bring doughnuts, and even wearing jeans on Fridays.

Ideally, a company's norms help the company achieve its values. For example, a new computer company whose culture is based on values of excellence and innovation may try to attain this high standard by encouraging workers to adopt norms about being creative, taking risks, and working hard now and looking long-term for rewards (this combination of values and norms leads to an *entrepreneurial* culture in a company). On the other hand, a bank or an insurance company that has values of stability and predictability may emphasize norms of cautiousness and obedience to authority (the result of adopting these values and norms would be a *stable, conservative* culture in a company).

Over time, members of a company learn from one another how to perceive and interpret various events that happen in the work setting and to respond to them in ways that reflect the company's guiding values and norms. This is why organizational culture is so important: When a strong and cohesive set of organizational values and norms is in place, employees focus on what is best for the organization in the long run—all their decisions and actions become oriented toward helping the organization perform well. For example, a teacher spends personal time after school, coaching and counseling students; an R&D scientist works 80 hours a week, evenings, and weekends to help speed up a late project; or a salesclerk at a department store runs after a customer who left a credit card at the cash register. Sometimes in a large company, allowing separate divisions to create their own values and ways to communicate can help the overall organization thrive, as discussed in the accompanying "Manager as a Person" feature.

MANAGER AS A PERSON

Pixar Chief Encourages Communication

Ed Catmull, cofounder of Pixar Studios, followed a different strategy when Disney and Pixar merged. He insisted that each company maintain its own organizational culture in an effort to encourage communication and employee creativity.

© Alberto E. Rodriguez/WireImage/Getty Images

What do Snow White, Buzz Lightyear, and Iron Man have in common? The studios that produced these movies are all owned by the Walt Disney Company. Disney owns several companies, including Walt Disney Animation Studios, Pixar Animation Studios, and Marvel Studios.

Although these three studios are owned by the same company and all do roughly the same thing, they have different stories and different organizational cultures. Walt Disney Animation Studios is the oldest of the three, established by Walt and Roy Disney under the name Disney Brothers Cartoon Studio in 1923.[78] Its first feature film was *Snow White and the Seven Dwarfs* in 1937. In 2013 it released its 53rd animated film, *Frozen,* which became the No. 1 animated film of all time.[79]

Marvel was founded in 1939 as Timely Publications. In 1941 it introduced the comic book *Captain America* with a cover picture of the hero punching Adolf Hitler.[80] In 1991 Marvel Studios was established as a film production unit.[81] Marvel has more than 8,000 characters, including the Avengers, Green Goblin, Iron Man, Spider-Man, and the X-Men. Most of these characters live in the Marvel universe, in fictional cities similar to New York and Los Angeles. The Walt Disney Company bought Marvel in 2009.[82]

In 2002 investor and then-owner of Marvel Ronald Perelman said, "It is a mini-Disney in terms of intellectual property. Disney's got much more highly recognized characters and softer characters, whereas our characters are termed action heroes. But at Marvel we are now in the business of the creation and marketing of characters."[83]

Pixar Animation Studios was founded in 1979 as Graphics Group. It was originally the computer division of Lucasfilm, and it became its own corporation in 1986 with funding from Apple cofounder Steve Jobs.[84] Its first feature film was *Toy Story* in 1995, which was nominated for several awards by the Academy of Motion Pictures Arts and Sciences.[85] The Walt Disney Company bought Pixar in 2006.[86]

Despite *Toy Story*'s success, Pixar cofounder Ed Catmull found there were structural issues within the company. Pixar had insisted that communication happen through proper vertical channels. This led to hard feelings between the creative and production departments. While working on *A Bug's Life,* the film that came after *Toy Story,* Pixar created a rule that anyone could talk to anyone else, regardless of level within the organization. The resulting communication structure helped Pixar foster a more creative culture.[87]

In his recent book, *Creativity, Inc.: Overcoming the Unseen Forces That Stand in the Way of True Inspiration,* Catmull, now president of Pixar and Walt Disney Animation Studios, discusses the merger of Disney and Pixar. He said that when two organizations merge, there is typically a push to consolidate workflows and to reduce redundancies. However, when Disney and Pixar came together, they did something different.

"We took the exact opposite approach, which was to say to each studio, 'You may look at the tools that the other has, you may use them if you want, but the choice is entirely yours.' They each have a development group that's coming up with different ideas, but because we said, 'You don't have to take ideas from anybody else,' they felt freer to talk with each other."[88]

Yet some lessons from Pixar were applied at Disney, according to Catmull. When Pixar joined Disney in 2006, Disney employees were demoralized by a few lackluster film projects, including *Chicken Little* and *Home on the Range*.[89] Pixar practices, such as creating an environment where workers can be candid and where innovative ideas can move forward, were implemented at Disney. After the ideas took hold, the studio produced several big hits, including *Tangled* and *Frozen*.[90]

"The one thing we were really adamant about was that the two studios not be integrated together. We established an absolute rule, which we still adhere to, that neither studio can do any production work for the other. For me, the local ownership is really important. We put in place mechanisms to keep each studio's culture unique," Catmull said. "It's a model that Bob's using at Marvel. Marvel has a completely different culture than Pixar does, or Disney Animation, and he lets them run it their way. You want to have mechanisms to bridge between them, but you don't interfere with that local culture."[91]

LO10-5 List the four sources of organizational culture, and explain why and how a company's culture can lead to competitive advantage.

Where Does Organizational Culture Come From?

In managing organizational architecture, some important questions arise: Where does organizational culture come from? Why do different companies have different cultures? Why might a culture that for many years helped an organization achieve its goals suddenly harm the organization?

Organizational culture is shaped by the interaction of four main factors: the personal and professional characteristics of people within the organization, organizational ethics, the nature of the employment relationship, and the design of its organizational structure (see Figure 10.9). These factors work together to produce different cultures in different organizations and cause changes in culture over time.

Figure 10.9

Sources of an Organization's Culture

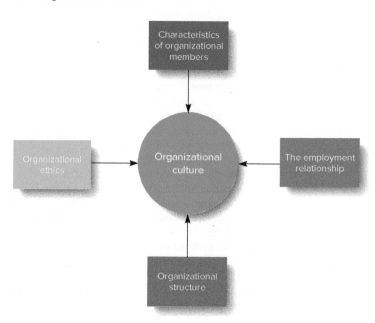

CHARACTERISTICS OF ORGANIZATIONAL MEMBERS   The ultimate source of organizational culture is the people who make up the organization. If you want to know why organizational cultures differ, look at how the characteristics of their members differ. Organizations A, B, and C develop distinctly different cultures because they attract, select, and retain people who have different values, personalities, and ethics.[92] Recall the attraction–selection–attrition model from Chapter 3. People may be attracted to an organization whose values match theirs; similarly, an organization selects people who share its values. Over time, people who do not fit in leave. The result is that people inside the organization become more similar, the values of the organization become more pronounced and clear-cut, and the culture becomes distinct from those of similar organizations.[93]

The fact that an organization's members become similar over time and come to share the same values may actually hinder their ability to adapt and respond to changes in the environment.[94] This happens when the organization's values and norms become so strong and promote so much cohesiveness in members' attitudes that the members begin to misperceive the environment.[95] Companies such as Ford, Google, Apple, and Microsoft need a strong set of values that emphasize innovation and hard work; they also need to be careful their success doesn't lead members to believe their company is the best in the business. Companies frequently make this mistake. One famous example is the CEO of Digital Equipment, who in the 1990s laughed off the potential threat posed by PCs to his powerful minicomputers, claiming, "Personal computers are just toys." This company no longer exists.

ORGANIZATIONAL ETHICS   The managers of an organization can set out purposefully to develop specific cultural values and norms to control how its members behave. One important class of values in this category stems from organizational ethics, which are the moral values, beliefs, and rules that establish the appropriate way for an organization and its members to deal with each other and with people outside the organization. Recall from Chapter 4 that ethical values rest on principles stressing the importance of treating organizational stakeholders fairly and equitably. Managers and employees are constantly making choices about the right, or ethical, thing to do; to help them make ethical decisions, top managers purposefully implant ethical values into an organization's culture.[96] Consequently, ethical values, and the rules and norms that embody them, become an integral part of an organization's culture and determine how its members will manage situations and make decisions.

organizational ethics The moral values, beliefs, and rules that establish the appropriate way for an organization and its members to deal with each other and with people outside the organization.

THE EMPLOYMENT RELATIONSHIP   A third factor shaping organizational culture is the nature of the employment relationship a company establishes with its employees via its human resource policies and practices. Recall from Chapter 1 our discussion of the changing relationship between organizations and their employees due to the growth of outsourcing and employment of contingent workers. Like a company's hiring, promotion, and layoff policies, human resource policies, along with pay and benefits, can influence how hard employees will work to achieve the organization's goals, how attached they will be to the organization, and whether they will buy into its values and norms.[97] As we discuss in Chapter 12, an organization's human resource policies are a good indicator of the values in its culture concerning its responsibilities to employees. Consider the effects of a company's promotion policy, for example: A company with a policy of promoting from within will fill higher-level positions with employees who already work for the organization. On the other hand, a company with a policy of promotion from without will fill its open positions with qualified outsiders. What does this say about each organization's culture?

Promoting from within will bolster strong values and norms that build loyalty, align employees' goals with the organization, and encourage employees to work hard to advance within the organization. If employees see no prospect of being promoted from within, they are likely to look for better opportunities elsewhere, cultural values and norms result in self-interested behavior, and cooperation and cohesiveness fall. The tech sector has gone through great turmoil in recent years, and over 2 million U.S. tech employees lost their jobs during the 2000s because of outsourcing and the recession. Apple, HP, and IBM—known for their strong employee-oriented values that emphasized long-term employment and respect for employees—were among the many companies forced to lay off employees, and their cultures have changed as a result. To rebuild their cultures and make their remaining employees feel like "owners," many companies have HRM pay policies that reward superior performance with bonuses and stock options.[98] For example, Southwest Airlines and Google established companywide stock option systems that encourage their employees to be innovative and responsive to customers. Other companies offer different perks, such as Airbnb's $2,000 annual stipend for each employee to travel and stay in an Airbnb listing anywhere in the world and PwC's $1,200 per year student loan debt reimbursement.[99]

ORGANIZATIONAL STRUCTURE   We have seen how the values and norms that shape employee work attitudes and behaviors derive from an organization's people, ethics, and HRM policies. A fourth source of cultural values comes from the organization's structure. *Different kinds of structure give rise to different kinds of culture;* thus, to create a certain culture, managers often need to design a particular type of structure. Tall and highly centralized structures give rise to totally different sets of norms, rules, and cultural values than do structures that are flat and decentralized. In a tall, centralized organization, people have little personal autonomy, and norms that focus on being cautious, obeying authority, and respecting traditions emerge because predictability and stability are desired goals. In a flat, decentralized structure, people have more freedom to choose and control their own activities, and norms that focus on being creative and courageous and taking risks appear, giving rise to a culture in which innovation and flexibility are desired goals.

Whether a company is centralized or decentralized also leads to the development of different kinds of cultural values. By decentralizing authority and empowering employees, an organization can establish values that encourage and reward creativity or innovation. In doing this, an organization signals employees that it's okay to be innovative and do things their own way—as long as their actions are consistent with the good of the organization. Conversely, in some organizations it is important that employees do not make decisions on their own and that their actions be open to the scrutiny of superiors. In cases like this, centralization can be used to create cultural values that reinforce obedience and accountability. For example, in nuclear power plants, values that promote stability, predictability, and obedience to authority are deliberately fostered to prevent disasters.[100] Through norms and rules, employees are taught the importance of behaving consistently and honestly, and they learn that sharing information with supervisors, especially information about mistakes or errors, is the only acceptable form of behavior.[101]

An organization that seeks to manage and change its culture must take a hard look at all four factors that shape culture: the characteristics of its members, its ethical values, its human resource policies, and its organizational structure. However, changing a culture can be difficult because of the way these factors interact and affect one another.[102] Often a major reorganization is necessary for a cultural change to occur, as we discuss in the next chapter.

Strong, Adaptive Cultures versus Weak, Inert Cultures

Many researchers and managers believe that employees of some organizations go out of their way to help the organization because it has a strong and cohesive organizational culture—an adaptive culture that controls employee attitudes and behaviors. *Adaptive cultures* are those whose values and norms help an organization to build momentum and to grow and change as needed to achieve its goals and be effective. By contrast, *inert cultures* are those whose values and norms fail to motivate or inspire employees; they lead to stagnation and, often, failure over time. What leads to a strong adaptive culture or one that is inert and hard to change?

Researchers have found that organizations with strong adaptive cultures, like 3M, UPS, Microsoft, and IBM, invest in their employees. They demonstrate their commitment to their members by, for example, emphasizing the long-term nature of the employment relationship and trying to avoid layoffs. These companies develop long-term career paths for their employees and spend a lot of money on training and development to increase employees' value to the organization. In these ways, terminal and instrumental values pertaining to the worth of human resources encourage the development of supportive work attitudes and behaviors.

In adaptive cultures employees often receive rewards linked directly to their performance and to the performance of the company as a whole. Sometimes employee stock ownership plans (ESOPs) are developed in which workers as a group are allowed to buy a significant percentage of their company's stock. Workers who are owners of the company have additional incentive to develop skills that allow them to perform highly and search actively for ways to improve quality, efficiency, and performance.

Some organizations, however, develop cultures with values that do not include protecting and increasing the worth of their human resources as a major goal. Their employment practices are based on short-term employment according to the needs of the organization and on minimal investment in employees who perform simple, routine tasks. Moreover, employees are not often rewarded on the basis of their performance and, thus, have little incentive to improve their skills or otherwise invest in the organization to help it achieve goals. If a company has an inert culture, poor working relationships frequently develop between the organization and its employees and instrumental values of noncooperation, laziness, and loafing and work norms of output restriction are common.

Moreover, an adaptive culture develops an emphasis on entrepreneurship and respect for the employee and allows the use of organizational structures, such as the cross-functional team structure, that empower employees to make decisions and motivate them to succeed. By contrast, in an inert culture, employees are content to be told what to do and have little incentive or motivation to perform beyond minimum work requirements. As you might expect, the emphasis is on close supervision and hierarchical authority, which result in a culture that makes it difficult to adapt to a changing environment.

Google is a good example of a company in which managers strive to create an adaptive culture that is based on values that emphasize creativity and innovation and where decision making is pushed right down to the bottom line to teams of employees who take up the challenge of developing the advanced software and hardware for which the company is known. Bureaucracy is kept to a minimum at Google; its adaptive culture is based on informal and personal relationships and norms of cooperation and teamwork. To help strengthen its culture, Google built a futuristic open-plan campus (called the Googleplex) in which its employees can work together to innovate advanced products and business solutions such as Google Maps, Google Drive, and Google AdWords.[103] Google's cultural values and norms can't be written down but are present in the work routines that cement people together and in the language and stories its members use to orient themselves to the company.

Another company with an adaptive culture is GlaxoSmithKline. Much of GSK's success can be attributed to its ability to recruit the best research scientists because its adaptive culture nurtures scientists and emphasizes values and norms of innovation. Scientists are given great freedom to pursue intriguing ideas even if the commercial payoff is questionable. Moreover, researchers are inspired to think of their work as a quest to alleviate human disease and suffering worldwide, and GSK has a reputation as an ethical company whose values put people above profits.

Although the experience of Google and GSK suggests that organizational culture can give rise to managerial actions that ultimately benefit the organization, this is not always the case. The cultures of some organizations become dysfunctional, encouraging managerial actions that harm the organization and discouraging actions that might improve performance.[104] For example, when Marissa Mayer left Google in 2012 to become Yahoo's new CEO, she jumped into a difficult situation. The company was already in decline, and several of her CEO predecessors had failed to make inroads into a dysfunctional culture or crystallize a solid business plan. Undaunted, Mayer tried to change the company's culture while acquiring several innovative start-up companies to help get Yahoo back on track—with mixed results. Now several activist investors have joined Yahoo's board and are demanding change, which may include Mayer's eventual ouster or resignation. Verizon recently announced plans to acquire Yahoo for nearly $5 billion, pending regulatory and shareholder approvals.[105]

Summary and Review

DESIGNING ORGANIZATIONAL STRUCTURE The four main determinants of organizational structure are the external environment, strategy, technology, and human resources. In general, the higher the

334   Chapter Ten

LO10-1   level of uncertainty associated with these factors, the more appropriate is a flexible, adaptable structure as opposed to a formal, rigid one.

LO10-2   **GROUPING TASKS INTO JOBS**   Job design is the process by which managers group tasks into jobs. To create more interesting jobs, and to get workers to act flexibly, managers can enlarge and enrich jobs. The job characteristics model is a tool that managers can use to measure how motivating or satisfying a particular job is.

LO10-3   **ORGANIZATIONAL STRUCTURE: GROUPING JOBS INTO FUNCTIONS AND DIVISIONS**   Managers can choose from many kinds of organizational structures to make the best use of organizational resources. Depending on the specific organizing problems they face, managers can choose from functional, product, geographic, market, matrix, product team, and hybrid structures.

LO10-4   **COORDINATING FUNCTIONS AND DIVISIONS**   No matter which structure managers choose, they must decide how to distribute authority in the organization, how many levels to have in the hierarchy of authority, and what balance to strike between centralization and decentralization to keep the number of levels in the hierarchy to a minimum. As organizations grow, managers must increase integration and coordination among functions and divisions. Four integrating mechanisms that facilitate this are liaison roles, task forces, cross-functional teams, and integrating roles.

LO10-5   **ORGANIZATIONAL CULTURE**   Organizational culture is the set of values, norms, and standards of behavior that control how individuals and groups in an organization interact with one another and work to achieve the organization's goals. The four main sources of organizational culture are member characteristics, organizational ethics, the nature of the employment relationship, and the design of organizational structure. How managers work to influence these four factors determines whether an organization's culture is strong and adaptive or inert and difficult to change.

Management in Action

Topics for Discussion and Action

Discussion

1. Would a flexible or a more formal structure be appropriate for these organizations? (a) a large department store, (b) a Big Four accounting firm, (c) a biotechnology company. Explain your reasoning. [LO10-1, 10-2]

2. Using the job characteristics model as a guide, discuss how a manager can enrich or enlarge subordinates' jobs. [LO10-2]

3. How might a salesperson's job or an administrative assistant's job be enlarged or enriched to make it more motivating? [LO10-2, 10-3]

4. When and under what conditions might managers change from a functional to (a) a product, (b) a geographic, or (c) a market structure? [LO10-1, 10-3]

5. How do matrix structure and product team structure differ? Why is product team structure more widely used? [LO10-1, 10-3, 10-4]

6. What is organizational culture, and how does it affect the way employees behave? [LO10-5]

Action

7. Find and interview a manager, and identify the kind of organizational structure that his or her organization uses to coordinate its people and resources. Why is the organization using that structure? Do you think a different structure would be more appropriate? Which one? [LO10-1, 10-3, 10-4]

8. With the same or another manager, discuss the distribution of authority in the organization. Does the manager think that decentralizing authority and empowering employees are appropriate? [LO10-1, 10-3]

9. Interview some employees of an organization, and ask them about the organization's values and norms, the typical characteristics of employees, and the organization's ethical values and socialization practices. Using this information, try to describe the organization's culture and the way it affects how people and groups behave. [LO10-1, 10-5]

Building Management Skills

Understanding Organizing [LO10-1, 10-2, 10-3]

Think of an organization with which you are familiar—perhaps one you have worked for, such as a store, a restaurant, an office, a church, or a school. Then answer the following questions:

1. Which contingencies are most important in explaining how the organization is organized? Do you think it is organized in the best way?

2. Using the job characteristics model, how motivating do you think the job of a typical employee is in this organization?

3. Can you think of any ways in which a typical job could be enlarged or enriched?

4. What kind of organizational structure does the organization use? If it is part of a chain, what kind of structure does the entire organization use? What other structures discussed in the chapter might allow the

organization to operate more effectively? For example, would the move to a product team structure lead to greater efficiency or effectiveness? Why or why not?

5. How many levels are in the organization's hierarchy? Is authority centralized or decentralized? Describe the span of control of the top manager and of middle or first-line managers.

6. Is the distribution of authority appropriate for the organization and its activities? Would it be possible to flatten the hierarchy by decentralizing authority and empowering employees?

7. What are the principal integrating mechanisms used in the organization? Do they provide sufficient coordination among individuals and functions? How might they be improved?

8. Now that you have analyzed the way this organization is structured, what advice would you give its managers to help them improve how it operates?

Managing Ethically [LO10-1, 10-3, 10-5]

Suppose an organization is downsizing and laying off many of its middle managers. Some top managers charged with deciding whom to terminate might decide to keep the subordinates they like and who are obedient to them, rather than the ones who are difficult or the best performers. They might also decide to lay off the most highly paid subordinates even if they are high performers. Think of the ethical issues involved in designing a hierarchy, and discuss the following issues.

Questions

1. What ethical rules (see Chapter 4) should managers use to decide which employees to terminate when redesigning their hierarchy?

2. Some people argue that employees who have worked for an organization for many years have a claim on the organization at least as strong as that of its shareholders. What do you think of the ethics of this position—can employees claim to "own" their jobs if they have contributed significantly to the organization's past success? How does a socially responsible organization behave in this situation?

Small Group Breakout Exercise

Bob's Appliances [LO10-1, 10-3]

Form groups of three or four people, and appoint one member as the spokesperson who will communicate your findings to the class when called on by the instructor. Then discuss the following scenario:

Bob's Appliances sells and services household appliances such as washing machines, dishwashers, ranges, and refrigerators. Over the years, the company has developed a good reputation for the quality of its customer service, and many local builders patronize the store. However, large retailers such as Best Buy, Walmart, and Costco are also providing an increasing range of appliances. Moreover, to attract more customers, these stores also carry a complete range of consumer electronics products—TVs, computers, and digital devices. Bob Lange, the owner of Bob's Appliances, has decided that if he is to stay in business, he must widen his product range and compete directly with the chains.

In 2016 he decided to build a 20,000-square-foot store and service center, and he is now hiring new employees to sell and service the new line of consumer electronics. Because of his company's increased size, Lange is not sure of the best way to organize the employees. Currently, he uses a functional structure; employees are divided into sales, purchasing and accounting, and repair. Bob is wondering whether selling and servicing consumer electronics is so different from selling and servicing appliances that he should move to a product structure (see the accompanying figure) and create separate sets of functions for each of his two lines of business.[106]

You are a team of local consultants whom Bob has called in to advise him as he makes this crucial choice. Which structure do you recommend? Why?

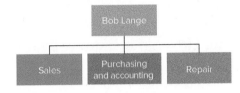

FUNCTIONAL STRUCTURE

Bob Lange

Sales | Purchasing and accounting | Repair

PRODUCT STRUCTURE

Bob Lange

Appliances | Consumer electronics

Sales | Purchasing and accounting | Repair | Sales | Purchasing and accounting | Repair

Exploring the World Wide Web [LO10-3]

Go to the website of Hitachi, a Japanese multinational engineering and electronics conglomerate (http://www.hitachi.com/about/corporate/organization/).

1. Look at the organizational chart. What type of structure does Hitachi have?

2. Click on the message from top management. What does this information tell you about how the structure might change or stay the same in the future?

3. Find the Hitachi Vision Book. How will the journey toward its vision affect the structure of Hitachi?

Be the Manager [LO10-1, 10-3, 10-5]

Speeding Up Website Design

You have been hired by a website design, production, and hosting company whose new animated website designs are attracting a lot of attention and many customers. Currently, employees are organized into different functions such as hardware, software design, graphic art, and website hosting, as well as functions such as marketing and human resources. Each function takes its turn to work on a new project from initial customer request to final online website hosting.

The problem the company is experiencing is that it typically takes one year from the initial idea stage to the time a website is up and running; the company wants to shorten this time by half to protect and expand its market niche. In talking to other managers, you discover that they believe the company's current functional structure is the source of the problem—it is not allowing employees to develop websites

fast enough to satisfy customers' demands. They want you to design a better structure.

Questions

1. Discuss how you can improve the way the current functional structure operates so it speeds website development.

2. Discuss the pros and cons of moving to a (a) multidivisional, (b) matrix, and (c) product team structure to reduce website development time.

3. Which of these structures do you think is most appropriate, and why?

4. What kind of culture would you help create to make the company's structure work more effectively?

Bloomberg Case in the News

Microsoft Pays $26 Billion for LinkedIn in Biggest Deal Yet [LO 10-1, 10-3, 10-4, 10-5]

Microsoft Corp. is acquiring the professional social network LinkedIn Corp. for $26.2 billion, one of the largest technology-industry deals on record, as the maker of Windows software attempts to put itself at the center of people's business lives.

The deal is a way for Microsoft, which largely missed out on the consumer Web boom dominated by the likes of Google and Facebook Inc., to sprint ahead in social tools—in this case, for professionals. While Chief Executive Officer Satya Nadella has drawn kudos for efforts to reshape the company and reignite sales growth, the board is urging an even faster shift toward software and services delivered over the Internet.

Microsoft will pay $196 per share in an all-cash transaction, including LinkedIn's net cash, a 49.5 percent premium to LinkedIn's closing price Friday. LinkedIn will retain its brand, culture and independence and Jeff Weiner will remain CEO of the social network, Microsoft said in a statement Monday. The price relative to LinkedIn's earnings makes the transaction the most expensive of any major deal this year, according to data compiled by Bloomberg.

"This is about the coming together of the leading professional cloud and the leading professional network," Nadella said in an interview. "This is the logical next step to take. We believe we can accelerate that by making LinkedIn the social fabric for all of Office."

The deal is the biggest ever for Microsoft as Nadella, 48, focuses on appealing to business customers with cloud-based services and productivity tools rather than regular customers. In a presentation announcing the deal, Redmond, Washington-based Microsoft outlined a vision in which a person's LinkedIn profile resides at the middle of other pieces of their work life, connecting with Windows, Outlook, Skype, Office productivity tools

like Excel and PowerPoint, and other Microsoft products.

Microsoft's Cortana digital assistant could provide users with information pulled from LinkedIn about participants in an upcoming meeting, for example, while a LinkedIn news feed will serve up articles based on projects that users are working on. Other products could include a kind of consulting service that will suggest an "expert" who might be able to help with a given project.

Microsoft could build LinkedIn, the largest global professional network, into a major customer relationship management software system for salespeople, pushing into an area dominated by Salesforce.com Inc., said Anurag Rana, a senior analyst for Bloomberg Intelligence. "LinkedIn could really become a really big competitor for Salesforce going forward," he said.

Building Relationships

LinkedIn's analytics will help power data tools for Microsoft's Dynamics, which competes with Salesforce in helping companies manage relationships with their customers.

While Nadella and Weiner had spoken many times about partnerships, they first met to discuss a potential acquisition deal in February. LinkedIn had just given a lower-than-expected revenue forecast that caused its stock to fall more than 40 percent in a day.

"In that very first meeting, we both got excited as we were brainstorming and riffing a bit about the things we could do in combination, combining the world's professional network and the world's professional cloud," Weiner said in an interview Monday.

Deal Dinners

What piqued Weiner's interest most was Nadella's idea for the structure of the organization—that LinkedIn could continue to operate independently like Facebook's WhatsApp or Google's

YouTube but still rely on Microsoft for a boost in potential customers. In April, several executives met for dinner, where they spent the evening discussing ways they could make their technologies work in concert. Attendees included the CEOs, as well as LinkedIn Chairman Reid Hoffman and Microsoft executive Qi Lu, who had worked with Weiner at Yahoo! Inc., according to people familiar with the matter.

A dinner Sunday night with both executive teams was more casual, with an icebreaker game to deepen their relationship. The attendees were asked to share something about themselves that was not on their LinkedIn profiles, the people said.

Shares Surge

LinkedIn shares surged 47 percent to $192.21 in New York, their biggest advance since 2011. They had declined 42 percent this year through Friday as investors began to question the company's long-term prospects. Microsoft fell 2.6 percent to $50.14. Twitter Inc. jumped as much as 9.1 percent amid speculation that it could be in play as well before paring some gains to close up 3.8 percent at $14.55.

The $26.2 billion offer values LinkedIn at about 91 times earnings before interest, taxes, depreciation and amortization, according to data compiled by Bloomberg. Excluding net cash, the multiple is about 84 times Ebitda [earnings before interest, taxes, depreciation, and amortization— indicator of a company's overall profitability]. That's the highest of any takeover valued at more than $5 billion this year, the data show. On a conference call, Microsoft said it's confident in the cash position it has and that the company will keep investing for growth.

However, the debt-financed LinkedIn deal gave Moody's Investors Service pause. The agency placed Microsoft's debt rating under review for downgrade, saying the purchase will increase Microsoft's gross debt to two times Ebitda, exceeding the 1.5 times leverage Moody's has said could pressure the rating. Microsoft and Johnson & Johnson are currently the only two U.S. companies with a AAA credit rating.

Viral Growth

Microsoft made several big acquisitions over recent years under previous CEO Steve Ballmer, though many of them have not panned out as hoped. Microsoft has largely written off its $9.5 billion purchase of Nokia Corp.'s mobile phone business, Skype hasn't matched the promise of integrating into other products after the $8.5 billion deal in 2011, and Yammer has been a mixed bag after the corporate social-network operator was bought in 2012. Nadella's 2014 purchase of Mojang AB, the maker of the Minecraft video game, has been a bright spot.

When assessing acquisitions, Nadella thinks about whether the target would expand market opportunity, ride the technology waves of the future and be at the core of Microsoft, he said in an interview with Bloomberg Television. Buying LinkedIn "checks all those boxes."

LinkedIn has long been valued for having the potential viral growth of a social network with the recurring revenues of a software-as-a-service business. But recently, growth has started to slow and it's been more difficult to get people to return to the site and pay for services. The company has been rethinking its strategy, redesigning its suite of mobile applications to make the product easier to use. Combining with Microsoft would give LinkedIn a boost in members with reasons to visit, making it more useful if people are sharing updates more frequently.

Questions for Discussion

1. Using the information in the article alone, how do you believe Microsoft is currently organized?

2. What impact do you think this acquisition will have on Microsoft's organizational culture? On LinkedIn's organizational culture?

3. Based on recent Microsoft acquisitions that have not appeared to be successful, do you think the LinkedIn deal makes sense from an organizational standpoint? Explain your reasoning.

Notes

1. G. Winfrey, "The Mistake That Turned Warby Parker into an Overnight Legend," *Inc.*, www.inc.com, May 2015.

2. D. Zax, "Fast Talk: How Warby Parker's Cofounders Disrupted the Eyewear Industry and Stayed Friends," *Inc.*, www.inc.com, accessed July 14, 2016.

3. Winfrey, "The Mistake That Turned Warby Parker into an Overnight Legend."

4. Ibid.

5. "We Have a Culture Crush on Warby Parker," *Big Spaceship*, http://www.bigspaceship.com, accessed July 14, 2016.

6. "Locations," www.warbyparker.com, accessed July 14, 2016; T. Novellino, "7 Warby Parker Secrets for a Talented, Happy Workforce," *New York Business Journal*, www.bizjournals.com, September 29, 2015.

7. Company Instagram account, "Words to Live and Work By: The Warby Parker Core Values," https://www.instagram.com, accessed July 14, 2016; M. West, "The Inside Story of How Zappos, IDEO, and Warby Parker Created Culture Manifestos—and How Your Company Can, Too," *Flox*, http://flox.works, October 27, 2015.

8. "Warby Parker: B Corporation," www.bcorporation.net, accessed July 14, 2016.

9. "Buy a Pair, Give a Pair," www.warbyparker.com, accessed July 14, 2016.

10. G. R. Jones, *Organizational Theory, Design, and Change: Text and Cases* (Upper Saddle River: Prentice-Hall, 2011).

11. J. Child, *Organization: A Guide for Managers and Administrators* (New York: Harper & Row, 1977).

12. P.R. Lawrence and J.W. Lorsch, *Organization and Environment* (Boston: Graduate School of Business Administration, Harvard University, 1967).

13. R. Duncan, "What Is the Right Organizational Design?" *Organizational Dynamics* (Winter 1979, 59–80).

14. T. Burns and G.R. Stalker, *The Management of Innovation* (London: Tavistock, 1966).

15. D. Miller, "Strategy Making and Structure: Analysis and Implications for Performance," *Academy of Management Journal* 30 (1987), 7–32.

16. A.D. Chandler, *Strategy and Structure* (Cambridge, MA: MIT Press, 1962).

17. J. Stopford and L. Wells, *Managing the Multinational Enterprise* (London: Longman, 1972).

18. C. Perrow, *Organizational Analysis: A Sociological View* (Belmont, CA: Wadsworth, 1970).

19. "First Lady Michelle Obama Announces Commitment by Subway® Restaurants to Promote Healthier Choices to Kids," The White House: Office of the First Lady, www.whitehouse.gov/the-press-office/2014/01/23/first-lady-michelle-obama-announces-commitment-subway-restaurants-promot, January 23, 2011.

20. F.W. Taylor, *The Principles of Scientific Management* (New York: Harper, 1911).

21. R.W. Griffin, *Task Design: An Integrative Approach* (Glenview, IL: Scott, Foresman, 1982).

22. V. Wong, "Let's Go to Wendy's and Cuddle by the Fireplace," *Bloomberg Businessweek*, www.businessweek.com/articles/2013-02-28/

340   Chapter Ten

lets-go-to-wendys-and-cuddle-by-the-fireplace, February 28, 2013.

23. Ibid.

24. Ibid.

25. P. Evans, "Meritage Is Ready for Another Helping," *Grand Rapids Business Journal,* www.grbj.com, November 27, 2015.

26. J. Daley, "Wendy's Franchise Owner Launches a Big Training Initiative," *Entrepreneur,* www.entrepreneur.com/article/227968#, September 27, 2013.

27. Ibid.

28. Ibid.

29. J.R. Hackman and G.R. Oldham, *Work Redesign* (Reading, MA: Addison-Wesley, 1980).

30. J.R. Galbraith and R.K. Kazanjian, *Strategy Implementation: Structure, System, and Process,* 2nd ed. (St. Paul, MN: West, 1986).

31. Lawrence and Lorsch, *Organization and Environment.*

32. Jones, *Organizational Theory.*

33. Lawrence and Lorsch, *Organization and Environment.*

34. R.H. Hall, *Organizations: Structure and Process* (Englewood Cliffs, NJ: Prentice-Hall, 1972); R. Miles, *Macro Organizational Behavior* (Santa Monica, CA: Goodyear, 1980).

35. Chandler, *Strategy and Structure.*

36. G.R. Jones and C.W.L. Hill, "Transaction Cost Analysis of Strategy-Structure Choice," *Strategic Management Journal* 9 (1988), 159–72.

37. "Our History," www.gsk.com, accessed July 14, 2016.

38. Ibid.

39. "GSK/Novartis Transaction," www.gsk.com, accessed July 14, 2016.

40. "Michael Baker International Selected for Pulaski Skyway Bridge Project," mbakercorp.com, March 13, 2014, www.mbakercorp.com/index.php?option=com_content&task=view&id=2577&Itemid=203.

41. E. Bader, "Michael Baker International Selected for Pulaski Skyway Bridge Project," NJBIZ, March 14, 2014, www.njbiz.com/article/20140314/NJBIZ01/140319874/Michael-Baker-International-selected-for-Pulaski-Skyway-Bridge-project.

42. "Michael Baker International Unveils New Organizational Structure for National and International Expansion," *Business Wire,* April 15, 2014, www.businesswire.com/news/home/20140415006475/en/Michael-Baker-International-Unveils-Organizational-Structure-National#.U1D5b1ehQV4.

43. "Mission Statement & Core Principles," www.mbakerint.com, accessed July 14, 2016.

44. "Michael Baker International Unveils New Organizational Structure for National and International Expansion," *Business Wire.*

45. C. Mortensen, "Jonathan Martin Went to Hospital," espn.go.com, espn.go.com/nfl/story/_/id/9936309/jonathan-martin-checked-hospital-leaving-miami-dolphins, November 8, 2013.

46. "Incognito, Others Tormented Martin," espn.go.com, espn .go.com/nfl/story/_/id/10455447/miami-dolphins-bullying-report-released-richie-incognito-others-responsible-harassment, February 15, 2014.

47. Ibid.

48. "Heads Roll Following Report on Miami Dolphins Bullying Scandal," *The Blaze,* www.theblaze.com/stories/2014/02/19/heads-roll-following-report-on-miami-dolphins-bullying-scandal/, February 19, 2014.

49. M. Maske, "Dolphins Make the Right Move in Hiring Adam Gase as Their Coach," *The Washington Post,* https://www.washingtonpost.com, January 9, 2016.

50. C. Orr, "Training Camp Preview: Will Dolphins Rise under Gase?" *Around the NFL,* www.nfl.com, July 8, 2016. K. Nogle, "Adam Gase Has Three Years to Fix the Dolphins," *SB Nation: The Phinsider,* www.thephinsider.com, February 15, 2016. M. Bianchi, "Dolphins Get It Wrong Again with Adam Gase," *Orlando Sentinel,* www.orlandosentinel.com, January 11, 2016.

51. S.M. Davis and P.R. Lawrence, *Matrix* (Reading, MA: Addison-Wesley, 1977); J.R. Galbraith, "Matrix Organization Designs: How to Combine Functional and Project Forms," *Business Hojizons* 14 (1971), 29–40.

52. L.R. Burns, "Matrix Management in Hospitals: Testing Theories of Matrix Structure and Development," *Administrative Science Quarterly* 34 (1989), 349–68.

53. C.W.L. Hill, *International Business* (Homewood, IL: Irwin, 2003).

54. Kotter International, "5 Innovation Secrets from Sealy," *Forbes,* www.forbes.com/sites/johnkotter/2012/10/10/5-innovation-secrets-from-sealy/, October 10, 2012.

55. Jones, *Organizational Theory.*

56. A. Farnham, "America's Most Admired Company," *Fortune,* February 7, 1994, 50–54.

57. "Leading Through Design and Innovation to Connect with Customers," http://design.newellbrands.com, accessed July 14, 2016.

58. P. Blau, "A Formal Theory of Differentiation in Organizations," *American Sociological Review* 35 (1970), 684–95.

59. "Leadership," www.aboutmcdonalds.com, accessed July 14, 2016.

60. Child, *Organization.*

61. C. S. Rugaber, "Robust Hiring Gain in June Points to a Resilient US Economy," *ABC News,* http://abcnews.go.com, July 8, 2016.

62. D. Novak, "What I've Learned after 20 Years on the Job," *CNBC,* www.cnbc.com, May 20, 2016. K. Kruse, "Leadership Secrets from Yum Brands CEO David Novak," *Forbes,* www.forbes.com, June 25, 2014.

63. "About Us," www.plexus.com, accessed July 14, 2016.

64. Ibid

65. P.M. Blau and R.A. Schoenherr, *The Structure of Organizations* (New York: Basic Books, 1971).

66. Jones, *Organizational Theory.*

67. S. Ballmer, "Steve Ballmer Email to Employees on New CEO," Microsoft News Center, www.microsoft.com/en-us/news/press/2014/feb14/02-04mail1.aspx, February 4, 2014.

68. "Satya Nadella, Chief of Microsoft, on His New Role," *The New York Times,* www.nytimes.com/2014/02/21/business/satya-nadella-chief-of-microsoft-on-his-new-role.html, February 20, 2014.

69. Ibid.

70. Ibid.

71. "Satya Nadella, Chief of Microsoft, on His New Role."

72. P. Sawers, "Microsoft Announces Up to 1,850 More Layoffs, Mostly a Result of Failed Nokia Acquisition," *Venture Beat,* http://venturebeat.com, May 25, 2016.

73. J. Greene, "Microsoft to Acquire LinkedIn for $26.2 Billion," *The Wall Street Journal,* www.wsj.com, June 14, 2016.

74. Lawrence and Lorsch, *Organization and Environment,* 50–55.

75. J.R. Galbraith, *Designing Complex Organizations* (Reading, MA: Addison-Wesley, 1977), chap. 1; Galbraith and Kazanjian, *Strategy Implementation,* chap. 7.

76. "What Is Food for Good?" https://www.pepsicofoodforgood.com, accessed July 14, 2016; "PepsiCo's Amy Chen: Doing Good for the Bottom Line—and the World," *Knowledge@Wharton,* http://knowledge.wharton.upenn.edu, March 9, 2015.

77. S.D.N. Cook and D. Yanow, "Culture and Organizational Learning." *Journal of Management Inquiry* 2 (1993), 373–90.

78. "Disney History," *D23,* https://d23.com, accessed July 14, 2016.

79. A. Stewart, "'Frozen' Reaches $1.219 Billion to Become Fifth-Highest Grossing Film Globally," *Variety,* http://variety.com, May 25, 2014.

80. "Captain America Comics," http://marvel.com, accessed July 14, 2016.

81. "About Marvel," http://marvel. disneycareers.com, accessed July 14, 2016.

82. Ibid.

83. "Excerpt from *Comic Wars*," www. randomhouse.com, accessed July 14, 2016.

84. "The Pixar Timeline: 1979 to Present," www.pixar.com, accessed July 14, 2016.

85. "Toy Story: Awards," *IMDb,* www.imdb .com, accessed July 14, 2016.

86. "The Pixar Timeline."

87. E. Catmull, "Building a Sense of Purpose at Pixar," *McKinsey Quarterly,* www. mckinsey.com, April 2014.

88. D. Price, "Managing Creativity: Lessons from Pixar and Disney Animation," *Harvard Business Review,* http://blogs .hbr.com, April 9, 2014.

89. "How Pixar Changed Disney Animation from Within," *CBC News,* www.cbc.ca, April 11, 2014.

90. E. Catmull, "Inside the Pixar Braintrust," *Fast Company,* www.fastcompany.com, March 13, 2014.

91. Price, "Managing Creativity."

92. B. Schneider, "The People Make the Place," *Personnel Psychology* 40 (1987), 437–53.

93. J.E. Sheriden, "Organizational Culture and Employee Retention," *Academy of Management Journal* 35 (1992), 657–92.

94. M. Hannan and J. Freeman, "Structural Inertia and Organizational Change," *American Sociological Review* 49 (1984), 149–64.

95. C.A. O'Reilly, J. Chatman, and D.F. Caldwell, "People and Organizational Culture: Assessing Person-Organizational Fit," *Academy of Management Journal* 34 (1991), 487–517.

96. T.L. Beauchamp and N.E. Bowie, eds., *Ethical Theory and Business* (Englewood Cliffs, NJ: Prentice-Hall, 1979); A. MacIntyre, *After Virtue* (Notre Dame, IN: University of Notre Dame Press, 1981).

97. A. Sagie and D. Elizur, "Work Values: A Theoretical Overview and a Model of Their Effects," *Journal of Organizational Behavior* 17 (1996), 503–14.

98. G.R. Jones, "Transaction Costs, Property Rights, and Organizational Culture: An Exchange Perspective," *Administrative Science Quarterly* 28 (1983), 454–67.

99. L. Dishman, "These Are the Best Employee Benefits and Perks," *Fast Company,* www.fastcompany.com, February 3, 2016.

100. C. Perrow, *Normal Accidents* (New York: Basic Books, 1984).

101. H. Mintzberg, *The Structuring of Organizational Structures* (Englewood Cliffs, NJ: Prentice-Hall, 1979).

102. G. Kunda, *Engineering Culture* (Philadelphia: Temple University Press, 1992).

103. "Google Careers Locations: Mountain View," https://www.google.com, accessed July 14, 2016.

104. K.E. Weick, *The Social Psychology of Organization* (Reading, MA: Addison-Wesley, 1979).

105. K. Kline, "Why Verizon Just Bought Yahoo Assets for Nearly $5 Billion," *Inc.,* www.inc.com, July 29, 2016; E. Kim, "What Other CEOs Can Learn from Marissa Mayer's Attempts to Turn Yahoo Around," *Inc.,* www.inc.com, April 28, 2016.

106. Copyright © 2006, Gareth R. Jones.

CHAPTER 12

Human Resource Management

Learning Objectives

After studying this chapter, you should be able to:

LO12-1 Explain why strategic human resource management can help an organization gain a competitive advantage.

LO12-2 Describe the steps managers take to recruit and select organizational members.

LO12-3 Discuss the training and development options that ensure organizational members can effectively perform their jobs.

LO12-4 Explain why performance appraisal and feedback are such crucial activities, and list the choices managers must make in designing effective performance appraisal and feedback procedures.

LO12-5 Explain the issues managers face in determining levels of pay and benefits.

LO12-6 Understand the role that labor relations play in the effective management of human resources.

© David Lees/Digital Vision/Getty Images RF

A MANAGER'S CHALLENGE

Treating Employees Well Pays Off for ACUITY

How can managers increase financial performance while reducing employee turnover? ACUITY is a property and casualty insurance company that does business in 24 states, has more than 1,200 employees, has over $1.3 billion in revenues that are produced by 1,000 independent agencies, and is head-quartered in Sheboygan, Wisconsin.[1] Founded in 1925 as the Mutual Automobile Insurance Company of the Town of Herman, the company changed its name to Heritage Insurance, and then to ACUITY in 2001. But a lot more has changed at ACUITY than its name. In the years prior to 2000, ACUITY's financial performance was somewhat lackluster and employee turnover was at 28 percent. When Ben Salzmann became president and chief executive officer of ACUITY in 1999, the organization was very formal and rigid. Employees were not allowed to personalize their work areas with photos and there was even a bell that rang to let employees know when to start work and when they could take a break for lunch or to use the restroom.[2]

Upon taking on the top post at ACUITY, Salzmann has dramatically transformed the company, increasing revenues and reducing turnover. In a 2016 press release, Salzmann indicated that "over the past 16 years, ACUITY has grown 250 percent faster than the insurance industry. In the past 48 months alone, our company added nearly $500 million to its top-line revenue."[3] Annual employee turnover at ACUITY is less than 2 percent and due to its growth, the company has been steadily creating new jobs.[4] How was Salzmann able to increase financial performance while reducing costly employee turnover? A key ingredient in Salzmann's successful transformation of ACUITY has been an emphasis on treating employees well and effectively managing human resources.

From the start, Salzmann sought to make ACUITY less formal and rigid, a place where employees would want to come to work. He first got rid of the bell, of course, but many more changes ensued. Key objectives of these changes are to provide employees with the training and development experiences that will enable them to reach their potential, making the workplace a happy and fun place to be, providing employees deserved recognition and positive feedback, and treating employees well in terms of pay and benefits. And, of course, making sure that managers at ACUITY recruit and select employees who will do well at the company is also emphasized.[5]

In terms of recruitment and selection, the human resources department attends job fairs and prospective employees can submit their cover letters and applications online. In assessing applications and conducting interviews with promising candidates, managers at ACUITY seek to determine if a candidate will be able to support ACUITY's core values and has the competencies needed for a given position.

10% CONTRIBUTION TO 401K!

Al Meyer
General Manager - Sales
With ACUITY for 11 years

ACUITY knows the importance of treating its employee well with benefits that include tuition reimbursement, onsite fitness facility, and a 10 percent contribution to employees' 401(k) plan.
Source: Acuity Insurance. "Acuity Insurance - Always a Great Place to Work." YouTube. February 2, 2016

ACUITY's core values include open communication, mutual trust and respect, honesty and integrity, teamwork, empowerment, providing opportunities for development, enjoying the workplace and having fun, maintaining excellence, and being innovative.[6]

ACUITY provides training and development opportunities for employees, including a leadership training program and professional development workshops, and it provides tuition reimbursement for employees who seek to further their education. Personal and professional lunch-and-learns foster an environment of open communication and provide important learning and networking opportunities. For example, several times a year employees have the opportunity to have lunch with a top manager in the company. These lunches usually have between 10 and 15 employees, who dine with a top manager from a different part of the company. If an employee has been with ACUITY for about two years, he or she will have had the chance to have lunch with all of the top managers who are part of the executive team. The lunches give everyone a chance to get to know each other and are forums for employees to make suggestions and air their opinions.[7]

In the "When Magic Happens" program, around 20 to 30 employees who have received positive feedback from an agent, a customer, or a coworker during the past month have their names and the comments listed outside the company cafeteria on a bulletin board. Each month, one of these recognized employees is chosen and the positive feedback that he or she received is sent to all ACUITY employees over voice mail and the employee is given a $100 gift card.[8]

ACUITY pays its employees fairly and has a generous set of benefits and perks. For example, the company has a variety of wellness programs that employees can take advantage of, including a 9,800-square-foot fitness facility, which is open to employees 24/7. It provides free scheduled classes, an outdoor walking path, and opportunities to participate in local athletic events and races. Employees who have been at the company under five years are able to partake of a variety of activities such as happy hours and kayaking excursions to enjoy themselves, meet other employees, and network.[9]

ACUITY contributes 8 percent to employees 401(k) plans regardless of the amount that employees contribute, and profit-sharing bonuses are distributed in terms of both bonus checks and a supplemental addition to the 401(k) accounts. For example, in recent years, the total annual contribution to the accounts has been around 10 percent. ACUITY pays 85 percent of the costs of health insurance for employees and their dependents. Other benefits and perks include subsidized lunches and free snacks, massage therapy, on-site banking and dry cleaning, free beverages, flex time, and paid holidays and vacations.[10]

The work environment at ACUITY embodies their core value of having fun with four Ping Pong tables and a popcorn machine outside the cafeteria. ACUITY also sponsors fun activities for employees and their families, including a summer family picnic, which includes rides, door prizes to the tune of $250, a casino for adults, and a game called Bossy Bingo, which yields a $5,000 payout for the winner.[11]

Given how well ACUITY treats its employees and its effective management of human resources, it is perhaps not surprising that ACUITY has been given awards for being a best place to work. For example, in 2016 ACUITY was ranked second in *Fortune* magazine's 100 Best Companies to Work For® list.[12] ACUITY has also been listed in rankings of best places to work for millennials and women.[13] Clearly, taking good care of employees and effectively managing human resources is a win–win situation for ACUITY.

Overview

Managers are responsible for acquiring, developing, protecting, and utilizing the resources an organization needs to be efficient and effective. One of the most important resources in all organizations is human resources—the people involved in producing and distributing goods and services. Human resources include all members of an organization, ranging from top managers to entry-level employees. Effective managers, like Ben Salzmann in "A Manager's Challenge," realize how valuable human resources are and take active steps to make sure their organizations build and fully utilize their human resources to gain a competitive advantage.

This chapter examines how managers can tailor their human resource management system to their organization's strategy and structure. We discuss in particular the major components of human resource management: recruitment and selection, training and development, performance appraisal, pay and benefits, and labor relations. By the end of this chapter you will understand the central role human resource management plays in creating a high-performing organization.

LO12-1 Explain why strategic human resource management can help an organization gain a competitive advantage.

Strategic Human Resource Management

human resource management (HRM) Activities that managers engage in to attract and retain employees and to ensure that they perform at a high level and contribute to the accomplishment of organizational goals.

strategic human resource management The process by which managers design the components of an HRM system to be consistent with each other, with other elements of organizational architecture, and with the organization's strategy and goals.

Organizational architecture (see Chapter 10) is the combination of organizational structure, control systems, culture, and a human resource management system that managers develop to use resources efficiently and effectively. **Human resource management (HRM)** includes all the activities managers engage in to attract and retain employees and to ensure that they perform at a high level and contribute to the accomplishment of organizational goals. These activities make up an organization's human resource management system, which has five major components: recruitment and selection, training and development, performance appraisal and feedback, pay and benefits, and labor relations (see Figure 12.1).

Strategic human resource management is the process by which managers design the components of an HRM system to be consistent with each other, with other elements of organizational architecture, and with the organization's strategy and goals.[14] The objective of strategic HRM is the development of an HRM system that enhances an organization's efficiency, quality, innovation, and responsiveness to customers—the four building blocks of competitive advantage.

Figure 12.1

Components of a Human Resource Management System

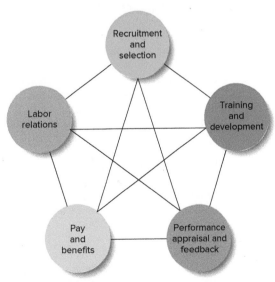

Each component of an HRM system influences the others, and all five must fit together.

As part of strategic human resource management, some managers have adopted Six Sigma quality improvement plans. These plans ensure that an organization's products and services are as free of errors or defects as possible through a variety of human resource–related initiatives. Jack Welch, former CEO of General Electric Company (GE), indicated that these initiatives saved GE millions of dollars; and other companies, such as Whirlpool and Motorola, also have implemented Six Sigma initiatives. For such initiatives to be effective, however, top managers have to be committed to Six Sigma, employees must be motivated, and there must be demand for the products or services of the organization in the first place. David Fitzpatrick, former head of Deloitte Consulting's Lean Enterprise Practice and currently a managing director at AlixPartners Professionals,[15] estimated that most Six Sigma plans are not effective because the conditions for effective Six Sigma are not in place. For example, if top managers are not committed to the quality initiative, they may not devote the necessary time and resources to make it work and may lose interest in it prematurely.[16]

Overview of the Components of HRM

Managers use *recruitment and selection,* the first component of an HRM system, to attract and hire new employees who have the abilities, skills, and experiences that will help an organization achieve its goals. Microsoft Corporation, for example, has the goal of remaining the premier computer software company in the world. To achieve this goal, managers at Microsoft realize the importance of hiring only the best software designers: Hundreds of highly qualified candidates are interviewed and rigorously tested. This careful attention to selection has contributed to Microsoft's competitive advantage. Microsoft has little trouble recruiting top programmers because candidates know they will be at the forefront of the industry if they work for Microsoft.[17]

After recruiting and selecting employees, managers use the second component, *training and development,* to ensure that organizational members develop the skills and abilities that will enable them to perform their jobs effectively in the present and the future. Training and development are an ongoing process, as is true at ACUITY in "A Manager's Challenge"; changes in technology and the environment, as well as in an organization's goals and strategies, often require that organizational members learn new techniques and ways of working. At Microsoft, newly hired program designers receive on-the-job training by joining small teams that include experienced employees who serve as mentors or advisers. New recruits learn firsthand from team members how to develop computer systems that are responsive to customers' programming needs.[18]

The third component, *performance appraisal and feedback,* serves two purposes in HRM. First, performance appraisal can give managers the information they need to make good human resources decisions—decisions about how to train, motivate, and reward organizational members.[19] Thus, the performance appraisal and feedback component is a kind of *control system* that can be used with management by objectives (discussed in Chapter 11). Second, feedback from performance appraisal serves a developmental purpose for members of an organization. When managers regularly evaluate their subordinates' performance, they can give employees valuable information about their strengths and weaknesses and the areas in which they need to concentrate.

On the basis of performance appraisals, managers distribute *pay* to employees, which is part of the fourth component of an HRM system. By rewarding high-performing organizational members with pay raises, bonuses, and the like, managers increase the likelihood that an organization's most valued human resources will be motivated to continue their high levels of contribution to the organization. Moreover, if pay is linked to performance, high-performing employees are more likely to stay with the organization, and managers are more likely to fill positions that become open with highly talented individuals. *Benefits* such as health insurance are important outcomes that employees receive by virtue of their membership in an organization.

Last but not least, *labor relations* encompass the steps that managers take to develop and maintain good working relationships with the labor unions that may represent their employees' interests. For example, an organization's labor relations component can help managers establish safe working conditions and fair labor practices in their offices and plants.

Managers must ensure that all five of these components fit together and complement their company's structure and control systems.[20] For example, if managers decide to decentralize authority and empower employees, they need to invest in training and development to ensure that lower-level employees have the knowledge and expertise they need to make the decisions that top managers would make in a more centralized structure.

Each of the five components of HRM influences the others (see Figure 12.1).[21] The kinds of people the organization attracts and hires through recruitment and selection, for example, determine (1) the kinds of training and development that are necessary, (2) the way performance is appraised, and (3) the appropriate levels of pay and benefits. Managers at Microsoft ensure that their organization has highly qualified program designers by (1) recruiting and selecting the best candidates, (2) guiding new hires with experienced team members, (3) appraising program designers' performance in terms of their individual contributions and their teams' performance, and (4) basing programmers' pay on individual and team performance.

Effectively managing human resources helps ensure that both customers and employees are satisfied and loyal, as illustrated in the accompanying "Managing Globally" feature.

MANAGING GLOBALLY

Managing Human Resources at Semco

Ricardo Semler was 21 years old (and one of the youngest graduates from the Harvard Business School MBA program) when he took his father's place as head of the family business, Semco, based in São Paolo, Brazil, in 1984.[22] His father, Antonio, had founded Semco in 1954 as a machine shop; the company went on to become a manufacturer of marine pumps for the shipbuilding industry, with $4 million a year in revenues when Ricardo Semler took over. Today Semco's revenues are over $200 million a year from a diverse set of businesses ranging from the development and manufacture of industrial mixing and refrigeration equipment to the provision of systems to manage communication, correspondence, and goods exchanges between an organization and its suppliers, customers, and partners.[23] Semco prides itself on being a premier provider of goods and services in its markets and has loyal customers.[24]

Semler is the first to admit that Semco's track record of success is due to its human resources—its employees. In fact, Semler so firmly believes in Semco's employees that he and the other top managers are reluctant to tell employees what to do. Semco has no rules, regulations, or organizational charts; hierarchy is eschewed; and workplace democracy rules the day. Employees have levels of autonomy unheard of in other companies, and flexibility and trust are built into every aspect of human resource management at Semco.[25]

Human resource practices at Semco revolve around maximizing the contributions employees make to the company, and this begins by hiring individuals who want to, can, and will contribute. Semco strives to ensure that all selection decisions are based on relevant and complete information. Job candidates are first interviewed as a group; the candidates meet many employees, receive a tour of the company, and interact with potential coworkers. This gives Semco a chance to size up candidates in ways more likely to reveal their true natures, and it gives the candidates a chance to learn about Semco. When finalists are identified from the pool, multiple Semco employees interview each finalist five or six more times to choose the best person(s) to be hired. The result is that both Semco and new hires make informed decisions and are mutually committed to making the relationship a success.[26]

Semco CEO Ricardo Semler is a firm believer in giving employees autonomy, flexibility, and the ability to change jobs often. This approach to human resource management helps ensure employees are loyal and turnover is low.
© James Leynse/Corbis via Getty Images

Once hired, entry-level employees participate in the Lost in Space program, in which they rotate through different positions and units of their own choosing for about a year.[27] In this way, the new hires learn about their options and can decide where their interests lie, and the units they work in learn about the new hires. At the end of the year, the new employees may be offered a job in one of the units in which they worked, or they may seek a position elsewhere in Semco. Seasoned Semco employees are also encouraged to rotate positions and work in different parts of the company to keep them fresh, energized, and motivated and to give them the opportunity to contribute in new ways as their interests change.[28]

Performance is appraised at Semco in terms of results; all employees and managers must demonstrate that they are making valuable contributions and deserve to be "rehired." For example, each manager's performance is anonymously appraised by all the employees who report to him or her, and the appraisals are made publicly available in Semco. Employees also can choose how they are paid from a combination of 11 different compensation options, ranging from fixed salaries, bonuses, and profit sharing to royalties on sales or profits and arrangements based on meeting annual self-set goals. Flexibility in compensation promotes risk taking and innovation, according to Semler, and maximizes returns to employees in terms of their pay and to the company in terms of revenues and profitability.[29] Flexibility, autonomy, the ability to change jobs often, and control of working hours and even compensation are some of the ways by which Semler strives to ensure that employees are loyal and involved in their work because they *want* to be; turnover at Semco is less than 1 percent annually.[30] And with human resource practices geared toward maximizing contributions and performance, Semco is well poised to continue to provide value to its customers.

The Legal Environment of HRM

In the rest of this chapter we focus in detail on the choices managers must make in strategically managing human resources to attain organizational goals and gain a competitive advantage. Effectively managing human resources is a complex undertaking for managers, and we provide an overview of some major issues they face. First, however, we need to look at how the legal environment affects human resource management.

The local, state, and national laws and regulations that managers and organizations must abide by add to the complexity of HRM. For example, the U.S. government's commitment to equal employment opportunity (EEO) has resulted in the creation and enforcement of a number of laws that managers must abide by. The goal of EEO is to ensure that all citizens have an equal opportunity to obtain employment regardless of their gender, race, country of origin, religion, age, or disabilities. Table 12.1 summarizes some of the major EEO laws affecting HRM. Other laws, such as the Occupational Safety and Health Act of 1970, require that managers ensure that employees are protected from workplace hazards and that safety standards are met.

equal employment opportunity (EEO) The equal right of all citizens to the opportunity to obtain employment regardless of their gender, age, race, country of origin, religion, or disabilities.

In Chapter 5 we explained how effectively managing diversity is an ethical and business imperative, and we discussed the many issues surrounding diversity. EEO laws and their enforcement make the effective management of diversity a legal imperative as well. The Equal Employment Opportunity Commission (EEOC) is the division of the Department of Justice that enforces most EEO laws and handles discrimination complaints. In addition, the EEOC issues guidelines for managers to follow to ensure that they are abiding by EEO laws. For example, the Uniform Guidelines on Employee Selection Procedures issued by the EEOC (in conjunction with the Departments of Labor and Justice and the Civil Service Commission) guide managers on how to ensure that the recruitment and selection component of human resource management complies with Title VII of the Civil Rights Act (which prohibits discrimination based on gender, race, color, religion, and national origin).[31]

Contemporary challenges that managers face related to the legal environment include how to eliminate sexual harassment (see Chapter 5 for an in-depth discussion of sexual harassment), how to accommodate employees with disabilities, how to deal with employees who have

Table 12.1

Major Equal Employment Opportunity Laws Affecting HRM

Year	Law	Description
1963	Equal Pay Act	Requires that men and women be paid equally if they are performing equal work.
1964	Title VII of the Civil Rights Act	Prohibits employment discrimination on the basis of race, religion, sex, color, or national origin; covers a wide range of employment decisions, including hiring, firing, pay, promotion, and working conditions.
1967	Age Discrimination in Employment Act	Prohibits discrimination against workers over the age of 40 and restricts mandatory retirement.
1978	Pregnancy Discrimination Act	Prohibits employment discrimination against women on the basis of pregnancy, childbirth, and related medical decisions.
1990	Americans with Disabilities Act	Prohibits employment discrimination against individuals with disabilities and requires that employers make accommodations for such workers to enable them to perform their jobs.
1991	Civil Rights Act	Prohibits discrimination (as does Title VII) and allows the awarding of punitive and compensatory damages, in addition to back pay, in cases of intentional discrimination.
1993	Family and Medical Leave Act	Requires that employers provide 12 weeks of unpaid leave for medical and family reasons, including paternity and illness of a family member.

substance abuse problems, and how to manage HIV-positive employees and employees with AIDS.[32] HIV-positive employees are infected with the virus that causes AIDS but may show no AIDS symptoms and may not develop AIDS in the near future. Often such employees are able to perform their jobs effectively, and managers must take steps to ensure that they are allowed to do so and are not discriminated against in the workplace.[33] Employees with AIDS may or may not be able to perform their jobs effectively, and, once again, managers need to ensure that they are not unfairly discriminated against.[34] Many organizations have instituted AIDS awareness training programs to educate organizational members about HIV and AIDS, dispel myths about how HIV is spread, and ensure that individuals infected with the HIV virus are treated fairly and are able to be productive as long as they can be while not putting others at risk.[35]

 LO12-2 Describe the steps managers take to recruit and select organizational members.

Recruitment and Selection

recruitment Activities that managers engage in to develop a pool of qualified candidates for open positions.

selection The process that managers use to determine the relative qualifications of job applicants and their potential for performing well in a particular job.

Recruitment includes all the activities managers engage in to develop a pool of qualified candidates for open positions.[36] **Selection** is the process by which managers determine the relative qualifications of job applicants and their potential for performing well in a particular job. Before actually recruiting and selecting employees, managers need to engage in two important activities: human resource planning and job analysis (see Figure 12.2).

Figure 12.2

The Recruitment and Selection System

Human Resource Planning

Human resource planning includes all the activities managers engage in to forecast their current and future human resource needs. Current human resources are the employees an organization needs today to provide high-quality goods and services to customers. Future human resource needs are the employees the organization will need at some later date to achieve its longer-term goals.

As part of human resource planning, managers must make both demand forecasts and supply forecasts. *Demand forecasts* estimate the qualifications and numbers of employees an organization will need, given its goals and strategies. *Supply forecasts* estimate the availability and qualifications of current employees now and in the future, as well as the supply of qualified workers in the external labor market.

As a result of their human resource planning, managers sometimes decide to **outsource** to fill some of their human resource needs. Instead of recruiting and selecting employees to produce goods and services, managers contract with people who are not members of their organization to produce goods and services. Managers in publishing companies, for example, frequently contract with freelance editors to copyedit books that they intend to publish. Kelly Services is an organization that provides the services of technical and professional employees to managers who want to use outsourcing to fill some of their human resource requirements in these areas.[37]

Two reasons human resource planning sometimes leads managers to outsource are flexibility and cost. First, outsourcing can give managers increased flexibility, especially when accurately forecasting human resource needs is difficult, human resource needs fluctuate over time, or finding skilled workers in a particular area is difficult. Second, outsourcing can sometimes allow managers to use human resources at a lower cost. When work is outsourced, costs can be lower for a number of reasons: The organization does not have to provide benefits to workers; managers can contract for work only when the work is needed; and managers do not have to invest in training. Outsourcing can be used for functional activities such as after-sales service on appliances and equipment, legal work, and the management of information systems.[38]

Outsourcing has disadvantages, however.[39] When work is outsourced, managers may lose some control over the quality of goods and services. Also, individuals performing outsourced work may have less knowledge of organizational practices, procedures, and goals and less commitment to an organization than regular employees. In addition, unions resist outsourcing because it has the potential to eliminate some of their members. To gain some of the flexibility and cost savings of outsourcing and avoid some of its disadvantages, a number of organizations, such as Microsoft and IBM, rely on a pool of temporary employees to, for example, debug programs.

A major trend reflecting the increasing globalization of business is the outsourcing of office work, computer programming, and technical jobs from the United States and countries in Western Europe, with high labor costs, to countries such as India and China, with low labor costs.[40] For example, computer programmers in India and China earn a fraction of what their U.S. counterparts earn. Outsourcing (or *offshoring,* as it is also called when work is outsourced to other countries) has also expanded into knowledge-intensive work such as engineering, research and development, and the development of computer software. According to a study conducted by The Conference Board and Duke University's Offshoring Research Network, more than half of U.S. companies surveyed have some kind of offshoring strategy related to knowledge-intensive work and innovation.[41] Why are so many companies engaged in offshoring, and why are companies that already offshore work planning to increase the extent of offshoring? While cost savings continue to be a major motivation for offshoring, managers also want to take advantage of an increasingly talented global workforce and be closer to the growing global marketplace for goods and services.[42]

Major U.S. companies often earn a substantial portion of their revenues overseas. For example, Hewlett-Packard, Caterpillar, and IBM earn over 60 percent of their revenues from overseas markets. And many large companies employ thousands of workers overseas. For example, IBM employs close to 100,000 workers in India; Hewlett-Packard, over 25,000.[43] Managers at some smaller companies have offshored work to Sri Lanka, Russia, and Egypt.[44]

Key challenges for managers who offshore are retaining sufficient managerial control over activities and employee turnover.[45] In recent times, there have been some interesting developments in outsourcing to other countries, as profiled in the accompanying "Managing Globally" feature.

MANAGING GLOBALLY

Recent Trends in Outsourcing

Countries in Latin America and Eastern Europe are becoming increasingly popular outsourcing destinations for skilled professional workers in the areas of finance, accounting, research, and procurement. For example, São Paulo, Brazil, has a sizable population of engineering and business school graduates who speak English and can perform a diverse set of tasks ranging from financial analysis to video game development.[46] A Brazilian trade group for technology, Brasscom,[47] indicates that there are more Java programmers in Brazil than in any other country and Brazil has the second highest number of COBOL programmers. Thus, perhaps it is not surprising that IBM's ninth research center is located in São Paulo.[48]

It typically costs more to outsource work to Latin American countries than to India. For example, outsourcing an entry-level accounting job to India costs around 51 percent less than hiring a worker in the United States; outsourcing the same job to Argentina costs about 13 percent less than hiring a U.S. worker.[49] However, if the Argentinian has a better understanding of business and is more skilled at interacting with clients, bearing the added costs might make sense. Additionally, if client interaction levels are high, it is advantageous for outsourcing countries and home countries to be in similar time zones. The time difference between New York and Argentina, for example, is much smaller than the time difference between New York and India.[50]

Copal Amba, an outsourcing/offshoring company that provides research and analytic services for global corporations and financial institutions, has offices in West Chester, Pennsylvania; Beijing, China; Gurgaon and Bangalore, India; Argentina; San Jose, Costa Rica; Prague, Czech Republic; and Colombo, Sri Lanka—in part because of the benefits of being in a closer time zone with clients.[51] As Rishi Khosla, the chairman and CEO of Copal Amba[52] put it, "If you're working with a hedge fund manager where you have to interact 10 to 15 times a day, having someone in about the same time zone is important."[53] Tata Consultancy Services, the Indian outsourcing giant, has over 8,000 employees in South American countries, including Peru and Paraguay.[54]

Countries in Eastern Europe are also seeing surges in outsourcing. For example, Microsoft, Ernst & Young, and IBM have all opened outsourcing facilities in Wroclaw, Poland. Ernst & Young actually has six outsourcing centers in cities in Poland that together have around 1,300 employees.[55] Young people in Poland are more likely to be college-educated than those in India, and they tend to be multilingual. Jacek Levernes—who managed outsourcing to Europe, Africa, and the Middle East for Hewlett-Packard's Wroclaw, Poland, facility—indicated that having 26 different languages spoken in the center was advantageous for interacting with clients in different countries in these regions. Guatemala is also an outsourcing destination for companies such

Indian office workers face a downswing in the amount of outsourced jobs from the United States. Argentina offers stiff competition with skilled workers whose hours are more closely aligned to the U.S. time zones but who can still be paid less than their U.S. counterparts.

© david pearson/Alamy

as Capgemini Consulting and Coca-Cola enterprises. Evidently, the trend toward "near-shoring" to countries closer to home has advantages.[56]

However, when it comes to the manufacturing of garments and clothing, new trends indicate that Africa is gaining attention as a potential location.[57] African countries can both be sources of cotton and then can process the cotton and manufacture garments. Costs are low in Africa and production times can be shorter because African countries can grow cotton. Thus, companies such as VF Corp. which own Lee, Timberland, and Wrangler, are looking to manufacture some of their garments in Ethiopia. PVH Corp., which owns Calvin Klein and Tommy Hilfiger, has been manufacturing some of its clothing in Kenya. Walmart, JC Penney, and Levi Strauss all outsource some of their work to sub-Sahara Africa.[58] Clearly, when it comes to outsourcing, there are multiple options.

Job Analysis

job analysis Identifying the tasks, duties, and responsibilities that make up a job and the knowledge, skills, and abilities needed to perform the job.

Job analysis is a second important activity that managers need to undertake prior to recruitment and selection.[59] **Job analysis** is the process of identifying (1) the tasks, duties, and responsibilities that make up a job (the *job description*) and (2) the knowledge, skills, and abilities needed to perform the job (the *job specifications*).[60] For each job in an organization, a job analysis needs to be done.

Job analysis can be done in a number of ways, including observing current employees as they perform the job or interviewing them. Often managers rely on questionnaires compiled by jobholders and their managers. The questionnaires ask about the skills and abilities needed to perform the job, job tasks and the amount of time spent on them, responsibilities, supervisory activities, equipment used, reports prepared, and decisions made.[61] The Position Analysis Questionnaire (PAQ) is a comprehensive, standardized questionnaire that many managers rely on to conduct job analyses.[62] It focuses on behaviors jobholders perform, working conditions, and job characteristics and can be used for a variety of jobs.[63] The PAQ contains 194 items organized into six divisions: (1) information input (where and how the jobholder acquires information to perform the job), (2) mental processes (reasoning, decision making, planning, and information processing activities that are part of the job), (3) work output (physical activities performed on the job and machines and devices used), (4) relationships with others (interactions with other people that are necessary to perform the job), (5) job context (the physical and social environment of the job), and (6) other job characteristics (such as work pace).[64] A trend, in some organizations, is toward more flexible jobs in which tasks and responsibilities change and cannot be clearly specified in advance. For these kinds of jobs, job analysis focuses more on determining the skills and knowledge workers need to be effective and less on specific duties.

After managers have completed human resource planning and job analyses for all jobs in an organization, they will know their human resource needs and the jobs they need to fill. They will also know what knowledge, skills, and abilities potential employees need to perform those jobs. At this point, recruitment and selection can begin.

External and Internal Recruitment

As noted earlier, recruitment is what managers do to develop a pool of qualified candidates for open positions.[65] They traditionally have used two main types of recruiting, external and internal, which are now supplemented by recruiting over the Internet.

EXTERNAL RECRUITING   When managers recruit externally to fill open positions, they look outside the organization for people who have not worked for the organization previously. There are multiple means through which managers can recruit externally: advertisements in newspapers and magazines, open houses for students and career counselors at high schools and colleges or on-site at the organization, career fairs at colleges, job fairs, and recruitment meetings with groups in the local community.

Many large organizations send teams of interviewers to college campuses to recruit new employees. External recruitment can also take place through informal networks, as occurs when current employees inform friends about open positions in their companies or recommend people they know to fill vacant spots. Some organizations use employment agencies for external recruitment, and some external recruitment takes place simply through walk-ins— job hunters going to an organization and inquiring about employment possibilities.

With all the downsizing and corporate layoffs that have taken place in recent years, you might think external recruiting would be a relatively easy task for managers. However, it often is not, because even though many people may be looking for jobs, many jobs that are open require skills and abilities that these job hunters do not have. Managers needing to fill vacant positions and job hunters seeking employment opportunities are increasingly relying on the Internet to connect with each other through employment websites such as Monster.com[66] and JobLine International.[67] Major corporations such as Coca-Cola, Cisco, Ernst & Young, Canon, and Telia have relied on JobLine to fill global positions.[68]

External recruiting has both advantages and disadvantages for managers. Advantages include having access to a potentially large applicant pool; being able to attract people who have the skills, knowledge, and abilities that an organization needs to achieve its goals; and being able to bring in newcomers who may have a fresh approach to problems and are up to date on the latest technology. These advantages have to be weighed against the disadvantages, including the relatively high costs of external recruitment. Employees recruited externally lack knowledge about the inner workings of the organization and may need to receive more training than those recruited internally. Finally, when employees are recruited externally, there is always uncertainty concerning whether they will actually be good performers. Nonetheless, managers can take steps to reduce some of the uncertainty surrounding external recruitment, as profiled in the accompanying "Information Technology Byte" feature.

INFORMATION TECHNOLOGY BYTE

Fog Creek Software's Approach to Recruiting

Fog Creek Software is a small, privately owned software company founded in 2000 by Joel Spolsky and Michael Pryor in a renovated loft in the Fashion District of New York City.[69] Fog Creek has earned a profit each year since its founding.[70] Hiring great computer software developers is essential for a company like Fog Creek; according to Spolsky, the top 1 percent of software developers outperform average developers by a ratio of around 10:1. And the top 1 percent are the inventive types who can successfully develop new products while being highly efficient.[71]

Fog Creek Software uses paid summer internships to help identify and attract promising software developers.
Courtesy of Fog Creek Software

Finding, never mind recruiting, the top 1 percent is a challenge for a small company like Fog Creek because many of these people already have great jobs and are not looking to switch employers. Realizing that the top 1 percent of developers might rarely apply for positions with Fog Creek (or any other company), Fog Creek uses paid summer internships to recruit over 50 percent of its developers while they are still in college; they are hired full-time after graduation.[72]

In the fall of every year, Fog Creek sends personalized letters to computer science majors across the country who have the potential to be top developers in the future, contacts professors at leading computer science programs for recommendations, and seeks applications through its website.[73] This process yields hundreds of applicants for internships, the best of whom are then given a phone interview. During the interview, the candidates describe themselves and their classes, are asked how they would go about solving a software development problem or challenge, and then can ask anything they want about the company or living in New York City.[74]

Those who do well in the phone interview are flown to New York for an all-expense-paid visit to Fog Creek—they are met at the airport in a limousine, stay in a hip hotel, receive welcoming gifts in their rooms, have a full day of interviews at Fog Creek, and then are given the option of staying two extra nights (at no cost to themselves) to get a feel for New York City. Typically, only one out of every three recruits who has an on-site visit receives an internship offer.[75]

Interns perform real software development work—several summers ago, a team of four interns developed a new, successful technology support product called Fog Creek Copilot.[76] This both motivates the interns and helps managers decide which interns they would like to hire. The interns are treated well—in addition to being paid, they receive free housing and are invited to outings, parties, and cultural events in New York City. At the conclusion of the internships, managers have a good sense of which interns are great programmers. These top programmers are offered jobs upon graduation with generous salaries, excellent working conditions, and great benefits. Although Fog Creek's approach to external recruitment is lengthy and expensive, it more than pays for itself by identifying and attracting top programmers. As Spolsky indicates, "An internship program creates a pipeline for great employees. It's a pretty long pipeline, so you need to have a long-term perspective, but it pays off in spades."[77]

INTERNAL RECRUITING When recruiting is internal, managers turn to existing employees to fill open positions. Employees recruited internally are either seeking **lateral moves** (job changes that entail no major changes in responsibility or authority levels) or promotions. Internal recruiting has several advantages. First, internal applicants are already familiar with the organization (including its goals, structure, culture, rules, and norms). Second, managers already know the candidates; they have considerable information about their skills, abilities, and actual behavior on the job. Third, internal recruiting can help boost levels of employee motivation and morale, both for the employee who gets the job and for other workers. Those who are not seeking a promotion or who may not be ready for one can see that promotion is a possibility in the future; or a lateral move can alleviate boredom once a job has been fully mastered and can be a useful way to learn new skills. Finally, internal recruiting is normally less time-consuming and expensive than external recruiting.

Given the advantages of internal recruiting, why do managers rely on external recruiting as much as they do? The answer lies in the disadvantages of internal recruiting—among them, a limited pool of candidates and a tendency among those candidates to be set in the organization's ways. Often the organization simply does not have suitable internal candidates. Sometimes even when suitable internal applicants are available, managers may rely on external recruiting to find the very best candidate or to help bring new ideas and approaches into their organization. When organizations are in trouble and performing poorly, external recruiting is often relied on to bring in managerial talent with a fresh approach.

HONESTY IN RECRUITING At times, when trying to recruit the most qualified applicants, managers may be tempted to paint rosy pictures of both the open positions and the organization as a whole. They may worry that if they are honest about advantages and disadvantages, they either will not be able to fill positions or will have fewer or less qualified applicants. A manager trying to fill a secretarial position, for example, may emphasize the high level of pay and benefits the job offers and fail to mention the fact that the position is usually a dead-end job offering few opportunities for promotion.

Research suggests that painting a rosy picture of a job and the organization is not a wise recruiting strategy. Recruitment is more likely to be effective when managers give potential applicants an honest assessment of both the advantages and the disadvantages of the job and organization. Such an assessment is called a **realistic job preview (RJP)**.[78] RJPs can

lateral move A job change that entails no major changes in responsibility or authority levels.

realistic job preview (RJP) An honest assessment of the advantages and disadvantages of a job and an organization.

reduce the number of new hires who quit when their jobs and organizations fail to meet their unrealistic expectations, and they help applicants decide for themselves whether a job is right for them.

Take the earlier example of the manager trying to recruit a secretary. The manager who paints a rosy picture of the job might have an easy time filling it but might hire a secretary who expects to be promoted quickly to an administrative assistant position. After a few weeks on the job, the secretary may realize that a promotion is unlikely no matter how good his or her performance, become dissatisfied, and look for and accept another job. The manager then has to recruit, select, and train another new secretary. The manager could have avoided this waste of valuable organizational resources by using a realistic job preview. The RJP would have increased the likelihood of hiring a secretary who was comfortable with few promotional opportunities and subsequently would have been satisfied to remain on the job.

The Selection Process

Once managers develop a pool of applicants for open positions through the recruitment process, they need to find out whether each applicant is qualified for the position and likely to be a good performer. If more than one applicant meets these two conditions, managers must further determine which applicants are likely to be better performers than others. They have several selection tools to help them sort out the relative qualifications of job applicants and appraise their potential for being good performers in a particular job. These tools include background information, interviews, paper-and-pencil tests, physical ability tests, performance tests, and references (see Figure 12.3).[79]

BACKGROUND INFORMATION   To aid in the selection process, managers obtain background information from job applications and from résumés. Such information might include the highest levels of education obtained, college majors and minors, type of college or university attended, years and type of work experience, and mastery of foreign languages. Background information can be helpful both to screen out applicants who are lacking key qualifications (such as a college degree) and to determine which qualified applicants are more promising than others. For example, applicants with a BS may be acceptable, but those who also have an MBA may be preferable.

Figure 12.3
Selection Tools

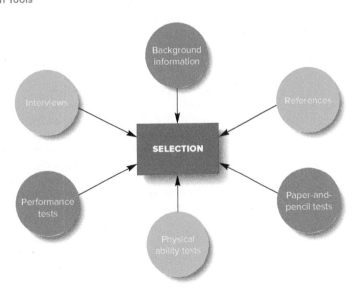

Increasing numbers of organizations are performing background checks to verify the background information prospective employees provide (and to uncover any negative information such as crime convictions).[80] According to Automatic Data Processing, Inc. (ADP), an outsourcing company that performs payroll and human resource functions for organizations, more and more companies are performing background checks on prospective employees and are uncovering inaccuracies, inconsistencies, and negative information not reported on applications.[81] According to ADP, about 30 percent of applicants provide some form of false information about their employment history.[82] And in some cases, background checks reveal prior convictions.[83]

INTERVIEWS   Virtually all organizations use interviews during the selection process, as is true at ACUITY in "A Manager's Challenge." Interviews may be structured or unstructured. In a *structured interview,* managers ask each applicant the same standard questions (such as "What are your unique qualifications for this position?" and "What characteristics of a job are most important to you?"). Particularly informative questions may be those that prompt an interviewee to demonstrate skills and abilities needed for the job by answering the question. Sometimes called *situational interview questions,* these often present interviewees with a scenario they would likely encounter on the job and ask them to indicate how they would handle it.[84] For example, applicants for a sales job may be asked to indicate how they would respond to a customer who complained about waiting too long for service, a customer who was indecisive, and a customer whose order was lost.

An *unstructured interview* proceeds more like an ordinary conversation. The interviewer feels free to ask probing questions to discover what the applicant is like and does not ask a fixed set of questions determined in advance. In general, structured interviews are superior to unstructured interviews because they are more likely to yield information that will help identify qualified candidates, are less subjective, and may be less influenced by the interviewer's biases.

Even when structured interviews are used, however, the potential exists for the interviewer's biases to influence his or her judgment. Recall from Chapter 5 how the similar-to-me effect can cause people to perceive others who are similar to themselves more positively than those who are different and how stereotypes can result in inaccurate perceptions. Interviewers must be trained to avoid these biases and sources of inaccurate perceptions as much as possible. Many of the approaches to increasing diversity awareness and diversity skills described in Chapter 5 are used to train interviewers to avoid the effects of biases and stereotypes. In addition, using multiple interviewers can be advantageous because their individual biases and idiosyncrasies may cancel one another out.[85]

When conducting interviews, managers cannot ask questions that are irrelevant to the job in question; otherwise, their organizations run the risk of costly lawsuits. It is inappropriate and illegal, for example, to inquire about an interviewee's spouse or to ask questions about whether an interviewee plans to have children. Because questions such as these are irrelevant to job performance, they are discriminatory and violate EEO laws (see Table 12.1). Thus, interviewers need to be instructed in EEO laws and informed about questions that may violate those laws.

Managers can use interviews at various stages in the selection process. Some use interviews as initial screening devices; others use them as a final hurdle that applicants must jump. Regardless of when they are used, managers typically use other selection tools in conjunction with interviews because of the potential for bias and for inaccurate assessments of interviewees. Even though training and structured interviews can eliminate the effects of some biases, interviewers can still come to erroneous conclusions about interviewees' qualifications. Interviewees, for example, who make a bad initial impression or are overly nervous in the first minute or two of an interview tend to be judged more harshly than less nervous candidates, even if the rest of the interview goes well.

PAPER-AND-PENCIL TESTS   The two main kinds of paper-and-pencil tests used for selection purposes are ability tests and personality tests; both kinds of tests can be administered in hard copy or electronic form. *Ability tests* assess the extent to which applicants possess the skills necessary for job performance, such as verbal comprehension or numerical skills. Autoworkers hired by General Motors, Chrysler, and Ford, for example, are typically tested for their ability to read and to do mathematics.[86]

Personality tests measure personality traits and characteristics relevant to job performance. Some retail organizations, for example, give job applicants honesty tests to determine how trustworthy they are. The use of personality tests (including honesty tests) for hiring purposes is controversial. Some critics maintain that honesty tests do not really measure honesty (that is, they are not valid) and can be faked by job applicants. Before using any paper-and-pencil tests for selection purposes, managers must have sound evidence that the tests are actually good predictors of performance on the job in question. Managers who use tests without such evidence may be subject to costly discrimination lawsuits.

PHYSICAL ABILITY TESTS   For jobs requiring physical abilities, such as firefighting, garbage collecting, and package delivery, managers use physical ability tests that measure physical strength and stamina as selection tools. Autoworkers are typically tested for mechanical dexterity because this physical ability is an important skill for high job performance in many auto plants.[87]

PERFORMANCE TESTS   *Performance tests* measure job applicants' performance on actual job tasks. Applicants for secretarial positions, for example, typically are required to complete a keyboarding test that measures how quickly and accurately they type. Applicants for middle and top management positions are sometimes given short-term projects to complete—projects that mirror the kinds of situations that arise in the job being filled—to assess their knowledge and problem-solving capabilities.[88]

Assessment centers, first used by AT&T, take performance tests one step further. In a typical assessment center, about 10 to 15 candidates for managerial positions participate in a variety of activities over a few days. During this time they are assessed for the skills an effective manager needs—problem-solving, organizational, communication, and conflict resolution skills. Some of the activities are performed individually; others are performed in groups. Throughout the process, current managers observe the candidates' behavior and measure performance. Summary evaluations are then used as a selection tool.

REFERENCES   Applicants for many jobs are required to provide references from former employers or other knowledgeable sources (such as a college instructor or adviser) who know the applicants' skills, abilities, and other personal characteristics. These individuals are asked to provide candid information about the applicant. References are often used at the end of the selection process to confirm a decision to hire. Yet the fact that many former employers are reluctant to provide negative information in references sometimes makes it difficult to interpret what a reference is really saying about an applicant.

In fact, several recent lawsuits filed by applicants who felt that they were unfairly denigrated or had their privacy invaded by unfavorable references from former employers have caused managers to be increasingly wary of providing any negative information in a reference, even if it is accurate. For jobs in which the jobholder is responsible for the safety and lives of other people, however, failing to provide accurate negative information in a reference does not just mean that the wrong person might get hired; it may also mean that other people's lives will be at stake.

THE IMPORTANCE OF RELIABILITY AND VALIDITY   Whatever selection tools a manager uses need to be both reliable and valid. **Reliability** is the degree to which a tool or test measures the same thing each time it is administered. Scores on a selection test should be similar if the same person is assessed with the same tool on two different days; if there is quite a bit of variability, the tool is unreliable. For interviews, determining reliability is more complex because the dynamic is personal interpretation. That is why the reliability of interviews can be increased if two or more qualified interviewers interview the same candidate. If the interviews are reliable, the interviewers should come to similar conclusions about the interviewee's qualifications.

Validity is the degree to which a tool measures what it purports to measure—for selection tools, it is the degree to which the test predicts performance on the tasks or job in question. Does a physical ability test used to select firefighters, for example, actually predict on-the-job

reliability The degree to which a tool or test measures the same thing each time it is used.

validity The degree to which a tool or test measures what it purports to measure.

performance? Do assessment center ratings actually predict managerial performance? Do keyboarding tests predict secretarial performance? These are all questions of validity. Honesty tests, for example, are controversial because it is not clear that they validly predict honesty in such jobs as retailing and banking.

Managers have an ethical and legal obligation to use reliable and valid selection tools. Yet reliability and validity are matters of degree rather than all-or-nothing characteristics. Thus, managers should strive to use selection tools in such a way that they can achieve the greatest degree of reliability and validity. For ability tests of a particular skill, managers should keep up to date on the latest advances in the development of valid paper-and-pencil tests and use the test with the highest reliability and validity ratings for their purposes. Regarding interviews, managers can improve reliability by having more than one person interview job candidates.

LO12-3 Discuss the training and development options that ensure organizational members can effectively perform their jobs.

Training and Development

Training and development help to ensure that organizational members have the knowledge and skills needed to perform jobs effectively, take on new responsibilities, and adapt to changing conditions, as is the case at ACUITY in "A Manager's Challenge." **Training** focuses primarily on teaching organizational members how to perform their current jobs and helping them acquire the knowledge and skills they need to be effective performers. **Development** focuses on building the knowledge and skills of organizational members so they are prepared to take on new responsibilities and challenges. Training tends to be used more frequently at lower levels of an organization; development tends to be used more frequently with professionals and managers.

Before creating training and development programs, managers should perform a **needs assessment** to determine which employees need training or development and what type of skills or knowledge they need to acquire (see Figure 12.4).[89]

training Teaching organizational members how to perform their current jobs and helping them acquire the knowledge and skills they need to be effective performers.

development Building the knowledge and skills of organizational members so they are prepared to take on new responsibilities and challenges.

needs assessment An assessment of which employees need training or development and what type of skills or knowledge they need to acquire.

Types of Training

There are two types of training: classroom instruction and on-the-job training.

CLASSROOM INSTRUCTION Through classroom instruction, employees acquire knowledge and skills in a classroom setting. This instruction may take place within the organization or outside it, such as through courses at local colleges and universities. Many organizations establish their own formal instructional divisions—some are even called "colleges"—to

Figure 12.4
Training and Development

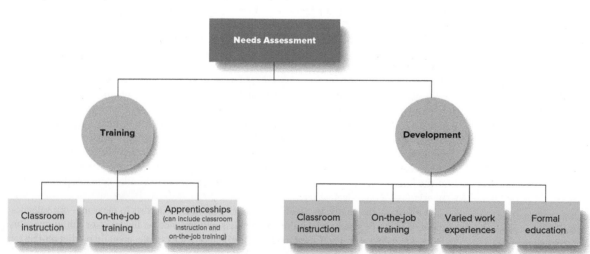

provide needed classroom instruction. For example, at Disney, classroom instruction and other forms of training and development are provided to employees at Disney University.[90]

Classroom instruction frequently uses videos and role-playing in addition to traditional written materials, lectures, and group discussions. *Videos* can demonstrate appropriate and inappropriate job behaviors. For example, by watching an experienced salesperson effectively deal with a loud and angry customer, inexperienced salespeople can develop skills in handling similar situations. During *role-playing,* trainees either directly participate in or watch others perform actual job activities in a simulated setting. At McDonald's Hamburger University, for example, role-playing helps franchisees acquire the knowledge and skills they need to manage their restaurants.

Simulations also can be part of classroom instruction, particularly for complicated jobs that require an extensive amount of learning and in which errors carry a high cost. In a simulation, key aspects of the work situation and job tasks are duplicated as closely as possible in an artificial setting. For example, air traffic controllers are trained by simulations because of the complicated nature of the work, the extensive amount of learning involved, and the very high costs of air traffic control errors.

on-the-job training Training that takes place in the work setting as employees perform their job tasks.

ON-THE-JOB TRAINING   In on-the-job training, learning occurs in the work setting as employees perform their job tasks. On-the-job training can be provided by coworkers or supervisors or can occur simply as jobholders gain experience and knowledge from doing the work. Newly hired waiters and waitresses in chains such as Red Lobster or the Olive Garden often receive on-the-job training from experienced employees. The supervisor of a new bus driver for a campus bus system may ride the bus for a week to ensure that the driver has learned the routes and follows safety procedures. Chefs learn to create new and innovative dishes by experimenting with different combinations of ingredients and cooking techniques. For all on-the-job training, employees learn by doing.

Managers often use on-the-job training on a continuing basis to ensure that their subordinates keep up to date with changes in goals, technology, products, or customer needs and desires. For example, sales representatives at Mary Kay Cosmetics Inc. receive ongoing training so they not only know about new cosmetic products and currently popular colors but also are reminded of Mary Kay's guiding principles. Mary Kay's expansion into Russia has succeeded in part because of the ongoing training that Mary Kay's Russian salespeople receive.[91]

Types of Development

Although both classroom instruction and on-the-job training can be used for development as well as training, development often includes additional activities such as varied work experiences and formal education.

At many restaurants, new employees receive on-the-job training by shadowing more experienced waiters and waitresses as they go about their work.
© Reza Estakhrian/Photographer's Choice/Getty Images

VARIED WORK EXPERIENCES   Top managers need to develop an understanding of, and expertise in, a variety of functions, products and services, and markets. To develop executives who will have this expertise, managers frequently make sure that employees with high potential have a wide variety of job experiences, some in line positions and some in staff positions. Varied work experiences broaden employees' horizons and help them think about the big picture. For example, one- to three-year stints overseas are being used increasingly to provide managers with international work experiences. With organizations becoming more global, managers need to understand the different values, beliefs, cultures, regions, and ways of doing business in different countries.

Another development approach is mentoring. (Recall from Chapter 5 that a *mentor* is an experienced member of an organization who provides advice and guidance to a less experienced member, called a *protégé.*) Having a mentor can help managers seek out work experiences and assignments that will contribute to their development and can enable them to gain the most possible from varied work experiences.[92] Although some mentors and protégés create relationships informally, organizations have found that formal mentoring programs can be valuable ways to contribute to the development of managers and all employees. For example, Goldman Sachs, Deloitte, and Time Inc. all have formal (and mandatory) mentoring programs.[93]

Formal mentoring programs ensure that mentoring takes place in an organization and structure the process. Participants receive training, efforts are focused on matching mentors and protégés so meaningful developmental relationships ensue, and organizations can track reactions and assess the potential benefits of mentoring. Formal mentoring programs can also ensure that diverse members of an organization receive the benefits of mentoring. A study conducted by David A. Thomas, a professor at the Harvard Business School, found that members of racial minority groups at three large corporations who were very successful in their careers had the benefit of mentors. Formal mentoring programs help organizations make this valuable development tool available to all employees.[94]

When diverse members of an organization lack mentors, their progress in the organization and advancement to high-level positions can be hampered. Ida Abott, a lawyer and consultant on work-related issues, presented a paper to the Minority Corporate Counsel Association in which she concluded, "The lack of adequate mentoring has held women and minority lawyers back from achieving professional success and has led to high rates of career dissatisfaction and attrition."[95]

Mentoring can benefit all kinds of employees in all kinds of work.[96] John Washko, a manager at the Four Seasons hotel chain, benefited from the mentoring he received from Stan Bromley on interpersonal relations and how to deal with employees; mentor Bromley, in turn, found that participating in the Four Seasons mentoring program helped him develop his own management style.[97] More generally, development is an ongoing process for all managers, and mentors often find that mentoring contributes to their own personal development.

FORMAL EDUCATION Many large corporations reimburse employees for tuition expenses they incur while taking college courses and obtaining advanced degrees. This is not just benevolence on the part of the employer or even a simple reward given to the employee; it is an effective way to develop employees who can take on new responsibilities and more challenging positions. For similar reasons, corporations spend thousands of dollars sending managers to executive development programs such as executive MBA programs. In these programs, experts teach managers the latest in business and management techniques and practices.

To save time and travel costs, some managers rely on *long-distance learning* to formally educate and develop employees. Using videoconferencing technologies, business schools such as the Harvard Business School, the University of Michigan, and Babson College teach courses on video screens in corporate conference rooms. Business schools also customize courses and degrees to fit the development needs of employees in a particular company and/or a particular geographic region.[98] Moreover, some employees and managers seek to advance their education through online degree programs.[99]

Transfer of Training and Development

Whenever training and development take place off the job or in a classroom setting, it is vital for managers to promote the transfer of the knowledge and skills acquired *to the actual work situation.* Trainees should be encouraged and expected to use their newfound expertise on the job.

LO12-4 Explain why performance appraisal and feedback are such crucial activities, and list the choices managers must make in designing effective performance appraisal and feedback procedures.

performance appraisal The evaluation of employees' job performance and contributions to their organization.

Performance Appraisal and Feedback

The recruitment/selection and training/development components of a human resource management system ensure that employees have the knowledge and skills needed to be effective now and in the future. Performance appraisal and feedback complement recruitment, selection, training, and development. Performance appraisal is the evaluation of employees' job performance and contributions to the organization.

performance feedback The process through which managers share performance appraisal information with subordinates, give subordinates an opportunity to reflect on their own performance, and develop, with subordinates, plans for the future.

Performance feedback is the process through which managers share performance appraisal information with their subordinates, give subordinates an opportunity to reflect on their own performance, and develop, with subordinates, plans for the future. Before performance feedback, performance appraisal must take place. Performance appraisal could take place without providing performance feedback, but wise managers are careful to provide feedback because it can contribute to employee motivation and performance.

Performance appraisal and feedback contribute to the effective management of human resources in several ways. Performance appraisal gives managers important information on which to base human resource decisions.[100] Decisions about pay raises, bonuses, promotions, and job moves all hinge on the accurate appraisal of performance. Performance appraisal can also help managers determine which workers are candidates for training and development and in what areas. Performance feedback encourages high levels of employee motivation and performance. It lets good performers know that their efforts are valued and appreciated. It also lets poor performers know that their lackluster performance needs improvement. Performance feedback can give both good and poor performers insight into their strengths and weaknesses and the ways in which they can improve their performance in the future.

Types of Performance Appraisal

Performance appraisal focuses on the evaluation of traits, behaviors, and results.[101]

TRAIT APPRAISALS When trait appraisals are used, managers assess subordinates on personal characteristics that are relevant to job performance, such as skills, abilities, or personality. A factory worker, for example, may be evaluated based on her ability to use computerized equipment and perform numerical calculations. A social worker may be appraised based on his empathy and communication skills.

Three disadvantages of trait appraisals often lead managers to rely on other appraisal methods. First, possessing a certain personal characteristic does not ensure that the personal characteristic will actually be used on the job and result in high performance. For example, a factory worker may possess superior computer and numerical skills but be a poor performer due to low motivation. The second disadvantage of trait appraisals is linked to the first. Because traits do not always show a direct association with performance, workers and courts of law may view them as unfair and potentially discriminatory. The third disadvantage of trait appraisals is that they often do not enable managers to give employees feedback they can use to improve performance. Because trait appraisals focus on relatively enduring human characteristics that change only over the long term, employees can do little to change their behavior in response to performance feedback from a trait appraisal. Telling a social worker that he lacks empathy says little about how he can improve his interactions with clients, for example. These disadvantages suggest that managers should use trait appraisals only when they can demonstrate that the assessed traits are accurate and important indicators of job performance.

BEHAVIOR APPRAISALS Through behavior appraisals, managers assess how workers perform their jobs—the actual actions and behaviors that workers exhibit on the job. Whereas trait appraisals assess what workers *are like,* behavior appraisals assess what workers *do.* For example, with a behavior appraisal, a manager might evaluate a social worker on the extent to which he looks clients in the eye when talking with them, expresses sympathy when they are upset, and refers them to community counseling and support groups geared toward the specific problems they are encountering. Behavior appraisals are especially useful when *how* workers perform their jobs is important. In educational organizations such as high schools, for example, the numbers of classes and students taught are important, but also important is how they are taught or the methods teachers use to ensure that learning takes place.

Behavior appraisals have the advantage of giving employees clear information about what they are doing right and wrong and how they can improve their performance. And because behaviors are much easier for employees to change than traits, performance feedback from behavior appraisals is more likely to lead to improved performance.

RESULTS APPRAISALS   For some jobs, *how* people perform the job is not as important as *what* they accomplish or the results they obtain. With results appraisals, managers appraise performance by the results or the actual outcomes of work behaviors. Take the case of two new car salespeople. One salesperson strives to develop personal relationships with her customers. She spends hours talking to them and frequently calls them to see how their decision-making process is going. The other salesperson has a much more hands-off approach. He is very knowledgeable, answers customers' questions, and then waits for them to come to him. Both salespersons sell, on average, the same number of cars, and the customers of both are satisfied with the service they receive, according to postcards the dealership mails to customers, asking for an assessment of their satisfaction. The manager of the dealership appropriately uses results appraisals (sales and customer satisfaction) to evaluate the salespeople's performance because it does not matter which behavior salespeople use to sell cars as long as they sell the desired number and satisfy customers. If one salesperson sells too few cars, however, the manager can give that person performance feedback about his or her low sales.

OBJECTIVE AND SUBJECTIVE APPRAISALS   Whether managers appraise performance in terms of traits, behaviors, or results, the information they assess is either *objective* or *subjective*. Objective appraisals are based on facts and are likely to be numerical—the number of cars sold, the number of meals prepared, the number of times late, the number of audits completed. Managers often use objective appraisals when results are being appraised because results tend to be easier to quantify than traits or behaviors. When *how* workers perform their jobs is important, however, subjective behavior appraisals are more appropriate than results appraisals.

Subjective appraisals are based on managers' perceptions of traits, behaviors, or results. Because subjective appraisals rest on managers' perceptions, there is always the chance that they are inaccurate (see Chapter 5). This is why both researchers and managers have spent considerable time and effort on determining the best way to develop reliable and valid subjective measures of performance.

Some of the more popular subjective measures such as the graphic rating scale, the behaviorally anchored rating scale (BARS), and the behavior observation scale (BOS) are illustrated in Figure 12.5.[102] When graphic rating scales are used, performance is assessed along a continuum with specified intervals. With a BARS, performance is assessed along a scale with clearly defined scale points containing examples of specific behaviors. A BOS assesses performance by how often specific behaviors are performed. Many managers may use both objective and subjective appraisals. For example, a salesperson may be appraised both on the dollar value of sales (objective) and the quality of customer service (subjective).

In addition to subjective appraisals, some organizations employ *forced rankings,* whereby supervisors must rank their subordinates and assign them to different categories according to their performance (which is subjectively appraised). For example, at LendingTree, managers and employees are ranked by their superiors as a "1" (top 15 percent based on individual performance and goals), "2" (middle 75 percent), or "3" (bottom 10 percent).[103] Although the forced ranking system was originally adopted at LendingTree to reward high performers and make it less likely that they would seek positions elsewhere, in tough times when housing and mortgage sales are down, the "3's" are the ones mostly likely to be laid off if layoffs take place.[104] Some managers are proponents of forced rankings, but others strongly oppose the practice. Proponents believe that forced rankings help ensure that human resource decisions are made based on merit, top performers are recognized, and all employees know where they stand relative to others. Opponents of forced ranking believe that forced rankings can be demoralizing, lead to a competitive environment unsupportive of cooperation and teamwork, and result in favoritism. And forced ranking schemes that force managers to group percentages of employees in certain predetermined categories might not make sense if the predetermined categories do not match the distribution of performance across the employees. For example, a forced ranking system might require a manager to "force" 20 percent of his or her subordinates into the bottom ranking designation when, in fact, most of the subordinates' performance is average or above average and only 5 to 10 percent of employees are poor performers. When forced rankings are applied on a regional basis, they can cause conflict and

objective appraisal An appraisal that is based on facts and is likely to be numerical.

subjective appraisal An appraisal that is based on perceptions of traits, behaviors, or results.

Figure 12.5

Subjective Measures of Performance

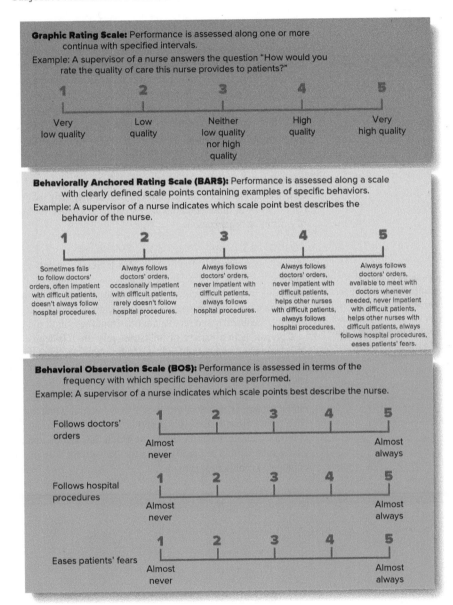

Graphic Rating Scale: Performance is assessed along one or more continua with specified intervals.

Example: A supervisor of a nurse answers the question "How would you rate the quality of care this nurse provides to patients?"

1	2	3	4	5
Very low quality	Low quality	Neither low quality nor high quality	High quality	Very high quality

Behaviorally Anchored Rating Scale (BARS): Performance is assessed along a scale with clearly defined scale points containing examples of specific behaviors.

Example: A supervisor of a nurse indicates which scale point best describes the behavior of the nurse.

1	2	3	4	5
Sometimes fails to follow doctors' orders, often impatient with difficult patients, doesn't always follow hospital procedures.	Always follows doctors' orders, occasionally impatient with difficult patients, rarely doesn't follow hospital procedures.	Always follows doctors' orders, never impatient with difficult patients, always follows hospital procedures.	Always follows doctors' orders, never impatient with difficult patients, helps other nurses with difficult patients, always follows hospital procedures.	Always follows doctors' orders, available to meet with doctors whenever needed, never impatient with difficult patients, helps other nurses with difficult patients, always follows hospital procedures, eases patients' fears.

Behavioral Observation Scale (BOS): Performance is assessed in terms of the frequency with which specific behaviors are performed.

Example: A supervisor of a nurse indicates which scale points best describe the nurse.

Follows doctors' orders

1	2	3	4	5
Almost never				Almost always

Follows hospital procedures

1	2	3	4	5
Almost never				Almost always

Eases patients' fears

1	2	3	4	5
Almost never				Almost always

political maneuvering among managers, each of whom wants to ensure that his or her subordinates are ranked in the better categories. Interestingly enough, while forced rankings were popularized, in part, by their use at General Electric under the leadership of Jack Welch, GE no longer uses a forced ranking system.

Who Appraises Performance?

We have been assuming that managers or the supervisors of employees evaluate performance. This is a reasonable assumption: Supervisors are the most common appraisers of performance.[105] Performance appraisal is an important part of most managers' job duties. Managers are responsible for not only motivating their subordinates to perform at a high level but also making many decisions hinging on performance appraisals, such as pay raises or promotions. Appraisals by managers can be usefully augmented by appraisals from other sources (see Figure 12.6).

SELF, PEERS, SUBORDINATES, AND CLIENTS When self-appraisals are used, managers supplement their evaluations with an employee's assessment of his or her own performance. Peer appraisals are provided by an employee's coworkers. Especially when subordinates work in groups or teams, feedback from peer appraisals can motivate team members while giving managers important information for decision making. A growing number of companies are having subordinates appraise their managers' performance and leadership as well. And sometimes customers or clients assess employee performance in terms of responsiveness to customers and quality of service. Although appraisals from these sources can be useful, managers need to be aware of issues that may arise when they are used. Subordinates may be inclined to inflate self-appraisals, especially if organizations are downsizing and they are worried about job security. Managers who are appraised by their subordinates may fail to take needed but unpopular actions out of fear that their subordinates will appraise them negatively. Some of these potential issues can be mitigated to the extent that there are high levels of trust in an organization.

360-DEGREE PERFORMANCE APPRAISALS To improve motivation and performance, some organizations include 360-degree appraisals and feedback in their performance appraisal systems, especially for managers. In a **360-degree appraisal** a variety of people, beginning with the manager and including peers or coworkers, subordinates, superiors, and sometimes even customers or clients, appraise a manager's performance. The manager receives feedback based on evaluations from these multiple sources.

Companies in a variety of industries rely on 360-degree appraisals and feedback.[106] For 360-degree appraisals and feedback to be effective, there has to be trust throughout an organization. More generally, trust is a critical ingredient in any performance appraisal and feedback procedure. In addition, research suggests that 360-degree appraisals should focus on behaviors rather than traits or results and that managers need to carefully select appropriate raters. Moreover, appraisals tend to be more honest when made anonymously and when raters have been trained in how to use 360-degree appraisal forms.[107] Additionally, managers need to think carefully about the extent to which 360-degree appraisals are appropriate for certain jobs and be willing to modify any appraisal system they implement if they become aware of unintended problems it creates.[108]

360-degree appraisal A performance appraisal by peers, subordinates, superiors, and sometimes clients who are in a position to evaluate a manager's performance.

Figure 12.6

Who Appraises Performance?

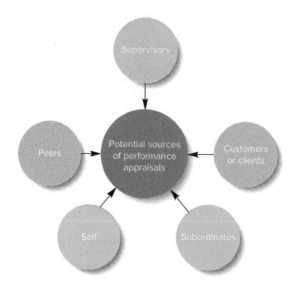

Even when 360-degree appraisals are used, it is sometimes difficult to design an effective process by which subordinates' feedback can be communicated to their managers; however, advances in information technology can solve this problem. For example, ImproveNow.com has online questionnaires that subordinates fill out to evaluate the performance of their managers and give the managers feedback. Each subordinate of a particular manager completes the questionnaire independently, all responses are tabulated, and the manager is given specific feedback on behaviors in a variety of areas, such as rewarding good performance, looking out for subordinates' best interests and being supportive, and having a vision for the future.[109]

Effective Performance Feedback

formal appraisal An appraisal conducted at a set time during the year and based on performance dimensions and measures that were specified in advance.

For the appraisal and feedback component of a human resource management system to encourage and motivate high performance, managers must give their subordinates feedback. To generate useful information to feed back to their subordinates, managers can use both formal and informal appraisals. Formal appraisals are conducted at set times during the year and are based on performance dimensions and measures that have been specified in advance. A salesperson, for example, may be evaluated by his or her manager twice a year on the performance dimensions of sales and customer service, sales being objectively measured from sales reports, and customer service being measured with a BARS (see Figure 12.5).

Managers in most large organizations use formal performance appraisals on a fixed schedule dictated by company policy, such as every six months or every year. An integral part of a formal appraisal is a meeting between the manager and the subordinate in which the subordinate is given feedback on performance. Performance feedback lets subordinates know which areas they are excelling in and which areas need improvement; it should also tell them *how* they can improve their performance. Realizing the value of formal appraisals, managers in many large corporations have committed substantial resources to updating their performance appraisal procedures and training low-level managers in how to use them and provide accurate feedback to employees.[110]

Formal performance appraisals supply both managers and subordinates with valuable information; however, subordinates often want more frequent feedback, and managers often want to motivate subordinates as the need arises. For these reasons many companies supplement formal performance appraisal with frequent informal appraisals, for which managers and their subordinates meet as the need arises to discuss ongoing progress and areas for improvement. Moreover, when job duties, assignments, or goals change, informal appraisals can give workers timely feedback concerning how they are handling their new responsibilities.

informal appraisal An unscheduled appraisal of ongoing progress and areas for improvement.

Managers often dislike providing performance feedback, especially when the feedback is negative, but doing so is an important managerial activity.[111] Here are some guidelines for giving effective performance feedback that contributes to employee motivation and performance:

- *Be specific and focus on behaviors or outcomes that are correctable and within a worker's ability to improve.* Example: Telling a salesperson that he is too shy when interacting with customers is likely to lower his self-confidence and prompt him to become defensive. A more effective approach would be to give the salesperson feedback about specific behaviors to engage in—greeting customers as soon as they enter the department, asking customers whether they need help, and volunteering to help customers find items.

- *Approach performance appraisal as an exercise in problem solving and solution finding, not criticizing.* Example: Rather than criticizing a financial analyst for turning in reports late, the manager helps the analyst determine why the reports are late and identify ways to better manage her time.

- *Express confidence in a subordinate's ability to improve.* Example: Instead of being skeptical, a first-level manager tells a subordinate that he is confident that the subordinate can increase quality levels.

- *Provide performance feedback both formally and informally.* Example: The staff of a preschool receives feedback from formal performance appraisals twice a year. The school director also provides frequent informal feedback such as complimenting staff members on creative ideas for special projects, noticing when they do a particularly good job handling a difficult child, and pointing out when they provide inadequate supervision.

- *Praise instances of high performance and areas of a job in which a worker excels.* Example: Rather than focusing on just the negative, a manager discusses the areas her subordinate excels in as well as the areas in need of improvement.

- *Avoid personal criticisms and treat subordinates with respect.* Example: An engineering manager acknowledges her subordinates' expertise and treats them as professionals. Even when the manager points out performance problems to subordinates, she refrains from criticizing them personally.

- *Agree to a timetable for performance improvements.* Example: A first-level manager and his subordinate decide to meet again in one month to determine whether quality levels have improved.

In following these guidelines, managers need to remember *why* they are giving performance feedback: to encourage high levels of motivation and performance. Moreover, the information that managers gather through performance appraisal and feedback helps them determine how to distribute pay raises and bonuses.

Pay and Benefits

Pay includes employees' base salaries, pay raises, and bonuses and is determined by a number of factors such as the characteristics of the organization and the job and levels of performance. Employee *benefits* are based on membership in an organization (not necessarily on the particular job held) and include sick days, vacation days, and medical and life insurance. In Chapter 13 we discuss how pay can motivate organizational members to perform at a high level, as well as the different kinds of pay plans managers can use to help an organization achieve its goals and gain a competitive advantage. As you will learn, it is important to link pay to behaviors or results that contribute to organizational effectiveness. Next we focus on establishing an organization's pay level and pay structure.

 LO12-5 Explain the issues managers face in determining levels of pay and benefits.

Pay Level

pay level The relative position of an organization's pay incentives in comparison with those of other organizations in the same industry employing similar kinds of workers.

Pay level is a broad, comparative concept that refers to how an organization's pay incentives compare, in general, to those of other organizations in the same industry employing similar kinds of workers. Managers must decide if they want to offer relatively high wages, average wages, or relatively low wages. High wages help ensure that an organization is going to be able to recruit, select, and retain high performers, but high wages also raise costs. Low wages give an organization a cost advantage but may undermine the organization's ability to select and recruit high performers and to motivate current employees to perform at a high level. Either of these situations may lead to inferior quality or inadequate customer service.

In determining pay levels, managers should take into account their organization's strategy. A high pay level may prohibit managers from effectively pursuing a low-cost strategy. But a high pay level may be worth the added costs in an organization whose competitive advantage lies in superior quality and excellent customer service. As one might expect, hotel and motel chains with a low-cost strategy, such as Days Inn and Hampton Inns, have lower pay levels than chains striving to provide high-quality rooms and services, such as the Four Seasons. In fact, the Four Seasons treats and pays its employees very well, as profiled in the accompanying "Management Insight" feature.

MANAGEMENT INSIGHT

Treating Employees Well Leads to Satisfied Customers

Four Seasons Hotels and Resorts is one of only around a dozen companies to be ranked one of the "100 Best Companies to Work For" every year since *Fortune* magazine started this annual ranking of companies (from 1998 to 2016).[112] And the Four Seasons often receives other awards and recognition such as having some of its properties included on the *Condé Nast Traveler* Gold List, the *Travel + Leisure* T + L 500 list, and Robb Report's World's Top 100 Hotels.[113] In an industry in which annual turnover rates are relatively high, the Four Seasons's turnover rate for full-time employees is 15 percent, which is among the lowest in the industry.[114] Evidently, employees and customers alike are satisfied with how they are treated at the Four Seasons. Understanding that the two are causally linked is perhaps the key to the Four Seasons's success. As the Four Seasons's founder and chairman of the board Isadore Sharp[115] suggested, "How you treat your employees is how you expect them to treat the customer."[116]

The Four Seasons was founded by Sharp in 1961 when he opened his first hotel, called the Four Seasons Motor Hotel, in a less-than-desirable area outside downtown Toronto. Whereas his first hotel had 125 inexpensively priced rooms appealing to the individual traveler, his fourth hotel was built to appeal to business travelers and conventions with 1,600 rooms, conference facilities, several restaurants, banquet halls, and shops in an arcade. Both these hotels were successful, but Sharp decided he could provide customers with a different kind of hotel experience by combining the best features of both kinds of hotel experiences—the sense of closeness and personal attention that a small hotel brings with the amenities of a big hotel to suit the needs of business travelers.[117]

Sharp sought to provide the kind of personal service that would really help business travelers on the road—giving them the amenities they have at home and in the office and miss when traveling on business. Thus, the Four Seasons was the first hotel chain to provide bathrobes, shampoo, round-the-clock room service, laundry and dry cleaning services, large desks in every room, two-line phones, and round-the-clock secretarial assistance.[118] While these are relatively concrete ways of personalizing the hotel experience, Sharp realized that how employees treat customers is just as, or perhaps even more, important. When employees view each customer as an individual with his or her own needs and desires, and empathetically try to meet these needs and desires and help customers both overcome any problems or challenges they face and truly enjoy their hotel experience, a hotel can indeed serve the purposes of a home away from home (and an office away from the office), and customers are likely to be both loyal and highly satisfied.[119]

Sharp always realized that for employees to treat customers well, the Four Seasons needs to treat its employees well. Salaries are relatively high at the Four Seasons by industry standards (between the 75th and 90th percentiles); employees participate in a profit-sharing plan; and the company contributes to their 401(k) plans. Four Seasons pays 78 percent of employees' health insurance premiums and provides free dental insurance.[120] All employees get free meals in the hotel cafeteria, have access to staff showers and a locker room, and receive an additional highly attractive benefit—once a new employee has worked for the Four Seasons for six months, he or she can stay for three nights free at any Four Seasons hotel or resort in the world. After a year of employment, this benefit increases to six free nights, and it continues to grow as tenure with the company increases. Employees like waitress Michelle De Rochemont love this benefit. As she indicated, "You're never treated like just an employee. You're a guest. . . . You come back from those trips on fire. You want to do so much for the guest."[121]

The Four Seasons also tends to promote from within.[122] For example, while recent college graduates may start out as assistant managers, those who do well and have high aspirations could become general managers in less than 15 years. This helps to ensure that managers have empathy and respect for those in lower-level positions as well as the ingrained ethos of treating others (employees, subordinates, coworkers, and customers) as they would like to be treated. All in all, treating employees well leads to satisfied customers at the Four Seasons.[123]

Pay Structure

pay structure The arrangement of jobs into categories, reflecting their relative importance to the organization and its goals, levels of skill required, and other characteristics.

After deciding on a pay level, managers have to establish a pay structure for the different jobs in the organization. A **pay structure** clusters jobs into categories, reflecting their relative importance to the organization and its goals, levels of skill required, and other characteristics managers consider important. Pay ranges are established for each job category. Individual jobholders' pay within job categories is then determined by factors such as performance, seniority, and skill levels.

There are some interesting global differences in pay structures. Large corporations based in the United States tend to pay their CEOs and top managers higher salaries than do their European or Japanese counterparts. Also, the pay differential between employees at the bottom of the corporate hierarchy and those higher up is much greater in U.S. companies than in European or Japanese companies.[124]

Concerns have been raised over whether it is equitable or fair for CEOs of large companies in the United States to be making millions of dollars in years when their companies are restructuring and laying off a large portion of their workforces.[125] Additionally, the average CEO in the United States typically earns over 360 times what the average hourly worker earns.[126] Is a pay structure with such a huge pay differential ethical? Shareholders and the public are increasingly asking this very question as well as asking large corporations to rethink their pay structures.[127] Also troubling are the millions of dollars in severance packages that some CEOs receive when they leave their organizations. When many workers are struggling to find and keep jobs and make ends meet, people are questioning whether it is ethical for some top managers to be making so much money.[128]

Benefits

Organizations are legally required to provide certain benefits to their employees, including workers' compensation, Social Security, and unemployment insurance. Workers' compensation helps employees financially if they become unable to work due to a work-related injury or illness. Social Security provides financial assistance to retirees and disabled former employees. Unemployment insurance provides financial assistance to workers who lose their jobs due to no fault of their own. The legal system in the United States views these three benefits as ethical requirements for organizations and thus mandates that they be provided.

Other benefits such as health insurance, dental insurance, vacation time, pension plans, life insurance, flexible working hours, company-provided day care, and employee assistance and wellness programs have traditionally been provided at the option of employers. The Health Care Reform Bill signed by President Barack Obama in March 2010 contains provisions whereby, starting in 2014, employers with 50 or more employees may face fines if they don't provide their employees with health insurance coverage.[129] Benefits enabling workers to balance the demands of their jobs and of their lives away from the office or factory are of growing importance for many workers who have competing demands on their scarce time and energy.

cafeteria-style benefit plan A plan from which employees can choose the benefits they want.

In some organizations, top managers determine which benefits might best suit the employees and organization and offer the same benefit package to all employees. Other organizations, realizing that employees' needs and desires might differ, offer **cafeteria-style benefit plans** that let employees choose the benefits they want. Cafeteria-style benefit plans sometimes help managers deal with employees who feel unfairly treated because they are unable to take advantage of certain benefits available to other employees who, for example, have children. Some organizations have success with cafeteria-style benefit plans; others find them difficult to manage.

As health care costs escalate and overstretched employees find it hard to take time to exercise and take care of their health, more companies are providing benefits and incentives to promote employee wellness. According to a survey conducted by Fidelity Investments and the National Business Group on Health, close to 90 percent of organizations provide some kind of incentive, prize, or reward to employees who take steps to improve their health.[130] For working parents, family-friendly benefits are especially attractive. For example, access to on-site child care, the ability to telecommute and take time off to care for sick children, and provisions for emergency back-up child care can be valued benefits for working parents with young children.

Same-sex domestic partner benefits are also being used to attract and retain valued employees. Gay and lesbian workers are reluctant to work for companies that do not provide the same kinds of benefits for their partners as those provided for partners of the opposite sex.[131]

Labor Relations

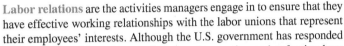

LO12-6 Understand the role that labor relations play in the effective management of human resources.

labor relations The activities managers engage in to ensure that they have effective working relationships with the labor unions that represent their employees' interests.

Labor relations are the activities managers engage in to ensure that they have effective working relationships with the labor unions that represent their employees' interests. Although the U.S. government has responded to the potential for unethical and unfair treatment of workers by creating and enforcing laws regulating employment (including the EEO laws listed in Table 12.1), some workers believe a union will ensure that their interests are fairly represented in their organizations.

Before we describe unions in more detail, let's take a look at some examples of important employment legislation. In 1938 the government passed the Fair Labor Standards Act, which prohibited child labor and provided for minimum wages, overtime pay, and maximum working hours to protect workers' rights. In 1963 the Equal Pay Act mandated that men and women performing equal work (work requiring the same levels of skill, responsibility, and effort performed in the same kind of working conditions) receive equal pay (see Table 12.1). In 1970 the Occupational Safety and Health Act mandated procedures for managers to follow to ensure workplace safety. These are just a few of the U.S. government's efforts to protect workers' rights. State legislatures also have been active in promoting safe, ethical, and fair workplaces.

Unions

Unions exist to represent workers' interests in organizations. Given that managers have more power than rank-and-file workers and that organizations have multiple stakeholders, there is always the potential for managers to take steps that benefit one set of stakeholders, such as shareholders, while hurting another, such as employees. For example, managers may decide to speed up a production line to lower costs and increase production in the hopes of increasing returns to shareholders. Speeding up the line, however, could hurt employees forced to work at a rapid pace and may increase the risk of injuries. Also, employees receive no additional pay for the extra work they are performing. Unions would represent workers' interests in a scenario such as this one.

Congress acknowledged the role that unions could play in ensuring safe and fair workplaces when it passed the National Labor Relations Act of 1935. This act made it legal for workers to organize into unions to protect their rights and interests and declared certain unfair or unethical organizational practices to be illegal. The act also established the National Labor Relations Board (NLRB) to oversee union activity. Currently, the NLRB conducts certification elections, which are held among the employees of an organization to determine whether they want a union to represent their interests. The NLRB also makes judgments concerning unfair labor practices and specifies practices that managers must refrain from.

Employees might vote to have a union represent them for any number of reasons.[132] They may think their wages and working conditions need improvement. They may believe managers are not treating them with respect. They may think their working hours are unfair or they need more job security or a safer work environment. Or they may be dissatisfied with management and find it difficult to communicate their concerns to their bosses. Regardless of the specific reason, one overriding reason is power: A united group inevitably wields more power than an individual, and this type of power may be especially helpful to employees in some organizations.

Although these would seem to be potent forces for unionization, some workers are reluctant to join unions. Sometimes this reluctance is due to the perception that union leaders are corrupt. Some workers may simply believe that belonging to a union might not do them much good while costing them money in membership dues. Employees also might not want to be forced into doing something they do not want to, such as striking because the union thinks it is in their best interest. Moreover, although unions can be a positive force in organizations, sometimes they also can be a negative force, impairing organizational effectiveness. For example, when union leaders resist needed changes in an organization or are corrupt, organizational performance can suffer.

The percentage of U.S. workers represented by unions today is smaller than it was in the 1950s, an era when unions were especially strong.[133] In the 1950s, around 35 percent of U.S. workers were union members; in 2015, 11.1 percent of workers were members of unions.[134] The American Federation of Labor–Congress of Industrial Organizations (AFL-CIO) includes 56 voluntary member unions representing 12.5 million workers.[135] Overall, approximately 14.8 million workers in the United States belong to unions.[136] Union influence in manufacturing and heavy industries has been on the decline; more generally, approximately 6.7 percent of private sector workers are union members.[137] However, around 35.2 percent of government workers belong to unions.[138] Unions have made inroads in other segments of the workforce, particularly the low-wage end. Garbage collectors in New Jersey, poultry plant workers in North Carolina, and janitors in Baltimore are among the growing numbers of low-paid workers who are currently finding union membership attractive. North Carolina poultry workers voted in a union partly because they thought it was unfair that they had to buy their own gloves and hairnets used on the job and had to ask their supervisors' permission to go to the restroom.[139]

Union membership and leadership, traditionally dominated by white men, are becoming increasingly diverse. For example, Linda Chavez-Thompson was the executive vice president of the AFL-CIO from 1995 to 2007 and was the first woman and Hispanic to hold a top management position in the federation.[140] Labor officials in Washington, DC, also are becoming increasingly diverse. Elaine L. Chao, the 24th U.S. Secretary of Labor,[141] was the first Asian-American woman to hold an appointment in a U.S. president's cabinet.[142] In terms of union membership, women now make up over 45 percent of unionized workers.[143]

Collective Bargaining

collective bargaining Negotiation between labor unions and managers to resolve conflicts and disputes about issues such as working hours, wages, benefits, working conditions, and job security.

Collective bargaining is negotiation between labor unions and managers to resolve conflicts and disputes about important issues such as working hours, wages, working conditions, and job security. Sometimes union members go on strike to drive home their concerns to managers. Once an agreement that union members support has been reached (sometimes with the help of a neutral third party called a *mediator*), union leaders and managers sign a contract spelling out the terms of the collective bargaining agreement. We discuss conflict and negotiation in depth in Chapter 17, but some brief observations are in order here because collective bargaining is an ongoing consideration in labor relations.

The signing of a contract, for example, does not finish the collective bargaining process. Disagreement and conflicts can arise over the interpretation of the contract. In such cases, a neutral third party called an *arbitrator* is usually called in to resolve the conflict. An important component of a collective bargaining agreement is a *grievance procedure* through which workers who believe they are not being fairly treated are allowed to voice their concerns and have their interests represented by the union. Workers who think they were unjustly fired in violation of a union contract, for example, may file a grievance, have the union represent them, and get their jobs back if an arbitrator agrees with them. Union members sometimes go on strike when managers make decisions that the members think will hurt them and are not in their best interests.

Summary and Review

STRATEGIC HUMAN RESOURCE MANAGEMENT   Human resource management (HRM) includes all the activities managers engage in to ensure that their organizations can attract, retain, and effectively use human resources. Strategic HRM is the process by which managers design the components of a human resource management system to be

LO12-1   consistent with each other, with other elements of organizational architecture, and with the organization's strategies and goals.

LO12-2 RECRUITMENT AND SELECTION Before recruiting and selecting employees, managers must engage in human resource planning and job analysis. Human resource planning includes all the activities managers engage in to forecast their current and future needs for human resources. Job analysis is the process of identifying (1) the tasks, duties, and responsibilities that make up a job and (2) the knowledge, skills, and abilities needed to perform the job. Recruitment includes all the activities managers engage in to develop a pool of qualified applicants for open positions. Selection is the process by which managers determine the relative qualifications of job applicants and their potential for performing well in a particular job.

LO12-3 TRAINING AND DEVELOPMENT Training focuses on teaching organizational members how to perform effectively in their current jobs. Development focuses on broadening organizational members' knowledge and skills so they are prepared to take on new responsibilities and challenges.

LO12-4 PERFORMANCE APPRAISAL AND FEEDBACK Performance appraisal is the evaluation of employees' job performance and contributions to the organization. Performance feedback is the process through which managers share performance appraisal information with their subordinates, give them an opportunity to reflect on their own performance, and develop with them plans for the future. Performance appraisal gives managers useful information for decision making. Performance feedback can encourage high levels of motivation and performance.

LO12-5 PAY AND BENEFITS Pay level is the relative position of an organization's pay incentives in comparison with those of other organizations in the same industry employing similar workers. A pay structure clusters jobs into categories according to their relative importance to the organization and its goals, the levels of skill required, and other characteristics. Pay ranges are then established for each job category. Organizations are legally required to provide certain benefits to their employees; other benefits are provided at the discretion of employers.

LO12-6 LABOR RELATIONS Labor relations include all the activities managers engage in to ensure that they have effective working relationships with the labor unions that represent their employees' interests. The National Labor Relations Board oversees union activity. Collective bargaining is the process through which labor unions and managers resolve conflicts and disputes and negotiate agreements.

Management in Action

Topics for Discussion and Action

Discussion

1. Discuss why it is important for human resource management systems to be in sync with an organization's strategy and goals and with each other. [LO12-1]

2. Discuss why training and development are ongoing activities for all organizations. [LO12-3]

3. Describe the type of development activities you think middle managers are most in need of. [LO12-3]

4. Evaluate the pros and cons of 360-degree performance appraisals and feedback. Would you like your performance to be appraised in this manner? Why or why not? [LO12-4]

5. Discuss why two restaurants in the same community might have different pay levels. [LO12-5]

6. Explain why union membership is becoming more diverse. [LO12-6]

Action

7. Interview a manager in a local organization to determine how that organization recruits and selects employees. [LO12-2]

Building Management Skills

Analyzing Human Resource Management Systems [LO12-1, 12-2, 12-3, 12-4, 12-5]

Think about your current job or a job you have had in the past. If you have never had a job, interview a friend or family member who is currently working. Answer the following questions about the job you have chosen:

1. How are people recruited and selected for this job? Are the recruitment and selection procedures the organization uses effective or ineffective? Why?

2. What training and development do people who hold this job receive? Are the training and development appropriate? Why or why not?

3. How is performance of this job appraised? Does performance feedback contribute to motivation and high performance on this job?

4. What levels of pay and benefits are provided on this job? Are these levels appropriate? Why or why not?

Managing Ethically [LO12-4, 12-5]

Some managers do not want to become overly friendly with their subordinates because they are afraid that doing so will impair their objectivity in conducting performance appraisals and making decisions about pay raises and promotions. Some subordinates resent it when they see one or more of their coworkers being very friendly with the boss; they are concerned about the potential for favoritism. Their reasoning runs something like this: If two subordinates are equally qualified for a promotion and one is a good friend of the boss and the other is a mere acquaintance, who is more likely to receive the promotion?

Questions

1. Either individually or in a group, think about the ethical implications of managers' becoming friendly with their subordinates.

2. Do you think managers should feel free to socialize and become good friends with their subordinates outside the workplace if they so desire? Why or why not?

Small Group Breakout Exercise

Building a Human Resource Management System [LO12-1, 12-2, 12-3, 12-4, 12-5]

Form groups of three or four people, and appoint one member as the spokesperson who will communicate your findings to the class when called on by the instructor. Then discuss the following scenario:

You and your three partners are engineers who minored in business at college and have decided to start a consulting business. Your goal is to provide manufacturing process engineering and other engineering services to large and small organizations. You forecast that there will be an increased use of outsourcing for these activities. You discussed with managers in several large organizations the services you plan to offer, and they expressed considerable interest. You have secured funding to start your business and now are building the HRM system. Your human resource planning suggests that you need to hire between five and eight experienced engineers with good communication skills, two clerical/secretarial workers, and two MBAs who between them have financial, accounting, and human resource skills. You are striving to develop your human resources in a way that will enable your new business to prosper.

1. Describe the steps you will take to recruit and select (a) the engineers, (b) the clerical/secretarial workers, and (c) the MBAs.

2. Describe the training and development the engineers, the clerical/secretarial workers, and the MBAs will receive.

3. Describe how you will appraise the performance of each group of employees and how you will provide feedback.

4. Describe the pay level and pay structure of your consulting firm.

Exploring the World Wide Web [LO12-2]

Go to www.net-temps.com, a website geared toward temporary employment. Imagine that you have to take a year off from college and are seeking a one-year position. Guided by your own interests, use this website to learn about your options and possible employment opportunities.

1. What are the potential advantages of online job searching and recruiting? What are the potential disadvantages?

2. Would you ever rely on a website like this to help you find a position? Why or why not?

Be the Manager [LO12-4]

You are Walter Michaels and have just received some disturbing feedback. You are the director of human resources for Maxi Vision Inc., a medium-size window and glass door manufacturer. You recently initiated a 360-degree performance appraisal system for all middle and upper managers at Maxi Vision, including yourself, but excluding the most senior executives and the top management team.

You were eagerly awaiting the feedback you would receive from the managers who report to you; you had recently implemented several important initiatives that affected them and their subordinates, including a complete overhaul of the organization's performance appraisal system. While the managers who report to you were evaluated based on 360-degree appraisals, their subordinates were evaluated using a 20-question BARS scale you recently created that focuses on behaviors. Conducted annually, appraisals are an important input into pay raise and bonus decisions.

You were so convinced that the new performance appraisal procedures were highly effective that you hoped your own subordinates would mention them in their feedback to you. And, boy, did they! You were amazed to learn that the managers and their subordinates thought the new BARS scales were unfair, inappropriate, and a waste of time. In fact, the managers' feedback to you was that their own performance was suffering, based on the 360-degree appraisals they received, because their subordinates hated the new appraisal system and partially blamed their bosses, who were part of management. Some managers even admitted giving all their subordinates approximately the same scores on the scales so their pay raises and bonuses would not be affected by their performance appraisals.

You couldn't believe your eyes when you read these comments. You spent so much time developing what you thought was the ideal rating scale for this group of employees. Evidently, for some unknown reason, they wouldn't give it a chance. Your own supervisor is aware of these complaints and said that it was a top priority for you to fix "this mess" (with the implication that you were responsible for creating it). What are you going to do?

Bloomberg Case in the News

Say Goodbye to the Annual Pay Raise [LO 12-1, 12-4, 12-5]

Annual pay raises don't work. The salary increase serves two purposes: to motivate workers and to keep employees from leaving for a better-paying job. In its current form, the traditional raise does neither of those things very well.

"You can't really do a lot with the annual raise," said Evren Esen, director of survey programs at the Society for Human Resource Management. When the economy is decent, annual pay adjustments come in at 1 percentage point or 2 percentage points ahead of inflation for a given year. That doesn't go far. Employees expect to get at least the cost of living adjustment, and a measly 2 percent increase in pay doesn't do much to encourage or change employee behavior. At best, the most stellar employees are getting a 5 percent raise, only slightly more than their average colleagues, who in 2016 can expect a 3.1 percent bump—if that. In the end, it's too small an increase to make a difference.

Historically, the best way to receive a significant raise is to either get a promotion or jump to a new company. With the job market tightening for certain white collar workers in competitive and growing industries, companies have started rethinking compensation packages to keep people around. That has not only resulted in a perks and benefits arms race but in new ways of thinking about pay increases. The yearly ritual of doling out incremental and somewhat disappointing salary increases is quietly disappearing. "The conventional process of giving an annual increase is being studied, reviewed—under siege, you might say," said Steve Gross, a senior partner at human resources consulting firm Mercer.

A once-a-year payment schedule is too infrequent to change someone's work ethic. In theory, money signals how good (or not) someone is at their job. But, it's impossible to give someone feedback on an entire year's worth of work with a nominal pay increase. Plus, it's rarely an indication of how well someone did the job over a full year. Managers don't remember how people performed all year long, and they admit to rating sub-par workers the same as standout employees. Workers also complain that hearing about their flaws once a year gives them no chance to respond and change behaviors.

Many companies, including Adobe Systems Inc., Accenture PLC, and Gap Inc., have already abandoned the annual performance review for those exact reasons. These organizations have ongoing review processes that, in theory, more accurately reflect someone's output on the job. As reviews become more frequent, so should raises. "If we have performance reviews all the time, we're not going to have annual increases," said Esen. As of now, 90 percent of companies give everyone raises on the same day, once a year, according to an annual compensation survey by Mercer. That is already changing.

GE Company, which recently moved away from the annual review, is considering scrapping annual compensation hikes. "We uncovered an opportunity to improve the way we reward people for their contributions," Janice Semper, GE's head of executive development, told Bloomberg. GE declined to elaborate on what its new system might look like, but Semper cited the vague goals of "being flexible and rethinking how we define rewards."

Other organizations are achieving such flexibility via bonuses. Variable pay has become an increasingly large part of pay packages, making up a record 12.7 percent of compensation, according to an Aon Hewitt survey from last year. It's a much more effective way to tell people they did a good job. "With bonuses, you're specifically rewarding someone for their behavior in a given year. And they're more able to directly see the line of sight between their performance and the reward for that performance," said Esen. "It gives companies the ability to really make a meaningful gesture to their top performers—to say you did well and you're getting this bonus."

Bonuses also help companies keep compensation costs down. It's hard not to give people raises, and it's even harder to cut people's salaries, but employers can give bonuses at will. If a company has a bad year, it doesn't have to give out bonuses. On an even more granular level, an employee who has a bad year might not get a bonus that year, either. Companies can use them as sticks or carrots, as needed.

The bonus is just one version of the changing nature of compensation. Whatever happens to the raise, it will become more granular and regular. "Companies are trying to break away from this old-school you get an annual increase," said Esen. "Nobody really values that increase that much because it's usually not that high."

Questions for Discussion

1. From a managerial perspective, what are some potential disadvantages of ongoing, informal performance reviews?

2. From an employee viewpoint, do you think replacing small annual increases with bonuses based on performance is equitable? Why or why not?

3. What can managers do to prepare their employees for a shift away from annual reviews and annual salary increases?

Notes

1. "ACUITY Insurance—Company Profile," http://www.acuity.com/acuityweb/abouts/compprofile.xhtml, March 11, 2016; "ACUITY in the News—ACUITY Grows to New Record in Revenue in 2015," https://www.acuity.com/acuityweb/media/newsarticle.xhtml?articleId=70A6275DF8CB45B486257F38005806E2, March 9, 2016.

2. "ACUITY in the News—ACUITY Celebrates 90th Anniversary," https://www.acuity.com/acuityweb/media/news-article.xhtml?articleId=4BD8C594168FB93986257E9D006584E1, March 10, 2016; "Acuity Cops New Attitude, Outpaces Competitors," http://www.bizjournals.com/milwaukee/stories/2003/03/17/focus1.html, March 11, 2016.

3. "ACUITY in the News—ACUITY Grows to New Record in Revenue in 2015."

4. "ACUITY Insurance—Company Profile."

5. "I Am ACUITY," https://www.acuity.com/public/i_am_acuity_brochure.pdf, March 10, 2016.

6. Ibid.; "Fortune.com 100 Best Companies to Work for 2016—ACUITY Insurance," http://fortune.com/best-companies/acuity-insurance-2/, March 9, 2016; ACUITY in the News—ACUITY Moves into the Top 2 in Fortune 100 Best Companies to Work For," https://www.acuity.com/acuityweb/media/newsarticle.xhtml?articleId=09E6642001EF08CD86257F6B00732C41, March 9, 2016; "ACUITY Insurance—Great Place to Work Reviews," http://reviews.greatplacetowork.com/acuity, March 9, 2016.

7. "I Am ACUITY"; "Fortune.com 100 Best Companies to Work for 2016—ACUITY Insurance"; "ACUITY in the News—ACUITY Moves into the Top 2 in Fortune 100 Best Companies to Work For"; "ACUITY Insurance—Great Place to Work Reviews."

8. "ACUITY Insurance—Great Place to Work Reviews."

9. "I Am ACUITY"; "Fortune.com 100 Best Companies to Work for 2016—ACUITY Insurance"; "ACUITY in the News—ACUITY Moves into the Top 2 in Fortune 100 Best Companies to Work For"; "ACUITY Insurance—Great Place to Work Reviews."

10. Ibid.

11. Ibid.

12. "ACUITY in the News—ACUITY Moves into the Top 2 in Fortune 100 Best Companies to Work For."

13. "ACUITY in the News—ACUITY Ranks as a Top Workplace for Women," https://www.acuity.com/acuityweb/media/newsarticle.xhtml?articleId=BC02B7D48C4FDE1D86257EDC0058A8E5, March 9, 2016; "ACUITY in the News—ACUITY Ranks as a Top Workplace for Millennials," https://www.acuity.com/acuityweb/media/newsarticle.xhtml?articleId=15194600B5E6981F86257E83004EACF5, March 10, 2016.

14. J.E. Butler, G.R. Ferris, and N.K. Napier, *Strategy and Human Resource Management* (Cincinnati: Southwestern, 1991); P.M. Wright and G.C. McMahan, "Theoretical Perspectives for Strategic Human Resource Management," *Journal of Management* 18 (1992), 295–320.

15. AlixPartners Professionals, "Fitzpatrick, David A.," http://www.alixpartners.com/en/Professionals/tabid/670/EmployeeBio/FitzpatrickDavidA/Id/1709/Default.aspx, April 23, 2014.

16. L. Clifford, "Why You Can Safely Ignore Six Sigma," *Fortune*, January 22, 2001, 140.

17. J.B. Quinn, P. Anderson, and S. Finkelstein, "Managing Professional Intellect: Making the Most of the Best," *Harvard Business Review*, March–April 1996, 71–80.

18. Ibid.

19. C.D. Fisher, L.F. Schoenfeldt, and J.B. Shaw, *Human Resource Management* (Boston: Houghton Mifflin, 1990).

20. Wright and McMahan, "Theoretical Perspectives for Strategic Human Resource Management."

21. L. Baird and I. Meshoulam, "Managing Two Fits for Strategic Human Resource Management," *Academy of Management Review* 14, 116–28; J. Milliman, M. Von Glinow, and M. Nathan, "Organizational Life Cycles and Strategic International Human Resource Management in Multinational Companies: Implications for Congruence Theory," *Academy of Management Review* 16 (1991), 318–39; R.S. Schuler and S.E. Jackson, "Linking Competitive Strategies with Human Resource Management Practices," *Academy of Management Executive* 1 (1987), 207–19; P.M. Wright and S.A. Snell, "Toward an Integrative View of Strategic Human Resource Management," *Human Resource Management Review* 1 (1991), 203–25.

22. "Who's in Charge Here? No One," *The Observer*, http://observer.guardian.co.uk/business/story/0,6903,944138,00.html, April 27, 2003; "Ricardo Semler, CEO, Semco SA," cnn.com, http://cnn.worldnews.printthis.clickability.com/pt/cpt&title5cnn.com, June 29, 2004; D. Kirkpatrick, "The Future of Work: An 'Apprentice' Style Office?" *Fortune*, www.fortune.com/fortune/subs/print/0,15935,611068,00.html, April 14, 2004; A. Strutt and R. Van Der Beek, "Report from HR2004," www.mce.be/hr2004/reportd2.htm, July 2, 2004; R. Semler, "Seven-Day Weekend Returns Power to Employees," workopolis.com, http://globeandmail.workopolis.com/servlet/content/qprinter/20040526/cabooks26, May 26, 2004; "SEMCO," http://semco.locaweb.com.br/ingles, May 31, 2006; "Ricardo Semler, Semco SA: What Are You Reading?" cnn.com, www.cnn.com/2004/BUSINESS/06/29/semler.profile/index.html, May 31, 2006; "About the Semco Group," SEMCO, http://www.semco.com.br/en/content.asp?content51&contentID5610, April 24, 2012.

23. "Group Companies: Semco Capital Goods Division," SEMCO, http://www.semco.com.br/en/content.asp?content57&contentID5611, April 24, 2012; "Group Companies: Pitney Bowes Semco," SEMCO, http://www.semco.com.br/en/content.asp?content57&contentID5612, April 24, 2012.

24. R. Semler, *The Seven-Day Weekend: Changing the Way Work Works* (New York: Penguin, 2003); "SEMCO"; Semco Partners, http://semco.com.br/en/, April 23, 2014; "Joint-Venture Catalysts for Expansion in Brazil—Semco Partners," http://www.semco.com.br/en/, March 11, 2016.

25. Semler, *The Seven-Day Weekend*; "SEMCO"; G. Hamel, *The Future of Management* (Cambridge, MA: Harvard Business Press, 2007).

26. A. Strutt, "Interview with Ricardo Semler," *Management Centre Europe*, www.mce.be/knowledge/392/35, April 2004.

27. Semler, *The Seven-Day Weekend*.

28. Ibid.

29. R. Semler, "How We Went *Digital* without a *Strategy*," *Harvard Business Review* 78, no. 5 (September–October 2000), 51–56.

30. Semler, *The Seven-Day Weekend*.

31. Equal Employment Opportunity Commission, "Uniform Guidelines on Employee Selection Procedures," *Federal Register* 43 (1978), 38290–315.

32. R. Stogdill II, R. Mitchell, K. Thurston, and C. Del Valle, "Why AIDS Policy Must Be a Special Policy," *BusinessWeek*, February 1, 1993, 53–54.

33. J.M. George, "AIDS/AIDS-Related Complex," in L. Peters, B. Greer, and S. Youngblood, eds., *The Blackwell Encyclopedic Dictionary of Human Resource*

410 Chapter Twelve

Management (Oxford, England: Blackwell, 1997).

34. Ibid.

35. Ibid.; Stogdill et al., "Why AIDS Policy Must Be a Special Policy"; K. Holland, "Out of Retirement and into Uncertainty," *The New York Times,* May 27, 2007, BU17.

36. S.L. Rynes, "Recruitment, Job Choice, and Post-Hire Consequences: A Call for New Research Directions," in M.D. Dunnette and L.M. Hough, eds., *Handbook of Industrial and Organizational Psychology,* vol. 2 (Palo Alto, CA: Consulting Psychologists Press, 1991), 399–444.

37. "Kelly Services—Background," http://www.kellyservices.com/web/global/services/en/pages/background.html, April 24, 2012.

38. R.L. Sullivan, "Lawyers a la Carte," *Forbes,* September 11, 1995, 44.

39. E. Porter, "Send Jobs to India? U.S. Companies Say It's Not Always Best," *The New York Times,* April 28, 2004, A1, A7.

40. D. Wessel, "The Future of Jobs: New Ones Arise; Wage Gap Widens," *The Wall Street Journal,* April 2, 2004, A1, A5; "Relocating the Back Office," *The Economist,* December 13, 2003, 67–69.

41. The Conference Board, "Offshoring Evolving at a Rapid Pace, Report Duke University and The Conference Board," http://www.conference-board.org/utilities/pressPrinterFriendly.cfm?press_ID53709, August 3, 2009, accessed February 24, 2010; S. Minter, "Offshoring by U.S. Companies Doubles," *Industry Week,* http://www.industryweek.com/PrintArticle.aspx?ArticleID519772&SectionID53, August 19, 2009, accessed February 24, 2010; AFP, "Offshoring by U.S. Companies Surges: Survey," http://www.google.com/hostednews/afp/article/ALeqM5iDaq1D2KZU16YfbKrMPdborD7 at. . ., August 3, 2009, accessed February 24, 2010; V. Wadhwa, "The Global Innovation Migration," *BusinessWeek,* http://www.businessweek.com/print/-technology/content/nov2009/tc2009119_331698.htm, November 9, 2009, accessed February 24, 2010; T. Heijmen, A.Y. Lewin, S. Manning, N. Perm-Ajchariyawong, and J.W. Russell, "Offshoring Research the C-Suite," 2007–2008 ORN Survey Report, *The Conference Board,* in collaboration with Duke University Offshoring Research Network.

42. The Conference Board, "Offshoring Evolving at a Rapid Pace"; Minter, "Offshoring by U.S. Companies Doubles"; AFP, "Offshoring by U.S. Companies Surges"; Wadhwa, "The Global Innovation Migration"; Heijmen et al., "Offshoring Research the C-Suite."

43. Wadhwa, "The Global Innovation Migration."

44. The Conference Board, "Offshoring Evolving at a Rapid Pace."

45. Ibid.; Minter, "Offshoring by U.S. Companies Doubles"; AFP, "Offshoring by U.S. Companies Surges"; Heijmen et al., "Offshoring Research the C-Suite."

46. "Outsourcing: A Passage Out of India," *Bloomberg Businessweek,* March 19–25, 2012.

47. BRASSCOM—Brazilian Association of Information Technology and Communication Companies, http://www.brasscomglobalitforum.com/index.php, April 24, 2014.

48. "Outsourcing: A Passage Out of India"; "IBM Research—Brazil," http://www.research.ibm.com/brazil/, April 25, 2012.

49. "Outsourcing: A Passage Out of India."

50. Ibid.

51. KPO Services, "'Knowledge Process Outsourcing—Copal Amba," http://www.copalamba.com/about-us; "Copal Amba," Wikipedia, the Free Encyclopedia, http://en.wikipedia.org/wiki/Copal_Amba, April 24, 2014.

52. KPO Services, "Knowledge Process Outsourcing."

53. "Outsourcing: A Passage Out of India"; "Senior Management—Copal Partners," http://www.copalpartners.com/Senior%20Management, April 25, 2012.

54. "Outsourcing: A Passage Out of India."

55. Ibid.

56. Ibid.

57. Christina Passariello and Suzanne Kapner, "Search for Cheaper Labor Leads to Africa," *The Wall Street Journal,* July 13, 2015.

58. Ibid.

59. R.J. Harvey, "Job Analysis," in M.D. Dunnette and L.M. Hough, eds., *Handbook of Industrial and Organizational Psychology,* vol. 2 (Palo Alto, CA: Consulting Psychologists Press, 1991), 71–163.

60. E.L. Levine, *Everything You Always Wanted to Know about Job Analysis: A Job Analysis Primer* (Tampa, FL: Mariner, 1983).

61. R.L. Mathis and J.H. Jackson, *Human Resource Management,* 7th ed. (Minneapolis: West, 1994).

62. E.J. McCormick, P.R. Jeannerette, and R.C. Mecham, *Position Analysis Questionnaire* (West Lafayette, IN: Occupational Research Center, Department of Psychological Sciences, Purdue University, 1969).

63. Fisher et al., *Human Resource Management;* Mathis and Jackson, *Human Resource Management;* R.A. Noe,

J.R. Hollenbeck, B. Gerhart, and P.M. Wright, *Human Resource Management: Gaining a Competitive Advantage* (Burr Ridge, IL: Irwin, 1994).

64. Fisher et al., *Human Resource Management;* E.J. McCormick, *Job Analysis: Methods and Applications* (New York: American Management Association, 1979); E.J. McCormick and P.R. Jeannerette, "The Position Analysis Questionnaire," in S. Gael, ed., *The Job Analysis Handbook for Business, Industry, and Government* (New York: Wiley, 1988); Noe et al., *Human Resource Management.*

65. Rynes, "Recruitment, Job Choice, and Post-Hire Consequences."

66. R. Sharpe, "The Life of the Party? Can Jeff Taylor Keep the Good Times Rolling at Monster.com?" *BusinessWeek,* June 4, 2001 (*BusinessWeek* Archives); D.H. Freedman, "The Monster Dilemma," *Inc.,* May 2007, 77–78; P. Korkki, "So Easy to Apply, So Hard to Be Noticed," *The New York Times,* July 1, 2007, BU16.

67. Jobline International, "Resume Vacancy Posting, Employment Resources, Job Searches," http://www.jobline.net, February 25, 2010.

68. www.jobline.org, press releases, May 8, 2001.

69. J. Spolsky, "There Is a Better Way to Find and Hire the Very Best Employees," *Inc.,* May 2007, 81–82; "About the Company," www.fogcreek.com, March 5, 2008; "Fog Creek Software," www.fogcreek.com, March 5, 2008; Fog Creek Software, "About the Company," http://fogcreek.com/About.html, February 25, 2010; "About Us—Fog Creek Software," http://www.fogcreek.com/about/, April 24, 2014; "About Us—Fog Creek Software," http://www.fogcreek.com/about/, March 11, 2016.

70. Spolsky, "Better Way to Find and Hire"; "Fog Creek Software"; "Careers and Internships—Fog Creek Software," http://www.fogcreek.com/careers/, April 24, 2014.

71. Spolsky, "Better Way to Find and Hire"; "Fog Creek Software."

72. Ibid.; "Intern in Software Development—Fog Creek Software," http://www.fogcreek.com/jobs/summerintern, June 10, 2016.

73. Spolsky, "Better Way to Find and Hire"; "Intern in Software Development."

74. Spolsky, "Better Way to Find and Hire."

75. Ibid.; "Fog Creek Software."

76. Spolsky, "Better Way to Find and Hire"; "About the Company"; "Fog Creek Software."

77. Spolsky, "Better Way to Find and Hire."

78. S.L. Premack and J.P. Wanous, "A Meta-Analysis of Realistic Job Preview

Experiments," *Journal of Applied Psychology* 70 (1985), 706–19; J.P. Wanous, "Realistic Job Previews: Can a Procedure to Reduce Turnover also Influence the Relationship between Abilities and Performance?" *Personnel Psychology* 31 (1978), 249–58; J.P. Wanous, *Organizational Entry: Recruitment, Selection, and Socialization of Newcomers* (Reading, MA: Addison-Wesley, 1980).

79. R.M. Guion, "Personnel Assessment, Selection, and Placement," in M.D. Dunnette and L.M. Hough, eds., *Handbook of Industrial and Organizational Psychology,* vol. 2 (Palo Alto, CA: Consulting Psychologists Press, 1991), 327–97.

80. T. Joyner, "Job Background Checks Surge," *Houston Chronicle,* May 2, 2005, D6.

81. Ibid.; "ADP News Releases: Employer Services: ADP Hiring Index Reveals Background Checks Performed More Than Tripled since 1997," Automatic Data Processing, Inc., www.investquest.com/iq/a/aud/ne/news/adp042505background.htm, June 3, 2006; "Employee Benefits Administration," ADP, http://www.adp.com/, April 25, 2012.

82. "Background Checks and Employment Screening from ADP," http://www.adpes.co.uk/employment-screening/?printpreview51, April 25, 2012.

83. "ADP News Releases."

84. Noe et al., *Human Resource Management;* J.A. Wheeler and J.A. Gier, "Reliability and Validity of the Situational Interview for a Sales Position," *Journal of Applied Psychology* 2 (1987), 484–87.

85. Noe et al., *Human Resource Management.*

86. J. Flint, "Can You Tell Applesauce from Pickles?" *Forbes,* October 9, 1995, 106–8.

87. Ibid.

88. "Wanted: Middle Managers, Audition Required," *The Wall Street Journal,* December 28, 1995, A1.

89. I.L. Goldstein, "Training in Work Organizations," in M.D. Dunnette and L.M. Hough, eds., *Handbook of Industrial and Organizational Psychology,* vol. 2 (Palo Alto, CA: Consulting Psychologists Press, 1991), 507–619.

90. The Walt Disney Company, "Disney Workplaces: Training & Development," 2010 Corporate Citizenship Report, http://corporate.disney.go.com/citizenship2010/disneyworkplaces/overview/trainingandde . . ., April 25, 2012.

91. N. Banerjee, "For Mary Kay Sales Reps in Russia, Hottest Shade Is the Color of Money," *The Wall Street Journal,* August 30, 1995, A8.

92. T.D. Allen, L.T. Eby, M.L. Poteet, E. Lentz, and L. Lima, "Career Benefits Associated with Mentoring for Protégés: A Meta-Analysis," *Journal of Applied Psychology* 89, no. 1 (2004), 127–36.

93. M. Khidekel, "The Misery of Mentoring Millennials," *Bloomberg Businessweek,* http://www.businessweek.com/printer/articles/102262-the-misery-of-mentoring-millennials, April 24, 2014.

94. P. Garfinkel, "Putting a Formal Stamp on Mentoring," *The New York Times,* January 18, 2004, BU10.

95. Ibid.

96. Allen et al., "Career Benefits Associated with Mentoring"; L. Levin, "Lesson Learned: Know Your Limits. Get Outside Help Sooner Rather Than Later," *BusinessWeek Online,* www.businessweek.com, July 5, 2004; "Family, Inc.," *BusinessWeek Online,* www.businessweek.com, November 10, 2003; J. Salamon, "A Year with a Mentor. Now Comes the Test," *The New York Times,* September 30, 2003, B1, B5; E. White, "Making Mentorships Work," *The Wall Street Journal,* October 23, 2007, B11.

97. Garfinkel, "Putting a Formal Stamp on Mentoring."

98. J.A. Byrne, "Virtual B-Schools," *BusinessWeek,* October 23, 1995, 64–68; "Michigan Executive Education Locations around the Globe," http://exceed.bus.umich.edu/InternationalFacilities/default.aspx, February 25, 2010.

99. "Top Distance Learning & Online MBA Programs," *Businessweek,* http://www.businessweek.com/bschools/rankings/distance_mba_profiles, April 24, 2014.

100. Fisher et al., *Human Resource Management.*

101. Ibid.; G.P. Latham and K.N. Wexley, *Increasing Productivity through Performance Appraisal* (Reading, MA: Addison-Wesley, 1982).

102. T.A. DeCotiis, "An Analysis of the External Validity and Applied Relevance of Three Rating Formats," *Organizational Behavior and Human Performance* 19 (1977), 247–66; Fisher et al., *Human Resource Management.*

103. L. Kwoh, "Rank and Yank," *The Wall Street Journal,* January 31, 2012, B6.

104. Ibid.

105. J.S. Lublin, "It's Shape-Up Time for Performance Reviews," *The Wall Street Journal,* October 3, 1994, B1, B2.

106. J.S. Lublin, "Turning the Tables: Underlings Evaluate Bosses," *The Wall Street Journal,* October 4, 1994, B1, B14; S. Shellenbarger, "Reviews from Peers Instruct—and Sting," *The Wall Street Journal,* October 4, 1994, B1, B4.

107. C. Borman and D.W. Bracken, "360 Degree Appraisals," in C.L. Cooper and C. Argyris, eds., *The Concise Blackwell Encyclopedia of Management* (Oxford, England: Blackwell, 1998), 17; D.W. Bracken, "Straight Talk about Multi-Rater Feedback," *Training and Development* 48 (1994), 44–51; M.R. Edwards, W.C. Borman, and J.R. Sproul, "Solving the Double Bind in Performance Appraisal: A Saga of Solves, Sloths, and Eagles," *Business Horizons* 85 (1985), 59–68.

108. M.A. Peiperl, "Getting 360 Degree Feedback Right," *Harvard Business Review,* January 2001, 142–47.

109. A. Harrington, "Workers of the World, Rate Your Boss!" *Fortune,* September 18, 2000, 340, 342; www.ImproveNow.com, June 2001.

110. Lublin, "It's Shape-Up Time for Performance Reviews."

111. S.E. Moss and J.I. Sanchez, "Are Your Employees Avoiding You? Managerial Strategies for Closing the Feedback Gap," *Academy of Management Executive* 18, no. 1 (2004), 32–46.

112. J.M. O'Brien, "100 Best Companies to Work For—A Perfect Season," *Fortune,* February 4, 2008, 64–66; "Four Seasons Employees Name Company to *Fortune* '100 Best Companies to Work For' List," www.fourseasons.com/about_us/press_release_280.html, February 22, 2008; "Four Seasons Hotels and Resort Named to *Fortune* List of the '100 Best Companies to Work For,'" http://press.fourseasons.com/news-releases/four-seasons-hotels-and-resorts-named-to-fortu . . ., February 24, 2010; "Four Seasons Hotels & Resorts—Best Companies to Work For 2012," *Fortune,* http://money.cnn.com/magazines/fortune/best-companies/2012/snapshots/85.html, April 23, 2012; "Employer of Choice: Four Seasons Hotels and Resorts Named to FORTUNE List of the '100 Best Companies to Work For' for 17th Consecutive Year," employer-of-choice-four-seasons-hotels-and-resorts-named-to-fortune-list-of-the-100-best-companies-to-work-for-fo-17th-consecutive-year, April 23, 2014; M. Moskowitz and R. Levering, "The 100 Best Companies to Work For," *Fortune,* February 3, 2014, 108–20; "Fortune.com 100 Best Companies to Work For 2016—Four Seasons Hotels & Resorts," http://fortune.com/best-companies/four-seasons-hotels-resorts-70/, March 14, 2016.

113. "Four Seasons Employees Name Company to *Fortune* '100 Best Companies to Work For' List"; "Employer of Choice: Four Seasons Hotels and Resorts Named to FORTUNE List of the '100 Best

Companies to Work For' for 17th Consecutive Year."

114. O'Brien, "100 Best Companies to Work
For—A Perfect Season"; "Four Seasons
Hotels & Resorts—Best Companies
to Work For 2012"; "Four Seasons
Hotels—100 Best Companies to Work
For 2014—Fortune," http://money.cnn
.com/magazines/fortune/best-
companies/2014/snapshots/91.html;
"Fortune.com 100 Best Companies to
Work For 2016—Four Seasons Hotels &
Resorts," http://fortune.com/best-
companies/four-seasons-hotels-
resorts-70/, March 14, 2016.

115. "Four Seasons Hotels and Resorts—
About Us: Corporate Bios," http://www.
fourseasons.com/about_us/corporate_
bios/, February 24, 2010; "Four Seasons
Hotels and Resorts Jobs / Hotel and
Resort Career Search Site," http://jobs
.fourseasons.com/Pages/Home.aspx,
April 26, 2012; "Four Seasons Holdings
Inc.: Private Company Information,"
BusinessWeek, http://investing.
businessweek.com/research/stocks/
private/snapshot.asp?privcapId=357114,
April 23, 2014; "Corporate Bios," http://
www.fourseasons.com/about_four_
seasons/corporate-bios/, March 14, 2016.

116. O'Brien, "100 Best Companies to Work
For—A Perfect Season."

117. Ibid.; "Creating the Four Seasons
Difference," www.businessweek
.com/print/innovate/content/jan2008/
id20080122_671354.htm, February 22,
2008.

118. Ibid.

119. Ibid.; "Four Seasons Employees Name
Company to *Fortune* '100 Best Companies to Work For' List."

120. M. Moskowitz, R. Levering, and
C. Tkaczyk, "The List," *Fortune,*
February 8, 2010, 75–88.

121. O'Brien, "100 Best Companies to Work
For—A Perfect Season."

122. Ibid.

123. Ibid.; "Creating the Four Seasons Differ-
ence"; "Four Seasons Employees Name
Company to *Fortune* '100 Best Compa-
nies to Work For' List"; "Employer of
Choice: Four Seasons Hotels and Resorts
Named to FORTUNE List of the '100
Best Companies to Work For' for 17th
Consecutive Year."

124. J. Flynn and F. Nayeri, "Continental
Divide over Executive Pay," *Business-
Week,* July 3, 1995, 40–41.

125. J.A. Byrne, "How High Can CEO Pay
Go?" *BusinessWeek,* April 22, 1996,
100–6.

126. A. Borrus, "A Battle Royal against Regal
Paychecks," *BusinessWeek,* February 24,
2003, 127; "Too Many Turkeys," *The
Economist,* November 26, 2005, 75–76;

G. Morgenson, "How to Slow Runaway
Executive Pay," *The New York Times,*
October 23, 2005, 1, 4; S. Greenhouse,
*The Big Squeeze: Tough Times for the
American Worker* (New York: Alfred
A. Knopf, 2008); "Trends in CEO
Pay," AFL-CIO, http://www.aflcio.org/
Corporate-Watch/CEO-Pay-and-the-99/
Trends-in-CEO-Pay, April 26, 2012.

127. "Executive Pay," *BusinessWeek,* April 19,
2004, 106–10.

128. "Home Depot Chief's Pay in 2007 Could
Reach $8.9m," *The New York Times,*
Bloomberg News, January 25, 2007, C7;
E. Carr, "The Stockpot," *The Economist,
A Special Report on Executive Pay,*
January 20, 2007, 6–10; E. Porter,
"More Than Ever, It Pays to Be the Top
Executive," *The New York Times,*
May 25, 2007, A1, C7.

129. K. Garber, "What Is (and Isn't) in the
Healthcare Bill," http://www.usnews.
com/articles/news/politics/2010/02/22/
what-is-and-isnt-in-the-healthca . . .,
March 29, 2010; S. Condon, "Health
Care Bill Signed by Obama," Political Hotsheet—CBS News, http://www.
cbsnews.com/8301-503544_162-
20000981-503544.html, March 29,
2010; T.S. Bernard, "For Consumers,
Clarity on Health Care Changes," *The
New York Times,* http://www.nytimes
.com/2010/03/22/your-money/health-
insurance/22consumer.html?sq5h . . .,
March 21, 2010; "Health Care Reform
Bill Summary: A Look At What's in
the Bill," CBSNews.com, http://www.
cbsnews.com/8301-503544_162-
20000846-503544.html, March 23,
2009; Reuters, "Factbox: Details of Final
Healthcare Bill," http://www.reuters
.com/article/idUSTRE62K11V20100321,
March 21, 2010.

130. J. Wieczner, "Your Company Wants to
Make You Healthy," "Pros and Cons of
Company Wellness Program Incentives,"
WSJ.com, http://online.wsj.com/news/
articles/SB1000142412788732339330457836025228415
1378, April 24, 2014.

131. S. Shellenbarger, "Amid Gay Marriage
Debate, Companies Offer More Benefits
to Same-Sex Couples," *The Wall Street
Journal,* March 18, 2004, D1.

132. S. Premack and J.E. Hunter, "Individual
Unionization Decisions," *Psychological
Bulletin* 103 (1988), 223–34.

133. M.B. Regan, "Shattering the AFL-CIO's
Glass Ceiling," *BusinessWeek,*
November 13, 1995, 46; S. Greenhouse,
"The Hard Work of Reviving Labor,"
The New York Times, September 16,
2009, B1, B7.

134. S. Greenhouse, "Survey Finds Deep
Shift in the Makeup of Unions," *The
New York Times,* November 11, 2009,
B5; "Union Members—2011," Union

Members Summary, http://www.bls.gov/
news.release/union2.nr0.htm, January 27,
2012; "Union Members Summary, Economic New Release"; "Union Members
Summary," http://www.bls.gov/news
.release/union2.nr0.htm, March 14,
2016.

135. www.aflcio.org, June 2001; "About Us,"
AFL-CIO, http://www.aflcio.org/
aboutus; S. Greenhouse, "Most U.S.
Union Members Are Working for the
Government, New Data Shows," *The
New York Times,* http://www.nytimes
.com/2010/01/23/business/23labor.
html?pagewanted5print, January 23,
2010; About the AFL-CIO, http://www.
aflcio.org/About; "About the AFL-CIO,"
http://www.aflcio.org/About, March 14,
2016.

136. Greenhouse, "Most U.S. Union Members Are Working for the Government";
"Union Members—2011," Union Members Summary, http://www.bls.gov/news
.release/union2.nr0.htm, January 27,
2012; Union Members Summary, Economic New Release, http://www.bls.gov/
news.release/union2.nr0.htm, March 14,
2016.

137. Greenhouse, "Survey Finds Deep Shift
in the Makeup of Unions"; "Union
Members—2011," Union Members
Summary, Economic New Release;
"Union Members Summary," http://
www.bls.gov/news.release/union2.nr0
.htm, March 14, 2016.

138. Greenhouse, "Most U.S. Union Members Are Working for the Government";
"Union Members Summary."

139. G.P. Zachary, "Some Unions Step Up
Organizing Campaigns and Get New
Members," *The Wall Street Journal,*
September 1, 1995, A1, A2; "Union
Members Summary, Economic New
Release," http://www.bls.gov/news.
release/union2.nr0.htm, April 24, 2014.

140. Regan, "Shattering the AFL-CIO's Glass
Ceiling"; www.aflcio.org, June 2001;
R.S. Dunham, "Big Labor: So Out
It's Off the Radar Screen," *Business-
Week,* March 26, 2001 (*BusinessWeek*
Archives); "Chavez-Thompson to
Retire as Executive Vice President,"
AFL-CIO Weblog, http://blog.aflcio.
org/2007/09/13/chavez-thompson-to-
retire-as-executive-vice-president/print/,
March 6, 2008.

141. U.S. Department of Labor—Office of
the Secretary of Labor Elaine L. Chao
(OSEC), "Secretary of Labor Elaine
L. Chao," www.dol.gov/_sec/welcome
.htm, March 6, 2008; S. Greenhouse,
"Departing Secretary of Labor Fends
Off Critics," *The New York Times,*
http://www.nytimes.com/2009/01/10/
washington/10chao.html?_r51&
pagewanted5print, February 25, 2010;

"Biography," http://www.elainechao
.com/index.php/biography/Print.html,
January 10, 2009, accessed April 27,
2012.

142. "The Honorable Elaine L. Chao, United
States Secretary of Labor," www.dol
.gov/dol/sec/public/aboutosec/chao.htm,
June 25, 2001.

143. Greenhouse, "Survey Finds Deep Shift
in the Makeup of Unions"; Bureau of
Labor Statistics (BLS), U.S. Department
of Labor, "Union Members—2011,"
news release, www.bls.gov/news
.release/pdf/union2.pdf, January 27,
2012, accessed April 27, 2012;
"Table 1. Union Affiliation of Employed

Wage and Salary Workers by Selected
Characteristics, Economic News
Release," http://www.bls.gov/news
.release/union2.t01.htm, April 24, 2014.

Harvard Business Review

www.hbrreprints.org

The first comprehensive look at what employees are thinking and feeling as they go about their work, why it matters, and how managers can use this information to improve job performance.

Inner Work Life
Understanding the Subtext of Business Performance

by Teresa M. Amabile and Steven J. Kramer

Included with this full-text *Harvard Business Review* article:

Reprint R0705D

Inner Work Life

Understanding the Subtext of Business Performance

The Idea in Brief

You've given your best employees pats on the back. You've injected light-hearted fun into the workplace. And you've provided emotional support when needed. So why aren't your people delivering *peak* performance?

Perhaps you've neglected their **inner work lives**—the complex interplay between employees' deeply private *perceptions* of what's happening around them, the *emotions* they experience as a result of those perceptions, and their level of *motivation* to do good work.

When people form negative perceptions—of their manager, organization, coworkers, work, or themselves—they feel frustrated and unhappy. Motivation shrivels. Performance suffers in the short *and* long run. But when employees form positive perceptions, the cycle turns from vicious to virtuous.

How to promote positive perceptions? Manipulate some simple levers, say Amabile and Kramer. In particular, **create conditions that enable people to get their work done**, and you'll create positive emotions, enhance motivation, and boost performance to unprecedented levels.

The Idea in Practice

Amabile and Kramer offer these suggestions for promoting positive inner work lives in your employees:

DEMYSTIFY THE INNER WORK LIFE SYSTEM

The interplay among employees' perceptions, emotions, and motivation form a complex system that can fuel—or kill—performance. This system operates all day long, unseen, within every employee—and in response to every event. Steps in the system include:

1. An event happens at work—for example, a manager fails to respond to an employee's e-mail, a worker solves a nagging technical problem, or top management announces a major layoff.

2. Each employee tries to figure out why the event happened and what its implications are.

3. If perceptions resulting from this "sense making" are negative, the person experiences feelings such as anger, sadness, and disgust. If perceptions are positive, an employee experiences positive emotions—including satisfaction, pride, and elation.

4. Positive emotions fuel people's motivation, which in turn drives performance along four key dimensions: **creativity** (ability to come up with novel and useful ideas), **productivity**, **commitment** to the work, and **collegiality** (contributions to team cohesiveness). Not surprisingly, negative emotions corrode motivation, so performance suffers.

ACTIVATE A VIRTUOUS CYCLE IN EMPLOYEES' INNER WORK LIVES

Typical management techniques such as praising subordinates, working collaboratively with them, and making the workplace fun or relaxing can all help establish a positive cycle in employees' inner work lives.

But the *single* most important lever is to give people the sense that they can make progress in their work. Success in achieving a goal,

accomplishing a task, or solving a problem—whether mundane or immense—evokes intense pleasure and even joy.

To enable your people to get their work done:

- Provide direct help.

- Give them adequate resources and time to do their jobs.

- React to successes and failures with a learning orientation rather than a purely evaluative one.

- Set clear goals—by explaining where the work is heading and why it matters to the team, the organization, and the company's customers.

The first comprehensive look at what employees are thinking and feeling as they go about their work, why it matters, and how managers can use this information to improve job performance.

Inner Work Life
Understanding the Subtext of Business Performance

by Teresa M. Amabile and Steven J. Kramer

If your organization demands knowledge work from its people, then you undoubtedly appreciate the importance of sheer brainpower. You probably recruit high-intellect people and ensure they have access to good information. You probably also respect the power of incentives and use formal compensation systems to channel that intellectual energy down one path or another. But you might be overlooking another crucial driver of a knowledge worker's performance—that person's inner work life. People experience a constant stream of emotions, perceptions, and motivations as they react to and make sense of the events of the workday. As people arrive at their workplaces they don't check their hearts and minds at the door. Unfortunately, because inner work life is seldom openly expressed in modern organizations, it's all too easy for managers to pretend that private thoughts and feelings don't matter.

As psychologists, we became fascinated a decade ago with day-to-day work life. But our research into inner work life goes well beyond intellectual curiosity about the complex operations of emotions, perceptions, and motivations. It addresses the very pragmatic managerial question of how these dynamics affect work performance. To examine this question, we constructed a research project that would give us a window into the inner work lives of a broad population of knowledge workers. Specifically, we recruited 238 professionals from 26 project teams and had them complete daily diary entries, in a standard format, for the duration of their projects. Nearly 12,000 diary entries later, we have discovered the dynamics of inner work life and the significant effect it can have on the performance of your people—and, by implication, your entire organization.

It may stun you, if you are a manager, to learn what power you hold. Your behavior as a manager dramatically shapes your employees' inner work lives. But the key levers in your hands for driving motivation and performance may not be the ones you'd suspect.

More Than Meets the Eye

Think about your own most recent day at the office, and try to recall it in some detail. What would hidden observers have been able to learn had they been watching you go through that day? They might have read e-mails you composed, looked over the numbers you plugged into spreadsheets, reviewed the reports you prepared. They would have noted your interactions, in formal meetings or hallway encounters, with colleagues, subordinates, and superiors and listened in on a presentation you delivered. They would have heard your end of various telephone conversations, perhaps with customers, suppliers, or consultants. Maybe they would have watched you sitting quietly for a while, looking off into space, jotting down a few notes.

But would these observers really understand your inner work life that day? Of course not. In having those conversations and writing those reports, you were not only dealing with the task at hand. As events unfolded, you were also forming and adjusting perceptions about the people you work with, the organization you are part of, the work you do, and even yourself. You were experiencing emotions, maybe mild states of satisfaction or irritation, maybe intense feelings of pride or frustration. And these perceptions and emotions were intertwining to affect your work motivation from moment to moment—with consequences for your performance that day.

This is what we mean by inner work life: the dynamic interplay among personal *perceptions*, ranging from immediate impressions to more fully developed theories about what is happening and what it means; *emotions*, whether sharply defined reactions (such as elation over a particular success or anger over a particular obstacle) or more general feeling states, like good and bad moods; and *motivation*—your grasp of what needs to be done and your drive to do it at any given moment. Inner work life is crucial to a person's experience of the workday but for the most part is imperceptible to others. Indeed, it goes largely unexamined even by the individual experiencing it.

In order to study inner work lives, we needed a level of access beyond that of an observer. Thus, we relied on the classic form of the personal diary. Every day, we sent a standard e-mail to every participant requesting a brief description, for our eyes only, of an event

that stood out in his or her mind from that workday. (See the sidebar "How We Studied State of Mind" for more details on the study.) Their remarks tended to make clear what they thought of the event—what it said to them about their work, their team, their organization, or themselves—and how it made them feel. Beyond that, we had participants rate themselves and each of their teammates monthly along various dimensions (creativity, work quality, commitment to the work, and contributions to team cohesiveness). Because whole teams participated in the study, we were able to triangulate responses from colleagues, strengthening our understanding of notable events and their effects. Finally, rather than relying solely on a team's diaries to assess its overall performance, we also included evaluations by knowledgeable people outside the team.

We were immediately rewarded with evidence of the richness and intensity of people's inner work lives and the proof that they were influenced strongly by the events of the day. What also emerged over time was evidence of the interplay among perceptions, emotions, and motivations—an inner work life system (See the exhibit "Processing Work Events: What Happens Inside.") This discovery fits well with what is already known about the human brain. Recent research in neuroscience has found that emotion and cognition (which includes perception of events) are tightly intertwined. Areas of the brain associated with rational thought and decision making have direct connections to areas associated with feelings. They do not exist in separate psychological compartments, and they interact in complex ways. Like any system, the brain cannot be understood simply by looking at each individual component. Inner work life functions the same way: It is crucial to consider all components and their interactions.

When something happens at work—some workday event—it immediately triggers cognitive, emotional, and motivational processes. People's minds start "sensemaking": They try to figure out why the event happened and what its implications are. These perceptions feed the emotions evoked by the event, and the emotions, in turn, feed the perceptions. Depending on what happens with these cognitive and emotional processes, motivation can shift, which, in turn, affects how people per-

Teresa M. Amabile is the Edsel Bryant Ford Professor of Business Administration at Harvard Business School, in Boston. **Steven J. Kramer** is an independent researcher and writer, based in Wayland, Massachusetts.

form their work. We discerned these processes in the diaries of every team we studied and in most of the people who worked on those teams.

Consider how the dynamics played out with Infomap, a nine-person team of information technologists at DataBrook, a subsidiary of DreamSuite Hotels, that we tracked through various projects across a five-month period. (We have disguised all names and other identifying information about the people and their company.) One urgent project, dubbed the "BigDeal" project, came up suddenly in the fourth month of our study and had enormous financial implications. DreamSuite was being sued for more than $145 million, and its legal department required a great deal of analysis of financial records in order to defend the company. Infomap had eight days to complete the work.

Perception. As the diary entries shown in the exhibit "The Reality Management Never Sees" reveal, the project had significant effects on the inner work lives of the team members. What first becomes clear in studying the diary entries is that people's "events of the day" caused them to form perceptions. Clark's diary entry for May 26, for example, describes the start of the project and the activity surrounding it. Clearly he is engaging in sensemaking, and he comes away with positive perceptions of the "extreme importance" of the work done in his office, the "problem-solving capability" of his team, and the "supportive" nature of management. We see the same kind of reflection by Chester as the project winds up on May 31. His sensemaking produces positive perceptions of the team's coleader (Ellen), the team itself, other groups in the organization, and top management. These perceptions were triggered by specific events—for example, the extraordinary efforts of Ellen, who rolled up her sleeves and worked alongside the team.

Emotion. We also see the impact of daily events on people's emotions. Helen is inordinately pleased when an upper manager brings refreshments to the team. Marsha reacts to an example of outstanding teamwork with great pleasure. The work atmosphere on May 31 is "happy and light," she notes—even though they were working on Memorial Day, which should have been a holiday for everyone. Chester's upbeat emotions on May 31 are likewise unmistakable.

There is evidence, too, even in the span of these few diary entries, of interplay between perceptions and emotions. When a high-level executive delivers bottled water and pizza to the people working after hours, not only does the event cause happy surprise, it also sends a real signal to the workers. That seemingly trivial event caused people on the BigDeal project to perceive their work and themselves as important and valued, which evoked additional positive emotions. Similar emotions arose when other colleagues and teams offered to pitch in, reinforcing the positive perceptions that team members had formed of those people—and leading, over time, to even more positive emotions.

Motivation. High levels of motivation are also on display in the BigDeal project diaries. The entry by Marsha on May 27, for example, reveals that she has just worked 15 hours straight. Yet she describes what she's just endured as "one of the best days I've had in months!!" She notes, in that entry, that "our entire office worked like a real team" and referred to their work as the "big project." Her previous diary entries allowed us to understand how her motivation on May 27 resulted from positive emotions and perceptions. We found, in those entries, that she often felt elated when the team worked closely together, and she perceived herself and her work as more valued when others in the organization signaled its importance. These effects of emotion and perception on motivation make perfect sense. If people are sad or angry about their work, they won't care about doing it well. If they are happy and excited about it, they will leap to the task and put great effort behind it. The same goes for perception. If people perceive the work, and themselves, as having high value, their motivation will be high. Just as important, if they perceive a clear path forward, with little ambiguity about what will constitute progress, motivation levels rise. The BigDeal project had all this going for it. People felt highly valued and certain about what needed to be accomplished. Ultimately, this translated to high performance on the project. Not only did the team get the work done on time, but its high quality made an immediate and measurable contribution to the company's success.

The BigDeal project is all the more striking in comparison with the other projects we

Would hidden observers watching you go through the day really understand your inner work life? Of course not.

Inner Work Life

tracked for this team. In other periods, we were able to see the same inner work life system operating—but in much less positive ways. Despite the experiences during the Big-Deal project, all was not rosy between the team and upper-level management. When, early in our study, an acquisition was announced, employees interpreted the event as a hostile takeover and reacted to it emotionally. Diary entries during that time used terms like "boneheaded" and "bigoted bunch of plantation owners" to describe top management. When layoffs were announced after the acquisition, the entire team perceived the process as unfair. They expressed considerable fear and anger in their diaries and a markedly decreased level of motivation ("People are walking around scared and afraid for their jobs" and "What kills me is, after this, they will turn around and wonder why everyone doesn't just throw themselves in front of a train for the company…what dopes"). In fact, during the entire time we studied the team—with the exception of the BigDeal project—the team members perceived their company's executive leaders as aloof and oblivious to the team's

good work and reacted with varying levels of sadness, anger, and disgust.

Were managers aware of the team's intensely positive perceptions, emotions, and motivations during the BigDeal project? Were they aware of its extremely negative inner work life at other times? Maybe. But when we met with the team, they made it clear that they generally displayed their emotions and described their perceptions only to each other or kept them entirely private. Our research suggests that most managers are not in tune with the inner work lives of their people; nor do they appreciate how pervasive the effects of inner work life can be on performance.

What Gets Done When People Have Good Days?

There is a long-standing debate among management scholars on the question of how work performance is influenced by people's subjective experiences at work. One side says that people perform better when they are happier and internally motivated by love of the work. Others assert that people do their best work under pressure and when externally

How We Studied State of Mind

Ten years ago, we set out on a quest to understand what really happens at work. As psychologists, we were fascinated by the unexplored territory of day-to-day life inside organizations and, more specifically, inside the hearts and minds of the professionals working in those organizations. Our aim was to explore daily inner work life—the emotions, perceptions, and motivations that people experience as they react to and make sense of the events of their workdays—and how it affects performance. Our questions were basic: What affects a person's inner work life? Is there anything predictable about how it is shaped by specific events unfolding in the workday and by the organizational context? Does inner work life affect performance? We decided that the best way to get to the heart of these questions was to collect daily diaries from the people themselves.

Over a period of three years, we recruited 238 professionals from 26 project teams in seven companies and three industries to

participate in our study. Over 80% of the participants were college educated, and all of the projects required complex, creative work for successful completion. Thus, the term "knowledge workers" fits our participants well. We e-mailed diary forms to the participants every day (Monday through Friday) during the entire course of their projects, asking them each to complete the forms privately at the end of the workday. The average project length was a bit over four months, but some were as long as eight or nine months. About 75% of the forms were returned to us completed and on time, yielding nearly 12,000 individual diary reports.

The diary form had several numerical questions, asking participants to rate their own perceptions of various aspects of the work environment, their mood, and their motivation that day, as well as their own work and the team's work that day. There was also an open-ended question asking people to list the main work tasks they engaged in that day. The most important ques-

tion was also open-ended; it asked people to briefly report one event that stood out in their minds from the workday.

Although this question simply asked for an event—a concrete description of something specific that happened and who was involved—we found that, very often, people didn't stop there. They told us, sometimes in great detail, about their perceptions of the event and the thoughts that it engendered. They told us about how the event made them feel. And sometimes they told us how it affected their motivation and performance that day. These were the data that led to our primary discoveries of how constant and pervasive inner work life is and how it operates as a complex system. Together with the numerical data we collected on the diary forms and many other sources of data on the participants, the teams, the projects, and the companies, the daily diary narratives served as the basis for our conclusions about inner work life, what affects it, and how, in turn, inner work life affects performance.

motivated by deadlines and competition with peers. There is research evidence to support each of these positions.

Having taken a microscope to this question, we believe strongly that performance is linked to inner work life and that the link is a positive one. People perform better when their workday experiences include more positive emotions, stronger intrinsic motivation (passion for the work), and more favorable perceptions of their work, their team, their leaders, and their organization. Moreover, these effects cannot be explained by people's different personalities or backgrounds—which we did account for in our analyses. Put simply, every moment that

they are performing their jobs, employees are "working under the influence" of their inner work lives.

So what do we mean by performance as it relates specifically to knowledge work? In settings where people must work collaboratively to solve vexing problems, high performance depends on four elements: creativity, productivity, commitment, and collegiality. We looked at each of these—using quantitative data from the monthly team ratings and the daily diary forms, as well as content analysis of the diary narratives—and mapped them against the three components of inner work life.

Processing Work Events:
What Happens Inside

Every worker's performance is affected by the constant interplay of perceptions, emotions, and motivations triggered by workday events, including managerial action—yet inner work life remains mostly invisible to management.

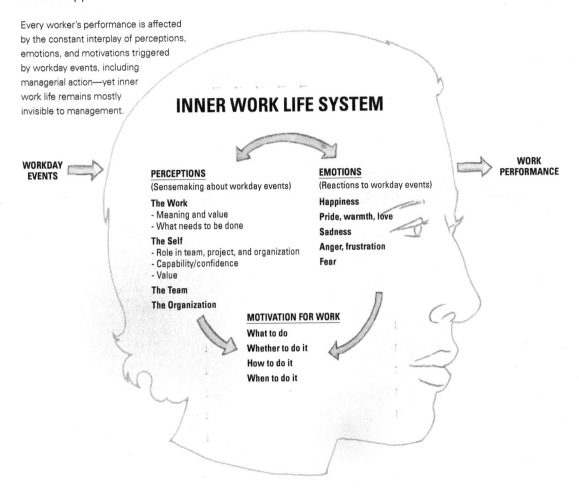

INNER WORK LIFE SYSTEM

WORKDAY EVENTS

PERCEPTIONS
(Sensemaking about workday events)

The Work
- Meaning and value
- What needs to be done

The Self
- Role in team, project, and organization
- Capability/confidence
- Value

The Team

The Organization

EMOTIONS
(Reactions to workday events)

Happiness
Pride, warmth, love
Sadness
Anger, frustration
Fear

WORK PERFORMANCE

MOTIVATION FOR WORK
What to do
Whether to do it
How to do it
When to do it

The Reality Management Never Sees

Most managers are unclear about what is going on in their employees' inner work lives and have even less of an idea of what events affect them. Consider these diary entries by the Infomap team at DataBrook, a subsidiary of DreamSuite Hotels. (We have disguised all names and company information. We've also edited the diary entries slightly for clarity and brevity.) This nine-person team of information technologists was tapped to work on an urgent assignment, dubbed "BigDeal," that had enormous financial implications. DreamSuite was being sued for more than $145 million, and its legal department required a great deal of analysis of financial records in order to defend the company. Infomap members worked long hours throughout the eight days they had been given to complete the project, including over a holiday weekend. Yet their spirits were remarkably upbeat. What was causing such a positive outlook despite the burdensome workload and schedule?

DataBrook upper management, which generally paid little attention to Infomap, spent time in the Infomap work area, checked frequently on the project's status, held back all other demands on the team's time, and provided encouragement and support in a number of small ways. Other groups within the organization cheerfully pitched in as needed. Ellen, the project manager and team coleader—who was recovering from surgery—not only did a great deal of the actual work but also served as a liaison between the team, upper management, and the internal clients. At the project's completion, although exhausted from the final five-day (and night) sprint, the team members were happy and pleased with the experience.

Clearly, management's engagement and behavior—even seemingly trivial and routine actions—made the difference. The diary excerpts tell the tale in people's own words.

Tuesday

I was called in to work on the BigDeal project. So DreamSuite has to go to court. So Big Deal. What about my vacation? **I'm angry about being called in. But I think I did some really good work under the pressure.** And I feel that I really supported the team. **HELEN**

TEAM MEMBER IS CALLED IN FROM VACATION

MAY 25TH

PROJECT KICKOFF

Wednesday

Today's significant team event was one that Tom and I were not involved in. Our office has been asked to produce some ad hoc data…[for the BigDeal project]. Our director, manager, and many users have been in the office all day to monitor our progress, while Ellen called Helen in from vacation to help address the problem. **While I was not involved, I've made this my event for the day because I was able to witness the extreme importance of the financial data that we handle in this office, the problem-solving capability of my team, and the supportive involvement of our immediate management.** It was a very positive experience. **CLARK**

MAY 26TH

Wednesday

More work today on the big DreamSuite lawsuit problem.

The boss's boss came by to offer encouragement. That was nice. He bought us bottled water! Not the cheap stuff I buy, either.

We are getting tired! Nobody's snapped yet, though. I have to admit that I love working under pressure. **HELEN**

Monday

I believe that the sense of accomplishment we felt after interacting so greatly throughout this entire ordeal is an event in itself.

From 05/25 through 05/30, I put in over 70 hours of work, and some other team members did the same – including Ellen, which was a constant worry for us due to her health. However, as usual, she was great. We ran into all sorts of unexpected problems and had to make all kinds of decisions. Several times, when we thought it was done, we would find a problem with the data, and sometimes almost start it all over again[....] This involved at least 5 members of our team, who worked around the clock, giving up holidays and even vacation. **It also involved people from other teams who were willing to help us (with a smile on their faces!), and what a fantastic help it was.** Looking on the bright side of things, this not only brought our team even closer, but our efforts were noticed by several other teams and top management as well, having them here with us over the weekend for support to the point of going out of their way to bring us food. **CHESTER**

Thursday

Hellzapoppin' around here the last week or so[....] People are working crazy hours, vice presidents are a dime a dozen in our office, and wonderful Miss Ellen is doing a great job keeping us going and still finding time to make a dozen status reports a day to every one of the VPs pestering her. Short-term, it's killing our productivity, but long-term, **Ellen is getting exposure under fire to some corporate bigwigs, which will enhance her career (and ours too,** by association, I suppose). **TOM**

Tuesday

Today my project manager attended a meeting at 9 AM to report to DreamSuite marketing the extraordinary efforts of our team over the last 5 days. We have worked 14 hours a day since last Thursday in order to attend to two major problems. The meeting went well and they commended our team effort. Today I get to go home at my normal time and work my normal hours. **The last 5 days are a blur and I am exhausted, but overall I'm feeling pretty good.** MARSHA

SENIOR MANAGEMENT VISITS PROJECT TEAM

MAY 27TH

MAY 31ST MEMORIAL DAY

PROJECT MANAGER REPORTS TO DREAMSUITES

JUNE 1ST

PROJECT COMPLETION

Thursday

We seem to be wearing down! My part of the project is almost finished – Thank God! Tonight's reward from the boss's boss – more bottled water and pizza! **HELEN**

Thursday

Today **our entire office worked like a real team again.** It was wonderful. We [...] have all worked around the clock to get a big project done. I have been here about 15 hours, but **it has been one of the best days I've had in months!!** MARSHA

Monday

I have been working straight through since Friday morning with just 7 or 8 hours off for sleep...I guess that's my event. I have been here with my project manager and one other team member. **I worked 14 hours Friday, 14 hours Saturday, 14 hours Sunday, and it looks like I will be here till midnight or later tonight.** The people I have been working with are wonderful, and **even though the hours have been stressful, the atmosphere has been happy and light.** MARSHA

Tuesday

Today, Ellen met with 20 to 30 people from DreamSuite Legal, DreamSuite Marketing, and DataBrook management to report the successful results of that activity. **When she returned, exhausted but happy, she told the worker-bees how well they had done, and we all applauded them.** Then she went home to get some sleep. **TOM**

First, we traced the influence of positive emotion on people's creativity—that is, their ability to come up with novel and useful ideas. Many previous studies, conducted as carefully controlled laboratory experiments, have demonstrated a causal relationship between emotion—also termed "affect" or "mood"—and creativity. Our diary study, which used real-world settings and a more naturalistic approach to measuring the effect of emotion on creativity, confirms that this is not merely a laboratory phenomenon. Positive emotion was tied to higher creativity, and negative emotion was tied to lower creativity. Across all 26 teams, people were over 50% more likely to have creative ideas on the days they reported the most positive moods than they were on other days. This finding is based not on people's self-ratings of creativity but on evidence in the diary narrative that they actually did creative thinking that day.

There was even a surprising carry-over effect. The more positive a person's mood on a given day, the more creative thinking he or she did the *next* day—and, to some extent, the day after that—even taking into account the person's mood on those later days. This was clearly the experience of Marsha on the Infomap team. Of her 68 diary entries, 20 contained evidence of creative thinking. Fully 80% of those creative-thinking days followed days on which Marsha's general mood was higher than average for her. Her negative emotions on the days preceding creative-thinking days were the mirror image. Her anger was below average on 75% of the preceding days, her fear was below average on 65%, and her sadness was below average on 60% of them.

Second, we looked at how people's perceptions of their work context affected creativity. Again, our diary study adds more detailed evidence to previous research findings. People in our study were more creative when they interpreted the goings-on in their organizations in a positive light—that is, when they saw their organizations and leaders as collaborative, cooperative, open to new ideas, able to evaluate and develop new ideas fairly, clearly focused on an innovative vision, and willing to reward creative work. They were less creative when they perceived political infighting and internal competition or an aversion to new ideas or to risk taking.

Finally, we analyzed the impact of motivation, the third aspect of inner work life, on creativity. Over the past 30 years, we have garnered a great deal of research evidence supporting what we call the intrinsic motivation principle of creativity: People are more creative when they are motivated primarily by the interest, enjoyment, satisfaction, and challenge of the work itself—not by external pressures or rewards. Most of this evidence comes from laboratory experiments. When intrinsic motivation is lowered, creativity dips as well. Our diary data add to the evidence. Our study participants were more creative in their individual work on the days when they were more highly intrinsically motivated. What's more, the projects distinguished by the greatest levels of creativity overall were the ones in which team members displayed the highest intrinsic motivation in their day-to-day work.

Our findings were quite similar when we shifted our focus from creativity to the other elements of performance: productivity, commitment to the work, and collegiality (specifically, contributions to team cohesiveness). People performed better on all these fronts when they were in a good mood and worse when they were in a bad mood. Productivity, commitment, and collegiality also increased when people held positive perceptions about their work context. At a "local" level, this meant perceiving that they were supported by their team leaders and colleagues, creatively challenged by their tasks, trusted to make decisions with reasonable autonomy, and given sufficient resources and time to complete assignments. More broadly, it meant they perceived the organizational context as collaborative and open, not rife with political game playing or crippling conservatism. Finally, intrinsic motivation levels predicted performance levels across the board. People were more productive, committed, and collegial when they were more motivated—especially by the satisfactions of the work itself.

Clearly, inner work life matters to performance—how creatively people will think, how productive they will be, how much commitment they will show to their work, how collegial they will be. And many of the events that shape inner work life are caused, directly or indirectly, by managers.

Most managers are not in tune with the inner work lives of their people; nor do they appreciate how pervasive the effects of inner work life can be on performance.

What Good Management Does

When we ask people in business to guess which events caused by managers have the greatest influence on inner work life, they often think of interpersonal events—the kinds of person-to-person encounters where, for example, the manager praises a subordinate, works collaboratively with a subordinate as a peer, makes things more fun and relaxing, or provides emotional support. Or the opposite. These sorts of events do, indeed, have a real impact on people's perceptions, emotions, and motivations. Recall what a difference they made to the BigDeal team.

But, interestingly, our research shows that the most important managerial behaviors don't involve giving people daily pats on the back or attempting to inject lighthearted fun into the workplace. Rather, they involve two fundamental things: enabling people to move forward in their work and treating them decently as human beings.

Enable progress. When we compared our study participants' best days (when they were most happy, had the most positive perceptions of the workplace, and were most intrinsically motivated) with their worst days, we found that the single most important differentiator was a sense of being able to make progress in their work. Achieving a goal, accomplishing a task, or solving a problem often evoked great pleasure and sometimes elation. Even making good progress toward such goals could elicit the same reactions.

Sometimes the successes were clearly important for the project. For example, when Louise (an Infomap software engineer coding a new version of a major program) solved a problem to bring her within reach of the goal, she wrote, "I figured out why something was not working correctly. I felt relieved and happy because this was a minor milestone for me. I am 90% complete with this version of enhancements." A few weeks later, she accomplished an important step on a different programming assignment: "Yippee! I think I completed part of a project that has been a pain in the butt! I am taking reports over to the user for their viewing pleasure." But even very mundane successes led to positive feelings. For instance, a diary entry by Tom, another Infomap programmer, said, "I smashed that bug that's been frustrating me for almost a calendar week. That may not be an event to you, but I live a very drab life, so I'm all hyped." This is the kind of joy that people feel when they can simply accomplish what they need to.

Not surprisingly, there is a flip side to this effect. Across our entire database, the worst days—the most frustrating, sad, and fearful days—were characterized by setbacks in the work. Again, the magnitude of the event is not important: Even seemingly small setbacks had a substantial impact on inner work life. On April 19, Tom's failure to make measurable progress in his work cast a pall on his day: "No event today, just the continuing frustration of the week—trying to install a fairly simple change in code to an enormously complicated method of installation and production execution. Honest, you don't want to hear the details." On April 12, Louise reported being irritable about an obstacle she couldn't get around. "I changed a program today and got a syntax error….I was angry with myself."

It was clear from the diary data that being able to make progress in the work is a very big deal for inner work life. The next question, then, is which managerial behaviors affect employees' ability to do so. Our research points to several: for example, providing direct help (versus hindrance), providing adequate resources and time (versus inadequate resources or unnecessary time pressure), and reacting to successes and failures with a learning orientation (versus a purely evaluative orientation). But one of the most important managerial behaviors turns out to be the setting of clear goals. People make more progress when managers clarify where the work is heading and why it matters. In our diary study, the teams that made greater progress had more events in which the project goals and the team members' individual work goals were clear or were changed carefully and where people knew why their work mattered to the team, the organization, and the organization's customers. By contrast, teams that made less progress reported more events that muddied, confused, or haphazardly changed the goals. Sometimes those teams would be given a goal by management, only to be assigned several other tasks that conflicted with that goal. Often, those teams had a sense of futility about their work, because of uncertainty about how or even whether their efforts would make a difference.

The people on the Infomap team generally made good progress in their work—on the

When we compared people's best days with their worst, the most important differentiator was being able to make progress in the work.

Inner Work Life

Because every employee's inner work life system is constantly operating, its effects are inescapable.

BigDeal project and others—and it was primarily because Ellen, the project manager and one of the team's leaders, relentlessly sought clarity from the team's clients about their needs and expectations. This clarity was sometimes hard to come by, and, in those instances, progress was impeded. Consider the following example, in which a client had requested a software development project with a firm deadline but with little more than a vague sense of what the final computer program was supposed to do. Repeatedly over several days, Ellen contacted the client manager to discuss specifics. Repeatedly, she was brushed off. Marsha, to whom Ellen had assigned the project, wrote in her April 6 diary:

> We had a meeting to discuss the CRR project that I have been working on; the meeting was with just Ellen and Helen. The users have never given us written requirements for the project, and yet they just sent us a note asking if we will make the May 6 deadline. I am just forging ahead and coding like crazy…here's hoping they like what they never have asked for. Ellen is trying very hard to get them to commit themselves.

Eventually, Ellen did manage to get specifications from the client team's manager, and, with a Herculean effort, Marsha did succeed in getting the project done well and on time. But all of Marsha's hard work before the specifications were nailed down was relatively directionless and based on supposition, which impeded both real progress and her own sense of accomplishment. By contrast, during the BigDeal project, the managers who needed the work done communicated in detail with Ellen from the outset to clarify the project goals, specify their needs, and explain to everyone involved why the project was so important. Although there were many technical problems to overcome, there was no ambiguity about the goal. The effects on progress were dazzling.

Managerial events facilitating or impeding progress may be so powerful because they have multiple direct and indirect effects on performance. The direct effects are fairly obvious. For example, when goals are not articulated clearly, work proceeds in wrong directions and performance suffers. Less directly, the frustration of spinning one's wheels sours inner work life, leading to lower motivation; people facing seemingly random

choices will be less inspired to act on any of them. And there is a further effect. When a manager's actions impede progress, that behavior sends a strong signal. People trying to make sense of why higher-ups would not do more to facilitate progress draw their own conclusions—perhaps that their work is unimportant or that their bosses are either willfully undermining them or hopelessly incompetent.

Manage with a human touch. None of this emphasis on the managerial behaviors that influence progress diminishes the importance of the interpersonal managerial events that we mentioned earlier—events in which people are or are not treated decently as human beings. Although such events weren't quite as important in distinguishing the best days from the worst days, they were a close second. We frequently observed interpersonal events working in tandem with progress events. Praise without real work progress, or at least solid efforts toward progress, had little positive impact on people's inner work lives and could even arouse cynicism. On the other hand, good work progress without any recognition—or, worse, with criticism about trivial issues—could engender anger and sadness. Far and away, the best boosts to inner work life were episodes in which people knew they had done good work and managers appropriately recognized that work.

•••

Peter Drucker once wrote, "So much of what we call management consists of making it difficult for people to do work." The truth of this has struck us as our ongoing analyses reveal more of the negative managerial behaviors that affect inner work life. But we have also been struck by the wealth of managerial opportunities for improving inner work life. Managers' day-to-day (and moment-to-moment) behaviors matter not just because they directly facilitate or impede the work of the organization. They're also important because they affect people's inner work lives, creating ripple effects on organizational performance. When people are blocked from doing good, constructive work day by day, for instance, they form negative impressions of the organization, their coworkers, their managers, their work, and themselves; they feel frustrated and unhappy; and they become demotivated in their work. Performance suffers in the short run, and in the longer run, too.

But when managers facilitate progress, every aspect of people's inner work lives are enhanced, which leads to even greater progress. This positive spiral benefits the individual workers—and the entire organization. Because every employee's inner work life system is constantly operating, its effects are inescapable.

Discovering how inner work life affects organizational performance is clearly valuable. But as researchers we hope we have also made progress on another front. Inner work lives matter deeply to the people living them. Studies of the modern workweek show that knowledge workers today, as compared with workers of past eras, spend more time in the office and more time focused on work issues while outside the office. As the proportion of time that is claimed by work rises, inner work life becomes a bigger component of life itself. People deserve happiness. They deserve dignity and respect. When we act on that realization, it is not only good for business. It affirms our value as human beings.

Reprint R0705D
To order, see the next page
or call 800-988-0886 or 617-783-7500
or go to www.hbrreprints.org

Inner Work Life

Understanding the Subtext of Business Performance

Further Reading

ARTICLES

How to Kill Creativity
by Teresa M. Amabile
Harvard Business Review
May 2000
Product no. 3499

In this earlier article by Amabile, the author focuses on creativity as one of the key dimensions of employee performance. Creativity gets smothered by managers much more often than it gets supported—though not intentionally. It's the business need for coordination and control that inadvertently undermines employees' ability to put existing ideas together in new and useful ways.

To foster creativity, you need to make people's work intrinsically motivating. How? Match people with assignments and teams that stretch them and present them with diverse perspectives. Give people freedom within the company's goals—by telling them what the goals are, but encouraging them to figure out how to achieve them. And let people know that what they do matters to you and the organization.

Building the Emotional Intelligence of Groups
by Vanessa Urch Druskat and
Steven B. Wolff
Harvard Business Review
March 2001
Product no. 620X

The quality of people's inner work lives is also influenced by their interactions with teammates and with other groups in your organization. You can promote positive inner work lives by helping your team strengthen its emotional intelligence (EI)—that powerful combination of self-management skills and ability to relate to others.

To build group EI, help your team be aware of and constructively regulate the emotions of 1) **individual team members**—by handling confrontation productively and treating one another in a caring way, 2) **the whole group**—by creating structures that let the group express its emotions and cultivating an affirmative environment, and 3) **other key groups**—by developing cross-boundary relationships to gain outsiders' confidence and showing your appreciation of other groups.

Harvard Business Review

To Order

For *Harvard Business Review* reprints and subscriptions, call 800-988-0886 or 617-783-7500. Go to www.hbrreprints.org

For customized and quantity orders of *Harvard Business Review* article reprints, call 617-783-7626, or e-mail customizations@hbsp.harvard.edu

Harvard Business Review
www.hbrreprints.org

U.S. and Canada
800-988-0886
617-783-7500
617-783-7555 fax

CHAPTER **1**

INTRODUCTION TO BUSINESS PROCESS MANAGEMENT

INTRODUCTION

In many organizations, businesses, nonprofits, and government agencies, the need for higher productivity, better quality, and speed has caused managers to look for techniques and methods to make improvements. This has prompted organizations to adopt methodologies such as Lean principles, Six Sigma, Lean Six Sigma, and Total Quality Management (TQM). While these techniques have led to significant improvements in some organizations, many others have been unable to sustain the momentum. The underlying problem relates to the disconnect between the execution of their strategy and the day-to-day processes that produce value for customers and returns to stakeholders. The primary reason for this disconnect is that these organizations fail to look at their interconnected processes as a whole. They only look at the software development process, or the business transaction process, or some other specific function of the business. It is important to improve the entire gamut of business processes to achieve the desired competitive edge.

The strategy of an organization provides it with *what* it should be doing. The processes of the organization provide it with *how* it should be doing that, or the tactical day-to-day operation of the organization. The solution to the problem of improvement can be found in creating a framework for the business processes. This framework must emphasize the capture and documentation of the business processes and the metrics defining the required

2   WHAT IS BPM?

level of performance for each of those business processes. In other words, the organization needs to focus on improving the maturity level of key business processes.

LINKAGE TO ORGANIZATIONAL PERFORMANCE

Most management teams believe that their organizations are process oriented, and they understand how their products or services are delivered to their customers. The reality is that they don't really understand how the work is actually performed. Business Process Management (BPM) is a methodology that provides the management team and the organization as whole with a clear perspective on how the work is actually performed.

Organizational performance requires managers to understand and execute strategy. The inability to execute strategy can be blamed on many factors:

- The economy
- The competition
- The traditional mind-set of the organization
- The marketplace

And so on. When this happens, managers embark upon all sorts of efforts, which are detailed in the current literature, to fix the problem. They might institute an initiative such as Six Sigma, Lean principles, or process reengineering, but if they don't have a clear picture of how their products or services are produced, they will get only marginal results. BPM provides management with a clear picture of how the work is performed.

WHERE BPM FITS

Business Process Management (BPM) consists of defining and managing the end-to-end, or value chain, processes of the orga-

INTRODUCTION TO BUSINESS PROCESS MANAGEMENT   **3**

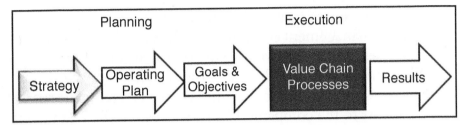

FIGURE 1-1.   The flow from strategy to results.

nization in order to achieve the outcome of improved execution. While this sounds very straightforward, the reality is that it either is not done or is poorly executed in most organizations. Figure 1-1 shows the flow of strategy to operational plans and indicates that the value stream processes are a gray area, but, when executed properly, they can provide the organization with the results required. BPM sounds simple, but it conflicts with traditional management thinking. The vast majority of management teams think of their organizations in terms of the functional organization chart. They have little or no understanding of how the work is actually accomplished.

Many organizations look at BPM as a means to automate their processes because they have made extensive investments in their software systems and have approached processes with automation tools that route data from one system to another, such as automated interfaces between enterprise resource planning (ERP), customer relationship management (CRM), and supply chain management (SCM) applications. However, executing a project to document business processes often requires more than just tying together these systems to create a "lights-out" automated process.

In reality, not all complex business processes can be fully automated, for the following reasons:

- People are an integral part of the process.

- Mistakes and exceptions occur unpredictably within the process.

- Complex process steps are not easily reduced to digital business rules.

4   WHAT IS BPM?

Any business process initiative needs to start with a strong process management component, such as BPM, to identify which processes require improvement, redesign, or reengineering to eliminate, or reduce, the steps that cause the greatest number of errors, result in wasted time or resources, or represent the most cost to the company. The processes may be automated, but as mentioned, the answer to process improvement is not always simply process automation. While it does incorporate process automation, this is not the sole purpose of BPM. Gaining control and managing your core business processes is the true objective of BPM.

The essential nature of any organization is people working together to achieve a common goal. For the overall effort to be successful, decisions and actions must be coordinated among individual contributors and between functional organizations.

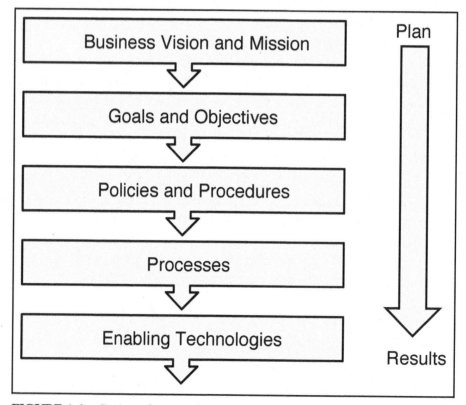

FIGURE 1-2.   Business framework.

They also must be consistent and yield satisfactory results at a reasonable cost. These factors are a result of the execution of business processes.

Generally, management teams follow an approach or work within a framework that is a top-down structure from planning to action, as illustrated in Figure 1-2, but it is typically focused on each functional organization, working in a silo. The real problem is that the processes that create value for customers are typically cross-functional in nature.

It should go without saying that the framework of most organizations also rests on an organizational commitment to quality. Six Sigma, Kaizen, Operations Excellence, Lean principles, Lean Six Sigma, and similar quality methodologies foster a continuous process improvement culture. The execution of these methodologies is typically performed in a functional organization setting. This tends to lead to suboptimizing processes that are, in reality, cross-functional in nature.

BPM FUNDAMENTALS

A simple definition of a business process is "a sequence of steps performed for a given purpose." Thus, a process is a predetermined course of action and a standing plan for people to follow in carrying out repetitive tasks in a systematic way. A process is a translation of general plans and policies into a standard pattern of decisions and actions. It establishes the actions required and the timing and sequence of activities. A business process can be described as a collection of related, structured activities or processes (a chain of events or activities) that produce a specific product or service for a particular customer or customers (internal or external to the organization). A business process usually cuts across several functions, for example, operations, logistics, sales, information technology (IT), finance, and legal.

BPM is a straightforward yet powerful method of looking beyond functional organizations and their activities and rediscovering the strategic or core business processes that actually make the business run—the value chain. It provides a discipline

6   What Is BPM?

that enables us to find our way through the complexity of the organizational structure and focus on the business processes that are truly the heart of the business. Figure 1-3 illustrates a typical organization chart for a business with examples of value chain processes shown horizontally to indicate their cross-functional nature.

The reason for applying BPM is to understand how the organization creates value for its customers through a collection of processes that make up the value chain. These business processes are the day-to-day activities that produce the products or services for customers and ultimately generate income and, ideally, profits. The management, improvement, and application of technology are the keys to success for any organization.

BPM provides a graphical representation of what needs to be managed, with an appreciation for the sequence of activities and a "right" level of detail. What is documented and measured is what

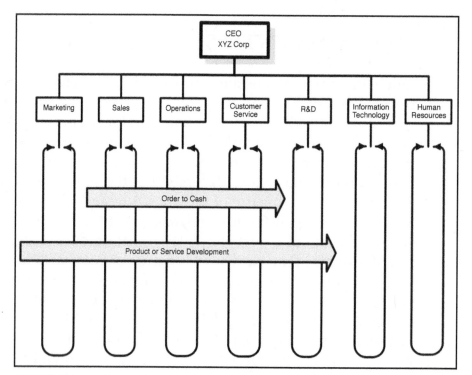

FIGURE 1-3.   A typical organization chart showing examples of value chain processes.

gets done in any organization. By using the measurement information, organizations can make decisions based upon facts, which leads to better decision making and smarter problem solving.

The benefits of BPM are that it:

- Provides a framework to identify the core business processes, the value chain, which directly creates value for customers and returns to shareholders
- Builds a graphical representation of the key business processes, the linkages between them, and the dependencies that allow shared understanding within the organization
- Defines how the day-to-day activities (work) are performed across the organization to deliver value to customers
- Offers insight into the way key organizational functions perform business processes and the cross-functional interdependencies
- Offers insight into what needs to be measured and how to measure it, as well as a linkage to a reward system
- Allows for optimal application of enabling technology once all of the preceding tasks have been accomplished

An organization can use BPM in several ways. The first and most important is to understand how business processes interact in a system. Once it has accomplished this task, the organization can use the BPM methodology to locate issues that are creating systemic problems. This allows the organization to evaluate which activities add value for its customers and identify business processes that need to be improved or redesigned. Management teams can now use any of the various process improvement methodologies available—Six Sigma, Lean principles, process redesign, reengineering, and so on. The net result is to mobilize employee teams to streamline, improve, and manage business processes in an efficient manner and to successfully initiate significant change that improves business results.

What is different about BPM is that it breaks down the traditional view of the organization, represented by the functional bias

8   WHAT IS BPM?

of the organization chart. Most managers believe that the work or activities of the organization are executed at the micro level, within their control. The reality is that the work is done horizontally across the organization—that is, cross-functionally—with many organizations contributing to the end product or service. The other problem encountered with this view is an "inside-out" perspective of the organization, whereby department focus is the preoccupation. BPM builds a system model of the way an organization actually operates. This model shows all of the interactions between the core, or value chain, processes and highlights the cross-functional nature of these activities. Putting the appropriate measurements in place sheds light on how the organization is performing from the customers' viewpoint.

BPM provides the organization with a method to align the processes (the value chain) across the enterprise and optimize their performance. Applying BPM allows the organization to model the flow of data, people, systems, and physical resources and thus model the processes in alignment with the business objectives and market needs. BPM practitioners consider the value chain processes of the organization a strategic asset that must be understood, managed, and improved to provide value-added products or services to the customers.

CONCLUSION

BPM differentiates itself as a management approach by focusing on aligning an organization with its customers through the execution of processes. It promotes efficiency and effectiveness by providing an understanding of how the core processes interact and by striving for continuous improvement and integration with enabling technology. BPM can be described as enabling the organization to be more efficient and effective by becoming a process-based organization rather than by using the traditional functionally managed approach.

CHAPTER   4

BPM LIFE CYCLE PHASES

DEFINING THE BUSINESS PROCESS MANAGEMENT PHASES

The value chain processes are a strategic asset of the organization, so they must be documented, measured, improved (when necessary), and managed like any other asset. By following the methodology outlined, managers have the added advantage of using enabling technology to help execute these processes more efficiently and effectively.

Business Process Management is a systematic approach to understanding, improving, and managing an organization. It is generally accepted to have four phases: document, assess, improve, and manage. (See Figure 4-1.)

THE FOUR BASIC PHASES IN THE BPM DISCIPLINE

- *Document*   *process modeling*
- *Assess*   *analysis and measurement*
- *Improve*   *design/redesign*
- *Manage*   *control*

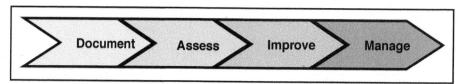

FIGURE 4-1.   Business Process Management life cycle phases.

24

DOCUMENT PHASE

The *document phase* focuses on several things:

1. Identifying the value chain processes
2. Creating a process inventory
3. Classifying processes as either core, support, or management
    - o   Core processes are the value chain processes.
    - o   Support processes are those needed to run the business but that do not directly add value to the product or service.
    - o   Management processes are those required to supervise and monitor business operations.

It is essential in this phase to keep the view of the processes at a high level. This is what might be called the 100,000-foot view, as though you are looking out the window of an airplane and see large blocks on the ground below. This phase seeks to identify between 5 and 10 value chain processes and should not become overly detailed. The number of processes needs to be manageable—an organization cannot sensibly manage over 100 processes. Also, when you get to this level of detail, you are falling back into the functional mind-set, because at this lower level of detail the process may be defined in terms of the work performed within only one functional organization. At the ground-level view of the processes you can get tied up in too much detail—work instructions, policies and procedures, business rules, and so on. (See Figure 4-2.)

Now that the value chain has been identified, the next step is to create a system-level map for the organization. This system-level map is a high-level graphical representation of the sequence of work as it flows through the organization. The primary interest is in the core processes or the value chain of the organization. An example of a system-level process map is shown in Figure 4-2.

26 WHAT IS BPM?

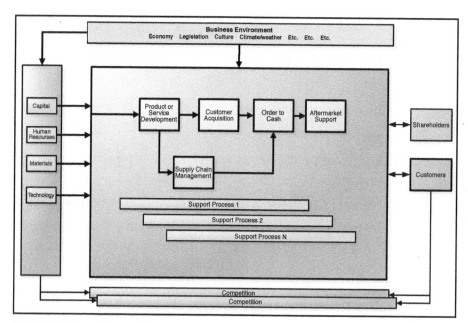

FIGURE 4-2. System-level process map.

The system-level process map shown in the central box of Figure 4-2 identifies the value chain processes. Although this diagram seems to identify generic processes, it does identify the five core processes of an organization. The names assigned to these core processes should not be the same as those of any functions on the organization chart.

There are several ways to go about developing the system-level map. The first is to adopt models that are available in the existing literature in this field or that can be found through various research groups. An example of such a model is the MIT Business Activity Model. The other method is to create the system-level map by working with the senior executives of the organization and facilitating a discussion about how the organization creates value for its customers. The rationale for identifying the core processes is simple: they function as a strategic weapon to achieve the organization's mission and vision by focusing on the critical business drivers. Identifying and assessing them can serve to clarify any inefficiency in the organization structure. We can then deploy improvement efforts against the critical goals of the business.

In order to identify the core processes, certain attributes must be identified:

- Strategic importance
  - o Processes that have a major impact on the organization and are crucial to its overall success.
  - o Processes that are relevant to the strategy, mission, and goals of the organization.
  - o Processes that, when executed efficiently and effectively, can provide a competitive advantage and that, conversely, can be a disadvantage if not performed efficiently or effectively.

- Attributes
  - o *Customer impact.* Processes that directly affect customers are always considered operational core processes. They are the value chain. Typical examples are customer acquisition, order to cash, and aftersales support.
  - o *Cross-functional.* These processes frequently cut across organizational boundaries and involve numerous functional, departmental, or even divisional business units.

Once the team members reach consensus on the system-level process map, they can proceed to creating core process maps.

DOCUMENTING THE CORE OR VALUE CHAIN BUSINESS PROCESSES

The goal of this phase is to document, review, and allow for detailed analysis of the way a given business process is currently performed in order to determine whether improvement is required.

1. Define the purpose:
   - o What is the primary result of the execution of this process?

28   WHAT IS BPM?

    o   What product or service is provided to the customer of this process?

    o   What constitutes an acceptable product or service?

2. Identify the boundaries:

    o   What is the starting point of this process?

    o   What is the trigger that starts this process?

    o   What is the end point of this process?

    o   How does the organization measure success?

3. Enlist the proper resources:

    o   Who are the employees that directly participate in these processes?

    o   Are these people who will speak freely about the actual performance?

    o   Do these people understand the day-to-day details of the execution of the process?

4. Control details: Work at the 50,000-foot level, taking it to the next level of detail (medium level, 20 to 25 process steps). Don't get bogged down in excessive detail.

5. Revise for accuracy:

    o   Review with other employees who did not participate in the original process documentation.

    o   Review with customers of the process. They may be external customers—those procuring the product or service. They can also be internal customers—other employees who use the output in order to perform their functions in other processes.

The actual development of the core process maps requires that you have a clear understanding of the sequence of steps in the process. The best source of information to create this level of detail is the employees who work in this process on a day-to-day basis. You need representation of the key people/stakeholders in all the functional organizations that participate in this process, in order to provide the needed information. The preferred format for a process map is called a *swimlane diagram*—a flowchart, with lanes for each functional organization that participates. The process steps are mapped according to the organization performing the work. An example of a swimlane diagram is shown in Figure 4-3. Here again the boundaries of the process must be clear: where it starts and ends, who and what are the triggers that start the process, and who is the ultimate customer for this product or service. In developing the sequence of events, the handoffs between the subprocesses must also be identified. A clear definition item for information handed off at each step and the recipient of that information is essential to having a usable process map.

This step generally requires some facilitation by professionals who can keep the discussion and level of detail on track. Trained facilitators with little or no direct knowledge of the existing process are ideal because they ask more probing questions and do not have any preconceived knowledge of the information being provided. The most effective way to develop this type of process map is by hanging a large roll of paper on a wall and using Post-it Notes to develop the process flow. This allows changes to be made easily, while providing a document for all participants to work with. Once the team has come to a consensus on the

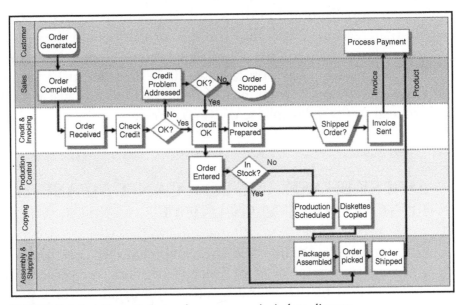

FIGURE 4-3. Cross-functional process map/swimlane diagram.

process flow, the process can be documented in an appropriate electronic format.

After the core process has been documented, there are a few more things that need to be done. First is to validate the process that was documented, which is accomplished by walking through the process. This is a critical step because it ensures that what has been documented is executed. This is where any work-arounds, undocumented procedures, shortcuts, unnecessary activities, and so on, may be found. Once any necessary adjustments have been made to the process map, the configuration of this document is locked down and placed in a safe repository for future use.

The next task is to identify the process owners for the core processes. The owners must be at a level where they will have total accountability for the end-to-end execution of the process. The rule of thumb is that the process owner for a core process should be the individual with the most to gain or lose from its proper execution. The biggest pitfall in assigning ownership is taking a functional bias. This is why the core processes should not have the same names as functional organizations. An example is the sample core process map in Figure 4-3. That process could have been named "Sales," which would then fall under the functional bias criteria. Realistically, this process was executed by several organizational entities and was named "Order to Cash" for that reason. Ownership for this process could be assigned to someone from any of the organizations—Sales, Finance, or Operations—as shown on the swimlane diagram in Figure 4-3. Once the process owner has been identified, you are ready to proceed to the assess phase of BPM.

ASSESS PHASE—"IF YOU CAN'T MEASURE IT, YOU CAN'T MANAGE IT"

Once you have documented the value chain or core processes, you need to develop a set of measurements or key process indicators (KPIs) to determine whether the organization's performance can or does meet its strategy, goals, and objectives. There are three fundamental types of measurements that you can make for these processes: efficiency, effectiveness, and outcome.

Efficiency, also called *process measures*, are typically measured within the process. These measures represent parameters that directly control the integration of the resources. The resources may be human resources, equipment, consumables, space, electricity, parts, and so on. Process measures always include the performance of subprocesses. The most important thing to recognize here is that process measures enable you to predict characteristics of the output before they are delivered to the customers. These process measures enable you to make adjustments to the process in a way that prevents errors or defects persisting to the end of the process, where correction is most expensive.

Efficiency is multifaceted and is focused in different areas:

- Cost measures are intended to minimize the amount of resources consumed in the process.

- Variation measures are intended to eliminate the waste associated with non-value-added activities and insert contingency into plans and designs that cushion uncertainty.

- Cycle time measures are intended to reduce the total elapsed time required to transform input into outputs.

Process effectiveness, or *output measures*, quantify the capability of the process to deliver products or services according to their specifications and/or customer requirements.

Process effectiveness is determined by examining products or services after they are produced, so essentially you are looking in the rearview mirror. If you wait until the process is complete and all of the required resources have been applied and then find a problem, it is the most costly place to make the correction. The worst-case scenario would be if the problem escapes detection and is discovered by the customer. Not only do you have an expensive problem to correct, but you have also caused a customer satisfaction issue, which can be costly in the long run.

32   WHAT IS BPM?

Process effectiveness measures quantify the likelihood of satisfying the customer's needs before the product or service is delivered. They are predictive in nature once you understand the customers' requirements and turn them into specifications.

Outcome, or *output (product or service) effectiveness measures*, determine how well the product or service performs for the customer by satisfying the needs and expectations of that customer. They are generally referred to as *measures of customer satisfaction*. Output effectiveness measures are retrospective and thus are obtained after the product or service is delivered to customers. They are necessary because they validate the process effectiveness measures that are being applied to control the day-to-day process activities.

Table 4-1 summarizes these three types of measures.

Now that you are acquainted with the types of measurements and the reasoning behind each type, you need to develop a set of process performance measurements, or key process indicators (KPIs). Here are the steps to follow:

1. Identify the output or outputs of the process.

2. Identify the customer base, and segment the customers when there are market or regional differences.

3. Learn the customers' requirements. Identify their needs and expectations by the various customer seg-

TABLE 4-1.   Measuring Performance

If you can't measure it, you can't manage it!

TERMINOLOGY	EXPLANATION
1. Process or efficiency	1. Resources consumed in the process relative to minimum possible levels
2. Output or effectiveness	2. Ability of a process to deliver products or services according to specifications
3. Outcome or customer satisfaction	3. Ability of outputs to satisfy the needs of customers

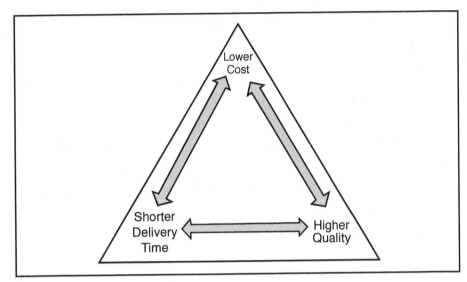

FIGURE 4-4.   What customers desire.

ments. (See Figure 4-4.) Listen to the voice of the customers. Customers typically want products or services:

o   Faster = shorter time

o   Better = higher quality

o   Cheaper = less cost

Translate the needs and requirements into operational terms. Ideally, they must be things that can be measured or that are critical to quality characteristics. It is better to have quantitative measures because they can be translated into the process measures that represent parameters that directly control the integration of the resources. That enables you to predict characteristics of the output before it is delivered to the customers.

The characteristics to consider when measuring output quality vary, depending on whether the output is a product or a service. The following lists identify the characteristics that are critical to product and service quality, respectively.

Dimensions of Product Quality

1.   Performance

2.   Features

34   WHAT IS BPM?

3. Reliability
4. Conformance
5. Durability
6. Serviceability
7. Aesthetics
8. Perceived quality or reputation of the organization

Determinants of Service Quality

1. Reliability
2. Responsiveness
3. Competence
4. Accessibility
5. Courtesy
6. Communication
7. Credibility
8. Security
9. Understanding of the customer
10. Tangibles

To reiterate: The output measures need to be quantitative. Product or service quality is characterized by its respective set of elements, shown in the preceding lists.

- Deliverables—attributes provided
- Interactions—customer experience

You need to ensure quality in both of these sets!

The objective of the *assess phase* is to determine measurements for the core processes. When an organization determines that there is an area where improvement is needed, management can direct improvement efforts to maximize benefit to the business. Process improvement is an organizational investment with a very nice payback, so you need to make the investment wisely. Chapter 5 contains a further discussion of process improvement.

In order to make decisions concerning process improvement or even automation, start with a quantitative assessment of the business's core processes. Then follow this procedure:

1. Create a gap analysis based upon these three criteria:
    1.1. Importance—what is the importance of making this improvement?
    1.2. Opportunity—how big is the opportunity if the improvement is successful (business case)?
    1.3. Feasibility—what is the likelihood of success? (This becomes critical in the initial stages of BPM implementation in order to create a model for further rollout.)

2. How to proceed:
    2.1. Rank the opportunities.
    2.2. Clarify the scope of improvement.
    2.3. Avoid suboptimization—don't improve one value chain process at the expense of another.
    2.4. Validate the choices.
    2.5. Differentiate product/service improvement from process improvement.

3. Develop and communicate an improvement/management plan.
    3.1. Create a shared understanding of beliefs, approach, and what needs to be done at the executive level and throughout the organization.
        3.1.1. Clearly state the vision.
        3.1.2. Clearly state beliefs, approach, and objectives.
        3.1.3. Communicate the business process framework and roles.
        3.1.4. Do it in multiple media.
        3.1.5. Do it frequently, clearly, and concisely.
        3.1.6. Create a sense of urgency.

36   WHAT IS BPM?

3.1.7. Focus on serving the customer.

3.1.8. Lead by example.

3.1.9. Don't overmanage.

IMPROVE PHASE

In a well-structured BPM initiative, the organization is driven by the need to efficiently and effectively satisfy the customers' needs and expectations. It is essential that the organization focus on customers and the processes that serve them—not on the CEO. This establishes process-oriented thinking, which is demonstrated in the organization's structure. You have identified process owners who are responsible and accountable for key processes. There is a drive to achieve excellence. The means and

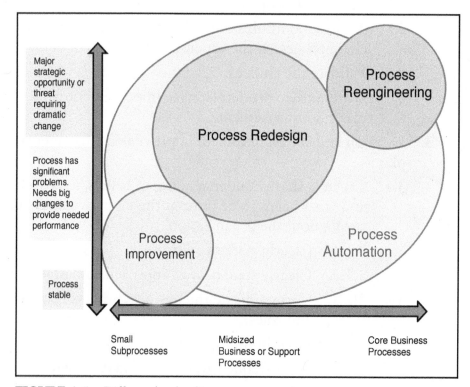

FIGURE 4-5.   Different levels of improvement projects.

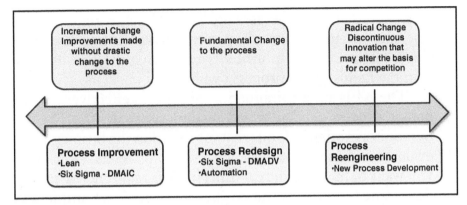

FIGURE 4-6.   Process and level of change.

systems are in place to move in the stated direction. Goals and objectives are clear and meaningful.

In the *improve phase*, the goal is to evaluate how an organization's resources can be used most efficiently. Typical objectives are reducing costs, shortening cycle time, and improving product or service quality. Implementing a redesigned process can have adverse effects in other parts of the business, so care must be taken to make the improvements with an understanding of the entire value chain. Good use of analytical tools is required to execute the improvements correctly.

There are several choices when it comes to selecting the process improvement tools. Six Sigma, Lean principles, Lean Six Sigma, process simulation, process redesign, and process reengineering provide the necessary analytical tools if properly applied to the problems. (See Figures 4-5 and 4-6.) A good understanding of these tools is required for process improvement. Chapter 5 examines the fundamentals of these tools and the differences in their application.

MANAGE PHASE

The *manage phase* of BPM encompasses the tracking of the core processes, so that their performance can be easily monitored. The key process indicators are tracked and reviewed periodically

38   WHAT IS BPM?

to ensure that the processes are performing as required, and, if not, appropriate actions take place to make the necessary corrections. The primary responsibility to see that these things happen is in the hands of the process owners.

The KPIs are a combination of process effectiveness or outcomes, process efficiency, and customer satisfaction. The degree of monitoring depends on what information the business wants to evaluate and analyze. Decisions need to be made about whether you want to measure in real time, in near real time, or over some determined period. Some of these decisions are influenced by the level of automation applied to the processes.

The role of the process owners is absolutely critical at this stage. Their accountabilities can be divided into four areas: leadership, documentation, performance, and improvement.

Leadership

1. Drives the alignment between corporate strategy and customer focus
2. Prioritizes improvement opportunities
3. Resolves process interdependency issues
4. Owns process education and training
5. Leads the change to a process-focused organization

Documentation

1. Maintains documentation of the inputs and outputs of the process
2. Maintains the process documentation and approves all changes
3. Prioritizes automation
4. Ensures controls are in place for accurate financial reporting
5. Audits process compliance

Performance

1. Implements KPIs and reports process performance on a regular basis

2. Achieves KPI targets, goals, and objectives
3. Prioritizes performance gaps
4. Ensures adequate process resources
5. Monitors data collection system for accuracy

Improvement
1. Analyzes performance gaps
2. Develops plans to close the gaps
3. Identifies the appropriate process improvement tools based upon the gap
4. Executes process improvement projects, across the process
5. Benchmarks and adopts best practices
6. Fosters new process improvement ideas

The role of the process owners is critical to any successful effort to apply BPM. This is why it is important that the selection process for ownership be kept at a high level—the executive level—and should not revert to the functional mind-set.

CHAPTER 5

PROCESS IMPROVEMENT (IMPROVE PHASE TOOLS)

FUNDAMENTAL CONCEPTS OF THE IMPROVE PHASE

When it comes to process improvement, there are many choices in terms of how to approach it. Most organizations adopt a particular methodology and use it for all improvement projects. This is not always the best answer. Process improvement should be approached as toolbox from which to choose the right tool to do the job. This toolbox contains many different tools and requires different levels of skills, training, and understanding. These tools include process mapping and improvement, process reengineering, Six Sigma, and Lean principles. Each has its strengths and weaknesses, determined by the problem to be solved. This chapter provides an overview of each of these methods and points out the respective strengths and weaknesses.

Process improvement activities come with a price. That is, you must expend resources to make an improvement. These resources include human resources—that is, people who would otherwise be performing their day-to-day job functions, specialists trained in process improvement, or even external consultants brought in to train personnel and execute the problem resolution. This can be expensive, but the payback from a well-executed process improvement can save many times the cost of the improvement effort.

40

PROCESS IMPROVEMENT (IMPROVE PHASE TOOLS)   **41**

Let's look at an example that illustrates the source of the cost savings. Figure 5-1 shows the basic concept of profit and loss in a business. The first bar shows the simple concept for a business: there is a cost to produce a product or service, and then there is a profit margin on top. Reality is better represented by the bars to the right in Figure 5-1. The second bar shows the cost to produce the product or service, profit margin, and the associated waste. This is realistically where most organizations operate, and one of the goals of process improvement is to reduce the waste. The third bar represents the result of competition in the market-place. To be competitive a business must lower its selling price. If the business lowers its price without taking action on its cost to produce and its waste, then it also reduces its profit. If the business is forced into a significant price reduction, the result could be a loss instead of a profit.

Process improvement activities are intended to reduce waste and improve the processes used to create a business's products or services. If the business acts on those effectively by using the various process improvement tools discussed in this chapter, then it's possible to achieve a result that resembles the bar on the far right in Figure 5-1. Not only can the business reduce the waste

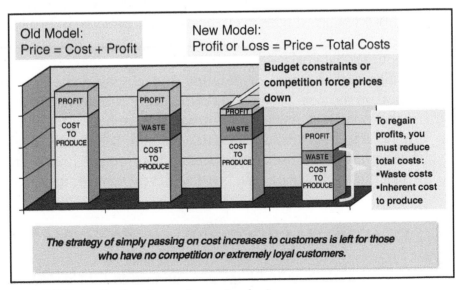

FIGURE 5-1. Profit or loss and waste in a business.

inherent in the process, it can also improve and simplify the process used to produce its products. This allows the business to maintain the profit margin and also potentially reduce prices and continue to be competitive in the marketplace.

Using process improvement tools in these areas creates opportunities for an organization to retain customers and provide them with what they want when they want it, as well as providing employees with the time and training to tackle work challenges.

Even a low percentage of defects or errors can result in numerous unhappy customers. Realistically, any organization wants to avoid any defects or errors that could result in the loss of revenue and poor customer satisfaction. Organizations might have been able to get away with high defect rates in the past, but it is definitely not a formula for long-term success. There has been a great deal of research suggesting that customers no longer sit around feeling sorry about their bad experiences with a product or service—they file a complaint and tell their friends and families about these negative transactions.

Keeping customers happy is good, and it is profitable for any organization. An increase in customer retention has been shown to increase profits by multiples of between 5 and 10. It has been shown that companies lose 15 to 20 percent of revenues each year to ineffective and inefficient processes—some suggest that this percentage might even be higher. Process improvement strives to make changes in order to meet short- and long-range organizational goals.

The earlier stages of defining and assessing the core processes of the organization operated at a relatively high level. At this point, the gaps in performance have been identified and the need to improve has been determined. It is time to start on the segments of those core processes that require improvement, which means moving to the "ground-level" view of the processes.

PROCESS MAPPING AND IMPROVEMENT

The goal of the methodology is to understand the current state, or "as-is," process, with the aim of documenting, reviewing, and analyzing the way a given business process is currently performed in order to improve upon it. The *current state process analysis* occurs in a team environment, using subject matter experts (SMEs) who work in this process. This serves as the basis for *future state process design* and *business case development.* When there are many critical areas that need attention, it is useful to develop a current state process map.

The current state process mapping session usually requires a facilitator (someone knowledgeable in process mapping and team dynamics) and a team of knowledgeable employees to work as a group to develop the current state process using the sequence laid out in the following list. Start the analysis at the 100,000-foot level, and then repeat the process for the identified 50,000-foot-level diagrams as needed for review of the situation and to clarify the gap identification.

- *100,000-foot level.* Low level of detail; provides a summary of a process at the system level. Captures the major phases of the value chain processes.

- *50,000-foot level.* Medium level of detail; breaks down a high-level process phase into the core process steps.

- *Ground level.* Captures process detail at the subgroup or even the individual level.

Figure 5-2 shows the high-level flow for this analysis effort. The steps in process mapping and improvement are as follows:

1. Identify the beginning and end of the process or the process segment associated with the need for improvement or gaps in performance.

2. Determine the key process participants and/or stakeholders.

3. Document the key process steps.

    3.1. Try to keep diagrams as simple and clear as possible.

    3.2. Make sure to document the process *as it actually is,* not how it should be.

44   WHAT IS BPM?

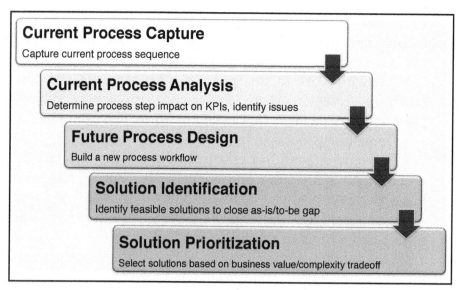

FIGURE 5-2.   Process mapping and improvement workflow.

4. Determine the activities and cycle times and other relevant KPIs. Business processes consist of three primary types of activities:

    o   *Value-adding activities* provide products or services to the customer.

    o   *Handoff activities* move work across organizational boundaries.

    o   *Control activities* provide a standard and measurement checkpoints in a process.

5. Determine the work and cycle time for each step in the process.

    o   Work time = labor hours directly attributable to process step

    o   Cycle time = elapsed time from step beginning to step end

6. Additionally, identify any relevant KPIs of the process. Examples could include:

    o   Number of units processed daily/monthly/yearly by the organization

    o   Number of units processed per person

PROCESS IMPROVEMENT (IMPROVE PHASE TOOLS)   45

o   Cost to process the unit or service

o   Customer or stakeholder satisfaction with the process

7. Start at measurable gaps in performance.

o   KPIs are measurable pains when they are not meeting goals.

o   Pains have *no quantitative value* if they cannot be measured.

8. Complete the process map with pains and indicators shown directly on it.

9. Vet the current state process map with the team.

10. Walk the process as documented, identifying pains and problems, stakeholders, and so on.

11. Future state process—design goal: to address key areas of improvement identified during the current state analysis.

12. Identify solutions:

12.1. Brainstorm solutions or process improvements and work with the group to narrow the list of solutions to those most valuable and most feasible.

12.2. Select and prioritize process improvements for inclusion in the "to-be" process.

12.3. Narrow the list of ideas, ranking them against the impact to address the problem and the overall implementation effort, considering such things as:

o   Ballpark cost, ballpark level of effort, degree to which the solution addresses the problem, degree of change management/estimated cultural acceptance

o   Type of value it would represent

o   Degree of difficulty to implement this solution

13. Develop the to-be process map using the subject matter experts and solution ideas generated.

14. Document the anticipated benefits of the process changes.

o   Use a level of detail necessary to fully communicate process pains or process improvement benefits.

14.1. Get early consensus for the "to-be" process maps.

15. Tailor the complexity of the implementation plan to the business's needs and expectations.
16. Execute the implementation plan.

SIMULATION

BPM provides the tools to create the model or flowchart of your critical business processes. It allows you to understand how the processes operate in your business. Once you have applied this methodology, the next logical step is to use this knowledge and add simulation to your tools.

Today's technology has provided an even more effective and useful tool: simulation modeling. If a picture (flowchart) is worth a thousand words, then one that logically simulates tasks and collects data has to be worth a million. Simulation models have the capability of considering complex interrelated tasks and structurally projected outcomes in a matter of seconds, providing users with validated, and reliable, results.

Simulation provides a less expensive means of experimenting with a detailed model of a real process to determine how the process will respond to changes in its structure, environment, or underlying assumptions. As you attempt to improve or streamline your processes to meet your current business conditions, simulation provides you with another tool. It allows for a better understanding of process changes with the goal of improving performance, while experiencing no disruption of normal business activity. Simulation modeling provides a structure and a method to evaluate, redesign, and measure process changes, while minimizing the amount of time spent, the resource utilization, and the risk.

When you combine BPM with process simulation, you have a powerful means by which to design, evaluate, and visualize new or existing processes without running the risks associated with conducting tests on a functioning business process. Dynamic process simulation allows organizations to study their processes from a systems perspective, thereby affording them a better

PROCESS IMPROVEMENT (IMPROVE PHASE TOOLS)   47

understanding of cause and effect, in addition to predicting out-comes. The strengths and capabilities of simulation make it an ideal tool for process redesign. It aids in evaluating, redesigning, and measuring, with the following benefits:

- Improved cycle time
- Effective use of resources/improved productivity
  - o   Non-value-added work
  - o   Wait times/queues
- Identification of critical process parameters
- Modification of critical process parameters
- Improved critical-to-quality parameters
- Improved customer satisfaction

During a process design or redesign project, simulation can assist in the following areas:

- Feasibility analyses
- Examining the viability of new processes while looking at various constraints
- Cost-benefit analysis or process evaluation
- Exploring the possibilities for the system in the future state
- Examining the performance metrics of a system in both current and future states
- Prototyping, once a future state vision for a redesigned process is generated
- Modeling implementation planning, risk assessment, and process design
- Disseminating information about the newly reengineered process to the organization

Simulation can assist in creative problem solving by provid-ing a less expensive way of testing ideas. Fear of the high cost of failure prevents people from coming up with creative ideas.

48   WHAT IS BPM?

Simulation allows for experimentation and testing, followed by selling the idea to management. The use of simulation can help to predict outcomes. For example, it could help in predicting the response to increases or decreases in market demands placed on a business process, analyzing how the existing infrastructure can handle the new demands placed on it. Simulation can help determine how resources may be effectively and efficiently allocated.

Conventional analytical methods, using static mathematical models, don't effectively address variation because calculations are made from constant values. Simulation looks at process variation, by taking into consideration the interaction among components, the appropriate statistical distribution, and time. It allows for a more sophisticated analysis of all the variables.

This approach used in simulation promotes total solutions by modeling the entire process. It provides insight into the capabilities of the process and the effect process changes will have on the inputs and outputs. The biggest bonus comes from using a simulation model for experimenting with process parameters without making changes to the functioning process as it exists. It allows practitioners to test more alternatives, lowering risk and increasing the probability of success, and it generates information for decision support.

The biggest plus in applying simulation can be cost effectiveness. As organizations try to respond quickly to rapid changes in their markets, a good working simulation model can be an excellent tool for prototyping and evaluating rapid changes. For example, a sudden change in market demand for a product or service can be modeled using a validated process model to determine whether the existing process can meet the new demand, either up or down.

Another use for simulation can be validating performance metrics. For example, the aim of a key business process may be to satisfy a customer within a specified time frame. Using a simulation model, this requirement could be translated to the time required to respond to a customer's request, which can then be designated as a key performance measure resulting in customer satisfaction. Simulation can help test the tradeoffs associated with process designs and allow for further analysis on parameters such as time to market, service levels, cycle time, production costs, inventory levels, and staffing levels. Simulation can provide a quantitative approach to establishing key performance metrics.

Simulation can also provide an effective communication tool. It can be used to introduce a new or redesigned process in a dynamic fashion. Using simulation to display the functioning process provides a powerful means of explaining the function of various components to those who will work in the new process; in turn, it helps them understand how it works and fits together in the big picture.

Businesses don't lose customers over typical performance; it is the extremes and variations in performance that make customers unhappy—for example, your business commits to answer the phone on or before the third ring 95 percent of the time, and it typically takes six to eight rings for a customer's call to be picked up. Simulation modeling is the most effective way to do the type of analysis required. It allows you to develop a staffing plan that enables you to answer the phone in three rings 95 percent of the time.

PROCESS REENGINEERING[1]

Business Process Reengineering (BPR) is radically redesigning an organization's existing processes. BPR, however, is an approach for redesigning the way work is done to better support the organization's mission and reduce costs. Reengineering typically starts with a high-level assessment of the organization's mission, strategic goals, and customer needs. Once the organization rethinks what it should be doing, it proceeds to rethink how best to radically redesign the processes.

Within the framework of this overall assessment of mission and goals, reengineering focuses on the organization's business processes—the steps and procedures that govern how resources are used to create products and services that meet the needs of

---

[1] Information in this section was compiled from Wikipedia and *GAO Business Process Reengineering Assessment Guide* (U.S. General Accounting Office, Version 3, May 1997).

50   WHAT IS BPM?

particular markets, market segments, or customers. As a structured ordering of work steps across time and place, a business process can be decomposed into specific activities, measured, modeled, and improved. It can also be completely redesigned or eliminated altogether. Reengineering identifies, analyzes, and redesigns an organization's core business processes with the aim of achieving dramatic improvements in critical performance measures, such as cost, quality, service, and speed.

Reengineering recognizes that an organization's business processes are usually fragmented into subprocesses and tasks that are carried out by various functional areas within the organization. As discussed earlier, there is no single process owner who is responsible for the overall performance of the entire process. Reengineering maintains that optimizing the performance of subprocesses can result in some benefits but cannot yield dramatic improvements if the process itself is fundamentally flawed. For that reason, reengineering focuses on radically redesigning the process as a whole in order to achieve the greatest possible benefits to the organization and its customers. This drive for realizing dramatic improvements by fundamentally rethinking how the organization's work should be done distinguishes reengineering from process improvement efforts that focus on functional or incremental improvement. Table 5-1 shows some of the areas of comparison between process improvement and process reengineering.

Process redesign using BPR principles generally starts with a clean slate. It is a great deal more complex, time consuming, and, above all, risky. BPR does not mean just change but, rather, dramatic change. What constitutes this drastic change is the remodeling of organizational structures, management systems, employee job responsibilities, performance measurements, incentive systems, skills development, and the application of IT. BPR can potentially impact every aspect of the way business is conducted today. Change on this scale can cause results ranging from enviable success to complete failure. There has been a great deal written in this area, and it is strongly recommended that before you embark down this path you apply some due diligence and investigate the successes and failures. Another effective method used to reengineer business processes is a Design for Six Sigma approach, which is discussed later in this chapter.

TABLE 5-1.   Differences between Process Improvement and Process
Reengineering

	PROCESS IMPROVEMENT	PROCESS REENGINEERING
LEVEL OF CHANGE	Incremental	Radical
STARTING POINT	Existing process	Clean slate
FREQUENCY OF CHANGE	Continuous	One-time
TIME REQUIRED	Short	Long
PARTICIPATION	Bottom-up	Top-down
TYPICAL SCOPE	Narrow, within functions	Broad, cross-functional
RISK	Moderate	High
PRIMARY ENABLER	Technology	Technology
TYPE OF CHANGE	Cultural/structural	Cultural/structural

SIX SIGMA

The roots of Six Sigma go back nearly 60 years, to the post–
World War II Japanese management breakthroughs and extend
through the "Total Quality" efforts in the 1970s and 1980s. Six
Sigma is a methodology that provides an organization with the
tools to improve the capability of its business processes. This
increase in performance and decrease in process variation can
lead to defect reduction and significant improvement in profits,
employee morale, and quality of product. Simply stated, the goal
of Six Sigma is to help people and processes deliver defect-free
products and services.

Three key characteristics separate Six Sigma from other
quality or process improvement initiatives. Six Sigma:

1. Is a customer-focused approach
2. Yields and tracks the returns on investment from projects
3. Changes how management functions

Six Sigma is just as much a business initiative as it is a quality
initiative. It's about preparing the entire organization to meet the
changing needs of markets, technologies, and customers.

52 WHAT IS BPM?

Six Sigma is a well-structured, data-driven methodology for eliminating defects, waste, or quality problems in all kinds of businesses—manufacturing or service, large or small—by making incremental process improvements. The methodology is based on the combination of well-established statistical process control techniques, data analysis methods, and the systematic training of personnel at every level in the organization involved in the processes targeted.

The following outlines the six major themes of Six Sigma.

1. *Focus on the customer.* Customer focus becomes the top priority. Improvement projects are measured by their impact on customer value and satisfaction.

2. *Fact- and data-driven management.* Rather than act on opinions and assumptions, Six Sigma clarifies what measures are necessary to gauge organizational performance, then gathers data and analyzes key variables. By doing this, problems can be more effectively defined, analyzed, and resolved permanently. These essential questions need to be answered to support data-driven decisions and solutions:

   o What information/data do I really need?

   o How do I use the information/data to its full potential?

   o Is my measurement system accurate enough for what I am doing?

3. *Processes are the key.* Improving processes is the way to build competitive advantage in delivering value to customers.

4. *Proactive management.* This methodology focuses on problem prevention and asking why things are done a certain way, rather than resorting to a reactive mode.

5. *Collaboration without boundaries.* By breaking down the barriers across organizational lines and between departments, Six Sigma works to negate competitiveness and miscommunication so that everyone can be working toward providing value to the customer.

PROCESS IMPROVEMENT (IMPROVE PHASE TOOLS)   53

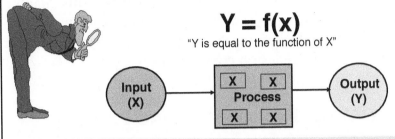

Y = f(x)
"Y is equal to the function of X"

Input (X) → X X Process X X → Output (Y)

•Inputs and processes (X's) have a profound effect on the output (Y)

•Controlling the inputs, their interactions and the processes will improve the output

•Attempting to manage results (Y) only causes increased costs due to rework, test, and inspection

FIGURE 5-3.   The essence of Six Sigma.

6. *Drive for perfection and tolerate failure.* If people see possible ways to come closer to perfection but are too afraid of the risks and consequences involved, they will never try. Any organization with Six Sigma as a goal must continue to strive for perfection, while being willing to manage and accept occasional setbacks.

There is a basic mathematical concept that states that Y (results) is equal to the function of X (inputs and processes). In business, we often expend all of our attention on the output (repair, redo, recycle), which always adds time and money.

Six Sigma forces us to look at the inputs and processes (function of X) as they affect the output (Y). Figure 5-3 shows a graphical representation of this concept. If we are able to control inputs and improve processes, the outcome will automatically improve without redoing anything.

When people say they are using Six Sigma, what do they mean? Which methodology are they using? The majority of the time they are using the DMAIC (Define, Measure, Analyze, Improve, Control) methodology because they already have existing products or services that are not performing up

54   WHAT IS BPM?

to expectations. Because it is more widespread, this chapter discusses DMAIC first, followed by a brief discussion of the other methodology—Design for Six Sigma (DFSS)—which can be used to design or redesign complete processes.

THE DMAIC PROBLEM-SOLVING PROCESS

DMAIC teams are created to solve process problems and to capitalize on opportunities. Led by a trained specialist, the teams usually contain 3 to 10 members representing the groups participating in the process being worked upon. The team will interact with the larger organization, interview customers, gather data, and talk to people whose work will be affected by the team's recommendations.

Steps in the DMAIC Life Cycle

- *Pinpoint and select the project.* Management reviews a list of possible projects and selects the most promising to be tackled by the team.

- *Structure the team.* A specialist (Black Belt or Green Belt) is selected. Management selects team members who have good working knowledge of the process but are not resistant to change.

- *Create the charter.* The charter includes the reason for pursuing the project, the goal, a basic project plan, the project scope, a business case, and a review of roles and responsibilities. It is the key document that provides the written guide to the problem and is drafted by the Champion and the team.

- *Train the team.* Training is carried out for the DMAIC tools and processes involved.

- *Perform DMAIC and implement solutions.* The team must develop pilots, training material, project plans, and procedures for their proposed solutions. The team is also responsible for implementation, measurement, and monitoring of the results for a meaningful set period of time.

- *Hand off the project.* Once the work of the DMAIC team is finished, the solution is handed off to the process owner. Often, some of the team members continue to work in the affected area to help manage the process or solution and drive it toward continued success. Other team members return to their regular jobs, but not without having learned some new skills and gained experience that can be applied elsewhere.

The DMAIC Problem-Solving Model

1. *Define the problem.* The team creates the charter that defines its focus and is the blueprint for the project. Next, the team identifies the customer. The team must listen to the customer and translate the customer's language into meaningful requirements. Then, a high-level diagram of the process is created. This diagram usually shows 5 to 10 major steps describing the current process. This diagram is meant to get all members of the team on the same page and to set the stage for the next major step in the process.

2. *Measure.* This step has two main objectives: to gather data to confirm and quantify the problem or opportunity and to begin searching for facts and numbers that offer clues about the causes of the problem. Also, the team looks at and analyzes the data collection system to ensure that the accuracy is statistically good enough to make the critical measurements. Three measures can be taken to determine the source of the problem:

    o *Input.* Anything that comes into the process to be changed into an output. Bad inputs lead to bad outputs.

    o *Process.* Anything that can be tracked and measured. These things usually help the team pinpoint and track the problem.

56   WHAT IS BPM?

o   *Output or outcome.* The end results of the process. End results focus on immediate results, such as deliveries, defects, or complaints, and more long-term impacts such as profits and satisfaction.

The team's first priority is the output measure. This baseline measure is the data used to complete the charter. Then a few input measures are targeted to begin getting data on potential causes. Once the team members have determined what to measure, they create a data collection plan, whereby they collect the data that is required. An initial sigma measure for the process being fixed should then be established.

3. *Analyze.* The team determines the root cause of existing problems. One of the principles of good problem solving is to consider many types of causes and to prevent biases or past experience from clouding judgment. Some of the common cause categories to be explored are procedures, techniques, machines, materials, measures, environmental elements, and people. The analysis begins by combining experience, data/measures, and a review of the process, and then forming an initial theory of the cause. The team then looks for more data and other evidence to see whether it fits with the suspected cause. This cycle of analysis continues, with the theory being rejected or refined until the true root cause is identified and verified with data.

4. *Improve.* A good team leader must recognize that many teams are tempted to jump right to this step from the start of the project. Solutions have to be carefully managed and tested. Changes have to be sold to the organization members whose participation is critical. Data must be gathered to track and verify the impact of the solution.

5. *Control.* The main goal of this step is to prevent the people and processes from reverting to old habits. There has to be long-term impact on the way people work. Specific control tasks that DMAIC teams must complete are:

o   Creating a monitoring process to keep track of the changes they have set out

PROCESS IMPROVEMENT (IMPROVE PHASE TOOLS)   57

o   Developing a response plan for dealing with problems that may arise

o   Selling the project through presentations and demonstrations

o   Focusing management's attention on a few critical measures that provide current information on the outcomes of the project

o   Ensuring support from management for the long-term goals of the project

o   Handing off project responsibilities to those who do the day-to-day work

The Six Sigma methodology for process improvement is DMAIC (Define, Measure, Analyze, Improve, and Control). This methodology is consistently used by organizations in all industries. Figure 5-4 provides a summary of some of the tools that may be used during this process improvement methodology.

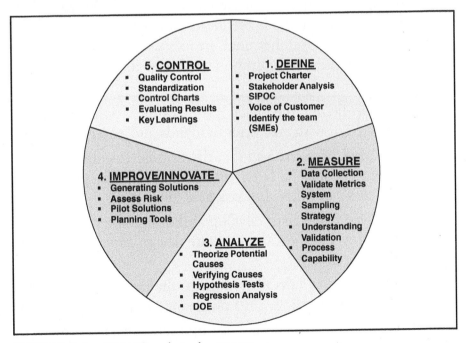

FIGURE 5-4.   DMAIC cycle tool summary.

58   WHAT IS BPM?

DESIGN FOR SIX SIGMA (DFSS)

DFSS is the methodology that is most commonly used by organizations that are redesigning or creating a new process. The steps or phases in DFSS are not as clearly defined as they are in DMAIC. DSFF is often defined differently by each organization that uses it. Producing such a low defect level for product or service launch means that customer needs and expectations must be completely understood before a design can be completed and implemented. There are many different acronyms that are used in performing DFSS. This section focuses on the most common ones.

Process design or redesign using Six Sigma is generally referred to as Design for Six Sigma (DFSS) or DMADV (Define, Measure, Analyze, Design, Verify). The objective is not to fix the process, as you would with DMAIC or Lean principles, but to replace it with a new and greatly improved one. The concept here is very similar to the concepts of process reengineering; that is, the process is beyond repair, and it needs replacement or at least a major redesign.

Process design/redesign is the creation of a new process to achieve exponential improvement and/or meet the changing demands of customers, technology, and competition. It must handle totally dysfunctional processes and reengineer them. DMADV is the most common road map followed for DFSS:

- *Define.* Define the goals of the design activity that are consistent with customer demands and enterprise strategy.

- *Measure.* Measure and identify critical-to-quality characteristics (CTQs), product capabilities, production process capability, and risk assessments.

- *Analyze.* Analyze to develop and design alternatives, create high-level design, and evaluate design capability to select the best design.

- *Design.* Design details, optimize the design, and plan for design verification. This phase may require simulations.

- *Verify.* Verify the design, set up pilot runs, implement the production process, and hand it over to the process owners.

LEAN PRINCIPLES

The core concept of Lean principles is to maximize customer value while minimizing waste. *Lean* means creating more value for customers with fewer resources. A lean organization understands customer value and focuses its key processes to continually increase it. The ultimate goal is to provide as close to perfect value as possible to the customer through the value creation process that has zero waste.

Process improvement using Lean concepts is a set of methods that focus on speed, efficiency, and elimination of waste. The goal is to maximize process speed by reducing waste. Waste is defined from the understanding of value from the standpoint of the customer. The key underlying concepts of the Lean approach are defined by the following five principles.

Five Lean Principles

1. Specify value from the standpoint of the customer—what is the customer willing to pay for?

2. Identify all steps in the value stream and eliminate those that do not create value. Identify the value-added, non-value-added, and business non-value-added work in the process.

3. Make value-creating steps occur in tight sequence.

4. As flow is introduced, let customers pull value from the next upstream activity.

5. As value is specified, value streams are identified, wasted steps are removed, and flow and pull are introduced, begin the process again and continue it until a state of perfection is reached in which perfect value is created with no waste.

In applying lean principles, you need to identify process steps and eliminate those that do not create value, ensuring that value-creating steps occur in tight sequence. Let customers pull value by producing at the rate of demand. Then do it all again.

Lean tools include several different things. The most important tool and the most closely related to BPM is *value stream map-*

60   WHAT IS BPM?

ping. This is a paper-and-pencil tool (which can later be stored electronically) that helps you to see and understand the *flow* of material and information as a product or service makes its way through the value stream. Looking at a process on a value stream map (VSM) allows you to see the process from end to end and identify steps where no real value is added (bottlenecks, delays, excess inventory, defects, and so on).

The goal of value stream mapping is to identify waste and provide a road map and an ongoing systematic approach for improvement in the value stream—it enables and optimizes flow. The originating VSM of a given process or product, often referred to as a *current state value stream*, becomes the baseline for improvement initiatives that eliminate non-value-added and wasteful activities and enable flow.

A VSM includes the materials, information, and processes required to design, produce, and provide a product or service for a customer. A VSM includes all elements (value-added, business non-value-added, and non-value-added) that occur to a product or service from its inception through delivery to the customer.

Value-added steps in a process are exactly that: work that is expended on a product or service for which a customer is willing to pay. Non-value-added work is the waste in the process. Business non-value-added work is the steps and activities in a process that the business is required to perform because of regulatory or business record-keeping requirements. In other words, this is work expended that does not add value to a product but must be done to meet other business requirements.

The VSM helps you visualize and optimize the whole rather than individual parts. It links material and information flows and shows total lead time, it identifies the ratio of value-added to non-value-added time, it provides a blueprint for implementation, it provides a framework for more quantitative tools, and it ties together Lean concepts and techniques.

Lean is all about learning how to reduce waste, or non-value–added, steps in a process. Typically 80 to 95 percent of lead time is non-value-added, or waste. Eliminate the waste in your process, and you will produce services more efficiently and more profitably. The acronym WORMPIIT is used to help you remem-

PROCESS IMPROVEMENT (IMPROVE PHASE TOOLS) **61**

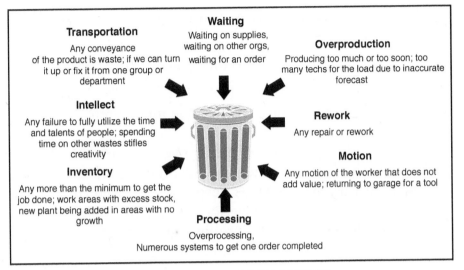

FIGURE 5-5. The eight types of waste—W.O.R.M.P.I.I.T.

ber the eight types of waste: waiting (W), overproduction (O), rework/defects (R), motion (M), [excess] processing (P), inventory (I), intellect (I), and transportation (T). See Figure 5-5 for examples of each category of waste.

KAIZEN

Another methodology, occasionally connected to Lean principles, is kaizen. In Japanese, the word *kaizen* means "change for the better." A kaizen event is intended as a relatively quick method to improve a process. The technique was developed for manufacturing, but it is now applied to service industries as well. It also takes advantage of the knowledge of the participants in the process to perform the analysis and recommend the changes and improvements. People who do the work are the ones who truly know how to improve it.

The cycle of kaizen activity can be described as follows:

1. Standardize an operation in the process.
2. Measure the standardized operation (find cycle time and amount of in-process inventory).

62   WHAT IS BPM?

3. Gauge measurements against requirements—look for the gaps in performance.
4. Innovate to meet requirements and increase productivity.
5. Standardize the new, improved operations.
6. Continue the improvement cycle indefinitely.

Table 5-2 provides a quick overview of the differences between the Lean approach and Six Sigma (DMAIC). The Lean approach does not delve as deeply into a problem and can be accomplished in a shorter period of time. Six Sigma tends to dig very deeply into a specific problem and can be time consuming due to the level of research and analysis required.

TABLE 5-2.   High-Level Comparison of Six Sigma (DMAIC) and Lean Principles

SIX SIGMA	LEAN
• Focus on subprocesses	• Remove waste, rework
• Remove variation	• Improve flow, velocity
• Research process problems	• Fast results
• Design more capable processes	• Focus on system
"An inch wide and a mile deep"	"A mile wide and an inch deep"

LEAN SIX SIGMA

Lean Six Sigma is a process improvement methodology that combines tools from both Lean and Six Sigma methodologies. The Lean methodology focuses on speed, and traditional Six Sigma focuses on quality. The combination of the two methodologies is intended to meld the two different tool sets into one, resulting in better quality faster. Figure 5-6 gives the highlights of the combination of the Lean and Six Sigma methodologies. Lean principles and DMAIC are directed toward redesigning and improving processes to meet the expectations of customers and to remain competitive. The Lean approach focuses on improving

PROCESS IMPROVEMENT (IMPROVE PHASE TOOLS)   63

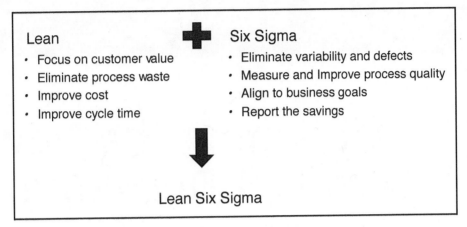

FIGURE 5-6   Lean Six Sigma.

the flow of products or services to the customer. DMAIC focuses on the quality of the product or service by reducing variation in the features and functions that the customer values. Nonvarying, predictable, reliable inputs to the process are necessary for process stability—a requirement before Lean principles can be rigorously applied to improve flow.

CONCLUSION

These process improvement tools are examples of how you can make the changes required in your business processes when they are not meeting the needs of the organization. They need to be applied by knowledgeable practitioners. As you look at the differing approaches in each of these methodologies it should be evident that each suits a specific purpose and it is not a one-size-fits-all approach to process improvement. These methodologies equip us with a toolbox from which to select the right tool for the right job.

Chapter **Eleven**

Managing the New Product Development Process

Skullcandy: Developing Extreme Headphones[a]

Founded in 2003 by Rick Alden, Skullcandy grew from a simple idea to a company with products distributed in approximately 80 countries and generating over $200 million in revenues annually. The company's core products, headphones with an extreme sport aesthetic, were sold in both specialty shops (e.g., skateboard, surf, and snowboard shops) and mass market channels such as Target, Best Buy, college bookstores, and more, and its iconic skull logo was recognizable by its core youth market worldwide. Rather than the simplistic and streamlined ear buds that dominated the headphone category throughout the 1990s, many of Skullcandy's designs had large ear cups with integrated amplifiers, akin to those worn by disc jockeys. As Alden notes, one of their first set of headphones, the Skullcrushers, provided sound that "rattles your head and bleeds through your eyes. It's a damage-your-hearing kind of bass."[b] The headphones also came in bold colors and patterns. Skullcandy had reinvented the headphone category from a commodity-like product to one that was highly differentiated and branded, with distinct designs that became as much about fashion and identity as functionality.

The Idea

In 2001, Rick Alden was riding up a ski lift and listening to music on an MP3 player when he heard his phone ringing, muffled in the pocket of his ski jacket. He fumbled around with his gloved hands, trying to get to the phone before it stopped ringing, and at that moment he thought "why not have headphones that connect to both a cell phone and an MP3 player?"[c] In January of 2002, he had his first prototype built by a Chinese manufacturer, and by January of 2003, he had taken out two mortgages on his home to launch his company, Skullcandy.[d]

Building an Action Sports Brand

Alden had an extensive background in the snowboarding industry, having previously founded National Snowboard Incorporated (one of the first companies to promote snowboarding) and having developed and marketed his own line of snowboard bindings. His father, Paul Alden, had played many roles in the industry, including serving as the president of the North American Snowboard Association, which helped open up ski resorts to snowboarders. His brother, David Alden, had been a professional snowboarder for Burton, and a sales representative for several snowboard lines. Thus, when Alden began creating an image and brand for the headphones, it only made sense to create a brand that would have the kind of dynamic edginess that would attract snowboarders and skateboarders. Alden could also use his deep connections in the snowboarding and skateboarding worlds to line up endorsements by pro riders and distribution by skate and snowboard shops. As Alden notes, "I'd walk into snowboarding and skateboarding shops that I'd sold bindings to or that I'd known for 15 years, and say, 'Hey, man, I think you ought to sell headphones.'"[e] Soon he was developing headphones that were integrated into Giro ski and snowboard helmets, and MP3-equipped backpacks and watches. The graphic imagery of the brand—which draws from hip-hop culture and features a prominent skull—helped to turned a once placid and commoditized product category into an exciting and important fashion accessory for action sports enthusiasts.

The company grew quickly. By 2005, the company broke $1 million in sales, and in the following year sold almost $10 million worth of headphones and accessories. By 2007, Skullcandy's products were selling in Best Buy, Target, Circuit City, and most college bookstores in addition to the core market of action sport retailers, for total revenues of $35 million, greatly exceeding even the stretch targets the company was shooting for. By the end of 2011, Skullcandy sales had reached $232.5 million—a 44 percent increase from its 2010 sales. In the same year, the company went public in an initial public offering that raised $188.8 million.

The company was careful in its approach to selling to the mass market, carefully distinguishing between products that were sold to the core channel versus to big box retailers.[f] Alden's philosophy was that "Conservative guys buy core products, but core guys will never buy conservative. In other words, we've got to be edgy and keep our original consumer happy, because without him, we'll lose people like me—old guys who want to buy cool young products too."[g]

In 2009, the company began to target the hip-hop music aficionado market by partnering with key music industry veterans such as Calvin "Snoop Dogg" Broadus and Michael "Mix Master Mike" Schwartz of the Beastie Boys. The collaboration with Snoop Dogg resulted in the "Skullcrusher"—a headphone with extreme bass amplification perfect for listening to rap music. The collaboration with Mix Master Mike was intended to produce the "ultimate DJ headphone."

Developing the Ultimate DJ Headphone

To begin designing a set of headphones that would uniquely target disc jockeys/turntablists, Skullcandy assembled a team that included Mix Master Mike (who would lend insight into the key factors that would make the "ideal" DJ headphone, as well as lending his own personal design inspirations), Skullcandy's Director of Industrial Design, Pete Kelly (who would translate the desired features into engineering specifications), an external industrial design company that could quickly transform the team's ideas into photo-realistic renderings, Product Manager Josh Poulsen (who would manage the project milestones and communicate directly to the factory in China where the product would be manufactured), and team members with backgrounds in graphic arts or fine arts who would explore the potential color palettes, materials and form factors to use.

The small size and informal atmosphere at Skullcandy ensured close contact between the team members, and between the team and other Skullcandy personnel. For example, the director of industrial design and the art director shared an office, and all of the graphic designers worked in a common bullpen.[h] The team would schedule face-to-face meetings with Mix Master Mike and the external industrial design company, and Josh Poulsen would travel to China to have similar face-to-face meetings with the manufacturer.

In the first phase, the team met to analyze what functionality would be key to making a compelling product. For the DJ headphones, the team identified the following key factors that would help to significantly improve headphone design:

- Tough, replaceable and/or washable ear pads made of antimicrobial materials (ear pads were prone to getting soiled or torn)
- Headphones that could be worn by "righty" or "lefty" DJs (DJs typically have a preference for leaning on one side while they work, and this side determines the optimal cable location)
- Sound quality that was not too clear, not too bass, and not too muddy (DJs typically were not looking for the clear quality of studio sound)
- Coiled cord or straight cord options (many DJs preferred coiled cords, whereas mass market consumers typically preferred straight cords)

Above all, the team had the mandate given by Alden to create "headphones that don't look like headphones."

The product's aesthetic design would be heavily influenced by Mix Master Mike. As noted by Dan Levine, "When you attach yourself to someone iconic, you try to figure out what inspires their form sensibilities. For example, Mike likes transformers, Japanese robots, Lamborghinis, furniture by B&B Italia . . . we use these design elements to build inspiration boards."[i] The team initially met for three straight days in Mix Master Mike's studio. Then, after the team had created 6–12 initial sketches, they worked to narrow the list down to three of the best and then fine-tuned those until they had one best sketch. The external industrial design firm created photorealistic renderings that precisely portrayed what the end product was to look like. At this point, marketing people could be brought into the team to begin developing a marketing strategy around the product. The marketing team used "sneak peaks" of renderings and nonfunctioning prototypes to gain initial sales contracts.

The next phase was an iterative process of commercialization and design refinement. According to Levine, "That's when it feels like you're swimming in glue because it never happens fast enough. The design phase is exciting. Once you have that design you get impatient for it to come to market, but you can only work as fast as manufacturing capabilities dictate, and building technical products takes time."[j] First, CAD files would be brought to China where a manufacturer would use a stereolithography apparatus (SLA) to create prototypes of each part of the headphone in a wax resin. As described by Alden, "you can't see the lasers—the part just rises up out of this primordial ooze. Then you can sand it down, paint it, and screw it to your other parts. This part will end up costing $300 compared to the 30 cents the part will eventually cost when it's mass-produced using injection molding, but it's worth creating these SLA parts to make sure that they're accurate."[k] SLA versions of the products were also often taken to the trade shows to solicit customer feedback and generate orders. Every week or two, the Product Manager would need to talk to the Chinese factory about building or modifying SLA parts, until eventually a 100 percent complete SLA product was achieved. At that point, it was time to begin "tooling" (the process of building molds that would be used to mass produce the product). This phase took four to six weeks to complete and was expensive. Several samples would be produced while final modifications were made, and then once a perfect sample was obtained, the tools would be hardened and mass production would begin. As Alden described, "after you've got everything in place—after you've made the first one, then it's just like making doughnuts."[l]

All of the steps of the project were scheduled using a Gantt chart (a type of chart commonly used to depict project elements and their deadlines). Project deadlines were determined by working backward from a target market release date and the time required to manufacture the product in China. In general, the firm sought to release new products in September (before the big Christmas sales season), which required having the tooling complete in July.

Every major design decision was passed up to Dan Levine for approval, and when the design was ready for "tooling" (being handed off to manufacturing), it had to be approved by Rick Alden, as this phase entailed large irreversible investments. Most of the people at Skullcandy were involved with many projects simultaneously. As Levine emphasized, "This is a lean organization. At Nike you can work on a single or a few projects; when you have a brand that's small and growing fast, you work on a tremendous number of projects, and you also hire outside talent for some tasks."[m] According to Rick Alden, "We used to try to manage everything in-house, but we just don't have enough bodies. We've discovered that the fastest way to expand our development capacity is to use outside developers for portions of the work. We'll develop the initial idea, and then bring it to one of our trusted industrial design firms to do the renderings, for example."[n]

Team members did not receive financial rewards from individual projects. Instead, their performance was rewarded through recognition at monthly "Skullcouncil" meetings, and through quarterly "one touch" reviews. For the quarterly reviews, each employee would prepare a one-page "brag sheet" about what they had accomplished in the previous quarter, what they intended to accomplish in the next quarter, and what their strengths and weaknesses were. These reviews would be used to provide feedback to the employee and to determine the annual bonus; 75 percent of the annual bonus was based on the individual's performance, and 25 percent was based on overall company performance. According to Rick Alden, "In the early days, we did things very differently than we do now. Everyone received bonuses based on overall performance—there were so few of us that we all had a direct attachment to the bottom line. Now with a bigger staff, we have to rely more on individual metrics, and we have to provide quarterly feedback so that the amount of the annual bonus doesn't come as a surprise."[o] The company also relied on some less conventional incentives. Each year the board of directors would set an overarching stretch target for revenues, and if the company surpassed it, Alden took the whole company on a trip. In 2006, he took everyone heliboarding (an extreme sport where snowboarders are brought to the top of a snow-covered peak by helicopter). When the company achieved nearly triple its 2007 sales goal (earning $35 million instead of the targeted $13 million), Alden took the entire staff and their families to Costa Rica to go surfing.[p]

According to Alden, the biggest challenge associated with new product development has been managing three different development cycles simultaneously. "You have your new stuff that you're coming out with that you haven't shown anyone yet—that's the really exciting stuff that everyone focuses on. Then you have the products you have just shown at the last show but that aren't done yet—maybe the manufacturing process isn't approved or the packaging isn't finished. You're taking orders but you haven't yet finished the development. Finally, you have all of the products you've been selling already but that require little improvements (e.g., altering how something is soldered, improving a cord, and changing the packaging). We have so little bandwidth in product development that the big challenge has been managing all of these cycles. We just showed a product in January of this year [2009] that we still haven't delivered and it's now May. We were just too excited to show it. But that's risky. If you don't deliver on time to a retailer, they get really angry and they won't keep your product on the shelf."[q]

Soon a flurry of new headphone brands had followed in Skullcandy's footsteps—including the wildly successful Beats by Dre. The functionality and style trends in headphones were relatively easy to quickly imitate. The key source of advantage, then, was to create brand loyalty among consumers and distributors. Alden noted that though he had initially patented some of the individual headphone models or technologies, given the time lag between patent application and patent granting, and the expense involved in using patent attorneys, patenting didn't make much sense in his industry—he preferred to just beat his competitors to market with great products.[r]

Discussion Questions

1. How does Skullcandy's new product development activities affect its ability to (a) maximize the fit with customer needs, (b) minimize development cycle time, and (c) control development costs?

2. What are some of the ways that Skullcandy's size and growth rate influence its development process?

3. What are the advantages of using Computer Aided Design (CAD) and stereo-lithography to create prototypes of Skullcandy's headphones?

4. If you were advising the top management of Skullcandy about new product development processes, what recommendations would you make?

[a] Skullcandy 10-K reports; www.hoovers.com
[b] Alden, R. "How I did it." *Inc.* (2008), September: 108–112.
[c] A. Osmond, "Rick Alden: Founder & CEO Skullcandy," Launch, March/April 2007 (http://issuu.com/lumin/docs/launch200703)
[d] Rick Alden interviewed by Melissa Schilling, May 5, 2009.
[e] Rick Alden interviewed by Melissa Schilling, May 5, 2009.
[f] Anonymous. 2008. Caught on tape: Rick Alden, CEO of Skullcandy. *Transworld Business*, October 24th.
[g] Alden, R. "How I did it." *Inc.* (2008), September: 108–112.
[h] Dan Levine, interviewed by Melissa Schilling, May 2, 2009.
[i] Dan Levine, interviewed by Melissa Schilling, May 2, 2009.
[j] Dan Levine, interviewed by Melissa Schilling, May 2, 2009.
[k] Rick Alden, interviewed by Melissa Schilling, May 5, 2009.
[l] Rick Alden, interviewed by Melissa Schilling, May 5, 2009.
[m] Dan Levine, interviewed by Melissa Schilling, May 2, 2009.
[n] Rick Alden, interviewed by Melissa Schilling, May 5, 2009.
[o] Rick Alden, interviewed by Melissa Schilling, February 20, 2012.
[p] Rick Alden, interviewed by Melissa Schilling, May 5, 2009.
[q] Rick Alden, interviewed by Melissa Schilling, May 5, 2009.
[r] Interview with Rick Alden, February 2012.

OVERVIEW

In many industries, the ability to develop new products quickly, effectively, and efficiently is now the single most important factor driving firm success. In industries such as computer hardware and software, telecommunications, automobiles, and consumer electronics, firms often depend on products introduced within the past five years for more than 50 percent of their sales. Yet despite the avid attention paid to new product development, the failure rates for new product development projects are still agonizingly high. By many estimates, more than 95 percent of all new product development projects fail to result in an economic return.[1] Many projects are never completed, and of those that are, many flounder in the marketplace. Thus, a considerable amount of research has been focused on how to make the new product development process more effective and more efficient. This chapter discusses some strategic imperatives for new product development processes that have emerged from the study of best—and worst—practices in new product development.

We will begin by looking at the three key objectives of the new product development process: maximizing fit with customer requirements, minimizing cycle time, and controlling development costs. We then will turn to methods of achieving these objectives, including adopting parallel development processes, using project champions, and involving customers and suppliers in the development process. Next we will look at a number of tools firms can utilize to improve the effectiveness and efficiency of the development process, including creating go/kill decision points with stage-gate processes, defining design targets with quality function deployment, reducing costs and development time with design for manufacturing and CAD/CAM systems, and using metrics to assess the performance of the new product development process.

OBJECTIVES OF THE NEW PRODUCT DEVELOPMENT PROCESS

For new product development to be successful, it must simultaneously achieve three sometimes-conflicting goals: (1) maximizing the product's fit with customer requirements, (2) minimizing the development cycle time, and (3) controlling development costs.

Maximizing Fit with Customer Requirements

For a new product to be successful in the marketplace, it must offer more compelling features, greater quality, or more attractive pricing than competing products. Despite the obvious importance of this imperative, many new product development projects fail to achieve it. This may occur for a number of reasons. First, the firm may not have a clear sense of which features customers value the most, resulting in the firm's overinvesting in some features at the expense of features the customer values more. Firms may also overestimate the customer's willingness to pay for particular features, leading them to produce feature-packed products that are too expensive to gain significant market penetration. Firms may also have difficulty resolving heterogeneity in customer demands; if some customer groups desire different features from other groups, the firm may end up producing a product that makes compromises between these conflicting demands, and the resulting product may fail to be attractive to any of the customer groups.

Numerous new products have offered technologically advanced features compared to existing products but have failed to match customer requirements and were subsequently rejected by the market. For example, consider Apple's Newton MessagePad, a relatively early entrant into the personal digital assistant market. The Newton was exceptional on many dimensions. It had a highly advanced ARM610 RISC chip for superior processing performance. Its operating system was object oriented (a feature that software programmers had been clamoring for), and Apple openly licensed the architecture to encourage rapid and widespread adoption by other vendors. Also, its weight, size, and battery life were better than many of the other early competitors. However, the Newton MessagePad was still much too large to be kept in a pocket, limiting its usefulness as a handheld device. Many corporate users thought the screen was too small to make the product useful for their applications. Finally, early problems with the handwriting recognition software caused many people to believe the product was fatally flawed.

Another example is Philips' attempt to enter the video game industry. In 1989, Philips introduced its Compact Disc Interactive (CD-i). The CD-i was a 32-bit system (introduced well before Sega's 32-bit Saturn or Sony's 32-bit PlayStation), and in addition to being a game player, it offered a number of educational programs and played audio CDs. However, Philips had overestimated how much customers would value (and be willing to pay for) these features. The CD-i was priced at $799, more than double the cost of Nintendo or Sega video game systems. Furthermore, the product was very complex, requiring a half-hour demonstration by a skilled sales representative. Ultimately, the product failed to attract many customers and Philips abandoned the product.

Minimizing Development Cycle Time

Even products that achieve a very close fit with customer requirements can fail if they take too long to bring to market. As discussed in Chapter Five, bringing a product to market early can help a firm build brand loyalty, preemptively capture scarce assets, and build customer switching costs. A firm that brings a new product to market late may find that customers are already committed to other products. Also, a company that is able to bring its product to market early has more time to develop (or encourage others to develop) complementary goods that enhance the value and attractiveness of the product.[2] Other things being equal, products that are introduced to the market earlier are likely to have an installed base and availability of complementary goods advantage over later offerings.

development cycle time
The time elapsed from project initiation to product launch, usually measured in months or years.

Another important consideration regarding **development cycle time** relates to the cost of development and the decreasing length of product life cycles. First, many development costs are directly related to time. Both the expense of paying employees involved in development and the firm's cost of capital increase as the development cycle lengthens. Second, a company that is slow to market with a particular generation of technology is unlikely to be able to fully amortize the fixed costs of development before that generation becomes obsolete. This phenomenon is particularly vivid in dynamic industries such as electronics where life cycles can be as short as 12 months (e.g., personal computers, semiconductors). Companies that are slow to market may find that by the time they have introduced their products, market demand has already shifted to the products of a subsequent technological generation.

Finally, a company with a short development cycle can quickly revise or upgrade its offering as design flaws are revealed or technology advances. A firm with a short development cycle can take advantage of both first-mover *and* second-mover advantages.

Some researchers have pointed out the costs of shortening the development cycle and rushing new products to market. For example, Dhebar points out that rapid product introductions may cause adverse consumer reactions; consumers may regret past purchases and be wary of new purchases for fear they should rapidly become obsolete.[3] Other researchers have suggested that speed of new product development may come at the expense of quality or result in sloppy market introductions.[4] Compressing development cycle time can result in overburdening the development team, leading to problems being overlooked in the product design or manufacturing process. Adequate product testing may also be sacrificed to meet development schedules.[5] However, despite these risks, most studies have found a strong positive relationship between speed and the commercial success of new products.[6]

Controlling Development Costs

Sometimes a firm engages in an intense effort to develop a product that exceeds customer expectations and brings it to market early, only to find that its development costs have ballooned so much that it is impossible to recoup the development expenses even if the product is enthusiastically received by the market. This highlights the fact that development efforts must be not only *effective*, but also *efficient*. Later in the chapter, ways to monitor and control development costs are discussed.

SEQUENTIAL VERSUS PARTLY PARALLEL DEVELOPMENT PROCESSES

Before the mid-1990s, most U.S. companies proceeded from one development stage to another in a sequential fashion (see Figure 11.1a). The process included a number of gates at which managers would decide whether to proceed to the next stage, send the project back to a previous stage for revision, or kill the project. Typically, R&D and marketing provided the bulk of the input in the opportunity identification and concept development stages, R&D took the lead in product design, and manufacturing took the lead in process design. According to critics, one problem with such a system emerges at the product design stage when R&D engineers fail to communicate directly with manufacturing engineers. As a result, product design proceeds without manufacturing requirements in mind. A sequential process has no early warning system to indicate that planned features are not manufacturable. Consequently, cycle time can lengthen as the project iterates back and forth between the product design and process design stages.[7]

FIGURE 11.1
Sequential versus Partly Parallel Development Processes

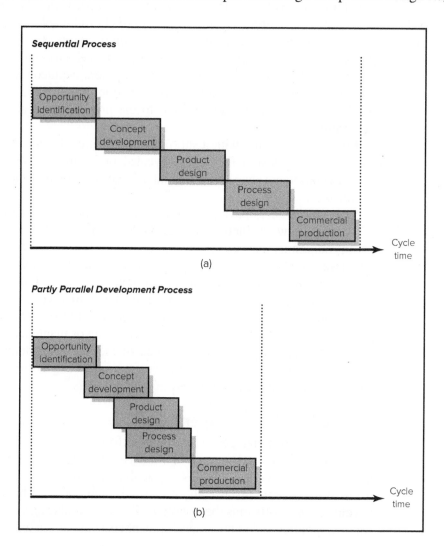

Theory in Action   The Development of Zantac

In the 1970s, Glaxo Holdings PLC of Great Britain was one of the larger health care conglomerates in the world, known principally for its baby food, but it needed a new hit product to stimulate sales. While contemplating research possibilities, the head of Glaxo's research laboratory, David Jack, attended a lecture by James Black, a Nobel Prize–winning scientist and researcher for U.S.-based SmithKline Beecham. During the lecture, Black described a new possibility for treating ulcers that involved compounds called H_2 blockers that would inhibit gastrointestinal cells from secreting acid. Jack was intrigued. Ulcers were a common problem, and thus represented a large market opportunity for an effective solution. Jack began experimenting with different compounds in pursuit of a formula that would be safe and effective. Unfortunately, researchers at SmithKline Beecham beat Glaxo to the finish line, introducing Tagamet in 1977. Tagamet revolutionized ulcer treatment, and sales grew phenomenally.[a]

Discouraged but not thwarted, Jack's team kept working. Other companies (including Merck and Eli Lilly) were also developing their own ulcer treatments, and Jack believed that beating them to market might still give the company a shot at a significant share. In that same year, the team came up with a compound based on ranitidine (Tagamet was based on a compound called cimetedine) that achieved the desired objectives. However, Jack realized that if Glaxo was going to beat Merck and Eli Lilly to market, it would need to radically shorten the typical 10-year testing period required to secure regulatory approval and bring the product to market. To achieve this, Jack proposed the first parallel development process used in the pharmaceutical industry. Instead of following the typical sequence of testing (e.g., from rats to monkeys, and from short-term toxicity to long-term toxicity), Jack proposed doing all of the tests concurrently.[b] This intensified development process could potentially cut the cycle time in half—to five years—however, it would also be expensive and risky. If the development efforts increased the research costs substantially, it would be much harder to recoup those expenses through sales of the drug.

Fortunately for Jack's team, Paul Girolami, Glaxo's director of finance, chose to champion the project. Girolami argued that the company should be willing to risk its range of decently profitable products for one potentially sensational drug, stating, "Having all your eggs in one basket concentrates the mind because you had better make sure it is a good basket."[c] Not only was he able to convince the company that it was worth investing in the shortened development process, but he also insisted that the product be modified so that it could be taken once a day (Tagamet required twice-a-day use) and so that the product would have fewer side effects than Tagamet. These features would help differentiate Zantac as a superior product, and it was hoped they would enable Glaxo to take share away from SmithKline Beecham. The development process was successful, and the product was ready for launch in 1982. To recoup its development costs, Girolami chose a premium pricing strategy for the product (one-third higher than Tagamet), arguing that its advantages would warrant its additional cost. He also insisted that the product be launched globally in all major markets, and he set up a distribution alliance with Hoffman-LaRoche to speed up the product's penetration of the U.S. market.

Girolami's strategies were successful, and by the end of the year, Zantac was stealing about 100,000 patients a month from Tagamet. By 1987, Zantac sales had exceeded Tagamet's, and by 1991 Zantac became the world's No. 1 selling prescription drug and the first drug ever to achieve $1 billion in U.S. sales.[d] Both David Jack and Paul Girolami were knighted, and Sir Paul Girolami was appointed chairman of Glaxo.[e]

[a] A. Corsig, T. Soloway, and R. Stanaro, "Glaxo Holdings PLC: Zantac," in New Product Success Stories, ed. R. Thomas (New York: John Wiley & Sons, Inc., 1995), pp. 242–52.

[b] Ibid.

[c] C. Kennedy, "Medicine Man to the World," Director 46, no. 4 (1992), pp. 106–10.

[d] "Anti-Ulcer Drugs: Too Much Acid," The Economist 318, no. 7700 (1991), pp. 82–84.

[e] Corsig, Soloway, and Stanaro, "Glaxo Holdings PLC: Zantac."

partly parallel development process
A development process in which some (or all) of the development activities at least partially overlap. That is, if activity A would precede activity B in a partly parallel development process, activity B might commence before activity A is completed.

To shorten the development process and avoid time-consuming and costly iterations between stages of the development cycle, many firms have adopted a **partly parallel development process**, as shown in Figure 11.1b.[8] Product design is initiated before concept development is complete, and process design is begun long before product design is finalized, enabling much closer coordination between the different stages and minimizing the chance that R&D will design products that are difficult or costly to manufacture. This should eliminate the need for time-consuming iterations between design stages and shorten overall cycle time. One type of parallel development process, **concurrent engineering**, involves not only conducting the typical product development stages simultaneously but also takes into account downstream stages of a product's lifecycle such as maintenance and disposal.

Parallel development processes are not universally endorsed, however. In some situations, using a parallel development process can substantially increase the risks or costs of the development process. If, for example, variations in product design require significant changes to the process design, beginning process design before product design is finalized can result in costly rework of the production process. Such risks are especially high in markets characterized by rapid change and uncertainty.[9] Furthermore, once process design has commenced, managers may be reluctant to alter the product design even if market testing reveals that the product design is suboptimal. It is precisely these risks that the stage-gate* process (discussed later in the chapter) attempts to minimize.

PROJECT CHAMPIONS

concurrent engineering
A design method in which stages of product development (e.g., concept development, product design, and process design) and planning for later stages of the product lifecycle (e.g., maintenance, disposal, and recycling) occur simultaneously.

A number of studies on new product development have suggested that firms should assign (or encourage) a senior member of the company to champion a new product development project.[10] Senior executives have the power and authority to support and fight for a project. They can facilitate the allocation of human and capital resources to the development effort, ensuring that cycle time is not extended by resource constraints, and help ensure that the project can sustain the necessary momentum to surmount the hurdles that inevitably will arise.[11] A senior project champion also can stimulate communication and cooperation between the different functional groups involved in the development process. Given that interfunctional communication and cooperation are necessary both to compress cycle time and to achieve a good fit between product attributes and customer requirements, the use of executive sponsors can improve the effectiveness of the development process. As of 2001, 68 percent of North American firms, 58 percent of European firms, and 48 percent of Japanese firms reported using senior managers to champion new product development projects.[12] An example of a successful use of project championing is described in the accompanying Theory in Action.

Risks of Championing

Vigorous project championing, however, also has its risks. A manager's role as champion may cloud judgment about the true value of the project. Optimism is the norm in product

*Note: Stage-Gate® is a registered trademark of Stage-Gate International Inc.

Research Brief   Five Myths about Product Champions

Stephen Markham and Lynda Aiman-Smith argue that a number of myths have become widely accepted about new product champions. While Markham and Aiman-Smith believe that product champions are critical to new product development, they also argue that for product champions to be effective, their role in the development process must be completely understood. Markham and Aiman-Smith conducted a systematic review of the theoretical and empirical literature on product champions and identified five popular myths:

Myth 1: *Projects with champions are more likely to be successful in the market.* Markham and Aiman-Smith's review of the empirical data on use of project champions found that projects with champions were just as likely to be market failures as market successes. Markham and Aiman-Smith point out that while champions may improve the likelihood of a project being completed, the factors determining its market success are often beyond the champion's control.[a]

Myth 2: *Champions get involved because they are excited about the project, rather than from self-interest.* Markham and Aiman-Smith report that empirical evidence suggests champions are more likely to support projects that will benefit the champion's own department.[b]

Myth 3: *Champions are more likely to be involved with radical innovation projects.* Empirical evidence from multiple large sample studies indicates that champions were equally likely to be involved with radical versus incremental innovation projects.

Myth 4: *Champions are more likely to be from high (or low) levels in the organization.* Markham and Aiman-Smith argue that there are myths about both high-level and low-level managers being more likely to be product champions. Though stories abound featuring prominent senior managers supporting projects, as do stories featuring low-level champions fighting vigorously for a project's success, empirical evidence suggests that champions may arise from any level in the organization. (Note that this research does not indicate champions from all levels of the firm are equally effective.)

Myth 5: *Champions are more likely to be from marketing.* Markham and Aiman-Smith argue that while anecdotal evidence may more often emphasize champions who have marketing backgrounds, an empirical study of 190 champions found that champions arose from many functions of the firm. Specifically, the study found that 15 percent of champions were from R&D, 14 percent were from marketing, 7 percent were from production and operations, and 6 percent were general managers. Interestingly, 8 percent of champions were potential users of the innovations.[c]

[a] S. Markham, S. Green, and R. Basu, "Champions and Antagonists: Relationships with R&D Project Characteristics and Management," *Journal of Engineering and Technology Management* 8 (1991), pp. 217–42; S. Markham and A. Griffin, "The Breakfast of Champions: Associations between Champions and Product Development Environments, Practices, and Performance," The *Journal of Product Innovation Management* 15 (1998), pp. 436–54; and S. Markham, "Corporate Championing and Antagonism as Forms of Political Behavior: An R&D Perspective," *Organization Science* 11 (2000), pp. 429–47.

[b] Markham, "Corporate Championing and Antagonism as Forms of Political Behavior."

[c] D. Day, "Raising Radicals: Different Processes for Championing Innovative Corporate Ventures," *Organization Science* 5 (1994), pp. 148–72.

development—surveys indicate a systematic upward bias in estimates of future cash flows from a project.[13] In the role of champion, this optimism is often taken to extreme levels. Managers may fall victim to escalating commitment and be unable (or unwilling) to admit that a project should be killed even when it is clear to many others in the organization that the project has gone sour, or the factors driving the project's original value are no longer relevant. While it is common to read stories about projects that succeed against all odds because of the almost fanatical zeal and persistence of their champions, bankruptcy courts are full of companies that should have been less zealous in pursuing some projects. Managers who have invested their reputations and years of their lives in development projects may find it very difficult to cut their losses, in much the same way that individuals tend to hold losing stocks much longer than they should due to the temptation to try to recoup what they have lost. Though the champion's seniority is an asset in gaining access to resources and facilitating coordination, this same seniority may also make others in the firm unwilling to challenge the project champion even if it has become apparent that the project's expected value has turned negative.[14]

Firms may benefit from also developing "antichampions" who can play the role of devil's advocate. Firms should also encourage a corporate culture open to the expression of dissenting opinion, and champions should be encouraged to justify their projects on the basis of objective criteria, without resorting to force of personality.[15] The accompanying Research Brief describes five myths that have become widely accepted about project champions.

INVOLVING CUSTOMERS AND SUPPLIERS IN THE DEVELOPMENT PROCESS

As mentioned previously, many products fail to produce an economic return because they do not fulfill customer requirements for performance and price, or because they take too long to bring to market. Both of these problems can be reduced by involving customers and suppliers in the development process.

Involving Customers

Firms often make decisions about projects on the basis of financial considerations and level of production and technical synergy achieved by the new product proposal rather than on marketing criteria. This can lead to an overemphasis on incremental product updates that closely fit existing business activities.[16] The screening decision should focus instead on the new product's advantage and superiority to the consumer, and the growth of its target market.[17] The customer is often the one most able to identify the maximum performance capabilities and minimum service requirements of a new product. Including the customer in the actual development team or designing initial product versions and encouraging user extensions can help the firm focus its development efforts on projects that better fit customer needs.[18]

Many firms use *beta testing* to get customer input early in the development process. A "beta version" of a product is an early working prototype of a product released to users for testing and feedback. Beta versions also enable a firm to signal the market about its product features before the product reaches the commercial production stage.

Other firms involve customers in the new product development process in even more extensive ways, such as enabling customers to "cocreate" the end product (this is discussed more in the section below on crowdsourcing).

Some studies suggest that firms should focus on the input of lead users in their development efforts rather than a large sample of customers. **Lead users** are those who face the same needs of the general marketplace but face them months or years earlier than the bulk of the market, and expect to benefit significantly from a solution to those needs.[19] According to a survey by the Product Development & Management Association, on average, firms report using the lead user method to obtain input into 38 percent of the projects they undertake. Not surprisingly, when customers help co-create an innovation, the resulting innovations tend to better fit their needs or expectations.[20] More detail on how firms use lead users is provided in the accompanying Theory in Action section.

lead users
Customers who face the same general needs of the marketplace but are likely to experience them months or years earlier than the rest of the market and stand to benefit disproportionately from solutions to those needs.

Involving Suppliers

Much of the same logic behind involving customers in the new product development process also applies to involving suppliers. By tapping into the knowledge base of its suppliers, a firm expands its information resources. Suppliers may be actual members of the product team or consulted as an alliance partner. In either case, they can contribute ideas for product improvement or increased development efficiency. For instance, a supplier may be able to suggest an alternative input (or configuration of inputs) that would achieve the same functionality but at a lower cost. Additionally, by coordinating with suppliers, managers can help to ensure that inputs arrive on time and that necessary changes can be made quickly to minimize development time.[21] Consistent with this argument, research has shown that many firms produce new products in less time, at a lower cost, and with higher quality by incorporating suppliers in integrated product development efforts.[22] For example, consider Chrysler. Beginning in 1989, Chrysler reduced its supplier base from 2,500 to 1,140, offering the remaining suppliers long-term contracts and making them integrally involved in the process of designing new cars. Chrysler also introduced an initiative called SCORE (Supplier Cost Reduction Effort) that encouraged suppliers to make cost-saving suggestions in the development process. The net result was $2.5 billion in savings by 1998.

Boeing's development of the 777 involved both customers and suppliers on the new product development team; United employees (including engineers, pilots, and flight attendants) worked closely with Boeing's engineers to ensure that the airplane was designed for maximum functionality and comfort. Boeing also included General Electric and other parts suppliers on the project team, so that the engines and the body of the airplane could be simultaneously designed for maximum compatibility.

Crowdsourcing

crowdsourcing
A distributed problem-solving model whereby a design problem or production task is presented to a group of people who voluntarily contribute their ideas and effort in exchange for compensation, intrinsic rewards, or a combination thereof.

Firms can also open up an innovation task to the public through crowdsourcing. Many crowdsourcing platforms such as InnoCentive, Yet2.com, and TopCoder present an innovation problem identified by a firm on a public Web platform, and provide rewards to participants who are able to solve them. Some crowdsourcing initiatives target people with special skills (e.g., TopCoder matches companies that need technical expertise such as software design with experienced specialists), while others solicit participation from the general public (e.g., Quirky allows individuals to share their

Theory in Action   The Lead User Method of Product Concept Development

Hilti AG, a European manufacturer of construction components and equipment, turned to the lead user method in its development of a pipe hanger (a steel support that fastens pipes to walls or ceilings of buildings). The firm first used telephone interviews to identify customers who had lead user characteristics (were ahead of market trends and stood to benefit disproportionately from the new solution). The lead users were invited to participate in a three-day product concept generation workshop to develop a pipe hanging system that would meet their needs. At the end of the workshop, a single pipe hanger design was selected as the one that best met all the lead users' objectives. The company then presented this design to 12 routine users (customers who were not lead users but who had a long, close relationship with Hilti). Ten of the 12 routine users preferred the new design to previously available solutions, and all but one of the 10 indicated they would be willing to pay a 20 percent higher price for the product. Not only was the project successful, but the lead user method was also faster and cheaper than the conventional market research methods the firm had used in the past to develop its product concepts. Hilti's typical process took 16 months and cost $100,000, but the lead user method took 9 months and cost $51,000.

Source: C. Herstatt and E. von Hippel, "Developing New Product Concepts via the Lead User Method: A Case Study in a Low-Tech Field," *Journal of Product Innovation Management* 9 (1992), pp. 213–21.

inventive ideas for others to review; companies or investors can then select the best ideas and help the inventor execute them). Many crowdsourcing programs offer some sort of prize to successful participants. For example, Ben & Jerry's asked its customers to invent their new varieties of ice cream flavors—the submitters of the best flavors were given a trip to the Dominican Republic to see a sustainable fair trade cocoa farm. However, individuals also often individuals participate for the sheer excitement and challenge of solving the problem,[23] or for social or reputational benefits.[24] For example, Fiat Brazil used crowdsourcing to develop a new concept car called the "Fiat Mio" ("My Fiat"). Fiat created a website inviting people to create the car of the future. More than 17,000 people from around the world submitted over 11,000 ideas—and not just in the design. Participants were invited to contribute solutions at every stage of the development process, including solving problems related to fuel efficiency and production. Participants received no rewards from their participation other than the pleasure they derived from interacting with Fiat and with each other, and the satisfaction they felt at having their ideas incorporated into the car. Hundreds of Fiat Mio's co-creators turned up at the unveiling of the car at a Sao Paulo motor show.

TOOLS FOR IMPROVING THE NEW PRODUCT DEVELOPMENT PROCESS

Some of the most prominent tools used to improve the development process include stage-gate processes, quality function deployment ("house of quality"), design for manufacturing, failure modes and effects analysis, and computer-aided design/computer-aided manufacturing. Using the available tools can greatly expedite the new product development process and maximize the product's fit with customer requirements.

Stage-Gate Processes

go/kill decision points
Gates established in the development process where managers must evaluate whether or not to kill the project or allow it to proceed.

As discussed in a previous section, escalating commitment can lead managers to support projects long after their expected value has turned negative, and the cost of pushing bad projects forward can be very high. To help avoid this, many managers and researchers suggest implementing tough **go/kill decision points** in the product development process. The most widely known development model incorporating such go/kill points is the stage-gate process developed by Robert G. Cooper.[25] The stage-gate process provides a blueprint for moving projects through different stages of development. Figure 11.2 shows a typical stage-gate process.

At each stage, a cross-functional team of people (led by a project team leader) undertakes parallel activities designed to drive down the risk of a development project. At each stage of the process, the team is required to gather vital technical, market,

FIGURE 11.2
Typical Stage-Gate Process, from Idea to Launch

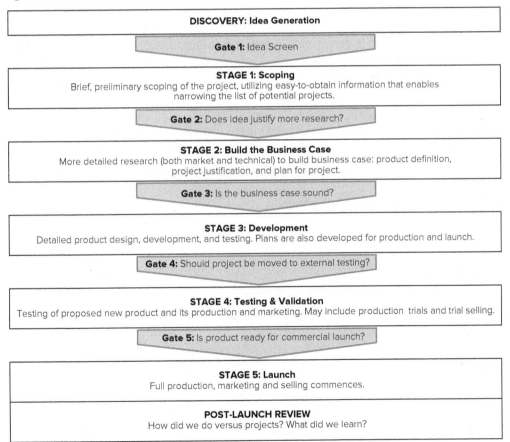

DISCOVERY: Idea Generation

Gate 1: Idea Screen

STAGE 1: Scoping
Brief, preliminary scoping of the project, utilizing easy-to-obtain information that enables narrowing the list of potential projects.

Gate 2: Does idea justify more research?

STAGE 2: Build the Business Case
More detailed research (both market and technical) to build business case: product definition, project justification, and plan for project.

Gate 3: Is the business case sound?

STAGE 3: Development
Detailed product design, development, and testing. Plans are also developed for production and launch.

Gate 4: Should project be moved to external testing?

STAGE 4: Testing & Validation
Testing of proposed new product and its production and marketing. May include production trials and trial selling.

Gate 5: Is product ready for commercial launch?

STAGE 5: Launch
Full production, marketing and selling commences.

POST-LAUNCH REVIEW
How did we do versus projects? What did we learn?

Source: R.G. Cooper, "Stage-Gate Idea to Launch System," *Wiley International Encyclopedia of Marketing: Product Innovation & Management* 5, B.L. Bayus (ed.), (West Sussex UK: Wiley, 2011).

and financial information to use in the decision to move the project forward (go), abandon the project (kill), hold, or recycle the project.

In Stage 1, the team does a quick investigation and conceptualization of the project. In Stage 2, the team builds a business case that includes a defined product, its business justification, and a detailed plan of action for the next stages. In Stage 3, the team begins the actual design and development of the product, including mapping out the manufacturing process, the market launch, and operating plans. In this stage, the team also defines the test plans utilized in the next stage. In Stage 4, the team conducts the verification and validation process for the proposed new product, and its marketing and production. At Stage 5, the product is ready for launch, and full commercial production and selling commence.[26]

Preceding each stage is a go/kill gate. These gates are designed to control the quality of the project and to ensure that the project is being executed in an effective and efficient manner. Gates act as the funnels that cull mediocre projects. Each gate has three components: *deliverables* (these are the results of the previous stage and are the inputs for the gate review), *criteria* (these are the questions or metrics used to make the go/kill decision), and *outputs* (these are the results of the gate review process and may include a decision such as go, kill, hold, or recycle; outputs should also include an action plan for the dates and deliverables of the next gate).

Because each stage of a development project typically costs more than the stage preceding it, breaking down the process into stages deconstructs the development investment into a series of incremental commitments. Expenditures increase only as uncertainty decreases. Figure 11.3 shows the escalation costs and cycle time for each stage of a typical development process in a manufacturing industry.

Many companies have adapted the stage-gate process to more specifically meet the needs of their firm or industry. For example, while managers at Exxon were strong advocates of using a stage-gate process to track and manage development projects, they also felt that the standard five-stage system did not adequately address the needs

FIGURE 11.3

Escalation of Development Time and Costs by Stage

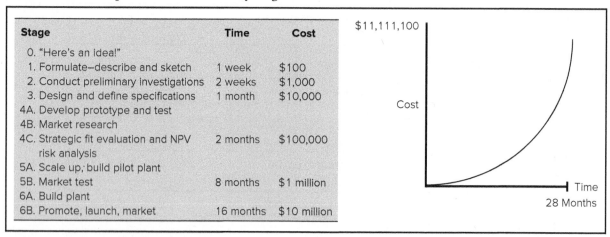

Stage	Time	Cost
0. "Here's an idea!"		
1. Formulate—describe and sketch	1 week	$100
2. Conduct preliminary investigations	2 weeks	$1,000
3. Design and define specifications	1 month	$10,000
4A. Develop prototype and test		
4B. Market research		
4C. Strategic fit evaluation and NPV risk analysis	2 months	$100,000
5A. Scale up; build pilot plant		
5B. Market test	8 months	$1 million
6A. Build plant		
6B. Promote, launch, market	16 months	$10 million

$11,111,100

Cost

Time
28 Months

Source: From Frederick D. Buggie, "Set the 'Fuzzy Front End' in Concrete," *Research Technology Management*, vol. 45, no. 4, July–August 2002. Reprinted with permission of Industrial Research Institute.

FIGURE 11.4
Exxon Research and Engineering's Stage-Gate System

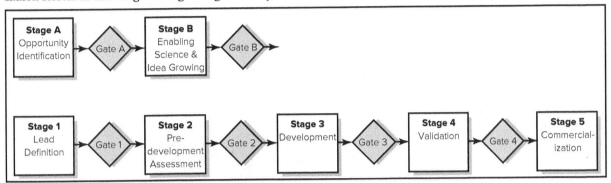

of a company in which basic research was a primary component in generating innovations. Exxon managers created their own extended stage-gate system to include directed basic research. The resulting stage-gate system included two basic research stages (Stages A and B in Figure 11.4) and five applied research and development stages. In Stage A, the company identifies the potential business incentives and competitive advantages of an envisioned technology. The company then develops a basic research plan that establishes specific scientific deliverables, the methods of achieving these deliverables, and the required resources. In Stage B, Exxon's research division begins to execute the plan developed in Stage A, using scientific methods to generate leads for addressing the business opportunity. Stage 1 then identifies the best leads, using "proof-of-principle" assessments to establish whether the leads are feasible.[27] Stages 2 through 5 proceed according to a typical stage-gate process.

According to studies by the Product Development and Management Association, nearly 60 percent of firms (including IBM, Procter & Gamble, 3M, General Motors, and Corning) use some type of stage-gate process to manage their new product development process. Corning has made the process mandatory for all information system development projects, and Corning managers believe that the process enables them to better estimate the potential payback of any project under consideration. They also report that the stage-gate process has reduced development time, allows them to identify projects that should be killed, and increases the ratio of internally developed products that result in commercial projects.[28]

Quality Function Deployment (QFD)—The House of Quality

QFD was developed in Japan as a comprehensive process for improving the communication and coordination among engineering, marketing, and manufacturing personnel.[29] It achieves this by taking managers through a problem-solving process in a very structured fashion. The organizing framework for QFD is the "house of quality" (see Figure 11.5). The house of quality is a matrix that maps customer requirements against product attributes. This matrix is completed in a series of steps.

1. The team must first identify customer requirements. In Figure 11.5, market research has identified five attributes that customers value most in a car door: it is easy to open and close, it stays open on a hill, it does not leak in the rain, it isolates the occupant from road noise, and it protects the passengers in the event of crashes.

FIGURE 11.5

Quality Function Deployment House of Quality for a Car Door

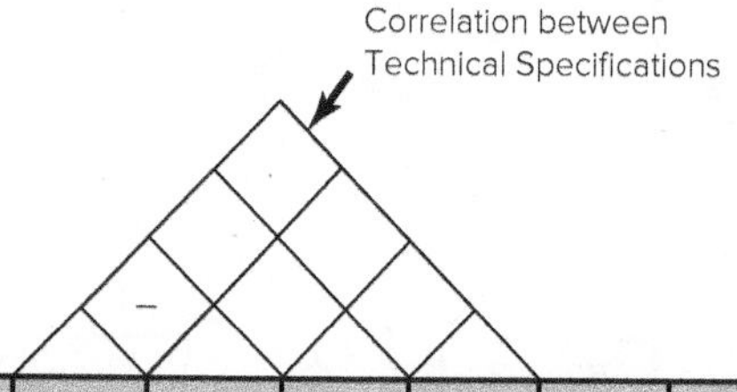

Customer Requirements	Engineering Attributes	Importance	Weight of Door	Stiffness of Hinge	Tightness of Door and Seal	Tightness of Window Seal	Competitor A	Competitor B	Evaluation of New Design
	Easy to Open	15	9	3			7	4	
	Stays Open on Hill	10	3	9			6	7	
	Does Not Leak	35			9	9	7	6	
	Isolates Occupant from Road Noise	20	1		9	9	4	7	
	Crash Protection	20	9				4	7	
Relative Importance of Each Engineering Attribute			365	135	495	495			
Design Targets									

2. The team weights the customer requirements in terms of their relative importance from a customer's perspective. This information might be obtained from focus group sessions or direct interaction with the customers. The weights are typically entered as percentages, so that the complete list totals 100 percent.

3. The team identifies the engineering attributes that drive the performance of the product—in this case the car door. In Figure 11.5, four attributes are highlighted: the weight of the door, the stiffness of the door hinge (a stiff hinge helps the door stay open on a hill), the tightness of the door seal, and the tightness of the window seal.

4. The team enters the correlations between the different engineering attributes to assess the degree to which one characteristic may positively or negatively affect another. The correlations are entered into the matrix that creates the peaked roof of the house. In this case, the negative sign between door weight and hinge stiffness indicates that a heavy door reduces the stiffness of the hinge.

5. The team fills in the body of the central matrix. Each cell in the matrix indicates the relationship between an engineering attribute and a customer requirement. A number (in this example, one, three, or nine) is placed in the cell located at the intersection of each row (customer requirements) with each column (engineering attributes), which represents the strength of relationship between them. A value of one indicates a weak relationship, a three indicates a moderate relationship and

a nine indicates a strong relationship. The cell is left blank if there is no relationship. The ease of opening the door, for example, is strongly related to the weight of the door and moderately related to the stiffness of the door hinge, but is not related to the tightness of the door seal or window seal.

6. The team multiplies the customer importance rating of a feature by its relationship to an engineering attribute (one, three, or nine). These numbers are then summed for each column, yielding a total for the relative importance of each engineering attribute. For example, the stiffness of the hinge influences how easy the door is to open, and whether the door stays open on a hill. Thus to calculate the relative importance of the stiffness of the hinge, the team multiplies the customer importance rating of how easy the door is to open by its relationship to the stiffness of the hinge ($15 \times 3 = 45$), then multiplies the customer importance rating of the door staying open on a hill by its relationship to the stiffness of the hinge ($10 \times 9 = 90$), and then adds these together for the total relative importance of the hinge stiffness ($45 + 90 = 135$). These scores indicate that the tightness of the door and window seals is the most important engineering attribute, followed by the weight of the door.

7. The team evaluates the competition. A scale of one to seven is used (one indicating a requirement is not addressed, and seven indicating a requirement is completely satisfied) to evaluate the competing products (in this case A and B) on each of the customer requirements. These scores go in the right-hand "room" of the house of quality.

8. Using the relative importance ratings established for each engineering attribute and the scores for competing products (from step 7), the team determines target values for each of the design requirements (for example, the door's optimal weight in pounds).

9. A product design is then created based on the design targets from step 8. The team then evaluates the new design that was created. The team assesses the degree to which each of the customer requirements has been met, entering a one to seven in the far right column of the house of quality, permitting it to compare the new design with the scores of the competing products.

The great strength of the house of quality is that it provides a common language and framework within which the members of a project team may interact. The house of quality makes the relationship between product attributes and customer requirements very clear, it focuses on design trade-offs, it highlights the competitive shortcomings of the company's existing products, and it helps identify what steps need to be taken to improve them. The house of quality is used in settings as diverse as manufacturing, construction, police service, and educational curriculum design.[30] Advocates of QFD maintain that one of its most valuable characteristics is its positive effect upon cross-functional communication and, through that, upon cycle time and the product/customer fit.[31]

Design for Manufacturing

Another method of facilitating integration between engineering and manufacturing, and of bringing issues of manufacturability into the design process as early as possible, is the use of design for manufacturing methods (DFM). Like QFD, DFM is simply a

FIGURE 11.6
Design Rules for Fabricated Assembly Products

Source: Adapted from M. A. Schilling and C. W. L. Hill, 1998, "Managing the New Product Development Process," *Academy of Management Executive*, vol. 12, no. 3, pp. 67–81.

Design Rule	Impact on Performance
Minimize the number of parts	Simplifies assembly; reduces direct labor; reduces material handling and inventory costs; boosts product quality
Minimize the number of part numbers (use common parts across product family)	Reduces material handling and inventory costs; improves economies of scale (increases volume through commonalty)
Eliminate adjustments	Reduces assembly errors (increases quality); allows for automation; increases capacity and throughput
Eliminate fasteners	Simplifies assembly (increases quality); reduces direct labor costs; reduces squeaks and rattles; improves durability; allows for automation
Eliminate jigs and fixtures	Reduces line changeover costs; lowers required investment

way of structuring the new product development process. Often this involves articulating a series of design rules. Figure 11.6 summarizes a set of commonly used design rules, along with their expected impact on performance.

As shown in Figure 11.6, the purpose of such design rules is typically to reduce costs and boost product quality by ensuring that product designs are easy to manufacture. The easier products are to manufacture, the fewer the assembly steps required, the higher labor productivity will be, resulting in lower unit costs. DEKA Research makes a point of bringing manufacturing into the design process early, because as founder Dean Kamen points out, "It doesn't make sense to invent things that ultimately are made of unobtanium or expensium."[32] In addition, designing products to be easy to manufacture decreases the likelihood of making mistakes in the assembly process, resulting in higher product quality.

The benefits of adopting DFM rules can be dramatic. Considering manufacturing at an early stage of the design process can shorten development cycle time. In addition, by lowering costs and increasing product quality, DFM can increase the product's fit with customer requirements. For example, when NCR used DFM techniques to redesign one of its electronic cash registers, it reduced assembly time by 75 percent, reduced the parts required by 85 percent, utilized 65 percent fewer suppliers, and reduced direct labor time by 75 percent.[33]

Failure Modes and Effects Analysis

Failure modes and effects analysis (FMEA) is a method by which firms identify potential failures in a system, classify them according to their severity, and put a plan into place to prevent the failures from happening.[34] First, potential failure modes are identified. For example, a firm developing a commercial aircraft might consider failure modes such as "landing gear does not descend," or "communication system experiences interference"; a firm developing a new line of luxury hotels might consider failure modes such as "a reservation cannot be found" or "guest experiences poor service by room service staff." Potential failure modes are then evaluated on three criteria of the risk they pose: severity, likelihood of occurrence, and inability of controls to detect it. Each criterion is given a score (e.g., one for lowest risk, five for highest risk), and then a composite risk priority number is created for each failure mode by multiplying its scores together (i.e., risk priority number = severity × likelihood of occurrence × inability of controls to detect). The firm can then prioritize its development efforts to target potential failure modes that pose the most composite risk. This means that rather than focus first on the failure modes that have the highest scores for severity of risk, the firm might find that it should focus first on failure modes that have less severe impacts, but occur more often and are less detectable.

FMEA was originally introduced in the 1940s by the U.S. Armed Forces and was initially adopted primarily for development projects in which the risks posed by failure were potentially very severe. For example, FMEA was widely used in the Apollo Space Program in its mission to put a man on the moon, and was adopted by Ford after its extremely costly experience with its Pinto model (the location of the gas tank in the Pinto made it exceptionally vulnerable to collisions, leading to fire-related deaths; Ford was forced to recall the Pintos to modify the fuel tanks, and was forced to pay out record-breaking sums in lawsuits that resulted from accidents).[35] Soon, however, FMEA was adopted by firms in a wide range of industries, including many types of manufacturing industries, service industries, and health care. A recent PDMA study found that firms report using FMEA in 40 percent of the projects they undertake.[36]

Computer-Aided Design Computer-Aided Engineering/ Computer-Aided Manufacturing

Computer-aided design (CAD) and computer-aided engineering (CAE) is the use of computers to build and test product designs. Rapid advances in computer technology have enabled the development of low-priced and high-powered graphics-based workstations. With these workstations, it is now possible to achieve what could previously be done only on a supercomputer: construct a three-dimensional "working" image of a product or subassembly. CAD enables the creation of a three-dimensional model; CAE makes it possible to virtually test the characteristics (e.g., strength, fatigue, and reliability) of this model. The combination enables product prototypes to be developed and tested in virtual reality. Engineers can quickly adjust prototype attributes by manipulating the three-dimensional model, allowing them to compare the characteristics of different product designs. Eliminating the need to build physical prototypes can reduce cycle time and lower costs as illustrated in the accompanying Theory in Action. Visualization tools and 3-D software are even being used to allow nonengineering customers to see and make minor alterations to the design and materials.

three-dimensional printing
A method whereby a design developed in a computer aided design program is printed in three dimensions by laying down thin strips of material until the model is complete.

Computer-aided manufacturing (CAM) is the implementation of machine-controlled processes in manufacturing. CAM is faster and more flexible than traditional manufacturing.[37] Computers can automate the change between different product variations and allow for more variety and customization in the manufacturing process.

A recent incarnation of computer-aided manufacturing is **three-dimensional printing** (also known as additive manufacturing), whereby a design developed in a computer aided design program is literally printed by laying down thin horizontal cross sections of material until the model is complete. Unlike traditional methods of constructing a model, which typically involve machining a mold that can take several

Theory in Action   Computer-Aided Design of an America's Cup Yacht

Team New Zealand discovered the advantages of using sophisticated computer-aided-design techniques in designing the team's 1995 America's Cup yacht. The team had traditionally relied on developing smaller-scale prototypes of the yacht and testing the models in a water tank. However, such prototypes took months to fabricate and test and cost about $50,000 per prototype. This greatly limited the number of design options the team could consider. However, by using computer-aided-design technologies, the team could consider many more design specifications more quickly and inexpensively. Once the basic design is programmed, variations on that design can be run in a matter of hours, at little cost, enabling more insight into design trade-offs. Computer-aided design also avoided some of the problems inherent in scaling up prototypes (some features of the scaled-down prototype boats would affect the flow of water differently from full-scale boats, resulting in inaccurate results in prototype testing). The team would still build prototypes, but only after considering a much wider range of design alternatives using computer-aided-design methods. As noted by design team member Dave Egan, "Instead of relying on a few big leaps, we had the ability to continually design, test, and refine our ideas. The team would often hold informal discussions on design issues, sketch some schematics on the back of a beer mat, and ask me to run the numbers. Using traditional design methods would have meant waiting months for results, and by that time, our thinking would have evolved so much that the reason for the experiment would long since have been forgotten."

Source: M. Iansiti and A. MacCormack, "Team New Zealand," Harvard Business School case no. 9-697-040, 1997.

days to complete, three-dimensional printing can generate a model in a few hours. By 2015, three-dimensional printing was being used to create products as diverse as food, clothing, jewelry, solid-state batteries, and even titanium landing gear brackets for supersonic jets.[38] Biotechnology firms were even using three-dimensional printing for use in creating organs by depositing layers of living cells onto a gel medium.[39] This method has recently begun rapidly replacing injection molding for products that are produced in relatively small quantities.

TOOLS FOR MEASURING NEW PRODUCT DEVELOPMENT PERFORMANCE

Many companies use a variety of metrics to measure the performance of their new product development process. In addition to providing feedback about a particular new product, such performance assessments help the company improve its innovation strategy and development processes. For example, evaluating the performance of its new product development process may provide insight into which core competencies the firm should focus on, how projects should be selected, whether or not it should seek collaboration partners, how it should manage its development teams, and so on.

Theory in Action   Postmortems at Microsoft

At Microsoft, almost all projects receive either a post-mortem discussion or a written postmortem report to ensure that the company learns from each of its development experiences. These postmortems tend to be extremely candid and can be quite critical. As noted by one Microsoft manager, "The purpose of the document is to beat yourself up." Another Microsoft manager notes that part of the Microsoft culture is to be very self-critical and never be satisfied at getting things "halfway right." A team will spend three to six months putting together a postmortem document that may number anywhere from less than 10 pages to more than 100. These postmortem reports describe the development activities and team, provide data on the product size (e.g., lines of code) and quality (e.g., number of bugs), and evaluate what worked well, what did not work well, and what the group should do to improve on the next project. These reports are then distributed to the team members and to senior executives throughout the organization.

Source: M. A. Cusumano and R. W. Selby, *Microsoft Secrets* (New York: Free Press, 1995).

Both the metrics used by firms and the timing of their use vary substantially across firms. In a survey by Goldense and Gilmore, 45 percent of companies reported using periodic reviews at calendar periods (e.g., monthly or weekly) and at predetermined milestones (e.g., after product definition, after process design, post launch, etc.).[40] Microsoft, for example, uses postmortems to measure new product development performance, as described in the accompanying Theory in Action. Measures of the success of the new product development process can help management to:

- Identify which projects met their goals and why.
- Benchmark the organization's performance compared to that of competitors or to the organization's own prior performance.
- Improve resource allocation and employee compensation.
- Refine future innovation strategies.[41]

Multiple measures are important because any measure used singly may not give a fair representation of the effectiveness of the firm's development process or its overall innovation performance. Also, the firm's development strategy, industry, and other environmental circumstances must be considered when formulating measures and interpreting results. For example, a firm whose capabilities or objectives favor development of breakthrough projects may experience long intervals between product introductions and receive a low score on measures such as cycle time or percent of sales earned on projects launched within the past five years, despite its success at its strategy. Conversely, a firm that rapidly produces new generations of products may receive a high score on such measures even if it finds its resources are overtaxed and its projects are overbudget. Additionally, the success rate of new product development can vary significantly by industry and project type. Some authors argue that even firms with excellent new product development processes should not expect to have a greater than 65 percent success rate for all new products launched.[42]

New Product Development Process Metrics

Many firms use a number of methods to gauge the effectiveness and efficiency of the development process. These measures capture different dimensions of the firm's ability to successfully shepherd projects through the development process. To use such methods it is important to first define a finite period in which the measure is to be applied in order to get an accurate view of the company's current performance; this also makes it easier for the manager to calculate a response. The following questions can then be asked:

1. What was the average cycle time (time to market) for development projects? How did this cycle time vary for projects characterized as breakthrough, platform, or derivative?
2. What percentage of development projects undertaken within the past five years met all or most of the deadlines set for the project?
3. What percentage of development projects undertaken within the past five years stayed within budget?
4. What percentage of development projects undertaken within the past five years resulted in a completed product?

Overall Innovation Performance

Firms also use a variety of methods to assess their overall performance at innovation. These measures give an overall view of the bang for the buck the organization is achieving with its new product development processes. Such measures include:

1. What is the firm's return on innovation? (This measure assesses the ratio of the firm's total profits from new products to its total expenditures, including research and development costs, the costs of retooling and staffing production facilities, and initial commercialization and marketing costs.)
2. What percentage of projects achieve their sales goals?
3. What percentage of revenues are generated by products developed within the past five years?
4. What is the firm's ratio of successful projects to its total project portfolio?

Summary of Chapter

1. Successful new product development requires achieving three simultaneous objectives: maximizing fit with customer requirements, minimizing time to market, and controlling development costs.
2. Many firms have adopted parallel development processes to shorten the development cycle time and to increase coordination among functions such as R&D, marketing, and manufacturing.
3. Many firms have also begun using project champions to help ensure a project's momentum and improve its access to key resources. Use of champions also has its risks, however, including escalating commitment and unwillingness of others in the organization to challenge the project.
4. Involving customers in the development process can help a firm ensure that its new products match customer expectations. In particular, research indicates that involving lead users can help the firm understand what needs are most important

to customers, helping the firm to identify its development priorities. Involving lead users in the development process can also be faster and cheaper than involving a random sample of customers in the development process.

5. Many firms use beta testing to get customer feedback, exploit external development of the product, and signal the market about the firm's upcoming products.

6. Firms can also involve suppliers in the development process, helping to minimize the input cost of a new product design and improving the likelihood that inputs are of appropriate quality and arrive on time.

7. Stage-gate processes offer a blueprint for guiding firms through the new product development process, providing a series of go/kill gates where the firm must decide if the project should be continued and how its activities should be prioritized.

8. Quality function deployment can be used to improve the development team's understanding of the relationship between customer requirements and engineering attributes. It can also be a tool for improving communication between the various functions involved in the development process.

9. Failure Modes and Effects Analysis can be used to help firms prioritize their development efforts in order to reduce the likelihood of failures that will have the greatest impact on the quality, reliability, and safety of a product or process.

10. Design for manufacturing and CAD/CAM are additional tools development teams can use to reduce cycle time, improve product quality, and control development costs.

11. Firms should use a variety of measures of their new product development effectiveness and overall innovation performance to identify opportunities for improving the new product development process and improving the allocation of resources.

Discussion Questions

1. What are some of the advantages and disadvantages of a parallel development process? What obstacles might a firm face in attempting to adopt a parallel process?

2. Consider a group project you have worked on at work or school. Did your group use mostly sequential or parallel processes?

3. Name some industries in which a parallel process would not be possible or effective.

4. What kinds of people make good project champions? How can a firm ensure that it gets the benefits of championing while minimizing the risks?

5. Is the stage-gate process consistent with suggestions that firms adopt parallel processes? What impact do you think using stage-gate processes would have on development cycle time and development costs?

6. What are the benefits and costs of involving customers and suppliers in the development process?

Suggested Further Reading

Classics

Clark, K. B., and S. C. Wheelwright, *Managing New Product and Process Development* (New York: Free Press, 1993).

Cooper, R., and E. J. Kleinschmidt, "New Product Processes at Leading Industrial Firms," *Industrial-Marketing-Management* 20, no. 2 (1991), pp. 137–48.

Griffin, A., and J. R. Hauser, "Patterns of Communication among Marketing, Engineering and Manufacturing," *Management Science* 38 (1992), pp. 360–73; and Kahn, K. B. *The PDMA Handbook of New Product Development* (2005), Hoboken, NJ: John Wiley & Sons.

Recent Work

Carnevalli, J. A., and P. C. Miguel, "Review, Analysis and Classification of the Literature on QFD—Types of Research, Difficulties and Benefits," *International Journal of Production Economics* 114 (2008), pp. 737–54.

Gattiker, T. F., and C. R. Carter, "Understanding Project Champions' Ability to Gain Intra-organizational Commitment for Environmental Projects," *Journal of Operations Management* 28 (2010), pp. 72–85.

Lawson, B., D. Krause, and A. Potter, "Improving Supplier New Product Development Performance: The Role of Supplier Development." *Journal of Product Innovation Management* 32 (2015), pp. 777–92.

Chesbrough, H. W., and A. R. Garman, "How Open Innovation Can Help You in Lean Times." *Harvard Business Review* 87 (2009), issue 12, pp. 68–76.

Loch, C., and S. Kavadias, *Handbook of New Product Development Management.* (Oxford, UK: Elsevier Ltd., 2008).

Endnotes

1. E. Berggren and T. Nacher, "Introducing New Products Can Be Hazardous to Your Company: Use the Right New-Solutions Delivery Tools," *Academy of Management Executive* 15, no. 3 (2001), pp. 92–101.

2. M. A. Schilling, "Technological Lockout: An Integrative Model of the Economic and Strategic Factors Driving Success and Failure," *Academy of Management Review* 23 (1998), pp. 267–84; and W. B. Arthur, *Increasing Returns and Path Dependence in the Economy* (Ann Arbor: University of Michigan Press, 1994).

3. A. Dhebar, "Speeding High-Tech Producer, Meet Balking Consumer," *Sloan Management Review,* Winter 1996, pp. 37–49.

4. M. C. Crawford, "The Hidden Costs of Accelerated Product Development," *Journal of Product Innovation Management* 9, no. 3 (1992), pp. 188–200.

5. G. Pacheco-de-Almeida and P. Zemsky, "The Creation and Sustainability of Competitive Advantage: Resource Accumulation with Time Compression Diseconomies," mimeo, Stern School of Business, 2003.

6. E. J. Nijssen, A. R. Arbouw, and H. R. Commandeur, "Accelerating New Product Development: A Preliminary Empirical Test of a Hierarchy of Implementation," *Journal of Product Innovation Management* 12 (1995), pp. 99–104; R. W. Schmenner, "The Merits of Making Things Fast," *Sloan Management Review,* Fall 1988, pp. 11–17; A. Ali, R. Krapfel, and D. LaBahn, "Product Innovativeness and Entry Strategy: Impact on Cycle Time and Break-Even Time," *Journal of Product Innovation Management* 12 (1995), pp. 54–69; and R. Rothwell, "Successful Industrial Innovation: Critical Factors for the 1990s," *R&D Management* 22, no. 3 (1992), pp. 221–39.

7. A. Griffin, "Evaluating QFD's Use in US Firms as a Process for Developing Products," *Journal of Product Innovation Management* 9 (1992), pp. 171–87; and C. H. Kimzey, *Summary of the Task Force Workshop on Industrial-Based Initiatives* (Washington, DC: Office of the Assistant Secretary of Defense, Production and Logistics, 1987).

8. A. De Meyer and B. Van Hooland, "The Contribution of Manufacturing to Shortening Design Cycle Times," *R&D Management* 20, no. 3 (1990), pp. 229–39; R. Hayes, S. G. Wheelwright, and K. B. Clark, *Dynamic Manufacturing* (New York: Free Press, 1988); R. G. Cooper, "The New Product Process: A Decision Guide for Managers," *Journal of Marketing Management* 3 (1988), pp. 238–55; and H. Takeuchi and I. Nonaka, "The New Product Development Game," *Harvard Business Review,* January–February 1986, pp. 137–46.

9. K. Eisenhardt and B. N. Tabrizi, "Accelerating Adaptive Processes: Product Innovation in the Global Computer Industry," *Administrative Science Quarterly* 40 (1995), pp. 84–110; and C. Terwiesch and C. H. Loch, "Measuring the Effectiveness of Overlapping Development Activities," *Management Science* 45 (1999), pp. 455–65.

10. B. J. Zirger and M. A. Maidique, "A Model of New Product Development: An Empirical Test," *Management Science* 36 (1990), pp. 867–83; R. Rothwell, C. Freeman, A. Horley, P. Jervis, A. B. Robertson, and J. Townsend, "SAPPHO Updates—Project SAPPHO, PHASE II," *Research Policy* 3 (1974), pp. 258–91; A. H. Rubenstein, A. K. Chakrabarti, R. D. O'Keffe, W. E. Souder, and H. C. Young, "Factors Influencing Innovation Success at the Project Level," *Research Management,* May 1976, pp. 15–20; F. A. Johne and P. A. Snelson, "Product Development Approaches in Established Firms," *Industrial Marketing Management* 18 (1989), pp. 113–24; and Y. Wind and V. Mahajan, "New Product Development Process: A Perspective for Reexamination," *Journal of Product Innovation Management* 5 (1988), pp. 304–10.

11. T. F. Gattiker and C. R. Carter, "Understanding project champions' ability to gain intra-organizational commitment for environmental projects," *Journal of Operations Management* 28 (2010), pp. 72–85.

12. E. Roberts, "Benchmarking Global Strategic Management of Technology," *Research Technology Management,* March–April 2001, pp. 25–36.

13. E. Rudden, "The Misuse of a Sound Investment Tool," *Wall Street Journal,* November 1, 1982.

14. M. Devaney, "Risk, Commitment, and Project Abandonment," *Journal of Business Ethics* 10, no. 2 (1991), pp. 157–60.

15. Devaney, "Risk, Commitment, and Project Abandonment."

16. F. A. Johne and P. A. Snelson, "Success Factors in Product Innovation," *Journal of Product Innovation Management* 5 (1988), pp. 114–28; and F. W. Gluck and R. N. Foster, "Managing Technological Change: A Box of Cigars for Brad," *Harvard Business Review* 53 (1975), pp. 139–50.

17. R. G. Cooper, "Selecting Winning New Product Projects: Using the NewProd System," *Journal of Product Innovation Management* 2 (1985), pp. 34–44.

18. J. E. Butler, "Theories of Technological Innovation as Useful Tools for Corporate Strategy," *Strategic Management Journal* 9 (1988), pp. 15–29.

19. C. Herstatt and E. von Hippel, "Developing New Product Concepts via the Lead User Method: A Case Study in a Low-Tech Field," *Journal of Product Innovation Management* 9 (1992), pp. 213–21.

20. D. Mahr, A. Lievens, and V. Blazevic. "The value of customer cocreated knowledge during the innovation process." *Journal of Product Innovation Management* 31 (2014), 599–615.

21. Asmus and Griffin found that firms that integrate their suppliers with engineering, manufacturing, and purchasing gain cost reductions, shortened lead times, lowered development risks, and tightened development cycles. D. Asmus and J. Griffin, "Harnessing the Power of Your Suppliers," *McKinsey Quarterly,* no. 3 (1993), pp. 63–79. Additionally, Bonaccorsi and Lipparini found that strategic alliances with suppliers lead to shorter product development cycles and better products, particularly in rapidly changing markets. A. Bonaccorsi and A. Lipparini, "Strategic Partnership in New Product Development: An Italian Case Study," *Journal of Product Innovation Management* 11, no. 2 (1994), pp. 134–46.

22. L. Birou and S. Fawcett, "Supplier Involvement in New Product Development: A Comparison of US and European Practices," *Journal of Physical Distribution and Logistics Management* 24, no. 5 (1994), pp. 4–15; and A. Ansari and B. Modarress, "Quality Function Deployment: The Role of Suppliers," *International Journal of Purchasing and Materials Management* 30, no. 4 (1994), pp. 28–36.

23. N. Franke and M. Schreier. "Why customers value self-designed products: The importance of process effort and enjoyment." *Journal of Product Innovation Management* 27 (2010), pp. 1020–1031.

24. W. D. Hoyer, R. Chandy, M. Dorotic, M. Krafft, and S. S. Singh, "Consumer cocreation in new product development," in *Journal of Service Research* 13 (2010), issue 3, 283–296.

25. R. Cooper and E. J. Kleinschmidt, "New Product Processes at Leading Industrial Firms," *Industrial-Marketing-Management* 20, no. 2 (1991), pp. 137–48; and R. G. Cooper, "Doing It Right," *Ivey Business Journal* 64, no. 6 (2000), pp. 54–61; and R.G. Cooper, "Stage-Gate Idea to Launch System," *Wiley International Encyclopedia of Marketing: Product Innovation & Management* 5, B.L. Bayus (ed.), (West Sussex UK: Wiley, 2011).

26. R.G. Cooper, "Stage-Gate Idea to Launch System," *Wiley International Encyclopedia of Marketing: Product Innovation & Management* 5, B.L. Bayus (ed.), (West Sussex UK: Wiley, 2011).

27. L. Y. Coyeh, P. W. Kamienski, and R. L. Espino, "Gate System Focuses on Industrial Basic Research," *Research Technology Management* 41, no. 4 (1998), pp. 34–37.

28. A. LaPlante and A. E. Alter, "Corning, Inc: The Stage-Gate Innovation Process," *Computerworld* 28, no. 44 (1994), p. 81.

29. J. J. Cristiano, J. K. Liker, and C. C. White, "Key Factors in the Successful Application of Quality Function Deployment (QFD)," *IEEE Transactions on Engineering Management* 48, no. 1 (2001), p. 81.

30. I. Bier, "Using QFD to Construct a Higher Education Curriculum," *Quality Progress* 34, no. 4 (2001), pp. 64–69; N. Eldin, "A Promising Planning Tool: Quality Function Deployment," *Cost Engineering* 44, no. 3 (2002), pp. 28–38; and W. J. Selen and J. Schepers, "Design of Quality Service Systems in the Public Sector: Use of Quality Function Deployment in Police Services," *Total Quality Management* 12, no. 5 (2001), pp. 677–87; J. A. Carnevalli and P. C. Miguel, "Review, analysis and classification of the literature on QFD—types of research, difficulties and benefits," *International Journal of Production Economics* 114 (2008), pp. 737–54.

31. K. B. Clark and S. C. Wheelwright, *Managing New Product and Process Development* (New York: Free Press, 1993); J. R. Hauser and D. Clausing, "The House of Quality," *Harvard Business Review,* May–June 1988, pp. 63–73; A. Griffin, "Evaluating QFD's Use in US Firms as a Process for Developing Products," *Journal of Product Innovation Management* 9 (1992), pp. 171–87; and A. Griffin and J. R. Hauser, "Patterns of Communication among Marketing, Engineering and Manufacturing," *Management Science* 38 (1992), pp. 360–73.

32. E. I. Schwartz, "The Inventor's Play-Ground," *Technology Review* 105, no. 8 (2002), pp. 68–73.

33. Clark and Wheelwright, *Managing New Product and Process Development.*

34. S. Kumar, E. C. Aquino, and E. Anderson, "Application of a Process Methodology and a Strategic Decision Model for Business Process Outsourcing," *Information Knowledge Systems Management* 6 (2007), pp. 323–42; and J. W. Langford, *Logistics: Principles and Applications* (New York: McGraw-Hill, 1995).

35. L. P. Chao and K. Ishii, "Design Error Classification and Knowledge Management," *Journal of Knowledge Management Practice,* May 2004; and P. Valdes-Dapena, "Tagged: 10 Cars with Bad Reputations," CNNMoney.com (accessed April 23, 2009).

36. G. Barczak, A. Griffin, and K. B. Kahn, "Trends and Drivers of Success in NPD Practices: Results of the 2003 PDMA Best Practices Study," *Journal of Product Innovation Management* 26 (2009), pp. 3–23.

37. M. R. Millson, S. P. Raj, and D. Wilemon, "A Survey of Major Approaches for Accelerating New Product Development," *Journal of Product Innovation Management* 9 (1992), pp. 53–69.

38. "The printed World," *The Economist (2011),* February 10, 2011; K. Lee, "Foodini 3D printer cooks up meals like the Star Trek food replicator," www.inhabitat.com (2013): December 9th; Fitzgerald, M. "With 3-D printing the shoe really fits." *MIT Sloan Management Review* (2013), www.sloanreview.mit.edu:May 15th.

39. J. Silverstein, "Organ Printing Could Drastically Change Medicine," ABC News, February 10, 2006.

40. B. L. Goldense and J. Gilmore, "Measuring Product Design," *Machine Design* 73, no. 14 (2001), pp. 63–67.

41. T. D. Kuczmarski, "Measuring Your Return on Innovation," *Marketing Management* 9, no. 1 (2000), pp. 24–32.

42. Ibid.

1

THE ENTREPRENEURIAL MIND-SET

1

To introduce the concept of entrepreneurship and explain the process of entrepreneurial action.

2

To describe how structural similarities enable entrepreneurs to make creative mental leaps.

3

To highlight bricolage as a source of entrepreneurs' resourcefulness.

4

To introduce effectuation as a way expert entrepreneurs sometimes think.

5

To develop the notion that entrepreneurs cognitively adapt.

6

To introduce sustainable entrepreneurship as a means of sustaining the natural environment and communities and developing gains for others.

OPENING PROFILE

EWING MARION KAUFFMAN

Born on a farm in Garden City, Missouri, Ewing Marion Kauffman moved to Kansas City with his family when he was eight years old. A critical event in his life occurred several years later when Kauffman was diagnosed with a leakage of the heart. His prescription was one year of complete bed rest; he was not even allowed to sit up.

www.kauffman.org

Kauffman's mother, a college graduate, came up with a solution to keep the active 11-year-old boy lying in bed—reading. According to Kauffman, he "sure read! Because nothing else would do, I read as many as 40 to 50 books every month. When you read that much, you read anything. So I read the biographies of all the presidents, the frontiersmen, and I read the Bible twice and that's pretty rough reading."

Another important early childhood experience centered on door-to-door sales. Since his family did not have a lot of money, Kauffman sold 36 dozen eggs collected from the farm or fish he and his father had caught, cleaned, and dressed. His mother was very encouraging during these formative school years, telling young Ewing each day, "There may be some who have more money in their pockets, but Ewing, there is nobody better than you."

During his youth, Kauffman worked as a laundry delivery person and was a Boy Scout. In addition to passing all the requirements to become an Eagle Scout and a Sea Scout, he sold twice as many tickets to the Boy Scout Roundup as anyone else in Kansas City, an accomplishment that enabled him to attend, for free, a two-week scout summer camp that his parents would not otherwise have been able to afford. According to Kauffman, "This experience gave me some of the sales techniques which came into play when subsequently I went into the pharmaceutical business."

Kauffman went to junior college from 8 to 12 in the morning and then walked two miles to the laundry where he worked until 7 p.m. Upon graduation, he went to work at the laundry full time for Mr. R. A. Long, who eventually became one of his role models. His job as route foreman involved managing 18 to 20 route drivers, where he would set up sales contests, such as challenging the other drivers to get more customers on a particular route than he could obtain. Kauffman says, "I got practice in selling and that proved to be beneficial later in life." R. A. Long made money not only at the laundry business but also on patents, one of which was a form fit for the collar of a shirt that would hold the shape of the shirt. He showed his young protégé that one could make money with brains as well as brawn. Kauffman commented, "He was quite a man and had quite an influence on my life."

Kauffman's sales ability was also useful during his stint in the Navy, which he joined shortly after Pearl Harbor on January 11, 1942. When designated as an apprentice seaman, a position that paid $21 per month, he responded, "I'm better than an apprentice seaman, because I have been a Sea Scout. I've sailed ships and I've ridden in whale boats." His selling ability convinced the Navy that he should instead start as a seaman first class, with a $54 monthly salary. Kauffman was assigned to the admiral's staff, where he became an outstanding signalman (a seaman who transmitted messages from ship to ship), in part because he was able to read messages better than anyone else due to his previous intensive reading. With his admiral's encouragement, Kauffman took a correspondence navigator's course and was given a deck commission and made a navigation officer.

After the war was over in 1947, Ewing Kauffman began his career as a pharmaceutical salesperson after performing better on an aptitude test than 50 other applicants. The job involved selling supplies of vitamin and liver shots to doctors. Working on straight commission, without expenses or benefits, he was earning pay higher than the president's salary by the end of the second year; the president promptly cut the commission. Eventually, when Kauffman was made Midwest sales manager, he made 3 percent of everything his salespeople sold and continued to make more money than the president. When his territory was cut, he eventually quit and in 1950 started his own company—Marion Laboratories. (Marion is his middle name.)

When reflecting on founding the new company, Ewing Kauffman commented, "It was easier than it sounds because I had doctors whom I had been selling office supplies to for several years. Before I made the break, I went to three of them and said, 'I'm thinking of starting my own company. May I count on you to give me your orders if I can give you the same quality and service?' These three were my biggest accounts and each one of them agreed because they liked me and were happy to do business with me."

Marion Laboratories started by marketing injectable products that were manufactured by another company under Marion's label. The company expanded to other accounts and other products and then developed its first prescription item, Vicam, a vitamin product. The second pharmaceutical product it developed, oyster shell calcium, also sold well.

To expand the company, Kauffman borrowed $5,000 from the Commerce Trust Company. He repaid the loan, and the company continued to grow. After several years, outside investors could buy $1,000 worth of common stock if they loaned the company $1,000 to be paid back in five years at $1,250, without any intermittent interest. This initial $1,000 investment, if held until 1993, would have been worth $21 million.

Marion Laboratories continued to grow and reached over $1 billion per year in sales, due primarily to the relationship between Ewing Kauffman and the people in the company, who were called associates, not employees. "They are all stockholders, they build this company, and they mean so much to us," said Kauffman. The concept of associates was also a part of the two basic philosophies of the company: Those who produce should share in the results or profits and treat others as you would like to be treated.

The company went public through Smith Barney on August 16, 1965, at $21 per share. The stock jumped to $28 per share immediately and has never dropped below that level, sometimes selling at a 50 to 60 price/earnings multiple. The associates of the company were offered a profit-sharing plan, where each could own stock in the company. In 1968, Kauffman brought Major League Baseball back to Kansas City by purchasing the Kansas City Royals. This boosted the city's economic base, community profile, and civic pride. When Marion Laboratories merged with Merrill Dow in 1989, there were 3,400 associates, 300 of whom became millionaires as a result of the merger. The new company, Marion Merrill Dow, Inc., grew to 9,000 associates and sales of $4 billion in 1998 when it was acquired by Hoechst, a European pharmaceutical company. Hoechst Marion Roussel became a world leader in pharmaceutical-based health care involved in the discovery, development, manufacture, and sale of pharmaceutical products. In late 1999, the company was again merged with Aventis Pharma, a global pharmaceutical company focusing on human medicines (prescription pharmaceuticals and vaccines) and animal health. In 2002, Aventis's sales reached $16.634 billion, an increase of 11.6 percent from 2001, while earnings per share grew 27 percent from the previous year.

Ewing Marion Kauffman was an entrepreneur, a Major League Baseball team owner, and a philanthropist who believed his success was a direct result of one fundamental philosophy: Treat others as you would like to be treated. "It is the happiest principle by which to live and the most intelligent principle by which to do business and make money," he said.

Ewing Marion Kauffman's philosophies of associates, rewarding those who produce, and allowing decision making throughout the organization are the fundamental concepts underlying what is now called *corporate entrepreneurship* in a company. He went even further and illustrated his belief in entrepreneurship and the spirit of giving back when he established the Kauffman Foundation, which supports programs in two areas: youth development and entrepreneurship. Truly a remarkable entrepreneur, Mr. K, as he was affectionately called by his employees, will now produce many more successful "associate entrepreneurs."

Like Ewing Marion Kauffman, many other entrepreneurs and future entrepreneurs frequently ask themselves, "Am I really an entrepreneur? Do I have what it takes to be a success? Do I have sufficient background and experience to start and manage a new venture?" As enticing as the thought of starting and owning a business may be, the problems and pitfalls inherent to the process are as legendary as the success stories. The fact remains that more new business ventures fail than succeed. To be one of the few successful entrepreneurs requires more than just hard work and luck. It requires the ability to think in an environment of high uncertainty, be flexible, and learn from one's failures.

THE NATURE OF ENTREPRENEURSHIP

Entrepreneurship plays an important role in the creation and growth of businesses, as well as in the growth and prosperity of regions and nations. These large-scale outcomes can have quite humble beginnings; entrepreneurial actions begin at the nexus of a lucrative opportunity and an enterprising individual.[1] *Entrepreneurial opportunities* are "those situations in which new goods, services, raw materials, and organizing methods can be introduced and sold at greater than their cost of production."[2] For example, an entrepreneurial opportunity could stem from introducing an existing technological product used in one market to create a new market. Alternatively, an entrepreneurial opportunity could be creating a new technological product for an existing market or creating both a new product/service and a new market. The recurring theme is that an entrepreneurial opportunity represents something new. However, such possibilities require an enterprising individual or a group of enterprising individuals to recognize, evaluate, and exploit these situations as possible opportunities. Therefore, entrepreneurship requires action— *entrepreneurial action* through the creation of new products/processes and/or the entry into new markets, which may occur through a newly created organization or within an established organization.

Entrepreneurs act on what they believe is an opportunity. Because opportunities exist in (or create and/or generate) high uncertainty, entrepreneurs must use their judgment about whether or not to act. However, doubt can undermine entrepreneurial action. Therefore, a key to understanding entrepreneurial action is being able to assess the amount of uncertainty perceived to surround a potential opportunity and the individual's willingness to bear that uncertainty. The individual's prior knowledge can decrease the amount of uncertainty, and his or her motivation indicates a willingness to bear uncertainty.

As illustrated in Figure 1.1, the McMullen-Shepherd model explains how knowledge and motivation influence two stages of entrepreneurial action. Signals of changes in the environment that represent possible opportunities will be noticed by some individuals but not others. Individuals with knowledge of markets and/or technology are more capable of detecting changes in the external environment, and if they are also motivated, they will allocate further attention to processing this information. Others, however, will remain ignorant of the possibility. The result of Stage 1 is an individual's realization that an opportunity exists for someone. The individual then needs to determine whether it represents an opportunity for him or her (Stage 2). This involves assessing whether it is feasible to successfully exploit the opportunity given one's knowledge and whether it is desirable given one's motivation. In other words, does this opportunity for someone (third-person opportunity belief) represent an opportunity for me (first-person opportunity belief)? If the individual overcomes enough doubt to form (1) the belief that the situation represents an opportunity for someone in general, and then (2) the belief that the opportunity for someone is an opportunity for himself or herself personally, this individual may act.

Therefore, to be an entrepreneur is to act on the possibility that one has identified an opportunity worth pursuing.[3] It involves *entrepreneurial thinking*—individuals' mental processes of overcoming ignorance to decide whether a signal represents an opportunity for someone and/or reducing doubt as to whether an opportunity for someone is also an opportunity for them specifically, and/or processing feedback from action steps taken. To explain these processes more fully, we now turn to different forms of entrepreneurial thinking.

---

entrepreneurial opportunities Those situations in which new goods, services, raw materials, and organizing methods can be introduced and sold at greater than their cost of production

entrepreneurial action Action through the creation of new products/processes and/or the entry into new markets, which may occur through a newly created organization or within an established organization

entrepreneurial thinking Individuals' mental processes of overcoming ignorance to decide whether a signal represents an opportunity for someone and/or reducing doubt as to whether an opportunity for someone is also an opportunity for them specifically, and/or processing feedback from action steps taken

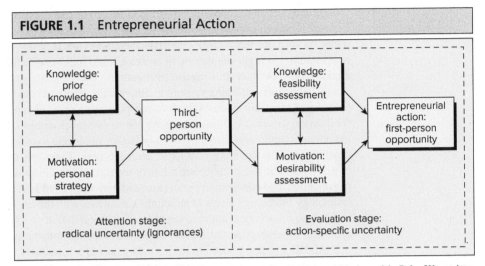

FIGURE 1.1 Entrepreneurial Action

Reprinted with permission from McMullen, J., and Shepherd, D. A. (2006). Entrepreneurial Action and the Role of Uncertainty in the Theory of the Entrepreneur. *Academy of Management Review.* 31: 132–142.

HOW ENTREPRENEURS THINK

Entrepreneurs think differently from nonentrepreneurs. Moreover, an entrepreneur in a particular situation may think differently from when faced with some other task or decision environment. Entrepreneurs must often make decisions in highly uncertain environments where the stakes are high, time pressures are immense, and there is considerable emotional investment. We all think differently in these strained environments than we do when the nature of a problem is well understood and we have time and rational procedures at hand to solve it. Given the nature of an entrepreneur's decision-making environment, he or she must sometimes (1) think structurally, (2) engage in bricolage, (3) effectuate, and (4) cognitively adapt.

Think Structurally

Forming opportunity beliefs often requires creative mental leaps. These creative mental leaps are launched from a source—one's existing knowledge. In the case of entrepreneurial opportunities, an example of a creative mental leap is from knowledge about existing markets to a new technology that could lead to products/services that satisfy that market. Alternatively, the creative mental leap could be from knowledge about a technology to a new market that could benefit from its introduction. Making these connections between a new product (or new service, new business model, or new technology) and a target market where it can be introduced is aided by the superficial and structural similarities between the source (e.g., the market) and the destination (e.g., technology). *Superficial similarities* exist when the basic (relatively easy to observe) elements of the technology resemble (match) the basic (relatively easy to observe) elements of the market. In contrast, *structural similarities* exist when the underlying mechanisms of the technology resemble (or match) the underlying mechanisms of the market. The entrepreneurial challenge often lies in making creative mental leaps based on *structural* similarities. This is best illustrated with an example based on a real case that Denis Gregoire from Syracuse University and me (Dean Shepherd from Indiana University) used as part of a study of entrepreneurial thinking.[4]

superficial similarities
Exist when the basic (relatively easy to observe) elements of the technology resemble (match) the basic (relatively easy to observe) elements of the market

structural similarities
Exist when the underlying mechanisms of the technology resemble (or match) the underlying mechanisms of the market

The example is a technology developed by space and computer engineers at NASA's Langley Research Center. It involves big and bulky flight simulators used by space shuttle pilots. As such, the technology's superficial elements are very similar to a market for airline pilots training in flight simulators. In contrast, it has little superficial similarity with a target market of K–12 school children and their parents. The technology underlying the superficial situations includes attaching sensors to individuals' forefingers to monitor the electric conductivity of their skin to send signals to computer processors in another machine with which the individual interacts. Ultimately, these one-to-one relationships (skin to sensor and sensor to computer) culminate into a network of higher-order relationships that reflect the overall capabilities of the technology, its aims, and/or its uses. Therefore, the technology is capable of helping shuttle pilots (or airline pilots or teenage drivers) improve their abilities to focus, pay attention, and concentrate for an extended period. Looked at in a new light, however, the technology shares high levels of structural similarities with the target market of parents who seek nonpharmaceutical alternatives to treat attention deficit (ADHD). This opportunity to apply the technology to the market of parents seeking nonpharmaceutical alternatives to treat ADHD was not obvious to individuals who were distracted from the deeper structural similarities by the superficial mismatch between the technology and the new market.

Thus, individuals who can see or create structural matches between a technology and a target market, especially in the presence of superficial mismatches, are more likely to recognize entrepreneurial opportunities. Knowledge specific to a technology and/or a market can facilitate this ability,[5] and the good news is that this skill can also be enhanced through practice and training.

Bricolage

bricolage Entrepreneurs making do by applying combinations of the resources at hand to new problems and opportunities

Entrepreneurs often lack resources. As a result, they either seek resources from others to provide the "slack" necessary to experiment and generate entrepreneurial opportunities or they engage in bricolage. By *bricolage* we mean that some entrepreneurs make "do by applying combinations of the resources at hand to new problems and opportunities."[6] This involves taking existing resources (those at hand) and experimenting, tinkering, repackaging, and/or reframing them so they can be used in a way for which they were not originally designed or conceived.[7] From this process of "making do," entrepreneurs can create opportunities. Baker and Nelson (2005: 341–42) offer the following example of bricolage.

Tim Grayson was a farmer whose land was crisscrossed by abandoned coal mines. He knew that the tunnels—a nuisance to farmers because of their tendency to collapse, causing mammoth sinkholes in fields—also contained large quantities of methane. Methane is another nuisance, a toxic greenhouse gas that poisons miners and persists in abandoned mines for generations. Grayson and a partner drilled a hole from Grayson's property to an abandoned mine shaft, then acquired a used diesel generator from a local factory and crudely retrofitted it to burn methane. During the conversion process, Grayson was repeatedly blown off his feet when the odorless, colorless gas exploded. His bricolage produced electricity, most of which he sold to the local utility company using scavenged switchgear. Because Grayson's generator also produced considerable waste heat, he built a greenhouse for hydroponic tomatoes, which he heated with water from the generator's cooling system. He also used electricity generated during off-peak hours to power special lamps to speed plant growth. With the availability of a greenhouse full of trenches of nutrient-rich water that were heated "for free," Grayson realized he might be able to raise tilapia, a tropical delicacy increasingly popular in the United States. He introduced the fish to the waters that bathed the tomato roots and used the fish waste as fertilizer. Finally, with abundant methane still at hand, Grayson began selling excess methane to a natural gas company. As you can see from this example, bricolage is a resourceful way of thinking and behaving that represents an important source of entrepreneurial opportunities.

Effectuation

As potential business leaders, you are trained to think rationally and perhaps admonished if you do not. This admonishment might be appropriate given the nature of the task, but it appears that there is an alternate way of thinking that entrepreneurs sometimes use, especially when thinking about opportunities. Professor Saras Sarasvathy (from Darden, University of Virginia) has found that entrepreneurs do not always think through a problem in a way that starts with a desired outcome and focuses on the means to generate that outcome. Such a process is referred to as a *causal process*. But, entrepreneurs sometimes use an *effectuation process*, which means they take what they have (who they are, what they know, and whom they know) and select among possible outcomes. Professor Sarasvathy is a great cook, so it is not surprising that her examples of these thought processes revolve around cooking.

causal process   A process that starts with a desired outcome and focuses on the means to generate that outcome

effectuation process   A process that starts with what one has (who they are, what they know, and whom they know) and selects among possible outcomes

Imagine a chef assigned the task of cooking dinner. There are two ways the task can be organized. In the first, the host or client picks out a menu in advance. All the chef needs to do is list the ingredients needed, shop for them, and then actually cook the meal. This is a process of causation. It begins with a given menu and focuses on selecting between effective ways to prepare the meal.

In the second case, the host asks the chef to look through the cupboards in the kitchen for possible ingredients and utensils and then cook a meal. Here, the chef has to imagine possible menus based on the given ingredients and utensils, select the menu, and then prepare the meal. This is a process of effectuation. It begins with given ingredients and utensils and focuses on preparing one of many possible desirable meals with them.[8]

Sarasvathy's Thought Experiment #1: Curry in a Hurry

In this example I [Sarasvathy] trace the process for building an imaginary Indian restaurant, "Curry in a Hurry." Two cases, one using causation and the other effectuation, are examined. For the purposes of this illustration, the example chosen is a typical causation process that underlies many economic theories today—theories in which it is argued that artifacts such as firms are inevitable outcomes, given the preference orderings of economic actors and certain simple assumptions of rationality (implying causal reasoning) in their choice behavior. The causation process used in the example here is typified by and embodied in the procedures stated by Philip Kotler in his *Marketing Management* (1991: 63, 263), a book that in its many editions is considered a classic and is widely used as a textbook in MBA programs around the world.

Kotler defines a market as follows: "A market consists of all the potential customers sharing a particular need or want who might be willing and able to engage in exchange to satisfy that need or want" (1991: 63). Given a product or a service, Kotler suggests the following procedure for bringing the product/service to market (note that Kotler assumes the market exists):

1. Analyze long-run opportunities in the market.
2. Research and select target markets.
3. Identify segmentation variables and segment the market.
4. Develop profiles of resulting segments.
5. Evaluate the attractiveness of each segment.
6. Select the target segment(s).
7. Identify possible positioning concepts for each target segment.
8. Select, develop, and communicate the chosen positioning concept.
9. Design marketing strategies.

10. Plan marketing programs.

11. Organize, implement, and control marketing effort.

This process is commonly known in marketing as the STP—segmentation, targeting, and positioning—process.

Curry in a Hurry is a restaurant with a new twist—say, an Indian restaurant with a fast food section. The current paradigm using causation processes indicates that, to implement this idea, the entrepreneur should start with a universe of all potential customers. Let us imagine that she wants to build her restaurant in Pittsburgh, Pennsylvania, which will then become the initial universe or market for Curry in a Hurry. Assuming that the percentage of the population of Pittsburgh that totally abhors Indian food is negligible, the entrepreneur can start the STP process.

Several relevant segmentation variables, such as demographics, residential neighborhoods, ethnic origin, marital status, income level, and patterns of eating out, could be used. On the basis of these, the entrepreneur could send out questionnaires to selected neighborhoods and organize focus groups at, say, the two major universities in Pittsburgh. Analyzing responses to the questionnaires and focus groups, she could arrive at a target segment—for example, wealthy families, both Indian and others, who eat out at least twice a week. That would help her determine her menu choices, decor, hours, and other operational details. She could then design marketing and sales campaigns to induce her target segment to try her restaurant. She could also visit other Indian and fast food restaurants and find some method of surveying them and then develop plausible demand forecasts for her planned restaurant.

In any case, the process would involve considerable amounts of time and analytical effort. It would also require resources both for research and, thereafter, for implementing the marketing strategies. In summary, the current paradigm suggests that we proceed inward to specifics from a larger, general universe—that is, to an optimal target segment from a predetermined market. In terms of Curry in a Hurry, this could mean something like a progression from the entire city of Pittsburgh to Fox Chapel (an affluent residential neighborhood) to the Joneses (specific customer profile of a wealthy family), as it were.

Instead, if our imaginary entrepreneur were to use processes of effectuation to build her restaurant, she would have to proceed in the opposite direction (note that effectuation is suggested here as a viable and descriptively valid alternative to the STP process—not as a normatively superior one). For example, instead of starting with the assumption of an existing market and investing money and other resources to design the best possible restaurant for the given market, she would begin by examining the particular set of means or causes available to her. Assuming she has extremely limited monetary resources—say $20,000—she should think creatively to bring the idea to market with as close to zero resources as possible. She could do this by convincing an established restaurateur to become a strategic partner or by doing just enough market research to convince a financier to invest the money needed to start the restaurant. Another method of effectuation would be to convince a local Indian restaurant or a local fast food restaurant to allow her to put up a counter where she would actually sell a selection of Indian fast food. Selecting a menu and honing other such details would be seat-of-the-pants and tentative, perhaps a process of satisficing.[9]

Several other courses of effectuation can be imagined. Perhaps the course the entrepreneur actually pursues is to contact one or two of her friends or relatives who work downtown and bring them and their office colleagues some of her food to taste. If the people in the office like her food, she might get a lunch delivery service going. Over time, she might develop enough of a customer base to start a restaurant or else, after a few weeks of trying to build the lunch business, she might discover that the people who said they enjoyed her food did not really enjoy it so much as they did her quirky personality and conversation, particularly her rather unusual life perceptions. Our imaginary entrepreneur might now decide to give up the lunch business and start writing a book, going on the lecture circuit and eventually building a business in the motivational consulting industry!

Given the exact same starting point—but with a different set of contingencies—the entrepreneur might end up building one of a variety of businesses. To take a quick tour of some possibilities, consider the following: Whoever first buys the food from our imaginary Curry in a Hurry entrepreneur becomes, by definition, the first target customer. By continually listening to the customer and building an ever-increasing network of customers and strategic partners, the entrepreneur can then identify a workable segment profile. For example, if the first customers who actually buy the food and come back for more are working women of varied ethnic origin, this becomes her target segment. Depending on what the first customer really wants, she can start defining her market. If the customer is really interested in the food, the entrepreneur can start targeting all working women in the geographic location, or she can think in terms of locating more outlets in areas with working women of similar profiles—a "Women in a Hurry" franchise?

Or, if the customer is interested primarily in the idea of ethnic or exotic entertainment, rather than merely in food, the entrepreneur might develop other products, such as catering services, party planning, and so on—"Curry Favors"? Perhaps, if the customers buy food from her because they actually enjoy learning about new cultures, she might offer lectures and classes, maybe beginning with Indian cooking and moving on to cultural aspects, including concerts and ancient history and philosophy, and the profound idea that food is a vehicle of cultural exploration—"School of Curry"? Or maybe what really interests them is theme tours and other travel options to India and the Far East—"Curryland Travels"?

In a nutshell, in using effectuation processes to build her firm, the entrepreneur can build several different types of firms in completely disparate industries. This means that the original idea (or set of causes) does not imply any one single strategic universe for the firm (or effect). Instead, the process of effectuation allows the entrepreneur to create one or more several possible effects irrespective of the generalized end goal with which she started. The process not only enables the realization of several possible effects (although generally one or only a few are actually realized in the implementation) but it also allows a decision maker to change his or her goals and even to shape and construct them over time, making use of contingencies as they arise.[10]

Our use of direct quotes from Sarasvathy on effectuation is not to make the case that it is superior to thought processes that involve causation; rather, it represents a way that entrepreneurs sometimes think. Effectuation helps entrepreneurs think in an environment of high uncertainty. Indeed organizations today operate in complex and dynamic environments that are increasingly characterized by rapid, substantial, and discontinuous change.[11] Given the nature of this type of environment, most managers of firms need to take on an entrepreneurial mind-set so that their firms can successfully adapt to environmental changes.[12] This *entrepreneurial mind-set* involves the ability to rapidly sense, act, and mobilize, even under uncertain conditions.[13] In developing an entrepreneurial mind-set, individuals must attempt to make sense of opportunities in the context of changing goals, constantly questioning the "dominant logic" in the context of a changing environment and revisiting "deceptively simple questions" about what is thought to be true about markets and the firm. For example, effective entrepreneurs are thought to continuously "rethink current strategic actions, organization structure, communications systems, corporate culture, asset deployment, investment strategies, in short every aspect of a firm's operation and long-term health."[14]

To be good at these tasks, individuals must develop a *cognitive adaptability*. Mike Haynie, a retired major of the U.S. Air Force and now professor at Syracuse University, and me (Dean Shepherd from Indiana University) have developed a number of models of cognitive adaptability and a survey for capturing it, to which we now turn.[15]

Cognitive Adaptability

Cognitive adaptability describes the extent to which entrepreneurs are dynamic, flexible, self-regulating, and engaged in the process of generating multiple decision frameworks focused on sensing and processing changes in their environments and then acting on them. Decision frameworks are organized on knowledge about people and situations that are used to help someone make sense of what is going on.[16] Cognitive adaptability is

---

entrepreneurial mind-set
Involves the ability to rapidly sense, act, and mobilize, even under uncertain conditions

cognitive adaptability
Describes the extent to which entrepreneurs are dynamic, flexible, self-regulating, and engaged in the process of generating multiple decision frameworks focused on sensing and processing changes in their environments and then acting on them

AS SEEN IN *BUSINESS NEWS*

DO ENTREPRENEURS BENEFIT FROM PARANOIA?

Some believe that paranoia is a psychological condition that causes dysfunction. But, at least in terms of business, Andrew Grove, president and CEO of Intel Corp., believes that "Only the Paranoid Survive." By placing yourself in a state of paranoia, you become highly concerned about, and sensitive to, threats to your company and you are motivated to take action to alleviate or eliminate those threats.

PRINCIPLES OF ACTING PARANOIA

Underlying paranoia is a recognition that others want to achieve success and are willing to take it away from you. They are watching your business and how you respond to changes in the competitive environment. Therefore, Andrew Grove worries about product defects, releasing products too early, factories not performing efficiently, having too much (or too little) capacity, and so on. The principles of paranoia are the following:

1. **Paranoia Means Not Resting on Your Laurels.** This simply means that even given your past successes there are still threats out there; you must be vigilant to notice and then respond to these threats. Andrew Grove calls this a *guardian attitude*—the attitude that is required to protect the firm from potential competitor moves or other environmental threats.

2. **Paranoia Means Being Detail Orientated.** This means attending to even the smallest details because this is a major line of defense against threats. This means attending both to the details internal to running the business and to those external including catering to the demands of your customers.

Paranoia is particularly important when the business environment is characterized in terms of high levels of competition and high number of opportunities.

THE DOWNSIDE OF PARANOIA

There may be such thing as too much paranoia—too much time and effort invested in noticing and responding to threats. One entrepreneur uses the examples of using $500 worth of accounting time to find a $5 error (which does not make sense unless there is information of a more systematic problem that led to the $5 error). Worrying "obsessively" could also be a warning sign, one that requires a remedy. Although entrepreneurs are known to often be thinking about their business, an inability to "turn it off," at least for short periods, can cause psychological and physical problems. That is, having some work life balance can be beneficial to the individual both as an entrepreneur and as a human being.

reflected in an entrepreneur's metacognitive awareness, that is, the ability to reflect upon, understand, and control one's thinking and learning.[17] Specifically, metacognition describes a higher-order cognitive process that serves to organize what individuals know and recognize about themselves, tasks, situations, and their environments to promote effective and *adaptable* cognitive functioning in the face of feedback from complex and dynamic environments.[18]

How cognitively adaptable are you? Try the survey in Table 1.1 and compare yourself to some of your classmates. A higher score means that you are more metacognitively aware, and this in turn helps provide cognitive adaptability. Regardless of your score, the good news is that you can learn to be more cognitively adaptable. This ability will serve you well in most new tasks, but particularly when pursuing a new entry and managing a firm in an uncertain environment. Put simply, it requires us to "think about thinking which requires, and helps provide, knowledge and control over our thinking and learning activities—it requires us to be self-aware, think aloud, reflect, be strategic, plan, have a plan in mind, know what to know, and self-monitor.[19] We can achieve this by asking ourselves a series of questions that relate to (1) comprehension, (2) connection, (3) strategy, and (4) reflection.[20]

Paranoia can also lead to fear, such as fear of failure. Fear of failure can constrict thinking and lead to inaction and inaction can make the entrepreneur's firm more vulnerable. One entrepreneur noted that if he was fearful then his business would never have got off the ground. Indeed, perhaps entrepreneurs are already so paranoid that any more paranoia may push them over the edge of what is healthy. They may be so paranoid about the business that their words and actions begin to discourage employees and customers. That is, paranoia that your employees or customers are out to get you may lead to them leaving and creating an actual (rather than an imagined) threat to the business. Indeed, for the entrepreneur's business to grow and achieve success, he or she may need to put some faith in the organization's employees and customers.

"CRITICAL EVALUATION" RATHER THAN PARANOIA

Perhaps the term *paranoia* is too loaded, and therefore care must be taken in advising entrepreneurs that they need to become more paranoid. But Andrew Grove's point is well taken. It might be better to talk about critical evaluation or critical analysis, which means to look at everything (suggests Stephen Markoitz, director of governmental and political relations of a small business association). He suggests that if the entrepreneur is paranoid then he or she is unable to look at everything. That is, the entrepreneur may be particularly good at noticing threats but miss opportunities. (But is it ever possible to see and evaluate everything?)

Whatever it is called, the point is that entrepreneurs are likely to keep worrying about their business, keep trying to attend to both threats and opportunities, and think constantly about how to enable their business to succeed.

ADVICE TO AN ENTREPRENEUR

A friend who has just become an entrepreneur has read the above article and comes to you for advice:

1. I worry about my business; does that mean I am paranoid?

2. What are the benefits of paranoia and what are the costs?

3. How do I know I have the right level of paranoia to effectively run the business and not put me in the hospital with a stomach ulcer?

4. Won't forcing myself to be more paranoid take the fun out of being an entrepreneur?

Source: "How Smart Entrepreneurs Harness the Power of Paranoia," by Mark Henricks, March 1997, *Entrepreneur* magazine: www.entrepreneur.com.

---

comprehension questions Questions designed to increase entrepreneurs' understanding of the nature of the environment

1. *Comprehension questions* are designed to increase entrepreneurs' understanding of the nature of the environment before they begin to address an entrepreneurial challenge, whether it be a change in the environment or the assessment of a potential opportunity. Understanding arises from recognition that a problem or opportunity exists, the nature of that situation, and its implications. In general, the questions that stimulate individuals to think about comprehension include: What is the problem all about? What is the question? What are the meanings of the key concepts? Specific to entrepreneurs, the questions are more likely to include: What is this market all about? What is this technology all about? What do we want to achieve by creating this new firm? What are the key elements to effectively pursuing this opportunity?

connection tasks Tasks designed to stimulate entrepreneurs to think about the current situation in terms of similarities to and differences from situations previously faced and solved

2. *Connection tasks* are designed to stimulate entrepreneurs to think about the current situation in terms of similarities to and differences from situations previously faced and solved. In other words, these tasks prompt the entrepreneur to tap into his or her knowledge and experience without overgeneralizing. Generally, connection tasks focus on questions like: How is this problem similar to problems I have already solved? Why? How is this problem different from what I have already solved? Why? Specific to entrepreneurs, the questions are more likely to include: How is this new environment

TABLE 1.1   Mike Haynie's "Measure of Adaptive Cognition"

How Cognitively Flexible Are You? On a scale of 1 to 10, where 1 is "not very much like me" and 10 is "very much like me," how do you rate yourself on the following statements?

Goal Orientation

I often define goals for myself.	Not very much—1 2 3 4 5 6 7 8 9 10—Very much like me like me
I understand how accomplishment of a task relates to my goals.	Not very much—1 2 3 4 5 6 7 8 9 10—Very much like me like me
I set specific goals before I begin a task.	Not very much—1 2 3 4 5 6 7 8 9 10—Very much like me like me
I ask myself how well I've accomplished my goals once I've finished.	Not very much—1 2 3 4 5 6 7 8 9 10—Very much like me like me
When performing a task, I frequently assess my progress against my objectives.	Not very much—1 2 3 4 5 6 7 8 9 10—Very much like me like me

Metacognitive Knowledge

I think of several ways to solve a problem and choose the best one.	Not very much—1 2 3 4 5 6 7 8 9 10—Very much like me like me
I challenge my own assumptions about a task before I begin.	Not very much—1 2 3 4 5 6 7 8 9 10—Very much like me like me
I think about how others may react to my actions.	Not very much—1 2 3 4 5 6 7 8 9 10—Very much like me like me
I find myself automatically employing strategies that have worked in the past.	Not very much—1 2 3 4 5 6 7 8 9 10—Very much like me like me
I perform best when I already have knowledge of the task.	Not very much—1 2 3 4 5 6 7 8 9 10—Very much like me like me
I create my own examples to make information more meaningful.	Not very much—1 2 3 4 5 6 7 8 9 10—Very much like me like me
I try to use strategies that have worked in the past.	Not very much—1 2 3 4 5 6 7 8 9 10—Very much like me like me
I ask myself questions about the task before I begin.	Not very much—1 2 3 4 5 6 7 8 9 10—Very much like me like me
I try to translate new information into my own words.	Not very much—1 2 3 4 5 6 7 8 9 10—Very much like me like me
I try to break problems down into smaller components.	Not very much—1 2 3 4 5 6 7 8 9 10—Very much like me like me
I focus on the meaning and significance of new information.	Not very much—1 2 3 4 5 6 7 8 9 10—Very much like me like me

Metacognitive Experience

I think about what I really need to accomplish before I begin a task.	Not very much—1 2 3 4 5 6 7 8 9 10—Very much like me like me
I use different strategies depending on the situation.	Not very much—1 2 3 4 5 6 7 8 9 10—Very much like me like me
I organize my time to best accomplish my goals.	Not very much—1 2 3 4 5 6 7 8 9 10—Very much like me like me

I am good at organizing information.	Not very much—1 2 3 4 5 6 7 8 9 10—Very much like me / like me
I know what kind of information is most important to consider when faced with a problem.	Not very much—1 2 3 4 5 6 7 8 9 10—Very much like me / like me
I consciously focus my attention on important information.	Not very much—1 2 3 4 5 6 7 8 9 10—Very much like me / like me
My "gut" tells me when a given strategy I use will be most effective.	Not very much—1 2 3 4 5 6 7 8 9 10—Very much like me / like me
I depend on my intuition to help me formulate strategies.	Not very much—1 2 3 4 5 6 7 8 9 10—Very much like me / like me

Metacognitive Choice

I ask myself if I have considered all the options when solving a problem.	Not very much—1 2 3 4 5 6 7 8 9 10—Very much like me / like me
I ask myself if there was an easier way to do things after I finish a task.	Not very much—1 2 3 4 5 6 7 8 9 10—Very much like me / like me
I ask myself if I have considered all the options after I solve a problem.	Not very much—1 2 3 4 5 6 7 8 9 10—Very much like me / like me
I re-evaluate my assumptions when I get confused.	Not very much—1 2 3 4 5 6 7 8 9 10—Very much like me / like me
I ask myself if I have learned as much as I could have after I finish the task.	Not very much—1 2 3 4 5 6 7 8 9 10—Very much like me / like me

Monitoring

I periodically review to help me understand important relationships.	Not very much—1 2 3 4 5 6 7 8 9 10—Very much like me / like me
I stop and go back over information that is not clear.	Not very much—1 2 3 4 5 6 7 8 9 10—Very much like me / like me
I am aware of what strategies I use when engaged in a given task.	Not very much—1 2 3 4 5 6 7 8 9 10—Very much like me / like me
I find myself analyzing the usefulness of a given strategy while engaged in a given task.	Not very much—1 2 3 4 5 6 7 8 9 10—Very much like me / like me
I find myself pausing regularly to check my comprehension of the problem or situation at hand.	Not very much—1 2 3 4 5 6 7 8 9 10—Very much like me / like me
I ask myself questions about how well I am doing while I am performing a novel task. I stop and re-read when I get confused.	Not very much—1 2 3 4 5 6 7 8 9 10—Very much like me / like me

Result—A higher score means that you are more aware of the way that you think about how you make decisions and are therefore more likely to be cognitively flexible.

Source: Reprinted with permission from M. Haynie and D. Shepherd, "A Measure of Adaptive Cognition for Entrepreneurship Research," *Entrepreneurship, Theory and Practice* 33, no. 3 (2009), pp. 695–714.

strategic tasks Tasks designed to stimulate entrepreneurs to think about which strategies are appropriate for solving the problem (and why) or pursuing the opportunity (and how)

similar to others in which I have operated? How is it different? How is this new organization similar to the established organizations I have managed? How is it different?

3. *Strategic tasks* are designed to stimulate entrepreneurs to think about which strategies are appropriate for solving the problem (and why) or pursuing the opportunity (and how). These tasks prompt them to think about the what, why, and how of their ap-

proach to the situation. Generally, these questions include: What strategy/tactic/principle can I use to solve this problem? Why is this strategy/tactic/principle the most appropriate one? How can I organize the information to solve the problem? How can I implement the plan? Specific to entrepreneurs, the questions are likely to include: What changes to strategic position, organizational structure, and culture will help us manage our newness? How can the implementation of this strategy be made feasible?

reflection tasks Tasks designed to stimulate entrepreneurs to think about their understanding and feelings as they progress through the entrepreneurial process

4. *Reflection tasks* are designed to stimulate entrepreneurs to think about their understanding and feelings as they progress through the entrepreneurial process. These tasks prompt entrepreneurs to generate their own feedback (create a feedback loop in their solution process) to provide the opportunity to change. Generally, reflection questions include: What am I doing? Does it make sense? What difficulties am I facing? How do I feel? How can I verify the solution? Can I use another approach for solving the task? Specific to the entrepreneurial context, entrepreneurs might ask: What difficulties will we have in convincing our stakeholders? Is there a better way to implement our strategy? How will we know success if we see it?

Entrepreneurs who are able to increase cognitive adaptability have an improved ability to (1) adapt to new situations—that is, it provides a basis by which a person's prior experience and knowledge affect learning or problem solving in a new situation; (2) be creative—that is, it can lead to original and adaptive ideas, solutions, or insights; and (3) communicate one's reasoning behind a particular response.[21] We hope that this section of the book has provided you not only a deeper understanding of how entrepreneurs can think and act with great flexibility but also an awareness of some techniques for incorporating cognitive adaptability in your life.

We have discussed how entrepreneurs make decisions in uncertain environments and how one might develop an ability to be more cognitively flexible. It is important to note that entrepreneurs not only think but they also intend to act.

THE INTENTION TO ACT ENTREPRENEURIALLY

Entrepreneurial action is most often intentional. Entrepreneurs intend to pursue certain opportunities, enter new markets, and offer new products—and this is rarely the process of unintentional behavior. Intentions capture the motivational factors that influence a behavior; they are indications of how hard people are willing to try and how much of an effort they are planning to exert to perform the behavior. As a general rule, the stronger the intention to engage in a behavior, the more likely should be its performance.[22] Individuals have stronger intentions to act when taking action is perceived to be *feasible* and *desirable*. *Entrepreneurial intentions* can be explained in the same way.

entrepreneurial intentions The motivational factors that influence individuals to pursue entrepreneurial outcomes

entrepreneurial self-efficacy The conviction that one can successfully execute the entrepreneurial process

The perception of feasibility has much to do with an entrepreneurial self-efficacy. *Entrepreneur's self-efficacy* refers to the conviction that one can successfully execute the behavior required; people who believe they have the capacity to perform (high self-efficacy) tend to perform well. Thus, it reflects the perception of a personal capability to do a particular job or set of tasks. High self-efficacy leads to increased initiative and persistence and thus improved performance; low self-efficacy reduces effort and thus performance. Indeed, people with high self-efficacy think differently and behave differently than people with low self-efficacy.[23] Self-efficacy affects the person's choice of action and the amount of effort exerted. Entrepreneurship scholars have found that self-efficacy is positively associated with the creation of a new independent organization.[24]

Not only must an individual perceive entrepreneurial action as feasible for entrepreneurial intention to be high, the individual must also perceive this course of action as

perceived desirability
The degree to which an individual has a favorable or unfavorable evaluation of the potential entrepreneurial outcomes

desirable. *Perceived desirability* refers to an individual's attitude toward entrepreneurial action—the degree to which he or she has a favorable or unfavorable evaluation of the potential entrepreneurial outcomes.[25] For example, creative actions are not likely to emerge unless they produce personal rewards that are perceived as relatively more desirable than more familiar behaviors.[26]

Therefore, the higher the perceived desirability and feasibility, the stronger the intention to act entrepreneurially. We next investigate the background characteristics of entrepreneurs to understand why some individuals are more likely to engage in entrepreneurship than other individuals. That is, we examine how background characteristics provide an indication of whether certain individuals are more or less likely to perceive entrepreneurial action as feasible and/or desirable and therefore whether they are more or less likely to intend to be entrepreneurs.

ENTREPRENEUR BACKGROUND AND CHARACTERISTICS
Education

Although some may feel that entrepreneurs are less educated than the general population, research findings indicate that this is clearly not the case. Education is important in the upbringing of the entrepreneur. Its importance is reflected not only in the level of education obtained but also in the fact that it continues to play a major role in helping entrepreneurs cope with the problems they confront. Although a formal education is not necessary for starting a new business—as is reflected in the success of such high school dropouts as Andrew Carnegie, William Durant, Henry Ford, and William Lear—it does provide a good background, particularly when it is related to the field of the venture. For example, entrepreneurs have cited an educational need in the areas of finance, strategic planning, marketing (particularly distribution), and management. The ability to communicate clearly with both the written and the spoken word is also important in any entrepreneurial activity.

Even general education is valuable because it facilitates the integration and accumulation of new knowledge, providing individuals with a larger opportunity set (i.e., a broader base of knowledge casts a wider net for the discovery or generation of potential opportunities), and assists entrepreneurs in adapting to new situations.[27] The general education (and experiences) of an entrepreneur can provide knowledge, skills, and problem-solving abilities that are transferable across many different situations. Indeed, it has been found that while education has a positive influence on the chance that a person will discover new opportunities, it does not necessarily determine whether he will create a new business to exploit the discovered opportunity.[28] To the extent that individuals believe that their education has made entrepreneurial action more feasible, they are more likely to become entrepreneurs.

Age

The relationship of age to the entrepreneurial career process also has been carefully researched.[29] In evaluating these results, it is important to differentiate between entrepreneurial age (the age of the entrepreneur reflected in his or her experience) and chronological age (years since birth). As discussed in the next section, entrepreneurial experience is one of the best predictors of success, particularly when the new venture is in the same field as the previous business experience.

In terms of chronological age, most entrepreneurs initiate their entrepreneurial careers between the ages of 22 and 45. A career can be initiated before or after these ages, as long as the entrepreneur has the necessary experience and financial support, and the high energy level needed to launch and manage a new venture successfully. Also, there are milestone ages every five years (25, 30, 35, 40, and 45) when an individual is more inclined to start an entrepreneurial career. As one entrepreneur succinctly stated, "I felt it was now or never in terms of starting a new venture when I approached 30." Generally, male entrepreneurs tend to start their first significant venture in their early 30s, while women entrepreneurs tend to do so in their middle 30s. However, an entrepreneurial career is quite popular later in life when the children have left home, there are fewer financial concerns, and individuals start to think about what they would really like to do with the rest of their lives.[30]

Work History

work history The past work experience of an individual

Work history can influence the decision to launch a new entrepreneurial venture, but it also plays a role in the growth and eventual success of the new venture. While dissatisfaction with various aspects of one's job—such as a lack of challenge or promotional opportunities, as well as frustration and boredom—often motivates the launching of a new venture, previous technical and industry experience is important once the decision to launch has been made. Experience in the following areas is particularly important: financing, product or service development, manufacturing, and the development of distribution channels.

As the venture becomes established and starts growing, managerial experience and skills become increasingly important. Although most ventures start with few (if any) employees, as the number of employees increases, the entrepreneur's managerial skills come more and more into play. In addition, entrepreneurial experiences, such as the start-up process, making decisions under high levels of uncertainty, building a culture from "scratch," raising venture capital, and managing high growth, are also important. Most entrepreneurs indicate that their most significant venture was not their first one. Throughout their entrepreneurial careers, they are exposed to many new venture opportunities and gather ideas for many more new ventures.

Finally, previous start-up experience can provide entrepreneurs with expertise in running an independent business as well as benchmarks for judging the relevance of information, which can lead to an understanding of the "real" value of new entry opportunities, speed up the business creation process, and enhance performance.[31] Previous start-up experience is a relatively good predictor of starting subsequent businesses.[32] To the extent that start-up experience provides entrepreneurs with a greater belief in their ability to successfully achieve entrepreneurial outcomes, this increased perceived feasibility will strengthen entrepreneurial intentions.

ROLE MODELS AND SUPPORT SYSTEMS

role models Individuals whose example an entrepreneur can aspire to and copy

One of the most important factors influencing entrepreneurs in their career path is their choice of a *role model*.[33] Role models can be parents, brothers or sisters, other relatives, or other entrepreneurs. Successful entrepreneurs frequently are viewed as catalysts by potential entrepreneurs. As one entrepreneur succinctly stated, "After evaluating Ted and his success as an entrepreneur, I knew I was much smarter and could do a better job. So I started my own business." In this way, role models can provide important signals that entrepreneurship is feasible for them.

Role models can also serve in a supportive capacity as mentors during and after the launch of a new venture. An entrepreneur needs a strong support and advisory system in every phase of the new venture. This support system is perhaps most crucial during the start-up phase, as it provides information, advice, and guidance on such matters as organizational structure, obtaining needed financial resources, and marketing. Since entrepreneurship is a social role embedded in a social context, it is important that an entrepreneur establish connections and eventually networks early in the new venture formation process.

As initial contacts and connections expand, they form a network with similar properties prevalent in a social network—density (the extensiveness of ties between the two individuals) and centrality (the total distance of the entrepreneur to all other individuals and the total number of individuals in the network). The strength of the ties between the entrepreneur and any individual in the network is dependent upon the frequency, level, and reciprocity of the relationship. The more frequent, in-depth, and mutually beneficial a relationship, the stronger and more durable the network between the entrepreneur and the individual.[34] Although most networks are not formally organized, an informal network for moral and professional support still greatly benefits the entrepreneur.

Moral-Support Network

moral-support network
Individuals who give psychological support to an entrepreneur

It is important for each entrepreneur to establish a *moral-support network* of family and friends—a cheering squad. This cheering squad plays a critical role during the many difficult and lonely times that occur throughout the entrepreneurial process. Most entrepreneurs indicate that their spouses are their biggest supporters and allow them to devote the excessive amounts of time necessary to the new venture.

Friends also play key roles in a moral-support network. Not only can friends provide advice that is often more honest than that received from other sources, but they also provide encouragement, understanding, and even assistance. Entrepreneurs can confide in friends without fear of criticism. Finally, relatives (children, parents, grandparents, aunts, and uncles) also can be strong sources of moral support, particularly if they are also entrepreneurs. As one entrepreneur stated, "The total family support I received was the key to my success. Having an understanding cheering squad giving me encouragement allowed me to persist through the many difficulties and problems."

Professional-Support Network

professional-support network   Individuals who help the entrepreneur in business activities

In addition to encouragement, the entrepreneur needs advice and counsel throughout the establishment of the new venture. This advice can be obtained from a mentor, business associates, trade associations, or personal affiliations—all members of a *professional-support network*.

Most entrepreneurs indicate that they have mentors. How does one find a mentor? This task sounds much more difficult than it really is. Since a mentor is a coach, a sounding board, and an advocate—someone with whom the entrepreneur can share both problems and successes—the individual selected needs to be an expert in the field. An entrepreneur can start the "mentor-finding process" by preparing a list of experts in various fields—such as in the fundamental business activities of finance, marketing, accounting, law, or management—who can provide the practical "how-to" advice needed. From this list, an individual who can offer the most assistance should be identified and contacted. If the selected individual is willing to act as a mentor, he or she should be periodically apprised of the progress of the business so that a relationship can gradually develop.

Another good source of advice can be cultivated by establishing a network of business associates. This group can be composed of self-employed individuals who have experienced starting a business; clients or buyers of the venture's product or service; experts such as consultants, lawyers, or accountants; and the venture's suppliers. Clients or buyers are a particularly important group to cultivate. This group represents the source of revenue to the venture and is the best provider of word-of-mouth advertising. There is nothing better than word-of-mouth advertising from satisfied customers to help establish a winning business reputation and promote goodwill.

Suppliers are another important component in a professional-support network. A new venture needs to establish a solid track record with suppliers to build a good relationship and to ensure the adequate availability of materials and other supplies. Suppliers also can provide good information on the nature of trends, as well as competition, in the industry.

In addition to mentors and business associates, trade associations can offer an excellent professional-support network. Trade association members can help keep the new venture competitive. Trade associations keep up with new developments and can provide overall industry data.

Finally, personal affiliations of the entrepreneur also can be a valuable part of a professional-support network. Affiliations developed with individuals through shared hobbies, participation in sporting events, clubs, civic involvements, and school alumni groups are excellent potential sources of referrals, advice, and information. Each entrepreneur needs to establish both moral and professional-support networks. These contacts provide confidence, support, advice, and information. As one entrepreneur stated, "In your own business, you are all alone. There is a definite need to establish support groups to share problems with and to obtain information and overall support for the new venture."

Therefore, it is important to recognize that entrepreneurial activity is embedded in networks of interpersonal relationships. These networks are defined by a set of actors (individuals and organizations) and a set of linkages between them, and they provide individuals access to a variety of resources necessary for entrepreneurial outcomes.[35] These resources may assist in efforts to discover and exploit opportunities, as well as in the creation of new independent organizations.[36] The trust embedded in some of these networks provides potential entrepreneurs the opportunity to access highly valuable resources. For example, business networks are composed of independent firms linked by common interests, friendship, and trust and are particularly important in facilitating the transfer of difficult-to-codify, knowledge-intensive skills that are expensive to obtain in other ways.[37] These networks also create opportunities for exchanging goods and services that are difficult to enforce through contractual arrangements, which facilitates the pursuit of opportunities.[38] To the extent that a network provides an individual greater belief in his or her ability to access resources critical to the successful achievement of entrepreneurial outcomes, this increased perceived feasibility will strengthen entrepreneurial intentions. This can include intentions for sustainable entrepreneurship.

SUSTAINABLE ENTREPRENEURSHIP

sustainable entrepreneurship
Entrepreneurship focused on preserving nature, life support, and community (sustainability) in the pursuit of perceived opportunities to bring future products, processes, and services into existence for gain (entrepreneurial action) where gain is broadly construed to include economic and noneconomic benefits to individuals, the economy, and society (development)

Sustainable development is perhaps the most important issue of our time, and entrepreneurship can have a positive impact on this issue. That is, entrepreneurial action can help us both sustain and develop. Specifically, *sustainable entrepreneurship* is focused on preserving nature, life support, and community (sustainability) in the pursuit of perceived opportunities to bring future products, processes, and services into existence for gain (entrepreneurial action) where gain is broadly construed to include economic and noneconomic benefits to individuals, the economy, and society (development).[39]

Based on the McMullen-Shepherd model, we know that entrepreneurial action is driven by knowledge and motivation. Those with greater knowledge of the natural environment—the physical world, including the earth, biodiversity, and ecosystems[40]—are more likely to notice changes in that environment that form opportunity beliefs than

 ETHICS

AN ORGANIZATION'S CODE OF ETHICS

There has been a litany of financial scandals, which have led to increased action by governments in an attempt to regulate against such actions. But companies themselves are placing higher priority on ethical behavior, and that goes for the organization's employees. One way that they have done this is to create a code of ethics for all employees (indeed, many schools in universities have created a student code of ethics).

There are some distinct advantages from creating and implementing an employee code of ethics. The first is that the code makes everyone within the organization aware of what represents ethical behavior (and, through deduction, what is unethical behavior). To the extent that employees understand what ethical behavior is, they are more likely to ensure that their behavior remains consistent with that expectation. But it should be noted that a code of ethics is not solely a formal statement delineating ethical from nonethical behavior but also an important positive statement about the beliefs and values of the organization. The code is part of a broader system, such as the following:

Leaders Are the "Walking Talking" Embodiment of the Ethical Values of the Organization: Having something in writing is good but not sufficient to encourage ethical behavior. Employees often take their cues from the organization's leaders. That is, they model the behaviors of their leaders, whether that behavior is ethical or unethical. Therefore, everyone within the organization needs to abide by the code of ethics, especially its managers. For example, even a simple transgression of the code by a manager can have a substantially negative impact on the code's effectiveness with the rest of those within the organization—they see a distinction between what is said should be done and the way things are really done within the organization. Of course, this completely undermines the code of ethics. Therefore, if managers do not always follow the code of ethics, they should not be surprised if the employees do not follow the code either.

Ethics Is One of the Organization's Core Values: Organizations known for the ethical actions of their managers and employees

have ethics as one of its core values—it is part of the organization's identity and reflected in the organizational culture. Being at the core of the organization's values, members of the organization realize that *ethical behavior* is "what we do around here." Indeed, this is reflected in hiring practices—organizations want to hire managers and employees who already share their core values including ethics. In one study (reported in this news article), 58 percent of managers indicated that what impressed them the most were candidates who displayed honesty and integrity.

Creating a Safe Environment for Employees to Voice Concerns: Part of creating an ethical climate within the organization involves creating a culture where employees feel psychologically safe to voice concerns about potentially unethical behavior. If they feel that they can voice concerns, then the management is able to become aware of ethical transgressions and fix them before the event blows out of control and/or before the ethical culture of the organization is destroyed. Both have a considerable negative impact on the organization. The key for managers is to notice and respond early to ethical issues, and one critical way for managers to notice these transgressions is to encourage employees to voice their concerns. Employees have to feel that in voicing their concerns they are not going to be penalized.

Once aware of ethical transgressions, no matter how small, managers must act. Action reinforces the code of ethics; inaction undermines it.

One way to ensure that organizational members understand and "buy into the code" is to involve them in the process of creating the code.

By implementing a code of ethics, having it reflected in the organization's core values, and reinforcing the code through words and actions, the organization can ensure ethical behavior, which is a critical basis of an entrepreneurial firm.

Source: Max Messmer, "Does Your Company Have a Code of Ethics?" *Strategic Finance*, April 2003.

those with less knowledge. However, we cannot underestimate the role of entrepreneurial knowledge of markets, technologies, and/or opportunity exploitation; without entrepreneurial knowledge, opportunities for sustainable development are unlikely to become a reality.

For entrepreneurial actions that preserve nature to be considered sustainable entrepreneurship, they must also develop gains for the entrepreneur, others, and/or society. It has long been accepted that entrepreneurs can generate economic wealth for themselves, but their impact on development can be far greater. They can generate gains for others that are economic, environmental, and social, including employment opportunities, improved access to quality/valuable goods, and revenues for the government(s). The environmental gain generated for others could be reduced air pollution, improved air quality, improved drinking-water quality, and other enhanced living conditions. The social gains include improved child survival rates, longer life expectancy, superior education, equal opportunity, and so on. For example, individuals who were knowledgeable about cooking practices in developing countries were able to recognize opportunities for hybrid stoves that substantially reduced particle pollutants in households but were consistent with traditional recipes.[41] It is not just the natural environment that can be sustained, though; communities also need to be preserved. Indeed, knowledge of indigenous groups' cultures has led to the pursuit of opportunities that serve to sustain these cultures.

We recognize that our explanation of sustainable entrepreneurship could be considered highly idealistic. However, it is consistent with thinking of entrepreneurial action as a tool (e.g., a hammer) that can be used for good (e.g., to build a community center) or for bad (e.g., as a weapon for harming others). Indeed, in a study of 83 entrepreneurs, the researchers found that while most entrepreneurs had positive attitudes toward the natural environment, under some conditions, they disengaged these values to decide to exploit an opportunity that caused harm to the natural environment.[42] We do believe, however, that there are many people in the world today who are motivated to use the tool of entrepreneurial action to sustain the natural environment and communities and develop gains for others. Perhaps you are one of these people.

IN REVIEW

SUMMARY

Entrepreneurship involves action. Before action, individuals use their knowledge and motivation to overcome ignorance to form a belief that there exists an opportunity for someone. They then need to determine if this opportunity for someone matches their knowledge and motivation—is it an opportunity for them? Individuals engaging in the entrepreneurial task think differently from those engaged in other tasks, such as managerial tasks. The process requires that the individual and the firm have an entrepreneurial mind-set. We started our discussion of this mind-set with the concepts of thinking structurally and effectually, which challenges traditional notions of the way that entrepreneurs think about their tasks.

By thinking structurally and not being distracted by superficial features, entrepreneurs are able to identify opportunities by making connections between a technology and a market that may not be obvious. Furthermore, although entrepreneurs think about some tasks in a causal way, they also are likely to think about some tasks effectually (and some entrepreneurs more so than other entrepreneurs). Rather than starting with the desired outcome in mind and then focusing on the means to achieving that outcome, entrepreneurs sometimes approach tasks by looking at what they have—their means—and selecting among possible outcomes. Who is to say whether the "causal chef" who starts with a menu or the "effectual chef" who starts with what is in the cupboard produces the best meal? But we can say that some expert entrepreneurs think effectually about opportunities. Thinking effectually helps entrepreneurs make decisions in uncertain environments. Entrepreneurs are often situated in resource-scarce environments but are able to make do with (and recombine) the resources they have at hand to create opportunities.

The external environment can also have an impact on performance and therefore the entrepreneur needs to be able to adapt to changes in the environment. In this chapter, we introduced the notion of cognitive flexibility and emphasized that it is something that can be measured and learned. By asking questions related to comprehension, connection, strategy, and reflection, entrepreneurs can maintain an awareness of their thought process and in doing so develop greater cognitive adaptability.

Individuals become entrepreneurs because they intend to do so. The stronger the intention to be an entrepreneur, the more likely it is that it will happen. Intentions become stronger as individuals perceive an entrepreneurial career as feasible and desirable. These perceptions of feasibility and desirability are influenced by one's background and characteristics, such as education, personal values, age and work history, role models and support systems, and networks.

The outcome of entrepreneurial action can be economic gain for the entrepreneur and his or her family. But this may not be the only motivation for the intention to be an entrepreneur. Some individuals exploit opportunities that sustain (the natural environment and/or communities) and generate gains for others. We call this process sustainable entrepreneurship.

RESEARCH TASKS

1. Speak to people from five different countries and ask what entrepreneurship means to them and how their national culture helps and/or hinders entrepreneurship.

2. Ask an entrepreneur about his or her business today and ask him or her to describe the decisions and series of events that led the business from start-up to its current form. Would you classify this process as causal, effectual, or both?

3. Ask two entrepreneurs and five students (not in this class) to fill out the Haynie-Shepherd "Measure of Adaptive Cognition" (see Table 1.1). How do you rate relative to the entrepreneurs? Relative to your fellow students?

4. When conducting a homework exercise for another class (especially a case analysis), ask yourself comprehension questions, connection questions, strategy questions, and reflection questions. What impact did this have on the outcome of the task?

5. What impact does entrepreneurship have on your natural environment? What impact does it have on sustaining local communities? Use data to back up your arguments.

24   PART 1   THE ENTREPRENEURIAL PERSPECTIVE

CLASS DISCUSSION

1. List the content that you believe is necessary for an entrepreneurship course. Be prepared to justify your answer.

2. Do you really think that entrepreneurs think effectually? What about yourself—do you sometimes think effectually? In what ways is it good? Then why are we taught in business classes to always think causally? Are there particular problems or tasks in which thinking causally is likely to be superior to effectuation? When might effectuation be superior to causal thinking?

3. To be cognitively flexible seems to require that the entrepreneur continually question himself or herself. Doesn't that create doubt that can be seen by employees and financiers such that success actually becomes more difficult to achieve? Besides, although flexibility is a good thing, if the firm keeps changing based on minor changes in the environment, the buyers are going to become confused about the nature of the firm. Is adaptation always a good thing?

4. Do you believe that sustainable development should be part of an entrepreneurship course, or did the textbook authors just include a section on it to be "politically correct"?

5. Provide some examples of the mental leaps that entrepreneurs have taken.

6. What excites you about being an entrepreneur? What are your major concerns?

SELECTED READINGS

Baker, Ted; and Reed Nelson. (2005). Something from Nothing: Resource Construction through Entrepreneurial Bricolage. *Administrative Science Quarterly,* vol. 50, no. 3, pp. 329–66.

> *In this article, the authors studied 29 firms and demonstrated that entrepreneurs differ in their responses to severe resource constraints. Some entrepreneurs were able to render unique services by recombining elements at hand for new purposes that challenged institutional definitions and limits. They introduce the concept of bricolage to explain many of these behaviors of creating something from nothing by exploiting physical, social, or institutional inputs that other firms rejected or ignored. Central to the study's contribution is the notion that companies engaging in bricolage refuse to enact the limitations imposed by dominant definitions of resource environments; rather, they create their opportunities. (from journal's abstract)*

Baron, Robert. (1998). Cognitive Mechanisms in Entrepreneurship: Why and When Entrepreneurs Think Differently Than Other People. *Journal of Business Venturing,* vol. 13, no. 4, pp. 275–95.

> *In this conceptual article, the author presents information on a study that examined the possible differences in the thinking of entrepreneurs and other people. This article offers a number of implications of a cognitive perspective for entrepreneurship research.*

Davidsson, Per; and Benson Honig. (2003). The Role of Social and Human Capital among Nascent Entrepreneurs. *Journal of Business Venturing,* vol. 18, pp. 301–31.

> *This study examines nascent entrepreneurship by comparing individuals engaged in nascent activities with a control group and finds that social capital is a robust predictor for nascent entrepreneurs, as well as for advancing through the start-up*

process. With regard to outcomes like first sale or showing a profit, only one aspect of social capital, viz., being a member of a business network, had a statistically significant positive effect. The study supports human capital in predicting entry into nascent entrepreneurship, but only weakly for carrying the start-up process toward successful completion.

Gaglio, Connie Marie; and Jerome Katz. (2001). The Psychological Basis of Opportunity Identification: Entrepreneurial Alertness. *Small Business Economics*, vol. 16, pp. 95–111.

In this article, the authors describe a model of entrepreneurial alertness and propose a research agenda for understanding opportunity identification. They investigate the origin of the entrepreneurial alertness concept and the notion of the psychological schema of alertness.

Gregoire, Denis; and Dean A. Shepherd. (2012). Technology Market Combinations and the Identification of Entrepreneurial Opportunities. *Academy of Management Journal*, vol. 55, no. 4, pp. 753–85.

Integrating theoretical work on the nature of entrepreneurial opportunities with cognitive science research on the use of similarity comparisons in making creative mental leaps, the authors develop a model of opportunity identification that examines the independent effects of an opportunity idea's similarity characteristics and the interaction of these characteristics with an individual's knowledge and motivation. They test this model with an experiment where they asked entrepreneurs to form beliefs about opportunity ideas for technology transfer. They found that the superficial and structural similarities of technology-market combinations impact the formation of opportunity beliefs, and that individual differences in prior knowledge and entrepreneurial intent moderate these relationships. (from journal's abstract)

Haynie, J. Michael; Dean A. Shepherd; Elaine Mosakowski; and Christopher Earley. (2010). A Situated Metacognitive Model of the Entrepreneurial Mindset. *Journal of Business Venturing*, vol. 25, no. 2, pp. 217–29.

The authors develop a framework to investigate the foundations of an "entrepreneurial mindset"—described by scholars as the ability to sense, act, and mobilize under uncertain conditions. They focus on metacognitive processes that enable the entrepreneur to think beyond or reorganize existing knowledge structures and heuristics, promoting adaptable cognitions in the face of novel and uncertain decision contexts. They integrate disparate streams of literature from social and cognitive psychology toward a model that specifies entrepreneurial metacognition as situated in the entrepreneurial environment. They posit that foundations of an entrepreneurial mindset are metacognitive in nature, and subsequently detail how, and with what consequence, entrepreneurs formulate and inform "higher-order" cognitive strategies in the pursuit of entrepreneurial ends. (from journal's abstract)

Haynie, J. Michael; and Dean A. Shepherd. (2011). Toward a Theory of Discontinuous Career Transition: Investigating Career Transitions Necessitated by Traumatic Life-Events. *Journal of Applied Psychology*, vol. 96, pp. 501–24.

Career researchers have focused on the mechanisms related to career progression. Although less studied, situations in which traumatic life events necessitate a discontinuous career transition are becoming increasingly prevalent. Employing a multiple case study method, the authors offer a deeper understanding of such transitions by studying an extreme case: soldiers and Marines disabled by wartime combat. Their study highlights obstacles to future employment that are counterintuitive and stem from the discontinuous and traumatic nature of job loss. Effective management of this type of transitioning appears to stem from efforts positioned to formulate a coherent narrative of the traumatic experience and thus reconstruct foundational assumptions about the world, humanity, and self. These foundational assumptions form the basis for enacting future-oriented career strategies, such that progress toward establishing a new career path is greatest for those who can orientate themselves away from the past (trauma), away from the present (obstacles to a new career), and toward an envisioned future career positioned to confer meaning and purpose through work. (from journal's abstract)

Hitt, Michael; Barbara Keats; and Samuel DeMarie. (1998). Navigating in the New Competitive Landscape: Building Strategic Flexibility and Competitive Advantage in the 21st Century. *Academy of Management Executive,* vol. 12, pp. 22–43.

The article cites the importance of building strategic flexibility and a competitive advantage for organizations to survive in the face of emerging technical revolution and increasing globalization. The nature of the forces in the new competitive landscape requires a continuous rethinking of current strategic actions, organization structure, communication systems, corporate culture, asset deployment, and investment strategies—in short, every aspect of a firm's operation and long-term health.

Hmieleski, Keith; and Andrew Corbett. (2006). Proclivity for Improvisation as a Predictor of Entrepreneurial Intentions. *Journal of Small Business Management,* vol. 44, pp. 45–63.

This study examines the relationship between improvisation and entrepreneurial intentions and finds that entrepreneurial intentions are associated with measures of personality, motivation, cognitive style, social models, and improvisation. The strongest relationship is found between entrepreneurial intentions and improvisation.

Keh, Hean; Maw Der Foo; and Boon Chong Lim. (2002). Opportunity Evaluation under Risky Conditions: The Cognitive Processes of Entrepreneurs. *Entrepreneurship: Theory and Practice,* vol. 27, pp. 125–48.

This study uses a cognitive approach to examine opportunity evaluation, as the perception of opportunity is essentially a cognitive phenomenon. The authors present a model that consists of four independent variables (overconfidence, belief in the law of small numbers, planning fallacy, and illusion of control), a mediating variable (risk perception), two control variables (demographics and risk propensity), and the dependent variable (opportunity evaluation). They find that illusion of control and belief in the law of small numbers are related to how entrepreneurs evaluate opportunities. Their results also indicate that risk perception mediates opportunity evaluation.

Krueger, Norris. (2000). The Cognitive Infrastructure of Opportunity Emergence. *Entrepreneurship: Theory and Practice,* vol. 24, pp. 5–23.

In this article, the author argues that seeing a prospective course of action as a credible opportunity reflects an intentions-driven process driven by known critical antecedents. On the basis of well-developed theory and robust empirical evidence, he proposes an intentions-based model of the cognitive infrastructure that supports or inhibits how individuals perceive opportunities. The author also shows the practical diagnostic power this model offers to managers.

Kuemmerle, Walter. (May 2002). A Test for the Fainthearted. *Harvard Business Review,* pp. 122–27.

Starting a business is rarely a dignified affair. The article discusses what really makes an entrepreneur; what characteristics set successful entrepreneurs apart, enabling them to start ventures against all odds and keep them alive even in the worst of times; and finally, whether, if you don't possess those characteristics, they can be developed.

McGrath, Rita; and Ian MacMillan. (2000). *The Entrepreneurial Mindset: Strategies for Continuously Creating Opportunity in an Age of Uncertainty.* Cambridge, MA: Harvard Business School Press.

> *In this book, the authors provide tips on how to achieve an entrepreneurial mind-set. For example, they discuss the need to focus beyond incremental improvements to entrepreneurial actions, assess a business's current performance to establish the entrepreneurial framework, and formulate challenging goals by using the components of the entrepreneurial framework.*

McMullen, Jeffery S.; and Dean Shepherd. (2006). Entrepreneurial Action and the Role of Uncertainty in the Theory of the Entrepreneur. *Academy of Management Review,* vol. 31, pp. 132–52.

> *By considering the amount of uncertainty perceived and the willingness to bear uncertainty concomitantly, the authors provide a conceptual model of entrepreneurial action that allows for examination of entrepreneurial action at the individual level of analysis while remaining consistent with a rich legacy of system-level theories of the entrepreneur. This model not only exposes limitations of existing theories of entrepreneurial action but also contributes to a deeper understanding of important conceptual issues, such as the nature of opportunity and the potential for philosophical reconciliation among entrepreneurship scholars.*

Mitchell, Ron; Lowell Busenitz; Theresa Lant; Patricia McDougall; Eric Morse; and Brock Smith. (2002). Toward a Theory of Entrepreneurial Cognition: Rethinking the People Side of Entrepreneurship Research. *Entrepreneurship: Theory and Practice,* vol. 27, no. 2, pp. 93–105.

> *In this article, the authors reexamine "the people side of entrepreneurship" by summarizing the state of play within the entrepreneurial cognition research stream, and by integrating the five articles accepted for publication in a special issue focusing on this ongoing narrative. The authors propose that the constructs, variables, and proposed relationships under development within the cognitive perspective offer research concepts and techniques that are well suited to the analysis of problems that require better explanations of the distinctly human contributions to entrepreneurship.*

Sarasvathy, Saras. (2006). *Effectuation: Elements of Entrepreneurial Expertise.* Cheltenham, UK: Edward Elgar Publishers.

> *This book gives the history of the development of effectuation and provides provocative new applications and future research directions.*

Sarasvathy, Saras. www.effectuation.org.

> *This Web site provides an up-to-date collection of works on effectuation.*

Shepherd, Dean A.; and Holger Patzelt. (2011). Sustainable Entrepreneurship: Entrepreneurial Action Linking "What Is to Be Sustained" with "What Is to Be Developed." *Entrepreneurship: Theory and Practice,* vol. 1, pp. 137–63.

> *Informed by the sustainable development and entrepreneurship literatures, the authors offer the following definition: Sustainable entrepreneurship is focused on the preservation of nature, life support, and community in the pursuit of perceived opportunities to bring into existence future products, processes, and services for gain, where gain is broadly construed to include economic and noneconomic gains to individuals, the economy, and society. (from journal's abstract)*

Shepherd, Dean A.; and Holger Patzelt. (2015). Harsh Evaluations of Entrepreneurs Who Fail: The Role of Sexual Orientation, Use of Environmentally Friendly Technologies, and Observers' Perspective Taking. *Journal of Management Studies,* vol. 52, pp. 253–84.

Although there is a pervasive anti-failure bias in society, we investigate why some entrepreneurs who fail are evaluated more harshly than others. Building on attribution theory and the literatures on prejudice, pro-social intentions, and perspective taking, we offer an evaluation model of entrepreneurial failure and test this model on 6,784 assessments made by 212 observers. We find that variance in the harshness of failure evaluations depends on both the attributes of the entrepreneur and the attributes of the observer, and the interaction between the two. Specifically, entrepreneurs who are homosexual are evaluated more harshly by some observers and entrepreneurs who use environmentally friendly technology are evaluated less harshly. Moreover, observers high in perspective taking are more "lenient" in their failure evaluations of those who use environmentally friendly technology than those low in perspective taking. (from journal's abstract)

Shepherd, Dean A.; Trenton A. Williams; and Holger Patzelt. (2015). Thinking about Entrepreneurial Decision Making Review and Research Agenda. *Journal of Management*, vol. 41, no. 1, pp. 11–46.

Judgment and decision-making research has a long tradition in management and represents a substantial stream of research in entrepreneurship. Despite numerous reviews of this topic in the organizational behavior, psychology, and marketing fields, this is the first review in the field of entrepreneurship. In this review, the authors inductively categorize the articles into decision-making topics arranged along the primary activities associated with entrepreneurship—opportunity assessment decisions, entrepreneurial entry decisions, decisions about exploiting opportunities, entrepreneurial exit decisions, heuristics and biases in the decision-making context, characteristics of the entrepreneurial decision maker, and environment as decision context. (from journal's abstract)

END NOTES

1. S. Venkataraman, "The Distinctive Domain of Entrepreneurship Research: An Editor's Perspective," in J. Katz and R. Brockhaus (eds.), *Advances in Entrepreneurship, Firm Emergence, and Growth* 3 (1997), pp. 119–38 (Greenwich, CT: JAI Press).
2. Scott Shane and S. Venkataraman, "The Promise of Entrepreneurship as a Field of Research," *The Academy of Management Review* 25, no. 1 (January 2000), pp. 217–26.
3. J. S. McMullen and D. A. Shepherd, "Entrepreneurial Action and the Role of Uncertainty in the Theory of the Entrepreneur," *The Academy of Management Review* 31, no. 1 (2006), pp. 132–52.
4. Denis Grégoire and Dean A. Shepherd, "Technology Market Combinations and the Identification of Entrepreneurial Opportunities," *Academy of Management Journal* 55, no. 4 (2012), pp. 753–85.
5. D. A. Grégoire, P. S. Barr, and D. A. Shepherd, "Cognitive Processes of Opportunity Recognition: The Role of Structural Alignment," *Organization Science* 21, no. 2 (2010), pp. 413–31.
6. T. Baker and R. E. Nelson, "Creating Something from Nothing: Resource Construction through Entrepreneurial Bricolage," *Administrative Science Quarterly* 50, no. 3 (2005), p. 329.
7. J. M. Senyard, T. Baker, and P. R. Steffens, "Entrepreneurial Bricolage and Firm Performance: Moderating Effects of Firm Change and Innovativeness," Presentation at 2010 Annual Meeting of the Academy of Management, Montreal, Canada (2010).

8. S. Sarasvathy, "Causation and Effectuation: Toward a Theoretical Shift from Economic Inevitability to Entrepreneurial Contingency," *Academy of Management Review* 26 (2001), p. 245.

9. H. A. Simon, "Theories of Decision Making in Economics and Behavioral Science," *American Economic Review* 49 (1959), pp. 253–83.

10. Sarasvathy, "Causation and Effectuation," pp. 245–47.

11. M. A. Hitt, "The New Frontier: Transformation of Management for the New Millennium," *Organizational Dynamics* 28, no. 3 (2000), pp. 7–17.

12. R. D. Ireland, M. A. Hitt, and D. G. Sirmon, "A Model of Strategic Entrepreneurship: The Construct and Its Dimensions," *Journal of Management* 29 (2003), pp. 963–90; and Rita McGrath and Ian MacMillan, *The Entrepreneurial Mindset: Strategies for Continuously Creating Opportunity in an Age of Uncertainty* (Cambridge, MA: Harvard Business School Press, 2000).

13. Ireland, Hitt, and Sirmon, "A Model of Strategic Entrepreneurship."

14. M. A. Hitt, B. W. Keats, and S. M. DeMarie, "Navigating in the New Competitive Landscape: Building Strategic Flexibility and Competitive Advantage in the 21st Century," *Academy of Management Executive* 12 (1998), pp. 22–43 (from page 26).

15. M. Haynie, D. A. Shepherd, E. Mosakowski, and C. Earley, "A Situated Metacognitive Model of the Entrepreneurial Mindset," *Journal of Business Venturing* 25, no. 2 (2010), pp. 217–29; and M. Haynie and D. A. Shepherd, "A Measure of Adaptive Cognition for Entrepreneurship Research," *Entrepreneurship: Theory and Practice* 33, no. 3 (2009), pp. 695–714.

16. Haynie and Shepherd, "A Measure of Adaptive Cognition for Entrepreneurship Research."

17. G. Schraw and R. Dennison, "Assessing Metacognitive Awareness," *Contemporary Educational Psychology* 19 (1994), pp. 460–75.

18. A. Brown, "Metacognition and Other Mechanisms," in F. E. Weinert and R. H. Kluwe (eds.), *Metacognition, Motivation, and Understanding* (Hillsdale, NJ: Lawrence Erlbaum Associates, 1987).

19. E. Guterman, "Toward a Dynamic Assessment of Reading: Applying Metacognitive Awareness Guiding to Reading Assessment Tasks," *Journal of Research in Reading* 25, no. 3 (2002), pp. 283–98.

20. Z. R. Mevarech and B. Kramarski, "The Effects of Metacognitive Training versus Worked-out Examples on Students' Mathematical Reasoning," *British Journal of Educational Psychology* 73, no. 4 (2003), pp. 449–71; and D. Shepherd, M. Haynie, and J. McMullen (working paper), "Teaching Management Students Metacognitive Awareness: Enhancing Inductive Teaching Methods and Developing Cognitive Adaptability."

21. Mevarech and Kramarski, "The Effects of Metacognitive Training."

22. J. Ajzen, "The Theory of Planned Behavior," *Organizational Behavior and Human Decision Processes* 50 (1991), pp. 179–211.

23. A. Bandura, *Self-Efficacy: The Exercise of Control* (New York: W. H. Freeman, 1997); and D. A. Shepherd and N. Krueger, "An Intentions-Based Model of Entrepreneurial Teams' Social Cognition," Special Issue on Cognition and Information Processing, *Entrepreneurship: Theory and Practice* 27 (2002), pp. 167–85.

24. N. F. J. Krueger and D. V. Brazael, "Entrepreneurial Potential and Potential Entrepreneurs," *Entrepreneurship: Theory and Practice* 18 (1994), pp. 91–104.

25. Shepherd and Krueger, "An Intentions-Based Model."

26. C. M. Ford and D. A. Gioia, *Creativity in Organizations: Ivory Tower Visions and Real World Voices* (Newbury Park, CA: Sage, 1995).

27. See J. Gimeno, T. Folta, A. Cooper, and C. Woo, "Survival of the Fittest? Entrepreneurial Human Capital and the Persistence of Underperforming Firms," *Administrative Science Quarterly* 42 (1997), pp. 750–83.

28. P. Davidsson and B. Honig, "The Role of Social and Human Capital among Nascent Entrepreneurs," *Journal of Business Venturing* 18 (2003), pp. 301–31. D. R. DeTienne, D. A. Shepherd, and J. O. De Castro, "The Fallacy of 'Only the Strong Survive': The Effects of Extrinsic Motivation on the Persistence Decisions for Under-Performing Firms," *Journal of Business Venturing* 23 (2008), pp. 528–46.

29. Much of this information is based on research findings in Robert C. Ronstadt, "Initial Venture Goals, Age, and the Decision to Start an Entrepreneurial Career," *Proceedings of the 43rd Annual Meeting of the Academy of Management*, August 1983, p. 472; and Robert C. Ronstadt, "The Decision Not to Become an Entrepreneur," *Proceedings, 1983 Conference on Entrepreneurship*, April 1983, pp. 192–212. See also M. Lévesque, D. A. Shepherd, and E. J. Douglas, "Employment or Self-Employment: A Dynamic Utility-Maximizing Model," *Journal of Business Venturing* 17 (2002), pp. 189–210.

30. See also Lévesque, Shepherd, and Douglas, "Employment or Self-Employment."

31. A. C. Cooper, T. B. Folta, and C. Woo, "Entrepreneurial Information Search," *Journal of Business Venturing* 10 (1995), pp. 107–20; and M. Wright, K. Robbie, and C. Ennew, "Venture Capitalists and Serial Entrepreneurs," *Journal of Business Venturing* 12, no. 3 (1997), pp. 227–49.

32. Davidsson and Honig, "The Role of Social and Human Capital."

33. The influence of role models on career choice is discussed in E. Almquist and S. Angrist, "Role Model Influences on College Women's Career Aspirations," *Merrill-Palmer Quarterly* 17 (July 1971), pp. 263–97; J. Strake and C. Granger, "Same-Sex and Opposite-Sex Teacher Model Influences on Science Career Commitment among High School Students," *Journal of Educational Psychology* 70 (April 1978), pp. 180–86; Alan L. Carsrud, Connie Marie Gaglio, and Kenneth W. Olm, "Entrepreneurs-Mentors, Networks, and Successful New Venture Development: An Exploratory Study," *Proceedings, 1986 Conference on Entrepreneurship*, April 1986, pp. 29–35; and Howard Aldrich, Ben Rosen, and William Woodward, "The Impact of Social Networks on Business Foundings and Profit: A Longitudinal Study," *Proceedings, 1987 Conference on Entrepreneurship*, April 1987, pp. 154–68.

34. A thoughtful development of the network concept can be found in Howard Aldrich and Catherine Zimmer, "Entrepreneurship through Social Networks," in *The Art and Science of Entrepreneurship* (Cambridge, MA: Ballinger, 1986), pp. 3–24.

35. H. Hoang and B. Antoncic, "Network-Based Research in Entrepreneurship: A Critical Review," *Journal of Business Venturing* 18 (2003), pp. 165–88.

36. S. Birley, "The Role of Networks in the Entrepreneurial Process," *Journal of Business Venturing* 1 (1985), pp. 107–17; A. Cooper and W. Dunkelberg, "Entrepreneurship and Paths to Business Ownership," *Strategic Management Journal* 7 (1986), pp. 53–68; and B. Johannisson, "Networking and Entrepreneurial Growth," in D. Sexton and H. Landström (eds.), *The Blackwell Handbook of Entrepreneurship* (Oxford, MA: Blackwell, 2000), pp. 26–44.

37. A. Larson, "Network Dyads in Entrepreneurial Settings: A Study of the Governance of Exchange Relationships," *Administrative Science Quarterly* 37 (1992), pp. 76–104; W. Powell, "Neither Market nor Hierarchy: Network Forms of Organization," in B. Staw and L. Cummings (eds.), *Research in Organizational Behavior* (Greenwich, CT: JAI Press, 1990); and B. Uzzi, "The Sources and Consequences of Embeddedness for the Economic Performance of Organizations: The Network Effect," *American Sociological Review* 61 (1996), pp. 674–98.

38. Uzzi, "The Sources and Consequences of Embeddedness."
39. Dean A. Shepherd and Holger Patzelt, "Sustainable Entrepreneurship: Entrepreneurial Action Linking 'What Is to Be Sustained' with 'What Is to Be Developed,'" *Entrepreneurship: Theory and Practice* 1 (2011), pp. 137–63.
40. T. M. Parris and R. W. Kates, "Characterizing and Measuring Sustainable Development," *Annual Review of Environment and Resources* 28, no. 1 (2003), pp. 559–86.
41. C. K. Prahalad, *The Fortune at the Bottom of the Pyramid: Eradicating Poverty through Profits* (Wharton, 2010).
42. D. Shepherd, H. Patzelt, and R. Baron, "'I Care about Nature, but…': Disengaging Values in Assessing Opportunities that Cause Harm," *Academy of Management Journal* 56, no. 5 (2013), pp. 1251–73.

2

CORPORATE ENTREPRENEURSHIP

1

To understand the causes of interest in corporate entrepreneurship.

2

To introduce the "entrepreneurial" mode of managing firms and distinguish it from the traditional mode.

3

To provide a scale for capturing the extent to which management adopts entrepreneurial or traditional behaviors.

4

To discuss how established firms can develop an entrepreneurial culture and the challenges of doing so.

5

To acknowledge that projects fail and people feel bad about it, and to introduce the dual process model for maximizing learning from failure experiences.

OPENING PROFILE

ROBERT MONDAVI

Robert G. Mondavi, the son of poor Italian immigrants, began making wine in California in 1943 when his family purchased the Charles Krug Winery in Napa Valley, where he served as a general manager. In 1966, at the age of 54, after a severe dispute over control of the family-owned winery, Robert Mondavi used his personal savings and loans from friends to start the flagship Robert Mondavi Winery in Napa Valley with his eldest son, Michael Mondavi. Robert's vision was to create wines in California that could successfully compete with the greatest wines of the world. As a result, Robert Mondavi Winery became the first in California to produce and market premium wines that were expected to compete with premium wines from France, Spain, Italy, and Germany.

www.mondavi.com

To achieve this objective, Robert believed that he needed to build a Robert Mondavi brand in the premium wine market segment. This resulted in the initial production of a limited quantity of premium wines using the best grapes, which brought the highest prices in the market and had the highest profit margins per bottle. However, he soon realized that this strategy, while establishing the brand, did not allow the company to generate enough cash flow to expand the business. To solve this problem, Robert decided to produce less expensive wines that he could sell in higher volumes. He dedicated time and effort to finding the best vineyards in Napa Valley for the company's production of grapes. In addition, he signed long-term contracts with growers in Napa Valley and worked closely with each grower to improve grape quality.

Robert Mondavi built a state-of-the-art winery that became a premium wine-making facility as well as conveying a unique sense of Mondavi wines to the visitors. Soon the new winery became a place where the best practices in the production of premium wines were developed, eventually establishing the standard in the wine industry. Robert Mondavi was the first winemaker to assemble experts with various backgrounds in the fields of viticulture and wine-making to give advice on the new wines. He also developed new technology that allowed special handling of grapes and the cold fermentation of white wines. Furthermore, Mondavi's company created process innovations, such as steel fermentation tanks, vacuum corking of bottles, and aging of wines in new French oak barrels. Dedicated to growing vines naturally, Robert

Mondavi introduced a natural farming and conservation program that allowed enhanced grape quality, environmental protection, and worker health. Moreover, from the very beginning, the company promoted the presentation of wine as part of a sociable way of everyday living. Robert Mondavi Winery was one of the first wineries to present concerts, art exhibitions, and culinary programs.

In his book, Robert Mondavi describes his search for innovation:

> From the outset, I wanted my winery to draw inspiration and methods from the traditional Old World chateaux of France and Italy, but I also wanted to become a model of state-of-the-art technology, a pioneer in research and a gathering place for the finest minds in our industry. I wanted our winery to be a haven of creativity, innovation, excitement, and that unbelievable energy you find in a start-up venture when everyone is committed, heart and soul, to a common cause and a common quest.

In 1972, Mondavi's hard work and dedication to his venture were formally recognized when the Los Angeles Times Vintners Tasting Event selected the 1969 Robert Mondavi Winery Cabernet Sauvignon as the top wine produced in California.

Despite Robert Mondavi's relentless efforts, things did not always go smoothly. A noticeable improvement in the quality and reputation of the Robert Mondavi wines during the 1970s did not spark the interest of reputable five-star restaurants and top wine shops across the country. So, for over a decade, Mondavi traveled throughout the country and abroad, promoting Napa Valley wines and the Robert Mondavi brand name. Often, while dining alone on business trips, Mondavi offered restaurant employees the opportunity to taste his wine. Slowly, Mondavi got his wines on the wine lists of the top five-star restaurants in the United States. By the end of the 1970s, restaurant owners, famous wine connoisseurs, and industry critics were eager to be introduced to Robert Mondavi products. Recognizing the increased popularity of his wines, Mondavi began slowly raising the prices of his wines to the price level of comparable French wines. Subsequently, the company expanded its capacity to produce 500,000 cases of premium wines annually.

About this time, Robert Mondavi started building a portfolio of premium wine brands to satisfy the needs of consumers in various price and quality segments of the domestic wine market. As a result, from the late 1970s until the 1980s, Robert Mondavi diversified its portfolio through acquisition and further growth of the Woodbridge, Byron, and Coastal brands of California wine. Most of these acquisitions were financed through long-term debt.

In the early 1990s, Robert Mondavi faced financial difficulties as a result of the rapid expansion; the increased competition; and a *phylloxera* infestation of several of the company's vineyards, which necessitated replanting. After contemplating the matter for several years, Robert Mondavi decided to raise enough capital to continue expansion of his company while maintaining family control of the company. On June 10, 1993, Robert Mondavi issued 3.7 million shares of stock at $13.50 a share and began trading on the NASDAQ as MOND. The initial public offering (IPO) raised approximately $49.95 million, bringing the company's market capitalization to $213.3 million.

The IPO was structured with two classes of stock: Class A common stock issued to the Mondavi family and Class B common stock offered to the public. Class A shares carried ten votes per share, and Class B shares carried one vote per share. This structure allowed the Mondavi family to retain 90 percent ownership of the company and, subsequently, to preserve control over the company's destiny. Robert Mondavi stock was trading at $8 a share a few days after the initial offering and at $6.50 a share six months later, slashing the company's value, and the Mondavi family's wealth, by half.

One factor affecting the price decrease in the stock was the difficulty that the investment community and analysts had in valuing Robert Mondavi due to a lack of information on the wine industry. There were only two other publicly traded wine companies, both in low-end wine categories. To help solve this problem, Robert Mondavi began educating investors, trying to convince them that it is possible to build a strong, globally recognized business selling premium wines. As part of his knowledge-building and awareness-creation campaign, Robert sent teams to New York, Boston, and Chicago, who brought wine presentations, receptions, and tastings to the investors. According to Robert Mondavi, "Well, we had to mount an effective campaign and take it right to them, and not just explain our approach but put our wines right in their hands! Let them taste, in their own mouths, our expertise and commitment to excellence."

At the same time, the company was continuing its innovating efforts, creating in 1994 a revolutionary, capsule-free, flange-top bottle design, which became widely accepted in the industry.

In the mid-1990s, the company started engaging in various multinational partnerships on a 50:50 basis: Its partnership with the Baron Philippe de Rothschild of Chateau Mouton Rothschild in Bordeaux, France, resulted in the creation of *Opus One* wine in 1979; with the Frescobaldi family of Tuscany, Italy, Mondavi launched *Luce*, *Lucente*, and *Danzante* wines in 1995; with the Eduardo Chadwick family of Chile, it introduced *Caliterra* wines in 1996; and with Australia's largest premium producer, Southcorp, it began producing and marketing new wines from Australia and California in 2001.

Today, the company continues to pursue its goals around the world with its unique cultural and innovative spirit and its consistent growth strategy, reaching revenue of over $441 million in 2002. The company produces 20 unique and separate labels representing more than 80 individual wines from California, Italy, Chile, and France and sells its wines in more than 80 countries. Some of the popular Robert Mondavi fine wine labels such as Robert Mondavi Winery, Robert Mondavi Coastal Private Selection, and Woodbridge Winery have gained enormous popularity among wine lovers in the United States as well as the rest of the world. The company remains a close family business.

Recognized as the global representative of California wines, Robert Mondavi has been a major force in leading the U.S. wine industry into the modern era and has devoted his life to creating a fine wine culture in America. Through hard work and a constant striving for excellence, he has achieved his goal of causing California wines to be viewed as some of the great wines of the world.

CAUSES FOR INTEREST IN CORPORATE ENTREPRENEURSHIP

Interest in entrepreneurship within established businesses has intensified due to a variety of events occurring on social, cultural, and business levels. On a social level, there is an increasing interest in "doing your own thing" and doing it on one's own terms. Individuals who believe strongly in their own talents frequently desire to create something of their own. They want responsibility and have a strong need for individual expression and freedom in their work environment. When this freedom is not there, frustration can cause that individual to become less productive or even leave the organization to achieve self-actualization elsewhere. This new search for meaning, and the impatience involved, has recently caused more discontent in structured organizations than ever before. When meaning is not provided within the organization, individuals often search for an institution that will provide it.

Corporate entrepreneurship is one method of stimulating, and then capitalizing on, individuals in an organization who think that something can be done differently and better. Most people think of Xerox as a large, bureaucratic Fortune 100 company. Although, in part, this may be true of the $23 billion giant company, Xerox has done something unique in trying to ensure that its creative employees do not leave like Steve Jobs did to form Apple Computer, Inc. In 1989, Xerox set up Xerox Technology Ventures (XTV) for the purpose of generating profits by investing in the promising technologies of the company, many of which would have otherwise been overlooked.[1] Xerox wanted to avoid mistakes of the past by having "a system to prevent technology from leaking out of the company," according to Robert V. Adams, president of XTV.

The fund has supported numerous start-ups thus far, similar to Quad Mark, the brainchild of Dennis Stemmle, a Xerox employee of 25 years. Stemmle's idea was to make a battery-operated, plain paper copier that would fit in a briefcase along with a laptop computer. Although Xerox's operating committee did not approve the idea for 10 years, it was finally funded by XTV and Taiwan's Advanced Scientific Corporation. As is the case with all the companies funded by XTV, the founder and key employees of a company own 20 percent of it. This provides an incentive for employees like Dennis Stemmle to take the risk, leave Xerox, and form a technology-based venture.

XTV provides both financial and nonfinancial benefits to its parent, Xerox. The funded companies provide profits to the parent company as well as the founders and employees, and now Xerox managers pay closer attention to employees' ideas as well as internal technologies. Is XTV a success? Apparently so, if replication is any indication. The XTV concept contains an element of risk in that Xerox employees forming new ventures are not guaranteed a management position if the new venture fails. This makes XTV different from most entrepreneurial ventures in companies. This aspect of risk and no guaranteed employment is the basis for AT&T Ventures, a fund modeled on XTV.

What Xerox recognized is what hundreds of executives in other organizations are also becoming aware of: It is important to keep, or instill, the entrepreneurial spirit in an organization to innovate and grow. This realization has revolutionized management thinking. In a large organization, problems often occur that thwart creativity and innovation, particularly in activities not directly related to the organization's main mission. The growth and diversification that can result from flexibility and creativity are particularly critical since large, vertically integrated, diversified corporations are often more efficient in a competitive market than smaller firms.

corporate
entrepreneurship
Entrepreneurial action
within an established
organization

The resistance against flexibility, growth, and diversification can, in part, be overcome by developing a spirit of entrepreneurship within the existing organization, called *corporate entrepreneurship.* An increase in corporate entrepreneurship reflects an increase in social, cultural, and business pressures toward entrepreneurial action. Hypercompetition has forced companies to have an increased interest in such areas as new product development, diversification, increased productivity, and decreasing costs by methods such as reducing the company's labor force.

Corporate entrepreneurship is most strongly reflected in entrepreneurial activities as well as in top management orientations in organizations. These entrepreneurial endeavors consist of the following four key elements: new business venturing, innovativeness, self-renewal, and proactiveness.[2]

New business venturing (sometimes called corporate venturing) refers to the creation of a new business within an existing organization. These entrepreneurial activities consist of creating something new of value either by redefining the company's current products or services, developing new markets, or forming more formally autonomous or semiautonomous units or firms. Formations of new corporate ventures are the most salient manifestations of corporate entrepreneurship. Organizational innovativeness refers to product and service innovation, with an emphasis on development and innovation in technology. It includes new product development, product improvements, and new production methods and procedures.

Self-renewal is the transformation of an organization through the renewal of the key ideas on which it is built. It has strategic and organizational change connotations and includes a redefinition of the business concept, reorganization, and the introduction of system-wide changes to increase innovation. Proactiveness includes initiative and risk taking, as well as competitive aggressiveness and boldness, which are particularly reflected in the orientations and activities of top management. A proactive organization tends to take risks by conducting experiments; it also takes initiative and is bold and aggressive in pursuing opportunities. Organizations with this proactive spirit attempt to lead rather than follow competitors in such key business areas as the introduction of new products or services, operating technologies, and administrative techniques.

In the previous chapter, we showed that acting entrepreneurially is something that people choose to do based on their perceptions of the desirability and feasibility of creating a new venture to pursue an opportunity. However, existing companies also can pursue opportunities, but this requires that the management of these firms create an environment that encourages employees to think and act entrepreneurially. Such an environment is one that helps people realize that entrepreneurial behavior within the firm is both personally desirable and feasible. This builds a strong entrepreneurial intention and, as discussed in the previous chapter, the general rule is that the stronger the intention to engage in entrepreneurial action, the more likely it will happen. To create such a culture requires a different perspective on how to manage the firm.

MANAGERIAL VERSUS ENTREPRENEURIAL DECISION MAKING

Howard Stevenson, a professor at Harvard University, believes that entrepreneurship represents a mode of managing an existing firm that is distinct from the way existing firms are traditionally managed. Entrepreneurial management is distinct from traditional management in terms of eight dimensions: (1) strategic orientation, (2) commitment to opportunity, (3) commitment of resources, (4) control of resources, (5) management structure, (6) reward philosophy, (7) growth orientation, and (8) entrepreneurial culture.[3] The nature of the differences among these dimensions is represented in Table 2.1 and described in greater detail below.[4]

Strategic Orientation and Commitment to Opportunity

The first two factors that help distinguish more entrepreneurially managed firms from those that are more traditionally managed relate to strategic issues—strategic orientation

TABLE 2.1   Distinguishing Entrepreneurially from Traditionally Managed Firms

Entrepreneurial Focus	Conceptual Dimension	Administrative Focus
Driven by perception of opportunity	Strategic orientation	Driven by controlled resources
Revolutionary with short duration	Commitment to opportunity	Evolutionary with long duration
Many stages with minimal exposure	Commitment of resources	A single stage with complete commitment out of decision
Episodic use or rent of required resources	Control of resources	Ownership or employment of required resources
Flat with multiple informal networks	Management structure	Hierarchy
Based on value creation	Reward philosophy	Based on responsibility and seniority
Rapid growth is top priority; risk accepted to achieve growth	Growth orientation	Safe, slow, and steady
Promoting broad search for opportunities	Entrepreneurial culture	Opportunity search restricted by controlled resources; failure punished

Source: This table is taken from T. Brown, P. Davidsson, and J. Wiklund, "An Operationalization of Stevenson's Conceptualization of Entrepreneurship as Opportunity-Based Firm Behavior," *Strategic Management Journal* 22 (2001), p. 955.

and commitment to opportunity. An emphasis on strategy in developing a deeper understanding of entrepreneurship at the firm level is not surprising because both entrepreneurship and strategy have important implications for the performance of the firm.

strategic orientation
A focus on those factors that are inputs into the formulation of the firm's strategy

Strategic orientation refers to those factors that are inputs into the formulation of the firm's strategy. We can think of it as the philosophy of the firm that drives its decision about strategy; the way that it looks at the world and the way it looks at itself and these perceptions are the driving factors behind the firm's strategy. The strategy of entrepreneurial management is driven by the presence or generation of opportunities for new entry and is less concerned about the resources that may be required to pursue such opportunities. Acquiring and marshaling the necessary resources represents a secondary step for the entrepreneurially managed firm and perhaps part of the thinking about the exploitation of discovered opportunities. Resources do not constrain the strategic thinking of an entrepreneurially managed firm. In contrast, the strategy of traditional management is to use the resources of the firm efficiently. Therefore, the type and the amount of resources that the firm has (or knows it can readily access) represent a key starting point for thinking strategically about the future of the firm. Only those opportunities that can be pursued effectively using existing resources are considered the appropriate domain of further strategic thinking.

Both entrepreneurship and strategy are more than simply thinking about the future of the firm, they are also concerned with the firm taking action. It is through its actions that a firm is judged, often by analysis of its financial and competitive performance. Entrepreneurially and traditionally managed firms can be distinguished in terms of their commitment to opportunity. More entrepreneurially managed firms have an *entrepreneurial orientation toward opportunity* in that they are committed to taking action on potential opportunities and therefore can pursue opportunities rapidly, making the most of windows of opportunity. They also are able to withdraw their resources from a particular opportunity and do so rapidly, such that if initial feedback from the pursuit of a potential opportunity provides information suggesting that it might not be the right opportunity for the firm, then management can "pull the plug," minimizing losses from the initial pursuit. In contrast, traditionally managed firms tend to place considerable emphasis on information; information is derived from data collection and analysis of that information to determine, say, the return

entrepreneurial orientation toward opportunity A commitment to taking action on potential opportunities

on resources to be deployed. If the traditionally managed firm chooses to pursue the given opportunity, it would be with a much larger initial investment and the intention of remaining in that line of business for a considerable time.

Commitment of Resources and Control of Resources

entrepreneurial orientation toward commitment of resources A focus on how to minimize the resources that would be required in the pursuit of a particular opportunity

It is important to note that entrepreneurs still care about the resources they must commit to the pursuit of an opportunity, but they have an *entrepreneurial orientation toward the commitment of resources* that is focused on the opportunity. Thoughts of resources turn more to how the firm can minimize the resources that would be required in the pursuit of a particular opportunity. By minimizing the resources that the firm must invest to initially pursue an opportunity, the amount of resources at risk if the opportunity does not "pan out" is also minimized. For example, entrepreneurially managed firms may "test the waters" by committing small amounts of resources in a multistep manner with minimal (risk) exposure at each step. These investments can be considered probes into the future that reveal information in an uncertain environment. Indeed, given the uncertainty surrounding these opportunities, these probes into the future reveal information that would not otherwise be available through traditional market research methods. Therefore, this small and incremental process of resource commitment provides the firm the flexibility to change direction rapidly as new information about the opportunity or the environment comes to light. Psychologically, these smaller sunk costs help stop entrepreneurially managed firms from becoming entrenched with a particular course of action, especially if that course of action turns out to be a losing one. In contrast, when traditionally managed firms decide to commit resources to an opportunity, they do so on a large scale. That is, rather than put a toe in to test the water, they make calculations based on the ambient temperature over the last week, the density of the water, and whether a pool cover has been used or not. If, based on that calculation, the water is theoretically deemed to be sufficiently warm, the traditional manager commits to that assessment with a full swan dive. Having made a large commitment of resources, the firm often feels compelled to justify the initial decision to commit, and so the initial commitment gains momentum that maintains the status quo of continual resource commitment. Therefore, a traditionally managed firm uses in-depth analysis of available information to go for it or not—and if they do go for it, then the investment of resources is not easily reversed.

entrepreneurial orientation toward control of resources A focus on how to access others' resources

entrepreneurial orientation toward management structure More organic focus—has few layers of bureaucracy between top management and the customer and typically has multiple informal networks

Over and above their commitment of resources, entrepreneurially and traditionally managed firms differ in their control of resources. Entrepreneurially managed firms are less concerned about the ownership of resources and more concerned about having access to others' resources, including financial capital, intellectual capital, skills, and competencies. Entrepreneurially managed firms operate from the standpoint, "Why do I need to control resources if I can access them from others?" Access to resources is possible to the extent that the opportunity allows the firm to effectively deploy others' resources for the benefit of the entrepreneurial firm and the owner of the invested resources. In contrast, traditionally managed firms focus on the ownership of resources and the accumulation of further resources. They believe that if they control their own resources then they are self-contained. For these firms, the control that comes with ownership means that resources can be deployed more effectively for the benefit of the firm.

Management Structure and Reward Philosophy

An *entrepreneurial orientation toward management structure* is organic. That is, the organizational structure has few layers of bureaucracy between top management and the customer and typically has multiple informal communication channels. In this way,

 E T H I C S

DO ENTREPRENEURS AND MANAGERS DIFFER IN ETHICAL CONDUCT?

Ethical conduct is of critical importance. It appears that this is even more so in the current hypercompetitive and global business environment in which most firms operate. In such environments, competitors act in ways that disrupt the status quo and attempt to change the "rules of the game" to suit them to disadvantage others. Although in such an environment the temptation is to respond in any way necessary to maintain the status quo and/or the firm's advantage, including unethical behavior, it appears that entrepreneurial firms are setting a high standard of ethical conduct, a standard that will hopefully motivate others to follow suit.

Investigating the decision making of 165 entrepreneurs and 128 managers, one study found little difference between managers and entrepreneurs in their ethical decision making. This provides some indication that the legal, cultural, and educational factors in which people (managers and entrepreneurs) are embedded has an influence on ethical conduct. Although managers and entrepreneurs were largely similar in their ethical decision making, the study did find that in some instances entrepreneurs were prone to hold more ethical standards. Specifically, managers faced the issue of needing to forgo their personal values for those of the organization, more than did

entrepreneurs. (This makes sense because entrepreneurs can create their organizations such that there is little, if any, discrepancy between the values of the organization and the entrepreneur.)

Entrepreneurs were also more ethical in terms of not taking longer than necessary to complete a task and not using company resources for personal use. Indeed, these results are consistent with the notion that entrepreneurs believe that the firm is part of their property and therefore treat it (and its operations) more fairly than managers who are less likely to view the organization as part of their personal property.

Consistent with this perspective is the prescription that by providing greater equity share for managers they are more likely to see the firm as their property and act more ethically as a result. In addition, as managers and entrepreneurs develop stronger relationships with customers and other stakeholders, they are likely to value these relationships more and, as a result, be more ethical in their conduct toward these communities.

Source: Branko Bucar and Robert Hisrich, "Ethics of Business Managers vs. Entrepreneurs," *Journal of Development Entrepreneurship* 6, no. 1 (2001), pp. 59–83.

---

entrepreneurially managed firms are able to capture and communicate more information from the external environment and are sufficiently "fluid" to be able to take quick action based on that information.

In addition, entrepreneurially managed firms are more structured to make use of both their internal networks (e.g., through informal communication channels at work) and external networks (with buyers, suppliers, and financial institutions), which provide information and other resources important in the discovery/generation and exploitation of opportunities. In contrast, the traditionally managed firm has a structure well suited for the internal efficiencies of allocating controlled resources. There is a formalized hierarchy with clear roles and responsibilities, highly routinized work, and layers of middle management to "manage" employees' use of the firm's resources. Traditionally managed firms have structures that are typically inwardly focused on efficiency rather than on detecting and rapidly acting on changes in the external environment.

Firms are organized not only by their structures but also by their reward philosophy. The entrepreneurially managed firm is focused on pursuing opportunities for new entry that represent new value for the firm (and hopefully for others, including society as a whole). It is not surprising then that entrepreneurially managed firms have an *entrepreneurial philosophy toward rewards* that compensates employees based on their contribution toward the

entrepreneurial philosophy toward rewards   One that compensates employees based on their contribution toward the discovery/generation and exploitation of opportunity

discovery/generation and exploitation of opportunity. Given the organic structure described earlier, employees often have the freedom to experiment with potential opportunities and are rewarded accordingly. The traditionally managed firm rewards management and employees based on their responsibilities, where responsibilities are typically determined by the amount of resources (assets and/or people) that each manager or employee controls. Promotion is a reward that provides a manager control of even more resources and, therefore, further scope for rewards.

Growth Orientation and Entrepreneurial Culture

entrepreneurial orientation toward growth A focus on rapid growth

In a firm that has an *entrepreneurial orientation toward growth*, there is a great desire to expand the size of the firm at a rapid pace. Although traditionally managed firms may also desire to grow, they prefer growth to be slow and at a steady pace. That is, they prefer a pace of growth that is more "manageable" in that it does not "unsettle the firm" by putting at risk the resources that the firm controls and thus does not put at risk the jobs and power of top management.

culture The environment of a particular organization

entrepreneurial orientation toward culture A focus on encouraging employees to generate ideas, experiment, and engage in other tasks that might produce opportunities

Culture also distinguishes entrepreneurially and traditionally managed firms. A firm with an *entrepreneurial orientation toward culture* encourages employees to generate ideas, experiment, and engage in other tasks that might produce creative output. Such output is highly valued by entrepreneurial management because it is often the source of opportunities for new entries. Opportunities are the focus of the entrepreneurially managed firm.

In contrast, the traditionally managed firm begins with an assessment of the resources that it controls, and this is reflected in its organizational culture. So while a traditionally managed firm is still interested in ideas, it is mostly interested in ideas that revolve around currently controlled resources. With only ideas considered that relate to currently controlled resources, the scope of opportunities discovered and generated by a traditionally managed firm is limited.

It is unlikely that there are many firms that are "purely" entrepreneurially managed or purely traditionally managed; most firms fall somewhere in between. Table 2.2 presents a scale for determining how entrepreneurially managed a particular firm is. The higher the score, the more entrepreneurially managed the firm is.

Establishing a Culture for Corporate Entrepreneurship

How can the culture for corporate entrepreneurship be established in an organization? In establishing an entrepreneurial environment within an established organization, certain factors and leadership characteristics need to be present.[5] The overall characteristics of a high entrepreneurial environment are summarized in Table 2.3. The first of these is that the organization operates on the frontiers of technology. Since research and development are key sources for successful new product ideas, the firm must operate on the cutting edge of the industry's technology, encouraging and supporting new ideas instead of discouraging them, as frequently occurs in firms that require a rapid return on investment and a high sales volume.

Second, entrepreneurial firms encourage experimentation to facilitate trial-and-error learning. Successful new products or services usually do not appear fully developed; they evolve. It took time and some product failures before the first smart phone appeared. A company wanting to establish an entrepreneurial spirit has to establish an environment that allows mistakes and failures in developing new and innovative products. This is in direct opposition to the established career and promotion system of the traditional organization.

TABLE 2.2   Scale to Capture How Entrepreneurially a Firm Is Managed

Strategic Orientation

As we define our strategies, our major concern is how to best utilize the sources we control.	1 2 3 4 5 6 7 8 9 10	We are not constrained by the resources at (or not at) hand.
We limit the opportunities we pursue on the basis of our current resources.	1 2 3 4 5 6 7 8 9 10	Our fundamental task is to pursue opportunities we perceive as valuable and then to acquire the resources to exploit them.
The resources we have significantly influence our business strategies.	1 2 3 4 5 6 7 8 9 10	Opportunities control our business strategies.

Resource Orientation

Since our objective is to use our resources, we will usually invest heavily and rapidly.	1 2 3 4 5 6 7 8 9 10	Since we do not need resources to commence the pursuit of an opportunity, our commitment of resources may be in stages.
We prefer to totally control and own the resources we use.	1 2 3 4 5 6 7 8 9 10	All we need from resources is the ability to use them.
We prefer to use only our own resources in our ventures.	1 2 3 4 5 6 7 8 9 10	We like to employ resources that we borrow or rent.
In exploiting opportunities, access to money is more important than just having the idea.	1 2 3 4 5 6 7 8 9 10	In exploiting opportunities, having the idea is more important than just having the money.

Management Structure

We prefer tight control of funds and operations by means of sophisticated control and information systems.	1 2 3 4 5 6 7 8 9 10	We prefer loose, informal control. There is a dependence on informal relations.
We strongly emphasize getting things done by following formal processes and procedures.	1 2 3 4 5 6 7 8 9 10	We strongly emphasize getting things done even if this means disregarding formal procedures.
We strongly emphasize holding to tried and true management principles and industry norms.	1 2 3 4 5 6 7 8 9 10	We strongly emphasize adapting freely to changing circumstances without much concern for past practices.
There is a strong insistence on a uniform management style throughout the firm.	1 2 3 4 5 6 7 8 9 10	Managers' operating styles are allowed to range freely from very formal to very informal.
There is a strong emphasis on getting line and staff personnel to adhere closely to their formal job descriptions.	1 2 3 4 5 6 7 8 9 10	There is a strong tendency to let the requirements of the situation and the personality of the individual dictate proper job behavior.

Reward Philosophy

Our employees are evaluated and compensated based on their responsibilities.	1 2 3 4 5 6 7 8 9 10	Our employees are evaluated and compensated based on the value they add to the firm.
Our employees are usually rewarded by promotion and annual raises.	1 2 3 4 5 6 7 8 9 10	We try to compensate our employees by devising ways that they can benefit from the increased value of the firm.
An employee's standing is based on the amount of responsibility he/she has.	1 2 3 4 5 6 7 8 9 10	An employee's standing is based on the value he/she adds.

	Growth Orientation	
Growth is not necessarily our top objective. Long-term survival may be at least as important.	1 2 3 4 5 6 7 8 9 10	It is generally known throughout the firm that growth is our top objective.
It is generally known throughout the firm that steady and sure growth is the best way to expand.	1 2 3 4 5 6 7 8 9 10	It is generally known throughout the firm that our intention is to grow as big and as fast as possible.
	Entrepreneurial Culture	
It is difficult to find a sufficient number of promising ideas to utilize all of our resources.	1 2 3 4 5 6 7 8 9 10	We have many more promising ideas than we have time and resources to pursue.
Changes in the society-at-large seldom lead to commercially promising ideas for our firm.	1 2 3 4 5 6 7 8 9 10	Changes in the society-at-large often give us ideas for new products and services.
It is difficult for our firm to find ideas that can be converted into profitable products/services.	1 2 3 4 5 6 7 8 9 10	We never experience a lack of ideas that we can convert into profitable products/services.

Source: This table is taken from T. Brown, P. Davidsson, and J. Wiklund, "An Operationalization of Stevenson's Conceptualization of Entrepreneurship as Opportunity-Based Firm Behavior," *Strategic Management Journal* 22 (2001), Appendix.

Yet without the opportunity to fail in an organization, few, if any, corporate entrepreneurial ventures will be developed. Almost every entrepreneur has experienced at least one failure in establishing a successful venture. The importance and the difficulty of learning from the experience are discussed in the last section of this chapter.

Third, entrepreneurial firms remove obstacles to creativity in the new product development process. Frequently in an organization, various "turfs" are protected, frustrating attempts by potential entrepreneurs to establish new ventures. In one Fortune 500 company, an attempt to establish an entrepreneurial environment ran into problems and eventually failed when the potential entrepreneurs were informed that a proposed new product and venture was not possible because it was in the domain of another division.

TABLE 2.3   Characteristics of an Entrepreneurial Environment

- Organization operates on frontiers of technology
- New ideas encouraged
- Trial and error encouraged
- Failures allowed
- No opportunity parameters
- Resources available and accessible
- Multidiscipline teamwork approach
- Long time horizon
- Volunteer program
- Appropriate reward system
- Sponsors and champions available
- Support of top management

Fourth, entrepreneurial firms make highly accessible resources for experimentation—they have slack resources such as money and time. As one corporate entrepreneur stated, "If my company really wants me to take the time, effort, and career risks to establish a new venture, then it needs to put money and people resources on the line." Often, insufficient funds are allocated not to creating something new, but instead to solving problems that have an immediate effect on the bottom line. Some companies—like Xerox, 3M, and AT&T—have recognized this problem and have established separate venture-capital areas for funding new internal as well as external ventures. Even when resources are available, all too often the reporting requirements become obstacles to obtaining them.

Fifth, entrepreneurial firms construct and encourage multidisciplinary teams to work on new ventures. This open approach, with participation by needed individuals regardless of area, is the antithesis of the typical corporate organizational structure. An evaluation of successful cases of corporate entrepreneurship indicated that one key to success was the existence of "skunkworks" involving relevant people. Developing the needed teamwork for a new venture is further complicated by the fact that a team member's promotion and overall career within the corporation are based on his or her job performance in the current position, not on his or her contribution to the new venture being created.

Besides encouraging teamwork, the corporate environment must establish a long time horizon for evaluating the success of the overall program as well as the success of each individual venture. If a company is not willing to invest money without a guarantee of return for 5–10 years, it should not attempt to create an entrepreneurial environment. This patient attitude toward money in the corporate setting is no different from the investment/return time horizon used by venture capitalists and others when they invest in an entrepreneurial effort.

Sixth, the spirit of corporate entrepreneurship cannot be forced upon individuals; it must be on a volunteer basis. There is a difference between corporate thinking and entrepreneurial thinking (discussed earlier and summarized in Table 2.1), with certain individuals performing much better on one side of the continuum or the other. Most managers in a corporation are not capable of being successful corporate entrepreneurs. Those who do emerge from this self-selection process must be allowed the latitude to carry a project through to completion. This is not consistent with most corporate procedures for new product development, where different departments and individuals are involved in each stage of the development process. An individual willing to spend the excess hours and effort to create a new venture needs the opportunity and the accompanying reward of completing the project. A corporate entrepreneur falls in love with the newly created internal venture and will do almost anything to help ensure its success.

Seventh, entrepreneurial firms create a reward system that encourages creativity, risk taking, and even failure. The corporate entrepreneur needs to be appropriately rewarded for all the energy, effort, and risk taking expended in the creation of the new venture. Rewards should be based on the attainment of established performance goals. An equity position in the new venture is one of the best rewards for motivating and eliciting the amount of activity and effort needed for success.

Eighth, an entrepreneurial firm develops sponsors, develops product champions, and matches the two. That is, a corporate environment favorable for corporate entrepreneurship has sponsors and champions throughout the organization who not only support the creative activity but also have the planning flexibility to establish new objectives and directions as needed. As one corporate entrepreneur stated, "For a new business venture to succeed, the corporate entrepreneur needs to be able to alter plans at will and not be concerned about how close they come to achieving the previously stated objectives." Corporate structures frequently measure managers on their ability to come close to objectives, regardless of the quality of performance reflected in this accomplishment.

Finally, and perhaps most importantly, an entrepreneurial firm is one that has a top management team that wholeheartedly supports and embraces the entrepreneurial actions of employees. That is, through their physical presence and allocating sufficient resources to new ventures, managers explicitly and implicitly send signals to the employees that their entrepreneurial endeavors are valued and supported. Without top management support, a successful entrepreneurial environment cannot be created.

Leadership Characteristics of Corporate Entrepreneurs

Within this overall corporate environment, certain individual characteristics have been identified that constitute a successful corporate entrepreneur. As summarized in Table 2.4, these include understanding the environment, being visionary and flexible, creating management options, encouraging teamwork, encouraging open discussion, building a coalition of supporters, and being persistent.

An entrepreneur needs to understand all aspects of the environment. Part of this ability is reflected in the individual's level of creativity. To establish a successful corporate venture, the individual must be creative and have a broad understanding of the internal and external environments of the corporation. The understanding of the environment is important because it enables the individual to notice signals of potential opportunity and those high in creativity are able to "connect the dots" to form an opportunity belief.

The person who is going to establish a successful new venture within the firm must also be a visionary leader—a person who dreams great dreams. Although there are many definitions of leadership, the one that best describes what is needed for corporate entrepreneurship is: "A leader is like a gardener. When you want a tomato, you take a seed, put it in fertile soil, and carefully water under tender care. You don't manufacture tomatoes; you grow them." Another good definition is that "leadership is the ability to dream great things and communicate these in such a way that people say yes to being a part of the dream." Martin Luther King, Jr., said, "I have a dream," and articulated that dream in such a way that thousands followed him in his efforts, in spite of overwhelming obstacles. Therefore, the notion of a dream is important because it encourages the individual to envisage a positive future, one that can eventually be enacted. To establish a successful new venture, the corporate entrepreneur must have a dream and overcome obstacles to achieving it by selling the dream to others.

The third necessary leadership characteristic is that the corporate entrepreneur must be flexible and create management options. A corporate entrepreneur does not "mind the store,"

TABLE 2.4 Leadership Characteristics of a Corporate Entrepreneur

- Understands the environment
- Is visionary and flexible
- Creates management options
- Encourages teamwork
- Encourages open discussion
- Builds a coalition of supporters
- Persists

but rather is open to and even encourages change. By challenging the beliefs and assumptions of the corporation, a corporate entrepreneur has the opportunity to create something new in the organizational structure. Indeed, rather than seeing a change from plans as a threat to the venture, an entrepreneurial individual will see the change as a potential opportunity. That is, he or she asks when confronted with a change "How can I turn this change into an opportunity, that is, turn this lemon into lemonade?"

The corporate entrepreneur needs a fourth characteristic: the ability to encourage teamwork and use a multidisciplined approach. This also violates the organizational practices and structures taught in most business schools that are apparent in established organizational structures. In forming a new venture, putting together a variety of skills requires crossing established departmental structure and reporting systems. To minimize disruption, the corporate entrepreneur must be a good diplomat.

Open discussion must be encouraged to develop a good team for creating something new. It is worth noting that there are two types of conflicts that occur in team interactions: (1) There is conflict over the nature of the task and this conflict reveals information for enhancing performance on the task and (2) there is relationship conflict where the discussion becomes personal and this obstructs performance on the task. With that in mind, it is important that in attempting to avoid relationship conflict, teams do not also avoid or eliminate task conflict. Indeed, many corporate managers have forgotten the frank, open discussions and disagreements that were a part of their educational process. Instead, they spend time building protective barriers and insulating themselves in their corporate empires. A successful new venture within an established firm can be formed only when the team involved feels free to disagree and to critique an idea to reach the best solution. The degree of openness among the team members depends on the degree of openness of the corporate entrepreneur.

Openness leads also to the establishment of a strong coalition of supporters and encouragers. The corporate entrepreneur must encourage and affirm each team member, particularly during difficult times. This encouragement is very important, as the usual motivators of career paths and job security are not operational in establishing a new corporate venture. A good corporate entrepreneur makes everyone a hero.

Last, but not least, is persistence. Throughout the establishment of any new venture, frustration and obstacles will occur. Only through the corporate entrepreneur's persistence will a new venture be created and successful commercialization result.

ESTABLISHING CORPORATE ENTREPRENEURSHIP IN THE ORGANIZATION

Over and above the creation of an organizational culture and the leadership characteristics discussed so far, an organization wanting to establish a more entrepreneurial firm must implement a procedure for its creation. Although this can be done internally, frequently it is easier to use someone outside to facilitate the process. This is particularly true when the organization's environment is very traditional and has a record of little change and few new products being introduced.

top management commitment Managers in an organization strongly supporting corporate entrepreneurship

The first step in this process is to secure a commitment to corporate entrepreneurship in the organization by top, upper, and middle management levels. Without *top management commitment*, the organization will never be able to go through all the cultural changes necessary for implementation. Once the top management of the organization has been committed to corporate entrepreneurship for a sufficient period of time (at least three years), the concept can be introduced throughout the organization. This is accomplished most effectively through seminars, where the aspects of corporate entrepreneurship are introduced and strategies are developed to transform the organizational culture into an entrepreneurial one. General guidelines need to be established for corporate venture development. Once the initial framework is established and the concept embraced, corporate entrepreneurs need to be identified, selected, and trained. This training needs to focus on identifying viable opportunities and their markets and developing the appropriate business plan.

Second, ideas and general areas that top management is interested in supporting should be identified, along with the amount of risk money that is available to develop the concept further. Overall program expectations and the target results of each corporate venture should be established. As much as possible, these should specify the time frame, volume, and profitability requirements for the new venture, as well as the impact of the organization. Along with entrepreneurial training, a mentor/sponsor system needs to be established. Without sponsors or champions, there is little hope that the culture of the organization can be transformed into an entrepreneurial one.

Third, a company needs to use technology to make itself more flexible. Technology has been used successfully for the past decade by small companies that behave like big ones.[6] How else could a small firm like Value Quest Ltd. compete against very large money management firms, except through a state-of-the-art personal computer and access to large data banks? Similarly, large companies can use technology to make themselves responsive and flexible like smaller firms.

Fourth, the organization should be a group of interested managers who will train employees as well as share their experiences. The training sessions should be conducted one day per month for a specified period of time. Informational items about corporate entrepreneurship in general—and about the specifics of the company's activities in developing ideas into marketable products or services that are the basis of new business venture units—should be well publicized. This will require the entrepreneurial team to develop a business plan, obtain customer reaction and some initial intentions to buy, and learn how to coexist within the organizational structure.

Fifth, the organization needs to develop ways to get closer to its customers. This can be done by tapping the database, hiring from smaller rivals, and helping the retailer.

Sixth, an organization that wants to become more entrepreneurial must learn to be more productive with fewer resources. This has already occurred in many companies that have downsized. Top-heavy organizations are out of date in today's hypercompetitive environment. To accommodate the large cutbacks in middle management, much more control has to be given to subordinates at all levels in the organization. Not surprisingly, the span of control may become as high as 30-to-1 in divisions of such companies. The concept of "lean and mean" needs to exist if corporate entrepreneurship is to prevail.

Seventh, the organization needs to establish a strong support structure for corporate entrepreneurship. This is particularly important since corporate entrepreneurship is usually a secondary activity in the organization. Since entrepreneurial activities do not immediately affect the bottom line, they can be easily overlooked and may receive little funding and support. To be successful, these ventures require flexible, innovative behavior, with the corporate entrepreneurs having total authority over expenditures and access to sufficient funds. When the corporate entrepreneur has to justify expenses on a daily basis, it is really not a new internal venture but merely an operational extension of the funding source.

Eighth, support also must involve tying the rewards to the performance of the entrepreneurial unit. This encourages the team members to work harder and compete more effectively since they will benefit directly from their efforts. Because the corporate venture is a part of the larger organization and not a totally independent unit, the equity portion of the compensation is particularly difficult to handle.

AS SEEN IN *BUSINESS NEWS*

OPPORTUNITY OR NOT?

THE TECHNOLOGY

Are you concerned that employees stop work during their lunch break or while preparing a coffee? If you are, then this fridge could be a boon for your business. LG Electronics has offered a multimedia fridge. This fridge has an Internet connection and LCD screen that allows employees to continue to research their projects and work on their e-mails while they enjoy their lunch. Wait, there is more. The fridge has a built-in television, video camera, and Web radio that can allow video-conference calls while enjoying a coffee. The video display can also be used to show training videos so that employees are learning during their breaks.

THE IMPORTANCE OF "SMALL-WORLD" TECHNOLOGY

Rick Snyder, CEO of Ardesta, believes in the business mantra of "smaller, faster, better." In this case, he is referring to small technology such as *nanotechnology*, *microtechnology*, and *microanalytical systems*. Because of its wide range of applications, it is somewhat difficult to put your finger on exactly what is nanotechnology. But we can start with the notion that nanotechnology "deals with matter at atomic and molecular levels—that is, with matter often described as being less the width of a human hair in size."

Presently, a lot of research and development is going on in the field of nanotechnology. Many of the businesses working in the area of nanotechnology are small entrepreneurial start-ups and new ventures spun out of research institutions such as universities. This is particularly apparent in the industries of life sciences and materials manufacturing. However, it seems that nanotechnology is moving in a direction such that it could be applicable in most industries. Nanotechnology is on its way to being a pervasive approach to technology. It is already widespread and in products that might surprise you, for example, tennis racquets and LCD screens.

Therefore, there are many reasons to be excited about the possibilities of nanotechnology (and the other small tech approaches), but it is important not to become too excited. It will take time before small tech becomes sufficiently feasible to enter more and more industries. Even then, we as customers may not be aware of its use, but rather simply experience its benefits in a form of ignorant bliss.

Source: Mike Hogan, "Employees Can Munch and Work on the Web at the Same Time with This Time Save," *Entrepreneur* (February 2003), pp. 18–22.

Finally, the organization needs to implement an evaluation system that allows successful entrepreneurial units to expand and unsuccessful ones to be eliminated. The organization can establish constraints to ensure that this expansion does not run contrary to the corporate mission statement. Similarly, corporate ventures that fail to show sufficient viability should not be allowed to exist just because of vested interests.

Problems and Successful Efforts

Corporate entrepreneurship is not without its problems. One study found that new ventures started within a corporation performed worse than those started independently by entrepreneurs.[7] The reasons cited were the corporation's difficulty in maintaining a long-term commitment, a lack of freedom to make autonomous decisions, and a constrained environment. Generally, independent, venture-capital-based start-ups by entrepreneurs tend to outperform corporate start-ups significantly. On average, not only did the independents become profitable twice as fast, but they ended up twice as profitable.[8]

These findings should not deter organizations from starting the process. There are numerous examples of companies that, having understood the environmental and entrepreneurial characteristics necessary, have adopted their own version of the implementation process to launch new ventures successfully. One of the best known of these firms is Minnesota Mining and Manufacturing (3M). Having had many entrepreneurial successes, 3M, in effect, allows employees to devote a percentage of their time to independent projects. This enables the divisions of the company to meet an important goal: to generate a significant percent of sales from new products introduced within the last five years. One of the most successful of these entrepreneurial activities was the development of Post-it Notes by entrepreneur Arthur Fry. This effort developed out of Fry's annoyance that pieces of paper marking his church hymnal constantly fell out while he was singing. As a 3M chemical engineer, Fry knew about the discovery by a scientist, Spencer Silver, of an adhesive with very low sticking power, which to the company was a poor product characteristic. However, this characteristic was perfect for Fry's problem; a marker with a light-sticking adhesive that would be easy to remove provided a good solution. Obtaining approval to commercialize the idea proved to be a monumental task until the samples distributed to secretaries within 3M, as well as to other companies, created such a demand that the company eventually began selling the product under the name Post-it.

IBM also decided that corporate entrepreneurship would help spur corporate growth. The company developed the independent business unit concept, in which each unit is a separate organization with its own mini-board of directors and autonomous decision-making authority on many manufacturing and marketing issues. The business units have developed such products as the automatic teller machine for banks, industrial robots, and the IBM personal computer. The latter business unit was given a blank check with a mandate to get IBM into the personal computer market. Corporate entrepreneur Philip Estridge led his group to develop and market the PCs, through both IBM's sales force and the retail market, breaking some of the most binding operational rules of IBM at that time.

These and other success stories indicate that the problems of corporate entrepreneurship are not insurmountable and that implementing corporate entrepreneurship can lead to new products, growth, and the development of an entirely new corporate environment and culture.

Learning from Failure

dual process model of coping with negative emotions Involves oscillation between a loss orientation and a restoration orientation

loss orientation An approach to negative emotions that involves working through, and processing, some aspect of the loss experience and, as a result of this process, breaking emotional bonds to the object lost

Entrepreneurial actions are shrouded in uncertainty because opportunities exist in (or create) such environments. They are essentially experiments with unknown outcomes. Whether it is a new project, new venture, or new business model, sometimes these entrepreneurial initiatives do not work out as expected—they fail to achieve their objectives and, as a result, are terminated. This represents an opportunity to learn. By learning why an entrepreneurial initiative failed, entrepreneurs can avoid such mistakes in the future and/or do a better job of managing the uncertainties associated with entrepreneurial action. While a common saying is that we learn more from our failures than our successes, doing so in practice can be quite difficult. In particular, such learning is made difficult when strong negative emotions are generated from the loss felt by the failure. The more important the entrepreneurial initiative is to an entrepreneur, the greater his or her negative emotional reaction to the loss of that initiative will be.[9] While these negative emotions can interfere with the learning process,[10] those individuals who can more quickly recover from the emotions of failure can more quickly and effectively learn from the experience and are often more motivated to try again.

Individuals who use a *dual process model of coping with negative emotions* or grief recovery can more quickly recover from the negative emotions generated by the failure of an entrepreneurial initiative. This dual process model requires oscillating (shifting back and forth) between two alternate approaches to loss. The first is a *loss orientation*, which involves focusing on the loss event to create an account of (i.e., a plausible story for) the failure. Entrepreneurs with a loss orientation might seek out friends, family, or psychologists to talk through the event and their negative emotions. As the individual gains a deeper understanding of the reasons underlying the failure, he or she is able to break the emotional bonds to the loss of the initiative. But by focusing on the failure event for an extended period, thoughts can shift to the emotions surrounding the failure event, making the current situation worse—escalating grief. This negative cycle can be broken by shifting to the second alternative—a *restoration orientation*. This orientation involves distracting oneself from thinking about the failure and focusing one's energy on addressing other (secondary) problems that have arisen as a result of the failure. The "distracting" reduces the short-term level of negative emotions and the proactiveness towards secondary problems helps reduce the "enormity" of the failure itself. However, without allocating attention to the events surrounding the failure, there is little opportunity to learn. Therefore, oscillation (moving backward and forward) between the two orientations means the entrepreneur can benefit from both orientations while minimizing the costs of maintaining either for too long.

restoration orientation
An approach to negative emotions based on both avoidance and a proactiveness toward secondary sources of stress arising from a major loss

The dual process of learning from failure has a number of practical implications. First, knowledge that the feelings and reactions being experienced by the entrepreneur are normal for someone dealing with such a loss may help reduce feelings of shame and embarrassment. This in turn might encourage the entrepreneur to articulate his or her feelings, possibly speeding the recovery process. Second, there are psychological and physiological outcomes caused by the feelings of loss. Realizing that these are "symptoms" can reduce secondary sources of stress and may also assist with the choice of treatment. Third, there is a process of recovery from failure to learn, which offers entrepreneurs some comfort that their current feelings of loss, sadness, and helplessness will eventually diminish. Fourth, the recovery and learning process can be enhanced by some degree of oscillation between a loss orientation and a restoration orientation. Finally, recovery from loss offers an opportunity to increase one's knowledge of entrepreneurship. This provides benefits to the individual and to society.

IN REVIEW

SUMMARY

Established firms can create environmental conditions to motivate individuals within their organizations to act entrepreneurially, that is, conditions that allow organizational members to perceive entrepreneurial outcomes as feasible and desirable. Within existing corporate structures, this entrepreneurial spirit and effort is called *corporate entrepreneurship*.

Corporate entrepreneurship requires an entrepreneurial management approach. To demonstrate this entrepreneurial approach, we contrasted entrepreneurially managed firms with traditionally managed firms on eight dimensions: (1) strategic orientation, (2) commitment to opportunity, (3) commitment of resources, (4) control of resources, (5) management structure, (6) reward philosophy, (7) growth orientation, and (8) entrepreneurial culture. Fortunately, three leading Swedish researchers developed a scale that enables us to assess firms in terms of where they fall on the scale between entrepreneurial and traditional management.

Organizations desiring an entrepreneurial culture need to encourage new ideas and experimental efforts, eliminate opportunity parameters, make resources available, promote a teamwork approach and voluntary corporate entrepreneurship, and enlist top management's support. The corporate entrepreneur also must have appropriate leadership characteristics. In addition to being creative, flexible, and visionary, the corporate entrepreneur must be able to work within the corporate structure. Corporate entrepreneurs need to encourage teamwork and work diplomatically across established structures. Open discussion and strong support of team members are also required. Finally, the corporate entrepreneur must be persistent to overcome the inevitable obstacles.

The process of establishing corporate entrepreneurship within an existing organization requires the commitment of management, particularly top management. The organization must carefully choose leaders, develop general guidelines for ventures, and delineate expectations before the entrepreneurial program begins. Training sessions are an important part of the process. As role models and entrepreneurial ventures are introduced, the organization must establish a strong organizational support system, along with a system of incentives and rewards to encourage team members. Finally, the organization should establish a system to expand successful ventures and eliminate unsuccessful ones.

It is important for individuals (and organizations) to learn from the projects that are terminated. However, learning from these failed projects is likely easier said than done. Those who invest their time and energy in the projects will feel bad when the project is terminated and these negative emotions can obstruct learning. The dual process of coping with negative emotions will help individuals recover more quickly and learn from their experiences.

RESEARCH TASKS

1. Interview three individuals employed within the research and development (R&D) departments of large, well-established companies. From the interview, gain an understanding of what the company does to foster corporate entrepreneurship, what it does to inhibit corporate entrepreneurship, and what it could be doing better toward further enhancing entrepreneurship throughout the whole organization.

2. Search the Internet for four accounts of successful corporate entrepreneurship. What key factors for success are common across all these accounts? Which are unique? If one company can foster an entrepreneurial culture within an existing firm, what stops another company from copying its process and taking away the initial advantage?

3. Request the participation of managers from two companies and then ask them to fill out an "entrepreneurial management" scale (see Table 2.2). Based on the scale, which firm is more entrepreneurially managed? Does this coincide with your "gut feel" about the businesses?

4. Interview three employees that have worked on projects that were terminated. Ask them how they felt about the project, how they felt after it was terminated, and how they feel today. How did they deal with the loss of the project?

CLASS DISCUSSION

1. Isn't "corporate entrepreneurship" an oxymoron? Do the characteristics of an established organization, such as its routines and structure, increase efficiency but at the same time kill any entrepreneurial spirit? Is there any way that a company can have the best of both worlds?

2. Is increasing the entrepreneurial orientation of a firm *always* a good thing? Or are there circumstances or environments in which the further pursuit of opportunities can diminish firm performance?

3. What does it mean to say that something is important to you? Who has lost something that was important to them? How did it feel? What did you do to recover from the loss?

SELECTED READINGS

Bradley, Steven W.; Johan Wiklund; and Dean A. Shepherd. (2011). Swinging a Double-Edged Sword: The Effect of Slack on Entrepreneurial Management and Growth. *Journal of Business Venturing*, vol. 26, no. 5, pp. 537–54.

Resource slack represents a double-edged sword, simultaneously fueling and hindering growth. Drawing on Penrose's growth theory and Stevenson's entrepreneurial management theory, we have developed and tested a conceptual model that provides a more nuanced account of the resource slack-growth relationship. Using a large dataset spanning six years, we have found that slack has a positive direct effect on growth but a negative effect on entrepreneurial management, and that entrepreneurial management has a positive effect on growth. Our empirical and conceptual findings are important to the development of firm growth theory and explicate causal mechanisms transforming slack into firm-level outcomes. (from journal's abstract)

Brown, Terence; Per Davidsson; and Johan Wiklund. (2001). An Operationalization of Stevenson's Conceptualization of Entrepreneurship as Opportunity-Based Firm Behavior. *Strategic Management Journal*, vol. 22, pp. 953–69.

This article describes a new instrument that was developed specifically for operationalizing Stevenson's conceptualization of entrepreneurial management. The instrument should open up opportunities for researchers to further evaluate entrepreneurship in existing firms.

Dess, Gregory; R. Duane Ireland; Shaker Zahra; Steven Floyd; Jay Janney; and Peter Lane. (2003). Emerging Issues in Corporate Entrepreneurship. *Journal of Management*, vol. 29, pp. 351–78.

In this article, the authors identify four major issues scholars can pursue to further our understanding about corporate entrepreneurship (CE). The issues explored include various forms of CE and their implications for organizational learning; the role of leadership and social exchange in the CE process; and key research opportunities relevant to CE in an international context. Throughout the article, the authors use the organizational learning theory as a means of integrating our discussion and highlighting the potential contributions of CE to knowledge creation and effective exploitation.

Ireland, R. Duane; Jeffrey G. Covin; and Don F. Kuratko. (2009). Conceptualizing Corporate Entrepreneurship Strategy. *Entrepreneurship: Theory and Practice*, vol. 33, pp. 19–46.

In this article, the authors conceptualize the components of corporate entrepreneurship (CE) to include (1) the individual entrepreneurial cognitions of the organization's members and external environmental conditions that invite entrepreneurial activity; (2) the top management's entrepreneurial strategic vision for the firm, organizational architectures that encourage entrepreneurial processes and behavior, and the generic forms of entrepreneurial process that are reflected in entrepreneurial behavior; and (3) the organizational outcomes resulting from entrepreneurial actions, including the development of competitive capability and strategic repositioning.

Kuratko, Donald; R. Duane Ireland; Jeffrey Covin; and Jeffrey Hornsby. (2005). A Model of Middle-Level Managers' Entrepreneurial Behavior. *Entrepreneurship: Theory and Practice,* vol. 29, pp. 699–716.

In this article, the authors integrate knowledge about corporate entrepreneurship and middle-level managers' behaviors to develop and explore a conceptual model. The model depicts the organizational antecedents of middle-level managers' entrepreneurial behavior, the entrepreneurial actions describing that behavior, and outcomes of that behavior, as well as factors influencing its continuance.

Morris, Michael H.; Donald F. Kuratko; and Jeffrey G. Covin. (2010). *Corporate Entrepreneurship and Innovation: Entrepreneurial Development within Organizations.* Mason, OH: Thompson Publishing.

This book provides an extensive account of how to introduce entrepreneurial action within an existing organization. The goal of the book is to explain how to develop an entrepreneurial mindset and is organized around a three-phase model to examine (1) the nature of entrepreneurship within established organizations, (2) how to create an organizational environment that supports entrepreneurship, and (3) how to sustain entrepreneurship, and its performance benefits, over time.

Shepherd, Dean A. (2003). Learning from Business Failure: Propositions about the Grief Recovery Process for the Self-Employed. *Academy of Management Review,* vol., 28, pp. 318–29.

This article employs the psychological literature on grief to explore the emotion of business failure. It suggests that the loss of a business due to failure can cause the self-employed to feel grief, which is a negative emotional response interfering with the ability to learn from the events surrounding that loss. Recovering from grief involves dealing with the loss, avoiding thinking about the loss, or a dual process that iteratively combines these two approaches. A dual process provides the speediest path to grief recovery enabling the self-employed to learn more from the events surrounding the loss of the business owing to a lack of emotional interference. Those who have not yet completed this process continue to feel negative emotions and remain in the recovery process. But even in the presence of grief, a dual process minimizes emotional interference enhancing the ability of the self-employed to learn from the loss of a business. An improved ability to learn from business failure is important for individuals and society.

Shepherd, Dean A. (2009). *Lemons to Lemonade: Squeezing the Most out of Your Mistakes.* Wharton School Press.

Learn More from Failure, Learn It Faster ... and Use Those Lessons to Achieve Breakthrough Success! We all fail. And we all want to learn from our failures. But learning from failure doesn't happen automatically. It requires very specific emotional and rational skills. You can learn those skills from this book. Drawing on leading-edge research with hundreds of failing and successful entrepreneurs, Dr. Dean A. Shepherd offers powerful strategies for managing the emotions generated by failure so failure becomes less devastating, learning happens faster, and you grow as much as possible from the experience. Shepherd shows how to clarify why you failed, so you can walk away with insights you can actually use ... how to eliminate "secondary" stresses that aggravate failure or make it more likely ... how to master the self-compassion you deserve in times of trouble ... and a whole lot more. Failing will never be easy or desirable. But this book will make it less catastrophic, and more instructive, so you can get back to success and get there fast. Mourn your failure faster, so you can learn from it sooner. Learn how to "undo" your emotional ties to failure. Grow from the experience of failure. Absorb the lessons that don't fit with your preconceptions. Discover when to "pull the plug" on a failure in progress. Know when to move on, so failure won't last longer or feel worse than it has to. Stay committed to excellence, no matter what. Keep focused on success, even in environments where multiple failures are commonplace. (from abstract)

Shepherd, Dean A.; Holger Patzelt; and Marcus Wolfe. (2011). Moving Forward from Project Failure: Negative Emotions, Affective Commitment, and Learning from the Experience. *Academy of Management Journal*, vol. 54, pp. 1229–59.

Project failures are common. We theorized and found that although time heals wounds (reduces the negative emotions from project failure), it heals differently depending on the strength of individuals' specific coping orientations. Further, wounds are shallower for those who perceive that their organization normalizes failure. We conjointly consider learning from failure and affective commitment to an organization as determining how individuals move forward from project failure. Findings suggest that studies framing moving forward solely as learning from failure will likely overstate the benefits of a "loss orientation" and understate the benefits of both a "restoration" and an "oscillation orientation."

Shepherd, Dean A.; Jeffrey G. Covin, and Donald F. Kuratko. (2009). Project Failure from Corporate Entrepreneurship: Managing the Grief Process. *Journal of Business Venturing*, vol. 24, pp. 588–600.

In this paper, the authors complement social cognitive theory with psychological theories on grief in their discussion of two approaches to grief management—grief regulation and grief normalization—that hold promise for enabling corporate entrepreneurs to cope with negative emotions induced by project failure. They propose that to the extent that organizational members have high self-efficacy for recovering from grief over project failure, or this coping self-efficacy can be built through the social support offered by the organizational environment, regulating rather than eliminating grief via normalization processes will explain superior learning and motivational outcomes.

Shepherd, Dean A.; and Melissa Cardon. (2009). Negative Emotional Reactions to Project Failure and the Self-Compassion to Learn from the Experience. *Journal of Management Studies*, vol. 46, pp. 923–49.

Project failure is likely to generate a negative emotional response for those involved in the project. But do all people feel the same way? And are some better able to regulate their emotions to learn from the failure experience? In this paper the authors develop an emotion framework of project failure that relies on self-determination to explain variance in the intensity of the negative emotions triggered by project failure and self-compassion to explain variance in learning from project failure. They discuss the implications of the model for research on entrepreneurial and innovative organizations, employees' psychological ownership, and personal engagement at work.

Shepherd, Dean A.; and Norris Krueger. (2002). An Intentions-Based Model of Entrepreneurial Teams' Social Cognition. *Entrepreneurship: Theory and Practice*, vol. 27, pp. 167–85.

In this article, the authors present an intentions-based model of how to promote entrepreneurial thinking in the domain of corporate entrepreneurship. They emphasize the importance of perceptions of desirability and feasibility and that these perceptions are from the team as well as the individual perspective.

Stevenson, Howard; and J. Carlos Jarillo. (1990). A Paradigm of Entrepreneurship: Entrepreneurial Management. *Strategic Management Journal*, vol. 11 (Special Issue), pp. 17–27.

In this article, the authors propose that the very concept of corporate entrepreneurship sounds to many entrepreneurship scholars like something of an oxymoron. They point out that there is no doubt that, of late, entrepreneurship in general has gained its status as a legitimate scholarly research subject, enjoying in addition much public interest. The authors offer a discussion of the concept of entrepreneurship within established firms.

END NOTES

1. For a discussion of XTV, see Larry Armstrong, "Nurturing an Employee's Brainchild," *BusinessWeek/Enterprise* (1993), p. 196.

2. For a discussion of corporate entrepreneurship elements and their measures, see G. T. Lumpkin and G. G. Dess, "Clarifying the Entrepreneurial Orientation Construct and Linking It to Performance," *Academy of Management Review* 12, no. 1 (1996), pp. 135–72; and B. Antoncic and R. D. Hisrich, "Intrapreneurship: Construct Refinement and Cross-Cultural Validation," *Journal of Business Venturing* 16, no. 61 (September 2001), pp. 495–527.

3. H. H. Stevenson and D. Gumpert, "The Heart of Entrepreneurship," *Harvard Business Review* 63, no. 2 (1985), pp. 85–94.

4. Based on T. Brown, P. Davidsson, and J. Wiklund, "An Operationalization of Stevenson's Conceptualization of Entrepreneurship as Opportunity-Based Firm Behavior," *Strategic Management Journal* 22 (2001), pp. 953–69 (table on page 955).

5. For a thorough discussion of the factors important in corporate entrepreneurship, see R. M. Kanter, *The Change Masters* (New York: Simon & Schuster, 1983); and G. Pinchot III, *Intrapreneuring* (New York: Harper & Row, 1985).

6. For a discussion of this aspect, see Peter Coy, "Start with Some High-Tech Magic … ," *BusinessWeek/Enterprise* (1993), pp. 24–25, 28, 32.

7. N. Fast, "Pitfalls of Corporate Venturing," *Research Management* (March 1981), pp. 21–24.

8. For complete information on the relative performance, see R. Biggadike, "The Risky Business of Diversification," *Harvard Business Review* (May–June 1979), pp. 103–11; L. E. Weiss, "Start-Up Business: A Comparison of Performances," *Sloan Management Review* (Fall 1981), pp. 37–53; and N. D. Fast and S. E. Pratt, "Individual Entrepreneurship and the Large Corporation," *Proceedings, Babson Research Conference*, April 1984, pp. 443–50.

9. D. A. Shepherd and M. Cardon, "Negative Emotional Reactions to Project Failure and the Self-Compassion to Learn from the Experience," *Journal of Management Studies* 46, no. 6 (September 2009), pp. 923–49.

10. D. A. Shepherd, "Learning from Business Failure: Propositions about the Grief Recovery Process for the Self-Employed," *Academy of Management Review* 28, no. 2 (2003), pp. 318–29.

part one Introduction and Overview

Globalization

1

LEARNING OBJECTIVES

After reading this chapter, you will be able to:

LO1-1   Understand what is meant by the term *globalization*.

LO1-2   Recognize the main drivers of globalization.

LO1-3   Describe the changing nature of the global economy.

LO1-4   Explain the main arguments in the debate over the impact of globalization.

LO1-5   Understand how the process of globalization is creating opportunities and challenges for business managers.

Medical Tourism and the Globalization of Health Care

OPENING CASE

You might think that health care is one of the industries least vulnerable to dislocation from globalization. Like many service businesses, surely health care is delivered where it is purchased? If an American goes to a hospital for an MRI scan, won't a local radiologist read that scan? If the MRI scan shows that surgery is required, surely the surgery will be done at a local hospital in the United States? Until recently, this was true, but we are now witnessing globalization in this traditionally most local of industries.

Consider the MRI scan: The United States has a shortage of radiologists, the doctors who specialize in reading and interpreting diagnostic medical images, including X-rays, CT scans, MRI scans, and ultrasounds. Demand for radiologists is reportedly growing twice as fast as the rate at which medical schools are graduating radiologists with the skills and qualifications required to read medical images. This imbalance between supply and demand means that radiologists are expensive; an American radiologist can earn as much as $400,000 a year. Back in the early 2000s, an Indian radiologist working at the prestigious Massachusetts General Hospital, Dr. Sanjay Saini, thought he had found a clever way to deal with the shortage and expense—send images over the Internet to India where they could be interpreted by radiologists. This would reduce the workload on America's radiologists and cut costs. A radiologist in India might earn one-tenth of his or her U.S. counterpart. Plus, because India is on the opposite side of the globe, the images could be interpreted while it was nighttime in the United States and be ready for the attending physician when he or she arrived for work the following morning.

As for the surgery, here too we are witnessing an outsourcing trend. Consider Howard Staab, a 53-year-old uninsured self-employed carpenter from North Carolina. Mr. Staab had surgery to repair a leaking heart valve—in India. Mr. Staab flew to New Delhi, had the operation, and afterward toured the Taj Mahal, the price of which was bundled with that of the surgery. The cost, including airfare, totaled $10,000. If Mr. Staab's surgery had been performed in the United States, the cost would have been $60,000 and there would have been no visit to the Taj Mahal.

Howard Staab is not alone. Driven by a desire to access low-cost health care, some 150,000 Westerners visit India every year for medical treatments. In general, medical procedures in India cost about 10–20% less than in the United States. The Indian industry generates $2 billion in revenues every year from foreign patients. In another example, after years of living in pain, Robert Beeney, a 64-year-old from San Francisco, was advised to get his hip joint replaced. After doing some research, Mr. Beeney elected instead for joint resurfacing, which was not covered by his insurance. Instead of going to a nearby hospital, he flew to Hyderabad in southern India and had the surgery done for $6,600, a fraction of the $25,000 the procedure would have cost in the United States.

Mr. Beeney had his surgery performed at a branch of the Apollo hospital chain. Apollo, which was founded by Dr. Prathap C. Reddy, a surgeon trained at Massachusetts General Hospital, runs a chain of 50 state-of-the-art hospitals throughout Asia. Eight of Apollo's hospitals have the highest level of international accreditation. Apollo's main hospitals in India are estimated to treat some 50,000 international patients from 55 countries every year, mainly from nations in Southeast Asia and the Persian Gulf, although a growing number are from western Europe and North America.

Will demand for American health services soon collapse as work moves offshore to places like India? That seems unlikely. Regulations, personal preferences, and practical considerations mean that the majority of health services will always be performed in the country where the patient resides. For example, the U.S. government–sponsored medical insurance program, Medicare, will not pay for services done outside the country.

Moreover, in an interesting countertrend, U.S. medical providers also seem to be benefiting from medical tourism, particularly from China, where health care services are poor and lag far behind U.S. levels. Over the past decade middle-class Chinese have flocked to South Korea for plastic surgery, and to the United States, Singapore, and India for treatment of life-threatening conditions. When Lin Tao was diagnosed with a lethal spinal tumor in 2012, rather than risk treatment in his native Hangzhou, China, he flew to San Francisco and paid $70,000 for treatment at UCSF Medical Center. UCSF Medical Center says that its Chinese population has grown by more than 25 percent in each of the past few years. Similarly, Massachusetts General Hospital is expecting its Chinese patients to more than double in 2015 over 2014. As China gets wealthier, ever more Chinese are apparently willing to spend more to get better treatment overseas, and America's world-class hospitals are benefiting from this trend.

Sources: G. Colvin, "Think Your Job Can't Be Sent to India?," *Fortune*, December 13, 2004, p. 80; A. Pollack, "Who's Reading Your X-Ray," *The New York Times*, November 16, 2003, pp. 1, 9; S. Rai, "Low Costs Lure Foreigners to India for Medical Care," *The New York Times*, April 7, 2005, p. C6; J. Solomon, "Traveling Cure: India's New Coup in Outsourcing," *The Wall Street Journal*, April 26, 2004, p. A1; J. Slater, "Increasing Doses in India," *Far Eastern Economic Review*, February 19, 2004, pp. 32–35; U. Kher, "Outsourcing Your Heart," *Time*, May 29, 2006, pp. 44–47; Anuradha Raghunathan, "The Reddy Sisters Have India's Apollo Hospitals Covered in Four Ways," *Forbes Asia*, January 8, 2014; Fanfan Wang, "Desperate Chinese Seek Medical Care Abroad," *The Wall Street Journal*, September 6, 2014; Apollo Hospital Group, Patients beyond Borders, **www.patientsbeyondborders.com/hospital/apollo-hospitals-group**, accessed April 2015.

Part 1   Introduction and Overview

Introduction

Over the past four decades a fundamental shift has been occurring in the world economy. We have been moving away from a world in which national economies were relatively self-contained entities, isolated from each other by barriers to cross-border trade and investment; by distance, time zones, and language; and by national differences in government regulation, culture, and business systems. We are moving toward a world in which barriers to cross-border trade and investment are declining; perceived distance is shrinking due to advances in transportation and telecommunications technology; material culture is starting to look similar the world over; and national economies are merging into an interdependent, integrated global economic system. The process by which this transformation is occurring is commonly referred to as *globalization.*

The rise of medical tourism discussed in the opening case is one illustration of the trend toward globalization. Twenty years ago almost all medical procedures were delivered in the country where the patient resided. This is now changing. A global marketplace for medical care is developing. MRI images from U.S. patients may be diagnosed by radiologists in India. Wealthy Chinese may go to South Korea for plastic surgery and America for state-of-the-art medical treatment for life-threatening conditions. Some Americans make the trek to India for surgeries that can be done in internationally accredited hospitals at a fraction of the cost in the United States. In all of these cases, the motive is to get less expensive or better treatment than is available in the patient's home nation.

More generally, globalization now has an impact on almost everything we do. The average American, for example, might drive to work in a car that was designed in Germany and assembled in Mexico by Ford from components made in the United States and Japan, which were fabricated from Korean steel and Malaysian rubber. He may have filled the car with gasoline at a Shell service station owned by a British-Dutch multinational company. The gasoline could have been made from oil pumped out of a well off the coast of Africa by a French oil company that transported it to the United States in a ship owned by a Greek shipping line. While driving to work, the American might talk to his stockbroker (using a hands-free, in-car speaker) on an Apple iPhone that was designed in California and assembled in China using chip sets produced in Japan and Europe, glass made by Corning in Kentucky, and memory chips from South Korea. He could tell the stockbroker to purchase shares in Lenovo, a multinational Chinese PC manufacturer whose operational headquarters is in North Carolina, and whose shares are listed on the New York Stock Exchange.

This is the world in which we live. It is a world where the volume of goods, services, and investments crossing national borders has expanded faster than world output for more than half a century. It is a world where more than $5 trillion in foreign exchange transactions are made every day, where $19 trillion of goods and $4.9 trillion of services were sold across national borders in 2014.[1] It is a world in which international institutions such as the World Trade Organization and gatherings of leaders from the world's most powerful economies have repeatedly called for even lower barriers to cross-border trade and investment. It is a world where the symbols of material and popular culture are increasingly global: from Coca-Cola and Starbucks to Sony PlayStations, Facebook, MTV shows, Disney films, IKEA stores, and Apple iPads and iPhones. It is also a world in which vigorous and vocal groups protest against globalization, which they blame for a list of ills from unemployment in developed nations to environmental degradation and the Americanization of local culture.

For businesses, this globalization process has produced many opportunities. Firms can expand their revenues by selling around the world and/or reduce their costs by producing in nations where key inputs, including labor, are cheap. The global expansion of enterprises has been facilitated by favorable political and economic trends. Since the collapse of communism a quarter of a century ago, the pendulum of public policy in nation after nation has swung toward the free market end of the economic spectrum. Regulatory and administrative barriers to doing business in foreign nations have been reduced, while those nations have often transformed their economies, privatizing state-owned enterprises, deregulating markets, increasing competition, and welcoming investment by foreign businesses. This has allowed businesses both large and small, from both advanced nations and developing nations, to expand internationally.

As globalization unfolds, it is transforming industries and creating anxiety among those who believed their jobs were protected from foreign competition. Historically, while many workers in manufacturing industries worried about the impact foreign competition might have on their jobs, workers in service industries felt more secure. Now, this too is changing. Advances in technology, lower transportation costs, and the rise of skilled workers in developing countries imply that many services no longer need to be performed where they are delivered. The opening case described how this is occurring with medical services. The same is true of some accounting services. Today, many individual U.S. tax returns are compiled in India. Indian accountants, trained in U.S. tax rules, perform work for U.S. accounting firms.[2] They access individual tax returns stored on computers in the United States, perform routine calculations, and save their work so that it can be inspected by a U.S. accountant, who then bills clients. As the best-selling author Thomas Friedman has argued, the world is becoming flat.[3] People living in developed nations no longer have the playing field tilted in their favor. Increasingly, enterprising individuals based in India, China, or Brazil have the same opportunities to better themselves as those living in western Europe, the United States, or Canada.

In this text, we will take a close look at the issues introduced here and many more. We will explore how changes in regulations governing international trade and investment, when coupled with changes in political systems and technology, have dramatically altered the competitive playing field confronting many businesses. We will discuss the resulting opportunities and threats and review the strategies that managers can pursue to exploit the opportunities and counter the threats. We will consider whether globalization benefits or harms national economies. We will look at what economic theory has to say about the outsourcing of manufacturing and service jobs to places such as India and China and look at the benefits and costs of outsourcing, not just to business firms and their employees but also to entire economies. First, though, we need to get a better overview of the nature and process of globalization, and that is the function of this first chapter.

What Is Globalization?

LO 1-1

Understand what is meant by the term *globalization*.

As used in this text, **globalization** refers to the shift toward a more integrated and interdependent world economy. Globalization has several facets, including the globalization of markets and the globalization of production.

THE GLOBALIZATION OF MARKETS

The **globalization of markets** refers to the merging of historically distinct and separate national markets into one huge global marketplace. Falling barriers to cross-border trade have made it easier to sell internationally. It has been argued for some time that the tastes and preferences of consumers in different nations are beginning to converge on some global norm, thereby helping create a global market.[4] Consumer products such as Citigroup credit cards, Coca-Cola soft drinks, video games, McDonald's hamburgers, Starbucks coffee, IKEA furniture, and Apple iPhones are frequently held up as prototypical examples of this trend. The firms that produce these products are more than just benefactors of this trend; they are also facilitators of it. By offering the same basic product worldwide, they help create a global market.

A company does not have to be the size of these multinational giants to facilitate, and benefit from, the globalization of markets. In the United States, for example, according to the International Trade Administration, more than 295,000 small and medium-size firms with less than 500 employees exported in 2013, accounting for 98 percent of the companies that exported that year. More generally, exports from small and medium-size companies accounted for 33 percent of the value of U.S. exports of manufactured goods in 2013.[5] Typical of these is

6

 Part 1   Introduction and Overview

B&S Aircraft Alloys, a New York company whose exports account for 40 percent of its $8 million annual revenues.[6] The situation is similar in several other nations. For example, in Germany, the world's largest exporter, a staggering 98 percent of small and midsize companies have exposure to international markets, via either exports or international production.[7]

---

globalEDGE INTERNATIONAL BUSINESS RESOURCES

globalEDGE offers the latest and most comprehensive international business and trade content for a wide range of topics. Whether conducting extensive market research, looking to improve your international knowledge, or simply browsing, you're sure to find what you need to sharpen your competitive edge in today's rapidly changing global marketplace. The easy, convenient, and free globalEDGE website's tagline is "Your Source for Global Business Knowledge." It was developed and is maintained by a 30-member team in the International Business Center at Michigan State University under the supervision of Tomas Hult, Tunga Kiyak, and Sarah Singer. For example, related to this chapter on globalization, take a look at the always up-to-date "Globalization" resources on the site at **globaledge. msu.edu/global-resources/globalization**. There is even a quick guide to the world history of globalization to browse!

Despite the global prevalence of Citigroup credit cards, McDonald's hamburgers, Starbucks coffee, and IKEA stores, it is important not to push too far the view that national markets are giving way to the global market. As we shall see in later chapters, significant differences still exist among national markets along many relevant dimensions, including consumer tastes and preferences, distribution channels, culturally embedded value systems, business systems, and legal regulations. These differences frequently require companies to customize marketing strategies, product features, and operating practices to best match conditions in a particular country.

The most global of markets are not typically markets for consumer products—where national differences in tastes and preferences can still be important enough to act as a brake on globalization—but markets for industrial goods and materials that serve universal needs the world over. These include the markets for commodities such as aluminum, oil, and wheat; for industrial products such as microprocessors, DRAMs (computer memory chips), and commercial jet aircraft; for computer software; and for financial assets from U.S. Treasury bills to Eurobonds and futures on the Nikkei index or the euro. That being said, it is increasingly evident that many newer high-technology consumer products, such as Apple's iPhone, are being successfully sold the same way the world over.

In many global markets, the same firms frequently confront each other as competitors in nation after nation. Coca-Cola's rivalry with PepsiCo is a global one, as are the rivalries between Ford and Toyota; Boeing and Airbus; Caterpillar and Komatsu in earthmoving equipment; General Electric and Rolls-Royce in aero engines; and Sony, Nintendo, and Microsoft in video-game consoles. If a firm moves into a nation not currently served by its rivals, many of those rivals are sure to follow to prevent their competitor from gaining an advantage.[8] As firms follow each other around the world, they bring with them many of the assets that served them well in other national markets—their products, operating strategies, marketing strategies, and brand names—creating some homogeneity across markets. Thus, greater uniformity replaces diversity. In an increasing number of industries, it is no longer meaningful to talk about "the German market," "the American market," "the Brazilian market," or "the Japanese market"; for many firms there is only the global market.

THE GLOBALIZATION OF PRODUCTION

The **globalization of production** refers to the sourcing of goods and services from locations around the globe to take advantage of national differences in the cost and quality of factors of production (such as labor, energy, land, and capital). By doing this, companies hope to lower their overall cost structure or improve the quality or functionality of their product offering, thereby allowing them to compete more effectively. For example, Boeing has made extensive use of outsourcing to foreign suppliers. Consider Boeing's 777: eight Japanese suppliers make parts for the fuselage, doors, and wings; a supplier in Singapore makes the doors for the nose landing gear; three suppliers in Italy manufacture wing flaps; and so on.[9] In total, some 30 percent of the 777, by value, is built by foreign companies. And, for its most recent jet airliner, the 787, Boeing has pushed this trend even further; some 65 percent of the total value of the aircraft is outsourced to foreign companies, 35 percent of which goes to three major Japanese companies.

Part of Boeing's rationale for outsourcing so much production to foreign suppliers is that these suppliers are the best in the world at their particular activity. A global web of suppliers yields a better final product, which enhances the chances of Boeing winning a greater share of total orders for aircraft than its global rival, Airbus. Boeing also outsources some production to foreign countries to increase the chance that it will win significant orders from airlines based in that country. For another example of a global web of activities, consider the example of Vizio profiled in the accompanying Management Focus.

Early outsourcing efforts were primarily confined to manufacturing activities, such as those undertaken by Boeing, Apple, and Vizio; increasingly, however, companies are taking advantage of modern communications technology, particularly the Internet, to outsource service activities to low-cost producers in other nations. The Internet has allowed hospitals to outsource some radiology work to India, where images from MRI scans and the like are read at night while U.S. physicians sleep; the results are ready for them in the morning (see the opening case). Many software companies, including IBM and Microsoft, now use Indian engineers to perform test functions on software designed in the United States. The time difference allows Indian engineers to run debugging tests on software written in the United States when U.S. engineers sleep, transmitting the corrected code back to the United States over secure Internet connections so it is ready for U.S. engineers to work on the following day. Dispersing value-creation activities in this way can compress the time and lower the costs required to develop new software programs. Other companies, from computer makers to banks, are outsourcing customer service functions, such as customer call centers, to developing nations where labor is cheaper. In another example from health care, workers in the Philippines transcribe American medical files (such as audio files from doctors seeking approval from insurance companies for performing a procedure). Some estimates suggest the outsourcing of many administrative procedures in health care, such as customer service and claims processing, could reduce health care costs in America by as much as $70 billion.[10]

Robert Reich, who served as secretary of labor in the Clinton administration, has argued that as a consequence of the trend exemplified by companies such as Boeing, Apple, IBM, and Vizio, in many cases it is becoming irrelevant to talk about American products, Japanese products, German products, or Korean products. Increasingly, according to Reich, the outsourcing of productive activities to different suppliers results in the creation of products that are global in nature, that is, "global products."[11] But as with the globalization of markets, companies must be careful not to push the globalization of production too far. As we will see in later chapters, substantial impediments still make it difficult for firms to achieve the optimal dispersion of their productive activities to locations around the globe. These impediments include formal and informal barriers to trade between countries, barriers to foreign direct investment, transportation costs, issues associated with economic and political risk, and the shear managerial challenge of coordinating a globally dispersed supply chain (which was an issue for Boeing with the 787, as discussed in the closing case). For example, government regulations ultimately limit the ability of hospitals to outsource the process of interpreting MRI scans to developing nations where radiologists are cheaper.

Nevertheless, the globalization of markets and production will probably continue. Modern firms are important actors in this trend, their very actions fostering increased globalization. These firms, however, are merely responding in an efficient manner to changing conditions in their operating environment—as well they should.

 **TEST PREP**

Use SmartBook to help retain what you have learned. Access your instructor's Connect course to check out SmartBook or go to learnsmartadvantage.com for help.

MANAGEMENT FOCUS

Vizio and the Market for Flat-Panel TVs

Operating sophisticated tooling in environments that must be kept absolutely clean, fabrication centers in South Korea, Taiwan, and Japan produce sheets of glass twice as large as king-size beds to exacting specifications. From there, the glass panels travel to Mexican plants located alongside the U.S. border. There, they are cut to size, combined with electronic components shipped in from Asia and the United States, assembled into finished flat-panel TVs, and loaded onto trucks bound for retail stores in the United States, where consumers spend more than $35 billion a year on flat-panel TVs.

The underlying technology for flat-panel displays was invented in the United States in the late 1960s by RCA. But after RCA and rivals Westinghouse and Xerox opted not to pursue the technology, the Japanese company Sharp made aggressive investments in flat-panel displays. By the early 1990s, Sharp was selling the first flat-panel screens, but as the Japanese economy plunged into a decade-long recession, investment leadership shifted to South Korean companies such as Samsung. Then the 1997 Asian crisis hit Korea hard, and Taiwanese companies seized leadership. Today, Chinese companies are elbowing their way into the flat-panel display manufacturing business.

As production for flat-panel displays migrates its way around the globe to low-cost locations, there are clear winners and losers. U.S. consumers have benefited from the falling prices of flat-panel TVs and are snapping them up. Efficient manufacturers have taken advantage of globally dispersed supply chains to make and sell low-cost, high-quality flat-panel TVs. Foremost among these

Vizio's flat-panel TVs are assembled in Mexico from components produced in many different countries.

Source: © Jin Lee/Bloomberg/Getty Images

has been the California-based company Vizio, founded by a Taiwanese immigrant. In just 10 years, sales of Vizio flat-panel TVs ballooned from nothing to around $3.1 billion by 2013. The privately held company is the largest provider to the U.S. market with an 18 to 19 percent share. Vizio, however, has reportedly fewer than 500 employees. Its focus is on final product design, sales, and customer service. Vizio outsources most of its engineering work, all of its manufacturing, and much of its logistics. For each of its models, Vizio assembles a team of supplier partners strung across the globe. Its 42-inch flat-panel TV, for example, contains a panel from South Korea, electronic components from China, and processors from the United States, and it is assembled in Mexico. Vizio's managers scour the globe continually for the cheapest manufacturers of flat-panel displays and electronic components. They sell most of their TVs to large discount retailers such as Costco and Sam's Club. Good order visibility from retailers, coupled with tight management of global logistics, allows Vizio to turn over its inventory every three weeks, twice as fast as many of its competitors, which allows major cost savings in a business where prices are falling continually.

Sources: D. J. Lynch, "Flat Panel TVs Display Effects of Globalization," *USA Today,* May 8, 2007, pp. 1B, 2B; P. Engardio and E. Woyke, "Flat Panels, Thin Margins," *BusinessWeek,* February 26, 2007, p. 50; B. Womack, "Flat TV Seller Vizio Hits $600 Million in Sales, Growing," *Orange County Business Journal,* September 4, 2007, pp. 1, 64; E. Taub, "Vizio's Flat Panel Display Sales Are Anything but Flat," *The New York Times Online,* May 12, 2009; Greg Tarr, "HIS: Samsung Dusts Vizio in Q4 LCD TV Share in the U.S.," *This Week in Consumer Electronics,* April 12, 2012, p. 12.

The Emergence of Global Institutions

As markets globalize and an increasing proportion of business activity transcends national borders, institutions are needed to help manage, regulate, and police the global marketplace and to promote the establishment of multinational treaties to govern the global business system. Over the past half century, a number of important global institutions have been created to help perform these functions, including the **General Agreement on Tariffs and Trade (GATT)** and its successor, the World Trade Organization; the International Monetary Fund and its sister institution, the World Bank; and the United Nations. All these institutions were created by voluntary agreement between individual nation-states, and their functions are enshrined in international treaties.

The **World Trade Organization (WTO)** (like the GATT before it) is primarily responsible for policing the world trading system and making sure nation-states adhere to the rules laid down in trade treaties signed by WTO member states. As of 2015, 160 nations that collectively accounted for 98 percent of world trade were WTO members, thereby giving the organization enormous scope and influence. The WTO is also responsible for facilitating the establishment of additional multinational agreements among WTO member states. Over its entire history, and that of the GATT before it, the WTO has promoted the lowering of barriers to cross-border trade and investment. In doing so, the WTO has been the instrument of its member states, which have sought to create a more open global business system unencumbered by barriers to trade and investment between countries. Without an institution such as the WTO, the globalization of markets and production is unlikely to have proceeded as far as it has. However, as we shall see in this chapter and in Chapter 7 when we look closely at the WTO, critics charge that the organization is usurping the national sovereignty of individual nation-states.

The **International Monetary Fund (IMF)** and the **World Bank** were both created in 1944 by 44 nations that met at Bretton Woods, New Hampshire. The IMF was established to maintain order in the international monetary system; the World Bank was set up to promote economic development. In the more than six decades since their creation, both institutions have emerged as significant players in the global economy. The World Bank is the less controversial of the two sister institutions. It has focused on making low-interest loans to cash-strapped governments in poor nations that wish to undertake significant infrastructure investments (such as building dams or roads).

The IMF is often seen as the lender of last resort to nation-states whose economies are in turmoil and whose currencies are losing value against those of other nations. During the past two decades, for example, the IMF has lent money to the governments of troubled states, including Argentina, Indonesia, Mexico, Russia, South Korea, Thailand, and Turkey. More recently, the IMF has taken a proactive role in helping countries cope with some of the effects of the 2008–2009 global financial crisis. IMF loans come with strings attached, however; in return for loans, the IMF requires nation-states to adopt specific economic policies aimed at returning their troubled economies to stability and growth. These requirements have sparked controversy. Some critics charge that the IMF's policy recommendations are often inappropriate; others maintain that by telling national governments what economic policies they must adopt, the IMF, like the WTO, is usurping the sovereignty of nation-states. We will look at the debate over the role of the IMF in Chapter 11.

The **United Nations (UN)** was established October 24, 1945, by 51 countries committed to preserving peace through international cooperation and collective security. Today, nearly every nation in the world belongs to the United Nations; membership now totals 193 countries. When states become members of the United Nations, they agree to accept the obligations of the UN Charter, an international treaty that establishes basic principles of international relations. According to the charter, the UN has four purposes: to maintain international peace and security, to develop friendly relations among nations, to cooperate in solving international problems and in promoting respect for human rights, and to be a center for harmonizing the actions of nations. Although the UN is perhaps best known for its peacekeeping role, one of the organization's central mandates is the promotion of higher standards of living, full employment, and conditions of economic and social progress and development—all issues that are central to the creation of a vibrant global economy. As much as 70 percent of the work of the UN system is devoted to accomplishing this mandate. To do so, the UN works closely with other international institutions such as the World Bank. Guiding the work is the belief that eradicating poverty and improving the well-being of people everywhere are necessary steps in creating conditions for lasting world peace.[12]

Another institution in the news is the Group of Twenty (G20). Established in 1999, the G20 comprises the finance ministers and central bank governors of the 19 largest economies in the world, plus representatives from the European Union and the European Central Bank. Collectively, the G20 represents 90 percent of global GDP and 80 percent of international global trade. Originally established to formulate a coordinated policy response to financial crises in developing nations, in 2008 and 2009 it became the forum through which major nations attempted to launch a coordinated policy response to the global financial crisis that started in America and then rapidly spread around the world, ushering in the first serious global economic recession since 1981.

Drivers of Globalization

LO 1-2

Recognize the main drivers of globalization.

Two macro factors underlie the trend toward greater globalization.[13] The first is the decline in barriers to the free flow of goods, services, and capital that has occurred since the end of World War II. The second factor is technological change, particularly the dramatic developments in recent decades in communication, information processing, and transportation technologies.

DECLINING TRADE AND INVESTMENT BARRIERS

During the 1920s and 1930s, many of the world's nation-states erected formidable barriers to international trade and foreign direct investment. International trade occurs when a firm exports goods or services to consumers in another country. Foreign direct investment (FDI) occurs when a firm invests resources in business activities outside its home country. Many of the barriers to international trade took the form of high tariffs on imports of manufactured goods. The typical aim of such tariffs was to protect domestic industries from foreign competition. One consequence, however, was "beggar thy neighbor" retaliatory trade policies, with countries progressively raising trade barriers against each other. Ultimately, this depressed world demand and contributed to the Great Depression of the 1930s.

Having learned from this experience, the advanced industrial nations of the West committed themselves after World War II to progressively reducing barriers to the free flow of goods, services, and capital among nations.[14] This goal was enshrined in the General Agreement on Tariffs and Trade. Under the umbrella of GATT, eight rounds of negotiations among member states worked to lower barriers to the free flow of goods and services. The most recent negotiations to be completed, known as the Uruguay Round, were finalized in December 1993. The Uruguay Round further reduced trade barriers; extended GATT to cover services as well as manufactured goods; provided enhanced protection for patents, trademarks, and copyrights; and established the World Trade Organization to police the international trading system.[15] Table 1.1 summarizes the impact of GATT agreements on average tariff rates for *manufactured* goods. As can be seen, average tariff rates have fallen significantly since 1950 and now stand at about 1.5 percent. Comparable tariff rates in 2014 for China and India were 4.8 and 7.1 percent, respectively.

In late 2001, the WTO launched a new round of talks aimed at further liberalizing the global trade and investment framework. For this meeting, it picked the remote location of Doha in the Persian Gulf state of Qatar. At Doha, the member states of the WTO staked

Globalization   **Chapter 1**   **11**

	1913	1950	1990	2014
France	21%	18%	5.9%	1.5%
Germany	20	26	5.9	1.5
Italy	18	25	5.9	1.5
Japan	30	—	5.3	1.3
Holland	5	11	5.9	1.5
Sweden	20	9	4.4	1.5
United Kingdom	—	23	5.9	1.5
United States	44	14	4.8	1.5

TABLE 1.1

Average Tariff Rates on Manufactured Products as Percentage of Value

Sources: The 1913–1990 data are from "Who Wants to Be a Giant?," *The Economist: A Survey of the Multinationals,* June 24, 1995, pp. 3–4. Copyright © The Economist Books, Ltd. The 2014 data are from World Development Indicators 2015, World Bank.

out an agenda. The talks were scheduled to last three years, but, as of 2015, the talks are effectively stalled due to opposition from several key nations. The Doha agenda includes further tariff reductions for industrial goods, services, and agricultural products; phasing out subsidies to agricultural producers; reducing barriers to cross-border investment; and limiting the use of antidumping laws. If the Doha talks are ever completed, the biggest gain may come from discussion on agricultural products; average agricultural tariff rates are still about 40 percent, and rich nations spend some $300 billion a year in subsidies to support their farm sectors. The world's poorer nations have the most to gain from any reduction in agricultural tariffs and subsidies; such reforms would give them access to the markets of the developed world.[16]

In addition to reducing trade barriers, many countries have also been progressively removing restrictions to foreign direct investment. According to the United Nations, some 80 percent of the 1,440 changes made worldwide between 2000 and 2013 in the laws governing foreign direct investment created a more favorable environment for FDI.[17]

Such trends have been driving both the globalization of markets and the globalization of production. The lowering of barriers to international trade enables firms to view the world, rather than a single country, as their market. The lowering of trade and investment barriers also allows firms to base production at the optimal location for that activity. Thus, a firm might design a product in one country, produce component parts in two other countries, assemble the product in yet another country, and then export the finished product around the world.

According to WTO, the volume world trade in merchandised goods has grown consistently faster than the growth rate in the world economy since since 1950. As a consequence, by 2013 the volume of world trade was 33 times larger than in 1950, whereas the world economy was 9 times larger (these figures are in *real* terms, adjusted for inflation). This trend has continued into the modern era. Between 2000 and 2013, the volume of world trade has increased 2.9 times whereas the world economy has increased 1.34 times after adjusting for inflation.[18] Since the mid-1980s, the value of international trade in services has also grown robustly and now accounts for about 20 percent of the value of all international trade. Increasingly, international trade in services has been driven by advances in communications, which allow corporations to outsource service activities to different locations around the globe. For example, many corporations in the developed world outsource customer service functions, from software testing to customer call centers, to developing nations where labor costs are lower.

The fact that the volume of world trade has been growing faster than world GDP implies several things. First, more firms are doing what Boeing does with the 777 and 787: dispersing parts of their production process to different locations around the globe to drive down production costs and increase product quality. Second, the economies of the world's nation-states are becoming ever more intertwined. As trade expands, nations are becoming increasingly dependent on each other for important goods and services. Third, the world has become significantly wealthier since 1990. The implication is that rising trade is the engine that has helped pull the global economy along.

Evidence also suggests that foreign direct investment is playing an increasing role in the global economy as firms increase their cross-border investments. The average yearly outflow of FDI increased from $14 billion in 1970 to $1.26 trillion in 2014.[19] Even though the 2014 figure was significantly below the peak of $1.9 billion in foreign direct investment recorded in 2007, the long-term trends remain positive. As a result of the strong FDI flow, by 2013 the global stock of FDI was about $25.5 trillion. More than 80,000 parent companies had more than 800,000 affiliates in foreign markets that collectively employed more than 71 million people abroad and generated value accounting for about 11 percent of global GDP. The foreign affiliates of multinationals had $34.5 trillion in global sales, higher than the value of global exports of goods and services, which stood at close to $23.4 trillion.[20]

The globalization of markets and production and the resulting growth of world trade, foreign direct investment, and imports all imply that firms are finding their home markets under attack from foreign competitors. This is true in China, where U.S. companies such as Apple, General Motors, and Starbucks are expanding their presence. It is true in the United States, where Japanese automobile firms have taken market share away from General Motors and Ford over the past three decades, and it is true in Europe, where the once-dominant Dutch company Philips has seen its market share in the consumer electronics industry taken by Japan's Panasonic and Sony and Korea's Samsung and LG. The growing integration of the world economy into a single, huge marketplace is increasing the intensity of competition in a range of manufacturing and service industries.

However, declining barriers to cross-border trade and investment cannot be taken for granted. As we shall see in subsequent chapters, demands for "protection" from foreign competitors are still often heard in countries around the world, including the United States. Although a return to the restrictive trade policies of the 1920s and 1930s is unlikely, it is not clear whether the political majority in the industrialized world favors further reductions in trade barriers. Indeed, the global financial crisis of 2008–2009 and the associated drop in global output that occurred led to more calls for trade barriers to protect jobs at home. If trade barriers decline no further, this may slow the rate of globalization of both markets and production.

THE ROLE OF TECHNOLOGICAL CHANGE

The lowering of trade barriers made globalization of markets and production a theoretical possibility. Technological change has made it a tangible reality. Since the end of World War II, the world has seen major advances in communication, information processing, and transportation technology, including the explosive emergence of the Internet.

Microprocessors and Telecommunications

Perhaps the single most important innovation has been development of the microprocessor, which enabled the explosive growth of high-power, low-cost computing, vastly increasing the amount of information that can be processed by individuals and firms. The microprocessor also underlies many recent advances in telecommunications technology. Over the past 30 years, global communications have been revolutionized by developments in satellite, optical fiber, wireless technologies, and the Internet. These technologies rely on the microprocessor to encode, transmit, and decode the vast amount of information that flows along these electronic highways. The cost of microprocessors continues to fall, while their power increases (a phenomenon known as **Moore's law**, which predicts that the power of microprocessor technology doubles and its cost of production falls in half every 18 months).[21]

Commercial jet travel has reduced the time needed to get from one location to another, effectively shrinking the globe.

Source: © Glow Images, RF

The Internet

The explosive growth of the Internet since 1994 when the first web browser was introduced is the latest expression of this development. In 1990, fewer than 1 million users were connected to the Internet. By 1995, the figure had risen to 50 million. By 2014, the Internet had 2.9 billion users.[22] The Internet has developed into the information backbone of the global economy. In North America alone, e-commerce retail sales reached $300 billion in 2014 (up from almost nothing in 1998), while global e-commerce sales surpassed $1 trillion for the first time in 2012.[23] Viewed globally, the Internet has emerged as an equalizer. It rolls back some of the constraints of location, scale, and time zones.[24] The Internet makes it much easier for buyers and sellers to find each other, wherever they may be located and whatever their size. It allows businesses, both small and large, to expand their global presence at a lower cost than ever before. Just as important, it enables enterprises to coordinate and control a globally dispersed production system in a way that was not possible 25 years ago.

Transportation Technology

In addition to developments in communications technology, several major innovations in transportation technology have occurred since World War II. In economic terms, the most important are probably the development of commercial jet aircraft and superfreighters and the introduction of *containerization*, which simplifies transshipment from one mode of transport to another. The advent of commercial jet travel, by reducing the time needed to get from one location to another, has effectively shrunk the globe. In terms of travel time, New York is now "closer" to Tokyo than it was to Philadelphia in the colonial days.

Containerization has revolutionized the transportation business, significantly lowering the costs of shipping goods over long distances. Because the international shipping industry is responsible for carrying about 90 percent of the *volume* of world trade in goods, this has been an extremely important development.[25] Before the advent of containerization, moving goods from one mode of transport to another was very labor intensive, lengthy, and costly. It could take days and several hundred longshore workers to unload a ship and reload goods onto trucks and trains. With the advent of widespread containerization in the 1970s and 1980s, the whole process can now be executed by a handful of longshore workers in a couple of days. As a result of the efficiency gains associated with containerization, transportation costs have plummeted, making it much more economical to ship goods around the globe, thereby helping drive the globalization of markets and production. Between 1920 and 1990, the average ocean freight and port charges per ton of U.S. export and import cargo fell from $95 to $29 (in 1990 dollars).[26] Today, the typical cost of transporting a 20-foot container from Asia to Europe carrying more than 20 tons of cargo is about the same as the economy airfare for a single passenger on the same journey. As a result, in 2012 the shipping cost of a $700 TV set was just $10 and that of a $150 vacuum cleaner just $1.[27] The cost of shipping freight per ton-mile on railroads in the United States also fell from 3.04 cents in 1985 to 2.3 cents in 2000, largely as a result of efficiency gains from the widespread use of containers.[28] An increased share of cargo now goes by air. Between 1955 and 1999, average air transportation revenue per ton-kilometer fell by more than 80 percent.[29] Reflecting the falling cost of airfreight, by the early 2000s air shipments accounted for 28 percent of the value of U.S. trade, up from 7 percent in 1965.[30]

Implications for the Globalization of Production

As transportation costs associated with the globalization of production have declined, dispersal of production to geographically separate locations has become more economical. As a result of the technological innovations discussed earlier, the real costs of information processing and communication have fallen dramatically in the past two decades.

14   **Part 1**   Introduction and Overview

These developments make it possible for a firm to create and then manage a globally dispersed production system, further facilitating the globalization of production. A world-wide communications network has become essential for many international businesses. For example, Dell uses the Internet to coordinate and control a globally dispersed production system to such an extent that it holds only three days' worth of inventory at its assembly locations. Dell's Internet-based system records orders for computer equipment as they are submitted by customers via the company's website and then immediately transmits the resulting orders for components to various suppliers around the world, which have a real-time look at Dell's order flow and can adjust their production schedules accordingly. Given the low cost of airfreight, Dell can use air transportation to speed up the delivery of critical components to meet unanticipated demand shifts without delaying the shipment of final product to consumers. Dell has also used modern communications technology to outsource its customer service operations to India. When U.S. customers call Dell with a service inquiry, they are routed to Bangalore in India, where English-speaking service personnel handle the call.

Implications for the Globalization of Markets

In addition to the globalization of production, technological innovations have facilitated the globalization of markets. Low-cost global communications networks, including those built on top of the Internet, are helping create electronic global marketplaces. As noted earlier, low-cost transportation has made it more economical to ship products around the world, thereby helping create global markets. In addition, low-cost jet travel has resulted in the mass movement of people between countries. This has reduced the cultural distance between countries and is bringing about some convergence of consumer tastes and preferences. At the same time, global communications networks and global media are creating a worldwide culture. U.S. television networks such as CNN, MTV, and HBO are now received in many countries, Hollywood films are shown the world over, while non-U.S. news networks such as the BBC and Al Jazeera also have a global footprint. In any society, the media are primary conveyors of culture; as global media develop, we must expect the evolution of something akin to a global culture. A logical result of this evolution is the emergence of global markets for consumer products. Clear signs of this are apparent. It is now as easy to find a McDonald's restaurant in Tokyo as it is in New York, to buy an iPad in Rio as it is in Berlin, and to buy Gap jeans in Paris as it is in San Francisco.

Despite these trends, we must be careful not to overemphasize their importance. While modern communications and transportation technologies are ushering in the "global village," significant national differences remain in culture, consumer preferences, and business practices. A firm that ignores differences among countries does so at its peril. We shall stress this point repeatedly throughout this text and elaborate on it in later chapters.

LO 1-3

Describe the changing nature of the global economy.

The Changing Demographics of the Global Economy

Hand in hand with the trend toward globalization has been a fairly dramatic change in the demographics of the global economy over the past 30 years. As late as the 1960s, four stylized facts described the demographics of the global economy. The first was U.S. dominance in the world economy and world trade picture. The second was U.S. dominance in world foreign direct investment. Related to this, the third fact was the dominance of large, multinational U.S. firms on the international business scene. The fourth was that roughly half the globe—the centrally planned economies of the communist world—was off-limits to Western international businesses. As will be explained here, all four of these qualities either have changed or are now changing rapidly.

Country	Share of World Output, 1960 (%)	Share of World Output, 2013 (%)	Share of World Exports, 2013 (%)
United States	38.3%	22.2%	9.7%
Germany	8.7	4.9	7.9
France	4.6	3.7	3.5
Italy	3.0	2.2	2.7
United Kingdom	5.3	3.5	3.3
Canada	3.0	2.4	2.3
Japan	3.3	6.5	3.6
China	NA	12.2	13.0

TABLE 1.2

The Changing Demographics of World Output and Trade

Sources: Output data from World Bank database, April, 2015. Trade data from WTO Statistical Database, 2015.

THE CHANGING WORLD OUTPUT AND WORLD TRADE PICTURE

In the early 1960s, the United States was still by far the world's dominant industrial power. In 1960, the United States accounted for 38.3 percent of world output, measured by gross domestic product (GDP). By 2012, the United States accounted for 23.1 percent of world output, still the world's largest industrial power but down significantly in relative size (see Table 1.2). Nor was the United States the only developed nation to see its relative standing slip. The same occurred to Germany, France, and the United Kingdom—all nations that were among the first to industrialize. This change in the U.S. position was not an absolute decline because the U.S. economy grew significantly between 1960 and 2012 (the economies of Germany, France, and the United Kingdom also grew during this time). Rather, it was a relative decline, reflecting the faster economic growth of several other economies, particularly in Asia. For example, as can be seen from Table 1.2, from 1960 to 2013, China's share of world output increased from a trivial amount to 12.2 percent, making it the world's second-largest economy. Other countries that markedly increased their share of world output included Japan, Thailand, Malaysia, Taiwan, Brazil, and South Korea.

By the end of the 1980s, the U.S. position as the world's leading trading nation was threatened. Over the past 30 years, U.S. dominance in export markets has waned as Japan, Germany, and a number of newly industrialized countries such as South Korea and China have taken a larger share of world exports. During the 1960s, the United States routinely accounted for 20 percent of world exports of manufactured goods. But as Table 1.2 shows, the U.S. share of world exports of goods and services had slipped to 9.7 percent by 2013, behind that of China.

As emerging economies such as China, India, Russia, and Brazil continue to grow, a further relative decline in the share of world output and world exports accounted for by the United States and other long-established developed nations seems likely. By itself, this is not bad. The relative decline of the United States reflects the growing economic development and industrialization of the world economy, as opposed to any absolute decline in the health of the U.S. economy.

Most forecasts now predict a rapid rise in the share of world output accounted for by developing nations such as China, India, Russia, Indonesia, Thailand, South Korea, Mexico, and Brazil, and a commensurate decline in the share enjoyed by rich industrialized countries such as Great Britain, Germany, Japan, and the United States. If current trends continue, the Chinese economy could ultimately be larger than that of the United States on a purchasing power parity basis, while the economy of India will approach that of Germany. The World Bank has estimated that today's developing nations may account

COUNTRY FOCUS

India's Software Sector

Some 25 years ago, a number of small software enterprises were established in Bangalore, India. Typical of these enterprises was Infosys Technologies, which was started by seven Indian entrepreneurs with about $1,000 among them. Infosys now has annual revenues of $8.25 billion and some 170,000 employees, but it is just 1 of more than 100 software companies clustered around Bangalore, which has become the epicenter of India's fast-growing information technology sector. From a standing start in the mid-1980s, by 2014–2015 this sector was generating export sales of almost $100 billion.

The growth of the Indian software sector has been based on four factors. First, the country has an abundant supply of engineering talent. Every year, Indian universities graduate some 400,000 engineers. Second, labor costs in the Indian software sector have historically been low. As recently as 2008, the cost to hire an Indian graduate was roughly 12 percent of the cost of hiring an American graduate (however, this gap is narrowing fast with pay in the sector now only 30–40 percent less than in the United States). Third, many Indians are fluent in English, which makes coordination between Western firms and India easier. Fourth, due to time differences, Indians can work while Americans sleep.

Initially, Indian software enterprises focused on the low end of the software industry, supplying basic software development and testing services to Western firms. But as the industry has grown in size and sophistication, Indian firms have moved up the market. Today, the leading Indian companies compete directly with the likes of IBM and EDS for large software development projects, business process outsourcing contracts, and information technology consulting services. Over the past 15 years, these markets have boomed, with Indian enterprises capturing a large slice of the pie. One response of Western firms to this emerging competitive threat has been to invest in India to garner the same kind of economic advantages that Indian firms enjoy. IBM, for example, has invested $2 billion in its Indian operations and now has 150,000 employees located there, more than in any other country. Microsoft, too, has made major investments in India, including a research and development (R&D) center in Hyderabad that employs 4,000 people and was located there specifically to tap into talented Indian engineers who did not want to move to the United States.

Sources: "America's Pain, India's Gain: Outsourcing," *The Economist,* January 11, 2003, p. 59; "The World Is Our Oyster," *The Economist,* October 7, 2006, pp. 9–10; "IBM and Globalization: Hungry Tiger, Dancing Elephant," *The Economist,* April 7, 2007, pp. 67–69; P. Mishra, "New Billing Model May Hit India's Software Exports," *Live Mint,* February 14, 2013; "India's Outsourcing Business: On the Turn," *The Economist,* January 19, 2013.

for more than 60 percent of world economic activity by 2025, while today's rich nations, which currently account for more than 55 percent of world economic activity, may account for only about 38 percent. Forecasts are not always correct, but these suggest that a shift in the economic geography of the world is now under way, although the magnitude of that shift is not totally evident. For international businesses, the implications of this changing economic geography are clear: Many of tomorrow's economic opportunities may be found in the developing nations of the world, and many of tomorrow's most capable competitors will probably also emerge from these regions. A case in point has been the dramatic expansion of India's software sector, which is profiled in the accompanying Country Focus.

THE CHANGING FOREIGN DIRECT INVESTMENT PICTURE

Reflecting the dominance of the United States in the global economy, U.S. firms accounted for 66.3 percent of worldwide foreign direct investment flows in the 1960s. British firms were second, accounting for 10.5 percent, while Japanese firms were a distant eighth, with only 2 percent. The dominance of U.S. firms was so great that books were written about the economic threat posed to Europe by U.S. corporations.[31] Several European governments, most notably France, talked of limiting inward investment by U.S. firms.

However, as the barriers to the free flow of goods, services, and capital fell, and as other countries increased their shares of world output, non-U.S. firms increasingly began

Globalization   **Chapter 1**   **17**

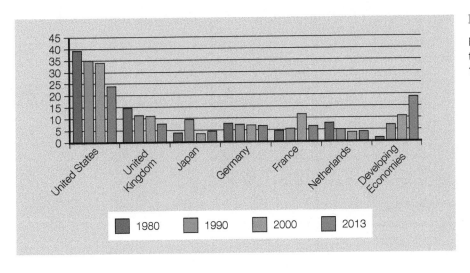

FIGURE 1.1

Percentage share of
total FDI stock,
1980–2013.

to invest across national borders. The motivation for much of this foreign direct investment by non-U.S. firms was the desire to disperse production activities to optimal locations and to build a direct presence in major foreign markets. Thus, beginning in the
1970s, European and Japanese firms began to shift labor-intensive manufacturing operations from their home markets to developing nations where labor costs were lower. In
addition, many Japanese firms invested in North America and Europe—often as a hedge
against unfavorable currency movements and the possible imposition of trade barriers.
For example, Toyota, the Japanese automobile company, rapidly increased its investment
in automobile production facilities in the United States and Europe during the late 1980s
and 1990s. Toyota executives believed that an increasingly strong Japanese yen would
price Japanese automobile exports out of foreign markets; therefore, production in the
most important foreign markets, as opposed to exports from Japan, made sense. Toyota
also undertook these investments to head off growing political pressures in the United
States and Europe to restrict Japanese automobile exports into those markets.

One consequence of these developments is illustrated in Figure 1.1, which shows how the
stock of foreign direct investment by the world's six most important national sources—
the United States, the United Kingdom, Germany, the Netherlands, France, and Japan—
changed between 1980 and 2013. [The **stock of foreign direct investment (FDI)** refers
to the total cumulative value of foreign investments.] Figure 1.1 also shows the stock accounted for by firms from developing economies. The share of the total stock accounted
for by U.S. firms declined from about 38 percent in 1980 to 24 percent in 2013. Meanwhile, the shares accounted for by the world's developing nations increased markedly.
The rise in the share of FDI stock accounted for by developing nations reflects a growing
trend for firms from these countries to invest outside their borders. In 2013, firms based
in developing nations accounted for 19 percent of the stock of foreign direct investment,
up from around 1 percent in 1980. Firms based in Hong Kong, South Korea, Singapore,
Taiwan, India, Brazil, and mainland China accounted for much of this investment.

Figure 1.2 illustrates two other important trends—the sustained growth in cross-border
flows of foreign direct investment that occurred during the 1990s and the increasing
importance of developing nations as the destination of foreign direct investment.
Throughout the 1990s, the amount of investment directed at both developed and developing nations increased dramatically, a trend that reflects the increasing internationaliza-
tion of business corporations. A surge in foreign direct investment from 1998 to 2000 was
followed by a slump from 2001 to 2003, associated with a slowdown in global economic
activity after the collapse of the financial bubble of the late 1990s and 2000. The growth

FIGURE 1.2

FDI inflows, 1980–2013.

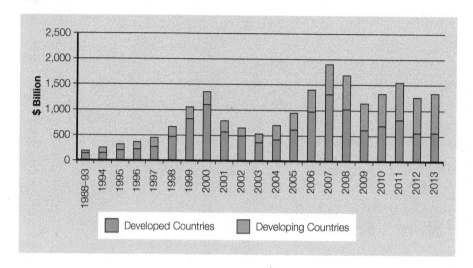

of foreign direct investment resumed in 2004 and continued through 2007, when it hit record levels, only to slow again in 2008 and 2009 as the global financial crisis took hold. However, throughout this time period the growth of foreign direct investment into developing nations remained robust. Among developing nations, the largest recipient has been China, which in 2004–2012 received $60 billion to $100 billion a year in inflows, followed by the likes of Brazil, Mexico, and India. As we shall see later in this text, the sustained flow of foreign investment into developing nations is an important stimulus for economic growth in those countries, which bodes well for the future of countries such as China, Mexico, and Brazil—all leading beneficiaries of this trend.

THE CHANGING NATURE OF THE MULTINATIONAL ENTERPRISE

A **multinational enterprise (MNE)** is any business that has productive activities in two or more countries. Since the 1960s, two notable trends in the demographics of the multinational enterprise have been (1) the rise of non-U.S. multinationals and (2) the growth of mini-multinationals.

Non-U.S. Multinationals

In the 1960s, global business activity was dominated by large U.S. multinational corporations. With U.S. firms accounting for about two-thirds of foreign direct investment during the 1960s, one would expect most multinationals to be U.S. enterprises. According to the data summarized in Figure 1.3, in 1973, 48.5 percent of the world's 260 largest multinationals were U.S. firms. The second-largest source country was the United Kingdom, with 18.8 percent of the largest multinationals. Japan accounted for 3.5 percent of the world's largest multinationals at the time. The large number of U.S. multinationals reflected U.S. economic dominance in the three decades after World War II, while the large number of British multinationals reflected that country's industrial dominance in the early decades of the twentieth century.

By 2012, things had shifted significantly. Some 22 of the world's 100 largest nonfinancial multinationals were U.S. enterprises; 14 were British, 14 French, 10 were German, and 7 were from Japan.[32] Although the 1973 data are not strictly comparable with the later data, they illustrate the trend (the 1973 figures are based on the largest 260 firms, whereas the later figures are based on the largest 100 multinationals). The globalization and growth of the world economy has resulted in a relative reduction in the dominance of U.S. firms in the global marketplace.

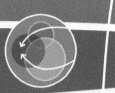

MANAGEMENT FOCUS

China's Hisense—an Emerging Multinational

Hisense is rapidly emerging as one of China's leading multi-nationals. Like many other Chinese corporations, Hisense traces its origins back to a state-owned manufacturer, in this case Qingdao No. 2 Radio Factory, which was established in 1969 with just 10 employees. In the 1970s, the state-owned factory diversified into the manufacture of TV sets; by the 1980s, it was one of China's leading manufacturers of color TVs, making sets designed by Matsushita under license. In 1992, a 35-year-old engineer named Zhou Houjian was appointed head of the enterprise. In 1994, the shackles of state owner-ship were relaxed when the Hisense Company Ltd. was es-tablished with Zhou as CEO (he is now board chairman).

Under Zhou's leadership, Hisense entered a period of rapid growth, product diversification, and global expan-sion. By 2013, the company had sales of more than $15 billion and had emerged as one of China's premier makers of TV sets, air conditioners, refrigerators, personal comput-ers, and telecommunications equipment. Hisense sold more than 10 million TV sets, 3 million air conditioners, 4 million CDMA wireless phones, 6 million refrigerators, and 1 million personal computers. International sales accounted for more than 15 percent of total revenue. The company had established overseas manufacturing subsidiaries in Algeria, Hungary, Iran, Pakistan, and South Africa and was growing rapidly in developing markets, where it was taking share away from long-established consumer electronics and appliance makers.

Hisense's ambitions are grand. It seeks to become a global enterprise with a world-class consumer brand. Al-though it is without question a low-cost manufacturer, Hisense believes its core strength is in rapid product innovation. The company believes that the only way to gain leadership in the highly competitive markets in which it competes is to continuously launch advanced, high-quality, and competitively priced products.

To this end, Hisense established its first R&D center in China in the mid-1990s. This was followed by a South African R&D center in 1997 and a European R&D center in 2007. The com-pany also has plans for an R&D center in the United States. By 2008, these R&D centers filed for more than 600 patents.

Hisense's technological prowess is evident in its digital TV business. It introduced set-top boxes in 1999, making it possi-ble to browse the Internet from a TV. In 2002, Hisense intro-duced its first interactive digital TV set, and in 2005 it developed China's first core digital processing chip for digital TVs, breaking the country's reliance on foreign chip makers for this core technology. In 2006, Hisense launched an innovative line of multimedia TV sets that integrated digital high-definition technology, network technology, and flat-panel displays.

Sources: Harold L. Sirkin, "Someone May Be Gaining on Us," *Barron's*, February 5, 2007, p. 53; "Hisense Plans to Grab More International Sales," *Sino Cast China IT Watch*, November 30, 2006; "Hisense's Wonder Chip," *Financial Times Information Limited—Asian Intelli-gence Wire*, October 30, 2006; Hisense's website, **www.hisense.com**.

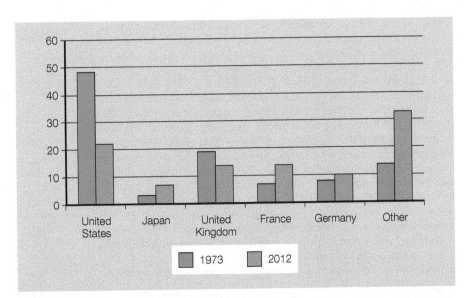

FIGURE 1.3

National share of largest multinationals, 1973 and 2012.

According to UN data, the ranks of the world's largest 100 multinationals are still dominated by firms from developed economies.[33] However, eight firms from developing economies had entered the UN's list of the 100 largest multinationals by 2012. The largest was Hutchison Whampoa of Hong Kong, China, which ranked 26th.[34] Firms from developing nations can be expected to emerge as important competitors in global markets, further shifting the axis of the world economy away from North America and western Europe and threatening the long dominance of Western companies. One such rising competitor, Hisense, one of China's premier manufacturers of consumer appliances and telecommunications equipment, is profiled in the accompanying Management Focus.

The Rise of Mini-Multinationals

Another trend in international business has been the growth of medium-size and small multinationals (mini-multinationals).[35] When people think of international businesses, they tend to think of firms such as ExxonMobil, General Motors, Ford, Panasonic, Procter & Gamble, Sony, and Unilever—large, complex multinational corporations with operations that span the globe. Although most international trade and investment are still conducted by large firms, many medium-size and small businesses are becoming increasingly involved in international trade and investment. The rise of the Internet is lowering the barriers that small firms face in building international sales.

Consider Lubricating Systems Inc. of Kent, Washington. Lubricating Systems, which manufactures lubricating fluids for machine tools, employs 25 people and generates sales of $6.5 million. It's hardly a large, complex multinational, yet more than $2 million of the company's sales are generated by exports to a score of countries, including Japan, Israel, and the United Arab Emirates. Lubricating Systems has also set up a joint venture with a German company to serve the European market.[36] Consider also Lixi Inc., a small U.S. manufacturer of industrial X-ray equipment; 70 percent of Lixi's $4.5 million in revenues comes from exports to Japan.[37] Or take G. W. Barth, a manufacturer of cocoa-bean roasting machinery based in Ludwigsburg, Germany. Employing just 65 people, this small company has captured 70 percent of the global market for cocoa-bean roasting machines.[38] International business is conducted not just by large firms but also by medium-size and small enterprises.

THE CHANGING WORLD ORDER

Between 1989 and 1991, a series of democratic revolutions swept the communist world. For reasons that are explored in more detail in Chapter 3, in country after country throughout eastern Europe and eventually in the Soviet Union itself, Communist Party governments collapsed. The Soviet Union receded into history, having been replaced by 15 independent republics. Czechoslovakia divided itself into two states, while Yugoslavia dissolved into a bloody civil war, now thankfully over, among its five successor states.

Many of the former communist nations of Europe and Asia seem to share a commitment to democratic politics and free market economics. For half a century, these countries were essentially closed to Western international businesses. Now, they present a host of export and investment opportunities. Two decades later, the economies of many of the former communist states are still relatively undeveloped, and their continued commitment to democracy and market-based economic systems cannot be taken for granted. Disturbing signs of growing unrest and totalitarian tendencies continue to be seen in several eastern European and central Asian states, including Russia, which has shown signs of shifting back toward greater state involvement in economic activity and authoritarian government.[39] Thus, the risks involved in doing business in such countries are high, but so may be the returns.

In addition to these changes, quieter revolutions have been occurring in China, other states in Southeast Asia, and Latin America. Their implications for international businesses may be just as profound as the collapse of communism in eastern Europe. China suppressed its own pro-democracy movement in the bloody Tiananmen Square massacre of 1989. Despite this, China continues to move progressively toward greater free market reforms. If what is occurring in China continues for two more decades, China may move from third-world to industrial superpower status even more rapidly than Japan did. If China's GDP per capita grows by an average of 6 to 7 percent, which is slower than the 8 to 10 percent growth rate achieved during the past decade, then by 2030 this nation of 1.3 billion people could boast an average GDP per capita of about $23,000, roughly the same as that of Chile or Poland today.

The potential consequences for international business are enormous. On the one hand, China represents a huge and largely untapped market. Reflecting this, between 1983 and 2014, annual foreign direct investment in China increased from less than $2 billion to $110 billion annually. On the other hand, China's new firms are proving to be very capable competitors, and they could take global market share away from Western and Japanese enterprises (e.g., see the Management Focus about Hisense). Thus, the changes in China are creating both opportunities and threats for established international businesses.

As for Latin America, both democracy and free market reforms have been evident there too. For decades, most Latin American countries were ruled by dictators, many of whom seemed to view Western international businesses as instruments of imperialist domination. Accordingly, they restricted direct investment by foreign firms. In addition, the poorly managed economies of Latin America were characterized by low growth, high debt, and hyperinflation—all of which discouraged investment by international businesses. In the past two decades, much of this has changed. Throughout most of Latin America, debt and inflation are down, governments have sold state-owned enterprises to private investors, foreign investment is welcomed, and the region's economies have expanded. Brazil, Mexico, and Chile have led the way. These changes have increased the attractiveness of Latin America, both as a market for exports and as a site for foreign direct investment. At the same time, given the long history of economic mismanagement in Latin America, there is no guarantee that these favorable trends will continue. Indeed, Bolivia, Ecuador, and most notably Venezuela have seen shifts back toward greater state involvement in industry in the past few years, and foreign investment is now less welcome than it was during the 1990s. In these nations, the government has seized control of oil and gas fields from foreign investors and has limited the rights of foreign energy companies to extract oil and gas from their nations. Thus, as in the case of eastern Europe, substantial opportunities are accompanied by substantial risks.

THE GLOBAL ECONOMY OF THE TWENTY-FIRST CENTURY

As discussed, the past quarter century has seen rapid changes in the global economy. Barriers to the free flow of goods, services, and capital have been coming down. As their economies advance, more nations are joining the ranks of the developed world. A generation ago, South Korea and Taiwan were viewed as second-tier developing nations. Now they boast large economies, and their firms are major players in many global industries, from shipbuilding and steel to electronics and chemicals. The move toward a global economy has been further strengthened by the widespread adoption of liberal economic policies by countries that had firmly opposed them for two generations or more. In short, current trends indicate the world is moving toward an economic system that is more favorable for international business.

But it is always hazardous to use established trends to predict the future. The world may be moving toward a more global economic system, but globalization is not inevitable. Countries may pull back from the recent commitment to liberal economic ideology if their experiences do not match their expectations. There are clear signs, for example, of a retreat from liberal economic ideology in Russia. If Russia's hesitation were to become more permanent and widespread, the liberal vision of a more prosperous global economy based on free market principles might not occur as quickly as many hope. Clearly, this would be a tougher world for international businesses.

22

    Part 1   Introduction and Overview

Also, greater globalization brings with it risks of its own. This was starkly demonstrated in 1997 and 1998 when a financial crisis in Thailand spread first to other East Asian nations and then to Russia and Brazil. Ultimately, the crisis threatened to plunge the economies of the developed world, including the United States, into a recession. We explore the causes and consequences of this and other similar global financial crises in Chapter 11. Even from a purely economic perspective, globalization is not all good. The opportunities for doing business in a global economy may be significantly enhanced, but as we saw in 1997–1998, the risks associated with global financial contagion are also greater. Indeed, during 2008–2009, a crisis that started in the financial sector of America, where banks had been too liberal in their lending policies to homeowners, swept around the world and plunged the global economy into its deepest recession since the early 1980s, illustrating once more that in an interconnected world a severe crisis in one region can affect the entire globe. Still, as explained later in this text, firms can exploit the opportunities associated with globalization while reducing the risks through appropriate hedging strategies.

LO 1-4

Explain the main arguments in the debate over the impact of globalization.

The Globalization Debate

Is the shift toward a more integrated and interdependent global economy a good thing? Many influential economists, politicians, and business leaders seem to think so.[40] They argue that falling barriers to international trade and investment are the twin engines driving the global economy toward greater prosperity. They say increased international trade and cross-border investment will result in lower prices for goods and services. They believe that globalization stimulates economic growth, raises the incomes of consumers, and helps create jobs in all countries that participate in the global trading system. The arguments of those who support globalization are covered in detail in Chapters 6, 7, and 8. As we shall see, there are good theoretical reasons for believing that declining barriers to international trade and investment do stimulate economic growth, create jobs, and raise income levels. Moreover, as described in Chapters 6, 7, and 8, empirical evidence lends support to the predictions of this theory. However, despite the existence of a compelling body of theory and evidence, globalization has its critics.[41] Some of these critics are vocal and active, taking to the streets to demonstrate their opposition to globalization. Here, we look at the nature of protests against globalization and briefly review the main themes of the debate concerning the merits of globalization. In later chapters, we elaborate on many of these points.

ANTIGLOBALIZATION PROTESTS

Popular demonstrations against globalization date to December 1999, when more than 40,000 protesters blocked the streets of Seattle in an attempt to shut down a World Trade Organization meeting being held in the city. The demonstrators were protesting against a wide range of issues, including job losses in industries under attack from foreign competitors, downward pressure on the wage rates of unskilled workers, environmental degradation, and the cultural imperialism of global media and multinational enterprises, which was seen as being dominated by what some protesters called the "culturally impoverished" interests and values of the United States. All of these ills, the demonstrators claimed, could be laid at the feet of globalization. The World Trade Organization was meeting to try to launch a new round of talks to cut barriers to cross-border trade and investment. As such, it was seen as a promoter of globalization and a target for the protesters. The protests turned violent, transforming the normally placid streets of Seattle into a running battle between "anarchists" and Seattle's bemused and poorly prepared police department. Pictures of brick-throwing protesters and armored police wielding their batons were duly recorded by the global media, which then circulated the images around the world. Meanwhile, the WTO meeting failed to reach agreement, and although

COUNTRY FOCUS

Protesting Globalization in France

One night in August 1999, 10 men under the leadership of local sheep farmer and rural activist José Bové crept into the town of Millau in central France and vandalized a McDonald's restaurant under construction, causing an estimated $150,000 in damage. These were no ordinary vandals, however, at least according to their supporters, for the "symbolic dismantling" of the McDonald's outlet had noble aims, or so it was claimed. The attack was initially presented as a protest against unfair American trade policies. The European Union had banned imports of hormone-treated beef from the United States, primarily because of fears that it might lead to health problems (although EU scientists had concluded there was no evidence of this). After a careful review, the World Trade Organization stated the EU ban was not allowed under trading rules that the EU and United States were party to and that the EU would have to lift it or face retaliation. The EU refused to comply, so the U.S. government imposed a 100 percent tariff on imports of certain EU products, including French staples such as foie gras, mustard, and Roquefort cheese. On farms near Millau, Bové and others raised sheep whose milk was used to make Roquefort. They felt incensed by the American tariff and decided to vent their frustrations on McDonald's.

Bové and his compatriots were arrested and charged. About the same time in the Languedoc region of France, California winemaker Robert Mondavi had reached agreement with the mayor and council of the village of Aniane and regional authorities to turn 125 acres of wooded hillside belonging to the village into a vineyard. Mondavi planned to invest $7 million in the project and hoped to produce top-quality wine that would sell in Europe and the United States for $60 a bottle. However, local environmentalists objected to the plan, which they claimed would destroy the area's unique ecological heritage. José Bové, basking in sudden fame, offered his support to the opponents, and the protests started. In May 2001, the socialist

mayor who had approved the project was defeated in local elections in which the Mondavi project had become the major issue. He was replaced by a communist, Manuel Diaz, who denounced the project as a capitalist plot designed to enrich wealthy U.S. shareholders at the cost of his villagers and the environment. Following Diaz's victory, Mondavi announced he would pull out of the project. A spokesperson noted, "It's a huge waste, but there are clearly personal and political interests at play here that go way beyond us."

So, are the French opposed to foreign investment? The experience of McDonald's and Mondavi seems to suggest so, as does the associated news coverage, but look closer and a different reality seems to emerge. Today McDonald's has more than 1,200 restaurants in France. McDonald's employs 69,000 workers in the country. France is the most profitable market for McDonald's after the United States. In short, 15 years after the protests, France is a major success story for McDonald's. Moreover, France has long been one of the most favored locations for inward foreign direct investment, receiving more than $660 billion of foreign investment between 2000 and 2013, which makes it one of the top destinations for foreign investment in Europe. American companies have always accounted for a significant percentage of this investment. French enterprises have also been significant foreign investors; some 1,100 French multinationals have about $1.1 trillion of assets in other nations. For all of the populist opposition to globalization, French corporations and consumers appear to be embracing it.

Sources: "Behind the Bluster," *The Economist*, May 26, 2001; "The French Farmers' Anti-global Hero," *The Economist*, July 8, 2000; C. Trueheart, "France's Golden Arch Enemy?" *Toronto Star*, July 1, 2000; J. Henley, "Grapes of Wrath Scare Off U.S. Firm," *The Economist*, May 18, 2001, p. 11; United Nations, *World Investment Report, 2014* (New York and Geneva: United Nations, 2011); Rob Wile, "The True Story of How McDonald's Conquered France," *Business Insider*, August 22, 2014.

the protests outside the meeting halls had little to do with that failure, the impression took hold that the demonstrators had succeeded in derailing the meetings.

Emboldened by the experience in Seattle, antiglobalization protesters now often turn up at major meetings of global institutions. Smaller-scale protests have occurred in several countries, such as France, where antiglobalization activists destroyed a McDonald's restaurant in 1999 to protest the impoverishment of French culture by American imperialism (see the accompanying Country Focus for details). While violent protests may give the antiglobalization effort a bad name, it is clear from the scale of the demonstrations that support for the cause goes beyond a core of anarchists. Large segments of the population in many countries believe that globalization has detrimental effects on living standards, wage rates, and the environment. The media have often fed on this fear. For example, former CNN news anchor Lou Dobbs ran TV shows that were highly critical of the trend by American companies to take advantage of globalization and "export jobs" overseas. As the world slipped into a recession in 2008, Dobbs stepped up his antiglobalization rhetoric (Dobbs left CNN in 2009).

Both theory and evidence suggest that many of these fears are exaggerated; both politicians and businesspeople need to do more to counter these fears. Many protests against globalization are tapping into a general sense of loss at the passing of a world in which barriers of time and distance, and significant differences in economic institutions, political institutions, and the level of development of different nations, produced a world rich in the diversity of human cultures. However, while the rich citizens of the developed world may have the luxury of mourning the fact that they can now see McDonald's restaurants and Starbucks coffeehouses on their vacations to exotic locations such as Thailand, fewer complaints are heard from the citizens of those countries, who welcome the higher living standards that progress brings.

GLOBALIZATION, JOBS, AND INCOME

One concern frequently voiced by globalization opponents is that falling barriers to international trade destroy manufacturing jobs in wealthy advanced economies such as the United States and western Europe. Critics argue that falling trade barriers allow firms to move manufacturing activities to countries where wage rates are much lower.[42] Indeed, due to the entry of China, India, and states from eastern Europe into the global trading system, along with global population growth, estimates suggest that the pool of global labor may have quadrupled between 1985 and 2005, with most of the increase occurring after 1990.[43] Other things being equal, we might conclude that this enormous expansion in the global labor force, when coupled with expanding international trade, would have depressed wages in developed nations.

This fear is often supported by anecdotes. For example, D. L. Bartlett and J. B. Steele, two journalists for the *Philadelphia Inquirer* who gained notoriety for their attacks on free trade, cite the case of Harwood Industries, a U.S. clothing manufacturer that closed its U.S. operations, where it paid workers $9 per hour, and shifted manufacturing to Honduras, where textile workers received 48 cents per hour.[44] Because of moves such as this, argue Bartlett and Steele, the wage rates of poorer Americans have fallen significantly over the past quarter of a century.

In the past few years, the same fears have been applied to services, which have increasingly been outsourced to nations with lower labor costs. The popular feeling is that when corporations such as Dell, IBM, or Citigroup outsource service activities to lower-cost foreign suppliers—as all three have done—they are "exporting jobs" to low-wage nations and contributing to higher unemployment and lower living standards in their home nations (in this case, the United States). Some U.S. lawmakers have responded by calling for legal barriers to job outsourcing.

Supporters of globalization reply that critics of these trends miss the essential point about free trade—the benefits outweigh the costs.[45] They argue that free trade will result in countries specializing in the production of those goods and services that they can produce most efficiently, while importing goods and services that they cannot produce as efficiently. When a country embraces free trade, there is always some dislocation—lost textile jobs at Harwood Industries or lost call-center jobs at Dell—but the whole economy is better off as a result. According to this view, it makes little sense for the United States to produce textiles at home when they can be produced at a lower cost in Honduras or China. Importing textiles from China leads to lower prices for clothes in the United States, which enables consumers to spend more of their money on other items. At the same time, the increased income generated in China from textile exports increases income levels in that country, which helps the Chinese purchase more products produced in the United States, such as pharmaceuticals from Amgen, Boeing jets, microprocessors made by Intel, Microsoft software, and Cisco routers.

The same argument can be made to support the outsourcing of services to low-wage countries. By outsourcing its customer service call centers to India, Dell can reduce its cost structure, and thereby its prices for PCs. U.S. consumers benefit from this development. As prices for PCs fall, Americans can spend more of their money on other goods and services. Moreover, the increase in income levels in India allows Indians to purchase more U.S. goods and services, which helps create jobs in the United States. In this manner, supporters of globalization argue that free trade benefits *all* countries that adhere to a free trade regime.

If the critics of globalization are correct, three things must be shown. First, the share of national income received by labor, as opposed to the share received by the owners of capital (e.g., stockholders and bondholders), should have declined in advanced nations as a result of downward pressure on wage rates. Second, even though labor's share of the economic pie may have declined, this does not mean lower living standards if the size of the total pie has increased sufficiently to offset the decline in labor's share—in other words, if economic growth and rising living standards in advanced economies have offset declines in labor's share (this is the position argued by supporters of globalization). Third, the decline in labor's share of national income must be due to moving production to low-wage countries, as opposed to improvement in production technology and productivity.

Several studies shed light on these issues.[46] First, the data suggest that over the past two decades, the share of labor in national income has declined. However, detailed analysis suggests the share of national income enjoyed by *skilled labor* has actually *increased,* suggesting that the fall in labor's share has been due to a fall in the share taken by *unskilled labor.* A study by the IMF suggested the earnings gap between workers in skilled and unskilled sectors has widened by 25 percent over the past two decades.[47] Another study that focused on U.S. data found that exposure to competition from imports led to a decline in real wages for workers who performed *unskilled* tasks, while having no discernible impact on wages in skilled occupations. The same study found that skilled and unskilled workers in sectors where exports grew saw an increase in their real wages.[48] These figures suggest that *unskilled labor* in sectors that have been exposed to more efficient foreign competition probably has seen its share of national income decline over the past three decades.

However, this does not mean that the *living standards* of unskilled workers in developed nations have declined. It is possible that economic growth in developed nations has offset the fall in the share of national income enjoyed by unskilled workers, raising their living standards. Evidence suggests that real labor compensation has expanded in most developed nations since the 1980s, including the United States. Several studies by the Organisation for Economic Co-operation and Development (OECD), whose members include the 34 richest economies in the world, conclude that while the gap between the poorest and richest segments of society in OECD countries has widened, in *most* countries real income levels have increased for all, including the poorest segment. In one study the OECD found that between 1985 and 2008, real household income (adjusted for inflation) increased by 1.7 percent annually among its member states. The real income level of the poorest 10 percent of the population increased at 1.4 percent on average, while that of the richest 10 percent increased by 2 percent annually (i.e., while everyone got richer, the gap between the most affluent and the poorest sectors of society widened). The differential in growth rates was more extreme in the United States than most other countries. The study found that the real income of the poorest 10 percent of the population grew by just 0.5 percent a year in the United States between 1985 and 2008, while that of the richest 10 percent grew by 1.9 percent annually.[49]

As noted earlier, globalization critics argue that the decline in unskilled wage rates is due to the migration of low-wage manufacturing jobs offshore and a corresponding reduction in demand for unskilled workers. However, supporters of globalization see a more complex picture. They maintain that the weak growth rate in real wage rates for unskilled workers owes far more to a technology-induced shift within advanced economies away from jobs where the only qualification was a willingness to turn up for work every day and toward jobs that require significant education and skills. They point out that many advanced economies report a shortage of highly skilled workers and an excess supply of unskilled workers. Thus, growing income inequality is a result of the wages for skilled workers being bid up by the labor market and the wages for unskilled workers being discounted. In fact, evidence suggests that technological change has had a bigger impact than globalization on the declining share of national income enjoyed by labor.[50] This suggests that a solution to the problem of slow real income growth among the unskilled is to be found not in limiting free trade and globalization, but in increasing society's investment in education to reduce the supply of unskilled workers.[51]

Finally, it is worth noting that the wage gap between developing and developed nations is closing as developing nations experience rapid economic growth. For example, one estimate suggests that wages in China will approach Western levels in two decades.[52] To the extent that this is the case, any migration of unskilled jobs to low-wage countries is a temporary phenomenon representing a structural adjustment on the way to a more tightly integrated global economy.

GLOBALIZATION, LABOR POLICIES, AND THE ENVIRONMENT

A second source of concern is that free trade encourages firms from advanced nations to move manufacturing facilities to less developed countries that lack adequate regulations to protect labor and the environment from abuse by the unscrupulous.[53] Globalization critics often argue that adhering to labor and environmental regulations significantly increases the costs of manufacturing enterprises and puts them at a competitive disadvantage in the global marketplace vis-à-vis firms based in developing nations that do not have to comply with such regulations. Firms deal with this cost disadvantage, the theory goes, by moving their production facilities to nations that do not have such burdensome regulations or that fail to enforce the regulations they have.

If this were the case, we might expect free trade to lead to an increase in pollution and result in firms from advanced nations exploiting the labor of less developed nations.[54] This argument was used repeatedly by those who opposed the 1994 formation of the North American Free Trade Agreement (NAFTA) among Canada, Mexico, and the United States. They painted a picture of U.S. manufacturing firms moving to Mexico in droves so that they would be free to pollute the environment, employ child labor, and ignore workplace safety and health issues, all in the name of higher profits.[55]

Supporters of free trade and greater globalization express doubts about this scenario. They argue that tougher environmental regulations and stricter labor standards go hand in hand with economic progress.[56] In general, as countries get richer, they enact tougher environmental and labor regulations.[57] Because free trade enables developing countries to increase their economic growth rates and become richer, this should lead to tougher environmental and labor laws. In this view, the critics of free trade have got it backward—free trade does not lead to more pollution and labor exploitation; it leads to less. By creating wealth and incentives for enterprises to produce technological innovations, the free market system and free trade could make it easier for the world to cope with pollution and population growth. Indeed, while pollution levels are rising in the world's poorer countries, they have been falling in developed nations. In the United States, for example, the concentration of carbon monoxide and sulfur dioxide pollutants in the atmosphere decreased by 60 percent between 1978 and 1997, while lead concentrations decreased by 98 percent—and these reductions have occurred against a background of sustained economic expansion.[58]

A number of econometric studies have found consistent evidence of a hump-shaped relationship between income levels and pollution levels (see Figure 1.4).[59] As an economy grows and income levels rise, initially pollution levels also rise. However, past some

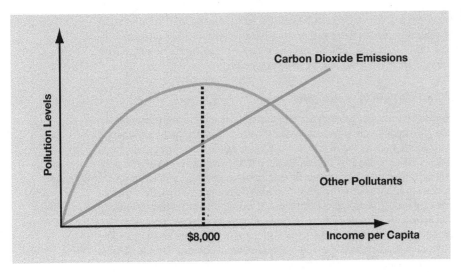

FIGURE 1.4

Income levels and
environmental pollution.

point, rising income levels lead to demands for greater environmental protection, and pollution levels then fall. A seminal study by Grossman and Krueger found that the turning point generally occurred before per capita income levels reached $8,000.[60]

While the hump-shaped relationship depicted in Figure 1.4 seems to hold across a wide range of pollutants—from sulfur dioxide to lead concentrations and water quality—carbon dioxide emissions are an important exception, rising steadily with higher-income levels. Given that carbon dioxide is a heat-trapping gas, and given that there is good evidence that increased atmospheric carbon dioxide concentrations are a cause of global warming, this should be of serious concern. The solution to the problem, however, is probably not to roll back the trade liberalization efforts that have fostered economic growth and globalization, but to get the nations of the world to agree to policies designed to limit carbon emissions.[61] Although UN-sponsored talks have had this as a central aim since the 1992 Earth Summit in Rio de Janeiro, there has been little success in moving toward the ambitious goals for reducing carbon emissions laid down in the Earth Summit and subsequent talks in Kyoto, Japan, in 1997 and in Copenhagen in 2009. In part, this is because the largest emitters of carbon dioxide, the United States and China, have failed to reach agreements about how to proceed. China, a country whose carbon emissions are increasing at a rapid rate, has shown little appetite to adopt tighter pollution controls. As for the United States, political divisions in Congress and a culture of denial have made it difficult for the country to even acknowledge, never mind move forward with, legislation designed to tackle climate change. On the other hand, in late 2014 America and China struck a historic deal under which both countries agreed to potentially significant reductions in carbon emissions. If this agreement holds, progress may be made on this important issue.

Notwithstanding this, supporters of free trade point out that it is possible to tie free trade agreements to the implementation of tougher environmental and labor laws in less developed countries. NAFTA, for example, was passed only after side agreements had been negotiated that committed Mexico to tougher enforcement of environmental protection regulations. Thus, supporters of free trade argue that factories based in Mexico are now cleaner than they would have been without the passage of NAFTA.[62]

They also argue that business firms are not the amoral organizations that critics suggest. While there may be some rotten apples, most business enterprises are staffed by managers who are committed to behave in an ethical manner and would be unlikely to move production offshore just so they could pump more pollution into the atmosphere or exploit labor. Furthermore, the relationship between pollution, labor exploitation, and production costs may not be that suggested by critics. In general, a well-treated labor force is productive, and it is productivity rather than base wage rates that often has the greatest influence on costs. The vision of greedy managers who shift production to low-wage countries to exploit their labor force may be misplaced.

GLOBALIZATION AND NATIONAL SOVEREIGNTY

Another concern voiced by critics of globalization is that today's increasingly interdependent global economy shifts economic power away from national governments and toward supranational organizations such as the World Trade Organization, the European Union, and the United Nations. As perceived by critics, unelected bureaucrats now impose policies on the democratically elected governments of nation-states, thereby undermining the sovereignty of those states and limiting the nation's ability to control its own destiny.[63]

The World Trade Organization is a favorite target of those who attack the headlong rush toward a global economy. As noted earlier, the WTO was founded in 1995 to police the world trading system established by the General Agreement on Tariffs and Trade. The WTO arbitrates trade disputes between the 160 states that are signatories to the GATT. The arbitration panel can issue a ruling instructing a member state to change trade policies that violate GATT regulations. If the violator refuses to comply with the ruling, the WTO allows other states to impose appropriate trade sanctions on the transgressor. As a result, according to one prominent critic, U.S. environmentalist, consumer rights advocate, and sometime presidential candidate Ralph Nader:

> Under the new system, many decisions that affect billions of people are no longer made by local or national governments but instead, if challenged by any WTO member nation, would be deferred to a group of unelected bureaucrats sitting behind closed doors in Geneva (which is where the headquarters of the WTO are located). The bureaucrats can decide whether or not people in California can prevent the destruction of the last virgin forests or determine if carcinogenic pesticides can be banned from their foods; or whether European countries have the right to ban dangerous biotech hormones in meat.... At risk is the very basis of democracy and accountable decision making.[64]

In contrast to Nader, many economists and politicians maintain that the power of supranational organizations such as the WTO is limited to what nation-states collectively agree to grant. They argue that bodies such as the United Nations and the WTO exist to serve the collective interests of member states, not to subvert those interests. Supporters of supranational organizations point out that the power of these bodies rests largely on their ability to persuade member states to follow a certain action. If these bodies fail to serve the collective interests of member states, those states will withdraw their support and the supranational organization will quickly collapse. In this view, real power still resides with individual nation-states, not supranational organizations.

GLOBALIZATION AND THE WORLD'S POOR

Critics of globalization argue that despite the supposed benefits associated with free trade and investment, over the past 100 years or so the gap between the rich and poor nations of the world has gotten wider. In 1870, the average income per capita in the world's 17 richest nations was 2.4 times that of all other countries. In 1990, the same group was 4.5 times as rich as the rest. In 2013, the 34 member states of the Organisation for Economic Co-operation and Development (OECD), which includes most of the world's rich economies, had an average gross national income (GNI) per person of $38,896, whereas the world's 40 least developed countries had a GNI of just $888 per capital—implying that income per capita in the world's 34 richest nations was 45 times that in the world's 40 poorest.[65]

While recent history has shown that some of the world's poorer nations are capable of rapid periods of economic growth—witness the transformation that has occurred in some Southeast Asian nations such as South Korea, Thailand, and Malaysia—there appear to be strong forces for stagnation among the world's poorest nations. A quarter of the countries with a GDP per capita of less than $1,000 in 1960 had growth rates of less than zero from 1960 to 1995, and a third had growth rates of less than 0.05 percent.[66] Critics argue that if globalization is such a positive development, this divergence between the rich and poor should not have occurred.

Although the reasons for economic stagnation vary, several factors stand out, none of which has anything to do with free trade or globalization.[67] Many of the world's poorest countries have suffered from totalitarian governments, economic policies that destroyed wealth rather than facilitated its creation, endemic corruption, scant protection for property rights, and prolonged civil war. A combination of such factors helps explain why countries such as Afghanistan, Cuba, Haiti, Iraq, Libya, Nigeria, Sudan, Syria, North Korea, and Zimbabwe have failed to improve the economic lot of their citizens during recent decades. A complicating factor is the rapidly expanding populations in many of these countries. Without a major change in government, population growth may exacerbate their problems. Promoters of free trade argue that the best way for these countries to improve their lot is to lower their barriers to free trade and investment and to implement economic policies based on free market economics.[68]

Many of the world's poorer nations are being held back by large debt burdens. Of particular concern are the 40 or so "highly indebted poorer countries" (HIPCs), which are home to some 700 million people. Among these countries, the average government debt burden has been as high as 85 percent of the value of the economy, as measured by gross domestic product, and the annual costs of serving government debt consumed 15 percent of the country's export earnings.[69] Servicing such a heavy debt load leaves the governments of these countries with little left to invest in important public infrastructure projects, such as education, health care, roads, and power. The result is the HIPCs are trapped in a cycle of poverty and debt that inhibits economic development. Free trade alone, some argue, is a necessary but not sufficient prerequisite to help these countries bootstrap themselves out of poverty. Instead, large-scale debt relief is needed for the world's poorest nations to give them the opportunity to restructure their economies and start the long climb toward prosperity. Supporters of debt relief also argue that new democratic governments in poor nations should not be forced to honor debts that were incurred and mismanaged long ago by their corrupt and dictatorial predecessors.

In the late 1990s, a debt relief movement began to gain ground among the political establishment in the world's richer nations.[70] Fueled by high-profile endorsements from Irish rock star Bono (who has been a tireless and increasingly effective advocate for debt relief), the Dalai Lama, and influential Harvard economist Jeffrey Sachs, the debt relief movement was instrumental in persuading the United States to enact legislation in 2000 that provided $435 million in debt relief for HIPCs. More important perhaps, the United States also backed an IMF plan to sell some of its gold reserves and use the proceeds to help with debt relief. The IMF and World Bank have now picked up the banner and have embarked on a systematic debt relief program.

For such a program to have a lasting effect, however, debt relief must be matched by wise investment in public projects that boost economic growth (such as education) and by the adoption of economic policies that facilitate investment and trade. Consistent with this, in June 2005, the finance ministers from several of the world's richest economies (including the United States) agreed to provide enough funds to the World Bank and IMF to allow them to cancel a further $55 billion in debt owed by the HIPCs. The goal was to enable the HIPCs to redirect resources from debt payments to health and education programs, and for alleviating poverty.

The richest nations of the world also can help by reducing barriers to the importation of products from the world's poorest nations, particularly tariffs on imports of agricultural products and textiles. High-tariff barriers and other impediments to trade make it difficult for poor countries to export more of their agricultural production. The World Trade Organization has estimated that if the developed nations of the world eradicated subsidies to their agricultural producers and removed tariff barriers to trade in agriculture,

30

 Part 1   Introduction and Overview

this would raise global economic welfare by $128 billion, with $30 billion of that going to poor nations, many of which are highly indebted. The faster growth associated with expanded trade in agriculture could significantly reduce the number of people living in poverty according to the WTO.[71]

Despite the large gap between the rich and poor nations, there is some evidence that progress is being made. In 2000 the United Nations adopted what were known as the *Millennium Goals.* These were eight economic and human development goals for the world. One of these goals was to cut in half the number of people living in extreme poverty, defined as less than $1.25 a day, between 1995 and 2015. This goal was actually achieved in 2010, five years ahead of schedule. Some 1.2 billion people were pulled out of poverty, the majority in China and India, two countries that have been rapidly integrated into the global economy. This represents the greatest reduction in extreme poverty in human history. It's hard to escape the conclusion that globalization and lower barriers to cross-border trade and investment were major factors behind this remarkable achievement.

✅ **TEST PREP**

Use SmartBook to help retain what you have learned. Access your instructor's Connect course to check out SmartBook or go to learnsmartadvantage.com for help.

LO 1-5

Understand how the process of globalization is creating opportunities and challenges for business managers.

Managing in the Global Marketplace

Much of this text is concerned with the challenges of managing in an international business. An **international business** is any firm that engages in international trade or investment. A firm does not have to become a multinational enterprise, investing directly in operations in other countries, to engage in international business, although multinational enterprises are international businesses. All a firm has to do is export or import products from other countries. As the world shifts toward a truly integrated global economy, more firms—both large and small—are becoming international businesses. What does this shift toward a global economy mean for managers within an international business?

As their organizations increasingly engage in cross-border trade and investment, managers need to recognize that the task of managing an international business differs from that of managing a purely domestic business in many ways. At the most fundamental level, the differences arise from the simple fact that countries are different. Countries differ in their cultures, political systems, economic systems, legal systems, and levels of economic development. Despite all the talk about the emerging global village, and despite the trend toward globalization of markets and production, as we shall see in this text, many of these differences are very profound and enduring.

Differences among countries require that an international business vary its practices country by country. Marketing a product in Brazil may require a different approach from marketing the product in Germany; managing U.S. workers might require different skills from managing Japanese workers; maintaining close relations with a particular level of government may be very important in Mexico and irrelevant in Great Britain; the business strategy pursued in Canada might not work in South Korea; and so on. Managers in an international business must not only be sensitive to these differences but also adopt the appropriate policies and strategies for coping with them. Much of this text is devoted to explaining the sources of these differences and the methods for successfully coping with them.

A further way in which international business differs from domestic business is the greater complexity of managing an international business. In addition to the problems that arise from the differences between countries, a manager in an international business is confronted with a range of other issues that the manager in a domestic business never confronts. The managers of an international business must decide where in the world to site production activities to minimize costs and to maximize value added. They must decide whether it is ethical to adhere to the lower labor and environmental standards found in many less developed nations. Then they must decide how best to coordinate and control globally dispersed production activities (which, as we shall see later in the text, is not a trivial problem). The managers in an international business also must decide which foreign markets to enter and which to avoid. They must choose the appropriate mode for entering a particular foreign country. Is it best to export its product to the foreign country? Should the firm allow a local company to produce its product under license in that country? Should the firm enter into a joint venture with a local firm to produce its product in that country? Or should the firm set up a wholly owned subsidiary to serve the market in that country? As we shall see, the choice of entry mode is critical because it has major implications for the long-term health of the firm.

Conducting business transactions across national borders requires understanding the rules governing the international trading and investment system. Managers in an international business must also deal with government restrictions on international trade and investment. They must find ways to work within the limits imposed by specific governmental interventions. As this text explains, even though many governments are nominally committed to free trade, they often intervene to regulate cross-border trade and investment. Managers within international businesses must develop strategies and policies for dealing with such interventions.

Cross-border transactions also require that money be converted from the firm's home currency into a foreign currency and vice versa. Because currency exchange rates vary in response to changing economic conditions, managers in an international business must develop policies for dealing with exchange rate movements. A firm that adopts the wrong policy can lose large amounts of money, whereas one that adopts the right policy can increase the profitability of its international transactions.

In sum, managing an international business is different from managing a purely domestic business for at least four reasons: (1) countries are different, (2) the range of problems confronted by a manager in an international business is wider and the problems themselves more complex than those confronted by a manager in a domestic business, (3) an international business must find ways to work within the limits imposed by government intervention in the international trade and investment system, and (4) international transactions involve converting money into different currencies.

In this text, we examine all these issues in depth, paying close attention to the different strategies and policies that managers pursue to deal with the various challenges created when a firm becomes an international business. Chapters 2, 3, and 4 explore how countries differ from each other with regard to their political, economic, legal, and cultural institutions. Chapter 5 takes a detailed look at the ethical issues that arise in international business. Chapters 6 through 9 look at the international trade and investment environment within which international businesses must operate. Chapters 10 through 12 review the international monetary system. These chapters focus on the nature of the foreign exchange market and the emerging global monetary system. Chapters 13 through 15 explore the organization and strategy of international businesses. Chapters 16 through 20 look at the management of various functional operations within an international business, including production, marketing, and human relations. By the time you complete this text, you should have a good grasp of the issues that managers working within international business have to grapple with on a daily basis, and you should be familiar with the range of strategies and operating policies available to compete more effectively in today's rapidly emerging global economy.

 TEST PREP

Use SmartBook to help retain what you have learned. Access your instructor's Connect course to check out SmartBook or go to learnsmartadvantage.com for help.

Key Terms

globalization, p. 5
globalization of markets, p. 5
globalization of production, p. 6
factors of production, p. 7
General Agreement on Tariffs and
    Trade (GATT), p. 9
World Trade Organization
    (WTO), p. 9

International Monetary Fund
    (IMF), p. 9
World Bank, p. 9
United Nations, p. 9
Group of Twenty (G20), p. 10
international trade, p. 10
foreign direct investment
    (FDI), p. 10

Moore's law, p. 12
stock of foreign direct
    investment (FDI), p. 17
multinational enterprise
    (MNE), p. 18
international business, p. 30

CHAPTER SUMMARY

This chapter has shown how the world economy is becoming more global and reviewed the main drivers of globalization, arguing that they seem to be thrusting nation-states toward a more tightly integrated global economy. It looked at how the nature of international business is changing in response to the changing global economy, discussed concerns raised by rapid globalization, and reviewed implications of rapid globalization for individual managers. The chapter made the following points:

1. Over the past three decades, we have witnessed the globalization of markets and production.

2. The globalization of markets implies that national markets are merging into one huge marketplace. However, it is important not to push this view too far.

3. The globalization of production implies that firms are basing individual productive activities at the optimal world locations for the particular activities. As a consequence, it is increasingly irrelevant to talk about American products, Japanese products, or German products because these are being replaced by "global" products.

4. Two factors seem to underlie the trend toward globalization: declining trade barriers and changes in communication, information, and transportation technologies.

5. Since the end of World War II, barriers to the free flow of goods, services, and capital have been lowered significantly. More than anything else, this has facilitated the trend toward the globalization of production and has enabled firms to view the world as a single market.

6. As a consequence of the globalization of production and markets, in the last decade world trade has grown faster than world output, foreign direct investment has surged, imports have penetrated more deeply into the world's industrial nations, and competitive pressures have increased in industry after industry.

7. The development of the microprocessor and related developments in communication and information processing technology have helped firms link their worldwide operations into sophisticated information networks. Jet air travel, by shrinking travel time, has also helped link the worldwide operations of international businesses.

These changes have enabled firms to achieve tight coordination of their worldwide operations and to view the world as a single market.

8. In the 1960s, the U.S. economy was dominant in the world, U.S. firms accounted for most of the foreign direct investment in the world economy, U.S. firms dominated the list of large multinationals, and roughly half the world—the centrally planned economies of the communist world—was closed to Western businesses.

9. By the 2000s, the U.S. share of world output had been cut in half, with major shares now being accounted for by western European and Southeast Asian economies. The U.S. share of worldwide foreign direct investment had also fallen by about two-thirds. U.S. multinationals were now facing competition from a large number of Japanese and European multinationals. In addition, the emergence of mini-multinationals was noted.

10. One of the most dramatic developments of the past 30 years has been the collapse of communism in eastern Europe, which has created enormous opportunities for international businesses. In addition, the move toward free market economies in China and Latin America is creating opportunities (and threats) for Western international businesses.

11. The benefits and costs of the emerging global economy are being hotly debated among businesspeople, economists, and politicians. The debate focuses on the impact of globalization on jobs, wages, the environment, working conditions, national sovereignty, and extreme poverty in the world's poorest nations.

12. Managing an international business is different from managing a domestic business for at least four reasons: (*a*) countries are different, (*b*) the range of problems confronted by a manager in an international business is wider and the problems themselves more complex than those confronted by a manager in a domestic business, (*c*) managers in an international business must find ways to work within the limits imposed by governments' intervention in the international trade and investment system, and (*d*) international transactions involve converting money into different currencies.

Critical Thinking and Discussion Questions

1. Describe the shifts in the world economy over the past 30 years. What are the implications of these shifts for international businesses based in Great Britain? North America? Hong Kong?

2. "The study of international business is fine if you are going to work in a large multinational enterprise, but it has no relevance for individuals who are going to work in small firms." Evaluate this statement.

3. How have changes in technology contributed to the globalization of markets and production? Would the globalization of production and markets have been possible without these technological changes?

4. "Ultimately, the study of international business is no different from the study of domestic business. Thus, there is no point in having a separate course on international business." Evaluate this statement.

5. How does the Internet affect international business activity and the globalization of the world economy?

6. If current trends continue, China may be the world's largest economy by 2030. Discuss the possible implications of such a development for

(a) the world trading system, (b) the world monetary system, (c) the business strategy of today's European and U.S.-based global corporations, and (d) global commodity prices.

7. Reread the Management Focus on Vizio and answer the following questions:

   a. Why is the manufacturing of flat-panel TVs migrating to different locations around the world?

   b. Who benefits from the globalization of the flat-panel display industry? Who are the losers?

   c. What would happen if the U.S. government required that flat-panel displays sold in the United States had to also be made in the United States? On balance, would this be a good or a bad thing?

   d. What does the example of Vizio tell you about the future of production in an increasingly integrated global economy? What does it tell you about the strategies that enterprises must adopt to thrive in highly competitive global markets?

globalEDGE research task globaledge.msu.edu

Use the globalEDGE website (**globaledge.msu.edu**) to complete the following exercises:

1. As the drivers of globalization continue to pressure both the globalization of markets and the globalization of production, we continue to see the impact of greater globalization on worldwide trade patterns. HSBC, a large global bank, analyzes these pressures and trends to identify opportunities across markets and sectors, through its *trade forecasts*. Visit the HSBC Global Connections site and use the trade forecast tool to identify which export routes are forecasted to see the greatest growth over the next 15 to 20 years. What patterns do you see? What types of countries dominate these routes?

2. You are working for a company that is considering investing in a foreign country. Investing in countries with different traditions is an important element of your company's long-term strategic goals. As such, management has requested a report regarding the attractiveness of alternative countries based on the potential return of FDI. Accordingly, the ranking of the top 25 countries in terms of FDI attractiveness is a crucial ingredient for your report. A colleague mentioned a potentially useful tool called the Foreign Direct Investment (FDI) Confidence Index. The FDI Confidence Index is a regular survey of global executives conducted by A.T. Kearney. Find this index, and provide additional information regarding how the index is constructed.

CLOSING CASE

Building the Boeing 787

Executives at the Boeing Corporation, America's largest exporter, like to say that building a large commercial jet aircraft like the 747 or 787 involves bringing together more than a million parts in flying formation. Forty-five years ago, when the early models of Boeing's venerable 737 and 747 jets were rolling off the company's Seattle area production lines, foreign suppliers accounted for only 5 percent of those parts on average. Boeing was vertically integrated and manufactured many of the major components that went into the planes. The largest parts produced by outside suppliers were the jet engines, where two of the three suppliers were American companies. The lone foreign engine manufacturer was the British company Rolls-Royce.

Fast-forward to the modern era, and things look very different. In the case of its latest aircraft, the super efficient 787 Dreamliner, 50 outside suppliers spread around the world account for 65 percent of the value of the aircraft. Italian firm Alenia Aeronautica makes the center fuselage and horizontal stabilizer. Kawasaki of Japan makes part of the forward fuselage and the fixed trailing edge of the wing. French firm Messier-Dowty makes the aircraft's landing gear. German firm Diehl Luftahrt Elektronik supplies the main cabin lighting. Sweden's Saab Aerostructures makes the access doors. Japanese company Jamco makes parts for the lavatories, flight deck interiors, and galleys. Mitsubishi Heavy Industries of Japan makes the wings. KAA of Korea makes the wing tips. And so on.

Why the change? One reason is that 80 percent of Boeing's customers are foreign airlines, and to sell into those nations, it often helps to be giving business to those nations. The trend started in 1974 when Mitsubishi of Japan was given contracts to produce inboard wing flaps for the 747. The Japanese reciprocated by placing big orders for Boeing jets. A second rationale was to disperse component part production to those suppliers who are the best in the world at their particular activity. Over the years, for example, Mitsubishi has acquired considerable expertise in the manufacture of wings, so it was logical for Boeing to use Mitsubishi to make the wings for the 787. Similarly, the 787 is the first commercial jet aircraft to be made almost entirely out of carbon fiber, so Boeing tapped Japan's Toray Industries, a world-class expert in sturdy but light carbon-fiber composites, to supply materials for the fuselage. A third reason for the extensive outsourcing on the 787 was that

Boeing wanted to unburden itself of some of the risks and costs associated with developing production facilities for the 787. By outsourcing, it pushed some of those risks and costs onto suppliers, who had to undertake major investments in capacity to ramp up to produce for the 787.

So what did Boeing retain for itself? Engineering design, marketing and sales, and final assembly are done at its Everett plant north of Seattle, all activities where Boeing maintains it is the best in the world. Of major component parts, Boeing made only the tail fin and wing to body fairing (which attaches the wings to the fuselage of the plane). Everything else was outsourced.

As the 787 moved through development in the 2000s, however, it became clear that Boeing had pushed the outsourcing paradigm too far. Coordinating a globally dispersed production system this extensive turned out to be very challenging. Parts turned up late, some parts didn't "snap together" the way Boeing had envisioned, and several suppliers ran into engineering problems that slowed down the entire production process. As a consequence, the date for delivery of the first jet was pushed back more than four years, and Boeing had to take millions of dollars in penalties for late deliveries. The problems at one supplier, Vought Aircraft in North Carolina, were so severe that Boeing ultimately agreed to acquire the company and bring its production in-house. Vought was co-owned by Alenia of Italy and made parts of the main fuselage.

There are now signs that Boeing is rethinking some of its global outsourcing policy. For its next jet, a new version of its popular wide-bodied 777 jet, the 777X, which will use the same carbon-fiber technology as the 787, Boeing will bring wing production back in-house. Mitsubishi and Kawasaki of Japan produce much of the wing structure for the 787, and for the original version of the 777. However, recently Japan's airlines have been placing large orders with Airbus, breaking with their traditional allegiance to Boeing. This seems to have given Boeing an opening to bring wing production back in-house. Boeing executives also note that Boeing has lost much of its expertise in wing production over the last 20 years due to outsourcing, and bringing it back in-house for new carbon-fiber wings might enable Boeing to regain these important core skills and strengthen the company's competitive position.

Sources: K. Epstein and J. Crown, "Globalization Bites Boeing," *Bloomberg Businessweek*, March 12, 2008; H. Mallick, "Out of Control Outsourcing Ruined Boeing's Beautiful Dreamliner," *The Star*, February 25, 2013; P. Kavilanz, "Dreamliner: Where in the World Its Parts Come From," *CNN Money*, January 18, 2013; S. Dubois, "Boeing's Dreamliner Mess: Simply Inevitable?," *CNN Money*, January 22, 2013; A. Scott and T. Kelly, "Boeing's Loss of a $9.5 Billion Deal Could Bring Jobs Back to the U.S.," *Business Insider*, October 14, 2013.

Case Discussion Questions

1. What are the benefits to Boeing of outsourcing manufacturing of components of the Boeing 787 to firms based in other countries?

2. What are the potential costs and risks to Boeing of outsourcing?

3. In addition to foreign subcontractors and Boeing, who else benefits from Boeing's decision to outsource component part manufacturing assembly to other nations? Who are the potential losers?

4. If Boeing's management decided to keep all production in America, what do you think the effect would be on the company, its employees, and the communities that depend on it?

5. On balance, do you think that the kind of outsourcing undertaken by Boeing is a good thing or a bad thing for the American economy? Explain your reasoning.

Endnotes

1. Figures from World Trade Organization, Statistics Database, 2013.

2. Thomas L. Friedman, *The World Is Flat* (New York: Farrar, Straus and Giroux, 2005).

3. Ibid.

4. T. Levitt, "The Globalization of Markets," *Harvard Business Review*, May–June 1983, pp. 92–102.

5. U.S. Department of Commerce, Internal Trade Administration, "Profile of U.S. Exporting and Importing Companies, 2012–2013," April 2015.

6. C. M. Draffen, "Going Global: Export Market Proves Profitable for Region's Small Businesses," *Newsday*, March 19, 2001, p. C18.

7. B. Benoit and R. Milne, "Germany's Best Kept Secret, How Its Exporters Are Betting the World," *Financial Times*, May 19, 2006, p. 11.

8. See F. T. Knickerbocker, *Oligopolistic Reaction and Multinational Enterprise* (Boston: Harvard Business School Press, 1973); R. E. Caves, "Japanese Investment in the U.S.: Lessons for the Economic Analysis of Foreign Investment," *The World Economy* 16 (1993), pp. 279–300.

9. I. Metthee, "Playing a Large Part," *Seattle Post-Intelligencer*, April 9, 1994, p. 13.

10. "Operating Profit," *The Economist*, August 16, 2008, pp. 74–76.

11. R. B. Reich, *The Work of Nations* (New York: Knopf, 1991).

12. United Nations, "The UN in Brief," **www.un.org/Overview/brief.html**.

13. J. A. Frankel, "Globalization of the Economy," National Bureau of Economic Research, working paper no. 7858, 2000.

14. J. Bhagwati, *Protectionism* (Cambridge, MA: MIT Press, 1989).

15. F. Williams, "Trade Round Like This May Never Be Seen Again," *Financial Times*, April 15, 1994, p. 8.

16. W. Vieth, "Major Concessions Lead to Success for WTO Talks," *Los Angeles Times*, November 14, 2001, p. A1; "Seeds Sown for Future Growth," *The Economist*, November 17, 2001, pp. 65–66.

17. United Nations, *World Investment Report, 2014* (New York and Geneva: United Nations, 2014).

18. World Trade Organization, *International Trade Statistics 2014* (Geneva: WTO, 2014).

19. United Nations Conference on Trade and Investment, "Global FDI Flows Declined in 2014," *Global Investment Trends Monitor*, January 29, 2015.

20. United Nations, *World Investment Report, 2014*.

21. Moore's law is named after Intel founder Gordon Moore.

22. Data compiled from various sources and listed at **www.internetworldstats.com/stats.htm**.

23. From **www.census.gov/mrts/www/ecomm.html**. See also S. Fiegerman, "Ecommerce Is Now a Trillion Dollar Industry," *Mashable Business*, February 5, 2013.

24. For a counterpoint, see "Geography and the Net: Putting It in Its Place," *The Economist,* August 11, 2001, pp. 18–20.

25. International Chamber of Shipping, Key Facts, **www.ics-shipping.org/shipping-facts/key-facts**.

26. Frankel, "Globalization of the Economy."

27. R. Wile, "Here's What It Costs to Ship 7 Everyday Goods across the Ocean," *Business Insider,* September 19, 2012.

28. Data from Bureau of Transportation Statistics, 2001.

29. John G. Fernald and Victoria Greenfield, "The Fall and Rise of the Global Economy," Chicago Fed Letter, April 2001, Number 164.

30. Data located at **www.bts.gov/publications/us_international_trade_and_freight_transportation_trends/2003/index.html**.

31. N. Hood and J. Young, *The Economics of the Multinational Enterprise* (New York: Longman, 1973).

32. United Nations, *World Investment Report, 2014.*

33. Ibid.

34. Ibid.

35. S. Chetty, "Explosive International Growth and Problems of Success among Small and Medium Sized Firms," *International Small Business Journal,* February 2003, pp. 5–28.

36. R. A. Mosbacher, "Opening Up Export Doors for Smaller Firms," *Seattle Times,* July 24, 1991, p. A7.

37. "Small Companies Learn How to Sell to the Japanese," *Seattle Times,* March 19, 1992.

38. W. J. Holstein, "Why Johann Can Export, but Johnny Can't," *BusinessWeek,* November 3, 1991, **www.businessweek.com/stories/1991-11-03/why-johann-can-export-but-johnny-cant**.

39. N. Buckley and A. Ostrovsky, "Back to Business—How Putin's Allies Are Turning Russia into a Corporate State," *Financial Times,* June 19, 2006, p. 11.

40. J. E. Stiglitz, *Globalization and Its Discontents* (New York: W. W. Norton, 2003); J. Bhagwati, *In Defense of Globalization* (New York: Oxford University Press, 2004); Friedman, *The World Is Flat.*

41. See, for example, Ravi Batra, *The Myth of Free Trade* (New York: Touchstone Books, 1993); William Greider, *One World, Ready or Not: The Manic Logic of Global Capitalism* (New York: Simon & Schuster, 1997); D. Radrik, *Has Globalization Gone Too Far?* (Washington, DC: Institution for International Economics, 1997).

42. E. Goldsmith, "The Winners and the Losers," in *The Case against the Global Economy,* ed. J. Mander and E. Goldsmith (San Francisco: Sierra Club, 1996); Lou Dobbs, *Exporting America* (New York: Time Warner Books, 2004).

43. For an excellent summary, see "The Globalization of Labor," Chapter 5, in *IMF, World Economic Outlook 2007* (Washington, DC: IMF, April 2007). Also see R. Freeman, "Labor Market Imbalances," Harvard University working paper, **www.bos.frb.org/economic/conf/conf51/conf51d.pdf**.

44. D. L. Bartlett and J. B. Steele, "America: Who Stole the Dream," *Philadelphia Inquirer,* September 9, 1996.

45. For example, see Paul Krugman, *Pop Internationalism* (Cambridge, MA: MIT Press, 1996).

46. For example, see B. Milanovic and L. Squire, "Does Tariff Liberalization Increase Wage Inequality?," National Bureau of Economic Research, working paper no. 11046, January 2005; B. Milanovic, "Can We Discern the Effect of Globalization on Income Distribution?," *World Bank Economic Review* 19 (2005), pp. 21–44. Also see the summary in Thomas Piketty, "The Globalization of Labor," in *Capital in the Twenty First Century* (Cambridge, MA: Harvard University Press, 2014).

47. See Piketty, "The Globalization of Labor."

48. A. Ebenstein, A. Harrison, M. McMillam, and S. Phillips, "Estimating the Impact of Trade and Offshoring on American Workers Using the Current Population Survey," *Review of Economics and Statistics* 67 (October 2014), pp. 581–95.

49. M. Forster and M. Pearson, "Income Distribution and Poverty in the OECD Area," *OECD Economic Studies* 34 (2002); Moffett, "Income Inequality Increases"; OECD, "Growing Income Inequality in OECD Countries," *OECD Forum,* May 2, 2011.

50. See Piketty, "The Globalization of Labor."

51. See Krugman, *Pop Internationalism;* D. Belman and T. M. Lee, "International Trade and the Performance of U.S. Labor Markets," in *U.S. Trade Policy and Global Growth,* ed. R. A. Blecker (New York: Economic Policy Institute, 1996).

52. Freeman, "Labor Market Imbalances."

53. E. Goldsmith, "Global Trade and the Environment," in *The Case against the Global Economy,* eds. J. Mander and E. Goldsmith (San Francisco: Sierra Club, 1996).

54. P. Choate, *Jobs at Risk: Vulnerable U.S. Industries and Jobs under NAFTA* (Washington, DC: Manufacturing Policy Project, 1993).

55. Ibid.

56. B. Lomborg, *The Skeptical Environmentalist* (Cambridge, UK: Cambridge University Press, 2001).

57. H. Nordstrom and S. Vaughan, *Trade and the Environment, World Trade Organization Special Studies No. 4* (Geneva: WTO, 1999).

58. Figures are from "Freedom's Journey: A Survey of the 20th Century. Our Durable Planet," *The Economist,* September 11, 1999, p. 30.

59. For an exhaustive review of the empirical literature, see B. R. Copeland and M. Scott Taylor, "Trade, Growth and the Environment," *Journal of Economic Literature,* March 2004, pp. 7–77.

60. G. M. Grossman and A. B. Krueger, "Economic Growth and the Environment," *Quarterly Journal of Economics* 110 (1995), pp. 353–78.

61. For an economic perspective on climate change see William Nordhouse, *The Climate Casino* (Yale University Press, Princeton, NJ, 2013).

62. Krugman, *Pop Internationalism.*

63. R. Kuttner, "Managed Trade and Economic Sovereignty," in *U.S. Trade Policy and Global Growth,* ed. R. A. Blecker (New York: Economic Policy Institute, 1996).

64. Ralph Nader and Lori Wallach, "GATT, NAFTA, and the Subversion of the Democratic Process," in *U.S. Trade Policy and Global Growth,* ed. R. A. Blecker (New York: Economic Policy Institute, 1996), pp. 93–94.

65. Lant Pritchett, "Divergence, Big Time," *Journal of Economic Perspectives* 11, no. 3 (Summer 1997), pp. 3–18. The data are from the World Bank's *World Development Indicators,* 2015.

66. Ibid.

67. W. Easterly, "How Did Heavily Indebted Poor Countries Become Heavily Indebted?" *World Development,* October 2002, pp. 1677–96; and J. Sachs, *The End of Poverty* (New York, Penguin Books, 2006).

68. See D. Ben-David, H. Nordstrom, and L. A. Winters, *Trade, Income Disparity and Poverty: World Trade Organization Special Studies No. 5* (Geneva: WTO, 1999).

69. William Easterly, "Debt Relief," *Foreign Policy,* November–December 2001, pp. 20–26.

70. Jeffrey Sachs, "Sachs on Development: Helping the World's Poorest," *The Economist,* August 14, 1999, pp. 17–20.

71. World Trade Organization, *Annual Report 2003* (Geneva: WTO, 2004).

CHAPTER 7

Strategies for Competing in International Markets

© Kenneth Batelman/Ikon Images/SuperStock

Learning Objectives

THIS CHAPTER WILL HELP YOU UNDERSTAND:

LO 1   The primary reasons companies choose to compete in international markets.

LO 2   How and why differing market conditions across countries influence a company's strategy choices in international markets.

LO 3   The five major strategic options for entering foreign markets.

LO 4   The three main strategic approaches for competing internationally.

LO 5   How companies are able to use international operations to improve overall competitiveness.

LO 6   The unique characteristics of competing in developing-country markets.

Our key words now are globalization, new products and businesses, and speed.

Tsutomu Kanai—*Former chair and president of Hitachi*

You have no choice but to operate in a world shaped by globalization and the information revolution. There are two options: Adapt or die.

Andy Grove—*Former chair and CEO of Intel*

A sharing of control with local partners will lead to a greater contribution from them, which can assist in coping with circumstances that are unfamiliar to the foreign partner.

Yanni Yan—*Business author and academic*

Any company that aspires to industry leadership in the 21st century must think in terms of global, not domestic, market leadership. The world economy is globalizing at an accelerating pace as ambitious, growth-minded companies race to build stronger competitive positions in the markets of more and more countries, as countries previously closed to foreign companies open up their markets, and as information technology shrinks the importance of geographic distance. The forces of globalization are changing the competitive landscape in many industries, offering companies attractive new opportunities and at the same time introducing new competitive threats. Companies in industries where these forces are greatest are therefore under considerable pressure to come up with a strategy for competing successfully in international markets.

This chapter focuses on strategy options for expanding beyond domestic boundaries and competing in the markets of either a few or a great many countries. In the process of exploring these options, we introduce such concepts as multidomestic, transnational, and global strategies; the Porter diamond of national competitive advantage; and profit sanctuaries. The chapter also includes sections on cross-country differences in cultural, demographic, and market conditions; strategy options for entering foreign markets; the importance of locating value chain operations in the most advantageous countries; and the special circumstances of competing in developing markets such as those in China, India, Brazil, Russia, and eastern Europe.

WHY COMPANIES DECIDE TO ENTER FOREIGN MARKETS

A company may opt to expand outside its domestic market for any of five major reasons:

LO 1

The primary reasons companies choose to compete in international markets.

1. *To gain access to new customers.* Expanding into foreign markets offers potential for increased revenues, profits, and long-term growth; it becomes an especially attractive option when a company encounters dwindling growth opportunities in its home market. Companies often expand internationally to extend the life cycle

of their products, as Honda has done with its classic 50-cc motorcycle, the Honda Cub (which is still selling well in developing markets, more than 50 years after it was first introduced in Japan). A larger target market also offers companies the opportunity to earn a return on large investments more rapidly. This can be particularly important in R&D-intensive industries, where development is fast-paced or competitors imitate innovations rapidly.

2. *To achieve lower costs through economies of scale, experience, and increased purchasing power.* Many companies are driven to sell in more than one country because domestic sales volume alone is not large enough to capture fully economies of scale in product development, manufacturing, or marketing. Similarly, firms expand internationally to increase the rate at which they accumulate experience and move down the learning curve. International expansion can also lower a company's input costs through greater pooled purchasing power. The relatively small size of country markets in Europe and limited domestic volume explains why companies like Michelin, BMW, and Nestlé long ago began selling their products all across Europe and then moved into markets in North America and Latin America.

3. *To gain access to low-cost inputs of production.* Companies in industries based on natural resources (e.g., oil and gas, minerals, rubber, and lumber) often find it necessary to operate in the international arena since raw-material supplies are located in different parts of the world and can be accessed more cost-effectively at the source. Other companies enter foreign markets to access low-cost human resources; this is particularly true of industries in which labor costs make up a high proportion of total production costs.

4. *To further exploit its core competencies.* A company may be able to extend a market-leading position in its domestic market into a position of regional or global market leadership by leveraging its core competencies further. H&M is capitalizing on its considerable expertise in online retailing to expand its reach internationally. By bringing its easy-to-use and mobile-friendly online shopping to 23 different countries, the company hopes to pave the way for setting up physical stores in these countries. Companies can often leverage their resources internationally by replicating a successful business model, using it as a basic blueprint for international operations, as Starbucks and McDonald's have done.[1]

5. *To gain access to resources and capabilities located in foreign markets.* An increasingly important motive for entering foreign markets is to acquire resources and capabilities that may be unavailable in a company's home market. Companies often make acquisitions abroad or enter into cross-border alliances to gain access to capabilities that complement their own or to learn from their partners.[2] In other cases, companies choose to establish operations in other countries to utilize local distribution networks, gain local managerial or marketing expertise, or acquire technical knowledge.

In addition, companies that are the suppliers of other companies often expand internationally when their major customers do so, to meet their customers' needs abroad and retain their position as a key supply chain partner. For example, when motor vehicle companies have opened new plants in foreign locations, big automotive parts suppliers have frequently opened new facilities nearby to permit timely delivery of their parts and components to the plant. Similarly, Newell-Rubbermaid, one of Walmart's biggest suppliers of household products, has followed Walmart into foreign markets.

WHY COMPETING ACROSS NATIONAL BORDERS MAKES STRATEGY MAKING MORE COMPLEX

Crafting a strategy to compete in one or more countries of the world is inherently more complex for five reasons. First, different countries have different home-country advantages in different industries; competing effectively requires an understanding of these differences. Second, there are location-based advantages to conducting particular value chain activities in different parts of the world. Third, different political and economic conditions make the general business climate more favorable in some countries than in others. Fourth, companies face risk due to adverse shifts in currency exchange rates when operating in foreign markets. And fifth, differences in buyer tastes and preferences present a challenge for companies concerning customizing versus standardizing their products and services.

LO 2

How and why differing market conditions across countries influence a company's strategy choices in international markets.

Home-Country Industry Advantages and the Diamond Model

Certain countries are known for their strengths in particular industries. For example, Chile has competitive strengths in industries such as copper, fruit, fish products, paper and pulp, chemicals, and wine. Japan is known for competitive strength in consumer electronics, automobiles, semiconductors, steel products, and specialty steel. Where industries are more likely to develop competitive strength depends on a set of factors that describe the nature of each country's business environment and vary from country to country. Because strong industries are made up of strong firms, the strategies of firms that expand internationally are usually grounded in one or more of these factors. The four major factors are summarized in a framework developed by Michael Porter and known as the *Diamond of National Competitive Advantage* (see Figure 7.1).[3]

Demand Conditions   The demand conditions in an industry's home market include the relative size of the market, its growth potential, and the nature of domestic buyers' needs and wants. Differing population sizes, income levels, and other demographic factors give rise to considerable differences in market size and growth rates from country to country. Industry sectors that are larger and more important in their home market tend to attract more resources and grow faster than others. For example, owing to widely differing population demographics and income levels, there is a far bigger market for luxury automobiles in the United States and Germany than in Argentina, India, Mexico, and China. At the same time, in developing markets like India, China, Brazil, and Malaysia, market growth potential is far higher than it is in the more mature economies of Britain, Denmark, Canada, and Japan. The potential for market growth in automobiles is explosive in China, where 2015 sales of new vehicles amounted to 26.4 million, surpassing U.S. sales of 17.2 million and making China the world's largest market for the sixth year in a row.[4] Demanding domestic buyers for an industry's products spur greater innovativeness and improvements in quality. Such conditions foster the development of stronger industries, with firms that are capable of translating a home-market advantage into a competitive advantage in the international arena.

FIGURE 7.1   The Diamond of National Competitive Advantage

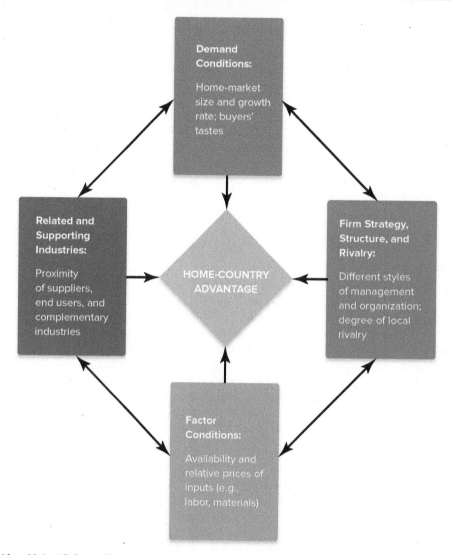

Source: Adapted from Michael E. Porter, "The Competitive Advantage of Nations," *Harvard Business Review,* March–April 1990, pp. 73–93.

Factor Conditions   Factor conditions describe the availability, quality, and cost of raw materials and other inputs (called *factors of production*) that firms in an industry require for producing their products and services. The relevant factors of production vary from industry to industry but can include different types of labor, technical or managerial knowledge, land, financial capital, and natural resources. Elements of a country's infrastructure may be included as well, such as its transportation, communication, and banking systems. For instance, in India there are efficient, well-developed national channels for distributing groceries, personal care items, and other packaged products to the country's 3 million retailers, whereas in China distribution is primarily local and there is a limited national network for distributing most products. Competitively strong industries and firms develop where relevant factor conditions are favorable.

Related and Supporting Industries   Robust industries often develop in locales where there is a cluster of related industries, including others within the same value chain system (e.g., suppliers of components and equipment, distributors) and the makers of complementary products or those that are technologically related. The sports car makers Ferrari and Maserati, for example, are located in an area of Italy known as the "engine technological district," which includes other firms involved in racing, such as Ducati Motorcycles, along with hundreds of small suppliers. The advantage to firms that develop as part of a related-industry cluster comes from the close collaboration with key suppliers and the greater knowledge sharing throughout the cluster, resulting in greater efficiency and innovativeness.

Firm Strategy, Structure, and Rivalry   Different country environments foster the development of different styles of management, organization, and strategy. For example, strategic alliances are a more common strategy for firms from Asian or Latin American countries, which emphasize trust and cooperation in their organizations, than for firms from North America, where individualism is more influential. In addition, countries vary in terms of the competitive rivalry of their industries. Fierce rivalry in home markets tends to hone domestic firms' competitive capabilities and ready them for competing internationally.

For an industry in a particular country to become competitively strong, all four factors must be favorable for that industry. When they are, the industry is likely to contain firms that are capable of competing successfully in the international arena. Thus the diamond framework can be used to reveal the answers to several questions that are important for competing on an international basis. First, it can help predict *where foreign entrants into an industry are most likely to come from*. This can help managers prepare to cope with new foreign competitors, since the framework also reveals something about the basis of the new rivals' strengths. Second, it can reveal the countries in which foreign rivals are likely to be weakest and thus can help managers decide *which foreign markets to enter first*. And third, because it focuses on the attributes of a country's business environment that allow firms to flourish, it reveals something about the advantages of conducting particular business activities in that country. Thus the diamond framework is an aid to deciding *where to locate different value chain activities most beneficially*—a topic that we address next.

Opportunities for Location-Based Advantages

Increasingly, companies are locating different value chain activities in different parts of the world to exploit location-based advantages that vary from country to country. This is particularly evident with respect to the location of manufacturing activities. Differences in wage rates, worker productivity, energy costs, and the like create sizable variations in manufacturing costs from country to country. By locating its plants in certain countries, firms in some industries can reap major manufacturing cost advantages because of lower input costs (especially labor), relaxed government regulations, the proximity of suppliers and technologically related industries, or unique natural resources. In such cases, the low-cost countries become principal production sites, with most of the output being exported to markets in other parts of the world. Companies that build production facilities in low-cost countries (or that source their products from contract manufacturers in these countries) gain a competitive advantage over rivals with plants in countries where costs are higher. The competitive role of low manufacturing costs is most evident in low-wage countries like China, India,

Pakistan, Cambodia, Vietnam, Mexico, Brazil, Guatemala, the Philippines, and several countries in Africa and eastern Europe that have become production havens for manufactured goods with high labor content (especially textiles and apparel). Hourly compensation for manufacturing workers in 2013 averaged about $1.46 in India, $2.12 in the Philippines, $3.07 in China, $6.82 in Mexico, $9.37 in Taiwan, $9.44 in Hungary, $10.69 in Brazil, $12.90 in Portugal, $21.96 in South Korea, $25.85 in New Zealand, $29.13 in Japan, $36.33 in Canada, $36.34 in the United States, $48.98 in Germany, and $65.86 in Norway.[5] China emerged as the manufacturing capital of the world in large part because of its low wages—virtually all of the world's major manufacturing companies now have facilities in China. This in turn has driven up their wages to nearly double the average wage offered in 2012.

For other types of value chain activities, input quality or availability are more important considerations. Tiffany & Co. entered the mining industry in Canada to access diamonds that could be certified as "conflict free" and not associated with either the funding of African wars or unethical mining conditions. Many U.S. companies locate call centers in countries such as India and Ireland, where English is spoken and the workforce is well educated. Other companies locate R&D activities in countries where there are prestigious research institutions and well-trained scientists and engineers. Likewise, concerns about short delivery times and low shipping costs make some countries better locations than others for establishing distribution centers.

The Impact of Government Policies and Economic Conditions in Host Countries

Cross-country variations in government policies and economic conditions affect both the opportunities available to a foreign entrant and the risks of operating within the host country. The governments of some countries are eager to attract foreign investments, and thus they go all out to create a business climate that outsiders will view as favorable. Governments eager to spur economic growth, create more jobs, and raise living standards for their citizens usually enact policies aimed at stimulating business innovation and capital investment; Ireland is a good example. They may provide such incentives as reduced taxes, low-cost loans, site location and site development assistance, and government-sponsored training for workers to encourage companies to construct production and distribution facilities. When new business-related issues or developments arise, "pro-business" governments make a practice of seeking advice and counsel from business leaders. When tougher business-related regulations are deemed appropriate, they endeavor to make the transition to more costly and stringent regulations somewhat business-friendly rather than adversarial.

On the other hand, governments sometimes enact policies that, from a business perspective, make locating facilities within a country's borders less attractive. For example, the nature of a company's operations may make it particularly costly to achieve compliance with a country's environmental regulations. Some governments provide subsidies and low-interest loans to domestic companies to enable them to better compete against foreign companies. To discourage foreign imports, governments may enact deliberately burdensome procedures and requirements regarding customs inspection for foreign goods and may impose tariffs or quotas on imports. Additionally, they may specify that a certain percentage of the parts and components used in manufacturing a product be obtained from local suppliers, require prior approval of capital spending projects, limit withdrawal of funds from the country, and require partial ownership of foreign company operations by local companies or investors. There are times when a government may place restrictions on exports to ensure adequate local supplies and regulate the prices of imported and locally produced goods. Such government actions make a country's business climate less attractive and in some cases may be sufficiently onerous as to discourage a company from locating facilities in that country or even selling its products there.

A country's business climate is also a function of the political and economic risks associated with operating within its borders. **Political risks** have to do with the instability of weak governments, growing possibilities that a country's citizenry will revolt against dictatorial government leaders, the likelihood of new onerous legislation or regulations on foreign-owned businesses, and the potential for future elections to produce corrupt or tyrannical government leaders. In industries that a government deems critical to the national welfare, there is sometimes a risk that the government will nationalize the industry and expropriate the assets of foreign companies. In 2012, for example, Argentina nationalized the country's top oil producer, YPF, which was owned by Spanish oil major Repsol. Other political risks include the loss of investments due to war or political unrest, regulatory changes that create operating uncertainties, security risks due to terrorism, and corruption. **Economic risks** have to do with instability of a country's economy and monetary system— whether inflation rates might skyrocket or whether uncontrolled deficit spending on the part of government or risky bank lending practices could lead to a breakdown of the country's monetary system and prolonged economic distress. In some countries, the threat of piracy and lack of protection for intellectual property are also sources of economic risk. Another is fluctuations in the value of different currencies—a factor that we discuss in more detail next.

> **CORE CONCEPT**
>
> **Political risks** stem from instability or weakness in national governments and hostility to foreign business. **Economic risks** stem from instability in a country's monetary system, economic and regulatory policies, and the lack of property rights protections.

The Risks of Adverse Exchange Rate Shifts

When companies produce and market their products and services in many different countries, they are subject to the impacts of sometimes favorable and sometimes unfavorable changes in currency exchange rates. The rates of exchange between different currencies can vary by as much as 20 to 40 percent annually, with the changes occurring sometimes gradually and sometimes swiftly. *Sizable shifts in exchange rates pose significant risks for two reasons:*

1. They are hard to predict because of the variety of factors involved and the uncertainties surrounding when and by how much these factors will change.
2. They create uncertainty regarding which countries represent the low-cost manufacturing locations and which rivals have the upper hand in the marketplace.

To illustrate the economic and competitive risks associated with fluctuating exchange rates, consider the case of a U.S. company that has located manufacturing facilities in Brazil (where the currency is *reals*—pronounced "ray-alls") and that exports most of the Brazilian-made goods to markets in the European Union (where the currency is euros). To keep the numbers simple, assume that the exchange rate is 4 Brazilian reals for 1 euro and that the product being made in Brazil has a manufacturing cost of 4 Brazilian reals (or 1 euro). Now suppose that the exchange rate shifts from 4 reals per euro to 5 reals per euro (meaning that the real has declined in value and that the euro is stronger). Making the product in Brazil is now more cost-competitive because a Brazilian good costing 4 reals to produce has fallen to only 0.8 euro at the new exchange rate (4 reals divided by 5 reals per euro = 0.8 euro). This clearly puts the producer of the Brazilian-made good *in a better position to compete* against the European makers of the same good. On the other hand, should the value of the Brazilian real grow stronger in relation to the euro—resulting in an exchange rate of 3 reals to 1 euro—the same Brazilian-made good formerly costing 4 reals (or 1 euro) to produce now has a cost of 1.33 euros (4 reals divided by 3 reals per euro = 1.33 euros), putting the producer of the Brazilian-made good in a weaker competitive position vis-à-vis the European producers. Plainly, the attraction of manufacturing a good in Brazil and selling it in Europe is far greater when the euro is strong (an exchange rate of 1 euro for 5 Brazilian reals) than when the euro is weak and exchanges for only 3 Brazilian reals.

But there is one more piece to the story. When the exchange rate changes from 4 reals per euro to 5 reals per euro, not only is the cost-competitiveness of the Brazilian manufacturer stronger relative to European manufacturers of the same item but the Brazilian-made good that formerly cost 1 euro and now costs only 0.8 euro can also be sold to consumers in the European Union for a lower euro price than before. In other words, the combination of a stronger euro and a weaker real acts to *lower the price of Brazilian-made goods* in all the countries that are members of the European Union, which is likely to *spur sales of the Brazilian-made good in Europe and boost Brazilian exports to Europe.* Conversely, should the exchange rate shift from 4 reals per euro to 3 reals per euro—which makes the Brazilian manufacturer less cost-competitive with European manufacturers of the same item—the Brazilian-made good that formerly cost 1 euro and now costs 1.33 euros will sell for a higher price in euros than before, thus weakening the demand of European consumers for Brazilian-made goods and acting to reduce Brazilian exports to Europe. Brazilian exporters are likely to experience (1) rising demand for their goods in Europe whenever the Brazilian real grows weaker relative to the euro and (2) falling demand for their goods in Europe whenever the real grows stronger relative to the euro. Consequently, from the standpoint of a company with Brazilian manufacturing plants, *a weaker Brazilian real is a favorable exchange rate shift* and *a stronger Brazilian real is an unfavorable exchange rate shift.*

It follows from the previous discussion that shifting exchange rates have a big impact on the ability of domestic manufacturers to compete with foreign rivals. For example, U.S.-based manufacturers locked in a fierce competitive battle with low-cost foreign imports benefit from a *weaker* U.S. dollar. There are several reasons why this is so:

- Declines in the value of the U.S. dollar against foreign currencies raise the U.S. dollar costs of goods manufactured by foreign rivals at plants located in the countries whose currencies have grown stronger relative to the U.S. dollar. A *weaker* dollar acts to reduce or eliminate whatever cost advantage foreign manufacturers may have had over U.S. manufacturers (and helps protect the manufacturing jobs of U.S. workers).

- A *weaker* dollar makes foreign-made goods more expensive in dollar terms to U.S. consumers—this curtails U.S. buyer demand for foreign-made goods, stimulates greater demand on the part of U.S. consumers for U.S.-made goods, and reduces U.S. imports of foreign-made goods.

- A *weaker* U.S. dollar enables the U.S.-made goods to be sold at lower prices to consumers in countries whose currencies have grown stronger relative to the U.S. dollar—such lower prices boost foreign buyer demand for the now relatively cheaper U.S.-made goods, thereby stimulating exports of U.S.-made goods to foreign countries and creating more jobs in U.S.-based manufacturing plants.

- A *weaker* dollar has the effect of increasing the dollar value of profits a company earns in foreign-country markets where the local currency is stronger relative to the dollar. For example, if a U.S.-based manufacturer earns a profit of €10 million on its sales in Europe, those €10 million convert to a larger number of dollars when the dollar grows weaker against the euro.

A weaker U.S. dollar is therefore an economically favorable exchange rate shift for manufacturing plants based in the United States. A decline in the value of the U.S. dollar strengthens the cost-competitiveness of U.S.-based manufacturing plants and boosts buyer demand for U.S.-made goods. When the value of the U.S. dollar is expected to remain weak for some time to come, foreign companies have an incentive to build manufacturing facilities in the United States to make goods for U.S. consumers rather than export the same goods to the United States from foreign plants where production costs in dollar terms have been driven up by the decline in the value of the dollar. Conversely, a *stronger* U.S. dollar is an *unfavorable exchange rate shift* for U.S.-based manufacturing plants because it makes such plants less cost-competitive with foreign plants and weakens foreign demand for U.S.-made goods. A strong dollar also weakens the incentive of foreign companies to locate manufacturing facilities in the United States to make goods for U.S. consumers. The same reasoning applies to companies that have plants in countries in the European Union where euros are the local currency. A weak euro versus other currencies enhances the cost-competitiveness of companies manufacturing goods in Europe vis-à-vis foreign rivals with plants in countries whose currencies have grown stronger relative to the euro; a strong euro versus other currencies weakens the cost-competitiveness of companies with plants in the European Union.

> Fluctuating exchange rates pose significant economic risks to a company's competitiveness in foreign markets. Exporters are disadvantaged when the currency of the country where goods are being manufactured grows stronger relative to the currency of the importing country.

> Domestic companies facing competitive pressure from lower-cost imports benefit when their government's currency grows *weaker* in relation to the currencies of the countries where the lower-cost imports are being made.

Cross-Country Differences in Demographic, Cultural, and Market Conditions

Buyer tastes for a particular product or service sometimes differ substantially from country to country. In France, consumers prefer top-loading washing machines, whereas in most other European countries consumers prefer front-loading machines. People in Hong Kong prefer compact appliances, but in Taiwan large appliances are more popular. Novelty ice cream flavors like eel, shark fin, and dried shrimp have more appeal to East Asian customers than they have for customers in the United States and in Europe. Sometimes, product designs suitable in one country are inappropriate in another because of differing local standards—for example, in the United States electrical devices run on 110-volt electric systems, but in some European countries the standard is a 240-volt electric system, necessitating the use of different electrical designs and components. Cultural influences can also affect consumer demand for a product. For instance, in South Korea many parents are reluctant to purchase PCs even when they can afford them because of concerns that their children will be distracted from their schoolwork by surfing the Web, playing PC-based video games, and becoming Internet "addicts."[6]

Consequently, companies operating in an international marketplace have to wrestle with *whether and how much to customize their offerings in each country market to match local buyers' tastes and preferences or whether to pursue a strategy of offering a mostly standardized product worldwide.* While making products that are closely matched to local tastes makes them more appealing to local buyers, customizing a company's products country by country may raise production and distribution costs due to the greater variety of designs and components, shorter production runs, and the complications of added inventory handling and distribution logistics. Greater standardization of a global company's product offering, on the other hand, can lead to scale economies and learning-curve effects, thus reducing per-unit production costs and contributing to the achievement of a low-cost advantage. *The tension between the market pressures to localize a company's product offerings country by country and the competitive pressures to lower costs is one of the big strategic issues that participants in foreign markets have to resolve.*

STRATEGIC OPTIONS FOR ENTERING INTERNATIONAL MARKETS

LO 3

The five major strategic options for entering foreign markets.

Once a company decides to expand beyond its domestic borders, it must consider the question of how to enter foreign markets. There are five primary strategic options for doing so:

1. Maintain a home-country production base and *export* goods to foreign markets.
2. *License* foreign firms to produce and distribute the company's products abroad.
3. Employ a *franchising* strategy in foreign markets.
4. Establish a *subsidiary* in a foreign market via acquisition or internal development.
5. Rely on *strategic alliances* or joint ventures with foreign companies.

Which option to employ depends on a variety of factors, including the nature of the firm's strategic objectives, the firm's position in terms of whether it has the full range of resources and capabilities needed to operate abroad, country-specific factors such as trade barriers, and the transaction costs involved (the costs of contracting with a partner and monitoring its compliance with the terms of the contract, for example). The options vary considerably regarding the level of investment required and the associated risks—but higher levels of investment and risk generally provide the firm with the benefits of greater ownership and control.

Export Strategies

Using domestic plants as a production base for exporting goods to foreign markets is an excellent initial strategy for pursuing international sales. It is a conservative way to test the international waters. The amount of capital needed to begin exporting is often minimal; existing production capacity may well be sufficient to make goods for export. With an export-based entry strategy, a manufacturer can limit its involvement in foreign markets by contracting with foreign wholesalers experienced in importing to handle the entire distribution and marketing function in their countries or regions of the world. If it is more advantageous to maintain control over these functions, however, a manufacturer can establish its own distribution and sales organizations in some or all of the target foreign markets. Either way, a home-based production and export strategy helps the firm minimize its direct investments in foreign countries. Such strategies are commonly favored by Chinese, Korean, and Italian companies—products are designed and manufactured at home and then distributed through local channels in the importing countries. The primary functions performed abroad relate chiefly to establishing a network of distributors and perhaps conducting sales promotion and brand-awareness activities.

Whether an export strategy can be pursued successfully over the long run depends on the relative cost-competitiveness of the home-country production base. In some industries, firms gain additional scale economies and learning-curve benefits from centralizing production in plants whose output capability exceeds demand in any one country market; exporting enables a firm to capture such economies. However, an export strategy is vulnerable when (1) manufacturing costs in the home country are substantially higher than in foreign countries where rivals have plants, (2) the costs of shipping the product to distant foreign markets are relatively high, (3) adverse shifts occur in currency exchange rates, and (4) importing countries impose tariffs or erect other trade barriers. Unless an exporter can keep its production and shipping costs competitive with rivals' costs, secure adequate local distribution and marketing support of its products, and effectively hedge against unfavorable changes in currency exchange rates, its success will be limited.

Licensing Strategies

Licensing as an entry strategy makes sense when a firm with valuable technical know-how, an appealing brand, or a unique patented product has neither the internal organizational capability nor the resources to enter foreign markets. Licensing also has the advantage of avoiding the risks of committing resources to country markets that are unfamiliar, politically volatile, economically unstable, or otherwise risky. By licensing the technology, trademark, or production rights to foreign-based firms, a company can generate income from royalties while shifting the costs and risks of entering foreign markets to the licensee. The big disadvantage of licensing is the risk of providing valuable technological know-how to foreign companies and thereby losing some degree of control over its use; monitoring licensees and safeguarding the company's proprietary know-how can prove quite difficult in some circumstances. But if the royalty potential is considerable and the companies to which the licenses are being granted are trustworthy and reputable, then licensing can be a very attractive option. Many software and pharmaceutical companies use licensing strategies to participate in foreign markets.

Franchising Strategies

While licensing works well for manufacturers and owners of proprietary technology, franchising is often better suited to the international expansion efforts of service and retailing enterprises. McDonald's, Yum! Brands (the parent of Pizza Hut, KFC, Taco Bell, and WingStreet), the UPS Store, Roto-Rooter, 7-Eleven, and Hilton Hotels have all used franchising to build a presence in foreign markets. Franchising has many of the same advantages as licensing. The franchisee bears most of the costs and risks of establishing foreign locations; a franchisor has to expend only the resources to recruit, train, support, and monitor franchisees. The problem a franchisor faces is maintaining quality control; foreign franchisees do not always exhibit strong commitment to consistency and standardization, especially when the local culture does not stress the same kinds of quality concerns. A question that can arise is whether to allow foreign franchisees to make modifications in the franchisor's product offering so as to better satisfy the tastes and expectations of local buyers. Should McDonald's give franchisees in each nation some leeway in what products they put on their menus?

Should franchised KFC units in China be permitted to substitute spices that appeal to Chinese consumers? Or should the same menu offerings be rigorously and unvaryingly required of all franchisees worldwide?

CORE CONCEPT

A **greenfield venture** (or internal startup) is a subsidiary business that is established by setting up the entire operation from the ground up.

Foreign Subsidiary Strategies

Very often companies electing to compete internationally or globally prefer to have direct control over all aspects of operating in a foreign market. Companies that want to direct performance of all essential value chain activities typically establish a wholly owned subsidiary, either by acquiring a local company or by establishing its own new operating organization from the ground up. A subsidiary business that is established internally from scratch is called an *internal startup* or a **greenfield venture.**

Acquiring a local business is the quicker of the two options; it may be the least risky and most cost-efficient means of hurdling such entry barriers as gaining access to local distribution channels, building supplier relationships, and establishing working relationships with government officials and other key constituencies. Buying an ongoing operation allows the acquirer to move directly to the task of transferring resources and personnel to the newly acquired business, redirecting and integrating the activities of the acquired business into its own operation, putting its own strategy into place, and accelerating efforts to build a strong market position.

One thing an acquisition-minded firm must consider is whether to pay a premium price for a successful local company or to buy a struggling competitor at a bargain price. If the buying firm has little knowledge of the local market but ample capital, it is often better off purchasing a capable, strongly positioned firm. However, when the acquirer sees promising ways to transform a weak firm into a strong one and has the resources and managerial know-how to do so, a struggling company can be the better long-term investment.

Entering a new foreign country via a greenfield venture makes sense when a company already operates in a number of countries, has experience in establishing new subsidiaries and overseeing their operations, and has a sufficiently large pool of resources and capabilities to rapidly equip a new subsidiary with the personnel and competencies it needs to compete successfully and profitably. Four other conditions make a greenfield venture strategy appealing:

- When creating an internal startup is cheaper than making an acquisition.
- When adding new production capacity will not adversely impact the supply–demand balance in the local market.
- When a startup subsidiary has the ability to gain good distribution access (perhaps because of the company's recognized brand name).
- When a startup subsidiary will have the size, cost structure, and capabilities to compete head-to-head against local rivals.

Greenfield ventures in foreign markets can also pose problems, just as other entry strategies do. They represent a costly capital investment, subject to a high level of risk. They require numerous other company resources as well, diverting them from other uses. They do not work well in countries without strong, well-functioning markets and institutions that protect the rights of foreign investors and provide other legal protections. Moreover, an important disadvantage of greenfield ventures relative to other means of international expansion is that they are the slowest entry route—particularly if the objective is to achieve a sizable market share. On the other hand, successful greenfield ventures may offer higher returns to compensate for their high risk and slower path.

Alliance and Joint Venture Strategies

Strategic alliances, joint ventures, and other cooperative agreements with foreign companies are a widely used means of entering foreign markets.[7] A company can benefit immensely from a foreign partner's familiarity with local government regulations, its knowledge of the buying habits and product preferences of consumers, its distribution-channel relationships, and so on.[8] Both Japanese and American companies are actively forming alliances with European companies to better compete in the 27-nation European Union (and the five countries that are candidates to become EU members). Many U.S. and European companies are allying with Asian companies in their efforts to enter markets in China, India, Thailand, Indonesia, and other Asian countries.

Another reason for cross-border alliances is to capture economies of scale in production and/or marketing. By joining forces in producing components, assembling models, and marketing their products, companies can realize cost savings not achievable with their own small volumes. A third reason to employ a collaborative strategy is to share distribution facilities and dealer networks, thus mutually strengthening each partner's access to buyers. A fourth benefit of a collaborative strategy is the learning and added expertise that comes from performing joint research, sharing technological know-how, studying one another's manufacturing methods, and understanding how to tailor sales and marketing approaches to fit local cultures and traditions. A fifth benefit is that cross-border allies can direct their competitive energies more toward mutual rivals and less toward one another; teaming up may help them close the gap on leading companies. And, finally, alliances can be a particularly useful way for companies across the world to gain agreement on important technical standards—they have been used to arrive at standards for assorted PC devices, Internet-related technologies, high-definition televisions, and mobile phones.

Cross-border alliances are an attractive means of gaining the aforementioned types of benefits (as compared to merging with or acquiring foreign-based companies) because they allow a company to preserve its independence (which is not the case with a merger) and avoid using scarce financial resources to fund acquisitions. Furthermore, an alliance offers the flexibility to readily disengage once its purpose has been served or if the benefits prove elusive, whereas mergers and acquisitions are more permanent arrangements.[9]

Alliances may also be used to pave the way for an intended merger; they offer a way to test the value and viability of a cooperative arrangement with a foreign partner before making a more permanent commitment. Illustration Capsule 7.1 shows how Walgreens pursued this strategy with Alliance Boots in order to facilitate its expansion abroad.

The Risks of Strategic Alliances with Foreign Partners   Alliances and joint ventures with foreign partners have their pitfalls, however. Sometimes a local partner's knowledge and expertise turns out to be less valuable than expected (because its knowledge is rendered obsolete by fast-changing market conditions or because its operating practices are archaic). Cross-border allies typically must overcome language and cultural barriers and figure out how to deal with diverse (or conflicting) operating practices. The transaction costs of working out a mutually agreeable

Collaborative strategies involving alliances or joint ventures with foreign partners are a popular way for companies to edge their way into the markets of foreign countries.

Cross-border alliances enable a growth-minded company to widen its geographic coverage and strengthen its competitiveness in foreign markets; at the same time, they offer flexibility and allow a company to retain some degree of autonomy and operating control.

ILLUSTRATION CAPSULE 7.1

Walgreens Boots Alliance, Inc.: Entering Foreign Markets via Alliance Followed by Merger

Walgreens pharmacy began in 1901 as a single store on the South Side of Chicago, and grew to become the largest chain of pharmacy retailers in America. Walgreens was an early pioneer of the "self-service" pharmacy and found success by moving quickly to build a vast domestic network of stores after the Second World War. This growth-focused strategy served Walgreens well up until the beginning of the 21st century, by which time it had nearly saturated the U.S. market. By 2014, 75 percent of Americans lived within five miles of a Walgreens. The company was also facing threats to its core business model. Walgreens relies heavily on pharmacy sales, which generally are paid for by someone other than the patient, usually the government or an insurance company. As the government and insurers started to make a more sustained effort to cut costs, Walgreens's core profit center was at risk. To mitigate these threats, Walgreens looked to enter foreign markets.

Walgreens found an ideal international partner in Alliance Boots. Based in the UK, Alliance Boots had a global footprint with 3,300 stores across 10 countries. A partnership with Alliance Boots had several strategic advantages, allowing Walgreens to gain swift entry into foreign markets as well as complementary assets and expertise. First, it gave Walgreens access to new markets beyond the saturated United States for its retail pharmacies. Second, it provided Walgreens with a new revenue stream in wholesale drugs. Alliance Boots held a vast European distribution network for wholesale drug sales; Walgreens could leverage that network and expertise to build a similar model in the United States. Finally, a merger with Alliance Boots would strengthen Walgreens's existing business by increasing the company's market position and therefore bargaining power

© Michael Nagle/Bloomberg via Getty Images

with drug companies. In light of these advantages, Walgreens moved quickly to partner with and later acquire Alliance Boots and merged both companies in 2014 to become Walgreens Boots Alliance. Walgreens Boots Alliance, Inc. is now one of the world's largest drug purchasers, able to negotiate from a strong position with drug companies and other suppliers to realize economies of scale in its current businesses.

The market has thus far responded favorably to the merger. Walgreens Boots Alliance's stock has more than doubled in value since the first news of the partnership in 2012. However, the company is still struggling to integrate and faces new risks such as currency fluctuation in its new combined position. Yet as the pharmaceutical industry continues to consolidate, Walgreens is in an undoubtedly stronger position to continue to grow in the future thanks to its strategic international acquisition.

Note: Developed with Katherine Coster.

Sources: Company 10-K Form, 2015, investor.walgreensbootsalliance.com/secfiling.cfm?filingID=1140361-15-38791&CIK=1618921; L. Capron and W. Mitchell, "When to Change a Winning Strategy," *Harvard Business Review,* July 25, 2012, hbr.org/2012/07/when-to-change-a-winning-strat; T. Martin and R. Dezember, "Walgreen Spends $6.7 Billion on Alliance Boots Stake," *The Wall Street Journal,* June 20, 2012.

arrangement and monitoring partner compliance with the terms of the arrangement can be high. The communication, trust building, and coordination costs are not trivial in terms of management time.[10] Often, partners soon discover they have conflicting objectives and strategies, deep differences of opinion about how to proceed, or important differences in corporate values and ethical standards. Tensions build, working relationships cool, and the hoped-for benefits never materialize.[11] It is not unusual for there to be little personal chemistry among some of the key people on whom the success or failure of the alliance depends—the rapport such personnel need to work well together may never emerge. And even if allies are able to develop productive personal relationships, they can still have trouble reaching mutually agreeable ways to deal with key issues or launching new initiatives fast enough to stay abreast of rapid advances in technology or shifting market conditions.

One worrisome problem with alliances or joint ventures is that a firm may risk losing some of its competitive advantage if an alliance partner is given full access to its proprietary technological expertise or other competitively valuable capabilities. There is a natural tendency for allies to struggle to collaborate effectively in competitively sensitive areas, thus spawning suspicions on both sides about forthright exchanges of information and expertise. It requires many meetings of many people working in good faith over a period of time to iron out what is to be shared, what is to remain proprietary, and how the cooperative arrangements will work.

Even if the alliance proves to be a win–win proposition for both parties, there is the danger of becoming overly dependent on foreign partners for essential expertise and competitive capabilities. Companies aiming for global market leadership need to develop their own resource capabilities in order to be masters of their destiny. Frequently, experienced international companies operating in 50 or more countries across the world find less need for entering into cross-border alliances than do companies in the early stages of globalizing their operations.[12] Companies with global operations make it a point to develop senior managers who understand how "the system" works in different countries, plus they can avail themselves of local managerial talent and know-how by simply hiring experienced local managers and thereby detouring the hazards of collaborative alliances with local companies. One of the lessons about cross-border partnerships is that they are more effective in helping a company establish a beachhead of new opportunity in world markets than they are in enabling a company to achieve and sustain global market leadership.

INTERNATIONAL STRATEGY: THE THREE MAIN APPROACHES

Broadly speaking, a firm's **international strategy** is simply its strategy for competing in two or more countries simultaneously. Typically, a company will start to compete internationally by entering one or perhaps a select few foreign markets—selling its products or services in countries where there is a ready market for them. But as it expands further internationally, it will have to confront head-on two conflicting pressures: the demand for responsiveness to local needs versus the prospect of efficiency gains from offering a standardized product globally. Deciding on the degree to vary its competitive approach to fit the specific market conditions and buyer preferences in each host country is perhaps the foremost strategic issue that must be addressed when a company is operating in two or more foreign markets.[13] Figure 7.2 shows a company's three options for resolving this issue: choosing a *multidomestic, global,* or *transnational* strategy.

LO 4

The three main strategic approaches for competing internationally.

CORE CONCEPT

An **international strategy** is a strategy for competing in two or more countries simultaneously.

FIGURE 7.2   Three Approaches for Competing Internationally

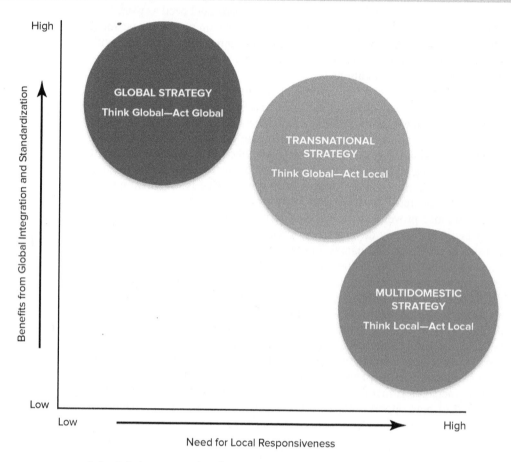

Multidomestic Strategies—a "Think-Local, Act-Local" Approach

CORE CONCEPT

A **multidomestic strategy** is one in which a company varies its product offering and competitive approach from country to country in an effort to be responsive to differing buyer preferences and market conditions. It is a **think-local, act-local** type of international strategy, facilitated by decision making decentralized to the local level.

A **multidomestic strategy** is one in which a company varies its product offering and competitive approach from country to country in an effort to meet differing buyer needs and to address divergent local-market conditions. It involves having plants produce different product versions for different local markets and adapting marketing and distribution to fit local customs, cultures, regulations, and market requirements. Castrol, a specialist in oil lubricants, produces over 3,000 different formulas of lubricants to meet the requirements of different climates, vehicle types and uses, and equipment applications that characterize different country markets. In the food products industry, it is common for companies to vary the ingredients in their products and sell the localized versions under local brand names to cater to country-specific tastes and eating preferences. Government requirements for gasoline additives that help reduce carbon monoxide, smog, and other emissions are almost never the same from country to country. BP utilizes localized strategies in its gasoline and service station business segment because of these cross-country formulation differences and because of customer familiarity with local brand names. For example, the company markets gasoline in the United States under its BP and Arco brands, but markets gasoline in Germany, Belgium, Poland, Hungary, and the Czech Republic under the Aral brand.

In essence, a multidomestic strategy represents a **think-local, act-local** approach to international strategy. A think-local, act-local approach to strategy making is most appropriate when the need for local responsiveness is high due to significant cross-country differences in demographic, cultural, and market conditions and when the potential for efficiency gains from standardization is limited, as depicted in Figure 7.2. A think-local, act-local approach is possible only when decision making is decentralized, giving local managers considerable latitude for crafting and executing strategies for the country markets they are responsible for. Giving local managers decision-making authority allows them to address specific market needs and respond swiftly to local changes in demand. It also enables them to focus their competitive efforts, stake out attractive market positions vis-à-vis local competitors, react to rivals' moves in a timely fashion, and target new opportunities as they emerge.[14]

Despite their obvious benefits, think-local, act-local strategies have three big drawbacks:

1. They hinder transfer of a company's capabilities, knowledge, and other resources across country boundaries, since the company's efforts are not integrated or coordinated across country boundaries. This can make the company less innovative overall.

2. They raise production and distribution costs due to the greater variety of designs and components, shorter production runs for each product version, and complications of added inventory handling and distribution logistics.

3. They are not conducive to building a single, worldwide competitive advantage. When a company's competitive approach and product offering vary from country to country, the nature and size of any resulting competitive edge also tends to vary. At the most, multidomestic strategies are capable of producing a group of local competitive advantages of varying types and degrees of strength.

Global Strategies—a "Think-Global, Act-Global" Approach

A **global strategy** contrasts sharply with a multidomestic strategy in that it takes a standardized, globally integrated approach to producing, packaging, selling, and delivering the company's products and services worldwide. Companies employing a global strategy sell the same products under the same brand names everywhere, utilize much the same distribution channels in all countries, and compete on the basis of the same capabilities and marketing approaches worldwide. Although the company's strategy or product offering may be adapted in minor ways to accommodate specific situations in a few host countries, the company's fundamental competitive approach (low cost, differentiation, best cost, or focused) remains very much intact worldwide and local managers stick close to the global strategy.

A **think-global, act-global** approach prompts company managers to integrate and coordinate the company's strategic moves worldwide and to expand into most, if not all, nations where there is significant buyer demand. It puts considerable strategic emphasis on building a *global* brand name and aggressively pursuing opportunities to transfer ideas, new products, and capabilities from one country to another. Global strategies are characterized by relatively centralized value chain activities, such as production and distribution. While there may be more than one manufacturing plant and distribution center to minimize transportation costs, for example, they tend to be few in number. Achieving the efficiency potential of a global strategy requires that resources and best practices be shared, value chain

CORE CONCEPT

A **global strategy** is one in which a company employs the same basic competitive approach in all countries where it operates, sells standardized products globally, strives to build global brands, and coordinates its actions worldwide with strong headquarters control. It represents a **think-global, act-global** approach.

activities be integrated, and capabilities be transferred from one location to another as they are developed. These objectives are best facilitated through centralized decision making and strong headquarters control.

Because a global strategy cannot accommodate varying local needs, it is an appropriate strategic choice when there are pronounced efficiency benefits from standardization and when buyer needs are relatively homogeneous across countries and regions. A globally standardized and integrated approach is especially beneficial when high volumes significantly lower costs due to economies of scale or added experience (moving the company further down a learning curve). It can also be advantageous if it allows the firm to replicate a successful business model on a global basis efficiently or engage in higher levels of R&D by spreading the fixed costs and risks over a higher-volume output. It is a fitting response to industry conditions marked by global competition.

Ford's global design strategy is a move toward a think-global, act-global strategy, involving the development and production of standardized models with country-specific modifications limited to what is required to meet local country emission and safety standards. The 2010 Ford Fiesta and 2011 Ford Focus were the company's first global design models to be marketed in Europe, North America, Asia, and Australia. Whenever country-to-country differences are small enough to be accommodated within the framework of a global strategy, a global strategy is preferable because a company can more readily unify its operations and focus on establishing a brand image and reputation that are uniform from country to country. Moreover, with a global strategy a company is better able to focus its full resources on securing a sustainable low-cost or differentiation-based competitive advantage over both domestic rivals and global rivals.

There are, however, several drawbacks to global strategies: (1) They do not enable firms to address local needs as precisely as locally based rivals can; (2) they are less responsive to changes in local market conditions, in the form of either new opportunities or competitive threats; (3) they raise transportation costs and may involve higher tariffs; and (4) they involve higher coordination costs due to the more complex task of managing a globally integrated enterprise.

Transnational Strategies—a "Think-Global, Act-Local" Approach

A **transnational strategy** (sometimes called *glocalization*) incorporates elements of both a globalized and a localized approach to strategy making. This type of middle-ground strategy is called for when there are relatively high needs for local responsiveness as well as appreciable benefits to be realized from standardization, as Figure 7.2 suggests. A transnational strategy encourages a company to use a **think-global, act-local** approach to balance these competing objectives.

Often, companies implement a transnational strategy with mass-customization techniques that enable them to address local preferences in an efficient, semi-standardized manner. McDonald's, KFC, and Starbucks have discovered ways to customize their menu offerings in various countries without compromising costs, product quality, and operating effectiveness. Unilever is responsive to local market needs regarding its consumer products, while realizing global economies of scale in certain functions. Otis Elevator found that a transnational strategy delivers better results than a global strategy when it is competing in countries like China, where local needs are highly differentiated. By switching from its customary single-brand approach to a multi-brand strategy aimed at serving different segments of the market, Otis was able to double its market share in China and increased its revenues sixfold over a nine-year period.[15]

As a rule, most companies that operate internationally endeavor to employ as global a strategy as customer needs and market conditions permit. Electronic Arts (EA) has two major design studios—one in Vancouver, British Columbia, and one in Los Angeles—and smaller design studios in locations including San Francisco, Orlando, London, and Tokyo. This dispersion of design studios helps EA design games that are specific to different cultures—for example, the London studio took the lead in designing the popular FIFA Soccer game to suit European tastes and to replicate the stadiums, signage, and team rosters; the U.S. studio took the lead in designing games involving NFL football, NBA basketball, and NASCAR racing.

A transnational strategy is far more conducive than other strategies to transferring and leveraging subsidiary skills and capabilities. But, like other approaches to competing internationally, transnational strategies also have significant drawbacks:

1. They are the most difficult of all international strategies to implement due to the added complexity of varying the elements of the strategy to situational conditions.

2. They place large demands on the organization due to the need to pursue conflicting objectives simultaneously.

3. Implementing the strategy is likely to be a costly and time-consuming enterprise, with an uncertain outcome.

Illustration Capsule 7.2 explains how Four Seasons Hotels has been able to compete successfully on the basis of a transnational strategy.

Table 7.1 provides a summary of the pluses and minuses of the three approaches to competing internationally.

TABLE 7.1 Advantages and Disadvantages of Multidomestic, Global, and Transnational Strategies

	Advantages	Disadvantages
Multidomestic (think local, act local)	• Can meet the specific needs of each market more precisely • Can respond more swiftly to localized changes in demand • Can target reactions to the moves of local rivals • Can respond more quickly to local opportunities and threats	• Hinders resource and capability sharing or cross-market transfers • Has higher production and distribution costs • Is not conducive to a worldwide competitive advantage
Global (think global, act global)	• Has lower costs due to scale and scope economies • Can lead to greater efficiencies due to the ability to transfer best practices across markets • Increases innovation from knowledge sharing and capability transfer • Offers the benefit of a global brand and reputation	• Cannot address local needs precisely • Is less responsive to changes in local market conditions • Involves higher transportation costs and tariffs • Has higher coordination and integration costs
Transnational (think global, act local)	• Offers the benefits of both local responsiveness and global integration • Enables the transfer and sharing of resources and capabilities across borders • Provides the benefits of flexible coordination	• Is more complex and harder to implement • Entails conflicting goals, which may be difficult to reconcile and require trade-offs • Involves more costly and time-consuming implementation

Four Seasons Hotels: Local Character, Global Service

© Stephen Hilger/Bloomberg via Getty Images

Four Seasons Hotels is a Toronto, Canada-based manager of luxury hotel properties. With 98 properties located in many of the world's most popular tourist destinations and business centers, Four Seasons commands a following of many of the world's most discerning travelers. In contrast to its key competitor, Ritz-Carlton, which strives to create one uniform experience globally, Four Seasons Hotels has gained market share by deftly combining local architectural and cultural experiences with globally consistent luxury service.

When moving into a new market, Four Seasons always seeks out a local capital partner. The understanding of local custom and business relationships this financier brings is critical to the process of developing a new Four Seasons hotel. Four Seasons also insists on hiring a local architect and design consultant for each property, as opposed to using architects or designers

it's worked with in other locations. While this can be a challenge, particularly in emerging markets, Four Seasons has found it is worth it in the long run to have a truly local team.

The specific layout and programming of each hotel is also unique. For instance, when Four Seasons opened its hotel in Mumbai, India, it prioritized space for large banquet halls to target the Indian wedding market. In India, weddings often draw guests numbering in the thousands. When moving into the Middle East, Four Seasons designed its hotels with separate prayer rooms for men and women. In Bali, where destination weddings are common, the hotel employs a "weather shaman" who, for some guests, provides reassurance that the weather will cooperate for their special day. In all cases, the objective is to provide a truly local experience.

When staffing its hotels, Four Seasons seeks to strike a fine balance between employing locals who have an innate understanding of the local culture alongside expatriate staff or "culture carriers" who understand the DNA of Four Seasons. It also uses global systems to track customer preferences and employs globally consistent service standards. Four Seasons claims that its guests experience the same high level of service globally but that no two experiences are the same.

While it is much more expensive and time-consuming to design unique architectural and programming experiences, doing so is a strategic trade-off Four Seasons has made to achieve the local experience demanded by its high-level clientele. Likewise, it has recognized that maintaining globally consistent operation processes and service standards is important too. Four Seasons has struck the right balance between thinking globally and acting locally—the marker of a truly transnational strategy. As a result, the company has been rewarded with an international reputation for superior service and a leading market share in the luxury hospitality segment.

Note: Developed with Brian R. McKenzie.

Sources: Four Seasons annual report and corporate website; interview with Scott Woroch, executive vice president of development, Four Seasons Hotels, February 22, 2014.

INTERNATIONAL OPERATIONS AND THE QUEST FOR COMPETITIVE ADVANTAGE

There are three important ways in which a firm can gain competitive advantage (or offset domestic disadvantages) by expanding outside its domestic market. First, it can use location to lower costs or achieve greater product differentiation. Second, it can transfer competitively valuable resources and capabilities from one country to another or share them across international borders to extend its competitive advantages. And third, it can benefit from cross-border coordination opportunities that are not open to domestic-only competitors.

LO 5

How companies are able to use international operations to improve overall competitiveness.

Using Location to Build Competitive Advantage

To use location to build competitive advantage, a company must consider two issues: (1) whether to concentrate each activity it performs in a few select countries or to disperse performance of the activity to many nations, and (2) in which countries to locate particular activities.

Companies that compete internationally can pursue competitive advantage in world markets by locating their value chain activities in whatever nations prove most advantageous.

When to Concentrate Activities in a Few Locations   It is advantageous for a company to concentrate its activities in a limited number of locations when:

- *The costs of manufacturing or other activities are significantly lower in some geographic locations than in others.* For example, much of the world's athletic footwear is manufactured in Asia (China and Korea) because of low labor costs; much of the production of circuit boards for PCs is located in Taiwan because of both low costs and the high-caliber technical skills of the Taiwanese labor force.

- *Significant scale economies exist in production or distribution.* The presence of significant economies of scale in components production or final assembly means that a company can gain major cost savings from operating a few super-efficient plants as opposed to a host of small plants scattered across the world. Makers of digital cameras and LED TVs located in Japan, South Korea, and Taiwan have used their scale economies to establish a low-cost advantage in this way. Achieving low-cost provider status often requires a company to have the largest worldwide manufacturing share (as distinct from brand share or market share), with production centralized in one or a few giant plants. Some companies even use such plants to manufacture units sold under the brand names of rivals to further boost production-related scale economies. Likewise, a company may be able to reduce its distribution costs by establishing large-scale distribution centers to serve major geographic regions of the world market (e.g., North America, Latin America, Europe and the Middle East, and the Asia-Pacific region).

- *Sizable learning and experience benefits are associated with performing an activity.* In some industries, learning-curve effects can allow a manufacturer to lower unit costs, boost quality, or master a new technology *more quickly* by concentrating production in a few locations. The key to riding down the learning curve is to concentrate production in a few locations to increase the cumulative volume at a plant (and thus the experience of the plant's workforce) as rapidly as possible.

- *Certain locations have superior resources, allow better coordination of related activities, or offer other valuable advantages.* Companies often locate a research unit or a sophisticated production facility in a particular country to take advantage of its pool of technically trained personnel. Samsung became a leader in memory chip technology by establishing a major R&D facility in Silicon Valley and transferring the know-how it gained back to its operations in South Korea. Where just-in-time inventory practices yield big cost savings and/or where an assembly firm has long-term partnering arrangements with its key suppliers, parts manufacturing plants may be clustered around final-assembly plants. A customer service center or sales office may be opened in a particular country to help cultivate strong relationships with pivotal customers located nearby.

When to Disperse Activities across Many Locations   In some instances, dispersing activities across locations is more advantageous than concentrating them. Buyer-related activities—such as distribution, marketing, and after-sale service—usually must take place close to buyers. This makes it necessary to physically locate the capability to perform such activities in every country or region where a firm has major customers. For example, firms that make mining and oil-drilling equipment maintain operations in many locations around the world to support customers' needs for speedy equipment repair and technical assistance. Large public accounting firms have offices in numerous countries to serve the foreign operations of their international corporate clients. Dispersing activities to many locations is also competitively important when high transportation costs, diseconomies of large size, and trade barriers make it too expensive to operate from a central location. Many companies distribute their products from multiple locations to shorten delivery times to customers. In addition, dispersing activities helps hedge against the risks of fluctuating exchange rates, supply interruptions (due to strikes, natural disasters, or transportation delays), and adverse political developments. Such risks are usually greater when activities are concentrated in a single location.

Even though global firms have strong reason to disperse buyer-related activities to many international locations, such activities as materials procurement, parts manufacture, finished-goods assembly, technology research, and new product development can frequently be decoupled from buyer locations and performed wherever advantage lies. Components can be made in Mexico; technology research done in Frankfurt; new products developed and tested in Phoenix; and assembly plants located in Spain, Brazil, Taiwan, or South Carolina, for example. Capital can be raised wherever it is available on the best terms.

Sharing and Transferring Resources and Capabilities across Borders to Build Competitive Advantage

When a company has competitively valuable resources and capabilities, it may be able to leverage them further by expanding internationally. If its resources retain their value in foreign contexts, then entering new foreign markets can extend the company's resource-based competitive advantage over a broader domain. For example, companies like Hermes, Prada, and Gucci have utilized their powerful brand names to extend their differentiation-based competitive advantages into markets far beyond their home-country origins. In each of these cases, the luxury brand name represents a valuable competitive asset that can readily be *shared* by all of the company's international stores, enabling them to attract buyers and gain a higher degree of market penetration over a wider geographic area than would otherwise be possible.

Another way for a company to extend its competitive advantage internationally is to *transfer* technological know-how or other important resources and capabilities from its operations in one country to its operations in other countries. For instance, if a company discovers ways to assemble a product faster and more cost-effectively at one plant, then that know-how can be transferred to its assembly plants in other countries. Whirlpool, the leading global manufacturer of home appliances, with 70 manufacturing and technology research centers around the world, uses an online global information technology platform to quickly and effectively transfer key product innovations and improved production techniques both across national borders and across various appliance brands. Walmart is expanding its international operations with a strategy that involves transferring its considerable resource capabilities in distribution and discount retailing to its retail units in 28 foreign countries.

Cross-border sharing or transferring resources and capabilities provides a cost-effective way for a company to leverage its core competencies more fully and extend its competitive advantages into a wider array of geographic markets. The cost of sharing or transferring already developed resources and capabilities across country borders is low in comparison to the time and considerable expense it takes to create them. Moreover, deploying them abroad spreads the fixed development costs over a greater volume of unit sales, thus contributing to low unit costs and a potential cost-based competitive advantage in recently entered geographic markets. Even if the shared or transferred resources or capabilities have to be adapted to local-market conditions, this can usually be done at low additional cost.

Consider the case of Walt Disney's theme parks as an example. The success of the theme parks in the United States derives in part from core resources such as the Disney brand name and characters like Mickey Mouse that have universal appeal and worldwide recognition. These resources can be freely shared with new theme parks as Disney expands internationally. Disney can also replicate its theme parks in new countries cost-effectively since it has already borne the costs of developing its core resources, park attractions, basic park design, and operating capabilities. The cost of replicating its theme parks abroad should be relatively low, even if the parks need to be adapted to a variety of local country conditions. By expanding internationally, Disney is able to enhance its competitive advantage over local theme park rivals. It does so by leveraging the differentiation advantage conferred by resources such as the Disney name and the park attractions. And by moving into new foreign markets, it augments its competitive advantage worldwide through the efficiency gains that come from cross-border resource sharing and low-cost capability transfer and business model replication.

Sharing and transferring resources and capabilities across country borders may also contribute to the development of broader or deeper competencies and capabilities—helping a company achieve *dominating depth* in some competitively valuable area. For example, the reputation for quality that Honda established worldwide began in motorcycles but enabled the company to command a position in both automobiles and outdoor power equipment in multiple-country markets. A one-country customer base is often too small to support the resource buildup needed to achieve such depth; this is particularly true in a developing or protected market, where competitively powerful resources are not required. By deploying capabilities across a larger international domain, a company can gain the experience needed to upgrade them to a higher performance standard. And by facing a more challenging set of international competitors, a company may be spurred to develop a stronger set of competitive capabilities. Moreover, by entering international markets, firms may be able to augment their capability set by learning from international rivals, cooperative partners, or acquisition targets.

However, cross-border resource sharing and transfers of capabilities are not guaranteed recipes for competitive success. For example, whether a resource or capability can confer a competitive advantage abroad depends on the conditions of rivalry in each particular market. If the rivals in a foreign-country market have superior resources and capabilities, then an entering firm may find itself at a competitive disadvantage even if it has a resource-based advantage domestically and can transfer the resources at low cost. In addition, since lifestyles and buying habits differ internationally, resources and capabilities that are valuable in one country may not have value in another. Sometimes a popular or well-regarded brand in one country turns out to have little competitive clout against local brands in other countries.

To illustrate, Netherlands-based Royal Philips Electronics, with 2012 sales of about €25 billion in more than 60 countries, is a leading seller of electric shavers, lighting products, small appliances, televisions, DVD players, and health care products. It has proven competitive capabilities in a number of businesses and countries and has been consistently profitable on a global basis. But the company's Philips and Magnavox brand names and the resources it has invested in its North American organization have proved inadequate in changing its image as a provider of low-end TVs and DVD players, recruiting retailers that can effectively merchandise its Magnavox and Philips products, and exciting consumers with the quality and features of its products. It has lost money in North America every year since 1988.

Benefiting from Cross-Border Coordination

Companies that compete on an international basis have another source of competitive advantage relative to their purely domestic rivals: They are able to benefit from coordinating activities across different countries' domains.[16] For example, an international manufacturer can shift production from a plant in one country to a plant in another to take advantage of exchange rate fluctuations, to cope with components shortages, or to profit from changing wage rates or energy costs. Production schedules can be coordinated worldwide; shipments can be diverted from one distribution center to another if sales rise unexpectedly in one place and fall in another. By coordinating their activities, international companies may also be able to enhance their leverage with host-country governments or respond adaptively to changes in tariffs and quotas. Efficiencies can also be achieved by shifting workloads from where they are unusually heavy to locations where personnel are underutilized.

CROSS-BORDER STRATEGIC MOVES

While international competitors can employ any of the offensive and defensive moves discussed in Chapter 6, there are two types of strategic moves that are particularly suited for companies competing internationally. Both involve the use of "profit sanctuaries."

Profit sanctuaries are country markets (or geographic regions) in which a company derives substantial profits because of a strong or protected market position. In most cases, a company's biggest and most strategically crucial profit sanctuary is its home market, but international and global companies may also enjoy profit sanctuary status in other nations where they have a strong position based on some type of competitive advantage. Companies that compete globally are likely to have more profit sanctuaries than companies that compete in just a few country markets; a domestic-only competitor, of course, can have only one profit sanctuary. Nike, which markets its products in 190 countries, has two major profit sanctuaries: North America and Greater China (where it earned $13.7 billion and $3.1 billion, respectively, in revenues in 2015).

Using Profit Sanctuaries to Wage a Strategic Offensive

Profit sanctuaries are valuable competitive assets, providing the financial strength to support strategic offensives in selected country markets and fuel a company's race for world-market leadership. The added financial capability afforded by multiple profit sanctuaries gives an international competitor the financial strength to wage a market offensive against a domestic competitor whose only profit sanctuary is its home market. The international company has the flexibility of lowballing its prices or launching high-cost marketing campaigns in the domestic company's home market and grabbing market share at the domestic company's expense. Razor-thin margins or even losses in these markets can be subsidized with the healthy profits earned in its profit sanctuaries—a practice called **cross-market subsidization.** The international company can adjust the depth of its price cutting to move in and capture market share quickly, or it can shave prices slightly to make gradual market inroads (perhaps over a decade or more) so as not to threaten domestic firms precipitously and trigger protectionist government actions. If the domestic company retaliates with matching price cuts or increased marketing expenses, it thereby exposes its entire revenue stream and profit base to erosion; its profits can be squeezed substantially and its competitive strength sapped, even if it is the domestic market leader.

> **CORE CONCEPT**
>
> **Cross-market subsidization**—supporting competitive offensives in one market with resources and profits diverted from operations in another market—can be a powerful competitive weapon.

When taken to the extreme, cut-rate pricing attacks by international competitors may draw charges of unfair "dumping." A company is said to be *dumping* when it sells its goods in foreign markets at prices that are (1) well below the prices at which it normally sells them in its home market or (2) well below its full costs per unit. Almost all governments can be expected to retaliate against perceived dumping practices by imposing special tariffs on goods being imported from the countries of the guilty companies. Indeed, as the trade among nations has mushroomed over the past 10 years, most governments have joined the World Trade Organization (WTO), which promotes fair trade practices among nations and actively polices dumping. Companies deemed guilty of dumping frequently come under pressure from their own government to cease and desist, especially if the tariffs adversely affect innocent companies based in the same country or if the advent of special tariffs raises the specter of an international trade war.

Using Profit Sanctuaries to Defend against International Rivals

Cross-border tactics involving profit sanctuaries can also be used as a means of defending against the strategic moves of rivals with multiple profit sanctuaries of their own. If a company finds itself under competitive attack by an international rival in one country market, one way to respond is to conduct a counterattack against the rival in one of its key markets in a different country—preferably where the rival is least protected and has the most to lose. This is a possible option when rivals compete against one another in much the same markets around the world.

For companies with at least one profit sanctuary, having a presence in a rival's key markets can be enough to deter the rival from making aggressive attacks. The reason for this is that the combination of market presence in the rival's key markets and a profit sanctuary elsewhere can send a signal to the rival that the company could quickly ramp up production (funded by the profit sanctuary) to mount a competitive counterattack if the rival attacks one of the company's key markets.

> **CORE CONCEPT**
>
> When the same companies compete against one another in multiple geographic markets, the threat of cross-border counterattacks may be enough to deter aggressive competitive moves and encourage **mutual restraint** among international rivals.

When international rivals compete against one another in multiple-country markets, this type of deterrence effect can restrain them from taking aggressive action against one another, due to the fear of a retaliatory response that might escalate the battle into a cross-border competitive war. **Mutual restraint** of this sort tends to stabilize the competitive position of multimarket rivals against one another. And while it may prevent each firm from making any major market share gains at the expense of its rival, it also protects against costly competitive battles that would be likely to erode the profitability of both companies without any compensating gain.

STRATEGIES FOR COMPETING IN THE MARKETS OF DEVELOPING COUNTRIES

LO 6

The unique characteristics of competing in developing-country markets.

Companies racing for global leadership have to consider competing in developing-economy markets like China, India, Brazil, Indonesia, Thailand, Poland, Mexico, and Russia—countries where the business risks are considerable but where the opportunities for growth are huge, especially as their economies develop and living standards climb toward levels in the industrialized world.[17] In today's world, a company that aspires to international market leadership (or to sustained rapid growth) cannot ignore the market opportunities or the base of technical and managerial talent such countries offer. For example, in 2015 China was the world's second-largest economy (behind the United States), based on purchasing power and its population of over 1.6 billion people. China's growth in demand for consumer goods has made it the fifth largest market for luxury goods, with sales greater than those in developed markets such as Germany, Spain, and the United Kingdom. Thus, no company that aspires to global market leadership can afford to ignore the strategic importance of establishing competitive market positions in the so-called BRIC countries (Brazil, Russia, India, and China), as well as in other parts of the Asia-Pacific region, Latin America, and eastern Europe.

Tailoring products to fit market conditions in developing countries, however, often involves more than making minor product changes and becoming more familiar with local cultures. McDonald's has had to offer vegetable burgers in parts of Asia and to rethink its prices, which are often high by local standards and affordable only by the well-to-do. Kellogg has struggled to introduce its cereals successfully because consumers in many less developed countries do not eat cereal for breakfast. Single-serving packages of detergents, shampoos, pickles, cough syrup, and cooking oils are very popular in India because they allow buyers to conserve cash by purchasing only what they need immediately. Thus, many companies find that trying to employ a strategy akin to that used in the markets of developed countries is hazardous.[18] Experimenting with some, perhaps many, local twists is usually necessary to find a strategy combination that works.

Strategy Options for Competing in Developing-Country Markets

There are several options for tailoring a company's strategy to fit the sometimes unusual or challenging circumstances presented in developing-country markets:

- *Prepare to compete on the basis of low price.* Consumers in developing markets are often highly focused on price, which can give low-cost local competitors the edge unless a company can find ways to attract buyers with bargain prices as well as better products. For example, in order to enter the market for laundry detergents in India, Unilever had to develop a low-cost detergent (named Wheel), construct new low-cost production facilities, package the detergent in single-use amounts so that it could be sold at a very low unit price, distribute the product to local merchants by handcarts, and craft an economical marketing campaign that included painted signs on buildings and demonstrations near stores. The new brand quickly captured $100 million in sales and by 2014 was the top detergent brand in India based dollar sales. Unilever replicated the strategy in India with low-priced packets of shampoos and deodorants and in South America with a detergent brand-named Ala.

- *Modify aspects of the company's business model to accommodate the unique local circumstances of developing countries.* For instance, Honeywell had sold industrial products and services for more than 100 years outside the United States and Europe using a foreign subsidiary model that focused international activities on sales only. When Honeywell entered China, it discovered that industrial customers in that country considered how many key jobs foreign companies created in China, in addition to the quality and price of the product or service when making purchasing decisions. Honeywell added about 150 engineers, strategists, and marketers in China to demonstrate its commitment to bolstering the Chinese economy. Honeywell replicated its "East for East" strategy when it entered the market for industrial products and services in India. Within 10 years of Honeywell establishing operations in China and three years of expanding into India, the two emerging markets accounted for 30 percent of the firm's worldwide growth.

- *Try to change the local market to better match the way the company does business elsewhere.* An international company often has enough market clout to drive major changes in the way a local country market operates. When Japan's Suzuki entered India, it triggered a quality revolution among Indian auto parts manufacturers. Local component suppliers teamed up with Suzuki's vendors in Japan and worked with Japanese experts to produce higher-quality products. Over the next two decades, Indian companies became proficient in making top-notch components for vehicles, won more prizes for quality than companies in any country other than Japan, and broke into the global market as suppliers to many automakers in Asia and other parts of the world. Mahindra and Mahindra, one of India's premier automobile manufacturers, has been recognized by a number of organizations for its product quality. Among its most noteworthy awards was its number-one ranking by J.D. Power Asia Pacific for new-vehicle overall quality.

- *Stay away from developing markets where it is impractical or uneconomical to modify the company's business model to accommodate local circumstances.* Home Depot's executive vice president and CFO, Carol Tomé, argues that there are few developing countries where Home Depot can operate successfully.[19] The company expanded successfully into Mexico, but it has avoided entry into other developing countries because its value proposition of good quality, low prices, and attentive customer service relies on (1) good highways and logistical systems to minimize store inventory costs, (2) employee stock ownership to help motivate store personnel to provide good customer service, and (3) high labor costs for housing construction and home repairs that encourage homeowners to engage in do-it-yourself projects. Relying on these factors in North American markets has worked spectacularly for Home Depot, but the company found that it could not count on these factors in China, from which it withdrew in 2012.

Company experiences in entering developing markets like Argentina, Vietnam, Malaysia, and Brazil indicate that profitability seldom comes quickly or easily. Building a market for the company's products can often turn into a long-term process that involves reeducation of consumers, sizable investments in advertising to alter tastes and buying habits, and upgrades of the local infrastructure

> Profitability in developing markets rarely comes quickly or easily—new entrants have to adapt their business models to local conditions, which may not always be possible.

(transportation systems, distribution channels, etc.). In such cases, a company must be patient, work within the system to improve the infrastructure, and lay the foundation for generating sizable revenues and profits once conditions are ripe for market takeoff.

DEFENDING AGAINST GLOBAL GIANTS: STRATEGIES FOR LOCAL COMPANIES IN DEVELOPING COUNTRIES

If opportunity-seeking, resource-rich international companies are looking to enter developing-country markets, what strategy options can local companies use to survive? As it turns out, the prospects for local companies facing global giants are by no means grim. Studies of local companies in developing markets have disclosed five strategies that have proved themselves in defending against globally competitive companies.[20]

1. *Develop business models that exploit shortcomings in local distribution networks or infrastructure.* In many instances, the extensive collection of resources possessed by the global giants is of little help in building a presence in developing markets. The lack of well-established local wholesaler and distributor networks, telecommunication systems, consumer banking, or media necessary for advertising makes it difficult for large internationals to migrate business models proved in developed markets to emerging markets. Emerging markets sometimes favor local companies whose managers are familiar with the local language and culture and are skilled in selecting large numbers of conscientious employees to carry out labor-intensive tasks. Shanda, a Chinese producer of massively multiplayer online role-playing games (MMORPGs), overcame China's lack of an established credit card network by selling prepaid access cards through local merchants. The company's focus on online games also protects it from shortcomings in China's software piracy laws. An India-based electronics company carved out a market niche for itself by developing an all-in-one business machine, designed especially for India's millions of small shopkeepers, that tolerates the country's frequent power outages.

2. *Utilize keen understanding of local customer needs and preferences to create customized products or services.* When developing-country markets are largely made up of customers with strong local needs, a good strategy option is to concentrate on customers who prefer a local touch and to accept the loss of the customers attracted to global brands.[21] A local company may be able to astutely exploit its local orientation—its familiarity with local preferences, its expertise in traditional products, its long-standing customer relationships. A small Middle Eastern cell phone manufacturer competes successfully against industry giants Samsung, Apple, Nokia, and Motorola by selling a model designed especially for Muslims— it is loaded with the Koran, alerts people at prayer times, and is equipped with a compass that points them toward Mecca. Shenzhen-based Tencent has become the leader in instant messaging in China through its unique understanding of Chinese behavior and culture.

3. *Take advantage of aspects of the local workforce with which large international companies may be unfamiliar.* Local companies that lack the technological capabilities of foreign entrants may be able to rely on their better understanding of the local labor force to offset any disadvantage. Focus Media is China's largest outdoor advertising firm and has relied on low-cost labor to update its more than 170,000 LCD displays and billboards in over 90 cities in a low-tech manner, while

international companies operating in China use electronically networked screens that allow messages to be changed remotely. Focus uses an army of employees who ride to each display by bicycle to change advertisements with programming contained on a USB flash drive or DVD. Indian information technology firms such as Infosys Technologies and Satyam Computer Services have been able to keep their personnel costs lower than those of international competitors EDS and Accenture because of their familiarity with local labor markets. While the large internationals have focused recruiting efforts in urban centers like Bangalore and Delhi, driving up engineering and computer science salaries in such cities, local companies have shifted recruiting efforts to second-tier cities that are unfamiliar to foreign firms.

4. *Use acquisition and rapid-growth strategies to better defend against expansion-minded internationals.* With the growth potential of developing markets such as China, Indonesia, and Brazil obvious to the world, local companies must attempt to develop scale and upgrade their competitive capabilities as quickly as possible to defend against the stronger international's arsenal of resources. Most successful companies in developing markets have pursued mergers and acquisitions at a rapid-fire pace to build first a nationwide and then an international presence. Hindalco, India's largest aluminum producer, has followed just such a path to achieve its ambitions for global dominance. By acquiring companies in India first, it gained enough experience and confidence to eventually acquire much larger foreign companies with world-class capabilities.[22] When China began to liberalize its foreign trade policies, Lenovo (the Chinese PC maker) realized that its long-held position of market dominance in China could not withstand the onslaught of new international entrants such as Dell and HP. Its acquisition of IBM's PC business allowed Lenovo to gain rapid access to IBM's globally recognized PC brand, its R&D capability, and its existing distribution in developed countries. This has allowed Lenovo not only to hold its own against the incursion of global giants into its home market but also to expand into new markets around the world.[23]

5. *Transfer company expertise to cross-border markets and initiate actions to contend on an international level.* When a company from a developing country has resources and capabilities suitable for competing in other country markets, launching initiatives to transfer its expertise to foreign markets becomes a viable strategic option. Televisa, Mexico's largest media company, used its expertise in Spanish culture and linguistics to become the world's most prolific producer of Spanish-language soap operas. By continuing to upgrade its capabilities and learn from its experience in foreign markets, a company can sometimes transform itself into one capable of competing on a worldwide basis, as an emerging global giant. Sundaram Fasteners of India began its foray into foreign markets as a supplier of radiator caps to General Motors—an opportunity it pursued when GM first decided to outsource the production of this part. As a participant in GM's supplier network, the company learned about emerging technical standards, built its capabilities, and became one of the first Indian companies to achieve QS 9000 quality certification. With the expertise it gained and its recognition for meeting quality standards, Sundaram was then able to pursue opportunities to supply automotive parts in Japan and Europe.

Illustration Capsule 7.3 discusses how a travel agency in China used a combination of these strategies to become that country's largest travel consolidator and online travel agent.

ILLUSTRATION CAPSULE 7.3

How Ctrip Successfully Defended against International Rivals to Become China's Largest Online Travel Agency

© Nelson Ching/Bloomberg via Getty Images

Ctrip has utilized a business model tailored to the Chinese travel market, its access to low-cost labor, and its unique understanding of customer preferences and buying habits to build scale rapidly and defeat foreign rivals such as Expedia and Travelocity in becoming the largest travel agency in China. The company was founded in 1999 with a focus on business travelers, since corporate travel accounts for the majority of China's travel bookings. The company initially placed little emphasis on online transactions because at the time there was no national ticketing system in China, most hotels did not belong to a national or international chain, and most consumers preferred paper tickets to electronic tickets. To overcome this infrastructure shortcoming and enter the online market, the company established its own central database of 5,600 hotels located throughout China and flight information for all major airlines operating in China. Ctrip set up a call center of 3,000 representatives that could use its proprietary database to provide travel information for up to 100,000 customers per day.

Because most of its transactions were not done over the Internet at the start, the company hired couriers in all major cities in China to ride by bicycle or scooter to collect payments and deliver tickets to Ctrip's corporate customers. Ctrip also initiated a loyalty program that provided gifts and incentives to the administrative personnel who arranged travel for business executives, who were more likely to use online services. By 2011, Ctrip.com held 60 percent of China's online travel market, having grown 40 percent every year since 1999, leading to a market cap coming close to those of some major U.S. online travel agencies.

However, the phenomenal growth of the Chinese market for such travel agency services, along with changing technological ability and preferences, has led to a new type of competition: online, and more pivotally, mobile travel booking. Dominance in the mobile space drove a competitor, Qunar, to experience a huge surge in growth. While this competition was a negative in the traditional financial sense for Ctrip, analysts believe that new technology has ended up benefiting the entire industry. Additionally, this has provided the two companies with the opportunity to utilize another important local strategy to grow and remain competitive against global firms—a partnership, which Ctrip and Qunar undertook in 2013, combining their unique advantages to cross-sell travel products. The solidity of this partnership was furthered in late 2015, when the two companies agreed to an alliance through the exchange of shares in one another's companies. Together, the two companies control more than 80 percent of China's hotel and air ticket markets. The long-term effects of the new agreement still have yet to be seen, but the success of Ctrip has demonstrated the potential benefits of an effective local-market strategy.

Note: Developed with Harold W. Greenstone.

Sources: Arindam K. Bhattacharya and David C. Michael, "How Local Companies Keep Multinationals at Bay," *Harvard Business Review* 86, no. 3 (March 2008), pp. 85–95; B. Perez, "Ctrip Likely to Gain More Business from Stronger Qunar Platform," *South China Morning Press* online, October 2, 2013 (accessed April 3, 2014); B. Cao, "Qunar Jumps on Mobile User Growth as Ctrip Tumbles," *Bloomberg* online, January 5, 2014 (accessed April 3, 2014); www.thatsmags.com/shanghai/article/detail/480/a-journey-with-ctrip; money.cnn.com/quote/quote.html?symb5EXPE (accessed March 28, 2012).

KEY POINTS

1. Competing in international markets allows a company to (1) gain access to new customers; (2) achieve lower costs through greater economies of scale, learning, and increased purchasing power; (3) gain access to low-cost inputs of production; (4) further exploit its core competencies; and (5) gain access to resources and capabilities located outside the company's domestic market.

2. Strategy making is more complex for five reasons: (1) Different countries have *home-country advantages* in different industries; (2) there are location-based advantages to performing different value chain activities in different parts of the world; (3) varying political and economic risks make the business climate of some countries more favorable than others; (4) companies face the risk of adverse shifts in exchange rates when operating in foreign countries; and (5) differences in buyer tastes and preferences present a conundrum concerning the trade-off between customizing and standardizing products and services.

3. The strategies of firms that expand internationally are usually grounded in home-country advantages concerning demand conditions; factor conditions; related and supporting industries; and firm strategy, structure, and rivalry, as described by the Diamond of National Competitive Advantage framework.

4. There are five strategic options for entering foreign markets. These include maintaining a home-country production base and *exporting* goods to foreign markets, *licensing* foreign firms to produce and distribute the company's products abroad, employing a *franchising* strategy, establishing a foreign *subsidiary via an acquisition or greenfield venture,* and using *strategic alliances or other collaborative partnerships.*

5. A company must choose among three alternative approaches for competing internationally: (1) a *multidomestic strategy*—a *think-local, act-local* approach to crafting international strategy; (2) a *global strategy*—a *think-global, act-global* approach; and (3) a combination *think-global, act-local* approach, known as a *transnational strategy.* A multidomestic strategy (think local, act local) is appropriate for companies that must vary their product offerings and competitive approaches from country to country in order to accommodate different buyer preferences and market conditions. The global strategy (think global, act global) works best when there are substantial cost benefits to be gained from taking a standardized, globally integrated approach and there is little need for local responsiveness. A transnational strategy (think global, act local) is called for when there is a high need for local responsiveness as well as substantial benefits from taking a globally integrated approach. In this approach, a company strives to employ the same basic competitive strategy in all markets but still customizes its product offering and some aspect of its operations to fit local market circumstances.

6. There are three general ways in which a firm can gain competitive advantage (or offset domestic disadvantages) in international markets. One way involves locating various value chain activities among nations in a manner that lowers costs or achieves greater product differentiation. A second way draws on an international competitor's ability to extend its competitive advantage by cost-effectively sharing, replicating, or transferring its most valuable resources and capabilities across borders. A third looks for benefits from cross-border coordination that are unavailable to domestic-only competitors.

7. Two types of strategic moves are particularly suited for companies competing internationally. Both involve the use of profit sanctuaries—country markets where a company derives substantial profits because of its strong or protected market position. Profit sanctuaries are useful in waging strategic offenses in international markets through *cross-subsidization*—a practice of supporting competitive offensives in one market with resources and profits diverted from operations in another market (the profit sanctuary). They may be used defensively to encourage *mutual restraint* among competitors when there is international *multimarket competition* by signaling that each company has the financial capability for mounting a strong counterattack if threatened. For companies with at least one profit sanctuary, having a presence in a rival's key markets can be enough to deter the rival from making aggressive attacks.

8. Companies racing for global leadership have to consider competing in developing markets like the BRIC countries—Brazil, Russia, India, and China—where the business risks are considerable but the opportunities for growth are huge. To succeed in these markets, companies often have to (1) compete on the basis of low price, (2) modify aspects of the company's business model to accommodate local circumstances, and/or (3) try to change the local market to better match the way the company does business elsewhere. Profitability is unlikely to come quickly or easily in developing markets, typically because of the investments needed to alter buying habits and tastes, the increased political and economic risk, and/or the need for infrastructure upgrades. And there may be times when a company should simply stay away from certain developing markets until conditions for entry are better suited to its business model and strategy.

9. Local companies in developing-country markets can seek to compete against large international companies by (1) developing business models that exploit shortcomings in local distribution networks or infrastructure, (2) utilizing a superior understanding of local customer needs and preferences or local relationships, (3) taking advantage of competitively important qualities of the local workforce with which large international companies may be unfamiliar, (4) using acquisition strategies and rapid-growth strategies to better defend against expansion-minded international companies, or (5) transferring company expertise to cross-border markets and initiating actions to compete on an international level.

ASSURANCE OF LEARNING EXERCISES

LO 1, LO 3   1. L'Oréal markets 32 brands of cosmetics, fragrances, and hair care products in 130 countries. The company's international strategy involves manufacturing these products in 40 plants located around the world. L'Oréal's international strategy is discussed in its operations section of the company's website (www.loreal.com/careers/who-you-can-be/operations) and in its press releases, annual reports, and presentations. Why has the company chosen to pursue a foreign subsidiary strategy? Are there strategic advantages to global sourcing and production in the cosmetics, fragrances, and hair care products industry relative to an export strategy?

2. Alliances, joint ventures, and mergers with foreign companies are widely used as a means of entering foreign markets. Such arrangements have many purposes, including learning about unfamiliar environments, and the opportunity to access the complementary resources and capabilities of a foreign partner. Illustration Capsule 7.1 provides an example of how Walgreens used a strategy of entering foreign markets via alliance, followed by a merger with the same entity. What was this entry strategy designed to achieve, and why would this make sense for a company like Walgreens?

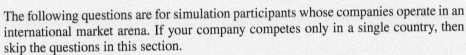

connect
LO 1, LO 3

3. Assume you are in charge of developing the strategy for an international company selling products in some 50 different countries around the world. One of the issues you face is whether to employ a multidomestic strategy, a global strategy, or a transnational strategy.

connect
LO 2, LO 4

   a. If your company's product is mobile phones, which of these strategies do you think it would make better strategic sense to employ? Why?

   b. If your company's product is dry soup mixes and canned soups, would a multidomestic strategy seem to be more advisable than a global strategy or a transnational strategy? Why or why not?

   c. If your company's product is large home appliances such as washing machines, ranges, ovens, and refrigerators, would it seem to make more sense to pursue a multidomestic strategy, a global strategy, or a transnational strategy? Why?

4. Using your university library's subscription to LexisNexis, EBSCO, or a similar database, identify and discuss three key strategies that Volkswagen is using to compete in China.

LO 5, LO 6

EXERCISE FOR SIMULATION PARTICIPANTS

The following questions are for simulation participants whose companies operate in an international market arena. If your company competes only in a single country, then skip the questions in this section.

1. To what extent, if any, have you and your co-managers adapted your company's strategy to take shifting exchange rates into account? In other words, have you undertaken any actions to try to minimize the impact of adverse shifts in exchange rates?

LO 2

2. To what extent, if any, have you and your co-managers adapted your company's strategy to take geographic differences in import tariffs or import duties into account?

LO 2

3. Which one of the following best describes the strategic approach your company is taking in trying to compete successfully on an international basis?

LO 4

   • Multidomestic or think-local, act-local approach.

   • Global or think-global, act-global approach.

   • Transnational or think-global, act-local approach.

   Explain your answer and indicate two or three chief elements of your company's strategy for competing in two or more different geographic regions.

ENDNOTES

[1] Sidney G. Winter and Gabriel Szulanski, "Getting It Right the Second Time," *Harvard Business Review* 80, no. 1 (January 2002), pp. 62–69.

[2] P. Dussauge, B. Garrette, and W. Mitchell, "Learning from Competing Partners: Outcomes and Durations of Scale and Link Alliances in Europe, North America and Asia," *Strategic Management Journal* 21, no. 2 (February 2000), pp. 99–126; K. W. Glaister and P. J. Buckley, "Strategic Motives for International Alliance Formation," *Journal of Management Studies* 33, no. 3 (May 1996), pp. 301–332.

[3] Michael E. Porter, "The Competitive Advantage of Nations," *Harvard Business Review,* March–April 1990, pp. 73–93.

[4] Tom Mitchell and Avantika Chilkoti, "China Car Sales Accelerate Away from US and Brazil in 2013," *Financial Times,* January 9, 2014, www.ft.com/cms/s/0/8c649078-78f8-11e3-b381-00144feabdc0.html#axzz2rpEqjkZO.

[5] U.S. Department of Labor, Bureau of Labor Statistics, "International Comparisons of Hourly Compensation Costs in Manufacturing 2012," August 9, 2013. (The numbers for India and China are estimates.)

[6] Sangwon Yoon, "South Korea Targets Internet Addicts; 2 Million Hooked," *Valley News,* April 25, 2010, p. C2.

[7] Joel Bleeke and David Ernst, "The Way to Win in Cross-Border Alliances," *Harvard Business Review* 69, no. 6 (November–December 1991), pp. 127–133; Gary Hamel, Yves L. Doz, and C. K. Prahalad, "Collaborate with Your Competitors—and Win," *Harvard Business Review* 67, no. 1 (January–February 1989), pp. 134–135.

[8] K. W. Glaister and P. J. Buckley, "Strategic Motives for International Alliance Formation," *Journal of Management Studies* 33, no. 3 (May 1996), pp. 301–332.

[9] Jeffrey H. Dyer, Prashant Kale, and Harbir Singh, "When to Ally and When to Acquire," *Harvard Business Review* 82, no. 7–8 (July–August 2004).

[10] Yves Doz and Gary Hamel, Alliance Advantage: *The Art of Creating Value through Partnering* (Harvard Business School Press, 1998); Rosabeth Moss Kanter, "Collaborative Advantage: The Art of the Alliance," *Harvard Business Review* 72, no. 4 (July–August 1994), pp. 96–108.

[11] Jeremy Main, "Making Global Alliances Work," *Fortune,* December 19, 1990, p. 125.

[12] C. K. Prahalad and Kenneth Lieberthal, "The End of Corporate Imperialism," *Harvard Business Review* 81, no. 8 (August 2003), pp. 109–117.

[13] Pankaj Ghemawat, "Managing Differences: The Central Challenge of Global Strategy," *Harvard Business Review* 85, no. 3 (March 2007).

[14] C. A. Bartlett and S. Ghoshal, *Managing across Borders: The Transnational Solution,* 2nd ed. (Boston: Harvard Business School Press, 1998).

[15] Lynn S. Paine, "The China Rules," *Harvard Business Review* 88, no. 6 (June 2010), pp. 103–108.

[16] C. K. Prahalad and Yves L. Doz, *The Multinational Mission: Balancing Local Demands and Global Vision* (New York: Free Press, 1987).

[17] David J. Arnold and John A. Quelch, "New Strategies in Emerging Markets," *Sloan Management Review* 40, no. 1 (Fall 1998), pp. 7–20.

[18] Tarun Khanna, Krishna G. Palepu, and Jayant Sinha, "Strategies That Fit Emerging Markets," *Harvard Business Review* 83, no. 6 (June 2005), p. 63; Arindam K. Bhattacharya and David C. Michael, "How Local Companies Keep Multinationals at Bay," *Harvard Business Review* 86, no. 3 (March 2008), pp. 94–95.

[19] www.ajc.com/news/business/home-depot-eschews-large-scale-international-expan/nSQBh/ (accessed February 2, 2014).

[20] Tarun Khanna and Krishna G. Palepu, "Emerging Giants: Building World-Class Companies in Developing Countries," *Harvard Business Review* 84, no. 10 (October 2006), pp. 60–69.

[21] Niroj Dawar and Tony Frost, "Competing with Giants: Survival Strategies for Local Companies in Emerging Markets," *Harvard Business Review* 77, no. 1 (January–February 1999), p. 122; Guitz Ger, "Localizing in the Global Village: Local Firms Competing in Global Markets," *California Management Review* 41, no. 4 (Summer 1999), pp. 64–84.

[22] N. Kumar, "How Emerging Giants Are Rewriting the Rules of M&A," *Harvard Business Review,* May 2009, pp. 115–121.

[23] H. Rui and G. Yip, "Foreign Acquisitions by Chinese Firms: A Strategic Intent Perspective," *Journal of World Business* 43 (2008), pp. 213–226.

CHAPTER 5

Managing Diverse Employees in a Multicultural Environment

Learning Objectives

After studying this chapter, you should be able to:

LO5-1 Discuss the increasing diversity of the workforce and the organizational environment.

LO5-2 Explain the central role that managers play in the effective management of diversity.

LO5-3 Explain why the effective management of diversity is both an ethical and a business imperative.

LO5-4 Discuss how perception and the use of schemas can result in unfair treatment.

LO5-5 List the steps managers can take to manage diversity effectively.

LO5-6 Identify the two major forms of sexual harassment and how they can be eliminated.

© Sam Edwards/age fotostock RF

A MANAGER'S CHALLENGE

Novartis and Sodexo Effectively Manage Diversity in Multiple Ways

What steps can organizations take to effectively manage an increasingly diverse workforce? By all counts, the diversity of the workforce is increasing. Effectively managing diversity is more than just ensuring that diverse members of organizations are treated fairly (itself a challenging task). When diversity is effectively managed, organizations can benefit from the diverse perspectives, points of view, experiences, and knowledge bases of their diverse members to produce better goods and services and be responsive to their increasingly diverse customer bases.

Extolling the benefits of effectively managing diversity is one thing; taking tangible steps to ensure that an organization continuously improves in this regard is another. Both organizationwide initiatives and the steps that each manager takes to effectively manage diversity have the potential for substantial payoffs in terms of both improving organizational effectiveness and maintaining a satisfied, committed, and motivated workforce.

Consider the steps that Novartis Pharmaceuticals Corporation has taken to effectively manage diversity. Novartis is the U.S. subsidiary of Novartis AG based in Basel, Switzerland. It conducts research to develop prescription medications to treat health issues, problems, and diseases such as those involved with the cardiovascular system, the central nervous system, ophthalmics, cancer, organ transplantation, and the respiratory system and manufactures and markets these prescription drugs. Headquartered in East Hanover, New Jersey, Novartis has over 7,100 employees in the U.S.[1] Effectively managing diversity is critical for developing innovative solutions to health care problems and making sure these medicines reach their

targeted audiences. Dr. Vijay Bhargava, corporate executive vice president and global head of drug metabolism and pharmacokinetics, indicates that effective management of diversity, diversity of thought, and studies of diverse populations help Novartis to develop new markets for drugs in developing countries.[2]

Support for diversity at Novartis starts at the top with Christi Shaw, U.S. country head and president.[3] Multiple roles throughout the organization support the effective management of diversity, including diversity champions, an executive diversity and inclusion council concerned with company goals and metrics, diversity and inclusion councils, and employee resource groups. Employee resource groups are voluntary groups of employees who have interests, perspectives, or experiences in common and provide opportunities for exchanging ideas, networking, developing creative solutions to problems, and facilitating professional and career growth and advancement. These groups help with recruitment and retention, mentoring,

Sodexo encourages managers to interact with diverse groups to gain a better appreciation and understanding of their experiences.
© Kris Tripplaar/Sipa USA/Newscom

multicultural awareness, understanding, respect, development of broader views and more innovative solutions, and community outreach and philanthropy. There are 19 employee resource groups, and over half the employees participate in them. The leaders of these groups have their roles and responsibilities for the groups included in their performance appraisals.[4]

At Novartis, the effective management of diversity and inclusion is not just directed inwardly but also extends to patients and customers through, for example, clinical trials and market approaches. As Christi Shaw puts it, "Novartis Pharmaceuticals Corporation is focused on creating products, services and solutions that help patients manage disease and live fuller lives. We believe that diversity and inclusion are directly linked to the achievement of these goals—and can help us create a culture where people can be authentic and courageous, where collaboration can flourish, and where greater patient and customer understanding can drive future breakthroughs and innovations."[5] Thus, it is perhaps not surprising that Novartis has been ranked no. 1 on Diversity Inc.'s Top 50 Companies for Diversity and is the first company ever to be in the no. 1 spot for two years in a row.[6]

In good company with Novartis is Sodexo Inc. Sodexo has been ranked in the top 5 on Diversity Inc.'s Top 50 Companies for Diversity for six years running.[7] Sodexo is a major food and facilities management company serving over 15 million customers per day in businesses, health care facilities, schools and universities, and government agencies in North America.[8] Sodexo encourages managers to interact with diverse groups to gain a better appreciation and understanding of their experiences.[9] Sodexo provides employees and managers with extensive diversity training, encourages managers to mentor and coach employees who are different from themselves, and bases 25 percent of top managers' bonuses on their performance on diversity initiatives, including hiring and training

diverse employees.[10] Managers are encouraged to sponsor employee business resource groups for employees who differ from themselves. For example, a male manager might sponsor a women's group, which provides a forum for female employees to connect with each other and address their mutual concerns. Sponsoring such groups helps managers become aware of and address concerns of some employee groups they might never have thought of otherwise.[11]

When Lorna Donatone, of Swedish and German ancestry and raised in Nebraska, managed a unit of Sodexo that provides food services for cruise companies, she sponsored Sodexo's Latino group and discovered a better way to serve her unit's customers. As a result, Donatone relied on more bilingual materials to promote the services she provided to cruise companies and their customers.[12] After holding a series of other positions at Sodexo, in 2016 Donatone was appointed Sodexo region chair for North America and CEO of schools worldwide, a position in which she oversees all Sodexo businesses in the United States, Canada, and Puerto Rico and schools worldwide, with over 3,500 client locations in 42 countries.[13]

Similar to Novartis, at Sodexo the commitment to diversity and inclusion starts at the top, with CEO George Chavel and Senior Vice President and Global Chief Diversity Officer Dr. Rohini Anand.[14] As Anand indicates, "To really engage people, you have to create a series of epiphanies and take leaders through those epiphanies."[15]

Sodexo is well-known for its mentoring program, in which all senior executives are required to participate. Mentors are paired with mentees and over 60 percent of the pairs are cross-cultural. Sodexo tracks the pairs and assesses engagement, retention, and promotion of mentees.[16] Sodexo also has a Diversity and Inclusion Business Advisory Board, which is made up of six leaders from outside the company who are experts on diverse communities and serve both an external relations function and an internal advisory function providing Sodexo with outside input on its initiatives and representing the company in communities. In 2016, members of the board included Eliza Byard (executive director of GLSEN, the Gay, Lesbian, and Straight Education Network), Cari Dominguez (former chair of the U.S. Equal Employment Opportunity Commission (EEOC) and a board member of Manpower, Inc.), Alexis Herman (former secretary of the Department of Labor and chairman

and CEO of New Ventures, Inc.), John Hofmeister (founder and CEO of Citizens for Affordable Energy), John D. Kemp (president and CEO of Abilities!), and Thomas S. Williamson Jr. (partner, Covington & Burling, and board member of the National Lawyers Committee for Civil Rights Under Law).[17] Sodexo also often helps its clients with their own managing diversity programs.[18]

All in all, Novartis and Sodexo are among the growing numbers of companies that are reaping the benefits of an increasingly diverse workforce.[19]

Overview

LO5-1 Discuss the increasing diversity of the workforce and the organizational environment.

diversity Dissimilarities or differences among people due to age, gender, race, ethnicity, religion, sexual orientation, socioeconomic background, education, experience, physical appearance, capabilities/disabilities, and any other characteristic that is used to distinguish between people.

As indicated in "A Manager's Challenge," effective management of diversity means more than hiring diverse employees. It means learning to appreciate and respond appropriately to the needs, attitudes, beliefs, and values that diverse people bring to an organization. It also means correcting misconceptions about why and how various kinds of employee groups differ from one another and finding the most effective way to use the skills and talents of diverse employees.

In this chapter we focus on the effective management of diversity in an environment that is becoming increasingly diverse in all respects. Not only are the diversity and integration of the global workforce increasing, but suppliers and customers are also becoming increasingly diverse. Managers need to manage diversity proactively to attract and retain the best employees and compete effectively in a global environment. For example, managers at the audit and consulting firm Deloitte & Touche have instituted a program to encourage minority suppliers to compete for its business, and the firm sponsors schools and colleges that supply a stream of well-trained recruits.[20]

Sometimes well-intentioned managers inadvertently treat various groups of employees differently, even though there are no performance-based differences between them. This chapter explores why differential treatment occurs and the steps managers and organizations can take to ensure that diversity, in all respects, is effectively managed for the good of all organizational stakeholders.

The Increasing Diversity of the Workforce and the Environment

One of the most important management issues to emerge over the last 40 years has been the increasing diversity of the workforce. **Diversity** is dissimilarities—differences—among people due to age, gender, race, ethnicity, religion, sexual orientation, socioeconomic background, education, experience, physical appearance, capabilities/disabilities, and any other characteristic that is used to distinguish between people (see Figure 5.1).

Diversity raises important ethical issues and social responsibility issues (see Chapter 4). It is also a critical issue for organizations—one that if not handled well can bring an organization to its knees, especially in our increasingly global environment. There are several reasons that diversity is such a pressing concern and an issue, both in the popular press and for managers and organizations:

- There is a strong ethical imperative in many societies that diverse people must receive equal opportunities and be treated fairly and justly. Unfair treatment is also illegal.

Figure 5.1

Sources of Diversity in the Workplace

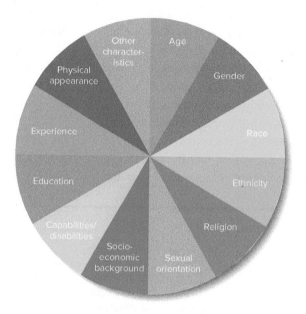

- Effectively managing diversity can improve organizational effectiveness.[21] When managers effectively manage diversity, they not only encourage other managers to treat diverse members of an organization fairly and justly but also realize that diversity is an important organizational resource that can help an organization gain a competitive advantage.

- There is substantial evidence that diverse individuals continue to experience unfair treatment in the workplace as a result of biases, stereotypes, and overt discrimination.[22] In one study, résumés of equally qualified men and women were sent to high-priced Philadelphia restaurants (where potential earnings are high). Though equally qualified, men were more than twice as likely as women to be called for a job interview and more than five times as likely to receive a job offer.[23] Findings from another study suggest that both women and men tend to believe that women will accept lower pay than men; this is a possible explanation for the continuing gap in pay between men and women.[24]

Other kinds of diverse employees may face even greater barriers. For example, the federal Glass Ceiling Commission Report indicated that African Americans have the hardest time being promoted and climbing the corporate ladder, that Asians are often stereotyped into technical jobs, and that Hispanics are assumed to be less well educated than other minority groups.[25] (The term **glass ceiling** alludes to the invisible barriers that prevent minorities and women from being promoted to top corporate positions.)[26]

Before we can discuss the multitude of issues surrounding the effective management of diversity, we must document just how diverse the U.S. workforce is becoming.

glass ceiling A metaphor alluding to the invisible barriers that prevent minorities and women from being promoted to top corporate positions.

Age

According to data from the U.S. Census Bureau and the CIA's World Fact Book, the median age of a person in the United States is the highest it has ever been, 37.8 years.[27] Moreover, it is projected that by 2030 close to 20 percent of the U.S. population will be 65 or over.[28] The Age Discrimination in Employment Act of 1967 prohibits age discrimination.[29] Although we discuss federal employment legislation in more depth in Chapter 12, major equal employment opportunity legislation that prohibits discrimination among diverse groups is summarized in Table 5.1.

The aging of the population suggests that managers need to be vigilant to ensure that employees are not discriminated against because of age. Moreover, managers need to ensure

Table 5.1

Major Equal Employment Opportunity Laws Affecting Human Resources Management

Year	Law	Description
1963	Equal Pay Act	Requires that men and women be paid equally if they are performing equal work.
1964	Title VII of the Civil Rights Act	Prohibits discrimination in employment decisions on the basis of race, religion, sex, color, or national origin; covers a wide range of employment decisions, including hiring, firing, pay, promotion, and working conditions.
1967	Age Discrimination in Employment Act	Prohibits discrimination against workers over the age of 40 and restricts mandatory retirement.
1978	Pregnancy Discrimination Act	Prohibits discrimination against women in employment decisions on the basis of pregnancy, childbirth, and related medical decisions.
1990	Americans with Disabilities Act	Prohibits discrimination against disabled individuals in employment decisions and requires that employers make accommodations for disabled workers to enable them to perform their jobs.
1991	Civil Rights Act	Prohibits discrimination (as does Title VII) and allows for the awarding of punitive and compensatory damages, in addition to back pay, in cases of intentional discrimination.
1993	Family and Medical Leave Act	Requires that employers provide 12 weeks of unpaid leave for medical and family reasons, including paternity and illness of a family member.

that the policies and procedures they have in place treat all workers fairly, regardless of their ages. Additionally, effectively managing diversity means employees of diverse ages are able to learn from each other, work well together, and take advantage of the unique perspective each has to offer.

Gender

Women and men both have substantial participation rates in the U.S. workforce (approximately 55.7 percent of the U.S. workforce is male and 44.3 percent female),[30] yet women's median weekly earnings are estimated to be $726 compared to $895 for men.[31] Thus, the gender pay gap appears to be as unfortunately real as the glass ceiling. According to the nonprofit organization Catalyst, which studies women in business, while women compose about 51.5 percent of the employees in managerial and professional positions,[32] only around 14.6 percent of executive officers in the 500 largest U.S. companies (that is, the *Fortune* 500) are women, and only 8.1 percent of the top-earner executive officers are women.[33] These women, such as Virginia Rometty, CEO of IBM, and Indra Nooyi, CEO of PepsiCo, stand out among their male peers and often receive a disparate amount of attention in the media. (We address this issue later when we discuss the effects of being salient.) Women are also very underrepresented on boards of directors—they currently hold 16.9 percent of the board seats of *Fortune* 500 companies.[34] However, as Sheila Wellington, former president of Catalyst, indicates, "Women either control or influence nearly all consumer purchases, so it's important to have their perspective represented on boards."[35]

Additionally, research conducted by consulting firms suggests that female executives outperform their male colleagues in skills such as motivating others, promoting good communication, turning out high-quality work, and being good listeners.[36] For example, the Hagberg Group performed in-depth evaluations of 425 top executives in a variety of industries, with each executive rated by approximately 25 people. Of the 52 skills assessed, women received higher ratings than men on 42 skills, although at times the differences were small.[37] Results of a study conducted by Catalyst found that organizations with higher proportions of women in

A female executive enjoying the company plane is not as rare a sight today as it used to be; nevertheless, the glass ceiling remains a real barrier to women in the business workforce.
© ColorBlind Images/Blend Images RF

top management positions had significantly better financial performance than organizations with lower proportions of female top managers.[38] Another study conducted by Catalyst found that companies with three or more women on their boards of directors performed better in terms of returns on equity, sales, and invested capital than companies with fewer or no women on their boards.[39] Studies such as these make one wonder why the glass ceiling continues to hamper the progress of women in business (a topic we address later in the chapter).

Race and Ethnicity

The U.S. Census Bureau distinguished among the following races in the 2010 census: American Indian or Alaska Native; Asian Indian; black, African-American, or Negro; Chinese; Filipino; Japanese; Korean; Vietnamese; other Asian; Native Hawaiian; Guamanian or Chamorro; Samoan; other Pacific Islander; white; and other races.[40] Although *ethnicity* refers to a grouping of people based on some shared characteristic such as national origin, language, or culture, the U.S. Census Bureau treats ethnicity in terms of whether a person is Hispanic, Latino, or of Spanish origin or not.[41] Hispanics, also referred to as Latinos, are people whose origins are in Spanish cultures such as those of Cuba, Mexico, Puerto Rico, and South and Central America. Hispanics can be of different races.[42] According to a recent poll, most Hispanics prefer to be identified by their country of origin (such as Mexican, Cuban, or Salvadoran) rather than by the overarching term *Hispanic*.[43]

The racial and ethnic diversity of the U.S. population is increasing quickly, as is the diversity of the workforce.[44] According to the U.S. Census Bureau, approximately one of every three U.S. residents belongs to a minority group (is not a non-Hispanic white).[45] More specifically, 16.3 percent of the population is Hispanic or Latino, 83.7 percent of the population is not Hispanic or Latino, and 63.7 percent of the population is white alone (that is, white and not Hispanic or Latino).[46] For those individuals self-identifying one race in the 2010 U.S. census, approximately 72.4 percent of the population is white, 12.6 percent is black or African-American, 0.9 percent is American Indian or Alaska Native, 4.8 percent is Asian, 0.2 percent is Native Hawaiian and other Pacific Islander, and 6.2 percent is another race; 2.9 percent of the population self-identifies two or more races.[47] According to projections released by the U.S. Census Bureau, the composition of the U.S. population in 2050 will be quite different from its composition today; in 2050 the U.S. population is projected to be 54 percent minority.[48]

The increasing racial and ethnic diversity of the workforce and the population as a whole underscores the importance of effectively managing diversity. Statistics compiled by the Bureau of Labor Statistics suggest that much needs to be done in terms of ensuring that diverse employees have equal opportunities. For example, median weekly earnings for black men are approximately 73.9 percent of median earnings for white men; median weekly earnings for black women are approximately 82.8 percent of median earnings for white women.[49] In the remainder of this chapter, we focus on the fair treatment of diverse employees and explore why this is such an important challenge and what managers can do to meet it. We begin by taking a broader perspective and considering how increasing racial and ethnic diversity in an organization's environment (such as customers and suppliers) affects decision making and organizational effectiveness.

At a general level, managers and organizations are increasingly being reminded that stakeholders in the environment are diverse and expect organizational decisions and actions to reflect this diversity. For example, the NAACP (National Association for the Advancement of Colored People) and Children Now (an advocacy group) have lobbied the entertainment industry to increase the diversity in television programming, writing, and producing.[50] The need for such increased diversity is more than apparent. For example, while Hispanics make up 17 percent of the U.S. population (53 million potential TV viewers), less than 5 percent of the characters in prime-time TV shows are Hispanics, according to a study conducted by

Children Now.[51] Moreover, less than 5 percent of the evening network TV news stories are reported by Hispanic correspondents, according to the Center for Media and Public Affairs.[52]

Pressure is mounting on networks to increase diversity for a variety of reasons revolving around the diversity of the population as a whole, TV viewers, and consumers. For example, home and automobile buyers are increasingly diverse, reflecting the increasing diversity of the population as a whole.[53] Moreover, managers have to be especially sensitive to avoid stereotyping different groups when they communicate with potential customers. For example, Toyota Motor Sales USA made a public apology to the Reverend Jesse Jackson and his Rainbow Coalition for using a print advertisement depicting an African-American man with a Toyota RAV4 sport utility image embossed on his gold front tooth.[54]

Religion

Title VII of the Civil Rights Act prohibits discrimination based on religion (as well as based on race/ethnicity, country of origin, and sex; see Table 5.1 and Chapter 12). In addition to enacting Title VII, in 1997 the federal government issued "The White House Guidelines on Religious Exercise and Expression in the Federal Workplace."[55] These guidelines, while technically applicable only in federal offices, also are frequently relied on by large corporations. The guidelines require that employers make reasonable accommodations for religious practices, such as observances of holidays, as long as doing so does not entail major costs or hardships.[56]

A key issue for managers in religious diversity is recognizing and being aware of different religions and their beliefs, with particular attention being paid to when religious holidays fall. For example, critical meetings should not be scheduled during a holy day for members of a certain faith, and managers should be flexible in allowing people to have time off for religious observances. According to Lobna Ismail, director of a diversity training company in Silver Spring, Maryland, when managers acknowledge, respect, and make even small accommodations for religious diversity, employee loyalty is often enhanced. For example, allowing employees to leave work early on certain days instead of taking a lunch break or posting holidays for different religions on the company calendar can go a long way toward making individuals of diverse religions feel respected and valued as well as enabling them to practice their faith.[57] According to research conducted by the Tanenbaum Center for Interreligious Understanding in New York, while only about 23 percent of employees who feel they are victims of religious discrimination actually file complaints, about 45 percent of these employees start looking for other jobs.[58]

Capabilities/Disabilities

The Americans with Disabilities Act (ADA) of 1990 prohibits discrimination against persons with disabilities and requires that employers make reasonable accommodations to enable these people to effectively perform their jobs. On the surface, few would argue with the intent of this legislation. However, as managers attempt to implement policies and procedures to comply with the ADA, they face a number of interpretation and fairness challenges.

On one hand, some people with real disabilities warranting workplace accommodations are hesitant to reveal their disabilities to their employers and claim the accommodations they deserve.[59] On the other hand, some employees abuse the ADA by seeking unnecessary accommodations for disabilities that may or may not exist.[60] Thus, it is perhaps not surprising that the passage of the ADA does not appear to have increased employment rates significantly for those with disabilities.[61] A key challenge for managers is to promote an environment in which employees needing accommodations feel comfortable disclosing their need while ensuring that the accommodations not only enable those with disabilities to effectively perform their jobs but also are perceived to be fair by those who are not disabled.[62]

In addressing this challenge, often managers must educate both themselves and their employees about the disabilities, as well as the real capabilities, of those who are disabled. For example, during a Disability Awareness Week, administrators at the University of Notre Dame sought to increase the public's knowledge of disabilities while heightening awareness of the abilities of persons who are disabled.[63] The University of Houston conducted a similar program, called "Think Ability."[64] According to Cheryl Amoruso, director of the University of Houston's Center for Students with Disabilities, many people are unaware of the prevalence of disabilities as well as misinformed about their consequences.[65] She suggests, for example, that although students may not be able to see, they can still excel in their coursework and have successful careers.[66] Accommodations enabling such students to perform up to their capabilities are covered under the ADA.

The ADA also protects employees with acquired immune deficiency syndrome (AIDS) from being discriminated against in the workplace. AIDS is caused by the human immunodeficiency virus (HIV) and is transmitted through sexual contact, infected needles, and contaminated blood products. HIV is not spread through casual, nonsexual contact. Yet out of ignorance, fear, or prejudice, some people wish to avoid all contact with anyone infected with HIV. Infected individuals may not necessarily develop AIDS, and some individuals with HIV are able to remain effective performers of their jobs while not putting others at risk.[67]

AIDS awareness training can help people overcome their fears and give managers a tool to prevent illegal discrimination against HIV-infected employees. Such training focuses on educating employees about HIV and AIDS, dispelling myths, communicating relevant organizational policies, and emphasizing the rights of HIV-positive employees to privacy and an environment that allows them to be productive.[68] The need for AIDS awareness training is underscored by some of the problems HIV-positive employees experience once others in their workplace become aware of their condition.[69] Moreover, organizations are required to make reasonable accommodations to enable people with AIDS to effectively perform their jobs.

Thus, managers have an obligation to educate employees about HIV and AIDS, dispel myths and the stigma of AIDS, and ensure that HIV-related discrimination is not occurring in the workplace. For example, Home Depot has provided HIV training and education to its store managers; such training was sorely needed, given that over half of the managers indicated it was the first time they had had the opportunity to talk about AIDS.[70] Moreover, advances in medication and treatment mean that more infected individuals are able to continue working or are able to return to work after their condition improves. Thus, managers need to ensure that these employees are fairly treated by all members of their organizations.[71] And managers and organizations that do not treat HIV-positive employees in a fair manner, as well as provide reasonable accommodations (such as allowing time off for doctor visits or to take medicine), risk costly lawsuits.

Socioeconomic Background

The term *socioeconomic background* typically refers to a combination of social class and income-related factors. From a management perspective, socioeconomic diversity (and, in particular, diversity in income levels) requires that managers be sensitive and responsive to the needs and concerns of individuals who might not be as well off as others. U.S. welfare reform in the middle to late 1990s emphasized the need for single mothers and others receiving public assistance to join or return to the workforce. In conjunction with a strong economy, this led to record declines in the number of families, households, and children living below the poverty level, according to the 2000 U.S. census.[72] However, the economic downturns in the early and late 2000s suggest that some past gains that lifted families out of poverty have been reversed. In a strong economy, it is much easier for poor people with few skills to find jobs; in a weak economy, when companies lay off employees in hard times, people who need their incomes the most are unfortunately often the first to lose their jobs.[73] And in recessionary times, it is difficult for laid-off employees to find new positions. For example, in December 2009 there were an average of 6.1 unemployed workers for every open position.[74]

According to statistics released by the U.S. Census Bureau, the official poverty rate in the United States in 2012 was 15.0 percent, or 46.5 million people; in 2009 the poverty rate was 14.3 percent, or 43.6 million people.[75] The Census Bureau relies on predetermined threshold income figures, based on family size and composition, adjusted annually for inflation, to determine the poverty level. Families whose income falls below the threshold level are considered poor.[76] For example, in 2012 a family of four was considered poor if their annual income fell below $23,492.[77] When workers earn less than $15 per hour, it is often difficult, if not impossible, for them to meet their families' needs.[78] Moreover, increasing numbers of families are facing the challenge of finding suitable child care arrangements that enable the adults to work long hours and/or through the night to maintain an adequate income level. New information technology has led to more businesses operating 24 hours a day, creating challenges for workers on the night shift, especially those with children.[79]

Hundreds of thousands of parents across the country are scrambling to find someone to care for their children while they are working the night shift, commuting several hours a day, working weekends and holidays, or putting in long hours on one or more jobs. This has led to the opening of day-care facilities that operate around the clock as well as to managers seeking ways to provide such care for children of their employees. For example, the Children's Choice Learning Center in Las Vegas, Nevada, operates around the clock to accommodate employees working nights in neighboring casinos, hospitals, and call centers. Randy Donahue, a security guard who works until midnight, picks up his children from the center when he gets off work; his wife is a nurse on the night shift.[80]

Judy Harden, who focuses on families and child care issues for the United Workers Union, indicates that the demands that families are facing necessitate around-the-clock and odd-hour child care options. Many parents simply do not have the choice of working at hours that allow them to take care of their children at night and/or on weekends, never mind when the children are sick.[81] Some parents and psychologists feel uneasy having children separated from their families for so much time and particularly at night. Most agree that, unfortunately for many families, this is not a choice but a necessity.[82]

Socioeconomic diversity suggests that managers need to be sensitive and responsive to the needs and concerns of workers who may be less fortunate than themselves in terms of income and financial resources, child care and elder care options, housing opportunities, and the existence of sources of social and family support. Moreover—and equally important—managers should try to give such individuals opportunities to learn, advance, and make meaningful contributions to their organizations while improving their economic well-being.

Sexual Orientation

According to research conducted by Gary Gates of the Williams Institute at the UCLA School of Law, approximately 3.5 percent of adults in the United States, or 9 million U.S. residents, self-identify as lesbian, gay, bisexual, or transgender (LGBT).[83] In 2015 the Equal Employment Opportunity Commission pronounced that workplace discrimination on the grounds of sexual orientation is illegal, according to federal law.[84] An increasing number of organizations recognize the minority status of LGBT employees, affirm their rights to fair and equal treatment, and provide benefits to same-sex partners of gay and lesbian employees.[85] For example, a majority of the *Fortune* 500 companies provide domestic partner benefits.[86] As indicated in the accompanying "Focus on Diversity" feature, managers can take many steps to ensure that sexual orientation is not used to unfairly discriminate among employees.

FOCUS ON DIVERSITY

Preventing Discrimination Based on Sexual Orientation

Although gays and lesbians have made great strides in attaining fair treatment in the workplace, much more needs to be done. In a study conducted by Harris Interactive Inc. (a research firm) and Witeck Communications Inc. (a marketing firm), over 40 percent of gay and lesbian employees indicated that they had been unfairly treated, denied a promotion, or pushed to quit their jobs because of their sexual orientation.[87] Given continued harassment and discrimination despite the progress that has been made,[88] many LGBT employees fear disclosing their sexual orientation in

Italian employees of Microsoft raise awareness at Milan's annual Pride Parade. Corporate support, such as displayed here, can go a long way toward making sure workplaces are safe and respectful for everyone.

© Tinxi/Shutterstock.com RF

the workplace and thus live a life of secrecy. While there are a few openly gay top managers, such as David Geffen, cofounder of DreamWorks SKG, and Allan Gilmour, former vice chairman and CFO of Ford and currently a member of the board of directors of DTE Energy Holding Company, many others choose not to disclose or discuss their personal lives, including long-term partners.[89]

Thus, it is not surprising that many managers are taking active steps to educate and train their employees about issues of sexual orientation. S.C. Johnson & Sons, Inc., maker of Raid insecticide and Glade air fresheners in Racine, Wisconsin, provides mandatory training to its plant managers to overturn stereotypes; and Merck & Co., Ernst & Young, and Toronto-Dominion Bank all train managers in how to prevent sexual orientation discrimination.[90] Other organizations such as Lucent Technologies, Microsoft, and Southern California Edison send employees to seminars conducted at prominent business schools. And many companies such as Raytheon, IBM, and Lockheed Martin assist their gay and lesbian employees through gay and lesbian support groups.[91] In 2016 Boeing, Google, Yahoo, Chevron, JP Morgan Chase, Goldman Sachs Group, and Bank of America were among the 407 companies recognized as "Best Places to Work for LGBT Equality" by the Human Rights Campaign, a nonprofit organization that advocates for the civil rights of LGBT people.[92]

The Chubb Group of Insurance Companies, a property and casualty insurance company, gives its managers a two-hour training session to help create work environments that are safe and welcoming for LGBT people.[93] The sessions are conducted by two Chubb employees; usually one of the trainers is straight and the other is gay. The sessions focus on issues that affect a manager's ability to lead diverse teams, such as assessing how safe and welcoming the workplace is for LGBT people, how to refer to gay employees' significant others, and how to respond if employees or customers use inappropriate language or behavior. The idea for the program originated from one of Chubb's employee resource groups. Managers rate the program highly and say they are better able to respond to the concerns of their LGBT employees while creating a safe and productive work environment for all.[94] In 2016 the Chubb Group was also recognized as one of the Best Places to Work for LGBT Equality by the Human Right Campaign.[95]

Other Kinds of Diversity

Other kinds of diversity are important in organizations, are critical for managers to deal with effectively, and are potential sources of unfair treatment. For example, organizations and teams need members with diverse backgrounds and experiences. This is clearly illustrated by the prevalence of cross-functional teams in organizations whose members might come from various departments such as marketing, production, finance, and sales (teams are covered in depth in Chapter 15). A team responsible for developing and introducing a new product, for example, often needs the expertise of employees not only from research and design and engineering but also from marketing, sales, production, and finance.

Other types of diversity can affect how employees are treated in the workplace. For example, employees differ from each other in how attractive they are (based on the standards of the cultures in which an organization operates) and in body weight. Whether individuals are attractive, unattractive, thin, or overweight in most cases has no bearing on their job performance unless they have jobs in which physical appearance plays a role, such as modeling. Yet sometimes these physical sources of diversity affect advancement rates and salaries. A study published in the *American Journal of Public Health* found that highly educated obese women earned approximately 30 percent less per year than women who were not obese and men (regardless of whether or not the men were obese).[96] Clearly, managers need to ensure that all employees are treated fairly, regardless of their physical appearance.

Managers and the Effective Management of Diversity

The increasing diversity of the environment—which, in turn, increases the diversity of an organization's workforce—increases the challenges managers face in effectively managing diversity. Each of the kinds of diversity just discussed presents a particular set of issues managers need to appreciate before they can respond to them effectively. Understanding these issues is not always a simple matter, as many informed managers have discovered. Research on how different groups are currently treated and the unconscious biases that might adversely affect them is vital because it helps managers become aware of the many subtle and unobtrusive ways in which diverse employee groups can come to be treated unfairly over time. Managers can take many more steps to become sensitive to the ongoing effects of diversity in their organizations, take advantage of all the contributions diverse employees can make, and prevent employees from being unfairly treated.

 LO5-2 Explain the central role that managers play in the effective management of diversity.

Critical Managerial Roles

In each of their managerial roles (see Chapter 1), managers can either promote the effective management of diversity or derail such efforts; thus, they are critical to this process. For example, in their interpersonal roles, managers can convey that the effective management of diversity is a valued goal and objective (figurehead role), can serve as a role model and institute policies and procedures to ensure that all organizational members are treated fairly (leader role), and can enable diverse individuals and groups to coordinate their efforts and cooperate with each other both inside the organization and at the organization's boundaries (liaison role). Table 5.2 summarizes ways in which managers can ensure that diversity is effectively managed as they perform their different roles.

Table 5.2

Managerial Roles and the Effective Management of Diversity

Type of Role	Specific Role	Example
Interpersonal	Figurehead	Conveys that the effective management of diversity is a valued goal and objective.
	Leader	Serves as a role model and institutes policies and procedures to ensure that diverse members are treated fairly.
	Liaison	Enables diverse individuals to coordinate their efforts and cooperate with one another.
Informational	Monitor	Evaluates the extent to which all employees are treated fairly.
	Disseminator	Informs employees about diversity policies and initiatives and the intolerance of discrimination.
	Spokesperson	Supports diversity initiatives in the wider community and speaks to diverse groups to interest them in career opportunities.
Decisional	Entrepreneur	Commits resources to develop new ways to effectively manage diversity and eliminate biases and discrimination.
	Disturbance handler	Takes quick action to correct inequalities and curtail discriminatory behavior.
	Resource allocator	Allocates resources to support and encourage the effective management of diversity.
	Negotiator	Works with organizations (e.g., suppliers) and groups (e.g., labor unions) to support and encourage the effective management of diversity.

Given the formal authority that managers have in organizations, they typically have more influence than rank-and-file employees. When managers commit to supporting diversity, as is the case at Novartis and Sodexo in "A Manager's Challenge," their authority and positions of power and status influence other members of an organization to make a similar commitment.[97] Research on social influence supports such a link: People are likely to be influenced and persuaded by others who have high status.[98]

Consider the steps that managers at PricewaterhouseCoopers (PwC) have taken to effectively manage diversity, as profiled in the accompanying "Focus on Diversity" feature.

FOCUS ON DIVERSITY

Effectively Managing Diversity at PricewaterhouseCoopers

PricewaterhouseCoopers (PwC), one of the largest private companies in the United States with revenues over $32 billion and over 180,000 employees, has taken multiple proactive steps to effectively manage diversity.[99] PwC renders audit and assurance, tax, and consulting services to clients in over 155 countries.[100] PwC's commitment to the effective management of diversity starts at the top and extends throughout the firm. Bob Moritz, chairman and senior partner of the U.S. firm of PwC and a PwC global network leadership team member, has long been an enthusiastic supporter and proponent of the effective management of diversity.[101] A long-tenured member of PwC, Moritz learned some valuable diversity lessons early in his career when he spent three years in PwC Tokyo assisting U.S. and European financial services firms doing business in Japan with audit and advisory services. Working in Japan opened Moritz's eyes to a host of diversity-related issues—what it felt like to be in the minority, to not speak the native language, and to experience discrimination. It also made him appreciate the value of cultural diversity, diversity of thought, and building trusting relationships with people who might be different from you on a number of dimensions.[102] As Moritz puts it, "Diverse and unexpected pools of talent are emerging around the world. To succeed in today's global economy requires organizations to have an inclusive culture that enables them to attract and retain diverse talent."[103]

Moritz gets together with diversity resource groups on a quarterly basis and ensures that executives and partners are working toward diversity and inclusion goals in a variety of areas such as recruiting and retention, engagement, promotions, and cross-cultural mentoring. All U.S. employees (the majority of whom are in management positions) are involved in mentoring programs (such as mentoring for newcomers, peer mentoring, and reverse mentoring), and over half of these mentoring relations involve a cross-cultural dyad.[104]

Maria Castañón Moats is an assurance partner at PwC and its chief diversity officer, leading its diversity strategy and initiatives.[105] She believes that effectively managing diversity includes providing all employees with

PricewaterhouseCoopers, which provides audit and consulting services to clients, is committed to the effective management of diversity and inclusion in areas such as recruiting, retention, engagement, promotion, and cross-cultural mentoring.
© Joe Fox/Radharc Images/Alamy

the chance to have a successful career; she also believes that everyone needs to work to understand people who are different from themselves and help each other to thrive. Diverse employees also help PwC to innovatively meet the needs of diverse clients.[106]

At PwC, multiple dimensions of diversity are valued and effectively managed, including ethnicity, gender, race, sexual orientation, religion, physical ability, and generation. A key focus of PwC's diversity initiatives is providing and maintaining an inclusive environment whereby diverse individuals not only feel welcome and supported but also have the opportunity to succeed and thrive. Thus, initiatives focus on ensuring that PwC has a good pipeline for hiring diverse employees and that these employees can make valuable contributions and achieve early success in their careers with PwC. Providing ongoing opportunities for development and advancement is also key, along with having a diverse leadership base.[107]

Initiatives and resources are in place for a variety of minority and majority employees. For example, working parents are supported in numerous ways such as through paid parental leave, child care provisions (discounts for child care, a nanny resource/referral service, and backup child care for emergencies), adoption assistance and leave, parenting circles, and groups for working parents. As another example, LGBT professionals are supported in multiple ways and have social networking and networking circles as well as access to full domestic partner benefit coverage and tax equalization. In fact, PwC is the only Big Four accounting firm that has a gay and lesbian partner advisory board composed of openly gay/lesbian partners, which advises PwC on LGBT concerns and issues and focuses on career development.[108]

Over 35 percent of newly hired employees at PwC are minorities (Latino/Hispanic, Native American, black/African-American, Asian/Pacific Islander, or multicultural), and PwC actively strives to ensure that these valuable employees are retained and advance in the firm. Diversity circles are professional forums whereby members of these and other diversity groupings can make contact with each other and provide learning, development, and mentoring experiences. The circles also give employees role models as they seek to advance in their careers. One of the most recent diversity circles established at PwC is the Special Needs Caregivers Circle, which seeks to provide a support network for professionals who have a disability or special need or have someone in their personal lives with a special need or disability.[109]

Recognizing that many employees, at some point in their careers and lives, need or want flexibility to balance professional demands with their personal lives, PwC has a variety of flexible work arrangements that employees can take advantage of. PwC also helps employees determine which type of flexible work arrangement might best meet their professional and personal needs.[110] This is just a sampling of the many diversity-related endeavors PwC has undertaken and continues to pursue. PwC continues to strive to effectively manage diversity in multiple ways for the good of its employees, its clients, the firm itself, and other stakeholders.[111]

When managers commit to diversity, their commitment legitimizes the diversity management efforts of others.[112] In addition, resources are devoted to such efforts, and all members of an organization believe that their diversity-related efforts are supported and valued. Consistent with this reasoning, top management commitment and rewards for the support of diversity are often cited as critical ingredients in the success of diversity management initiatives.[113] Additionally, seeing managers express confidence in the abilities and talents of diverse employees causes other organizational members to be similarly confident and helps reduce any prejudice they have as a result of ignorance or stereotypes.[114]

Two other important factors emphasize why managers are so central to the effective management of diversity. The first factor is that women, African-Americans, Hispanics, and other minorities often start out at a slight disadvantage due to how they are perceived by others in organizations, particularly in work settings where they are a numerical minority. As Virginia Valian, a psychologist at Hunter College who studies gender, indicates, "In most

144   Chapter Five

organizations women begin at a slight disadvantage. A woman does not walk into the room with the same status as an equivalent man, because she is less likely than a man to be viewed as a serious professional."[115]

The second factor is that research suggests that slight differences in treatment can accumulate and result in major disparities over time. Even small differences—such as a small favorable bias toward men for promotions—can lead to major differences in the number of male and female managers over time.[116] Thus, while women and other minorities are sometimes advised not to make "a mountain out of a molehill" when they perceive they have been unfairly treated, research conducted by Valian and others suggests that molehills (slight differences in treatment based on irrelevant distinctions such as race, gender, or ethnicity) can turn into mountains over time (major disparities in important outcomes such as promotions) if they are ignored.[117] Once again, managers have the obligation, from both an ethical and a business perspective, to prevent any disparities in treatment and outcomes due to irrelevant distinctions such as race or ethnicity.

LO5-3 Explain why the effective management of diversity is both an ethical and a business imperative.

distributive justice A moral principle calling for fair distribution of pay, promotions, and other organizational resources based on meaningful contributions that individuals have made and not personal characteristics over which they have no control.

The Ethical Imperative to Manage Diversity Effectively

Effectively managing diversity not only makes good business sense (which is discussed in the next section) but also is an ethical imperative in U.S. society. Two moral principles guide managers in their efforts to meet this imperative: distributive justice and procedural justice.

DISTRIBUTIVE JUSTICE   The principle of distributive justice dictates fair distribution of pay, promotions, job titles, interesting job assignments, office space, and other organizational resources among members of an organization. These outcomes should be distributed according to the meaningful contributions that individuals have made to the organization (such as time, effort, education, skills, abilities, and performance levels) and not irrelevant personal characteristics over which individuals have no control (such as gender, race, or age).[118] Managers have an obligation to ensure that distributive justice exists in their organizations. This does not mean that all members of an organization receive identical or similar outcomes; rather, it means that members who receive more favorable outcomes than others have made substantially higher or more significant contributions to the organization.

Is distributive justice common in organizations in corporate America? Probably the best way to answer this question is to say things are getting better. Fifty years ago, overt discrimination against women and minorities was common; today organizations are inching closer toward the ideal of distributive justice. Statistics comparing the treatment of women and minorities with the treatment of other employees suggest that most managers need to take a proactive approach to achieve distributive justice in their organizations.[119] For example, across occupations, women consistently earn less than men (see Table 5.3), according to

Table 5.3

Median Weekly Earnings for Full-Time Workers by Sex and Occupation in 2013

Occupation	Men	Women	Women's Earnings as a Percentage of Men's
Management, professional, and related	$1,383	$996	72
Service	585	463	79
Sales and office	777	627	81
Natural resources, construction, and maintenance	770	580	75
Production, transportation, and material moving	704	512	73

Source: "Household Data; Annual Averages; 39. Median Weekly Earnings of Full-Time Wage and Salary Workers by Detailed Occupation and Sex," www.bls.gov/cps/cpsaat39.pdf, February 25, 2016.

data collected by the U.S. Bureau of Labor Statistics.[120] Even in occupations dominated by women, such as sales and office occupations, men tend to earn more than women.[121]

In many countries, managers have not only an ethical obligation to strive to achieve distributive justice in their organizations but also a legal obligation to treat all employees fairly. They risk being sued by employees who believe they are not being fairly treated. That is precisely what six African-American Texaco employees did when they experienced racial bias and discrimination.[122]

procedural justice A moral principle calling for the use of fair procedures to determine how to distribute outcomes to organizational members.

PROCEDURAL JUSTICE   The principle of procedural justice requires that managers use fair procedures to determine how to distribute outcomes to organizational members.[123] This principle applies to typical procedures such as appraising subordinates' performance, deciding who should receive a raise or a promotion, and deciding whom to lay off when an organization is forced to downsize. Procedural justice exists, for example, when managers (1) carefully appraise a subordinate's performance; (2) take into account any environmental obstacles to high performance beyond the subordinate's control, such as lack of supplies, machine breakdowns, or dwindling customer demand for a product; and (3) ignore irrelevant personal characteristics such as the subordinate's age or ethnicity. Like distributive justice, procedural justice is necessary not only to ensure ethical conduct but also to avoid costly lawsuits.

Effectively Managing Diversity Makes Good Business Sense

Diverse organizational members can be a source of competitive advantage, helping an organization provide customers with better goods and services.[124] The variety of points of view and approaches to problems and opportunities that diverse employees provide can improve managerial decision making. Suppose the Budget Gourmet frozen food company is trying to come up with creative ideas for new frozen meals that will appeal to health-conscious, time-conscious customers tired of the same old frozen fare. Which group do you think is likely to come up with the most creative ideas: a group of white women with marketing degrees from Yale University who grew up in upper-middle-class families in the Northeast or a racially mixed group of men and women who grew up in families with varying income levels in different parts of the country and attended a variety of geographically dispersed business schools? Most people would agree that the diverse group is likely to have a wider range of creative ideas. Although this example is simplistic, it underscores one way in which diversity can lead to a competitive advantage.

Just as the workforce is becoming increasingly diverse, so are the customers who buy an organization's goods or services. In an attempt to suit local customers' needs and tastes, organizations like Target often vary the selection of products available in stores in different cities and regions.[125]

Diverse members of an organization are likely to be attuned to what goods and services diverse segments of the market want and do not want. Automakers, for example, are increasingly assigning women to their design teams to ensure that the needs and desires of female customers are taken into account in new car design.

For Darden Restaurants, the business case for diversity rests on market share and growth. Darden seeks to satisfy the needs and tastes of diverse customers by providing menus in Spanish in communities with large Hispanic populations.[126] Similarly, market share and growth and the identification of niche markets led Tracey Campbell to cater to travelers with disabilities.[127] She heads InnSeekers, a telephone and online listing resource for bed and breakfasts. Nikki Daruwala works for the Calvert Group in Bethesda, Maryland, a mutual fund that emphasizes social responsibility and diversity. She indicates that profit alone is more than enough of an incentive to effectively manage diversity. As she puts it, "You can look at an automaker. There are more women making decisions about car buying or home buying . . . $3.72 trillion per year are spent by women."[128]

Another way that effective management of diversity can improve profitability is by increasing retention of valued employees, which decreases the costs of hiring replacements for those who quit as well as ensures that all employees are highly motivated. In terms of retention, given the current legal environment, more and more organizations are attuned to the need to emphasize the importance of diversity in hiring. Once hired, if diverse employees think they are being unfairly treated, however, they will be likely to seek opportunities elsewhere. Thus, recruiting diverse employees has to be followed with ongoing effective management of diversity to retain valued organizational members.

If diversity is not effectively managed and turnover rates are higher for members of groups who are not treated fairly, profitability will suffer on several counts. Not only are the future contributions of diverse employees lost when they quit, but the organization also has to bear the costs of hiring replacement workers. According to the Employment Management Association, on average it costs more than $10,000 to hire a new employee; other estimates are significantly higher. For example, Ernst & Young estimates it costs about $1.2 million to replace 10 professionals, and the diversity consulting firm Hubbard & Hubbard estimates replacement costs average one-and-a-half times an employee's annual salary.[129] Moreover, additional costs from failing to effectively manage diversity stem from time lost due to the barriers diverse members of an organization perceive as thwarting their progress and advancement.[130]

Effectively managing diversity makes good business sense for another reason. More and more, managers and organizations concerned about diversity are insisting that their suppliers also support diversity.[131]

Finally, from both business and ethical perspectives, effective management of diversity is necessary to avoid costly lawsuits such as those settled by Advantica (owner of the Denny's chain) and The Coca-Cola Company. In 2000 Coca-Cola settled a class action suit brought by African-American employees at a cost of $192 million. The damage such lawsuits cause goes beyond the monetary awards to the injured parties; it can tarnish a company's image. One positive outcome of Coca-Cola's 2000 settlement is the company's recognition of the need to commit additional resources to diversity management initiatives. Coca-Cola is increasing its use of minority suppliers, instituting a formal mentoring program, and instituting days to celebrate diversity with its workforce.[132] These efforts have paid off, and Coca-Cola has appeared on *DiversityInc.*'s list of the "Top 50 Companies for Diversity."

In 2013 Merrill Lynch agreed to settle a racial discrimination lawsuit, brought by 700 black brokers, which spent around eight years in the U.S. federal court system; the settlement cost was $160 million.[133] After the suit was initially filed, Merrill Lynch was bought by Bank of America. As part of the settlement, Merrill Lynch agreed to change its policies, take proactive steps to ensure that discrimination does not take place, and ensure that black brokers have fair opportunities to be successful. This three-year initiative is being overseen by a committee composed of black brokers.[134] Also in 2013, Bank of America agreed to settle a discrimination lawsuit brought by female employees of Merrill Lynch for $39 million; from around 1998 to 2013, Merrill Lynch paid close to $500 million to settle discrimination claims.[135] As part of the settlement, Merrill Lynch consented to alter its policies to help ensure that women have fair opportunities to be successful.[136] Initiatives undertaken as a result of both of these lawsuits should help ensure that Merrill Lynch effectively manages diversity.

By now it should be clear that effectively managing diversity is a necessity on both ethical and business grounds. This brings us to the question of why diversity presents managers and all of us with so many challenges—a question we address in the next section, on perception.

Perception

Most people tend to think that the decisions managers make in organizations and the actions they take are the result of objective determination of the issues involved and the surrounding situation. However, each manager's interpretation of a situation or even of another person is precisely that—an interpretation. Nowhere are the effects of perception more likely to lead to different interpretations than in the area of diversity. This is because each person's interpretation of a situation, and subsequent response to it, is affected by his or her own age, race, gender, religion, socioeconomic status, capabilities, and sexual orientation. For example, different managers may see the same 21-year-old black male, gay, gifted, and talented subordinate in different ways: One may see a creative maverick with a great future in the organization, while another may see a potential troublemaker who needs to be watched closely.

LO5-4 Discuss how perception and the use of schemas can result in unfair treatment.

perception The process through which people select, organize, and interpret what they see, hear, touch, smell, and taste to give meaning and order to the world around them.

Perception is the process through which people select, organize, and interpret sensory input—what they see, hear, touch, smell, and taste—to give meaning and order to the world around them.[137] All decisions and actions of managers are based on their subjective perceptions. When these perceptions are relatively accurate—close to the true nature of what is actually being perceived—good decisions are likely to be made and appropriate actions taken. Managers of fast-food restaurant chains such as McDonald's, Pizza Hut, and Wendy's accurately perceived that their customers were becoming more health-conscious in the 1980s and 1990s and added salad bars and low-fat entries to their menus. Managers at Kentucky Fried Chicken, Jack-in-the-Box, and Burger King took much longer to perceive this change in what customers wanted.

One reason that McDonald's is so successful is that its managers go to great lengths to make sure their perceptions of what customers want are accurate. McDonald's has over 21,000 restaurants outside the United States that generate billions of dollars in annual revenues.[138] Key to McDonald's success in these diverse markets are managers' efforts to perceive accurately a country's culture and taste in food and then to act on these perceptions. For instance, McDonald's serves veggie burgers in Holland and black currant shakes in Poland.[139]

When managers' perceptions are relatively inaccurate, managers are likely to make bad decisions and take inappropriate actions that hurt organizational effectiveness. Bad decisions concerning diversity for reasons of age, ethnicity, or sexual orientation include (1) not hiring qualified people, (2) failing to promote top-performing subordinates, who subsequently may take their skills to competing organizations, and (3) promoting poorly performing managers because they have the same "diversity profile" as the manager or managers making the decision.

Factors That Influence Managerial Perception

Several managers' perceptions of the same person, event, or situation are likely to differ because managers differ in personality, values, attitudes, and moods (see Chapter 3). Each of these factors can influence how someone perceives a person or situation. An older middle manager who is high on openness to experience is likely to perceive the recruitment of able young managers as a positive learning opportunity; a similar middle manager who is low on openness to experience may perceive able younger subordinates as a threat. A manager who has high levels of job satisfaction and organizational commitment may perceive a job transfer to another department or geographic location that has very different employees (age, ethnicity, and so on) as an opportunity to learn and develop new skills. A dissatisfied, uncommitted manager may perceive the same transfer as a demotion.

Managers' and all organizational members' perceptions of one another also are affected by their past experiences with and acquired knowledge about people, events, and situations—information that is organized into preexisting schemas. Schemas are abstract knowledge structures stored in memory that allow people to organize and interpret information about a person, an event, or a situation.[140] Once a person develops a schema for a kind of person or event, any newly encountered person or situation that is related to the schema activates it, and information is processed in ways consistent with the information stored in the schema. Thus, people tend to perceive others by using the expectations or preconceived notions contained in their schemas.[141] Once again, these expectations are derived from past experience and knowledge.

schema An abstract knowledge structure that is stored in memory and makes possible the interpretation and organization of information about a person, an event, or a situation.

People tend to pay attention to information that is consistent with their schemas and to ignore or discount inconsistent information. Thus, schemas tend to be reinforced and strengthened over time because the information attended to is seen as confirming the schemas. This also results in schemas being resistant to change.[142] This does not mean schemas never change; if that were the case, people could never adapt to changing conditions and learn from their mistakes. Rather, it suggests that schemas are slow to change and that for people to change their schemas, they need to encounter a considerable amount of contradictory information.

Schemas that accurately depict the true nature of a person or situation are functional because they help people make sense of the world around them. People typically confront so much information that it is not possible to make sense of it without relying on schemas.

Schemas are dysfunctional when they are inaccurate because they cause managers and all members of an organization to perceive people and situations inaccurately and assume certain things that are not necessarily true.

Psychologist Virginia Valian refers to inaccurate preconceived notions of men and women as gender schemas. Gender schemas are a person's preconceived notions about the nature of men and women and their traits, attitudes, behaviors, and preferences.[143] Research suggests that among white middle-class Americans, the following gender schemas are prevalent: Men are action-oriented, assertive, independent, and task-focused; women are expressive, nurturing, and oriented toward and caring of other people.[144] Any schemas such as these—which assume that a single visible characteristic such as gender causes a person to possess specific traits and tendencies—are bound to be inaccurate. For example, not all women are alike and not all men are alike, and many women are more independent and task-focused than men. Gender schemas can be learned in childhood and are reinforced in a number of ways in society. For instance, while young girls may be encouraged by their parents to play with toy trucks and tools (stereotypically masculine toys), boys generally are not encouraged to, and sometimes are actively discouraged from, playing with dolls (stereotypically feminine toys).[145] As children grow up, they learn that occupations dominated by men have higher status than occupations dominated by women.

gender schemas Preconceived beliefs or ideas about the nature of men and women and their traits, attitudes, behaviors, and preferences.

Perception as a Determinant of Unfair Treatment

Even though most people would agree that distributive justice and procedural justice are desirable goals, diverse organizational members are sometimes treated unfairly, as previous examples illustrate. Why is this problem occurring? One important overarching reason is inaccurate perceptions. To the extent that managers and other members of an organization rely on inaccurate information, such as gender schemas, to guide their perceptions of each other, unfair treatment is likely to occur.

stereotype Simplistic and often inaccurate belief about the typical characteristics of particular groups of people.

Gender schemas are a kind of stereotype, which is composed of simplistic and often inaccurate beliefs about the typical characteristics of particular groups of people. Stereotypes are usually based on a visible characteristic such as a person's age, gender, or race.[146] Managers who allow stereotypes to influence their perceptions assume erroneously that a person possesses a whole host of characteristics simply because the person happens to be an Asian woman, a white man, or a lesbian, for example. African-American men are often stereotyped as good athletes, Hispanic women as subservient.[147] Obviously, there is no reason to assume that every African-American man is a good athlete or that every Hispanic woman is subservient. Stereotypes, however, lead people to make such erroneous assumptions. A manager who accepts stereotypes might, for example, decide not to promote a highly capable Hispanic woman into a management position because the manager thinks she will not be assertive enough to supervise others.

A recent study suggests that stereotypes might hamper the progress of mothers in their organizations when they are seeking to advance in positions that are traditionally held by men. According to the study, based on gender stereotypes, people tend to view mothers as less competent in terms of skills and capabilities related to advancing in such positions.[148]

People with disabilities might also be unfairly treated due to stereotypes.[149] Although the ADA requires (as mentioned previously) that organizations provide disabled employees with accommodations, employment rates of people with disabilities tend to be low. That is, around 34 percent of people with disabilities are employed compared to 74 percent of people without disabilities. In a recent study, when fictitious cover letters and résumés were sent for thousands of accounting openings, letters disclosing a disability were 26 percent less likely to yield an expression of interest from employers (the cover letters and résumés were identical except for whether or not a disability was disclosed in the cover letter).[150] However, as profiled in the accompanying "Ethics in Action" feature, a number of organizations have not only provided employment opportunities for adults with disabilities but also have benefited from their valuable contributions.[151]

ETHICS IN ACTION

Disabled Employees Make Valuable Contributions

Some large organizations, like McDonald's, Walmart, Home Depot, and Walgreens, actively recruit employees with disabilities to work in positions such as cashiers, maintenance workers, greeters, shelf stockers, and floor workers who help customers find items. Home Depot, for example, works with a nonprofit agency called Ken's Krew, Inc., founded by parents of disabled adults, to recruit and place employees with disabilities in its stores.[152] Thus far, working with Ken's Krew has enabled Home Depot to recruit and place disabled adults in over 60 of its stores.[153]

Often, when given the opportunity, employees with disabilities make valuable contributions to their organizations. Walgreens opened an automated distribution center in Anderson, South Carolina, in which more than 40 percent of its 264 employees have disabilities.[154] For disabled employees like Harrison Mullinax, who has autism and checks in merchandise to be distributed to drugstores with a bar code scanner, having a regular job is a godsend. Randy Lewis, senior vice president of distribution and logistics at Walgreens, thought about hiring workers with disabilities when Walgreens was considering using technology to increase automation levels in a distribution center. Lewis, the father of a young adult son who has autism, was aware of how difficult it can be for young adults like his son to find employment. Various accommodations were made, such as redesigning workstations and computer displays to suit employees' needs, and employees received appropriate training in how to do their jobs. Some days, disabled employees are actually the most productive in the center. As Lewis puts it, "One thing we found is they can all do the job. . . . What surprised us is the environment that it's created. It's a building where everybody helps each other out."[155]

Walgreens is a large organization, but small organizations also have benefited from the valuable contributions of disabled employees. Habitat International Inc., founded by current CEO David Morris and his father, Saul, over 30 years ago, is a manufacturer and contractor of indoor–outdoor carpet and artificial grass and a supplier to home improvement companies, like Lowe's and Home Depot.[156] Habitat's profits have steadily increased over the years, and the factory's defect rate is less than 0.5 percent.[157]

Morris attributes Habitat's success to its employees, 75 percent of whom have either a physical or a mental disability, or both.[158] Habitat has consistently provided employment opportunities to people with disabilities such as Down syndrome, schizophrenia, or cerebral palsy.[159] The company has also hired the homeless, recovering alcoholics, and non-English-speaking refugees from other countries. And these employees were relied on by plant manager Connie Presnell when she needed to fill a rush order by assigning it to a team of her fastest workers.[160] Habitat pays its employees regionally competitive wages and has low absence and turnover rates. Employees who need accommodations to perform their jobs are provided them, and Habitat has a highly motivated, satisfied, and committed workforce.[161]

While Habitat has actually gained some business from clients who applaud its commitment to diversity, Habitat's ethical values and social responsibility have

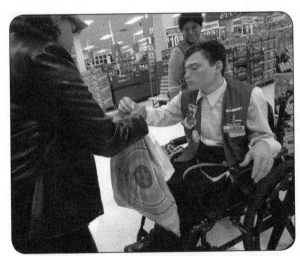

Working through his training as a greeter, Jamie Heal embraces his job at Walmart with gusto. His new found independence became a catalyst for life changes (going by the name Cameron was one) as well as a deeper sense of self-respect.
© Tannis Toohey/Toronto Star/ZUMAPRESS/Newscom

also led the company to forgo a major account when stereotypes reared their ugly heads. Several years ago CEO Morris dropped the account of a distribution company because its representatives had made derogatory comments about his employees. Although it took Habitat two years to regain the lost revenues from this major account, Morris had no regrets.[162] Habitat's commitment to diversity and fair treatment is a win–win situation; the company is thriving, and so are its employees.[163]

---

bias The systematic tendency to use information about others in ways that result in inaccurate perceptions.

Inaccurate perceptions leading to unfair treatment of diverse members of an organization also can be due to biases. Biases are systematic tendencies to use information about others in ways that result in inaccurate perceptions. Because of the way biases operate, people often are unaware that their perceptions of others are inaccurate. There are several types of biases.

The *similar-to-me effect* is the tendency to perceive others who are similar to ourselves more positively than we perceive people who are different.[164] The similar-to-me effect is summed up by the saying "Birds of a feather flock together." It can lead to unfair treatment of diverse employees simply because they are different from the managers who are perceiving them, evaluating them, and making decisions that affect their future in the organization.

Managers (particularly top managers) are likely to be white men. Although these managers may endorse the principles of distributive and procedural justice, they may unintentionally fall into the trap of perceiving other white men more positively than they perceive women and minorities. This is the similar-to-me effect. Being aware of this bias as well as using objective information about employees' capabilities and performance as much as possible in decision making about job assignments, pay raises, promotions, and other outcomes can help managers avoid the similar-to-me effect.

Social status—a person's real or perceived position in a society or an organization—can be the source of another bias. The *social status effect* is the tendency to perceive individuals with high social status more positively than we perceive those with low social status. A high-status person may be perceived as smarter and more believable, capable, knowledgeable, and responsible than a low-status person, even in the absence of objective information about either person.

Imagine being introduced to two people at a company holiday party. Both are white men in their late thirties, and you learn that one is a member of the company's top management team and the other is a supervisor in the mailroom. From this information alone, you might assume that the top manager is smarter, more capable, more responsible, and even more interesting than the mailroom supervisor. Because women and minorities have traditionally had lower social status than white men, the social status effect may lead some people to perceive women and minorities less positively than they perceive white men.

Have you ever stood out in a crowd? Maybe you were the only man in a group of women, or maybe you were dressed formally for a social gathering but everyone else was in jeans. Salience (that is, conspicuousness) is another source of bias. The *salience effect* is the tendency to focus attention on individuals who are conspicuously different from others in a group; the salience effect results in extra attention being focused on a person who stands out from the group mold. When people are salient, they often feel as though all eyes are watching them, and this perception is not far from the mark. Salient individuals are more often the object of attention than are other members of a work group, for example. A manager who has six white subordinates and one Hispanic subordinate reporting to her may inadvertently pay more attention to the Hispanic in group meetings because of the salience effect. Individuals who are salient are often perceived to be primarily responsible for outcomes and operations and are evaluated more extremely in either a positive or a negative direction.[165] Thus, when the Hispanic subordinate does a good job on a project, she receives excessive praise, and when she misses a deadline, she is excessively chastised. Part of being a good manager includes being aware of these sorts of tendencies and actively working against them.

Overt Discrimination

overt discrimination Knowingly and willingly denying diverse individuals access to opportunities and outcomes in an organization.

Inaccurate schemas and perceptual biases can lead well-meaning managers and organizational members to unintentionally discriminate against others. On the other hand, overt discrimination, or knowingly and willingly denying diverse individuals access to opportunities and outcomes in an organization, is intentional and deliberate. Overt discrimination is both unethical and illegal. Unfortunately, just as some managers steal from their organizations, others engage in overt discrimination.

Overt discrimination is a clear violation of the principles of distributive and procedural justice. Moreover, when managers are charged with overt discrimination, costly lawsuits can ensue. Organizations including the Adam's Mark chain of luxury hotels, Texaco, Ford Motor Company, Johnson & Johnson, BellSouth, Coca-Cola, Merrill Lynch, the National Football League, General Electric, Walmart, and Nike either have settled or face pending lawsuits alleging overt workplace discrimination.[166] Whereas in the past, lawsuits due to overt workplace discrimination focused on unfair treatment of women and minority group members, given the aging of the U.S. workforce, increasing numbers of discrimination cases are being brought by older workers who believe they were unfairly dismissed from their jobs due to their age.[167]

Despite all the advances that have been made, allegations of overt discrimination based on gender, race, age, and other forms of diversity continue to occur in the United States. For example, Nike settled a class action lawsuit filed on behalf of 400 African-American employees of its Chicago Niketown store.[168] Employees claimed that managers used racial slurs when referring to African-American employees and customers, gave African-American employees lower-paying jobs, made unwarranted accusations of theft, and had security personnel monitor employees and customers based on race.[169] Although Nike denied the allegations, as part of the settlement, Nike agreed to pay current and former employees $7.6 million and to promote effective management of diversity, partly by providing diversity training to all managers and supervisors in the store.[170]

Overt discrimination continues to be a problem in other countries as well. For example, although Japan passed its first Equal Employment Opportunity Law in 1985 and Japanese women are increasingly working in jobs once dominated by men, professional Japanese women have continued to find it difficult to advance in their careers and assume managerial positions.[171] Women make up almost half of the Japanese workforce, but only around 10 percent of managerial positions in business and government are occupied by women, according to the International Labor Organization agency of the United Nations.[172]

According to the United Nations Development Program's gender empowerment measure, which assesses the participation of women in a country's politics and economy, Japan is the most unequal of the world's wealthy nations when it comes to women.[173] Takako Ariishi witnessed women's struggle in Japan firsthand. As an employee of a family-owned manufacturing business that supplies parts to Nissan,[174] Ariishi was fired by her own father (who was then president of the company) when she had a son (her father claimed that her son would be his successor as president). Nonetheless, when Ariishi's father died, she took over as company president. Her company is 1 of 160 Nissan suppliers in Japan, and the heads of these companies meet twice a year; Ariishi is the only woman among the 160 presidents, and the first time the group met, she was asked to wait in a separate room with the secretaries. Miiko Tsuda, an employee of a tutoring company, indicated that she is paid less than her male coworkers, and she is often asked to push elevator buttons and make tea for male coworkers. Only 5 of the company's 300 management employees are women.[175]

Overt discrimination also can be a potential problem when it comes to layoff decisions. Organizational restructurings, a weak economy, and the recession that began in December 2007[176] led to record numbers of U.S. employees being laid off from 2007 to 2010. Although it is always a challenge for managers to decide who should be let go when layoffs take place, some laid-off employees felt that factors that should be irrelevant to this tough decision played a role in the layoffs at their former employers. And while many workers who believe they were unfairly discriminated against do not pursue legal remedies, some filed lawsuits alleging discrimination in layoff decisions.

Age-related discrimination complaints have been at record highs in recent times.[177] According to a press release issued in 2012 by the EEOC, "the number of age discrimination charges filed with the Commission increased by 50% since 2000."[178] Although this might be due to the fact that there were more older employees in the workforce than in previous years, David Grinberg, speaking on behalf of the EEOC, suggests that the rise in age discrimination allegations could also be due to the fact that older workers tend to be paid more and have better benefits.[179] For example, Joan Zawacki, in her late fifties, was laid off from her position as a vice president at the Cartus division of Realogy Corp. after having worked at the company for over 30 years. According to Zawacki, senior managers such as herself were told to talk discreetly with older workers in a friendly manner and suggest that they inquire with human resources about early retirement packages while protecting the jobs of younger workers. Zawacki indicates that she was laid off after not having convinced an older employee in her department to retire. A company spokesperson disputed the allegations in Zawacki's age discrimination lawsuit. In addition, over 90 employees at the Lawrence Livermore National Laboratory filed complaints alleging age discrimination in layoffs. Eddy Stappaerts, a 62-year-old senior scientist who had worked at the lab for 11 years and has a PhD from Stanford University, says, "A week before I was laid off, my boss said my contributions were essential."[180] He alleges that some of the work he did was given to a younger employee.[181]

Some women laid off from their jobs in the financial industry filed lawsuits alleging gender discrimination. Laid-off female executives at Citigroup, Merrill Lynch, Bank of America, and Bank of Tokyo have claimed that gender played a role in their firings.[182] In some cases, the women had done very well in their early years with the firms, were transferred to less desirable positions after becoming pregnant and taking maternity leaves, and ultimately were let go. Some of these women suggest that they were laid off even though they were just as qualified as men who were able to keep their jobs.[183]

Four former human resource managers at Dell filed a class action lawsuit alleging that Dell's massive layoffs discriminated against women and employees over age 40 and that women had been unfairly treated in pay and promotions.[184] Dell agreed to settle the lawsuit for $9.1 million while not admitting any wrongdoing.[185] Although many companies charged with discrimination allege that no discrimination took place, these are matters for the courts to decide.[186]

How to Manage Diversity Effectively

Various kinds of barriers arise to managing diversity effectively in organizations. Some barriers originate in the person doing the perceiving; others are based on the information and schemas that have built up over time concerning the person being perceived. To overcome these barriers and effectively manage diversity, managers (and other organizational members) must possess or develop certain attitudes and values as well as the skills needed to change other people's attitudes and values.

LO5-5 List the steps managers can take to manage diversity effectively.

Steps in Managing Diversity Effectively

Managers can take a number of steps to change attitudes and values and promote the effective management of diversity. Here we describe these steps (listed in Table 5.4), some of which we have referred to previously.

SECURE TOP MANAGEMENT COMMITMENT As mentioned earlier in the chapter, top management's commitment to diversity is crucial for the success of any diversity-related initiatives. Top managers need to develop the correct ethical values and performance- or business-oriented attitudes that allow them to make appropriate use of their human resources.

STRIVE TO INCREASE THE ACCURACY OF PERCEPTIONS One aspect of developing the appropriate values and attitudes is to take steps to increase the accuracy of perceptions. Managers should consciously attempt to be open to other points of view and perspectives, seek them out, and encourage their subordinates to do the same.[187] Organizational members

Table 5.4

Promoting the Effective Management of Diversity

- Secure top management commitment.
- Increase the accuracy of perceptions.
- Increase diversity awareness.
- Increase diversity skills.
- Encourage flexibility.
- Pay close attention to how employees are evaluated.
- Consider the numbers.
- Empower employees to challenge discriminatory behaviors, actions, and remarks.
- Reward employees for effectively managing diversity.
- Provide training, utilizing a multipronged, ongoing approach.
- Encourage mentoring of diverse employees.

who are open to other perspectives put their own beliefs and knowledge to an important reality test and will be more inclined to modify them when necessary. Managers should not be afraid to change their views about a person, an issue, or an event; moreover, they should encourage their subordinates to be open to changing their views in the light of disconfirming evidence. Additionally, managers and all other members of an organization should strive to avoid making snap judgments about people; rather, judgments should be made only when sufficient and relevant information has been gathered.[188]

INCREASE DIVERSITY AWARENESS   It is natural for managers and other members of an organization to view other people from their own perspective because their own feelings, thoughts, attitudes, and experiences guide their perceptions and interactions. The ability to appreciate diversity, however, requires that people become aware of other perspectives and the various attitudes and experiences of others. Many diversity awareness programs in organizations strive to increase managers' and workers' awareness of (1) their own attitudes, biases, and stereotypes and (2) the differing perspectives of diverse managers, subordinates, coworkers, and customers. Diversity awareness programs often have these goals:[189]

- Providing organizational members with accurate information about diversity
- Uncovering personal biases and stereotypes
- Assessing personal beliefs, attitudes, and values and learning about other points of view
- Overturning inaccurate stereotypes and beliefs about different groups
- Developing an atmosphere in which people feel free to share their differing perspectives and points of view
- Improving understanding of others who are different from oneself

Sometimes simply taking the time to interact with someone who is different in some way can increase awareness. Often when employees and managers are at social functions or just having lunch with a coworker, they interact with the people with whom they feel most comfortable. If all members of an organization make an effort to interact with people they ordinarily would not, mutual understanding is likely to be enhanced.[190]

In large organizations, top managers are often far removed from entry-level employees—they may lack an understanding and appreciation for what these employees do day in and day out, the challenges and obstacles they face, and the steps that can be taken to improve effectiveness. Recognizing this fact, some managers have taken concrete steps to improve their understanding of the experiences, attitudes, and perspectives of frontline employees, as indicated in the accompanying "Management Insight" feature.

Top Execs Improve Their Understanding of the Front Line

A growing number of organizations are implementing programs whereby top managers spend time performing the jobs of frontline employees to improve their understanding of the challenges these employees face and ways to improve their working conditions.[191] For example, DaVita Inc., a major provider of kidney dialysis services in the United States, has a program called "Reality 101," through which senior executives who have never worked in a dialysis clinic spend time working as clinic technicians.[192] Dialysis helps patients whose kidneys are not working properly to eliminate waste from their bloodstream. Treatments last around four hours, and patients often require multiple treatments per week.[193]

An executive meets with those who report to her to gain a better understanding of their jobs and the challenges they face.
© Digital Vision/Getty Images RF

Carolyn Kibler, a senior executive at DaVita who oversaw 48 clinics and around 750 employees, gained a much better understanding of the challenges technicians face, the nature of their jobs, and how best to manage them as a result of her participation in Reality 101. A former nurse, Kibler was surprised at how physically and emotionally demanding the job was and the high levels of stress it entailed. She also gained an appreciation of the high levels of empathy technicians have for their patients—trying to make them as comfortable as possible, helping them deal with their frustrations, and mourning the loss of those who die as a result of their often multiple medical problems.[194]

Realizing how hard technicians work and how hectic and stressful the clinics can be, Kibler became more understanding when paperwork was submitted late due to staff shortages, gave positive feedback to those who might have to miss meetings or conference calls to treat patients, tried to avoid giving clinics last-minute requests and deadlines for reports, and was more forthcoming with praise for clinic staff. More fully appreciating how patient care is the top priority and the nature of work on the clinic floor, Kibler was also more sensitive to how her own initiatives might affect these frontline employees and the patients they serve. As she indicated, "I am more conscious of the power of my words and my actions and the impact they have down in the organization."[195]

As part of its "Now Who's Boss Day," senior executives at Loews Hotels perform entry-level jobs one day per year to appreciate and understand the challenges in these jobs and ways to make performing them easier while improving customer service.[196] This program originated when Loews Hotels then CEO and current chairman Jonathan Tisch[197] took part in a reality TV show called *Now Who's Boss?* and performed the jobs of pool attendant, housekeeper, and bellman at a Florida hotel. He perspired so much in the polyester uniform people in these jobs were required to wear that he changed the uniform. As a result of another manager's experience in the trenches, handlebars were installed on room service carts so they weren't as difficult to push.[198]

Clearly, the jobs frontline employees perform are essential for organizational functioning. When top managers, who are far removed from these jobs, gain a better understanding of these jobs and the employees who perform them, they are in a better position to manage them effectively.

INCREASE DIVERSITY SKILLS   Efforts to increase diversity skills focus on improving how managers and their subordinates interact with each other and improving their ability to work with different kinds of people.[199] An important issue here is being able to communicate with diverse employees. Diverse organizational members may have different communication styles, may differ in their language fluency, may use words differently, may differ in the nonverbal signals they send through facial expressions and body language, and may differ in how they perceive and interpret information. Managers and their subordinates must learn to communicate effectively with one another if an organization is to take advantage of the skills and abilities of its entire workforce. Educating organizational members about differences in ways of communicating is often a good starting point.

Diversity education can help managers and subordinates gain a better understanding of how people may interpret certain kinds of comments. Diversity education also can help employees learn how to resolve misunderstandings. Organizational members should feel comfortable enough to solve communication difficulties and misunderstandings as they occur rather than letting problems grow and fester without acknowledgment.

ENCOURAGE FLEXIBILITY   Managers and their subordinates must learn how to be open to different approaches and ways of doing things. This does not mean organizational members have to suppress their personal styles. Rather, it means they must be open to, and not feel threatened by, different approaches and perspectives and must have the patience and flexibility to understand and appreciate diverse perspectives.[200]

To the extent feasible, managers should also be flexible enough to incorporate the differing needs of diverse employees. Earlier we mentioned that religious diversity suggests that people of certain religions might need time off for holidays that are traditionally workdays in the United States; managers need to anticipate and respond to such needs with flexibility (perhaps letting people skip the lunch hour so they can leave work early). Moreover, flexible work hours, the option to work from home, and cafeteria-style benefit plans (see Chapter 12) are just a few of the many ways in which managers can respond to the differing needs of diverse employees while enabling those employees to be effective contributors to an organization.

PAY CLOSE ATTENTION TO HOW ORGANIZATIONAL MEMBERS ARE EVALUATED   Whenever feasible, it is desirable to rely on objective performance indicators (see Chapter 12) because they are less subject to bias. When objective indicators are not available or are inappropriate, managers should ensure that adequate time and attention are focused on the evaluation of employees' performance and that evaluators are held accountable for their evaluations.[201] Vague performance standards should be avoided.[202]

CONSIDER THE NUMBERS   Looking at the numbers of members of different minority groups and women in various positions, at various levels in the hierarchy, in locations that differ in their desirability, and in any other relevant categorizations in an organization can tell managers important information about potential problems and ways to rectify them.[203] If members of certain groups are underrepresented in particular kinds of jobs or units, managers need to understand why this is the case and resolve any problems they uncover.

EMPOWER EMPLOYEES TO CHALLENGE DISCRIMINATORY BEHAVIORS, ACTIONS, AND REMARKS   When managers or employees witness another organizational member being unfairly treated, they should be encouraged to speak up and rectify the situation. Top managers can make this happen by creating an organizational culture (see Chapter 3) that has zero tolerance for discrimination. As part of such a culture, organizational members should feel empowered to challenge discriminatory behavior, whether the behavior is directed at them or they witness it being directed at another employee.[204]

REWARD EMPLOYEES FOR EFFECTIVELY MANAGING DIVERSITY   If effective management of diversity is a valued organizational objective, then employees should be rewarded for their contributions to this objective.[205] For example, after settling a major race discrimination lawsuit, The Coca-Cola Company now ties managers' pay to their achievement of diversity goals. Examples of other organizations that do so include American Express and Bayer Corporation.[206]

PROVIDE TRAINING UTILIZING A MULTIPRONGED, ONGOING APPROACH   Many managers use a multipronged approach to increase diversity awareness and skills in their organizations; they use films and printed materials supplemented by experiential exercises to uncover hidden biases and stereotypes. Sometimes simply providing a forum for people to learn about and discuss their differing attitudes, values, and experiences can be a powerful means of increasing awareness. Also useful are role-plays that enact problems resulting from lack of awareness and show the increased understanding that comes from appreciating others' viewpoints. Accurate information and training experiences can debunk stereotypes. Group exercises, role-plays, and diversity-related experiences can help organizational members develop the skills they need to work effectively with a variety of people. Many organizations hire outside consultants to provide diversity training, in addition to utilizing their own in-house diversity experts.[207]

United Parcel Service (UPS), a package delivery company, developed an innovative community internship program to increase the diversity awareness and skills of its managers and, at the same time, benefit the wider community. Upper and middle managers participating in the program take one month off the job to be community interns.[208] They work in community organizations helping people who, in many instances, are very different from themselves—such organizations include a detention center in McAllen, Texas, for Mexican immigrants; homeless shelters; AIDS centers; Head Start programs; migrant farmworker assistance groups; and groups aiming to halt the spread of drug abuse in inner cities.

Interacting with and helping diverse people enhances the interns' awareness of diversity because they experience it firsthand. Bill Cox, a UPS division manager who spent a month in the McAllen detention center, summed up his experience of diversity: "You've got these [thousands of] migrant workers down in McAllen . . . and they don't want what you have. All they want is an opportunity to earn what you have. That's a fundamental change in understanding that only comes from spending time with these people."[209]

Many managers who complete the UPS community internship program have superior diversity skills as a result of their experiences. During their internships, they learn about different cultures and approaches to work and life; they learn to interact effectively with people whom they ordinarily do not come into contact with; and they are forced to learn flexibility because of the dramatic differences between their roles at the internship sites and their roles as managers at UPS.

ENCOURAGE MENTORING OF DIVERSE EMPLOYEES   Unfortunately, African-Americans and other minorities continue to be less likely to attain high-level positions in their organizations, and for those who do attain them, the climb up the corporate ladder typically takes longer than it does for white men. David Thomas, a professor at the Harvard Business School, has studied the careers of minorities in corporate America. One of his major conclusions is that mentoring is very important for minorities, most of whom have reached high levels in their organizations by having a solid network of mentors and contacts.[210] **Mentoring** is a process by which an experienced member of an organization (the mentor) provides advice and guidance to a less experienced member (the protégé) and helps the less experienced member learn how to advance in the organization and in his or her career.

According to Thomas, effective mentoring is more than providing instruction, offering advice, helping build skills, and sharing technical expertise. Of course, these aspects of mentoring are important and necessary. However, equally important is developing a high-quality, close, and supportive relationship with the protégé. Emotional bonds between a mentor and a protégé can enable a protégé, for example, to express fears and concerns, and sometimes even reluctance to follow a mentor's advice. The mentor can help the protégé build his or her confidence and feel comfortable engaging in unfamiliar work behaviors.[211]

mentoring A process by which an experienced member of an organization (the mentor) provides advice and guidance to a less experienced member (the protégé) and helps the less experienced member learn how to advance in the organization and in his or her career.

Sexual Harassment

Sexual harassment seriously damages both the people who are harassed and the reputation of the organization in which it occurs. It also can cost organizations large amounts of money. In 1995, for example, Chevron Corporation agreed to pay $2.2 million to settle a sexual harassment

LO5-6 Identify the two major forms of sexual harassment and how they can be eliminated.

lawsuit filed by four women who worked at the Chevron Information Technology Company in San Ramon, California. One woman involved in the suit said she had received violent pornographic material through the company mail. Another, an electrical engineer, said she had been asked to bring pornographic videos to Chevron workers at an Alaska drill site.[212] In 2001 TWA spent $2.6 million to settle a lawsuit that alleged female employees were sexually harassed at JFK International Airport in New York. According to the EEOC, not only was sexual harassment tolerated at TWA but company officials did little to curtail it when it was brought to their attention.[213]

Unfortunately, the events at Chevron and TWA are not isolated incidents.[214] In 2011 two lawsuits were filed against American Apparel and its founder and CEO, Dov Charney, alleging sexual harassment.[215] Of the 607 women surveyed by the National Association for Female Executives, 60 percent indicated that they had experienced some form of sexual harassment.[216] In a Society for Human Resource Management survey of 460 companies, 36 percent indicated that within the last 24 months, one or more employees had claimed that they had been sexually harassed.[217] Sexual harassment victims can be women or men, and their harassers do not necessarily have to be of the opposite sex.[218] However, women are the most frequent victims of sexual harassment, particularly those in male-dominated occupations or those who occupy positions stereotypically associated with certain gender relationships, such as a female secretary reporting to a male boss. Though it occurs less frequently, men can also be victims of sexual harassment. For instance, several male employees at Jenny Craig filed a lawsuit claiming they were subject to lewd and inappropriate comments from female coworkers and managers.[219] Sexual harassment is not only unethical but also illegal. Managers have an ethical obligation to ensure that they, their coworkers, and their subordinates never engage in sexual harassment, even unintentionally.

Forms of Sexual Harassment

quid pro quo sexual harassment Asking or forcing an employee to perform sexual favors in exchange for receiving some reward or avoiding negative consequences.

hostile work environment sexual harassment Telling lewd jokes, displaying pornography, making sexually oriented remarks about someone's personal appearance, and other sex-related actions that make the work environment unpleasant.

There are two basic forms of sexual harassment: quid pro quo sexual harassment and hostile work environment sexual harassment. Quid pro quo sexual harassment occurs when a harasser asks or forces an employee to perform sexual favors to keep a job, receive a promotion, receive a raise, obtain some other work-related opportunity, or avoid receiving negative consequences such as demotion or dismissal.[220] This "Sleep with me, honey, or you're fired" form of harassment is the more extreme type and leaves no doubt in anyone's mind that sexual harassment has taken place.[221]

Hostile work environment sexual harassment is more subtle. It occurs when organizational members face an intimidating, hostile, or offensive work environment because of their sex.[222] Lewd jokes, sexually oriented comments or innuendos, vulgar language, displays of pornography, displays or distribution of sexually oriented objects, and sexually oriented remarks about one's physical appearance are examples of hostile work environment sexual harassment.[223] A hostile work environment interferes with organizational members' ability to perform their jobs effectively and has been deemed illegal by the courts. Managers who engage in hostile work environment harassment or allow others to do so risk costly lawsuits for their organizations. For example, in February 2004 a federal jury awarded Marion Schwab $3.24 million after deliberating on her sexual harassment case against FedEx.[224] Schwab was the only female tractor-trailer driver at the FedEx facility serving the Harrisburg International Airport vicinity in Middletown, Pennsylvania, from 1997 to 2000. During that period she was the target of sexual innuendos, was given inferior work assignments, and was the brunt of derogatory comments about her appearance and the role of women in society. On five occasions the brakes on her truck were tampered with. The federal EEOC sued FedEx, and Schwab was part of the suit.[225]

The courts have recently recognized other forms of hostile work environment harassment in addition to sexual harassment. For example, in June 2006 a California jury awarded $61 million in punitive and compensatory damages to two FedEx Ground drivers. The drivers, of Lebanese descent, indicated that they had faced a hostile work environment and high levels of stress because a manager had harassed them with racial slurs for two years.[226]

Steps Managers Can Take to Eradicate Sexual Harassment

Managers have an ethical obligation to eradicate sexual harassment in their organizations. There are many ways to accomplish this objective. Here are four initial steps managers can take to deal with the problem:[227]

- *Develop and clearly communicate a sexual harassment policy endorsed by top management.* This policy should include prohibitions against both quid pro quo and hostile work environment sexual harassment. It should contain (1) examples of types of behavior that are unacceptable, (2) a procedure for employees to use to report instances of harassment, (3) a discussion of the disciplinary actions that will be taken when harassment has taken place, and (4) a commitment to educate and train organizational members about sexual harassment.

- *Use a fair complaint procedure to investigate charges of sexual harassment.* Such a procedure should (1) be managed by a neutral third party, (2) ensure that complaints are dealt with promptly and thoroughly, (3) protect and fairly treat victims, and (4) ensure that alleged harassers are fairly treated.

- *When it has been determined that sexual harassment has taken place, take corrective actions as soon as possible.* These actions can vary depending on the severity of the harassment. When harassment is extensive, prolonged, of a quid pro quo nature, or severely objectionable in some other manner, corrective action may include firing the harasser.

- *Provide sexual harassment education and training to all organizational members, including managers.* The majority of *Fortune* 500 firms currently provide this education and training for their employees. Managers at DuPont, for example, developed DuPont's "A Matter of Respect" program to help educate employees about sexual harassment and eliminate its occurrence. The program includes a four-hour workshop in which participants are given information that defines sexual harassment, sets forth the company's policy against it, and explains how to report complaints and access a 24-hour hotline. Participants watch video clips showing actual instances of harassment. One clip shows a saleswoman having dinner with a male client who, after much negotiating, seems about to give her company his business when he suddenly suggests that they continue their conversation in his hotel room. The saleswoman is confused about what to do. Will she be reprimanded if she says no and the deal is lost? After watching a video, participants discuss what they have seen, why the behavior is inappropriate, and what organizations can do to alleviate the problem.[228] Throughout the program, managers stress to employees that they do not have to tolerate sexual harassment or get involved in situations in which harassment is likely to occur.

Barry S. Roberts and Richard A. Mann, experts on business law and authors of several books on the topic, suggest a number of additional factors that managers and all members of an organization need to keep in mind about sexual harassment:[229]

- Every sexual harassment charge should be taken seriously.

- Employees who go along with unwanted sexual attention in the workplace can be sexual harassment victims.

- Employees sometimes wait before they file complaints of sexual harassment.

- An organization's sexual harassment policy should be communicated to each new employee and reviewed with current employees periodically.

- Suppliers and customers need to be familiar with an organization's sexual harassment policy.

- Managers should give employees alternative ways to report incidents of sexual harassment.

- Employees who report sexual harassment must have their rights protected; this includes being protected from any potential retaliation.

- Allegations of sexual harassment should be kept confidential; those accused of harassment should have their rights protected.

- Investigations of harassment charges and any resultant disciplinary actions need to proceed in a timely manner.

- Managers must protect employees from sexual harassment from third parties they may interact with while performing their jobs, such as suppliers or customers.[230]

Summary and Review

THE INCREASING DIVERSITY OF THE WORKFORCE AND THE ENVIRONMENT Diversity is dissimilarity or differences among people. Diversity is a pressing concern for managers and organizations for business and ethical reasons. There are multiple forms of diversity such as age, gender, race and ethnicity, religion, capabilities/disabilities, socioeconomic background, sexual orientation, and physical appearance.

LO5-1

LO5-2, 5-3 **MANAGERS AND THE EFFECTIVE MANAGEMENT OF DIVERSITY** Both the workforce and the organizational environment are increasingly diverse, and effectively managing this diversity is an essential component of management. In each of their managerial roles, managers can encourage the effective management of diversity, which is both an ethical and a business imperative.

LO5-4 **PERCEPTION** Perception is the process through which people select, organize, and interpret sensory input to give meaning and order to the world around them. It is inherently subjective. Schemas guide perception; when schemas are based on a single visible characteristic such as race or gender, they are inaccurate stereotypes that lead to unfair treatment. Unfair treatment also can result from biases and overt discrimination.

LO5-5 **HOW TO MANAGE DIVERSITY EFFECTIVELY** Managers can take many steps to manage diversity effectively, an ongoing process that requires frequent monitoring.

LO5-6 **SEXUAL HARASSMENT** Two forms of sexual harassment are quid pro quo sexual harassment and hostile work environment sexual harassment. Steps that managers can take to eradicate sexual harassment include development and communication of a sexual harassment policy endorsed by top management, use of fair complaint procedures, prompt corrective action when harassment occurs, and sexual harassment training and education.

Management in Action

Topics for Discussion and Action

Discussion

1. Discuss why violations of the principles of distributive and procedural justice continue to occur in modern organizations. What can managers do to uphold these principles in their organizations? [LO5-2, 5-3, 5-4, 5-5]

2. Why are workers who test positive for HIV sometimes discriminated against? [LO5-1, 5-4]

3. Why would some employees resent the accommodations made for employees with disabilities that are dictated by the Americans with Disabilities Act? [LO5-1, 5-4]

4. Discuss the ways in which schemas can be functional and dysfunctional. [LO5-4]

5. Discuss an occasion when you may have been treated unfairly because of stereotypical thinking. What stereotypes were applied to you? How did they result in your being treated unfairly? [LO5-4]

6. How does the similar-to-me effect influence your own behavior and decisions? [LO5-4]

7. Why is mentoring particularly important for minorities? [LO5-5]

8. Why is it important to consider the numbers of different groups of employees at various levels in an organization's hierarchy? [LO5-5]

9. Think about a situation in which you would have benefited from mentoring but a mentor was not available. What could you have done to try to get the help of a mentor in this situation? [LO5-5]

Action

10. Choose a *Fortune* 500 company not mentioned in the chapter. Conduct research to determine what steps this organization has taken to manage diversity effectively and eliminate sexual harassment. [LO5-2, 5-5, 5-6]

Building Management Skills

Solving Diversity-Related Problems [LO5-1, 5-2, 5-3, 5-4, 5-5, 5-6]

Think about the last time that you (1) were treated unfairly because you differed from a decision maker on a particular dimension of diversity or (2) observed someone else being treated unfairly because that person differed from a decision maker on a particular dimension of diversity. Then answer these questions:

1. Why do you think the decision maker acted unfairly in this situation?

2. In what ways, if any, were biases, stereotypes, or overt discrimination involved in this situation?

3. Was the decision maker aware that he or she was acting unfairly?

4. What could you or the person who was treated unfairly have done to improve matters and rectify the injustice on the spot?

5. Was any sexual harassment involved in this situation? If so, what kind was it?

6. If you had authority over the decision maker (that is, if you were his or her manager or supervisor), what steps would you take to ensure that the decision maker stops treating people unfairly?

Managing Ethically [LO5-1, 5-2, 5-3, 5-5]

Some companies require that their employees work long hours and travel extensively. Employees with young children, employees taking care of elderly relatives, and employees who have interests outside the workplace sometimes find that their careers are jeopardized if they try to work more reasonable hours or limit their work-related travel. Some of these employees feel that it is unethical for their managers to expect so much of them in the workplace and not understand their needs as parents and caregivers.

Questions

1. Either individually or in a group, think about the ethical implications of requiring long hours and extensive amounts of travel for some jobs.

2. What obligations do you think managers and companies have to enable employees to have balanced lives and meet nonwork needs and demands?

Small Group Breakout Exercise

Determining If a Problem Exists [LO5-1, 5-2, 5-3, 5-4, 5-5]

Form groups of three or four people, and appoint one member as the spokesperson who will communicate your findings to the whole class when called on by the instructor. Then discuss the following scenario:

You and your partners own and manage a local chain of restaurants, with moderate to expensive prices, that are open for lunch and dinner during the week and for dinner on weekends. Your staff is diverse, and you believe that you are managing diversity effectively. Yet on visits to the different restaurants, you have noticed that your African-American employees tend to congregate together and communicate mainly with each other. The same is true for your Hispanic employees and your white employees. You are meeting with your partners today to discuss this observation.

1. Discuss why the patterns of communication that you observed might be occurring in your restaurants.

2. Discuss whether your observation reflects an underlying problem. If so, why? If not, why not?

3. Discuss whether you should address this issue with your staff and in your restaurants. If so, how and why? If not, why not?

Exploring the World Wide Web [LO5-1, 5-2, 5-3, 5-5, 5-6]

Go to the U.S. government websites that deal with employment issues, diversity, and sexual harassment, such as the websites of the Equal Employment Opportunity Commission (EEOC) and the Bureau of Labor Statistics. After reviewing these websites, develop a list of tips to help managers manage diversity effectively and avoid costly lawsuits.

Be the Manager [LO5-1, 5-2, 5-3, 5-4, 5-5]

You are Maria Herrera and have been recently promoted to the position of director of financial analysis for a medium-sized consumer goods firm. During your first few weeks on the job, you took the time to have lunch with each of your subordinates to try to get to know him or her better. You have 12 direct reports, junior and senior financial analysts who support different product lines. Susan Epstein, one of the female financial analysts you had lunch with, made the following statement: "I'm so glad we finally have a woman in charge. Now, hopefully, things will get better around here." You pressed Epstein to elaborate, but she clammed up. She indicated that she didn't want to unnecessarily bias you and

that the problems were pretty self-evident. In fact, Epstein was surprised that you didn't know what she was talking about and jokingly mentioned that perhaps you should spend some time undercover, observing her group and their interactions with others.

You spoke with your supervisor and the former director, who had been promoted and had volunteered to be on call if you had any questions. Neither man knew of any diversity-related issues in your group. In fact, your supervisor's response was, "We've got a lot of problems, but fortunately that's not one of them."

What are you going to do to address this issue?

Bloomberg Case in the News [LO 5-1, 5-2, 5-3, 5-4, 5-5]

At Biotech Party, Gender Diversity Means Cocktail Waitresses

Outside the Exploratorium, an airy event space on San Francisco's waterfront, a long line of mostly male biotechnology investors and executives waited to get into a party.

"There are the models!" one man yelled.

And, yes, there they were, in matching short, tight, black dresses with shoulder cutouts. It was the second year in a row that New York-based financial communications firm LifeSci Advisors had thrown the party, balancing out a shortage of women in town for the annual **J.P. Morgan Healthcare Conference** with ones who'd been hired to mingle and hold champagne.

"It's clearly not how women should be portrayed," Anna Protopapas, chief executive officer at Mersana Therapeutics Inc., said in San Francisco, as she wrapped up a series of meetings. She'd been invited to the LifeSci party, but had instead gone to one of a number of women-only events that have sprung up around the conference in recent years.

Andrew McDonald, founding partner at LifeSci, said that about 1,000 people attended the firm's bash—a much bigger crowd than last year, the first time they had the models.

"Last year, people were just coming to a cocktail party, and the buzz was generated during the party and afterward," McDonald said in an interview Tuesday. "Obviously for this event this year, people knew what to expect."

Industry Gathering

The J.P. Morgan conference, held each January, is the health-care sector's biggest gathering for investors and companies, with 9,000 attendees this year. Biotech is a major focus—the industry is considered a cradle of innovation, where daring medical entrepreneurs change patients' lives, and make fortunes.

Yet the event also offers a revealing look at the industry's lack of gender diversity. The ballrooms of the Westin St. Francis hotel were packed with rows of men in blue and gray suits. Outside the hotel, where attendees gather for coffee, was about the same—of 47 people sitting on one side of the square outside the conference hotel, two were women. Of those, one was in media relations. There was no line for the women's bathroom.

LifeSci's McDonald says it's just reality that the industry and its investors skew male. That's why he hired the models.

"When you think about going to a party, when you don't have any models, it's going to be 90/10, or even greater, male-to-female," he said. "Adding in some females changes the dynamic quite a bit."

No Complaints

McDonald said he got "zero" complaints from anyone offended, and that he's sensitive to any concerns his clients might have raised. He said there are many women in business development roles in the industry, many of whom asked for invitations. Other clients asked if they could bring their wives. "I made a point to talk to female guests," he said.

He also said his firm held an event in June when they hired male models in an effort for gender equality. It didn't go well.

"It was really awkward," he said. "The male models were just standing around talking to themselves, and they were relatively young relative to the other men at the party. It created a bizarre feeling they didn't anticipate."

A spokeswoman for JPMorgan Chase & Co. declined to comment. The LifeSci Advisors party isn't affiliated with the conference and is held off-site.

Few Female Executives

While women earned 39 percent of undergraduate bioengineering and biomedical engineering degrees, and 38 percent of doctorates in those fields in 2011, according to Catalyst, a New York-based research and advocacy group for executive women, it hasn't translated into top jobs.

Women occupy only 20 of 112 senior management roles at the 10 highest-valued companies in the industry. At small, young companies, it's not much better—of the 10 biotech startups that raised the most money in 2014, 19 percent of top executives are women, and their boards are 8 percent female, according to an August editorial in the journal Nature.

"Having the network is so critical," said Rachel King, CEO of GlycoMimetics Inc. and former chairwoman of the of Biotechnology Industry Organization, or BIO, the industry's trade group. "We need all kind of diversity in this industry not just because it's the right thing to do but because that's how we achieve excellence."

Top Roles

Illumina Inc. CEO Jay Flatley said his company has struggled to fill top roles with women. The San Diego-based genetics company, worth about $24 billion, lists no female members of its senior management team and just one on the board.

"The frustrating part is that we have had a reasonable amount of senior roles that open up in our company, and the number of women that become candidates is very small," he said in an interview. "It's hard."

The same is true of board seats, Flatley said. When the company tried to find a female director three years ago, he was told it would have a tough time competing with Fortune 500 companies that could pay qualified female candidates lucrative salaries.

"Really, talent is hard to find?" said Wende Hutton, a partner at venture capital firm Canaan Partners, which manages assets worth $4.2 billion.

"Well, try some more!" She was in town meeting with large drugmakers about her firm's portfolio companies.

Women have a difficult time advancing in biotech companies because there's little support structure for them, said director of research. They often lack women mentors or role models, or are hired for with the same qualifications, and for lower pay. As a result, they're more likely to leave for other industries.

'Unwelcoming'

"Executives often use the excuse that women aren't in the pipeline because they lack the right educational credentials, when in fact these companies are unwelcoming to women," Beninger said. "When they look above them they see hardly any women who've advanced."

Judy Lieberman is a professor at Harvard Medical School and a member of the scientific advisory board at the biotechnology company Alnylam Pharmaceuticals Inc. Her lab studies one of the hottest areas in biotech—the immune system's role in cancer, and how the genetic code's messenger system may play a role in disease. Yet when she tried to found her own company, it was hard to get an interested audience from mostly male investors, she said.

"When you do something like start a company, if you're not part of the network, or if people don't view you as a good boy, they don't take what you say with the same amount of credibility," she said. Lieberman got a grant from the National Institutes of Health to continue the work.

No Fishing Trips

Still, there are signs things are changing. Hutton was planning to attend a women-only dinner at the meeting with 85 venture capital executives. That's quite a change from not long ago, when at an earlier firm she was the only woman among the partners. When the others planned a ski retreat, she wasn't invited because they thought she'd feel strange as the lone woman.

At Canaan, Hutton said that of the firm's eight current life-science investors, four are female.

"We don't plan rental lodge fishing trips," she said.

Source: Damouni, Sasha, Doni Bloomfield, and Caroline Chen, "At Biotech Party, Gender Diversity Means Cocktail Waitresses," *Bloomberg*, January 13, 2016. Used with permission of Bloomberg. Copyright © 2016. All rights reserved.

Questions for Discussion

1. Why do you think there is a lack of diversity in the biotech industry?

2. In what ways might stereotypes and biases contribute to a lack of diversity in the biotech industry?

3. What are some steps that decision makers and managers in the health sciences field can take to increase diversity?

Notes

1. "About Novartis Pharmaceuticals," http://www.pharma.us.novartis.com/info/about-us/about-us.jsp, February 22, 2016; "Company Overview of Novartis Pharmaceuticals Corporation," http://www.bloomberg.com/research/stocks/private/snapshot.asp?privcapId=4276705, February 22, 2016; "No. 1—Novartis Pharmaceuticals Corporation—DiversityInc Top 50," http://www.diversityinc.com/novartis-pharmaceticals-corporation/, February 23, 2016.

2. "No. 1—Novartis Pharmaceuticals Corporation—DiversityInc Top 50."

3. "Novartis Pharmaceuticals Corporation Is First Company to Receive Number One Ranking Two Years in a Row on DiversityInc Top 50 Companies for Diversity List," http://www.pharma.us.novartis.com/info/newsroom/news-description.jsp?id=137225, February 22, 2016.

4. "Diversity and Inclusion," http://www.pharma.us.novartis.com/info/about-us/diversity-and-inclusion.jsp, February 22, 2016; "Diversity Champions," http://www.pharma.us.novartis.com/info/about-us/diversity-and-inclusion/diversity-champions.jsp, February 22, 2016.

5. "No. 1—Novartis Pharmaceuticals Corporation—DiversityInc Top 50."

6. "Novartis Pharmaceuticals Corporation Is First Company to Receive Number One Ranking Two Years in a Row on DiversityInc Top 50 Companies for Diversity List."

7. "No. 5—Sodexo—DiversityInc Top 50," http://www.diversityinc.com/sodexo/, February 22, 2016; "The Diversity Inc Top 50 Companies for Diversity 2014," 2014 Diversity Inc., 27–80.

8. P. Dvorak, "Firms Push New Methods to Promote Diversity," *The Wall Street Journal,* December 18, 2006, B3; www.sodexhousa.com/, About Us, http:/www.sodexousa.com/usen/aboutus/aboutus.asp, February 7, 2008, accessed February 8, 2010; "Catalyst Honors Initiatives at Sodexo and Commonwealth Bank of Australia with the 2012 Catalyst Award," http://www.sodexousa.com/usen/newsroom/press/press12/sodexo_catalyst_award.asp, January 24, 2012, accessed April 5, 2012; "About Us—Sodexo in the USA," http://sodexousa.com/usen/about_us/sodexo_in_usa.aspx, February 24, 2016.

9. Dvorak, "Firms Push New Methods to Promote Diversity."

10. Ibid.

11. Ibid.

12. Ibid.

13. "Lorna C. Donatone to Lead Sodexo's Business in North America and Its Schools Operations Globally," http://sodexousa.com/usen/print-page.aspx, February 22, 2016.

14. "Sodexo Diversity & Inclusion," http://sodexousa.com/usen/corporate_responsibility/responsible_employer/diversity_inclusion/diversity_inclusion.aspx, February 23, 2016.

15. Dvorak, "Firms Push New Methods to Promote Diversity"; "Sodexo Executive

164   Chapter Five

Dr. Rohini Anand Honored with Mosaic Woman Leadership Award," http://www.sodexousa.com/usen/newsroom/press/press11/rohinianandmosaicaward.asp, November 17, 2011, accessed April 5, 2012.

16. "No. 5—Sodexo—DiversityInc Top 50," http://www.diversityinc.com/sodexo/, February 22, 2016.

17. "Sodexo Diversity & Inclusion."

18. Ibid.

19. "No. 1—Novartis Pharmaceuticals Corporation—DiversityInc Top 50"; "No. 5—Sodexo—DiversityInc Top 50."

20. D. McCracken, "Winning the Talent War for Women," *Harvard Business Review,* November–December 2000, 159–67.

21. W.B. Swann, Jr., J.T. Polzer, D.C. Seyle and S. J. Ko, "Finding Value in Diversity: Verification of Personal and Social Self-Views in Diverse Groups," *Academy of Management Review* 29, no. 1 (2004), 9–27.

22. "Usual Weekly Earnings Summary," *News: Bureau of Labor Statistics,* www.bls.gov/news.release/whyeng.nr0.htm, April 16, 2004; "Facts on Affirmative Action in Employment and Contracting," *Americans for a Fair Chance,* fairchance.civilrights.org/research_center/details.cfm?id518076, January 28, 2004; "Household Data Annual Averages," www.bls.gov, April 28, 2004.

23. "Prejudice: Still on the Menu," *Business-Week,* April 3, 1995, 42.

24. "She's a Woman, Offer Her Less," *BusinessWeek,* May 7, 2001, 34.

25. "Glass Ceiling Is a Heavy Barrier for Minorities, Blocking Them from Top Jobs," *The Wall Street Journal,* March 14, 1995, A1.

26. "Catalyst Report Outlines Unique Challenges Faced by African-American Women in Business," *Catalyst* news release, February 18, 2004.

27. C. Gibson, "Nation's Median Age Highest Ever, but 65-and-Over Population's Growth Lags, Census 2000 Shows," *U.S. Census Bureau News,* www.census.gov, May 30, 2001; "U.S. Census Press Releases: Nation's Population One-Third Minority," *U.S. Census Bureau News,* www.census.gov/Press-Release/www/releases/archives/population/006808.html, May 10, 2006; Central Intelligence Agency, "The World Factbook," https://www.cia.gov/library/publications/the-world-factbook/fields/2177.html, April 5, 2012; Central Intelligence Agency, "The World Factbook," https://www.cia.gov/library/publications/the-world-factbook/fields/2177.html, April 1, 2014; "The World Factbook—Central Intelligence Agency," https://www.cia.gov/library/publications/resources/the-world-factbook/index.html, February 24, 2016.

28. "Table 2: United States Population Projections by Age and Sex: 2000–2050," *U.S. Census Board, International Data Base, 94,* www.census.gov/ipc/www.idbprint.html, April 28, 2004; "An Older and More Diverse Nation by Midcentury," Newsroom: Population, http://www.census.gov/newsroom/releases/archives/population/cb08-123.html, Auust 14, 2008.

29. U.S. Equal Employment Opportunity Commission, "Federal Laws Prohibiting Job Discrimination—Questions and Answers," www.eeoc.gov, June 20, 2001.

30. "Sex by Industry by Class of Worker for the Employed Civilian Population 16 Years and Over," *American FactFinder,* factfinder.census.gov, October 15, 2001; "2002 Catalyst Census of Women Corporate Officers and Top Earners in the *Fortune* 500," www.catalystwomen.org, August 17, 2004; "WB—Statistics & Data," http://www.dol.gov/wb/stats/main.htm?PrinterFriendly5true&, February 9, 2010; "Statistical Overview of Women in the Workplace," *Catalyst,* http://www.catalyst.org/publication/219/statistical-overview-of-women-in-the-workplace, December 2011, accessed April 4, 2012; Bureau of Labor Statistics, U.S. Department of Labor, "Usual Weekly Earnings of Wage and Salary Workers Fourth Quarter 2013," http://www.bls.gov/news.release/pdf/wkyemg.pdf, January 22, 2014, accessed April 1, 2014; "Table 7. Median Usual Weekly Earnings of Full-Time Wage and Salary Workers by Selected Characteristics, Annual Averages," http://www.bls.gov/news.release/wkyeng.t07.htm, February 24, 2016.

31. "Profile of Selected Economic Characteristics: 2000," *American FactFinder,* factfinder.census.gov, October 15, 2001; "Usual Weekly Earnings Summary," www.bls.gov/news.release, August 17, 2004; "WB—Statistics & Data," http://www.dol.gov/wb/stats/main.htm?PrinterFriendly5true&, February 9, 2010; Bureau of Labor Statistics, U.S. Department of Labor, "Usual Weekly Earnings of Wage and Salary Workers Fourth Quarter 2011," http://www.bls.gov/news.release/pdf/-wkyeng.pdf, January 24, 2012, accessed April 5, 2012; Bureau of Labor Statistics, U.S. Department of Labor, "Usual Weekly Earnings of Wage and Salary Workers Fourth Quarter 2013," http://www.bls.gov/news.release/pdf/wkyemg.pdf, January 22, 2014, accessed April 1, 2014; "Table 7. Median Usual Weekly Earnings of Full-Time Wage and Salary Workers by Selected Characteristics, Annual Averages."

32. "Women in Management in the United States, 1960–Present," *Catalyst,* http://www.catalyst.org/-publication/207/women-in-management-in-the-united-

states-1960-p, July 2011, accessed April 5, 2012; "Statistical Overview of Women in the Workplace," Knowledge Center—Catalyst.org, http://www.catalyst.org/knowledge/statistical—overview-women-workplace, March 3, 2014, accessed April 1, 2014.

33. "2000 Catalyst Census of Women Corporate Officers and Top Earners of the *Fortune* 500," www.catalystwomen.org, October 21, 2001; S. Wellington, M. Brumit Kropf, and P.R. Gerkovich, "What's Holding Women Back?" *Harvard Business Review,* June 2003, 18–19; D. Jones, "The Gender Factor," USA Today.com, December 30, 2003; "2002 Catalyst Census of Women Corporate Officers and Top Earners in the *Fortune* 500," www.catalystwomen.org, August 17, 2004; "2007 Catalyst Census of Women Corporate Officers and Top Earners of the *Fortune* 500," www.catalyst.org/-knowledge/titles/title.php?page5cen_COTE_07, February 8, 2008; "No News Is Bad News: Women's Leadership Still Stalled in Corporate America," *Catalyst,* http://www.catalyst.org/press-release/199/no-news-is-bad-news—womens-leadership-still-sta . . . , December 14, 2011, accessed April 5, 2012; "Statistical Overview of Women in the Workplace," Knowledge Center—Catalyst.org, http://www.catalyst.org/knowledge/statistical—overview-women-workplace, March 3, 2014, accessed April 1, 2014; "Fortune 500 Executive Officer Top Earner Positions Held by Women," Knowledge Center—Catalyst.org, http://www.catalyst.org/knowledge/women-executive-officer-top-earners-fortune-500-0, April 1, 2014.

34. T. Gutner, "Wanted: More Diverse Directors," *BusinessWeek,* April 30, 2001, 134; "2003 Catalyst Census of Women Board Directors," www.catalystwomen.org, August 17, 2004; "2007 Catalyst Census of Women Board Directors of the *Fortune* 500," www.catalyst.org/knowledge/titles/title.php?page1cen_WBD_07, February 8, 2008; "Statistical Overview of Women in the Workplace," *Catalyst,* http://www.catalyst.org/publication/219/statistical-overview-of-women-in-the-workplace, December 2011, accessed April 4, 2012; "Statistical Overview of Women in the Workplace," Knowledge Center—Catalyst.org, http://www.catalyst.org/knowledge/statistical-overview-women-workplace, March 3, 2014, accessed April 1, 2014.

35. Gunter, "Wanted: More Diverse Directors"; "2003 Catalyst Census of Women Board Directors."

36. R. Sharpe, "As Leaders, Women Rule," *BusinessWeek,* November 20, 2000, 75–84.

37. Ibid.

38. "New Catalyst Study Reveals Financial Performance Is Higher for Companies with More Women at the Top," *Catalyst* news release, January 26, 2004.

39. P. Sellers, "Women on Boards (NOT!)," *Fortune*, October 15, 2007, 105.

40. U.S. Census 2010, U.S. Department of Commerce, U.S. Census Bureau; K.R. Hums, N.A. Jones, and R.R. Ramirez, "Overview of Race and Hispanic Original: 2010," *2010 Census Briefs*, http://www.census.gov/prod/cen2010/briefs/c2010br-02.pdf, March 2011, accessed April 5, 2012.

41. U.S. Census 2010.

42. B. Guzman, "The Hispanic Population," U.S. Census Bureau, May 2001; U.S. Census Bureau, "Profiles of General Demographic Characteristics," May 2001; U.S. Census Bureau, "Revisions to the Standards for the Classification of Federal Data on Race and Ethnicity," November 2, 2000, 1–19.

43. L. Chavez, "Just Another Ethnic Group," *The Wall Street Journal*, May 14, 2001, A22.

44. Bureau of Labor Statistics, "Civilian Labor Force 16 and Older by Sex, Age, Race, and Hispanic Origin, 1978, 1988, 1998, and Projected 2008," stats.bls.gov/emp, October 16, 2001.

45. "An Older and More Diverse Nation by Midcentury"; Humes, Jones, and Ramirez, "Overview of Race and Hispanic Original: 2010."

46. Humes, Jones, and Ramirez, "Overview of Race and Hispanic Original: 2010."

47. "U.S. Census Bureau, Profile of General Demographic Characteristics: 2000," *Census 2000*, www.census.gov; "U.S. Census Press Releases: Nation's Population One-Third Minority," *U.S. Census Bureau News*, www.census.gov/Press-Release/www/releases/archives/population/006808.html, May 10, 2006; Humes, Jones, and Ramirez, "Overview of Race and Hispanic Original: 2010."

48. "An Older and More Diverse Nation by Midcentury."

49. Bureau of Labor Statistics, U.S. Department of Labor (BLS), "Usual Weekly Earnings of Wage and Salary Workers Fourth Quarter 2011"; Bureau of Labor Statistics, U.S. Department of Labor (BLS), "Usual Weekly Earnings of Wage and Salary Workers Fourth Quarter 2013."

50. J. Flint, "NBC to Hire More Minorities on TV Shows," *The Wall Street Journal*, January 6, 2000, B13.

51. J. Poniewozik, "What's Wrong with This Picture?" *Time*, www.Time.com, June 1, 2001; "Hispanic Heritage Month 2013: Sept. 15–Oct. 15," U.S. Census Bureau News, https://www.census.gov/newsroom/releases/pdf/cb13ff-19-hispanicheritage.pdf.

52. Poniewozik, "What's Wrong with This Picture?"

53. National Association of Realtors, "Real Estate Industry Adapting to Increasing Cultural Diversity," *PR Newswire*, May 16, 2001.

54. "Toyota Apologizes to African Americans over Controversial Ad," *Kyodo News Service*, Japan, May 23, 2001.

55. J.H. Coplan, "Putting a Little Faith in Diversity," *BusinessWeek Online*, December 21, 2000.

56. Ibid.

57. Ibid.

58. K. Holland, "When Religious Needs Test Company," *The New York Times*, February 25, 2007, BU17.

59. J.N. Cleveland, J. Barnes-Farrell, and J.M. Ratz, "Accommodation in the Workplace," *Human Resource Management Review* 7 (1997), 77–108; A. Colella, "Coworker Distributive Fairness Judgments of the Workplace Accommodations of Employees with Disabilities," *Academy of Management Review* 26 (2001), 100–16.

60. Colella, "Coworker Distributive Fairness Judgments of the Workplace Accommodations of Employees with Disabilities"; D. Stamps, "Just How Scary Is the ADA," *Training* 32 (1995), 93–101; M.S. West and R.L. Cardy, "Accommodating Claims of Disability: The Potential Impact of Abuses," *Human Resource Management Review* 7 (1997), 233–46.

61. G. Koretz, "How to Enable the Disabled," *BusinessWeek*, November 6, 2000 (*BusinessWeek* Archives).

62. Colella, "Coworker Distributive Fairness Judgments of the Workplace Accommodations of Employees with Disabilities."

63. "Notre Dame Disability Awareness Week 2004 Events," www.nd.edu/~bbuddies/daw.html, April 30, 2004.

64. P. Hewitt, "UH Highlights Abilities, Issues of the Disabled," *Houston Chronicle*, October 22, 2001, 24A.

65. Center for Students with DisAbilities (CSD)—University of Houston, http://www.uh.edu/csd/about_us/staff.html, April 1, 2014.

66. "Notre Dame Disability Awareness"; Hewitt, "UH Highlights Abilities, Issues of the Disabled."

67. J.M. George, "AIDS/AIDS-Related Complex," in L.H. Peters, C.R. Greer, and S.A. Youngblood, eds., *The Blackwell Encyclopedic Dictionary of Human Resource Management* (Oxford, UK: Blackwell, 1997), 6–7.

68. J.M. George, "AIDS Awareness Training," in L.H. Peters, C.R. Greer, and S.A. Youngblood, eds., *The Blackwell Encyclopedic Dictionary of Human Resource Management* (Oxford, UK: Blackwell, 1997), 6.

69. S. Armour, "Firms Juggle Stigma, Needs of More Workers with HIV," *USA Today*, September 7, 2000, B1.

70. Ibid.

71. Ibid.; S. Vaughn, "Career Challenge; Companies' Work Not Over in HIV and AIDS Education," *Los Angeles Times*, July 8, 2001.

72. R. Brownstein, "Honoring Work Is Key to Ending Poverty," *Detroit News*, October 2, 2001, 9; G. Koretz, "How Welfare to Work Worked," *BusinessWeek*, September 24, 2001 (*BusinessWeek* Archives).

73. "As Ex-Welfare Recipients Lose Jobs, Offer Safety Net," *Atlanta Constitution*, October 10, 2001, A18.

74. C.S. Rugaber, "Job Openings in a Squeeze," *Houston Chronicle*, February 10, 2010, D1.

75. U.S. Census Bureau, "Income, Poverty and Health Insurance Coverage in the United States: 2008," http://www.census.gov/Press-Release/www/releases/archives/income_wealth/014227.html, February 8, 2010; "The 2009 HHS Poverty Guidelines," http://aspe.hhs.gov/poverty/09poverty.shtml, February 8, 2010; "Income, Poverty and Health Insurance Coverage in the United States: 2010," http://www.census.gov/newsroom/releases/archives/income_wealth/cb11-157.html, September 13, 2011, accessed April 5, 2012; "About Poverty—Highlights—U.S. Census Bureau," http://www.census.gov/hhes/www/-poverty/about/overview/index.html, April 1, 2014.

76. U.S. Census Bureau, "Poverty—How the Census Bureau Measures Poverty," *Census 2000*, September 25, 2001; "How the Census Bureau Measures Poverty," http://www.census.gov/hhes/www/poverty/about/o-verview/measure.html, April 1, 2014.

77. U.S. Census Bureau, "Income, Poverty and Health Insurance Coverage in the United States: 2008"; U.S. Census Bureau, "The 2009 HHS Poverty Guidelines"; "Income, Poverty and Health Insurance Coverage in the United States: 2010," http://www.census.gov/-newsroom/releases/archives/income_wealth/cb11-157.html, September 13, 2011, accessed April 5, 2012; "Income, Poverty and Health Insurance Coverage in the United States: 2012," http://www.census.gov/newsroom/releases/archives/income_wealth/cb13-165.html, April 1, 2014.

78. I. Lelchuk, "Families Fear Hard Times Getting Worse/$30,000 in the Bay Area Won't Buy Necessities, Survey Says," *San Francisco Chronicle*, September 26, 2001, A13; S.R. Wheeler, "Activists: Welfare-to-Work Changes Needed," *Denver Post*, October 10, 2001, B6.

79. B. Carton, "Bedtime Stories: In 24-Hour Workplace, Day Care Is Moving to the Night Shift," *The Wall Street Journal*, July 6, 2001, A1, A4.

80. Carton, "Bedtime Stories"; "Mission, Core Values, and Philosophy," *Children's Choice Features,* http://childrenschoice .com/AboutUs/MissionCoreValuesand Philosophy/tabid/59/Default.aspx, February 9, 2010.

81. Carton, "Bedtime Stories."

82. Ibid.

83. G.J. Gates, "How Many People Are-Lesbian, Gay, Bisexual, and Transgender?" The Williams Institute, http:// williamsinstitute.law.ucla.edu/wp-content/uploads/Gates-How-Many—People-LGBT-Apr-2011.pdf, April 2011, accessed April 5, 2012.

84. N. Scheiber, "U.S. Agency Rules for Gays in Workplace Discrimination," *The New York Times,* July 18, 2015, B1, B2.

85. K. Fahim, "United Parcel Service Agrees to Benefits in Civil Unions," *The New York Times,* July 31, 2007, A19.

86. J. Hempel, "Coming Out in Corporate America," *BusinessWeek,* December 15, 2003, 64–72; Human Rights Campaign, "LGBT Equality at the Fortune 500," http://www.hrc.org/resources/entry/lgbt-equality-at-the-fortune-500, April 5, 2012.

87. Hempel, "Coming Out in Corporate America."

88. J. Files, "Study Says Discharges Continue under 'Don't Ask, Don't Tell,'" *The New York Times,* March 24, 2004, A14; J. Files, "Gay Ex-Officers Say 'Don't Ask' Doesn't Work," *The New York Times,* December 10, 2003, A14.

89. Hempel, "Coming Out in Corporate America"; "DreamWorks Animation SKG Company History," www. dreamworksanimation.com/dwa/opencms/ company/history/index.html, May 29, 2006; J. Chng, "Allan Gilmour: Former Vice-Chairman of Ford Speaks on Diversity," www.harbus.org/media/storage/ paper343/news/2006/04/18/News/Allan .Gilmour.Former.ViceChairman.Of.Ford .Speaks.On.Diversity-1859600.html?nore write200606021800&sourcedomain5 www.harbus.org, April 18, 2006; "Allan D. Gilmour Profile," Forbes.com, http://people.forbes.com/profile/print/ allan-d-gilmour/27441, April 11, 2012; Allan Gilmour—Forbes, http://www. forbes.com/profile/allan-gilmour/, April 1, 2014.

90. Needleman, "More Programs Move to Halt Bias"; "A History of Respect—Diversity and Inclusion at SC Johnson," https://www.scjohnson.com/en/ commitment/diversity/17Years.aspx, April 1, 2014.

91. Hempel, "Coming Out in Corporate America."

92. D. Kopecki, "JPMorgan, Goldman Rank Among Best Workplaces for Gays, Lesbians," *Bloomberg Businessweek,* http://www.businessweek.com/

news/2011-12-09/jpmorgan-goldman-rank-among-best-work . . . , December 9, 2011, accessed April 5, 2012; "Best Places to Work 2012," http://www. hrc.org/resources/entry/best-places-to-work-2012, April 5, 2012; Human Rights Campaign, "Award for Workplace Equality Innovation," http://www.hrc.org/ resources/entry/award-for-workplace-equality-innovation, April 5, 2012; "Best Places to Work 2014—Resources—Human Rights Campaign," http://hrc .org/resources/entry/best-places-to-work-2014, April 1, 2014; "The 304 Best Places to Work for LGBT Equality in America—Human Rights Campaign," http://www.hrc.org/blog/entry/the-304-best-places-to-work-for-lgbt-equality-in-american, April 1, 2014; "HRC's 2016 Corporate Equality Index—Human Rights Campaign," http://www.hrc.org/ campaigns/corporate-equality-index, February 24, 2016.

93. S. E. Needleman, "More Programs Move to Halt Bias against Gays." *The Wall Street Journal,* November 26, 2007, B3.

94. Ibid.

95. "Best Places to Work 2012"; "Best Places to Work 2014—Resources—Human Rights Campaign."

96. "For Women, Weight May Affect Pay," *Houston Chronicle,* March 4, 2004, 12A.

97. V. Valian, *Why So Slow? The Advancement of Women* (Cambridge, MA: MIT Press, 2000).

98. S.T. Fiske and S.E. Taylor, *Social Cognition,* 2nd ed. (New York: McGraw-Hill, 1991); Valian, *Why So Slow?*

99. "PricewaterhouseCoopers on the Forbes America's Largest Private Companies List," http://www.forbes.com/companies/ pricewaterhousecoopers/, March 25, 2014; "Facts and Figures: PwC," http:// www.pwc.com/gx/en/about-pwc/facts-and-figures.jhtml, March 25, 2014; "PwC: Business Services, Audit, Assurance, Tax and Advisory for the US and the Globe," http://www.pwc.com/us/en/ about-us/index.jhtml, March 26, 2014; "PwC Business Services, Audit, Assurance, Tax and Advisory for the US," http://www.pwc .com/us/en/about-us.html, February 24, 2016.

100. "PricewaterhouseCoopers on the Forbes America's Largest Private Companies List"; "PwC: Business Services, Audit, Assurance, Tax and Advisory for the US and the Globe."

101. "PwC—Bob Moritz," http://www. pwc.com/us/en/about-us/leadership/ bob-moritz.jhtml, March 26, 2014; A. Bryant, "Bob Moritz, on How to Learn about Diversity," *The New York Times,* http://www. nytimes.com/2013/09/15/-business/

bob-moritz-on-how-to-learn-about—diversity.html?_r50, September 14, 2013, accessed March 24, 2014.

102. "PwC—Bob Moritz"; Bryant, "Bob Moritz, on How to Learn about Diversity."

103. "The 2012 DiversityInc Top 50 Companies for Diversity List," *DiversityInc,* June 2012, 44–74.

104. Ibid.; "The DiversityInc Top 50," *DiversityInc,* June 2013, 29–76.

105. "Leveraging the Power of Our Differences," PwC, http://www.pwc.com/us/ en/about-us/diversity.jhtml, May 2013, accessed March 27, 2014; "Maria Castañón Moats," http://www.pwc.com/ us/en/about-us/leadership/maria-moats .html, February 24, 2016.

106. "The 2012 DiversityInc Top 50 Companies for Diversity List"; "The DiversityInc Top 50,"

107. "Leveraging the Power of Our Differences."

108. Ibid.

109. Ibid.

110. Ibid.

111. Ibid.

112. Valian, *Why So Slow?*

113. S. Rynes and B. Rosen, "A Field Survey of Factors Affecting the Adoption and Perceived Success of Diversity Training," *Personnel Psychology* 48 (1995), 247–70; Valian, *Why So Slow?*

114. V. Brown and F.L. Geis, "Turning Lead into Gold: Leadership by Men and Women and the Alchemy of Social Consensus," *Journal of Personality and Social Psychology* 46 (1984), 811–24; Valian, *Why So Slow?*

115. Valian, *Why So Slow?*

116. J. Cole and B. Singer, "A Theory of Limited Differences: Explaining the Productivity Puzzle in Science," in H. Zuckerman, J.R. Cole, and J.T. Bruer, eds., *The Outer Circle: Women in the Scientific Community* (New York: Norton, 1991), 277–310; M.F. Fox, "Sex, Salary, and Achievement: Reward Dualism in Academia," *Sociology of Education* 54 (1981), 71–84; J.S. Long, "The Origins of Sex Differences in Science," *Social Forces* 68 (1990), 1297–315; R.F. Martell, D.M. Lane, and C. Emrich, "Male–Female Differences: A Computer Simulation," *American Psychologist* 51 (1996), 157–58; Valian, *Why So Slow?*

117. Ibid.

118. R. Folger and M.A. Konovsky, "Effects of Procedural and Distributive Justice on Reactions to Pay Raise Decisions," *Academy of Management Journal* 32 (1989), 115–30; J. Greenberg, "Organizational Justice: Yesterday, Today, and

Tomorrow," *Journal of Management* 16 (1990), 399–402; O. Janssen, "How Fairness Perceptions Make Innovative Behavior More or Less Stressful," *Journal of Organizational Behavior* 25 (2004), 201–15.

119. Catalyst, "The Glass Ceiling in 2000: Where Are Women Now?" www.catalystwomen.org, October 21, 2001; Bureau of Labor Statistics, 1999, www.bls.gov; Catalyst, "1999 Census of Women Corporate Officers and Top Earners," www.catalystwomen.org; "1999 Census of Women Board Directors of the *Fortune* 1000," www.catalystwomen.org; Catalyst, "Women of Color in Corporate Management: Opportunities and Barriers, 1999," www.catalystwomen.org, October 21, 2001.

120. "Household Data Annual Averages," www.bls.gov, April 28, 2004; U.S. Bureau of Labor Statistics, Economic News Release, Table 7. *Median Usual Weekly Earnings of Full-Time Wage and Salary Workers by Occupation and Sex, Annual Averages,* http://data.bls.gov/cgi-bin/print.pl/news.release/wkyeng.t07.htm, February 9, 2010; "Household Data Annual Averages: 39. Median Weekly Earnings of Full-Time Wage and Salary Workers by Detailed Occupation and Sex," http://www.bls.gov/cps/cpsaat39.pdf, April 11, 2012; "Household Data Annual Averages 39. Median Weekly Earnings of Full-Time Wage Salary Workers by Detailed Occupation and Sex," http://www.bls.gov/cps/cpsaat39.htm, April 1, 2014; "Household Data—Annual Averages—39. Weekly Earnings of Full-Time Wage Salary Workers by Detailed Occupation and Sex," www.bls.gov/cps/cpsaat39.pdf, February 25, 2016.

121. Bureau of Labor Statistics, Labor Force Statistics from the Current Population Survey, "Household Data Annual Averages 39. Median Weekly Earnings of Full-Time Wage Salary Workers by Detailed Occupation and Sex," http://www.bls.gov/cps/cpsaat39.htm, April 1, 2014.

122. A.M. Jaffe, "At Texaco, the Diversity Skeleton Still Stalks the Halls," *The New York Times,* December 11, 1994, sec. 3, p. 5.

123. Greenberg, "Organizational Justice"; M.G. Ehrhart, "Leadership and Procedural Justice Climate as Antecedents of Unit-Level Organizational Citizenship Behavior," *Personnel Psychology* 57 (2004), 61–94; A. Colella, R.L. Paetzold, and M.A. Belliveau, "Factors Affecting Coworkers' Procedural Justice Inferences of the Workplace Accommodations of Employees with Disabilities," *Personnel Psychology* 57 (2004), 1–23.

124. G. Robinson and K. Dechant, "Building a Case for Business Diversity," *Academy of Management Executive* 3 (1997), 32–47.

125. A. Patterson, "Target 'Micromarkets' Its Way to Success; No 2 Stores Are Alike," *The Wall Street Journal,* May 31, 1995, A1, A9.

126. "The Business Case for Diversity: Experts Tell What Counts, What Works," DiversityInc.com, October 23, 2001.

127. B. Hetzer, "Find a Niche—and Start Scratching," *BusinessWeek,* September 14, 1998 (*BusinessWeek* Archives).

128. K. Aaron, "Woman Laments Lack of Diversity on Boards of Major Companies," *Times Union,* www.timesunion.com, May 16, 2001.

129. "The Business Case for Diversity."

130. B. Frankel, "Measuring Diversity Is One Sure Way of Convincing CEOs of Its Value," DiversityInc.com, October 5, 2001.

131. A. Stevens, "Lawyers and Clients," *The Wall Street Journal,* June 19, 1995, B7.

132. J. Kahn, "Diversity Trumps the Downturn," *Fortune,* July 9, 2001, 114–16.

133. K. Weise, "The Man Who Took on Merrill," *Bloomberg Businessweek,* November 28, 2013, 56–61.

134. Weise, "The Man Who Took on Merrill"; P. McGeehan, "Merrill Lynch in Big Payout for Bias Case," *The New York Times,* August 28, 2013.

135. P. McGeehan, "Bank of America to Pay $39 Million in Gender Bias Case," *The New York Times,* September 6, 2013.

136. McGeehan, "Bank of America to Pay $39 Million in Gender Bias Case."

137. H.R. Schiffmann, *Sensation and Perception: An Integrated Approach* (New York: Wiley, 1990).

138. McDonald's Corporation, "2008 Annual Report"; "McDonald's 2013 Financial Information Workbook.xlsx," http://www.aboutmcdonalds.com/med/-investors/financial_highlights.html, April 3, 2014.

139. A.E. Serwer, "McDonald's Conquers the World," *Fortune,* October 17, 1994, 103–16.

140. S.T. Fiske and S.E. Taylor, *Social Cognition* (Reading, MA: Addison-Wesley, 1984).

141. J.S. Bruner, "Going beyond the Information Given," in H. Gruber, G. Terrell, and M. Wertheimer, eds., *Contemporary Approaches to Cognition* (Cambridge, MA: Harvard University Press, 1957); Fiske and Taylor, *Social Cognition.*

142. Fiske and Taylor, *Social Cognition.*

143. Valian, *Why So Slow?*

144. D. Bakan, *The Duality of Human Existence* (Chicago: Rand McNally, 1966); J.T. Spence and R.L. Helmreich, *Masculinity and Femininity: Their Psychological Dimensions, Correlates, and Antecedents* (Austin: University of Texas Press, 1978); J.T. Spence and L.L. Sawin, "Images of Masculinity and Femininity: A Reconceptualization," in V.E. O'Leary, R.K. Unger, and B.B. Wallston, eds., *Women, Gender, and Social Psychology* (Hillsdale, NJ: Erlbaum, 1985), 35–66; Valian, *Why So Slow?*

145. Valian, *Why So Slow?*

146. Serwer, "McDonald's Conquers the World"; P.R. Sackett, C.M. Hardison, and M.J. Cullen, "On Interpreting Stereotype Threat as Accounting for African American–White Differences on Cognitive Tests," *American Psychologist* 59, no. 1 (January 2004), 7–13; C.M. Steele and J.A. Aronson, "Stereotype Threat Does Not Live by Steele and Aronson," *American Psychologist* 59, no. 1 (January 2004), 47–55; P.R. Sackett, C.M. Hardison, and M.J. Cullen, "On the Value of Correcting Mischaracterizations of Stereotype Threat Research," *American Psychologist* 59, no. 1 (January 2004), 47–49; D.M. Amodio, E. Harmon-Jones, P.G. Devine, J.J. Curtin, S.L. Hartley, and A.E. Covert, "Neural Signals for the Detection of Unintentional Race Bias," *Psychological Science* 15, no. 2 (2004), 88–93.

147. M. Loden and J.B. Rosener, *Workforce America! Managing Employee Diversity as a Vital Resource* (Burr Ridge, IL: Irwin, 1991).

148. M.E. Heilman and T.G. Okimoto, "Motherhood: A Potential Source of Bias in Employment Decisions," *Journal of Applied Psychology* 93, no. 1 (2008), 189–98.

149. L. Roberson, B.M. Galvin, and A.C. Charles, "Chapter 13, When Group Identities Matter: Bias in Performance Appraisal," in J.P. Walsh and A.P. Brief, eds., *The Academy of Management Annals* 1 (New York: Erlbaum, 2008), 617–50.

150. N. Scheiber, "Study Using Fake Job Letters Exposes Bias against Disabled," *The New York Times,* November 2, 2015, B1, B2.

151. A. Stein Wellner, "The Disability Advantage," *Inc.,* October 2005, 29–31.

152. Ken's Krew Inc.—Home, http://-kenskrew.org, April 3, 2014.

153. A. Merrick, "Erasing 'Un' from 'Unemployable,'" *The Wall Street Journal,* August 2, 2007, B6; "2012 Spirit of Social Work Awards Luncheon–Public Citizen of the Year Award / Online...," http://www.event.com/events/2012-spirit-of-social-work-awards-luncheon/custom-19-a3be..., April 11, 2012; http://kenskrew.org/partners.htm, April 3, 2014.

154. Merrick, "Erasing 'Un' from 'Unemployable.'"

155. Ibid.

156. "Habitat International: Our Products," www.habitatint.com/products.htm, April 6, 2006; "Habitat International, Inc. Home Page," www.habitatint.com, April 6, 2006; "Habitat International, Inc. Home Page," http://www.habitatint .com/, April 11, 2012; Habitat International, Inc. Home Page, http://www. habitatint.com/, April 3, 2014; "Habitat International, Inc. Home Page," http:// habitatint.com/, February 25, 2016.

157. Wellner, "The Disability Advantage."

158. "Habitat International: Our People," Habitat International—Our People, http://www.habitatint.com/people.htm, February 10, 2010.

159. Wellner, "The Disability Advantage."

160. "Habitat International: Our People"; Wellner, "The Disability Advantage."

161. Ibid.

162. Ibid.

163. Ibid.

164. E.D. Pulakos and K.N. Wexley, "The Relationship among Perceptual Similarity, Sex, and Performance Ratings in Manager Subordinate Dyads," *Academy of Management Journal* 26 (1983), 129–39.

165. Fiske and Taylor, *Social Cognition.*

166. "Hotel to Pay $8 Million in Settlement," *Houston Chronicle,* March 22, 2000, 3A; M. France and T. Smart, "The Ugly Talk on the Texaco Tape," *BusinessWeek,* November 18, 1996, 58; J.S. Lublin, "Texaco Case Causes a Stir in Boardrooms," *The Wall Street Journal,* November 22, 1996, B1, B6; T. Smart, "Texaco: Lessons from a Crisis-in-Progress," *BusinessWeek,* December 2, 1996, 44; "Ford Settling Bias Case, Will Hire More Women, Minorities," *Houston Chronicle,* February 19, 2000, 8C; C. Salter, "A Reformer Who Means Business," *Fast Company,* April 2003, 102–11; A. Zimmerman, "Walmart Appeals Bias-Suit Ruling," *The Wall Street Journal,* August 8, 2005, B5: C.H. Deutsch, "Chief of Unit Files Lawsuit Accusing G.E. of Racial Bias," *The New York Times,* May 18, 2005, C3; "Nike Settles Discrimination Suit for $7.6 Million," *The Wall Street Journal,* July 31, 2007, B9; R. Parloff, "The War over Unconscious Bias," *Fortune,* October 15, 2007, 90–102.

167. N. Alster, "When Gray Heads Roll, Is Age Bias at Work?" *The New York Times,* January 30, 2005, BU3.

168. "Nike Settles Discrimination Suit for $7.6 Million," *The Wall Street Journal,* July 31, 2007, B9.

169. Ibid.

170. Ibid.

171. M. Fackler, "Career Women in Japan Find a Blocked Path," *The New York Times,* August 6, 2007, A6; "Japan Values Women Less—As It Needs Them More," Inter Press Service, January 31, 2013, http://www.ipsnews.net/2013/01/ japan-values-women-less-as-it-needs-them-more/, April 3, 2014.

172. Fackler, "Career Women in Japan Find a Blocked Path"; www.un.org, February 11, 2008.

173. Fackler, "Career Women in Japan Find a Blocked Path."

174. www.nissanusa.com.

175. Fackler, "Career Women in Japan Find a Blocked Path."

176. U.S. Census Bureau, "Income, Poverty and Health Insurance Coverage in the United States: 2008," http://www. census.gov/Press-Release/www/releases/ archives/income_wealth/014227.html, February 8, 2010.

177. Jennifer Levitz, "More Workers Cite Age Bias during Layoffs," *The Wall Street Journal,* March 11, 2009, D1–2; U.S. Equal Employment Opportunity Commission, "Age Discrimination in Employment Act (ADEA) Charges," http://www1.eeoc.gov/eeoc/statistics/- enforcement/adea.cfm?renderforprint51, April 12, 2012; "What It Takes to Win an Age Discrimination Suit," *Forbes,* http://www.forbes.com/sites/n-extave- nue/2013/04/30/what-it-takes-to-win-an- age-discrimination-suit/, April 3, 2014.

178. "EEOC Issues Final Rule on 'Reasonable Factors Other Than Age' under the ADEA," http://www1.eeoc.gov/eeoc/ newsroom/release/3-29-12.cfm? renderforprint51, April 12, 2012.

179. Levitz, "More Workers Cite Age Bias."

180. Ibid.

181. Ibid.

182. A. Raghavan, "Terminated: Why the Women of Wall Street Are Disappearing," Forbes.com—Magazine Article, *ForbesWoman,* http://forbes.com/ forbes/2009/0316-072_t-erminated_ women_print.html, March 16, 2009, accessed February 10, 2010.

183. Raghavan, "Terminated."

184. G. Gross, "Dell Hit with Discrimination Class-Action Lawsuit," *The New York Times,* http://www.nytimes.com/external/ idg/2008/10/29/29idg-Dell-hit-with-d .html?pagewanted . . . , October 29, 2008.

185. A. Shah, "Dell Settles Discrimination Suit for $9.1 Million," *PC World,* http:// www.pcworld.com/printable/article/ id,169046/printable.html, July 24, 2009, accessed April 12, 2012; "Dell Settles Discrimination Lawsuit for $9.1M," http://www.bizjournals.com/austin/ stories/2009/07/27/daily1.html?s5print, July 27, 2009, accessed April 12, 2012.

186. A. Gonsalves, "Dell Denies Discrimination in Layoffs," *Information- Week,* http://www.-informationweek. com/shared/-printableArticleSrc. jhtml;jsessionid5 5RQQTNK . . . , November 3, 2008, accessed February 11, 2010.

187. A.G. Greenwald and M. Banaji, "Implicit Social Cognition: Attitudes, Self-Esteem, and Stereotypes," *Psychological Review* 102 (1995), 4–27.

188. A. Fisher, "Ask Annie: Five Ways to Promote Diversity in the Workplace," *Fortune,* www.fortune.com/fortune/subs/ print/0,15935,455997,00.html, April 23, 2004; E. Bonabeau, "Don't Trust Your Gut," *Harvard Business Review,* May 2003, 116–23.

189. A.P. Carnevale and S.C. Stone, "Diversity: Beyond the Golden Rule," *Training & Development,* October 1994, 22–39.

190. Fisher, "Ask Annie."

191. J.S. Lublin, "Top Brass Try Life in the Trenches," *The Wall Street Journal,* June 25, 2007, B1, B3; J.S. Lublin, "How to Be a Better Boss? Spend Time on the Front Lines," *Wall Street Journal,* http://online.wsj.com/article/SB1000142 4052970203824904577212951446826014.html, February 9, 2012.

192. www.davita.com, accessed February 11, 2008; "Company—About DaVita," http://www.davita.com/about/, February 11, 2010; Lublin, "How to Be a Better Boss?"

193. Lublin, "Top Brass Try Life in the Trenches"; "Developing Leaders— Community Care—DaVita," http://www. davita.com/community-care/helping- teammates/leadership-development, April 3, 2014.

194. Ibid.

195. Lublin, "Top Brass Try Life in the Trenches."

196. Ibid.; www.loews.com/loews.nsf/ governance.htm, February 7, 2008; "Lowes Hotel—Resorts," http:// www.loewshotels.com/en/default .aspx?cm_mmc5Google-_-National-_- Paid%20Sea . . . , February 11, 2010.

197. B. De Lollis, "Lowes Hotels' New CEO Advised Virgin Hotels," USAToday.com, http://travel.usatoday.com/hotels/post/ 2012/01/virgin-hotels-director-to-become- ceo-loews . . . , January 4, 2012, accessed April 12, 2012; "Jonathan M. Tisch— Leadership & BOD at Loews Corporation," http://www.loews.com/leadership/ jonathan-m-tisch/, April 3, 2014.

198. Lublin, "Top Brass Try Life in the Trenches."

199. B.A. Battaglia, "Skills for Managing Multicultural Teams," *Cultural Diversity at Work* 4 (1992); Carnevale and Stone, "Diversity."

200. Swann, Polzer, Seyle and Ko, "Finding Value in Diversity."

201. Valian, *Why So Slow?*

202. A.P. Brief, R.T. Buttram, R.M. Reizenstein, S.D. Pugh, J.D. Callahan, R.L. McCline, and J.B. Vaslow, "Beyond Good Intentions: The Next Steps toward Racial Equality in the American Workplace," *Academy of Management Executive*, November 1997, 59–72.

203. Ibid.

204. Ibid.

205. Ibid.

206. Y. Cole, "Linking Diversity to Executive Compensation," *Diversity Inc.*, August–September 2003, 58–62.

207. B. Mandell and S. Kohler-Gray, "Management Development That Values Diversity," *Personnel*, March 1990, 41–47.

208. B. Leak, "Online Extra: UPS Delivers an Eye-Opener," *BusinessWeek*, http://www.businessweek.com/print/magazine/content/05_41/b3954012.htm?chan5gl, October 10, 2005, accessed February 11, 2010; Community Internship-Program—UPS Corporate Responsibility, "Community Internship Program," http://www.-community.ups.com/Community/Community1Internship1Program, February 11, 2010.

209. B. Filipczak, "25 Years of Diversity at UPS," *Training*, August 1992, 42–46.

210. D.A. Thomas, "Race Matters: The Truth about Mentoring Minorities," *Harvard Business Review*, April 2001, 99–107.

211. Ibid.

212. "Chevron Settles Claims of 4 Women at Unit as Part of Sex Bias Suit," *The Wall Street Journal*, January 22, 1995, B12.

213. D.K. Berman, "TWA Settles Harassment Claims at JFK Airport for $2.6 Million," *The Wall Street Journal*, June 25, 2001, B6.

214. A. Lambert, "Insurers Help Clients Take Steps to Reduce Sexual Harassment," *Houston Business Journal*, Houston.bizjournals.com/-Houston/stories/2004/03/22/focus4.html, March 19, 2004.

215. L.M. Holson, "Chief of American Apparel Faces Second Harassment Suit," *The New York Times*, March 24, 2011, B2.

216. T. Segal, "Getting Serious about Sexual Harassment," *BusinessWeek*, November 9, 1992, 78–82.

217. J. Green, "The Silencing of Sexual Harassment," *Bloomberg Businessweek*, November 21–27, 2011, 27–28.

218. U.S. Equal Employment Opportunity Commission, "Facts about Sexual Harassment," www.eeoc.gov/facts/fs-sex.html, May 1, 2004.

219. B. Carton, "Muscled Out? At Jenny Craig, Men Are Ones Who Claim Sex Discrimination," *The Wall Street Journal*, November 29, 1994, A1, A7.

220. R.L. Paetzold and A.M. O'Leary-Kelly, "Organizational Communication and the Legal Dimensions of Hostile Work Environment Sexual Harassment," in G.L. Kreps, ed., *Sexual Harassment: Communication Implications* (Cresskill, NJ: Hampton Press, 1993).

221. M. Galen, J. Weber, and A.Z. Cuneo, "Sexual Harassment: Out of the Shadows," *Fortune*, October 28, 1991, 30–31.

222. A.M. O'Leary-Kelly, R.L. Paetzold, and R.W. Griffin, "Sexual Harassment as Aggressive Action: A Framework for Understanding Sexual Harassment," paper presented at the annual meeting of the Academy of Management, Vancouver, August 1995.

223. B.S. Roberts and R.A. Mann, "Sexual Harassment in the Workplace: A Primer," www3.uakron.edu/lawrev/robert1.html, May 1, 2004.

224. "Former FedEx Driver Wins EEOC Lawsuit," *Houston Chronicle*, February 26, 2004, 9B.

225. Ibid.

226. J. Robertson, "California Jury Awards $61M for Harassment," http://news.Yahoo.com, June 4, 2006.

227. S.J. Bresler and R. Thacker, "Four-Point Plan Helps Solve Harassment Problems," *HR Magazine*, May 1993, 117–24.

228. "Du Pont's Solution," *Training*, March 1992, 29.

229. Ibid.

230. Ibid.

The Environment of Management | **part 2**

CHAPTER 4

Ethics and Social Responsibility

Learning Objectives

After studying this chapter, you should be able to:

LO4-1 Explain the relationship between ethics and the law.

LO4-2 Differentiate between the claims of the different stakeholder groups that are affected by managers and their companies' actions.

LO4-3 Describe four rules that can help companies and their managers act in ethical ways.

LO4-4 Discuss why it is important for managers to behave ethically.

LO4-5 Identify the four main sources of managerial ethics.

LO4-6 Distinguish among the four main approaches toward social responsibility that a company can take.

© Chris Ryan/age fotostock **RF**

A MANAGER'S CHALLENGE

TOMS Adds Clean Water and Bullying to Its Social Agenda

Can ethical and socially responsible management be good for the bottom line?

One for One—that is the trademark at TOMS. In 2006 the company began selling shoes, and for every pair of shoes purchased, it gave a pair of new shoes to a person in need. In 2011 the company did the same with eyeglasses, donating a pair of glasses for every pair of sunglasses and optical frames purchased. In 2014 TOMS got into the coffee business and now donates one week of water to one person for every bag of coffee purchased. And in 2015 the company added bullying to its social agenda by offering a special selection of Standup backpacks for sale and partnering with the Crisis Text Line and No Bully. For each backpack sold, TOMS gives a donation to its social partners to help provide training for school staff and crisis counselors to help prevent and respond to instances of bullying.[1]

How can TOMS afford to do this? It is estimated that the TOMS shoes cost $9 to manufacture. The "best sellers" in the shoe area on the TOMS website cost $48. Another best seller on the website is a $179 pair of sunglasses. Twelve ounces of TOMS coffee beans cost $12.99, almost the same price as 16 ounces of Starbucks coffee beans. And the new backpack costs $50.[2]

TOMS operates by identifying a global need and creating a product to help address it. It began when Blake Mycoskie, TOMS founder, was traveling in Argentina and found that many children had no shoes. In response, he established a company that donates a pair of shoes for every purchased pair of shoes. Since then more than 60 million pairs of shoes have been purchased, and 60 million pairs have been donated. TOMS are sold at more than 500 stores globally and on the company's website at TOMS.com.

The next global need Mycoskie identified was eyesight. TOMS partnered with the Seva Foundation to provide eyeglasses and surgeries to the millions of people who are visually impaired in the world. Whenever a pair of TOMS sunglasses or an optical frame is purchased, help is given to restore sight and support sustainable community-based eye care

Blake Mycoskie, founder of TOMS, demonstrates his belief in social responsibility via the company's One for One program. He began with shoes, expanded to eyeglasses, and jumped into coffee roasting to help supply clean water. In 2016, TOMS added bullying to its social agenda—making donations when consumers purchased certain TOMS backpacks.
© Nick Ut/AP Images

programs. More than 400,000 people have received eyeglasses or surgery through the One for One program since 2011. TOMS sunglasses, made in Italy, have three hand-painted stripes that symbolize the three elements of One for One: the buyer, the person being helped, and TOMS.[3]

In 2014 the global need identified was clean water. Mycoskie announced that the company would apply its One for One business model to help provide clean drinking water. To do so, TOMS went into the coffee business. For every bag of TOMS beans sold, a person in need will get clean water for a week. TOMS is partnering with Water for People, an international charity based in Denver, to deliver the water to the regions from which the beans are sourced, including Peru, Honduras, Rwanda, Malawi, and Guatemala. To date, TOMS Roasting Company purchases have helped provide more than 335,000 weeks of safe water for people in need.[4]

In 2015 TOMS identified bullying as one of the social needs the company wanted to address. In the United States, nearly one out of every three students between the ages of 12 and 18 reports being bullied—a statistic TOMS and its partners hope to change. One of TOMS's partners, Crisis Text Line (CTL), focuses specifically on how to respond to bullying by providing real-time emotional support to teens in crisis. A person in need of help can text CTL anytime about any crisis. A trained specialist responds quickly to the text and helps the person stay safe with effective crisis counseling and referrals—all done through texting. No Bully is an organization that partners with schools around the country to train staff on how to interrupt bullying and how to bring students together as a "solution team" when bullying or harassment occurs. These teams empower other students to become leaders in their schools, building empathy for bullied students and working together to find ways to treat everyone with more respect and compassion.[5]

TOMS recently celebrated its 10th anniversary, and Mycoskie remains the face of the organization, although people still ask about "Tom." According to him, there is no Tom—the company's name stands for Mycoskie's vision of selling a pair of shoes today, giving away a pair tomorrow. The word *tomorrow* wouldn't fit on the tag that goes in the shoes, so he shortened it to TOMS. Regardless of the name, TOMS has made a significant contribution to the lives and social well-being of people around the world—starting with one pair of shoes at a time.[6]

Overview

As TOMS's "One for One" campaign illustrates, management decision making can have far-reaching implications when it comes to doing business in a socially responsible manner. TOMS's recent antibullying campaign may be targeted to children and teens, but the campaign affects parents, schools, communities, and many other groups. But globally, nations, companies, and managers differ enormously in their commitment to these people, or *stakeholders*—various groups of people who may benefit or be harmed by how managers make decisions that affect them. Managers of some companies make the need to behave ethically toward stakeholders their main priority. Managers of other companies pursue their own self-interest at the expense of their stakeholders and do harm to them—such as the harm done to the millions of people around the world who work in dangerous, unsanitary conditions or who work for a pittance.

In this chapter we examine the obligations and responsibilities of managers and the companies they work for toward the people and society that are affected by their actions. First we examine the nature of ethics and the sources of ethical problems. Next we discuss the major stakeholder groups that are affected by how companies operate. We also look at four rules or guidelines managers can use to decide whether a specific business decision is ethical or unethical. Finally, we consider the sources of managerial ethics and the reasons why it is important for a company to behave in a socially responsible manner. By the end of this chapter you will understand the central role of ethics in shaping the practice of management and the life of a people, society, and nation.

The Nature of Ethics

Suppose you see a person being mugged. Will you act in some way to help even though you risk being hurt? Will you walk away? Perhaps you might not intervene, but will you call the police? Does how you act depend on whether the person being mugged is a fit male, an elderly person, or a homeless person? Does it depend on whether other people are around so you can tell yourself, "Oh, well, someone else will help or call the police. I don't need to"?

Ethical Dilemmas

ethical dilemma The quandary people find themselves in when they have to decide if they should act in a way that might help another person or group even though doing so might go against their own self-interest.

The situation just described is an example of an ethical dilemma, the quandary people find themselves in when they have to decide if they should act in a way that might help another person or group and is the right thing to do even though doing so might go against their own self-interest.[7] A dilemma may also arise when a person has to choose between two different courses of action, knowing that whichever course he or she selects will harm one person or group even though it may benefit another. The ethical dilemma here is to decide which course of action is the lesser of two evils.

People often know they are confronting an ethical dilemma when their moral scruples come into play and cause them to hesitate, debate, and reflect upon the rightness or goodness of a course of action. Moral scruples are thoughts and feelings that tell a person what is right or wrong; they are a part of a person's ethics. Ethics are the inner guiding moral principles, values, and beliefs that people use to analyze or interpret a situation and then decide what is the right or appropriate way to behave. Ethics also indicate what is inappropriate behavior and how a person should behave to avoid harming another person.

ethics The inner guiding moral principles, values, and beliefs that people use to analyze or interpret a situation and then decide what is the right or appropriate way to behave.

The essential problem in dealing with ethical issues, and thus solving moral dilemmas, is that no absolute or indisputable rules or principles can be developed to decide whether an action is ethical or unethical. Put simply, different people or groups may dispute which actions are ethical or unethical depending on their personal self-interest and specific attitudes, beliefs, and values—concepts we discussed in Chapter 3. How are we and companies and their managers and employees to decide what is ethical and, so, act appropriately toward other people and groups?

Ethics and the Law

LO4-1 Explain the relationship between ethics and the law.

The first answer to this question is that society as a whole, using the political and legal process, can lobby for and pass laws that specify what people can and cannot do. Many different kinds of laws govern business—for example, laws against fraud and deception and laws governing how companies can treat their employees and customers. Laws also specify what sanctions or punishments will follow if those laws are broken. Different groups in society lobby for which laws should be passed based on their own personal interests and beliefs about right and wrong. The group that can summon the most support can pass laws that align with its interests and beliefs. Once a law is passed, a decision about what the appropriate behavior is with regard to a person or situation is taken from the personally determined ethical realm to the societally determined legal realm. If you do not conform to the law, you can be prosecuted; and if you are found guilty of breaking the law, you can be punished. You have little say in the matter; your fate is in the hands of the court and its lawyers.

In studying the relationship between ethics and law, it is important to understand that *neither laws nor ethics are fixed principles* that do not change over time. Ethical beliefs change as time passes; as they do so, laws change to reflect the changing ethical beliefs of a society. It was seen as ethical, and it was legal, for example, to acquire and possess slaves in ancient Rome and Greece and in the United States until the late 19th century. Ethical views regarding whether slavery was morally right or appropriate changed, however. Slavery was made illegal in the United States when those in power decided that slavery degraded the meaning of being human. Slavery makes a statement about the value or worth of human beings and about their right to life, liberty, and the pursuit of happiness. And if we deny these rights to other people, how can we claim to have any natural rights to these things?

Moreover, what is to stop any person or group that becomes powerful enough to take control of the political and legal process from enslaving us and denying us the right to be free and to own property? In denying freedom to others, one risks losing it oneself, just as stealing from others opens the door for them to steal from us in return. "Do unto others as you would have them do unto you" is a common ethical or moral rule that people apply in such situations to decide what is the right thing to do.

Changes in Ethics over Time

There are many types of behavior—such as murder, theft, slavery, rape, and driving while intoxicated—that most people currently believe are unacceptable and unethical and should therefore be illegal. However, the ethics of many other actions and behaviors are open to dispute. Some people might believe a particular behavior—for example, smoking tobacco or possessing guns—is unethical and, so, should be made illegal. Others might argue that it is up to the individual or group to decide if such behaviors are ethical and thus whether a particular behavior should remain legal.

As ethical beliefs change over time, some people may begin to question whether existing laws that make specific behaviors illegal are still appropriate. They might argue that although a specific behavior is deemed illegal, this does not make it unethical and thus the law should be changed. In 25 states, for example, it is illegal to possess or use marijuana (cannabis). To justify this law, it is commonly argued that smoking marijuana leads people to try more dangerous drugs. Once the habit of taking drugs has been acquired, people can get hooked on them. More powerful drugs such as heroin and other narcotics are addictive, and most people cannot stop using them without help. Thus, the use of marijuana, because it might lead to further harm, is an unethical practice.

It has been documented medically, however, that marijuana use can help people with certain illnesses. For example, for cancer sufferers who are undergoing chemotherapy and for those with AIDS who are on potent medications, marijuana offers relief from many treatment side effects, such as nausea and lack of appetite. Yet in the United States it is illegal in some states for doctors to prescribe marijuana for these patients, so their suffering continues. Since 1996, however, 25 states have made it legal to prescribe marijuana for medical purposes; nevertheless, the federal government has sought to stop such state legislation. The U.S. Supreme Court ruled in 2005 that only Congress or the states could decide whether medical marijuana use should be made legal, and people in many states are currently lobbying for a relaxation of state laws against its use for medical purposes.[8] In Canada there has been a widespread movement to decriminalize marijuana. While not making the drug legal, decriminalization removes the threat of prosecution even for uses that are not medically related and allows the drug to be taxed. Initiatives are under way in several states to decriminalize the possession of small amounts of marijuana for personal use as well as to make it more widely available to people legally for medical purposes. A major ethical debate is currently raging over this issue in many states and countries.

The important point to note is that while ethical beliefs lead to the development of laws and regulations to prevent certain behaviors or encourage others, laws themselves change or even disappear as ethical beliefs change. In Britain in 1830 a person could be executed for over 350 different crimes, including sheep stealing. Today the death penalty is no longer legal in Britain. Thus, both ethical and legal rules are *relative:* No absolute or unvarying standards exist to determine how we should behave, and people are caught up in moral dilemmas all the time. Because of this, we have to make ethical choices.

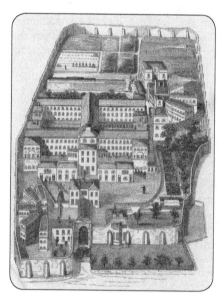

Coldbath Fields Prison, London, circa 1810. The British criminal justice system around this time was severe: A person could be executed for 350 different crimes, including sheep stealing. As ethical beliefs change over time, so do laws.
© Hulton Archive/Getty Images

The previous discussion highlights an important issue in understanding the relationship among ethics, law, and business. Throughout the 2010s many scandals plagued major companies such as J.P. Morgan Chase, HSBC, Standard Chartered Bank, ING, Barclays, and Capital One. Managers at some of these companies engaged in risky trades, interest rate manipulation, illegal trade facilitation, drug money laundering, and deception of customers.

In other cases no laws were broken, yet outrage was expressed over perceptions of unethical actions. One example of this is the Occupy Wall Street movement, a protest that began on September 17, 2011, in a park close to New York City's Wall Street financial district. The movement was prompted in part by the perceived unethical influence of the financial services sector on the government. On its web page (occupywallstreet.org), the organization says it is "fighting back against the corrosive power of major banks and multinational corporations over the democratic process, and the role of Wall Street in creating an economic collapse that has caused the greatest recession in generations." It also raised issues of social and economic inequality.

Some of the goals of this protest were to reduce the influence of corporations on government and allow a more balanced distribution of income. While the protesters did not allege that what financial institutions were doing was illegal, they asserted that the actions of financial institutions were not congruent with ethical business practices.

In 2011 President Barack Obama commented on Occupy Wall Street's concerns about the way policies are influenced by the financial sector: "It expresses the frustrations that the American people feel that we had the biggest financial crisis since the Great Depression, huge collateral damage all throughout the country, all across Main Street. And yet you're still seeing some of the same folks who acted irresponsibly trying to fight efforts to crack down on abusive practices that got us into this problem in the first place."[9]

Stakeholders and Ethics

Just as people have to work out the right and wrong ways to act, so do companies. When the law does not specify how companies should behave, their managers must decide the right or ethical way to behave toward the people and groups affected by their actions. Who are the people or groups that are affected by a company's business decisions? If a company behaves in an ethical way, how does this benefit people and society? Conversely, how are people harmed by a company's unethical actions?

The people and groups affected by how a company and its managers behave are called its stakeholders. **Stakeholders** supply a company with its productive resources; as a result, they have a claim on and a stake in the company.[10] Because stakeholders can directly benefit or be harmed by its actions, the ethics of a company and its managers are important to them. Who are a company's major stakeholders? What do they contribute to a company, and what do they claim in return? Here we examine the claims of these stakeholders—stockholders; managers; employees; suppliers and distributors; customers; and community, society, and nation-state as Figure 4.1 depicts.

stakeholders The people and groups that supply a company with its productive resources and, so, have a claim on and a stake in the company.

LO4-2 Differentiate between the claims of the different stakeholder groups that are affected by managers and their companies' actions.

Stockholders

Stockholders have a claim on a company because when they buy its stock or shares they become its owners. When the founder of a company decides to publicly incorporate the business to raise capital, shares of the stock of that company are issued. This stock grants its buyers ownership of a certain percentage of the company and the right to receive any future stock dividends. For example, in 2005 Microsoft decided to pay the owners of its 5 billion shares a special dividend payout of $32 billion. Bill Gates received $3.3 billion in dividends based on his stockholding, and he donated this money to the Bill and Melinda Gates Foundation, to which he has reportedly donated over $28 billion to date, with the promise of much more to come; and Warren Buffet committed to donate at least $30 billion to the Gates Foundation over the next decade. The two richest people in the world have decided to give away a large part of their wealth to serve global ethical causes—in particular to address global health concerns such as malnutrition, malaria, tuberculosis, and AIDS. Gates is also donating about $1.8 billion to the Gates Foundation to help eradicate polio as part of the Polio Eradication & Endgame Strategic Plan 2013–2018.[11]

Figure 4.1

Types of Company Stakeholders

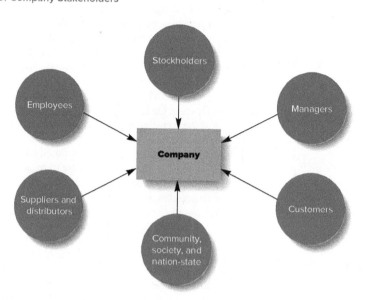

Stockholders are interested in how a company operates because they want to maximize the return on their investment. Thus, they watch the company and its managers closely to ensure that management is working diligently to increase the company's profitability.[12] Stockholders also want to ensure that managers are behaving ethically and not risking investors' capital by engaging in actions that could hurt the company's reputation. No company wants the reputation described by the Occupy Wall Street protesters, who alleged that business organizations value money over people and work in the self-interest of a privileged few. However, experts warn businesses not to ignore the movement. Harvard bloggers say the persistence of Occupy Wall Street is "a signal that there is authentic, deep-seated unhappiness with the failings of the U.S. economic system. It's an indicator that economic inequality is perceived as an important issue—one requiring businesses' immediate attention."[13]

Managers

Managers are a vital stakeholder group because they are responsible for using a company's financial, capital, and human resources to increase its performance and thus its stock price.[14] Managers have a claim on an organization because they bring to it their skills, expertise, and experience. They have the right to expect a good return or reward by investing their human capital to improve a company's performance. Such rewards include good salaries and benefits, the prospect of promotion and a career, and stock options and bonuses tied to company performance.

Managers are the stakeholder group that bears the responsibility to decide which goals an organization should pursue to most benefit stakeholders and how to make the most efficient use of resources to achieve those goals. In making such decisions, managers frequently must juggle the interests of different stakeholders, including themselves.[15] These sometimes difficult decisions challenge managers to uphold ethical values because some decisions that benefit certain stakeholder groups (managers and stockholders) harm other groups (individual workers and local communities). For example, in economic downturns or when a company experiences performance shortfalls, layoffs may help cut costs (thus benefiting shareholders) at the expense of the employees laid off. Many U.S. managers have recently faced this difficult decision. Until the 2009 financial crisis sent unemployment soaring over 10 percent, on average about 1.6 million U.S. employees out of a total labor force of 140 million were affected by mass layoffs each year; and over 3 million jobs from the United States, Europe, and Japan have been outsourced to Asia since 2005. Layoff decisions are always difficult: They not only take a heavy toll on workers, their families, and local communities but also

Layoff decisions are always difficult. Bank of America recently announced plans to reduce the workforce in its consumer-banking unit by thousands, as more and more customers are using mobile technology to do their banking.
© Steve Debenport/E+/Getty Images

mean the loss of the contributions of valued employees to an organization. In 2016, Bank of America announced plans to reduce the workforce in its consumer-banking unit by thousands, explaining that more and more customers are using mobile and online technology instead of local bank branches to do their banking.[16]

As we discussed in Chapter 1, managers must be motivated and given incentives to work hard in the interests of stockholders. Their behavior must also be scrutinized to ensure they do not behave illegally or unethically, pursuing goals that threaten stockholders and the company's interests.[17] Unfortunately, we have seen in the 2010s how easy it is for top managers to find ways to ruthlessly pursue their self-interest at the expense of stockholders and employees because laws and regulations are not strong enough to force them to behave ethically.

In a nutshell, the problem has been that in many companies corrupt managers focus not on building the company's capital and stockholders' wealth but on maximizing their own personal capital and wealth. In an effort to prevent future scandals, the Securities and Exchange Commission (SEC), the government's top business watchdog, has begun to rework the rules governing a company's relationship with its auditor, as well as regulations concerning stock options, and to increase the power of outside directors to scrutinize a CEO. The SEC's goal is to outlaw many actions that were previously classified as merely unethical. For example, companies are now forced to reveal to stockholders the value of the stock options they give their top executives and directors and when they give them these options; this shows how much such payments reduce company profits. Managers and directors can now be prosecuted if they disguise or try to hide these payments. In the 2010s the SEC announced many new rules requiring that companies disclose myriad details of executive compensation packages to investors; already the boards of directors of many companies have stopped giving CEOs perks such as free personal jet travel, membership in exclusive country clubs, and luxury accommodations on "business trips." Also, in 2010 Congress passed new laws preventing the many unethical and illegal actions of managers of banks and other financial institutions that led to the 2009 financial crisis. One of these regulations, the "Volcker Rule," seeks to reduce the chances that banks will put depositors' money at risk.[18]

Indeed, many experts argue that the rewards given to top managers, particularly the CEO and COO, grew out of control in the 2000s. Top managers are today's "aristocrats," and through their ability to influence the board of directors and raise their own pay, they have amassed personal fortunes worth hundreds of millions of dollars. For example, according to a study by the Federal Reserve, U.S. CEOs now get paid about 600 times what the average worker earns, compared to about 40 times in 1980—a staggering increase. In 2016 the median CEO compensation was $10.8 million.[19] We noted in Chapter 1 that besides their salaries, top managers often receive tens of millions in stock bonuses and options—even when their companies perform poorly.

Is it ethical for top managers to receive such vast amounts of money from their companies? Do they earn it? Remember, this money could have gone to shareholders in the form of dividends. It could also have reduced the huge salary gap between those at the top and those at the bottom of the hierarchy. Many people argue that the growing disparity between the rewards given to CEOs and to other employees is unethical and should be regulated. CEO pay has skyrocketed because CEOs are the people who set and control one another's salaries and bonuses; they can do this because they sit on the boards of other companies as outside directors. Others argue that because top managers play an important role in building a company's capital and wealth, they deserve a significant share of its profits. Some recent research has suggested that the companies whose CEO compensation includes a large percentage of stock options tend to experience big share losses more often than big gains, and on average, company performance improves as stock option use declines.[20] The debate over how much money CEOs and other top managers should be paid is still raging, particularly because the financial crisis beginning in 2009 showed how much money the CEOs of troubled financial companies earned even as their companies' performance and stock prices collapsed. For example, Countrywide Mortgage, which pioneered the subprime business, suffered losses of over $1.7 billion in 2007, and its stock fell 80 percent, yet its CEO, Angelo Mozilo, still received $20 million in stock awards and sold stock options worth $121 million before the company's price collapsed.

Ethics and Nonprofit Organizations

The issue of what is fair compensation for top managers is not limited to for-profit companies; it is one of many issues facing nonprofits. The many ethics scandals that have plagued companies in the 2010s might suggest that the issue of ethics is important only for profit-seeking companies, but this is untrue. There are almost 2 million private nonprofit charitable and philanthropic organizations in the United States, and charges that their managers have acted in unethical and even illegal ways have grown in the 2010s. For example, many states and the federal government are investigating the huge salaries that the top executives of charitable institutions earn.

One impetus for this was the revelation that the NYSE, which is classified as a charitable organization, paid its disgraced top executive, Richard A. Grasso, over $187 million in pension benefits. It turns out that over 80 nonprofits pay their top executives more than $1 million a year in salary, bonus, and other benefits, and the boards of trustees or directors of many of these organizations also enjoy lavish perks and compensation for attendance at board meetings. And unlike for-profit companies, which are required by law to provide detailed reports of their operations to their shareholders, nonprofits do not have shareholders, so the laws governing disclosure are far weaker. As a result, the board and its top managers have considerable latitude to decide how they will spend a nonprofit's resources, and little oversight exists.

To remedy this situation, many states and the federal government are considering new laws that would subject nonprofits to strict Sarbanes-Oxley-type regulations that force the disclosure of issues related to managerial compensation and financial integrity. There are also efforts in progress to strengthen the legal power of the IRS to oversee nonprofits' expenditures so that it has more authority to examine how these organizations spend their resources on managerial and director compensation and perks.

Experts hope that the introduction of new rules and regulations to monitor and oversee how nonprofits spend their funds will result in much more value being created from the funds given by donors. After all, every cent that is spent administering a nonprofit is a cent not being used to help the people or cause for which the money was intended. Ethical issues are involved because some badly run charities spend 70 cents of every dollar on administration costs. And charges have been leveled against charities such as the Red Cross for mishandling the hundreds of millions of dollars they received in donations after Hurricane Katrina struck; changes have been made in the Red Cross to address these issues. Clearly, the directors and managers of all organizations need to carefully consider the ethical issues involved in their decision making.

Employees

A company's employees are the hundreds of thousands of people who work in its various departments and functions, such as research, sales, and manufacturing. Employees expect to receive rewards consistent with their performance. One principal way that a company can act ethically toward employees and meet their expectations is by creating an occupational structure that fairly and equitably rewards employees for their contributions. Companies, for example, need to develop recruitment, training, performance appraisal, and reward systems that do not discriminate against employees and that employees believe are fair.

Suppliers and Distributors

No company operates alone. Every company is in a network of relationships with other companies that supply it with the inputs (such as raw materials, components, contract labor, and clients) that it needs to operate. It also depends on intermediaries such as wholesalers and retailers to distribute its products to the final customers. Suppliers expect to be paid fairly and promptly for their inputs; distributors expect to receive quality products at agreed-upon prices. Once again, many ethical issues arise in how companies contract and interact with their suppliers and distributors. Important issues concerning safety specifications are governed by the contracts a company signs with its suppliers and distributors, for example; however, lax oversight can have tragic consequences, as the accompanying "Ethics in Action" feature shows.

ETHICS IN ACTION

Keeping Garment Industry Workers Safe

Why have more than 220 international brands and retailers, including Abercrombie & Fitch, American Eagle Outfitters, Fruit of the Loom, and PVH, signed the Accord on Fire and Building Safety in Bangladesh? The accord is a five-year agreement stating that the signing companies and organizations commit to meet the minimum safety standards for the textile industry in Bangladesh.

Could it be that the buying power of consumers in their mid-twenties—consumers very concerned about the plight of the global worker—encouraged brands and retailers to sign the agreement? Sébastien Breteau, founder and chief executive officer of AsiaInspection, a quality control service provider of supplier audits, product inspections, and lab testing for consumer goods and food importers, believes young people have raised awareness of social accountability in global supply chain management. "This generation cares a lot about transparency," he said. "They want to know that what they are buying doesn't kill the planet."[21] This means that organizations that do not monitor their suppliers carefully risk paying a steep price with young consumers.

Several industrial accidents in 2013 catalyzed social accountability in global supply chain management, according to Breteau's firm. Probably the most tragic of the tipping points was the collapse of the Rana Plaza in Dhaka, Bangladesh. The collapse of the eight-story commercial building killed 1,132 workers and injured more than 2,500 on April 24, 2013. The day before the collapse, building inspectors had found cracks in the structure and warned business owners to evacuate. A few shops and a bank heeded the warning, but owners of garment factories in the building ordered employees to come to work. The collapse was the deadliest disaster in the history of the garment industry worldwide.

There are parallels between the collapse of Rana Plaza and a tragedy in the history of American garment factories. In 1911 a fire destroyed the Triangle Shirtwaist Factory and killed 146 garment workers. The factory was on the top floors of a building in Greenwich Village, New York City. When the fire broke out, workers found the exit doors locked from the outside, a common practice at the time to stop theft and unauthorized breaks. Many workers died by jumping out the windows to escape the flames. The outrage that followed the Triangle fire was a catalyst for change in factory conditions, much like the outrage that followed the Rana Plaza collapse. In the aftermath of the fire, the Factory Investigating Commission was formed and, much like the Accord on Fire and Building Safety in Bangladesh, began factory inspections. Many factories in New York City were found to have the same conditions that caused the Triangle fire, such as flammable materials, locked exit doors, and inadequate fire alarms and fire suppression systems. Between 1911 and 1913, 60 new laws were passed to improve factory conditions.

In March 2014 engineering teams organized through the accord issued inspection reports on 10 Bangladesh factories. The reports indicated many factories did not have adequate fire alarm and sprinkler systems and that some fire exits were locked.[22] Also, many factories had dangerously high weight loads on floors, which is believed to be a cause of the Rana Plaza collapse.

Following the Rana Plaza collapse, clients of Breteau's inspection firm have become less reluctant to commit to the creation and enforcement of programs to audit factory working conditions. "Suddenly, we saw a switch in our clients' attitude to social accountability," according to Breteau. "They became very serious about running audit programs through their supply chains."[23] The company's audit programs include quality management standards according to the ISO 9001 or U.S. C-TPAT standards, social compliance according to SA 8000 standards, and ethical trading according to Sedex Ethical Trade Audits.

Will this change in attitudes toward social accountability in global supply chains have a lasting impact? *Forbes* blogger Robert Bowman, managing editor of Supply-ChainBrain, a website and magazine covering global supply chains, names several reasons that retailers have failed to take aggressive action to stop unsafe working conditions in the past. From the retailers' point of view, it can be difficult to keep track of complex supply chains. Multiple layers of suppliers and subcontractors in some supply chains make it complicated to know exactly how and where goods are being produced, Bowman says. From the consumer's point of view, shocking revelations of poor labor practices cause temporary indignation. After headlines and media stories about sweatshops and safety violations, shoppers quickly return to being indifferent about how clothing is produced, Bowman says. However, the shocking collapse of Rana Plaza and the resulting signatures on the Accord on Fire and Building Safety in Bangladesh bode well for change in global supply chain ethics.

Many other issues depend on business ethics. For example, numerous products sold in U.S. stores have been outsourced to countries that do not have U.S.-style regulations and laws to protect the workers who make these products. All companies must take an ethical position on the way they obtain and make the products they sell. Commonly, this stance is published on a company's website. Table 4.1 presents part of the Gap's statement about its approach to global ethics (www.gapinc.com).

Customers

Customers are often regarded as the most critical stakeholder group because if a company cannot attract them to buy its products, it cannot stay in business. Thus, managers and employees must work to increase efficiency and effectiveness in order to create loyal customers and attract new ones. They do so by selling customers quality products at a fair price and providing good after-sales service. They can also strive to improve their products over time and provide guarantees to customers about the integrity of their products, like the Soap Dispensary, profiled in the accompanying "Ethics in Action" feature.

Community, Society, and Nation

The effects of the decisions made by companies and their managers permeate all aspects of the communities, societies, and nations in which they operate. *Community* refers to physical locations like towns or cities or to social milieus like ethnic neighborhoods in which companies are located. A community provides a company with the physical and social infrastructure that allows it to operate; its utilities and labor force; the homes in which its managers and employees live; the schools, colleges, and hospitals that serve their needs; and so on.

Through the salaries, wages, and taxes it pays, a company contributes to the economy of its town or region and often determines whether the community prospers or declines. Similarly, a company affects the prosperity of a society and a nation and, to the degree that a company is involved in global trade, all the countries it operates in and thus the prosperity of the global economy. We have already discussed the many issues surrounding global outsourcing and the loss of jobs in the United States, for example.

Table 4.1

Some Principles from the Gap's Code of Vendor Conduct

As a condition of doing business with Gap Inc., each and every factory must comply with this Code of Vendor Conduct. Gap Inc. will continue to develop monitoring systems to assess and ensure compliance. If Gap Inc. determines that any factory has violated this Code, Gap Inc. may either terminate its business relationship or require the factory to implement a corrective action plan. If corrective action is advised but not taken, Gap Inc. will suspend placement of future orders and may terminate current production.

I. General Principles

Factories that produce goods for Gap Inc. shall operate in full compliance with the laws of their respective countries and with all other applicable laws, rules, and regulations.

II. Environment

Factories must comply with all applicable environmental laws and regulations. Where such requirements are less stringent than Gap Inc.'s own, factories are encouraged to meet the standards outlined in Gap Inc.'s statement of environmental principles.

III. Discrimination

Factories shall employ workers on the basis of their ability to do the job, without regard to race, color, gender, nationality, religion, age, maternity, or marital status.

IV. Forced Labor

Factories shall not use any prison, indentured, or forced labor.

V. Child Labor

Factories shall employ only workers who meet the applicable minimum legal age requirement or are at least 15 years of age, whichever is greater. Factories must also comply with all other applicable child labor laws. Factories are encouraged to develop lawful workplace apprenticeship programs for the educational benefit of their workers, provided that all participants meet both Gap Inc.'s minimum age standard of 15 and the minimum legal age requirement.

VI. Wages & Hours

Factories shall set working hours, wages, and overtime premiums in compliance with all applicable laws. Workers shall be paid at least the minimum legal wage or a wage that meets local industry standards, whichever is greater. While it is understood that overtime is often required in garment production, factories shall carry out operations in ways that limit overtime to a level that ensures humane and productive working conditions.

ETHICS IN ACTION

Helping to Keep the Soap Market Green

Soap consumption is not as clean a business as you might think. First, soap is often packaged in plastic, and that's beyond the bar: dishwashing detergent, clothing detergent, shampoos, body washes, liquid hand soaps—they're all in plastic containers. With over 33 million tons of plastic being discarded yearly by Americans, only about 14 percent is recycled or sent to waste-to-energy facilities. The rest goes to landfills, where it may leak pollutants into the soil and water, or into the ocean, where an estimated 100 million tons of plastic debris already threatens the health of marine life.[24]

Second, many soaps have chemicals that contain suspected or known carcinogens (cancer-causing agents). One study of 25 household products found that many of their fragrances emitted hazardous chemicals.[25] One such chemical is triclosan, which is commonly found in soap products. Triclosan is toxic to aquatic plants and animals. When it reacts with chlorine in water, it can cause cancer, nerve disorders, and immune system disorders. It also contributes to antibiotic resistance in bacteria that cause infection in humans.

108   Chapter Four

At the Soap Dispensary in Vancouver, owner
Linh Truong sells biodegradable household and
personal products free from fillers, dyes, and perfumes. Customers bring their own containers to
refill over and over again, and Linh tracks the savings to the environment with each bottle refilled.
© Liang Sen Xinhua News Agency/Newscom

To combat the dirty residue of soap consumption, stores like the Soap Dispensary in Vancouver, Canada, are popping up. The Soap Dispensary is a refill store specializing in soaps, household cleaners, and personal care products that are not harmful to humans or the environment. Instead of harsh chemicals, the Soap Dispensary's products are selected to be as free as possible from fillers, dyes, and synthetic perfumes. The products are also biodegradable and animal cruelty–free, and some are vegan certified.

Customers take their own containers back to the store again and again to refill instead of throwing them away, or they can pay a small deposit fee to obtain a reusable container from the store. The store also sells ingredients customers can use to make their own soaps (as well as other products) and conducts classes to teach customers how to make them at home. Classes range from simple soap making to aromatherapy. Besides soap, the store sells nonplastic cleaning supplies, reusable razors, natural beeswax candles, repurposed fabric, and other environmentally friendly items.

Linh Truong and Stewart Lampe, owners of the Soap Dispensary, estimate that in the first two years of the store's existence, it kept more than 12,000 plastic containers from being thrown away.

The store also has provided a venue where customers can purchase locally made products. Among the local brands sold at the Soap Dispensary are Curiosities Tallow Soap and Sadie's Soap. Curiosities Tallow Soap's ingredients include beef fat collected from local butcher shops, and Sadie's Soap's ingredients include hops from locally crafted beer.[26] These locally made soaps and their locally acquired ingredients make a short supply chain that is easier on the environment than a national or international one. When locally owned businesses provide supplies for other locally owned businesses, less fuel and other energy is spent on transportation, creating less pollution in the environment.[27]

The Soap Dispensary tracks the savings to the environment of each bottle refilled, which Truong uses to inspire her customers to keep conserving. Refill stores like the Soap Dispensary make a difference by focusing on one feasible aspect of sustainability. Truong also achieves her mission of reducing waste by encouraging her suppliers to switch to more sustainable packaging and by washing out some delivery containers to return to suppliers for reuse.

"Refilling soap is just one way to do it," she said. "It's just the art of shifting consumers' mentality. Once you start that shift, it can be applied to lots of other things in their lives, and also to how a business is run."[28]

Although the individual effects of the way each McDonald's restaurant operates might be small, for instance, the combined effects of how all McDonald's and other fast-food companies do business are enormous. In the United States alone, more than 3 million people work in the fast-food industry, and many thousands of suppliers, like farmers, paper cup manufacturers, and builders, depend on it for their livelihood. Small wonder, then, that the ethics of the fast-food business are scrutinized closely. This industry was the major lobbyer against attempts to raise the national minimum wage (which was raised to $7.25 an hour in 2009, where it remains in 2016, up from $5.15—a figure that had not changed since 1997), for example, because a higher minimum wage would substantially increase its operating costs. However, responding to protests about chickens raised in cages where they cannot move, McDonald's—the largest egg buyer in the United States—issued new ethical guidelines concerning cage size and related matters that its egg suppliers must abide by if they are to retain its business. What ethical rules does McDonald's use to decide its stance toward minimum pay or minimum cage size?

Business ethics are also important because the failure of a company can have catastrophic effects on a community; a general decline in business activity affects a whole nation.

The decision of a large company to pull out of a community, for example, can threaten the community's future. Some companies may attempt to improve their profits by engaging in actions that, although not illegal, can hurt communities and nations. One of these actions is pollution. For example, many U.S. companies reduce costs by trucking their waste to Mexico, where it is legal to dump waste in the Rio Grande. The dumping pollutes the river from the Mexican side, but the U.S. side of the river is increasingly experiencing pollution's negative effects.

Rules for Ethical Decision Making

LO4-3 Describe four rules that can help companies and their managers act in ethical ways.

When a stakeholder perspective is taken, questions on company ethics abound.[29] What is the appropriate way to manage the claims of all stakeholders? Company decisions that favor one group of stakeholders, for example, are likely to harm the interests of others.[30] High prices charged to customers may bring high returns to shareholders and high salaries to managers in the short run. If in the long run customers turn to companies that offer lower-cost products, however, the result may be declining sales, laid-off employees, and the decline of the communities that support the high-priced company's business activity.

When companies act ethically, their stakeholders support them. For example, banks are willing to supply them with new capital, they attract highly qualified job applicants, and new customers are drawn to their products. Thus, ethical companies grow and expand over time, and all their stakeholders benefit. The results of unethical behavior are loss of reputation and resources, shareholders selling their shares, skilled managers and employees leaving the company, and customers turning to the products of more reputable companies.

When making business decisions, managers must consider the claims of all stakeholders.[31] To help themselves and employees make ethical decisions and behave in ways that benefit their stakeholders, managers can use four ethical rules or principles to analyze the effects of their business decisions on stakeholders: the *utilitarian, moral rights, justice,* and *practical* rules (Figure 4.2).[32] These rules are useful guidelines that help managers decide on the appropriate way to behave in situations where it is necessary to balance a company's self-interest

Figure 4.2

Four Ethical Rules

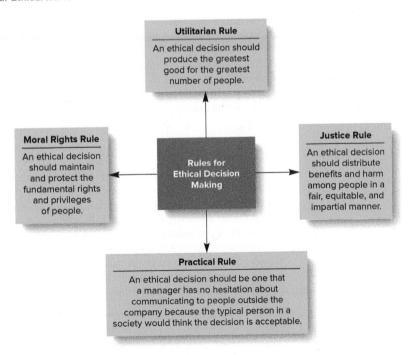

and the interests of its stakeholders. Remember, the right choices will lead resources to be used where they can create the most value. If all companies make the right choices, all stakeholders will benefit in the long run.[33]

UTILITARIAN RULE   The **utilitarian rule** is that an ethical decision is a decision that produces the greatest good for the greatest number of people. To decide which is the most ethical course of business action, managers should first consider how different possible courses of business action would benefit or harm different stakeholders. They should then choose the course of action that provides the most benefits, or, conversely, the one that does the least harm, to stakeholders.[34]

The ethical dilemma for managers is this: How do you measure the benefit and harm that will be done to each stakeholder group? Moreover, how do you evaluate the rights of different stakeholder groups, and the relative importance of each group, in coming to a decision? Because stockholders own the company, shouldn't their claims be held above those of employees? For example, managers might face a choice of using global outsourcing to reduce costs and lower prices or continuing with high-cost production at home. A decision to use global outsourcing benefits shareholders and customers but will result in major layoffs that will harm employees and the communities in which they live. Typically, in a capitalist society such as the United States, the interests of shareholders are put above those of employees, so production will move abroad. This is commonly regarded as being an ethical choice because in the long run the alternative, home production, might cause the business to collapse and go bankrupt, in which case greater harm will be done to all stakeholders.

MORAL RIGHTS RULE   Under the **moral rights rule**, an ethical decision is one that best maintains and protects the fundamental or inalienable rights and privileges of the people affected by it. For example, ethical decisions protect people's rights to freedom, life and safety, property, privacy, free speech, and freedom of conscience. The adage "Do unto others as you would have them do unto you" is a moral rights principle that managers should use to decide which rights to uphold. Customers must also consider the rights of the companies and people who create the products they wish to consume.

From a moral rights perspective, managers should compare and contrast different courses of business action on the basis of how each course will affect the rights of the company's different stakeholders. Managers should then choose the course of action that best protects and upholds the rights of *all* stakeholders. For example, decisions that might significantly harm the safety or health of employees or customers would clearly be unethical choices.

The ethical dilemma for managers is that decisions that will protect the rights of some stakeholders often will hurt the rights of others. How should they choose which group to protect? For example, in deciding whether it is ethical to snoop on employees, or search them when they leave work to prevent theft, does an employee's right to privacy outweigh an organization's right to protect its property? Suppose a coworker is having personal problems and is coming in late and leaving early, forcing you to pick up the person's workload. Do you tell your boss even though you know this will probably get that person fired?

JUSTICE RULE   The **justice rule** is that an ethical decision distributes benefits and harms among people and groups in a fair, equitable, or impartial way. Managers should compare and contrast alternative courses of action based on the degree to which they will fairly or equitably distribute outcomes to stakeholders. For example, employees who are similar in their level of skill, performance, or responsibility should receive similar pay; allocation of outcomes should not be based on differences such as gender, race, or religion.

The ethical dilemma for managers is to determine the fair rules and procedures for distributing outcomes to stakeholders. Managers must not give people they like bigger raises than they give to people they do not like, for example, or bend the rules to help their favorites. On the other hand, if employees want managers to act fairly toward them, then employees need to act fairly toward their companies by working hard and being loyal. Similarly, customers need to act fairly toward a company if they expect it to be fair to them.

PRACTICAL RULE   Each of these rules offers a different and complementary way of determining whether a decision or behavior is ethical, and all three rules should be used to sort out the ethics of a particular course of action. Ethical issues, as we just discussed, are

practical rule An ethical decision is one that a manager has
no reluctance about communicating to people outside the
company because the typical
person in a society would
think it is acceptable.

seldom clear-cut, however, because the rights, interests, goals, and incentives of different stakeholders often conflict. For this reason many experts on ethics add a fourth rule to determine whether a business decision is ethical: The **practical rule** is that an ethical decision is one that a manager has no hesitation or reluctance about communicating to people outside the company because the typical person in a society would think it is acceptable. A business decision is probably acceptable on ethical grounds if a manager can answer yes to each of these questions:

1. Does my decision fall within the accepted values or standards that typically apply in business activity today?

2. Am I willing to see the decision communicated to all people and groups affected by it—for example, by having it reported on TV or via social media?

3. Would the people with whom I have a significant personal relationship, such as family members, friends, or even managers in other organizations, approve of the decision?

Applying the practical rule to analyze a business decision ensures that managers are taking into account the interests of all stakeholders.[35] After applying this rule, managers can judge if they have chosen to act in an ethical or unethical way, and they must abide by the consequences.

LO4-4 Discuss why it is important for managers to behave ethically.

Why Should Managers Behave Ethically?

Why is it so important that managers, and people in general, act ethically and temper their pursuit of self-interest by considering the effects of their actions on others? The answer is that the relentless pursuit of self-interest can lead to a collective disaster when one or more people start to profit from being unethical because this encourages other people to act in the same way.[36] More and more people jump onto the bandwagon, and soon everybody is trying to manipulate the situation to serve their personal ends with no regard for the effects of their action on others. This is called the "tragedy of the commons."

Suppose that in an agricultural community there is common land that everybody has an equal right to use. Pursuing self-interest, each farmer acts to make the maximum use of the free resource by grazing his or her own cattle and sheep. Collectively, all the farmers overgraze the land, which quickly becomes worn out. Then a strong wind blows away the exposed topsoil, so the common land is destroyed. The pursuit of individual self-interest with no consideration of societal interests leads to disaster for each individual and for the whole society because scarce resources are destroyed.[37] Consider digital piracy: The tragedy that would result if all people were to steal digital media would be the disappearance of music, movie, and book companies as creative people decided there was no point in working hard to produce original songs, stories, and so on.

We can look at the effects of unethical behavior on business activity in another way. Suppose companies and their managers operate in an unethical society, meaning one in which stakeholders routinely try to cheat and defraud one another. If stakeholders expect each other to cheat, how long will it take them to negotiate the purchase and shipment of products? When they do not trust each other, stakeholders will probably spend hours bargaining over fair prices, and this is a largely unproductive activity that reduces efficiency and effectiveness.[38] The time and effort that could be spent improving product quality or customer service are lost to negotiating and bargaining. Thus, unethical behavior ruins business commerce, and society has a lower standard of living because fewer goods and services are produced, as Figure 4.3 illustrates.

On the other hand, suppose companies and their managers operate in an ethical society, meaning stakeholders believe they are dealing with others who are basically moral and honest. In this society stakeholders have a greater reason to trust others. **Trust** is the willingness of one person or group to have faith or confidence in the goodwill of another person, even though this puts them at risk (because the other might act in a deceitful way). When trust exists, stakeholders are likely to signal their good intentions by cooperating and providing information that makes it easier to exchange and price goods and services. When one person acts in a trustworthy way, this encourages others to act in the same way. Over time, as greater trust between stakeholders develops, they can work together more efficiently and effectively,

trust The willingness of one
person or group to have faith
or confidence in the goodwill of another person, even
though this puts them at risk.

Figure 4.3

Some Effects of Ethical and Unethical Behavior

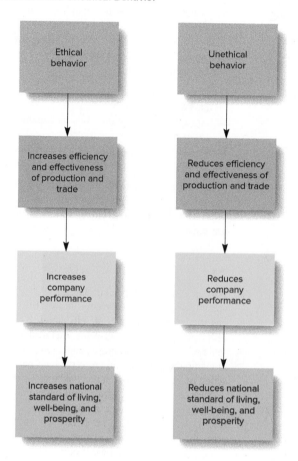

which raises company performance (see Figure 4.3). As people see the positive results of acting in an honest way, ethical behavior becomes a valued social norm, and society in general becomes increasingly ethical.

As noted in Chapter 1, a major responsibility of managers is to protect and nurture the resources under their control. Any organizational stakeholders—managers, workers, stockholders, suppliers—who advance their own interests by behaving unethically toward other stakeholders, either by taking resources or by denying resources to others, waste collective resources. If other individuals or groups copy the behavior of the unethical stakeholder, the rate at which collective resources are misused increases, and eventually few resources are available to produce goods and services. Unethical behavior that goes unpunished creates incentives for people to put their unbridled self-interests above the rights of others.[39] When this happens, the benefits that people reap from joining together in organizations disappear quickly.

An important safeguard against unethical behavior is the potential for loss of reputation.[40] Reputation, the esteem or high repute that people or organizations gain when they behave ethically, is an important asset. Stakeholders have valuable reputations, which they must protect because their ability to earn a living and obtain resources in the long run depends on how they behave.

If a manager misuses resources and other parties regard that behavior as being at odds with acceptable standards, the manager's reputation will suffer. Behaving unethically in the short run can have serious long-term consequences. A manager who has a poor reputation will have difficulty finding employment with other companies. Stockholders who

reputation The esteem or high repute that individuals or organizations gain when they behave ethically.

see managers behaving unethically may refuse to invest in their companies, and this will decrease the stock price, undermine the companies' reputations, and ultimately put the managers' jobs at risk.[41]

All stakeholders have reputations to lose. Suppliers who provide shoddy inputs find that organizations learn over time not to deal with them, and eventually they go out of business. Powerful customers who demand ridiculously low prices find that their suppliers become less willing to deal with them, and resources ultimately become harder for them to obtain. Workers who shirk responsibilities on the job find it hard to get new jobs when they are fired. In general, if a manager or company is known for being unethical, other stakeholders are likely to view that individual or organization with suspicion and hostility, creating a poor reputation. But a manager or company known for ethical business practices will develop a good reputation.[42]

In summary, in a complex, diverse society, stakeholders, and people in general, need to recognize they are part of a larger social group. How they make decisions and act not only affects them personally but also affects the lives of many other people. Unfortunately, for some people, the daily struggle to survive and succeed or their total disregard for others' rights can lead them to lose that bigger connection to other people. We can see our relationships to our families and friends, school, church, and so on. But we must go further and keep in mind the effects of our actions on other people—people who will be judging our actions and whom we might harm by acting unethically. Our moral scruples are like those "other people" but are inside our heads.

Ethics and Social Responsibility

Some companies, like UPS, PepsiCo, Kellogg, Marriott International, and Aflac, are know for their ethical business practices.[43] Other companies such as Enron, which is out of business, or WorldCom, Tyco, and Siemens, which have been totally restructured, repeatedly engaged in unethical and illegal business activities. What explains such differences between the ethics of these companies and their managers?

There are four main determinants of differences in ethics among people, employees, companies, and countries: *societal* ethics, *occupational* ethics, *individual* ethics, and *organizational* ethics—especially the ethics of a company's top managers.[44] (See Figure 4.4.)

Figure 4.4
Sources of Ethics

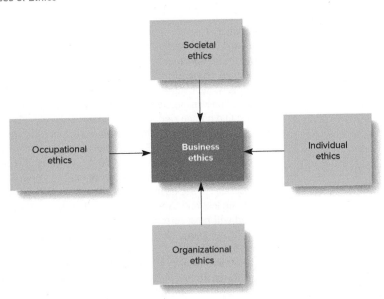

LO4-5 Identify the four main sources of managerial ethics.

societal ethics Standards that govern how members of a society should deal with one another in matters involving issues such as fairness, justice, poverty, and the rights of the individual.

Societal Ethics

Societal ethics are standards that govern how members of a society should deal with one another in matters involving issues such as fairness, justice, poverty, and the rights of the individual. Societal ethics emanate from a society's laws, customs, and practices and from the unwritten values and norms that influence how people interact with each other. People in a particular country may automatically behave ethically because they have *internalized* (made a part of their morals) certain values, beliefs, and norms that specify how they should behave when confronted with an ethical dilemma.

Societal ethics vary among societies. Countries like Germany, Japan, Sweden, and Switzerland are known as being some of the most ethical countries in the world, with strong values about social order and the need to create a society that protects the welfare of all their citizens. In other countries the situation is different. In many economically poor countries, bribery is standard practice to get things done—such as getting a telephone installed or a contract awarded. In the United States and other economically advanced countries, bribery is considered unethical and has been made illegal.

German engineering firm Siemens reported its involvement in a price-fixing cartel in Brazil so that it could build the Sao Paolo Metro.[45] Brazil ranks 76 out of 168 countries in the corruption perceptions index compiled by Transparency International.[46] However, that perception could soon change. In 2014 Brazil began imposing harsh penalties on any organization operating in Brazil that engages in corruption through its Law to Combat Corruption. The 2016 Olympic Games took place in Brazil, and companies working on the Games were subject to abiding by the new anti-corruption laws.[47]

Countries also differ widely in their beliefs about appropriate treatment for their employees. In general, the poorer a country is, the more likely employees are to be treated with little regard. One issue of concern is how an organization uses the resources of another country. The accompanying "Ethics in Action" feature discusses how the jewelry company Tiffany works to be ethical in its sourcing.

ETHICS IN ACTION

Finding Diamonds in a Rough Ethical Landscape

Tiffany & Co., an American multinational luxury jewelry and specialty retailer, has a stated commitment to "obtaining precious metals and gemstones and crafting our jewelry in ways that are socially and environmentally responsible." On its website the company recognizes the challenges of living up to that commitment. According to the company, the biggest concern is the impact of large, industrial-scale mining activities. These concerns include air, water, and soil contamination; the destruction of cultural sites; and human rights abuses.

"I would like to think that the majority of consumers are genuinely concerned about ethical sourcing," says Michael J. Kowalski, then chairman of the board and CEO. ". . . I do believe that Tiffany customers trust, either explicitly or through assumption, that Tiffany—as part of our brand promise—has in fact attended to those concerns. . . . For many of our customers those promises may be implicit, but it makes them no less real. And should we fail to deliver on those promises, the damage to our brand will most certainly be real."[48]

The company, along with the Jewelers of America and other organizations, has founded the Initiative for Responsible Mining Assurance (IRMA) to help ensure that ethical mining practices are followed. IRMA is creating a certification system for environmentally and socially responsible mining, which took effect in 2015.

The vision statement of IRMA calls for practices that "respect human rights and aspirations of affected communities, provide safe, healthy and respectful workplaces, avoid or minimize harm to the environment and leave positive legacies."[49] IRMA believes that most negative social and environmental impacts can be avoided if responsible mining practices are followed. These practices include careful choice of mine location to preserve ecologically and culturally significant areas, reduction of environmental impact from habitat loss and pollution, informed consent of indigenous peoples for mining, health and safety provisions, and transparency in revenue and corporate governance.[50]

In other ethical sourcing efforts, Tiffany & Co. purchases diamonds only from countries that use the Kimberley Process Certification Scheme (KPCS). This process was established by a United Nations General Assembly Resolution to stop the smuggling of "conflict diamonds" or diamonds that are sold to support violence, war efforts, or other malevolent activities. While the company believes the Kimberley Process has made a difference, it would like to see the definition of "conflict diamonds" expanded to include diamond-related human rights abuses.[51]

"While we certainly have a deep moral commitment to act responsibly—a commitment which emanates not just from myself or the senior management group but from all our Tiffany colleagues around the world—we also believe we have a business imperative to act responsibly," Kowalski said. "We have always prided ourselves on managing Tiffany & Co. for the long term. Witness our storied 177-year history. And over the long term, we have no doubt whatsoever that consumers will increasingly demand responsible behavior, and that effectively meeting that demand will be a source of brand differentiation and ultimately lead to the creation of long-term shareholder value."[52]

Occupational Ethics

occupational ethics
Standards that govern how members of a profession, trade, or craft should conduct themselves when performing work-related activities.

Occupational ethics are standards that govern how members of a profession, trade, or craft should conduct themselves when performing work-related activities.[53] For example, medical ethics govern how doctors and nurses should treat their patients. Doctors are expected to perform only necessary medical procedures and to act in the patient's interest, not their own self-interest. The ethics of scientific research require that scientists conduct their experiments and present their findings in ways that ensure the validity of their conclusions. Like society at large, most professional groups can impose punishments for violations of ethical standards.[54] Doctors and lawyers can be prevented from practicing their professions if they disregard professional ethics and put their own interests first.

Within an organization, occupational rules and norms often govern how employees such as lawyers, researchers, and accountants should make decisions to further stakeholder interests. Employees internalize the rules and norms of their occupational group (just as they do those of society) and often follow them automatically when deciding how to behave. Because most people tend to follow established rules of behavior, people frequently take ethics for granted. However, when occupational ethics are violated, such as when scientists fabricate data to disguise the harmful effects of products, ethical issues come to the forefront. For example, in 2014 Toyota said it had deceived "U.S. consumers by concealing and making deceptive statements about two safety issues involving its vehicles."[55] Millions of Toyota and Lexus vehicles had problems with unintended acceleration. As part of the $1.2 billion settlement with the Justice Department, Toyota's procedures and practices will be assessed by an independent monitor. As of 2016, this is still the largest criminal penalty ever levied against a U.S. automobile company—surpassing GM's $900 million fine for a defective ignition switch in 2015.[56] Table 4.2 lists some failures or lapses in professional ethics according to type of functional manager.

Table 4.2

Some Failures in Professional Ethics

For manufacturing and materials management managers:
- Releasing products that are not of a consistent quality because of defective inputs
- Producing product batches that may be dangerous or defective and harm customers
- Compromising workplace health and safety to reduce costs (for example, to maximize output, employees are not given adequate training to maintain and service machinery and equipment)

For sales and marketing managers:
- Knowingly making unsubstantiated product claims
- Engaging in sales campaigns that use covert persuasive or subliminal advertising to create customer need for the product
- Marketing to target groups such as the elderly, minorities, or children to build demand for a product
- Having ongoing campaigns of unsolicited junk mail, spam, door-to-door, or telephone selling

For accounting and finance managers:
- Engaging in misleading financial analysis involving creative accounting or "cooking the books" to hide salient facts
- Authorizing excessive expenses and perks to managers, customers, and suppliers
- Hiding the level and amount of top management and director compensation

For human resource managers:
- Failing to act fairly, objectively, and in a uniform way toward different employees or kinds of employees because of personal factors such as personality and beliefs
- Excessively encroaching on employee privacy through non-job-related surveillance or personality, ability, and drug testing
- Failing to respond to employee observations and concerns surrounding health and safety violations, hostile workplace issues, or inappropriate or even illegal behavior by managers or employees

---

Individual Ethics

individual ethics Personal standards and values that determine how people view their responsibilities to others and how they should act in situations when their own self-interests are at stake.

Individual ethics are personal standards and values that determine how people view their responsibilities to other people and groups and, thus, how they should act in situations when their own self-interests are at stake.[57] Sources of individual ethics include the influence of one's family, peers, and upbringing in general. The experiences gained over a lifetime— through membership in social institutions such as schools and religions, for example—also contribute to the development of the personal standards and values that a person uses to evaluate a situation and decide what is the morally right or wrong way to behave. However, suppose you are the son or daughter of a mobster, and your upbringing and education take place in an organized crime context; this affects how you evaluate a situation. You may come to believe that it is ethical to do anything and perform any act, up to and including murder, if it benefits your family or friends. These are your ethics. They are obviously not the ethics of the wider society and, so, are subject to sanction. In a similar way, managers and employees in an organization may come to believe that actions they take to promote or protect their organization are more important than any harm these actions may cause other stakeholders. So they behave unethically or illegally, and when this is discovered, they also are sanctioned—as happened to New York's cab drivers.

In 2009 the New York City taxi commission, which regulates cab fares, began an investigation after it found that one cab driver from Brooklyn, Wasim Khalid Cheema, overcharged 574 passengers in just one month. The taxi drivers' scheme, the commission said, involved 1.8 million rides and cost passengers an average of $4 to $5 extra per trip. The drivers pressed a button on the taxi's payment meter that categorized the fare as a Code No. 4, which is charged for trips outside the city to Nassau or Westchester and is twice the rate of

Code No. 1, which is charged for rides within New York City limits. Passengers can see which rate is being charged by looking at the meter, but few bother to do so; they rely on the cab driver's honesty.

After the commission discovered the fraud, it used GPS data, collected in every cab, to review millions of trips within New York City and found that in 36,000 cabs the higher rates were improperly activated at least once; in each of about 3,000 cabs it was done more than 100 times; and 35,558 of the city's roughly 48,000 drivers had applied the higher rate. This scheme cost New York City riders more than $8 million plus all the higher tips they paid as a result of the higher charges. The fraud ranks as one of the biggest in the taxi industry's history, and New York City Mayor Michael R. Bloomberg said criminal charges could be brought against cab drivers.

As a result of the scandal, a notification system in taxicabs now alerts passengers if the higher rate is activated. The message is displayed on a television screen in the back seat of the cab and encourages riders to call the city to report any suspected abuse. Also, officials said taxi companies would eventually be forced to use meters based on a GPS system that would automatically set the charge based on the location of the cab, and drivers would no longer be able to manually activate the higher rate—and cheat their customers. In 2011, 630 taxi drivers had their licenses revoked.

In general, many decisions or behaviors that one person finds unethical, such as using animals for cosmetics testing, may be acceptable to another person. If decisions or behaviors are not illegal, individuals may agree to disagree about their ethical beliefs, or they may try to impose their own beliefs on other people and make those ethical beliefs the law. In all cases, however, people should develop and follow the ethical criteria described earlier to balance their self-interests against those of others when determining how they should behave in a particular situation.

Organizational Ethics

organizational ethics The guiding practices and beliefs through which a particular company and its managers view their responsibility toward their stakeholders.

Organizational ethics are the guiding practices and beliefs through which a particular company and its managers view their responsibility toward their stakeholders. The individual ethics of a company's founders and top managers are especially important in shaping the organization's code of ethics. Organizations whose founders had a vital role in creating a highly ethical code of organizational behavior include UPS, Procter & Gamble, Johnson & Johnson, and the Prudential Insurance Company. Johnson & Johnson's code of ethics—its credo—reflects a well-developed concern for its stakeholders (see Figure 4.5). Company credos, such as that of Johnson & Johnson, are meant to deter self-interested, unethical behavior; to demonstrate to managers and employees that a company will not tolerate people who, because of their own poor ethics, put their personal interests above the interests of other organizational stakeholders and ignore the harm they are inflicting on others; and to demonstrate that those who act unethically will be punished.

Managers or workers may behave unethically if they feel pressured to do so by the situation they are in and by unethical top managers. People typically confront ethical issues when weighing their personal interests against the effects of their actions on others. Suppose a manager knows that promotion to vice president is likely if she can secure a $100 million contract, but getting the contract requires bribing the contract giver with $1 million. The manager reasons that performing this act will ensure her career and future, and what harm would it do, anyway? Bribery is common and she knows that, even if she decides not to pay the bribe, someone else surely will. So what to do? Research seems to suggest that people who realize they have the most at stake in a career sense or a monetary sense are the ones most likely to act unethically. And it is exactly in this situation that a strong code of organizational ethics can help people behave in the right or appropriate way. *The New York Times* detailed code of ethics, for example, was crafted by its editors to ensure the integrity and honesty of its journalists as they report sensitive information.

If a company's top managers consistently endorse the ethical principles in its corporate credo, they can prevent employees from going astray. Employees are much more likely to act unethically when a credo does not exist or is disregarded. Arthur Andersen, for example, did not follow its credo at all; its unscrupulous partners ordered middle managers to shred records

Figure 4.5

Johnson & Johnson's Credo

Our Credo

We believe our first responsibility is to the doctors, nurses and patients, to mothers and fathers and all others who use our products and services. In meeting their needs everything we do must be of high quality. We must constantly strive to reduce our costs in order to maintain reasonable prices. Customers' orders must be serviced promptly and accurately. Our suppliers and distributors must have an opportunity to make a fair profit.

We are responsible to our employees, the men and women who work with us throughout the world. Everyone must be considered as an individual. We must respect their dignity and recognize their merit. They must have a sense of security in their jobs. Compensation must be fair and adequate, and working conditions clean, orderly and safe. We must be mindful of ways to help our employees fulfill their family responsibilities. Employees must feel free to make suggestions and complaints. There must be equal opportunity for employment, development and advancement for those qualified. We must provide competent management, and their actions must be just and ethical.

We are responsible to the communities in which we live and work and to the world community as well. We must be good citizens — support good works and charities and bear our fair share of taxes. We must encourage civic improvements and better health and education. We must maintain in good order the property we are privileged to use, protecting the environment and natural resources.

Our final responsibility is to our stockholders. Business must make a sound profit. We must experiment with new ideas. Research must be carried on, innovative programs developed and mistakes paid for. New equipment must be purchased, new facilities provided and new products launched. Reserves must be created to provide for adverse times. When we operate according to these principles, the stockholders should realize a fair return.

Johnson & Johnson

Source: © Johnson & Johnson. Used with permission.

that showed evidence of their wrongdoing. Although the middle managers knew this was wrong, they followed the orders because they responded to the personal power and status of the partners and not the company's code of ethics. They were afraid they would lose their jobs if they did not behave unethically, but their actions cost them their jobs anyway.

Top managers play a crucial role in determining a company's ethics. It is clearly important, then, that when making appointment decisions, the board of directors should scrutinize the reputations and ethical records of top managers. It is the responsibility of the board to decide whether a prospective CEO has the maturity, experience, and integrity needed to head a company and be entrusted with the capital and wealth of the organization, on which the fate of all its stakeholders depends. Clearly, a track record of success is not enough to decide whether a top manager is capable of moral decision making; a manager might have achieved this success through unethical or illegal means. It is important to investigate prospective top managers and examine their credentials. Although the best predictor of future behavior is often past behavior, the board of directors needs to be on guard against unprincipled executives who use unethical means to rise to the top of the organizational hierarchy. For this reason it is necessary that a company's directors continuously monitor the behavior of top executives. In the 2000s this increased scrutiny led to the dismissal of many top executives for breaking ethical rules concerning issues such as excessive personal loans, stock options, inflated expense accounts, and even sexual misconduct. As illustrated in the accompanying "Ethics in Action" feature, the tone set by the founder and leader of an organization can set its ethical tone and business model.

ETHICS IN ACTION

Michelle Obama Leads Challenge to Get Kids Moving

Childhood obesity is an ongoing concern in the United States. According to the U.S. government, more than 33 percent of children are overweight or obese. To help combat the problem, First Lady Michelle Obama started the Let's Move! campaign to end childhood obesity in a generation's time.[58]

There are several causes for the rising numbers of overweight children. Children used to play outside, where they would run around and burn calories. However, with television and video games providing enticing entertainment, children now do their playing mostly indoors on a mobile device. Sugars and fats are much more prevalent in foods, and what we eat today is more processed than ever before, robbing our kids of vital nutrients. Being overweight is unhealthy, especially in children. It may lead to serious health problems such as type 2 diabetes or heart disease. In addition to health risks, being overweight or obese can make children the targets of social discrimination. And the chances that a child will "grow out of it" are small—obese children are likely to become obese adults.[59]

To bring awareness and activism to the problem, Mrs. Obama's campaign targets not just parents and caregivers but the community at large, too. Let's Move! has five pillars: (1) Create a healthy start for children; (2) empower parents and caregivers; (3) provide healthful food in schools; (4) improve access to healthful, affordable foods; and (5) increase physical activity. Mrs. Obama says the movement will continue even after her husband leaves office and she is no longer First Lady.

Some accomplishments of the movement so far include the MyPlate and MiPlato icon, which makes it easy to understand healthful food choices; the closing of city streets to create areas where children can be active without worrying about traffic; and higher standards for nutrition and fitness in schools.[60]

Let's Move! collaborates with the Partnership for a Healthier America (PHA), which works with government agencies on industry-specific solutions to fight obesity. Partnership for a Healthier America aims to bring together leaders from all sectors to reduce childhood obesity.

Many food companies also have joined the Let's Move! campaign. For example, Darden, which owns popular restaurant chains such as Olive Garden, has pledged to offer a fruit or vegetable and low-fat milk with every kid's meal and to reduce the amount of calories and

First Lady Michelle Obama tends the White House garden with a group of children as part of the *Let's Move!* campaign to end childhood obesity.
© Evan Vucci/AP Images

sodium in its menu items by 20 percent over the next 10 years. Walmart committed to lowering the cost of fruits, vegetables, and other healthful options and to work with manufacturers to reduce the amount of sugar and sodium in products throughout the store.

In 2010 the Healthy Weight Commitment Foundation agreed with Let's Move! and PHA to cut 1.5 trillion calories in food products over the next five years. The companies developed lower-calorie options, reduced calories in existing products, and made portion sizes smaller. An independent evaluator announced that by 2014 the foundation had exceeded its goal and removed 6.4 trillion calories from food products.

Being socially responsible can also help the bottom line. As the demand for healthier food items continues to rise, studies are being conducted to see how companies are faring. According to the Hudson Institute, "better-for-you" foods made up about 40 percent of sales for the companies studied but created 70 percent or more in sales growth over a four-year span. The report concludes that "sound strategic planning with a commitment to growing sales of better-for-you foods is good business."[61]

Approaches to Social Responsibility

LO4-6 Distinguish among the four main approaches toward social responsibility that a company can take.

social responsibility The way a company's managers and employees view their duty or obligation to make decisions that protect, enhance, and promote the welfare and well-being of stakeholders and society as a whole.

A company's ethics are the result of differences in societal, organizational, occupational, and individual ethics. In turn, a company's ethics determine its stance on social responsibility. A company's stance on social responsibility is the way its managers and employees view their duty or obligation to make decisions that protect, enhance, and promote the welfare and well-being of stakeholders and society as a whole. As we noted earlier, when no laws specify how a company should act toward stakeholders, managers must decide the right, ethical, and socially responsible thing to do. Differences in business ethics can lead companies to diverse positions or views on their responsibility toward stakeholders.

Many kinds of decisions signal a company's beliefs about its obligations to make socially responsible business decisions (see Table 4.3). The decision to spend money on training and educating employees—investing in them—is one such decision; so is the decision to minimize or avoid layoffs whenever possible. The decision to act promptly and warn customers when a batch of defective merchandise has been accidentally sold is another one. Companies that try to hide such problems show little regard for social responsibility. In the past both GM and Ford tried to hide the fact that several of their vehicles had defects that made them dangerous to drive; the companies were penalized with hundreds of millions of dollars in damages for their unethical behavior, and today they move more quickly to recall vehicles to fix problems. In 2014 General Motors CEO Mary Barra admitted that the automaker did not react fast enough when fault was found with an ignition switch that triggered the recall of eventually more than 10 million cars worldwide.[62] On the other side, also in 2014, Fitbit voluntarily recalled its activity tracking wrist band, the Fitbit Force, due to skin rash issues. The company offered to send consumers a return kit and promised a reimbursement check or exchange within two to six weeks of receipt.[63] The way a company announces business problems or admits its mistakes provides strong clues about its stance on social responsibility.

Four Different Approaches

obstructionist approach Companies and their managers choose *not* to behave in a socially responsible way and instead behave unethically and illegally.

The strength of companies' commitment to social responsibility can range from low to high (see Figure 4.6). At the low end of the range is an obstructionist approach, in which companies and their managers choose *not* to behave in a socially responsible way. Instead they behave unethically and often illegally and do all they can to prevent knowledge of their behavior from reaching other organizational stakeholders and society at large. Managers at the Manville Corporation adopted this approach when they sought to hide evidence that asbestos causes lung damage; so, too, did tobacco companies when they sought to hide evidence that cigarette smoking causes lung cancer. In 2010 it was revealed that the managers of Lehman Brothers, whose bankruptcy helped propel the 2008–2009 financial crisis, used

Table 4.3

Forms of Socially Responsible Behavior

Managers are being socially responsible and showing their support for their stakeholders when they

- Provide severance payments to help laid-off workers make ends meet until they can find another job.
- Give workers opportunities to enhance their skills and acquire additional education so they can remain productive and do not become obsolete because of changes in technology.
- Allow employees to take time off when they need to and provide health care and pension benefits for employees.
- Contribute to charities or support various civic-minded activities in the cities or towns in which they are located (Target and Levi Strauss both contribute 5 percent of their profits to support schools, charities, the arts, and other good works).
- Decide to keep open a factory whose closure would devastate the local community.
- Decide to keep a company's operations in the United States to protect the jobs of American workers rather than move abroad.
- Decide to spend money to improve a new factory so it will not pollute the environment.
- Decline to invest in countries that have poor human rights records.
- Choose to help poor countries develop an economic base to improve living standards.

loopholes in U.K. law to hide billions of dollars of worthless assets on its balance sheet to disguise its poor financial condition. The fall of Lehman Brothers has been recorded in several films, including the 2009 British television film *The Last Days of Lehman Brothers*, the 2011 American independent film *Margin Call*, and the 2011 HBO movie *Too Big to Fail*. It is also referenced in the 2010 animated film *Despicable Me*. In that film the criminal mastermind Gru goes into a building called the "Bank of Evil," which displays a small banner with the words "Formerly Lehman Brothers."

Top managers at Enron also acted in an obstructionist way when they prevented employees from selling Enron shares in their pension funds while they sold hundreds of millions of dollars' worth of their own Enron stock. Most employees lost all their retirement savings. Senior partners at Arthur Andersen who instructed their subordinates to shred files chose an obstructionist approach that caused not only a loss of reputation but devastation for the organization and for all stakeholders involved. These companies are no longer in business.

defensive approach
Companies and their managers behave ethically to the degree that they stay within the law and strictly abide by legal requirements.

A defensive approach indicates at least some commitment to ethical behavior.[64] Defensive companies and managers stay within the law and abide strictly by legal requirements but make no attempt to exercise social responsibility beyond what the law dictates; thus, they can and often do act unethically. These are the kinds of companies, like Computer Associates, WorldCom, and Merrill Lynch, that gave their managers large stock options and bonuses even as company performance was declining rapidly. The managers are the kind who sell their stock in advance of other stockholders because they know their company's performance is about to fall. Although acting on inside information is illegal, it is often hard to prove because top managers have wide latitude regarding when they sell their shares. The founders of most dot-com companies took advantage of this legal loophole to sell billions of dollars of their dot-com shares before their stock prices collapsed. When making ethical decisions, such managers put their own interests first and commonly harm other stakeholders.

accommodative approach
Companies and their managers behave legally and ethically and try to balance the interests of different stakeholders as the need arises.

An accommodative approach acknowledges the need to support social responsibility. Accommodative companies and managers agree that organizational members ought to behave legally and ethically, and they try to balance the interests of different stakeholders so the claims of stockholders are seen in relation to the claims of other stakeholders. Managers adopting this approach want to make choices that are reasonable in the eyes of society and want to do the right thing.

This approach is the one taken by the typical large U.S. company, which has the most to lose from unethical or illegal behavior. Generally, the older and more reputable a company, the more likely its managers are to curb attempts by their subordinates to act unethically.

Figure 4.6

Four Approaches to Social Responsibility

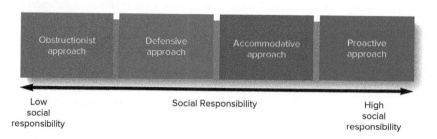

Large companies, like GM, Intel, DuPont, and Dell, seek every way to build their companies' competitive advantage. Nevertheless, they rein in attempts by their managers to behave unethically or illegally, knowing the grave consequences such behavior can have on future profitability. Sometimes they fail, however, such as in 2013 when SAC Capital Advisors (among others) agreed to pay $1.8 billion and plead guilty to criminal insider trading charges. To date, this is the biggest insider trading settlement in history.[65]

proactive approach
Companies and their managers actively embrace socially responsible behavior, going out of their way to learn about the needs of different stakeholder groups and using organizational resources to promote the interests of all stakeholders.

Companies and managers taking a **proactive approach** actively embrace the need to behave in socially responsible ways. They go out of their way to learn about the needs of different stakeholder groups and are willing to use organizational resources to promote the interests not only of stockholders but also of the other stakeholders such as their employees and communities. U.S. steelmaker Nucor is one such company. In 1977 its visionary CEO Ken Iverson announced that throughout its history Nucor had never laid off one employee, and even though a major recession was raging, it did not plan to start now. In 2009 Nucor CEO Daniel R. DiMicco announced that Nucor again would not start layoffs despite the fact its steel mills were operating at only 50 percent of capacity (compared to 95 percent just months earlier) because customers had slashed orders due to the recession. While rivals laid off thousands of employees, Nucor remained loyal to its employees. However, even though there were no layoffs, both managers and employees took major cuts in pay and bonuses to weather the storm together, as they always had, and they searched for ways to reduce operating costs so they would all benefit when the economy recovered, and by 2012 their sacrifice had paid off: Nucor was doing well again. By 2014, it had reported above-expected earnings per share. In 2015 Nucor paid out an increased cash dividend for the 43rd year in a row.[66]

Proactive companies are often at the forefront of campaigns for causes such as a pollution-free environment; recycling and conservation of resources; the minimization or elimination of the use of animals in drug and cosmetics testing; and the reduction of crime, illiteracy, and poverty. For example, companies such as McDonald's, Google, REI, Whole Foods, and Target all have reputations for being proactive in the support of stakeholders such as their suppliers or the communities in which they operate.

Why Be Socially Responsible?

Several advantages result when companies and their managers behave in a socially responsible manner. First, demonstrating its social responsibility helps a company build a good reputation. Reputation is the trust, goodwill, and confidence others have in a company that lead them to want to do business with it. The rewards for a good company reputation are increased business and improved ability to obtain resources from stakeholders.[67] Reputation thus can enhance profitability and build stockholder wealth, and behaving responsibly socially is the economically right thing to do because companies that do so benefit from increasing business and rising profits.

A second major reason for companies to act responsibly toward employees, customers, and society is that, in a capitalist system, companies as well as the government, have to bear the costs of protecting their stakeholders, providing health care and income, paying taxes, and so on. So if all companies in a society act responsibly, the quality of life as a whole increases.

Moreover, how companies behave toward their employees determines many of a society's values and norms and the ethics of its citizens, as already noted. It has been suggested that if all organizations adopted a caring approach and agreed that their responsibility is to promote the interests of their employees, a climate of caring would pervade the wider society. Experts point to Japan, Sweden, Germany, the Netherlands, and Switzerland as countries where organizations are highly socially responsible and where, as a result, crime, poverty, and unemployment rates are relatively low, literacy rates are relatively high, and sociocultural values promote harmony between different groups of people. Business activity affects all aspects of people's lives, so how business behaves toward stakeholders affects how stakeholders behave toward business. You "reap what you sow," as the adage goes.

The Role of Organizational Culture

Although an organization's code of ethics guides decision making when ethical questions arise, managers can go one step further by ensuring that important ethical values and norms are key features of an organization's culture. For example, Herb Kelleher and Coleen Barrett created Southwest Airlines's culture in which promoting employee well-being is a main company priority; this translates into organizational values and norms dictating that layoffs should be avoided and employees should share in the profits the company makes.[68] Google, UPS, and Toyota are among the many companies that espouse similar values. When ethical values and norms such as these are part of an organization's culture, they help organizational members resist self-interested action because they recognize that they are part of something bigger than themselves.[69]

Managers' roles in developing ethical values and standards in other employees are important. Employees naturally look to those in authority to provide leadership, just as a country's citizens look to its political leaders, and managers become ethical role models whose behavior is scrutinized by subordinates. If top managers are perceived as being self-interested and not ethical, their subordinates are not likely to behave in an ethical manner. Employees may think that if it's all right for a top manager to engage in dubious behavior, it's all right for them, too, and for employees this might mean slacking off, reducing customer support, and not taking supportive actions to help their company. The actions of top managers such as CEOs and the president of the United States are scrutinized so closely for ethical improprieties because their actions represent the values of their organizations and, in the case of the president, the values of the nation.

Managers can also provide a visible means of support to develop an ethical culture. Increasingly, organizations are creating the role of ethics officer, or **ethics ombudsperson**, to monitor their ethical practices and procedures. The ethics ombudsperson is responsible for communicating ethical standards to all employees, designing systems to monitor employees' conformity to those standards, and teaching managers and employees at all levels of the organization how to respond to ethical dilemmas appropriately.[70] Because the ethics ombudsperson has organizationwide authority, organizational members in any department can communicate instances of unethical behavior by their managers or coworkers without fear of retribution. This arrangement makes it easier for everyone to behave ethically. In addition, ethics ombudspeople can provide guidance when organizational members are uncertain about whether an action is ethical. Some organizations have an organizationwide ethics committee to provide guidance on ethical issues and help write and update the company code of ethics.

Ethical organizational cultures encourage organizational members to behave in a socially responsible manner. As mentioned earlier in this chapter, one company epitomizing an ethical, socially responsible firm is Johnson & Johnson (J&J). The ethical values and norms in Johnson & Johnson's culture, along with its credo, have guided its managers to make the right decision in difficult situations for decades.

ethics ombudsperson
A manager responsible for communicating and teaching ethical standards to all employees and monitoring their conformity to those standards.

Summary and Review

THE NATURE OF ETHICS Ethical issues are central to how companies and their managers make decisions, and they affect not only the efficiency and effectiveness of company operations but also the prosperity of the nation. The result of ethical behavior is a general increase in company performance and in a nation's standard of living, well-

LO4-1 being, and wealth. An ethical dilemma is the quandary people find themselves in when they have to decide if they should act in a way that might help another person or group and is the right thing to do, even though it might go against their own self-interest. Ethics are the inner guiding moral principles, values, and beliefs that people use to analyze or interpret a situation and then decide what is the right or appropriate way to behave.

Ethical beliefs alter and change as time passes, and as they do so, laws change to reflect the changing ethical beliefs of a society.

LO4-2, 4-4 **STAKEHOLDERS AND ETHICS** Stakeholders are people and groups who have a claim on and a stake in a company. The main stakeholder groups are stockholders, managers, employees, suppliers and distributors, customers, and the community, society, and nation. Companies and their managers need to make ethical business decisions that promote the well-being of their stakeholders and avoid doing them harm.

LO4-3, 4-5 **ETHICS AND DECISION MAKING** To determine whether a business decision is ethical, managers can use four ethical rules to analyze it: the utilitarian, moral rights, justice, and practical rules. Managers should behave ethically because this avoids the tragedy of the commons and results in a general increase in efficiency, effectiveness, and company performance. The main determinants of differences in a manager's, company's, and country's business ethics are societal, occupational, individual, and organizational.

LO4-6 **ETHICS AND SOCIAL RESPONSIBILITY** A company's stance on social responsibility is the way its managers and employees view their duty or obligation to make decisions that protect, enhance, and promote the welfare and well-being of stakeholders and society as a whole.

LO4-6 **ETHICS AND SOCIAL RESPONSIBILITY** There are four main approaches to social responsibility: obstructionist, defensive, accommodative, and proactive. The rewards from behaving in a socially responsible way are a good reputation, the support of all organizational stakeholders, and thus superior company performance.

Management in Action

Topics for Discussion and Action

Discussion

1. What is the relationship between ethics and the law? [LO4-1]

2. Why do the claims and interests of stakeholders sometimes conflict? [LO4-2]

3. Why should managers use ethical criteria to guide their decision making? [LO4-3]

4. As an employee of a company, what are some of the most unethical business practices that you have encountered in its dealings with stakeholders? [LO4-4]

5. What are the main determinants of business ethics? [LO4-5]

Action

6. Find a manager and ask about the most important ethical rules he or she uses to make the right decisions. [LO4-3]

7. Find an example of (a) a company that has an obstructionist approach to social responsibility and (b) one that has an accommodative approach. [LO4-6]

Building Management Skills

Dealing with Ethical Dilemmas [LO4-1, 4-4]

Use the chapter material to decide how you, as a manager, should respond to each of the following ethical dilemmas:

1. You are planning to leave your job to go work for a competitor; your boss invites you to an important meeting where you will learn about new products your company will be bringing out next year. Do you go to the meeting?

2. You're the manager of sales in an expensive sports car dealership. A young executive who has just received a promotion comes in and wants to buy a car that you know is out of her price range. Do you encourage the executive to buy it so you can receive a big commission on the sale?

3. You sign a contract to manage a young rock band, and that group agrees to let you produce their next five records, for which they will receive royalties of 5 percent. Their first record is a smash hit and sells millions. Do you increase their royalty rate on future records?

Managing Ethically [LO4-3, 4-5]

Apple Juice or Sugar Water?

In the early 1980s Beech-Nut, a maker of baby foods, was in grave financial trouble as it tried to compete with Gerber Products, the market leader. Threatened with bankruptcy if it could not lower its operating costs, Beech-Nut entered an agreement with a low-cost supplier of apple juice concentrate. The agreement would save the company over $250,000 annually when every dollar counted. Soon one of Beech-Nut's food scientists became concerned about the quality of the concentrate. He believed it was not made from apples alone but contained large quantities of corn syrup and cane sugar. He brought this information to the attention of top managers at Beech-Nut, but they were obsessed with the need to keep costs down and chose to ignore his concerns. The company continued to produce and sell its product as pure apple juice.[71]

Eventually, investigators from the U.S. Food and Drug Administration (FDA) confronted Beech-Nut with evidence that the concentrate was adulterated. The top managers issued denials and quickly shipped the remaining stock of apple juice to the market before their inventory could be seized. The scientist who had questioned the purity of the apple juice had resigned from Beech-Nut, but he decided to blow the whistle on the company. He told the FDA that Beech-Nut's top management had known of the problem with the concentrate and had acted to maximize company profits rather than to inform customers about the additives in the apple juice. In 1987 the company pleaded guilty to charges that it had deliberately sold adulterated juice and was fined over $2 million. Its top managers were also found guilty and were sentenced to prison terms. The company's reputation was ruined, and it was eventually sold to Ralston Purina, now owned by Nestlé, which installed a new management team and a new ethical code of values to guide future business decisions.

Questions

1. Why is it that an organization's values and norms can become too strong and lead to unethical behavior?

2. What steps can a company take to prevent this problem—to stop its values and norms from becoming so inwardly focused that managers and employees lose sight of their responsibility to their stakeholders?

Small Group Breakout Exercise

Is Chewing Gum the "Right" Thing to Do? [LO4-1, 4-3]

Form groups of three or four people, and appoint one member as the spokesperson who will communicate your findings to the class when called on by the instructor. Then discuss the following scenario:

In the United States, the right to chew gum is taken for granted. Although it is often against the rules to chew gum in a classroom, church, and so on, it is legal to do so on the street. If you possess or chew gum on a street in Singapore, you can be arrested. Chewing gum has been made illegal in Singapore because those in power believe it creates a mess on pavements and feel that people cannot be trusted to dispose of their gum properly and, thus, should have no right to use it.

1. What makes chewing gum acceptable in the United States but unacceptable in Singapore?

2. Why can you chew gum on the street but not in a church?

3. How can you use ethical principles to decide when gum chewing is ethical or unethical and if and when it should be made illegal?

Exploring the World Wide Web [LO4-2, 4-5]

Check out *Fortune*'s list of the World's Most Admired Companies (http://fortune.com/worlds-most-admired-companies/). *Fortune* puts this list together each year based on ratings from executives, directors, and analysts.

1. Select a company on the list and go to that company's web page. How would you describe the company's organizational ethics?

2. What do you believe are the occupational ethics of the people who work at the company?

Be the Manager [LO4-3]

Creating an Ethical Code

You are an entrepreneur who has decided to go into business and open a steak and chicken restaurant. Your business plan requires that you hire at least 20 people as chefs, waiters, and so on. As the owner, you are drawing up a list of ethical principles that each of these people will receive and must agree to when he or she accepts a job

offer. These principles outline your view of what is right or acceptable behavior and what will be expected both from you and from your employees.

Create a list of the five main ethical rules or principles you will use to govern how your business operates. Be sure to spell out how these principles relate to your stakeholders; for example, state the rules you intend to follow in dealing with your employees and customers.

Bloomberg Case in the News

Can a Bunch of Doctors Keep an $8 Billion Secret? Not on Twitter [LO4-1, 4-3, 4-6]

In New Orleans Monday, a major medical organization attempted a feat perhaps as hard as treating the disease doctors were there to discuss. They asked a packed convention hall of attendees not to tweet the confidential, market-moving data they had flown in to see.

It didn't work.

In an unusual arrangement, the American Diabetes Association let hundreds, if not thousands, of in-person attendees see new data on Novo Nordisk A/S's blockbuster diabetes treatment Victoza more than an hour before its official release to the public and the markets. That's atypical for such sensitive data, which are usually shared only with journalists and researchers who have agreed to abide by strict terms, under threat of losing future access.

As the Monday afternoon presentation neared, attendees posted on Twitter pictures of the packed hall, of the crowds waiting to get in, and of the projection screens touting the trial's name: "LEADER."

After warning attendees not to share the information they were about to post, presenters in the hall put up slides showing that Bagsvaerd, Denmark-based Novo's drug, cut heart attacks and strokes by 13 percent and improved survival, while also lowering blood sugar rates and a host of other complications. While good news for diabetics, it was less than investors had hoped.

Tweets

Within minutes, some Twitter accounts were posting pictures of the charts, including key slides that showed the drug's success in reducing deaths. And as fast as the posts went up, the medical society's communications team issued online pleas for them to stop.

"#2016ADA slides include unpublished data and are the intellectual property of the presenters," the association tweeted at accounts who posted the data. "Please delete immediately."

"Wow—that was fast. Just got slammed for posting embargoed data from the session. Better stop :-(" was posted by the account @Loenborg-Madsen, which put up several pictures containing slides [of] the presentation. Attempts to get a person associated with the account to comment were unsuccessful.

It was too little, too late. Some of the tweets had already been re-tweeted by others, making it impossible to scrub the information from the web. One account, @AndyBiotech, whose online description claims he's an investor, retweeted the images to his more than 18,000 followers. An attempt to reach the person behind the account wasn't immediately successful.

Shares Drop

On Tuesday, Novo's shares fell 5.6 percent to 343 kroner, for their biggest one-day drop since February—confirmation of how important the information was to the market. The decline represented about a 52 billion kroner ($7.77 billion) decline in market value.

Officials from the ADA and Novo Nordisk didn't respond to requests for comment on the way the events of the day unfolded. Earlier Monday, a Novo spokeswoman said a detailed press release after the embargo lifted was sufficient, since the company had previously communicated the general results of the study.

The meeting organizers appeared aware of the potential for a leak. The moderator at the session, Matthew Riddle, an endocrinologist from Oregon Health & Science University in Portland, announced the embargo date and time at the start of the session, and the restrictions on sharing the data were noted on multiple slides.

Not the First Time

It's not the first time medical meeting organizers have tried to restrict the distribution of information from the event they are running, said Ivan Oransky, global editorial director of MedPage Today. Oransky runs the Embargo Watch website, which tracks leaks of confidential medical and scientific data. While the ADA in particular has improved in recent years, Monday's events were a backslide, he said in a telephone interview.

"You can't embargo something that is being discussed publicly," Oransky said. "Why are they trying to control the flow of information, especially in this case where the results could influence public health and the markets? Hopefully other organizations won't take this as a signal they can do the same thing."

Questions for Discussion

1. Do you think it was unethical that the attendees tweeted out information about the new drug and results of the study? Why or why not?

2. How have social media platforms such as Twitter and Facebook changed the discussion about confidentiality and social responsibility? Explain.

3. Suppose you were the marketing director at a pharmaceutical company that had just received promising results about a new drug still in the development stage. What ethical responsibilities do you have to keep the information confidential?

Notes

1. "Preventing Bullying in Schools with No Bully" and "Responding to Bullying with Crisis Text Line," www.toms.com, accessed June 15, 2016.

2. "Best Sellers: Backpacks," www.toms.com, accessed June 15, 2016.

3. "Giving Sight," www.toms.com, accessed June 15, 2016; "TOMS Introduces TOMS Eyewear, the Next One for One Product," *PR Newswire,* www.prnewswire.com, June 7, 2011.

4. "Giving Water," www.toms.com, accessed June 15, 2016.

5. A. Morris, "How Crisis Text Line Founder Nancy Lublin Is Saving Lives, Text by Text," *Glamour,* www.glamour .com, June 19, 2015 "Preventing Bullying in Schools with No Bully."

6. M. Isaza, "Founder of Shoe Giveaway Company TOMS Looks Back on 10 Years," Associated Press, http:// bigstory.ap.org, May 6, 2016.

7. www.apple.com, press release, 2012.

8. E. G. Brosious, "At Least 20 States Could Vote on Marijuana Legalization in 2016," *Sun Times Network,* http://national .suntimes.com, February 19, 2016.

9. "About Occupy Wall Street," http:// occupywallst.org, accessed June 15, 2016; M. Bruce, "Obama Says Wall St. Protests Voice Widespread Frustrations," *ABC News,* http://abcnews.go, October 6, 2011.

10. R.E. Freeman, *Strategic Management: A Stakeholder Approach* (Marshfield, MA: Pitman, 1984).

11. "Foundation Fact Sheet: Who We Are," www.gatesfoundation.org, accessed June 15, 2016; S. Bianchi, "Bill Gates Seeks $1.5 Billion More to Eradicate Polio by 2018," *Bloomberg,* www. bloomberg.com, April 25, 2012.

12. J.A. Pearce, "The Company Mission as a Strategic Tool," *Sloan Management Review,* Spring 1982, 15–24.

13. H. Bapuji and S. Riaz, "Occupy Wall Street: What Businesses Need to Know," *Harvard Business Review,* blogs.hbr .org/2011/10/occupy-wall-street-what-business/, October 14, 2011.

14. C.I. Barnard, *The Functions of the Executive* (Cambridge, MA: Harvard University Press, 1948).

15. Freeman, *Strategic Management.*

16. R. Rothacker, "Bank of America Plans to Reduce Consumer Workforce by Thousands More," *The Charlotte Observer,* www.charlotteobserver.com, June 15, 2016.

17. P.S. Adler, "Corporate Scandals: It's Time for Reflection in Business Schools,"

Academy of Management Executive 16 (August 2002), 148–50.

18. K. To, "The Volcker Rule: More Work to Be Done," Global Association of Risk Professionals, www.garp.org, November 6, 2015; C. Main, "Volcker Rule, EU Bank Deadlock, Deutsche Bank Risk: Compliance," *Bloomberg,* www.bloomberg.com, December 10, 2013.

19. Equilar, "Equilar/Associated Press S&P 500 CEO Pay Study 2016," www.equilar .com, May 25, 2016.

20. W.G. Sanders and D.C. Hambrick, "Swinging for the Fences: The Effects of CEO Stock Options on Company Risk Taking and Performance," *Academy of Management Journal* 53, no. 5 (2007), 1055–78.

21. K. Smith, "Who Has Signed the Bangladesh Safety Accord—Update," *Just-Style,* www.just-style.com, February 8, 2016; R. Bowman, Is This the Year When Supply Chains Become Socially Responsible?" *Forbes,* www.forbes.com, March 14, 2011.

22. S. Greenhouse, "Bangladesh Inspections Find Gaps in Safety," *The New York Times,* www.nytimes.com, March 11, 2014.

23. Ibid.

24. R. Cho, "What Happens to All That Plastic?" blogs.ei.columbia.edu/2012 /01/31/what-happens-to-all-that-plastic/, January 31, 2012.

25. A.C. Steinemann, I.C. MacGregor, S.M. Gordon, L.G. Gallagher, A.L. Davis, D.S. Ribeiro, et al., "Fragranced Consumer Products: Chemicals Emitted, Ingredients Unlisted," *Environ Impact Review* 31 (2011), 328–33.

26. The Soap Dispensary, www.facebook .com/pages/The-Soap-Dispensary/ 266253066720178, March 5, 2014.

27. N. Yeh, "Rethink, Re-Use," *Pacific Rim Magazine,* http://langaraprm.com, May 2, 2016.

28. N. Burg, "How One Business Diverted 8,000 Plastic Bottles from Landfills," *Forbes,* www.forbes.com, March 16, 2014.

29. T.L. Beauchamp and N.E. Bowie, eds., *Ethical Theory and Business* (Englewood Cliffs, NJ: Prentice-Hall, 1929); A. MacIntyre, *After Virtue* (South Bend, IN: University of Notre Dame Press, 1981).

30. R.E. Goodin, "How to Determine Who Should Get What," *Ethics,* July 1975, 310–21.

31. E.P. Kelly, "A Better Way to Think about Business" (book review), *Academy of Management Executive* 14 (May 2000), 127–29.

32. T.M. Jones, "Ethical Decision Making by Individuals in Organization: An Issue Contingent Model," *Academy of Management Journal* 16 (1991), 366–95; G.F. Cavanaugh, D.J. Moberg, and M. Velasquez, "The Ethics of Organizational Politics," *Academy of Management Review* 6 (1981), 363–74.

33. L.K. Trevino, "Ethical Decision Making in Organizations: A Person-Situation Interactionist Model," *Academy of Management Review* 11 (1986), 601–17; W.H. Shaw and V. Barry, *Moral Issues in Business,* 6th ed. (Belmont, CA: Wadsworth, 1995).

34. T.M. Jones, "Instrumental Stakeholder Theory: A Synthesis of Ethics and Economics," *Academy of Management Review* 20 (1995), 404–37.

35. B. Victor and J.B. Cullen, "The Organizational Bases of Ethical Work Climates," *Administrative Science Quarterly* 33 (1988), 101–25.

36. D. Collins, "Organizational Harm, Legal Consequences and Stakeholder Retaliation," *Journal of Business Ethics* 8 (1988), 1–13.

37. R.C. Solomon, *Ethics and Excellence* (New York: Oxford University Press, 1992).

38. T.E. Becker, "Integrity in Organizations: Beyond Honesty and Conscientiousness," *Academy of Management Review* 23 (January 1998), 154–62.

39. S.W. Gellerman, "Why Good Managers Make Bad Decisions," in K.R. Andrews, ed., *Ethics in Practice: Managing the Moral Corporation* (Boston: Harvard Business School Press, 1989).

40. J. Dobson, "Corporate Reputation: A Free Market Solution to Unethical Behavior," *Business and Society* 28 (1989), 1–5.

41. M.S. Baucus and J.P. Near, "Can Illegal Corporate Behavior Be Predicted? An Event History Analysis," *Academy of Management Journal* 34 (1991), 9–36.

42. Trevino, "Ethical Decision Making in Organizations."

43. "The World's Most Ethical Companies 2016 Honorees," Ethisphere Institute, http://worldsmostethicalcompanies .ethisphere.com, accessed June 15, 2016.

44. A.S. Waterman, "On the Uses of Psychological Theory and Research in the Process of Ethical Inquiry," *Psychological Bulletin* 103, no. 3 (1988), 283–98.

45. A. Knobloch, "Siemens Bribery Case Spreads to Brazilian Politics," *DW,* www.dw.de/siemens-bribery-case-spreads-to-brazilian-politics/a-17268276, March 12, 2012.

46. "2015 Corruption by Country/Territory: Brazil," Transparency International, https://www.transparency.org, accessed June 15, 2016.

47. I. Watson and V. Cotovio, "Rio Mayor Welcomes Federal Olympic Investigation," *CNN,* www.cnn.com, May 26, 2016.

48. R. Kanani, "CEO of Tiffany & Co. on Ethical Sourcing, Responsible Mining, and Leadership," *Forbes,* www.forbes.com/sites/rahimkanani/2014/01/19/ceo-of-tiffany-co-on-ethical-sourcing-responsible-mining-and-leadership/, January 19, 2014.

49. "About IRMA," www.responsiblemining.net, accessed June 15, 2016.

50. Ibid.

51. "About KP Basics," https://www.kimberleyprocess.com, accessed June 15, 2016.

52. "CEO of Tiffany & Co. on Ethical Sourcing, Responsible Mining, and Leadership."

53. M.S. Frankel, "Professional Codes: Why, How, and with What Impact?" *Ethics* 8 (1989), 109–15.

54. J. Van Maanen and S.R. Barley, "Occupational Communities: Culture and Control in Organizations," in B. Staw and L. Cummings, eds., *Research in Organizational Behavior,* vol. 6 (Greenwich, CT: JAI Press, 1984), 287–365.

55. M. Maynard, "The Steep Cost of Toyota's Settlement with the U.S. Government," *Forbes,* www.forbes.com/sites/michelinemaynard/2014/03/19/the-steep-cost-of-toyotas-settlement-with-the-u-s-government/, March 19, 2014.

56. B. Snyder, "GM's $900 Million Settlement Isn't the Biggest in History," *Fortune,* http://fortune.com, September 17, 2015.

57. Jones, "Ethical Decision Making."

58. "About Let's Move," www.letsmove.gov, accessed June 15, 2016.

59. Ibid.

60. K. Thompson and T. Carman, "A Healthful Legacy: Michelle Obama Looks to the Future of 'Let's Move,'" *The Washington Post,* https://www.washingtonpost.com, May 3, 2015.

61. H. Cardello, "Better-for-You Foods: It's Just Good Business,"www.hudson.org, October 13, 2011.

62. "GM: Steps to a Recall Nightmare," *CNN Money,* http://money.cnn.com, accessed June 15, 2016.

63. "Fitbit Force Skin Irritation FAQs," *fitbithelp,* February 26, 2014, https://help.fitbit.com/customer/portal/articles/1425569.

64. M. Friedman, "A Friedman Doctrine: The Social Responsibility of Business Is to Increase Its Profits," *The New York Times Magazine,* September 13, 1970, 33.

65. P. Hurtado and M. Keller, "How the Feds Pulled Off the Biggest Insider-Trading Investigation in U.S. History," *Bloomberg,* www.bloomberg.com, June 9, 2016.

66. "2015 Annual Report," www.nucor.com, accessed June 15, 2016.

67. P. Engardio and M. Arndt, "What Price Reputation?" July 9, 2007, www.businessweek.com.

68. "2015 Southwest Airlines One Report," www.southwest.com, accessed June 15, 2016.

69. G.R. Jones, *Organizational Theory: Text and Cases* (Englewood Cliffs, NJ: Prentice-Hall, 2008).

70. P.E. Murphy, "Creating Ethical Corporate Structure," *Sloan Management Review,* Winter 1989, 81–87.

71. R. Johnson, "Ralston to Buy Beechnut, Gambling It Can Overcome Apple Juice Scandal," *The Wall Street Journal,* September 18, 1989, B11.